COPY 1

Everyman's Eng   ary,
 containing o   r-
 national pho
Daniel Jones   C.
Gimson. -- London . Dent, 19
 xlvi, 544 p. : ill. -- (Everyman's
reference Library).
 1917 ed. has title : An English pronouncing
dictionary, by Daniel Jones.

0460030159   (Continued on next card)

Everyman's

ENGLISH PRONOUNCING DICTIONARY

A volume in
EVERYMAN'S REFERENCE LIBRARY

Everyman's Reference Library

CLASSICAL ATLAS

CLASSICAL DICTIONARY

CONCISE ENCYCLOPAEDIA OF ARCHITECTURE

DICTIONARY OF ABBREVIATIONS

DICTIONARY OF DATES

DICTIONARY OF ECONOMICS

DICTIONARY OF EUROPEAN WRITERS

DICTIONARY OF FICTIONAL CHARACTERS

DICTIONARY OF LITERARY BIOGRAPHY:
ENGLISH AND AMERICAN

DICTIONARY OF MUSIC

DICTIONARY OF NON-CLASSICAL MYTHOLOGY

DICTIONARY OF PICTORIAL ART (2 volumes)

DICTIONARY OF QUOTATIONS AND PROVERBS

DICTIONARY OF SHAKESPEARE QUOTATIONS

EVERYMAN'S ASTRONOMY

EVERYMAN'S ENCYCLOPAEDIA (12 volumes)

ENCYCLOPAEDIA OF GARDENING

ENGLISH PRONOUNCING DICTIONARY

FRENCH-ENGLISH—ENGLISH-FRENCH DICTIONARY

THESAURUS OF ENGLISH WORDS AND PHRASES

Other Works by Daniel Jones

Those marked * are pamphlets

The Phoneme: its Nature and Use. By D. JONES. Heffer, Cambridge, 3rd ed., 1967.

* The History and Meaning of the Term Phoneme. By D. JONES. International Phonetic Association, 1957. Obtainable from the Dept of Phonetics, University College, London.

* The Aims of Phonetics. By D. JONES. International Phonetic Association, 1938.

An Outline of English Phonetics. By D. JONES. 8th edition (revised, modernized and reset), Heffer, Cambridge, 9th ed., 1960 (7th edition, Teubner, Leipzig, 1949).

The Pronunciation of English. By D. JONES. Cambridge University Press. 4th edition revised, and with new texts, 1956.

Phonetic Readings in English. By D. JONES. Winter, Heidelberg. New and improved edition, 1956.

Colloquial French. by E. M. STEPHAN and D. JONES. A Complete Course (586 pp.). H.M.V. Gramophone Co., London. With 15 double-sided gramophone records and Key Book for Exercises. Pupils' Book for class use. 1927.

100 Poésies Enfantines, recueillies et transcrites phonétiquement par D. JONES. Illustrations par E. M. PUGH. Teubner, Leipzig, 1907.

Intonation Curves. By D. JONES. Teubner, Leipzig, 1909.

* Shakespeare in the Original Pronunciation. Texts in phonetic transcription with notes. By D. JONES. Pages 36–45 of *English Pronunciation through the Centuries*, published by the Linguaphone Institute, London. Accompanies a double-sided gramophone record of passages from Shakespeare in the original pronunciation, spoken by D. JONES and E. M. EVANS. Linguaphone Institute, London.

Cardinal Vowels. Double-sided gramophone records of the primary and secondary Cardinal Vowels spoken by D. JONES. Linguaphone Institute, London. With leaflet giving the texts of the records with explanations of the use of Cardinal Vowels.

* Some Thoughts on the Phoneme. By D. JONES. Philological Society, 1944. Offprints obtainable from the Dept of Phonetics, University College, London.

* Dhe Fonetik Aspekt ov Speling Reform. By D. JONES. Simplified Spelling Society, c/o I. J. Pitman & Sons 29 Parker St, London, W.C.2.

* Concrete and Abstract Sounds. By D. JONES. In the *Proceedings of the Third International Congress of Phonetic Sciences*. Ghent, 1938. Offprints obtainable from the Dept of Phonetics, University College, London.

* On 'Received Pronunciation'. By D. JONES. International Phonetic Association, 1937.

* A Passage of Chaucer in Phonetic Transcription (reconstructed pronunciation). By D. JONES. International Phonetic Association, 1938.

* The Great English Vowel Shift (Chart). By D. JONES and C. L. WRENN. Obtainable from the Dept of Phonetics, University College, London.

* The Problem of a National Script for India. By D. JONES. 1942. Obtainable from the Dept. of Phonetics, University College, London.

A Colloquial Sinhalese Reader. By D. JONES and H. S. PERERA. Manchester University Press, 1919.

A Sechuana Reader. By D. JONES and S. T. PLAATJE. University of London Press, 1916.

The Tones of Sechuana Nouns. By D. JONES. International African Institute, 10 Fetter Lane, London, E.C.4, 1927.

A Cantonese Phonetic Reader. By D. JONES and KWING TONG WOO. University of London Press, 1912. Supplement, Texts in Chinese character.

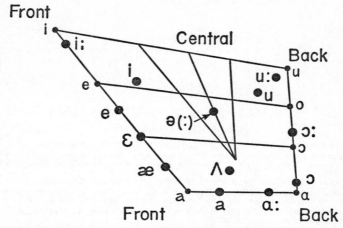

A. Diagrammatic representation of approximate tongue-positions of average English Vowels compared with those of Cardinal Vowels. (The dots indicate roughly the positions of the highest point of the tongue.)

Cardinal Vowels *small dots.*
English Vowels *large dots.*

(It is to be assumed that there is a small dot as well as a large one at the point « ε »)

TONGUE-POSITIONS OF VOWELS

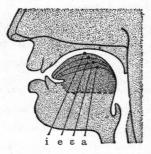

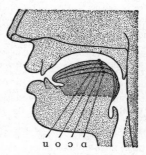

B. Tongue-positions of Front Cardinal Vowels

C. Tongue-positions of Back Cardinal Vowels

Note. The positions for cardinal « i, a, ɑ » and « u » are copied from X-ray photographs (reproduced in the frontispiece to my book *The Pronunciation of English*, third and subsequent editions). The positions for cardinal « e, ε, ɔ » and « o » are drawn approximately.

D. J.

Everyman's
ENGLISH PRONOUNCING DICTIONARY

CONTAINING OVER 58,000 WORDS IN
INTERNATIONAL PHONETIC TRANSCRIPTION

By

DANIEL JONES

M.A. (Cambridge), Dr Phil. h.c. (Zürich), Hon. LL.D (Edinb.)
Professor Emeritus of Phonetics in the University of London
Corresponding Member of the German Academy of Sciences, Berlin
Honorary Member of the Royal Irish Academy

THIRTEENTH EDITION

Edited by

A. C. GIMSON

Professor of Phonetics in the University of London

LONDON: J. M. DENT & SONS LTD
NEW YORK: E. P. DUTTON & CO. INC.

Made in Great Britain
at the
Aldine Press · Letchworth · Herts
for
J. M. DENT & SONS LTD
Aldine House · Albemarle Street · London
First published 1917
Reprinted 1919, 1921, 1922
Second Edition (revised, with Supplement) 1924
Third Edition (with revised Introduction) 1926
Reprinted 1927, 1928, 1930, 1931, 1932 (twice), 1934, 1935
Fourth Edition (revised, enlarged and reset) 1937
Fifth Edition 1940
Sixth Edition 1944
Seventh Edition (with Supplement) 1945
Eighth Edition 1947
Ninth Edition 1948
Tenth Edition 1949
Reprinted 1950, 1952, 1953, 1954 (twice), 1955
Eleventh Edition (completely revised, enlarged, brought
up to date and reset) 1956
Reprinted (with minor corrections) 1957
Reprinted (with minor corrections and
short supplement) 1958
Reprinted 1960
Twelfth Edition (revised, with new Supplement, and
with Glossary of Phonetic Terms) 1963
Reprinted (with corrections and
minor revisions by A. C. Gimson) 1964
© Thirteenth Edition (revised, enlarged and reset) 1967
Reprinted (with corrections) 1969
Reprinted (with corrections) 1972
Reprinted (with corrections) 1974
Reprinted 1975
First paperback edition 1975

Feb— 8/77

Hardback ISBN: 0 460 03015 9
Paperback ISBN: 0 460 02181 8

EDITOR'S PREFACE TO THE
THIRTEENTH EDITION (1967)

1. THIS Dictionary, first published in 1917, retains in the present thirteenth edition the essential form developed by Daniel Jones over the last fifty years. However, 468 completely new words have been added in this edition, and 17 words, which appear to be no longer in common use, have been deleted. Moreover I have thought it correct to introduce certain changes which take into account the type of reader who nowadays makes use of the Dictionary and which reflect the present state of the kind of English described (Received Pronunciation: see Introduction, sections 3–9).

2. It has become increasingly clear that a very high percentage of those who consult this Dictionary do not have English as their first language. For such readers, a somewhat simplified account of RP would seem to be called for, containing a minimum of allophonic and other variants as are of interest and utility mainly to the minority of users having English as a mother tongue. I have concentrated, therefore, on indicating those variants which are of a phonemic, i.e. distinctive, kind, and have excluded many allophonic, i.e. non-distinctive, variants previously shown.

3. I have also taken into account the evolution of RP.[1] There seems little doubt that this type of English speech has evolved considerably since this Dictionary was first conceived. Since the turn of the century, RP has become less and less the property of an exclusive social class. Its extension throughout a wider section of the population has doubtless led to some dilution of the earlier form. As a result of this and the natural evolution of a phonological system, the quality of some sounds and the accentual patterns of some words appear to have changed sufficiently in the last half-century for the fact to be noted. Many changes, which formerly were only incipient, are now generally established. When several pronunciations of a word exist, the ordering of their usage has often changed. In order to discover how far such changes had become established and to provide some statistical basis for an assessment, a questionnaire containing nearly 300 crucial words was sent out to some 100 colleagues engaged in linguistic work who were likely to be able to make an objective judgment on the present state of RP. As a result important amendments were made to many entries, e.g. those under **actual, bankrupt, Biarritz, frontier, issue, retch,** etc.

4. A dictionary of this kind is largely descriptive in intent, but it also fulfils for a majority of its readers a prescriptive function. It has, therefore, to be cautious and not seek to anticipate events and recommend pronunciations which may not become thoroughly established and general for the span of another generation. Thus, the word **controversy**, given in most dictionaries with a recommended accentual pattern '----, emerges from the questionnaire as having -'--- (given as a less common variant in previous editions of this Dictionary) for some 40 per cent of the replies. But more than 90 per cent of some

---

[1] A. C. Gimson, *Introduction to the Pronunciation of English*, 2nd ed. 1970 (Arnold), §6.32.

500 students questioned on this point used only -'---. The pattern -'--- may well, therefore, supersede '---- by the turn of the century. At the moment it would seem appropriate to list both variants as equally representative.

5. As a result of the various considerations mentioned above, the changes made in this edition may be summarized as follows:

(a) The detail of the Frontispiece diagram, showing the relationship of the English vowels, has been modified in order to take account of recent changes, i.e. /ʌ/ has been advanced, /ɔ:/ and /ə/ raised, and [o] deleted.[1]

(v) The diphthong formerly transcribed as /ou/ is now shown as /əu/, for two reasons:

  (i) [ə] more correctly indicates the present-day starting point of the RP diphthong and underlines its affinity with /ə:/.[2] Such a consideration is important for foreign learners;

  (ii) often, in weakly stressed positions, e.g. in the first syllable of **November,** the choice is between /ə/ or /əu/, and this can be stated economically in the form /nəu'vembə*/. The selection of /ə/ or /əu/ will usually depend on the style and speed of utterance or on the familiarity of the word, e.g. **November** tends to have /əu/ in slower or more formal speech, and **allopath** is more likely to have /əu/ in the second syllable, whereas the more common **allocate** usually has /ə/. The allophonic variant [o] replacing the diphthong in cases such as **November** or in pre-vocalic situations as in **going** or **slower** is discarded as obsolescent. (In such words as **going, slower** the full diphthong /əu/ is given.)

(c) Allophonic, i.e. non-distinctive, variants have not been shown. Thus, the variants [oə] for /uə/, [ç] for /hj/, [ɱ] for /m/ or /n/ before /f/ or /v/, [æ:] for /æ/, and the insertion of [ʔ] where /r/ has been omitted (e.g. in **over-eat**) have been deleted, on the grounds that, if the above are kept, many other predictable allophonic variants should be shown. The symbols in question are, however, retained where necessary for the transcription of exclamations and foreign words.

(d) The variant /jə:/ for /iə/, e.g. in **dear,** is deleted as obsolescent.

(e) The variant /jə:/ for /juə/, shown in previous editions in such a word as **curious,** is extended to many other entries of the same type, e.g. **endurance, furious,** as becoming increasingly common.

(f) In the final sequence vowel + /n/ + /l/, e.g. in **panel, final,** /l/ is not marked as syllabic, in accordance with Explanations, Section XVIII (p. xxviii).

6. In addition to the developments already mentioned, it seems probable that the first pronunciation of such words as **fire** and **power** will have, in an early edition, to be shown with a diphthong or monophthong rather than with a sequence of three vowels (see Explanations, Section XXIII (4), p. xxxii). The reduced forms have existed for at least a century and are probably the most common nowadays amongst RP speakers (the form /ɑ:/ being extremely widespread for such a word as **our**). The acknowledgment of the pronunciations [aə] or [ɑə] and [a:] or [ɑ:] will, however, involve a restatement of the system of English vowels.

7. As far as foreign readers are concerned, the essential qualitative distinction between /i:/–/i/ and /u:/–/u/ needs to be emphasized (see Explanations, Section XXIV, p. xxxii). It also needs to be borne in mind by foreign readers that long vowels and diphthongs are very much reduced in length before syllable-final /p, t, k, tʃ, f, θ, s, ʃ/. Thus, /i:/ in **bead** is considerably longer than /i:/ in **beat,** which has approximately the same length as the /i/ (of different quality) in **bid.**[3]

---

[1] See my *Introduction*, §§ 7.13, 7.16, 7.19, 7.20, 7.25. In this Preface, I follow the usual convention of distinguishing phonetic and phonemic symbols by the use of [ ] and //.

[2] *Introduction to the Pronunciation of English*, § 7.25.

[3] See my *Introduction to the Pronunciation of English*, § 7.04.

8. The Introduction written by Daniel Jones remains unchanged. It expresses the philosophy which has guided the Dictionary since the time of its first compilation. All the items and definitions contained in the more recent Glossary of Phonetic Terms have also been retained. However, the Explanations on p. xxii, et seq., have been amended, where necessary, to conform to the modifications in approach which I have felt to be justified. Paragraphs amended in this way are indicated by a notice in brackets.

A. C. G.

January 1967.

ACKNOWLEDGMENTS

I continue to remember with gratitude those who rendered service in connexion with former editions, and especially those whose names were recorded in previous prefaces. Here it must suffice if I make special mention of my late friend Walter Ripman whose death in 1947 deprived the world of a very remarkable linguist, teacher and authority on modern methods in education. His help with this Dictionary dated from the time wh en the book was in contemplation about fifty years ago. Its original plan was settled largely in consultation with him; he revised all the proofs of the first edition, and he never failed subsequently to assist me with his experience and advice as long as he was able. I am glad to take this opportunity of recalling with gratitude and affection all the help that he so generously bestowed on this work.

D. J.

February 1963.

(For the Thirteenth Edition)

I must above all thank Professor Daniel Jones for entrusting this present edition to my care and for his unfailing help and encouragement during the many months of preparation. My sincere thanks are also due to Mr. G. F. Arnold, my colleague at University College, London, for undertaking the heavy task of checking all the proofs of this revised edition. In addition, I must express my gratitude to all those colleagues and correspondents from all over the world who have suggested corrections and new entries and who have given most valuable advice. I am especially grateful to Professor D. Abercrombie, Mr. S. S. Eustace, Mr. R. Furuskog, Mr. L. Guierre, Mr. L. A. Hill, Dr. W. R. Lee, Mr. J. W. Lewis, Mr. P. A. D. MacCarthy, Mr. K. P. Mayer, Miss G. M. Miller (and the Pronunciation Unit of B.B.C.), Mr. V. Petti, Mr. J. Posthumus, Dr. J. T. Pring, Mrs. H. J. Uldall, and to all those colleagues who painstakingly completed the long and tedious questionnaire which I sent them.

A. C. G.

January 1967

NUMBER OF THE WORDS RECORDED IN THE DICTIONARY

THE fourth printing (1960) of the eleventh edition of this Dictionary recorded the pronunciation of some 58,101 words, comprising:

Ordinary Words [1]	43,378
Proper Names [2] and Abbreviations . .	14,723

The twelfth edition added about 200 more words. The present (thirteenth) edition contains 556 new words (including 88 previously printed as a supplement), of which 387 are ordinary words and 169 proper names and abbreviations. Seventeen entries have been deleted. The present total therefore reaches 58,840 words (excluding the inflected forms).

---

[1] Ordinary words include all head-words and those grouped under head-words with such terminations as **-ly, -ness, -er, -or, -ment.** Not included in the total (except when they occur as head-words with specific meanings) are plurals of nouns, similar forms without plural meaning (e.g. **athletics**), comparatives and superlatives of adjectives, inflected forms of verbs, verbal forms derived from words other than verbs (e.g. **blanketing**), proper names of plural form grouped under the corresponding singular form (e.g. **Ayre, -s**). Words of different meaning but the same pronunciation and spelling have a single entry (e.g. **bear**).

[2] The term 'proper name' is taken to include all words written with a capital initial letter.

CONTENTS

Frontispiece (diagram showing the tongue positions of English Vowels compared with those of Cardinal Vowels) . . . iv
Editor's Preface to the Thirteenth Edition vii
Acknowledgments xi
Number of Words Recorded in the Dictionary xiii

INTRODUCTION:
    Object of this Book xvii
    The Pronunciation xvii
    Utility of this Book in Practical Linguistic Teaching . . xix
    The Phonetic Transcription xix

EXPLANATIONS:
    I. How to read the Entries xxii
    II. Meaning of [ ] xxii
    III. Rare Pronunciations xxii
    IV. Meaning of Italic Letters xxii
    V. Meaning of (:) xxiii
    VI. Meaning of (') xxiii
    VII. Combinations of Variant Forms xxiii
    VIII. Variant Spellings xxiv
    IX. Proper Names Identical with Ordinary Words . xxiv
    X. Proper Names pronounced Differently but spelt the Same xxiv
    XI. Words grouped under Head-words . . . xxv
    XII. Stress of Derived Words xxv
    XIII. Variations of Stress xxvi
    XIV. Abbreviated Spellings xxvi
    XV. Linking « r » and Intrusive « r » . . . xxvi
    XVI. Meaning of * xxviii
    XVII. Incomplete Plosive Consonants . . . xxviii
    XVIII. Syllabic Consonants xxviii
    XIX. Syllable Separation, Use of the Hyphen . xxviii
    XX. Disyllabic « i-ə », « u-ə », etc. xxx
    XXI. Strong and Weak Forms xxx
    XXII. Variant Pronunciations of the Unstressed Terminations, *-less, -ness*, etc. xxxi
    XXIII. Other Variants of Sound-distribution occurring in RP but not as a rule noted in this Dictionary . xxxi

CONTENTS

XXIV. Values of the Phonetic Symbols . . . xxxii

    A. Table of Sounds xxxii

    B. Diphthongs xxxv

    C. Digraphs xxxv

    D. Allophonic Variants xxxvi

    E. Diaphonic Variants xxxvii

    F. Foreign Sounds xxxix

    G. Special Symbols for Interjections . . xlii

    H. Diacritical Marks and Other Signs . xlii

XXV. Abbreviations xliii

XXVI. Key-words for English Phonetic Symbols . xliv

SOME USEFUL BOOKS FOR THE STUDY OF ENGLISH PRONUNCIATION xlv

DICTIONARY 1

GLOSSARY OF PHONETIC TERMS USED IN THE INTRODUCTION
AND EXPLANATIONS 541

INTRODUCTION

by Daniel Jones

OBJECT OF THIS BOOK

1. THE purpose of the present Dictionary is to record, with as much accuracy as is necessary for practical linguistic purposes, the pronunciation used by a considerable number of typical Southern English people (see § 3) in ordinary conversation.

2. The book is a record of *facts*, not of theories or personal preferences. No attempt is made to decide how people *ought* to pronounce; all that the dictionary aims at doing is to give a faithful record of the manner in which certain people *do* pronounce.

THE PRONUNCIATION

3. The pronunciation represented in this book is that which I believe to be very usually heard in everyday speech in the families of Southern English people who have been educated at the public schools.[1] This pronunciation is also used (sometimes with modifications) by those who do not come from Southern England, but who have been educated at these schools. The pronunciation may also be heard, to an extent which is considerable though difficult to specify, from natives of Southern England who have not been educated at these schools. It is probably accurate to say that a majority of Londoners who have had a university education, use either this pronunciation or a pronunciation not differing greatly from it.[2]

4. I believe that the pronunciation above referred to is readily understood in most parts of the English-speaking world. This result is perhaps due to the boarding-school system of education prevalent in England. For centuries past, boys from all parts of Great Britain have been educated together in boarding-schools. If a boy in such a school has a marked local peculiarity in his pronunciation, it generally disappears or is modified during his school career under the influence of the different mode of speaking which he hears continually around him; he consequently emerges from school with a pronunciation similar to that of the other boys. Similar considerations apply to modern boarding-schools for girls.

5. In day schools local pronunciations do not disappear nearly as readily as in the boarding-schools, because the pupils continually hear

---

[1] 'Public school' in the English sense, not in the American sense.
[2] The pronunciation is in the main that which I use myself. I have, however, put my pronunciation in a secondary place in all cases where another form appears to me to be in more frequent use. Readers may like to know that my father and mother were both Londoners, and that I have lived all my life in or near London. I was educated at Radley College (Abingdon), University College School (London) and King's College, Cambridge.

the local pronunciation used around them. Nevertheless the fact remains that people in every important centre often have opportunities of hearing the above-mentioned pronunciation either from people who have had a public school education, or through the constant intercommunication with London, or through the school teachers or through broadcasting. For these reasons I think it probable that this form of speech is more widely understood with ease in Great Britain than any other form would be. It is often called 'Received Pronunciation' (abbreviation RP), for want of a better term. I should like it to be understood, however, that RP means merely 'widely understood pronunciation', and that I do not hold it up as a standard which everyone is recommended to adopt.

6. RP is, as far as I have been able to ascertain, also easily understood in South Africa, Australia and New Zealand, and by English-speaking Canadians. Even in the United States, where so many varieties of pronunciation are to be heard, it seems that this pronunciation is fairly universally understood without difficulty—a curious fact considering that American speech is not by any means always understood in England. When I was in America in 1925, several American teachers (mostly from New York and the North-Eastern part of the United States) informed me, somewhat to my surprise, that RP or RP with slight modifications would be a suitable standard for teaching in American schools. This view is probably no longer held. In any case, I cannot think that any attempt to introduce this pronunciation into America is likely to meet with success.

7. The fact that RP and approximations to it are easily *understood* almost everywhere in the English-speaking world does not mean that RP is *used* by a majority of English-speaking people. On the contrary, it is used by a rather small minority. There exist countless other ways of pronouncing English, some of them being used by large communities. Whether broadcasting will in the long run alter this state of things remains to be seen.

8. I would add here that I do not regard RP as intrinsically 'better' or more 'beautiful' than any other form of pronunciation. I have recorded it because it happens to be the only type of English pronunciation about which I am in a position to obtain full and accurate information.

9. I wish also to state that I have no intention of becoming either a reformer of pronunciation or a judge who decides what pronunciations are 'good' and what are 'bad'. My aim is to observe and record accurately, and I do not believe in the feasibility of imposing one particular form of pronunciation on the English-speaking world. I take the view that people should be allowed to speak as they like. And if the public wants a standardized pronunciation, I have no doubt that some appropriate standard will evolve itself. If there are any who think otherwise, it must be left to them to undertake the invidious task of deciding what is to be approved and what is to be condemned. This book will provide them with some of the materials they will require as a basis to work upon.

9a. Useful further information relating to RP will be found in Chapter IV of *Problems and Principles* by David Abercrombie (published by Longmans).

(1) *Utility in General*

10. This Dictionary will, it is hoped, prove useful to anyone who wishes to find out an existing pronunciation of words or proper names which he has seen written but never heard.[1] In addition it will be found to have the following special uses depending on the normal speech of the student.

(2) *Utility to the English Student who speaks with RP*

11. A study of this pronunciation will help such a student to realize what sounds he uses when he speaks. This knowledge is indispensable to him if he is called upon to teach his own pronunciation of English. It may also be of value to him if he is learning to speak a foreign language, and finds it necessary to compare his native speech habits with those of speakers of the language he wishes to acquire.

(3) *Utility to the English-speaking Student whose Pronunciation differs from that here recorded*

12. A study of RP will bring home to such a student the important fact, which is fundamental to all linguistic study, that great variations of pronunciation exist, and are to be expected.

13. If he is a teacher of English, it is desirable that he should be familiar with the main features of other types of English speech besides his own.

(4) *Utility to Foreign Learners*

14. Many foreign learners will no doubt consider one form of RP to be a suitable pronunciation for them to acquire, for the practical reasons that it is widely understood in the English-speaking world and that books dealing with it are easily accessible.

THE PHONETIC TRANSCRIPTION

15. The phonetic alphabet used in this Dictionary is that of the *Association Phonétique Internationale* (generally known in English as the IPA). For full particulars of this alphabet and the manner of using the symbols readers are referred to the Association's brochure *The Principles of the International Phonetic Association*, 1949 and subsequent editions; it is obtainable from the Secretary of the Association, Department of Phonetics, University College, London, W.C.1 (price 6s. 6d.).

16. Various types of phonetic transcription are possible within the framework of this or any other system. Their constructions depend upon the purposes for which the transcriptions are needed. Some

---

[1] Its use is thus the contrary of that of the *English Phonetic Dictionary* by H. Michaelis and myself (Carl Meyer, Hanover, 1912). That work was designed for those who wish to find out the current spelling of words they have heard but not seen written.

types are very simple, and comprise relatively few letters and marks; in such types many existing shades of sound are not designated by particular symbols, but are implied by conventions. Other types are more elaborate, and contain more symbols; some or many of the minuter distinctions of sound are shown by means of special symbols, with the result that there are fewer conventions.

17. The simplest kind of phonetic transcription is one which represents one definite form of the language and which is both linguistically and typographically 'broad'. By 'linguistically broad' is meant 'phonemic', i.e. based on the principle 'one symbol per phoneme'.[1] By 'typographically broad' is meant 'using the minimum number of letter shapes of simplest Romanic form'.[2] More elaborate kinds of transcription comprise additional symbols or marks introduced for one or more of the following purposes:
(1) to denote particular 'allophones',[3] (2) to show that sounds of the language transcribed differ from analogous sounds of one or more other languages or dialects, (3) to make the system adaptable to more than one way of pronouncing the language transcribed. When a system introduces special symbols for purpose (1) above, it is said to be 'allophonic' or 'linguistically narrow'. When it introduces special symbols for purpose (2), it is said to be 'comparative' or 'typographically narrow'. When it comprises symbols for purpose (3), it is said to be 'inclusive'.[4]

18. For the general theory of types of phonetic transcription and the terminology applicable to the various types, readers are referred to Appendix A in the 1956 and subsequent editions of my *Outline of English Phonetics* (published by Heffer, Cambridge), in which the subject is discussed in considerable detail, and to the article 'Phonetic Transcriptions' by D. Abercrombie in *Le Maître Phonétique*, July–December 1953.

19. The form of phonetic transcription of English used in this Dictionary is of an intermediate type. If the book had been designed solely for the use of the foreign learner needing a representation of one particular kind of English pronunciation which he can take as a model, a simpler notation might have been used. Very suitable for such a purpose is the 'Simplified IPA Transcription' employed, for instance, in my book *The Phoneme*, in the books for foreign learners by MacCarthy, Scott and Tibbitts, in Hornby and Parnwell's *English-Reader's Dictionary* and in numerous articles by myself and others which have appeared in *Le Maître Phonétique* since 1930.[5] The present Dictionary, however, covers a wider field. It is intended as a work of reference for English-speaking people as well as for foreign learners, and is designed both for those who take interest in phonetics as a subject and for those who desire informa-

---

[1] For the term 'phoneme' see various books on phonetics, e.g. my *Outline of English Phonetics* (9th ed., 1960), pp. 49, 50, and *The Pronunciation of English* (4th ed., 1956), p. 165, or in greater detail *The Phoneme* (3rd ed., 1967), and K. L. Pike's *Phonemics* (University of Michigan Press, 1947).
[2] See *Outline of English Phonetics* (9th ed., 1960), Appendix A, §§ 5, 13.
[3] i.e. 'members of phonemes'. See *Outline of English Phonetics* (1956), §197, or *The Pronunciation of English* (4th ed., 1956), § 497, or *The Phoneme*, § 24.
[4] See *Outline of English Phonetics* (9th ed., 1960), Appendix A, §§ 24–27.
[5] Simplified IPA Transcription represents adequately one type of Southern English without recourse to the special vowel letters « ɛ », « æ », « ɑ » and « ɔ » used in this Dictionary.

tion not only on one particular form of English but also on the most important varieties of pronunciation which may be considered as coming within the range of RP.

20.[1] To this end the present phonetic transcription has to be more 'inclusive' than the Simplified IPA Transcription (see (3) in § 17 above). In particular the following variants (which are unimportant from the point of view of the foreign learner) are shown by means of it:

(1) the occasional lengthening of « æ »,
(2) the reduction of the sequences « eiə », « ouə », « oui » to diphthongs « eə », « oə », « oi » (distinct from « ɛə », « ɔə », « ɔi »),
(3) the use of a monophthongal « o »-sound (distinct from « ɔ ») in various unstressed syllables where either « ou » or « ə » or sometimes « u » are also possible.

The transcription is moreover 'internally comparative' to the extent of providing a special symbol « a » (separate from « æ » and « ɑ ») to denote the beginning parts of the diphthongs « ai » and « au ».

21. Four other variant pronunciations are demonstrable by the transcription used here, but it has not seemed to me necessary to include them. They are the occasional lengthening of the traditionally short « e » and « ʌ », and the reduction of « aiə » to a diphthong « aə » or to a monophthongal « a: » (distinct from « ɑ: »). Yet other variants which might be considered to come within the range of RP exist, but they are not shown in this Dictionary because their inclusion would necessitate a considerable elaboration of the transcription. There are, for instance, many Southern English people who at times lengthen the traditionally short « i », « u » and « ɔ », and there are some who reduce « auə » to a diphthong of the « aə »-type (distinct from the corresponding reduction of « aiə ») or to a monophthong of the « a: »-type (distinct from « ɑ: » and also distinct from the reduction of « aiə »). To represent these variants would necessitate the introduction and use throughout the book of four further phonetic symbols, which would I believe seriously impair the legibility and therefore the value of the transcripts.

22. For the same reason I have judged it inadvisable to narrow the transcription (as some have urged me to do) by indicating a third degree of length, or by using a special sign for 'dark' « l », or by introducing a special vowel-letter to denote the ordinary English short « e » on the ground that it differs from the French sounds of *é* and *è*.

---

[1] [Certain of the variants mentioned in this paragraph have been omitted from the present edition: in particular, « ou » is now replaced by « əu », and the monophthongal « o » no longer used. See Editor's Preface, p. viii—A. C. G.]

EXPLANATIONS

I. How to read the Entries

ALL entries in this Dictionary are to be taken as facts ascertained, or in some cases expressions of opinion, by the author. Thus the entry

celluloid 'seljulɔid

is to be taken to mean 'The word written in conventional spelling **celluloid** is, in my opinion, generally pronounced « 'seljulɔid » in ordinary conversation by the people referred to in § 3 of the Introduction, subject to variations referred to in the notes in Section XXIV of these Explanations (pp. xxxii–xliii). Similarly the entry

Batho 'bæθəu, 'beiθəu

means that I have ascertained that some people with the name spelt **Batho** pronounce « 'bæθəu » and others pronounce « 'beiθəu ».

II. Meaning of [ ]

Where two (or more) pronunciations of a word are current among the people referred to in § 3 of the Introduction, and neither (or none) of the forms can be considered rare (relatively to the frequency of the word), both (or all) are as a rule given, the less frequent form (or forms) being enclosed in square brackets [ ]. The only common variants not included are those mentioned in the Introduction, § 21 (p. xxi), and in Sections XXIII and XXIV of these Explanations (pp. xxxi, xxxii). Thus the entry

dynastic di'næstik [dai'n-]

is to be taken to mean that the forms « di'næstik » and « dai'næstik » both occur in RP, « di'næstik » being in my opinion the more frequent.

In a few cases for convenience, and especially where it was particularly difficult to form an idea of the relative frequency of variants, the forms have simply been separated by commas. This is done, for instance, in the entries **into, Rand,** and interjections like **humph, phew.**

III. Rare Pronunciations

Pronunciations which are undoubtedly rare (relatively to the frequency of the word) in the speech of those referred to in § 3 of the Introduction are not as a rule included in the Dictionary. In cases where for some special reason it has been thought desirable to mention the existence of such rarer forms, the fact that they are not of the same degree of commonness as other variants has been shown by the addition of '*rarely*', '*old-fashioned*', or some other qualifying term.

IV. Meaning of Italic Letters

When two pronunciations of a word are distinguished by the insertion or omission of a single sound, and both forms appear to be of approximately equal frequency, the fact is indicated by printing the symbol of the optional sound in italics. Thus the entry

defamatory di'fæmətəri

is to be taken to mean that the forms « di'fæmətəri » and « di'fæmətri » both occur in RP, the two forms being, as far as I am able to judge, of approximately equal frequency.

In the case of « ei*ə* » the use of italic « *i* » is to be taken to mean not only that the words transcribed with this symbol are said either with the disyllabic sequence « eiə » or with the diphthong « eə », but also that they may be said with the disyllabic sequence « e-ə ». See Explanations XX and XXIV B below. Thus the entry

player 'plei*ə**

implies three pronunciations of the word, viz. « 'pleiə* », « pleə* », « 'ple-ə* ». [Amended. A. C. G.]

V. MEANING OF (:)

When two variant pronunciations are distinguished by the use of « i: » and « i », « u: » and « u », or « ə: » and « ə », and the two forms appear to be of fairly equal frequency, the notation « i(:) », « u(:) », « ə(:) » has been adopted. Thus the entries

trio 'tri(:)əu
duplicity dju(:)'plisiti
interpenetrate ,intə(:)'penitreit

are to be taken to mean that the forms « 'tri:əu » and « 'triəu » both occur in RP, and seem to be of approximately equal frequency; and similarly with « dju:'plisiti » and « dju'plisiti », « ,intə:'penitreit » and « ,intə'penitreit ».

When (:) intervenes between « i » and « ə », it is to be understood that besides having pronunciations with « i:ə » and the diphthong « iə », the word can also be pronounced with a sequence « iə » said in a disyllabic manner (phonetically « i-ə », see Explanations XX, p. xxx). The same applies to (:) intervening between « u » and « ə ». Thus the entries

seer 'si(:)ə*
truant 'tru(:)ənt

are to be interpreted to mean that there exist not only the pronunciations « 'si:ə* », « siə* », « 'tru:ənt », « truənt » but also « 'si-ə* », « 'tru-ənt ».

VI. MEANING OF (')

The notation (') means that the syllable following is sometimes pronounced with strong stress and sometimes not, and that the two pronunciations appear to be of nearly equal frequency. Thus the entry

inclemency in'klemənsi ['in'k-, (')iŋ'k-]

is to be understood to mean that in addition to the pronunciations « in'klemənsi » and « 'in'klemənsi » there exist less usual forms « iŋ'klemənsi » and « 'iŋ'klemənsi », and that, as far as I can judge, the two stressings of the pronunciations with « ŋ » are of about equal frequency.

VII. COMBINATIONS OF VARIANT FORMS

When two or more variant pronunciations are indicated, it is to be understood that the forms may be combined in so far as they may be compatible with each other. Thus the entry

Australia ɔs'treiljə [ɔ:s-, -liə]

is to be taken to mean that the four forms « ɔs'treiljə », « ɔ:s'treiljə », « ɔs'treiliə », « ɔ:s'treiliə », all occur in RP, « ɔs'treiljə » being probably the most frequent.

Similarly the entry

distinction dis'tiŋ*k*ʃən

is to be taken to mean that the four forms « dis'tiŋkʃən », « dis'tiŋʃən », « dis-'tiŋkʃn », « dis'tiŋʃn », all occur in RP, and are of approximately equal frequency.

VIII. Variant Spellings

Square brackets [ ] are also used to show variant spellings of words written in conventional spelling in more than one way, but the use of these brackets has in this case no reference to the frequency of either spelling. Thus the two spellings **iron-gray, iron-grey** are grouped together under the notation

iron-gray [-grey]

Variations of spelling distinguished by the presence or absence of a single letter are shown, when convenient, by enclosing that letter in round brackets ( ). Thus the two spellings **zincky, zinky** are grouped together under the notation **zin(c)ky.**

In like manner, proper names which have the same pronunciation, but spellings differing by the presence or absence of a single letter, are often combined by enclosing that letter in round brackets ( ). Thus the entry

Ham(m)ond 'hæmənd

is to be taken to mean that the proper names **Hammond** and **Hamond** are both pronounced « 'hæmənd ».

The above devices are not resorted to when the two spellings would be widely separated from each other in the alphabetical order of the words, as in the case of **coloration** and **colouration.**

IX. Proper Names Identical with Ordinary Words

When a proper name is identical with an ordinary word both in conventional spelling and in pronunciation, the fact is indicated by placing a capital letter in round brackets ( ) after the ordinary spelling of the word. Thus the entry

hay (H.) hei

is to be taken to mean that the noun **hay** and the proper name **Hay** are both pronounced « hei ».

When two proper names exist, one of which is identical in spelling and pronunciation with the singular and the other with the plural of an ordinary noun, the one bracketed capital letter placed after the singular noun is to be understood to cover also the name having the plural form. Thus the (G.) in the entry

gibbon (G.), -s 'gibən, -z

is to be taken to show that **Gibbons** is pronounced « 'gibənz » as well as that **Gibbon** is pronounced « 'gibən ». Where, however, a name of plural form has a different pronunciation from that of the plural noun, it is given as a separate entry (*e.g.* **Gillies**).

X. Proper Names Pronounced Differently but Spelt the Same

When two differently pronounced proper names happen to have the same conventional spelling, the different pronunciations are separated by commas. Thus the entry

Bowden 'bəudn, 'baudn

is to be taken to mean that there is a proper name **Bowden** pronounced « 'bəudn » and another proper name **Bowden** pronounced « 'baudn ».

Similarly with **Batho, Jaques, Laing, Powell, Rowan,** and many others.

XI. Words grouped under Head-words

The pronunciations of all plurals of nouns are shown under the singulars; all comparatives and superlatives of adjectives and inflected forms of verbs are given under the simple words from which they are derived. Likewise nouns formed from other words by means of the terminations **-er, -ing, -ment, -or** or **-ness,** and adverbs formed by adding the termination **-ly** will as a rule be found under the words from which they may be considered to be derived. Thus **talker, meeting** (noun), **annulment,** will be found under **talk, meet, annul.**

Other derivatives are also grouped under simple words, when no difficulty in finding them is caused thereby. Thus **refractive** will be found under **refract, motherhood** and **motherless** under **mother.**

The derived forms of words are not as a rule written out in full, but the terminations to be added are each preceded by a hyphen and divided by a comma, or sometimes by a semicolon, from what precedes. Thus the entry

afford, -s, -ing, -ed ə'fɔːd, -z, -iŋ, -id

is to be taken to mean that in RP the words **afford, affords, affording, afforded** are pronounced « ə'fɔːd », « ə'fɔːdz », « ə'fɔːdiŋ », « ə'fɔːdid ».

When the final part of the spelling of a head-word is not repeated before adding a termination, the part to be repeated is marked off by a vertical line | (see, for instance, **addendum, fade**). The same thing is done when the final part undergoes some alteration in pronunciation, though not in spelling, in an inflected form (see, for instance, **house, nocturnal,** where | precedes the **-se** and the **-al**).

Words not grammatically connected (and especially proper names) are often similarly grouped together, with or without the use of the mark |, where no difficulty in finding the words is caused thereby. Thus the entry.

Ruther|ford, -glen 'rʌðə|fəd, -glen

is to be taken to mean that in RP **Rutherford** is pronounced « 'rʌðəfəd » and **Rutherglen** « 'rʌðəglen ».

The mark / is often used to indicate derivatives of words grouped under a head-word. Thus the entry

elegan|ce, -t/ly 'eligən|s, -t/li

is to be taken to mean that in RP the words **elegance, elegant, elegantly** are pronounced « 'eligəns », « 'eligənt », « 'eligəntli ».

When one or more derived words are grouped under a head-word as explained above, and a variant pronunciation of the head-word is given, that variant is to be taken to apply to all the derived words in so far as this may be possible. Thus it is to be understood from the entry

Galt, -on gɔːlt [gɔlt], -ən

that **Galton** as well as **Galt** is subject to the variant pronunciation with « ɔ ».

XII. Stress of Derived Words

When the head-word is a monosyllable, and a termination for forming a derived word adds another syllable, it is to be understood that the derived word has a strong stress on the root-syllable. Thus from the entry

nine, -s, -fold nain, -z, -fəuld

it is to be understood that **ninefold** has single stress (on the first syllable). And from the entry

ewe, -s; -lamb/s juː, -z; -'læm/z

it is to be understood that in **ewe-lamb** both syllables have strong stress.

When a head-word is a *compound* of which the second element is a weakly stressed monosyllable, and a termination for forming a derived word adds yet another syllable, it is to be understood that the derived word has secondary stress on the first syllable of the second element, except when otherwise indicated. Thus from the entries

> **greenhou|se, -ses** 'gri:nhau|s, -ziz
> **shockhead, -s, -ed** 'ʃɔkhed, -z, -id

it is to be understood that **greenhouses** and **shockheaded** are pronounced « 'gri:n,hauziz », « 'ʃɔk,hedid ».

It is shown, however, under **tea-cup** that **tea-cupful** has secondary stress on the final syllable, thus « 'ti:kʌp,ful ».

XIII. Variations of Stress

Variations of stress are indicated in many cases by representing the syllables of the word in question by hyphens, instead of writing the word out in its entirety. Thus in the entry

> **Waterloo** ,wɔ:tə'lu: ['--'-, '---]

the indications '--'-, '--- signify the pronunciations « 'wɔ:tə'lu: », « 'wɔ:təlu: ». Sometimes (as in this case) a note is appended stating in what circumstances or by whom the variants are used.

XIV. Abbreviated Spellings

A certain number of common abbreviations (such as **Bros., Chas., cwt., E.C., MSS., q.v., V.I.P.**) are included in the Dictionary. These are arranged in alphabetical order according to the letters composing them.

XV. Linking « r » and Intrusive « r »

When a word ending in « ə » (including « iə », « ɛə », etc.), « ɑ: » « ɔ: » or « ə: » is immediately followed in a connected sentence by a word beginning with a vowel in close grammatical connexion with it, the sound « r » is very often inserted at the end of it, joining it to the next word. (There are two common exceptions to this general rule: (1) The insertion of « r » is unusual if a pause is possible between the words, even if no pause is actually made. (2) Words ending in « -rə » (« -riə », « -rɛə », etc.), « -rɑ: », « -rɔ: », « -rə: », are exceptional and are very often not pronounced with this added « r ». For examples see the end of the third paragraph of this Section.)

When the ordinary spelling of the word ends in the letter **r** (or **-re** in some words, such as **are, more, centre**), the inserted « r »-sound is called a 'linking « r »'. When there is no written **r** in the spelling, the inserted « r »-sound is called an 'intrusive « r »'. [1]

---

[1] It is the origin of the added « r » which determines whether it is called 'linking' or 'intrusive'. 'Linking « r »' is a relic of the old pronunciation of English when all written *r*'s were pronounced, that is to say when *r*'s were sounded finally and before consonants as well as before vowels—as they still are in many forms of the language. 'Intrusive « r »' is a comparatively recent innovation. It has evidently been brought about by analogy, and dates doubtless from the time when « r » ceased to be sounded in final positions. It is believed that a dropping of final « r » began in the fifteenth century and became general in south-eastern England in the course of the seventeenth. It is reasonable to suppose that the analogical 'intrusive « r »' came into existence at the same time. Its existence was mentioned by some late eighteenth-century writers, who called it a vulgarism (see Jespersen, *Modern English Grammar*, Vol. I, § 13.42).

The following are examples of 'linking « r »'. The words **order, bear, clear, hour, far, more, incur** when said by themselves contain no « r »-sound in RP; they are pronounced « 'ɔ:də », « beə », « kliə », « auə », « fɑ: », « mɔ: » or « mɔə », « in'kə: ». But in such expressions as **order of merit, bear up, clear it away, an hour or two, far off, more effective, to incur a debt** it is usual in RP to insert the sound « r », thus « 'ɔ:dər əv 'merit », « 'beər 'ʌp », « 'kliər it ə'wei », « ən'auər ɔ: tu: », « 'fɑ:r 'ɔf », « 'mɔ:r i'fektiv » or « 'mɔər i'fektiv », « tu in'kə:r ə 'det ». Instances of cases where 'linking « r »' is not as a rule inserted, as mentioned in the first paragraph of this section, are (1) **he opened the door and walked in, we'll go there later if there's time** (« hi: 'əupnd ðə 'dɔ: ənd 'wɔ:kt 'in », « wi: l 'gəu ðeə 'leitə if ðeə z 'taim »), (2) **an error of judgment, a roar of laughter** (« ən 'erə əv 'dʒʌdʒmənt », « ə 'rɔ: əv 'lɑ:ftə »).

The following are examples of 'intrusive « r »'. The words **sofa, Asia, idea, papa, jackdaw** likewise contain no « r »-sound when said in isolation; they are normally pronounced « 'səufə », « 'eiʃə », « ai'diə », « pə'pɑ: », « 'dʒækdɔ: ». But it is quite common to hear people of the type referred to in § 3 of the Introduction add the sound « r » in such expressions as **the sofa over there, Asia and Africa, the idea of it, Papa isn't here, the Jackdaw of Rheims**, thus « ðə 'səufər əuvə 'ðeə », « 'eiʃər ənd 'æfrikə », « ði ai'diər əv it », « pə'pɑ:r iznt 'hiə », « ðə 'dʒækdɔ:r əv 'ri:mz ».[1]

'Linking « r »' is never added to vowel-sounds other than « ə », « ɑ: », « ɔ: » or « ə: », and 'intrusive « r »' is never added to vowel-sounds other than « ə », « ɑ: » or « ɔ: »

The use of linking « r » and intrusive « r » is a very noteworthy feature of south-eastern English. There is, however, much variation in the way different people employ them. Many use them both consistently, some employ linking « r » consistently but do not use intrusive « r », some (especially younger people) do not use either; others again use one or the other or both irregularly.

There are four types of consistent pronouncers: (1) those who never use intrusive « r » at all but who always insert linking « r » in the circumstances described in the first paragraph of this Section, (2) those who always insert linking « r » in these circumstances and who introduce an intrusive « r » regularly after words ending in « ə » and « iə » in the same circumstances, (3) those who use linking « r » similarly but who insert intrusive « r » regularly after « ɑ: » and « ɔ: » as well as after « ə » and « iə », (4) those who never use intrusive « r » and either never employ linking « r » at all or confine its use to a few stock expressions such as **for instance, as a matter of fact, later on** (« fər 'instəns », « əz ə 'mætr ə 'fækt », « 'leitər 'ɔn »).

My own pronunciation used to be, and generally still is, of type (1). In recent years, however, I have occasionally found myself using intrusive « r » after « ə », though not in accordance with any system. I do not use intrusive « r » after « ɑ: » or « ɔ: ».

Those whose pronunciation is of type (4) say not only « ðə 'səufə əuvə 'ðeə », « 'eiʃə ənd 'æfrikə », etc., like those whose pronunciation is of type (1), but also « 'ɔ:də əv 'merit », « 'beə 'ʌp », « 'kliə it ə'wei », etc.

It does not seem possible to estimate which, if any, of these ways of pronouncing is the commonest among those who speak with RP. When teaching English to foreign learners, I find it convenient to recommend them to speak as type (1).

---

[1] This last pronunciation was used whenever **jackdaw** was followed by a word beginning with a vowel throughout a fine BBC broadcast of the poem in 1953.

XVI. MEANING OF *

In this Dictionary an asterisk * is placed at the end of every word to which linking « r » is added in appropriate contexts by those whose pronunciation is of the type (1) described in the seventh paragraph of Section XV. Words ending in « ə », « ɑ: » or « ɔ: » which have no asterisk do not take intrusive « r » in the speech of those who pronounce as type (1); they are said with intrusive « r » in the above-mentioned contexts by those who pronounce as type (3).

The asterisk is to be dropped in the transcription of derivatives of words marked with it. Thus the entry

flatter, -s, -ing/ly, -ed, -er/s 'flætə*, -z, -rɪŋ/li, -d, -rə*/z

is to be taken to mean that in RP the words **flatter, flatters, flattering, flatteringly, flattered, flatterer, flatterers** are pronounced « 'flætə », « 'flætəz », « 'flætərɪŋ », « 'flætərɪŋli », « 'flætəd », « 'flætərə », « 'flætərəz ». And the entry

tar (s. v.), **-s, -ring, -red** tɑ:*, -z, -rɪŋ, -d

is to be taken to mean that in RP the words **tar, tars, tarring, tarred** are pronounced « tɑ: », « tɑ:z », « 'tɑ:rɪŋ », « tɑ:d ».

XVII. INCOMPLETE PLOSIVE CONSONANTS

It is to be understood throughout that when two plosive consonants occur next to each other in a word, as in **act** (« ækt »), **bedtime** (« bedtaim »), the first is pronounced by most people without plosion, or with the least possible plosion. Cases of unexploded stop not coming under this general rule are indicated by placing the sign ° immediately after the consonant symbol (as in « nəup° » a variant pronunciation of the interjection **no**).

XVIII. SYLLABIC CONSONANTS

The fact that a consonant is syllabic is marked (by placing the mark ˌ under the letter) only when there might be ambiguity. Thus the syllabic « l » is specially marked in « 'flænl̩i » (**flannelly**), because « flænli » would indicate a pronunciation rhyming with **Hanley**. It is not needful to mark the syllabicity of the « l » in such a word as **bottle** « 'bɔtl », since the sound cannot be other than syllabic in this situation.

XIX. SYLLABLE SEPARATION, USE OF THE HYPHEN AS A PHONETIC SIGN

It is necessary in phonetic notation to have a means of showing 'syllable separation' for use in all circumstances where the absence of suitable marking might lead to ambiguity in the interpretation of a phonetically transcribed word. An indication of a place of syllable separation does not mean that there is any cessation of sound at that place. It means that the sound preceding the place of separation is pronounced as if it were final, and that the sound following is pronounced as if it were initial. This in turn may imply that the syllable preceding the place of separation is said with particular 'allophones' and degrees of length appropriate to final positions, and that the syllable following begins with allophones appropriate to initial positions.

When the second of two consecutive syllables bears a stress (primary or secondary), the place of separation between the syllables is shown by the stress-mark. For instance, the position of the ˌ in « 'ʃi:tˌæŋkə* » (given as the pronunciation of **sheet-anchor** in this Dictionary) shows that there is syllable separation between the « t » and the « æ ». It would be possible to pronounce the same sequence of phonemes with syllable separation between the « i: » and the « t », thus « 'ʃi:ˌtæŋkə* », though a word pronounced like this does not happen to exist. This pronunciation would differ markedly in sound from « 'ʃi:tˌæŋkə* ». In « 'ʃi:ˌtæŋkə* » the « i: » would be fully long and the « t » would be strong and aspirated, but in « 'ʃi:tˌæŋkə* » the « i: » is not very long and the « t » is weak and lacking in aspiration. The principles underlying these differences are explained in my *Outline of English Phonetics*, 1960, §§ 512, 866.

So also if we compare the separated « tr » of « aut'reidʒəs » (**outrageous**) from the non-separated « tr » of « ə'træktiv » (**attractive**), we find that the « t » of « aut'reidʒəs » is weak and the « r » is fully voiced, whereas in « ə'træktiv » the « t » is strong and the « r » is partially or wholly breathed. Again, many English people (including myself) distinguish the « r » of « ˌəuvər'ɔ:d » (**overawed**) from that of « ˌəuvə'rɔ:t » (**overwrought**). The « r » of « ˌəuvə'rɔ:t » is either the common fricative or the common ' frictionless continuant' sound, but the « r » of « ˌəuvər'ɔ:d » is or may be the 'flapped' variety described in *Outline of English Phonetics*, §§ 750, 753.

When the second of two consecutive syllables does not need a stress-mark, essential syllable separation has to be shown by a special mark. A hyphen is convenient for this purpose, and is used in the present Dictionary.

Thus the hyphen in « 'bai-plein » (**biplane**) shows (1) that the « ai » is treated as if it were final and is therefore fully long, in accordance with the principle formulated in *Outline of English Phonetics*, § 866, and (2) that the « p » is treated as if it were initial and that in consequence the « l » following it is breathed or only partially voiced, as explained in *Outline*, § 845 (i)*a*. The word « 'bai-plein » may be compared with « 'paip-lain » (**pipe-line**), in which the syllable separation is between the « p » and the « l ». Here the position of the hyphen shows (1) that the « p » preceding it is treated as if it were final and that in consequence the « ai » is rather short, in accordance with the principle formulated in *Outline*, § 866, and (2) that the « l », being treated as if it were initial, is fully voiced.

Similarly the hyphen inserted in the transcription « 'ʃel-fiʃ » (**shell-fish**) shows that the « l » is treated as if it were final and is consequently pronounced long as explained in *Outline*, § 881, while the absence of any hyphen in « 'selfiʃ » (**selfish**) implies that the « l » is not so treated, but is short on account of the presence of the following « f ». « 'bi:-stiŋz » (**bee-stings,** stings of bees) is distinguished from « 'bi:stiŋz » (**beestings,** first milk of a cow) in a similar way ; the hyphen in « 'bi:-stiŋz » shows that the « i: » is fully long, while the absence of hyphen in « 'bi:stiŋz » implies that the vowel is rather short in consequence of the presence of the following « s ».

Further examples illustrating the necessity for hyphens as markers of syllable separation are « 'təu-stræp » (**toe-strap**), which should be compared with « 'maus-træp » (**mouse-trap**) and with « 'təust-ræk » (**toast-rack**) ; « 'wilt-ʃə » (**Wiltshire**) which may be compared with « 'piltʃəd » (**pilchard**). Many others will be found in *Outline of English Phonetics*, 1960, Chap. XXXII.

In the form of transcription used in this Dictionary « tʃ » is always to be taken to be a 'digraph' with the 'affricate' value when the two letters are not separated by a hyphen. See Section XXIV C, p. xxxv.

The presence of a phonetic hyphen will be assumed, wherever necessary, in front of the terminations of derivatives and other words grouped under a head-word. Thus it is to be understood in « 'delft-wɛə* » (**Delft-ware**), « 'gəul-pəust » (**goal-post**), since the transcriptions « 'delftwɛə* », « 'gəulpəust » might be thought to stand for the non-existent pronunciations « 'delf-twɛə* », « 'gəulp-əust ».

For the use of - in « i-ə », « u-ə », « ai-ə », « au-ə », etc., see next Section.

EXPLANATIONS

XX. Disyllabic « i-ə », « u-ə », etc.

It is possible to pronounce sequences of « i » and « ə », « u » and « ə », « e » and « ə », « u » and « i » in a disyllabic manner as well as in the gliding (diphthongal) manner. The disyllabic way of pronouncing is sometimes used in English, especially in slow utterance of certain classes of words. It may be represented in phonetic transcription by inserting hyphens, thus « i-ə », « u-ə », « e-ə », etc. This notation is employed for explanatory purposes in these Explanations, but except in the cases of « ai-ə » and « au-ə » it is not used in the body of this Dictionary. The reason for this is that these disyllabic sequences « i-ə », « u-ə », etc., are always alternatives to other pronunciations, and their occurrences may be deduced from the following facts:

(1) « i-ə » and « u-ə » are always possible alternatives to the 'rising' diphthongs « ĭə » and « ŭə » (for which see Explanations XXIV B, p. xxxv). For instance, « 'glɔːrĭəs (**glorious**), « 'ɑːdjŭəs » (**arduous**) may also be pronounced « 'glɔːri-əs », « 'ɑːdju-əs ».

(2) « i-ə » and « u-ə » are always possible alternatives to the common 'falling' diphthongs « iə » and « uə » in the words which have variant pronunciations with « iːə » and « uːə », such as **seer, freer, Fleance, doer, fewer, truant** (see Explanations V, p. xxiii. [Amended. A. C. G.]

(3) « e-ə » and « u-i » are always possible alternatives to the diphthongs « eə » (as in **gayer**) and « ui » (as in **screwing**). For « e-ə », see also Explanations IV, p. xxiii. [Amended. A. C. G.]

(4) The notation « ai-ə » is employed when « ai » is fully pronounced and « ə » follows it forming a definite separate syllable. This sequence, which may be heard in such words as « 'ʃai-ə* » (**shyer**), « 'flai-ə* » (**flyer**), is distinct from the common « aiə » of « 'ʃaiə* » (**shire**), « 'faiəri » (**fiery**), etc., which is nearly a monosyllable and which has monosyllabic variants « aə » and « aː ». Similarly « au-ə » is used to denote the definitely disyllabic sequence heard in « 'plau-ə* » (**plougher**). This sequence is distinct from the common « auə » of « 'flauə* » (**flour**), which is nearly monosyllabic and which is replaceable by monosyllabic forms of the type « aə » and « aː ». See Explanations XXIII (4), p. xxxii; also *Outline of English Phonetics*, 1960, §§ 414, 415, 434. [Amended. A. C. G.]

XXI. Strong and Weak Forms

The mention '*strong form*' appended to a pronunciation means that the form in question is one used when the word is stressed. The designation '*weak form*' means that (in the absence of a special statement to the contrary) the form in question occurs only in unstressed positions.

It is to be understood that circumstances exist in which strong forms occur unstressed, but that weak forms do not bear strong stress except in a few rare instances where special mention is made of the possibility of such stressing (see for instance **because, just**).

Unless the term '*weak form*' is amplified by some such qualification as '*occasional*' it is to be understood that the weak form (or one or other of the weak forms, when several are given) is the pronunciation most usually heard when the word is unstressed.

XXII. Variant Pronunciations of the Unstressed Terminations -less, -ness, etc.

The unstressed terminations **-less** (as in **helpless**), **-ness** (as in **goodness**), **-ess** (as in **hostess**), **-est** (as in **quickest**), **-et** (as in **ticket**), **-es** (as in **places**), **-ed** (as in **waited**), **-age** (as in **village**) are recorded in this Dictionary as having the vowel « i »; thus « 'helplis », « 'gudnis », « 'həustis », etc. This is the pronunciation I use, and is I believe that most commonly employed by non-dialectal southern English speakers. It must be observed, however, that there do exist well-educated English people who speak in most respects with RP but who use the vowel « ə » in some, or possibly all, of these terminations. I have the impression that such speakers have had their speech influenced by contacts with people from northern or eastern parts of England (including Essex), and that these special features of their pronunciation cannot properly be regarded as coming within the limits of what should be included in this Dictionary.

The same probably holds good for those words ending in **-en, -ain** and the substantival and adjectival **-ate** which are not shown in this Dictionary as having « -ən », « -ən », « -ət ». Such are **linen** (« 'linin »), **chicken** (« 'tʃikin »), **bargain** (« 'bɑ:gin »), **delicate** (« 'delikit »). Pronunciations with « ə » are given in the case of a few words with these terminations (e.g. **barren, stricken, chieftain, immediate**), where these forms appear to me to be usual in the type of English with which this Dictionary is concerned.[1]

XXIII. Other Variants of Sound-distribution occurring in RP but not as a rule noted in this Dictionary

It has for practical reasons not been possible to include in the body of the Dictionary *all* the variant pronunciations of every word. We give below some examples of the chief variants which it is possible to represent without recourse to a still 'narrower' system of phonetic notation, but which have generally been omitted from this Dictionary on practical grounds. All these varieties may be heard from the people referred to in § 3 of the Introduction.

(1) Omissions of « t » and « d » from various consonant sequences such as « nts », « ndz », « stn », e.g. « hins » for « hints » (**hints**), « saunz » for « saundz » (**sounds**), « 'stedfəsnis » for « 'stedfəstnis » (**steadfastness**).

---

[1] Examples of the use of « ə » in some of the above-mentioned terminations are to be found here and there in published phonetic texts. L. E. Armstrong used this vowel in **-less, -ness, -est, -en, -ain**, in the substantival and adjectival **-ate**, and in most though not all of the words ending in **-et**; thus we find in her *English Phonetic Reader* (University of London Press, 1923) **cutlet** written as « 'kʌtlət » and **carelessness** as « 'keələsnəs ». In her preface to that book she mentioned that these forms with « ə » were due to northern influence in her speech. She pronounced **-es, -ed** and **-age** with « i ».

More recently J. D. O'Connor, considering it useful that foreign learners should be aware of the existence of the variants « -ləs » and « -nəs », recorded these forms in two of the texts in his *New Phonetic Readings* (Francke, Berne, 1948). In his other texts he wrote « -lis », « -nis ». He moreover pronounces the substantival and adjectival **-ate** as « -ət », and has shown this pronunciation throughout. The other terminations mentioned above are transcribed by him with « i ». There are traces of northern influence in his speech.

Most of the other eminent English phoneticians (e.g. Sweet, Wyld, Ripman, Palmer, MacCarthy, Scott, Pring) have written all the terminations in question with « i » in their transcripts.

(2) Insertion of « t » between « n » and « s », or of « d » between « n » and « z », e.g. « fents » for « fens » (**fence**), « 'frendzi » for « 'frenzi » (**frenzy**).

(3) Very numerous assimilations and reductions due to the proximity of other words. Such are: « dʒʌʃ » for « dʒʌst » (often heard in **just shut the door**), « ðiʃ » for « ðis » (often heard in **this shop**), « dʌʒ » for « dʌz » (often heard in **does she**), « l̥'au », « ɲi » for «ə'lau», « 'eni » (often heard in **we're not allowed to, they haven't got any more**), « ri'main » for « ri'maind » (generally heard in **remind me**), « rɑːðr » for « 'rɑːðər » (often heard in **rather a good thing**) « 'daum bi'ləu » for « 'daun bi'ləu » (**down below**), « gu » for « gud » (as in **a good deal**).

(4) Reductions of « aiə » to « aə », « ɑə », « aː » or « ɑː », e.g. « di'zaərəbl » or « di'zɑərəbl » or « di'zaːrəbl » or « di'zɑːrəbl » for « di'zaiərəbl » (**desirable**), and « auə » to « ɑə » or « aə » or « ɑː », e.g. « 'kɔliflɑə » or « 'kɔliflaə » or « 'kɔliflɑː » for « 'kɔliflauə » (**cauliflower**).

(5) Many instances of possible reduction of final unstressed « -uː » to « -u », e.g. « 'reskju » for « 'reskjuː », a pronunciation which is frequent especially when another word follows, as in « 'reskju ðəm » (**rescue them**).

(6) Similar reductions of final « -ei » to « -e » in cases like « ə 'de ə tuː » (**a day or two**). [Amended. A. C. G.]

(7) The use of « -əti » for « -iti » in words like **necessity, quality** (exceptions being the words ending in **-bility**).

(8) The common use of the glottal stop in place of « t » and « k » in words like **department, tightly, quickly** (« di'pɑːʔmənt », « 'taiʔli », « 'kwiʔli »). See *Outline*, § 555, note 15; also *The Pronunciation of English*, 1956, §§ 234, 250, 258.

(9) Substitution of « m̩ », « n̩ », « ŋ̩ » for « p », « t », « k » in such words as **encampment, ointment, embankment** (« in'kæmm̩mənt », « 'ɔinŋ̩mənt », « im'bæŋŋ̩mənt »).

(10) Variations of stress and sound due to a desire to emphasize one part of a word, e.g. the form « 'kɔ'miʃən » (**commission**) which is sometimes used when the word is contrasted with **omission**.

(11) Reinforcement of secondary stress on the first syllable of a word for the purpose of giving greater emphasis to the whole word, e.g. « 'fʌndə'mentl » for « ˌfʌndə'mentl » (**fundamental**), « 'rekə'mend » for « ˌrekə'mend » (**recommend**), « 'stændədai'zeiʃən » for « ˌstændədai-'zeiʃən « (**standardization**).

(12) Variants with disyllabic « i-ə », « u-ə » « e-ə », « u-i ». See Explanations IV, V, XX, XXIV B. [Amended. A. C. G.]

For variants of sound-*formation* see next Section.

XXIV. Values of the Phonetic Symbols

A. *Table of Sounds*

The Table opposite shows the manner of forming the principal English speech-sounds. The descriptions (indicated by the technical terms) of the sounds denoted by the consonant-letters are of the 'norms' or 'principal

TABLE OF THE PRINCIPAL ENGLISH SOUNDS

	LABIAL		DENTAL	ALVEOLAR	POST-ALVEOLAR	PALATO-ALVEOLAR	PALATAL	VELAR	GLOTTAL
	Bi-labial	Labio-dental							
Plosive	p b			t d				k g	
Affricate						tʃ dʒ			
Nasal	m			n				ŋ	
Lateral				l					
Fricative		f v	θ ð	s z	r	ʃ ʒ		x	h
Semi-vowel	w						j	(w)	

CONSONANTS

Close	(uː) (u)
Half-close	
Half-open	(ɔː) (ɔ)
Open	

VOWELS

The secondary articulations of sounds having two places of articulation are shown by the symbols in ( ).

members' of the respective phonemes.[1] The positions of the vowel-letters in the Table give a rough idea of the tongue-positions taken up when the commonest vowel-sounds of RP are uttered. When there is lip action in addition to tongue action, the secondary articulation is shown by the symbol enclosed in round brackets ( ).

The arrangement of the vowel-symbols in the Table is a very simplified one, but it is nevertheless a convenient one to work with in the practical teaching of pronunciation. An arrangement of greater precision is shown in the Frontispiece. In that chart the nature of the commonest vowels of RP is demonstrated by comparisons with a set of eight suggested Cardinal Vowels. The IPA symbols for these cardinal vowels are

i	e	ε	a	ɑ	ɔ	o	u
1	2	3	4	5	6	7	8

The manner of their selection is described in *Outline of English Phonetics*, § 131 ff. The student who has in his mind the acoustic qualities of these Cardinal Vowels can estimate by ear and by muscular sensations the values to be attributed to symbols placed at different points on the chart. For instance if he knows the sounds of Cardinals 2 and 3 (shown by dots in the Frontispiece), he can judge what is meant by the English « e » (shown by a large dot in the Frontispiece), which is half way between the two.[2]

The shape of the Frontispiece chart and the placing on it of the dots indicating the relations between the different vowels were arrived at after much research. The relative positions of Cardinals 1, 4, 5 and 8 were ascertained by X-ray photography; the photographs from which the measurements were taken are reproduced in the frontispiece of my *Pronunciation of English* (1956 and subsequent editions). The placings of the other Cardinal Vowels and of all the English vowels on the quadrilateral figure thus obtained were judged by ear and muscular sensations. The chart is thus in the nature of a convenient compromise between scientifically ascertained facts and the practical needs of the language teacher.

The English vowels shown on the Frontispiece chart are the 'average' sounds described in Sub-section E below.

For full details as to the formation of English sounds, as also for the meanings of the technical terms, readers are referred to the various books on the phonetics of English. A few notes on the sounds and on the values to be attributed to the symbols are, however, subjoined here; and some short explanations of the chief technical terms are given in the Glossary at the end of this book.

---

[1] For the meaning of 'phoneme' see my *Outline of English Phonetics* (1956 and subsequent editions), Chapter X, or *The Pronunciation of English* (1956 and subsequent editions), § 492 ff., or in greater detail *The Phoneme, its Nature and Use* (3rd ed., 1967).

[2] The Cardinal Vowels should be learnt, if possible, from a teacher who knows them (see *Outline of English Phonetics*, § 140). Gramophone records have been made of them, and may be utilized by students who have not access to such a teacher. One such record is No. ENG 252–3, published by the Linguaphone Institute, 207 Regent Street, London, W.1. See further *Outline*, §§ 140, 141 and footnote 7 on p. 34.

Tape recordings of these Cardinal Vowels said on various pitches by twelve reliable phoneticians have been made by Dr P. Ladefoged, when he was Lecturer in Phonetics in the University of Edinburgh, as part of a research programme. Copies of these recordings can be made available for linguistic research institutions. (Particulars on application to the Secretary, Dept of Phonetics, Minto House, Chambers St, Edinburgh.)

The sound « x » shown in the Table facing p. xxxiii is only occasionally used, as a variant pronunciation, e.g. for the Scottish sound of **ch** in **loch**. [Amended. A. C. G.]

B. *Diphthongs*

Thirteen diphthongal sounds are recorded in this Dictionary. They cannot conveniently be entered in the Table, but their values can be judged fairly well from the letters used in their representation. Eleven of them (« ei », « ai », « ɔi », « ui », « au », « əu », « iə », « eə », « ɛə », « ɔə », « uə ») are 'falling' diphthongs, i.e. their beginnings have greater prominence than their endings. Two of them (« ïə » and « ŭə », as in **happier, influence**) are 'rising' diphthongs, i.e. their endings have greater prominence than their beginnings. In most of the diphthongs the falling or rising character is the natural result of the inherent sonorities of the vowel sounds of which they are composed. In « iə » (as in **clear**) and « uə » (as in **gourd**), however, the initial prominence is effected by a certain degree of special stress on the initial parts, since the inherent sonority of « ə » is greater than that of « i » and « u ». For a full discussion of the nature of « ïə » and « ŭə », and the differences between them and « iə », « uə », see *Outline of English Phonetics* (1956 and subsequent editions), §§ 466a–466u. [Amended. A. C. G.]

For the disyllabic sequences « i-ə », « u-ə », « e-ə », « u-i », see Explanations XX, p. xxx. See also my article 'Falling and Rising Diphthongs in Southern English' in *Miscellanea Phonetica* II, 1954, published by the IPA.[1] [Amended. A. C. G.]

For the 'levelling' of « aiə » and « auə » see *Outline of English Phonetics* (1956 and subsequent editions), §§ 414, 415, 430, 434.

C. *Digraphs*

A 'digraph' is a sequence of two letters used to represent a 'single sound'. The digraphs employed in this Dictionary are « tʃ », « dʒ », « hw », « ei », « əu », « ai » and the other sequences denoting diphthongs.

« tʃ » and « dʒ » are convenient symbols for representing the affricate consonants which we denote in ordinary spelling by **ch** (as in **church**) and **j** (as in **join**). Their use obviates the introduction of two additional phonetic symbols. In words where the sounds « t » and « ʃ » occur in juxtaposition and belong to different syllables, the letters are separated by a hyphen (see end of Section XIX, p. xxviii).

« hw » is a convenient digraph to denote 'voiceless « w »'. In this Dictionary it is to be taken to mean either this or alternatively the sequence « h » + « w ».

The diphthongs (« ei », « əu », « ai », etc.) are considered by some, including myself, to be 'single sounds', i.e. gliding sounds which begin with one vowel and glide towards another. Some authorities regard them as sequences of two sounds, namely the initial vowel and the glide. Whichever view is taken, it is convenient to represent them phonetically by sequences of two letters; if the first view is held, these sequences are digraphs.

---

[1] Obtainable from the Secretary of the International Phonetic Association, Department of Phonetics, University College, London, W.C.1.

D. *Allophonic Variants*

The values of most phonetic symbols vary to some extent according to the *phonetic context*. For instance the sound denoted by « k » in « ki: » (**key**) is not the same as that in « ku:l » (**cool**), and this again differs from the « k »-sound in « 'kɔtidʒ » (**cottage**). The sound used in each case is conditioned unambiguously by the phonetic environment, and the three sounds together with various other shades are said to 'belong to a single phoneme' or to be 'allophones' (or 'particular members') of one phoneme. Transcriptions of the above words are unambiguous if all the members of the phoneme are written with the same letter « k ».

Similar considerations apply to other symbols. A single letter denotes all the allophones of a phoneme unambiguously, as long as the conditions under which each allophone occurs are known and understood by conventions.

The following are a few particularly noteworthy examples of phonemes in English which contain allophones differing considerably from the 'norm' (principal member).

Both 'clear' and 'dark' varieties of « l » are met with in the speech of most of those referred to in § 3 of the Introduction. The majority of these speakers use a 'clear' or 'medium' type of « l » whenever a vowel follows (as in **leaf, lock**) and a 'dark' variety when the sound is final or followed by a consonant-sound (as in **feel, people, field**). The variety of « l » used in each case is conditioned unambiguously by its phonetic environment: the different varieties accordingly belong to a single phoneme, and the single letter « l » is consequently adequate for representing them all.

In the speech of many users of RP there are three distinct kinds of « r »-sound. The commonest is the voiced fricative entered in the Table facing p. xxxii. Another is the corresponding breathed sound, which is used by many after a voiceless consonant beginning a stressed syllable, as in « kri:m » (**cream**). Yet another is a 'flapped' « r » which occurs in the speech of many in unstressed positions between vowels as in **heritage, orator, overawe** (« 'əuvər'ɔː »). (In the speech of these people the « r » in « 'əuvər'ɔː » is different from the one in **overwrought** (« 'əuvə'rɔːt »,) which begins a stressed syllable.)

There are voiced kinds of « h » occurring as allophones of the « h »-phoneme. They occur between other voiced sounds; e.g. in **adhere, boyhood,** especially in rapid speaking.

The value to be attributed to the symbol « ə » varies considerably according to the phonetic context. A particularly 'open' variety is used in final positions, as when such words as **china, paper** are said by themselves or occur at the end of a sentence.[1]

In other phonetic contexts several other varieties of « ə » occur; the varieties used are conditioned by the nature of the adjacent sounds. The varieties extend from a sound near to « ʌ » (see Frontispiece) to a half-close central « ə » and in some cases (especially when next to « k » or « g ») to a still 'closer' sound. Three different varieties of « ə » may be heard in the words « 'tʃainə » (**china**) and « kə'θiːdrəl » (**cathedral**); in the latter word the first « ə » is a rather 'close' one, and the second is 'opener' and 'retracted' though distinct from the « ə » of **china**.[2]

---

[1] Some people indeed substitute the sound « ʌ » for it in this situation, pronouncing « 'tʃainʌ », « 'peipʌ ». This « ʌ » is not an allophone of the « ə »-phoneme; people who pronounce in this way substitute the « ʌ »-phoneme for the « ə »-phoneme in final positions.

[2] The subject of the allophones of the « ə »-phoneme is dealt with in greater detail in my *Outline of English Phonetics*, 1956, and subsequent editions, §§ 342, 355–70, and in *The Phoneme*, §§ 197–202.

None of the above-mentioned allophonic variants are shown by special symbols in this Dictionary. The precise sounds employed in each case are deducible from the phonetic contexts.

When a phonetic transcription contains a special symbol to denote a subsidiary member of a phoneme (i.e. an allophone other than the norm), it is said to be 'allophonic'. [Amended. A. C. G.]

Descriptions of allophones of phonemes other than those mentioned in this sub-section are to be found in the books on English phonetic theory.

E. *Diaphonic Variants*

The sounds used in particular words by *different people* are not always identical; there are often variations as between one speaker and another. If, for instance, a number of Southern English people are asked one after another to say the expression **get ready for breakfast** («'get 'redi fə 'brekfəst»), it will generally be found that several varieties of « e » are used. Some of the speakers will employ what may be termed an 'average' southern « e »,[1] others will use a somewhat 'closer' vowel,[2] others an 'opener' one,[3] some possibly a 'retracted' variety,[4] and so on. Quite a number of deviations from the 'average' sound are in fact accepted as belonging to RP. There are, of course, limits to such deviations; a very wide deviation from the 'average' sound would cause the speaker's pronunciation to be considered dialectal or unusual. For instance, the use of a very open « e »—'opener' than Cardinal 3—is a sign of northern speech or of northern influence in the speech of a southerner.

A family of sounds consisting of an 'average' sound used by many speakers in a given word together with deviations from this used as equivalents by other speakers may be called a 'diaphone'. Thus the family of « e »-sounds described in the preceding paragraph is a diaphone. Each variety of sound contained in a diaphone may be termed a 'diaphonic variant' or a 'free variant'. ('Diaphonic' or 'free' variants have to be distinguished from allophones, which are 'conditioned variants'.)

The symbol « e » can thus be taken in this Dictionary to mean any member of the diaphone described above, that is to say it may be interpreted either as the 'average' sound or as any one of a number of sounds near to this. Similar considerations apply in a greater or less degree to most of the other vowel symbols, and especially to the diphthongal symbols « ei », « əu », « ai » and « au »; also to some consonant symbols, especially « s », « z » and « r ».

The positions of the large dots in the Frontispiece indicate in a rough manner the 'average' values of the English vowels.

A member of a diaphone may be one of a set of allophones, i.e. of variants conditioned by phonetic context. Thus corresponding to each member of the above-mentioned « e » diaphone there is a 'lowered' variety occurring as an allophone when 'dark « l »' follows (as in **help, well**).

---

[1] i.e. a sound about half way between Cardinal Vowels 2 and 3 in the system of eight Cardinal Vowels.

[2] i.e. a sound nearer to Cardinal 2.

[3] i.e. a sound nearer to Cardinal 3.

[4] i.e. a slightly « ə »-like variety of « e ».

The chief diaphonic variants found in RP are summarized below. For more detailed information readers must consult the books on the phonetics of English.

i: is commonly monophthongal, but many people substitute a diphthong consisting of an 'opener' « i » followed by a 'closer' one. Some transcribers use the notation « ij » to represent this variant.

i 'average' value (when stressed) about as shown in Frontispiece, but there is a modern tendency to use an 'opener' variety. It is instructive to listen to radio announcers pronouncing the word **visibility** in the weather reports.

e see first paragraph of Explanations XXIV E (p. xxxvii).

ɑ: 'average' value as shown in Frontispiece, but a more retracted variety is not uncommon.

ɔ: is subject to slight diaphonic variations, more especially in the matter of the amount of lip-rounding.

u is likewise subject to diaphonic variations in the amount of lip-rounding.

u: is commonly monophthongal, but many people substitute a diphthong consisting of an 'opener' « u » followed by a 'closer' one. This variant is written « uw » by some transcribers.

ʌ is most commonly now an open central vowel, but more 'advanced' as well as more 'retracted' variants are heard. [Amended. A. C. G.]

ə: 'average' value probably as shown in Frontispiece, but there are several diaphonic variants, some 'opener' and some 'closer' than this.

ei 'average' value may be taken to begin about half way between Cardinal « e » and « ɛ », but diaphonic variants of the types « ɛi » and « ɛe » are common.

əu 'average' value probably begins in a mid-central position, without lip-rounding. Diaphonic variants include a more 'retracted' and rounded starting point, a monophthong of the type « ə: » and a more 'advanced' unrounded starting point. [Amended. A. C. G.]

ai 'average' value begins at about Cardinal 4; there are diaphonic variants, some of which are « æi »-like and some « ɑi »-like.

au 'average' value begins at a point slightly back from Cardinal 4. There are 'fronter' and 'backer' diaphonic variants; the latter might be denoted by « ɑu ».

ɛə has a diaphonic variant « æə ».[1]

The vowels « æ » and « ɔ » and the diphthongs « ɔi », « ui », « iə », « eə », « ɔə » and « uə » do not have diaphonic variants differing to any great extent from the 'average' values. (« iə », « eə » and « ɛə » have *allophonic* variants with a very open final element, near to « ʌ »; they are used in final positions.[1] « uə » is, in the speech of many, replaced by the phonemes « ɔə » or « ɔ: » or « ə: » in certain words; these variants are shown in the body of this Dictionary. They are not diaphonic variants; they are other phonemes which many people use in place of « uə ».)

---

[1] Note that « æə » is a *diaphonic* variant of « ɛə » (used by particular people), but that « ɛʌ » is an *allophonic* variant of « ɛə » (used in final position in place of the « ɛə » used elsewhere).

F. *Foreign Sounds*

Those English people who speak foreign languages well often use the foreign pronunciations, or approximations to them, in the modern foreign words which are used in English. The foreign pronunciations are therefore entered in this Dictionary as possible pronunciations; they are shown in round brackets ( ). It is to be understood that the phonetic symbols used in transcribing them have appropriate foreign values, or approximations to them. Thus when a short « i » occurs in a phonetically transcribed French word, as for instance in « tapi » **(tapis)**, it is to be taken to have its French 'tense' value, and not the value of English short « i ».

The languages which are sufficiently well known to some English people to justify including the foreign pronunciations are French, German, Italian, Spanish, Russian and Hindustani. The (North) Welsh pronunciation of most of the Welsh names is also shown, and in a few instances transcriptions of other native pronunciations (e.g. Scottish English, Hungarian, Afrikaans) have been given when it seemed likely that the information thus conveyed might be of particular interest or help to users of the Dictionary.

For the values of the letters used in transcribing foreign pronunciations readers are referred to the books on the languages concerned, e.g. for French Armstrong's *The Phonetics of French*,[1] for German Viëtor's *Die Aussprache des Schriftdeutschen* [2] and Egan's *German Phonetic Reader*,[3] for Italian Camilli's *Italian Phonetic Reader*,[3] for Spanish Stirling's *The Pronunciation of Spanish*,[4] for Russian Boyanus's *Russian Pronunciation* [5] and various 'broad' Russian texts in *Le Maître Phonétique*,[6] for Hindustani Harley's *Colloquial Hindustani*,[7] and for Welsh Stephen Jones's *Welsh Phonetic Reader*.[3] Short particulars of the sounds of these languages are to be found in the 1949 edition of *The Principles of the International Phonetic Association*.[8]

In transcribing the native pronunciations of German, Spanish and Russian words in this Dictionary, I have found it advisable to simplify slightly the forms of transcription used in the above-mentioned books on these languages, as shown in the three following paragraphs.

In the transcriptions of German words, the short 'open' « i » and « u » sounds are denoted simply by « i » and « u », as they are in English words, and not with special letters such as those employed by Viëtor.

In the transcriptions of Spanish words, « b », « d » and « g » are to be interpreted in the Spanish way. This means that they are nearly always to be understood to have 'frictionless continuant' values—values which would be written in 'comparative' transcription by the special letters « β », « ð », and « ɣ ». The exceptions are when they follow a nasal consonant, and when « d » follows « l », in which cases they have 'plosive' values. Thus they have 'frictionless continuant' values in the Spanish renderings of **Oviedo** and

---

[1] Bell, London.
[2] Reisland, Leipzig.
[3] University of London Press.
[4] Cambridge University Press.
[5] Lund Humphries, London.
[6] e.g. in the January numbers of 1950, 1951, 1952, 1953, 1954.
[7] Kegan Paul.
[8] Obtainable from the Secretary of the International Phonetic Association, Department of Phonetics, University College, London, W.C.1.

Guadalquivir (« o'bjedo », « gwadalki'bir »), but « d » has 'plosive' value in the Spanish renderings of **Santander** and **Calderon** (« santan'der », « kalde'ron »).

Russian pronunciations are written here in a style of transcription which is 'broad' except in two points, namely that the 'retracted' allophone of « i » (used after 'hard' consonants) is denoted by the special symbol « ɨ », and the 'obscured' allophone of « a » (used in all unstressed positions except pre-tonic ones, and initial ones when two unstressed syllables follow) is written with « ə ». Thus the symbol « ɨ » is used in the Russian rendering of **Kuibyshev** (« 'kujbɨʃɨf »), and « ə » is used in the Russian rendering of **Ladoga** (« 'ladəgə »). « a » is, however, written in **Onega** (« a'njegə »), where the first vowel, though unstressed, is pre-tonic; also in the first syllable of **Vladivostok** (« vladjiva-'stok »), where the first syllable is followed by two weak syllables. The affricate and palatalized consonants are represented 'digraphically', thus « ts », « tʃ », « pj », « dj », etc., as in the Russian text in the *Principles of the International Phonetic Association*, 1949, and in the above-mentioned texts in *Le Maître Phonétique*.

The mode of transcribing Hindustani words in this Dictionary is the 'World Orthography' employed in Harley's book, with two modifications, namely that the **j** and consonantal **y** of WO are replaced by the IPA « ʝ » and « j ». Users of this Dictionary should note the following conventions in the Hindustani transcriptions. « a » has a sound resembling English « ɑ: ». « e » and « o » resemble the vowels in the Scottish pronunciation of **day** and **go**. « i » and « u » represent 'close' varieties. The 'open' varieties (which resemble the English short « i » and « u ») are represented by « y » and « w ». Hindustani « ə » is a 'central' ('obscure') vowel resembling « ʌ ». « əy » and « əw » are digraphs denoting slightly diphthongal sounds, the first roughly intermediate in sound between « ai » and a long « æ: », and the second intermediate between « au » and « ɔ: ». « t » and « d » have dental articulation. « v » is to be interpreted as a labio-dental frictionless continuant.

In renderings of Scottish pronunciation the 'open' « i » is written with the special symbol « ɨ »; thus the Scottish pronunciation of **Lerwick** is entered as « 'lɛrwɨk ». This is because in Scottish English the 'close' « i » is generally pronounced short and not long as in Southern English, the word **week** for instance being said with a 'close' « i » which is quite short. Consequently the vowel-sounds of the words **week** and **wick** are distinguished by quality only, and must therefore be distinguished in transcription by separate symbols. The « ɨ » in such Scottish transcriptions is to be taken to have the same value as the English short « i ». « e », « a », « ɔ » and « o » are to be taken to have cardinal or nearly cardinal values in the transcriptions of Scottish pronunciation, and « ɛ » is to be interpreted as a sound near to Southern English « e ».

« ɨ » in transcriptions of Russian pronunciation denotes a sound near to an 'unrounded' « u », i.e. the sound obtained by trying to say a close « u » with the lips placed as for « i ». In transcriptions of Welsh words the same symbol denotes a vowel intermediate between this and « i ».

« gw » preceding « l » or « r » in Welsh words denotes a 'labialized' « g ». « gwrɨːx » (the Welsh form of **Gwrych**) thus constitutes a single syllable.

No stress is marked in the phonetic rendering of French and Hindustani words, since these languages make no use of lexically significant word-stress. It is to be understood that there is a certain stress on the final syllables of French words of more than one syllable, but that stress for intensity may be applied to other syllables in accordance with the principles enunciated in Armstrong's *The Phonetics of French*, Chapter XVII. It is also to be understood that there is no particular stress on any syllables of Hindustani words, though there is generally 'prominence' (by length) on every « i », « e », « a », « o » and « u » in that language, and on the diphthongs « əy » and « əw ».

The additional symbols used in phonetic transcriptions of foreign or other unusual pronunciations are as follows:

ṭ   'retroflex' « t ».

ḍ   'retroflex' « d ».

c   Hindustani sound resembling English sound of **ch** (« tʃ »).

ɟ   Hindustani sound resembling English sound of **j** (« dʒ »).

m̥   breathed (voiceless) « m ».

ɲ   French 'n mouillé' (sound of **gn** as in **signe**).

ṇ   'retroflex' « n » (occurs only in Sanskrit words; it is used by Indian scholars, but ordinary Hindustani speakers replace it by « n »).

l̥   breathed (voiceless) « l ».

ṭ   'retroflex' « r ».

ɹ   'retroflex fricative', as in **draw**; also used to denote 'retroflex continuants', as in American pronunciation of **fur**.

ʎ   Italian sound of **gl** in **gli**.

r̥   breathed (voiceless) « r ».

ɸ   bi-labial « f ».

ṣ   'retroflex' « s » (occurs only in Sanskrit words; it is used by Indian scholars, but ordinary Hindustani speakers replace it by « ʃ » or « s »).

ç   the sound of **ch** in German **ich**.

x   the sound of **ch** in Scottish **loch**, German **ach**.

ɣ   voiced consonant corresponding to « x ».

ɥ   the sound of **u** in French **nuit**.

y   normally the sound of **u** in French **lune**. For special use of « y » in Hindustani see above (p. xl).

ø   the sound of **eu** in French **peu**.

œ   the sound of **eu** in French **neuf**.

ɛ̃   the sound of **in** in French **vin**.

ã   a nasalized « a ».

ɑ̃   the sound of **an** in French **blanc**.

ɔ̃   the sound of **on** in French **bon**.

œ̃   the sound of **un** in French **brun**.

    the North Welsh sound of **u** in **Llandudno** (« ɬanˈdɨdno »), Russian sound of ы. Also used to denote ordinary 'open' « i » in transcriptions of Scottish pronunciation.

ɯ   'unrounded' « u », a vowel resembling the Russian « i » (sound of ы).

ɐ   an 'open' variety of « ə », as in Portuguese **para**.

ʇ   alveolar or dental click.

ʖ   lateral click (the sound used for urging on a horse).

G. *Special Symbols for Interjections*

There are some interjections which, though they have spellings, can hardly be regarded as real words. Such are **humph, phew, pshaw, ugh.** They are not generally sounded in the manner the spelling suggests; they are as a rule sounded as grunts or other noises made up mostly of peculiar sounds which do not belong to ordinary language. Some of these noises are representable by phonetic symbols; others are not. Those which are capable of phonetic representation are entered in this Dictionary. The transcription of such noises sometimes involves the use of special phonetic symbols not needed for any other purpose in this Dictionary. These are:

ÿ   French « y » (sound of **u**) pronounced with breath instead of voice.

ə̃   nasalized « ə ».

ʌ: a lengthened « ʌ ».

H. *Diacritical Marks and other Signs*

:   means that the sound represented by the preceding letter is long. In the case of the English 'long' vowels « i: », « ɔ: ». « u: » and « ə: » this sign also implies the differences of quality between them and the corresponding 'short' vowels. For bracketed (:) see Explanations V (p. xxiii).

ı   placed below a consonant-letter (thus « n̩ », « l̩ », « r̩ ») means that the consonant is syllabic. This generally implies that the sound is rather long. See Explanations XVIII (p. xxviii).

₀   placed below the symbol of a voiced sound means that the sound is breathed (voiceless). Thus « u̥ » means a devoiced « u ». When the letter has a descending tail, it is usual to place the ° on the top of it (e.g. « ÿ »).

°   placed in raised position after the symbol of a plosive consonant means that the sound consists of 'stop' only, i.e. it is not finished off with a plosion. See Explanations XVII (p. xxviii).

*   at the end of a word means that « r » is generally inserted when a word beginning with a vowel follows. See, however, Explanations XV (p. xxvi).

~   placed over a letter denotes nasalization.

ᴐ   placed under a letter means that the sound is pronounced with inhaling of breath.

˘   over a vowel letter denotes the less prominent part of a diphthong. For conventions concerning the use of ˘ in « ĭə » and « ŭə » see Explanations XX (1) (p. xxx) and XXIV B (p. xxxv).

ˈ   means that the following syllable has strong stress.

ˌ   means that the following syllable has secondary stress.

-     used as a phonetic sign marks syllable separation. See Explanations XIX (p. xxviii), also IV, V, XX, XXIII (12), XXIV B.

[]   encloses less frequent pronunciations. See Explanations II (p. xxii). Also VIII (p. xxiv).

()   encloses foreign pronunciations. See Explanations XXIV F (p. xxxix). Also used to show alternative spellings and pronunciations. See Explanations V (p. xxiii), VI (p. xxiii), VIII (p. xxiv) and IX (p. xxiv).

| marks off the part of a word which is repeated in derivatives or other words grouped under a head-word. See Explanations XI (p. xxv).

/   marks off derivatives of derivatives. See Explanations XVII (p. xxviii).

XXV. ABBREVIATIONS

abbrev.	means	abbreviation
accus.	,,	accusative
adj.	,,	adjective
adv.	,,	adverb
aux., auxil.	,,	auxiliary
compar.	,,	comparative
conj.	,,	conjunction
cp.	,,	compare
demonstr.	,,	demonstrative
E.	,,	East
esp.	,,	especially
fem.	,,	feminine, female
freq.	,,	frequently
Heb.	,,	Hebrew
Hind.	,,	Hindustani
Hung.	,,	Hungarian
interj.	,,	interjection
IPA	,,	International Phonetic Association
N.	,,	North
opp.	,,	as opposed to
p.	,,	past
partic.	,,	participle
plur.	,,	plural
Port.	,,	Portuguese
prep.	,,	preposition
pres.	,,	present
pron.	,,	pronoun, pronunciation
RP	,,	Received Southern English Pronunciation (see § 3 and onwards in the Introduction)
s.	,,	substantive (noun)
S.	,,	South
sing.	,,	singular
v.	,,	verb
W.	,,	West
WO	,,	'World Orthography'
zoolog.	,,	zoological

XXVI. Key-words for English Phonetic Symbols
[Amended. A. C. G.]

Key words are not required for the following consonant-letters, since they have their customary English sounds:

p, b, t, d, k, m, n, l, r, f, v, s, z, h, w.

Below are key-words for the remaining English sounds, including the affricate consonants and the diphthongs. The sounds marked † occur only as variants of other pronunciations.

It is to be understood that the key-words illustrate the sounds in question when pronounced by many, but not necessarily by all, of the people referred to in § 3 of the Introduction.

Consonants

g *g*ive	ʃ *sh*ip
tʃ *ch*in	ʒ mea*s*ure
dʒ *j*am	†x lo*ch*
ŋ lo*ng*	j *y*es
θ *th*in	ļ tunn*ell*ing
ð *th*en	ņ butt*on*ing
	†ŗ temp*or*ary

Vowels

i: s*ee*	ɔ: s*aw*
i *it*	u p*u*t
e g*e*t	u: t*oo*
æ c*a*t	ʌ *u*p
ɑ: f*a*ther	ə: b*ir*d
ɔ h*o*t	ə chin*a*, c*a*thedr*a*l

Diphthongs

ei d*ay*	iə h*ere*
əu g*o*	iə happ*ier*
ai fl*y*	ɛə th*ere*
au h*ow*	†ɔə f*our*
ɔi b*oy*	uə g*our*d
†ui r*ui*n	ŭə infl*ue*nce
	†eə th*ey're*

When a letter is printed in italics in a phonetic transcription, it means that the sound is sometimes pronounced and sometimes omitted (see Explanations IV, p. xxii).

SOME USEFUL BOOKS FOR THE STUDY
OF ENGLISH PRONUNCIATION

*In the books marked * the pronunciation represented is substantially the same
as that recorded in this Dictionary.*
*In the books marked § the pronunciation is shown by means of the Alphabet
of the Association Phonétique Internationale. Those marked † use a form of
transcription 'narrower' than that of this Dictionary. Those marked ‡ use
Simplified IPA Transcription (see Introduction, § 19).*

1. BOOKS ON PHONETIC THEORY

* § D. JONES, *An Outline of English Phonetics* (Heffer, Cambridge, new
  edition, 1956; reprinted with frontispiece and minor corrections, 1960).
* § —, *The Pronunciation of English* (Cambridge University Press, 4th
  edition, revised and enlarged, 1958). Contains phonetic texts.
* § ‡ —, *The Phoneme, its Nature and Use* (Heffer, Cambridge, 1950; 2nd
  edition, 1962; 3rd edition, 1967).
* § † A. C. GIMSON, *An Introduction to the Pronunciation of English* (Edward
  Arnold, 1962; 2nd edition, 1970).
* § ‡ P. A. D. MACCARTHY, *English Pronunciation*, a practical handbook for
  the foreign learner (Heffer, Cambridge, 4th edition, 1952).
* § † I. C. WARD, *The Phonetics of English* (Heffer, Cambridge).
* § ‡ —, *Speech Defects, their Nature and Cure* (Dent, London).
* H. SWEET, *The Sounds of English* (Oxford University Press).
* —, *Primer of Spoken English* (Oxford University Press). Contains
  phonetic texts.
* § † L. E. ARMSTRONG and I. C. WARD, *Handbook of English Intonation*
  (Teubner, Leipzig and Heffer, Cambridge).
* § J. T. PRING, *Colloquial English Pronunciation* (Longmans, 1959).
  R. KINGDON, *The Groundwork of English Stress* (Longmans, 1958).
  —, *The Groundwork of English Intonation* (Longmans, 1958).
  —, *English Intonation Practice* (Longmans, 1958).
  J. D. O'CONNOR and G. F. ARNOLD, *Intonation of Colloquial English*
  (Longmans, 1961).
* § H. E. PALMER, *Grammar of Spoken English* (Heffer, Cambridge).
* § —, *English Intonation* (Heffer, Cambridge).
  H. KLINGHARDT and G. KLEMM, *Übungen im englischen Tonfall* (Quelle &
  Meyer, Leipzig).
* § † A. LLOYD JAMES, *Talks on English Speech: A Short Gramophone Course
  of English Pronunciation* (Linguaphone Institute).
  —, *Our Spoken Language* (Nelson).
* § † BULLARD and LINDSAY, *Speech at Work* (Longmans, 1951).
  § † A. G. MITCHELL, *The Pronunciation of English in Australia* (Angus &
  Robertson, Sydney, 1946).

§ J. S. KENYON, *American Pronunciation* (George Wahr, Ann Arbor, Michigan).

§ C. K. THOMAS, *Introduction to the Phonetics of American English* (Ronald Press Company, New York, 2nd edition, 1958).

K. L. PIKE, *The Intonation of American English* (University of Michigan Press, Ann Arbor, 1949).

LADO and FRIES, *English Pronunciation* (University of Michigan Press, 1954).

§ C. M. WISE, *Applied Phonetics* (Prentice-Hall Inc., Englewood Cliffs, N.J., 1957).

H. A. GLEASON, *Introduction to Descriptive Linguistics* (Henry Holt & Co., New York, 1956).

§ R.-M. S. HEFFNER, *General Phonetics* (University of Wisconsin Press, 1952).

2. PHONETIC READERS

* § D. JONES, *Phonetic Readings in English* (Winter, Heidelberg, new improved edition, 1956).

* § J. D. O'CONNOR, *New Phonetic Readings* (Francke, Berne, 1948).

* § ‡ N. C. SCOTT, *English Conversations*, in simplified phonetic transcription (Heffer, Cambridge, 1942; 2nd edition, 1965).

* § ‡ E. L. TIBBITTS, *Phonetic Reader for Foreign Learners of English* (Heffer, Cambridge, 1947).

* § ‡ P. A. D. MACCARTHY, *English Conversation Reader* (Longmans, 1956).

J. T. PRING and R. GERMER, *A New English Phonetic Reader*, with intonation-marks (Verlag Lambert Lensing, Dortmund, 1962).

E. L. TIBBITTS, *Practice Material for the English Sounds* (Heffer, Cambridge, 1963).

* § D. ABERCROMBIE, *English Phonetic Texts* (Faber, 1964).

* § † G. F. ARNOLD and A. C. GIMSON, *English Pronunciation Practice*, (University of London Press, 1965).

* § † W. RIPMAN, *Specimens of English*, revised version (Dent, London).

* § † L. E. ARMSTRONG, *An English Phonetic Reader* (University of London Press).

* § H. E. PALMER, *100 English Substitution Tables* (Heffer, Cambridge).

* § † H. E. PALMER and F. G. BLANDFORD, *Everyday Sentences in Spoken English* (Heffer, Cambridge, 5th edition, 1935, reprinted 1953).

* § † G. L. BROOK, *An English Phonetic Reader* (Manchester University Press).

* § G. SCHERER, *Englische Texte in Lautschrift* (Cornelsen, Berlin-Bielefeld).

§ R. GERHARD, *General American Pronunciation* (Sanseidō, Tōkyō, 1954).

§ *Le Maître Phonétique*, the Journal of the International Phonetic Association, founded by P. PASSY, present editor A. C. GIMSON, University College, London.

See also the books by JONES, SWEET, ARMSTRONG and WARD, mentioned in the preceding section.

A

A (*the letter*), -'s ei, -z
a (*indefinite article*) ei (*strong form*), ə (*weak form*)
aardvark, -s 'ɑːdvɑːk, -s
Aaron, -s 'ɛərən, -z
aback ə'bæk
Abaco (*in Bahamas*) 'æbəkəu
abacus, -es 'æbəkəs, -iz
Abadan (*in Persia*) ,æbə'dɑːn [-'dæn]
Abaddon ə'bædən [-dn]
abaft ə'bɑːft
abandon (*s.*) ə'bændən (abãdɔ̃)
abandon (*v.*), -s, -ing, -ed/ly, -ment
    ə'bændən, -z, -iŋ, -d/li, -mənt
abas|e, -es, -ing, -ed, -ement ə'beis,
    -iz, -iŋ, -t, -mənt
abash, -es, -ing, -ed ə'bæʃ, -iz, -iŋ, -t
abatab|le, -ly ə'beitəb|l, -li
abat|e, -es, -ing, -ed, -ement/s ə'beit,
    -s, -iŋ, -id, -mənt/s
abatis (*sing.*) 'æbətis [-tiː]
abatis (*plur.*) 'æbəti:z
abatises (*plur.*) 'æbətisiz
abattis, -es ə'bætis, -iz
abattoir, -s 'æbətwɑ:* [-twɔ:*], -z
Abba 'æbə
abbac|y, -ies 'æbəs|i, -iz
Abbas 'æbəs [-bæs]
abbé, -s 'æbei (abe), -z
abbess, -es 'æbis [-bes], -z
Abbeville (*in France*) 'æbviːl (abvil),
    (*in U.S.A.*) 'æbivil
abbey (A.), -s 'æbi, -z
abbot (A.), 'æbət, -s
Abbotsford 'æbətsfəd
abbotship, -s 'æbət-ʃip, -s
Abbott 'æbət
abbreviat|e, -es, -ing, -ed, -or/s ə'briː-
    vieit [vjeit], -s, -iŋ, -id, -ə*/z
abbreviation, -s ə,briːvi'eiʃən, -z
abbreviatory   ə'briːvjətəri   [-viət-
    -vieit-]
abc, -'s 'eibiː'siː, -z
Abdera æb'diərə
abdicant, -s 'æbdikənt, -s
abdicat|e, -es, -ing, -ed 'æbdikeit, -s,
    -iŋ, -id
abdication, -s ,æbdi'keiʃən, -z
Abdiel 'æbdiəl [-djəl]

abdomen, -s 'æbdəmen [æb'dəumen,
    -min, -mən], -z
    Note.—æb'dəumen [-min] *is the form
    generally used by members of the
    medical profession.*
abdomin|al, -ally æb'dɔmin|l [əb-], əli
abduct, -s, -ing, -ed, -or/s æb'dʌkt
    [əb-], -s, -iŋ, -id, -ə*/z
abduction, -s æb'dʌkʃən [əb-], -z
Abdulla, -s æb'dʌlə [əb-], -z
Abdy 'æbdi
abeam ə'biːm
abecedarian ,eibi(ː)siː(ː)'dɛərïən
A Becket ə'bekit
abed ə'bed
Abednego ,æbed'niːgəu [ə'bednigəu]
Abel (*biblical name, English name*)
    'eibəl, (*foreign name*) 'ɑːbəl
Abell 'eibəl
Abelmeholah 'eibəlmi'həulə [-mə'h-]
Aberavon ,æbə'rævən [-bə:'r-] (*Welsh*
    aber'avon)
Aberbrothock ,æbə'brɔθək [-bə:'b-]
    *Note.—This place-name has to be
    pronounced incorrectly ,æbəbrə-
    'θɔk [-bə:b-] in Southey's 'Inch-
    cape Rock.'*
Abercorn 'æbəkɔːn [-bəː'k-]
Abercrombie [-by] 'æbəkrʌmbi [-bəː'k-,
    -krɔm-, ,--'--]
Aberdare ,æbə'dɛə* [-bə:'d-] (*Welsh*
    aber'da:r)
Aberdeen,   -shire   ,æbə'diːn   [-bə:'d-,
    '--'-], -ʃiə* [-ʃə*]
aberdevine, -s ,æbədə'vain [-bə:d-], -z
Aberdonian, -s ,æbə'dəunjən [-bə:'d-,
    -nïən], -z
Aberdour ,æbə'dauə* [-bə:'d-]
Aberdovey ,æbə'dʌvi [-bə:'d-] (*Welsh*
    aber'dəvi)
Abergavenny (*family name*) ,æbə'geni
    [-bə:'g-], (*place*) ,æbəgə'veni (*Welsh*
    aberga'veni)
Abergele ,æbə'geli [-bə:'g-] (*Welsh*
    aber'gele)
Abernethy ,æbə'neθi [-bə:'n-, *in the S.
    also* -'niːθi]
aberran|ce, -cy, -t æ'berən|s [ə'b-], -si,
    -t

aberrat|e, -es, -ing, -ed 'æbəreit [-ber-], -s, -iŋ, -id

abberration, -s ˌæbə'reiʃən [-be'r-], -z

Abersychan ˌæbə'sikən [-bə:'s-] (Welsh aber'səxan)

Abert 'eibə:t

Abertillery ˌæbəti'lɛəri (Welsh abertəl'eri)

Aberystwyth ˌæbə'ristwiθ (Welsh aber'əstuiθ)

abet, -s, -ting, -ted, -tor/s, -ment ə'bet, -s, -iŋ, -id, -ə*/z, -mənt

abeyance ə'beiəns

abhor, -s, -ring, -red, -rer/s əb'hɔ:*, -z, -riŋ, -d, -rə*/z

abhorren|ce, -t əb'hɔrən|s, -t

Abia (biblical name) ə'baiə, (city) 'æbïə

Abiathar ə'baiəθə*

Abib 'eibib ['ɑ:bib]

abid|e, -es, -ing, abode ə'baid, -z, -iŋ, ə'bəud

abies 'æbii:z ['eib-]

abigail, -s 'æbigeil, -z

Abigail 'æbigeil [with some Jews ˌæbi'geil]

Abijah ə'baidʒə

Abilene (in Syria) ˌæbi'li:ni, (in U.S.A.) 'æbili:n

abilit|y, -ies ə'bilit|i [-lət-], -iz

Abi|melech, -nadab ə'bi|mələk, -nədæb

Abingdon 'æbiŋdən

Abinger 'æbindʒə*

ab initio ˌæbi'niʃiəu [-'nitiəu, -'nisiəu]

Abinoam ə'binəuæm [with some Jews ˌæbi'nəuəm]

abiogenesis ˌeibaiəu'dʒenisis

Abishai æ'biʃeiai [ə'b-, 'æbiʃai, ˌɑ:bi-'ʃeiai]

abject, -ly, -ness 'æbdʒekt, -li, -nis

abjection æb'dʒekʃən

abjudicat|e, -es, -ing, -ed æb'dʒu:di-keit [əb-], -s, iŋ, -id

abjuration, -s ˌæbdʒuə'reiʃən, [-dʒɔə'r-, -dʒɔ:'r-], -z

abjur|e, -es, -ing, -ed, -er/s əb'dʒuə* [æb-, -'dʒɔə*, -'dʒɔ:*], -z, -riŋ, -d, -rə*/z

ablation æb'leiʃən [əb-]

ablatival ˌæblə'taivəl

ablative (s. adj.), -s 'æblətiv, -z

ablaut, -s 'æblaut ('aplaut), -s

ablaze ə'bleiz

ab|le, -ler, -lest, -ly 'eib|l, -lə*, -list, li

able-bodied 'eibl'bɔdid ['eibl,b-]

ablution, -s ə'blu:ʃən, -z

abnegat|e, -es, -ing, -ed 'æbnigeit [-neg-], -s, -iŋ, -id

abnegation, -s ˌæbni'geiʃən [-ne'g-], -z

Abner 'æbnə*

abnorm|al, -ally æb'nɔ:m|əl [əb-, 'æb'n-], -əli

abnormalit|y, -ies ˌæbnɔ:'mælit|i, -iz

abnormit|y, -ies æb'nɔ:mit|i [əb-], -iz

aboard ə'bɔ:d [-'bɔəd]

abode (s. v.), -s ə'bəud, -z

abolish, -es, -ing, -ed, -er/s ə'bɔliʃ, -iz, -iŋ, -t, -ə*/z

abolition, -s ˌæbəu'liʃən [-bu'l-], -z

abolitioni|sm, -st/s ˌæbəu'liʃəni/zəm [-bu'l-, -ʃni-], -st/s

abominab|le, -ly, -leness ə'bɔminəb|l, -li, -lnis

abominat|e, -es, -ing, -ed ə'bɔmineit, -s, -iŋ, -id

abomination, -s əˌbɔmi'neiʃən, -z

aborigin|al, -ally ˌæbə'ridʒən|l [-bɔ'r-, -dʒin-], -əli

aborigines ˌæbə'ridʒini:z [-bɔ'r-]

abort, -s, -ing, -ed ə'bɔ:t, -s, iŋ, -id

abortion, -s ə'bɔ:ʃən, -z

abortive, -ly, -ness ə'bɔ:tiv, -li, -nis

Aboukir, ˌæbu(:)'kiə* [ˌɑ:b-]

abound, -s, -ing, -ed ə'baund, -z, -iŋ, -id

about ə'baut

above ə'bʌv

above-board ə'bʌv'bɔ:d [-'bɔəd, -'--]

above - mentioned ə'bʌv'menʃənd [when attributive also -'-,--]

abracadabra, -s ˌæbrəkə'dæbrə, -z

abrad|e, -es, -ing, -ed ə'breid, -z, -iŋ, -id

Abraham 'eibrəhæm [-həm, as a biblical name freq. also 'ɑ:b-]

Abrahams 'eibrəhæmz

Abram 'eibrəm [-ræm, as a biblical name freq. also 'ɑ:b-]

abrasion, -s ə'breiʒən, -z

abrasive ə'breisiv

abraxus ə'bræksəs

abreast ə'brest

abridg|e, -es, -ing, -ed, -(e)ment/s ə'bridʒ, -iz, -iŋ, -d, -mənt/s

abroad ə'brɔ:d

abrogat|e, -es, -ing, -ed 'æbrəugeit [-rug-], -s, -iŋ, -id

abrogation, -s ˌæbrəu'geiʃən [-ru'g-], -z

A'Brook ə'bruk

abrupt, -est, -ly, -ness ə'brʌpt, -ist, -li, -nis

Abruzzi ə'brutsi(:)

Absalom 'æbsələm

abscess, -es 'æbsis [-ses], -iz

absciss|a, -ae, -as æb'sis|ə [əb-], -i:, -əz

abscission, -s æb'siʒən [-'siʃən], -z

abscond, -s, -ing, -ed əb'skɔnd [æb-], -z, -iŋ, -id

absence, -s 'æbsəns, -iz
absent (adj.), -ly 'æbsənt, -li
absent (v.), -s, -ing, -ed æb'sent [əb-], -s, -iŋ, -id
absentee, -s, -ism ‚æbsən'ti: [-sen-], -z -izəm
absent-minded, -ly, -ness 'æbsənt-'maindid [also '—,—, ,—'—, according to sentence-stress], -li, -nis
absinth, 'æbsinθ
absolute, -st, -ness 'æbsəlu:t [-lju:t], -ist, -nis
absolutely 'æbsəlu:tli [-lju:-, emphatic-ally also '—'—, predicatively also ,—'—]
Note.—Some people use the form '— meaning 'completely' and '—'— meaning 'certainly.'
absolution, -s ‚æbsə'lu:ʃən [-'lju:-], -z
absoluti|sm, -st/s 'æbsəlu:ti|zəm [-lju:-], -st/s
absolv|e, -es, -ing, -ed, -er/s əb'zɔlv, -z, -iŋ, -d, -ə*/z
absorb, -s, -ing/ly, -ed, -edly; -able; -ent/ly əb'sɔ:b [əb'zɔ:b], -z, -iŋ/li, -d, -idli; -əbl; -ənt/li
absorption əb'sɔ:pʃən [əb'zɔ:-]
absorptive əb'sɔ:ptiv [əb'zɔ:-]
abstain, -s, -ing, -ed, -er/s əb'stein [æb-], -z, -iŋ, -d, -ə*/z
abstemious, -ly, -ness æb'sti:mjəs [əb-, -miəs], -li, -nis
abstention, -s əb'stenʃən [æb-], -z
abstergent (s. adj.), -s əb'stə:dʒənt, -s
abstinen|ce, -t 'æbstinən|s, -t
abstract (s. adj.), -s, -ly, -ness 'æbs-trækt, -s, -li [-'—], -nis [-'—]
abstract (v.), -s, -ing, -ed/ly, -edness æb'strækt [əb-], -s, -iŋ, -id/li, -idnis
abstraction, -s æb'strækʃən [əb-], -z
abstruse, -ly, -ness æb'stru:s [əb-], -li, -nis
absurd, -est, -ly, -ness; -ity, -ities əb'sə:d, -ist, -li, -nis; -iti, -itiz
Abu 'ɑ:bu:
Abukir ‚æbu(:)'kiə* [‚ɑ:b-]
abundan|ce, -t/ly ə'bʌndən|s, -t/li
Abury 'eibəri
abuse (s.), -s ə'bju:s, -iz
abus|e (v.), -es, -ing, -ed, -er/s ə'bju:z, -iz, -iŋ, -d, -ə*/z
abusive, -ly, -ness ə'bju:siv, -li, -nis
abut, -s, -ting, -ted, -ment/s; -tal ə'bʌt, -s, -iŋ, -id, -mənt/s; -l
abutilon, -s ə'bju:tilən, -z
Abydos ə'baidɔs
abysm, -s ə'bizəm, -z
abysm|al, -ally ə'bizm|əl, -əli

abyss, -es ə'bis, -iz
Abyssinia, -n/s ‚æbi'sinjə [-bə's-, -niə], -n/z
acacia, -s ə'keiʃə, -z
academic, -al, -ally ‚ækə'demik, -əl, -əli
academician, -s ə‚kædə'miʃən [-de'm-, -di'm-], -z
academ|y, -ies ə'kædəm|i, -iz
Acadia, -n/s ə'keidjə [-diə], -n/z
acajou, -s 'ækəʒu:, -z
acanth|us, -i, -uses, -ine ə'kænθ|əs, -ai, -əsiz, -ain
acatalectic æ‚kætə'lektik [ə‚k-]
acatalepsy æ'kætəlepsi [ə'k-]
acataleptic æ‚kætə'leptik [ə‚k-]
Accad 'ækæd
Accadia, -n/s ə'keidjə [-diə], -n/z
acced|e, -es, -ing, -ed, -er/s æk'si:d [ək-], -z, -iŋ, -id, -ə*/z
accelerando æk‚selə'rændəu [ək-, ə‚tʃel-]
accelerat|e, -es, -ing, -ed ək'seləreit [æk-], -s, -iŋ, -id
acceleration, -s ək‚selə'reiʃən [æk-], -z
accelerative ək'selərətiv [æk-, -reit-]
accelerator, -s ək'seləreitə* [æk-], -z
accent (s.), -s 'æksənt [-sent], -s
accent (v.), -s, -ing, -ed æk'sent [ək-], -s, -iŋ, -id
accentual, -ly æk'sentjŭəl [ək-, -tjwəl, -tjul, -tʃŭəl], -i
accentuat|e, -es, -ing, -ed æk'sentjueit [ək-, -tʃueit], -s, -iŋ, -id
accentuation, -s æk‚sentju'eiʃən [ək-, -tʃu-], -z
accept, -s, -ing, -ed, -er/s, -or/s ək'sept [æk-], -s, -iŋ, -id, -ə*/z, -ɔ*/z
acceptability ək‚septə'biliti [æk-, -lət-]
acceptab|le, -ly, -leness ək'septəb|l [æk-], -li, -lnis
acceptan|ce, -ces, -cy, -t/s ək'septən|s [æk-], -siz, -si, -t/s
acceptation, -s ‚æksep'teiʃən, -z
access 'ækses
accessar|y, -ies ək'sesər|i [æk-], -iz
accessibility ək‚sesi'biliti [æk-, -sə'b-, -lət-]
accessible ək'sesəbl [æk-, -sib-]
accession, -s æk'seʃən [ək-], -z
accessit, -s æk'sesit [ək-], -s
accessor|y (s. adj.), -ies ək'sesər|i [æk-], -iz
accidence 'æksidəns
accident, -s 'æksidənt, -s
accident|al, -ally ‚æksi'dent|l, -əli [-li]
acclaim, -s, -ing, -ed ə'kleim, -z, -iŋ, -d
acclamation, -s ‚æklə'meiʃən, -z
acclamatory ə'klæmətəri
acclimatation ə‚klaimə'teiʃən
acclimation ‚æklai'meiʃən

acclimatization [-isa-] ə‚klaimətai'zei-ʃən [-ti'z-]

acclimatiz|e [-is|e], -es, -ing, -ed ə'klaimətaiz, -iz, -iŋ, -d

acclivit|y-, ies ə'klivit|i [æ'k-], -iz

accolade, -s 'ækəʊleid [-lɑːd, ‚--'-], -z

accommodat|e, -es, -ing/ly, -ed, -or/s; -ive/ly ə'kɔmədeit, -s, -iŋ/li, -id, -ə*/z; -iv/li

accommodation, -s ə‚kɔmə'deiʃən, -z

accompaniment, -s ə'kʌmpənimənt, -s

accompanist, -s ə'kʌmpənist, -s

accompan|y, -ies, -ying, -ied, -ier/s; -yist/s ə'kʌmpən|i, -iz, -iiŋ, -id, -iə*/z; -iist/s

accomplice, -s ə'kɔmplis [-'kʌm-], -iz

accomplish, -es, -ing, -ed, -ment/s ə'kʌmpliʃ [-'kɔm-], -iz, -iŋ, -t, -mənt/s

accord (s. v.), -s, -ing, -ed ə'kɔːd, -z, -iŋ, -id

accordan|ce, -t ə'kɔːdən|s, -t

according, -ly ə'kɔːdiŋ, -li

accordion, -s ə'kɔːdjən [-diən], -z

accost, -s, -ing, -ed ə'kɔst, -s, -iŋ, -id

accouchement, -s ə'kuːʃmɑ̃ːŋ [-mɔ̃ːŋ, -mɔŋ] (akuʃmɑ̃), -z

accoucheur, -s ‚æku:'ʃə:* [ə'kuːʃəː*] (akuʃœːr), -z

accoucheuse, -s ‚æku:'ʃəːz (akuʃøːz), -iz

account (s. v.), -s, -ing, -ed ə'kaunt, -s, -iŋ, -id

accountability ə‚kauntə'biliti [-lət-]

accountab|le, -ly, -leness ə'kauntəb|l, -li, -lnis

accountan|cy, -t/s ə'kauntən|si, -t/s

account-book, -s ə'kauntbuk, -s

accou|tre, -tres, -tring, -tred; -tre-ment/s ə'kuː|tə*, -təz, -təriŋ [-triŋ], -təd; -təmənt/s [-trəmənt/s]

Accra (in Ghana) ə'krɑː [æ'k-]

accredit, -s, -ing, -ed ə'kredit, -s, -iŋ, -id

accretion, -s æ'kriːʃən [ə'k-], -z

accretive æ'kriːtiv [ə'k-]

Accrington 'ækriŋtən

accru|e, -es, -ing, -ed ə'kruː, -z, -iŋ [ə'kruiŋ]

accumulat|e, -es, -ing, -ed, -or/s ə'kjuːmjuleit [-mjəl-], -s, -iŋ, -id, -ə*/z

accumulation, -s ə‚kju:mju'leiʃən [-mjə'l-], -z

accumulative ə'kjuːmjulətiv [-mjəl-, -leit-]

accuracy 'ækjurəsi [-kjər-, -risi]

accur|ate, -ately, -ateness 'ækjur|it [-kjər-], -itli [-ətli], -itnis [-ətnis]

accursed, -ly ə'kəːsid, -li

accusal, -s ə'kjuːzəl, -z

accusation, -s ‚ækju(ː)'zeiʃən, -z

accusatival ə‚kjuːzə'taivəl

accusative (s. adj.), -s ə'kjuːzətiv, -z

accusatory ə'kjuːzətəri

accus|e, -es, -ing, -ed, -er/s ə'kjuːz, -iz, -iŋ, -d, -ə*/z

accustom, -s, -ing, -ed/ness ə'kʌstəm, -z, -iŋ, -d/nis

ace, -s eis, -iz

Aceldama ə'keldəmə [ə'sel-]

acerbity ə'səːbiti

Acestes ə'sestiːz

acetate 'æsiteit [-tit]

acetic ə'siːtik [æ's-, -'set-]

aceti|fy, -fies, -fying, -fied ə'seti|fai [æ's-], -faiz, -faiiŋ, -faid

acetone 'æsitəun

acet|ose, -ous 'æsitəus, -əs

acetyl 'æsitil

acetylene ə'setiliːn [æ's-, -təl-]

Achaea, -n/s ə'kiː(ː)ə, -n/z

Achaia ə'kaiə

Achan 'eikæn

Achates ə'keitiːz

ach|e (s. v.) (pain), -es, -ing, -ed, -er/s eik, -s, -iŋ, -t, -ə*/z

ache (letter H), -s eitʃ, -iz

Achernar (star) 'eikənɑː*

Acheron 'ækərɔn [-rən]

Acheson 'ætʃisn

achiev|e, -es, -ing, -ed, -ement/s; -able ə'tʃiːv, -z, -iŋ, -d, -mənt/s; -əbl

Achil(l) 'ækil

Achilles ə'kiliːz

Achille Serre 'æʃil'seə* [-ʃiːl-] (aʃilseːr)

Achin ə'tʃiːn

Achish 'eikiʃ

Achonry 'ækənri

Achray ə'krei [ə'xrei]

achromatic, -ally ‚ækrəʊ'mætik [-kru'm-], -əli

achromatism ə'krəumətizəm [æ'k-]

achromatiz|e [-is|e], -es, -ing, -ed ə'krəumətaiz [æ'k-], -iz, -iŋ, -d

acid (s. adj.), -s, -est, -ly, -ness 'æsid, -z, -ist, -li, -nis

acidi|fy, -fies, -fying, -fied ə'sidi|fai [æ's-], -faiz, -faiiŋ, -faid

acidity ə'siditi [æ's-]

acidiz|e [-is|e], -es, -ing, -ed 'æsidaiz, -iz, -iŋ, -d

acidosis ‚æsi'dəusis

acidulat|e, -es, -ing, -ed ə'sidjuleit [æ's-], -s, -iŋ, -id

Acis 'eisis

ack æk

ack-ack 'æk'æk

Ackerman(n) 'ækəmən [-kə:m-, -mæn]
**acknowledg|e, -es, -ing, -ed, -(e)ment/s;
-eable** ək'nɔlidʒ [æk-], -iz, -iŋ, -d,
-mənt/s; -əbl
Note.—There is also a rare form
-'nəul-.
Ackroyd 'ækrɔid
Acland 'æklənd
acme, -s 'ækmi, -z
acne 'ækni
Acol (*road in London, system of bridge*
playing) 'ækəl
acolyte, -s 'ækəulait, -s
Acomb 'eikəm
Aconcagua ˌækɔŋ'kɑ:gwə [-'kægjŭə]
aconite, -s 'ækənait, -s
acorn, -s; -shell/s 'eikɔ:n, -z; -ʃel/z
acotyledon, -s æˌkɔti'li:dən [ə,k-], -z
acoustic, -ally, -s ə'ku:stik [*old-
fashioned* -'kaus-], əli, -s
acquaint, -s, -ing, -ed; -ance/s
ə'kweint, -s, -iŋ, -id; -əns/iz
acquaintanceship, -s ə'kweintənʃip
[-nsʃ-, -nʃʃ-], -s
acquest, -s æ'kwest [ə'k-], -s
acquiesc|e, -es, -ing, -ed; -ence, -ent
ˌækwi'es, -iz, -iŋ, -t; -ns, -nt
acquir|e, -es, -ing, -ed, -ement/s; -able
ə'kwaiə*, -z, -riŋ, -d, -mənt/s; -rəbl
acquisition, -s ˌækwi'ziʃən, -z
acquisitive ə'kwizitiv [æ'k-]
acquit, -s, -ting, -ted; -tal/s ə'kwit, -s,
-iŋ, -id; -l/z
acre (A.), **-s; -age|s** 'eikə*, -z; -ridʒ/iz
acrid, -ly, -ness 'ækrid, -li, -nis
acridity æ'kriditi [ə'k-]
acrimonious, -ly, -ness ˌækri'məunjəs
[-nïəs], -li, -nis
acrimon|y, -ies 'ækrimənˌi, -iz
acritude 'ækritju:d
acrobat, -s; -ism 'ækrəbæt, -s; -izəm
acrobatic, -s, -ally ˌækrəu'bætik, -s, -əli
Acroceraunia ˌækrəuke'rɔ:njə
Acrocorinthus ˌækrəukə'rinθəs [-kɔ'r-]
acronym, -s 'ækrəunim, -z
acropolis, -es ə'krɔpəlis [-pļis], -iz
across ə'krɔs [-'krɔ:s]
acrostic, -s ə'krɔstik, -s
Acrux (*star*) 'ei-krʌks
act (s. v.), **-s, -ing, -ed, -or/s** ækt, -s, -iŋ,
-id, -ə*/z
acta 'æktə
A.C.T.H. 'ei-si:ti:'eitʃ [ækθ]
actinic æk'tinik
actinium æk'tinïəm [-njəm]
action, -s 'ækʃən, -z
actionable 'ækʃnəbl [-ʃnəb-, -ʃənəb-]
Actium 'æktïəm [-tjəm]

activable 'æktivəbl
activat|e, -es, -ing, -ed 'æktiveit, -s,
-iŋ, -id
active, -ly, -ness 'æktiv, -li, -nis
activist, -s 'æktivist, -s
activit|y, -ies æk'tivitˌi, -iz
Acton 'æktən
actor, -s 'æktə*, -z
actress, es 'æktris, -iz
actual, -ly 'æktʃŭəl [-tjwəl, -tjul, -tjŭəl,
-tʃwəl, -tʃul], -i
actualit|y, -ies ˌæktʃu'ælitˌi [-tju-], -iz
actualiz|e [-is|e], -es, -ing, -ed 'æk-
tʃŭəlaiz [-tjwəl-, -tjŭəl-, -tʃwəl-], -iz,
-iŋ, -d
actuarial ˌæktju'ɛərïəl [-tʃu-]
actuar|y, -ies 'æktjŭər|i [-tjwər-, -tʃŭər-,
-tʃwər-], -iz
actuate, -es, -ing, -ed 'æktjueit
[-tʃu-], -s, -iŋ, -id
actuation, -s ˌæktju'eiʃən [-tʃu-], -z
acuity ə'kju(:)iti
acumen ə'kju:men ['ækjumen]
acute, -r, -st, -ly, -ness ə'kju:t, -ə*, -ist,
-li, -nis
A.D. 'ei'di: ['ænəu'dɔminai]
ad æd
Ada 'eidə
adage, -s 'ædidʒ, -iz
adagio, -s ə'dɑ:dʒiəu [-dʒjəu], -z
Adair ə'dɛə*
Adalbert 'ædəlbə:t
Adam 'ædəm
adamant 'ædəmənt [-mænt]
adamantine ˌædə'mæntain
adamite (A.), **-s** 'ædəmait, -s
Adams 'ædəmz
Adamson 'ædəmsn
Adamthwaite 'ædəmθweit
Adana (*in Turkey*) 'ædənə
adapt, -s, -ing, -ed, -er/s ə'dæpt, -s, -iŋ,
-id, -ə*/z
adaptability əˌdæptə'biliti [-lət-]
adaptable, -ness ə'dæptəbl, -nis
adaptation, -s ˌædæp'teiʃən [-dəp-], -z
Adar 'eidɑ:*
Adare ə'dɛə*
Adastral ə'dæstrəl
Adcock 'ædkɔk
add, -s, -ing, -ed æd, -z, -iŋ, -id
addend|um, -a ə'dend|əm [æ'd-], -ə
adder, -s; -'s-tongue, -wort 'ædə*, -z;
-ztʌn, -wə:t
addict (s.), **-s** 'ædikt, -s
addict (v.), **-s, -ing, -ed/ness** ə'dikt, -s,
-iŋ, -id/nis
addiction, -s ə'dikʃən, -z
Addington 'ædiŋtən

Addis Ababa 'ædis'æbəbə [-'ɑːb-]
Addiscombe 'ædiskəm
Addison 'ædisn
addition, -s ə'diʃən, -z
addi|tional, -tionally ə'di|ʃənl [-ʃnəl, -ʃn̩l, -ʃn̩l, -ʃənəl], -ʃn̩əli [-ʃnəli, -ʃn̩li, -ʃn̩li, -ʃənəli]
additive, -s 'æditiv, -z
add|le (adj. v.), **-les, -ling, -led** 'æd|l, -lz, -liŋ [-liŋ], -ld
addle|headed, -pated 'ædl|,hedid, -,peitid ['--'--]
Addlestone 'ædlstən
address (s. v.), **-es, -ing, -ed** ə'dres, -iz, -iŋ, -t
addressee, -s ,ædre'siː, -z   [-s
addressograph, -s ə'dresougrɑːf [-græf],
adduc|e, -es, -ing, -ed, -er/s; -ible ə'djuːs [æ'd-], -iz, -iŋ, -t, -ə*/z; -ibl [-əbl]
Adeane ə'diːn
Adel (in Yorks.) 'ædl
Adela (English name) 'ædilə, (foreign name) ə'deilə
Adelaide (in Australia) 'ædəleid [-dil-, -lid], (Christian name, road in London) 'ædəleid [-dil-]
Note.—The pronunciation in Australia is with -leid.
Adelina ,ædi'liːnə [-də'l-]
Adeline 'ædiliːn [-dəl-, -lain]
Adelphi ə'delfi
Aden (in Arabia) 'eidn, (in Aberdeenshire) 'ædn
adenoid, -s 'ædinɔid [-dən-], -z
adenoidal, ,ædi'nɔidl [-də'n-]
adept (s.), **-s** 'ædept [ə'dept, æ'd-, rarely 'eidept], -s
adept (adj.) 'ædept [ə'd-, æ'd-]
adequacy 'ædikwəsi
adequate, -ly, -ness 'ædikwit, -li ['ædikwətli], -nis ['ædikwətnis]
adher|e, -es, -ing, -ed, -er/s əd'hiə* [æd-], -z, -riŋ, -d, -rə*/z
adheren|ce, -t/s əd'hiərən|s [æd-], -t/s
adhesion, -s əd'hiːʒən [æd-], -z
adhesive, -ly, -ness əd'hiːsiv [æd-, -'hiːziv], -li, -nis
ad hoc 'æd'hɔk [-'həuk]
Adie 'eidi
adieu, -s ə'djuː:, -z
adipocere, ,ædipəu'siə*
adipose 'ædipəus
Adirondack, -s ,ædi'rɔndæk, -s
adit, -s 'ædit, -s
adjacen|cy, -t/ly ə'dʒeisən|si, -t/li
adjectiv|al, -ally ,ædʒek'taiv|əl [-dʒik-], -əli

adjective, -s 'ædʒiktiv [-dʒekt-], -z
adjoin, -s, -ing, -ed ə'dʒɔin, -z, -iŋ, -d
adjourn, -s, -ing, -ed, -ment/s ə'dʒəːn, -z, -iŋ, -d, -mənt/s
adjudg|e, -es, -ing, -ed, -ment/s ə'dʒʌdʒ [æ'dʒ-], -iz, -iŋ, -d, -mənt/s
adjudicat|e, -es, -ing, -ed, -or/s ə'dʒuː-dikeit, -s, -iŋ, -id, -ə*/z
adjudication, -s ə,dʒuːdi'keiʃən, -z
adjunct, -s, -ly 'ædʒʌŋkt, -s, -li [ə'dʒʌŋktli]
adjuration, -s ,ædʒuə'reiʃən, -z
adjuratory ə'dʒuərətəri
adjur|e, -es, -ing, -ed ə'dʒuə*, -z, -riŋ, -d
adjus|t, -ts, -ting, -ted, -tment/s ə'dʒʌs|t, -ts, -tiŋ, -tid, -tmənt/s
adjutage 'ædʒutidʒ [ə'dʒuːt-]
adjutan|cy, -t/s 'ædʒutən|si [-dʒət-], Adlai 'ædlei   [-t/s
Adler 'ædlə*, 'ɑːdlə*
ad lib. 'æd'lib
ad-man 'ædmæn
admass 'ædmæs
admeasur|e, -es, -ing, -ed, -ement/s æd'meʒə* [əd-], -z, -riŋ, -d, -mənt/s
administ|er, -ers, -ering, -ered əd-'minist|ə*, -əz, -əriŋ, -əd
administr|able, -ant/s əd'ministr|əbl, -ənt/s
administration, -s əd,minis'treiʃən, -z
administrative əd'ministrətiv [-treit-]
administrator, -s, -ship/s əd'minis-treitə*, -z, -ʃip/s
administratri|x, -xes, -ces əd'minis-treitri|ks, -ksiz, -siːz
admirab|le, -ly, -leness 'ædmərəb|l, -li, -lnis
admiral, -s 'ædmərəl, -z
admiralt|y, -ies 'ædmərəlt|i, -iz
admiration ,ædmə'reiʃən [-mi'r-]
admir|e, -es, -ing/ly, -ed, -er/s əd'maiə*, -z, -riŋ/li, -d, -rə*/z
admissibility əd,misə'biliti [-si'b-, -lət-]
admissible əd'misəbl [-sib-]
admission, -s əd'miʃən, -z
admit, -s, -ting, -ted/ly; -tance/s əd'mit, -s, -iŋ, -id/li; -əns/iz
admix, -es, -ing, -ed; -ture/s əd'miks [æd-], -iz, -iŋ, -t; -tʃə*/z
admonish, -es, -ing, -ed, -ment/s əd'mɔniʃ, -iz, -iŋ, -t, -mənt/s
admonition, -s ,ædməu'niʃən, -z
admonitory əd'mɔnitəri [æd-]
ado ə'duː
adobe, -s ə'dəubi [ə'dəub], -z
adolescen|ce, -t/s ,ædəu'lesn|s, -t/s
Adolf (English name) 'ædɔlf, (German name) 'ɑːdɔlf ['æd-] ('ɑːdɔlf)

Adolphus ə'dɔlfəs
Adonais ˌædəu'neiis
Adonijah ˌædəu'naidʒə
Adonis ə'dəunis
adopt, -s, -ing, -ed; -ive ə'dɔpt, -s, -iŋ, -id; -iv
adoption, -s ə'dɔpʃən, -z
adorab|le, -ly, -leness ə'dɔ:rəb|l, -li, -lnis
adoration, -s ˌædɔ:'reiʃən [-də'r-], -z
ador|e, -es, -ing/ly, -ed, -er/s ə'dɔ:* ['dɔə*], -z, -riŋ/li, -d, -rə*/z
adorn, -s, -ing, -ed, -ment/s ə'dɔ:n, -z, -iŋ, -d, -mənt/s
adrenal ə'dri:nl
adrenalin ə'drenəlin
Adria, -n 'eidriə, -n
Adrianople ˌeidriə'nəupl [ˌæd-]
Adriatic ˌeidri'ætik [ˌæd-]
adrift ə'drift
adroit, -est, -ly, -ness ə'drɔit, -ist, -li, -nis
adsorb, -s, -ing, -ed æd'sɔ:b [əd-], -z, -iŋ, -d
adsum 'ædsʌm [-sum, -səm]
adulation, -s ˌædju'leiʃən, -z
adulatory 'ædjuleitəri [-lət-, ˌ--'--]
Adullam, -ite/s ə'dʌləm, -ait/s
adult (s. adj.), -s 'ædʌlt [ə'dʌlt], -s
adulterat|e, -es, -ing, -ed, -or/s ə'dʌltəreit, -s, -iŋ, -id, -ə*/z
adulteration, -s əˌdʌltə'reiʃən, -z
adulter|er/s, -ess/es ə'dʌltər|ə*/z, -is/iz [-es/iz]
adulterous, -ly ə'dʌltərəs, -li
adulter|y, -ies ə'dʌltər|i, -iz
adumbrat|e, -es, -ing, -ed 'ædʌmbreit [-dəm-], -s, -iŋ, -id
adumbration, -s ˌædʌm'breiʃən [-dəm-], -z
advaita əd'vaitə (Hind. ədvəyta)
ad valorem 'ædvə'lɔ:rem [-væ'l-, -rəm]
advanc|e (s. adj. v.), -es, -ing, -ed, -ement/s əd'vɑ:ns, -iz, -iŋ, -t, -mənt/s
advantage, -s əd'vɑ:ntidʒ, -iz
advantageous, -ly, -ness ˌædvən-'teidʒəs [-vɑ:n-, -væn-], -li, -nis
adven|e, -es, -ing, -ed æd'vi:n [əd-], -z, -iŋ, -d
advent (A.), -s 'ædvənt [-vent], -s
adventitious, -ly ˌædven'tiʃəs [-vən-], -li
advent|ure (s. v.), -ures, -uring, -ured, -urer/s, -uress/es əd'ventʃ|ə*, -əz, -əriŋ, -əd, -ərə*/z, -əris/iz
adventuresome əd'ventʃəsəm
adventurous, -ly, -ness əd'ventʃərəs, -li, -nis
adverb, -s 'ædvə:b, -z

adverbial, -ly əd'və:bjəl [æd-, -bɪəl], -i
adversar|y, -ies 'ædvəsər|i, -iz
adversative əd'və:sətiv [æd-]
adverse, -ly 'ædvə:s, -li [æd'və:sli, 'æd'və:sli]
adversit|y, -ies əd'və:sit|i, -iz
advert (advertisement), -s 'ædvə:t, -s
advert (v.), -s, -ing, -ed əd'və:t [æd-], -s, -iŋ, -id
adverten|ce, -cy, -t/ly əd'və:tən|s, -si, -t/li
advertis|e, -es, -ing, -ed, -er/s 'ædvə-taiz, -iz, -iŋ, -d, -ə*/z
advertisement,   -s   əd'və:tismənt [-tizm-], -s
advice, -s əd'vais, -iz
advisability əd,vaizə'biliti [-lət-]
advisab|le, -ly, -leness əd'vaizəb|l, -li, -lnis
advis|e, -es, -ing, -ed, -edly, -edness, -er/s, -or/s; -ory əd'vaiz, -iz, -iŋ, -d, -idli, -idnis, -ə*/z, -ə*/z; -əri
advocacy 'ædvəkəsi [-vuk-]
advocate (s.), -s 'ædvəkit [-vuk-, -keit, -kət], -s
advocat|e (v.), -es, -ing, -ed, -or/s 'ædvəkeit [-vuk-], -s, -iŋ, -id, -ə*/z
advocation ˌædvə'keiʃən [-vu'k-]
advowson, -s əd'vauzən, -z
Adye 'eidi
adynamic ˌædai'næmik [-di'n-]
adz|e (s. v.), -es, -ing, -ed ædz, -iz, -iŋ, -d
Aeacus 'i:əkəs
Aeaea i:'i:ə
aedile, -s; -ship/s 'i:dail, -z; -ʃip/s
Aeetes i:'i:ti:z
Aegean i(:)'dʒi:ən [-iən]
Aegeus 'i:dʒju:s [-dʒjəs, -dʒɪəs]
Aegina i(:)'dʒainə
aegis 'i:dʒis
aegrotat, -s i(:)'grəutæt ['i:grəut-], -s
Aelfric 'ælfrik
Aemilius i(:)'miliəs [-ljəs]
Aeneas i(:)'ni:æs ['i:niæs]
Aeneid, -s 'i:niid [-njid], -z
Aeneus 'i:nju:s ['i:njəs, -niəs]
Aeolia, -n/s i(:)'əuljə [-lɪə], -n/z
Aeolic i(:)'ɔlik
Aeolus 'i(:)əuləs
aeon, -s 'i:ən ['i:ɔn], -z
aerat|e, -es, -ing, -ed, -or/s 'eiəreit ['eər-], -s, -iŋ, -id, -ə*/z
aeration ˌeiə'reiʃən [eə'r-]
aerial (s. adj.), -s, -ly 'eəriəl, -z, -i
aerie, -s 'eəri ['iəri], -z
aeri|fy, -fies, -fying, -fied 'eəri|fai, -faiz, -faiiŋ, -faid
aero 'eərəu

aerodrome, -s 'ɛərədrəum, -z
aerodynamic, -s 'ɛərəudai'næmik ['eiər-, -di'n-], -s
aerodyne, -s 'ɛərəudain, -z
aerolite, -s 'ɛərəulait ['eiər-], -s
aerolith, -s 'ɛərəuliθ ['eiər-], -s
aerological ˌɛərəu'lɔdʒikəl [ˌeiər-]
aerolog|ist/s, -y ɛə'rɔlədʒ|ist/s [ˌeiə'r-], -i
aeronaut, -s 'ɛərənɔ:t, -s
aeronautic, -al, -s ˌɛərə'nɔ:tik, -əl, -s
aerophone, -s 'ɛərəfəun, -z
aeroplane, -s 'ɛərəplein, -z
aerosol, -s 'ɛərəusɔl, -z
aerostat, -s 'ɛərəustæt ['eiər-], -s
aertex 'ɛəteks
aeruginous iə'ru:dʒinəs
aer|y (s.) (= aerie), -ies 'ɛər|i ['iər|i], -iz
aery (adj.) 'eiəri ['ɛəri]
Aeschines 'i:skini:z
Aeschylus 'i:skiləs
Aesculapius ˌi:skju'leipjəs [-p²əs]
Aesop 'i:sɔp
aesthete, -s 'i:sθi:t ['es-], -s
aesthetic, -al, -ally, -s i:s'θetik [is-, es-], -əl, -əli, -s
aesthetici|sm, -st/s i:s'θetisi|zəm [is-, es-], -st/s
aestival i:s'taivəl
Aethelstan 'æθəlstən
aether 'i:θə*
Aethiopia, -n/s ˌi:θi'əupjə [-p²ə], -n/z
aetiology ˌi:ti'ɔlədʒi
Aetna 'etnə
afar ə'fɑ:*
afeard ə'fiəd
affability ˌæfə'biliti [-lət-]
affab|le, -ly, -leness 'æfəb|l, -li, -lnis
affair, -s ə'fɛə*, -z
affect, -s, -ing/ly, -ed/ly, -edness ə'fekt, -s, -iŋ/li, -id/li, -idnis
affectation, -s ˌæfek'teiʃən [-fik-], -z
affection, -s ə'fekʃən, -z
affectionate, -ly, -ness ə'fekʃnit [-ʃnit, -ʃənit], -li, -nis
afferent 'æfərənt
affettuoso əˌfetju'əuzəu [æˌf-, -tu-]
affianc|e, -es, -ing, -ed ə'faiəns, -iz, -iŋ, -t
affidavit, -s ˌæfi'deivit, -s
affiliat|e, -es, -ing, -ed ə'filieit, -s, -iŋ, -id
affiliation, -s əˌfili'eiʃən, -z
affinit|y, -ies ə'finit|i, -iz
affirm, -s, -ing, -ed; -able ə'fə:m, -z, -iŋ, -d; -əbl
affirmation, -s ˌæfə:'meiʃən [-fə'm-], -z
affirmative, -ly ə'fə:mətiv, -li

affirmatory ə'fə:mətəri
affix (s.), -es 'æfiks, -iz
affix (v.), -es, -ing, -ed ə'fiks [æ'f-], -iz, -iŋ, -t
afflatus ə'fleitəs
afflict, -s, -ing, -ed; -ive ə'flikt, -s, -iŋ, -id; -iv
affliction, -s ə'flikʃən, -z
affluen|ce, -t/s, -tly 'æfluən|s [-flwən-], -t/s, -tli
afflux, -es 'æflʌks, -iz
afford, -s, -ing, -ed ə'fɔ:d, -z, -iŋ, -id
afforest, -s, -ing, -ed æ'fɔrist [ə'f-], -s, -iŋ, -id
afforestation, -s æˌfɔris'teiʃən [əˌf-, -res-], -z
affranchis|e, -es, -ing, -ed ə'fræntʃaiz [æ'f-], -iz, -iŋ, -d
affray, -s ə'frei, -z
affricate (s. adj.), -s 'æfrikit [-keit], -s
affricated 'æfrikeitid
affrication ˌæfri'keiʃən
affricative (s. adj.), -s æ'frikətiv [ə'f-], -z
affright, -s, -ing, -ed/ly ə'frait, -s, -iŋ, -id/li
affront (s. v.), -s, -ing, -ed ə'frʌnt, -s, -iŋ, -id
Afghan, -s 'æfgæn, -z
Afghanistan æf'gænistæn [-tən, æfˌgænis'tæn, æfˌgænis'tɑ:n]
afield ə'fi:ld
afire ə'faiə*
Aflalo ə'flɑ:ləu
aflame ə'fleim
afloat ə'fləut
afoot ə'fut
afore, -said, -thought, -time ə'fɔ:* [-'fɔə*], -sed, -θɔ:t, -taim
a fortiori 'ei,fɔ:ti'ɔ:rai [-ˌfɔ:ʃi-, 'ɑ:ˌfɔ:-ti'ɔ:ri:]
afraid ə'freid
afreet, -s 'æfri:t, -s
afresh ə'freʃ
Afric 'æfrik
Africa, -n/s 'æfrikə, -n/z
Africander, -s ˌæfri'kændə*, -z
Africanus ˌæfri'kɑ:nəs [-'kein-]
Afridi, -s æ'fri:di [ə'f-], -z
Afrikaans ˌæfri'kɑ:ns
afrit, -s 'æfri:t, -s
aft ɑ:ft
after 'ɑ:ftə*
after-birth, -s 'ɑ:ftəbə:θ, -s
after-crop, -s 'ɑ:ftə-krɔp, -s
afterglow, -s 'ɑ:ftə-gləu, -z
after-guard, -s 'ɑ:ftəgɑ:d, -z
aftermath, -s 'ɑ:ftəmæθ [-mɑ:θ], -s
afternoon, -s 'ɑ:ftə'nu:n [ˌɑ:ftə'n-, attributively 'ɑ:ftənu:n], -z

after-piece, -s 'ɑːftəpiːs, -iz
afterthought, -s 'ɑːftəθɔːt, -s
afterward, -s 'ɑːftəwəd, -z
Aga 'ɑːgə
Agag 'eigæg
again, -st ə'gen [-'gein], -st
Agamemnon ˌægə'memnən [-nəun, -nɔn]
agape (s.), -s 'ægəpi(ː), -z
agape (adj. adv.) ə'geip
agapemone ˌægə'piːməni [-'pem-]
Agar 'eigɑː*, 'eigə*
agaric (s.), -s 'ægərik [ə'gærik], -s
agaric (adj.) æ'gærik [ə'g-]
Agassiz (Swiss-Amer. geologist) 'ægəsi(ː), (town in Brit. Columbia) ˌægə'si:
Agassizhorn ə'gæsihɔːn
agate (stone), -s 'ægət [-git], -s
Agate (surname) 'eigət, 'ægət
Agatha 'ægəθə
Agathocles ə'gæθəʊkliːz
agave, -s ə'geivi ['ægeiv], -z
agaze ə'geiz
age (s. v.), -s, -ing, -d (p. tense and partic.) eidʒ, -iz, -iŋ, -d
aged (adj.) (old) 'eidʒid, (of the age of) eidʒd
agedness 'eidʒidnis
ageless 'eidʒlis
agelong 'eidʒlɔŋ
agenc|y, -ies 'eidʒəns|i, -iz
agenda, -s ə'dʒendə, -z
agene 'eidʒiːn
Agenor ə'dʒiːnɔː*
agent, -s 'eidʒənt, -s
agent provocateur 'æʒɑ̃ːŋ prəˌvɔkə'təː* [-ɔŋ-] (aʒɑ̃ prɔvɔkatœːr)
Ager 'eidʒə*
Agesilaus əˌdʒesi'leiəs
Aggie 'ægi
agglomerate (s. adj.), -s ə'glɔmərit [-reit], -s
agglomerat|e (v.), -es, -ing, -ed ə'glɔməreit, -s, -iŋ, -id
agglomeration, -s əˌglɔmə'reiʃən, -z
agglutinate (adj.) ə'gluːtinit [-neit]
agglutinat|e (v.), -es, -ing, -ed ə'gluː-tineit, -s, -iŋ, -id
agglutination, -s əˌgluːti'neiʃən, -z
agglutinative ə'gluːtinətiv [-neit-]
aggrandiz|e [-is|e], -es, -ing, -ed ə'grændaiz ['ægrəndaiz], -iz, -iŋ, -d
aggrandizement [-ise-] ə'grændizmənt
aggravat|e, -es, -ing/ly, -ed 'ægrəveit, -s, -iŋ/li, -id
aggravation, -s ˌægrə'veiʃən, -z
aggregate (s. adj.), -s 'ægrigit [-geit], -s

aggregat|e (v.), -es, -ing, -ed 'ægrigeit, -s, -iŋ, -id
aggregation, -s ˌægri'geiʃən, -z
aggress, -es, -ing, -ed, -or/s ə'gres [æ'g-], -iz, -iŋ, -t, -ə*/z
aggression, -s ə'greʃən [æ'g-], -z
aggressive, -ly, -ness ə'gresiv [æ'g-], -li, -nis [-d
aggriev|e, -es, -ing, -ed ə'griːv, -z, -iŋ,
Aggy 'ægi
aghast ə'gɑːst [-nis
agile, -st, -ly, -ness 'ædʒail, -ist, -li,
agility ə'dʒiliti
Agincourt 'ædʒinkɔːt
agiotage 'ædʒətidʒ
agitat|e, -es, -ing, -ed, -or/s 'ædʒiteit, -s, -iŋ, -id, -ə*/z
agitation, -s ˌædʒi'teiʃən, -z
agitato ˌædʒi'tɑːtəu
aglow ə'gləu
agnail, -s 'ægneil, -z
agnate 'ægneit
agnation æg'neiʃən
Agnes 'ægnis
Agnew 'ægnjuː
agnomen, -s æg'nəumen ['æg'n-], -z
agnostic, -s æg'nɔstik [əg-], -s
agnosticism æg'nɔstisizəm [əg-]
Agnus Dei, -s 'ɑːgnus'deɪi: ['ægnəs-'diːai], -z
ago ə'gəu
agog ə'gɔg
agone ə'gɔn
Agonistes ˌægəʊ'nistiːz
agonistic, -ally, -s ˌægəʊ'nistik, -əli, -s
agoniz|e [-is|e], -es, -ing/ly, -ed 'ægənaiz, -iz, -iŋ/li, -d
agon|y, -ies 'ægən|i, -iz
agor|a, -ae, -as 'ægər|ə [-gɔr-], -iː, -əz
agouti, -s ə'guːti, -z
Agra 'ɑːgrə
agrarian, -s, -ism ə'grɛərɪən [ei'g-], -z, -izəm
agree, -s, -ing, -d ə'griː, -z, -iŋ, -d
agreeab|le, -ly, -leness ə'griəb|l, -li, -lnis
agreement, -s ə'griːmənt, -s
agrestic ə'grestik [æ'g-]
Agricola ə'grikəulə
agricultur|al, -alist/s ˌægri'kʌltʃər|əl [-tʃur-], -əlist/s
agriculture 'ægrikʌltʃə*
agriculturist, -s ˌægri'kʌltʃərist, -s
agrimony 'ægriməni
Agrippa ə'gripə
agronomy ə'grɔnəmi
aground ə'graund
ague, -s 'eigjuː, -z

Aguecheek 'eigju:tʃi:k
Aguilar ə'gwilə* [æ'g-]
Agutter ə'gʌtə*
ah ɑ:
aha ɑ(:)'hɑ: [ə'h-]
Ahab 'eihæb
Ahasuerus ə,hæzju'iərəs   [ei,hæz-,
    esp. by Jews]
Ahaz 'eihæz
Ahaziah ,eiħə'zaiə
ahead ə'hed
aheap ə'hi:p
ahem m'm̩m [m̩m, hm]
A'Hern 'eihə:n
Aherne ə'hə:n
Ahijah ə'haidʒə
Ahimelech ə'himələk
Ahithophel ə'hiθəʊfel
Ahmed 'ɑ:med
ahoy ə'hɔi
ahungered ə'hʌŋgəd
Ai 'eiai [rarely ei, ai]
aid (s. v.), -s, -ing, -ed, -er/s eid, -z, -iŋ,
    -id, -ə*/z
Aïda ai'i:də
aide-de-camp, -s 'eiddə'kɑ̃:ŋ [-'kɔ̃:ŋ,
    -'kɔŋ] (eddəkɑ̃), -z
aides-de-camp   'eidzdə'kɑ̃:ŋ   [-kɔ̃:ŋ,
    -'kɔŋ] (eddəkɑ̃)
aigrette, -s 'eigret [ei'gret], -s
aiguille, -s 'eigwi:l [-wi:] (egɥi:j, ɛg-), -z
Aik|en, -in 'eik|in, -in
ail, -s, -ing, -ed, -ment/s eil, -z, -iŋ, -d,
    -mənt/s
Aileen 'eili:n
aileron, -s 'eilərɔn, -z
Ailesbury 'eilzbəri
Ailsa 'eilsə
aim (s. v.), -s, -ing, -ed; -less eim, -z,
    -iŋ, -d; -lis
Ainger 'eindʒə*
Ainsl|ey, -ie 'einzl|i, -i
Ainsworth 'einzwə:θ [-wəθ]
ain't eint
Ainu, -s 'ainu:, -z
air (s. v.), -s, -ing/s, -ed ɛə*, -z, -riŋ/z,
    -d
air-arm, -s 'ɛər-ɑ:m ['ɛəɑ:m], -z
air-base, -s 'ɛəbeis, -iz
air-ba|th, -ths 'ɛəbɑ:|θ ['ɛə'b-], -ðz
air-bladder, -s 'ɛə,blædə*, -z
airborne 'ɛəbɔ:n, [-bɔən]
air-carrier, -s 'ɛə,kærɪə*, -z
air-cell, -s 'ɛə-sel, -z
air-chamber, -s 'ɛə,tʃeimbə*, -z
air-condi|tion, -tions, -tioning, -tioned
    'ɛə-kən,di|ʃən, -ʃənz, -ʃəniŋ, [-ʃn̩iŋ,
    -ʃniŋ], -ʃənd

air-cooled 'ɛə-ku:ld
aircraft 'ɛə-krɑ:ft
aircraft|man, -men 'ɛə-krɑ:ft|mən, -mən
aircraft|woman, -women 'ɛə-krɑ:ft|-
    ,wumən, -,wimin
air-cushion, -s 'ɛə,kuʃən ['ɛə'k-, -ʃin], -z
Aird ɛəd
airdrome, -s 'ɛədrəum, -z
Airedale, -s 'ɛədeil, -z
air-engine, -s 'ɛər,endʒin ['ɛə,en-], -z
Airey 'ɛəri
airfield, -s 'ɛə-fi:ld, -z
airgraph, -s 'ɛəgrɑ:f [-græf], -s
air-gun, -s 'ɛəgʌn, -z
air-hole, -s 'ɛəhəul, -z
air-hostess, -es 'ɛə,həustis [-stes], -iz
airless 'ɛəlis
Airlie 'ɛəli
air-letter, -s 'ɛə,letə*, -z
air-lift, -s 'ɛəlift, -s
airline, -s 'ɛə-lain, -z
air-lock, -s 'ɛəlɔk, -s
air|man, -men 'ɛə|mən [-mæn], -men
    [-mən]
air-mail, -s 'ɛəmeil, -z
air-minded 'ɛə,maindid
air-plane, -s 'ɛə-plein, -z
air-pocket, -s 'ɛə,pɔkit, -s
airport, -s 'ɛə-pɔ:t, -s
air-pump, -s 'ɛə-pʌmp, -s
air-raid, -s 'ɛə-reid, -z
air-route, -s 'ɛə-ru:t, -s
air-shaft, -s 'ɛə-ʃɑ:ft, -s
airship, -s 'ɛə-ʃip, -s
air-sick 'ɛə-sik
air-sickness 'ɛə,siknis
air-space 'ɛə-speis
air-strip, -s 'ɛə-strip, -s
air-terminal, -s 'ɛə,tə:minl, -z
airtight 'ɛə-tait
airway, -s 'ɛəwei, -z
airworth|y, -iness 'ɛə,wə:ði|i, -inis
air|y (A.), -ier, -iest, -ily, -iness 'ɛər|i,
    -iə*, -iist, -ili, -inis
Aisgill 'eisgil
Aislaby (in Yorks.) 'eizləbi [locally
    'eizlbi]
aisle, -s, -d ail, -z, -d
aitch (letter H), -es eitʃ, -iz
aitchbone, -s 'eitʃbəun, -z
Aitchison 'eitʃisn
Aith eiθ
Aitken 'eitkin [-kən], 'eik-
Aix eiks (ɛks)
Aix-la-Chapelle 'eikslɑ:ʃæ'pel [-ʃə'p-]
    (ɛkslaʃapɛl)
Aix - les - Bains 'eikslei'bɛ̃:ŋ [-'bæŋ]
    (ɛkslebɛ̃)

Ajaccio ə'jætʃiəu [ə'dʒæsiəu]
ajar ə'dʒɑ:*
Ajax, -es 'eidʒæks, -iz
ajutage 'ædʒutidʒ [ə'dʒu:t-]
Akaba 'ækəbə
Akbar 'ækbɑ:* ['ʌkbə*] (Hind. əkbər)
Akenside 'eikinsaid [-kən-]
Akerman 'ækəmən
Akers 'eikəz
akimbo ə'kimbəu
akin ə'kin
Akkad 'ækæd
Akkra 'ækrə
Akond of Swat (former title of the
   Wali of Swat territory in Pakistan)
   ə'ku:ndəv'swɔt, (fancy name in poem
   by E. Lear) 'ækəndəv'swɔt
Akron 'ækrɔn [-rən]
Akroyd 'ækrɔid
Al æl
à la ɑ:lɑ: (ala)
Alabama ˌælə'bæmə [-'bɑ:mə]
alabaster 'æləbɑ:stə* [-bæs-]
Alabaster 'æləbɑ:stə*
alack ə'læk
alackaday ə'lækədei
alacrity ə'lækriti
Aladdin ə'lædin
Alamein 'æləmein
Alan 'ælən
Aland 'ɑ:lənd ['ɔ:l-]
aland (adv.) ə'lænd
alar 'eilə*
Alaric 'ælərik
alarm (s. v.), -s, -ing/ly, -ed; -ist/s
   ə'lɑ:m, -z, -iŋ/li, -d; -ist/s
alarum, -s ə'lɛərəm [-'lɑ:r-, -'lær-], -z
alas ə'læs [-'lɑ:s]
Alaska ə'læskə
Alastair 'æləstə*
Alastor ə'læstɔ:* [æ'l-]
alate (winged) 'eileit
alb, -s ælb, -z
Alba 'ælbə
Alban 'ɔ:lbən ['ɔl-]
Albani æl'bɑ:ni
Albania, -n/s æl'beinjə [ɔ:l-, -nĭə], -n/z
Albano æl'bɑ:nəu
Albany (in London) 'ɔ:lbəni ['ɔl-, 'æl-],
   (in Australia) 'æl-, (in U.S.A.) 'ɔ:l-
   ['ɔl-]
albatross, -es 'ælbətrɔs, -iz
albeit ɔ:l'bi:it
Albemarle 'ælbimɑ:l [-bəm-]
Alberic 'ælbərik
albert (A.), -s 'ælbət [-bə:t], -s
Alberta æl'bə:tə
albescent æl'besənt

Albigenses ˌælbi'gensi:z [-'dʒensi:z]
Albin 'ælbin
albinism 'ælbinizəm
albino, -s æl'bi:nəu, -z
Albion 'ælbjən [-bĭən]
Alboni æl'bəuni
Albrecht 'ælbrekt ('albreçt)
Albright 'ɔ:lbrait ['ɔl-]
Albrighton 'ɔ:braitn ['ɔ:lb-, 'ɔlb-]
Albrow 'ɔ:lbrau
albugineous ˌælbju(:)'dʒinĭəs [-njəs]
Albula 'ælbjulə
album, -s 'ælbəm, -z
albumen 'ælbjumin [æl'bju:min, -men]
albumin 'ælbjumin [æl'bju:min]
albumin|oid/s, -ous æl'bju:min|ɔid/z,
   -əs
alburnum, -s æl'bə:nəm, -z
Albury (surname, town in Australia)
   'ɔ:lbəri ['ɔl-]
Alcaeus æl'si(:)əs
alcaic, -s æl'keiik, -s
Alcazar (Spanish palace) ˌælkə'zɑ:,
   (al'kaθar), (music hall) æl'kæzə*
Alcester 'ɔ:lstə* ['ɔl-]
Alcestis æl'sestis
alchemic, -al æl'kemik, -əl
alchem|ist/s, -y 'ælkim|ist/s, -i
Alcibiades ˌælsi'baiədi:z
Alcides æl'saidi:z
Alcinous æl'sinəuəs
Alcmene ælk'mi:ni(:)
Alcock 'ælkɔk, 'ɔ:lkɔk ['ɔl-]
   Note.—The family of Sir Walter
   Alcock, late organist of Salisbury
   Cathedral, pronounces 'ælkɔk.
alcohol, -s, -ism 'ælkəhɔl, -z, -izəm
alcoholic ˌælkə'hɔlik
alcoholomet|er/s, -ry ˌælkəhɔ'lɔmit|-
   ə*/z, -ri
Alcoran ˌælkɔ'rɑ:n [-kɔ:'r-, -kə'r-]
Alcorn 'ɔ:lkɔ:n ['ɔl-]
Alcott 'ɔ:lkət ['ɔl-]
alcove, -s, -d 'ælkəuv, -z, -d
Alcuin 'ælkwin
Alcyone æl'saiəni
Aldborough (in Yorks.) 'ɔ:ldbərə ['ɔl-,
   locally 'ɔ:lbrə], (in Suffolk) 'ɔ:ldbərə
   ['ɔl-]
Aldbury 'ɔ:ldbəri ['ɔl-]
Aldebaran æl'debərən [-ræn]
Aldeburgh 'ɔ:ldbərə ['ɔl-]
aldehyde, -s 'ældihaid, -z
Alden 'ɔ:ldən ['ɔl-]
Aldenham 'ɔ:ldnəm ['ɔl-, -dnəm]
alder (A.), -s 'ɔ:ldə* ['ɔl-], -z
alder|man (A.), -men, -manly 'ɔ:ldə-
   mən ['ɔl-], -mən, -mənli

aldermanic ˌɔːldə'mænik [ˌɔl-]
aldern 'ɔːldə(ː)n ['ɔl-]
Alderney 'ɔːldəni ['ɔl-]
Aldersgate 'ɔːldəzgit ['ɔl-, -geit]
Aldershot 'ɔːldəʃɔt ['ɔl-]
Alderwasley ˌældəwəz'liː
Aldgate 'ɔːldɡit ['ɔl-, -geit]
Aldine 'ɔːldain ['ɔl-, -diːn]
Aldis 'ɔːldis ['ɔl-]
Aldous 'ɔːldəs ['ɔl-], 'ældəs
Aldred 'ɔːldrid ['ɔl-, -dred]
Aldrich 'ɔːldritʃ ['ɔl-, -idʒ]
Aldridge 'ɔːldridʒ ['ɔl-]
Aldsworth 'ɔːldzwə(ː)θ ['ɔl-]
Aldus 'ɔːldəs ['ɔl-, 'æl-]
Aldwych 'ɔːldwitʃ ['ɔl-]
ale (A.), -s eil, -z
Alec(k) 'ælik [-lek]
alehou|se, -ses 'eilhau|s, -ziz
Alemannic ˌæli'mænik [-le'm-]
alembic, -s ə'lembik, -s
Aleppo ə'lepəu
alert (s. adj.), -s, -est, -ly, -ness ə'ləːt, -s, -ist, -li, -nis
Alessandria ˌæli'sændrɪə [-le's-, -'sɑː-]
Alethea ˌælə'θiə
Aletsch 'ælitʃ ['ɑːl-, -letʃ]
Aleutian ə'luːʃjən [-'lju:-, -ʃiən, -ʃən]
alewi|fe, -ves 'eilwai|f, -vz
Alexand|er, -ra, -ria, -rian/s ˌælig'zɑːnd|ə* [-leg-, -'zæn-, -k's-], -rə, -rɪə, -rɪən/z
Alexandrina ˌæligzɑːn'driːnə [-leg-, -zæn-, -ks-]
alexandrine, -s ˌælig'zændrain [-leg-, -'zɑːn-, -k's-], -z
Alexis ə'leksis
alfalfa æl'fælfə
Alfonso æl'fɔnzəu [-nsəu]
Alford 'ɔːlfəd ['ɔl-]
Alfred 'ælfrid
Alfreda æl'friːdə
Alfredian æl'friːdjən [-dɪən]
Alfree 'ɔːlfri ['ɔl-]
alfresco æl'freskəu
Alfreton 'ɔːlfritən ['ɔl-]
Alfric 'ælfrik
Alfriston (in Sussex) ɔːl'fristən [ɔl-]
al|ga, -gae 'æl|gə, -dʒiː [-gi:]
algebra, -s 'ældʒibrə, -z
algebraic, -al, -ally ˌældʒi'breiik, -əl, -əli
algebraist, -s ˌældʒi'breiist ['----], -s
Algeciras ˌældʒi'siərəs [-dʒə's-, -dʒe's-, -'saiər-]
Alger 'ældʒə*
Algeria, -n/s æl'dʒiərɪə, -n/z
Algernon 'ældʒənən
Algiers æl'dʒiəz [rarely '--]

Algoa æl'gəuə
Algol 'ælgɔl
Algonquin æl'gɔŋkwin [-kin]
algorithm, -s 'ælgəriðm, -z
algorithmic ˌælgə'riðmik
Algy 'ældʒi
Alhambra æl'hæmbrə [əl-]
alhambresque ˌælhæm'bresk
alias, -es 'eiliæs [-ljæs, -lïəs, -ljəs], -iz
Ali Baba 'æli'bɑːbə ['ɑːl-, -'bɑːbɑː]
alibi, -s 'ælibai, -z
Alicant 'ælikænt
Alicante, -s ˌæli'kænti, -z
Alice 'ælis
Alicia ə'liʃɪə [-ʃjə, -ʃə]
Alick 'ælik
alien (s. adj. v.), -s, -ing, -ed; -able, -age 'eiljən [-lïən], -z, -iŋ, -d; -əbl, -idʒ
Aliena ˌæli'iːnə
alienat|e, -es, -ing, -ed, -or/s 'eiljəneit [-lïən-], -s, -iŋ, -id, -ə*/z
alienation, -s ˌeiljə'neiʃən [-lïə'n-], -z
alienee, -s ˌeiljə'niː [ˌeilïə-], -z
alieni|sm, -st/s 'eiljəni|zəm [-lïən-], st/s
alight (adj. v.), -s, -ing, -ed ə'lait, -s, -iŋ, -id
align, -s, -ing, -ed, -ment/s ə'lain, -z, -iŋ, -d, -mənt/s
alike ə'laik
aliment, -s 'ælimənt, -s
aliment|al, -ary ˌæli'ment|l, -əri
alimentation ˌælimen'teiʃən
alimon|y, -ies 'ælimən|i, -iz
alin|e, -es, -ing, -ed ə'lain, -z, -iŋ, -d
Aline æ'liːn [ə'l-], 'æliːn
alineation, -s əˌlini'eiʃən, -z
Alington 'æliŋtən
Ali Pasha 'ɑːli'pɑːʃə ['æl-, rarely -'pæʃə, -pə'ʃɑː]
aliqu|ant, -ot 'ælikw|ənt, -ɔt
Alison 'ælisn
Alist|air, -er 'ælist|ə*, -ə*
alive ə'laiv
alizarin ə'lizərin
alkahest 'ælkəhest
alkalescen|ce, -cy, -t ˌælkə'lesn|s, -si, [-t
alkali, -(e)s 'ælkəlai, -z
alkali|fy, -fies, -fying, -fied 'ælkəli|fai [æl'kæl-], -faiz, -faiiŋ, -faid
alkaline 'ælkəlain
alkalinity ˌælkə'liniti
alkaloid, -s 'ælkəlɔid, -z
Alkoran ˌælkɔ'rɑːn [-kɔː'r-, -kə'r-]
all ɔːl
Allah 'ælə [-lɑː]
Allahabad ˌæləhə'bɑːd [-'bæd] (Hind. allahabad)

Allan 'ælən
Allan-a-Dale 'ælənə'deil
Allandale 'æləndeil
Allard 'ælɑːd [-ləd]
Allardice 'ælədais
allay, -s, -ing, -ed ə'lei, -z, -iŋ, -d
Allbright 'ɔːlbrait ['ɔl-]
Allbutt 'ɔːlbət ['ɔl-]
Allchin 'ɔːlʃin ['ɔl-]
Allcorn 'ɔːlkɔːn ['ɔl-]
Allcroft 'ɔːlkrɔft ['ɔl-, 'ɔːlkrɔːft]
allegation, -s ˌæli'geiʃən [-le'g-], -z
alleg|e, -es, -ing, -ed ə'ledʒ, -iz, -iŋ, -d
Alleghany 'æligeini
Allegheny 'æligeini
allegian|ce, -t ə'liːdʒən|s, -t
allegoric, -al, -ally ˌæli'gɔrik [-le'g-],
   -əl, -əli
allegorist, -s 'æligərist [-leg-], -s
allegoriz|e [-is|e], -es, -ing, -ed 'æli-
   gəraiz [-leg-], -iz, -iŋ, -d
allegor|y, -ies 'æligər|i [-leg-], -iz
allegretto, -s ˌæli'gretəu [-le'g-], -z
allegro, -s ə'leigrəu [æ'l-, -'leg-, rarely
   'æligrəu], -z
Allegwash 'æligwɔʃ
Allein(e) 'ælin
alleluia (A.), -s ˌæli'luːjə, -z
allemande, -s 'ælmã:nd [-mɔ̃:nd,
   -mɑːnd, -mɔːnd, -mɔnd] (almã:d), -z
Allen 'ælin
Allenby 'ælənbi
Allendale 'ælindeil [-lən-]
Allentown 'ælintaun [-lən-]
allergic ə'ləːdʒik
allergy 'ælədʒi
Allerton 'ælətən
alleviat|e, -es, -ing, -ed, -or/s ə'liːvieit,
   [-vjeit], -s, -iŋ, -id, -ə*/z
alleviation əˌliːvi'eiʃən
alley, -s 'æli, -z   ['ælin
Alleyn (founder of Dulwich College)
Alleyne æ'liːn, 'ælin, 'ælein
Alleynian, -s ə'leinjən [æ'l-, -nĭən], -z
All-Fools'-Day, -s 'ɔːl'fuːlzdei, -z
all-fours 'ɔːl'fɔːz [-'fɔəz]
Allfrey 'ɔːlfri ['ɔl-]
all-hail 'ɔːl'heil [ɔːl'h-]
All-Hallows 'ɔːl'hæləuz
Allhusen æl'hjuːzən
alliance, -s ə'laiəns, -iz
Allies 'ælaiz [ə'laiz]
alligator, -s 'æligeitə*, -z
allineation, -s əˌlini'eiʃən [æ,l-], -z
Allingham 'æliŋəm
Allison 'ælisn
alliterat|e, -es, -ing, -ed ə'litəreit [æ'l-],
   -s, -iŋ, -id

alliteration, -s əˌlitə'reiʃən [æ,l-], -z
alliterative ə'litərətiv [æ'l-, -reit-]
Allman 'ɔːlmən
Alloa 'æləuə
Allobroges ə'lɔbrədʒiːz [æ'l-, -brəudʒ-,
   ˌælə'brəudʒ-]
allocat|e, -es, -ing, -ed 'æləukeit, -s, -iŋ,
   -id
allocation, -s ˌæləu'keiʃən, -z
allochrone, -s 'æləkrəun [-ləu-], -z
allocution, -s ˌæləu'kjuːʃən, -z
allodi|al/s, -um ə'ləudj|əl/z [-dĭ|-], -əm
allomorph, -s 'æləmɔːf [-ləu-], -s
Allon 'ælən
allopath, -s 'æləupæθ, -s
allopathic ˌæləu'pæθik
allopath|ist/s, -y ə'lɔpəθ|ist/s [æ'l-], -i
allophone, -s 'æləfəun [-ləuf-], -z
allophonic ˌælə'fɔnik [-ləu'f-]
allot, -s, -ting, -ted, -ment/s ə'lɔt, -s,
   -iŋ, -id, -mənt/s
allotone, -s 'ælətəun [-ləut-], -z
allotropic ˌæləu'trɔpik
allow, -s, -ing, -ed ə'lau, -z, -iŋ, -d
allowab|le, -ly, -leness ə'lauəb|l,
   -li, -lnis
allowanc|e (s. v.), -es, -ing, -ed
   ə'lauəns, -iz, -iŋ, -t
Alloway 'æləwei ['æləuei]
alloy (mixture of metals), -s 'ælɔi
   [ə'lɔi], -z, (figurative sense) ə'lɔi
alloy (v.), -s, -ing, -ed ə'lɔi, -z, -iŋ, -d
Allpress 'ɔːlpres
All-Saints'-Day, -s 'ɔːl'seintsdei, -z
Allsop(p) 'ɔːlsɔp ['ɔl-, -səp]
All-Souls'-Day, -s 'ɔːl'səulzdei, -z
allspice 'ɔːl-spais
Allt (surname) ɔːlt
allud|e, -es, -ing, -ed ə'luːd [-'ljuːd],
   -z, -iŋ, -id
allur|e, -es, -ing/ly, -ed, -ement/s
   ə'ljuə* [-'luə*, -'ljɔə*, -'ljɔː*, -'ljə:*],
   -z, -riŋ/li, -d, -mənt/s
allusion, -s ə'luːʒən [-'ljuː-], -z
allusive, -ly, -ness ə'luːsiv [-'ljuː-],
   -li, -nis
alluvi|al, -on/s, -um/s, -a ə'luːvj|əl
   [-'ljuː-, -vĭ|əl], -ən/z, -əm/z, -ə
Allworth 'ɔːlwə(:)θ
Allworthy 'ɔːlˌwəːði
all|y (party to alliance), -ies 'ælai
   [ə'lai], -z
all|y (marble), -ies 'æl|i, -iz
all|y (v.), -ies, -ying, -ied ə'l|ai [æ'l-,
   'ælai], -aiz, -aiiŋ, -aid ['ælaid]
   Note.—allied is generally pronounced
   'ælaid when attributive.
Ally 'æli

Alma 'ælmə
Almack 'ɔːlmæk ['ɔl-]
almagest, -s 'ælmədʒest, -s [-z
Alma Mater, -s 'ælmə'mɑːtə* [-'meitə*,

almanac(k), -s 'ɔːlmənæk ['ɔl-], -s
Almanzor æl'mænzɔ:* [-zə*]
Alma-Tadema 'ælmə'tædimə
Almeria, -s æl'miərïə, -z
Almesbury 'ɑːmzbəri
almight|y (A.), -ily, -iness ɔːl'mait|i,
  -ili, -inis
almner, -s 'ɑːmnə*, -z
almoi(g)n 'ælmɔin
Almon 'ælmən
almond (A.), -s 'ɑːmənd, -z
Almondbury (in Yorks.) 'ælməndbəri
  ['ɑːmənd-, 'ɔːmbəri, 'eimbəri]
Almondsbury 'ɑːməndzbəri
almoner, -s 'ɑːmənə* ['ælm-], -z
almon|ry, -ies 'ɑːmənr|i ['ælm-], -iz
almost 'ɔːlməust ['ɔl-, -məst]
Almroth 'ælmrəuθ
alms ɑːmz
almsgiv|er/s, -ing 'ɑːmz,giv|ə*/z, -iŋ
almshou|se, -ses 'ɑːmzhau|s, -ziz
Alne (in Yorks., Warw.) ɔːn
Alnmouth 'ælnmauθ
Alnwick 'ænik
aloe, -s 'æləu, -z
aloft ə'lɔft [-'lɔːft]
alone, -ness ə'ləun, -nis
along, -side ə'lɔŋ, -'said
aloof, -ness ə'luːf, -nis
Alor Star 'ælɔ:'stɑ:*
aloud ə'laud
Aloysius ,æləu'iʃəs [-'isïəs]
alp (A.), -s ælp, -s
alpaca, -s æl'pækə, -z
alpenrose, -s 'ælpənrəuz [-pin-], -iz
alpenstock, -s 'ælpinstɔk [-pən-], -s
Alperton 'ælpətən
alpestrian æl'pestrïən
alpha, -s 'ælfə, -z
alphabet, -s 'ælfəbit [-bet], -s
alphabetic, -al, -ally ,ælfə'betik, -əl, -əli
Alphaeus æl'fi(:)əs
Alphonso æl'fɔnzəu [-nsəu]
alpine 'ælpain
alpinist, -s 'ælpinist, -s
already ɔːl'redi [ɔl-, also '-,-- when followed by a stress]
Alresford 'ɔːlrisfəd [locally 'ɔːlsfəd]
Alsace 'ælsæs [-lzæs] (alzas)
Alsager (in Cheshire) 'ɔːlsidʒə* [-sədʒ-],
  ɔːl'seidʒə
Alsa|tia, -tian/s æl'sei|ʃjə [-ʃïə, -ʃə],
  -ʃjən/z [-ʃïən/z, -ʃən/z]

also 'ɔːlsəu ['ɔl-]
Alsop(p) 'ɔːlsɔp ['ɔl-, -səp]
Alston 'ɔːlstən ['ɔl-]
alt ælt
Altai æl'teïai [-'tai]
Altaic æl'teiik
Altair æl'tɛə* ['æltɛə*]
altar, -s 'ɔːltə* ['ɔl-], -z
altar|-cloth, -cloths 'ɔːltə|klɔθ ['ɔl-,
  'ɔːltəklɔ:θ], -klɔθs ['ɔːltəklɔ:ðz,
  'ɔːltəklɔ:θs]
altar-piece, -s 'ɔːltəpi:s ['ɔl-], -iz
altar-rail, -s 'ɔːltə-reil ['ɔl-], -z
altazimuth, -s ælt'æziməθ, -s
alt|er, -ers, -ering, -ered; -erable;
  -erant/s 'ɔːlt|ə* ['ɔl-], -əz, -əriŋ, -əd;
  -ərəbl; -ərənt/s
alteration, -s ,ɔːltə'reiʃən [,ɔl-], -z
alterative 'ɔːltərətiv ['ɔl-, -reit-]
altercat|e, -es, -ing, -ed 'ɔːltəkeit
  ['ɔl-, -tə:k-], -s, -iŋ, -id
altercation, -s ,ɔːltə'keiʃən [,ɔl-, -tə:'k-],
  -z
alternance, -s ɔːl'tə:nəns [ɔl-, rarely
  æl-], -iz
alternant, -s ɔːl'tə:nənt [ɔl-, rarely æl-],
  -s
alternate (adj.), -ly, -ness ɔːl'tə:nit
  [ɔl-, rarely æl-], -li, -nis
alternat|e (v.), -es, -ing, -ed 'ɔːltəneit
  ['ɔl-, -tə:n-, rarely 'æl-], -s, -iŋ, -id
alternation, -s ,ɔːltə'neiʃən [,ɔl-, -tə:'n-,
  rarely ,æl-], -z
alternative (s. adj.), -s, -ly ɔːl'tə:nətiv
  [ɔl-, rarely æl-], -z, -li
Althorp 'ɔːlθɔ:p ['ɔl-], 'ɔːltrəp ['ɔl-]
  Note.—Viscount Althorp pronounces
  'ɔːltrəp.
although ɔːl'ðəu [ɔl-]
altimeter, -s 'æltimi:tə* ['ɔːl-], -z
altimetry æl'timitri [rarely ɔːl-, ɔl-]
altissimo æl'tisiməu
altitude, -s 'æltitjuːd, -z
alto, -s 'æltəu [rarely 'ɑːl-], -z
altogether ,ɔːltə'geðə* [,ɔl-, -tu'g-,
  '--'--, also sometimes '---- when
  attributive]
Alton 'ɔːltən ['ɔl-]
Altona (in Germany) 'æltəunə,
  ('alto:na:), (in U.S.A.) æl'təunə
alto-relievo 'æltəuri'li:vəu
alto-rilievo 'æltəurili'eivəu
Altrincham 'ɔːltriŋəm ['ɔl-]
altrui|sm, -st/s 'æltrui|zəm, -st/s
altruistic, -ally ,æltru'istik, -əli
alum (A.), -s 'æləm, -z
alumina ə'ljuːminə [æ'l-, -'luː-]
aluminium ,ælju'minjəm [-nïəm]

aluminous ə'lju:minəs [æ'l-, -'lu:-]
alumn|a, -ae ə'lʌmn|ə, -i:
alumn|us, -i ə'lʌmn|əs, -ai
Alva 'ælvə
Alvar 'ælvɑ:* [-və*]
Alvary 'ælvəri
Alvechurch 'ɔ:lvtʃə:tʃ
alveolar, -s æl'viələ* [ˌælvi'əulə*, 'ælviələ*], -z
alveole, -s 'ælviəul, -z
alveol|us, -i æl'viəl|əs [ˌælvi'əul-, 'ælviəl-], -ai [-i:]
Alverstone 'ɔ:lvəstən ['ɔl-]
Alvescot 'ælviskɔt [-kət, locally 'ɔ:lskət]
Alveston (in Glos.) 'ælvistən
Alwar 'ælwə* ['ʌl-] (Hind. əlvər)
alway 'ɔ:lwei
always 'ɔ:lweiz [-wəz, -wiz]
Alwyn 'ælwin
alyssum 'ælisəm
a.m. 'ei'em [ei'em when preceded by a stress]   [forms]
am, æm (strong form), əm, m (weak
Amabel 'æməbel
Amadis 'æmədis
amadou 'æmədu:
amain ə'mein
Amalek 'æmələk
Amalekite, -s ə'mælakait, -s
amalgam, -s ə'mælgəm, -z
amalgamat|e, -es, -ing, -ed ə'mælgə-meit, -s, -iŋ, -id
amalgamation, -s ə,mælgə'meiʃən, -z
Aman 'æmən
Amanda ə'mændə
amandine ə'mændain
Amantia ə'mænʃïə [-ʃjə]
amanuens|is, -es ə,mænju'ens|is, -i:z
Amara ə'mɑ:rə
amaranth, -s 'æmərænθ, -s
amaranthine ˌæmə'rænθain
amaryllis (A.), -es ˌæmə'rilis, -iz
Amasa 'æməsə [ə'meisə]
Amasis ə'meisis
amass, -es, -ing, -ed ə'mæs, -iz, -iŋ, -t
Amata ə'meitə
amateur, -s 'æmətə(:)* [-tjuə*, -tjɔə*, -tjɔ:*, -tʃə*, ˌæmə'tə:*], -z
amateurish, -ly, -ness ˌæmə'tə:riʃ [-'tjuər-, -'tjɔər-, -'tjɔ:r-, 'æmət-, -tʃə-], -li, -nis
Amati, -s ə'mɑ:ti [æ'm-], -z
amative, -ness 'æmətiv, -nis
amatol 'æmətɔl
amatory 'æmətəri
amaurosis ˌæmɔ:'rəusis
Amaury ə'mɔ:ri
amaz|e, -es, -ing/ly, -ed, -edly, -edness,

-ement/s ə'meiz, -iz, -iŋ/li, -d, -idli, -idnis, -mənt/s
Amaziah ˌæmə'zaiə
amazon (A.), -s 'æməzən, -z
amazonian, ˌæmə'zəunjən [-nïən]
ambage, -s 'æmbidʒ, æm'beidʒi:z ['æmbidʒiz]
ambassador, -s æm'bæsədə* [-sid-], -z
ambassadorial æm,bæsə'dɔ:rïəl [ˌæmb-, -si'd-]
ambassadress, -es æm'bæsədris [-sid-, -dres], -iz
ambe, -s 'æmbi, -z
amber 'æmbə*
ambergris 'æmbəgri(:)s
ambidexter, -s 'æmbi'dekstə* [ˌæm-], -z
ambidexterity 'æmbideks'teriti [ˌæm-]
ambidextrous 'æmbi'dekstrəs [ˌæm-]
ambience, -s 'æmbïəns [-bjəns], -iz
ambient 'æmbïənt [-bjənt]
ambiguit|y, -ies ˌæmbi'gju(:)it|i, -iz
ambiguous, -ly, -ness æm'bigjŭəs [-gjwəs], -li, -nis
Ambiorix æm'baiəriks
ambit, -s 'æmbit, -s
ambition, -s æm'biʃən, -z
ambitious, -ly, -ness æm'biʃəs, -li, -nis
ambivalen|ce, -t 'æmbi'veilən|s [æm'bivələns], -t [æm'bivələnt]
amb|le, -les, -ling, -led, -ler/s 'æmb|l, -lz, -liŋ [-lïŋ], -ld, -lə*/z [-|ə*/z]
Ambler 'æmblə*
Ambleside 'æmblsaid
amboyna (A.) æm'bɔinə
Ambree 'æmbri
Ambrose 'æmbrəuz [-əus]
ambrosia, -l, -lly, -n æm'brəuzjə [-zïə, -ʒjə, -ʒïə], -l, -li, -n
ambr|y, -ies 'æmbr|i, -iz
ambs-ace 'eimzeis ['æm-]
ambulance, -s 'æmbjuləns, -iz
ambulant 'æmbjulənt
ambulat|e, -es, -ing, -ed 'æmbjuleit, -s, -iŋ, -id
ambulation, -s ˌæmbju'leiʃən, -z
ambulator|y (s. adj.), -ies 'æmbjulə-tər|i [-leit-], -iz
ambuscad|e (s. v.), -es, -ing, -ed ˌæmbəs'keid, -z, -iŋ, -id
ambush (s. v.), -es, -ing, -ed 'æmbuʃ, -iz, -iŋ, -t
Amelia ə'mi:ljə [-lïə]
ameliorat|e, -es, -ing, -ed ə'mi:ljəreit [-lïər-, -lïɔ:r-, -ljɔ:r-], -s, -iŋ, -id
amelioration, -s ə,mi:ljə'reiʃən [-lïə'r-, -lïɔ:'r-, -ljɔ:'r-], -z
ameliorative ə'mi:ljərətiv [-lïər-, -lïɔ:r-, -ljɔ:r-, -reit-]

amen, -s (*liturgical*) 'ɑː'men [-'-], (*in ordinary spoken language*) 'ɑː'men ['ei'men, -'-], -z
amenability ə,miːnə'biliti [-lət-]
amenab|le, -ly, -leness ə'miːnəb|l, -li, -lnis
Amen Corner 'eimen 'kɔːnə*
amen|d, -ds, -ding, -ded, -dment/s ə'men|d, -dz, -diŋ, -did, -dmənt/s
Amen House 'eimen 'haus
amenit|y, -ies ə'miːnit|i [-'men-], -iz
amerc|e, -es, -ing, -ed, -ement/s ə'məːs, -iz, -iŋ, -t, -mənt/s
America, -n/s ə'merikə, -n/z
Americana ə,meri'kɑːnə
americanism, -s ə'merikənizəm, -z
americanization [-isa-] ə,merikənai'zeiʃən [-ni'z-]
americaniz|e [-is|e], -es, -ing, -ed ə'merikənaiz, -iz, -iŋ, -d
americium ,æmə'risiəm [-sjəm, -ʃiəm, -ʃjəm]
Amerindian, -s ,æmər'indjən [-diən], -z
Amersham 'æməʃəm
Amery 'eiməri
Ames, -bury eimz, -bəri
amethyst, -s 'æmiθist [-meθ-], -s
amethystine ,æmi'θistain [-me'θ-]
Amharic æm'hærik
Amherst 'æməst, 'æmhəːst
amiability ,eimjə'biliti [-miə-, -lət-]
amiab|le, -ly, -leness 'eimjəb|l [-miə-], -li, -lnis
Amias 'eimiəs [-mjəs]
amicability ,æmikə'biliti [-lət-]
amicab|le, -ly, -leness 'æmikəb|l, -li, -lnis
amice, -s 'æmis, -iz
Amice, 'eimis
amid ə'mid
Amidas 'æmidæs
amide, -s 'æmaid, -z
amidships ə'midʃips
amidst ə'midst [-itst]
Amiel 'æmiəl ['eim-, -mjəl]
Amiens (*French city*) 'æmjɛ̃ːŋ [-miɛ̃ːŋ, -miæŋ, -miənz, -mjənz] (amjɛ̃), (*Shakespearian character*) 'æmiənz [-mjənz], (*street in Dublin*) 'eimjənz [-miənz]
Amies 'eimiz
amir, -s ə'miə* [æ'm-, -'æmiə*], -z
Amis 'eimis
amiss ə'mis
amity 'æmiti
Amlwch 'æmluk [-lux] (*Welsh* 'amlux)
Amman ə'mɑːn
ammeter, -s 'æmitə*, -z

Ammon 'æmən [-mɔn]
ammonia ə'məunjə [-niə]
ammoniac ə'məuniæk, [-njæk]
ammoniacal ,æməu'naiəkəl
ammoniated ə'məunieitid [-njei-]
ammonite (A.), -s 'æmənait, -s
ammonium ə'məunjəm [-niəm]
ammunition ,æmju'niʃən
amnesia æm'niːzjə [-zіə]
amnest|y, -ies 'æmnist|i [-nəs-, -nes-], -iz
Amnon 'æmnɔn
amoeb|a, -ae, -as, -ic ə'miːb|ə, -iː, -əz, -ik
amok ə'mɔk ['ɑːməu]
  Note.—'ɑːməu *is the pronunciation used in Malaya.*
among, -st ə'mʌŋ, -st [ə'mʌŋkst]
amontillado (A.) ə,mɔnti'lɑːdəu [-i'ljɑː-]
Amoore 'eimuə*
amoral ,ei'mɔrəl [ə'm-, æ'm-]
amorist, -s 'æmərist, -s
Amorite, -s 'æmərait, -s
amorous, -ly, -ness 'æmərəs, -li, -nis
amorpha, -s ə'mɔːfə, -z
amorph|ism, -ous ə'mɔːf|izəm, -əs
amortization [-isa-], -s ə,mɔːti'zeiʃən, [,æmɔːt-, ,æmət-], -z
amortiz|e, -es, -ing, -ed ə'mɔːtaiz [-tiz], -iz, -iŋ, -d
Amory 'eiməri
Amos 'eimɔs [-s, -iŋ, -id
amount (*s. v.*), -s, -ing, -ed ə'maunt, amour, -s ə'muə* [æ'm-], -z
amour-propre 'æmuə'prɔpr̩ [-'prɔpə*] (amurprɔpr̩)
Amoy ə'mɔi
amp, -s æmp, -s
ampelopsis ,æmpi'lɔpsis
ampère [-pere], -s 'æmpɛə*, -z
Ampère 'æmpɛə* (ɑ̃pɛːr)
ampersand, -s 'æmpəsænd, -z
amphibi|a, -an/s, -ous æm'fibi|ə [-bj|ə], -ən/z, -əs
amphibole (*mineral*) 'æmfibəul
amphibole (*net*), -s æm'fibəli, -z
amphibology ,æmfi'bɔlədʒi
amphibol|y, -ies æm'fibəl|i, -iz
amphibrach, -s 'æmfibræk, -s
Amphictyon, -s æm'fiktiɔn [-tjən], -z
amphictyonic æm,fikti'ɔnik
Amphimedon æm'fimidən [-dəun]
Amphion æm'faiən
Amphipolis æm'fipəlis
amphiscian, -s æm'fiʃiən [-ʃjən], -z
amphitheatre, -s 'æmfi,θiətə* [-θi,etə*], -z
Amphitrite 'æmfitraiti

Amphitryon æm'fitrɪən

amphor|a, -ae, -as 'æmfər|ə, -i:, -əz

amphoric æm'fɔrik

amp|le, -ler, -lest, -ly, -leness 'æmp|l,
  -lə*, -list, -li, -lnis

amplification, -s ,æmplifi'keiʃən, -z

amplificatory 'æmplifikeitəri [,---'---]

ampli|fy, -fies, -fying, -fied, -fier/s 'æm-
  pli|fai, -faiz, -faiiŋ, -faid, -faiə*/z

amplitude, -s 'æmplitju:d, -z

ampoule, -s 'æmpu:l, -z

Ampthill 'æmpthil

ampull|a, -ae æm'pul|ə, -i:

amputat|e, -es, -ing, -ed 'æmpjuteit, -s,
  -iŋ, -id

amputation, -s ,æmpju'teiʃən, -z

Amram 'æmræm

Amritsar æm'ritsə* (Hind. əmrytsər)

Amsterdam 'æmstə'dæm [-mps-, ,--'-,
  '--,-]

amuck ə'mʌk

amulet, -s 'æmjulit [-let], -s

Amulree ,æmə'l'ri:

Amundsen 'ɑ:mundsən [-mən-]

Amur ə'muə* [æ'm-, 'æmuə*]

amus|e, -es, -ing/ly, -ingness, -ed,
  -ement/s ə'mju:z, -iz, -iŋ/li, -iŋnis,
  -d, -mənt/s

Amy 'eimi

Amyas 'eimjəs [-mɪəs]

amygdaloid ə'migdələid [æ'm-]

amyl 'æmil

amytal 'æmitæl

an æn (strong form), ən, n (weak forms)

ana 'ɑ:nə

anabapti|sm, -st/s ,ænə'bæpti|zəm, -st/s

anabaptistic ,ænəbæp'tistik ['ænə-
  bæp't-]

anabas|is, -es ə'næbəs|is, -i:z

anabolism ə'næbəulizəm

anachorism, -s ə'nækərizəm, -z

anachron|ism/s, -ous/ly ə'nækrən|-
  izəm/z, əs/li

anachronistic ə,nækrə'nistik [-krɔ'n-]

anacoluth|on, -a ,ænəkəu'lu:θ|ɔn [-næk-,
  -'lju:-, -θ|ən], -ə

anaconda, -s ,ænə'kɔndə, -z

Anacreon ə'nækrɪən

anacrus|is, -es ,ænə'kru:s|is, -i:z

Anadin 'ænədin

anaemia ə'ni:mjə [æ'n-, -mɪə]

anaemic ə'ni:mik [æ'n-]

anaesthesia ,ænis'θi:zjə [-ni:s-, -nəs-,
  -zɪə, -ʒjə, -ʒɪə, -ʒə]

anaesthetic, -s, -ally ,ænis'θetik [-ni:s-,
  -nəs-], -s, -əli

anaesthetist, -s æ'ni:sθitist [ə'n-, -θət-],
  -s

anaesthetiz|e [-is|e], -es, -ing, -ed
  æ'ni:sθitaiz [ə'n-, -θət-], -iz, -iŋ, -d

anagogic, -s, -al, -ally ,ænə'gɔdʒik, -s,
  -əl, -əli

anagogy 'ænəgɔdʒi [-gɔgi, -gəudʒi]

anagram, -s 'ænəgræm, -z

anagrammatic, -al, -ally ,ænəgrə-
  'mætik, -əl, -əli

Anak 'einæk [rarely 'ænæk]

Anakim 'ænəkim [rarely ə'nɑ:kim]

anal 'einəl

analects 'ænəlekts

analgesia ,ænæl'dʒi:zjə [-i:zɪə, -i:sjə,
  -i:sɪə]

analgesic ,ænæl'dʒesik [-'dʒi:sik]

analogic, -al, -ally ,ænə'lɔdʒik, -əl, -əli

analogist, -s ə'nælədʒist, -s

analogous, -ly, -ness ə'næləgəs, -li, -nis

analogue, -s 'ænəlɔg, -z

analog|y, -ies ə'nælədʒ|i, -iz

analphabetic, -al, -ally 'ænælfə'betik
  [,æn-], -əl, -əli

analysable 'ænəlaizəbl

analys|e, -es, -ing, -ed 'ænəlaiz, -iz, -iŋ,
  -d

analys|is, -es, ə'næləs|is [-lis-], -i:z

analyst, -s 'ænəlist, -s

analytic, -s, -al, -ally ,ænə'litik, -s, -əl,
  -əli

Anam 'ænæm

anamorphosis ,ænə'mɔ:fəsis

anana, -s (plur.) ə'nɑ:nə, -z

ananas (sing.), -es ə'nɑ:nəs, -iz

Ananias ,ænə'naiəs

anapaest, -s 'ænəpi:st [-pest], -s

anapaestic ,ænə'pi:stik [-'pest-]

anaphora, -s ə'næfərə, -z

anarch, -s 'ænɑ:k, -s

anarchic, -al, -ally æ'nɑ:kik [ə'n-], əl,
  -əli

anarch|ism, -ist/s, -y 'ænək|izəm,
  -ist/s, -i

Anastasia (English Christian name)
  ,ænəs'teizjə [-zɪə], (foreign name)
  ,ænəs'tɑ:z-

anastigmat, -s ə'næstigmæt [æ'n-], -s

anastomosis ,ænəstə'məusis [,ænæs-]

anastrophe, -s ə'næstrəfi [æ'n-], -z

anathema, -s ə'næθimə [-θəm-], -z

anathematization [-isa-], -s ə,næθi-
  mətai'zeiʃən [-θəm-, -ti'z-], -z

anathematiz|e [-is|e], -es, -ing, -ed
  ə'næθimətaiz [-θəm-], -iz, -iŋ, -d

Anatolia, -n/s ,ænə'təuljə [-lɪə], -n/z

anatomic, -al, -ally ,ænə'tɔmik, -əl, -əli

anatomist, -s ə'nætəmist, -s

anatomiz|e [-is|e], -es, -ing, -ed ə'nætə-
  maiz, -iz, -iŋ, -d

anatom|y, -ies ə'nætəm|i, -iz
anatto ə'nætəu
Anaxagoras ˌænæk'sægəræs [-rəs]
ancestor, -s 'ænsistə* [-ses-, -səs-], -z
ancestral æn'sestrəl
ancestress, -es 'ænsistris [-ses-, -səs-], -iz
ancestr|y, -ies 'ænsistr|i [-ses-, -səs-], -iz
Anchises æŋ'kaisi:z [æn'k-]
Ancholme 'æŋkhəum
anchor (s. v.), -s, -ing, -ed 'æŋkə*, -z, -riŋ, -d
anchorage, -s 'æŋkəridʒ, -iz
anchoress, -es 'æŋkəris [-res], -iz
anchoret, -s 'æŋkəret [-rit], -s
anchorhold, -s 'æŋkəhəuld, -z
anchorite, -s 'æŋkərait [-kɔr-], -s
anchov|y, -ies 'æntʃəv|i [æn'tʃəuv-], -iz
anchylosis ˌæŋkai'ləusis [ˌænk-]
ancient, -est, -ly, -s 'einʃənt, -ist, -li, -s
ancillary æn'siləri
ancipit|al, -ous æn'sipit|l, -əs
Ancren Riwle 'æŋkrin'riuli [-kren-, -krən-, -lə]
ancress, -es 'æŋkris [-kres], -iz
Ancyra æn'saiərə
and ænd (strong form), ənd, ən, nd, n, m, ŋ (weak forms)
  Note.—The form m only occurs next to p or b, and the form ŋ only occurs next to k or g.
Andalusia ˌændə'lu:zjə [-u:zïə, -u:ʒjə, -u:ʒïə, -u:sjə, -u:sïə, -u:ʃjə, -u:ʃïə]
Andaman 'ændəmæn [-mən]
andante, -s æn'dænti, -z
Ander|sen, -son 'ændə|sn, -sn
Andes 'ændi:z
andiron, -s 'ændaiən, -z
Andorra æn'dɔrə
Andover 'ændəuvə*
Andow (surname) 'ændau
Andrade (English surname) 'ændreid
Andrassy æn'dræsi
Andreas 'ændriæs [-ïəs]
Andrew 'ændru:
Andrewatha (Cornish family) æn-'dru:θə, (Plymouth family) æn-'dru:əθə, ˌændru:'ɔθə
Andrews 'ændru:z
Andria 'ændrïə
Androcles 'ændrəukli:z
Androclus æn'drɔkləs
androgynous, æn'drɔdʒinəs
android, -s 'ændrɔid, -z
Androm|ache, -eda æn'drɔm|əki, -idə
Andronicus (Byzantine emperors and other figures in ancient history) ˌændrə'naikəs [æn'drɔnikəs], (in Shakespeare's Titus A.) æn'drɔnikəs

Andros 'ændrɔs
anecdotal ˌænek'dəutl [-nik-]
anecdote, -s 'ænikdəut [-nek-], -s
anecdotic, -al, -ally ˌænek'dɔtik [-nik-], -əl, -əli
anechoic ˌæni'kəuik
Anelay (surname) 'einli
anelectric, -s ˌæni'lektrik, -s
anelectrode, -s ˌæni'lektrəud, -z
anemomet|er/s, -ry ˌæni'mɔmit|ə*/z, -ri
anemometric ˌæniməu'metrik
anemone, -s ə'neməni, -z
anemoscope, -s ə'neməskəup, -s
anent ə'nent
aneroid, -s 'ænərɔid, [-nir-], -z
aneurin 'ænjuərin
Aneurin ə'naiərin (Welsh a'nəïrin)
aneurism, -s 'ænjuərizəm, -z
anew ə'nju:
anfractuosity ˌænfræktju'ɔsiti
Angear 'æŋgïə*
angel (A.), -s 'eindʒəl, -z
Angela 'ændʒələ [-dʒil-]
Angeles 'ændʒili:z ['æŋgil-, -liz, -lis]
angelic, -al, -ally æn'dʒelik, -əl, -əli
angelica (A.) æn'dʒelikə
Angelina ˌændʒi'li:nə [-dʒe'l-, -dʒə'l-]
Angelo 'ændʒiləu
angelus, -es 'ændʒiləs [-dʒəl-], -iz
anger (s. v.), -s, -ing, -ed 'æŋgə*, -z, -riŋ, -d
Angevin 'ændʒivin
Angier 'ændʒïə*
angina, -s æn'dʒainə, -z
ang|le (s. v.) (A.), -les, -ling, -led, -ler/s 'æŋg|l, -lz, -liŋ, -ld, -lə*/z
angledozer, -s 'æŋgl,dəuzə*, -z
Angle|sea, -sey 'æŋgl|si, -si
Anglia, -n/s 'æŋglïə [-gljə], -n/z
Anglic|an, -anism 'æŋglik|ən/z, -ənizəm
anglice 'æŋglisi
anglici|sm/s, -st/s 'æŋglisi|zəm/z, -st/s
anglicization [-isa-] ˌæŋglisai'zeiʃən
angliciz|e [-is|e], -es, -ing, -ed 'æŋgli-saiz, -iz, -iŋ, -d
Anglo-French 'æŋgləu'frentʃ
anglomania 'æŋgləu'meinjə [-nïə]
Anglo-Norman 'æŋgləu'nɔ:mən
anglophile, -s 'æŋgləufail, -z
anglophobe, -s 'æŋgləufəub, -z
anglophobia ˌæŋgləu'fəubjə [-bïə]
Anglo-Saxon, -s 'æŋgləu'sæksən, -z
Anglo-Saxondom 'æŋgləu'sæksəndəm
Anglo-Saxonism, -s 'æŋgləu'sæksənizəm [-sŋi-], -z
Angmering 'æŋməriŋ
Angola æŋ'gəulə

Angora (*old form of* **Ankara** *in Turkey*)
'æŋgərə [æŋ'gɔ:rə]
Note.—*English residents in Turkey
formerly pronounced* 'æŋgərə.
Angora (*cat, rabbit, cloth*), **-s** æŋ'gɔ:rə, -z
Angostura ˌæŋgɔs'tjuərə [-gəs-, -'tjɔərə,
-'tjɔ:rə, -'stjə:rə]
angr|y, -ier, -iest, -ily, -iness 'æŋgr|i,
-iə*, -iist, -ili, -inis
angstrom, -s 'æŋstrəm, -z
anguine 'æŋgwin
anguish, -ed 'æŋgwiʃ, -t
angular 'æŋgjulə*
angularit|y, -ies ˌæŋgju'lærit|i, -iz
angulate 'æŋgjuleit [-lit]
angulated 'æŋgjuleitid
Angus 'æŋgəs
Angustura ˌæŋgəs'tjuərə [-'tjɔərə,
-'tjɔ:rə, -'stjə:rə]
anharmonic 'ænhɑ:'mɔnik
anhungered ən'hʌŋgəd
anhydr|ide/s, -ite, -ous æn'haidr|aid/z,
-ait, -əs
anil 'ænil
anile 'einail ['æn-]
aniline 'ænili:n [-lin, *rarely* -lain]
anility æ'niliti [ə'n-]
animadversion, -s ˌænimæd'və:ʃən
[-məd-], -z
animadvert, -s, -ing, -ed ˌænimæd'və:t
[-məd-], -s, -iŋ, -id
animal, -s 'æniml, -z
animalcular ˌæni'mælkjulə*
animalcule, -s ˌæni'mælkju:l, -z
animalism 'æniməlizəm [-m|i-]
animate (*adj.*) 'ænimit [-mət, -meit]
animat|e (*v.*), **-es, -ing, -ed/ly, -or/s**
'ænimeit, -s, -iŋ, -id|li, -ə*/z
animation ˌæni'meiʃən
animism 'ænimizəm
animosit|y, -ies ˌæni'mɔsit|i, -iz
animus 'æniməs
anion, -s 'ænaiən, -z
anise 'ænis
aniseed 'ænisi:d
anisette ˌæni'zet [-'set]
Anita ə'ni:tə
Anjou ɑ̃:ŋ'ʒu: [ɔ̃:ŋ-, ɔŋ-] (ãʒu)
Ankara (*in Turkey*) 'æŋkərə
nker, -s 'æŋkə*, -z
nkh, -s æŋk, -s
nkle, -s 'æŋkl, -z
nklet, -s 'æŋklit, -s
Ann æn
nna (**A.**), **-s** 'ænə, -z
nnabel 'ænəbel
nnabella ˌænə'belə
nnagh æ'nɑ: ['ænɑ:]

Annakin 'ænəkin
annalist, -s 'ænəlist, -s
annals 'æn|z
Annaly 'ænəli
Annam æn'æm ['ænæm]
Annamese ˌænə'mi:z
Annan, -dale 'ænən, -deil
Annapolis ə'næpəlis [æ'n-]
Annas 'ænæs [-nəs]
annatto ə'nætəu [æ'n-]
Anne æn
anneal, -s, -ing, -ed ə'ni:l, -z, -iŋ, -d
Annesley 'ænzli
annex (*s.*), **-es** 'æneks, -iz
annex (*v.*), **-es, -ing, -ed, -ment/s**
ə'neks [æ'n-], -iz, -iŋ, -t, -mənt/s
annexation, -s ˌænek'seiʃən, -z
annexe, -s 'æneks, -iz
Annie 'æni
annihilat|e, -es, -ing, -ed, -or/s ə'naiə-
leit [-'naiil-, *rarely* 'æniəl-], -s, -iŋ,
-id, -ə*/z
annihilation, -s ə,naiə'leiʃən [-,naii'l-,
rarely ,æniə'l-], -z
Anning 'æniŋ
Anniston 'ænistən
anniversar|y, -ies ˌæni'və:sər|i, -iz
Anno Domini 'ænəu'dɔminai
annotat|e, -es, -ing, -ed, -or/s 'ænəu-
teit, -s, -iŋ, -id, -ə*/z
annotation, -s ˌænəu'teiʃən, -z
**announc|e, -es, -ing, -ed, -er/s,
-ement/s** ə'nauns, -iz, -iŋ, -t, -ə*/z,
-mənt/s
annoy, -s, -ing/ly, -ed; -ance/s ə'nɔi,
-z, -iŋ/li, -d; -əns/iz
annual (*s. adj.*), **-s, -ly** 'ænjuəl [-njwəl,
-njul], -z, -i
annuit|y, -ies, -ant/s ə'nju(:)it|i, -iz,
-ənt/s
annul, -s, -ling, -led, -ment/s ə'nʌl, -z,
-iŋ, -d, -mənt/s
annul|ar, -ate, -ated 'ænjul|ə*, -eit [-it],
-eitid
annunciat|e, -es, -ing, -ed ə'nʌnʃieit
[-nʃjeit, -nsieit, -nsjeit], -s, -iŋ, -id
annunciation (**A.**), **-s** ə,nʌnsi'eiʃən, -z
anode, -s 'ænəud, -z
anodyne, -s 'ænəudain, -z
anoint, -s, -ing, -ed, -ment/s ə'nɔint,
-s, -iŋ, -id, -mənt/s
anomalous, -ly ə'nɔmələs, -li
anomal|y, -ies ə'nɔməl|i, -iz
anon ə'nɔn
anonym, -s 'ænənim [-nɔn-], -z
anonymity ˌænə'nimiti [-nɔ'n-]
anonymous, -ly ə'nɔniməs, -li
anopheles ə'nɔfili:z [-fəl-]

anorak, -s 'ænəræk, -s
another ə'nʌðə*
Anouilh 'ænu:i(:) (anu:j)
Anrias 'ænriæs
Anselm 'ænselm
anserine 'ænsərain
An|sley, -son 'æn|zli, -sn
Ansonia æn'səunjə [-nɪə]
Ansted 'ænsted [-tid]
Anster 'ænstə*
Anstey 'ænsti
Anstruther 'ænstrʌðə*
answ|er (s. v.), -ers, ering, -ered,
  -erer/s 'ɑ:ns|ə*, -əz, -ərɪŋ, -əd, -ərə*/z
answerab|le, -ly 'ɑ:nsərəb|l, -li
ant, -s ænt [rarely ɑ:nt], -s
an't (= am not) ɑ:nt
antacid (s. adj.), -s 'ænt'æsid ['ænt,æ-],
  -z
Antaeus æn'ti(:)əs
antagoni|sm/s, -st/s æn'tægəni|zəm/z,
  -st/s
antagonistic, -ally æn,tægə'nistik
  ['-,--'--], -əli
antagoniz|e [-is|e], -es, -ing, -ed
  æn'tægənaiz, -iz, -iŋ, -d
Antananarivo 'æntə,nænə'ri:vəu [,æn-]
Antarctic ænt'ɑ:ktik ['-'--, '-,--]
Antares æn'tɛəri:z
ant-bear, -s 'ænt'bɛə* [rarely 'ɑ:nt-], -z
ant-eater, -s 'ænt,i:tə* [rarely 'ɑ:nt-],
  -z
anteceden|ce, -t/ly, -ts ,ænti'si:dən|s
  ['ænti's-, 'ænti,s-], -t/li, -ts
antechamber, -s 'ænti,tʃeimbə*, -z
antechapel, -s 'ænti,tʃæpəl, -z
antedat|e, -es, -ing, -ed 'ænti'deit ['---],
  -s, -iŋ, -id
antediluvi|an/s, -al/ly 'æntidi'lu:-
  vj|ən/z [,æn-, -dai'l-, -'lju:-, -vɪ|ə-],
  -əl/i
antelope, -s 'æntiləup, -s
antemeridian 'æntimə'ridɪən [,æn-,
  -djən]
antenatal 'ænti'neitl
antenn|a, -ae, -al, -ary æn'ten|ə, -i:, -l,
  -əri
Antenor æn'ti:nɔ:*
antenuptial 'ænti'nʌpʃəl
antepenult, -s 'æntipi'nʌlt [-pe'n-,
  -pə'n-], -s
antepenultimate, -s 'æntipi'nʌltimit
  [-pe'n-, -pə'n-], -s
anteprandial 'ænti'prændjəl [-dɪəl]
anterior, -ly, -ness æn'tiərɪə*, -li, -nis
anteroom, -s 'æntirum [-ru:m], -z
Anthaea æn'θiə [-'θi:ə, 'ænθiə, 'ænθjə]
ant-heap, -s 'ænthi:p [rarely 'ɑ:nt-], -s

antheli|on/s, -a æn'θi:lj|ən/z [-lɪ|ə-], -ə
anthelix, -es æn'θi:liks ['ænθiliks], -iz
anthem, -s 'ænθəm [-θem], -z
anther, -s 'ænθə*, -z
anthill, -s 'ænθil [rarely 'ɑ:nt-], -z
anthological ,ænθə'lɒdʒikəl [-θəu'l-]
antholog|y, -ies æn'θɒlədʒ|i, -iz
Anthon 'ænθən
Anthony 'æntəni, 'ænθəni
anthracic æn'θræsik
anthracite 'ænθrəsait
anthracitic ,ænθrə'sitik
anthrax 'ænθræks
anthropoid (s. adj.), -s 'ænθrəupɔid
  [æn'θrəupɔid], -z
anthropoidal ,ænθrəu'pɔidl
anthropologic|al, -ally ,ænθrəpə'lɒdʒ-
  ik|əl [-θrəup-], -əli
anthropolog|ist/s, -y ,ænθrə'pɒlədʒ|-
  ist/s [-θrəu'p-], -i
anthropometric ,ænθrəupəu'metrik
anthropometry ,ænθrə'pɒmitri [-θrəu'p-,
  'ænθrəpəmetri, 'ænθrəupəmetri,
  'ænθrəpəumetri, 'ænθrəupəumetri]
anthropomorph|ic, -ism, -ist/s, -ous
  ,ænθrəpəu'mɔ:f|ik [-θrəup-], -izəm,
  -ist/s, -əs
anthropophagi ,ænθrəu'pɒfəgai [-fədʒai]
anthropopha|gous, -gy ,ænθrəu'pɒfə|gəs,
  -dʒi
anthroposoph|ist/s, -y ,ænθrəu'pɒsəf|-
  ist/s, -i
anti- 'ænti-
  Note.—Numerous compounds may be
  formed by prefixing anti- to other
  words. Those not entered below have
  double stress. Thus anti-vivisection
  is pronounced 'ænti,vivi'sekʃən
anti-aircraft 'ænti'ɛə-krɑ:ft
antibilious 'ænti'biljəs [-lɪəs]
antibiotic (s. adj.), -s 'æntibai'ɒtik, -s
antibod|y, -ies 'ænti,bɒd|i, -iz
antic, -s 'æntik, -s
anticatholic, -s 'ænti'kæθəlik [-'kɑ:θ-,
  -θ|ik], -s
Antichrist, -s 'æntikraist, -s
antichristian, -s (opposing Christianity)
  'ænti'kristjən [-tɪən, -tʃən], (pertaining to Antichrist) 'ænti,k-, -z
anticipant, -s æn'tisipənt, -s
anticipat|e, -es, -ing, -ed; -ive/ly
  æn'tisipeit, -s, -iŋ, -id; -iv/li
anticipation, -s æn,tisi'peiʃən [,ænti-], -z
anticipator|y, -ily æn'tisipeitər|i [-pət-],
  -ili
anticiz|e [-is|e], -es, -ing, -ed 'æntisaiz,
  -iz, -iŋ, -d
anticlerical 'ænti'klerikl

anticlimax, -es 'ænti'klaimæks [*in con-trast* 'ænti₁klaimæks], -iz
anticyclone, -s 'ænti'saikləun ['ænti₁s-], -z
anticyclonic ₁æntisai'klɔnik
antidotal 'æntidəutl [₁ænti'd-]
antidote, -s 'æntidəut, -s
antifat 'ænti'fæt
antifebrile 'ænti'fi:brail [-'feb-]
anti-freeze 'æntifri:z
Antigon|e, -us æn'tigən|i, -əs
Antigua æn'ti:gə
anti|helix, -helixes, -helices 'ænti|'hi:-liks, -'hi:liksiz, -'hi:lisi:z [-'helisi:z]
anti-icer, -s 'ænti'aisə*, -z
Antilles æn'tili:z
antilog|y, -ies æn'tiləd₃|i, -iz
antimacassar, -s 'æntimə'kæsə* [₁æn-], -z
Antimachus æn'timəkəs
antimonarchical 'æntimɔ'nɑ:kikəl [₁æn-, -mə'n-]
antimonarchist, -s 'ænti'mɔnəkist, -s
antimonial, -s ₁ænti'məunjəl [-niəl], -z
antimonic ₁ænti'mɔnik
antimony 'æntiməni
anti-national 'ænti'næʃənl [-ʃnəl, -ʃŋl, ʃnl, -ʃənəl]
antinomic, -al, -ally ₁ænti'nɔmik, -əl, -əli
antinom|y, -ies æn'tinəm|i, -iz
Antinous æn'tinəuəs
Antioch 'æntiɔk [-tjɔk]
Antiochian, -s ₁ænti'əukjən [-kïən], -z
Antiochus æn'taiəkəs
Antioquia ₁æntiəu'ki(:)ə
Antipas 'æntipæs
Antipater æn'tipətə*
antipathetic ₁æntipə'θetik [-₁--'--]
antipath|y, -ies æn'tipəθ|i, -iz
antiphlogistic 'æntifləu'd₃istik
antiphlogistine ₁æntifləu'd₃isti:n [-flɔ'd₃-, -tin]
antiphon, -s 'æntifən [-fɔn], -z
antiphon|al/s, -er/s æn'tifən|l/z [-əl/z], -ə*/z
antiphonic, -al, -ally ₁ænti'fɔnik, -əl, -əli
antiphon|y, -ies æn'tifən|i, -iz
antipodal æn'tipədl
antipodean æn₁tipə'di(:)ən [₁æntip-, -pəu'd-]
antipodes æn'tipədi:z
antipope, -s 'æntipəup, -s
antipyretic, -s 'æntipai'retik [-paiə'r-, -pi'r-], -s
antipyrin ₁ænti'paiərin
antiquarian, -s, -ism ₁ænti'kwɛərïən, -z, -izəm
antiquar|y, -ies 'æntikwər|i, -iz

antiquate (*adj.*) 'æntikwit [-kweit]
antiquated 'æntikweitid
antique (*s. adj.*), -s, -ly, -ness æn'ti:k, -s, -li, -nis
antiquit|y, -ies æn'tikwit|i, -iz
antirrhinum, -s ₁ænti'rainəm [-tə'r-], -z
antiscorbutic, -s 'ænti-skɔ:'bju:tik, -s
antiseptic (*s. adj.*), -s, -ally ₁ænti'septik, -s, -əli
antisocial 'ænti'səuʃəl
antisocialist, -s 'ænti'səuʃəlist [-ʃli-], -s
antistrophe, -s æn'tistrəfi, -z
antistrophic ₁ænti'strɔfik
antithes|is, -es æn'tiθis|is [-θəs-], -i:z
antithetic, -ally ₁ænti'θetik, -əli
antitoxi|c, -n/s 'ænti'tɔksi|k, -n/z
anti-trade, -s 'ænti'treid, -z
antiviral 'ænti'vairəl
antler, -s, -ed 'æntlə*, -z, -d
ant-lion, -s 'ænt₁laiən [*rarely* 'ɑ:nt-], -z
Antoinette ₁æntwɑ:'net [₁ɑ:n-, -twə'n-] (ātwanɛt)
Antonia æn'təunjə [-nïə]
Antonine, -s 'æntənain, -z
Antoninus ₁æntəu'nainəs
Antonio æn'təuniəu [-njəu]
Antonius æn'təunjəs [-nïəs]
Antony 'æntəni
antonym, -s 'æntəunim, -z
Antrim 'æntrim
Antrobus 'æntrəubəs
antr|um, -ums, -a 'æntr|əm, -əmz, -ə
antrycide 'æntrisaid
Antwerp 'ænt-wə:p
anus, -es 'einəs, -iz
anvil, -s 'ænvil, -z
Anwick 'ænik
anxiet|y, -ies æŋ'zaiət|i [-ŋg'z-], -iz
anxious, -ly, -ness 'æŋkʃəs, -li, -nis
any 'eni (*normal form*), əni (*occasional weak form*), ŋi (*occasional weak form after* t *or* d)
anybody 'eni₁bɔdi [-bədi]
anyhow 'enihau
anyone 'eniwʌn [-wən]
anything 'eniθiŋ
anyway 'eniwei
anywhere 'eniwɛə* [-hwɛə*]
anywise 'eniwaiz
Anzac, -s 'ænzæk, -s
Aonia, -n/s ei'əunjə [-nïə], -n/z
aorist, -s 'eərist ['eïər-], -s
aort|a/s, -al, -ic ei'ɔ:t|ə/z, -əl, -ik
Aosta ɑ:'ɔstə
apace ə'peis
Apache (*American tribesman*), -s ə'pætʃi, -z ⌈(apaʃ), -iz
apache (*ruffian*), -s ə'pæʃ [æ'p-, -'pɑ:ʃ]

apart, -ness ə'pɑːt, -nis
apartheid ə'pɑːtheit [-eid] (Afrikaans a'partheit)
apartment, -s ə'pɑːtmənt, -s
apathetic, -al, -ally ˌæpə'θetik, -əl, -əli
apath|y, -ies 'æpəθ|i, -iz
ap|e (s. v.), -es, -ing, -ed eip, -s, -iŋ, -t
apehood 'eiphud
Apelles ə'peliːz
Apennines 'æpinainz [-pen-]
aperçu, -s ˌæpəː'sju: [-'su:] (apɛrsy), -z
aperient, -s ə'piəriənt, -s
aperitive, -s ə'peritiv, -z
aperture, -s 'æpətjuə* [-tʃuə*, -tʃə*], -z
aper|y, -ies 'eipər|i, -iz
apex, -es, apices 'eipeks, -iz, 'eipisi:z ['æpisi:z]
aphasia æ'feizjə [ə'f-, -zïə, -ʒjə, -ʒïə, -ʒə]
aphasic ə'feizik
apheli|on, -a æ'fi:lj|ən [-lï|ən], -ə
apheresis æ'fiərisis
aphesis 'æfisis
aphid 'eifid
aphidian, -s ei'fidïən [æ'f-, -djən], -z
aph|is, -ides, -ises 'eif|is ['æf-], -idi:z, -ïsi:z
aphonia æ'fəunjə [ə'f-, ei'f-, -nïə] -isiz
aphonic æ'fonik [ə'f-, ei'f-]
aphony 'æfəni
aphori|sm/s, -st/s 'æfəri|zəm/z [-fɔr-], -st/s
aphoristic, -ally ˌæfə'ristik [-fɔ'r-], -əli
aphoriz|e [-is|e], -es, -ing, -ed, -er/s 'æfəraiz [-fɔr-], -iz, -iŋ, -d, -ə*/z
aphrodis|iac/s, -ian ˌæfrəu'diz|iæk/s, -ïən [-jən]
Aphrodite ˌæfrəu'daiti
aphtha 'æfθə
apian 'eipjən [-pïən]
apiarian, -s ˌeipi'ɛərïən, -z
apiar|y, -ies, -ist/s 'eipjər|i [-pïər-], -iz, -ist/s
apic|al, -ally 'æpik|əl ['eip-], -əli
apices (plur. of apex) 'eipisi:z ['æp-]
apiculture 'eipikʌltʃə*
apiece ə'pi:s
apis (bee) 'eipis
Apis 'ɑːpis ['eipis]
apish, -ly, -ness 'eipiʃ, -li, -nis
aplomb ə'plɔm ['æplɔ̃:ŋ, -plɔ̃:m] (aplɔ̃)
apocalyp|se/s (A.), -st/s, -t/s ə'pɔkə-lip|s/iz, -st/s, -t/s
apocalypti|c, -st/s əˌpɔkə'lipti|k, -st/s
apocopate (adj.) ə'pɔkəupit [-peit]
apocopat|e (v.), -es, -ing, -ed ə'pɔkəu-peit, -s, -iŋ, -id
apocopation, -s əˌpɔkəu'peiʃən, -z
apocope, -s ə'pɔkəupi, -z

apocryph|a/s, -al ə'pɔkrif|ə/z, -əl
apodeictic, -al, -ally ˌæpəu'daiktik, -əl, -əli
apodos|is, -es ə'pɔdəus|is, -i:z
apogee, -s 'æpəudʒi:, -z
Apollinaris əˌpɔli'nɛəris [-'nɑːr-]
Apollo ə'pɔləu
Apollodorus əˌpɔlə'dɔːrəs
Apolloni|a, -an, -us ˌæpə'ləunj|ə [-pɔ'l-, -nï|ə], -ən, -əs
Apollos ə'pɔlɔs
Apollyon ə'pɔljən [-lïən]
apologetic, -al, -ally, -s əˌpɔlə'dʒetik, -əl, -əli, -s
apologist, -s ə'pɔlədʒist, -s
apologiz|e [-is|e], -es, -ing, -ed, -er/s ə'pɔlədʒaiz, -iz, -iŋ, -d, -ə*/z
apologue, -s 'æpəlɔg [-pəul-, -ləug], -z
apolog|y, -ies ə'pɔlədʒ|i, -iz
apophthegm, -s 'æpəuθem, -z
apoplectic, -al, -ally ˌæpəu'plektik, -əl, -əli
apoplex|y, -ies 'æpəupleks|i, -iz
aposiopes|is, -es ˌæpəusaiəu'pi:s|is, -i:z
apostas|y, -ies ə'pɔstəs|i, -iz
apostate, -s ə'pɔstit [-teit], -s
apostatic, -al ˌæpəus'tætik, -əl
apostatiz|e [-is|e], -es, -ing, -ed ə'pɔstətaiz, -iz, -iŋ, -d
a posteriori 'ei-pɔsˌteri'ɔːrai [-ˌtiər-, 'ɑː-pɔsˌteri'ɔːri:]
apostigmat, -s 'æpəustigmæt, -s
apostil, -s ə'pɔstil, -z
apostle, -s, -ship ə'pɔsl, -z, -ʃip
apostolate, -s ə'pɔstəulit [-leit], -s
apostolic, -al, -ally ˌæpəs'tɔlik, -əl, -əli
apostolicism ˌæpəs'tɔlisizəm
apostrophe, -s ə'pɔstrəfi, -z
apostrophiz|e [-is|e], -es, -ing, -ed ə'pɔstrəfaiz, -iz, -iŋ, -d
apothecar|y, -ies ə'pɔθikər|i [-θək-], -iz
apotheos|is, -es əˌpɔθi'əus|is [ˌæpəuθ-], -i:z
apotheosiz|e [-is|e], -es, -ing, -ed ə'pɔθiəusaiz [-θïəs-, ˌæpəu'θiəusaiz], -iz, -iŋ, -d
appal, -s, -ling/ly, -led ə'pɔːl, -z, -iŋ/li, -d
Appalachian ˌæpə'leitʃjən [-tʃïən]
appanage, -s 'æpənidʒ, -iz
apparatus, -es ˌæpə'reitəs, -iz
apparatus (alternative plur. of apparatus) ˌæpə'reitəs
appar|el (s. v.), -els, -elling, -elled ə'pær|əl, -əlz, -əliŋ [-liŋ], -əld
apparent, -ly, -ness ə'pærənt [-'pɛər-], -li, -nis

apparition, -s ˌæpəˈriʃən, -z
apparitor, -s əˈpæritɔ:* [-tə*], -z
appassionata (*Beethoven sonata*) əˌpæsjəˈnɑːtə [-sïə-]
appeal (*s. v.*), -s, -ing/ly, -ingness, -ed, -er/s əˈpiːl, -z, -iŋ/li, -iŋnis, -d, -ə*/z
appear, -s, -ing, -ed, -er/s; -ance/s əˈpiə*, -z, -riŋ, -d, -rə*/z; -rəns/iz
appeas|e, -es, -ing/ly, -ed; -able əˈpiːz, -iz, -iŋ/li, -d; -əbl
appellant, -s əˈpelənt, -s
appellate əˈpelit [æˈp-, -leit]
appellation, -s ˌæpəˈleiʃən [-piˈl-, -peˈl-], -z
appellative, -ly, -ness əˈpelətiv [æˈp-], -li, -nis
append, -s, -ing, -ed; -age/s əˈpend, -z, -iŋ, -id; -idʒ/iz
appendicitis əˌpendiˈsaitis
append|ix, -ixes, -ices əˈpend|iks, -iksiz, -isi:z
apperception ˌæpə(ː)ˈsepʃən
Apperley ˈæpəli
appertain, -s, -ing, -ed ˌæpəˈtein [-pəːˈt-], -z, -iŋ, -d
appertinent əˈpəːtinənt [æˈp-]
appeten|ce, -cy, -t ˈæpitən|s, -si, -t
appetite, -s ˈæpitait, -s
appetiz|e, -es, -ing/ly, -ed, -er/s ˈæpitaiz, -iz, -iŋ/li, -d, -ə*/z
Appi|an, -us ˈæpï|ən [-pjˈl-], -əs
applaud, -s, -ing/ly, -ed, -er/s əˈplɔːd, -z, -iŋ/li, -id, -ə*/z
applause əˈplɔːz
apple, -s; -blight ˈæpl, -z; -blait
apple-blossom ˈæpl,blɔsəm
Appleby ˈæplbi
Appledore ˈæpldɔ:* [-dɔə*]
Appleford ˈæplfəd
Applegate ˈæplgeit [-git]
apple|-pie/s, -sauce ˈæpl|ˈpai/z, -ˈsɔːs
Appleton ˈæpltən
apple-tree, -s ˈæpltri:, -z
appliable, -ness əˈplaiəbl, -nis
appliance, -s əˈplaiəns, -iz
applicability ˌæplikəˈbiliti [əˌplik-, -lət-]
applicab|le, -ly, -leness ˈæplikəb|l [əˈplik-], -li, -lnis
applicant, -s ˈæplikənt, -s
applicate ˈæplikit [-keit]
application, -s ˌæpliˈkeiʃən, -z
appliqué, -s æˈpliːkei [əˈp-] (apˌlike), -z
appl|y, -ies, -ying, -ied əˈpl|ai, -aiz, aiiŋ, -aid
appoggiatura, -s əˌpɔdʒəˈtuərə [-dʒjə-, -dʒïə-, -ˈtjuər-, -ˈtjɔər-, -ˈtjɔːr-], -z
appoint, -s, -ing, -ed, -ment/s əˈpoint, -s, -iŋ, -id, -mənt/s

appointee, -s, əpɔinˈti: [ˌæpɔinˈt-], -z
apport, -s, -ing, -ed əˈpɔːt, -s, -iŋ, -id
apporti|on, -ons, -oning, -oned, -onment/s əˈpɔːʃ|ən, -ənz, -ŋiŋ [-niŋ, -əniŋ], -ənd, -ənmənt/s
appos|e, -es, -ing, -ed æˈpəuz, -iz, -iŋ, -d
apposite, -ly, -ness ˈæpəuzit, -li, -nis
apposition, -s, ˌæpəuˈziʃən [-puˈz-], -z
appositional ˌæpəuˈziʃənl [-puˈz-, -ʃnəl, -ʃn̩l, -ʃn̩l, -[ənəl]
apprais|e, -es, -ing, -ed, -er/s, -ement/s; -able, -al/s əˈpreiz, -iz, -iŋ, -d, -ə*/z, -mənt/s; -əbl, -əl/z
appreciab|le, -ly əˈpri:ʃəb|l [-ʃəb-, -ʃïəb-], -li
appreciat|e, -es, -ing/ly, -ed, -or/s əˈpri:ʃieit [-ʃjeit, -i:sieit, -i:sjeit], -s, -iŋ/li, -id, -ə*/z
appreciation, -s əˌpri:ʃiˈeiʃən [-i:si-], -z
appreciative, -ly, -ness əˈpri:ʃjətiv [-ʃïət-, -ʃieit-], -li, -nis
appreciatory əˈpri:ʃjətəri [-ʃïət-, -ʃieit-]
apprehend, -s, -ing, -ed ˌæpriˈhend, -z, -iŋ, -id
apprehensibility ˈæpriˌhensiˈbiliti [-sə'b-, -lət-]
apprehensible ˌæpriˈhensəbl [-sib-]
apprehension, -s ˌæpriˈhenʃən, -z
apprehensive, -ly, -ness ˌæpriˈhensiv, -li, -nis
apprentic|e (*s. v.*), -es, -ing, -ed əˈprentis, -iz, -iŋ, -t
apprenticeship, -s əˈprentiʃip [-tisʃip, -tiʃʃip], -s
appris|e, -es, -ing, -ed əˈpraiz, -iz, -iŋ, -d
appriz|e, -es, -ing, -ed, -er/s əˈpraiz, -iz, -iŋ, -d, -ə*/z
approach (*s. v.*), -es, -ing, -ed; -able əˈprəutʃ, -iz, -iŋ, -t; -əbl
approachability əˌprəutʃəˈbiliti [-lət-]
approbat|e, -es, -ing, -ed; -ive ˈæprəubeit [-prub-], -s, -iŋ, -id; -iv
approbation, -s ˌæprəuˈbeiʃən [-pruˈb-], -z
appro|priate (*adj.*), -priately, -priateness əˈprəu|priit, -priitli [-prïətli], -priitnis [-prïətnis]
appropriat|e (*v.*), -es, -ing, -ed, -or/s əˈprəuprieit, -s, -iŋ, -id, -ə*/z
appropriation, -s əˌprəupriˈeiʃən, -z
approv|e, -es, -ing/ly, -ed, -er/s; -able, -al/s əˈpru:v, -z, -iŋ/li, -d, -ə*/z; -əbl, -əl/z
approximate (*adj.*), -ly əˈprɔksimit, -li [-mətli]
approximat|e (*v.*), -es, -ing, -ed əˈprɔksimeit, -s, -iŋ, -id
approximation, -s əˌprɔksiˈmeiʃən, -z

approximative ə'prɔksimətiv
appui æ'pwi: [ə'p-] (apɥi)
Appuldurcombe ˌæpldə'ku:m
appulse, -s æ'pʌls [ə'pʌls, 'æpʌls], -iz
appurtenan|ce, -ces, -t ə'pə:tinən|s
　[-tŋə-], -siz, -t
apricot, -s 'eiprikɔt, -s
April, -s 'eiprəl [-ril], -z
a priori 'ei-prai'ɔ:rai ['ɑ:-pri(:)'ɔ:ri:]
apriority ˌei-prai'ɔriti
apron, -s, -ed 'eiprən, -z, -d
apropos 'æprəpou [ˌ-'-]
apse, -s æps, -iz
apsidal 'æpsidl
apsis, apsides 'æpsis, æp'saidi:z ['æp-
　sidi:z]
Apsley 'æpsli
apt, -er, -est, -ly, -ness æpt, -ə*, -ist,
　-li, -nis
apter|al, -ous 'æptər|əl, -əs
apteryges æp'teridʒi:z
apteryx, -es 'æptəriks, -iz
aptitude, -s 'æptitju:d, -z
Apulia, -n/s ə'pju:ljə [-liə], -n/z
apyretic ˌæpai'retik [-paiə'r-, -pi'r-]
aqua-fortis 'ækwə'fɔ:tis
aqua-lung, -s 'ækwəlʌŋ, -z
aquamarine, -s ˌækwəmə'ri:n, -z
aqua-plane, -s 'ækwəplein, -z
aqua-regia 'ækwə'ri:dʒə [-dʒiə]
aquarell|e, -es; -ist/s ˌækwə'rel, -z;
　-ist/s
aquarist, -s 'ækwərist, -s
aquari|um, -ums, -a ə'kwɛəri|əm, -əmz,
　-ə
Aquari|us, -an/s ə'kwɛəri|əs, -ən/z
aquatic (s. adj.), -s ə'kwætik [-'kwɔt], -s
aquatint, -s 'ækwətint, -s
aqua-vitae 'ækwə'vaiti: [-ti]
aqueduct, -s 'ækwidʌkt, -s
aqueous, -ly 'eikwiəs ['æk-], -li
Aquila 'ækwilə [as constellation also
　ə'kwilə]
aquilegia, -s ˌækwi'li:dʒə [-dʒiə], -z
aquiline 'ækwilain
Aquinas ə'kwainæs [æ'k-, -nəs]
Aquitaine ˌækwi'tein
Aquitania ˌækwi'teinjə [-niə]
Arab, -s 'ærəb, -z
Arabella ˌærə'belə
arabesque, -s, -d ˌærə'besk, -s, -t
Arabia, -n/s ə'reibjə [-biə], -n/z
Arabic (of Arabia) 'ærəbik, (name of
　ship) 'ærəbik [ə'ræb-]
arabis 'ærəbis
arable 'ærəbl ['ɛər-]
Araby 'ærəbi
Arachne ə'rækni

arachnid, -a, -s ə'ræknid, -ə, -z
arachnologist, -s ˌæræk'nɔlədʒist
　[-rək-], -s
Aragon 'ærəgən
aragonite ə'rægənait
Aral 'ɑ:rəl ['ɛər-]
Aram (biblical name) 'ɛəræm [-rəm],
　(surname) 'ɛərəm
Aramai|c, -sm ˌærə'meii|k, -zəm
Aramean, -s ˌærə'mi(:)ən, -z
Aramite, -s 'ærəmait ['ɛəræm-], -s
Aran 'ærən
Ararat 'ærəræt
Araucania ˌærɔ:'keinjə [-niə]
araucaria, -s ˌærɔ:'kɛəriə, -z
Arber 'ɑ:bə*
Arberry 'ɑ:bəri
arbiter, -s 'ɑ:bitə*, -z
arbitrage (arbitration) 'ɑ:bitridʒ
arbitrage (of stocks, etc.) ˌɑ:bi'trɑ:ʒ
　['ɑ:bitridʒ]
arbitrament, -s ɑ:'bitrəmənt [-trim-], -s
arbitrar|y, -ily, -iness 'ɑ:bitrər|i, -ili,
　-inis
arbitrat|e, -es, -ing, -ed, -or/s 'ɑ:bitreit,
　-s, -iŋ, -id, -ə*/z
arbitration, -s ˌɑ:bi'treiʃən, -z
arbitress, -es 'ɑ:bitris [-tres], -iz
Arblay 'ɑ:blei
arbor (tree) 'ɑ:bɔ:* [-bə*]
arbor (axle, arbour), -s 'ɑ:bə*, -z
Arbor 'ɑ:bə*
arboraceous ˌɑ:bə'reiʃəs [-bɔ:'r-]
arbore|al, -ous ɑ:'bɔ:ri|əl, -əs
arborescen|ce, -t ˌɑ:bə'resn|s [-bɔ:'r-],
　-t
arboretum, -s ˌɑ:bə'ri:təm [-bɔ:'r-], -z
arboriculture 'ɑ:bərikʌltʃə* [-bɔ:r-]
arbor-vitae, -s 'ɑ:bə'vaiti [-ti:], -z
arbour, -s 'ɑ:bə*, -z
Arbroath ɑ:'brouθ
Arbuthnot(t) ɑ:'bʌθnət [ə'b-]
arbutus, -es ɑ:'bju:təs, -iz
arc (A.), -s ɑ:k, -s
arcade, -s ɑ:'keid, -z
Arcadia, -n/s ɑ:'keidjə [-diə], -n/z
arcan|um, -a ɑ:'kein|əm, -ə
arch (s. v.), -es, -ing, -ed ɑ:tʃ, -iz, -iŋ, -t
arch (adj.), -est, -ly, -ness ɑ:tʃ, -ist, -li,
　-nis
archaean ɑ:'ki(:)ən
archaeologic|al, -ally ˌɑ:kiə'lɔdʒik|əl
　[-kjə-], -əli
archaeolog|ist/s, -y ˌɑ:ki'ɔlədʒ|ist/s, -i
archaeopteryx, -es ˌɑ:ki'ɔptəriks, -iz
archaic, -ally ɑ:'keiik, -əli
archaism, -s 'ɑ:keiizəm, -z
archangel, -s 'ɑ:kˌeindʒəl ['ɑ:k'ein-], -z

Archangel 'ɑːkˌeindʒəl [ɑːk'ein-]
archbishop, -s 'ɑːtʃ'biʃəp [also '-ˌ--,
-'-- according to sentence stress], -s
archbishopric, -s ɑːtʃ'biʃəprik ['ɑːtʃ'b-],
-s
Arch|bold, -dale 'ɑːtʃ|bəuld, -deil
archdeacon, -s 'ɑːtʃ'diːkən [also '-ˌ--,
-'-- according to sentence stress], -z
archdeaconr|y, -ies 'ɑːtʃ'diːkənr|i
[ɑːtʃ'd-], -iz
archdiocese, -s 'ɑːtʃ'daiəsis [-siːs], -iz
archducal 'ɑːtʃ'djuːkəl [-'--]
archduchess, -es 'ɑːtʃ'dʌtʃis, -iz
archduch|y, -ies 'ɑːtʃ'dʌtʃ|i, -iz
archduke, -s 'ɑːtʃ'djuːk ['--], -s
archdukedom, -s ɑːtʃ'djuːkdəm ['-'--], -z
Archelaus ˌɑːki'leiəs
arch-enem|y, -ies 'ɑːtʃ'enim|i [-nəm-],
-iz
archer (A.), -s 'ɑːtʃə*, -z
archeress, -es 'ɑːtʃəris [-res], -iz
archery 'ɑːtʃəri
archetype, -s 'ɑːkitaip, -s
arch-fiend (A.), -s 'ɑːtʃ'fiːnd, -z
arch-heretic, -s 'ɑːtʃ'herətik [-rit-], -s
Archibald 'ɑːtʃibəld [-bɔːld]
archidiaconal ˌɑːkidai'ækənl [-di'æk-,
-kɳl]
Archie 'ɑːtʃi
archiepiscop|acy, -al, -ate ˌɑːkii'pis-
kəp|əsi [-kie'p-], -əl, -it [-eit]
Archilochus ɑː'kiləkəs
Archimage 'ɑːkimeidʒ
archimandrite, -s ˌɑːki'mændrait, -s
Archimedean ˌɑːki'miːdjən [-dïən,
ˌɑːkimi(ː)'di(ː)ən]
Archimedes ˌɑːki'miːdiːz
archipelago, -(e)s ˌɑːki'peligəu [-ləg-], -z
archiphoneme, -s 'ɑːkiˌfəuniːm, -z
architect, -s 'ɑːkitekt, -s
architectonic ˌɑːkitek'tɔnik
architec|tural, -turally ˌɑːki'tek|tʃərəl
[-tʃurəl], -tʃərəli [-tʃərli, -tʃurəli]
architecture 'ɑːkitektʃə*
architrave, -s, -d 'ɑːkitreiv, -z, -d
archival ɑː'kaivəl
archive, -s 'ɑːkaiv, -z
archivist, -s 'ɑːkivist, -s
archon, -s 'ɑːkən [-kɔn], -z
arch-prelate, -s 'ɑːtʃ'prelit [-lət], -s
arch-priest, -s 'ɑːtʃ'priːst, -s
arch-traitor, -s 'ɑːtʃ'treitə*, -z
archway (A.), -s 'ɑːtʃwei, -z
archwise 'ɑːtʃwaiz
Archyll 'ɑːkil
Archytas ɑː'kaitæs [-təs]
Arcite 'ɑːsait
Arcot ɑː'kɔt

arctic 'ɑːktik
Arcturus ɑːk'tjuərəs [-'tjɔər-, -'tjɔːr-]
arcuate 'ɑːkjuit [-kjueit]
arcuated 'ɑːkjueitid
Arcy 'ɑːsi
Ardagh 'ɑːdə [-dɑː]
Ardee ɑː'diː
Arden 'ɑːdn
arden|cy, -t/ly 'ɑːdən|si, -t/li
Ardennes ɑː'den [-'denz]
Ardeshir ɑː'deiʃiə* [ˌɑːdə'ʃiə*] (Hind.
ərdeʃyr)
Ardilaun ˌɑːdi'lɔːn
Arding 'ɑːdiŋ
Ardingly (in Sussex) 'ɑːdiŋlai
Ardlamont ɑːd'læmənt
Ard|leigh, -ley 'ɑːd|li, -li
Ardoch 'ɑːdɔk [-ɔx]
ardour 'ɑːdə*
Ardrishaig ɑː'driʃig
Ardrossan ɑː'drɔsən
Arduin 'ɑːdwin
arduous, -ly, -ness 'ɑːdjʊəs [-djwəs], -li,
-nis
Ardwick 'ɑːdwik
are (surface measure), -s ɑː*, -z
are (from be) ɑː* (strong form), ə*
(weak form), r (occasional weak form
before vowels)
area, -s 'ɛəriə, -z
areca, -s 'ærikə [æ'riːkə, ə'riːkə], -z
are|fy, -fies, -fying, -fied 'æri|fai, -faiz,
-faiiŋ, -faid
arena, -s ə'riːnə, -z
Arendt 'ærənt ['ɑːr-]
aren't ɑːnt
areol|a, -as, -ae æ'riəul|ə [ə'r-], -əz, -iː
areomet|er/s, -ry ˌæri'ɔmit|ə*/z [ˌɛər-],
-ri
Areopagite, -s ˌæri'ɔpəgait [-ədʒait], -s
areopagitic, -a ˌæriɔpə'dʒitik, -ə
Areopagus ˌæri'ɔpəgəs
Arequipa ˌæri'kiːpə [-re'k-] (are'kipa)
Ares 'ɛəriːz
arête, -s æ'reit [ə'r-] (arɛːt), -s
Arete ə'riːti(ː) [æ'r-]
Arethusa ˌæri'θjuːzə [-re'θ-]
Argalus 'ɑːgələs
argand (A.), -s 'ɑːgænd [-gənd], -z
argent 'ɑːdʒənt
argentiferous ˌɑːdʒən'tifərəs [-dʒen't-]
Argentina ˌɑːdʒən'tiːnə [-dʒen't-]
argentine 'ɑːdʒəntain
Argentine 'ɑːdʒəntain [-tiːn]
argil 'ɑːdʒil
argillaceous ˌɑːdʒi'leiʃəs
Argive, -s 'ɑːgaiv, -z
Argo 'ɑːgəu

argol 'ɑːgɔl
Argolis 'ɑːgəlis
argon 'ɑːgɔn [-gən]
Argonaut, -s 'ɑːgənɔːt, -s
Argonautic ˌɑːgəˈnɔːtik
Argos 'ɑːgɔs
argos|y, -ies 'ɑːgəs|i, -iz
argot, -s 'ɑːgəu (argo), -z
arg|ue, -ues, -uing, -ued, -uer/s; -uable 'ɑːg|juː, -juːz, -juiŋ [-jwiŋ], -juːd, -jŭə*/z [-jwə*/z]; -jŭəbl [-jwəbl]
argument, -s 'ɑːgjumənt, -s
argumental ˌɑːgjuˈmentl
argumentation, -s ˌɑːgjumenˈteiʃən [-mən't-], -z
argumentative, -ly, -ness ˌɑːgjuˈmentətiv, -li, -nis
argus (A.), -es 'ɑːgəs, -iz
Argyle ɑːˈgail
Argyll ɑːˈgail [attributively also '--]
Argyllshire ɑːˈgail|iə* [-ʃə]
arhat, -s 'ɑːhət (Hind. ərhət), -s
aria, -s 'ɑːriə, -z
Ariadne ˌæriˈædni
Arian, -s, -ism 'ɛəriən, -z, -izəm
arianiz|e [-is|e], -es, -ing, -ed 'ɛəriənaiz, -iz, -iŋ, -d
arid, -ly, -ness 'ærid, -li, -nis
aridity æˈriditi [əˈr-]
ariel (A.), -s 'ɛəriəl, -z
Aries (constellation) 'ɛəriːz ['ɛəriiːz, 'æriiːz]
arietta, -s ˌæriˈetə, -z
aright əˈrait
Arimathaea ˌæriməˈθiə [-ˈθiːə]
Arion əˈraiən [æˈr-]
arioso ˌɑːriˈəuzəu [ˌær-]
Ariosto ˌæriˈɔstəu
aris|e, -es, -ing, arose, arisen əˈraiz, -iz, -iŋ, əˈrəuz, əˈrizn
Ariss 'ɛəris
Aristaeus ˌærisˈti(ː)əs
Aristarch 'æristɑːk
Aristarchus ˌærisˈtɑːkəs
Aristides ˌærisˈtaidiːz
aristocrac|y, -ies ˌærisˈtɔkrəs|i, -iz
aristocrat, -s 'æristəkræt [æ'ris-, əˈris-], -s
aristocratic, -al, -ally ˌæristəˈkrætik, -əl, -əli
aristocratism ˌærisˈtɔkrətizəm
Aristogiton ˌæristəuˈdʒaitn
Aristophanes ˌærisˈtɔfəniːz [-fɲiːz]
aristophanic ˌæristəuˈfænik [-tɔ'f-]
aristotelian, -s ˌæristɔˈtiːljən [-təuˈt-, -liən], -z
Aristotle 'æristɔtl
Aristoxenus ˌærisˈtɔksinəs [-sən-]

arithmetic (s.), -s əˈriθmətik [-mit-], -s
arithmetic (adj.), -al, -ally ˌæriθ-ˈmetik, -əl, -əli
arithmetician, -s əˌriθməˈtiʃən [ˌæriθ-, -miˈt-], -z
Arius 'ɛəriəs [əˈraiəs]
Arizona ˌæriˈzəunə
ark (A.), -s ɑːk, -s
Arkansas (state, city, river) 'ɑːkənsɔː [ɑːˈkænzəs]
  Note.—The most usual pronunciation in U.S.A. appears to be ('ɑːkənsɔː), but (ɑːˈkænzəs) is also in use locally.
Ark|low, -wright 'ɑːk|ləu, -rait
Arlberg 'ɑːlbəːg
Arlington 'ɑːliŋtən
arm (s. v.), -s, -ing, -ed ɑːm, -z, -iŋ, -d
armada (A.), -s ɑːˈmɑːdə [old-fashioned -ˈmeid-], -z
Armadale 'ɑːmədeil
armadillo, -s ˌɑːməˈdiləu, -z
Armageddon ˌɑːməˈgedn
Armagh ɑːˈmɑː
armament, -s 'ɑːməmənt, -s
armature, -s 'ɑːmətjuə* [-tʃuə*], -z
armchair, -s 'ɑːmˈtʃɛə* [-ˈ-- when preceded by a stress, also '-- esp. when followed by a stress], -z
Armenia, -n/s ɑːˈmiːnjə [-nĭə], -n/z
Armes ɑːmz
Armfield 'ɑːmfiːld
armful, -s 'ɑːmful, -z
armhole, -s 'ɑːmhəul, -z
armiger (A.), -s 'ɑːmidʒə*, -z
arm-in-arm 'ɑːminˈɑːm
Arminian, -s ɑːˈminiən [-njən], -z
Armistead 'ɑːmisted [-tid]
armistice, -s 'ɑːmistis [-ˈ--], -iz
Armitage 'ɑːmitidʒ
armless 'ɑːmlis
armlet, -s 'ɑːmlit, -s
armorial ɑːˈmɔːriəl
Armoric ɑːˈmɔrik
Armorica, -n/s ɑːˈmɔrikə, -n/z
armor|y, -ies = armour-
armour (A.), -s 'ɑːmə*, -z
armour-bearer, -s 'ɑːməˌbɛərə*, -z
armourer, -s 'ɑːmərə*, -z
armour-plat|e, -es, -ing, -ed 'ɑːmə-pleit ['ɑːməˈp-], -s, -iŋ, -id
armour|y, -ies 'ɑːmər|i, -iz
armpit, -s 'ɑːmpit, -s
Armstead 'ɑːmsted [-stid]
Armstrong 'ɑːmstrɔŋ
arm|y, -ies 'ɑːm|i, -iz
army-corps (sing.) 'ɑːmikɔː*, (plur.) -kɔːz
Arnald 'ɑːnəld

Arne ɑ:n
Arnhem 'ɑ:nhem, 'ɑ:nəm
arnica 'ɑ:nikə
Arno 'ɑ:nəu
Arnold, -son 'ɑ:nəld, -sn
Arnot(t) 'ɑ:nət [-nɔt]
Arolla ə'rɔlə
aroma, -s ə'rəumə, -z
aromatic (s. adj.), -s ‚ærəu'mætik, -s
arose (from arise) ə'rəuz
around ə'raund
arous|e, -es, -ing, -ed; -al/s ə'rauz,
 -iz, -iŋ, -d; -əl/z
arpeggio, -s ɑ:'pedʒiəu, -z
arquebus, -es 'ɑ:kwibəs, -iz
arquebusier, -s ‚ɑ:kwibə'siə*, -z
arrack, 'ærək
arrah 'ærə
arraign, -s, -ing, -ed, -er/s, -ment/s
 ə'rein, -z, -iŋ, -d, -ə*/z, -mənt/s
Arran 'ærən
arrang|e, -es, -ing, -ed, -ement/s
 ə'reindʒ, -iz, -iŋ, -d, -mənt/s
arrant, -ly 'ærənt, -li
arras, -es 'ærəs, -iz
Arras (French town) 'ærəs (ɑrɑ:s)
array (s. v.), -s, -ing, -ed ə'rei, -z, -iŋ, -d
arrear, -s, -age ə'riə*, -z, -ridʒ
arrest (s. v.), -s, -ing, -ed, -ment/s;
 -able ə'rest, -s, -iŋ, -id, -mənt/s; -əbl
arrestation, -s ‚æres'teiʃən, -z
Arrian 'æriən
arrière-ban, -s 'æriəə'bæn, -z
'Arriet 'æriət
arris, -es 'æris, -iz
arriv|e, -es, -ing, -ed; -al/s ə'raiv, -z,
 -iŋ, -d; -əl/z
arrogan|ce, -cy, -t/ly 'ærəugən|s [-rug-],
 -si, -t/li
arrogat|e, -es, -ing, -ed 'ærəugeit
 [-rug-], -s, -iŋ, -id
arrogation, -s ‚ærəu'geiʃən [-ru'g-], -z
arrow, -s 'ærəu, -z
arrow-head, -s 'ærəuhed, -z
Arrowpoint 'ærəupɔint
arrowroot 'ærəuru:t
Arrowsmith 'ærəu-smiθ
arrowy 'ærəui
'Arry, -ish 'æri, -iʃ
Ars ɑ:z
arse, -s ɑ:s, -iz
arsenal, -s 'ɑ:sinl [-sənl, -sn̩l, -snl]], -z
arsenate, -s 'ɑ:sinit [-sən-, -sn̩it, -snit,
 -eit], -s
arsenic (s.) 'ɑ:snik
arsenic (adj.), -al ɑ:'senik, -əl
arsenious ɑ:'si:njəs [-nɪəs]
arsenite 'ɑ:sinait [-sən-]

ars|is, -es 'ɑ:s|is, -i:z
arson 'ɑ:sn
art (s.), -s ɑ:t, -s
art (from be) ɑ:t (normal form), ət
 (occasional weak form)
Artaxerxes ‚ɑ:təg'zə:ksi:z ['ɑ:t-, -ək'sə:-,
 -ə'zə:-]
artefact, -s 'ɑ:tifækt, -s
Artegal 'ɑ:tigəl
Artemis 'ɑ:timis [-təm-]
Artemus 'ɑ:timəs
arterial ɑ:'tiəriəl
arterio-sclerosis   ɑ:'tiəriəu-skliə'rəusis
 [-skljə'r-, -skli'r-, -sklə'r-]
arteritis ‚ɑ:tə'raitis
arter|y, -ies 'ɑ:tər|i, -iz
artesian ɑ:'ti:zjən [-zïən, -ʒən, -ʒïən,
 -ʒən]
art|ful, -fully, -fulness 'ɑ:t|ful, -fuli
 [-fəli], -fulnis
arthritic (s. adj.), -s ɑ:'θritik, -s
arthritis ɑ:'θraitis
Arthur 'ɑ:θə*
Arthurian ɑ:'θjuərïən [-jɔər-, -jɔ:r-]
artichoke, -s 'ɑ:titʃəuk, -s
artic|le (s. v.), -les, -ling, -led 'ɑ:tik|l,
 -lz, -liŋ, -ld
articular ɑ:'tikjulə*
articulate (adj.), -ly, -ness ɑ:'tikjulit,
 -li, -nis
articulat|e (v.), -es, -ing, -ed, -or/s
 ɑ:'tikjuleit, -s, -iŋ, id, -ə*/z
articulation, -s ɑ:‚tikju'leiʃən, -z
articulatory   ɑ:'tikjulətəri   [-leit-,
 ɑ:‚tikju'leitəri]
artifact, -s 'ɑ:tifækt, -s
artifice, -s 'ɑ:tifis, -iz
artificer, -s ɑ:'tifisə* ['----], -z
artifici|al, -ally, -alness ‚ɑ:ti'fiʃ|əl, -əli
 [-li], -əlnis
 Note.—When used attributively, the
  word is sometimes pronounced
  'ɑ:tifiʃəl (esp. in the expression
  artificial silk).
artificialit|y, -ies ‚ɑ:tifiʃi'ælit|i, -iz
artificializ|e [-is|e], -es, -ing, -ed
 ‚ɑ:ti'fiʃəlaiz [-ʃaiz], -iz, -iŋ, -d
artiller|y, -ies, -ist/s ɑ:'tilər|i, -iz, -ist/s
artillery-|man, -men ɑ:'tiləri|mən
 [-mæn], -mən [-men]
artisan, -s ‚ɑ:ti'zæn ['ɑ:tiz-], -z
artist, -s 'ɑ:tist, -s
artiste, -s ɑ:'ti:st (artist), -s
artistic, -al, -ally ɑ:'tistik, -əl, -əli
artistry 'ɑ:tistri
artless, -ly, -ness 'ɑ:tlis, -li, -nis
art-school, -s 'ɑ:t-sku:l, -z
arts|man, -men 'ɑ:ts|mæn, -men

arty 'ɑːti
arum, -s 'ɛərəm, -z
Arun 'ærən
Arundel 'ærəndl
Arundell 'ærəndel [-dl]
Aryan, -s, -ism 'ɛərïən ['ɑːr-], -z, -izəm
arytenoid (s. adj.), -s ˌæri'tiːnɔid, -z
as (s.), (coin), -es æs, -iz
as (conj.), æz (strong form), əz, z (weak forms)
Asa (biblical name) 'eisə ['ɑːsə], (as modern Christian name) 'eizə
asafoetida ˌæsə'fetidə [-'fiːt-]
Asaph 'æsəf
asbest|ic, -os, -ous æz'best|ik [əz-, æs-, əs-]ˌ -ɔs [-əs], -əs
Ascalon 'æskələn [-lən]
Ascanius æs'keinjəs [-nïəs]
ascend, -s, -ing, -ed ə'send, [æ's-], -z, -iŋ, -id
ascendan|ce, -cy, -t ə'sendən|s [æ's-], -si, -t
ascenden|ce, -cy, -t ə'sendən|s [æ's-], -si, -t
ascension (A.), -s ə'senʃən, -z
ascensional ə'senʃənl [-ʃnəl, -ʃn̩l, -ʃnl̩, -ʃnəl]
Ascension-day, -s ə'senʃəndei, -z
ascent, -s ə'sent [æ's-], -s
ascertain, -s, -ing, -ed, -ment; -able ˌæsə'tein [-sə-'t-], -z, -iŋ, -d, -mənt; -əbl
ascetic (s. adj.), -al, -ally, -s ə'setik [æ's-], -əl, -əli, -s
asceticism ə'setisizəm [æ's-]
Ascham 'æskəm
ascian, -s 'æsïən [-ʃən], -z
asclepiad, -s æs'kliːpiæd [-pjæd, -pïəd, -pjəd], -z
ascorbic əs'kɔːbik [æs-]
Ascot, -s 'æskət, -s
ascrib|e, -es, -ing, -ed; -able əs'kraib, -z, -iŋ, -d; -əbl
ascription əs'kripʃən [æs-]
asdic, -s 'æzdik, -s
asepsis æ'sepsis [ei's-, ə's-] [-s
aseptic (s. adj.), -s æ'septik [ei's-, ə's-],
asexual æ'seksjʊəl [ei's-, ə's-, -ksjwəl, -ksjul, -kʃʊəl, -kʃwəl, -kʃul]
Asgard 'æsgɑːd
Asgill 'æsgil
ash (A.), -es æʃ, -iz
Asham 'æʃəm
asham|ed, -edly, -edness ə'ʃeim|d, -ïdli, -ïdnis
Ashanti, -s ə'ʃænti, -z
Ashbee 'æʃbi

Ashbourne 'æʃbɔːn [-bɔən, -buən, -bəːn]
Ashburne 'æʃbəːn
Ashbur|nham, ton 'æʃbə:|nəm, -tn
Ash|bury, -by 'æʃ|bəri, -bi
Ashby - de - la - Zouch 'æʃbidələ:'zuːʃ
Ashcombe 'æʃkəm [[-delə-]
Ashdod 'æʃdɔd
Ashdown 'æʃdaun
Ashe æʃ
ashen 'æʃn
Asher 'æʃə*
asher|y, -ies 'æʃər|i, -iz
Ash|field, -ford 'æʃ|fiːld, -fəd
ash-heap, -s 'æʃhiːp, -s
Ashkelon 'æʃkilən [-kəl-, -lɔn]
Ashland 'æʃlənd
ashlar 'æʃlə*
Ash|ley, -mole 'æʃ|li, -məul
Ashmolean æʃ'məuljən [-lïən]
Ashmore 'æʃmɔː* [-mɔə*]
Ashopton 'æʃəptən
ashore ə'ʃɔː* [-'ʃɔə*]
Ashover 'æʃəuvə*
ash-pan, -s 'æʃpæn, -z
Ashtaroth 'æʃtərɔθ
Ashton 'æʃtən
Ashtoreth 'æʃtəreθ [-tɔr-]
Ash-Wednesday, -s 'æʃ'wenzdi [-'wednz-, -dei], -z
Ash|well, -worth 'æʃ|wəl [-wel], -wəːθ
ash|y, -ier, -iest, -iness 'æʃ|i, -ïə*, -iist, -inis
Asia 'eiʃə [rarely 'eiʒə]
Asian, -s 'eiʃən ['eiʃjən, 'eiʃïən, 'eisïən, 'eisjən, rarely 'eizïən, 'eizjən, 'eiʒən]
Asiatic, -s ˌeiʃi'ætik [ˌeisi-, rarely ˌeiʒi-], -s
aside (s. adv.), -s ə'said, -z
asinine 'æsinain
asininit|y, -ies ˌæsi'ninit|i, -iz
ask (s.) (newt), -s æsk, -s
ask (v.), -s, -ing, -ed ɑːsk, -s, -iŋ, -t [also ɑːst in familiar speech]
askance əs'kæns [-'kɑːns]
askant əs'kænt
Aske æsk
Askelon 'æskilən [-kəl-, -lɔn]
askew əs'kjuː
Askew 'æskjuː
Ask|rigg, -with 'æsk|rig, -wiθ
aslant ə'slɑːnt
asleep ə'sliːp
Asmodeus æs'məudjəs [-dïəs]
    Note.—The name must be pronounced ˌæsməu'diːəs in Milton, 'Paradise Lost', iv, 168.

Asoka ə'səukə [ə'ʃəu-] (*Hind*, əʃoka)
asp, -s æsp [ɑ:sp], -s
asparagus əs'pærəgəs
Aspasia æs'peiʒiə [-ʒiə, -zjə, -ziə]
aspect, -s 'æspekt, -s
aspectable æs'pektəbl
aspen, -s 'æspən ['ɑ:s-, -pen, -pin], -z
asper 'æspə*
asperg|e, -es, -ing, -ed əs'pə:dʒ [æs-],
  -iz, -iŋ, -d
asperges (*religious service*) æs'pə:dʒi:z
  [əs-]
aspergill, -s 'æspədʒil, -z
asperit|y, -ies æs'perit|i [əs'p-], -iz
aspers|e, -es, -ing, -ed əs'pə:s [æs-], -iz,
  -iŋ, -t
aspersion, -s əs'pə:ʃən [æs-], -z
asphalt (*s.*), -s 'æsfælt, -s
asphalt (*v.*), -s, -ing, -ed 'æsfælt
  [æs'fælt], -s, -iŋ, -id
asphaltic æs'fæltik
asphodel, -s 'æsfədel [-fɔd-], -z
asphyxia æs'fiksiə [əs-, -sjə]
asphyxiat|e, -es, -ing, -ed, -or/s æs-
  'fiksieit [əs-], -s, -iŋ, -id, -ə*/z
asphyxiation, -s æs,fiksi'eiʃən [əs-], -z
asphyx|y, -ies æs'fiks|i, -iz
aspic 'æspik
aspidistra, -s ,æspi'distrə, -z
Aspinall 'æspinl [-nɔ:l]
Aspinwall 'æspinwɔ:l
aspirant, -s əs'paiərənt ['æspirənt], -s
aspirate (*s. adj.*), -s 'æspərit, -s
aspirat|e (*v.*), -es, -ing, -ed, -or/s
  'æspəreit [-pir-], -s, -iŋ, -id, -ə*/z
aspiration, -s ,æspə'reiʃən [-pi'r-], -z
aspir|e, -es, -ing/ly, -ingness, -ed, -er/s
  əs'paiə*, -z, -riŋ/li, -riŋnis, -d, -rə*/z
aspirin, -s 'æspərin [-pir-], -z
aspirine, -s 'æspəri:n [-pir-], -z
asplenium, -s æs'pli:njəm [ə's-, -niəm],
Asquith 'æskwiθ   [-z
ass, -es æs [ɑ:s, *esp. as term of contempt*], -iz
assagai, -s 'æsəgai, -z
assail, -s, -ing, -ed; -able, -ant/s
  ə'seil, -z, -iŋ, -d; -əbl, -ənt/s
Assam 'æsæm [æ'sæm]
Assamese ,æsæ'mi:z [-sə'm-]
assassin, -s ə'sæsin, -z
assassinat|e, -es, -ing, -ed, -or/s
  ə'sæsineit [-sŋeit], -s, -iŋ, -id, -ə*/z
assassination, -s ə,sæsi'neiʃən, -z
assault (*s. v.*), -s, -ing, -ed, -er/s
  ə'sɔ:lt [-'sɔlt], -s, -iŋ, -id, -ə*/z
assay (*s. v.*), -s, -ing, -ed, -er/s ə'sei
  [æ's-], -z, -iŋ, -d, -ə*/z

Assaye æ'sei
assay-master, -s ə'sei,mɑ:stə* [æ's-], -z
Assche æʃ
assegai, -s 'æsigai, -z
assemblage, -s ə'semblidʒ, -iz
assemb|le, -les, -ling, -led ə'semb|l, -lz,
  -liŋ, -ld
assembl|y, -ies ə'sembl|i, -iz   [-z
assembly-room, -s ə'semblirum [-ru:m],
assent (*s. v.*), -s, -ing/ly, -ed ə'sent
  [æ's-], -s, -iŋ/li, -id
Asser 'æsə*
assert, -s, -ing, -ed, -er/s, or/s; -able
  ə'sə:t, -s, -iŋ, -id, -ə*/z, -ə*/z; -əbl
assertion, -s ə'sə:ʃən, -z
assertive, -ly, -ness ə'sə:tiv, -li, -nis
assess, -es, -ing, -ed, -or/s, -ment/s;
  -able ə'ses, -iz, -iŋ, -t,- ə*/z, -mənt/s;
  -əbl
asset, -s 'æset [-sit], -s
assever, -s, -ing, -ed æ'sevə* [ə's-], -z,
  -riŋ, -d
asseverat|e, -es, -ing/ly, -ed ə'sevəreit
  [æ's-], -s, -iŋ/li, -id
asseveration, -s ə,sevə'reiʃən [æ,s-], -z
Assheton 'æʃtən
assibilated ə'sibileitid [æ's-]
assibilation, -s ə,sibi'leiʃən [æ,s-], -z
assiduit|y, -ies ,æsi'dju(:)it|i, -iz
assiduous, -ly, -ness ə'sidjūəs [-djwəs],
  -li, -nis
assign (*s. v.*), -s, -ing, -ed, -er/s,
  -ment/s; -able ə'sain, -z, -iŋ, -d,
  -ə*/z, -mənt/s; -əbl
assignat, -s ,æsin'jɑ: (asiɲa), -z ['æsig-
  -næt, -s]
assignation, -s ,æsig'neiʃən, -z
assignee, -s ,æsi'ni: [-sai'n-], -z
assimilat|e, -es, -ing, -ed ə'simileit, -s,
  -iŋ, -id
assimilation, -s ə,simi'leiʃən, -z
assimilative ə'similətiv [-leit-]
assimilatory ə'similətəri [ə,simi'leitəri]
Assiniboine ə'siniboin
Assisi ə'si:zi [æ's-]
assist, -s, -ing, -ed, -er/s ə'sist, -s, -iŋ,
  -id, -ə*/z
assistan|ce/s, -t/s ə'sistən|s/iz, -t/s
Assiut æ'sju:t
assiz|e, -es, -er/s ə'saiz, -iz, -ə*/z
associable ə'səuʃjəbl [-ʃiə-, -ʃə-, -sjə-,
  -siə-]
associate (*s.*), -s ə'səuʃiit [-ʃjit, -ʃjət,
  -ʃiət, -siit, -sjit, -sjət, -siət, -ʃieit,
  -ʃjeit], -s
associat|e (*v.*), -es, -ing, -ed ə'səuʃieit
  -[ʃjeit, -əusi-, -əusj-], -s, -iŋ, -id

association, -s ə,səusi'eiʃən [-əuʃi-], -z
associative ə'səuʃjətiv [-ʃïət-, -ʃieit-,
-ʃjeit-, -əusjət-, -əusïət-, -əusieit-,
-əusjeit-]
assoilzie (s. v.), -s, -ing, -d ə'sɔilji [-li],
-z, -iŋ, -d
assonan|ce/s, -t 'æsəunən|s/iz [-sṇə-],
-t
assonat|e, -es, -ing, -ed 'æsəuneit,
-s, -iŋ, -id
assort, -s, -ing, -ed, -ment/s ə'sɔːt, -s,
-iŋ, -id, -mənt/s
Assouan ,æsu'æn ['æsuæn, esp. when
attributive, as in Assouan dam]
assuag|e, -es, -ing, -ed, -ement ə'sweidʒ,
-iz, -iŋ, -d, -mənt
assum|e, -es, -ing/ly, -ed, -edly ; -able,
-ably ə'sjuːm [-'suːm], -z, -iŋ/li, -d,
-idli ; -əbl, -əbli
assumpsit ə'sʌmpsit
assumption (A.), -s ə'sʌmpʃən, -z
assumptive ə'sʌmptiv
assur|e, -es, -ing, -ed, -edly, -edness,
-er/s ; -ance/s ə'ʃuə*, [-'ʃɔə*, -'ʃɔː*,
-'ʃə:*], -z, -riŋ, -d, -ridli, -dnis
[-ridnis], -rə*/z ; -rəns/iz
Assynt 'æsint
Assyria, -n/s ə'siriə, -n/z
assyriolog|ist/s, -y ə,siri'ɔlədʒ|ist/s, -i
Astarte æs'tɑːti
Astbury 'æstbəri
aster, -s 'æstə* [rarely 'ɑːs-], -z
asterisk, -s 'æstərisk, -s
asterism, -s 'æstərizəm, -z
astern əs'təːn
asteroid, -s 'æstərɔid, -z
asthenia æs'θiːnjə [-nïə, rarely
,æsθi'naiə]
asthenic, -al æs'θenik, -əl
asthma 'æsmə [rarely 'æsθm-, 'æstm-]
asthmatic, -al, -ally, -s æs'mætik [rarely
æsθ'm-, æst'm-, əs-], -əl, -əli, -s
Asti æsti(ː)
astigmatic ,æstig'mætik
astigmatism æs'tigmətizəm [əs-]
astir ə'stəː*
Astle 'æsl
Astley 'æstli
Aston 'æstən
astonish, -es, -ing/ly, -ed/ly, -ment
əs'tɔniʃ, -iz, -iŋ/li, -t/li, -mənt
Astor 'æstə*, 'æstɔː*
Astoria æs'tɔːrïə [əs-]
astound, -s, -ing, -ed əs'taund, -z, -iŋ,
astraddle ə'strædl   [-id
astragal, -s 'æstrəgəl, -z
astrakhan (A.) ,æstrə'kæn

astr|al, -ally 'æstr|əl, -əli
astray ə'strei
astride ə'straid   [-d
astring|e, -es, -ing, -ed ə'strindʒ, -iz, -iŋ,
astringen|cy, -t/s, -tly ə'strindʒən|si,
-t/s, -tli
astrolabe, -s 'æstrəuleib, -z
astrologer, -s əs'trɔlədʒə*, -z
astrologic, -al, -ally ,æstrə'lɔdʒik, -əl, -əli
astrology əs'trɔlədʒi
astromet|er/s, -ry æs'trɔmit|ə*/z, -ri
astronaut, -s 'æstrənɔːt, -s
astronomer, -s əs'trɔnəmə*, -z
astronomic, -al, -ally ,æstrə'nɔmik, -əl,
-əli
astronom|y, -ies əs'trɔnəm|i, -iz
Astrophel 'æstrəufel
astrophysics 'æstrəu'fiziks
Asturias æs'tuəriæs [-'tjuər-, -'tjɔər-,
-'tjɔːr-, -rïəs]
astute, -r, -st, -ly, -ness əs'tjuːt [æs-],
-ə*, -ist, -li, -nis
Astyanax əs'taiənæks [æs-]
Asuncion ə,sunsi'əun [-'ɔn]
asunder ə'sʌndə*
asylum, -s ə'sailəm, -z
asymmetric, -al, -ally ,æsi'metrik
[,eisi'm-], -əl, -əli
asymmetry æ'simitri ['æ'sim-, 'ei'sim-]
asymptote, -s 'æsimptəut, -s
asymptotic, -al, -ally ,æsimp'tɔtik, -əl,
-əli
asyndet|on, -a æ'sindit|ən [ə's-], -ə
At (member of A.T.S.), -s æt, -s
at (prep.) æt (strong form), ət (weak
Atalanta ,ætə'læntə   [form)
Atall 'ætɔːl
Ataturk 'ætətɔːk [,--'-]
atavism 'ætəvizəm
atavistic ,ætə'vistik
ataxia ə'tæksïə [æ't-, ei't-]
atax|y, -ies ə'tæks|i, -iz
Atbara æt'bɑːrə
Atcheen ə'tʃiːn
Atchison 'ætʃisn, 'eitʃisn
Ate (s.) 'ɑːti ['eiti]
ate (from eat) et [eit]
atelier, -s 'ætəliei ['ætel-, æ'tel-, -ljei]
(ətəlje), -z
Atfield 'ætfiːld
Athabasca ,æθə'bæskə
Athaliah ,æθə'laiə
Athanase 'æθəneiz
Athanasian ,æθə'neiʃən [-θṇ'ei-, -ʃjən,
-ʃïən, -sjən, -sïən]
Athanasius ,æθə'neiʃəs [-θṇ'ei-, -ʃjəs,
-ʃïəs, -sjəs, -sïəs]

Athawes (*surname*) 'æthɔːz
atheism, -st/s 'eiθiiǀzəm [-θjiǀ-], -st/s
atheistic, -al, -ally ˌeiθiˈistik, -əl, -əli
atheling (A.), -s 'æθiliŋ [-θəl-], -z
Athelney 'æθəlni
Athelstan 'æθəlstən (*Old Eng.*
'æðəlstɑːn)
Athena əˈθiːnə
Athenaeum, -s ˌæθiˈni(ː)əm, -z
Athene əˈθiːni(ː)
Athenian, -s əˈθiːnjən [-nǐən], -z
Athenry ˌæθinˈrai [-θən-]
Athens 'æθinz
Atherley 'æθəli
Atherǀston, -ton 'æθəǀstən, -tən
athirst əˈθəːst
athlete, -s 'æθliːt, -s
athletic, -al, -ally, -s æθˈletik [əθ-], -əl,
-əli, -s
athleticism æθˈletisizəm [əθ-]
Athlone æθˈləun [*also* '— *when attributive, as in* the Athlone Press]
Athlumney æθˈlʌmni
Athole 'æθəl
Atholl 'æθəl
at home, -s ətˈhəum [əˈtəum], -z
Athos 'æθɔs ['eiθ-]
athwart əˈθwɔːt
Athy əˈθai
Atkinǀs, -son 'ætkinǀz, -sn
Atlanta ətˈlæntə [ætˈlæn-, əˈtlæn-]
atlantean ˌætlænˈtiːən [-lən-, -ˈtiən,
ətˈlæntǐən, ætˈlæntǐən, ətˈlæntjən,
ætˈlæntjən, əˈtlænt-]
Atlantes (*statues*) ətˈlæntiːz [ætˈlæn-,
əˈtlæn-], (*in Ariosto's 'Orlando
Furioso'*) ətˈlæntes [æt-]
Atlantic ətˈlæntik [əˈtlæn-]
Atlantis ətˈlæntis [ætˈlæn-, əˈtlæn-]
atlas, -es 'ætləs, -iz
Atlas 'ætləs [-læs]
atmometer, -s ætˈmɔmitə*, -z
atmosphere, -s 'ætməsfiə*, -z
atmospheric, -al, -ally, -s ˌætməsˈferik,
əl, -əli, -s
atoll, -s 'ætɔl [əˈtɔl], -z
atom, -s 'ætəm, -z
atomic əˈtɔmik
atomistic ˌætəuˈmistik
atomization [-isa-] ˌætəumaiˈzeiʃən
atomizǀe [-isǀe], -es, -ing, -ed, -er/s
'ætəumaiz, -iz, -iŋ, -d, -ə*/z
atonal eiˈtəunl [æˈt-, əˈt-]
atonǀe, -es, -ingǀly, -ed, -er/s, -ement/s
əˈtəun, -z, -iŋǀli, -d, -ə*/z, -mənt/s
atonic (*s. adj.*), -s æˈtɔnik [əˈt-], -s
atony 'ætəni

atrabilious ˌætrəˈbiljəs [-lǐəs]
Atreus 'eitriuːs [-truːs, -trjuːs, -trǐəs]
atriǀum, -a 'ɑːtriǀəm ['eit-], -ə
atrocious, -ly, -ness əˈtrəuʃəs, -li, -nis
atrocitǀy, -ies əˈtrɔsitǀi, -iz
atrophic æˈtrɔfik [əˈt-]
atrophǀy (*s. v.*), -ies, -ying, -ied 'ætrəfǀi
[-truf-], -iz, -iiŋ, -id
atropine 'ætrəpin [-trup-, -piːn]
Atropos 'ætrəpɔs [-trup-]
attach, -es, -ing, -ed, -ment/s; -able
əˈtætʃ, -iz, -iŋ, -t, -mənt/s; -əbl
attaché, -s əˈtæʃei [æˈt-] (ataʃe), -z
attaché-case, -s əˈtæʃikeis [-ʃei-], -iz
attack (*s. v.*), -s, -ing, -ed, -er/s əˈtæk,
-s, -iŋ, -t, -ə*/z
attain, -s, -ing, -ed, -ment/s; -able
əˈtein, -z, -iŋ, -d, -mənt/s; -əbl
attainability ˌteinəˈbiliti [-lət-]
attainder, -s əˈteində*, -z
attaint (*s. v.*), -s, -ing, -ed əˈteint, -s,
-iŋ, -id
attar 'ætə*
attemper, -s, -ing, -ed əˈtempə* [æˈt-],
-z, -riŋ, -d
attempt (*s. v.*), -s, -ing, -ed, -er/s;
-able əˈtempt, -s, -iŋ, -id, -ə*/z; -əbl
Attenborough 'ætnbrə [-bərə, -bʌrə]
attend, -s, -ing, -ed, -er/s; -ance/s,
-ant/s əˈtend, -z, -iŋ, -id, -ə*/z;
-əns/iz, -ənt/s
attention, -s əˈtenʃən, -z
attentive, -ly, -ness əˈtentiv, -li, -nis
attenuate (*adj.*) əˈtenjuit [-njueit]
attenuatǀe (*v.*), -s, -ing, -ed əˈtenjueit,
-s, -iŋ, -id
attenuation, -s əˌtenjuˈeiʃən, -z
attenuator, -s əˈtenjueitə*, -z
Atterǀbury, -cliffe 'ætəǀbəri, -klif
attest (*s. v.*), -s, -ing, -ed, -or/s; -able
əˈtest, -s, -iŋ, -id, -ə*/z; -əbl
attestation, -s ˌætesˈteiʃən, -z
Attfield 'ætfiːld
attic, -s 'ætik, -s
Attica 'ætikə
atticism, -s 'ætisizəm, -z
atticizǀe [-isǀe], -es, -ing, -ed 'ætisaiz,
-iz, -iŋ, -d
Attila 'ætilə
attirǀe (*s. v.*), -es, -ing, -ed, -ement
əˈtaiə*, -z, -riŋ, -d, -mənt
attitude, -s 'ætitjuːd, -z
attitudinal ˌætiˈtjuːdinl
attitudinarian, -s ˌætitjuːdiˈnɛəriən, -z
attitudinizǀe [-isǀe], -es, -ing, -ed, -er/s
ˌætiˈtjuːdinaiz, -iz, -iŋ, -d, -ə*/z
Attleborough 'ætlbrə [-bərə, -bʌrə]

Attlee 'ætli

Attock ə'tɔk (*Hind.* əṭək)

attorn, -s, -ing, -ed ə'tɔ:n, -z, -iŋ, -d

attorney, -s ; -ship/s ə'tə:ni, -z; -ʃip/s

attract, -s, -ing/ly, -ed, -or/s; -able
ə'trækt, -s, -iŋ/li, -id, -ə*/z; -əbl

attractability ə,træktə'biliti [-lət-]

attraction, -s ə'trækʃən, -z

attractive, -ly, -ness ə'træktiv, -li, -nis

attrahent ə'treiənt ['ætrəhənt, 'ætriənt]

attributable ə'tribjutəbl

attribute (*s.*), -s 'ætribju:t, -s

attrib|ute (*v.*), -utes, -uting, -uted
ə'trib|ju(:)t, -ju(:)ts, -jutiŋ, -jutid

attribution, -s ,ætri'bju:ʃən, -z

attributive, -ly ə'tribjutiv, -li

Attride 'ætraid

attrition ə'triʃən [æ't-]

attun|e, -es, -ing, -ed ə'tju:n [æ't-], -z,
-iŋ, -d

Attwood 'ætwud

At|water, -wood 'æt|,wɔ:tə*, -wud

atypical ,ei'tipikəl

aubade, -s əu'ba:d, -z

auberge, -s əu'beəʒ ['əub-] (obɛrʒ), -iz

aubergine, -s 'əubəʒi:n [-dʒi:n, ,əubə-
'ʒi:n, ,əubə'dʒi:n, ,əubeə'ʒi:n], -z

Aubrey 'ɔ:bri

aubrietia, -s ɔ:'bri:ʃjə [-ʃiə, -ʃə], -z

auburn (A.) 'ɔ:bən [-bə:n]

Aucher 'ɔ:kə*

Auchindachie ,ɔ:kin'dæki [,ɔ:xin'dæxi]
(*Scottish* ,ɔxin'daxi)

Auchinleck ,ɔ:kin'lek ['---, ,ɔ:x-] (*Scottish* ,ɔxin'lek)

Auchmuty ɔ:k'mju:ti

Auchtermuchty ,ɔ:ktə'mʌkti [,ɔ:xtə-
'mʌxti] (*Scottish* ,ɔxtər'mʌxtɨ)

Auckland 'ɔ:klənd

aucti|on (*s. v.*), -ons, -oning, -oned
'ɔ:kʃ|ən ['ɔk-], -ənz, -əniŋ [-ṇiŋ], -ənd

auctionary 'ɔ:kʃənəri ['ɔk-, -ʃṇə-]

auctioneer, -s ,ɔ:kʃə'niə* [,ɔk-, -ʃṇ'iə*], -z

audacious, -ly, -ness ɔ:'deiʃəs, -li, -nis

audacit|y, -ies ɔ:'dæsit|i, -iz

Auden 'ɔ:dn [-dən]

audibility ,ɔ:di'biliti [-də'b-, -lət-]

audib|le, -ly, -leness 'ɔ:dəb|l [-dib-], -li,
-lnis

audience, -s 'ɔ:djəns [-diəns], -iz

audiometer, -s ,ɔ:di'ɔmitə*, -z

audiometry ,ɔ:di'ɔmitri

audio-visual 'ɔ:diəu'vizjuəl [-ʒuəl, -ʒwəl,
-zjwəl, -zjəl, -ʒul, -ʒəl]

audiphone, -s 'ɔ:difəun, -z

audit (*s. v.*), -s, -ing, -ed, -or/s 'ɔ:dit,
-s, -iŋ, -id, -ə*/z

audition, -s ɔ:'diʃən, -z

auditorium, -s ,ɔ:di'tɔ:riəm, -z

auditorship, -s 'ɔ:ditəʃip, -s

auditor|y (*s. adj.*), -ies 'ɔ:ditər|i, -iz

Aud|ley, -rey 'ɔ:d|li, -ri

au fait ,əu 'fei (o fɛ)

Augean ɔ:'dʒi(:)ən

Augeas ɔ:'dʒi:æs ['ɔ:dʒiæs]

Augener (*music publisher*) 'augənə*

auger, -s 'ɔ:gə*, -z

Aughrim 'ɔ:grim

aught ɔ:t

augment (*s.*), -s 'ɔ:gmənt, -s

augment (*v.*), -s, -ing, -ed ; -able
ɔ:g'ment, -s, -iŋ, -id; -əbl

augmentation, -s ,ɔ:gmen'teiʃən
[-mən-], -z

augmentative ɔ:g'mentətiv

au gratin ,əu 'grætɛ̃ŋ [-tæŋ, -tæn]
(o gratɛ̃)

augur (*s. v.*), -s, -ing, -ed 'ɔ:gə*, -z,
-riŋ, -d

augural 'ɔ:gjurəl

augur|y, -ies 'ɔ:gjur|i [-jər-], -iz

August (*s.*), -s 'ɔ:gəst, -s

august (*adj.*), -est, -ly, -ness ɔ:'gʌst,
-ist, -li, -nis

August|a, -an ɔ:'gʌst|ə [ə'g-], -ən

Augustine (*Saint*) ɔ:'gʌstin [ə'g-, *rarely*
'ɔ:gəstin]

Augustinian ,ɔ:gəs'tiniən [-njən]

Augustus ɔ:'gʌstəs [ə'g-]

auk, -s ɔ:k, -s

aul|a, -ae 'ɔ:l|ə, ['aulə], -i: [-lai, -lei]

auld lang syne 'ɔ:ldlæŋ'sain

Ault ɔ:lt

aumbr|y, -ies 'ɔ:mbr|i, -iz

Aumonier əu'məniei [-'məun-, -njei]
(omɔnje)

Aungier (*street in Dublin*) 'eindʒə*

aunt, -s ; -ie/s ɑ:nt, -s; -i/z

au pair ,əu 'pɛə* (o pɛ:r)

aura, -s 'ɔ:rə, -z

aur|al, -ally 'ɔ:r|əl, -əli

aurate, -s 'ɔ:reit [-rit], -s

aureate 'ɔ:riit [-ieit, -ɨət]

Aureli|a, -an, -us ɔ:'ri:lj|ə [-lɨ|ə], -ən, -əs

aureola, -s ɔ:'riəulə, -z

aureole, -s 'ɔ:riəul, -z

aureomycin ,ɔ:riəu'maisin

au revoir ,əu rə'vwɑ:* [ri-] (o rəvwa:r)

auric 'ɔ:rik

auricle, -s 'ɔ:rikl, -z

auricula, -s ə'rikjulə [ɔ:'r-, u'r-, -jələ], -z

auricular, -ly ɔ:'rikjulə*, -li

auricul|ate, -ated ɔ:'rikjul|it [u'r-, -eit],
-eitid

auriferous ɔ:'rifərəs
Auriga ɔ:'raigə
Aurignacian ˌɔ:rig'neiʃən [-ʃjən, -ʃïən]
aurist, -s 'ɔ:rist, -s
aurochs, -es 'ɔ:rɔks, -iz   [-əz, -əl
auror|a (A.), -as, -al ɔ:'rɔ:r|ə [ə'r-],
Aurung|zeb, -zebe 'ɔ:rʌŋ|'zeb ['aur-,
    -rəŋ-], -'zi:b
auscultat|e, -es, -ing, -ed 'ɔ:skəlteit
    ['ɔs-, -kʌl-], -s, -iŋ, -id
auscultation, -s ˌɔ:skəl'teiʃən [ˌɔs-,
    -kʌl-], -z   [-z
auscultator, -s 'ɔ:skəlteitə* ['ɔs-, -kʌl-],
auspice, -s 'ɔ:spis ['ɔs-], -iz
auspicious, -ly, -ness ɔ:s'piʃəs [ɔs-],
    -li, -nis
Austell 'ɔ:stəl ['ɔs-, local Cornish pro-
    nunciation 'ɔ:sl]
Aussie, -s 'ɔzi ['ɔsi], -z
Austen 'ɔstin ['ɔ:s-]
Auster 'ɔ:stə*
austere, -r, -st, -ly, -ness ɔs'tiə* [ɔ:s-],
    -rə*, -rist, -li, -nis
austerit|y, -ies ɔs'terit|i [ɔ:s-], -iz
Austerlitz 'ɔ:stəlits
Austin, -s 'ɔstin ['ɔ:s-], -z
austral 'ɔ:strəl
Australasia ˌɔstrə'leiʒjə [ˌɔ:s-, -ʒïə, -ʒə,
    -zjə, -zïə, -ʃjə, -ʃïə, -ʃə]
Australasian, -s ˌɔstrə'leiʒjən [ˌɔ:s-,
    -ʒïən, -ʒən, -zjən, -zïən, -ʃjən, -ʃïən,
    -ʃən], -z
Australia, -n/s ɔs'treiljə [ɔ:s-, -lïə], -n/z
Austria, -n/s 'ɔstrïə ['ɔ:s-], -n/z
Austro|-German, -Hungarian 'ɔstrəu|-
    'dʒɑ:mən ['ɔ:s-], -hʌŋ'gɛərïən
authentic, -al, -ally ɔ:'θentik, -əl, -əli
authenticat|e, -es, -ing, -ed ɔ:'θentikeit,
    -s, -iŋ, -id
authentication, -s ɔ:ˌθenti'keiʃən, -z
authenticit|y, -ies ˌɔ:θen'tisit|i [-θən-],
    -iz
author, -s; -ess/es 'ɔ:θə*, -z; -ris/iz
    [-res/iz]
authoritative, -ly, -ness ɔ:'θɔritətiv
    [ɔ'θ-, ə'θ-, -teit-], -li, -nis
authorit|y, -ies ɔ:'θɔrit|i [ɔ'θ-, ə'θ-], -iz
authorization [-isa-], -s ˌɔ:θərai'zeiʃən
    [-ri'z-], -z
authoriz|e [-is|e], -es, -ing, -ed; -able
    'ɔ:θəraiz, -iz, -iŋ, -d; -əbl
authorship 'ɔ:θəʃip
autism 'ɔ:tizm
autistic ɔ:'tistik
autobahn, -s 'ɔ:təubɑ:n ['aut-], -z
autobiograph|er/s, -y, -ies ˌɔ:təubai-
    'ɔgrəf|ə*/z [-bi'ɔg-], -i, -iz

autobiographic, -al, -ally 'ɔ:təuˌbaiəu-
    'græfik [ˌɔ:t-], -əl, -əli
auto-car, -s 'ɔ:təukɑ:*, -z
autochthon, -s ɔ:'tɔkθən [-θɔn, 'ɔ:tək-],
    -z
autochthonous ɔ:'tɔkθənəs [-θŋəs]
autocrac|y, -ies ɔ:'tɔkrəs|i, -iz
autocrat, -s 'ɔ:təukræt, -s
autocratic, -al, -ally ˌɔ:təu'krætik, -əl,
    -əli
auto-da-fé, -s 'ɔ:təudɑ:'fei ['aut-], -z
autogiro [-gyro], -s 'ɔ:təu'dʒaiərəu, -z
autograph, -s 'ɔ:təgrɑ:f [-græf], -s
autographic, -al, -ally ˌɔ:təu'græfik, -əl,
    -əli
autography ɔ:'tɔgrəfi
autogyro, -s 'ɔ:təu'dʒaiərəu, -z
Autolycus ɔ:'tɔlikəs
automatic, -al, -ally ˌɔ:tə'mætik, -əl, -əli
automation ˌɔ:tə'meiʃən
automati|sm, -st/s ɔ:'tɔməti|zəm, -st/s
automat|on, -ons, -a ɔ:'tɔmət|ən, -ənz,
    -ə
automobile, -s 'ɔ:təməubi:l [-tum-,
    -mub-, ˌ---'-, ˌɔ:tə'məubi:l, -təu'm-,
    -tu'm-, 'ɔ:təˌməubi:l, -təu,m-, -tu,m-],
autonomic ˌɔ:təu'nɔmik   [-z
autonom|ous, -y, -ies ɔ:'tɔnəm|əs, -i, -iz
autonym, -s 'ɔ:tənim, -z
autops|y, -ies 'ɔ:təps|i [-tɔp-], -iz
autos-da-fé (plur. of auto-da-fé)
    'ɔ:təuzdɑ:'fei ['aut-]
auto - suggestion 'ɔ:təusə'dʒestʃən
    [-eʃtʃən]
autotyp|e (s. v.), -es, -ing, -ed 'ɔ:təutaip,
    -s, -iŋ, -t
autotypography ˌɔ:təutai'pɔgrəfi
autumn, -s 'ɔ:təm, -z
autumn|al, -ally ɔ:'tʌmn|əl [-ḷ], -əli
Auvergne əu'vɛən [-'və:n] (ovɛrŋ, ɔv-)
auxiliar|y (s. adj.), -ies ɔ:g'ziljər|i
    [ɔ:k'sil-, ɔg'zil-, ɔk'sil-, -lïər-], -iz
Ava 'ɑ:və
avail (s. v.), -s, -ing/ly, -ed ə'veil, -z,
    -iŋ/li, -d
availability əˌveilə'biliti [-lət-]
availab|le, -ly, -leness ə'veiləb|l, -li,
    -lnis
avalanche, -s 'ævəlɑ:nʃ [-lɑ:ntʃ, -lɔ:ntʃ],
Avalon 'ævəlɔn   [-iz
avant-courier, -s 'ævɑ̃:ŋ'kurïə* [-vɔ̃:ŋ'k-,
    -vɑ:ŋ'k-, -vɔ(:)ŋ'k-, -vənt'k-,] -z
avant-garde 'ævɑ̃:ŋ 'gɑ:d [-vɔ̃:ŋ, -vɔ:ŋ,
    -vɔŋ, -vəŋ] (avɑ̃ gard)
avarice 'ævəris
avaricious, -ly, -ness ˌævə'riʃəs, -li, -nis
avast ə'vɑ:st

avatar, -s ˌævə'tɑ:* ['---] (Hind. əwtar), -z

avaunt ə'vɔ:nt

ave (prayer), -s 'ɑ:vi, -z

Avebury 'eivbəri

Aveling 'eivliŋ

Ave Maria (prayer), -s 'ɑ:vimə'riə [-'ri:ə], -z

Ave Maria Lane 'ɑ:vimə'riə'lein [formerly 'eivimə'raiə'lein]

aveng|e, -es, -ing, -ed, -er/s; -eful ə'vendʒ, -iz, -iŋ, -d, -ə*/z; -ful

avengeress, -es ə'vendʒəris [-res], -iz

avenue, -s 'ævinju:, -z

aver, -s, -ring, -red, -ment/s ə'və:*, -z, -riŋ, -d, -mənt/s

averag|e (s. adj. v.), -es, -ing, -ed 'ævəridʒ, -iz, -iŋ, -d

averruncat|e, -es, -ing, -ed ˌævə'rʌŋkeit [-vi'r-, -ve'r-], -s, -iŋ, -id

averruncator, -s ˌævə'rʌŋkeitə* [-vi'r-, -ve'r-], -z

averse, -ly, -ness ə'və:s, -li, -nis

aversion, -s ə'və:ʃən, -z

avert, -s, -ing, -ed; -ible ə'və:t, -s, -iŋ, -id; -əbl [-ibl]

avertin ə'və:tin

Avery 'eivəri

Avesta ə'vestə [-i, -iz

aviar|ist/s, -y, -ies 'eivjər|ist/s [-viə-],

aviation ˌeivi'eiʃən [ˌæv-]

aviator, -s 'eivieitə*, -z

Avice (fem. name) 'eivis

Avicenna ˌævi'senə

aviculture 'eivikʌltʃə*

avid 'ævid

avidity ə'viditi [æ'v-]

Aviemore ˌævi'mɔ:* [-'mɔə*]

Avilion æ'viliən [-ljən]

aviso, -s ə'vaizəu [-'vi:z-], -z

Avoca ə'vəukə

avocado, -s ˌævəu'kɑ:dəu, -z

avocation, -s ˌævəu'keiʃən, -z

avocet, -s 'ævəuset, -s

Avoch ɔ:k [ɔ:x] (Scottish ɔx)

avoid, -s, -ing, -ed; -able, -ance/s ə'vɔid, -z, -iŋ, -id; -əbl, -əns/iz

avoirdupois ˌævədə'pɔiz

Avon (in Warw., etc.) 'eivən, (in Devon) 'ævən (in Banffshire) ɑ:n

Avondale 'eivəndeil

Avonmouth 'eivənmauθ [-məθ]

Avory 'eivəri

avouch, -es, -ing, -ed ə'vautʃ, -iz, -iŋ, -t

avow (s. v.), -s, -ing, -ed, -edly; -al/s ə'vau, -z, -iŋ, -d, -idli; ə'vau-əl/z

avuncular ə'vʌŋkjulə*

await, -s, -ing, -ed ə'weit, -s, -iŋ, -id

awak|e (adj. v.), -es, -ing, -ed, awoke ə'weik, -s, -iŋ, -t, ə'wəuk

awak|en, -ens, -ening, -ened, -enment/s ə'weik|ən, -ənz, -niŋ [-ŋiŋ, -əniŋ], -ənd, -ənmənt/s

awakening (s.), -s ə'weikniŋ, -z

award (s. v.), -s, -ing, -ed; -able ə'wɔ:d, -z, -iŋ, -id; -əbl

aware ə'wɛə*

awash ə'wɔʃ

away ə'wei

aw|e (s. v.) (A.), -es, -ing, -ed ɔ:, -z, -iŋ, -d

awe-inspiring 'ɔ: in,spaiəriŋ

aweless, -ness 'ɔ:lis, -nis

awesome, -ness 'ɔ:səm, -nis

awe-stricken 'ɔ:,strikən

awe-struck 'ɔ:-strʌk

awful, -ness (terrible) 'ɔ:ful [-fl], -nis, (great, considerable) 'ɔ:fl

awfully (terribly) 'ɔ:fuli, (very) 'ɔ:fli

awhile ə'wail [ə'hw-]

awkward, -s, -est, -ly, -ness, -ish 'ɔ:kwəd, -z, -ist, -li, -nis, -iʃ

awl, -s ɔ:l, -z

awn, -s, -ed ɔ:n, -z, -d

awning, -s 'ɔ:niŋ, -z

awoke (from awake) ə'wəuk

awry ə'rai

axe, -s æks, -iz

axes (plur. of axis) 'æksi:z

Axholm(e) 'ækshəum [-səm]

axial, -ly 'æksiəl [-sjəl], -i

axil, -s 'æksil, -z

axill|a, -ae; -ar, -ary æk'sil|ə, -i:; -ə*, -əri

axiom, -s 'æksiəm [-sjəm], -z

axiomatic, -al, -ally ˌæksiəu'mætik [-sjə'm-, -sjəu'm-], -əl, -əli

ax|is, -es 'æks|is, -i:z

axle, -s, -d 'æksl, -z, -d

axle-tree, -s 'æksltri:, -z

Axminster, -s 'æksminstə*, -z

axolotl, -s ˌæksə'lɔtl, -z

ay (yes), -es ai, -z

ayah, -s 'aiə ['ɑ:jə], -z

aye (ever), ei

aye (yes), -s ai, -z

aye-aye (animal), -s 'aiai, -z

Ayer, -s ɛə*, -z

Ayerst 'aiəst, 'eiəst

Aylesbury 'eilzbəri

Aylesford 'eilzfəd [-lsf-]

Ayliffe 'eilif

Ayling 'eiliŋ

Aylmer 'eilmə*

Aylsham 'eilʃəm
Aylward 'eilwəd
Aylwin 'eilwin
Aymer 'eimə*
Ayot 'eiət
Ayr, -shire ɛə*, -ʃiə* [-ʃə*]
Ayre, -s ɛə*, -z
Ayrton 'ɛətn
Ayscough 'æskə, 'æskju:, 'eiskəf
Ayscue 'eiskju:
Ayt|on, -oun 'eit|n, -n
azalea, -s ə'zeiljə [-liə], -z
Azariah ˌæzə'raiə
Azaziel ə'zeizjəl [-ziəl]
azimuth, -s 'æziməθ, -s
Azof 'ɑːzɔf

azoic ə'zəuik [æ'z-]
Azores ə'zɔːz [-'zɔəz]
   Note.—*It is customary to pronounce*
   ə'zɔːriz (*or* ə'zɔəriz *or* -rez) *in*
   reciting Tennyson's poem 'The
   Revenge'.
azote ə'zəut [æ'z-, 'æzəut]
azotic ə'zɔtik [æ'z-]
Azov 'ɑːzɔv
Azrael 'æzreiəl [-reil, -rïəl]
Aztec, -s 'æztek, -s
azure 'æʒə* ['eiʒ-, -ʒuə*, -ʒuə*, -ʒjə*, -zjuə*]
azur|ine/s, -ite 'æʒur|ain/z ['æʒər-, 'æʒuər-, 'æʒjur-, 'æʒjuər-, 'æzjur-, 'æzjuər-], -ait

B

B *(the letter)*, -'s biː, -z
ba *(note in Tonic Sol-fa)*, -s bei, -z
baa *(s. v.)*, -s, -ing, -ed bɑː, -z, -iŋ, -d
Baal 'beiəl ['beiæl, *Jewish pronunciation* bɑːl]
baa-lamb, -s 'bɑːlæm, -z
Baalim 'beiəlim [*Jewish pronunciation*
'bɑːlim]
Baal Schem 'bɑːl'ʃem
baas, -es bɑːs, -iz
Babbage 'bæbidʒ
babb|le, -les, -ling, -led, -ler/s, -le-
ment/s 'bæb|l, -lz, -liŋ [-liŋ], -ld,
-lə*/z [-lə*/z], -lmənt/s
Babcock 'bæbkɔk
babe, -s beib, -z
babel (B.), -s 'beibəl, -z
Bab-el-Mandeb 'bæbel'mændeb
Babington 'bæbiŋtən
baboo (B.), -s 'bɑːbuː, -z
baboon, -s bə'buːn, -z
babooner|y, -ies bə'buːnər|i, -iz
babu (B.), -s 'bɑːbuː, -z
bab|y (B.), -ies 'beib|i, -iz
baby-farmer, -s 'beibi,fɑːmə*, -z
babyhood 'beibihud
babyish, -ly, -ness 'beibiiʃ [-bjiʃ], -li, -nis
Babylon 'bæbilən
Babylonia, -n/s ,bæbi'ləunjə [-nïə], -n/z
baby-sitt|er/s, -ing 'beibi,sit|ə*/z, -iŋ
baccalaureate, -s ,bækə'lɔːriit [-rïət], -s
baccara(t) 'bækərɑː [,bækə'r-]
Bacchae 'bækiː
bacchanal, -s 'bækənl [-næl], -z
bacchanalian, -s ,bækə'neiljən [-lïən], -z
bacchant, -s 'bækənt, -s
bacchante, -s bə'kænti, -z [bə'kænt, -s]
bacchic 'bækik
Bacchus 'bækəs
Bacchylides bæ'kilidiːz [bə'k-]
baccy 'bæki
Bach *(English surname)* beitʃ, bætʃ,
(German composer) bɑːx [bɑːk] (bax)
Bache beitʃ
bachelor (B.), -s; -hood, -ship 'bætʃələ*
[-tʃil-], -z; -hud, -ʃip
bacill|us, -i bə'sil|əs, -ai
back *(s. v. adv.)* (B.), -s, -ing, -ed,
-er/s bæk, -s, -iŋ, -t, -ə*/z

backache, -s 'bækeik, -s
back-bencher, -s 'bæk'bentʃə*, -z
backbit|e, -es, -ing, backbit, backbitten
'bækbait, -s, -iŋ, 'bækbit, 'bæk,bitn
backbiter, -s 'bæk,baitə*, -z
backboard, -s 'bækbɔːd [-bɔəd], -z
backbone, -s 'bækbəun, -z
back-door, -s 'bæk'dɔː* [-'dɔə*], -z
backfir|e, -es, -ing, -ed 'bæk'faiə* ['--],
-z, -riŋ, -d
backgammon bæk'gæmən ['bæk,g-]
background, -s 'bækgraund, -z
back-hair 'bæk'heə*
back-hand, -s, -ed, -er/s 'bækhænd
['bæk'h-], -z, -id, -ə*/z
Backhouse 'bækhaus
backing *(s.)*, -s 'bækiŋ, -z
backlog, -s 'bæklɔg, -z
back-room 'bæk'ruːm [-'rum, '--]
backsheesh [-shish] 'bækʃiːʃ
backside, -s 'bæk'said ['bæk-said], -z
backslid|e, -es, -ing, backslid, back-
slider/s 'bæk'slaid, -z, -iŋ, 'bæk'slid,
'bæk'slaidə*/z
backstairs 'bæk'stɛəz ['bæk-stɛəz]
backstay, -s 'bæk-stei, -z
backstitch, -es 'bæk-stitʃ, -iz
backstrap, -s 'bæk-stræp, -s
backward, -s, -ly, -ness 'bækwəd, -z, -li,
-nis
backwash, -es 'bækwɔʃ, -iz
backwater, -s 'bæk,wɔːtə*, -z
backwoods, -man, -men 'bækwudz,
-mən, -mən
back-yard, -s 'bæk'jɑːd, -z
bacon 'beikən [-kŋ]
Bacon 'beikən [-kn]
Baconian, -s bei'kəunjən [bə'k-, -nïən],
-z
bacteriological bæk,tiərïə'lɔdʒikəl
bacteriolog|ist/s, -y bæk,tiəri'ɔlədʒ|-
ist/s [,bæktiəri'ɔ-], -i
bacteri|um, -a, -al bæk'tiərï|əm, -ə, -əl
Bactria, -n/s 'bæktrïə, -n/z
Bacup 'beikəp
bad; bad|ly, -ness bæd; 'bæd|li, -nis
Badajoz 'bædəhɔz (bada'xoθ)
Badam, -s 'bædəm, -z
Baddeley 'bædəli, 'bædli

baddish 'bædiʃ
bade (*from* bid) bæd [beid]
Badely 'bædli
Baden (*in Germany*) 'bɑːdn
Baden-Powell 'beidn'pəuel [-'pəuil, -'pəuəl, -'pauəl]
Bader (*Scottish surname*) 'bɑːdə*, beidə*
badg|e (s. v.), -es, -ing, -ed bædʒ, -iz, -iŋ, -d
badger (s. v.) (B.), -s, -ing, -ed 'bædʒə*, -z, -riŋ, -d
badger-baiting 'bædʒə,beitiŋ
badger-dog, -s 'bædʒədɔg, -z
Badham 'bædəm
badinage 'bædinɑːʒ [ˌ--'-] (badinɑːʒ)
badminton (B.) 'bædmintən
Baeda 'biːdə
Baedeker, -s 'beidikə*, -z
Baffin 'bæfin
baff|le (s. v.), -les, -ling, -led, -ler/s 'bæf|l, -lz, -liŋ [-liŋ], -ld, -lə*/z [-lə*/z]
bag (s.), -s bæg, -z
bag (v.), -s, -ging, -ged bæg, -z, -iŋ, -d
bagatelle, -s; -board/s ˌbægə'tel, -z; -bɔːd/z [-bɔəd/z]
Bagdad (*in Iraq*) bæg'dæd ['-'-, '--], (*in Tasmania, Florida*) 'bægdæd
Bagehot 'bædʒət
baggage, -s 'bægidʒ, -iz
baggage|man, -men 'bægidʒ|mæn [-mən], -men [-mən]
Baggallay 'bægəli
bagg|y, -ier, -iest, -ily, -iness 'bæg|i, -iə*, -iist, -ili, -inis
Baghdad bæg'dæd ['-'-, '--]
bag|man, -men 'bæg|mən, -mən
Bagnall 'bægnəl [-nl, -nɔːl]
Bagnell 'bægnəl [-nl]
bagnio, -s 'bɑːnjəu [-niəu], -z
Bagot 'bægət
bagpipe, -s, -r/s 'bægpaip, -s, -ə*/z
Bagrie 'bægri
Bagsh|aw(e), -ot 'bægʃ|ɔː, -ɔt
Bagworthy (*in Devon*) 'bædʒəri
bah bɑː
bahadur, -s bə'hɑːdə*, -z
Bahama, -s bə'hɑːmə, -z
Bahia bə'hiːə [-'hiə]
Baiae 'baii
baignoire, -s 'beinwɑː* [-wɔː*], -z
bail (s. v.), -s, -ing, -ed, -er/s; -able beil, -z, -iŋ, -d, -ə*/z; -əbl
bail-bond, -s 'beilbɔnd ['beil'b-], -z
bailee, -s bei'liː: ['bei'liː], -z
Bailey 'beili
Bailhache 'beilhæʃ
bailie (B.), -s 'beili, -z

bailiff, -s 'beilif, -s
bailiwick, -s 'beiliwik, -s
bailment, -s 'beilmənt, -s
Baily 'beili
Bain, -es bein, -z
Bainbridge 'beinbridʒ ['beimb-]
Baird bɛəd
bairn, -s bɛən, -z
bait (s. v.), -s, -ing, -ed, beit, -s, -iŋ, -id
baize, -s beiz, -iz
bak|e, -es, -ing, -ed, -er/s beik, -s, -iŋ, -t, -ə*/z
bakehou|se, -ses 'beikhau|s, -ziz
bakelite 'beikəlait
Baker 'beikə*
Bakerloo 'beikə'luː: [ˌ--'-]
baker|y, -ies 'beikər|i, -iz
baking-powder 'beikiŋˌpaudə*
baksheesh 'bækʃiːʃ
Bala (*in Wales*) 'bælə (*Welsh* 'bala)
balaam (B.), -s 'beilæm [-ləm], -z
balaclava (B.), -s ˌbælə'klɑːvə, -z
Balakirev bə'lækirev [-'lɑːk-] (ba'lakirjif)
balalaika, -s ˌbælə'laikə, -z
balanc|e (s. v.), -es, -ing, -ed 'bæləns, -iz, -iŋ, -t
balance-sheet, -s 'bælənsʃiːt [-nʃʃiːt, nʃiːt], -s
Balbriggan bæl'brigən
Balbus 'bælbəs
Balcarres bæl'kæris
Balchin 'bɔːltʃin ['bɔl-]
balcon|y, -ies 'bælkən|i, -iz
bald, -er, -est, -ly, -ness bɔːld, -ə*, -ist, -li, -nis
baldachin, -s 'bɔːldəkin, -z
balderdash 'bɔːldədæʃ
bald-head, -s 'bɔːldhed, -z
bald-headed 'bɔːld'hedid [*also* 'bɔːldˌh- *when attributive*]
Baldock 'bɔːldɔk
baldric, -s 'bɔːldrik, -s
Baldry 'bɔːldri
Baldwin 'bɔːldwin
bal|e (s. v.), -es, -ing, -ed beil, -z, -iŋ, -d
Bâle (*in Switzerland*) bɑːl
Balean (*surname*) 'bælin
Balearic ˌbæli'ærik
baleen, -s bə'liːn [bæ'l-], -z
bale|ful, -fully, -fulness 'beil|ful, -fuli [-fəli], -fulnis
baler, -s 'beilə*, -z
Balfour 'bælfə* [-fuə*, -fɔə*, -fɔː*]
Balgony bæl'gəuni
Balguy 'bɔːlgi
Balham 'bæləm
Baliol 'beiljəl [-liəl]
balk (s. v.), -s, -ing, -ed bɔːk [bɔːlk], -s,

Balkan, -s 'bɔːlkən ['bɔl-], -z
ball (B.), -s bɔːl, -z
ballad, -s 'bæləd, -z
ballade, -s bæ'lɑːd (balad), -z
Ballan|tine, -tyne 'bælən|tain, -tain
Ballarat ‚bælə'ræt] ['--'-, '---]
Ballard 'bæləd, -lɑːd
ballast, -s 'bæləst, -s
Ballater 'bælətə*
ball-cock, -s 'bɔːl-kɔk, -s
Balleine (surname in Channel Islands) bæ'len
ballerina, -s ‚bælə'riːnə, -z
ballet, -s 'bælei [-li], -z
ballet-dancer,-s 'bæli‚dɑːnsə* [-lei,d-], -z
ballet-girl, -s 'bæligəːl [-leig-], -z
balletomane, -s 'bælitəumein [-lət-, -let-], -z
Balliol 'beiljəl [-lɪəl]
ballistic bə'listik
balloon, -s, -ist/s bə'luːn, -z, -ist/s
ballot (s. v.), -s, -ing, -ed ; -age 'bælət, -s, -iŋ, -id; -idʒ
ballot-box, -es 'bælətbɔks, -iz
ball-point, -s, -ed 'bɔːl-pɔint, -s, -id
ball-proof 'bɔːl-pruːf
ball-room, -s 'bɔːlrum [-ruːm], -z
bally 'bæli
Bally|castle, -mena, -money ‚bæli|-'kɑːsl, -'miːnə, -'mʌni
ballyrag, -s, -ging, -ged 'bæliræg, -z, -iŋ, -d
balm, -s bɑːm, -z
Balm(e) bɑːm
Balmoral bæl'mɔrəl
balm|y, -ier, -iest, -ily, -iness 'bɑːm|i, -ɪə* [-jə*], -iist [-jist], -ili, -inis
baloney bə'ləuni
balsam, -s 'bɔːlsəm ['bɔl-], -z
balsamic bɔːl'sæmik [bæl-, bɔl-]
Balta (in Ukraine) 'bæltə
Balthazar (in Shakespeare) ‚bælθə'zɑː* ['---], (otherwise) bæl'θæzə*
Baltic 'bɔːltik ['bɔl-]
baltimore (B.), -s 'bɔːltimɔː* ['bɔlt--mɔə*], -z
Baluchistan bə'luːtʃistɑːn [-tæn, -,--'-]
baluster, -s, -ed 'bæləstə*, -z, -d
balustrade, -s ‚bæləs'treid, -z
Baly 'beili
Balzac 'bælzæk (balzak)
bamboo, -s bæm'buː, -z
bambooz|le, -les, -ling, -led bæm'buːz|l, -lz, -ļiŋ [-liŋ], -ld
Bamborough 'bæmbərə
Bam|field, -ford 'bæm|fiːld, -fəd
bamfooz|le, -les, -ling, -led bæm'fuːz|l, -lz, -ļiŋ [-liŋ], -ld

Bamfyld 'bæmfiːld
ban (s. v.), -s, -ning, -ned bæn, -z, -iŋ, -d
banal bə'nɑːl [bæ'n-, 'beinl]
Banal 'bænəl [-nl]
banalit|y, -ies bə'nælit|i [bæ'n-], -iz
banana, -s bə'nɑːnə, -z
Banaras bə'nɑːrəs (Hind. bənarəs)
Banbury 'bænbəri ['bæmbəri]
Banchory 'bæŋkəri
banco 'bæŋkəu
Bancroft 'bænkrɔft ['bæŋ-k-, -krɔːft]
band (s.), -s bænd, -z
band (v.), -s, -ing, -ed bænd, -z, -iŋ, -id
bandag|e (s. v.), -es, -ing, -ed 'bændidʒ, -iz, -iŋ, -d
bandana, -s bæn'dɑːnə [-'dænə], -z
bandanna, -s bæn'dænə, -z
bandbox, -es 'bændbɔks, -iz
bandeau, -x 'bændəu, -z
banderole, -s 'bændərəul, -z
bandicoot, -s 'bændikuːt, -s
bandit, -s 'bændit, -s
banditti bæn'diti(ː)
bandmaster, -s 'bænd‚mɑːstə*, -z
bandog, -s 'bændɔg, -z
bandoleer [-lier], -s ‚bændəu'liə*, -z
bandoline 'bændəuliːn
bands|man, -men 'bændz|mən, -mən [-men]
bandstand, -s 'bændstænd ['bæn-stænd], -z
band|y (adj. v.), -ier, -iest ; -ies, -ying, -ied 'bænd|i, -ɪə* [-jə*], -iist [-jist]; -iz, -iiŋ [-jiŋ], -id
bandy-legged 'bændilegd
bane, -s bein, -z
bane|ful, -fully, -fulness 'bein|ful, -fuli [-fəli], -fulnis
Banff, -shire bæmf [bænf], -ʃiə* [-ʃə*]
Banfield 'bænfiːld
bang (s. v.), -s, -ing, -ed bæŋ, -z, -iŋ, -d
Bangalore ‚bæŋgə'lɔː* [-'lɔə*]
Banger 'beindʒə*
Bangkok bæŋ'kɔk ['-'-, 'bæŋ-kɔk]
bangle, -s, -d 'bæŋgl, -z, -d
Bangor (in Wales) 'bæŋgə* (Welsh 'baŋgor), (in U.S.A.) 'bæŋgɔː*
Banham 'bænəm   [-z
banian, -s 'bæniən [-njən, -niæn, -njæn],
banish, -es, -ing, -ed, -ment/s 'bæniʃ, -iz, -iŋ, -t, -mənt/s
banister, -s 'bænistə*, -z
banjo, -s 'bændʒəu [-'-, '-'-], -z
bank (s. v.), -s, -ing, -ed, -er/s bæŋk, -s, -iŋ, -t [bæŋt], -ə*/z
Bankes bæŋks
bank-holiday, -s 'bæŋk'hɔlədi [-lid-, -dei], -z

bank-note, -s 'bæŋk-nəut ['bæŋk'n-], -s
bank-rate, -s 'bæŋk-reit, -s
bankrupt, -s 'bæŋkrʌpt [-rəpt], -s
bankruptc|y, -ies 'bæŋkrəp*t*s|i, -iz
Banks bæŋks
banksia, -s 'bæŋksiə [-sjə], -z
Bannatyne 'bænətain
banner (B.), -s 'bænə*, -z
Bannerman 'bænəmən
Banning 'bæniŋ
Bannister 'bænistə*
bannock, -s 'bænək, -s
Bannockburn 'bænəkbə:n
banns bænz
banquet (s. v.), -s, -ing, -ed 'bæŋkwit, -s, -iŋ, -id
banqueting-hall, -s 'bæŋkwitiŋhɔ:l, -z
banquette, -s bæŋ'ket, -s
Banquo 'bæŋkwəu
banshee, -s bæn'ʃi: ['bæn'ʃi:], -z
bant, -s, -ing, -ed bænt, -s, -iŋ, -id
bantam (B.), -s 'bæntəm, -z
banter (s. v.), -s, -ing, -ed 'bæntə*, -z, -riŋ, -d
Banting 'bæntiŋ
bantling, -s 'bæntliŋ, -z
Bantry 'bæntri
Bantu 'bæn'tu: ['bɑ:n't-, also '--, -'- according to sentence stress]
banyan, -s 'bæniən [-njən, -niæn, -njæn], -z
baobab, -s 'beiəubæb, -z
baptism, -s 'bæptizəm, -z
baptism|al, -ally bæp'tizm|əl, -əli
baptist, -s 'bæptist, -s
baptister|y, -ies 'bæptistər|i, -iz
baptistr|y, -ies 'bæptistr|i, -iz
baptiz|e, -es, -ing, -ed bæp'taiz, -iz, -iŋ, -d
bar (s. v. prep.), -s, -ring, -red bɑ:*, -z, -riŋ, -d
Barabbas bə'ræbəs
Barak 'beəræk [-rək]
Barat 'bærət
barb (s. v.), -s, -ing, -ed bɑ:b, -z, -iŋ, -d
Barbad|os, -ian bɑ:'beid|əuz, -iən [-jən]
Barbara 'bɑ:bərə
barbarian, -s bɑ:'beəriən, -z
barbaric bɑ:'bærik
barbarism, -s 'bɑ:bərizəm, -z
barbarit|y, -ies bɑ:'bærit|i, -iz
barbariz|e [-ise], -es, -ing, -ed 'bɑ:bə-raiz, -iz, -iŋ, -d
Barbarossa ‚bɑ:bə'rɔsə
barbarous, -ly, -ness 'bɑ:bərəs, -li, -nis
Barbary 'bɑ:bəri
barbate 'bɑ:beit [-bit]
barbated 'bɑ:beitid [bɑ:'beitid]

barbecu|e (s. v.), -es, -ing, -ed 'bɑ:bikju:, -z, -iŋ [-kjuiŋ], -d
barber (B.), -s 'bɑ:bə*, -z
barberr|y, -ies 'bɑ:bər|i, -iz
barbette, -s bɑ:'bet, -s
barbican (B.), -s 'bɑ:bikən, -z
Barbirolli ‚bɑ:bi'rɔli
barbitone, -s 'bɑ:bitəun, -z
barbiturate, -s bɑ:'bitjurit [-reit], -s
barbituric ‚bɑ:bi'tjuərik ['tjɔər-, -'tjɔ:r-, ‚bɑ:'bitjurik]
Barbour 'bɑ:bə*
Barca 'bɑ:kə
barcarolle, -s 'bɑ:kərəul [-rɔl, ‚—'-], -z
Barcelona ‚bɑ:si'ləunə
Barclay 'bɑ:kli [-lei]
Barcroft 'bɑ:-krɔft [-krɔ:ft]
bard (B.), -s, -ic bɑ:d, -z, -ik
Bardell bɑ:'del, 'bɑ:dəl [-del, -d'l]
Note.—In 'Pickwick' general1y pronounced bɑ:'del.
Bard|olph, -sley 'bɑ:d|ɔlf, -zli
Bardswell 'bɑ:dzwəl [-wel]
Bardwell 'bɑ:dwəl [-wel]
bare (adj.), -r, -st, -ly, -ness beə*, -rə*, -rist, -li, -nis
bare (archaic p. tense of bear) beə*
bareback, -ed 'beəbæk, -t
Barebones 'beəbəunz
barefac|ed, -edly, -edness 'beəfeis|t, -tli [-idli], -tnis
barefoot 'beəfut
barefooted 'beə'futid ['beə‚f-]
bare-headed 'beə'hedid ['beə‚h-]
Bareilly bə'reili (Hind. bərylli)
bare-legged 'beə'legd ['beəlegd, -'legid]
bare-necked 'beə'nekt ['beənekt]
Barfield 'bɑ:fi:ld
bargain (s. v.), -s, -ing, -ed, -er/s 'bɑ:gin, -z, -iŋ, -d, -ə*/z
barge, -s bɑ:dʒ, -z
bargee, -s bɑ:'dʒi: ['bɑ:'dʒi:], -z
barge|man, -men 'bɑ:dʒ|mən [-mæn], -mən [-men]
Barger 'bɑ:dʒə*
Bargery 'bɑ:dʒəri
Bargh bɑ:dʒ, bɑ:f
Bargrave 'bɑ:greiv
Barham (surname) 'bærəm, 'bɑ:rəm, (in Kent) 'bærəm
Baring 'beəriŋ, 'bæriŋ
baritone, -s 'bæritəun, -z
barium 'beəriəm
Barjesus 'bɑ:‚dʒi:zəs
bark (s. v.), -s, -ing, -ed, -er/s bɑ:k, -s, -iŋ, -t, -ə*/z
Barker 'bɑ:kə*
Barkston 'bɑ:kstən
barley 'bɑ:li

barleycorn (B.), -s 'bɑːlikɔːn, -z
barley-sugar 'bɑːli'ʃugə* ['--,--]
barley-water 'bɑːli,wɔːtə*
Barlow(e) 'bɑːləu
barm bɑːm
barmaid, -s 'bɑːmeid, -z
bar|man, -men 'bɑː|mən [-mæn], -mən [-men]
Barmby 'bɑːmbi
Barmecide 'bɑːmisaid
Barmouth 'bɑːməθ
barm|y, -ier, -iest 'bɑːm|i, -ɪə*, -iist
barn, s bɑːn, -z
Barnab|as, -y 'bɑːnəb|əs [-æs], -i
barnacle, -s 'bɑːnəkl, -z
Barnard 'bɑːnəd
Barnardiston ,bɑːnəˈdistən
Barnardo bɑːˈnɑːdəu [bəˈn-]
Barnby 'bɑːnbi
barn-door (s.), -s 'bɑːnˈdɔː* [-ˈdɔə*], -z
barndoor (adj.) 'bɑːndɔː* [-dɔə*]
Barnea 'bɑːniə ['bɑːnɪə, bɑːˈniə]
Barnes bɑːnz
Barnet(t) 'bɑːnit
Barney 'bɑːni
Barnham 'bɑːnəm
Barnicott 'bɑːnikət [-kɔt]
Barnoldswick (in Yorks.) bɑːˈnəuldzwik
Barnsley 'bɑːnzli
Barnstaple 'bɑːnstəpl [locally -əbl]
barnstormer, -s 'bɑːn,stɔːmə*, -z
Barnum 'bɑːnəm
Baroda bəˈrəudə (Gujarati vəɖodra)
barograph, -s 'bærəugrɑːf [-græf], -s
Barolong (Bechuana tribe) ,bɑːrəuˈləuŋ [,bær-, -ˈlɔŋ]
baromet|er/s, -ry bəˈrɔmit|ə*/z, -ri
barometric, -al, -ally ,bærəuˈmetrik, -əl, -əli
baron (B.), -s 'bærən, -z
baron|age/s, -ess/es 'bærən|idʒ/iz [-rn̩-], -is/iz [-es/iz]
baronet, -s 'bærənit [-rn̩it, -et], -s
baronetage, -s 'bærənitidʒ [-rn̩-], -iz
baronetc|y, -ies 'bærənits|i [-rn̩-, -et-], -iz
baronial bəˈrəunjəl [-nɪəl]
baron|y, -ies 'bærən|i [-rn̩-], -iz
baroque bəˈrɔk [-ˈrəuk]
barouche, -s bəˈruːʃ [bæˈr-], -iz
barque, -s bɑːk, -s
Barr bɑː*
barrack (s. v.), -s, -ing, -ed 'bærək, -s, -iŋ, -t
Barraclough 'bærəklʌf
barrage, -s 'bærɑːʒ [bæˈrɑːʒ, -rɑːdʒ], -iz
barratry 'bærətri
Barrat(t) 'bærət

barrel, -s 'bærəl, -z
barrel-organ, -s 'bærəl,ɔːgən [-rl̩-], -z
barr|en, -enest, -enly, -enness 'bær|ən, -ənist [-n̩ist], -ənli, -ənnis
Barrett 'bærət [-ret, -rit]
barricad|e (s. v.), -es, -ing, -ed ,bæri'keid [-rəˈk-], -z, -iŋ, -id
Barrie 'bæri
barrier (B.), -s 'bærɪə*, -z
barring 'bɑːriŋ
Barrington 'bæriŋtən
barrister, -s 'bæristə*, -z
barrister - at - law, barristers - at - law 'bæristərət'lɔː, 'bæristəzət'lɔː
barristerial ,bærisˈtiərɪəl
Barron 'bærən
barrow (B.), -s 'bærəu, -z
Barrow-in-Furness 'bærəuinˈfəːnis [-nes]
Barry 'bæri
Barrymore 'bærimɔː* [-mɔə*]
bart. (B.), barts bɑːt, -s
Bartelot 'bɑːtilət [-lɔt]
barter (B.) (s. v.), -s, -ing, -ed 'bɑːtə*, -z, -riŋ, -d
Bartholomew bɑːˈθɔləmjuː [bəˈθ-]
Bartimeus [-maeus] ,bɑːtiˈmi(ː)əs
Bartle 'bɑːtl
Bartlett 'bɑːtlit
Bartolozzi ,bɑːtəˈlɔtsi
Barton 'bɑːtn
Bart's bɑːts
Baruch (biblical name) 'bɑːruk ['bɛər-, -rək], (modern surname) bəˈruːk
Barugh (surname, place in Yorks.) bɑːf
Barum 'bɛərəm
Barwick 'bærik
barytone, -s =b-barit-
basal 'beisl
basalt 'bæsɔːlt ['bæsəlt, bəˈsɔːlt, bəˈsɔlt]
basaltic bəˈsɔːltik [-ˈsɔl-]
basan 'bæzən
Basan 'beisæn
bascule, -s 'bæskjuːl, -z
bas|e (s. adj. v.), -es; -er, -est, -ely, -eness; -ing, -ed beis, -iz; -ə*, -ist, -li, -nis; -iŋ, -t
base-ball 'beisbɔːl
base-born 'beisbɔːn
basecourt, -s 'beis-kɔːt [-kɔət], -s
Baseden 'beizdən
baseless, -ly, -ness 'beislis, -li, -nis
basement, -s 'beismənt, -s
bases (from base) 'beisiz, (plur. of basis) 'beisiːz
Basford (in Notts.) 'beisfəd, (in Staffs.) 'bæsfəd
bash, -es, -ing, -ed bæʃ, -iz, -iŋ, -t
Basham (surname) 'bæʃəm

Bashan 'beiʃæn
Bashford 'bæʃfəd
bash|ful, -fullest, -fully, -fulness 'bæʃ|-
 fu𝑙, -fulist [-fəlist, -flist], -fuli [-fəli,
 -fli], -fu𝑙nis
basic (B.), -ally 'beisik, -əli
basil (B.), bæzl [-zil]
basilica, -s, -n bə'zilikə [-'sil-], -z, -n
basilisk, -s 'bæzilisk [-zļi-], -s
basin, -s 'beisn, -z
Basingstoke 'beizinstəuk
bas|is, -es 'beis|is, -i:z
bask, -s, -ing, -ed ba:sk, -s, -iŋ, -t
Basker (surname) 'ba:skə*
Baskervill(e) 'bæskəvil
basket, -s, -ful/s 'ba:skit, -s, -ful/z
basket-ball, 'ba:skitbɔ:l
basket-work 'ba:skit-wə:k
Basle ba:l
basque (B.), -s bæsk [ba:sk], -s
Basra(h) 'bæzrə ['bʌzrə, 'bæsrə]
bas-relief,-s 'bæsri,li:f['ba:r-, 'ba:sr-],-s
bass (fish, fibre) (B.) bæs
bass (in music), -es beis, -iz
Bassanio bə'sa:niəu [bæ's-, -njəu]
basset, -s 'bæsit, -s
basset-horn, -s 'bæsithɔ:n ['bæsit'h-], -z
Basset(t) 'bæsit
bassinet(te), -s ,bæsi'net, -s
basso, -s 'bæsəu, -z
bassoon, -s bə'su:n [bə'zu:n], -z
bass-wood 'bæswud
bast bæst
Bastable 'bæstəbl
bastard, -s, -y 'bæstəd ['ba:s-], -z, -i
bastardiz|e [-is|e], -es, -ing, -ed 'bæst-
 ədaiz ['ba:s-], -iz, -iŋ, -d
bast|e, -es, -ing, -ed beist, -s, -iŋ, -id
bastille (B.), -s bæs'ti:l (basti:j), -z
bastinad|o (s. v.), -oes, -oing, -oed
 ,bæsti'neid|əu [-'na:d-], -əuz, -əuiŋ,
 -əud
bastion, -s, -ed 'bæstiən [-tjən], -z, -d
Basuto, -s bə'su:təu [bə'zu:-], -z
Basutoland bə'su:təulænd [bə'zu:-]
bat (s. v.), -s, -ting, -ted bæt, -s, -iŋ, -id
Batavia bə'teivjə [-viə]
Batavier ,bætə'viə*
batch, -es bætʃ, -iz
Batchell|ar, -or 'bætʃi𝑙|ə* [-tʃəl-], -ə*
bat|e (B.), -es, -ing, -ed beit, -s, -iŋ,
 -id
Bate|man, -s, -son 'beit|mən, -s, -sn
Batey 'beiti
ba|th (s.) (B.), -ths ba:|θ, -ðz
bath (v.), -s, -ing, -ed ba:θ, -s, -iŋ, -t
bath-brick, -s 'ba:θbrik, -s
bath-chair, -s 'ba:θ'tʃɛə*, -z

bath|e (s. v.), -es, -ing, -ed, -er/s beið,
 -z, -iŋ, -d, -ə*/z
Batho 'bæθəu, 'beiθəu
bat-horse, -s 'bæthɔ:s, -iz
bathos 'beiθɔs
bathroom, -s 'ba:θru(:)m, -z
Bathsheba 'bæθʃibə
bath-stone 'ba:θstəun
Bathurst 'bæθə(:)st
bathyscaphe, -s 'bæθiskæf, -s
batik 'bætik
batiste bæ'ti:st [bə't-] (batist)
bat|man (military), -men 'bæt|mən,
 -mən
batman (oriental weight), -s 'bætmən, -z
baton, -s 'bætən [-tɒn, -tɔ̃:ŋ] (batɔ̃), -z
Baton Rouge 'bætən'ru:ʒ
batrachian, -s bə'treikjən [-kiən], -z
bats bæts
bats|man, men 'bæts|mən, -mən
battalion, -s bə'tæljən, -z
battels 'bætlz
batt|en (s. v.), -ens, -ening, -ened 'bæt|n,
 -nz, -ṇiŋ [-niŋ], -nd
Battenberg 'bætnbə:g
batter (s. v.), -s, -ing, -ed 'bætə*, -z,
 -riŋ, -d
battering-ram, -s 'bætəriŋræm, -z
Battersby 'bætəzbi
Battersea 'bætəsi
batter|y, -ies 'bætər|i, -iz
batting (s.) 'bætiŋ
Battishill 'bætiʃil [-ʃl]
batt|le (s. v.) (B.), -les, -ling, -led
 'bæt|l, -lz, -ļiŋ [-liŋ], -ld
battle-axe, -s 'bætlæks, -iz
battle-cruiser, -s 'bætl,kru:zə*, -z
battle-cr|y, -ies 'bætlkr|ai, -aiz
battledore [-door], -s 'bætldɔ:* [-dɔə*], -z
battle-dress, -es 'bætldres, -iz
battlefield, -s 'bætlfi:ld, -z
battle-ground, -s 'bætlgraund, -z
battlement, -s, -ed 'bætlmənt, -s, -id
battle-royal, -s 'bætl'rɔiəl, -z
battleship, -s 'bætlʃip, -s
battue, -s bæ'tu: [-'tju:, '--] (baty), -z
Battye 'bæti
Batum ba:'tu:m
Baty 'beiti
bauble, -s 'bɔ:bl, -z
Baucis 'bɔ:sis
Bauer 'bauə*
Baugh bɔ:
Baughan bɔ:n
Baughurst 'bɔ:ghə:st
baulk (s. v.), -s, -ing, -ed bɔ:k [bɔ:lk], -s,
 -iŋ, -t
bauxite 'bɔ:ksait

Bavaria, -n/s bə'vɛərɪə, -n/z
bawbee, -s bɔ:'bi: ['bɔ:'bi:], -z
bawd, -s; -ry, -y bɔ:d, -z; -ri, -i
bawdy-hou|se, -ses 'bɔ:dihau|s, -ziz
bawl, -s, -ing, -ed, -er/s bɔ:l, -z, -iŋ, -d, -ə*/z
Bax bæks
Baxandall 'bæksəndɔ:l
Baxter 'bækstə*
bay (s. adj. v.) (B.), -s, -ing, -ed, bei, -z, -iŋ, -d
bayard (B.) (horse), -s 'beiəd, -z
Bayard (surname) 'beiɑ:d
Bayard (airship), -s bei'ɑ:d ['beiɑ:d, 'beiəd] (bajɑ:r), -z
Bayeux bai'jə: [bai'ə:, old-fashioned bei'ju:] (bajø)
Bayl(e)y 'beili
Bayliss 'beilis
Baynes beinz
bayonet, -s 'beiənit ['bɛən-], -s
Bayreuth 'bairɔit (bai'rɔyt)
bay-salt 'bei'sɔ:lt [-'sɔlt]
Bayswater 'beiz,wɔ:tə*
bay-tree, -s 'bei-tri:, -z
bay-window, -s 'bei'windəu, -z
bazaar, -s bə'zɑ:*, -z
Bazalgette 'bæzəldʒit [-dʒet]
bazooka, -s bə'zu:kə, -z
B.B.C. 'bi:bi:'si:
B.C. 'bi:'si:
B.C.G. 'bi:-si:'dʒi:
bdellium 'delɪəm [-ljəm]
be; being, been bi: (strong form), bi (weak form); 'bi:iŋ, bi:n [bin]
Note.—Some speakers use bin only as a weak form; others use it always.
B.E.A. 'bi:i:'ei
Beacall 'bi:kɔ:l
beach (s. v.) (B.), -es, -ing, -ed bi:tʃ, -iz, -iŋ, -t
beachcomber (B.), -s 'bi:tʃ,kəumə*, -z
beachhead, -s 'bi:tʃhed, -z
beach-la-mar 'bi:tʃlə'mɑ:*
beachy (B.) 'bi:tʃi
beacon, -s 'bi:kən, -z
Beaconsfield (place in Bucks.) 'bekənz-fi:ld, (title of B. Disraeli) 'bi:k-
bead, -s, -ing/s, -ed, -er/s bi:d, -z, -iŋ/z, -id, -ə*/z
beadle (B.), -s 'bi:dl, -z
Beadnall 'bi:dnəl [-nḷ]
Beadon 'bi:dn
bead|y, -ier, -iest, -iness 'bi:d|i, -ɪə*, -iist, -inis
beagle, -s 'bi:gl, -z
beak, -s, -ed bi:k, -s, -t
beaker, -s 'bi:kə*, -z

Beal(e) bi:l
beam (s. v.), -s, -ing, -ed bi:m, -z, -iŋ, -d
beam-ends 'bi:m'endz ['--]
beam-engine, -s 'bi:m,endʒin, -z
Beaminster 'beminstə* [locally also 'bemistə*]
Note.—'bi:m- is sometimes heard from people unfamiliar with the place.
Beamish 'bi:miʃ
beam|y, -ily, -iness 'bi:m|i, -ili, -inis
bean, -s bi:n, -z
beanfeast, -s, -er/s 'bi:nfi:st, -s, -ə*/z
beano, -s 'bi:nəu, -z
beanstalk, -s 'bi:n-stɔ:k, -s
bear (s. v.), -s, -ing, bore, born(e), bearer/s bɛə*, -z, -riŋ, bɔ:* [bɔə*], bɔ:n, 'bɛərə*/z
bearab|le, -ly, -leness 'bɛərəb|l, -li, -lnis
bear-baiting 'bɛə,beitiŋ
beard (B.), -s, -ed biəd, -z, -id
Beard|er, -sley 'biəd|ə*, -zli
beardless 'biədlis
Beare biə*
bear-garden, -s 'bɛə,gɑ:dn, -z
bearing (s.), -s 'bɛəriŋ, -z
bearing-rein, -s 'bɛəriŋrein, -z
bearish, -ly, -ness 'bɛəriʃ, -li, -nis
Bearsden (in Scotland) bɛəz'den
bearskin, -s 'bɛə-skin, -z
Beasley 'bi:zli
beast, -s bi:st, -s
beastl|y, -ier, -iest, -iness 'bi:stḷ|i, -ɪə* [-jə*], -iist, [-jist], -inis
beat (s. v.), -s, -ing/s, -en bi:t, -s, -iŋ/z, -n
beatific, -al, -ally ,bi:ə'tifik [biə't-], -əl, -əli
beatification, -s bi(:),ætifi'keiʃən, -z
beati|fy, -fies, -fying, -fied bi(:)'æti|fai, -faiz, -faiiŋ, -faid
beatitude, -s bi(:)'ætitju:d, -z
beatnik, -s 'bi:tnik, -s
Beatri|ce, -x 'biətri|s, -ks
Beatt|ie, -y 'bi:t|i, -i
beau, -s bəu, -z
Beauchamp 'bi:tʃəm
Beau|clerc, -clerk 'bəu|klɛə*, -klɛə*
Beaufort 'bəufət [-fɔ:t]
Beaufoy 'bəufɔi
Beaujolais 'bəuʒəlei [-ʒɔ-] (boʒɔlɛ)
Beaulieu (in Hants) 'bju:li
Beaumaris bəu'mæris [bju:'m-] (Welsh biu'maris)
Beaumont 'bəumənt
Beaune bəun
beauteous, -ly, -ness 'bju:tjəs [-tɪəs], -li, -nis

beautiful 'bjuːtəfʊl [-tif-]

beautifully 'bjuːtəfli [-tif-, -fuli, -fəli]

beauti|fy, -fies, -fying, -fied, -fier/s 'bjuːti|fai, -faiz, -faiiŋ, -faid, -faiə*/z

beaut|y, -ies 'bjuːt|i, -iz

beauty-sleep 'bjuːti-sliːp

beauty-spot, -s 'bjuːti-spɔt, -s

Beav|an, -en 'bev|ən, -ən

beaver (B.), -s 'biːvə*, -z

Beaverbrook 'biːvəbruk

beaver|y, -ies 'biːvər|i, -iz

Beavis 'biːvis

Beavon 'bevən

Beaworthy 'biːˌwəːði

Beazley 'biːzli

becalm, -s, -ing, -ed bi'kɑːm [bə'k-], -z, -iŋ, -d

became (from become) bi'keim [bə'k-]

because bi'kɔz [bə'kɔz, bikəz, rarely bi'kɔːz, colloquially also kɔz, kəz]
    Note.—The use of bikəz and its abbreviated form kəz is becoming very common.

Beccles 'beklz

Becher 'biːtʃə*

Bechstein, -s 'bekstain, -z

Bechuana, -s, -land ˌbetʃu'ɑːnə [be'tʃwɑː-], -z, -lænd

beck (B.), -s bek, -s

Becke bek

Beckenham 'bekŋəm [-knəm]

Becket(t) 'bekit

Beckles 'beklz

Beckley 'bekli

beck|on, -ons, -oning, -oned 'bek|ən, -ənz, -ŋiŋ [-əniŋ, -niŋ], -ənd

Beck|ton, -with 'bek|tən, -wiθ

Becky 'beki

becloud, -s, -ing, -ed bi'klaud [bə'k-], -z, -iŋ, -id

becom|e, -es, -ing/ly, -ingness, became bi'kʌm [bə'k-], -z, -iŋ/li, -iŋnis, bi'keim [bə'k-]

Becontree 'bekəntriː

bed (s. v.), -s, -ding, -ded bed, -z, -iŋ, -id

bedad bi'dæd [bə'd-]

Bedales 'biːdeilz

bedaub, -s, -ing, -ed bi'dɔːb [bə'd-], -z, -iŋ, -d

bedchamber, -s 'bedˌtʃeimbə*, -z

bedclothes 'bedkləuðz [old-fashioned -kləuz]

bedder, -s 'bedə*, -z

Beddgelert beð'gelə(ː)t (Welsh beː'ð-'gelert)

bedding (s.) 'bediŋ

Beddoes 'bedəuz

Bede biːd

bedeck, -s, -ing, -ed bi'dek [bə'd-], -s, -iŋ, -t

Bedel 'biːdl, bi'del [bə'd-]

bedel(l), -s be'del [bi'd-, bə'd-], -z

bed|ew, -ews, -ewing, -ewed bi'd|juː [bə'd-], -juːz, -ju(ː)iŋ, -juːd

bedfellow, -s 'bedˌfeləu, -z

Bedford, -shire 'bedfəd, -ʃiə* [-ʃə*]

bedim, -s, -ming, -med bi'dim [bə'd-], -z, -iŋ, -d

Bedivere 'bediviə*

bediz|en, -ens, -ening, -ened bi'daiz|n [bə'd-, -'diz-], -nz, -ŋiŋ, -nd

Bedlam 'bedləm

Bedlamite, -s 'bedləmait, -s

bedmaker, -s 'bedˌmeikə*, -z

Bedouin, -s 'beduin, -z

bedplate, -s 'bedpleit, -s

bedpost, -s 'bedpəust, -s

bedragg|le, -les, -ling, -led bi'dræg|l [bə'd-], -lz, -liŋ [-liŋ], -ld

bed-ridden 'bedˌridn

bedrock, -s 'bed'rɔk ['bed-rɔk], -s

bedroom, -s 'bedru(ː)m, -z

Bedruthan bi'drʌðən [bə'd-]

Beds. bedz

bedside 'bedsaid

bed-sore, -s 'bedsɔː* [-sɔə*], -z

bedspread, -s 'bedspred, -z

bedstead, -s 'bedsted [-stid], -z

bedstraw, -s 'bedstrɔː, -z

bedtime 'bedtaim

Bedwell 'bedwəl [-wel]

bee (B.), -s biː, -z

Beeby 'biːbi

beech (B.), -es biːtʃ, -iz

Beecham 'biːtʃəm

Beecher 'biːtʃə*

Beeching 'biːtʃiŋ

beechnut, -s 'biːtʃnʌt, -s

bee-eater, -s 'biːˌiːtə*, -z

bee|f, -ves biː|f, -vz

beefeater, -s 'biːfˌiːtə*, -z

beefsteak, -s 'biːf'steik [also '— when attributive], -s

beef-tea 'biːf'tiː

beef|y, -ier, -iest, -ily, -iness 'biːf|i, -ɪə*, -iist, -ili, -inis

bee-hive, -s 'biːhaiv, -z

bee-line, -s 'biːlain ['biː'lain], -z

Beelzebub bi(ː)'elzibʌb

been (from be) biːn [bin]
    Note.—Some speakers use bin only as a weak form; others use it always.

beer (B.), -s biə*, -z

Beerbohm 'biəbəum

beer-hou|se, -ses 'biəhau|s, -ziz

beer-money 'biəˌmʌni

Beersheba biə'ʃi:bə ['biəʃibə]
beer|y, -ier, -iest, -ily, -iness 'biər|i,
-iə*, -iist, -ili, -inis
Beesl(e)y 'bi:zli
bee-sting, -s 'bi:-stiŋ, -z
beestings 'bi:stiŋz
beeswax 'bi:zwæks
beeswing 'bi:zwiŋ
beet, -s bi:t, -s
Beetham 'bi:θəm
Beethoven (musical composer) 'beit-
həuvn, (square in London) 'bi:thəuvn
beet|le (s. v.), -les, -ling, -led 'bi:t|l, -lz,
-liŋ [-liŋ], -ld
Beeton 'bi:tn
beetroot, -s 'bi:tru:t, -s
beeves (plur. of beef) bi:vz
be|fall, -falls, -falling, -fell, -fallen
bi|'fɔ:l [bə|-], -'fɔ:lz, -fɔ:liŋ, -'fel,
-'fɔ:lən
befit, -s, -ting/ly, -ted bi'fit [bə'f-], -s,
-iŋ/li, -id
before bi'fɔ:* [bə'f-, -'fɔə*]
beforehand bi'fɔ:hænd [bə'f-, -'fɔəh-]
before - mentioned   bi'fɔ:,menʃənd
[-'fɔə,m-]
beforetime bi'fɔ:taim [bə'f-, -'fɔə-t-]
befoul, -s, -ing, -ed bi'faul [bə'f-], -z,
-iŋ, -d
befriend, -s, -ing, -ed bi'frend [bə'f-], -z,
-iŋ, -id
beg, -s, -ging, -ged beg, -z, -iŋ, -d
begad bi'gæd [bə'g-]
began (from begin) bi'gæn [bə'g-]
be|get, -gets, -getting, -gat, -gotten
bi|'get [bə|-], -'gets, -'getiŋ, -'gæt,
-'gɔtn
beggar, -s 'begə*, -z
beggarl|y, -iness 'begəl|i, -inis
beggar-my-neighbour 'begəmi'neibə*
beggary 'begəri
Beggs begz
be|gin, -gins, -ginning/s, -gan, -gun,
-ginner/s   bi|'gin [bə|-], -'ginz,
-'giniŋ/z, -'gæn, -'gʌn, -'ginə*/z
begone bi'gɔn [bə'g-]
begonia, -s bi'gəunjə [bə'g-, -nɪə], -z
begorra bi'gɔrə [bə'g-]
begot, -ten (from beget) bi'gɔt [bə'g-], -n
begrim|e, -es, -ing, -ed bi'graim [bə'g-],
-z, -iŋ, -d
begrudge, -es, -ing, -ed bi'grʌdʒ [bə'g-],
-iz, -iŋ, -d
beguil|e, -es, -ing, -ed bi'gail [bə'g-], -z,
-iŋ, -d
Begum, -s 'beigəm [old-fashioned 'bi:g-],
-z
begun (from begin) bi'gʌn [bə'g-]

behalf bi'hɑ:f [bə'h-]
Behar (surname)   'bi:hɑ*,   (former
spelling of Bihar, q.v.) bi'hɑ:*
behav|e, -es, -ing, -ed bi'heiv [bə'h-],
-z, -iŋ, -d
behaviour, -s bi'heivjə* [bə'h-], -z
behaviouri|sm,   -st/s   bi'heivjəri|zəm
[bə'h-], -st/s
behead, -s, -ing, -ed bi'hed [bə'h-], -z,
-iŋ, -id
beheld (from behold) bi'held [bə'h-]
behemoth (B.) bi'hi:mɔθ ['bi:himəuθ]
behest, -s bi'hest [bə'h-], -s
behind, -hand bi'haind [bə'h-], -hænd
be|hold, -holds, -holding, -held, -hol-
der/s   bi|'həuld   [bə|-],   -'həuldz,
-'həuldiŋ, -'held, -'həuldə*/z
beholden bi'həuldən [bə'h-]
behoof bi'hu:f [bə'h-]
behov|e, -es, -ing, -ed bi'həuv [bə'h-],
-z, -iŋ, -d
Behrens (English name), 'bɛərənz
beige beiʒ [beidʒ]
being (s.), -s 'bi:iŋ, -z
being (from be) 'bi:iŋ
Beira 'baiərə (Port. 'beirɐ)
Beirut bei'ru:t ['-'-]
Beit bait
Beith bi:θ
bejan, -s 'bi:dʒən, -z
bejewel, -s, -led, bejewelling bi'dʒu:əl
[-'dʒuəl, -'dʒu:l, -'dʒu(:)il], -z, -d,
bi'dʒu:əliŋ [bi'dʒuəliŋ, bi'dʒu(:)iliŋ]
bel, -s bel, -z
belab|our, -ours, -ouring, -oured
bi'leib|ə* [bə'l-], -əz, -əriŋ, -əd
belated, -ly, -ness bi'leitid [bə'l-], -li,
-nis
belaud, -s, -ing, -ed bi'lɔ:d [bə'l-], -z, -iŋ,
-id
Belaugh 'bi:lɔ:
belay, -s, -ing, -ed bɪ'lei [bə'l-], -z, -iŋ, -d
belch, -es, -ing, -ed, -er/s beltʃ [belʃ],
-iz, -iŋ, -t, -ə*/z
Belcher 'beltʃə*, 'belʃə*
beldam(e), -s 'beldəm, -z
beleaguer, -s, -ing, -ed, -er/s bi'li:gə*
[bə'l-], -z, -riŋ, -d, -rə*/z
belemnite, -s 'beləmnait, -s
Belfast bel'fɑ:st ['bel'fɑ:st, also '--, esp.
when attributive]
belfr|y, -ies 'belfr|i, -iz
Belg|ian/s, -ic 'beldʒ|ən/z, -ik
Belgium 'beldʒəm
Belgrade bel'greid
Belgrave 'belgreiv
Belgravia, -n bel'greivjə [-vɪə], -n
Belial 'bi:ljəl [-lɪəl]

bel|ie, -ies, -ying, -ied bi'l|ai [bə'l-], -aiz, -aiiŋ, -aid

belief, -s bi'li:f [bə'l-], -s

believ|e, -es, -ing/ly, -ed, -er/s; -able bi'li:v [bə'l-], -z, -iŋ/li, -d, -ə*/z; -əbl

belike bi'laik [bə'l-]

Belinda bi'lində [be'l-, bə'l-]

Belisha bi'li:ʃə [be'l-, bə'l-]

belitt|le, -les, -ling, -led bi'lit|l [bə'l-], -lz, -liŋ, [-liŋ], -ld

Belize be'li:z [bə'l-]

bell (s. v.) (B.), -s, -ing, -ed bel, -z, -iŋ, -d

Bella 'belə

belladonna, ,belə'dɔnə

Bellamy 'beləmi

Bellatrix (star) 'belətriks [be'leitriks, bə'leit-]

bell-buoy, -s 'belbɔi, -z

belle (B.), -s bel, -z

Belleisle be'li:l

Belle Isle 'bel'ail

Bellerophon bə'lerəfən [bi'l-]

belles lettres 'bel'letr [-'letə*] (bɛllɛtr̩)

Belle Tout 'bel'tu:t ['bel-tu:t, bel'tu:t]

Bellevue 'bel'vju: ['belvju:]

Bellew 'belju:

bell-founder, -s 'bel,faundə*, -z

bell-glass, -es 'belglɑ:s, -iz

bell-hanger, -s 'bel,hæŋə*, -z

bellicose, -ly 'belikəus, -li

bellicosity ,beli'kɔsiti

belligerency bi'lidʒərənsi [be'l-, bə'l-, -dʒrən-]

belligerent, -s bi'lidʒərənt [be'l-, bə'l-, -dʒrənt], -s

Bellingham (in Northumb.) 'belindʒəm, (surname) 'belindʒəm, 'beliŋəm

bell|man, men 'bel|mən [-mæn], -mən [-men]

bell-metal 'bel,metl

Belloc 'belɔk

Bellot be'lɔt

bellow, -s, -ing, -ed 'beləu, -z, -iŋ, -d

bellows (s.) 'beləuz [-ləz]

Bellows 'beləuz

bell-ringer, -s 'bel,riŋə*, -z

bell-rope, -s 'belrəup, -s

bell-shaped 'bel-ʃeipt

bell-tent, -s 'bel-tent, -s

bell-tower, -s 'bel,tauə*, -z

bell-wether, -s 'bel,weðə*, -z

bell|y (s. v.), -ies, -ying, -ied 'bel|i, -iz, -iiŋ, -id

belly-band, -s 'belibænd, -z

bellyful, -s 'beliful, -z

Belmont 'belmɔnt [-mənt]

Beloe 'bi:ləu

belong, -s, -ing/s, -ed bi'lɔŋ [bə'l-], -z, -iŋ/z, -d

beloved (used predicatively) bi'lʌvd [bə'l-], (used attributively or as noun) bi'lʌvd [bə'l-, -vid]

below bi'ləu [bə'l-]

Belsh|am, -aw 'belʃ|əm, -ɔ:

Belshazzar bel'ʃæzə*

Belsize 'belsaiz

Belstead 'belstid [-sted]

belt (B.), -s, -ed belt, -s, -id

Belteshazzar, ,belti'ʃæzə*

belting, -s 'beltiŋ, -z

Beltingham (in Northumb.) 'beltindʒəm

Belton 'beltən

Beluchistan bə'lu:tʃistɑ:n [be'l-, bi'l-, -tæn, -,-'-]

belvedere (B.), -s 'belvidiə* ['belvi'd-, ,belvi'd-], -z

Belvoir (castle) 'bi:və*, (in names of streets, etc.) 'belvwɔ:* [-vɔiə*, -vɔə*, -vɔ:*]

bema, -s, -ta 'bi:mə, -z, -tə

Beman 'bi:mən

Bembridge 'bembridʒ

Bemerton 'bemətən [-tn]

bemoan, -s, -ing, -ed bi'məun [bə'm-], -z, -iŋ, -d

bemus|e, -es, -ing, -ed bi'mju:z [bə'm-], -iz, -iŋ, -d

Ben ben

Benares (old form of Banaras, q.v.) bi'nɑ:riz [be'n-, bə'n-]

Benbow 'benbəu

bench, -es bentʃ, -iz

bencher, -s 'bentʃə*, -z

bend (s. v.), -s, -ing, -ed, bent bend, -z, -iŋ, -id, bent

beneath bi'ni:θ [bə'n-]   [tʃiti], -z

Benedicite, -s ,beni'daisiti [,bene'di:-

Benedick, -s 'benidik, -s

Benedict 'benidikt, 'benit

benedictine (liqueur), -s ,beni'dikti:n, -z

Benedictine (monk), -s ,beni'diktin [-tain], -z

Note.—Members of the Order pronounce -tin.

benediction, -s ,beni'dikʃən, -z

Benedictus, -es ,beni'diktəs [,bene-'diktus], -iz

benefaction, -s ,beni'fækʃən ['benif-], -z

benefactor, -s 'benifæktə* [,beni'f-], -z

benefactress, -es 'benifæktris [,beni'f-], -iz

benefic bi'nefik

benefice, -s, -d 'benifis, -iz, -t

beneficen|ce, -t/ly bi'nefisən|s [bə'n-], -t/li

benefici|al, -ally, -alness ˌbeni'fiʃ|əl, -əli, -əlnis
beneficiar|y, -ies ˌbeni'fiʃər|i [-ʃïə-, -ʃjə-], -iz
benefit (s. v.), -s, -ing, -ed 'benifit, -s, -iɳ, -id
Benelux 'benilʌks
Benenden 'benəndən
Bene't 'benit
Benet 'benit
Benét (American surname) be'nei
benevolen|ce, -t/ly bi'nevələn|s [bə'n-, -vḷ-, -vul-], -t/li
Bengal beɳ'gɔːl [ben'g-, '-'-, occasionally also '-- when followed by a stress]
Bengali, -s beɳ'gɔːli [ben'g-], -z
bengal-light, -s 'beɳgɔːl'lait ['beng-], -s
Benge (surname) bendʒ
Benger (food) 'bendʒə* ['beɳgə*]
Benhadad ben'heidæd [-dəd, 'benədæd]
Benham 'benəm
Benians 'beniənz [-njənz]
benighted bi'naitid [bə'n-]
benign, -est, -ly bi'nain [bə'n-], -ist, -li
benignan|cy, -t/ly bi'nignən|si [bə'n-], -t/li
benignity bi'nigniti [bə'n-]
Benin be'nin [bi'n-, bə'n-]
benison, -s 'benizn [-isn], -z
Benis(s)on 'benisn
Benjamin 'bendʒəmin [-mən]
Benjamite, -s 'bendʒəmait, -s
Bennet(t) 'benit
Bennette be'net [bə'n-]
Ben Nevis ben'nevis
Bennington 'beniɳtən
Benoliel ˌbenə'liəl [-'liːl]
Bensham (near Newcastle) 'benʃəm
Bensley 'benzli
Benson 'bensn
bent (s.), -s bent, -s
bent (from bend) bent
Benten 'bentən
Bentham 'bentəm [-nθəm]
Bentinck (surname) 'bentiɳk, old-fashioned 'bentik, (as name of street) 'bentiɳk
Bentley, -s 'bentli, -z
Benton 'bentən
benumb, -s, -ing, -ed bi'nʌm [bə'n-], -z, -iɳ, -d
benzene 'benziːn [-'-]
benzine 'benziːn [-'-]
benzoic ben'zəuik ['benzəuik]
benzoin 'benzəuin
benzol 'benzɔl
benzoline 'benzəuliːn

Beowulf 'beiəuwulf
bequea|th, -ths, -thing, -thed bi'kwiː|ð [bə'k-, -iː|θ], -ðz [-θs], -ðiɳ, -ðd [-θt]
bequest, -s bi'kwest [bə'k-], -s
Berber, -s 'bəːbə*, -z
Bere biə*
Berea bə'riə [bi'r-]
bereav|e, -es, -ing, -ed, bereft bi'riːv [bə'r-], -z, -iɳ, -d, bi'reft [bə'r-]
bereavement, -s bi'riːvmənt [bə'r-], -s
bereft (from bereave) bi'reft [bə'r-]
Berengaria ˌberiɳ'geəriə [-reɳ-, -rəɳ-]
Berenice (in ancient Egypt, etc.) ˌberi'naisi(ː), (opera by Handel) ˌberi'niːtʃi
Beresford 'berizfəd [-isf-]
beret, -s 'berei ['beri], -z ['berit, -s]
berg, -s bəːg, -z
bergamot, -s 'bəːgəmɔt [-mət], -s
Bergen 'bəːgən ['beəg-]
Berger (English surname) 'bəːdʒə*
beriberi 'beri'beri
Bering 'beriɳ ['biər-, 'beər-]
Berkeleian bɑː'kli(ː)ən
Berkeley (in England) 'bɑːkli [rarely 'bəːk-], (in U.S.A.) 'bəːkli
berkelium 'bəːkliəm
Berkhamsted [-mpstead] 'bəːkəmpstid [-sted, less commonly 'bɑːk-]
Note.—The usual pronunciation is 'bəːk-, but the form 'bɑːk- is used by some residents, esp. members of county families.
Berks. bɑːks [rarely bəːks]
Berkshire 'bɑːkʃiə* [-ʃə*, rarely 'bəːk-]
Berlin (in Germany) bəː'lin [ˈ-'-, occasionally also '-- when attributive], (surname) 'bəːlin, bəː'lin, (town in U.S.A.) 'bəːlin
Berlioz (composer) 'beəliəuz ['bəːl-] (bɛrljoːz)
Berlitz 'bəːlits [-'-]
Bermondsey 'bəːməndzi
Bermuda, -s bə(ː)'mjuːdə, -z
Bernard (Christian name) 'bəːnəd, (surname) bəː'nɑːd, 'bəːnəd
Bern(e) bəːn [bɛən]
Berners 'bəːnəz
Bernese bəː'niːz ['-'-, also '-- when attributive]
Bernice (biblical name) bə:'naisi(ː), (modern Christian name) 'bəːnis, (surname) 'bəːnis, bə:'niːs
Berowne bə'rəun
Berridge 'beridʒ
berr|y (B.), -ies 'ber|i, -iz
bersaglieri ˌbeəsɑːli'eəri(ː) (bersaʎˈʎeːri)
berserk, -s, -er/s bə(ː)'səːk, -s, -ə*/z
berth (s.), -s bəːθ, -s [bəːðz]

berth (v.), -s, -ing, -ed bə:θ, -s, -iŋ, -t
Bertha 'bə:θə
Berthold 'bə:thəuld
Bertie (Christian name) 'bə:ti, (surname) 'bɑ:ti, 'bə:ti
Bertram 'bə:trəm
Berwick, -shire 'berik, -ʃiə* [-ʃə*]
beryl (B.), -s 'beril, -z
beryllium be'riljəm [bə'r-, -lïəm]
Besant 'besənt, 'bezənt, bi'zænt [bə'z-]
  Note.—Pronounced 'besənt or 'bezənt
  in the case of Mrs Annie Besant
  (she herself pronounced 'bes-); pronounced bi'zænt or bə'zænt in the
  case of Sir Walter Besant and A.
  Digby Besant.
beseech, -es, -ing/ly, besought bi'si:tʃ
  [bə's-], -iz, -iŋ/li, bi'sɔ:t [bə's-]
beseem, -s, -ing, -ed bi'si:m [bə's-], -z,
  -iŋ, -d
beset, -ting bi'set [bə's-], -s, -iŋ
beshrew bi'ʃru: [bə'ʃ-]
beside, -s bi'said [bə's-], -z
besieg|e, -es, -ing, -ed, -er/s bi'si:dʒ
  [bə's-], -iz, -iŋ, -d, -ə*/z
Besley 'bezli   [-riŋ, -d
besmear, -s, -ing, -ed bi'smiə* [bə's-], -z,
besmirch, -es, -ing, -ed bi'smə:tʃ [bə's-],
  -iz, -iŋ, -t
besom, -s 'bi:zəm ['biz-], -z
besotted, -ly, -ness bi'sɔtid [bə's-], -li,
  -nis
besought (from beseech) bi'sɔ:t [bə's-]
bespang|le, -les, -ling, -led bi'spæŋg|l
  [bə's-], -lz, -liŋ [-l̩iŋ], -ld
bespatter, -s, -ing, -ed bi'spætə* [bə's-],
  -z, -riŋ, -d
bespeak, -s, -ing, bespoke, bespoken
  bi'spi:k [bə's-], -s, -iŋ, bi'spəuk
  [bə's-], bi'spəukən [bə's-]
bespectacled bi'spektəkld [-tik-]
besprink|le, -les, -ling, -led bi'spriŋk|l
  [bə's-], -lz, -liŋ [-l̩iŋ], -ld
Bess bes
Bessarabia ,besə'reibjə [-bïə]
Bessborough 'bezbrə
Bessemer 'besimə*
Besses o' th' Barn 'besizəð'bɑ:n
Bessie 'besi
best (adj. adv. v.) (B.), -s, -ing, -ed best,
  -s, -iŋ, -id
bestial, -ly, -ism 'bestjəl [-tïəl], -i, -izəm
bestialit|y, -ies ,besti'ælit|i, -iz
bestiar|y, -ies 'bestïər|i [-tjə-], -iz
bestir, -s, -ring, -red bi'stə:* [bə's-], -z,
  -riŋ, -d
best|ow, -ows,-owing, -owed bi'st|əu
  [bə's-], -əuz, -əuiŋ, -əud

bestowal, -s bi'stəuəl [bə's-], -z
bestrid|e, -es, -ing, bestrode, bestridden
  bi'straid [bə's-], -z, -iŋ, bi'strəud
  [bə's-], bi'stridn [bə's-]
bet (s. v.) (B.), -s, -ting, -ted, -tor/s bet,
  -s, -iŋ, -id, -ə*/z
beta, -s 'bi:tə, -z
be|take, -takes, -taking, -took, -taken
  bi|'teik [bə-], -'teiks, -'teikiŋ, -'tuk,
  -'teikən
betel, -nut/s 'bi:təl, -nʌt/s
Betelgeuse ,bi:tl'ʒə:z [,bet-, 'betldʒu:z]
bête noire, -s 'beit'nwɑ:* [-'nwɔ:*]
  (bɛ:tnwɑ:r), -z
Bethany 'beθəni [-θn̩i]
Bethel 'beθəl [be'θel]
  Note.—When used to denote a nonconformist chapel, the pronunciation
  is 'beθəl.
Bethesda be'θezdə [bi'θ-, bə'θ-]
bethink, -s, -ing, bethought bi'θiŋk
  [bə'θ-], -s, -iŋ, bi'θɔ:t [bə'θ-]
Bethlehem 'beθlihem [-lïəm, -ljəm]
Bethnal 'beθnəl [-n̩l]
Bethphage 'beθfədʒi
Bethsaida beθ'seidə [-'saidə]
Bethune (surname) 'bi:tn, (in names of
  streets, etc.) be'θju:n [bi'θ-, bə'θ-]
Béthune (French town) be'θju:n [bi'θ-,
  bə'θ-, -'tju:n, -'tu:n] (betyn)
betide bi'taid [bə't-]
betimes bi'taimz [bə't-]
Betjeman 'betʃəmən [-tjə-]
betok|en, -ens, -ening, -ened bi'təuk|ən
  [bə't-], -ənz, -n̩iŋ [-əniŋ], -ənd
betony 'betəni
betook (from betake) bi'tuk [bə't-]
betray, -s, -ing, -ed, -er/s bi'trei
  [bə't-], -z, -iŋ, -d, -ə*/z [-'treə*/z]
betrayal, -s bi'treiəl [bə't-, -'treil], -z
betro|th, -ths, -thing, -thed bi'trəu|ð
  [bə't-, əu|θ], -ðz [-θs], -ðiŋ, -ðd [-θt]
betrothal, -s bi'trəuðəl [bə't-], -z
Betsy 'betsi
Betteley 'betəli
better (s. adj. v.), -s, -ing, -ed 'betə*, -z,
  -riŋ, -d
betterment 'betəmənt
betting, -s 'betiŋ, -z
Bettws 'betəs (Welsh 'betus)
Bettws-y-Coed 'betəsi'kɔid [-tusi-, -təzi-,
  -'kəuid] (Welsh 'betusə'kɔid)
Betty 'beti
between bi'twi:n [bə't-]
betweentimes bi'twi:n-taimz [bə't-]
betwixt bi'twikst [bə't-]
Beulah 'bju:lə
Beurle bə:l

beurré (*pear*), -s 'bjuəri, -z
Beuthin 'bju:θin
Bevan 'bevən
bev|el (*s. v.*), -els, -elling, -elled 'bev|əl,
    -əlz, -liŋ [-əliŋ], -əld
Beven 'bevən
beverage, -s 'bevəridʒ, -iz
Beveridge 'bevəridʒ
Beverley 'bevəli
Beves 'bi:vis
Bevin 'bevin
Bevis 'bi:vis, 'bevis
bev|y, -ies 'bev|i, -iz
bewail, -s, -ing, -ed bi'weil [bə'w-], -z,
    -iŋ, -d
beware bi'wɛə* [bə'w-]
Bewick(e) 'bju(:)ik
bewild|er,   -ers,   -ering/ly,   -ered,
    -erment/s bi'wild|ə* [bə'w-], -əz,
    -əriŋ/li, -əd, -əmənt/s
bewitch, -es, -ing/ly, -ed, -ment/s
    bi'witʃ [bə'w-], -iz, -iŋ/li, -t, -mənt/s
Bewley 'bju:li
bewrayeth bi'reiiθ [bə'r-]
Bexhill 'beks'hil [-'-]
Bexley 'beksli
Bey, -s bei, -z
beyond bi'jɔnd [bi'ɔnd]
Beyrout(h) (*former spelling of* Beirut)
    bei'ru:t ['-'-]
Beyts beits
bezant, -s 'bezənt, -s
bezel, -s 'bezl, -z
bezique bi'zi:k [be'z-, bə'z-]
bheest|y, -ies 'bi:st|i, -iz
Biarritz biə'rits ['--] (bjarits)
bias (*s. v.*), -(s)es, -(s)ing, -(s)ed 'baiəs,
    -iz, -iŋ, -t   [[-jəl]
biax|al, -ial bai'æks|əl ['bai'æ-], -ɪəl
bib, -s bib, -z
Bibby 'bibi
Bible, -s 'baibl, -z
biblic|al, -ally 'biblik|əl, -əli
bibliograph|er/s,   -y,   -ies   ˌbibli'ɔ-
    grəf|ə*/z, -i, -iz
bibliolat|er/s, -ry ˌbibli'ɔlət|ə*/z, -ri
bibliomania ˌbibliə*u'meinjə [-nɪə]
bibliomaniac,   -s   ˌbibliə*u'meiniæk
    [-njæk], -s
bibliophile, -s 'bibliə*ufail [-ljəf], -z
bibulous 'bibjuləs
bicarbonate, -s bai'kɑ:bənit ['bai'k-
    -bn̩it, -bnit, -eit], -s
bice bais
Bice 'bi:tʃi
bicentenar|y (*s. adj.*), -ies ˌbai-sen'ti:-
    nər|i ['bai-sen't-, -'ten-, bai'sentin-],
    -iz

bicentennial ˌbai-sen'tenjəl ['bai-sen't-,
    -nɪəl]
biceps, -es 'baiseps, -iz
Bicester 'bistə*
bichloride 'bai'klɔ:raid
bichromate 'bai'krəumit [-meit]
bicker, -s, -ing/s, -ed, -er/s 'bikə*, -z,
    -riŋ/z, -d, -rə*/z
Bickerstaff 'bikəstɑ:f
Bickersteth 'bikəsteθ [-stiθ]
Bickerton 'bikətn
Bickford 'bikfəd
Bick|leigh, -ley 'bik|li, -li
Bicknell 'biknəl [-n̩l]
bicuspid, -s bai'kʌspid [bi'k-], -z
bicyc|le (*s. v.*), -les, -ling, -led 'baisik|l,
    -lz, -liŋ, -ld
bicyclist, -s 'baisiklist, -s
bid (*s.*), -s bid, -z
bid (*v.*) (*at auction*), -s, -ding, -der/s bid,
    -z, -iŋ, -ə*/z
bid (*v.*) (*command*), -s, -ding, bade,
    -bidden bid, -z, -iŋ, bæd [beid], 'bidn
Bidder 'bidə*
Biddle 'bidl
Biddulph 'bidʌlf [-dəlf]
bid|e (B.), -es, -ing, -ed baid, -z, -iŋ, -id
Bideford 'bidifəd
Biden 'baidn
bidet, -s 'bi:dei, -z (bidɛ)
biennial, -ly bai'enɪəl [-njəl], -i
bier, -s biə*, -z
biff (*s. v.*), -s, -ing, -ed bif, -s, -iŋ, -t
bifocal (*s. adj.*), -s 'bai'fəukəl [-'--], -z
bifurcat|e, -es, -ing, -ed 'baifə:keit, -s,
    -iŋ, -id
bifurcation, -s ˌbaifə:'keiʃən, -z
big, -ger, -gest, -ness big, -ə*, -ist, -nis
bigamist, -s 'bigəmist, -s
bigamous, -ly 'bigəməs, -li
bigam|y, -ies 'bigəm|i, -iz
Bigelow 'bigiləu [-gəl-]
Bigge big
biggish 'bigiʃ
Big|gs, -ham big|z, -əm
bight, -s bait, -s
Bignell 'bignəl [-n̩l]
Bigod 'baigəd
bigot, -s, -ed; -ry 'bigət, -s, -id; -ri
bigraph, -s 'baigrɑ:f [-græf], -s
bigwig, -s 'bigwig, -z
Bihar bi'hɑ:* (*Hind.* byhar)
bijou, -s 'bi:ʒu:, -z
bik|e (*s. v.*), -es, -ing, -ed baik, -s, -iŋ, -t
bikini (B.), -s bi'ki:ni, -z
bilabial (*s. adj.*), -s bai'leibjəl ['bai'l-,
    bɪəl], -z
bilater|al, -ally bai'lætər|əl ['bai'l-], -əli

Bilbao bil'bɑːəu [-'beiəu]
bilberr|y, -ies 'bilbər|i, -iz
Bilborough 'bilbərə
Bilbrough 'bilbrə
bile bail
bilg|e (s. v.), -es, -ing, -ed bildʒ, -iz, -iŋ, -d
bilge-pump, -s 'bildʒpʌmp, -s
bilge-water 'bildʒ,wɔːtə*
bilgy 'bildʒi
biliary 'biljəri [-lïər-]
bilingual, -ism bai'liŋgwəl ['bai'l-], -izəm
bilious, -ly, -ness 'biljəs, [-lïəs], -li, -nis
biliteral bai'litərəl ['bai'l-]
bilk, -s, -ing, -ed bilk, -s, -iŋ, -t
bill (B.), -s bil, -z
Billerica 'bilrikə
Billericay ,bilə'riki   [-id
billet (s. v.), -s, -ing, -ed 'bilit, -s, -iŋ,
billet-doux (sing.) 'bilei'duː [-li'd-], (plur.) -z
bill-hook, -s 'bilhuk, -s
billiard, -s; -ball/s, -cue/s, -marker/s, -room/s, -table/s 'biljəd, -z; -bɔːl/z, -kjuː/z, -,mɑːkə*/z, -rum/z [-ruːm/z], -,teibl/z
Billing, -s, -hurst 'biliŋ, -z, -həːst
Billingsgate 'biliŋzgit [-geit]
Billington 'biliŋtən
billion, -s, -th/s 'biljən, -z, -θ/s
bill-of-fare, -s 'biləv'fɛə* [,bil-, -lə'fɛə*], -z
bill|ow, -ows, -owy 'bil|əu, -əuz, -əui
bill-poster, -s 'bil,pəustə*, -z
bill-stick|er/s, -ing 'bil,stik|ə*/z, -iŋ
bill|y (B.), -ies 'bil|i, -iz
billycock, -s 'bilikɔk, -s
billy-goat, -s 'biligəut, -s
Bilston(e) 'bilstən
Bilton 'biltən
biltong 'biltɔŋ
bimestrial bai'mestrïəl
bimetalli|sm,   -st/s   bai'metəli|zəm ['bai'm-, -t̬i-], -st/s
bi-monthl|y, -ies 'bai'mʌnθl|i, -iz
bin, -s bin, -z
binary 'bainəri
binaural bain'ɔːrəl [bin-]
bind (s. v.), -s, -ing, bound, binder/s baind, -z, -iŋ, baund, 'baində*/z
bindweed 'baindwiːd
Binegar 'binigə*
Bing|ham, -ley 'biŋ|əm, -li
bingo 'biŋgəu
Bink(e)s biŋks
binnacle, -s 'binəkl, -z
Binn|ey, -ie 'bin|i, -i

Binns binz
binocle, -s 'binɔkl ['bain-, -nəkl], -z
binocular (s.), -s bi'nɔkjulə* [bai'n-, -kjəl-], -z
binocular (adj.) bai'nɔkjulə* [bi'n-, -kjəl-]
binomial bai'nəumjəl [-mïəl]
Binste(a)d 'binstid [-sted]
Binyon 'binjən
biochemist, -s, -ry 'baiəu'kemist, -s, -ri
biogenesis 'baiəu'dʒenisis
biograph, -s 'baiəugrɑːf [-græf], -s
biographer, -s bai'ɔgrəfə* [bi'ɔ-], -z
biographic, -al, -ally ,baiəu'græfik [,biəu'g-, biə'g-], -əl, -əli
biograph|y, -ies bai'ɔgrəf|i [bi'ɔ-], -iz
biologic, -al, -ally ,baiəu'lɔdʒik, əl, -əli
biolog|ist/s, -y bai'ɔlədʒ|ist/s, -i
biometry bai'ɔmitri
bioscope, -s 'baiəskəup, -s
biparous 'bipərəs
bipartite bai'pɑːtait ['bai,pɑːtait]
biped, -s 'baiped, -z
bipedal 'bai,pedl
biplane, -s 'bai-plein, -z
biquadratic (s. adj.), -s ,baikwɔ'dɪætik ['baikwɔ'd-, -kwə'd-], -s
birch (s. v.) (B.), -es, -ing, -ed bəːtʃ, -iz, -iŋ, -t
birchen 'bəːtʃən
Birchenough 'bəːtʃinʌf
bird (B.), -s bəːd, -z
bird-cage (B.), -s 'bəːdkeidʒ, -iz
bird-call, -s 'bəːdkɔːl, -z
bird-fancier, -s 'bəːd,fænsïə* [-sjə*], -z
bird-lime 'bəːdlaim
bird-nest, -s, -ing, -ed 'bəːdnest, -s, -iŋ, -id
birdseed 'bəːdsiːd
bird's-eye (s. adj.), -s 'bəːdzai, -z
Birdseye 'bəːdzai
bird's-nest (s. v.), -s, -ing, -ed 'bəːdznest, -s, -iŋ, -id
bireme, -s 'bairiːm ['baiər-], -z
biretta, -s bi'retə, -z
Birkbeck (surname) 'bəːbek, 'bəːkbek, (college in London) 'bəːkbek
Birkenhead (in Cheshire) 'bəːkənhed [locally ,bəːkən'hed], (Earl) 'bəːkənhed
Birkett 'bəːkit
Birley 'bəːli
Birling 'bəːliŋ
Birmingham 'bəːmiŋəm
Birnam 'bəːnəm
biro, -s 'baiərəu, -z
Biron (modern surname) 'baiərən
    Note.—The name must be pronounced
    bi'ruːn in 'Love's Labour's Lost'.

Birrell 'birəl
birth, -s bə:θ, -s
birthday, -s 'bə:θdei [-di], -z
birthmark, -s 'bə:θmɑːk, -s
birthplace, -s 'bə:θpleis, -iz
birth-rate, -s 'bə:θ-reit, -s
birthright, -s 'bə:θ-rait, -s
Birtwistle 'bə:t,wisl
bis bis
Biscay 'biskei [-ki]
biscuit, -s 'biskit, -s
bisect, -s, -ing, -ed, -or/s bai'sekt, -s, -iŋ, -id, -ə*/z
bisection, -s bai'sekʃən, -z
bisexual 'bai'seksjŭəl [bai's-, -ksjwəl, -ksjul, -kʃjŭəl, -kʃwəl, -kʃul]
bishop (B.), -s; -ric/s 'biʃəp, -s; -rik/s
Bishopsgate 'biʃəpsgeit [-git]
Bishop's Stortford 'biʃəps'stɔːfəd [-ɔːtf-]
Bishopst|oke, -on 'biʃəpst|əuk, -ən
Bisley, -s 'bizli, -z
Bismarck 'bizmɑːk ('bismark)
bismuth 'bizməθ
bison, -s 'baisn, -z
Bispham (surname) 'bisfəm, 'bispəm, (place) 'bispəm
bisque, -s bisk, -s
Bisseker 'bisikə*
Bissell 'bisl
bissextile, -s bi'sekstail, -z
bistour|y, -ies 'bistur|i [-tər-], -iz
bistre 'bistə*
bistro(t), -s 'biːstrəu, -z (bistro)
bisulph|ate, -ite bai'sʌlf|eit ['bai's-, -fit], -ait
bisurated 'bisjuəreitid
bit, -s bit, -s
bit (from bite) bit
bitch, -es bitʃ, -iz
bit|e (s. v.), -es, -ing, bit, bitten, biter/s bait, -s, -iŋ, bit, 'bitn, 'baitə*/z
Bithell bi'θel, 'biθəl
Bithynia bi'θiniə [bai'θ-, -njə]
bitter, -er, -est, -ly, -ness 'bitə*, -rə*, -rist, -li, -nis
bittern, -s 'bitə(ː)n, -z
bitters 'bitəz
bittersweet 'bitə-swiːt
bitumen, -s 'bitjumin [-men, -mən, bi'tjuːm-], -z
bituminous bi'tjuːminəs
bivalen|ce, -t 'bai,veilən|s ['bai'v-], -t
bivalve, -s 'baivælv, -z
bivouac (s. v.), -s, -king, -ked 'bivuæk [-vwæk], -s, -iŋ, -t
bi-weekly (s. adv.), -ies 'bai'wiːkl|i [bai'w-], -iz
bizarre bi'zɑː* (biza:r)

blab, -s, -bing, -bed, -ber/s blæb, -z, -iŋ, -d, -ə*/z
Blachford 'blæʃfəd
black (s. adj. v.) (B.), -s; -er, -est, -ish, -ly, -ness; -ing, -ed blæk, -s; -ə*, -ist, -iʃ, -li, -nis; -iŋ, -t
blackamoor, -s 'blækəmuə* [-mɔə*, -mɔː*], -z
blackball (v.), -s, -ing, -ed 'blækbɔːl, -z, -iŋ, -d
blackbeetle, -s 'blæk'biːtl, -z
blackberr|y, -ies 'blækbər|i [-,ber-], -iz
blackberrying 'blæk,beriiŋ [-bər-]
blackbird, -s 'blækbəːd, -z
blackboard, -s 'blækbɔːd [-bɔəd], -z
Blackburn(e) 'blækbəːn
blackcap, -s 'blækkæp, -s
black-cattle 'blæk'kætl
blackcock, -s 'blækkɔk, -s
black-currant, -s 'blæk'kʌrənt, -s
black-draught 'blæk'drɑːft
black|en, -ens, -ening, -ened 'blæk|ən, -ənz, -ɲiŋ [-əniŋ, -niŋ], -ənd
Blackett 'blækit
black-eye, -s 'blæk'ai, -z
black-eyed 'blækaid
Blackford 'blækfəd
Blackfriars 'blæk'fraiəz ['blæk,f-, esp. when attributive]
blackgame 'blækgeim
blackguard, -s, -ly 'blægɑːd, -z, -li
Blackheath 'blæk'hiːθ [also '--, -'-, according to sentence-stress]
Blackie 'blæki, in the N. also 'bleiki
blacking (s.), -s 'blækiŋ, -z
blacklead (s. v.), -s, -ing, -ed 'blæk'led, -z, -iŋ, -id
blackleg -s 'blækleg, -z
black-letter 'blæk'letə* ['blæk,l-]
Blackley (Manchester) 'bleikli, (surname) 'blækli
black-list (s. v.), -s, -ing, -ed 'blæklist, -s, -iŋ, -id
blackmail (s. v.), -s, -ing, -ed, -er/s 'blækmeil, -z, -iŋ, -d, -ə*/z
Blackman 'blækmən
Blackmoor 'blækmuə* [-mɔə*, -mɔː*]
Blackmore 'blækmɔː* [-mɔə*]
black-out, -s 'blækaut ['-'-], -s
Blackpool 'blækpuːl
Blackpudlian, -s blæk'pʌdliən [-ljən], -z
Blackrock 'blækrɔk
black-rod, -s 'blæk'rɔd, -z
blacksmith, -s 'blæksmiθ, -s
Blackston(e) 'blækstən
blackthorn, -s 'blækθɔːn, -z
Blackwall 'blækwɔːl
blackwater (B.) 'blæk,wɔːtə*

Blackwell 'blækwəl [-wel]
Blackwood (*surname*) 'blækwud, (*place in Monmouthshire*) 'blæk'wud
bladder, -s 'blædə*, -z
bladderwort, -s 'blædəwə:t, -s
blade, -s bleid, -z
blade-bone, -s 'bleidbəun, -z
blaeberr|y, -ies 'bleibər|i, -iz
Blagrave 'blægreiv
Blagrove 'bleigrəuv
blah-blah 'bla:'bla:
Blaikie 'bleiki
Blaikley 'bleikli
blain, -s blein, -z
Blair blɛə*
Blair-Atholl 'blɛər'æθəl
Blake, -ney bleik, -ni
Blakiston 'blækistən, 'bleik-
blamab|le, -ly, -leness 'bleiməb|l, -li, -lnis
blam|e (*s. v.*), -es, -ing, -ed bleim, -z, -iŋ, -d
blameless, -ly, -ness 'bleimlis, -li, -nis
blameworth|y, -iness 'bleim‚wə:ð|i, -inis
Blamires blə'maiəz
Blanc (*Mont*) blɑ̃:ŋ [blɔ̃:ŋ, blɑ:ŋ, blɔ:ŋ, blɒŋ] (blɑ̃)
blanch, -es, -ing, -ed blɑ:ntʃ, -iz, -iŋ, -t
Blanchard 'blæntʃəd [-tʃɑ:d]
Blanche blɑ:ntʃ
blanc-mange, -s blə'mɔnʒ [-'mɔ̃:nʒ, -'mɑ:nʒ], -iz
blanco 'blæŋkəu
bland (B.), -er, -est, -ly, -ness blænd, -ə*, -ist, -li, -nis ['blænnis]
Blandford 'blændfəd
blandish, -es, -ing, -ed, -ment/s 'blændiʃ, -iz, -iŋ, -t, -mənt/s
Blandy 'blændi
blank (*s. adj. v.*), -s ; -er, -est, -ly, -ness ; -ing, -ed blæŋk, -s ; -ə*, -ist, -li, -nis ; -iŋ, -t
blanket, -s, -ing 'blæŋkit, -s, -iŋ
Blankley 'blæŋkli
blank-verse 'blæŋk'və:s
Blantyre blæn'taiə*
blar|e (*s. v.*), -es, -ing, -ed blɛə*, -z, -riŋ, -d
blarney (B.) 'blɑ:ni
blasé 'blɑ:zei (blaze)
blasphem|e, -es, -ing/ly, -ed, -er/s blæs'fi:m [blɑ:s-], -z, -iŋ/li, -d, -ə*/z
blasphemous, -ly 'blæsfiməs ['blɑ:s-, -fəm-, -fm̩-], -li
blasphem|y, -ies 'blæsfim|i ['blɑ:s-, -fəm-, -fm̩-], -iz
blast (*s. v.*), -s, -ing, -ed blɑ:st, -s, -iŋ, -id
blast-furnace, -s 'blɑ:st'fə:nis ['-‚--], -iz

blastoderm, -s 'blæstəudə:m, -z
blast-pipe, -s 'blɑ:stpaip, -s
blatan|cy, -t/ly 'bleitən|si, -t/li
Blatchford 'blætʃfəd
blather, -s, -ing, -ed 'blæðə*, -z, -riŋ, -d
Blawith (*in Lancs.*) 'blɑ:iθ, (*road at Harrow*) 'bleiwiθ
Blaydes bleidz
blaz|e (*s. v.*), -es, -ing, -ed bleiz, -iz, -iŋ, -d
blazer, -s 'bleizə*, -z   [-d
Blazes 'bleiziz
Blazey 'bleizi
blaz|on, -ons, -oning, -oned 'bleiz|n [*in original heraldic sense also* 'blæz-], -nz, -ŋiŋ [-əniŋ, -niŋ], -nd
bleach, -es, -ing, -ed bli:tʃ, -iz, -iŋ, -t
bleaching-powder 'bli:tʃiŋ‚paudə*
bleak, -er, -est, -ly, -ness bli:k, -ə*, -ist, -li, -nis
blear, -eyed bliə*, -r-aid
blear|y, -ier, -iest, -iness 'bliər|i, -iə*, -iist, -inis
bleat (*s. v.*), -s, -ing, -ed bli:t, -s, -iŋ, -id
bleb, -s bleb, -z
bled bled
Bledisloe 'bledisləu
bleed, -s, -ing, bled bli:d, -s, -iŋ, bled
blemish (*s. v.*), -es, -ing, -ed 'blemiʃ, -iz, -iŋ, -t
blench, -es, -ing, -ed blentʃ, -iz, -iŋ, -t
Blencowe blen'kəu
blend (*s. v.*), -s, -ing, -ed, -er/s blend, -z, -iŋ, -id, -ə*/z
blende blend
Blenheim 'blenim [-nəm]
Blenkinsop 'bleŋkinsɔp
Blennerhassett ‚blenə'hæsit
Blériot, -s 'bleriəu ['bliər-] (blerjo), -z
bless, -es, -ing, -ed (*p. tense, p. partic.*), blest bles, -iz, -iŋ, -t, blest
blessed (*adj.*), -ly, -ness 'blesid, -li, -nis
blessing (*s.*), -s 'blesiŋ, -z
blest (*from* bless) blest
Bletchley 'bletʃli
bleth|er, -ers, -ering, -ered 'bleð|ə*, -əz, -əriŋ, -əd
blew (*from* blow) blu:
Blew|ett, -itt 'blu(:)|it, -it
Bligh blai
blight (*s. v.*), -s, -ing, -ed blait, -s, -iŋ, -id
blighter, -s 'blaitə*, -z
Blighty 'blaiti
blimey 'blaimi
blimp, -s blimp, -s
blind (*s. adj. v.*), -er, -est, -ly, -ness ; -s, -ing, -ed blaind, -ə*, -ist, -li, -nis ['blainnis] ; -z, -iŋ, -id

blindfold (adj. v.), -s, -ing, -ed 'blaind-fəuld, -z, -iŋ, -id
blindman's-buff 'blaindmænz'bʌf
blindworm, -s 'blaindwə:m, -z
blink (s. v.), -s, -ing, -ed bliŋk, -s, -iŋ, -t [bliŋt]
blinker, -s 'bliŋkə*, -z
bliss (B.) blis
Blissett 'blisit
bliss|ful, -fully, -fulness 'blis|fʊl, -fuli [-fəli], -fʊlnis
blist|er (s. v.), -ers, -ering, -ered 'blist|ə*, -əz, -əriŋ, -əd
blithe, -r, -st, -ly, -ness blaið, -ə*, -ist, -li, -nis
blith|er (v.), -ers, -ering, -ered, -erer/s 'blið|ə*, -əz, -əriŋ, -əd, -ərə*/z
blithesome, -ly, -ness 'blaiðsəm, -li, -nis
blitz (s. v.), -es, -ing, -ed blits, -iz, -iŋ, -t
blitzkrieg, -s 'blitskri:g, -z
blizzard, -s 'blizəd, -z
bloat, -s, -ing, -ed/ness bləut, -s, -iŋ, -id/nis
bloater, -s 'bləutə*, -z
blob, -s blɔb, -z
bloc, -s blɔk, -s
block (s. v.) (B.), -s, -ing, -ed, -er/s blɔk, -s, -iŋ, -t, -ə*/z
blockad|e (s. v.), -es, -ing, -ed, -er/s blɔ'keid [blə'k-], -z, -iŋ, -id, -ə*/z
blockhead, -s 'blɔkhed, -z
blockhou|se, ses 'blɔkhau|s, -ziz
Bloemfontein 'blu:mfəntein [-fɔn-]
Blois blwɑ: [surname blɔis] (blwa, blwɑ)
bloke, -s bləuk, -s
Blom (surname) blɔm
Blomefield 'blu:mfi:ld
Blomfield 'blɔmfi:ld, 'blum-, 'blʌm-, 'blu:m-
blond(e), -s blɔnd, -z
Blondel(l) 'blʌndl, 'blɔndl, blɔn'del
Blondin (French tight-rope walker) 'blɔndin (blɔ̃dɛ̃)
blood, -s blʌd, -z
bloodcurdling 'blʌd,kə:dliŋ
blood-guiltiness 'blʌd,giltinis
bloodheat 'blʌdhi:t
blood-horse, -s 'blʌdhɔ:s, -iz
bloodhound, -s 'blʌdhaund, -z
bloodless, -ly, -ness 'blʌdlis, -li, -nis
blood-money 'blʌd,mʌni
bloodpoisoning 'blʌd,pɔizniŋ [-zniŋ]
blood-red 'blʌd'red [also '-- when attributive]
blood-relation, -s 'blʌdri'leiʃən [-ri,l-], -z
blood|shed, -shot 'blʌd|ʃed, -ʃɔt
bloodstain, -s, -ed 'blʌdstein, -z, -d

blood-stone, -s 'blʌdstəun, -z
blood-sucker, -s 'blʌd,sʌkə*, -z
bloodthirst|y, -ier, -iest, -ily, -iness 'blʌd,θə:st|i, -iə* [-jə*], -iist [-jist], -ili, -inis
blood-vessel, -s 'blʌd,vesl, -z
blood|y, -ier, -iest, -ily, -iness 'blʌd|i, -iə*, -iist, -ili, -inis
bloom (s. v.), -s, -ing, -ed blu:m, -z, -iŋ, -d
bloomer (B.), -s 'blu:mə*, -z
Bloomfield 'blu:mfi:ld
Bloomsbury 'blu:mzbəri
Blore blɔ:* [blɔə*]
blossom (s. v.) (B.), -s, -ing, -ed 'blɔsəm, -z, -iŋ, -d
blot (s. v.), -s, -ting, -ted blɔt, -s, -iŋ, -id
blotch (s. v.), -es, -ing, -ed blɔtʃ, -iz, -iŋ, -t
blotch|y, -ier, -iest, -ily, -iness 'blɔtʃ|i, -iə*, -iist, -ili, -inis
blotter, -s 'blɔtə*, -z
blotting-paper, -s 'blɔtiŋ,peipə*, -z
blotto 'blɔtəu
Blougram 'bləugrəm ['blau-]
Bloundelle 'blʌndl
Blount blʌnt
blouse, -s blauz, -iz
blow (s. v.) (B.), -s, -ing, blew, blow|n, -ed, -er/s bləu, -z, -iŋ, blu:, bləu|n, -d, -ə*/z
blow-fl|y, -ies 'bləu-fl|ai, -aiz
blow-hole, -s 'bləuhəul, -z
blow-lamp, -s 'bləu-læmp, -s
blown (from blow) bləun
blow-out, -s 'bləu'aut ['--], -s
blowpipe, -s 'bləu-paip, -s
blow|y, -ier, -iest, -ily, -iness 'bləu|i, -iə*, -iist, -ili, -inis
blowz|y, -ier, -iest, -iness 'blauz|i, -iə*, -iist, -inis
Blox(h)am 'blɔksəm
blub, -s, -bing, -bed blʌb, -z, -iŋ, -d
blubber (s. v.), -s, -ing, -ed, -er/s 'blʌbə*, -z, -riŋ, -d, -rə*/z
blucher, -s 'blu:tʃə*, -z
Blücher 'blu:kə* [-u:tʃə*] ('blyçər)
bludg|eon (s. v.), -eons, -eoning, -eoned 'blʌdʒ|ən, -ənz, -ŋiŋ [-əniŋ], -ənd
blue (s. adj. v.), -s; -r, -st; -ing, -d blu:, -z; -ə* [bluə*], -ist [bluist]; -iŋ [bluiŋ], -d
Bluebeard 'blu:biəd
bluebell, -s 'blu:bel, -z
blue-black 'blu:'blæk ['--]
blue-blooded 'blu:'blʌdid ['-,--]
blue-book, -s 'blu:buk, -s
bluebottle, -s 'blu:,bɔtl, -z

blue-devils 'blu:'devlz
blue-coat, -s 'blu:-kəut, -s
blue-jacket, -s 'blu:‚dʒækit, -s
blue-john 'blu:dʒɔn
blue-light, -s 'blu:'lait, -s
blueness 'blu:-nis
blue-penc|il, -ils, -illing, -illed 'blu:-
  'pens|l, -lz, -liŋ [-əliŋ], -ld
blue-pill, -s 'blu:'pil, -z
blue-print, -s 'blu:print ['blu:'print], -s
bluestocking, -s 'blu:‚stɔkiŋ, -z
Bluett 'blu:it [bluit]
bluey 'blu:i [blui]
bluff (s. adj. v.), -s; -er, -est, -ly, -ness;
  -ing, -ed blʌf, -s; -ə*, -ist, -li, -nis;
  -iŋ, -t
bluish 'blu(:)iʃ
Blundell 'blʌndl
blund|er (s. v.), -ers, -ering, -ered,
  -erer/s 'blʌnd|ə*, -əz, -əriŋ, -əd,
  -ərə*/z
blunderbuss, -es 'blʌndəbʌs, -iz
Blunn blʌn
blunt (adj. v.) (B.), -er, -est, -ly, -ness;
  -s, -ing, -ed blʌnt, -ə*, -ist, -li, -nis;
  -s, -iŋ, -id
blur, -s, -ring, -red blə:*, -z, -riŋ, -d
blurb, -s blə:b, -z
blurt, -s, -ing, -ed blə:t, -s, -iŋ, -id
blush (s. v.), -es, -ing/ly, -ed, -er/s
  blʌʃ, -iz, -iŋ/li, -t, -ə*/z
blust|er, -ers, -ering/ly, -ered, -erer/s
  'blʌst|ə*, -əz, -əriŋ/li, -əd, -ərə*/z
Bly blai
Blyth blai, blaiθ, blaið
Blythborough 'blaibərə
Blythe blaið
Blyton 'blaitn
boa, -s 'bəuə [bɔə, bɔ:], -z
B.O.A.C. 'bi: əu ei 'si:
Boadicea ‚bəuədi'siə
Boag bəug
Boanas 'bəunəs
Boanerges ‚bəuə'nə:dʒi:z
boar, -s bɔ:* [bɔə*], -z
board (s. v.), -s, -ing, -ed, -er/s bɔ:d
  [bəəd], -z, -iŋ, -id, -ə*/z
boarding-hou|se, -ses 'bɔ:diŋhau|s
  ['bəəd-], -ziz
boarding-school, -s 'bɔ:diŋ-sku:l
  ['bəəd-], -z
boardroom, -s 'bɔ:drum [-ru:m], -z
board-school, -s 'bɔ:dsku:l ['bəəd-], -z
board-wages 'bɔ:d'weidʒiz ['bəəd-]
boar-hound, -s 'bɔ:haund ['bəəh-], -z
boarish 'bɔ:riʃ ['bəər-]
Boas 'bəuæz, 'bəuəz
Boase bəuz

boast (s. v.), -s, -ing, -ed, -er/s bəust, -s,
  -iŋ, -id, -ə*/z
boast|ful, -fully, -fulness 'bəust|ful,
  -fuli, [-fəli], -fulnis
boat, -s; -er/s bəut, -s; -ə*/z
boat-hook, -s 'bəuthuk, -s
boat-hou|se, -ses 'bəuthau|s, -ziz
boating 'bəutiŋ
boat|man, -men 'bəut|mən, -mən
boat-race, -s 'bəut-reis, -iz
boatswain, -s 'bəusn ['bəutswein], -z
Boaz 'bəuæz
bob (s. v.) (B.), -s, -bing, -bed bɔb, -z,
  -iŋ, -d
bobbin, -s 'bɔbin, -z
bobbish, -ly, -ness 'bɔbiʃ, -li, -nis
bobb|y (B.), -ies 'bɔb|i, -iz
bobbysox, -er/s 'bɔbisɔks, -ə*/z
bobolink, -s 'bɔbəliŋk [-bəul-], -s
bobsleigh, -s 'bɔbslei, -z
bobstay, -s 'bɔbstei, -z
bobtail, -s 'bɔbteil, -z
bob-wig, -s 'bɔb'wig ['bɔbwig], -z
Boccaccio bɔ'kɑ:tʃiəu [bə'k-, -'kætʃ-,
  -tʃjəu) (bɔ'kattʃo)
Bochaton 'bɔkətən
Bockett 'bɔkit
Bodd|ington, -y 'bɔd|iŋtən, -i
bod|e (B.), -es, -ing, -ed bəud, -z, -iŋ, -id
bodega (B.), -s bəu'di:gə, -z
Bodey 'bəudi
Bodiam 'bəudjəm [-dɪəm]
bodice, -s 'bɔdis, -iz
Bodie 'bəudi
Bodilly bə'dili [bɔ'd-, bəu'd-]
bodily 'bɔdili
bodkin (B.), -s 'bɔdkin, -z
Bodleian bɔd'li(:)ən ['bɔdliən, esp.
  when attributive]
Bod|ley, -min 'bɔd|li, -min
bod|y, -ies 'bɔd|i, -iz
bodyguard, -s 'bɔdigɑ:d, -z
body-snatcher, -s 'bɔdi‚snætʃə*, -z
Boeing 'bəuiŋ
Boeo|tia, -tian/s bi'əu|ʃjə [-ʃiə, -ʃə],
  -ʃjən/z [-ʃiən/z, -ʃən/z]
Boer, -s 'bəuə* [bɔə*, bɔ:*, buə*], -z
Boethius bəu'i:θjəs [-θɪəs]
boffin (B.), -s 'bɔfin, -z
Bofors 'bəufəz
bog, -s 'bɔg, -z
bogey, -s 'bəugi, -z
bogey|man, -men 'bəugi|mæn, -men
bogg|le, -les, -ling, -led, -ler/s 'bɔg|l,
  -lz, -liŋ [-liŋ], -ld, -lə*/z [-lə*/z]
bogg|ly, -ier, -iest, -iness 'bɔg|i, -iə*,
  -iist, -inis
bogie, -s 'bəugi, -z

bogie-engine, -s 'bəugi,endʒin, -z
bogie-wheel, -s 'bəugiwi:l [-ihw-], -z
Bognor 'bɔgnə*
bog-oak 'bɔg'əuk
Bogotá (in Colombia) ,bɔgəu'tɑ: [,bəug-]
Bogota (in New Jersey) bə'gəutə
bogus 'bəugəs
bog|y, -ies 'bəug|i, -iz
bohea bəu'hi:
Bohemia, -n/s bəu'hi:mjə [-mǐə], -n/z
Bohn bəun
Bohun 'bəuən, bu:n
Note.—bu:n in B. Shaw's ' You never can tell.'
boil (s. v.), -s, -ing, -ed, -er/s bɔil, -z, -iŋ, -d, -ə*/z
boiling-point, -s 'bɔiliŋpɔint, -s
Bois bɔiz
Boisragon 'bɔrəgən
boisterous, -ly, -ness 'bɔistərəs, -li, -nis
Boivie (English surname) 'beivi
Bojador ,bɔhə'dɔ:* [,bgzə-]
Bokhara bəu'kɑ:rə
Bolander 'bəulændə*
bolas, -es 'bəuləs, -iz
bold, -er, -est, -ly, -ness bəuld, -ə*, -ist, -li, -nis
bold-faced 'bəuldfeist
Boldre 'bəuldə*
bole, -s bəul, -z
bolero, -s (dance) bə'lɛərəu [bɔ'l-, -'liə-], (garment) 'bɔlərəu, -z
Boleyn 'bulin [bu'lin, bu'li:n]
Bolingbroke 'bɔliŋbruk [old-fashioned 'bul-]
Bolinger 'bəulindʒə*
Bolitho bə'laiθəu [bɔ'l-]
Bolivar (S. American general) bɔ'li:vɑ:* (bo'libar), (places in U.S.A.) 'bɔlivə* [-vɑ:*]
Bolivia, -n/s bə'liviə [bɔ'l-, -vjə], -n/z
boll, -s, -ed bəul [bɔl], -z, -d
bollard, -s 'bɔləd, -z
Bolling 'bəuliŋ
Bollinger (in U.S.A.) 'bɔlindʒə*
bolo, -s 'bəuləu, -z
Bologna bə'ləunjə (bo'loɲɲa)
bolometer, -s bəu'lɔmitə*, -z
boloney bə'ləuni
Bolshevi|k/s, -st/s 'bɔlʃivi|k/s [-ʃəv-, -ʃev-], -st/s
bolshie, -s 'bɔlʃi, -z
bolshy 'bɔlʃi, -z
Bolsover (surname, street in London) 'bɔlsəvə* [-səuvə*], (in Derbyshire) 'bəulzəuvə*

bolst|er (s. v.), -ers, -ering, -ered 'bəulst|ə*, -əz, -əriŋ, -əd
bolt (s. v.) (B.), -s, -ing, -ed bəult, -s, -iŋ, -id
bolter (B.), -s 'bəultə*, z-
Bolton 'bəultən
bolt-upright 'bəult'ʌprait
bolus, -es 'bəuləs, -iz
bomb (s. v.), -s, -ing, -ed bɔm, -z, -iŋ, -d
bombard (s.), -s 'bɔmbɑ:d, -z
bombard (v.), -s, -ing, -ed, -ment/s bɔm'bɑ:d [bəm-], -z, -iŋ, -id, -mənt/s
bombardier, -s ,bɔmbə'diə* [,bʌm-, -bɑ:'d-], -z
bombardon, -s bɔm'bɑ:dn, -z
bombasine 'bɔmbəsi:n [-əzi:n, ,--'-]
bombast 'bɔmbæst
bombastic bɔm'bæstik
Bombay bɔm'bei ['bɔm'bei, also 'bɔmbei when attributive]
bombe, -s bɔ̃:mb [bɔmb] (bɔ̃:b), -z
bomber, -s 'bɔmə*, -z
bomb-proof 'bɔm-pru:f
bombshell, -s 'bɔm-ʃel, -z
Bompas 'bʌmpəs
bon bɔn (bɔ̃)
bona fide 'bəunə'faidi
bonanza, -s bəu'nænzə, -z
Bonapart|e, -ist/s 'bəunəpɑ:t, -ist/s
Bonar 'bɔnə*
bon-bon, -s 'bɔnbɔn ['bɔmbɔn, 'bɔmbɔ̃, bɔ̃:mbɔ̃:ŋ, 'bɔ:mbɔ:ŋ] (bɔ̃bɔ̃), -z
Bonchurch 'bɔn-tʃə:tʃ
bond (s. v.) (B.), -s, -ing, -ed ; -age bɔnd, -z, -iŋ, -id ; -idʒ
bond-holder, -s 'bɔnd,həuldə*, -z
bondmaid, -s 'bɔndmeid, -z
bond|man, -men 'bɔnd|mən, -mən [-men]
bonds|man, -men 'bɔndz|mən, -mən [-men]
bonds|woman, -women 'bɔndz|-,wumən, -,wimin
bond|woman, -women 'bɔnd|,wumən, -,wimin
bon|e (s. v.), -es, -ing, -ed bəun, -z, -iŋ, -d
bone-ash 'bəun-æʃ
Bonella bəu'nelə
bone-setter, -s 'bəun,setə*, -z
bone-shaker, -s 'bəun,ʃeikə*, -z
Bo'ness bəu'nes ['bəu'nes]
bonfire, -s 'bɔn,faiə*, -z
Bonham 'bɔnəm
bonhomie 'bɔnɔmi: [-nəm-]
Boniface 'bɔnifeis
Bonn bɔn
bonne-bouche, -s 'bɔn'bu:ʃ (bɔnbuʃ), -iz

Bonner 'bɔnə*

bonnet (s. v.), -s, -ing, -ed 'bɔnit, -s, -iŋ, -id

Bonnett 'bɔnit

bonn|y, -ier, -iest, -ily, -iness 'bɔn|i, -ïə*, -iist, -ili, -inis

Bonsor 'bɔnsə*

Bonthron 'bɔnθrən

bonus, -es 'bəunəs, -iz

bon|y, -ier, -iest, -iness 'bəun|i, -ïə* [-jə*], -iist [-jist], -inis

Bonython bə'naiθən [bɔ'n-]

bonze, -s bɔnz, -iz

boo (v. interj,), -s, -ing, -ed, -er/s bu:, -z, -iŋ, -d, -ə*/z

boob|y, -ies, -yish 'bu:b|i, -iz, -iiʃ [-jiʃ]

booby-prize, -s 'bu:bi-praiz, -iz

booby-trap, -s 'bu:bi-træp, -s

boodle (B.) 'bu:dl

Boog bəug

boogie-woogie 'bu:gi,wu:gi

book (s. v.), -s, -ing, -ed, -er/s buk, -s, -iŋ, -t, -ə*/z

bookable 'bukəbl

bookbind|er/s, -ing 'buk,baind|ə*/z, -iŋ

bookcase, -s 'bukkeis [rarely 'bukeis], -iz

book-club, -s 'bukklʌb, -z

book-debt, -s 'bukdet, -s

Booker 'bukə*

bookie, -s 'buki, -z

booking, -s 'bukiŋ, -z

booking-office, -s 'bukiŋ,ɔfis, -iz

bookish, -ly, -ness 'bukiʃ, -li, -nis

book-keep|er/s, -ing 'buk,ki:p|ə*/z, -iŋ

bookland 'buklænd

book-learning 'buk,lə:niŋ

booklet, -s 'buklit, -s

book-mak|er/s, -ing 'buk,meik|ə*/z, -iŋ

book|man, -men 'buk|mən, -mən

book-mark, -s 'bukmɑ:k, -s

book-muslin 'buk,mʌzlin

bookplate, -s 'bukpleit, -s

book-post 'bukpəust

book-sell|er/s, -ing 'buk,sel|ə*/z, -iŋ

book-shel|f, -ves 'bukʃel|f, -vz

book-shop, -s 'bukʃɔp, -s

book-stall, -s 'bukstɔ:l, -z

bookstand, -s 'bukstænd, -z

bookwork 'bukwə:k

bookworm, -s 'bukwə:m, -z

boom (s. v.), -s, -ing, -ed bu:m, -z, -iŋ, -d

boomerang, -s 'bu:məræŋ, -z

boon, -s bu:n, -z

Boon(e) bu:n

ɔoor, -s buə*, -z

Boord bə:d

ɔoorish, -ly, -ness 'buəriʃ, -li, -nis

Boosey 'bu:zi

boost (s. v.), -s, -ing, -ed, -er/s bu:st, -s, -iŋ, -id, -ə*/z

boot (s. v.) (B.), -s, -ing, -ed bu:t, -s, -iŋ, -id

bootblack, -s 'bu:tblæk, -s

bootee, -s 'bu:ti: ['-'-, -'-], -z

Boötes bəu'əuti:z

booth (B.), -s bu:ð, -z

Boothby 'bu:ðbi

Boothe bu:ð

bootjack, -s 'bu:tdʒæk, -s

bootlace, -s 'bu:t-leis, -iz

Bootle 'bu:tl

bootlegg|er/s, -ing 'bu:t,leg|ə*/z, -iŋ

bootless, -ly, -ness 'bu:tlis, -li, -nis

boots (hotel servant) (sing.) bu:ts, (plur.) bu:ts ['bu:tsiz]

Boots bu:ts

boot-tree, -s 'bu:ttri:, -z

booty 'bu:ti

booz|e, -es, -ing, -er/s bu:z, -iz, -iŋ, -d, -ə*/z

booz|y, -ier, -iest 'bu:z|i, -ïə* [-jə*], -iist [-jist]

Bo-peep bəu'pi:p

boracic bə'ræsik [bɔ'r-]

borage 'bɔridʒ ['bʌr-]

borate, -s 'bɔ:reit, [-rit], -s

borax 'bɔ:ræks

Bord bɔ:d

Bordeaux bɔ:'dəu (bɔrdo)

bord|er (s. v.), -ers, -ering, -ered, -erer/s 'bɔ:d|ə*, -əz, -əriŋ, -əd, -ərə*/z

borderland, -s 'bɔ:dəlænd, -z

borderline, -s 'bɔ:dəlain, -z

bordure, -s 'bɔ:djuə* [-djə*], -z

bor|e (s. v.), -es, -ing, -ed, -er/s bɔ:* [bɔə*], -z, -riŋ, -d, -rə*/z

borealis ,bɔ:ri'eilis [,bɔri-]

Boreas 'bɔriæs ['bɔ:r-]

boredom 'bɔ:dəm ['bɔəd-]

Boreham 'bɔ:rəm ['bɔər-]

Borgia 'bɔ:dʒə [-dʒïə, -dʒə]

boric 'bɔ:rik ['bɔrik]

Boris 'bɔris

Borland 'bɔ:lənd

born (from bear, bring forth) bɔ:n

borne (from bear, carry) bɔ:n

Borneo 'bɔ:niəu

boron 'bɔ:rɔn [-rən]

borough, -s 'bʌrə, -z

borough-English 'bʌrə'iŋgliʃ

borough-reeve, -s 'bʌrə'ri:v, -z

borrow (B.), -s, -ing, -ed, -er/s 'bɔrəu, -z, -iŋ, -d, -ə*/z

Borrowdale 'bɔrəudeil

Borstal 'bɔ:stl

Borthwick 'bɔ:θwik

Borwick 'bɔrik
borzoi, -s 'bɔːzɔi, -z
Bosanquet 'bəʊznkit
boscage, -s 'bɔskidʒ, -iz
Boscastle 'bɔsˌkɑːsl
Boscawen bɔs'kəʊən [-'kəuin], -'kɔːin
bosh bɔʃ
Bosham (in Sussex) 'bɔzəm ['bɔsəm]
   Note.—A new pron. 'bɔʃəm is now
   sometimes heard.
Bosher 'bəʊʒə*
Bosinney bɔ'sini [bə's-]
bosky 'bɔski
Bosnia, -n/s 'bɔznɪə [-njə], -n/z
bosom, -s 'buzəm, -z
Bosphorus 'bɔsfərəs ['bɔspə-]
Bosporus 'bɔspərəs
boss (s. v.) (B.), -es, -ing, -ed bɔs, -iz,
   -iŋ, -t
boss-eyed 'bɔsaid
Bossiney bɔ'sini [bə's-]
boss|y, -ier, -iest, -ily, -iness 'bɔs|i,
   -ɪə*, -iist, -ili, -inis
Bostock 'bɔstɔk
Boston 'bɔstən
Bostonian, -s bɔs'təunjən [-nɪən], -z
bo'sun, -s 'bəʊsn, -z
Boswell 'bɔzwəl [-wel]
Bosworth 'bɔzwə(ː)θ
botanic, -al, -ally bə'tænik [bɔ't-], -əl,
   -əli
botanist, -s 'bɔtənist [-tn̩i-], -s
botaniz|e [-is|e], -es, -ing, -ed 'bɔtənaiz
   [-tn̩aiz], -iz, -iŋ, -d
botany 'bɔtəni [-tn̩i]
botch (s. v.), -es, -ing, -ed, -er/s bɔtʃ,
   -iz, -iŋ, -t, -ə*/z
both bəʊθ
Botha 'bəʊtə
Botham 'bɔðəm
both|er (s. v.), -ers, -ering, -ered 'bɔð|ə*,
   -əz, -əriŋ, -əd
botheration ˌbɔðə'reiʃən
bothersome 'bɔðəsəm
Bothnia 'bɔθnɪə [-njə]
Bothwell 'bɔθwəl [-ɔðw-, -wel]
both|y, -ies 'bɔθ|i, -iz
Botolph 'bɔtɔlf [-təlf]
Botswana bɔ'tswɑːnə [bə-]
Botticelli, -s ˌbɔti'tʃeli, -z
bottine, -s bɔ'tiːn, -z
bott|le, (s. v.), -les, -ling, -led, -ler/s
   'bɔt|l, -lz, -liŋ [-liŋ], -ld, -lə*/z
   [-lə*/z]
bottle-green 'bɔtlgriːn ['bɔtl'g-]
bottleneck, -s 'bɔtlnek, -s
bottle-nose, -s, -d 'bɔtlnəuz, -iz, -d
bottle-wash|er/s, -ing 'bɔtlˌwɔʃ|ə*/z, -iŋ

bottom (s. v.) (B.), -s, -ing, -ed 'bɔtəm,
   -z, -iŋ, -d
Bottome (surname) bə'təum
bottomless 'bɔtəmlis
Bottomley 'bɔtəmli
bottomry 'bɔtəmri
botulism 'bɔtjulizəm
Boucicault 'buːsikəu
Boudicca bəu'dikə
boudoir, -s 'buːdwɑː* [-wɔː*], -z
bouffe buːf
Bougainville 'buːgənvil
bougainvillea, -s ˌbuːgən'vilɪə [-gein-],
bough, -s bau, -z   [-z
Boughey 'bəui
bought (from buy) bɔːt
Boughton 'bɔːtn, 'bautn
bougie, -s 'buːʒiː, -z
bouillon 'buːjɔ̃:ŋ (bujɔ̃)
Boulby 'bəulbi
boulder, -s 'bəuldə*, -z
boulevard, -s 'buːlvɑː* [-liv-, -ləv-,
   -vɑːd] (bulvaːr), -z
Boulger 'bəuldʒə*
Boulogne bu'lɔin [bə'l-, -'ləun] (bulɔɲ)
Boult bəult
Boulter 'bəultə*
Boulton 'bəultən
Bouly 'buːli, 'bauli
Boumphrey 'bʌmfri
bounc|e (s. v.), -es, -ing, -ed, -er/s
   bauns, -iz, -iŋ, -t, -ə*/z
Bouncer 'baunsə*
bound (s. v.), -s, -ing, -ed baund, -z, -iŋ,
   -id
bound (from bind) baund
boundar|y, -ies 'baundər|i, -iz
bounden 'baundən
bounder, -s 'baundə*, -z
boundless, -ly, -ness 'baundlis, -li, -nis
bounteous, -ly, -ness 'bauntɪəs [-tjəs],
   -li, -nis
bounti|ful, -fully, -fulness 'baunti|-
   ful, -fuli [-fəli], -fulnis
bount|y, -ies 'baunt|i, -iz
bouquet, -s bu(ː)'kei ['bu(ː)kei, bəu'kei],
   -z
Bourbon, -s 'buəbən [-bɔn] (burbɔ̃), -z
bourbon (drink) 'bəːbən ['buə-, -bɔn]
Bourchier (English surname) 'bautʃə*
Bourdillon (English surname) bə'diljən
   bɔː'diljən [bɔə'd-], bɔː'dilən [bɔə'd-]
bourdon, -s 'buədn ['bɔəd-, 'bɔːd-], -z
bourgeois (middle class) 'buəʒwɑː
   (burʒwa)
bourgeois (printing type) bə'dʒɔis
bourgeoisie ˌbuəʒwɑː'ziː: [-ʒwə'z-]
   (burʒwazi)

Bourke bəːk
bourn(e), -s buən [bɔən, bɔːn], -z
Bourne buən [bɔən, bɔːn], *as surname*
   also bəːn
Bournemouth 'bɔːnməθ ['bɔən-, 'buən-,
   rarely -mauθ]
Bournville 'bɔːnvil ['bɔən-, 'buən-]
bourrée, -s 'burei (bure), -z
bourse, -s buəs, -iz
bous|e (*drink*), -es, -ing, -ed buːz
   [bauz], -iz, -iŋ, -d
bous|e (*nautical term*), -es, -ing, -ed
   bauz, -iz, -iŋ, -d
Bousfield 'bausfiːld
boustrophedon ,baustrə'fiːdən
bout, -s baut, -s
boutique, -s buː'tiːk, -s (butik)
bouts-rimés 'buː'riːmei [-eiz] (burime)
Bouverie 'buːvəri
Bovey (*place*) 'bʌvi, (*surname*) 'buːvi,
   'bəuvi, 'bʌvi
Bovill 'bəuvil
bovine 'bəuvain
Bovingdon (*in Herts.*) 'bʌviŋdən ['bɒv-]
   Note.—Locally 'bʌv-.
bovril 'bɒvril [-rəl]
bow (*s.*) (*bending, fore end of ship*), -s
   bau, -z
bow (*s.*) (*for shooting, etc., knot*) (B.), -s
   bəu, -z
bow (*v.*) (*bend*), -s, -ing, -ed bau, -z, -iŋ
   -d
bow (*v.*) (*in playing the violin, etc.*), -s,
   -ing/s, -ed bəu, -z, -iŋ/z, -d
Bowater (*surname*)   'bəu,wɔːtə*,
   'bauətə*
Bowden 'bəudn, 'baudn
Bowdler 'baudlə*
bowdlerization [-isa-] ,baudlərai'zeiʃən
bowdleriz|e [-is|e], -es, -ing, -ed
   'baudləraiz, -iz, -iŋ, -d
Bowdoin 'bəudn
bowel, s 'bauəl [-il, -el, baul], -z
Bowen 'bəuin
bower (B.), -s 'bauə*, -z
Bowering 'bauəriŋ
bowery (B.) 'bauəri
Bowes, -Lyon bəuz, -'laiən
Bowie (*Scottish surname*) 'baui
bowie-kni|fe, -ves 'bəuinai|f ['--'-], -vz
Bowker 'baukə*
bow-knot, -s 'bəunɔt ['bəu'n-], -s
bowl (*s. v.*), -s, -ing, -ed, -er/s bəul, -z,
   -iŋ, -d, -ə*/z
Bowland 'bəulənd
bow-legged 'bəulegd [-,legid]
bowler (B.), -s 'bəulə*, -z
Bowles bəulz

bowline, -s 'bəulin, -z
Bowling 'bəuliŋ
bowling-green, -s 'bəuliŋgriːn, -z
Bowlker 'bəukə*
bow|man (B.), -men 'bəu|mən, -mən
   [-men]
Bowmer 'bəumə*
Bown baun
Bowness bəu'nes ['bəu'nes]
Bowra 'baurə ['bauərə]
Bowring 'bauriŋ ['bauər-]
Bowron 'baurən ['bauər-]
bowshot, -s 'bəu-ʃɔt, -s
bowsprit, -s 'bəu-sprit, -s
bowstring, -s 'bəu-striŋ, -z
Bowtell bəu'tel
bow-window, -s 'bəu'windəu, -z
bow-wow, -s (*interj.*) 'bau'wau, (*s., dog*)
   'bauwau, -z
Bowyer 'bəujə*
box (*s. v.*) (B.), -es, -ing, -ed, -er/s bɒks,
   -iz, -iŋ, -t, -ə*/z
box-bed, -s 'bɒks'bed ['bɒksb-], -z
box-cloth 'bɒksklɔθ [-klɔːθ]
Boxer, -s 'bɒksə*, -z
Boxing-day, -s 'bɒksiŋdei, -z
boxing-glove, -s 'bɒksiŋglʌv, -z
boxing-match, -es 'bɒksiŋmætʃ, -iz
Boxmoor 'bɒksmuə* [-mɔə*, -mɔː*, *also
   locally* -'-]
box-room, -s 'bɒksrum [-ruːm], -z
boxwood 'bɒkswud
boy, -s bɔi, -z
Boyce bɔis
boycott (*s. v.*) (B.), -s, -ing, -ed, -er/s
   'bɔikət [-kɔt], -s, -iŋ, -id, -ə*/z
Boyd bɔid
Boyet (*Shakespearian character*) bɔi'et
   ['--]
boyhood, -s 'bɔihud, -z
boyish, -ly, -ness 'bɔiiʃ, -li, -nis
Boy|le, -ne bɔi|l, -n
Boyton 'bɔitn
Boz bɒz [*rarely* bəuz]
   *Note.—This pen-name of Charles
   Dickens was originally pronounced
   bəuz, but this pronunciation is not
   often heard now.*
Bozman 'bɒzmən
bra, -s brɑː, -z
Brabant brə'bænt
Brabantio (*Shakespearian character*)
   brə'bæntiəu [-nʃiəu, -nʃjəu]
Brabazon 'bræbəzən
Brabourne (*place*) 'breibɔːn [-bɔən],
   (*family name*) 'breibən, -bɔːn [-bɔən]
brac|e (*s. v.*) (B.), -es, -ing, -ed breis, -iz,
   -iŋ, -t

bracelet, -s 'breislit, -s
brach, -es bræt∫, -iz
Bracher 'breit∫ə*
brachial 'breikjəl [-kĭəl]
brachycephalic ˌbrækike'fælik [-kiki'f-, -kise'f-, -kisi'f-]
brack, -s bræk, -s
bracken 'brækən
Brackenbury 'brækənbəri
bracket (s. v.), -s, -ing, -ed 'brækit, -s, -iŋ, -id
brackish, -ness 'brækiʃ, -nis
Bracknell 'bræknəl [-nļ]
brad, -s bræd, -z
bradawl, -s 'brædɔ:l, -z
Bradbury 'brædbəri
Braddon 'brædn
Braden breidn
Brad|field, -ford 'bræd|fi:ld, -fəd
Bradgate 'brædgit [-geit]
Brading 'breidiŋ
Bradlaugh 'brædlɔ:
Brad|law, -ley, -shaw 'bræd|lɔ:, -li, -ʃɔ:
Bradwardine 'brædwədi:n
Brady 'breidi
brae, -s brei, -z
Braemar brei'mɑ:*
Braeriach ˌbreiə'riək [-əx]   [-d
brag, -s, -ging/ly, -ged bræg, -z, -iŋ/li,
Bragg bræg
braggadocio, -s ˌbrægə'dəutʃiəu [-tʃjəu], -z
braggart, -s 'brægət [-gɑ:t], -s
Braham 'breiəm
Brahan brɔ:n
Brahe (Danish astronomer) 'brɑ:ə ['brɑ:hə, 'brɑ:i, 'brɑ:hi]
brahma (B.), -s 'brɑ:mə, -z
Brahman, -s, -ism 'brɑ:mən, -z, -izəm
Brahmaputra ˌbrɑ:mə'pu:trə (Hind. brəhməpwtra)
Brahmin, -s, -ism 'brɑ:min, -z, -izəm
brahminical brɑ:'minikəl
Brahms brɑ:mz [brɑ:ms]
braid (s. v.) (B.), -s, -ing, -ed breid, -z, -iŋ, -id
brail, -s breil, -z
Braille (writing for the blind) breil
Brailsford 'breilsfəd
brain (B.), -s brein, -z
brain|-fag, -fever 'brein|fæg, -ˌfi:və* [-'fi:və*]
brainless, -ness 'breinlis, -nis
brainsick 'brein-sik
brainstorm, -s 'brein-stɔ:m, -z
Braintree 'brein-tri: [locally -tri]
brainwash, -es, -ing, -ed 'breinwɔʃ, -iz, -iŋ, -t

brainwave, -s 'breinweiv, -z
brain|y, -ier, -iest 'brein|i, -ĭə* [-jə*], -iist [-jist]
brais|e, -es, -ing, -ed breiz, -iz, -iŋ, -d
Braithwaite 'breiθweit
brake, (s.), -s breik, -s
Brakenridge 'brækənridʒ
brake-van, -s 'breikvæn, -z
Bralsford 'brælsfəd
Bramah 'brɑ:mə
bramble, -s; -bush/es 'bræmbl, -z; -buʃ/iz
brambly 'bræmbli
Bramley, -s 'bræmli, -z
Brampton 'bræmptən
Bramwell 'bræmwəl [-wel]
bran bræn
brancard, -s 'bræŋkəd [-kɑ:d], -z
branch (s. v.) (B.), -es, -ing, -ed brɑ:ntʃ, -iz, -iŋ, -t
bran|chia, -chiae 'bræŋ|kĭə, -kii:
branchiate 'bræŋkieit [-kiit]
brand (s. v.) (B.), -s, -ing, -ed brænd, -z, -iŋ, -id
Brandenburg 'brændənbə:g
branding-iron, -s 'brændiŋˌaiən, -z
brandish, -es, -ing, -ed 'brændiʃ, -iz, -iŋ, -t
brand-new 'brænd'nju:
Brandon 'brændən
Brandram 'brændrəm
brand|y, -ies, -ied 'brænd|i, -iz, -id
brandy-snap, -s 'brændi-snæp, -s
brank, -s bræŋk, -s
Branksome 'bræŋksəm
bran-mash 'bræn'mæʃ
bran-pie, -s 'bræn'pai, -z
Branson 'brænsn
Branston 'brænstən
brant, -s brænt, -s
Brant (surname) brɑ:nt
brant|-goose, -geese 'brænt|'gu:s, -'gi:s
Braque brɑ:k [bræk]
Brasenose 'breiznəuz
brash (s. adj.), -es bræʃ, -iz
brasier, -s 'breizjə* [-zĭə*, -ʒjə*, -ʒĭə*, -ʒə*], -z
brass, -es brɑ:s, -iz
brassard, -s 'bræsɑ:d [bræ'sɑ:d], -z
brass-band, -s 'brɑ:s'bænd, -z
Brassey 'bræsi
brass-founder, -s 'brɑ:sˌfaundə*, -z
brass-hat, -s 'brɑ:s'hæt, -s
brassière, -s 'bræsĭə* [-sjə*, -siɛə*, 'bræzĭə*, -zjə*], -z
brass|y [-ie] (golf club), -ies 'brɑ:s|i, -iz
brass|y (adj.), -ier, -iest 'brɑ:s|i, -ĭə*, -iist

Brasted 'breistid ['bræ-]
rat, -s bræt, -s
Bratislava ˌbræti'slɑːvə
ratt|le, -les, -ling, -led 'bræt|l, -lz, -liŋ [-liŋ], -ld
Brattleboro 'brætlbərə
Braughing 'bræfiŋ
Braun (English surname) broːn
ravado, -(e)s brə'vɑːdəu, -z
rav|e (adj. v.), -er, -est, -ely; -es, -ing, -ed breiv, -ə*, -ist, -li; -z, -iŋ, -d
raver|y, -ies 'breivər|i, -iz
Bravington 'bræviŋtən
ravo (s. interj.), -(e)s 'brɑː'vəu [brɑː'v-], -z
ravura brə'vuərə [-'vjuər-]
rawl (s. v.), -s, -ing, -ed, -er/s brɔːl, -z, -iŋ, -d, -ə*/z
rawn brɔːn
Brawne brɔːn
rawn|y, -ier, -iest, -iness 'brɔːn|i, -ïə* [-jə*], -iist [-jist], -inis
Braxton 'brækstən
raxy 'bræksi   [-d
ray (s. v.), (B.), -s, -ing, -ed brei, -z, -iŋ,
Brayley 'breili
raz|e, -es, -ing, -ed breiz, -iz, -iŋ, -d
razen, -ly, -ness 'breizn, -li, -nis
razen-faced 'breiznfeist
razier, -s 'breizjə* [-zïə*, -ʒjə*, -ʒïə, -ʒə*], -z
Brazier (surname) 'breiʒə*
Brazil (country) brə'zil [bri'z-], (English surname) 'bræzil [-zl]
Brazilian, -s brə'ziljən [bri'z-, -liən], -z
Brazil-nut, -s brə'zil'nʌt [bri'z-, -'--], -s
reach (s. v.), -es, -ing, -ed briːtʃ, -iz, -iŋ, -t
read, -s bred, -z
Breadalbane (Earl) brə'dɔːlbən, (place) brə'dælbən [-'dɔː-]
read-basket, -s 'bredˌbɑːskit, -s
readcrumb, -s 'bredkrʌm, -z
read-fruit 'bredfruːt
read-stuff, -s 'bredstʌf, -s
readth, -s bredθ [bretθ], -s
readth|ways,   -wise   'bredθ|weiz ['bretθ-], -waiz
read-winner, -s 'bredˌwinə*, -z
reak (s. v.), -s, -ing, broke, broken breik, -s, -iŋ, brəuk, 'brəukən
reakable, -s 'breikəbl, -z
reakage, -s 'breikidʒ, -iz
reak-away, -s 'breikəwei ['--'-], -z
reakdown, -s 'breikdaun ['-'-], -z
reaker, -s 'breikə*, -z
reakfast (s. v.), -s, -ing, -ed 'brekfəst, -s, -iŋ, -id

breakfast-set, -s 'brekfəsˌtset, -s
break-neck 'breiknek
Breakspear 'breik-spiə*
break-through, -s 'breikθru: ['-'-], -z
break-up, -s 'breik'ʌp ['breikʌp], -s
breakwater, -s 'breikˌwɔːtə*, -z
bream (B.), -s briːm, -z
Breamore 'bremə*
breast (s. v.), -s, -ing, -ed brest, -s, -iŋ, -id
breast-bone, -s 'brestbəun, -z
breast|-deep, -high 'brest|'diːp, -'hai
breast-plate, -s 'brestpleit, -s
breastsummer, -s 'bresəmə*, -z
breastwork, -s 'brest-wəːk, -s
breath, -s breθ, -s
breath|e, -es, -ing, -ed briːð, -z, -iŋ, -d
breathed (phonetic term) breθt [briːðd]
breather, -s 'briːðə*, -z
breath-group, -s 'breθgruːp, -s
breathiness 'breθinis
breathing-space, -s 'briːðiŋ-speis, -iz
breathless, -ly, -ness 'breθlis, -li, -nis
breath|y, -ier, -iest 'breθ|i, -ïə*, -iist
Brebner 'brebnə*
Brechin (in Scotland) 'briːkin ['briːxin]
Breckenridge [-kin-] 'breknridʒ
Brecknock, -shire 'breknɔk [-nək], -ʃiə* [-ʃə*]
Brecon 'brekən
bred (from breed) bred
Bredon 'briːdən
bree bri:
breech (s.) (of a gun, etc.), -es, -ed briːtʃ, -iz, -t
breeches (garment) 'britʃiz
breeching, -s 'britʃiŋ, -z
breech-loader, -s 'briːtʃˌləudə*, -z
breed (s. v.), -s, -ing, bred briːd, -z, -iŋ, bred
breeder, -s 'briːdə*, -z
breeder-reactor, -s 'briːdə-ri(ː)ˌæktə*, -z
breeks briːks
breeze, -s briːz, -iz
breez|y, -ier, -iest, -ily, -iness 'briːz|i, -ïə* [-jə*], -iist [-jist], -ili, -inis
Breingan 'briŋən
Bremen 'breimən ('breːmən)
Brennan 'brenən
Brent brent
Brentford 'brentfəd
brent|-goose, -geese 'brent|'guːs, -'giːs
Brer brə:*
Brereton 'briətn
Breslau 'brezlau ('breslau)
Brest brest
brethren (archaic plur. of brother) 'breðrin [-rən]

Breton, -s 'bretən (brətʒ, -z)
Bret(t) bret
Brettagh 'bretə
Bretwalda bret'wɔ:ldə ['bret‚w-, -ɔl-]
Breughel (*Flemish artist*) 'brɔigəl ['brə:g-, 'bru:g-]
breve, -s bri:v, -z
brevet (*s. v.*), -s, -ing, -ed 'brevit, -s, -iŋ, -id
breviar|y, -ies 'bri:vjər|i [-vĭə-], -iz
breviate, -s 'bri:viit [-vjit], -s
brevier brə'vĭə* [bri'v-]
brevity 'breviti
brew (*s. v.*) (B.), -s, -ing, -ed, -er/s bru:, -z, -iŋ [bruiŋ], -d, -ə*/z [bruə*/z]
Brewer 'bru(:)ə*
brewer|y, -ies 'bruər|i ['bru:ər-], -iz
Brewster 'bru:stə*
Brian 'braiən
briar, -s 'braiə*, -z
Briareus brai'ɛəriəs
brib|e (*s. v.*), -es, -ing, -ed, -er/s braib, -z, -iŋ, -d, -ə*/z
briber|y, -ies 'braibər|i, -iz
bric-à-brac 'brikəbræk
Brice brais
brick, -s brik, -s
brickbat, -s 'brikbæt, -s
brick-dust 'brik'dʌst ['--]
brick-field, -s 'brikfi:ld, -z
brick-kiln, -s 'brikkiln [-kil], -z
   Note.—The pronunciation -kil is used chiefly by those concerned with the working of kilns.
bricklayer, -s 'brik‚leiə*, -z
bricklaying 'brik‚leiiŋ
brickmak|er/s, -ing 'brik‚meik|ə*/z, -iŋ
brickwork 'brikwə:k
bridal 'braidl
bride, -s braid, -z
bride-chamber, -s 'braid‚tʃeimbə*, -z
bridegroom, -s 'braidgrum [-gru:m], -z
bridesmaid, -s 'braidzmeid, -z
brides|man, -men 'braidz|mən, -mən [-men]
Bridewell 'braidwəl [-wel]
bridg|e (*s. v.*) (B.), -es, -ing, -ed bridʒ, -iz, -iŋ, -d
bridgehead, -s 'bridʒhed, -z
Bridgenorth 'bridʒnɔ:θ
Bridger 'bridʒə*
Bridgerule 'bridʒru:l
Bridges 'bridʒiz
Bridget 'bridʒit
Bridgetown 'bridʒtaun
Bridgewater 'bridʒ‚wɔ:tə*
Bridgnorth 'bridʒnɔ:θ
Bridgwater 'bridʒ‚wɔ:tə*

bridie (B.), -s 'braidi, -z
brid|le (*s. v.*), -les, -ling, -led 'braid|l, -lz, -liŋ [-liŋ], -ld
bridle-pa|th, -ths 'braidlpɑ:|θ, -ðz
Bridlington 'bridliŋtən
bridoon, -s bri'du:n, -z
Bridport 'bridpɔ:t
Bridson 'braidsn
brief (*s. adj. v.*), -s, -er, -est, -ly, -ness; -ing, -ed bri:f, -s, -ə*, -ist, -li, -nis; -iŋ, -t
briefcas|e, -es 'bri:fkeis, -iz
briefless 'bri:flis
brier, -s 'braiə*, -z
Brierley 'braiəli
brig, -s brig, -z
brigade, -s bri'geid, -z
brigadier, -s ‚brigə'diə* [*attributively also* 'brigədiə*], -z   [-z
brigadier-general, -s 'brigədiə'dʒenərəl,
brigand, -s, -age 'brigənd, -z, -idʒ
brigantine, -s 'brigəntain [-ti:n], -z
Brigg, -s brig, -z
Brigham 'brigəm
bright (B.), -er, -est, -ly, -ness brait, -ə*, -ist, -li, -nis
bright|en, -ens, -ening, -ened 'brait|n, -nz, -niŋ [-niŋ], -nd
Brightlingsea 'braitliŋsi:
Brighton 'braitn
Brigid 'bridʒid
Brigstock(e) 'brigstɔk
brill (B.), -s bril, -z
brillian|ce, -cy 'briljən|s, -si
brilliant (*s. adj.*), -s, -ly, -ness 'briljənt, -s, -li, -nis
brilliantine ‚briljən'ti:n ['--'-, '---]
brim (*s. v.*), -s, -ming, -med brim, -z, -iŋ, -d
brimful 'brim'ful ['brim-ful]   [-iŋ,-d
brimstone 'brimstən
Brind brind
Brindisi 'brindizi [-zi:]
brindle (B.)₉ -s, -d 'brindl, -z, -d
brine brain
bring, -s, -ing, brought, bringer/s briŋ, -z, -iŋ, brɔ:t, 'briŋə*/z
brink, -s briŋk, -s
brinkmanship 'briŋkmənʃip
Brinsley 'brinzli
Brinsmead, -s 'brinzmi:d, -z
brin|y, -iness 'brain|i, -inis
bri-nylon ‚brai'nailən [-lɔn]
brio 'bri(:)əu
brioche, -s 'bri(:)ɔʃ [-i(:)əuʃ] (briɔʃ), -iz
briquette, -s bri'ket, -s
Brisbane 'brizbən [-bein]
   Note.—'brizbən is the pronunciation in Australia.

brisk, -er, -est, -ly, -ness brisk, -ə*, -ist, -li, -nis

brisket, -s 'briskit, -s

brist|le (s. v.), -les, -ling, -led 'bris|l, -lz, -liŋ [-liŋ], -ld

brist|ly, -liness 'bris|li [-l̩i], -linis [-l̩inis]

Bristol 'bristl

Bristow(e) 'bristəu

Britain 'britn [-tən]

Britannia bri'tænjə

Britannic, -a bri'tænik, -ə

briticism, -s 'britisizəm, -z

British, -er/s 'britiʃ, -ə*/z

britishism, -s 'britiʃizəm, -z

Briton, -s 'britn [-tən], -z

Brittain (surname) bri'tein, 'britn [-tən]

Brittany 'britəni [-tn̩i]

Britten 'britn [-tən]

britt|le, -ler, -lest, -leness 'britt|l, -l̩ə*, -l̩ist, -nis

Britton 'britən   [-l̩ist, -nis

Brixton 'brikstən

Brno 'bə:nəu, brə'nəu

broach, -es, -ing, -ed brəutʃ, -iz, -iŋ, -t

broad, -er, -est, -ly, -ness brɔ:d, -ə*, -ist, -li, -nis

Broad, -s brɔ:d, -z

broad-arrow, -s 'brɔ:d'ærəu, -z

Broadbent 'brɔ:dbent

broadbrimmed 'brɔ:d'brimd [also '— when attributive]

broadcast (s. adj. v.), -s, -ing, -er/s 'brɔ:dka:st, -s, -iŋ, -ə*/z

broadcloth 'brɔ:dklɔθ [-klɔ:θ]

broad|en, -ens, -ening, -ened 'brɔ:d|n, -nz, -n̩iŋ [-niŋ], -nd

broad-gauge 'brɔ:dgeidʒ

Broadhurst 'brɔ:dhə:st

broadloom 'brɔ:dlu:m

broad-minded 'brɔ:d'maindid ['-,—]

broad-mindedness 'brɔ:d'maindidnis

Broadmoor 'brɔ:dmuə* [-mɔə*, -mɔ:*]

broadsheet, -s 'brɔ:dʃi:t, -s

broadside, -s 'brɔ:dsaid, -z

Broadstairs 'brɔ:dstɛəz

broadsword, -s 'brɔ:dsɔ:d [-sɔəd], -z

Broad|way, -wood/s 'brɔ:d|wei, -wud/z

Brobdingnag 'brɔbdiŋnæg

Brobdingnagian, -s ,brɔbdiŋ'nægïən, -z

brocade, -s, -d brəu'keid [bru'k-], -z, -id

brocard, -s 'brəukəd [-ka:d], -z

broccoli 'brɔkəli [also -lai, esp. in country districts]

brochure, -s 'brəuʃə* [-ʃjuə*, -ʃuə*, brɔ'ʃjuə*, brɔ'ʃuə*], -z

brock (B.), -s brɔk, -s

Brocken 'brɔkən

Brockenhurst 'brɔkənhə:st

Brocklehurst 'brɔklhə:st

Brock|ley, -man 'brɔk|li, -mən

Brockwell 'brɔkwəl

brocoli 'brɔkəli [also -lai, esp. in country districts]

Brod(e)rick 'brɔdrik

Brodie 'brəudi

brogue, -s brəug, -z

broil (s. v.), -s, -ing, -ed brɔil, -z, -iŋ, -d

brok|e (v.), -es, -ing, -ed brəuk, -s, -iŋ, -t

broke (from break), -n/ly brəuk, -ən/li

Broke bruk

broken-down 'brəukən'daun [also '— — when attributive]

broken-hearted 'brəukən'ha:tid ['—,— when attributive]

broken-winded 'brəukən'windid

broker, -s; -age, -y 'brəukə*, -z; -ridʒ, -ri

broll|y, -ies 'brɔl|i, -iz

Bromage 'brʌmidʒ

bromate, -s 'brəumeit [-mit], -s

brome (grass), -s brəum [rarely bru:m], -z

Brome (surname) bru:m

Bromham 'brɔməm

bromic 'brəumik

bromide, -s 'brəumaid, -z

bromine 'brəumi:n [-min]

Bromley 'brɔmli ['brʌm-]

Brompton 'brɔmᵖtən ['brʌm-]

Bromsgrove 'brɔmzgrəuv ['brʌm-]

Bromwich (in Castle B., district of Birmingham) 'brɔmidʒ ['brʌm-, -itʃ], (in West B., Staffs.) 'brɔmidʒ ['brʌm-, -itʃ], (surname) 'brʌmidʒ

bron|chia, -chiae 'brɔŋ|kïə [-kjə], -kii: [-kji:]

bronchial 'brɔŋkjəl [-kïəl]

bronchitic brɔŋ'kitik [brɔn'k-]

bronchitis brɔŋ'kaitis [brɔn'k-]

broncho-pneumonia 'brɔŋkəunju(:)-'məunjə [-nïə]

bronch|us, -i 'brɔŋk|əs, -ai

bronco, -s 'brɔŋkəu, -z

Brontë 'brɔnti

brontosaur|us, -uses, -i ,brɔntə'sɔ:r|əs ['—'—], -əsiz, -ai

Bronx brɔŋks

bronz|e (s. v.), -es, -ing, -ed; -y brɔnz, -iz, -iŋ, -d; -i

brooch, -es brəutʃ, -iz

brood (s. v.), -s, -ing, -ed bru:d, -z, -iŋ, -id

brood|y, -ily, -iness 'bru:d|i, -ili, -inis

brook (s. v.), -s, -iŗg, -ed bruk, -s, -iŋ, -t

Brook(e), -s bruk, -s

Brookfield 'brukfi:ld

Brookland, -s 'bruklənd, -z

brooklet, -s 'bruklit, -s

Brookline 'bruklain
Brooklyn 'bruklin
Brooksmith 'bruksmiθ
Brookwood 'brukwud
broom (*shrub*), -s bru:m [brum], -z
broom (*for sweeping*), -s bru:m [brum], -z
  Note.—Some people pronounce bru:m *normally, but* -brum *when the word occurs unstressed as the second element of a compound (as in* carpet-broom).
Broom(e) bru:m
Broomfield 'bru:mfi:ld ['brum-]
broomstick, -s 'brum-stik ['bru:m-], -s
Bros. 'brʌðəz [*sometimes facetiously* brɔs, brɔz]
Brosnahan 'brɔznəhən ['brɔs-]
broth, -s brɔθ [brɔ:θ], brɔθs [brɔ:ðz, brɔ:θs]
brothel, -s 'brɔθl, -z
brother, -s 'brʌðə*, -z
brotherhood, -s 'brʌðəhud, -z
broth|er-in-law, -ers-in-law 'brʌð|ərin-lɔ:, -əzinlɔ:
brotherl|y, -iness 'brʌðəl|i, -inis
Brough brʌf
brougham, -s 'bru(:)əm [*old-fashioned* bru:m], -z
Brougham brum [bru:m], 'bru:əm, 'brəuəm
  Note.—The present baron pronounces brum.
Brougham and Vaux 'brumən'vɔ:ks
brought (*from* bring) brɔ:t
Broughton (*in Northants.*) 'brautn, (*all others in England*) 'brɔ:tn
Broughty 'brɔ:ti
brow, -s brau, -z
browbeat, -s, -ing, -en 'braubi:t, -s, -iŋ, -n
brown (*s. adj. v.*) (B.), -s; -er, -est, -ness; -ing, -ed braun, -z; -ə*, -ist, -nis; -iŋ, -d
Browne braun
brownie, -s 'brauni, -z
browning (B.) 'brauniŋ
brownish 'brauniʃ
Brownrigg 'braunrig
Brownsmith 'braun-smiθ
brows|e, -es, -ing, -ed brauz, -iz, -iŋ, -d
Browse brauz
Bruce, -smith bru:s, -smiθ
Bruges bru:ʒ (bry:ʒ)
bruin 'bru(:)in, -z
bruis|e (*s. v.*), -es, -ing, -ed, -er/s bru:z, -iz, -iŋ, -d, -ə*/z
bruit (*s. v.*), -s, -ing, -ed bru:t, -s, -iŋ, -id

brume bru:m
Brummagem 'brʌmədʒəm
Brunei 'bru:nai
Brunel bru'nel [bru:'n-]
brunette, -s bru:'net [bru'n-] (brynɛt), -s
Brünnhilde brun'hildə ['brun,h-] (bryn-'hildə)
Brunswick 'brʌnzwik
brunt brʌnt
Brunton 'brʌntən
brush (*s. v.*), -es ,-ing, -ed brʌʃ, -iz, -iŋ, -t
brushwood 'brʌʃwud
brusque, -ly, -ness brusk [bru:sk, brʌsk] (brysk), -li, -nis
Brussels 'brʌslz
Brussels-sprouts 'brʌsl'sprauts
brut|al, -ally 'bru:t|l, -əli [-li]
brutalit|y, -ies bru:'tælit|i [bru't-], -iz
brutaliz|e [-is|e], -es, -ing, -ed 'bru:tə-laiz [-t|aiz], -iz, -iŋ, -d
brute, -s bru:t, -s
brutish, -ly, -ness 'bru:tiʃ, -li, -nis
Brutnell 'bru:tnel [-nəl]
Bruton 'bru:tən
Brutus 'bru:təs
Bryan, -s, -t 'braiən, -z, -t
Bryce brais
Brydson 'braidsn
Bryers 'braiəz
Brynmawr (*in Wales*) brin'mauə* (*Welsh* brin'maur)
Bryn Mawr (*in U.S.A.*) brin'mɔ:*
Brynmor 'brinmɔ:* (*Welsh* 'brinmor)
bryony 'braiəni
Bryson 'braisn
bubb|le (*s. v.*), -les, -ling, -led 'bʌb|l, -lz, -liŋ [-liŋ], -ld
bubble-and-squeak 'bʌb|ən'skwi:k
bubble-gum 'bʌbl,gʌm
bubbly 'bʌbli [-li]
bubo, -es 'bju:bəu, -z
bubonic bju(:)'bɔnik
buccal 'bʌkəl
buccaneer, -s ,bʌkə'niə, -z
Buccleuch bə'klu:
Bucephalus bju(:)'sefələs
Buchan 'bʌkən ['bʌxən]
Buchanan bju(:)'kænən
Bucharest ,bju:kə'rest [,bu:-, '---]
Buchel 'bju:ʃəl
buck (*s. v.*) (B.), -s, -ing, -ed bʌk, -s, -iŋ, -t
buckboard, -s 'bʌkbɔ:d [-bɔəd], -z
bucket, -s 'bʌkit, -s
bucketful, -s 'bʌkitful, -z
buckhorn 'bʌkhɔ:n
buckhound, -s 'bʌkhaund, -z

Buckhurst 'bʌkhə:st ['bʌkə:st]

Buckingham, -shire 'bʌkiŋəm, -ʃiə* [-ʃə*]

Buckland 'bʌklənd

buck|le (s. v.) (B.), -les, -ling, -led 'bʌk|l, -lz, -l̩iŋ [-liŋ], -ld

buckler, -s 'bʌklə*, -z

Buckley 'bʌkli

Buckmaster 'bʌk,mɑ:stə*

Buckn|all, -ell 'bʌkn|əl [-l̩], -əl [-l̩]

Bucknill 'bʌknil

buck-passing 'bʌk,pɑ:siŋ

buckram, -s 'bʌkrəm, -z

Bucks. bʌks

buckshot 'bʌkʃɔt

buckskin, -s 'bʌk-skin, -z

Buckston 'bʌkstən

buckwheat 'bʌkwi:t [-khw-]

bucolic, -al, -ally bju(:)'kɔlik, -əl, -əli

bud (s. v.), -s, -ding, -ded bʌd, -z, -iŋ, -id

Budapest 'bju:də'pest ['bu:-, ‚--'-]

Budd bʌd

Buddha 'budə (Hind. bwddha)

buddhi|c, -sm, -st/s 'budi|k, -zəm, -st/s

buddleia, -s 'bʌdlïə, -z

Bude bju:d

budg|le (B.), -es, -ing, -ed bʌdʒ, -iz, -iŋ, -d

budgerigar, -s 'bʌdʒəriga:*, -z

budget (s. v.), -s, -ing, -ed 'bʌdʒit, -s, -iŋ, -id

Budleigh 'bʌdli

Buenos Aires 'bwenəs'aiəriz ['buin-, 'bəuin-, 'bəun-, -nə'zaiəriz, -nə'zɛəriz, -ris, -nə'zɛəz] ('bwenos'aires)

Buesst bju:st

buff bʌf

buffalo, -es 'bʌfələu [-fl̩əu], -z

buffer, -s 'bʌfə*, -z

buffet (s.) (blow, sideboard), -s 'bʌfit, -s

buffet (s.) (refreshment bar), -s 'bufei (byfɛ), -z

buffet (v.) (strike), -s, -ing, -ed 'bʌfit, -s, -iŋ, -id

buffo, -s 'bufəu, -z

buffoon, -s bə'fu:n [bʌ'f-], -z

buffooner|y, -ies bə'fu:nər|i [bʌ'f-], -iz

Buffs bʌfs

bug, -s bʌg, -z

Bug (river) bu:g [bʌg]

bugaboo, -s 'bʌgəbu:, -z

Buganda bu'gændə

bugbear, -s 'bʌgbɛə*, -z

bugger (s. v.), -s, -ing, -ed; -y 'bʌgə*, -z, -riŋ, -d; -ri

Buggs (surname) bju:gz, bʌgz

bugg|y, -ies 'bʌg|i, -iz

bugle (B.), -s 'bju:gl, -z

bugler, -s 'bju:glə*, -z

bugloss 'bju:glɔs

buhl bu:l

Buick, -s 'bju(:)ik, -s

build, -s, -ing, built, builder/s bild, -z, -iŋ, bilt, 'bildə*/z

build-up, -s 'bildʌp ['bild'ʌp], -s

Builth bilθ

Buist bju:st

Bukarest ‚bju:kə'rest [‚bu:-, '---]

Bulawayo ‚bulə'weiəu [-'waiəu]

bulb, -s bʌlb, -z

bulbaceous bʌl'beiʃəs

bulbous 'bʌlbəs

bulbul, -s 'bulbul, -z

Bulgar, -s 'bʌlgɑ:*, -z

Bulgaria, -n/s bʌl'gɛərïə, -n/z

bulg|e (s. v.), -es, -ing, -ed bʌldʒ, -iz, -iŋ, -d

bulg|y, -iness 'bʌldʒ|i, -inis

bulk (s. v.), -s, -ing, -ed bʌlk, -s, -iŋ, -t

bulkhead, -s 'bʌlkhed, -z

bulk|y, -ier, -iest, -ily, -iness 'bʌlk|i, -ïə* [-ïə*], -iist [-jist], -ili, -inis

bull (s. v.) (B.), -s, -ing, -ed bul, -z, -iŋ, -d

bullace, -s 'bulis, -iz

Bullard 'bulɑ:d

bull-baiting 'bul‚beitiŋ

bull-cal|f, -ves 'bul'kɑ:|f ['bul-kɑ:|f], -vz

bulldog, -s 'buldɔg, -z

bulldozer, -s 'bul‚dəuzə*, -z

Bulleid 'buli:d

Bull|en, -er 'bul|in [-ən], -ə*

bullet, -s 'bulit, -s

bulletin, -s 'bulitin [-lət-], -z

bullet-proof 'bulitpru:f

bullfight, -s 'bul-fait, -s

bullfinch, -es 'bul-fintʃ, -iz

bull-frog, -s 'bul-frɔg, -z

bullion, -ist/s 'buljən [-lïən], -ist/s

bullish 'buliʃ

bullock (B.), -s 'bulək, -s

Bullokar 'buləkɑ:* [-lɔk-]

Bullough 'buləu

bull-ring, -s 'bulriŋ, -z

bull's-eye, -s 'bulzai, -z

bull|y (s. v.), -ies, -ying, -ied 'bul|i, -iz, -iiŋ, -id

Bulmer 'bulmə*

bulrush, -es 'bulrʌʃ, -iz

bulsh bulʃ

Bulstrode 'bulstrəud, 'bʌl-

Bultitude 'bʌltitju:d

bulwark, -s 'bulwək [-wə:k], -s

Bulwer 'bulwə*

bum, -s bʌm, -z

bumble-bee, -s 'bʌmblbi:, -z
bumblepuppy 'bʌmbl̩ˌpʌpi
bumboat, -s 'bʌmbəut, -s
bumkin, -s 'bʌmkin [-mpk-], -z
bummaree, -s ˌbʌmə'ri: ['---], -z
bummel 'buməl [-ml, 'bʌm-]
bump (s. v.), -s, -ing, -ed bʌmp, -s, -iŋ,
    -t [bʌmt]
bumper, -s 'bʌmpə*, -z
bumpkin, -s 'bʌmpkin, -z
bumptious, -ly, -ness 'bʌmpʃəs, -li, -nis
Bumpus 'bʌmpəs
bump|y, -ier, -iest, -iness 'bʌmp|i, -iə*
    [-jə*], -iist [-jist], -inis
bun, -s bʌn, -z
bunch (s. v.) (B.), -es, -ing, -ed bʌntʃ,
    -iz, -iŋ, -t
buncombe (B.) 'bʌŋkəm
bund|le (s. v.), -les, -ling, -led 'bʌnd|l,
    -lz, -liŋ [-l̩iŋ], -ld
bung (s. v.), -s, -ing, -ed bʌŋ, -z, -iŋ, -d
bungaloid 'bʌŋgələid
bungalow, -s 'bʌŋgələu [-gləu], -z
Bungay 'bʌŋgi
Bunge 'bʌŋi
bung|le (s. v.), -les, -ling, -led, -ler/s
    'bʌŋg|l̩, -lz, -liŋ [-l̩iŋ], -ld, -lə*/z
    [-l̩ə*/z]
bunion, -s 'bʌnjən, -z
bunk (s. v.), -s, -ing, -ed bʌŋk, -s, -iŋ, -t
    [bʌŋt]
bunker (s. v.) (B.), -s, -ing, -ed 'bʌŋkə*,
    -z, -riŋ, -d
bunkum 'bʌŋkəm
Bunnett 'bʌnit
bunn|y, -ies 'bʌn|i, -iz
Bunsen 'bunsn ['bʌn-]
bunsen burner, -s 'bʌnsn'bə:nə*, -z
bunt, -s bʌnt, -s
bunting (B.), -s 'bʌntiŋ, -z
buntline, -s 'bʌntlain, -z
Bunyan 'bʌnjən
buoy (s. v.), -s -ing, -ed bɔi, -z, -iŋ, -d
buoyan|cy, -t/ly 'bɔiən|si, -t/li
bur, -s bə:*, -z
Burbage 'bə:bidʒ
Burberr|y, -ies 'bə:bər|i, -iz
Burbey 'bə:bi
Burbury 'bə:bəri
Burch, -ell bə:tʃ, -əl
burd|en (s. v.) (B.), -ens, -ening, -ened
    'bə:d|n, -nz, -niŋ [-niŋ], -nd
burdensome 'bə:dnsəm
Burdett bə(:)'det
Burdett-Coutts 'bə:det'ku:ts [bə(:)'det-
    'ku:ts]
burdock, -s 'bə:dɔk, -s
Burdon 'bə:dn

bureau, -s 'bjuərəu ['bjə:rəu, bjuə'rəu],
    -z
bureaucrac|y, -ies bjuə'rɔkrəs|i [bjə'r-,
    -'rəuk-], -iz
bureaucrat, -s 'bjuərəukræt ['bjə:r-], -s
bureaucratic ˌbjuərəu'krætik [ˌbjə:r-]
burette, -s bjuə'ret, -s
Burford 'bə:fəd
burg, -s bə:g, -z
Burgclere 'bə:klɛə*
Burge, -s bə:dʒ, -iz
burgee, -s 'bə:dʒi:, -z
burge|on (s. v.), -ons, -oning, -oned
    'bə:dʒ|ən, -ənz, -əniŋ [-niŋ], -ənd
burgess (B.), -es 'bə:dʒis [-dʒes], -iz
burgh, -s 'bʌrə, -z
Burgh (Hubert de) bə:g, (James) 'bʌrə,
    (Heath, in Surrey) 'bʌrə, (in Lincs.)
    'bʌrə, (in Suffolk) bə:g ['bʌrə]
burghal 'bə:gəl
Burghclere 'bə:klɛə*
burgher, -s 'bə:gə*, -z
Burghersh 'bə:gəʃ
Burghley 'bə:li
Burgin 'bə:gin, 'bə:dʒin
burglar, -s 'bə:glə*, -z
burglarious, -ly bə:'glɛəriəs, -li
burglar|y, -ies 'bə:glər|i, -iz
burg|le, -les, -ling, -led 'bə:g|l, -lz, -liŋ
    [-l̩iŋ], -ld
burgomaster, -s 'bə:gəuˌmɑ:stə*, -z
Burgoyne 'bə:gɔin, bə:'gɔin
burgund|y (B.), -ies 'bə:gənd|i, -iz
burial, -s; -ground/s, -place/s 'beriəl,
    -z; -graund/z, -pleis/iz
burin, -s 'bjuərin, -z
burk|e (B.), -es, -ing, -ed bə:k, -s, -iŋ,
    -t
burlap 'bə:læp
Burleigh 'bə:li
burlesqu|e (s. v.), -es, -ing, -ed bə:'lesk,
    -s, -iŋ, -t
Burley 'bə:li
Burlington 'bə:liŋtən
burl|y (B.), -ier, -iest, -iness 'bə:l|i, -iə*
    [-jə*], -iist [-jist], -inis
Burma 'bə:mə
Burman, -s 'bə:mən, -z
Burmese 'bə:'mi:z [bə:'m-]
burn (s. v.), -s, -ing, -ed, burnt bə:n, -z,
    -iŋ, -d, bə:nt
Burnaby 'bə:nəbi
Burnand bə(:)'nænd
Burne, -Jones bə:n, -'dʒəunz
burner, -s 'bə:nə*, -z
burnet (B.), -s 'bə:nit, -s
Burnett bə(:)'net, 'bə:nit
Burney 'bə:ni

Burnham 'bə:nəm
burning|-glass, -glasses 'bə:niŋ|glɑ:s,
  -,glɑ:siz
burnish, -es, -ing, -ed, -er/s 'bə:niʃ,
  -iz, -iŋ, -t, -ə*/z
burnous, -es bə:'nu:s, -iz
burnouse, -s bə:'nu:z, -iz
Burns bə:nz
Burnside 'bə:nsaid
burnt (from burn) bə:nt
Burntisland bə:nt'ailənd
burr (B.), -s bə:*, -z
Burrell 'bʌrəl
Burrough(e)s 'bʌrəuz
burr|ow (s. v.), -ows, -owing, -owed
  'bʌr|əu, -əuz, -əuiŋ, -əud
Burrows 'bʌrəuz
bursar, -s 'bə:sə*, -z
bursarship, -s 'bə:səʃip, -s
bursar|y, -ies 'bə:sər|i, -iz
Burslem 'bə:zləm*
burst (s. v.), -s, -ing bə:st, -s, -iŋ
Burt bə:t
Burtchaell 'bə:tʃəl
burthen, -s 'bə:ðən, -z
Burton 'bə:tn
Burundi bu'rundi
bur|y, -ies, -ying, -ied 'ber|i, -iz, -iiŋ, -id
Bury (place) 'beri, (surname) 'bjuəri,
  'beri
burying-ground, -s 'beriiŋgraund, -z
burying-place, -s 'beriiŋpleis, -iz
bus, -es bʌs, -iz
bus-conductor, -s 'bʌs-kən,dʌktə*, -z
bush (s. v.) (B.), -es, -ing, -ed buʃ, -iz,
  -iŋ, -t
bushel, -s 'buʃl, -z
Bushell 'buʃl
Bushey 'buʃi
Bushire bju(:)'ʃaiə*
bush|man (B.), -men 'buʃ|mən, -mən
  [-men]
Bushmills 'buʃmilz
Bushnell 'buʃnəl [-n̩l]
bushranger, -s 'buʃ,reindʒə*, -z
bush|y (B.), -ily, -iness 'buʃ|i, -ili, -inis
business (profession, etc.), -es 'biznis
  [-ɲis], -iz
business-like 'biznislaik
busk (s. v.) (B.), -s, -ing, -ed bʌsk, -s, -iŋ,
  -t
buskin, -s, -ed 'bʌskin, -z, -d
bus|-man, -men 'bʌs|mən [-mæn], -mən
  [-men]
Busoni bju(:)'səuni [-'zəu-]
buss (s. v.) (B.), -es, -ing, -ed bʌs, -iz,
  -iŋ, -t
bust (s.), -s bʌst, -s

bust (s. v.) (burst), -s, -ing bʌst, -s, -iŋ
bustard, -s 'bʌstəd, -z
buster (B.), -s 'bʌstə*, -z
bust|le (s. v.), -les, -ling, -led 'bʌs|l, -lz,
  -liŋ [-liŋ], -ld
Busvine 'bʌzvain
bus|y, -ier, -iest, -ily 'biz|i, -iə*, -iist, -ili
busybod|y, -ies 'bizi,bɔd|i, -iz
busyness (state of being busy) 'bizinis
Buszard 'bʌzəd
but bʌt (strong form), bət (weak form)
butane 'bju:tein
butcher (s. v.) (B.), -s, -ing, -ed 'butʃə*,
  -z, -riŋ, -d
butcher|y, -ies 'butʃər|i, -iz
Bute bju:t
butler (B.), -s 'bʌtlə*, -z
butler|age; -y, -ies 'bʌtlər|idʒ; -i, -iz
Butlin 'bʌtlin
butt (s. v.) (B.), -s, -ing, -ed bʌt, -s, -iŋ,
Buttar bə'tɑ:*   [-id
butt-end, -s 'bʌt'end ['bʌtend], -z
butter, -s 'bʌtə*, -z
butter-boat, -s 'bʌtəbəut, -s
buttercup, -s 'bʌtəkʌp, -s
butter-dish, -es 'bʌtədiʃ, -iz
Butterfield 'bʌtəfi:ld
butter-fingers 'bʌtə,fiŋgəz
butterfl|y, -ies 'bʌtəfl|ai, -aiz
Butterick 'bʌtərik
butter-kni|fe, -ves 'bʌtənai|f, -vz
Butter|leigh, -ley 'bʌtə|li, -li
buttermilk 'bʌtəmilk
butternut, -s 'bʌtənʌt, -s
butterscotch 'bʌtə-skɔtʃ ['bʌtə's-]
Butterwick 'bʌtərik, 'bʌtəwik
Butterworth 'bʌtəwə(:)θ
butter|y (s. adj.), -ies 'bʌtər|i, -iz
buttery-hatch, -es 'bʌtəri'hætʃ, -iz
buttock, -s 'bʌtək, -s
butt|on (s. v.) (B.), -ons, -oning, -oned
  'bʌt|n, -nz, -niŋ [-niŋ], -nd
button-hol|e (s. v.), -es, -ing, -ed 'bʌtn-
  həul, -z, -iŋ, -d
button-hook, -s 'bʌtnhuk, -s
buttress, -es 'bʌtris [-rəs], -iz
butyric bju:'tirik [bju't-]
buxom, -ness 'bʌksəm, -nis
Buxton 'bʌkstən
buy, -s, -ing, bought bai, -z, -iŋ, bɔ:t
buyable 'bai-əbl
buyer, -s 'bai-ə* ['baiə*], -z
Buzfuz 'bʌzfʌz
buzz (s. v.), -es, -ing, -ed, -er/s bʌz, -iz,
  -iŋ, -d, -ə*/z
buzzard, -s 'bʌzəd, -z
by bai (normal form), bi, bə (occasional
  weak forms)

by-and-by 'baiən*d*'bai [-əm'b-]
Byard 'baiəd
Byas(s) 'baiəs
bye, -s bai, -z
bye-bye (*sleep*), **-s** 'baibai, -z
bye-bye (*goodbye*) 'bai'bai
bye-law, -s 'bailɔ:, -z
by-election, -s 'baii‚lekʃən, -z
Byends 'baiendz
Byers 'baiəz
Byfleet 'bai-fli:t
bygone, -s 'baigɔn [-gɔ:n], -z
by-law, -s 'bailɔ:, -z
Byles bailz
Byng biŋ
Bynoe 'bainəu
by-pass, -es 'bai-pɑ:s, -iz
by-pa|th, -ths 'bai-pɑ:|θ, -ðz
by-play 'bai-plei

by-product, -s 'bai‚prɔdʌkt [-dəkt], -s
Byrd bə:d
byre, -s 'baiə*, -z
Byrne bə:n
by-road, -s 'bairəud, -z
Byron 'baiərən
Byronic, -ally bai'rɔnik [‚baiə'r-], -əli
Bysshe biʃ
byssus 'bisəs
bystander, -s 'bai‚stændə*, -z
by-street, -s 'bai-stri:t, -s
Bythesea 'biðəsi:
by|way/s, -word/s 'bai|wei/z, -wə:d/z
Byzantian bi'zæntïən [bai'z-, -ntjən, -nʃïən, -nʃjən]
Byzantine bi'zæntain [bai'z-, 'bizən-tain, -ti:n]
Byzantium bi'zæntïəm [bai'z-, -ntjəm, -nʃïəm, -nʃjəm]

C

C (*the letter*), -'s si:, -z
cab, -s kæb, -z
cabal, -s kə'bæl, -z
Cabala kə'bɑːlə [kæ'b-]
cabalistic, -al, -ally ˌkæbə'listik, -əl, -əli
cabaret, -s 'kæbərei, -z
cabbage, -s 'kæbidʒ, -iz
cabbage-rose, -s 'kæbidʒrəuz, -iz
Cabbala kə'bɑːlə [kæ'b-]
cabbalistic, -al, -ally ˌkæbə'listik, -əl,
cabb|y, -ies 'kæb|i, -iz   [-əli
Cabell 'kæbəl
caber, -s 'keibə*, -z
cabin, -s; -boy/s 'kæbin, -z; -bɔi/z
cabinet, -s; -maker/s 'kæbinit [-bn̩it],
  -s; -ˌmeikə*/z
cab|le (*s. v.*), -les, -ling, -led 'keib|l, -lz,
  -liŋ, [-liŋ], -ld
cablegram, -s 'keiblgræm, -z
cab|man, -men 'kæb|mən, -mən [-men]
caboodle kə'buːdl
caboose, -s kə'buːs, -iz
cabot, -s 'kæbəu, -z
Cabot 'kæbət
cabotage 'kæbətɑːʒ [-tidʒ]
cab|-stand/s, -tout/s 'kæb|stænd/z,
  -taut/s
cacao kə'kɑːəu [-'keiəu]
cachalot, -s 'kæʃəlɔt, -s
cache, -s kæʃ, -iz
cachet, -s 'kæʃei (kaʃɛ), -z
cachinnat|e, -es, -ing, -ed 'kækineit, -s,
  -iŋ, -id
cachinnation ˌkæki'neiʃən
cachou, -s 'kæʃuː, [kæ'ʃuː, kə-] -z
cachucha, -s kə'tʃuːtʃə, -z
cacique, -s kæ'siːk [kɑ's-], -s
cack|le (*s. v.*), -les, -ling, -led, -ler/s
  'kæk|l, -lz, -liŋ [-liŋ], -ld, -lə*/z
  [-lə*/z]
cacodyl 'kækəudail [-dil]
cacoepy 'kækəuepi
cacographic ˌkækəu'græfik
cacography kæ'kɔgrəfi [kə'k-]
cacology kæ'kɔlədʒi [kə'k-]
cacophonic, -al, -ally ˌkækəu'fɔnik, -əl,
  -əli
cacophonous kæ'kɔfənəs [kə'k-]
cacophon|y, -ies kæ'kɔfən|i [kə'k-], -iz

cactus, -es, cacti 'kæktəs, -iz, 'kæktai
cacuminal (*s. adj.*), -s kæ'kjuːminl
  [kə'k-], -z
cad, -s kæd, -z
cadastral kə'dæstrəl
cadaver, -s kə'deivə*, -z
cadaveric kə'dævərik
cadaverous, -ness kə'dævərəs, -nis
Cad|bury, -by 'kæd|bəri, -bi
Caddell kə'del
caddice 'kædis
caddie, -s 'kædi, -z
caddis; -fly, -flies 'kædis; -flai, -flaiz
caddish, -ly, -ness 'kædiʃ, -li, -nis
cadd|y, -ies 'kæd|i, -iz
cade (C.), -s keid, -z
Cadell 'kædl, kə'del
caden|ce/s, -cy 'keidən|s/iz, -si
cadenza, -s kə'denzə, -z
Cader Idris 'kædər'idris [ˌkæ-, -də'i-]
cadet, -s kə'det, -s
cadet-corps (*sing.*) kə'detkɔː*, (*plur.*) -z
cadetship, -s kə'det-ʃip, -s
cadg|e, -es, -ing, -ed, -er/s kædʒ, -iz, -iŋ,
  -d, -ə*/z
cadi, -s 'kɑːdi ['keidi], -z
Cadillac, -s 'kædilæk ['kædl̩æk], -s
Cadiz (*in Spain*) kə'diz ['keidiz]
  ('kadiθ), (*in Philippines*) 'kɑːdiːs, (*in
  U.S.A.*) 'kædiz, 'keidiz
Cadman 'kædmən
Cadmean kæd'mi(ː)ən
cadmium 'kædmiəm [-mjəm]
Cadmus 'kædməs
Cadogan kə'dʌgən
cadre, -s 'kɑːdə* [kɑːdr, 'kædri],
  'kɑːdəz ['kædriz]
caduce|us, -i kə'djuːsj|əs [-sǐ|əs, -ʃj|əs,
  -ʃǐ|əs], -ai
caec|um, -a 'siːk|əm, -ə
Caedmon 'kædmən
Caen (*French town*) kɑ̃ːŋ [kɔ̃ːŋ] (kɑ̃)
Caen (*in* Caen stone) kein
Caerleon kɑː'li(ː)ən [kə'l-]
Caernarvon, -shire kə'nɑːvən, -ʃiə* [-ʃə*]
Caerphilly kɑː'fili [kɛə'f-, kə'f-] (*Welsh*
  kar'fili, kair'fili)
Caesar, -s 'siːzə*, -z
Caesarea ˌsiːzə'riə

Caesarean (of Caesarea) ˌsiːzəˈriən
caesarean (of Caesar) si(ː)ˈzɛəriən
caesium ˈsiːzjəm [-zĭəm]
caesura, -s si(ː)ˈzjuərə [-ˈzjɔər-, -ˈzjɔːr-, -ˈzjəːr-, -ˈʒj-], -z
café, -s ˈkæfei [ˈkæfi] (kafe), -z
café chantant, -s ˈkæfei ˈʃɑː*ntɑ̃ː*ŋ [-ˈʃɔ̃ː*n*tɔ̃ːŋ, -ˈʃɑːntɑːŋ, -ˈʃɔːntɔːŋ, -ˈʃɔntɔŋ] (kafeʃɑ̃tɑ̃), -z
cafeteria, -s ˌkæfiˈtiəriə [-fəˈt-], -z
caffeine ˈkæfiːn [-fiːːn]
cag|e (s. v.), -es, -ing, -ed keidʒ, -iz, -iŋ, -d
cageling, -s ˈkeidʒliŋ, -z
Cagliari kæˈljɑːri [ˌkæliˈɑː-] (ˈkaʎʎari)
Cagliostro kæˈljɔstrəu [ˌkæliˈɔ-]
Cahan (surname) kɑːn
Cahill ˈkɑːhil, ˈkeihil
Caiaphas ˈkaiəfæs [-fəs]
Caillard (English name) ˈkeiləd
Cain(e) kein
Cainite, -s ˈkeinait, -s
caique, -s kaiˈiːk [kɑːˈiːk], -s
Cairene ˈkaiəriːn
cairn, -s kɛən, -z   [-z
cairngorm (C.), -s ˈkɛənˈgɔːm [ˈkɛəng-],
Cairns kɛənz
Cairo (in Egypt) ˈkaiərəu, (in U.S.A.) ˈkɛərəu
caisson, -s kəˈsuːn [ˈkeisən], -z
    Note.—Engineers pronounce kəˈsuːn.
Caithness ˈkeiθnes [-nəs, ˈkeiθˈnes]
caitiff, -s ˈkeitif, -s
Caius (Roman name, character in Shakespeare's 'Merry Wives') ˈkaiəs, (Cambridge College) kiːz
cajol|e, -es, -ing, -ed, -er/s kəˈdʒəul, -z, -iŋ, -d, -ə*/z
cajoler|y, -ies kəˈdʒəulər|i, -iz
Cajun ˈkeidʒən
cak|e (s. v.), -es, -ing, -ed; -y keik, -s, -iŋ, -t; -i
cakewalk, -s ˈkeik-wɔːk, -s
Calabar ˌkæləˈbɑː* [ˈkæləb-]
calabash, -es ˈkæləbæʃ, -iz
Calabria, -n/s kəˈlæbriə [-ˈlɑːb-, old-fashioned -ˈleib-], -n/z
Calais ˈkælei [ˈkæli, old-fashioned ˈkælis] (kalɛ, kalɛ)
calamine ˈkæləmain
calamitous, -ly, -ness kəˈlæmitəs, -li, -nis
calamit|y, -ies kəˈlæmit|i, -iz
calamus ˈkæləməs
calash, -es kəˈlæʃ, -iz
calcareous, -ness kælˈkɛəriəs, -nis
calces (plur. of calx) ˈkælsiːz

calciferous kælˈsifərəs
calcification ˌkælsifiˈkeiʃən
calci|fy, -fies, -fying, -fied ˈkælsiˌfai, -faiz, -faiiŋ, -faid
calcimine ˈkælsimain
calcination ˌkælsiˈneiʃən
calcin|e, -es, -ing, -ed ˈkælsain, -z, -iŋ, -d
calcite ˈkælsait
calcium ˈkælsiəm [-sjəm]
Calcot (near Reading) ˈkælkət
Calcott ˈkɔːlkət [ˈkɔl-]
calculable ˈkælkjuləbl [-kjəl-]
calculat|e, -es, -ing, -ed, -or/s ˈkælkjuleit [-kjəl-], -s, -iŋ, -id, -ə*/z
calculation, -s ˌkælkjuˈleiʃən [-kjə'l-], -z
calculative ˈkælkjulətiv [-kjəl-, -leitiv]
calcul|us, -uses, -i ˈkælkjul|əs [-kjəl-], -əsiz, -ai
Calcutt (surname) ˈkælkʌt
Calcutta kælˈkʌtə
Caldcleugh ˈkɑːldklʌf
Caldecote (in Herts.) ˈkɔːldikət
Caldecott ˈkɔːldəkət [ˈkɔl-, -dik-]
Calder ˈkɔːldə* [ˈkɔl-]
Calderara ˌkældəˈrɑːrə
Calderon (English name) ˈkɔːldərən [ˈkɔl-, ˈkæl-], (Spanish name) ˌkældəˈron (kaldeˈron)
caldron, -s ˈkɔːldrən [ˈkɔl-], -z
Caldwell ˈkɔːldwəl [ˈkɔl-, -wel]
Caleb ˈkeileb
Caledon ˈkælidən
Caledonia, -n/s ˌkæliˈdəunjə [-nĭə], -n/z
calefaction ˌkæliˈfækʃən
calefactor|y, -ies ˌkæliˈfæktər|i, -iz
calendar, -s ˈkælində* [-lən-], -z
calend|er (s. v.), -ers, -ering, -ered ˈkælind|ə* [-lən-], -əz, -əriŋ, -əd
calends ˈkælindz [-lendz, -ləndz]
calenture, -s ˈkæləntjuə* [-tʃuə*, -tʃə*], -z
cal|f, -ves kɑː|f, -vz
calf's-foot (jelly) ˈkɑːvzfut [ˈkɑːfsfut]
calf-skin ˈkɑːfskin
Calgary ˈkælgəri
Calhoun kælˈhəun, kəˈhuːn
Caliban ˈkælibæn [-bən]
calibrat|e, -es, -ing, -ed ˈkælibreit, -s, -iŋ, -id
calibration ˌkæliˈbreiʃən
calibre, -s ˈkælibə* [kəˈliːbə*], -z
calicle, -s ˈkælikl, -z
calico, -(e)s ˈkælikəu, -z
Calicut ˈkælikət
calif = caliph
California, -n/s ˌkæliˈfɔːnjə [-nĭə], -n/z
Caligula kəˈligjulə

calipash 'kælipæʃ
calipee 'kælipi: [ˌkæli'pi:]
caliper, -s 'kælipə*, -z
caliph, -s 'kælif ['keil-, 'kɑ:l-], -s
caliphate, -s 'kælifeit [-fit], -s
Calippus kə'lipəs
calisthenic, -s ˌkælis'θenik, -s
calk (s. v.), -s, -ing, -ed kɔ:k, -s, -iŋ, -t
calkin, -s 'kælkin ['kɔ:kin], -z
call (s. v.), -s, -ing, -ed, -er/s kɔ:l, -z, -iŋ, -d, -ə*/z
Callaghan 'kæləhən, 'kæləgən
Callander 'kæləndə*
call-boy, -s 'kɔ:lbɔi, -z
Callcott 'kɔ:lkət ['kɔl-]
Callender 'kælində* [-lən-]
Caller 'kælə*
Callicrates kə'likrəti:z [kæ'l-]
Callie 'kɔ:li
calligraph|er/s, -ist/s, -y kə'ligrəf|ə*/z [kæ'l-], -ist/s, -i
calligraphic, -al, -ally ˌkæli'græfik, -əl, -əli
calling (s.), -s 'kɔ:liŋ, -z
Calliope kə'laiəpi [kæ'l-]
calliper, -s 'kælipə*, -z
Callirrhoe kæ'lirəui(:) [kə'l-]
Callisthenes kæ'lisθəni:z [kə'l-]
callisthenic, -s ˌkælis'θenik, -s
Callistratus kæ'listrətəs [kə'l-]
call-office, -s 'kɔ:lˌɔfis, -iz
callosit|y, -ies kæ'lɔsit|i [kə'l-], -iz
callous, -ly, -ness 'kæləs, -li, -nis
call|ow (C.), -ower, -owest 'kæl|əu, -əuə*, -əuist
calm (s. adj. v.), -s; -er, -est, -ly, -ness; -ing, -ed kɑ:m, -z; -ə*, -ist, -li, -nis; -iŋ, -d
calmative, -s 'kælmətiv ['kɑ:m-], -z
Calne kɑ:n
calomel 'kæləumel
calor 'kælə*
caloric kə'lɔrik ['kælərik]
calorie, -s 'kæləri, -z
calorific ˌkælə'rifik [-lɔ:'r-, -lɔ'r-]
calorification kəˌlɔrifi'keiʃən [ˌkælər-, ˌkælɔ:r-, ˌkælɔr-]
calorimet|er/s, -ry ˌkælə'rimit|ə*/z [-lɔ:'r-, -lɔ'r-], -ri
calotte, -s kə'lɔt, -s
caloyer, -s 'kælɔiə*, -z
Calpurnia kæl'pə:njə [-niə]
Calshot (in Hants) 'kælʃɔt
Calthorpe (district in Birmingham) 'kælθɔ:p, (surname) 'kɔ:lθɔ:p ['kɔl-], 'kælθɔ:p
Note.—Baron Calthorpe pronounces 'kɔ:lθɔ:p.

Calton (Edinburgh) 'kɑ:ltən ['kæl-, 'kɔ:l-, 'kɔl-]
caltrop, -s 'kæltrəp, -s
calumet, -s 'kæljumet, -s
calumniat|e, -es, -ing, -ed, -or/s kə'lʌmnieit [-njeit], -s, -iŋ, -id, -ə*/z
calumniation, -s kəˌlʌmni'eiʃən, -z
calumn|y, -ies 'kæləmn|i, -iz
calvar|y (C.), -ies 'kælvər|i, -iz
calv|e, -es, -ing, -ed kɑ:v, -z, -iŋ, -d
Calverley (surname) 'kælvəli, (place in Yorks.) 'kɑ:vəli ['kɔ:vəli]
Calvert 'kælvə(:)t, 'kɔ:lvət
calves'-foot 'kɑ:vzfut
Calvin, -ism, -ist/s 'kælvin, -izəm, -ist/s
calvinistic, -al, -ally ˌkælvi'nistik, -əl, -əli
cal|x, -ces, -xes kæl|ks, -si:z, -ksiz [-əli
calycle, -s 'kælikl, -z
Calydon 'kælidən
caly|x, -ces, -xes 'keili|ks ['kæl-], -si:z, cam (C.), -s kæm, -z [-ksiz
Camalodunum ˌkæmələu'dju:nəm
camaraderie ˌkæmə'rɑ:dəri(:) [-'ræd-]
camarilla, -s ˌkæmə'rilə, -z
camber, -s 'kæmbə*, -z
Camberley 'kæmbəli [-bli]
Camberwell 'kæmbəwəl [-wel]
Cambodia, -n kæm'bəudjə [-diə], -n
Camborne 'kæmbɔ:n [-bən]
Cambria, -n/s 'kæmbriə, -n/z
cambric 'keimbrik
Cambridge 'keimbridʒ
Cambridgeshire 'keimbridʒʃiə* [-bridʒʃə*, -bridʃiə*, -bridʃə*]
Cambs. kæmbz
Cambyses kæm'baisi:z
Camden 'kæmdən
came (from come) keim
camel, -s 'kæməl, -z
cameleer, -s ˌkæmi'liə* [-mə'l-], -z
Camelford 'kæməlfəd
camellia, -s kə'mi:ljə [-'mel-, -liə], -z
camel|man, -men 'kæməl|mæn [-mən], -men [-mən]
camelopard, -s (giraffe) 'kæmiləpɑ:d [kə'meləpɑ:d, -ləup-], (facetiously applied to a person) 'kæməl'lepəd, -z
Camelot 'kæmilɔt
Camembert 'kæməmbɛə* (kamɑ̃bɛːr)
cameo, -s 'kæmiəu, -z
camera, -s 'kæmərə, -z
camera|-man, -men 'kæmərə|mæn, -men
Cameron 'kæmərən
Cameronian, -s ˌkæmə'rəunjən [-niən], -z
Cameroon, -s 'kæməru:n [ˌkæmə'r-], -z
cami-knickers ˌkæmi'nikəz ['--ˌ--]
Camilla kə'milə
camisole, -s 'kæmisəul, -z

Camlachie (Glasgow) kæm'læki [-'læxi]
camomile 'kæməumail
camorra, -s kə'mɔrə, -z
camouflag|e (s. v.), -es, -ing, -ed 'kæmuflɑ:ʒ [-məf-], -iz, -iŋ, -d
Camoys kə'mɔiz
camp (s. v.), -s, -ing, -ed kæmp, -s, -iŋ, -t [kæmt]
Campagna kæm'pɑ:njə (kam'paŋŋa)
campaign (s. v.), -s, -ing, -ed, -er/s kæm'pein, -z, -iŋ, -d, -ə*/z
campanile, -s ,kæmpə'ni:li, -z
campanolog|ist/s, -y ,kæmpə'nɔlədʒ|ist/s, -i
campanula, -s kəm'pænjulə [-njələ], -z
camp-bed, -s 'kæmp'bed, -z
Campbell, -s 'kæmbl, -z
Campbellite, -s 'kæmbəlait [-bḷait], -s
Campden 'kæmpdən
Campeachy kæm'pi:tʃi
Camperdown 'kæmpədaun
camp-follower, -s 'kæmp,fɔləuə*, -z
camphor, -s, -ated 'kæmfə*, -z, -reitid
camphoric kæm'fɔrik
campion (C.) 'kæmpjən [-pïən]
camp-stool, -s 'kæmp-stu:l, -z
campus, -es 'kæmpəs, -iz
camstairy kæm'stɛəri
camstone 'kæm-stəun
cam-wood 'kæmwud
can (s.), -s kæn, -z
can (auxil. v.) kæn (strong form), kən, kn, kŋ (weak forms)
Note.—The form kŋ occurs only before words beginning with k or g.
can (v.) (put in cans), -s, -ning, -ned kæn, -z, -iŋ, -d
Cana 'keinə
Canaan 'keinən [-njən, -nïən, Jewish pronunciation kə'neiən]
Canaanite, -s 'keinənait [-njən-, -nïən-, Jewish pronunciation kə'neiənait], -s
Canada 'kænədə
Canadian, -s kə'neidjən [-dïən], -z
canal, -s kə'næl, -z [[-li'z-]
canalization [-isa-] ,kænəlai'zeiʃən
canaliz|e [-is|e], -es, -ing, -ed 'kænəlaiz, -iz, -iŋ, -d
Cananite, -s 'kænənait ['kein-], -s
canard, -s kæ'nɑ:d [kə'nɑ:d, 'kænɑ:d] (kana:r), -z
Canarese ,kænə'ri:z
canar|y (C.), -ies kə'nɛər|i, -iz
canasta kə'næstə
canaster, -s kə'næstə*, -z
Canberra 'kænbərə
canc|el, -els, -elling, -elled 'kæns|əl, -əlz, -əliŋ [-ḷiŋ, -liŋ], -əld

cancellation, -s ,kænsə'leiʃən [-se'lei-, -si'lei-, -s|'ei-], -z
cancer, -s 'kænsə*, -z
Cancer (constellation) 'kænsə*
cancerous 'kænsərəs
Candace kæn'deisi
candelabr|a, -as, -um, ,kændi'lɑ:br|ə [-də'l-, -'læb-, -'leib-], -z, -əm
Candia 'kændiə [-djə]
candid, -ly, -ness 'kændid, -li, -nis
Candida 'kændidə
candidate, -s 'kændidit [-deit], -s
candidature, -s 'kændiditʃə* [-dətʃ-, -deitʃ-, -tʃuə*, -tjuə*], -z
candied 'kændid
candle, -s 'kændl, -z
candle-light 'kændllait
Candlemas 'kændlməs [-mæs]
candlepower, -s 'kændl,pauə*, -z
candlestick, -s 'kændlstik, -s
candour 'kændə*
cand|y (s. v.) (C.), -ies, -ying, -ied 'kænd|i, -iz, -iiŋ [-jiŋ], -id
candy-floss 'kændiflɔs
candytuft 'kænditʌft
cane (C.), -s kein, -z
Canford 'kænfəd
canicular kə'nikjulə* [kæ'n-]
canine (adj.) (in zoology and general use) 'keinain ['kæn-]
canine (s. adj.) (in dentistry), -s 'kænain ['kein-], -z
Canis (constellation) 'keinis
canister, -s 'kænistə*, -z [-riŋ, -d
canker (s.v.), -s, -ing, -ed 'kæŋkə*, -z, cankerous 'kæŋkərəs
canna, -s 'kænə, -z
cannabis 'kænəbis
Cannan 'kænən
canner|y, -ies 'kænər|i, -iz
cannibal, -s 'kænibəl, -z
cannibalism 'kænibəlizəm [-bḷi-]
cannibalistic ,kænibə'listik
cannibaliz|e [-is|e], -es, -ing, -ed 'kænibəlaiz, -iz, -iŋ, -d
cannikin, -s 'kænikin, -z
Cann|ing, -ock 'kæn|iŋ, -ək
cannon (C.), -s 'kænən, -z
cannonad|e (s. v.), -es, -ing, -ed ,kænə'neid, -z, -iŋ, -id
cannon-ball, -s 'kænənbɔ:l, -z
cannoneer, -s ,kænə'niə*, -z
cannon-proof 'kænənpru:f
cannonry 'kænənri
cannon-shot, -s 'kænənʃɔt, -s
cannot 'kænɔt [-nət]
Note.—This word is commonly contracted to kɑ:nt. See can't.

cannula, -s 'kænjulə, -z
cann|y, -ier, -iest, -ily, -iness 'kæn|i, -iə*, -iist, -ili, -inis
canoe (s. v.), -s, -ing, -d kə'nu:, -z, -iŋ [kə'nuiŋ], -d
canon, -s 'kænən, -z
cañon, -s 'kænjən, -z
canoness, -es 'kænənis [-nes], -iz
canonic, -al/s, -ally kə'nɔnik, -əl/z, -əli
canonization [-isa-], -s ,kænənai'zeiʃən [-ni'z-], -z
canoniz|e [-is|e], -es, -ing, -ed 'kænə- naiz, -iz, -iŋ, -d
canon|ry, -ies 'kænənr|i, -iz
Canopus kə'nəupəs
canop|y, -ies 'kænəp|i, -iz
canst (from can) kænst (strong form), kənst (weak form)
cant (s. v.) (C.), -s, -ing, -ed, -er/s kænt, -s, -iŋ, -id, -ə*/z
can't kɑ:nt
Cantab. 'kæntæb
cantabile kæn'tɑ:bili
Cantabrian kæn'teibrïən
Cantabrigian, -s ,kæntə'bridʒïən [-dʒjən], -z
cantaloup, -s 'kæntəlu:p, -s
cantankerous, -ly, -ness kæn'tæŋkərəs [kən-], -li, -nis
cantata, -s kæn'tɑ:tə [kən-], -z
cantatrice, -s 'kæntətri:s, -iz
canteen, -s kæn'ti:n, -z
cant|er (s. v.), -ers, -ering, -ered 'kænt|ə*, -əz, -əriŋ, -əd
Canterbury 'kæntəbəri [-beri]
cantharides kæn'θæridi:z [kən-]
canticle, -s 'kæntikl, -z
cantilever, -s 'kæntili:və*, -z
Cantire kæn'taiə*
Cantling 'kæntliŋ
canto, -s 'kæntəu, -z
canton (Swiss state) 'kæntən [-'-], (in heraldry) 'kæntən, -z
Canton (in China) kæn'tən ['kæn't-], (in Wales, surname) 'kæntən
canton (v.) (divide into portions or districts), -s, -ing, -ed kæn'tən, -z, -iŋ, -d
canton (v.) (quarter soldiers), -s, -ing, -ed; -ment/s kən'tu:n [kæn-], -z, -iŋ, -d; -mənt/s
cantonal 'kæntənəl [kæn'tɔnl]
Cantonese ,kæntə'ni:z [-tə'n-]
cantor, -s 'kæntɔ:*, -z
cantoris kæn'tɔ:ris
Cantuar. 'kæntjuɑ:*
Cantuarian ,kæntju'ɛərïən
Canute kə'nju:t

canvas, -es 'kænvəs, -iz
canvas-back, -s 'kænvəsbæk, -s
canvass (s. v.), -es, -ing, -ed, -er/s 'kænvəs, -iz, -iŋ, -t, -ə*/z
Canvey 'kænvi
canyon, -s 'kænjən [-nïən], -z
canzone, -s kæn'tsəuni [-n'zəu-], -z
canzonet, -s ,kænzəu'net -s
caoutchouc 'kautʃuk [-tʃu:k, -tʃu:]
cap (s. v.), -s, -ping, -ped kæp, -s, -iŋ, -t
capabilit|y, -ies ,keipə'bilit|i [-lət-], -iz
capab|le, -ly, -leness 'keipəb|l, -li, -lnis
capacious, -ly, -ness kə'peiʃəs, -li, -nis
capacitat|e, -es, -ing, -ed kə'pæsiteit, -s, -iŋ, -id
capacit|y, -ies kə'pæsit|i, -iz
cap-à-pie ,kæpə'pi:
caparis|on (s. v.), -ons, -oning, -oned kə'pæris|n, -nz, -ŋiŋ, -nd
cape (C.), -s keip, -s
Capel (in Surrey) 'keipəl, (in Wales) 'kæpəl (Welsh 'kapel)
Capel Curig 'kæpəl'kirig (Welsh 'kapel'kerig, -'kïrig)
Capell 'keipəl
capel(l)et, -s 'kæpəlet [-lit], -s
cap|er (s. v.), -ers, -ering, -ered, -erer/s 'keip|ə*, -əz, -əriŋ, -əd, -ərə*/z
caper (capercailzie), -s 'kæpə*, -z
capercailzie [-caillie], -s,kæpə'keilji[-lzi], -z
Capernaum kə'pə:njəm [-nïəm] [-z
Cape Town [Capetown] 'keiptaun ['-'-]
capias, -es 'keipiæs [-pjæs, -pjəs, -pïəs], -iz
capillaire ,kæpi'lɛə* [-iz
capillarity ,kæpi'læriti
capillary kə'piləri
capit|al (s. adj.), -als, -ally 'kæpit|l, -lz, -li [-li]
capitali|sm, -st/s 'kæpitəli|zəm [kə'pit-, kæ'pit-, -t]i-], -st/s
capitalization [-isa-], -s ,kæpitəlai'zei- ʃən [kæ,p-, kə,p-, -t]ai-], -z
capitaliz|e [-is|e], -es, -ing, -ed 'kæpitə- laiz [kæ'p-, kə'pi-, -tʃaiz], -iz, -iŋ, -d
capitation, -s ,kæpi'teiʃən, -z
capitol (C.), -s 'kæpitl, -z
capitolian ,kæpi'təuljən [-lïən]
capitoline kə'pitəulain
capitular (s. adj.), -s kə'pitjulə*, -z
capitular|y, -ies kə'pitjulərli, -iz
capitulat|e, -es, -ing, -ed kə'pitjuleit, -s, -iŋ, -id
capitulation kə,pitju'leiʃən, -z
capivi kə'paivi
capon, -s 'keipən, -z
caporal (cigarette), -s ,kæpə'rɑ:l, -z
capot (s. v.), -s, -ting, -ted kə'pɔt, -s, [-iŋ, -id
capote, -s kə'pəut, -s

Cappado|cia, -cian/s ˌkæpə'dəu|sjə [-sĭə, -ʃĭə, -ʒə], -ʃən/z [-sĭən/z, -ʃjən/z, -ʃĭən/z, -ʃən/z]
Capper 'kæpə*
Capri 'kæpri(:) ['kɑːp-] ('kaːpri)
capric 'kæprik
capriccio, -s kə'pritʃĭəu [-tʃjəu], -z
capriccioso kəˌpritʃi'əuzəu [-'əusəu]
caprice, -s kə'priːs, -iz
capricious, -ly, -ness kə'priʃəs, -li, -nis
Capricorn (constellation), -us 'kæprikɔːn, ˌkæpri'kɔːnəs
capriol|e (s. v.), -es, -ing, -ed 'kæprĭəul, -z, -iŋ, -d
Capron 'keiprən
capsicum 'kæpsikəm
capsiz|e, -es, -ing, -ed kæp'saiz, -iz, -iŋ, -d
capstan, -s 'kæpstən, -z
capsular 'kæpsjulə*
capsule, -s 'kæpsjuːl, -z
captain, -s 'kæptin, -z
captainc|y, -ies 'kæptins|i, [-tən-], -iz
caption, -s 'kæpʃən, -z
captious, -ly, -ness 'kæpʃəs, -li, -nis
captivat|e, -es, -ing, -ed 'kæptiveit, -s, -iŋ, -id
captive, -s 'kæptiv, -z
captivit|y, -ies kæp'tivit|i, -iz
captor, -s 'kæptə* [-tɔ:*], -z
capt|ure (s. v.), -ures, -uring, -ured 'kæptʃ|ə*, -əz, -əriŋ, -əd
Capua (Italian town) 'kæpjŭə ['kɑːpŭə] ('kaːpua)
capuche, -s kə'puːʃ, -iz
capuchin, -s 'kæpjuʃin [-tʃin], -z
Capulet 'kæpjulet [-lit]
car, -s kɑ:*, -z
carabineer, -s ˌkærəbi'nĭə*, -z
caracal, -s 'kærəkæl, -z
Caracas kə'rækəs [-'rɑ:k-]
caracole, -s 'kærəkəul, -z
Caractacus kə'ræktəkəs
Caradoc kə'rædək
carafe, -s kə'ræf [-'rɑ:f], -s
caramel, -s 'kærəmel, -z
carapace, -s 'kærəpeis, -iz
carat, -s 'kærət, -s
Caratacus ˌkærə'tɑ:kəs
caravan, -s 'kærəvæn ['kærə'v-, ˌkærə'v-], -z
caravanserai, -s ˌkærə'vænsərai [-rei, -ri], -z
caravanser|y, -ies ˌkærə'vænsər|i, -iz
caraway, -s 'kærəwei, -z
caraway-seed, -s 'kærəweiˌsiːd, -z
Carbery 'kɑ:bəri
carbide, -s 'kɑ:baid, -z

carbine, -s 'kɑ:bain, -z
carbineer, -s ˌkɑ:bi'nĭə*, -z
carbohydrate, -s 'kɑ:bəu'haidreit [-rit], -s
carbolic kɑ:'bɔlik [kə'b-]
carbon, -s (substance) 'kɑ:bən [-bɔn, -bn], (in typewriting, photography, etc.) 'kɑ:bən [-bn], -z
carbonaceous ˌkɑ:bəu'neiʃəs
carbonate, -s 'kɑ:bənit [-bɲit], -s
carbonated 'kɑ:bəneitid
carbonic kɑ:'bɔnik
carboniferous ˌkɑ:bə'nifərəs
carbonization [-isa-] ˌkɑ:bənai'zeiʃən [-bɲai-]
carboniz|e [-is|e], -es, -ing, -ed 'kɑ:bənaiz, -iz, -iŋ, -d
carborundum ˌkɑ:bə'rʌndəm
carboy, -s 'kɑ:bɔi, -z
carbuncle, -s 'kɑ:bʌŋkl, -z
carburet (s. v.), -s, -ting, -ted 'kɑ:bjuret [-bər-, ˌ--'-], -s, -iŋ, -id
carburett|er/s, -or/s 'kɑ:bjuret|ə*/z [-bər-, ˌ--'--], -ə*/z
carcase, -s 'kɑ:kəs, -iz
carcass, -es 'kɑ:kəs, -iz
Carchemish 'kɑ:kimiʃ [-kəm-]
carcinoma, -s ˌkɑ:si'nəumə, -z
card (s. v.), -s, -ing, -ed kɑ:d, -z, -iŋ, -id
cardamom [-mum] 'kɑ:dəməm
cardboard 'kɑ:dbɔːd [-bɔəd]
card-case, -s 'kɑ:dkeis, -iz
Cardew 'kɑ:dju:
cardiac 'kɑ:diæk [-djæk]
cardiacal kɑ:'daiəkl
Cardiff 'kɑ:dif
cardigan, -s 'kɑ:digən, -z
Cardigan, -shire 'kɑ:digən, -ʃĭə* [-ʃə*]
cardinal (s. adj.), -s; -ship/s 'kɑ:dinl [-dɲl, -dnl], -z; -ʃip/s
cardioid, -s 'kɑ:diɔid, -z
cardiolog|ist/s, -y ˌkɑ:di'ɔlədʒ|ist/s, -i
cardiometer, -s ˌkɑ:di'ɔmitə*, -z
card-sharper, -s 'kɑ:dˌʃɑ:pə*, -z
card-table, -s 'kɑ:dˌteibl, -z
Card|well, -y 'kɑ:d|wəl [-wel], -i
car|e (s. v.), -es, -ing, -ed kɛə*, -z, -riŋ, -d
careen, -s, -ing, -ed kə'ri:n, -z, -iŋ, -d
career (s. v.), -s, -ing, -ed kə'rĭə*, -z, -riŋ, -d
careerist, -s kə'rĭərist, -s
care|ful, -fullest, -fully, -fulness 'kɛə|ful, -flist, [-fļist, -fəlist, -fulist], -fli [-fļi, -fəli, -fuli], -fulnis
careless, -ly, -ness 'kɛəlis, -li, -nis
caress (s. v.), -es, -ing, -ed kə'res, -iz, -iŋ, -t

caret, -s 'kærət, -s
caretaker, -s 'kɛə,teikə*, -z
Carew kə'ru:, 'kɛəri, see also Pole Carew
careworn 'kɛəwɔ:n
Carey 'kɛəri
Carfax 'ka:-fæks
car-ferry, -ies 'ka:,feri, -z
Cargill 'ka:gil, ka:'gil
cargo, -es 'ka:gəu, -z
Caria 'kɛərïə
Carib, -s 'kærib, -z
Caribbean ,kæri'bi(:)ən [kə'ribïən]
Caribbees 'kæribi:z
caribou (C.), -s 'kæribu:, -z
caricatur|e (s. v.), -es, -ing, -ed ,kærikə-
  'tjuə* [-'tjɔə*, -'tjɔ:*, -'tʃuə*, '----],
  -z, -riŋ, -d
caricaturist, -s ,kærikə'tjuərist [-'tjɔər-,
  -'tjɔ:r-, -'tʃuər-], -s
caries 'kɛərii:z
carillon, -s 'kæriljən [-lɔn, kə'riljən], -z
Carinthia kə'rinθïə [-θjə]
carious 'kɛərïəs
Carisbrooke 'kærisbruk [-izb-]
Carl ka:l
Carleton 'ka:ltən
Carlile ka:'lail ['ka:'lail]
Carlisle ka:'lail ['ka:'lail, locally '--]
Carlist, -s 'ka:list, -s
Carlos 'ka:lɔs
Carlovingian ,ka:ləu'vindʒïən [-dʒjən,
  -dʒən]
Carlow 'ka:ləu
Carlsbad (K-) 'ka:lzbæd
Carlsruhe (K-) 'ka:lz,ru:ə [-ruə]
Carlton 'ka:ltən
Carluke ka:'lu:k
Carlyle ka:'lail ['ka:'lail]
Carlyon ka:'laiən
car|man, -men 'ka:|mən, -mən [-men]
Carmarthen, -shire kə'ma:ðən, -ʃïə*
  [-ʃə*]
Carmel 'ka:mel [-məl]
Carmelite, -s 'ka:milait [-məl-, -mel-], -s
Carmen 'ka:men
Carmichael ka:'maikəl
carminative (s. adj.), -s 'ka:minətiv, -z
carmine 'ka:main
Carnaby 'ka:nəbi
Carnac 'ka:næk
carnage 'ka:nidʒ
Carnaghan 'ka:nəgən
carn|al, -ally 'ka:n|l, -əli
carnality ka:'næliti
Carnarvon, old spelling of Caernarvon,
  q.v.
Carnatic ka:'nætik
carnation, -s ka:'neiʃən, -z

Carnegie ka:'negi, -'neigi
carnelian, -s kə'ni:ljən [ka:'n-, -lïən], -z
Carnforth 'ka:nfɔ:θ
carnival, -s 'ka:nivəl, -z
carnivore, -s 'ka:nivɔ:* [-vɔə*], -z
carnivorous ka:'nivərəs
Carnochan 'ka:nəkən [ka:'nɔ-, -xən]
Carnwath 'ka:nwəθ, ka:n'wɔθ
car|ol (s. v.) (C.), -ols, -olling, -olled
  'kær|əl, -əlz, -əliŋ [-liŋ], -əld
Carolina ,kærə'lainə
Caroline 'kærəlain [-r,ain], less freq.
  -rəlin [-r,in]
carolus (C.), -es 'kærələs [-r,əs], -iz
Carothers kə'rʌðəz
carotid, -s kə'rɔtid, -z
carous|e (s. v.), -es, -ing, -ed; -al/s
  kə'rauz, -iz, -iŋ, -d; -əl/z
car(r)ousel ,kæru:'zel
carp (s. v.), -s, -ing, -ed, -er/s ka:p, -s,
  -iŋ, -t, -ə*/z
car-park, -s 'ka:-pa:k, -s
Carpathian, -s ka:'peiθjən [-θïən, -ðjən,
  -ðïən], -z
carpel, -s 'ka:pel, -z
Carpentaria ,ka:pən'tɛərïə [-pen't-]
carpent|er (s. v.) (C.), -ers, -ering, -ered
  'ka:pint|ə* [-pən-, -pn-], -əz, -ərïŋ, -əd
carpentry 'ka:pintri [-pən-, -pn-]
carpet (s. v.), -s, -ing, -ed 'ka:pit, -s, -iŋ,
carpet-bag, -s 'ka:pitbæg, -z   [-id
carpet-beat|er/s, -ing 'ka:pit,bi:t|ə*/z,
  -iŋ
carpet-broom, -s 'ka:pitbrum [-bru:m],
  -z
carpet-sweeper, -s 'ka:pit,swi:pə*, -z
Carpmael 'ka:pmeil
Carr ka:*
carrag(h)een 'kærəgi:n
Carrara kə'ra:rə
carraway, -s 'kærəwei, -z
Carrhae 'kæri:
carriage, -s 'kæridʒ, -iz
carriage-dog, -s 'kæridʒdɔg, -z
carriage-drive, -s 'kæridʒdraiv, -z
carriage-folk 'kæridʒfəuk
carriage-horse, -s 'kæridʒhɔ:s, -iz
carriage-way 'kæridʒwei
carrick (C.) 'kærik
Carrickfergus ,kærik'fə:gəs
Carrington 'kæriŋtən
carrion; -crow/s 'kærïən; -'krəu/z
Carrodus 'kærədəs
Carroll 'kærəl
carrot, -s, -y 'kærət, -s, -i
Carruthers kə'rʌðəz
carr|y, -ies, -ying, -ied, -ier/s 'kær|i, -iz,
  -iiŋ, -id, -ïə*/z

carryings-on 'kæriiŋz'ɔn
Carshalton kə'ʃɔːltən [kɑː'ʃ-, old-fashioned local pronunciations keis-'hɔːltən, keis'hɔːtn, kei'ʃɔːtn]
Carson 'kɑːsn
Carstairs 'kɑː-stɛəz
cart (s. v.) (C.), -s, -ing, -ed, -er/s; -age kɑːt, -s, -iŋ, -id, -ə*/z; -idʒ
Carta 'kɑːtə
Cartagena ˌkɑːtə'dʒiːnə
carte (C.) kɑːt
carte blanche 'kɑːt'blɑ̃ːnʃ [-'blɔ̃ːnʃ, -'blɑːnʃ, -'blɔːnʃ] (kartblɑ̃ːʃ)
carte-de-visite, -s 'kɑː:tdəvi(ː)'ziːt (kartdəvizit), -s
cartel, -s (business combine) kɑː'tel, (other senses) kɑː'tel ['kɑːtl] , -z
Carter 'kɑːtə*
Carteret (surname) 'kɑːtəret [-rit], (Amer. place name) ˌkɑːtə'ret
Cartesian kɑː'tiːzjən [-zïən, -ʒjən, -ʒïən, -ʒən]
Carthage 'kɑːθidʒ
Carthaginian, -s ˌkɑːθə'dʒinïən [-njən], -z
cart-horse, -s 'kɑːthɔːs, -iz
Carthusian, -s kɑː'θjuːzjən [-'θuː-, -zïən], -z
cartilage, -s 'kɑːtilidʒ [-təl-], -iz
cartilaginous ˌkɑːti'lædʒinəs [-dʒŋəs]
cart-load, -s 'kɑːt-ləud, -z
Cartmel(e) 'kɑːtmel
cartography kɑː'tɔgrəfi
cartomancy 'kɑːtəumænsi
carton, -s 'kɑːtən [-tn], -z
cartoon, -s, -ist/s kɑː'tuːn, -z, -ist/s
cartouche, -s kɑː'tuːʃ, -iz
cartridge, -s 'kɑːtridʒ, -iz
cartridge-paper 'kɑːtridʒˌpeipə*
cart-track, -s 'kɑːttræk, -s
cart-wheel, -s 'kɑːt-wiːl [-thw-], -z
cartwright (C.), -s 'kɑːt-rait, -s
caruncle, -s 'kærəŋkl [kə'rʌŋkl], -z
Carus 'kɛərəs
Caruso kə'ruːzəu [-'ruːsəu]
Caruthers kə'rʌðəz
carv|e, -es, -ing, -ed, -er/s (C.) kɑːv, -z, -iŋ, -d, -ə*/z
carving-kni|fe, -ves 'kɑːviŋnai|f, -vz
Carwardine 'kɑːwədiːn
Cary 'kɛəri
caryatid, -s, -es ˌkæri'ætid, -z, -iːz
Caryll 'kærɪl
Carysfort 'kærisfɔːt
Casabianca 'kæsəbi'æŋkə [ˌkæs-, -æzə-, -'bjæ-]
Casablanca ˌkæsə'blæŋkə
Casanova ˌkæzə'nəuvə

cascade, -s kæs'keid, -z
cascara, -s kæs'kɑːrə [kəs-], -z
cascarilla ˌkæskə'rilə [-iŋ, -t
cas|e (s. v.) (C.), -es, -ing, -ed keis, -iz, case-ending, -s 'keisˌendiŋ, -z
case-hardened 'keisˌhɑːdnd
casein 'keisiːin [-siin]
case-kni|fe, -ves 'keis-nai|f, -vz
case-law 'keis-lɔː
casemate, -s 'keis-meit, -s
casement, -s 'keismənt [old-fashioned 'keizm-], -s
Casement 'keismənt
casern, -s kə'zəːn, -z
case-shot 'keisʃɔt ['keiʃʃɔt]
case-worm, -s 'keis-wəːm, -z
Casey 'keisi
cash (s. v.), -es, -ing, -ed kæʃ, -iz, -iŋ, -t
cash-account, -s 'kæʃə'kaunt ['--ˌ-], -s
cash-book, -s 'kæʃbuk, -s
cash-box, -es 'kæʃbɔks, -iz
cashew, -s kæ'ʃu: [kə'ʃ-, 'kæʃu:], -z
cashier (s.), -s kæ'ʃïə*, -z
cashier (v.), -s, -ing, -ed, -er/s kə'ʃïə* [kæ'ʃ-], -z, -riŋ, -d, -rə*/z
cashmere (C.), -s kæʃ'mïə* ['-'-, also '-- when attributive], -z
casing (s.), -s 'keisiŋ, -z
casino, -s kə'siːnəu [kə'ziː-], -z
cask (s. v.), -s, -ing, -ed kɑːsk, -s, -iŋ, -t
casket, -s 'kɑːskit, -s
Caslon 'kæzlən
Caspar 'kæspə* [-pɑː*]
Caspian 'kæspïən [-pjən]
casque, -s kæsk, -s
Cassandra kə'sændrə
cassation, -s kæ'seiʃən [kə's-], -z
cassava kə'sɑːvə
Cassel(l) 'kæsl
casserole, -s 'kæsərəul, -z
cassia 'kæsïə [-sjə]
Cassidy 'kæsidi
Cassil(l)is 'kæslz ['kɑː-s-]
Cassio 'kæsïəu
Cassiopeia ˌkæsïəu'pi(ː)ə [as name of constellation also ˌkæsi'əupjə, -'əupïə]
Cassius 'kæsïəs [-sjəs]
Cassivelaunus ˌkæsivi'lɔːnəs
cassock, -s, -ed 'kæsək, -s, -t
cassowar|y, -ies 'kæsəwɛər|i [-wər-], -iz
cast (s. v.), -s, -ing kɑːst, -s, -iŋ
Castalia, -n/s kæs'teiljə [-lïə], -n/z
castanet, -s ˌkæstə'net ['--'-], -s
castaway, -s 'kɑːstəwei, -z
caste, -s kɑːst, -s
castellated 'kæsteleitid [-til-, -təl-]
Castelnau (road in S.W. London) 'kɑːslnɔː [-nəu]

caster, -s 'kɑ:stə*, -z
castigat|e, -es, -ing, -ed, -or/s 'kæstigeit,
    -s, -iŋ, -id, -ə*/z
castigation, -s ˌkæsti'geiʃən, -z
Castile kæs'ti:l
Castilian, -s kæs'tiliən [-ljən], -z
casting (s.), -s 'kɑ:stiŋ, -z
casting-net, -s 'kɑ:stiŋnet, -s
casting-vote, -s 'kɑ:stiŋ'vout ['---], -s
cast-iron 'kɑ:st'aiən [also 'kɑ:stˌaiən
    when attributive]
castle, -s 'kɑ:sl, -z
Castlebar 'kɑ:sl'bɑ:* [ˌkɑ:-]
Castlenau (engineering firm) 'kɑ:slnɔ:
Castlerea(gh) 'kɑ:slrei
Castleton 'kɑ:sltən
cast-off, -s 'kɑ:st'ɔf ['ɔ:f, also '— esp.
    when attributive], -s
castor (C.), -s 'kɑ:stə*, -z
castor-oil 'kɑ:stər'ɔil [-tə'ɔil]
castrametation ˌkæstrəme'teiʃən [-mi't-]
castrat|e, -es, -ing, -ed kæs'treit
    ['kæstreit], -s, -iŋ, -id
castration, -s kæs'treiʃən, -z
Castro 'kæstrəu
casual, -ly 'kæʒjŭəl [-ʒjwəl, -ʒjul, -ʒŭəl,
    -ʒwəl, -ʒul, -zjŭəl, -zjwəl, -zjul], -i
casualt|y, -ies 'kæʒjŭəlt|i [-ʒjwəl-, -ʒjul-,
    -ʒŭəl-, -ʒwəl-, -ʒul-, -zjŭəl-, -zjwəl-,
    -zjul-], -iz
casuist, -s, -ry 'kæzjuist ['kæʒju-,
    'kæʒu-], -s, -ri
casuistic, -al ˌkæzju'istik [ˌkæʒju-,
    ˌkæʒu-], -əl
casus belli 'kɑ:sus'beli: ['keisəs'belai]
Caswell 'kæzwəl [-wel]
cat, -s kæt, -s
cataclysm, -s 'kætəklizəm, -z
catacomb, -s 'kætəku:m [-kəum], -z
catafalque, -s 'kætəfælk, -s
Catalan, -s 'kætələn [-læn], -z
catalectic ˌkætə'lektik
caleps|y, -ies 'kætəleps|i, -iz
cataleptic ˌkætə'leptik
catalogu|e (s. v.), -es, -ing, -ed 'kætəlɔg,
    -z, -iŋ, -d
Catalonia, -n/s ˌkætə'ləunjə [-niə], -n/z
catalpa, -s kə'tælpə, -z
catalysis kə'tælisis [-ləs-]
catalytic ˌkætə'litik
catamaran, -s ˌkætəmə'ræn, -z
Catania kə'teinjə [-niə]
cataplasm, -s 'kætəplæzəm, -z
catapult, -s 'kætəpʌlt, -s
cataract, -s 'kætərækt, -s
catarrh, -s, -al kə'tɑ:* [kæ't-], -z, -rəl
catasta, -s kə'tæstə, -z
catastas|is, -es kə'tæstəs|is, -i:z

catastrophe, -s kə'tæstrəfi, -z
catastrophic ˌkætə'strɔfik
catawba (C.) kə'tɔ:bə
catbird, -s 'kætbə:d, -z
catboat, -s 'kætbəut, -s
catcall, -s 'kætkɔ:l, -z
catch (s. v.), -es, -ing, caught, catcher/s
    kætʃ, -iz, -iŋ, kɔ:t, 'kætʃə*/z
catching (adj.) 'kætʃiŋ
catchpenn|y, -ies 'kætʃˌpen|i, -iz
catchpole, -s 'kætʃpəul, -z
catchpoll, -s 'kætʃpəul, -z
catchword, -s 'kætʃwə:d, -z
catch|y, -iness 'kætʃ|i, -inis
Catcott 'kætkət
catechetic, -al, -ally ˌkæti'ketik [-te'k-,
    -tək-], -əl, -əli
catechi|sm/s, -st/s 'kætiki|zəm/z, -st/s
catechiz|e [-is|e], -es, -ing, -ed, -er/s
    'kætikaiz, -iz, -iŋ, -d, -ə*/z
catechu 'kætitʃu:
catechumen, -s ˌkæti'kju:men [-min], -z
categoric|al, -ally ˌkæti'gɔrik|əl [-te'g-,
    -tə'g-], -əli
categoriz|e [-is|e], -es, -ing, -ed 'kæti-
    gəraiz [-teg-], -iz, -iŋ, -d
categor|y, -ies 'kætigər|i [-teg-], -iz
catena, -s kə'ti:nə, -z
catenar|y, -ies kə'ti:nər|i, -iz
catenat|e, -es, -ing, -ed 'kætineit, -s, -iŋ,
    -id
catenation, -s ˌkæti'neiʃən, -z
cateniz|e [-is|e], -es, -ing, -ed 'kætinaiz,
    -iz, -iŋ, -d
cat|er (C.), -ers, -ering, -ered, -erer/s
    'keit|ə*, -əz, -əriŋ, -əd, -ərə*/z
cater-cousin, -s 'keitəˌkʌzn, -z
Caterham 'keitərəm
Caterina ˌkætə'ri:nə
caterpillar, -s 'kætəpilə*, -z
caterwaul (s. v.), -s, -ing, -ed 'kætəwɔ:l,
    [-z, -iŋ, -d
Catesby 'keitsbi
cat-eyed 'kætaid
catfish, -es 'kætfiʃ, -iz
Catford 'kætfəd
catgut 'kætgʌt [-gət]
Catharine 'kæθərin
cathari|sm, -st/s 'kæθəri|zəm, -st/s
catharsis kə'θɑ:sis [kæ'θ-]
cathartic, -s kə'θɑ:tik [kæ'θ-], -s
Cathay kæ'θei [kə'θ-]
Cathcart 'kæθkət [-kɑ:t], kæθ'kɑ:t
    [kəθ-]
cathead, -s 'kæthed, -z
cathedra, -s kə'θi:drə [-'θed-], -z
cathedra (in phrase ex cathedra)
    kə'θi:drə [kæ'tedrɑ:, kæ'θed-, kə'ted-,
    kə'θed-]

cathedral, -s kə'θi:drəl, -z
Cather 'kæðə*
Catherine 'kæθərin
catherine-wheel, -s 'kæθərinwi:l [-nhw-], -z
catheter, -s 'kæθitə*, -z
cathetometer, -s ˌkæθi'tɔmitə*, -z
cathode, -s 'kæθəud, -z
cat-hole, -s 'kæthəul, -z
catholic (C.), -s 'kæθəlik ['kɑ:θ-, -θ‖ik, -θlik], -s
catholicism kə'θɔlisizəm
catholicity ˌkæθəu'lisiti
catholiciz|e [-is|e], -es, -ing, -ed kə'θɔlisaiz, -iz, -iŋ, -d
cat-ice 'kætais
Catiline 'kætilain [-təl-]
cation, -s 'kætaiən, -z
catkin, -s 'kætkin, -z
catlike 'kætlaik
catmint 'kætmint
Cato 'keitəu
cat-o'-nine-tails 'kætə'nain-teilz [ˌkæt-]
Cator 'keitə*
Catriona kə'triənə [kæ't-, -'tri:nə, rarely ˌkætri'əunə]
cat's-cradle 'kæts,kreidl
cat's-eye, -s 'kæts-ai, -z
cat's-meat 'kæts-mi:t
cat's-paw, -s 'kæts-pɔ:, -z
catsup, -s 'kætsəp ['kætʃəp, 'ketʃəp], -s
Cattanach 'kætənæk [-nɑ:x]
Cattegat 'kætigæt
Cattell kæ'tel [kə't-]
Cattermole 'kætəməul
cattish 'kætiʃ
cattle 'kætl
cattle-pen, -s 'kætlpen, -z
cattle-show, -s 'kætlʃəu, -z
cattle-truck, -s 'kætltrʌk, -s
catt|y, -ier, -iest, -ily, -iness 'kæt|i, -iə*, -iist, -ili, -inis
Catullus kə'tʌləs
Caucasia kɔ:'keizjə [-zïə, -ʒjə, -ʒïə, -ʒə]
Caucasian, -s kɔ:'keizjən [-eizïən, -eiʒjən, -eiʒïən, -eiʒən], -z
Caucasus 'kɔ:kəsəs
caucus, -es 'kɔ:kəs, -iz
caudal 'kɔ:dl
Caudine 'kɔ:dain
caudle (C.) 'kɔ:dl
caught (from catch) kɔ:t
caul, -s kɔ:l, -z
cauldron, -s 'kɔ:ldrən ['kɔl-], -z
cauliflower, -s 'kɔliflauə*, -z
caulk, -s, -ing, -ed kɔ:k, -s, -iŋ, -t
caulker, -s 'kɔ:kə*, -z
caus|al, -ally 'kɔ:z|əl, -əli

causality kɔ:'zæliti
causation kɔ:'zeiʃən
causative, -ly 'kɔ:zətiv, -li [-d
caus|e (s. v.), -es, -ing, -ed kɔ:z, -iz, -iŋ, causeless, -ly 'kɔ:zlis, -li
causerie, -s 'kəuzəri(:) (kozri), -z
causeway, -s 'kɔ:zwei, -z
caustic, -al, -ally 'kɔ:stik ['kɔs-], -əl, -əli
causticity kɔ:s'tisiti [kɔs-]
cauterization [-isa-], -s ˌkɔ:tərai'zeiʃən [-ri'z-], -z
cauteriz|e [-is|e], -es, -ing, -ed 'kɔ:təraiz, -iz, -iŋ, -d
cauter|y, -ies 'kɔ:tər|i, -iz
cauti|on (s. v.), -ons, -oning, -oned, -oner/s 'kɔ:ʃ|ən, -ənz, -ŋiŋ [-əniŋ, -niŋ], -ənd, -nə*/z [-ənə*/z, -nə*/z]
cautionary 'kɔ:ʃŋəri [-ʃənə-, -ʃnə-]
caution-money 'kɔ:ʃən,mʌni
cautious, -ly, -ness 'kɔ:ʃəs, -li, -nis
cavalcade, -s ˌkævəl'keid, -z
cavalier, -s ˌkævə'liə*, -z
Cavalleria Rusticana kəˌvælə'ri(:)ə-ˌrusti'kɑ:nə [ˌkævəl-]
cavalr|y, -ies 'kævəlr|i, -iz
cavalry|man, -men 'kævəlri|mən [-mæn], -mən [-men]
Cavan 'kævən
Cavanagh 'kævənə
Cavanaugh 'kævənɔ:
cavatina, -s ˌkævə'ti:nə, -z
cav|e (s. v.) (C.), -es, -ing, -ed keiv, -z, -iŋ, -d
cave (beware) 'keivi
caveat, -s 'keiviæt ['kæv-], -s
cave-dweller, -s 'keiv,dwelə*, -z
Cavell 'kævl, kə'vel
Note.—The family of Nurse Edith Cavell pronounces 'kævl.
cave|man, -men 'keiv|mæn, -men
Cavendish 'kævəndiʃ
cavern, -s, -ous 'kævən [-və:n], -z, -əs
Caversham 'kævəʃəm
caviar(e) 'kæviɑ:* [ˌkævi'ɑ:*]
cavil (s. v.), -s, -ling, -led, -ler/s 'kævil, -z, -iŋ, -d, -ə*/z
cavillation, -s ˌkævi'leiʃən, -z
cavit|y, -ies 'kævit|i, -iz
cavort, -s, -ing, -ed kə'vɔ:t, -s, -iŋ, -id
cav|y, -ies 'keiv|i, -z
caw, -s, -ing, -ed kɔ:, -z, -iŋ, -d
Caw|dor, -ley 'kɔ:|də*, -li
Cawnpore (old spelling of Kanpur) kɔ:n'pɔ:* [-'pɔə*] (Hind. kanpwr)
Cawse kɔ:z
Caxton 'kækstən
cayenne (C.) kei'en [but 'keien in Cayenne pepper]

Cayley 'keili
cayman (C.), -s 'keimən, -z
Cearns kɛənz
ceas|e, -es, -ing, -ed si:s, -iz, -iŋ, -t
ceaseless, -ly, -ness 'si:slis, -li, -nis
Cecil (Christian name, surname) 'sesl
  [-sil], 'sisl [-sil]
  Note.—The family name of the Marquess of Exeter is 'sesl [-sil]; that
  of the Marquess of Salisbury is
  'sisl [-sil].
Cecile (Christian name) 'sesil [-sl], 'sesi:l
Cecilia si'siljə [sə's-, -'si:-, -lïə]
Cecily 'sisili, 'sesili
cedar, -s 'si:də*, -z
ced|e, -es, -ing, -ed si:d, -z, -iŋ, -id
cedilla, -s si'dilə, -z
Cedric 'si:drik, 'sedrik
ceil, -s, -ing, -ed si:l, -z, -iŋ, -d
ceilidh, -s 'keili, -z
ceiling (s.), -s 'si:liŋ, -z
celadon 'selədɔn [-dən]
celandine, -s 'seləndain, -z
celanese ˌselə'ni:z
Celebes se'li:biz [si'l-]
celebrant, -s 'selibrənt, -s
celebrat|e, -es, -ing, -ed, -or/s 'selibreit,
  -s, -iŋ, -id, -ə*/z
celebration, -s ˌseli'breiʃən, -z
celebrit|y, -ies si'lebrit|i [sə'l-], -iz
celeriac si'leriæk [sə'l-, 'seləriæk]
celerity si'leriti [sə'l-]
celery 'seləri
celeste, -s si'lest [sə'l-], -s
celestial (C.), -ly si'lestjəl [sə'l-, -tïəl], -i
celestine (mineral) 'selistain
Celestine, -s 'selistain [si'lestain, si'les-
  tin], -z
Celia 'si:ljə [-lïə]
celibacy 'selibəsi
celibatarian, -s ˌselibə'tɛərïən, -z
celibate, -s 'selibit, -s
cell, -s sel, -z
cellar, -s; -age, -er/s 'selə*, -z; -ridʒ,
  -rə*/z
cellaret, -s ˌselə'ret ['seləret], -s
cellarist, -s 'selərist, -s
cellar|man, -men 'selə|mən [-mæn],
  -mən [-men]
cellist, -s 'tʃelist, -s
cello, -s 'tʃeləu, -z
cellophane 'seləufein
cellular 'seljulə*
cellule, -s 'selju:l, -z
celluloid 'seljulɔid
cellulose 'seljuləus
Celsius 'selsjəs [-sïəs]
celt, -s selt, -s

Celt, -s (as generally used) kelt [rarely
  selt], (member of football team) selt, -s
Celtic (as generally used) 'keltik [rarely
  'seltik], (in names of football teams)
  'seltik
Cely 'si:li
cembalo, -s 'tʃembələu, -z
cement (s. v.), -s, -ing, -ed si'ment
  [sə'm-], -s, -iŋ, -id
cementation, -s ˌsi:men'teiʃən, -z
cementium si'menfjəm [-ʃïəm]
cemeter|y, -ies 'semitr|i, -iz
Cenci (poem by Shelley) 'tʃentʃi
Cenis sə'ni: [se'n-] (səni)
cenobite, -s 'si:nəubait, -s
cenotaph, -s 'senəutɑ:f [-tæf], -s
cens|e, -es, -ing, -ed sens, -iz, -iŋ, -t
censer, -s 'sensə*, -z
cens|or (s. v.), -ors, -oring, -ored
  'sens|ə*, -əz, -əriŋ, -əd
censorial, -ly sen'sɔ:rïəl, -i
censorian sen'sɔ:rïən
censorious, -ly, -ness sen'sɔ:rïəs, -li, -nis
censorship, -s 'sensəʃip, -s
censurable 'senʃərəbl
censur|e (s. v.), -es, -ing, -ed 'senʃə*, -z,
  -riŋ, -d
census, -es 'sensəs, -iz
census-paper, -s 'sensəsˌpeipə*, -z
cent, -s sent, -s
centage 'sentidʒ
cental, -s 'sentl, -z
centaur, -s 'sentɔ:*, -z
centaur|y, -ies 'sentɔ:r|i, -iz
centenarian, -s ˌsenti'nɛərïən, -z
centenar|y, -ies sen'ti:nər|i [-'ten-,
  'sentinər|i], -iz
centennial sen'tenjəl [-nïəl]
center (s. v.), -s, -ing, -ed 'sentə*, -z,
  -riŋ, -d
centesim|al, -ally sen'tesim|əl, -əli
centigrade 'sentigreid
centigramme, -s 'sentigræm, -z
centilitre, -s 'sentiˌli:tə*, -z
centime, -s 'sɑ̃:nti:m ['sɔ̃:nt-, 'sɑ:nt-,
  'sɔ:nt-, 'sɔnt-] (sɑ̃tim), -z
centimetre, -s 'sentiˌmi:tə*, -z
centipede, -s 'sentipi:d, -z
centner, -s 'sentnə* ('tsɛntnər), -z
cento, -s 'sentəu, -z
centr|al, -ally 'sentr|əl, -əli
centrality sen'træliti
centralization [-isa-] ˌsentrəlai'zeiʃən
  [-tr]ai'z-, -trəli'z-, -trˌli'z-]
centraliz|e [-is|e], -es, -ing, -ed, 'sentrə-
  laiz [-trˌl-], -iz, -iŋ, -d
cent|re (s. v.), -res, -ring, -red 'sent|ə*,
  -əz, -əriŋ, -əd

centre-bit, -s 'sentəbit, -s
centre-piece, -s 'sentəpi:s, -iz
centric, -al, -ally 'sentrik, -əl, -əli
centrifugal sen'trifjugəl ['sentrifju:g-,
 ˌsentri'fju:g-]
centripetal sen'tripitl ['sentripi:t-,
 ˌsentri'pi:t-]
centr|um, -a 'sentr|əm, -ə
centumvir, -s sen'tʌmvə(:)* [ken'tum-],
 -z
centumvirate, -s sen'tʌmvirit [-vər-], -s
centuple 'sentjupl
centurion, -s sen'tjuəriən [-'tjɔər-,
 -'tjɔ:r-, -'tʃuər], -z
centur|y, -ies 'sentʃur|i [-tjur-, -tʃər-,
 'senʃər-], -iz
cephalic ke'fælik [ki'f-, se'f-, si'f-]
 Note.—Members of the medical profession usually pronounce ke'f- or
 ki'f-.
cephalopod, -s 'sefələupɒd, -z
cephalopoda ˌsefə'lɒpədə
Cephas 'si:fæs
Cepheid, -s 'si:fiid, -z
Cepheus 'si:fju:s [-fjəs, -fïəs]
ceramic, -s si'ræmik [se'r-, sə'r-, ki'r-,
 ke'r-, kə'r-], -s
cerastes si'ræsti:z [se'r-, sə'r-]
cerate, -s 'siərit [-reit], -s
Cerberus 'sə:bərəs
cerca|ria, -riae sə:'kɛə|rïə, -rii:
cer|e (s. v.), -es, -ing, -ed siə*, -z, -riŋ, -d
cereal, -s 'siəriəl, -z
cerebell|um, -ums, -a ˌseri'bel|əm, -əmz,
cerebos 'seribɒs   [-ə
cerebral (s. adj.), -s 'seribrəl, -z
cerebration ˌseri'breiʃən
cerebr|um, -a 'seribr|əm, -ə
cere|-cloth, -cloths 'siə|klɒθ [-klɔ:θ],
 -klɔθs [-klɔ:ðz, -klɔ:θs]
cerement, -s 'siəmənt, -s
ceremonial (s. adj.), -s, -ly ; -ism
 ˌseri'məunjəl [-nïəl], -z, -i; -izəm
ceremonious, -ly, -ness ˌseri'məunjəs
 [-nïəs], -li, -nis
ceremon|y, -ies 'serimən|i, -iz
cereous 'siəriəs
Ceres 'siəri:z
cerif [ser-], -s 'serif, -s
cerise sə'ri:z [si'r-, -'ri:s]
ceroplastic 'siərəu'plæstik
certain, -ly 'sə:tn [-tən, -tin], -li
certaint|y, -ies 'sə:tnt|i [-tən-, -tin-], -iz
certes 'sə:tiz [sə:ts]
certifiabl|e, -ly 'sə:tifaiəb|l [ˌ-ˌ-'---], -li
certificate (s.), -es sə'tifikit [sə:'t-], -s
certificat|e (v.), -es, -ing, -ed sə'tifikeit
 [sə:'t-], -s, -iŋ, -id [sə'tifikitid]

certification, -s (act of certifying) ˌsə:ti-
 fi'keiʃən, (providing with a certificate)
 ˌsə:tifi'keiʃən [sə,t-], -z
certificatory sə'tifikətəri [sə:'t-, -keit-]
certi|fy, -fies, -fying, -fied, -fier/s 'sə:-
 ti|fai, -faiz, -faiiŋ, -faid, -faiə*/z
certiorari, -s ˌsə:tiɔ:'rɛərai [-tïə'r-], -z
certitude 'sə:titju:d
cerulean si'ru:ljən [siə'r-, -lïən]
cerumen si'ru:men
ceruse 'siəru:s [si'ru:s, sə'r-]
Cervantes sə:'væntiz [-ti:z]
cervical sə(:)'vaikəl ['sə:vikəl]
cervine 'sə:vain
César 'seizɑ:* [-zə*] (seza:r)
Cesarewitch (Russian prince) si'zɑ:rə-
 vitʃ [-riv-], (race) si'zærəwitʃ [-'zɑ:r-,
 -riw-]
Cesario si:'zɑ:riəu [-'zær-]
cess, -es ses, -iz
cessation, -s se'seiʃən, -z
cession, -s 'seʃən, -z
cessionar|y, -ies 'seʃənər|i [-ʃŋər-], -iz
cesspool, -s 'sespu:l, -z
Cestrian 'sestrïən
cestui que trust, -s 'setiki'trʌst, -s
cestui que vie, -s 'setiki'vi:, -z
cestuis que trust 'setizki'trʌst
cestuis que vie 'setizki'vi:
cest|us, -i 'sest|əs, -ai
ceta|cea, -cean/s si'tei|ʃjə [se't-, -ʃïə,
 -ʃə, -sïə, -sïə], -ʃjən/z [-ʃïən/z, -ʃən/z,
 -sjən/z, -sïən/z]
cetaceous si'teiʃjəs [se't-, -ʃïəs, -ʃəs,
 -sjəs, -sïəs]
cetane 'si:tein
Cetewayo ketʃ'waiəu [ˌketi'waiəu,
 -'wa:jəu, old-fashioned ˌseti'weiəu]
 (Zulu ˌtetʃ'wa:jɔ)
Cet(t)inje tse'tinji [se't-]
Ceuta 'sju:tə
Cévennes si'ven [sə'v-, -enz] (sevɛn)
Ceylon si'lɒn
Ceyx 'si:iks
Cézanne sei'zæn [si-, se-] (sezan)
cf. kəm'pɛə* [kɒn'fɔ:*, 'si:'ef]
Chablis 'ʃæbli(:) (ʃabli)
chaconne, -s ʃə'kɒn [ʃæ'k-] (ʃakɔn), -z
Chad tʃæd
Chadwick 'tʃædwik
chaf|e, -es, -ing, -ed tʃeif, -s, -iŋ, -t
chafer, -s 'tʃeifə*, -z
chaff (s. v.), -s, -ing/ly, -ed, -er/s tʃɑ:f,
 -s, -iŋ/li, -t, -ə*/z
chaff-cutter, -s 'tʃɑ:f,kʌtə*, -z
chaffer (v.), -s, -ing, -ed 'tʃæfə*, -z, -riŋ,
 -d
Chaffey 'tʃeifi

chaffinch, -es 'tʃæfintʃ, -iz
chaff|y, -iness 'tʃɑːf|i, -inis
chafing-dish, -es 'tʃeifiŋdiʃ, -iz
chagrin (s.) 'ʃægrin
chagrin (v.), -s, -ing, -ed 'ʃægrin
  [ʃə'griːn], -z, -iŋ, -d
Chaim haim (Heb. 'xajim, xa'jiːm)
chain (s. v.), -s, -ing, -ed tʃein, -z, -iŋ, -d
chain-armour 'tʃein'ɑːmə* ['tʃein‚ɑː-]
chain-bridge, -s 'tʃein'bridʒ ['--], -iz
chain-gang, -s 'tʃeingæŋ, -z
chainless 'tʃeinlis
chain-mail 'tʃein'meil ['--]
chainstitch 'tʃein-stitʃ
chain-stores 'tʃein-stɔːz [-stɔəz]
chainwork 'tʃeinwəːk
chair (s. v.), -s, -ing, -ed tʃɛə*, -z, -riŋ, -d
chair-bed, -s 'tʃɛə'bed, -z
chair|man, -men 'tʃɛə|mən, -mən
chairmanship, -s 'tʃɛəmənʃip, -s
chaise, -s ʃeiz, -iz
Chalcedon 'kælsidən [-dn, -dɔn]
chalcedony kæl'sedəni
chalcedonyx, -es ‚kælsi'dɔniks, -iz
Chalcis 'kælsis
chalcography kæl'kɔgrəfi
Chaldaic kæl'deiik
Chaldea, -n/s kæl'di(ː)ə, -n/z
Chaldee, -s kæl'diː, -z
chaldron, -s 'tʃɔːldrən, -z
chalet, -s 'ʃælei ['ʃæli] (ʃɑlɛ), -z
Chalfont (in Bucks.) 'tʃælfənt [-fɔnt]
  [old-fashioned 'tʃɑːfənt]
Chaliapin ‚ʃæli'ɑːpin (ʃa'ljapjin)
chalice, -s, -d 'tʃælis, -iz, -t
chalk (s. v.) (C.), -s, -ing, -ed tʃɔːk, -s,
Chalkis 'kælkis   [-iŋ, -t
chalk-pit, -s 'tʃɔːkpit, -s
chalk-stone, -s 'tʃɔːk-stəun, -z
chalk|y, -ier, -iest, -ily, -iness 'tʃɔːk|i,
  -iə* [-jə*], -iist [-jist], -ili, -inis
Challen 'tʃælin
challeng|e (s. v.), -es, -ing, -ed -er/s
  'tʃælindʒ, -iz, -iŋ, -d, -ə*/z
Challenor 'tʃælinə*
challis 'ʃælis ['ʃæli]
Challoner 'tʃælənə*
Chalmers 'tʃɑːməz
Chaloner 'tʃælənə*
chalybeate kə'libiit [kæ'l-, -bjit]
Cham kæm
chamade, -s ʃə'mɑːd, -z
chamber, -s, -ed 'tʃeimbə*, -z, -d
Chamberlain 'tʃeimbəlin [-bl̩in, -lən],
  -bəlein
chamberlain, -s 'tʃeimbəlin [-bl̩in], -z
chamberlainship, -s 'tʃeimbəlinʃip
  [-bl̩in-], -s

chamber-maid, -s 'tʃeimbəmeid, -z
Chambers 'tʃeimbəz
chameleon, -s kə'miːljən, [-lïən], -z
chamfer, -s 'tʃæmfə* ['ʃæm-], -z
chamois (sing.) 'ʃæmwɑː [-wɔː] [in
  chamois leather often 'ʃæmi], (plur.) -z
Chamonix 'ʃæməni
champ, -s, -ing, -ed tʃæmp, -s, -iŋ, -t
  [tʃæmt]
champagne, -s ʃæm'pein ['-'-, also '--
  when attributive], -z
champaign, -s 'tʃæmpein, -z
champerty 'tʃæmpə(ː)ti
champignon, -s tʃæm'pinjən (ʃɑ̃piɲɔ̃), -z
champion (s. adj. v.) (C.), -s, -ing, -ed ;
  -ship/s 'tʃæmpjən, -z, -iŋ, -d; -ʃip/s
chanc|e (s. v.), -es, -ing, -ed tʃɑːns, -iz,
  -iŋ, -t
chancel, -s 'tʃɑːnsəl, -z
chanceller|y, -ies 'tʃɑːnsələr|i [-slə-],
  -iz
chancellor (C.), -s ; -ship/s 'tʃɑːnsələ*
  [-slə*, -silə*], -z; -ʃip/s
chancer|y (C.), -ies 'tʃɑːnsər|i, -iz
chancre 'ʃæŋkə*
chanc|y, -ier, -iest 'tʃɑːns|i, -iə [-jə], -iist
  [-jist]
chandelier, -s ‚ʃændi'liə* [-də'l-], -z
chandler, -s 'tʃɑːndlə*, -z
Chandos 'ʃændɔs, 'tʃændɔs
  Note.—Lord Chandos pronounces
  'ʃæn-. Chandos Street in London is
  generally pronounced with 'tʃ-.
chang|e (s. v.), -es, -ing, -ed, -er/s
  tʃeindʒ, -iz, -iŋ, -d, -ə*/z
changeability ‚tʃeindʒə'biliti [-lət-]
changeab|le, -ly, -leness 'tʃeindʒəb|l̩,
  -li, -lnis
changeless 'tʃeindʒlis
changeling, -s 'tʃeindʒliŋ, -z
chann|el (s. v.), -els, -elling, -elled
  'tʃæn|l̩, -lz, -l̩iŋ [-əliŋ], -ld
Channell 'tʃænl
Channing 'tʃæniŋ
chant (s. v.) (C.), -s, -ing, -ed, -er/s
  tʃɑːnt, -s, -iŋ, -id, -ə*/z
Chanter 'tʃɑːntə*
chanterelle, -s ‚tʃæntə'rel, -z
chanticleer, -s ‚tʃænti'kliə* [‚tʃɑːnt-,
  '---], -z
Chantilly ʃæn'tili [ʃɑ̃ːn't-, ʃɔ̃ːn't-, ʃɑːn't-,
  ʃɔːn't-, ʃɔn't-] (ʃɑ̃tiji)
Chantrey 'tʃɑːntri
chantr|y, -ies 'tʃɑːntr|i, -iz
chant|y, -ies 'tʃɑːnt|i, -iz
chaos 'keiɔs
chaotic kei'ɔtik   [-t
chap (s. v.), -s, -ping, -ped tʃæp, -s, -iŋ,

chap-book, -s 'tʃæpbuk, -s
chape, -s tʃeip, -s
chapel, -s 'tʃæpəl, -z
Chapel - en - le - Frith 'tʃæplənlə'friθ [-pḷen-]
chapelr|y, -ies 'tʃæpəlr|i, -iz
chaperon (s. v.), -s, -ing, -ed; -age 'ʃæpərəun, -z, -iŋ, -d; -idʒ
chapfallen 'tʃæp,fɔːlən
chaplain, -s 'tʃæplin, -z
chaplainc|y, -ies 'tʃæplins|i [-lən-], -iz
chaplet, -s 'tʃæplit, -s
Chap|lin, -man 'tʃæp|lin, -mən
Chapp|ell, -le 'tʃæp|əl, -l
chappiness 'tʃæpinis
chap|py (s. adj.), -ies 'tʃæp|i, -iz
chapter, -s 'tʃæptə*, -z
chapter-hou|se, -ses 'tʃæptəhau|s, -ziz
char (s. v.), -s, -ring, -red tʃɑː*, -z, -riŋ, -d
char-à-banc, -s 'ʃærəbæŋ [-bãːŋ, -bɔ̃ːŋ, -bɑːŋ, -bɔːŋ, -bɔŋ] (ʃarabã, as if French), -z
character, -s 'kæriktə* [-rək-], -z
characteristic, -s, -al, -ally ,kæriktə'ristik [-rək-], -s, -əl, -əli
characterization [-isa-], -s ,kæriktərai'zeiʃən [-rək-, -ri'z-], -z
characteriz|e [-is|e], -es, -ing, -ed 'kæriktəraiz [-rək-], -iz, -iŋ, -d
charade, -s ʃə'rɑːd, -z
charcoal 'tʃɑːkəul
Chard tʃɑːd
char|e, -es, -ing, -ed tʃɛə*, -z, -riŋ, -d
charg|e (s. v.), -es, -ing, -ed tʃɑːdʒ, -iz, -iŋ, -d
chargeab|le, -ly, -leness 'tʃɑːdʒəb|l, -li, -lnis
chargé(s) d'affaires (sing.) 'ʃɑːʒeidæ'fɛə* [-də'f-] (ʃarʒedafɛːr), (plur.) -z
charger, -s 'tʃɑːdʒə*, -z
Charig 'tʃærig
Charing Cross 'tʃæriŋ'krɔs ['tʃɛər-, -'krɔːs]
chariot, -s 'tʃæriət, -s
charioteer, -s ,tʃæriə'tiə*, -z
charitab|le, -ly, -leness 'tʃæritəb|l, -li, -lnis
charit|y, -ies 'tʃærit|i, -iz
charivari, -s 'ʃɑːri'vɑːri [,ʃɑː-], -z
charivaria ,ʃɑːri'vɑːriə
charlad|y, -ies 'tʃɑː,leid|i, -iz
charlatan, -s 'ʃɑːlətən [-tæn], -z
charlatan|ism/s, -ry 'ʃɑːlətən|izəm/z [-tṇ|-], -ri
Charlecote 'tʃɑːlkəut
Charlemagne 'ʃɑːləmein [-'main, ,--'-] (ʃarləmaɲ)

Charlemont 'tʃɑːlmənt
Charles tʃɑːlz
Charleston 'tʃɑːlstən
Charlestown 'tʃɑːlztaun
Charlesworth 'tʃɑːlzwəːθ
Charl|ey, -ie 'tʃɑːl|i, -i
charlock 'tʃɑːlɔk
charlotte (C.), -s 'ʃɑːlət, -s
Charlottenburg ʃɑː'lɔtnbəːg
Charlton 'tʃɑːltən
charm (s. v.), -s, -ing/ly, -ed, -er/s tʃɑːm, -z, -iŋ/li, -d, -ə*/z
Charmian 'tʃɑːmjən [-mɪən]
charnel 'tʃɑːnl
charnel-hou|se, -ses 'tʃɑːnlhau|s, -ziz
Charnock 'tʃɑːnɔk [-nək]
Charon 'kɛərən [-rɔn]
Charrington 'tʃæriŋtən
chart, -s tʃɑːt, -s
chart|er (s. v.), -ers, -ering, -ered, -erer/s 'tʃɑːt|ə*, -əz, -əriŋ, -əd, -ərə*/z
Charterhouse 'tʃɑːtəhaus
Charteris 'tʃɑːtəz, 'tʃɑːtəris
charter-part|y, -ies 'tʃɑːtə,pɑːt|i, -iz
charti|sm, -st/s 'tʃɑːti|zəm, -st/s
Chartreuse, -s ʃɑː'trəːz (ʃartrøːz), -iz
char|woman, -women 'tʃɑː|,wumən, -,wimin
char|y, -ier, -iest, -ily, -iness 'tʃɛər|i, -ɪə*, -iist, -ili, -inis
Charybdis kə'ribdis
Chas. tʃɑːlz [rarely tʃæs]
chas|e (s. v.) (C.), -es, -ing, -ed, -er/s tʃeis, -iz, -iŋ, -t, -ə*/z
chasm, -s 'kæzəm, -z
chasmy 'kæzmi [-zəmi]
chassé, -s 'ʃæsei (ʃase), -z
chasseur, -s ʃæ'sə:* (ʃasœːr), -z
chassis (sing.) 'ʃæsi [-siː], (plur.) 'ʃæsiz [-siːz]
chaste, -ly, -ness tʃeist, -li, -nis
chast|en, -ens, -ening, -ened 'tʃeis|n, -nz, -ṇiŋ [-niŋ], -nd
chastis|e, -es, -ing, -ed, -er/s tʃæs'taiz, -iz, -iŋ, -d, -ə*/z
chastisement, -s 'tʃæstizmənt, -s
chastity 'tʃæstiti
Chastney 'tʃæsni
chasuble, -s 'tʃæzjubl, -z
chat (s. v.), -s, -ting, -ted tʃæt, -s, -iŋ, -id
Chataway 'tʃætəwei
château, -x 'ʃætəu ['ʃɑː-t] (ʃato), -z
Château d'Oex 'ʃætəu'dei ['ʃɑː-t] (ʃatode)
chatelain(e), -s 'ʃætəlein [-til-], -z
Chater 'tʃeitə*
Chatham 'tʃætəm
Chatsworth 'tʃætswə(:)θ

chattel, -s 'tʃætl, -z
chatter, -s, -ing, -ed, -er/s 'tʃætə*, -z, -riŋ, -d, -rə*/z
chatterbox, -es 'tʃætəbɒks, -iz
Chatteris 'tʃætəris
Chatterton 'tʃætətn
Chatto 'tʃætəu
chatt|y, -ier, -iest, -ily, -iness 'tʃætl|i, -ïə*, -iist, -ili, -inis
Chaucer 'tʃɔ:sə*
Chaucerian tʃɔ:'siərïən
chaudron, -s 'tʃɔ:drən, -z
chauffer, -s 'tʃɔ:fə*, -z
chauffeur, -s 'ʃəufə* [ʃəu'fə:*], -z
Chauncey 'tʃɔ:nsi
chauvini|sm, -st/s 'ʃəuvini|zəm, -st/s
chaw, -s, -ing, -ed tʃɔ:, -z, -iŋ, -d
Chawner 'tʃɔ:nə*
Chaworth 'tʃɑ:wə:θ
Chaytor 'tʃeitə*
cheap, -er, -est, -ly, -ness tʃi:p, -ə*, -ist, -li, -nis
cheap|en, -ens, -ening, -ened 'tʃi:p|ən, ənz, -niŋ [-niŋ], -ənd
cheap-jack, -s 'tʃi:pdʒæk, -s
Cheapside 'tʃi:p'said ['tʃi:p-said]
cheat (s. v.), -s, -ing, -ed tʃi:t, -s, -iŋ, -id
Cheatham 'tʃi:təm
check (s. v. interj.), -s, -ing, -ed tʃek, -s, -iŋ, -t
checkers 'tʃekəz
checkmat|e (s. v. interj.), -es, -ing, -ed 'tʃekmeit [tʃek'm-], -s, -iŋ, -id
check-rein, -s 'tʃek-rein ['tʃek'r-], -z
check-weigher, -s 'tʃek,weiə*, -z
Cheddar 'tʃedə*
cheek (s. v.), -s, -ing, -ed tʃi:k, -s, -iŋ, -t
cheekbone, -s 'tʃi:kbəun, -z
Cheeke tʃi:k
cheek|y, -ier, -iest, -ily, -iness 'tʃi:k|i, -ïə* [-jə*], -iist [-jist], -ili, -inis
cheep, -s, -ing, -ed tʃi:p, -s, -iŋ, -t
cheer (s. v.), -s, -ing, -ed tʃiə*, -z, -riŋ, -d
cheer|ful, -fully, -fulness 'tʃiə|ful, -fuli [-fəli], -fulnis
cheerio 'tʃiəri'əu
cheerless, -ly, -ness 'tʃiəlis, -li, -nis
cheer|y, -ier, -iest, -ily, -iness 'tʃiər|i, -ïə*, -iist, -ili, -inis
Cheeryble 'tʃiəribl
cheese, -s tʃi:z, -iz
cheesecake, -s 'tʃi:zkeik, -s
Cheeseman 'tʃi:zmən
cheesemonger, -s 'tʃi:z,mʌŋgə*, -z
cheese-paring 'tʃi:z,pɛəriŋ
Cheesewright 'tʃezrait
chees|y, -iness 'tʃi:z|i, -inis
cheetah, -s 'tʃi:tə, -z

Cheetham 'tʃi:təm
chef, -s ʃef, -s
chef-d'œuvre, -s ʃei'də:vr [-və*] (ʃedœ:vr), -z
cheiromancy 'kaiərəumænsi
Cheke tʃi:k
chel|a (claw), -ae 'ki:l|ə, -i:
chela (disciple), -s 'tʃeilə ['tʃi:lə], -z
Chelmsford 'tʃelmsfəd [old-fashioned local pronunciation 'tʃem-, tʃɔm-]
Chelsea 'tʃelsi
Cheltenham 'tʃeltnəm [-tnəm]
chemic, -al, -ally, -als 'kemik, -əl, -əli, -əlz
chemise, -s ʃə'mi:z [ʃi'm-], -iz
chemisette, -s ˌʃemi(:)'zet, -s
chemist, -s, -ry 'kemist, -s, -ri
Note.—These words were formerly pronounced with 'kim-, and this pronunciation was fairly frequent among old-fashioned speakers in the early part of the twentieth century. It is now probably obsolete, or nearly so.
Chemnitz 'kemnits   Kɑvl-ɴɑvx-stɪeɪt
Chemosh 'ki:mɔʃ
Chenevix 'ʃeniviks [-nəv-], 'tʃen-
Cheney 'tʃi:ni, 'tʃeini
Chenies (in Bucks.) 'tʃeiniz ['tʃi:n-], (street in London) 'tʃi:niz
chenille ʃə'ni:l
Cheops 'ki:ɔps
Chepstow 'tʃepstəu
cheque, -s tʃek, -s
cheque-book, -s 'tʃekbuk, -s
chequer (s. v.), -s, -ing, -ed 'tʃekə*, -z, -riŋ, -d
Chequers 'tʃekəz
Cherbourg 'ʃɛəbuəg ['ʃə:b-, -bə:g] (ʃɛrbu:r)
cherish, -es, -ing, -ed 'tʃeriʃ, -iz, -iŋ, -t
Cherith 'kiəriθ ['ker-]
Cherokee ˌtʃerə'ki: ['---]
cheroot, -s ʃə'ru:t [ʃi'r-], -s
cherr|y, -ies 'tʃer|i, -iz
cherry-brand|y, -ies 'tʃeri'brænd|i, -iz
cherry-pie, -s 'tʃeri'pai, -z
cherry-stone, -s 'tʃeri-stəun, -z
Chersonese 'kə:sɔni:s
Chertsey 'tʃə:tsi
cherub, -s 'tʃerəb, -z
cherubic tʃe'ru:bik [tʃi'r-, tʃə'r-]
cherubim 'tʃerəbim [-rub-]
Cherubini ˌkeru'bi:ni(:) [-rə'b-]
chervil 'tʃə:vil
Cherwell (river, Lord) 'tʃɑ:wəl
Chesapeake 'tʃesəpi:k
Chesebro(ugh) 'tʃi:zbrə

Chesham 'tʃeʃəm [old-fashioned local pronunciation 'tʃesəm]
Cheshire 'tʃeʃə*
Cheshunt 'tʃesnt
Chesney 'tʃesni, 'tʃezni
chess tʃes
chessboard, -s 'tʃesbɔːd [-bəəd], -z
chess|-man, -men 'tʃes|mæn, -men
chest, -s, -ed tʃest, -s, -id
Chester 'tʃestə*
chesterfield (C.), -s 'tʃestəfiːld, -z
Chester-le-Street 'tʃestəli'striːt
Chesterton 'tʃestətən [-tn]
chest-note, -s 'tʃestnəut, -s
chestnut, -s 'tʃesnʌt [-stn-, -nət], -s
Chetham 'tʃetəm
Chet|wode, -wynd 'tʃet|wud, -wind
cheval-glass, -es ʃə'vælglɑːs, -iz
chevalier, -s ˌʃevə'liə*, -z
Chevalier (surname) ʃə'væljei [ʃi'v-]
Chevening (in Kent) 'tʃiːvniŋ
Chevenix 'ʃeviniks [-vən-]
cheveril 'ʃevəril
Cheves tʃiːvz
Cheviot (hills, sheep) 'tʃevïət [-vjət, also 'tʃiv-, 'tʃiːv- mostly by people accustomed to Scottish pronunciation], (cloth) 'tʃevïət [-vjət]
Chevis 'tʃevis
Chevrolet 'ʃevrəulei [ˌ--'-]
chevron, -s 'ʃevrən, -z
chev|y (s. v.) (C.), -ies, -ying, -ied 'tʃev|i, -iz, -iiŋ, -id
chew, -s, -ing, -ed tʃuː, -z, -iŋ [tʃuiŋ], -d
chewing-gum 'tʃu(ː)iŋɡʌm
Cheyenne ʃai'æn [-'en]
Cheylesmore 'tʃeilzmɔː* [-mɔə*], 'tʃil-
Cheyne 'tʃeini, tʃein
   Note.–In Cheyne Walk some say 'tʃeini and others tʃein. The Lady Jane Cheyne (who gave her name to Cheyne Walk) was always called 'tʃeini, and this pronunciation is still generally used in speaking of her. Otherwise the surname is now generally pronounced tʃein.
Cheyney 'tʃeini
chianti (C.) ki'ænti
chiaroscuro ki'ɑːrəs'kuərəu [-rɔs-, -'kjuə-]
chic ʃiːk [ʃik]
Chicago ʃi'kɑːɡəu [tʃi-, also -'kɔːɡəu in imitation of one American pronunciation]
chican|e (s. v.), -es, -ing, -ed, -er/s ʃi'kein [tʃi-], -z, -iŋ, -d, -ə*/z
chicaner|y, -ies ʃi'keinər|i, -iz
Chichele 'tʃitʃili

Chichester 'tʃitʃistə*
chi-chi 'ʃiːʃiː
chick (C.), -s tʃik, -s
chickabidd|y, -ies 'tʃikə,bid|i, -iz
chicken, -s 'tʃikin, -z
chicken-hearted 'tʃikin,hɑːtid
chicken-pox 'tʃikinpɔks
chickweed 'tʃik-wiːd
chicory 'tʃikəri
Chiddingly (in Sussex) 'tʃidiŋ'lai ['---]
chid|e, -es, -ing, chid tʃaid, -z, -iŋ, tʃid
chief (s. adj.), -s, -ly tʃiːf, -s, -li
chieftain, -s 'tʃiːftən [-tin], -z
chieftanc|y, -ies 'tʃiːftəns|i [-tin-], -iz
Chiene ʃiːn
chiff-chaff, -s 'tʃif-tʃæf, -s
chiffon, -s 'ʃifɔn, -z
chiffonier, -s ˌʃifə'niə*, -z
chignon, -s 'ʃiːnjɔ̃ːŋ [-njɔːŋ, -njɔŋ, old-fashioned ʃi'nɔn], -z
chilblain, -s 'tʃilblein, -z
child (C.), -ren tʃaild, 'tʃildrən ['tʃuldr-, 'tʃldr-]
child|bed, -birth 'tʃaild|bed, -bəːθ
Childe tʃaild
Childermas 'tʃildəmæs [-məs]
childhood 'tʃaildhud
childish, -ly, -ness 'tʃaildiʃ, -li, -nis
child|less, -like 'tʃaild|lis, -laik
Chile [-ili] 'tʃili
Chilean, -s 'tʃiliən [-ljən], -z
chilia|sm, -st/s 'kiliæ|zəm, -st/s
chiliad, -s 'kiliæd ['kail-, -ljæd], -z
chilia|sm, -st/s 'kiliæ|zəm, -st/s
chill (s. adj. v.), -s, -ing, -ed, -ness tʃil,
chilli, -s 'tʃili, -z
Chillingham (in Northumb.) 'tʃiliŋəm
Chillingworth 'tʃiliŋwə(ː)θ
Chillon 'ʃiːlɔ̃ːŋ ['ʃiːjɔ̃ːŋ, -ɔːŋ, old-fashioned 'ʃilən, 'ʃilɔn, ʃi'lɔn] (ʃijɔ)
   Note.–In reading Byron's 'Castle of Chillon' it is usual to pronounce 'ʃilən or 'ʃilɔn.
chill|y, -ier, -iest, -iness 'tʃil|i, -ïə*, -iist, -inis
Chiltern 'tʃiltə(ː)n
Chilton 'tʃiltən
Chimborazo ˌtʃimbə'rɑːzəu [-bɔ'r-]
chim|e (s. v.), -es, -ing, -ed, -er/s tʃaim, -z, -iŋ, -d, -ə*/z
chimera, -s kai'miərə [ki'm-], -z
chimere, -s tʃi'miə* [ʃi-], -z
chimeric, -al, -ally kai'merik [ki'm-], -əl, -əli
chimney, -s 'tʃimni, -z
chimney-corner, -s 'tʃimni,kɔːnə*, -z
chimney-piece, -s 'tʃimnipiːs, -iz
chimney-pot, -s 'tʃimnipɔt, -s

chimney-stack, -s 'tʃimni-stæk, -s
chimney-sweep, -s 'tʃimni-swiːp, -s
chimney-sweeper, -s 'tʃimni,swiːpə*, -z
chimpanzee, -s ,tʃimpən'ziː [-pæn-], -z
chin, -s tʃin, -z
china (C.) 'tʃainə
china-clay 'tʃainə'klei
China|man, -men 'tʃainə|mən, -mən
chinchilla -s tʃin'tʃilə, -z
Chindau tʃin'dau
chin-deep 'tʃin'diːp
Chindit 'tʃindit
chin|e (s. v.), -es, -ing, -ed tʃain, -z, -iŋ, -d
Chinee, -s tʃai'niː, -z
Chinese 'tʃai'niːz [also '--, -'- according
    to sentence-stress]
Chingford 'tʃiŋfəd
chink, -s tʃiŋk, -s
Chinnereth 'tʃinərəθ
Chinnock 'tʃinək
Chinnor 'tʃinə*
Chinook tʃi'nuk
chintz, -es tʃints, -iz
Chios 'kaiɔs
chip (s. v.), -s, -ping, -ped tʃip, -s, -iŋ, -t
chipmuck, -s 'tʃipmʌk, -s
chipmunk, -s 'tʃipmʌŋk, -s
chipolata, -s ,tʃipə'lɑːtə, -z
Chipp, -endale, -enham tʃip, -əndeil,
    -nəm [-ənəm]
Chippewa, -s 'tʃipiwɑ: [-wə], -z
Chipping 'tʃipiŋ   [-iist, -inis
chipp|y, -ier, -iest, -iness 'tʃip|i, -iə*,
chirograph, -s 'kaiərəugrɑːf ['kair-,
    -græf], -s
chirographer,-s ,kaiə'rɔgrəfə* [kai'r-], -z
chirographic ,kaiərəu'græfik [,kair-]
chirograph|ist/s, -y ,kaiə'rɔgrəf|ist/s
    [kai'r-], -i
Chirol 'tʃirəl
chiromancer, -s 'kaiərəumænsə*, -z
chiromancy 'kaiərəumænsi ['kair-]
Chiron (centaur) 'kaiərən ['kair-]
chiropod|ist/s, -y ki'rɔpəd|ist/s [ʃi'r-,
    tʃi'r-, old-fashioned ,kaiə'r-], -i
chirp (s. v.), -s, -ing, -ed; -y, -ier, -iest,
    -ily, -iness tʃəːp, -s, -iŋ, -t; -i, -iə*
    [-jə*], -iist [-jist], -ili, -inis
Chirrol 'tʃirəl   [-t
chirrup (s. v.), -s, -ing, -ed 'tʃirəp, -s, -iŋ,
chis|el (s. v.), -els, -elling, -elled 'tʃiz|l,
    -lz, -liŋ [-liŋ], -ld
Chisholm 'tʃizəm
Chislehurst 'tʃizlhəːst
Chiswick 'tʃizik
chit, -s tʃit, -s
chit-chat 'tʃittʃæt
chitin 'kaitin

Chittenden 'tʃitndən
Chitty 'tʃiti
chivalric 'ʃivəlrik [old-fashioned 'tʃiv-]
chivalrous, -ly, -ness 'ʃivəlrəs [old-
    fashioned 'tʃiv-], -li, -nis
chivalry 'ʃivəlri [old-fashioned 'tʃiv-]
chive, -s tʃaiv, -z
Chivers 'tʃivəz
chiv|y (s. v.), -ies, -ying, -ied 'tʃiv|i, -iz,
    -iiŋ, -id
Chladni 'klædni
chlamy|s, -des 'klæmi|s ['kleim-], -diːz
Chloe 'kləui
chloral 'klɔːrəl
chlorate, -s 'klɔːrit [-reit], -s
chloric 'klɔːrik ['klɔr-]
chloride, -s 'klɔːraid, -z
chlorine 'klɔːriːn
Chloris 'klɔːris ['klɔr-]
chlorite, -s 'klɔːrait, -s
chlorodyne 'klɔrədain ['klɔːr-]
chloroform (s. v.), -s, -ing, -ed 'klɔrə-
    fɔːm ['klɔːr-], -z, -iŋ, -d
chloromycetin ,klɔːrəumai'siːtin [,klɔr-]
chlorophyll 'klɔrəfil ['klɔːr-]
chlorous 'klɔːrəs
Choate tʃəut
chock, -s; -full tʃɔk, -s; -'ful
chock-a-block 'tʃɔkə'blɔk
chocolate, -s 'tʃɔkəlit, -s
choice (s. adj.), -s, -r, -st, -ly, -ness
    tʃɔis, -iz, -ə*, -ist, -li, -nis
choir, -s 'kwaiə*, -z
choir-organ,   -s   'kwaiər,ɔːgən,
    ['kwaiə,ɔː-], -z
choir-screen, -s 'kwaiə-skriːn, -z
chok|e, -es, -ing, -ed tʃəuk, -s, -iŋ, -t
choke-damp 'tʃəukdæmp
chok|y, -ier, -iest, -iness 'tʃəuk|i, -iə*,
    [-jə*], -iist [-jist], -inis
Cholderton (near Salisbury) 'tʃəuldətən
choler 'kɔlə*   [[-tn]
cholera 'kɔlərə
choleraic ,kɔlə'reiik
choleric 'kɔlərik [kɔ'lerik]
cholesterol kə'lestərɔl [kɔ-, -tiər-]
choliamb, -s 'kəuliæmb, -z
choliambic ,kəuli'æmbik
Cholmeley 'tʃʌmli
Cholmondeley 'tʃʌmli
Cholsey 'tʃəulzi
Chomley 'tʃʌmli
Chomolhari ,tʃɔmɔl'hʌri [,tʃəuməl-
    'hɑːri]
Chomolungma ,tʃəuməu'luŋmɑ:
choos|e, -es, -ing, chose, chosen,
    chooser/s tʃuːz, -iz, -iŋ, tʃəuz,
    'tʃəuzn, 'tʃuːzə*/z

choos|y, -ier, -iest, -iness 'tʃuːz|i, -iə* [-jə*], -iist [-jist], -inis
chop (s. v.), -s, -ping, -ped tʃɔp, -s, -iŋ, -t
chop-hou|se, -ses 'tʃɔphau|s, -ziz
Chopin 'ʃɔpɛ̃ːŋ ['ʃəup-, -pæŋ] (ʃɔpɛ̃)
chopper, -s 'tʃɔpə*, -z
chopp|y, -ier, -iest, -ily, -iness 'tʃɔp|i, -iə*, -iist, -ili, -inis
chop-stick, -s 'tʃɔp-stik, -s
chor|al, -ally 'kɔːr|əl ['kɔr-], -əli
chorale, -s kɔ'rɑːl [kə'r-, kɔː'r-, -'rɑːli], -z
Chorazin kɔ'reizin [kə'r-]
chord, -s kɔːd, -z
chore, -s tʃɔː* [tʃɔə*], -z
chorea kɔ'riə [kɔː'r-]
choreg|us, -i kɔ'riːg|əs [kɔː'r-, kə'r-], -ai
choreographer, -s ˌkɔri'ɔgrəfə* [ˌkɔːr-], -z
choreographic ˌkɔriə'græfik [ˌkɔːr-, -riəu'g-]
choreography ˌkɔri'ɔgrəfi [ˌkɔːr-]
choriamb, -s 'kɔriæmb ['kɔːr-], -z
choriambic ˌkɔri'æmbik [ˌkɔːr-]
choric 'kɔrik
chorister, -s 'kɔristə*, -z
Chorley 'tʃɔːli
chort|le, -les, -ling, -led 'tʃɔːt|l, -lz, -liŋ [-liŋ], -ld
chorus (s. v.), -es, -ing, -ed 'kɔːrəs, -iz, -iŋ, -t
chose (legal term) ʃəuz
chose (from choose), -n tʃəuz, -n
Chosen tʃəu'sen ['-'-]
Chou-en-Lai 'tʃəuen'lai
chough, -s tʃʌf, -s
chouse, -s tʃaus, -iz
chow, -s tʃau, -z
chow-chow, -s 'tʃau'tʃau ['--], -z
chowder, -s 'tʃaudə*, -z
Chowles tʃəulz
chrestomath|y, -ies kres'tɔməθ|i, -iz
chrism 'krizəm
chrisom, -s 'krizəm, -z
Christ, -s kraist, -s
Christabel 'kristəbel [-bəl],
Christchurch 'kraist-tʃɔːtʃ
Christ-cross-row, -s 'kriskrɔs'rəu [-krɔːs-], -z
Christdom 'kraistdəm
christ|en, -ens, -ening, -ened 'kris|n, -nz, -ŋiŋ [-niŋ], -nd
Christendom 'krisndəm
christening, -s 'krisŋiŋ [-niŋ], -z
Christi (in Corpus Christi) 'kristi
Christian, -s 'kristjən [-tiən, -tʃən], -z
Christiana ˌkristi'ɑːnə
Christiania ˌkristi'ɑːnjə [-niə]

Christianism 'kristjənizəm [-tiən-, -tʃən-, -tʃŋ-]
Christianity ˌkristi'æniti [kris'tjæn-]
christianiz|e [-is|e], -es, -ing, -ed 'kristjənaiz [-tiən-, -tʃən-, -tʃŋ-], -iz, -iŋ, -d
christianly 'kristjənli [-tiən-, -tʃən-]
Christian name, -s 'kristjənneim [-tʃən-], -z
Christie 'kristi ˌ[-z
Christina kris'tiːnə
Christine 'kristiːn, kris'tiːn
Christlike 'kraistlaik
Christliness 'kraistlinis
Christmas, -es 'krisməs [-stm-], -iz
Christmas-box, -es 'krisməsbɔks [-stm-], -iz
Christmas-card, -s 'krisməs-kɑːd [-stm-], -z
Christmas-tree, -s 'krisməs-triː [-stm-], -z
Christminster 'kristminstə*
Christopher 'kristəfə*
Christopherson kris'tɔfəsn
Christy 'kristi
chromate, -s 'krəumit [-meit], -s
chromatic, -ally krəu'mætik, -əli
chrome krəum
chromic 'krəumik
chromite, -s 'krəumait, -s
chromium 'krəumjəm [-miəm]
chromium-plated 'krəumjəm'pleitid [-miəm-, '--,--]
chromium-plating 'krəumjəm'pleitiŋ [-miəm-, '--,--]
chromolithograph, -s 'krəuməu'liθəugrɑːf [-græf], -s
chromolithography 'krəuməuli'θɔgrəfi
chromosome, -s 'krəuməsəum, -z
chromosphere, -s 'krəuməsfiə*, -z
chromotype 'krəuməutaip
chroneme, -s 'krəuniːm, -z
chronemic krəu'niːmik
chronic, -al, -ally 'krɔnik, -əl, -əli
chronic|le (s. v.), -les, -ling, -led, -ler/s 'krɔnik|l, -lz, -liŋ, -ld, -lə*/z
chronogram, -s 'krɔnəugræm, -z
chronograph, -s 'krɔnəugrɑːf [-græf], -s
chronologic, -al, -ally ˌkrɔnə'lɔdʒik, -əl, -əli
chronolog|ist/s, -y, -ies krə'nɔlədʒ|ist/s [krɔ'n-], -i, -iz
chronomet|er/s, -ry krə'nɔmit|ə*/z, -ri
chronometric, -al, -ally ˌkrɔnəu'metrik, -əl, -əli
chronopher, -s 'krɔnəfə*, -z
chrysalis, -es, chrysalides 'krisəlis [-sil-, -sl-], -iz, kri'sælidiːz
chrysanthemum, -s kri'sænθəməm [-i'zæ-, -θim-], -z

chryselephantine ˌkriseli'fæntain
Chrysler, -s 'kraizlə*, -z
chrysolite, -s 'krisəulait, -s
chrysoprase, -s 'krisəupreiz, -iz
chrysoprasus, -es kri'sɔprəsəs, -iz
Chrysostom 'krisəstəm
chub, -s tʃʌb, -z
Chubb tʃʌb
chubb|y, -ier, -iest, -ily, -iness 'tʃʌb|i,
  -ĭə*, -iist, -ili, -inis
chuck (s. v.), -s, -ing, -ed tʃʌk, -s, -iŋ, -t
chucker-out, chuckers-out 'tʃʌkər'aut
  [-ə'aut], 'tʃʌkəz'aut
chuck|le (s. v.), -les, -ling, -led 'tʃʌk|l,
  -lz, -liŋ [-l̩iŋ], -ld
Chudleigh 'tʃʌdli
chuff, -s tʃʌf, -s
Chuffey 'tʃʌfi
chukker, -s 'tʃʌkə*, -z
chum (s. v.), -s, -ming, -med tʃʌm, -z,
  -iŋ, -d
Chumalhari ˌtʃuməl'hʌri [-'hɑ:ri]
Chumbi 'tʃumbi
chumm|y, -ier, -iest, -ily, -iness 'tʃʌm|i,
  -ĭə*, -iist, -ili, -inis
chump, -s tʃʌmp, -s
Chungking tʃuŋ'kiŋ [tʃʌŋ-, '-'-]
chunk, -s tʃʌŋk, -s
church, -es tʃə:tʃ, -iz
Churchdown (near Gloucester) 'tʃə:tʃdaun
  Note.—There was until recently a local
    pronunciation 'tʃəuzn, which is
    now probably obsolete as far as the
    village is concerned. It is preserved
    as the name of a hill near by,
    which is now written Chosen.
church-goer, -s 'tʃə:tʃˌgəuə*, -z
Churchill 'tʃə:tʃil
churching, -s 'tʃə:tʃiŋ, -z
church|man (C.), -men 'tʃə:tʃ|mən, -mən
church-rate, -s 'tʃə:tʃ-reit, -s
churchwarden, -s 'tʃə:tʃ'wɔ:dn, -z
church|y, -ier, -iest, -ily, -iness 'tʃə:tʃ|i,
  -ĭə*, -iist, -ili, -inis
churchyard, -s 'tʃə:tʃ'jɑ:d [also '—, -'-
  according to sentence-stress], -z
  Note.—Some people always pronounce
  '—.
Churchyard (surname) 'tʃə:tʃəd
churl, -s tʃə:l, -z
churlish, -ly, -ness 'tʃə:liʃ, -li, -nis
churn (s. v.), -s, -ing, -ed tʃə:n, -z, -iŋ, -d
Churton 'tʃə:tn
chut ꞁ [tʃt, ʃ:t, tʃʌt]
chute, -s ʃu:t, -s
Chute ʃu:t
Chuter 'tʃu:tə*
chutney [-nee], -s 'tʃʌtni, -z

Chuzzlewit 'tʃʌzlwit
chyle kail
chyme kaim
Cibber 'sibə*
cibori|um/s, -a si'bɔ:rĭ|əm/z, -ə
cicada, -s si'kɑ:də [-'keid-], -z
cicala, -s si'kɑ:lə, -z
cicatrice, -s 'sikətris, -iz
cicatrices (Latin plur. of cicatrix)
  ˌsikə'traisi:z
cicatrix 'sikətriks
cicatriz|e [-is|e], -es, -ing, -ed 'sikətraiz,
  -iz, -iŋ, -d
Cicely 'sisĭli
Cicero 'sisərəu
cicerone, -s ˌtʃitʃə'rəuni [ˌsisə'r-], -z
Ciceronian ˌsisə'rəunjən [-nĭən]
cicisbe|o, -i ˌtʃitʃiz'bei|əu, -ĭ:
cider, -s 'saidə*, -z
cider-cup, -s 'saidəkʌp ['saidə'k-], -s
cigar, -s si'gɑ:*, -z
cigarette, -s ˌsigə'ret, -s
cigarette-holder, -s ˌsigə'ret,həuldə*, -z
cigar-shaped si'gɑ:-ʃeipt
cilia 'silĭə [-ljə]
ciliary 'silĭəri [-ljə-]
cilice, -s 'silis, -iz
Cilicia sai'liʃĭə [si'l-, -ʃjə, -sĭə, -sjə]
cill, -s sil, -z
Cilla 'silə
Cimabue ˌtʃimə'bu(:)i [ˌtʃi:m-, -'bu(:)ei]
Cimmer|ian, -ii si'miər|ĭən, -iai
cinch, -es sintʃ, -iz
cinchona, -s siŋ'kəunə, -z
Cincinnati, ˌsinsi'næti [-'nɑ:ti]
cincture, -s 'siŋktʃə* [-tʃuə*], -z
cinder, -s 'sində*, -z
Cinderella ˌsində'relə
cinder-pa|th, -ths 'sindəpɑ:|θ, -ðz
cinder-sifter, -s 'sindəˌsiftə*, -z
cinder-track, -s 'sində-træk, -s
cinecamera, -s 'siniˌkæmərə ['—'——], -z
cinema, -s 'sinəmə [-ni-, -mɑ:], -z
cinematograph, -s ˌsinə'mætəgrɑ:f
  [-ni'm-, -græf], -s
cinematographic ˌsinəˌmætə'græfik
  [-niˌm-]
cinematography ˌsinəmə'tɔgrəfi [-ni-]
cinerama ˌsinə'rɑ:mə [-ni-]
cineraria, -s ˌsinə'rɛərĭə, -z
cinerarium, -s ˌsinə'rɛərĭəm, -z
cinerary 'sinərəri
cineration ˌsinə'reiʃən
Cingalese ˌsiŋgə'li:z ['—'-]
cinnabar 'sinəbɑ:*
cinnamon 'sinəmən
cinque (C.) siŋk
cinquefoil 'siŋkfɔil

cinzano sin'zɑːnəu
ciph|er (s. v.), -ers, -ering, -ered 'saif|ə*, -əz, -əriŋ, -əd
cipher-key, -s 'saifəki:, -z
Cipriani ˌsipri'ɑːni
circa 'səːkə
Circassia, -n/s səː'kæsɪə [-sjə, -ʃɪə, -ʃjə], -n/z
Circe 'səːsi
circ|le (s. v.), -les, -ling, -led 'səːk|l, -lz, -liŋ [-ḷiŋ], -ld
circlet, -s 'səːklit, -s
circuit, -s 'səːkit, -s
circuitous, -ly, -ness sə(ː)'kju(ː)itəs, -li, -nis
circular (s. adj.), -s 'səːkjulə* [-kjəl-], -z
circulariz|e [-is|e], -es, -ing, -ed 'səːkjuləraiz [-kjəl-], -iz, -iŋ, -d
circulat|e, -es, -ing, -ed, -or/s 'səːkju-leit [-kjəl-], -s, -iŋ, -id, -ə*/z
circulation, -s ˌsəːkju'leiʃən [-kjə'l-], -z
circulatory ˌsəːkju'leitəri ['səːkjulətəri]
circumambient ˌsəːkəm'æmbiənt [-bjənt]
circumambulat|e, -es, -ing, -ed ˌsəːk-əm'æmbjuleit, -s, -iŋ, -id
circumcis|e, -es, -ing, -ed 'səːkəmsaiz, -iz, -iŋ, -d
circumcision, -s ˌsəːkəm'siʒən, -z
circumference, -s sə'kʌmfərəns, -iz
circumflex, -es 'səːkəmfleks, -iz
circumlocution, -s ˌsəːkəmlə'kjuːʃən, -z
circumlocutory ˌsəːkəm'lɔkjutəri
circumnavigat|e, -es, -ing, -ed, -or/s ˌsəːkəm'nævigeit, -s, -iŋ, -id, -ə*/z
circumnavigation, -s 'səːkəmˌnævi-'geiʃən [ˌsəː-], -z
circumpolar 'səːkəm'pəulə* [ˌsə-ː-]
circumscrib|e, -es, -ing, -ed 'səːkəm-skraib [ˌsəːkəm'skraib], -z, -iŋ, -d
circumscription, -s ˌsəːkəm'skripʃən, -z
circumspect, -ly, -ness 'səːkəmspekt, -li, -nis
circumspection ˌsəːkəm'spekʃən
circumstance, -s, -d 'səːkəmstəns, -iz ['səːkəmstænsiz], -t
circumstanti|al, -ally ˌsəːkəm'stænʃ|əl, -əli
circumstantiality 'səːkəmˌstænʃi'æliti [ˌsəː-]
circumstantiat|e, -es, -ing, -ed ˌsəːkəm-'stænʃieit [-ʃjeit], -s, -iŋ, -id
circumvallation, -s ˌsəːkəmvə'leiʃən [-væ'l-], -z
circumvent, -s, -ing, -ed ˌsəːkəm'vent, -s, -iŋ, -id
circumvention, -s ˌsəːkəm'venʃən, -z
circus, -es 'səːkəs, -iz

Cirencester 'saiərənsestə* ['sisitə*, 'sisistə*]
Note.—Members of county families generally pronounce 'sisitə*, but the pronunciation most usually heard in the town is 'saiərənsestə* (or -stər with the dialectal retroflex r). An older pronunciation 'sizitər may still be heard in the country round.
Ciriax 'siriæks
cirque, -s səːk [siək], -s
cirrhosis si'rəusis
cirro-cumulus 'sirəu'kuːmjuləs [-mjəl-]
cirro-stratus 'sirəu'strɑːtəs [-'streit-]
cirrous 'sirəs
cirrus 'sirəs
Cisalpine sis'ælpain
Cissie 'sisi
cissoid, -s 'sisɔid, -z
Cissy 'sisi
cist, -s sist, -s
Cistercian, -s sis'təːʃjən [-ʃɪən, -ʃən], -z
cistern, -s 'sistən, -z
cistus, -es 'sistəs, -iz
citadel, -s 'sitədl [-tid-, -dəl], -z
citation, -s sai'teiʃən [si't-], -z
citatory 'saitətəri ['sit-, sai'teitəri]
cit|e, -es, -ing, -ed sait, -s, -iŋ, -id
cithar|a, -ae 'siθər|ə, -i:
cither, -s 'siθə*, -z
cithern, -s 'siθən [-θə:n, 'siðən], -z
citizen, -s; -ship 'sitizn, -z; -ʃip
citole, -s si'təul, -z
citrate, -s 'sitrit ['sait-, -treit], -s
citrated 'sitreitid ['sait-]
citric 'sitrik
Citrine si'triːn
Citroën, -s 'sitrəuən [si't-, -əuin, -əuen] (sitrɔen), -z
citron, -s 'sitrən, -z
citr|ous, -us 'sitr|əs, -əs
cittern, -s 'sitəːn [-tən], -z
cit|y, -ies 'sit|i, -iz
civet, -s 'sivit, -s
civic, -s 'sivik, -s
civ|il, -illy 'siv|l ['siv|il], -ili
civilian, -s si'viljən [-lɪən], -z
civilit|y, -ies si'vilit|i, -iz
civilizable [-isa-] 'sivilaizəbl
civilization [-isa-], -s ˌsivilai'zeiʃən [-vḷai'z-, -vili'z-, -vḷi'z-], -z
civiliz|e [-is|e], -es, -ing, -ed 'sivilaiz [-vḷ-], -iz, -iŋ, -d
clack (s. v.), -s, -ing, -ed klæk, -s, -iŋ, -t
Clackmannan klæk'mænən
clack-valve, -s 'klækvælv, -z
Clacton 'klæktən

clad (*from* clothe) klæd
claim (*s. v.*), -s, -ing, -ed kleim, -z, -iŋ, -d
claimant, -s 'kleimənt, -s
claimer, -s 'kleimə*, -z
clairaudien|ce, -t klɛər'ɔ:djən|s [-dïə-], -t
clairvoyan|ce, -cy, -t/s, -te/s klɛə-'vɔiən|s, -si, -t/s, -t/s
clam, -s klæm, -z
clamant 'kleimənt
clamb|er, -ers, -ering, -ered 'klæmb|ə*, -əz, -*əriŋ, -əd
clamm|y, -ier, -iest, -ily, -iness 'klæm|i, -ïə*, -iist, -ili, -inis
clamorous, -ly, -ness 'klæmərəs, -li, -nis
clamour (*s. v.*), -s, -ing, -ed 'klæmə*, -z, -riŋ, -d
clamp (*s. v.*), -s, -ing, -ed klæmp, -s, -iŋ, -t [klæmt]
clan, -s klæn, -z
clandestine, -ly klæn'destin [-tain], -li
clang (*s. v.*), -s, -ing, -ed klæŋ, -z, -iŋ, -d
clangorous, -ly 'klæŋgərəs [-ŋə-], -li
clangour 'klæŋgə* [-ŋə*]
clank (*s. v.*), -s, -ing, -ed klæŋk, -s, -iŋ, -t [klæŋt]
Clanmaurice klæn'mɔris
Clanmorris klæn'mɔris
clannish, -ly, -ness 'klæniʃ, -li, -nis
Clanricarde klæn'rikəd ['klæn,rikəd]
Note.—The second pronunciation may often be heard from residents in the neighbourhood of Clanricarde Gardens, London.
clanship 'klæn-ʃip
clans|man, -men 'klænz|mən, -mən
clap (*s. v.*), -s, -ping, -ped klæp, -s, -iŋ, -t
clapboard, -s 'klæpbɔ:d [-bɔəd], -z
Clapham 'klæpəm [-pm]
clapper, -s 'klæpə*, -z
Clapton 'klæptən
clap-trap 'klæp-træp
claque, -s klæk, -s
Clara 'klɛərə
clarabella (C.), -s ,klærə'belə, -z
Clare klɛə*
Claremont 'klɛəmɔnt [-mənt]
Clarence 'klærəns
Clarenc(i)eux 'klærənsu: [-sju:]
clarendon (C.) 'klærəndən
claret, -s 'klærət, -s
claret-cup 'klærətkʌp ['klærət'k-]
Clarges (*street*) 'klɑ:dʒiz
Claridge, -'s 'klæridʒ, -iz
clarification ,klærifi'keiʃən
clari|fy, -fies, -fying, -fied, -fier/s 'klæri|fai, -faiz, -faiiŋ, -faid, -faiə*/z
Clarina klə'rainə

clarinet, -s ,klæri'net, -s
clarinettist, -s ,klæri'netist, -s
clarion, -s 'klærïən, -z
Clarissa klə'risə
clarity 'klæriti
Clark(e) klɑ:k
clarkia, -s 'klɑ:kjə [-kïə], -z
Clarkson 'klɑ:ksn
clash (*s. v.*), -es, -ing, -ed klæʃ, -iz, -iŋ, -t
clasp (*s. v.*), -s, -ing, -ed klɑ:sp, -s, -iŋ, -t
clasp-kni|fe, -ves 'klɑ:spnai|f ['-'-], -vz
class (*s. v.*), -es, -ing, -ed klɑ:s, -iz, -iŋ, -t
Classen 'klæsn
classic, -s, -al, -ally, -alness 'klæsik, -s, -əl, -əli, -əlnis
classicism, -s 'klæsisizəm, -z
classifiable 'klæsifaiəbl
classification, -s ,klæsifi'keiʃən, -z
classificatory ,klæsifi'keitəri ['klæsifi-kətəri]
classi|fy, -fies, -fying, -fied, -fier/s 'klæsi|fai, -faiz, -faiiŋ, -faid, -faiə*/z
class|man, -men 'klɑ:s|mæn [-mən], -men [-mən]
classroom, -s 'klɑ:srum [-ru:m], -z
class|y, -ier, -iest, -iness 'klɑ:s|i, -ïə* [-jə*], -iist [-jist], -inis
clatter (*s. v.*), -s, -ing, -ed 'klætə*, -z, -riŋ, -d
Claud(e) klɔ:d
Claudia, -n 'klɔ:djə [-dïə], -n
Claudius 'klɔ:djəs [-dïəs]
clause, -s klɔ:z, -iz
claustral 'klɔ:strəl
claustrophobia ,klɔ:strə'fəubjə [-bïə]
clave (*archaic past of* cleave) kleiv
clavecin, -s 'klævisin, -z
Claverhouse 'kleivəhaus
clavichord, -s 'klævikɔ:d, -z
clavicle, -s 'klævikl, -z
clavicular klə'vikjulə* [klæ'v-]
clavier (*keyboard*), -s 'klævïə* [-vjə*], -z
clavier (*instrument*), -s klə'vïə* ['klævïə*, 'klævjə*], -z
claw (*s. v.*), -s, -ing, -ed klɔ:, -z, -iŋ, -d
Claxton 'klækstən
clay (C.), -s klei, -z
clayey 'kleii
Clayhanger 'klei,hæŋə*
claymore, -s 'kleimɔ:* [-mɔə*], -z
Clayton 'kleitn
clean (*s. adj. v.*), -s; -er, -est, -ly (*adv.*), -ness; -ing, -ed, -er/s kli:n, -z; -ə*, -ist, -li, -nis; -iŋ, -d, -ə*/z
clean-cut 'kli:n'kʌt [*also* '-- *when attributive*]

cleanl|y (adj.), -ier, -iest, -iness 'klenl|i, -iə* [-jə*], -iist [-jist], -inis

cleans|e, -es, -ing, -ed, -er/s; -able klenz, -iz, -iŋ, -d, -ə*/z; -əbl

clean-up, -s 'kli:n'ʌp ['--], -s

clear (adj. v.) (C.), -er, -est, -ly, -ness; -s, -ing, -ed kliə*, -rə*, -rist, -li, -nis; -z, -riŋ, -d

clearage 'kliəridʒ

clearance, -s 'kliərəns, -iz

clear-cut 'kliə'kʌt [also '-- when attributive]

clear-headed 'kliə'hedid [also '-,-- when attributive]

clearing-hou|se, -ses 'kliəriŋhau|s, -ziz

clear-sighted 'kliə'saitid [also '-,-- when attributive]

clear-sighted|ly, -ness 'kliə'saitid|li, -nis

clearstor|y, -ies 'kliəstər|i [-stɔ:r-], -iz

cleat, -s kli:t, -s

Cleather 'kleðə*

cleavage, -s 'kli:vidʒ, -iz

cleav|e, -es, -ing, -ed, clove, cleft, cloven kli:v, -z, -iŋ, -d, kləuv, kleft, 'kləuvn

cleaver (C.), -s 'kli:və*, -z

cleek (s. v.), -s, -ing, -ed kli:k, -s, -iŋ, -t

Cleethorpe, -s 'kli:θɔ:p, -s

clef, -s klef, -s

cleft (s.), -s kleft, -s

cleft (from cleave) kleft

cleg, -s kleg, -z

Clegg kleg

Cleishbotham 'kli:ʃbɔðəm

clematis 'klemətis [kli'meitis, klə'meit-, kle'meit-]

Clemence 'klemens

clemen|cy, -t/ly 'klemən|si, -t/li

Clemens 'klemənz

Clement, -s 'klemənt, -s

Clementi kli'menti [klə'm-]

Clementina ,klemən'ti:nə

Clementine 'kleməntain, -ti:n

clench, -es, -ing, -ed klentʃ, -iz, -iŋ, -t

Clendenin klen'denin

Cleo 'kliəu ['kli:-, 'kleiəu]

Cleobury (in Norfolk) 'klibəri ['kleb-]

Cleopatra kliə'pætrə [,kliəu'p-, -'pɑ:t-]

clepsydr|a, -ae 'klepsidr|ə [klep's-], -i:

clerestor|y, -ies 'kliəstər|i [-stɔ:r-], -iz

clergy 'klə:dʒi

clergy|man, -men 'klə:dʒi|mən, -mən

cleric (s. adj.), -s, -al/s, -ally 'klerik, -s, -əl/z, -əli

clerihew (C.) 'klerihju:

clerk (C.), -s klɑ:k, -s

Clerke klɑ:k

Clerkenwell 'klɑ:kənwəl [-wel]

clerkship, -s 'klɑ:kʃip, -s

Clermont (towns in Ireland, village in Norfolk) 'klɛəmɔnt [-mənt], (in U.S.A.) 'klɛəmɔnt, 'klə:mɔnt

Clery 'kliəri

Clevedon 'kli:vdən

Cleveland 'kli:vlənd

clever, -er, -est, -ly, -ness, -ish 'klevə*, -rə*, -rist, -li, -nis, -riʃ

Cleverdon 'klevədən

Cleves kli:vz

clew (s. v.), -s, -ing, -ed klu:, -z, -iŋ [kluiŋ], -d

cliché, -s 'kli:ʃei (kliʃe), -z

click (s. v.), -s, -ing, -ed klik, -s, -iŋ, -t

client, -s 'klaiənt, -s

clientèle, -s ,kli:ã:n'tel [-ɔ:n't-, -ɑ:n't-, -ɔ:n't-, -ɔn't-, -'teil] (kliãtɛl), -z

cliff, -s klif, -s

Cliff(e) klif

Clifford 'klifəd

cliffy 'klifi

clift, -s klift, -s

Clifton 'kliftən

climacteric, -s klai'mæktərik [,klai-mæk'terik], -s

climacterical ,klaimæk'terikəl

climactic, -al, -ally klai'mæktik, -əli, -əli

climate, -s 'klaimit, -s

climatic, -al, -ally klai'mætik, -əl, -əli

climatolog|ist/s, -y ,klaimə'tɔlədʒ|ist/s, -i

climax, -es 'klaimæks, -iz

climb (s. v.), -s, -ing, -ed, -er/s klaim, -z, -iŋ, -d, -ə*/z

clime, -s klaim, -z

clinch (C.), -es, -ing, -ed, -er/s klintʃ, -iz, -iŋ, -t, -ə*/z

cline, -s klain, -z

cling, -s, -ing, clung kliŋ, -z, -iŋ, klʌŋ

clingy 'kliŋi

clinic, -s, -al, -ally 'klinik, -s, -əl, -əli

clink (s. v.), -s, -ing, -ed kliŋk, -s, -iŋ, -t [kliŋt]

clinker, -s 'kliŋkə*, -z

clinomet|er/s, -ry klai'nɔmit|ə*/z [kli'n-], -ri

clinometric ,klainəu'metrik

clinquant 'kliŋkənt

Clinton 'klintən

Clio 'klaiəu

clip, -s, -ping, -ped klip, -s, -iŋ, -t

clipper, -s 'klipə*, -z

clippie, -s 'klipi, -z

clipping (s. adj.), -s 'klipiŋ, -z

clique, -s kli:k, -s

cliquish 'kli:kiʃ

cliqu|y, -ier, -iest, -iness 'kli:k|i, -iə*
[-jə*], -iist [-jist], -inis
Clissold 'klisəld [-səuld]
Clitheroe 'kliðərəu
Clive klaiv
Cliveden (in Bucks.) 'klivdən ['kli:v-]
cloac|a/s, -ae kləu'eik|ə/z, -i:
cloacal kləu'eikəl
cloak (s. v.) (C.), -s, -ing, -ed kləuk, -s,
-iŋ, -t
cloak-room, -s 'kləuk-rum [-ru:m], -z
Cloan kləun
clock, -s klɔk, -s
clock-face, -s 'klɔkfeis, -iz
clock-maker, -s 'klɔk,meikə*, -z
clock|wise, -work 'klɔk|waiz, -wə:k
clod, -s, -dy klɔd, -z, -i
clodhopp|er/s, -ing 'klɔd,hɔp|ə*/z, -iŋ
Cloete kləu'i:ti, 'klu:ti
clog (s. v.), -s, -ging, -ged klɔg, -z, -iŋ,
-d
clogg|y, -ier, -iest, -ily, -iness 'klɔg|i,
-iə*, -iist, -ili, -inis
Clogher 'klɔhə* ['klɔxə*], 'klɔ:ə*, klɔ:*
[klɔə*]
cloist|er (s. v.), -ers, -ering, -ered
'klɔist|ə*, -əz, -əriŋ, -əd
cloistral 'klɔistrəl
Clonbrock klɔn'brɔk
Clonmel klɔn'mel ['klɔnmel]
Cloomber 'klu:mbə*
close (s.) (enclosure, yard), -s kləus, -iz
close (s.) (end), -s kləuz, -iz
Close kləus
close (adj.), -r, -st, -ly, -ness kləus, -ə*,
-ist, -li, -nis
clos|e (v.), -es, -ing, -ed, -er/s kləuz, -iz,
-iŋ, -d, -ə*/z
close-fisted 'kləus'fistid ['kləus,f- when
attributive]
close-grained 'kləus'greind ['kləusg-
when attributive]
close-hauled 'kləus'hɔ:ld
close-season, -s 'kləus,si:zn, -z
closet (s. v.), -s, -ing, -ed 'klɔzit, -s, -iŋ,
-id
close-time, -s 'kləus-taim, -z
close-up (picture), -s 'kləusʌp ['kləus'ʌp],
closure, -s 'kləuʒə*, -z   [-s
clot (s. v.), -s, -ting, -ted klɔt, -s, -iŋ, -id
Cloten 'kləutn
cloth, -s klɔθ [klɔ:θ], klɔθs [klɔ:ðz, klɔ:θs]
Note.—The plural forms klɔ:ðz, klɔ:θs
are only used by those who
pronounce klɔ:θ in the singular.
The variant klɔ:θs is frequent in
the sense of 'kinds of cloth' but
not in the sense of 'pieces of cloth'.

cloth|e, -es, -ing, -ed, clad kləuð, -z, -iŋ,
-d, klæd
clothes (s.) kləuðz [old-fashioned kləuz]
clothes-basket, -s 'kləuðz,ba:skit [old-
fashioned 'kləuz-], -s
clothes-brush, -es 'kləuðzbrʌʃ [old-
fashioned 'kləuz-], -iz
clothes-horse, -s 'kləuðzhɔ:s [old-
fashioned 'kləuz-], -iz
clothes-line, -s 'kləuðzlain [old-fashioned
'kləuz-], -z
clothes-peg, -s 'kləuðzpeg [old-fashioned
'kləuz-], -z
clothier, -s 'kləuðiə* [-ðiə*, -ðjə*], -z
clothing (s.) 'kləuðiŋ
Clotho 'kləuθəu
cloth-yard, -s 'klɔθ'jɑ:d ['klɔ:θ-, also '--
when followed by a stress], -z
cloud (s. v.), -s, -ing, -ed klaud, -z, -iŋ,
-id
cloudberr|y, -ies 'klaud,ber|i, -iz
cloud-burst, -s 'klaudbə:st, -s
cloud-capt 'klaudkæpt
Cloudesley 'klaudzli
cloudless, -ly, -ness 'klaudlis, -li, -nis
cloud|y, -ier, -iest, -ily, -iness 'klaud|i
-iə* [-jə*], -iist [-jist], -ili, -inis
clough, -s klʌf, -s
Clough klʌf, klu:
Clouston 'klu:stən, 'klaustən
clout (s. v.), -s, -ing, -ed klaut, -s, -iŋ,
-id
clove (s.), -s kləuv, -z
clove (from, cleave), -n kləuv, -n
Clovelly klə'veli
cloven-footed 'kləuvn'futid ['kləuvn,f-]
clover, -s 'kləuvə*, -z
Clovis 'kləuvis
Clow (surname) kləu
Clowes (in Norfolk) klu:z, (surname)
klauz, klu:z
clown, -s klaun, -z
clownish, -ly, -ness 'klauniʃ, -li, -nis
cloy, -s, -ing, -ed klɔi, -z, -iŋ, -d
club (s. v.), -s, -bing, -bed klʌb, -z, -iŋ, -d
clubbable 'klʌbəbl
club-f|oot, -eet 'klʌb'f|ut ['--], -i:t
club-footed 'klʌb'futid ['-,--]
club-hou|se, ses 'klʌbhau|s ['-'-], -ziz
clubland 'klʌblænd
club-law 'klʌb'lɔ: ['--]
club|man. -men 'klʌb|mən [-mæn], -mən
[-men]
club-moss, -es 'klʌb'mɔs ['--], -iz
club-room, -s 'klʌb'rum [-'ru:m, '--], -z
club-shaped 'klʌbʃeipt
cluck (s. v.), -s, -ing, -ed klʌk, -s, -iŋ, -t
clue, -s klu:, -z

clump (s. v.), -s, -ing, -ed klʌmp, -s, -iŋ, -t [klʌmt]
clumpy 'klʌmpi
clums|y, -ier, -iest, -ily, -iness 'klʌmz|i, -ĭə* [-jə*], -iist [-jist], -ili, -inis
clunch klʌntʃ
clung (from cling) klʌŋ
Cluse klu:z, klu:s
clust|er (s. v.), -ers, -ering, -ered 'klʌst|ə*, -əz, -əriŋ, -əd
clutch (s. v.), -es, -ing, -ed klʌtʃ, -iz, -iŋ, -t
clutter, -s, -ing, -ed 'klʌtə*, -z, -riŋ, -d
Clutterbuck 'klʌtəbʌk
Clutton 'klʌtn
Clwyd 'klu:id (Welsh kluɨd)
Clyde, -bank klaid, -bæŋk
Clymene 'klimini [-məni]
clyp|eus, -ei 'klip|ĭəs, -iai
clyster, s- 'klistə*, -z
Clytemnestra ˌklaitim'nestrə [-ti:m-, -tem-]
Clytie (nymph in Greek mythology) 'klitii: ['klaiti:], (modern Christian name, chignon) 'klaiti [-ti:]
Cnidus 'naidəs ['kn-]
Cnut kə'nju:t
Co. kəu ['kʌmpəni]
coach (s. v.), -es, -ing, -ed kəutʃ, -iz, -iŋ, -t
coach-dog, -s 'kəutʃdɔg, -z
coach-horse, -s 'kəutʃhɔ:s, -iz
coach|man, -men 'kəutʃ|mən, -mən
coac|tion, -tive kəu'æk|ʃən, -tiv
coadjacent ˌkəuə'dʒeisnt
coadjutor, -s kəu'ædʒutə* [-dʒət-], -z
co-administrator, -s 'kəuəd'ministreitə*, -z
coagulat|e, -es, -ing, -ed kəu'ægjuleit, -s, -iŋ, -id
coagulation, -s kəuˌægju'leiʃən, -z
coal (s. v.), -s, -ing, -ed kəul, -z, -iŋ, -d
coal-bed, -s 'kəulbed, -z
coal-black 'kəul'blæk ['— when attributive]
coalesc|e, -es, -ing, -ed ˌkəuə'les, -iz, -iŋ, -t
coalescen|ce, -t ˌkəuə'lesn|s, -t
coal-field, -s 'kəul-fi:ld, -z
coal-gas 'kəulgæs ['-'-]
coal-heaver, -s 'kəulˌhi:və*, -z
coal-hole, -s 'kəulhəul, -z
coal-hou|se, -ses 'kəulhau|s, -ziz
coaling-station, -s 'kəuliŋˌsteiʃən, -z
coalite 'kəulait
coalition, -s ˌkəuə'liʃən, -z
coal|-man, -men 'kəul|mæn [-mən], -men [-mən]

coal-measure, -s 'kəulˌmeʒə*, -z
coal-mine, -s 'kəulmain, -z
coal-owner, -s 'kəulˌəunə*, -z
coal-pit, -s 'koul-pit, -s
coal-scuttle, -s 'kəulˌskʌtl, -z
coal-tar 'kəul'tɑ:* ['kəul-tɑ:* esp. when attributive]
coal-tit, -s 'kəul-tit, -s
coarse, -r, -st, -ly, -ness kɔ:s [kɔəs], -ə*, -ist, -li, -nis
coarse-grained 'kɔ:sgreind ['kɔəs-]
coars|en, -ens, -ening, -ened 'kɔ:s|n ['kɔəs-], -nz, -ɲiŋ [-niŋ], -nd
coast (s. v.), -s, -ing, -ed kəust, -s, -iŋ, -id
coaster, -s 'kəustə*, -z
coast-guard, -s 'kəusṭgɑ:d, -z
coast-line, -s 'kəust-lain, -z
coastwise 'kəust-waiz
coat (s. v.), -s, -ing, -ed kəut, -s, -iŋ, -id
Coatbridge 'kəutbridʒ
coatee, -s 'kəuti: ['kəu'ti:, kəu'ti:], -z
Coat(e)s kəuts
coat-hanger, -s 'kəut,hæŋə*, -z
coaᴛung, -s 'kəutiŋ, -z
coat-of-arms, coats-of-arms 'kəutəv-ˈɑ:mz, 'kəutsəv'ɑ:mz
coax (s. v.), -es, -ing/ly, -ed, -er/s kəuks, -iz, -iŋ/li, -t, -ə*/z
co-axial 'kəu'æksiəl [-sjəl]
cob, -s kɔb, -z
cobalt kəu'bɔ:lt [-'bolt, 'kəubɔ:lt]
Cobb, -ett kɔb, -it
cobb|le (s. v.), -les, -ling, -led, -ler/s 'kɔb|l, -lz, -liŋ [-liŋ], -ld, -lə*/z
cobbler's-wax 'kɔbləzwæks
cobble-stone, -s 'kɔblstəun, -z
Cobbold 'kɔbəuld [-bld]
Cobden 'kɔbdən
Cobh kəuv
Cobham 'kɔbəm
Coblenz (K-) kəu'blenṭs ['kəublenṭs]
cob-nut, -s 'kɔbnʌt, -s
cobra, -s 'kəubrə ['kɔ-], -z
Coburg (K-), -s 'kəubə:g, -z
cobweb, -s 'kɔbweb, -z
coca 'kəukə
cocaine kə'kein [kɔ'k-]
cocciferous kɔk'sifərəs
coc|cus, -ci 'kɔk|əs, -ai ['kɔksai]
coccyx, -es 'kɔksiks, -iz
Cochin (in India) 'kəutʃin ['kəu'tʃin]
Cochin-China 'kɔtʃin'tʃainə
cochineal 'kɔtʃini:l
cochl|ea, -eas, -eae 'kɔkl|ĭə, -ĭəz, -ii:
Cochran 'kɔkrən
Cochrane 'kɔkrin [-rən]
cock (s. v.), -s, -ing, -ed kɔk, -s, -iŋ, -t

cockade, -s kɔ'keid, -z
cock-a-doodle-doo 'kɔkədu:dl'du:
cock-a-hoop 'kɔkə'hu:p ['—]
Cockaigne kɔ'kein [kə'k-]
cockalorum, -s ˌkɔkə'lɔ:rəm, -z
cockatoo, -s ˌkɔkə'tu: ['kɔkə't-], -z
cockatrice, -s 'kɔkətrais [-tris], -iz
Cockburn 'kəubə:n
cockchafer, -s 'kɔkˌtʃeifə*, -z
Cockcroft 'kəukkrɔft, 'kɔkkrɔft
cock-cr|ow, -owing 'kɔkkr|əu, -əuiŋ
Cocke (place) kɔk, (surname) kəuk, kɔk
Cockell 'kɔkl
cocker (C.), -s 'kɔkə*, -z
cockerel, -s 'kɔkərəl, -z
Cockerell 'kɔkərəl
Cockermouth 'kɔkəməθ [-mauθ]
  Note.—Locally -məθ.
cock-eye, -d 'kɔkai, -d
cock-fight, -s, -ing 'kɔkfait, -s, -iŋ
Cockfosters 'kɔk'fɔstəz [-'—]
cock-horse, -s 'kɔk'hɔ:s ['—, also -'-
  when preceded by a stress], -iz
cock|le (s. v.) (C.), -les, -ling, -led 'kɔk|l,
  -lz, -liŋ [-liŋ], -ld
cockleshell, -s 'kɔkl|ʃel, -z
cockney (C.), -s 'kɔkni, -z
cockneyism, -s 'kɔkniizəm [-njiz-], -z
cock-pit, -s 'kɔkpit, -s
cockroach, -es 'kɔkrəutʃ, -iz
Cockroft 'kəu-krɔft ['kəuk-rɔft, kɔk-]
cockscomb, -s 'kɔkskəum, -z
Cocksedge 'kɔksidʒ [-sedʒ], 'kɔsidʒ,
  'kəusidʒ
Cockshott 'kɔkʃɔt
cock-sh|y, -ies 'kɔkʃ|ai, -aiz
Cockspur 'kɔkspə:* [-pə*]
cock-sure 'kɔk'ʃuə* [-'ʃɔə*, -'ʃɔ:*, -'ʃə:*,
  also -'- when preceded by a stress]
cocktail, -s 'kɔkteil, -z
Cockwood (in Devon) 'kɔkwud
  Note.—There exists also a local pronunciation 'kɔkud, which seems
  likely to become obsolete before long.
cock|y, -ier, -iest, -ily, -iness 'kɔk|i, -iə*,
  -iist, -ili, -inis
cocky-leeky 'kɔki'li:ki
Cocles 'kɔkli:z
coco, -s 'kəukəu, -z
cocoa, -s 'kəukəu, -z
coco(a)nut, -s 'kəukənʌt, -s
cocoon, -s kə'ku:n [kɔ'k-], -z
Cocytus kəu'saitəs
cod, -s kɔd, -z
Coddington 'kɔdiŋtən
codd|le, -les, -ling, -led 'kɔd|l, -lz, -liŋ
  [-liŋ], -ld
code, -s kəud, -z

codeine 'kəudi:n [-di:n]
cod|ex, -exes, -ices 'kəud|eks, -eksiz,
  -isi:z ['kɔdisi:z]
cod-fish|er/s, -ing 'kɔdˌfiʃ|ə*/z, -iŋ
cod-fisher|y, -ies 'kɔdˌfiʃər|i, -iz
codger, -s 'kɔdʒə*, -z
codicil, -s 'kɔdisil, -z
codicillary ˌkɔdi'siləri
Codicote 'kəudikəut
codification, -s ˌkɔdifi'keiʃən [ˌkəud-], -z
codi|fy, -fies, -fying, -fied 'kɔdi|fai
  ['kəud-], -faiz, -faiiŋ, -faid
codling, -s 'kɔdliŋ, -z
cod-liver-oil 'kɔdlivər'ɔil [-və'ɔil]
Codrington 'kɔdriŋtən
Cody 'kəudi
Coe kəu
co-ed 'kəu'ed
coeducation 'kəuˌedju(:)'keiʃən
coeducational 'kəuˌedju(:)'keiʃənl
  [-dʒu(:)-, -ʃnəl, -ʃnl̩, -ʃnl̩, -ʃənəl]
coefficient, -s ˌkəui'fiʃənt, -s
coelacanth, -s 'si:ləkænθ, -s
Coelesyria ˌsi:li'siriə
coemption kəu'empʃən
coenobite, -s 'si:nəubait, -s
coequ|al, -ally kəu'i:kw|əl, -əli
coequality ˌkəui(:)'kwɔliti
coerc|e, -es, -ing, -ed kəu'ə:s, -iz, -iŋ, -t
coercib|le, -ly kəu'ə:sib|l [-səb-], -li
coercion kəu'ə:ʃən
coercionist, -s kəu'ə:ʃnist [-ʃənist], -s
coercive, -ly kəu'ə:siv, -li
co-eternal ˌkəui(:)'tə:nl
Cœur de Lion ˌkə:də'li:ɔ̃:ŋ [-'li:ɔ:ŋ,
  -'li:ɔŋ] (kœrdəljɔ̃)
coeval kəu'i:vəl
co-executor, -s 'kəuig'zekjutə* [-eg-,
  -kjət-], -z
co-exist, -s, -ing, -ed 'kəuig'zist [-eg-],
  -s, -iŋ, -id
co-existen|ce, -t 'kəuig'zistəns [-eg-], -t
co-extend, -s, -ing, -ed 'kəuiks'tend
  [-ek-], -z, -iŋ, -id
co-extension, -s 'kəuiks'tenʃən [-ek-], -z
co-extensive 'kəuiks'tensiv [-ek-]
coffee, -s 'kɔfi, -z
coffee-bar, -s 'kɔfibɑ:*, -z
coffee-bean, -s 'kɔfibi:n ['—'-], -z
coffee-cup, -s 'kɔfikʌp, -s
coffee-hou|se, -ses 'kɔfihau|s, -ziz
coffee-mill, -s 'kɔfimil, -z
coffee-pot, -s 'kɔfipɔt, -s
coffee-room, -s 'kɔfirum [-ru:m], -z
coffer, -s 'kɔfə*, -z
coffin (s. v.) (C.), -s, -ing, -ed 'kɔfin, -z,
  -iŋ, -d
cog (s. v.), -s, -ging, -ged kɔg, -z, -iŋ, -d

cogen|ce, -cy, -t/ly 'kəudʒən|s, -si, -t/li
Coggeshall (in Essex) 'kɔgiʃəl, (surname) 'kɔgzɔːl
Coggin 'kɔgin
Coghill 'kɔgil [-hil]
cogitat|e, -es, -ing, -ed, -or/s 'kɔdʒiteit, -s, -iŋ, -id, -ə*/z
cogitation, -s ˌkɔdʒi'teiʃən, -z
cogitative 'kɔdʒitətiv [-teit-]
cognac, -s 'kɔnjæk ['kəun-] (kɔɲak), -s
cognate (s. adj.), -s 'kɔgneit, -s
cognation kɔg'neiʃən
cognition, -s kɔg'niʃən, -z
cognizable [-isa-] 'kɔgnizəbl ['kɔn-]
cognizan|ce [-isa-], -ces, -t 'kɔgnizən|s ['kɔn-], -siz, -t
cogniz|e [-is|e], -es, -ing, -ed kɔg'naiz ['--], -iz, -iŋ, -d
cognomen, -s kɔg'nəumen, -z
cognominal kɔg'nəuminl [-'nɔm-]
cognoscent|e, -i ˌkɔnjəu'ʃent|i [ˌkɔnəu-, ˌkɔgnəu-], -i: [-i]
cognovit, -s kɔg'nəuvit, -s
cogwheel, -s 'kɔgwiːl [-ghw-], -z
cohabit, -s, -ing, -ed kəu'hæbit, -s, -iŋ, -id
cohabitant, -s kəu'hæbitənt, -s
cohabitation ˌkəuhæbi'teiʃən [kəuˌhæ-]
co-heir, -s 'kəu'ɛə* ['kəuɛə*], -z
co-heiress, -es 'kəu'ɛəris, -iz
Cohen 'kəuin
coher|e, -es, -ing, -ed kəu'hiə*, -z, -riŋ, -d
coheren|ce, -cy, -t/ly kəu'hiərən|s, -si, -t/li
cohesion kəu'hiːʒən
cohesive, -ly, -ness kəu'hiːsiv, -li, -nis
Cohorn 'kəuhɔːn
cohort, -s 'kəuhɔːt, -s
coif (s. v.), -s, -ing, -ed kɔif, -s, -iŋ, -t
coiffé, -s, -ing, -d 'kwɑːfei ['kwæf-, 'kwɔf-] (kwafe), -z, -iŋ, -d
coiffeur, -s kwɑː'fəː* [kwæ'f-, kwɔ'f-] (kwafœːr), -z
coiffure, -s kwɑː'fjuə* [kwæ'f-, kwɔ'f-] (kwafyːr), -z
coign, -s kɔin, -z
coil (s. v.), -s, -ing, -ed kɔil, -z, -iŋ, -d
Coimbra kəu'imbrə
coin (s. v.), -s, -ing, -ed, -er/s kɔin, -z, -iŋ, -d, -ə*/z
coinage, -s 'kɔinidʒ, -iz
coincid|e, -es, -ing, -ed ˌkəuin'said, -z, -iŋ, -id
coinciden|ce, -ces, -t/ly kəu'insidən|s, -siz, -t/li
coincident|al, -ally kəuˌinsi'dent|l [ˌkəuin-], -əli
co-inheritor, -s 'kəuin'heritə*, -z

coir 'kɔiə*
coition kəu'iʃən
coitus 'kəuitəs
coke kəuk
Coke kəuk, kuk
    Note.—Members of the Essex family pronounce kuk. So also the present Earl of Leicester.
Coker 'kəukə*
col, -s kɔl, -z
Col. 'kəːnl
cola 'kəulə
colander, -s 'kʌləndə* ['kɔl-], -z
Colby 'kəulbi
Colchester 'kəultʃistə*
colchicum 'kɔltʃikəm [-lki-]
Colchis 'kɔlkis
Colcleugh 'kəulklu:
Colclough 'kəukli, 'kɔlklʌf, 'kəulklʌf
cold (s. adj.), -s, -er, -est, -ly, -ness kəuld, -z, -ə*, -ist, -li, -nis
cold-blooded, -ly, -ness 'kəuld'blʌdid [',-- when attributive], -li, -nis
cold-cream 'kəuld'kriːm
cold-hearted 'kəuld'hɑːtid ['-,--]
coldish 'kəuldiʃ
cold-shoulder, -s, -ing, -ed 'kəuld-'ʃəuldə*, -z, -riŋ, -d
Coldstream 'kəuldstriːm
cole (C.), -s kəul, -z
Colebrook(e) 'kəulbruk
Coleby 'kəulbi
Coleclough 'kəulklau
Coleford 'kəulfəd
Coleman 'kəulmən
Colenso kə'lenzəu
coleopter|a, -al ˌkɔli'ɔptər|ə, -əl
Coleraine kəul'rein
Coleridge 'kəulridʒ
Coles kəulz
Colet 'kɔlit
cole-tit, -s 'kəul-tit, -s
Colgate 'kɔlgeit ['kəul-, -git]
colic 'kɔlik
Colin, -dale 'kɔlin, -deil
Coling 'kəuliŋ
Coliseum ˌkɔli'siəm [-'siːəm]
colitis kɔ'laitis [kəu'l-]
collaborat|e, -es, -ing, -ed, -or/s kə'læbəreit [kɔ'l-], -s, -iŋ, -id, -ə*/z
collaboration, -s kəˌlæbə'reiʃən [kɔˌl-], -z
collaps|e (s. v.), -es, -ing, -ed kə'læps, -iz, -iŋ, -t
collapsible kə'læpsəbl [-sib-]
collar (s. v.), -s, -ing, -ed 'kɔlə*, -z, -riŋ, -d
collar-bone, -s 'kɔləbəun, -z
Collard 'kɔləd

Collas 'kɔləs
collat|e, -es, -ing, -ed, -or/s kɔ'leit [kə'l-], -s, -iŋ, -id, -ə*/z
collater|al/s, -ally kɔ'lætər|əl/z [kə'l-], -əli
collation, -s kɔ'leiʃən [kə'l-], -z
colleague, -s 'kɔli:g, -z
collect (s.), **-s** 'kɔlekt [-likt], -s
collect (v.), **-s, -ing, -ed, -er/s** kə'lekt, -s, -iŋ, -id, -ə*/z
collectanea ‚kɔlek'tɑːnjə [-'tein-, -nɪə]
collected (adj.), **-ly, -ness** kə'lektid, -li, -nis
collection, -s kə'lekʃən, -z
collective, -ly kə'lektiv, -li
collectivi|sm, -st/s kə'lektivi|zəm, -st/s
collector, -s kə'lektə*, -z
colleen, -s 'kɔli:n [in Ireland kɔ'li:n], -z
college, -s; -r/s 'kɔlidʒ, -iz; -ə*/z
collegian, -s kə'li:dʒən [kɔ'l-, -dʒɪən], -z
collegiate kə'li:dʒiit [kɔ'l-, -dʒjit, -dʒjət, -dʒɪət]
Collen 'kɔlin
Colles 'kɔlis
collet (C.), -s 'kɔlit, -s
collid|e, -es, -ing, -ed kə'laid, -z, -iŋ, -id
collie (C.), -s 'kɔli, -z
collier (C.), -s 'kɔlɪə* [-ljə*], -z
collier|y, -ies 'kɔljər|i, -iz
collimat|e, -es, -ing, -ed 'kɔlimeit, -s, -iŋ, -id
collimation ‚kɔli'meiʃən
collimator, -s 'kɔlimeitə*, -z
collinear kɔ'linjə* [kə'l-, 'kɔ'l-, -nɪə*]
Collingham 'kɔliŋəm
Collingwood 'kɔliŋwud
Collin|s, -son 'kɔlin|z, -sn
Collis 'kɔlis
collision, -s kə'liʒən, -z
collocat|e, -es, -ing, -ed 'kɔləukeit, -s, -iŋ, -id
collocation, -s ‚kɔləu'keiʃən, -z
collodion kə'ləudjən [-dɪən]
colloid, -s 'kɔlɔid, -z
collop, -s 'kɔləp, -s
colloquial, -ly, -ism/s kə'ləukwɪəl [-kwjəl], -i, -izəm/z
colloquium kə'ləukwɪəm
colloqu|y, -ies 'kɔləkw|i, -iz
collotype, -s 'kɔləutaip, -s
Colls kɔlz
collud|e, -es, -ing, -ed, -er/s kə'lu:d [kɔ'l-, -'lju:d], -z, -iŋ, -id, -ə*/z
collusion, -s kə'lu:ʒən [-'lju:-], -z
collusive, -ly kə'lu:siv [-'lju:-], -li
Collyns 'kɔlinz
collywobbles 'kɔli‚wɔblz
Colman 'kəulmən

Colmekill 'kəulmkil
Colnaghi kɔl'nɑːgi
Colnbrook 'kəulnbruk ['kəun-]
Colne kəun, kəuln
Colney 'kəuni
Cologne kə'ləun
Colombia, -n/s kə'lɔmbɪə [-'lʌm-, -bjə], -n/z
Colombo kə'lʌmbəu [-'lɔm-]
colon (punctuation mark), **-s** 'kəulən, -z
colon (intestine), **-s** 'kəulən [-lɔn], -z
Colon kɔ'lɔn
colonel, -s; -cy, -cies, -ship/s 'kəːnl, -z; -si, -siz, -ʃip/s
colonial (s. adj.), **-s** kə'ləunjəl [-nɪəl], -z
colonist, -s 'kɔlənist, -s
colonization [-isa-] ‚kɔlənai'zeiʃən [-ni'z-]
coloniz|e [-is|e], -es, -ing, -ed, -er/s 'kɔlənaiz, -iz, -iŋ, -d, -ə*/z
colonnade, -s ‚kɔlə'neid, -z
Colonus kə'ləunəs
colon|y, -ies 'kɔlən|i [-lŋ|i], -iz
colophon, -s 'kɔləfən [-fɔn], -z
Colorado ‚kɔlə'rɑːdəu
coloration ‚kʌlə'reiʃən
coloratura ‚kɔlərə'tuərə [-'tjuər-, -'tjəːr-]
colorific ‚kɔlə'rifik
colossal kə'lɔsl
Colosseum ‚kɔlə'siəm [-'siːəm]
Colossian, -s kə'lɔʃən [-ɔsɪən, -ɔsjən, -ɔʃɪən, -ɔʃjən], -z
coloss|us, -i kə'lɔs|əs, -ai
colour (s. v.), **-s, -ing, -ed** 'kʌlə*, -z, -riŋ, -d
colourab|le, -ly 'kʌlərəb|l, -li
colouration ‚kʌlə'reiʃən
colour-bar, -s 'kʌləbɑː*, -z
colour-blin|d, -dness 'kʌləblain|d ['kʌlə'b-], -dnis
colour|ful, -less 'kʌlə|ful, -lis
colour|man, -men 'kʌlə|mən [-mæn], -mən [-men]
colour-proc|ess, -esses 'kʌlə‚prəus|es [rarely -‚prɔs-], -esiz [-isiz]
colour-sergeant, -s 'kʌlə‚sɑːdʒənt, -s
colporteur, -s 'kɔl‚pɔːtə* [‚kɔlpɔː'təː*], -z
Colquhoun kə'huːn
Cols. 'kəːnlz
Colson 'kəulsn
Colston 'kəulstən
colt, -s kəult, -s
coltsfoot, -s 'kəultsfut, -s
coluber, -s 'kɔljubə*, -z
colubrine 'kɔljubrain
Columba kə'lʌmbə
columbarium, -s ‚kɔləm'bɛərɪəm, -z
Columbia, -n/s kə'lʌmbɪə [-bjə], -n/z

columbine, -s 'kɔləmbain, -z
Columbus kə'lʌmbəs
columell|a, -ae ˌkɔlju'mel|ə, -i:
column, -s, -ed 'kɔləm, -z, -d
column|al, -ar kə'lʌmn|l̩, -ə*
columnist, -s 'kɔləmnist [-əmist], -s
colure, -s kə'ljuə*, -z
Colwyn 'kɔlwin
Colyton 'kɔlitn
colza 'kɔlzə
coma (deep sleep), -s 'kəumə, -z
com|a (tuft), -as, -ae 'kəum|ə, -əz, -i:
Coma Berenices 'kəumə ˌberi'naisi:z
comatose 'kəumətəus
comb (s. v.), -s, -ing/s, -ed kəum, -z, -iŋ/z, -d
comb|at (s. v.), -ats, -ating, -ated 'kɔmb|ət ['kʌm-, -æt], -əts [-æts], -ətiŋ, -ətid
combatant, -s 'kɔmbətənt ['kʌm-], -s
combative, -ly, -ness 'kɔmbətiv ['kʌm-], -li, -nis
combe (C.), -s ku:m, -z
comber (combing machine), -s 'kəumə*, -z
comber (fish) (C.), -s 'kɔmbə*, -z
combination, -s; -room/s ˌkɔmbi'neiʃən, -z; -rum/z [-ru:m/z]
combinative 'kɔmbinətiv [-neit-]
combinatory 'kɔmbinətəri [ˌkɔmbi'neitəri]
combine (s.), -s 'kɔmbain [kəm'bain], -z
combin|e (v.), -es, -ing, -ed kəm'bain, -z, -iŋ, -d
combust kəm'bʌst
combustibility kəmˌbʌstə'biliti [-ti'b-, -lət-]
combustible, -ness kəm'bʌstəbl [-tib-], -nis
combustion, -s kəm'bʌstʃən, -z
com|e, -es, -ing, came kʌm, -z, -iŋ, keim
  Note.—The command Come on said to a dog or other animal is often pronounced 'kum'ɔn or kəm'ɔn instead of 'kʌm'ɔn.
come-at-able kʌm'ætəbl
come-back, -s 'kʌmbæk, -s
comedian, -s kə'mi:djən [-diən], -z
comédienne, -s kəˌmeidi'en [ˌkɔm-, kəˌmi:d-] (kɔmedjɛn), -z
come-down, -s 'kʌmdaun ['-'-], -z
comed|y, -ies 'kɔmid|i, -iz
comel|y, -ier, -iest, -iness 'kʌml|i, -iə* [-jə*], -iist [-jist], -inis
Comenius kə'meinjəs [kɔ'm-, -niəs]
comestible, -s kə'mestibl, -z
comet, -s; -ary 'kɔmit, -s; -əri

comfit, -s 'kʌmfit ['kɔm-], -s
comfort (s. v.), -s, -ing, -ed, -er/s 'kʌmfət, -s, -iŋ, -id, -ə*/z
comfortab|le, -ly 'kʌmfətəb|l̩, -li
comforter (scarf), -s 'kʌmfətə*, -z
comfortless 'kʌmfətlis
comfrey 'kʌmfri
comf|y, -ier, -iest, -ily, -iness 'kʌmf|i -iə* [-jə*], -iist [-jist], -ili, -inis
comic, -al, -ally, -alness 'kɔmik, -əl, -əli, -əlnis
Comin 'kʌmin
Cominform 'kɔminfɔ:m ['--'-]
Comintern 'kɔmintə:n ['--'-]
comity 'kɔmiti
comma, -s 'kɔmə, -z
Commager 'kɔmədʒə*
command (s. v.), -s, -ing/ly, -ed, -er/s kə'mɑ:nd, -z, -iŋ/li, -id, -ə*/z
commandant, -s ˌkɔmən'dænt [-'dɑ:nt, '---], -s
commandantship, -s ˌkɔmən'dænt-ʃip [-'dɑ:nt-], -s
commandeer, -s, -ing, -ed ˌkɔmən'diə*, -z, -riŋ, -d
commander-in-chief, commanders-in-chief kə'mɑ:ndərin'tʃi:f [-dəin-], kə'mɑ:ndəzin'tʃi:f
commandership, -s kə'mɑ:ndəʃip, -s
commandment, -s kə'mɑ:ndmənt, -s
commando, -(e)s kə'mɑ:ndəu, -z
commemorat|e, -es, -ing, -ed, -or/s kə'meməreit [-mur-], -s, -iŋ, -id, -ə*/z
commemoration, -s kəˌmemə'reiʃən [-mu'r-], -z
commemorative kə'memərətiv [-mur-, -reit-]
commenc|e, -es, -ing, -ed, -ement/s kə'mens, -iz, -iŋ, -t, -mənt/s
commend, -s, -ing, -ed kə'mend, -z, -iŋ, -id
commendab|le, -ly, -leness kə'mend-əb|l̩, -li, -lnis
commendation, -s ˌkɔmen'deiʃən [-mən-], -z
commendatory kɔ'mendətəri [kə'm-]
commensurability kəˌmenʃərə'biliti [-sjər-, -sjur-, -ʃur-, -lət-]
commensurab|le, -ly, -leness kə'men-ʃərəb|l̩ [-ʃur-, -sjər-, -sjur-], -li, -lnis
commensurate, -ly, -ness kə'menʃərit [-ʃur-, -sjər-, -sjur-], -li, -nis
comment (s.), -s 'kɔment, -s
comment (v.), -s, -ing, -ed 'kɔment [-mənt, rarely kɔ'ment, kə'ment], -s, -iŋ, -id
commentar|y, -ies 'kɔməntər|i, -iz

commentator, -s 'kɔmenteitə* [-mən-], -z

commerce 'kɔmə(:)s

commerci|al, -ally kə'mə:ʃ|əl, -əli [-l̩i]

commercialese kə,mə:ʃə'li:z

commerciali|sm, -st/s kə'mə:ʃəli|zəm [-ʃli-], -st/s

commerciality kə,mə:ʃi'æliti

commercializ|e [-is|e], -es, -ing, -ed kə'mə:ʃəlaiz [-ʃlaiz], -iz, -iŋ, -d

comminat|e, -es, -ing, -ed 'kɔmineit, -s, -iŋ, -id

commination, -s ,kɔmi'neiʃən, -z

comminatory 'kɔminətəri [-neit-]

comming|le, -les, -ling, -led kɔ'miŋg|l [kə'm-], -lz, -liŋ [-l̩iŋ], -ld

comminut|e, -es, -ing, -ed 'kɔminju:t, -s, -iŋ, -id

comminution ,kɔmi'nju:ʃən

commiserat|e, -es, -ing, -ed kə'mizəreit [kɔ'm-], -s, -iŋ, -id

commiseration kə,mizə'reiʃən [kɔ,m-]

commissar, -s ,kɔmi'sɑ:* ['---], -z

commissarial ,kɔmi'sɛərɪəl

commissariat ,kɔmi'sɛərɪət [-'sær-, -riæt]

commissar|y, -ies 'kɔmisər|i [kə'mis-], -iz

commissi|on (s. v.), -ons, -oning, -oned, -oner/s kə'miʃ|ən, -ənz, -n̩iŋ [-əniŋ], -ənd, -n̩ə*/z [-ənə*/z, -nə*/z]

commission-agent, -s kə'miʃn̩,eidʒənt [-ʃən,ei-], -s

commissionaire, -s kə,miʃə'nɛə* [-ʃn̩'ɛə*, -sjə'nɛə*], -z

commissure, -s 'kɔmisjuə* [-iʃuə*], -z

commit, -s, -ting, -ted, -ter/s, -ment/s kə'mit, -s, -iŋ, -id, -ə*/z, -mənt/s

committal, -s kə'mitl, -z

committee (council), -s kə'miti, -z

committee (of a lunatic), -s ,kɔmi'ti:, -z

committor, -s ,kɔmi'tɔ:*, -z

commix, -es, -ing, -ed kɔ'miks, -iz, -iŋ, -t

commode, -s kə'məud, -z

commodious, -ly, -ness kə'məudjəs [-dɪəs], -li, -nis

commodit|y, -ies kə'mɔdit|i, -iz

commodore, -s 'kɔmədɔ:* [-dɔə*], -z

common (s. adj.), -s; -er, -est, -ly, -ness 'kɔmən, -z; -ə*, -ist, -li, -nis

commonage 'kɔmənidʒ

commonalt|y, -ies 'kɔmən|t|i, [-nəl-], -iz

Commondale 'kɔməndeil

commoner, -s 'kɔmənə*, -z

common law 'kɔmənlɔ:

commonplace (s. adj.), -s 'kɔmənpleis, -iz [-z

common-room, -s 'kɔmənrum [-ru:m],

commons (C.) 'kɔmənz

commonwealth, -s 'kɔmənwelθ, -s

commotion, -s kə'məuʃən, -z

communal 'kɔmjunl [kə'mju:nl]

commune (s.), -s 'kɔmju:n, -z

commun|e (v.), -es, -ing, -ed kə'mju:n ['kɔmju:n], -z, -iŋ ['kɔmjuniŋ], -d

communicab|le, -ly, -leness kə'mju:ni-kəb|l [-'mjun-], -li, -lnis

communicant, -s kə'mju:nikənt [-'mjun-], -s

communicat|e, -es, -ing, -ed, -or/s kə'mju:nikeit [-'mjun-], -s, -iŋ, -id, -ə*/z

communication, -s kə,mju:ni'keiʃən [-,mjun-], -z

communicative, -ness kə'mju:nikətiv [-'mjun-, -keit-], -nis

communion, -s kə'mju:njən [-nɪən], -z

communiqué, -s kə'mju:nikei [kɔ'm-, -'mjun-] (kɔmynike), -z

communi|sm, -st/s 'kɔmjuni|zəm [-mju:n-, -mjən-], -st/s

communit|y, -ies kə'mju:nit|i, -iz

commutability kə,mju:tə'biliti [-lət-]

commutable kə'mju:təbl

commutation, -s ,kɔmju(:)'teiʃən, -z

commutative, -ly kə'mju:tətiv ['kɔm-ju(:)teitiv], -li

commutator, -s 'kɔmju(:)teitə*, -z

commut|e, -es, -ing, -ed, -er/s kə'mju:t [kɔ'm-], -s, -iŋ, -id, -ə*/z

Como 'kəuməu

Comont 'kəumɔnt

Comorin 'kɔmərin

comose 'kəuməus

compact (s.), -s 'kɔmpækt, -s

compact (adj. v.), -er, -est, -ly, -ness; -s, -ing, -ed kəm'pækt, -ə*, -ist, -li, -nis; -s, -iŋ, -id

companion, -s, -ship kəm'pænjən, -z, -ʃip

companionable, -ness kəm'pænjənəbl, -nis

companionate kəm'pænjənit

companion-way, -s kəm'pænjənwei, -z

compan|y, -ies 'kʌmpən|i, -iz

comparability ,kɔmpərə'biliti [-lət-]

comparab|le, -ly, -leness 'kɔmpərəb|l, -li, -lnis

comparative (s. adj.), -s, -ly kəm-'pærətiv, -z, -li

compar|e (s. v.), -es, -ing, -ed kəm'pɛə*, -z, -riŋ, -d

comparison, -s kəm'pærisn, -z

compartment, -s kəm'pɑ:tmənt, -s

compass (s. v.), -es, -ing, -ed 'kʌmpəs, -iz, -iŋ, -t

compassion kəm'pæʃən

compassionate, -ly, -ness kəm'pæʃənit [-ʃṇit, -ʃṇit], -li, -nis

compatibility kəm,pætə'biliti [-ti'b-, -lət-]

compatib|le, -ly, -leness kəm'pætəb|l [-tib-], -li, -lnis

compatriot, -s kəm'pætrɪət [kɔm-], -s

compeer, -s kɔm'pɪə* ['kɔmpɪə*], -z

compel, -s, -ling, -led; -lable kəm'pel, -z, -ɪŋ, -d; -əbl

compendious, -ly, -ness kəm'pendɪəs [-djəs], -li, -nis

compendium, -s kəm'pendɪəm [-djəm], -z

compensat|e, -es, -ing, -ed 'kɔmpenseit [-pən-], -s, -ɪŋ, -id

compensation, -s ,kɔmpen'seiʃən [-pən-], -z

compensative kəm'pensətiv ['kɔmpenseit-, 'kɔmpənseit-]

compensatory kəm'pensətəri ['kɔmpenseitəri, 'kɔmpənseitəri]

comper|e (s. v.), -es, -ing, -ed 'kɔmpɛə*, -z, -rɪŋ, -d

compet|e, -es, -ing, -ed kəm'piːt, -s, -ɪŋ, -id

competen|ce, -cy, -t/ly 'kɔmpitən|s, -si, -t/li

competition, -s ,kɔmpi'tiʃən, -z

competitive kəm'petitiv [-tət-]

competitor, -s kəm'petitə*, -z

compilation, -s ,kɔmpi'leiʃən [-pai'l-], -z

compil|e, -es, -ing, -ed, -er/s kəm'pail, -z, -ɪŋ, -d, -ə*/z

complacen|ce, -cy, -t/ly kəm'pleisn|s, -si, -t/li

complain, -s, -ing, -ed, -er/s kəm'plein, -z, -ɪŋ, -d, -ə*/z

complainant, -s kəm'pleinənt, -s

complaint, -s kəm'pleint, -s

complaisan|ce, -t/ly kəm'pleizən|s, -t/li

complement (s.), -s 'kɔmplimənt, -s

complement (v.), -s, -ing, -ed 'kɔmpliment [,kɔmpli'ment], -s, -ɪŋ, -id

complement|al, -ary ,kɔmpli'ment|l, -əri

complet|e (adj. v.), -est, -ely -eness; -es, -ing, -ed kəm'pliːt, -ist, -li, -nis; -s, -ɪŋ, -id

completion kəm'pliːʃən

complex (s. adj.), -es 'kɔmpleks, -iz

complexion, -s, -ed kəm'plekʃən, -z, -d

complexit|y, -ies kəm'pleksit|i [kɔm-], -iz

complian|ce, -ces, -t/ly kəm'plaiən|s, -siz, -t/li

complicat|e, -es, -ing, -ed 'kɔmplikeit, -s, -ɪŋ, -id

complication, -s ,kɔmpli'keiʃən, -z

complicity kəm'plisiti [kɔm-]

compliment (s.), -s 'kɔmplimənt, -s

compliment (v.), -s, -ing, -ed 'kɔmpliment [,kɔmpli'ment], -s, -ɪŋ, -id

complimentar|y (s. adj.), -ies ,kɔmpli'mentər|i, -iz

complin, -s 'kɔmplin, -z

compline, -s 'kɔmplin [-lain], -z

compl|y, -ies, -ying, -ied kəm'pl|ai, -aiz, -aiɪŋ, -aid

compo 'kɔmpəu

component, -s kəm'pəunənt, -s

comport, -s, -ing, -ed, -ment kəm'pɔːt, -s, -ɪŋ, -id, -mənt

compos|e, -es, -ing, -ed, -er/s kəm'pəuz, -iz, -ɪŋ, -d, -ə*/z

compos|ed (adj.), -edly, -edness kəm'pəuz|d, -idli, -idnis

composite, -ly, -ness 'kɔmpəzit [-sit, -zait, -sait], -li, -nis

composition, -s ,kɔmpə'ziʃən, -z

compositor, -s kəm'pɔzitə*, -z

compost, -s 'kɔmpost, -s

composure kəm'pəuʒə*

compote, -s 'kɔmpot [-pəut] (kɔ̃pɔt), -s

compound (s. adj.), -s 'kɔmpaund, -z

compound (v.), -s, -ing, -ed kəm'paund [kɔm-], -z, -ɪŋ, -id

comprehend, -s, -ing, -ed ,kɔmpri'hend, -z, -ɪŋ, -id

comprehensibility 'kɔmpri,hensə'biliti [,kɔm-, -si'b-, -lət-]

comprehensib|le, -ly, -leness ,kɔmpri'hensəb|l [-sib-], -li, -lnis

comprehension ,kɔmpri'henʃən

comprehensive, -ly, -ness ,kɔmpri'hensiv, -li, -nis

compress (s.), -es 'kɔmpres, -iz

compress (v.), -es, -ing, -ed, -or/s kəm'pres, -iz, -ɪŋ, -t, -ə*/z

compressibility kəm,presi'biliti [-sə'b-, -lət-]

compressible, -ness kəm'presəbl [-sib-], -nis

compression, -s kəm'preʃən, -z

compressive kəm'presiv

compris|e, -es, -ing, -ed; -able kəm'praiz, -iz, -ɪŋ, -d; -əbl

compromis|e (s. v.), -es, -ing, -ed, -er/s 'kɔmprəmaiz [-prum-], -iz, -ɪŋ, -d, -ə*/z

comptometer, -s kɔmp'tɔmitə*, -z

Compton 'kɔmptən, 'kʌm-

   Note.—As surname more often 'kʌm-; as place-name more often 'kɔm-; London street generally 'kɔm-.

comptroller, -s kən'trəulə*, -z

compulsion kəm'pʌlʃən
compulsor|y, -ily kəm'pʌlsər|i, -ili
compunction kəm'pʌŋkʃən
compunctious kəm'pʌŋkʃəs
compurgation ‚kɔmpəː'geiʃən
compurgator, -s 'kɔmpəːgeitə*, -z
computable kəm'pjuːtəbl ['kɔmpjutəbl]
computation, -s ‚kɔmpju(ː)'teiʃən, -z
computator, -s 'kɔmpju(ː)teitə*, -z
comput|e, -es, -ing, -ed, -er/s kəm'pjuːt,
  -s, -iŋ, -id, -ə*/z
computist, -s kəm'pjuːtist, -s
comrade, -s, -ship 'kɔmrid ['kʌmrid,
  'kɔmreid], -z, -ʃip
Comte kɔ̃ːnt [kɔːnt] (kɔ̃ːt)
Comti|sm, -st/s 'kɔ̃ːnti|zəm ['kɔːnt-],
  -st/s
Comus 'kəuməs
Comyn 'kʌmin
con (s. v.), -s, -ning, -ned kɔn, -z, -iŋ, -d
Conan (personal name) 'kəunən, 'kɔnən,
  (place in Scotland) 'kɔnən
  Note.—The members of the family of
  Sir Arthur Conan Doyle pronounce
  'kəunən.
Conant 'kɔnənt
conation kəu'neiʃən
conative 'kəunətiv
concatenat|e, -es, -ing, -ed kɔn'kætineit
  [kən-], -s, -iŋ, -id
concatenation, -s kɔn‚kæti'neiʃən [kən-,
  ‚kɔnkæt-], -z
concave 'kɔn'keiv ['kɔnkeiv, 'kɔŋk-,
  kɔn'k-]
  Note.—The form kɔn'keiv is not used
  attributively.
concavit|y, -ies kɔn'kævit|i [kən-], -iz
conceal, -s, -ing, -ed, -ment/s; -able
  kən'siːl, -z, -iŋ, -d, -mənt/s; -əbl
conced|e, -es, -ing, -ed kən'siːd, -z, -iŋ,
  -id
conceit, -s kən'siːt, -s
conceited, -ly, -ness kən'siːtid, -li, -nis
conceivab|le, -ly, -leness kən'siːvəb|l, -li,
  -lnis
conceiv|e, -es, -ing, -ed kən'siːv, -z, -iŋ,
  -d
concent kən'sent [kɔn-]
concentrat|e, -es, -ing, -ed 'kɔnsəntreit
  [-sin-, -sen-], -s, -iŋ, -id
concentration, -s ‚kɔnsən'treiʃən [-sin-,
  -sen-], -z
concentrative 'kɔnsəntreitiv [-sin-,
  -sen-]
concent|re, -res, -ring, -ering, -red kɔn-
  'sent|ə*, -əz, -riŋ, -əriŋ, -əd
concentric, -ally kɔn'sentrik [kən-], -əli
concept, -s 'kɔnsept, -s

conception, -s kən'sepʃən, -z
conceptual kən'septjuəl [-tjwəl, -tʃuəl]
concern (s. v.), -s, -ing, -ed, -ment/s
  kən'səːn, -z, -iŋ, -d, -mənt/s
concern|ed (adj.), -edly, -edness kən-
  'səːn|d, -idli, -idnis
concert (s.) (musical entertainment),
  -s 'kɔnsət, -s
concert (C.) (union), -s 'kɔnsə(ː)t, -s
concert (v.), -s, -ing, -ed kən'səːt, -s, -iŋ,
  -id
concertina, -s ‚kɔnsə'tiːnə, -z
concerto, -s kən'tʃəːtəu [-'tʃɛət-], -z
concession, -s kən'seʃən, -z
concessionaire, -s kən‚seʃə'nɛə* [-ʃn'ɛə*]
  -z
concessionary kən'seʃnəri [-ʃənə-]
concessive kən'sesiv
conch, -s kɔntʃ, -iz [kɔŋk, -s]
concha, -s 'kɔŋkə, -z
conchoid, -s 'kɔŋkɔid, -z
concholog|ist/s, -y kɔŋ'kɔlədʒ|ist/s
  [kɔn'k], -i
concierge, -s ‚kɔ̃ːnsi'ɛəʒ [‚kɔːns-, ‚kɔns-,
  '---] (kɔ̃sjɛrʒ), -iz
conciliat|e, -es, -ing, -ed -or/s kən-
  'silieit, -s, -iŋ, -id, -ə*/z
conciliation kən‚sili'eiʃən
conciliative kən'siliətiv [-ljət-, -lieit-]
conciliatory kən'siliətəri [-ljə-, -lieitəri]
concise, -r, -st, -ly, -ness kən'sais, -ə*,
  -ist, -li, -nis
concision, -s kən'siʒən, -z
conclave, -s 'kɔnkleiv ['kɔŋk-], -z
conclud|e, -es, -ing, -ed kən'kluːd
  [kəŋ'k-], -z, -iŋ, -id
conclusion, -s kən'kluːʒən [kəŋ'k-], -z
conclusive, -ly, -ness kən'kluːsiv
  [kəŋ'k-], -li, -nis
concoct, -s, -ing, -ed, -er/s kən'kɔkt
  [kəŋ'k-], -s, -iŋ, -id, -ə*/z
concoction, -s kən'kɔkʃən [kəŋ'k-], -z
concomitan|ce, -cy, -t/ly kən'kɔmitən|s,
  -si, -t/li
concord (s.), -s 'kɔŋkɔːd ['kɔnk-], -z
concord (v.), -s, -ing, -ed kən'kɔːd
  [kəŋ'k-], -z, -iŋ, -id
concordan|ce, -ces, -t/ly kən'kɔːdən|s
  [kəŋ'k-], -siz, -t/li
concordat, -s kɔn'kɔːdæt [kən'k-, kəŋ'k-],
  -s
concourse, -s 'kɔŋkɔːs ['kɔnk-, -kɔəs],
  -iz
concrete (s. adj.) 'kɔnkriːt ['kɔŋk-]
concret|e (v.) (cover with concrete), -es,
  -ing, -ed 'kɔnkriːt ['kɔŋk-], -s, -iŋ, -id
concret|e (v.) (coalesce, cause to coalesce),
  -es, -ing, -ed kən'kriːt [kəŋ'k-], -s,
  -iŋ, -id

concrete|ly, -ness 'kɔnkri:t|li ['kɔŋk-,
  kɔn'k-], -nis
concretion, -s kən'kri:ʃən [kəŋ-, kɔn-], -z
concretiz|e (-is|e), -es, -ing, -ed 'kɔn-
  kri(:)taiz ['kɔŋk-], -iz, -iŋ, -d
concubinage kɔn'kju:binidʒ [kən-]
concubine, -s 'kɔŋkjubain ['kɔnk-], -z
concupiscen|ce,   -t   kən'kju:pisən|s
  [,kɔnkju(:)'p-], -t
concur, -s, -ring, -red kən'kə:* [kəŋ'k-],
  -z, -riŋ, -d
concurren|ce,   -cy,   -t/ly kən'kʌrən|s
  [kəŋ'k-], -si, -t/li
concuss, -es, -ing, -ed kən'kʌs [kəŋ'k-],
  -iz, -iŋ, -t
concussion, -s kən'kʌʃən [kəŋ'k-], -z
concyclic kɔn'saiklik [kən-]
condemn, -s, -ing, -ed; -able kən'dem,
  -z, -iŋ, -d; -nəbl
condemnation,   -s   ,kɔndem'neiʃən
  [-dəm-], -z
condemnatory kən'demnətəri
condensation, -s ,kɔnden'seiʃən [-dən-],
  -z
condens|e, -es, -ing, -ed; -able kən-
  'dens, -iz, -iŋ, -t; -əbl
condenser, -s kən'densə*, -z
condescend, -s, -ing, -ed ,kɔndi'send, -z,
  -iŋ, -id
condescension ,kɔndi'senʃən
condign, -ly, -ness kən'dain, -li, -nis
condiment, -s 'kɔndimənt, -s
conditi|on (s. v.), -ons, -oning, -oned
  kən'diʃ|ən, -ənz, -ɲiŋ [-əniŋ, -niŋ],
  -ənd
condi|tional, -tionally kən'diʃənl [-ʃnəl,
  -ʃɲl, -ʃnl, -ʃənəl], -ʃɲəli [-ʃnəli, -ʃɲli,
  -ʃɲli, -ʃənəli]
condol|e, -es, -ing, -ed, -ement/s kən-
  'dəul, -z, -iŋ, -d, -mənt/s
condolence, -s kən'dəuləns ['kɔndələns],
  -iz
condolent kən'dəulənt
condominium, -s 'kɔndə'miniəm [,kɔn-,
  -njəm], -z
condonation, -s ,kɔndəu'neiʃən, -z
condon|e, -es, -ing, -ed kən'dəun, -z,
  -iŋ, -d
condor, -s 'kɔndɔ:* [-də*], -z
conduc|e, -es, -ing, -ed, -ement/s
  kən'dju:s, -iz, -iŋ, -t, -mənt/s
conducive, -ly, -ness kən'dju:siv, -li, -nis
conduct (s.), -s 'kɔndʌkt [-dəkt], -s
conduct (v.), -s, -ing, -ed, -or/s kən-
  'dʌkt, -s, -iŋ, -id, -ə*/z
conductibility kən,dʌkti'biliti [-tə'b-,
  -lət-]
conductible kən'dʌktəbl [-tib-]

conduction kən'dʌkʃən
conductive kən'dʌktiv
conductivity ,kɔndʌk'tiviti [-dək-]
conductress, -es kən'dʌktris, -iz
conduit, -s 'kɔndit [old-fashioned 'kʌndit,
  as an electrical term also 'kɔndjuit and
  'kɔndwit], -s
Conduit (Street) 'kɔndit ['kʌn-]
Condy 'kɔndi
condyle, -s 'kɔndil [-dail], -z
cone, -s kəun, -z
coney (C.), -s 'kəuni, -z
confab, -s 'kɔnfæb [kɔn'fæb], -z
confabulat|e, -es, -ing, -ed kən'fæbju-
  leit [kɔn-], -s, -iŋ, -id
confabulation, -s kən,fæbju'leiʃən [kɔn-],
  -z
confect (s.), -s 'kɔnfekt, -s
confect (v.), -s, -ing, -ed kən'fekt, -s,
  -iŋ, -id
confecti|on (s. v.), -ons, -oning, -oned,
  -oner/s kən'fekʃ|ən, -ənz, -ɲiŋ [-əniŋ],
  -ənd, -nə*/z [-ɲə*/z, -ənə*/z]
confectionery   kən'fekʃɲəri [-ʃənəri,
  -ʃnəri, -ʃənri]
confederac|y, -ies kən'fedərəs|i, -iz
confederate (s. adj.), -s kən'fedərit, -s
confederat|e (v.), -es, -ing, -ed kən-
  'fedəreit, -s, -iŋ, -id
confederation, -s kən,fedə'reiʃən, -z
confer, -s, -ring, -red; -able kən'fə:*,
  -z, -riŋ, -d; -rəbl
conference, -s 'kɔnfərəns, -iz
confess, -es, -ing, -ed, -edly, -or/s
  kən'fes, -iz, -iŋ, -t, -idli, -ə*/z
  Note.—Some Catholics pronounce
  confessor as 'kɔnfesə* or 'kɔnfesə:*.
confession, -s kən'feʃən, -z
confessional, -s kən'feʃənl [-ʃnəl, -ʃɲl,
  -ʃnl, -ʃənəl], -z
confetti kən'feti(:) [kɔn-]
confidant(e), -s ,kɔnfi'dænt ['kɔnfidænt]
  -s
confid|e, -es, -ing/ly, -ed, -er/s kən-
  'faid, -z, -iŋ/li, -id, -ə*/z
confiden|ce, -ces, -t/ly 'kɔnfidən|s,
  -siz, -t/li
confidenti|al, -ally ,kɔnfi'denʃ|əl, -əli
configuration,   -s   kən,figju'reiʃən
  [,kɔnfig-, -gjuə'r-, -gjə'r-], -z
confine (s.) 'kɔnfain, -z
confin|e (v.), -es, -ing, -ed, -ement/s
  kən'fain, -z, -iŋ, -d, -mənt/s
confirm, -s, -ing, -ed, -er/s kən'fə:m, -z,
  -iŋ, -d, -ə*/z
confirmation, -s ,kɔnfə'meiʃən [-fɲ'ei-],
  -z

confirmat|ive, -ory kən'fə:mət|iv, -əri
confiscable kɔn'fiskəbl [kən-]
confiscat|e, -es, -ing, -ed, -or/s 'kɔn-
fiskeit, -s, -iŋ, -id, -ə*/z
confiscation, -s ˌkɔnfis'keiʃən, -z
confiscatory   kən'fiskətəri   [kɔn'f-,
'kɔnfiskeitəri]
confiserie, -s kɔn'fi:zəri: [-ri], -z
confiteor, -s kɔn'fitiɔ:* [kən-], -z
conflagration, -s ˌkɔnflə'greiʃən, -z
conflict (s.), -s 'kɔnflikt, -s
conflict (v.), -s, -ing, -ed kən'flikt, -s,
-iŋ, -id
confluen|ce, -ces, -t/ly, -t/s 'kɔnflūən|s
[-flwən-], -siz, -t/li, -t/s
conform, -s, -ing, -ed, -er/s kən'fɔ:m,
-z, -iŋ, -d, -ə*/z
conformability kənˌfɔ:mə'biliti [-lət-]
conformab|le, -ly kən'fɔ:məb|l, -li
conformation, -s ˌkɔnfɔ:'meiʃən [-fə'm-],
-z
conformist, -s kən'fɔ:mist, -s
conformit|y, -ies kən'fɔ:mit|i, -iz
confound, -s, -ing, -ed/ly kən'faund
[as oath also 'kɔn'faund], -z, -iŋ, -id/li
confraternit|y, -ies ˌkɔnfrə'tə:nit|i, -iz
confrère, -s 'kɔnfrɛə* (kɔ̃frɛ:r), -z
confront, -s, -ing, -ed kən'frʌnt, -s, -iŋ,
-id
Confucian, -s kən'fju:ʃjən [-ʃiən, -ʃən], -z
Confuciani|sm, -st/s kən'fju:ʃjəni|zəm
[-ʃiəni-, -ʃəni-, -ʃni-], -st/s
Confucius kən'fju:ʃjəs [-ʃiəs, -ʃəs]
confus|e, -es, -ing, -ed, -edly, -edness
kən'fju:z, -iz, -iŋ, -ed, -idli, -idnis
confusion, -s kən'fju:ʒən, -z
confutable kən'fju:təbl
confutation, -s ˌkɔnfju:'teiʃən [-fju't-], -z
confut|e, -es, -ing, -ed kən'fju:t, -s, -iŋ,
-id
conga, -s 'kɔŋgə, -z
congé, -s 'kɔ̃:nʒei ['kɔ:nʒ-, 'kɔnʒ-]
(kɔ̃ʒe), -z
congeal, -s, -ing, -ed; -able kən'dʒi:l,
-z, -iŋ, -d; -əbl
congee, -s 'kɔndʒi:, -z
congelation ˌkɔndʒi'leiʃən
congener, -s 'kɔndʒinə* [kən'dʒi:n-], -z
congenial, -ly kən'dʒi:njəl [-niəl], -i
congeniality kənˌdʒi:ni'æliti
congenit|al, -ally kən'dʒenit|l [kɔn-],
-əli [-l̥i]
conger, -s 'kɔŋgə*, -z
conger-eel, -s 'kɔŋgər'i:l [-gə'i:l], -z
congeries kɔn'dʒiəri:z [-'dʒiəriz, -'dʒiə-
rii:z, -'dʒerii:z, 'kɔndʒəriz]
congest, -s, -ing, -ed; -ive kən'dʒest, -s,
-iŋ, -id; -iv

congestion, -s kən'dʒestʃən [-eʃtʃ-], -z
Congleton 'kɔŋgltən
conglobat|e (adj. v.), -es, -ing, -ed
'kɔngləubeit ['kɔŋg-], -s, -iŋ, -id
conglobation ˌkɔngləu'beiʃən [ˌkɔŋg-]
conglomerate (s. adj.), -s kən'glɔmərit
[kəŋ-, kɔn-], -s
conglomerat|e (v.), -es, -ing, -ed kən-
'glɔməreit [kəŋ-, kɔn-], -s, -iŋ, -id
conglomeration,   -s   kənˌglɔmə'reiʃən
[kɔnˌglɔm-, ˌkəŋglɔm-, ˌkɔŋglɔm-], -z
Congo 'kɔŋgəu
Congolese ˌkɔŋgəu'li:z
congratulat|e, -es, -ing, -ed, -or/s kən-
'grætjuleit [kəŋ'g-, -tʃul-, -tʃəl-], -s,
-iŋ, -id, -ə*/z
congratulation,   -s   kənˌgrætju'leiʃən
[kəŋˌg-, -tʃu'l-, -tʃə'l-], -z
congratulatory kən'grætjulətəri [kəŋ'g-,
-tʃul-, -tʃəl-, -leitəri]
congregat|e, -es, -ing, -ed 'kɔŋgrigeit,
-s, -iŋ, -id
congregation, -s ˌkɔŋgri'geiʃən, -z
congregational   ˌkɔŋgri'geiʃənl   [-ʃnəl,
-ʃn̥l, -ʃn̩l, -ʃənəl]
congregationali|sm, -st/s ˌkɔŋgri'gei-
ʃnəli|zəm[-ʃn̥əli-,-ʃn̥li-,-ʃn̩li-,-ʃənəli-],
-st/s
congress, -es 'kɔŋgres, -iz
congressional kəŋ'greʃənl [kɔŋ-, -ʃnəl,
-ʃn̥l, -ʃn̩l, -ʃənəl]
congress|man, -men 'kɔŋgres|mən, -mən
[-men]
Congreve 'kɔŋgri:v
congruen|ce/s, -cy, -cies, -t/ly 'kɔŋ-
grūən|s/iz [-grwən-], -si, -siz, -t/li
congruit|y, -ies kɔŋ'gru(:)it|i [kən-,
kəŋ-], -iz
congruous, -ly, -ness 'kɔŋgrūəs [-grwəs],
-li, -nis
conic, -s, -al, -ally, -alness 'kɔnik, -s, -əl,
-əli, -əlnis
conifer, -s 'kəunifə* ['kɔn-], -z
coniferous kəu'nifərəs
coniform 'kəunifɔ:m
Coningham 'kʌniŋəm
Conisbee 'kɔnisbi
Conisbrough 'kɔnisbrə, 'kʌn-
Coniston 'kɔnistən
conjecturable kən'dʒektʃərəbl
conjectur|al,   -ally   kən'dʒektʃər|əl
[-tʃur-], -əli
conject|ure (s. v.), -ures, -uring, -ured
kən'dʒektʃ|ə*, -əz, -əriŋ, -əd
conjoin, -s, -ing, -ed kən'dʒɔin [kɔn-]
-z, -iŋ, -d
conjoint,   -ly   'kɔndʒɔint   ['kɔn'dʒ-,
kɔn'dʒ-, kən'dʒ-], -li

conjug|al, -ally 'kɔndʒug|əl [-dʒəg-],
  -əli
conjugality ˌkɔndʒu'gæliti
conjugate (s. adj.), -s 'kɔndʒugit
  [-dʒəg-, -geit], -s
conjugat|e (v.), -es, -ing, -ed 'kɔndʒu-
  geit [-dʒəg-], -s, -iŋ, -id
conjugation, -s ˌkɔndʒu'geiʃən [-dʒə'g-],
  -z
conjunct, -ly kən'dʒʌŋkt [kɔn'dʒ-,
  'kɔn'dʒ-, 'kɔndʒ-], -li
conjunction, -s kən'dʒʌŋkʃən, -z
conjunctiva ˌkɔndʒʌŋk'taivə
conjunctive, -ly kən'dʒʌŋktiv, -li
conjunctivitis kənˌdʒʌŋkti'vaitis
conjuncture, -s kən'dʒʌŋktʃə*, -z
conjuration, -s ˌkɔndʒuə'reiʃən, -z
conjur|e (charge solemnly), -es, -ing, -ed
  kən'dʒuə*, -z, -riŋ, -d
conj|ure (invoke a spirit, do things as
  if by magic), -ures, -uring, -ured,
  -urer/s, -uror/s 'kʌndʒ|ə*, -əz, -əriŋ,
  -əd, -ərə*/z, -ərə*/z
conk, -s kɔŋk, -s
Conn. (1) = Connecticut, (2) = Connaught
Connally 'kɔnəli
connate 'kɔneit
Connaught 'kɔnɔːt
connect, -s, -ing, -ed/ly kə'nekt, -s, -iŋ,
  -id/li
connectible kə'nektəbl [-tib-]
Connecticut kə'netikət
connection, -s kə'nekʃən, -z
connective (s. adj.), -s, -ly kə'nektiv,
  -z, -li
Connemara ˌkɔni'mɑːrə
connexion, -s kə'nekʃən, -z
Connie 'kɔni
conning-tower, -s 'kɔniŋˌtauə*, -z
connivance kə'naivəns
conniv|e, -es, -ing, -ed kə'naiv, -z, -iŋ,
  -d
connoisseur, -s ˌkɔnə'sə:* [ˌkɔni-,
  -'sjuə*], -z
Connolly 'kɔnəli
Connor 'kɔnə*
connotat|e, -es, -ing, -ed 'kɔnəuteit, -s,
  -iŋ, -id
connotation, -s ˌkɔnəu'teiʃən, -z
connotative 'kɔnəuteitiv [kə'nəutətiv]
connot|e, -es, -ing, -ed kɔ'nəut [kə'n-],
  -s, -iŋ, -id
connubial, -ly kə'nju:bjəl [kɔ'n-, -bïəl], -i
connubiality kəˌnju:bi'æliti [kɔˌn-]
conoid, -s 'kəunɔid, -z
conoidal kəu'nɔidl
Conolly 'kɔnəli

conqu|er, -ers, -ering, -ered, -eror/s;
  -erable 'kɔŋk|ə*, -əz, -əriŋ, -əd,
  -ərə*/z; -ərəbl
conquest (C.), -s 'kɔŋkwest, -s
Conrad 'kɔnræd
consanguine kɔn'sæŋgwin
consanguin|eous, -ity ˌkɔnsæŋ'gwin|ïəs,
  -iti
conscience, -s 'kɔnʃəns, -iz
conscientious, -ly, -ness ˌkɔnʃi'enʃəs
  [kɔn'ʃjen-], -li, -nis
conscionab|le, -ly, -leness 'kɔnʃŋəb|l
  [-ʃnə-, -ʃənə-], -li, -lnis
conscious, -ly, -ness 'kɔnʃəs, -li, -nis
conscrib|e, -es, -ing, -ed kən'skraib, -z,
  -iŋ, -d
conscript (s.), -s 'kɔnskript, -s
conscript (v.), -s, -ing, -ed kən'skript,
  -s, -iŋ, -id
conscription, -s kən'skripʃən, -z
consecrat|e, -es, -ing, -ed, -or/s 'kɔnsi-
  kreit, -s, -iŋ, -id, -ə*/z
consecration, -s ˌkɔnsi'kreiʃən, -z
consecutive, -ly, -ness kən'sekjutiv, -li,
  -nis
consensus kən'sensəs [kɔn-]
consent (s. v.), -s, -ing, -ed kən'sent, -s,
  -iŋ, -id
consequen|ce/s, -t/ly 'kɔnsikwən|s/iz,
  -t/li
consequenti|al, -ally ˌkɔnsi'kwenʃ|əl,
  -əli
conservable kən'sə:vəbl
conservanc|y, -ies kən'sə:v|əns|i, -iz
conservation ˌkɔnsə(:)'veiʃən
conservatism kən'sə:vətizəm
conservative, -s, -ly, -ness kən'sə:vətiv,
  -z, -li, -nis
conservatoire, -s kən'sə:vɑ:twa:* ['kɔn-
  -'sɛəv-, -twɔ:*], -z
conservator (preserver), -s 'kɔnsə(:)-
  veitə*, -z
conservator (official guardian), -s kən-
  'sə:vətə*, -z
conservator|y, -ies kən'sə:vətr|i, -iz
conserve (s.), -s kən'sə:v ['kɔnsə:v], -z
conserv|e (v.), -es, -ing, -ed kən'sə:v, -z,
  -iŋ, -d
consid|er, -ers, -ering, -ered kən'sid|ə*,
  -əz, -əriŋ, -əd
considerab|le, -ly, -leness kən'sidər-
  əb|l, -li, -lnis
considerate, -ly, -ness kən'sidərit, -li,
  -nis
consideration, -s kənˌsidə'reiʃən, -z
consign, -s, -ing, -ed, -er/s, -ment/s;
  -able kən'sain, -z, -iŋ, -d, -ə*/z,
  -mənt/s; -əbl

consignation ˌkɔnsai'neiʃən

consignee, -s ˌkɔnsai'ni: [-'si'ni:], -z

consist, -s, -ing, -ed kən'sist, -s, -iŋ, -id

consisten|ce, -cy, -cies, -t/ly kən-'sistən|s, -si, -siz, -t/li

consistorial ˌkɔnsis'tɔ:riəl

consistor|y, -ies kən'sistər|i, -iz

consolable kən'səuləbl

consolation, -s ˌkɔnsə'leiʃən [-sl̩'eiʃ-, -səu-], -z

consolatory kən'sɔlətəri [-'səul-]

console (s.), -s 'kɔnsəul, -z

consol|e (v.), -es, -ing, -ed, -er/s kən-'səul, -z, -iŋ, -d, -ə*/z

consolidat|e, -es, -ing, -ed, -or/s; -ive kən'sɔlideit, -s, -iŋ, -id, -ə*/z; -iv

consolidation, -s kən,sɔli'deiʃən, -z

consols kən'sɔlz [kɔn'sɔlz, 'kɔnsɔlz]

consommé kən'sɔmei (kõsɔme) [-iz

consonance, -s 'kɔnsənəns [-sŋə-, -snə-]

consonant (s. adj.), -s, -ly 'kɔnsənənt [-sŋə-, -snə-], -s, -li

consonant|al, -ally ˌkɔnsə'nænt|l [-sŋ'æ-], -əli

consort (s.), -s 'kɔnsɔ:t, -s

consort (v.), -s, -ing, -ed kən'sɔ:t [kɔn's-], -s, -iŋ, -id

consortium, -s kən'sɔ:tjəm [-tïəm], -z

conspectus, -es kən'spektəs, -iz

conspicuous, -ly, -ness kən'spikjuəs [-kjwəs], -li, -nis

conspirac|y, -ies kən'spirəs|i, -iz

conspirator, -s kən'spirətə* [-rit-], -z

conspir|e, -es, -ing, -ed, -er/s kən-'spaiə*, -z, -riŋ, -d, -rə*/z

onstable, -s 'kʌnstəbl ['kɔn-], -z

onstable (surname) 'kʌnstəbl, in Scotland 'kɔn-

constabular|y, -ies kən'stæbjulər|i, -iz

Constance 'kɔnstəns

constancy 'kɔnstənsi

constant (s. adj.), -s, -ly, -ness 'kɔn-stənt, -s, -li, -nis

Constantine 'kɔnstəntain

Constantinople ˌkɔnstænti'nəupl ['kɔnsˌtænti'n-]

constellation, -s ˌkɔnstə'leiʃən [-te'l-, -ti'l-], -z

consternat|e, -es, -ing, -ed 'kɔnstə(:)-neit, -s, -iŋ, -id

consternation ˌkɔnstə(:)'neiʃən

constipat|e, -es, -ing, -ed 'kɔnstipeit, -s, -iŋ, -id

constipation ˌkɔnsti'peiʃən

constituen|cy, -cies, -t/s kən'stitjŭən|si [-tjwən-], -siz, -t/s

constitut|e, -es, -ing, -ed 'kɔnstitju:t, -s, -iŋ, -id

constitution, -s ˌkɔnsti'tju:ʃən, -z

constitu|tional, -tionally ˌkɔnsti'tju:-ʃənl [-ʃnəl, -ʃŋl̩, -ʃnl̩, -ʃənəl], -ʃŋəli [-ʃnəli, -ʃŋl̩i, -ʃnl̩i, -ʃənəli]

constitutionali|sm, -st/s ˌkɔnsti'tju:-ʃŋəli|zəm [-ʃnəli-,-ʃŋl̩i-,-ʃnl̩i-,-ʃənəli-], -st/s

constitutionaliz|e [-is|e], -es, -ing, -ed ˌkɔnsti'tju:ʃŋəlaiz [-ʃnəl-, -ʃŋl̩-, -ʃnl̩-, -ʃənəl-], -iz, -iŋ, -d

constitutive 'kɔnstitju:tiv [kən'stitju(:)-]

constrain, -s, -ing, -ed, -edly; -able kən'strein, -z, -iŋ, -d, -idli; -əbl

constraint, -s kən'streint, -s

constrict, -s, -ing, -ed, -or/s; -ive kən-'strikt, -s, -iŋ, -id, -ə*/z; -iv

constriction, -s kən'strikʃən, -z

construct, -s, -ing, -ed, -or/s kən-'strʌkt, -s, -iŋ, -id, -ə*/z

construction, -s kən'strʌkʃən, -z

construc|tional, -tionally kən'strʌk|ʃənl [-ʃnəl, -ʃŋl̩, -ʃnl̩, -ʃənəl], -ʃŋəli [-ʃnəli, -ʃŋl̩i, -ʃnl̩i, -ʃənəli]

constructive, -ly, -ness kən'strʌktiv, -li, -nis

constr|ue (s. v.), -ues, -uing, -ued kən'str|u: ['kɔnst-], -u:z, -u(:)iŋ, -u:d

consubstanti|al, -ally ˌkɔnsəb'stænʃ|əl [-bz't-], -əli [-li]

consubstantiat|e, -es, -ing, -ed ˌkɔn-səb'stænʃieit [-bz't-, -ʃjeit], -s, -iŋ, -id

consubstantiation 'kɔnsəbˌstænʃi'eiʃən [-bz,t-, -nsi-]

consul, -s; -ship/s 'kɔnsəl, -z; -ʃip/s

consular 'kɔnsjulə* [-sjəl-]

consulate, -s 'kɔnsjulit [-sjəl-], -s

consult, -s, -ing, -ed kən'sʌlt, -s, -iŋ, -id

consultant, -s kən'sʌltənt [-tnt], -s

consultation, -s ˌkɔnsəl'teiʃən [-sʌl-], -z

consultative kən'sʌltətiv

consultatory kən'sʌltətəri

consultee, -s ˌkɔnsʌl'ti: [-səl-], -z

consum|e, -es, -ing, -ed, -er/s kən-'sju:m [-'su:m], -z, -iŋ, -d, -ə*/z

consummate (adj.), -ly kən'sʌmit, -li

consummat|e (v.), -es, -ing, -ed, -or/s 'kɔnsəmeit [-sʌm-, -sju-], -s, -iŋ, -id, -ə*/z

consummation, -s ˌkɔnsə'meiʃən [-sʌ'm-, -sju-], -z

consummative 'kɔnsəmeitiv [-sʌm-, -sju-, kən'sʌmətiv]

consumption kən'sʌmpʃən

consumptive (s. adj.), -s, -ly, -ness kən'sʌmptiv, -z, -li, -nis

contact (s.), -s 'kɔntækt, -s

contact (v.), -s, -ing, -ed kən'tækt [kɔn'tækt, 'kɔntækt], -s, -iŋ, -id

contagion, -s kən'teidʒən [-dʒjən, -dʒïən], -z
contagious, -ly, -ness kən'teidʒəs, -li, -nis
contain, -s, -ing, -ed, -er/s; -able kən'tein, -z, -iŋ, -d, -ə*/z; -əbl
contaminat|e, -es, -ing, -ed, -er/s kən-'tæmineit, -s, -iŋ, -id, -ə*/z
contamination, -s kən,tæmi'neiʃən, -z
contaminative kən'tæminətiv [-neit-]
contango, -s kən'tæŋgəu [kɔn-], -z
contemn, -s, -ing, -ed, -er/s kən'tem, -z, -iŋ, -d, -ə*/z [-nə*/z]
contemplat|e, -es, -ing, -ed, -or/s 'kɔn-templeit [-təm-], -s, -iŋ, -id, -ə*/z
contemplation, -s ,kɔntem'pleiʃən [-təm-], -z
contemplative (pensive), -ly, -ness 'kɔn-templeitiv [-təm-, kən'templət-], -li, -nis
contemplative (of religious orders) kən'templətiv
contemporaneity kən,tempərə'ni:iti [kɔn-, -'ni(:)əti, -'neiiti]
contemporaneous, -ly, -ness kən,tem-pə'reinjəs [kɔn-, -nïəs], -li, -nis
contemporar|y (s. adj.), -ies, -ily kən-'tempərər|i, -iz, -ili
contempt kən'tempt
contemptibility kən,temptə'biliti [-ti'b-, -lət-]
contemptib|le, -ly, -leness kən'temp-təb|l [-tib-], -li, -lnis
contemptuous, -ly, -ness kən'temp-tjŭəs [-tjwəs], -li, -nis
contend, -s, -ing, -ed, -er/s kən'tend, -z, -iŋ, -id, -ə*/z
content (s.) (what is contained) 'kɔntent, (contentment) kən'tent
content (adj. v.), -s, -ing, -ed/ly, -edness, -ment kən'tent, -s, -iŋ, -id/li, -idnis, -mənt
contention, -s kən'tenʃən, -z
contentious, -ly, -ness kən'tenʃəs, -li, -nis
contents (s.) 'kɔntents [kən't-]
Note.—Always 'kɔntents in contents-bill.
contermin|al, -ous kɔn'tə:min|l [kən-], -əs
contest (s.), -s 'kɔntest, -s
contest (v.), -s, -ing, -ed; -able kən-'test, -s, -iŋ, -id; -əbl
contestant, -s kən'testənt, -s
contestation, -s ,kɔntes'teiʃən, -z
context, -s 'kɔntekst, -s
contextual, -ly kɔn'tekstjŭəl [kən-, -tjwəl, -tjul, -tʃŭəl, -tʃwəl, -tʃul], -i

contiguity ,kɔnti'gju(:)iti
contiguous, -ly, -ness kən'tigjŭəs [kɔn-, -gjwəs], -li, -nis
continen|ce, -cy 'kɔntinən|s, -si
continent (s. adj.), -s, -ly 'kɔntinənt, -s, -li
continental ,kɔnti'nentl
contingen|ce, -cy, -cies kən'tindʒən|s, -si, -siz
contingent (s. adj.), -s, -ly kən'tindʒənt, -s, -li
continual, -ly kən'tinjŭəl [-njwəl, -njul], -i
continuan|ce, -t/s kən'tinjŭən|s [-njwən-], -t/s
continuation, -s kən,tinju'eiʃən, -z
continuative kən'tinjŭətiv [-njwət-]
continuator, -s kən'tinjueitə*, -z
contin|ue, -ues, -uing, -ued, -uer/s kən-'tin|ju(:), -ju(:)z, -juiŋ [-jwiŋ], -ju(:)d, -jŭə*/z [-jwə*/z]
continuity ,kɔnti'nju(:)iti
continuous, -ly, -ness kən'tinjŭəs [-njwəs], -li, -nis
continu|um, -a kən'tinjŭ|əm [-njw|əm], -ə
conto, -s 'kɔntəu, -z
contoid, -s 'kɔntɔid, -z
contort, -s, -ing, -ed kən'tɔ:t, -s, -iŋ, -id
contortion, -s kən'tɔ:ʃən, -z
contortionist, -s kən'tɔ:ʃnist [-ʃəni-], -s
contour (s. v.), -s, -ing, -ed 'kɔntuə*, -z, -riŋ, -d
contra 'kɔntrə
contraband; -ist/s 'kɔntrəbænd; -ist/s
contrabass, -es 'kɔntrə'beis ['kɔntrəb-], -iz
contraception ,kɔntrə'sepʃən
contraceptive, -s ,kɔntrə'septiv, -z
contract (s.), -s 'kɔntrækt, -s
contract (v.), -s, -ing, -ed, -or/s; -ive kən'trækt, -s, -iŋ, -id, -ə*/z; -iv
contractibility kən,træktə'biliti [-ti'b-, -lət-]
contractib|le, -ly, -leness kən'træktəb|l [-tib-], -li, -lnis
contractile kən'træktail
contraction, -s kən'trækʃən, -z
contradict, -s, -ing, -ed ,kɔntrə'dikt, -s, -iŋ, -id
contradiction, -s ,kɔntrə'dikʃən, -z
contradictor|y, -ily, -ness ,kɔntrə-'diktər|i, -ili, -inis
contradistinc|tion, -tive ,kɔntrədis-'tiŋk|ʃən ['—'—], -tiv
contradistinguish, -es, -ing, -ed ,kɔn-trədis'tiŋgwiʃ ['kɔntrədis't-], -iz, -iŋ, -t

contralto, -s kən'trælteu [-'traːl-], -z

contraposition ˌkɔntrəpə'ziʃən ['kɔn-trəpə'z-, -pu'z-]

contraption, -s kən'træpʃən, -z

contrapuntal ˌkɔntrə'pʌntl

contrapuntist, -s 'kɔntrəpʌntist, -s

contrariant, -s kən'trɛəriənt, -s

contrariety ˌkɔntrə'raiəti [-aiiti]

contrari|ness, -wise 'kɔntrəri|nis [kən-'trɛəri-], -waiz

contrar|y, -ies, -ily 'kɔntrər|i [also kən'trɛər- in sense of 'obstinate'], -iz, -ili

contrast (s.), -s 'kɔntrɑːst, -s

contrast (v.), -s, -ing, -ed kən'trɑːst, -s, -iŋ, -id

contrastive kən'trɑːstiv

contraven|e, -es, -ing, -ed ˌkɔntrə'viːn, -z, -iŋ, -d

contravention, -s ˌkɔntrə'venʃən, -z

contretemps (sing.) 'kɔ̃ːntrətɑ̃ːŋ ['kɔːnt-, 'kɔnt-, -tɔ̃ːŋ, -tɑːŋ, -tɔːŋ, -tɔŋ] (kɔ̃trətɑ̃), (plur.) -z

contrib|ute, -utes, -uting, -uted, -utor/s kən'trib|ju(ː)t ['kɔntribjuːt], -ju(ː)ts, -jutiŋ, -jutid, -jutə*/z

contribution, -s ˌkɔntri'bjuːʃən, -z

contribut|ive, -ory kən'tribjut|iv, -əri

contrite, -ly, -ness 'kɔntrait, -li, -nis

contrition kən'triʃən

contrivance, -s kən'traivəns, -iz

contriv|e, -es, -ing, -ed, -er/s kən-'traiv, -z, -iŋ, -d, -ə*/z

control (s.), -s kən'trəul [in machinery also 'kɔntrəul], -z

control (v.), -s, -ling, -led, -ler/s; -lable kən'trəul, -z, -iŋ, -d, -ə*/z; -əbl

controversi|al, -ally ˌkɔntrə'və:ʃ|əl [-tru'v-], -əli [-ʃi]

controversialist, -s ˌkɔntrə'və:ʃəlist [-tru'v-, -ʃli-], -s

controvers|y, -ies 'kɔntrəvə:s|i, kən-'trɔvəs|i [-truv-, -vəs-], -iz

controvert, -s, -ing, -ed 'kɔntrəvə:t ['kɔntruv-, '--'-, ,--'-], -s, -iŋ, -id

controvertib|le, -ly 'kɔntrəvə:təb|l ['kɔntruv-, -tib-, ,--'---], -li

contumacious, -ly, -ness ˌkɔntju(ː)-'meiʃəs, -li, -nis

contumacity ˌkɔntju(ː)'mæsiti

contumacy 'kɔntjuməsi

contumelious, -ly, -ness ˌkɔntju(ː)'miː-ljəs [-liəs], -li, -nis

contumel|y, -ies 'kɔntju(ː)ml|i ['kɔn-tjumil-, rarely kən'tju:mil|i], -iz

contus|e, -es, -ing, -ed kən'tju:z, -iz, -iŋ, -d

contusion, -s kən'tju:ʒən, -z

conundrum, -s kə'nʌndrəm, -z

conurbation, -s ˌkɔnə:'beiʃən, -z

convalesc|e, -es, -ing, -ed ˌkɔnvə'les, -iz, -iŋ, -t

convalescen|ce, -t/s ˌkɔnvə'lesn|s, -t/s

convection kən'vekʃən

convector, -s kən'vektə*, -z

convenance, -s 'kɔ̃:ŋvinɑ̃:ns ['kɔ̃:nv-, 'kɔ:nv-, 'kɔnv-, -vən-, -nɔ̃:ns, -nɑːns, -nɔ:ns] (kɔ̃vnɑ̃:s), -iz

conven|e, -es, -ing, -ed, -er/s kən'vi:n, -z, -iŋ, -d, -ə*/z

convenien|ce/s, -t/ly kən'vi:njən|s/iz [-niən-], -t/li

convent, -s 'kɔnvənt [rarely -vent], -s

conventicle, -s kən'ventikl, -z

convention, -s kən'venʃən, -z

conven|tional, -tionally kən'ven|ʃənl [-ʃnəl, -ʃṇl, -ʃnl, -ʃənəl], -ʃnəli [-ʃnəli, -ʃṇli, -ʃnli, -ʃənəli]

conventionali|sm, -st/s kən'venʃnəli|-zəm [-ʃnəl-, -ʃṇl-, -ʃnl-, -ʃənəl-], -st/s

conventionalit|y, -ies kənˌvenʃə'nælit|i [-ʃṇ'æl-], -iz

conventionaliz|e [-is|e], -es, -ing, -ed kən'venʃnəlaiz [-ʃnəl-, -ʃṇl-, -ʃnl-, -ʃənəl-], -iz, -iŋ, -d

conventual, -s kən'ventjŭəl [-tjwəl, -tjul, -tʃŭəl, -tʃwəl, -tʃul], -z

converg|e, -es, -ing, -ed kən'və:dʒ [kɔn-], -iz, -iŋ, -d

convergen|ce, -cy, -t/ly kən'və:dʒən|s [kɔn-], -si, -t/li

conversable kən'və:səbl

conversan|ce, -cy kən'və:sən|s ['kɔnvəs-], -si

conversant, -ly kən'və:sənt ['kɔnvəs-], -li

conversation, -s ˌkɔnvə'seiʃən, -z

conversa|tional, -tionally ˌkɔnvə'sei|ʃənl [-ʃnəl, -ʃṇl, -ʃnl, -ʃənəl], -ʃnəli [-ʃnəli, -ʃṇli, -ʃnli, -ʃənəli]

conversationalist, -s ˌkɔnvə'seiʃṇəlist [-ʃnəl-, -ʃṇl-, -ʃnl-, -ʃənəl-], -s

conversazione, -s 'kɔnvəˌsætsi'əuni [ˌkɔn-], -z

converse (s. adj.), -s, -ly 'kɔnvə:s, -iz, -li ['kɔn'və:sli, kɔn'və:sli]

convers|e (v.), -es, -ing, -ed kən'və:s, -iz, -iŋ, -t

conversion, -s kən'və:ʃən, -z

convert (s.), -s 'kɔnvə:t, -s

convert (v.), -s, -ing, -ed, -er/s kən'və:t, -s, -iŋ, -id, -ə*/z [-lət-]

convertibility kənˌvə:tə'biliti [-ti'b-, -vət-]

convertib|le, -ly kən'və:təb|l [-tib-], -li

convex, -ly 'kɔn'veks ['kɔnv-, kɔn'v-], -li
Note.—The form kɔn'veks is not used attributively.

convexit|y, -ies kɔn'veksit|i [kən-], -iz
convey, -s, -ing, -ed, -er/s; -able
 kən'vei, -z, -iŋ, -d, -ə*/z [-'veə*/z],
 -əbl [-'veəbl]
conveyance, -s kən'veiəns, -iz
conveyanc|er/s, -ing kən'veiəns|ə*/z,
 -iŋ
convict (s.), -s 'kɔnvikt, -s
convict (v.), -s, -ing, -ed kən'vikt, -s, -iŋ,
 -id
conviction, -s kən'vikʃən, -z
convinc|e, -es, -ing/ly, -ed kən'vins, -iz,
 -iŋ/li, -t
convincible kən'vinsəbl [-sib-]
convivial, -ly kən'viviəl [-vjəl], -i
conviviality kən,vivi'æliti
convocation, -s ,kɔnvəu'keiʃən, -z
convok|e, -es, -ing, -ed kən'vəuk, -s, -iŋ,
 -t
convolute, -d 'kɔnvəlu:t [-lju:t], -id
convolution, -s ,kɔnvə'lu:ʃən [-'lju:-], -z
convolv|e, -es, -ing, -ed kən'vɔlv, -z, -iŋ,
 -d
convolvul|us, -i, -uses kən'vɔlvjul|əs
 [-vjəl-], -ai, -əsiz
convoy (s. v.), -s, -ing, -ed 'kɔnvɔi, -z,
 -iŋ, -d
convuls|e, -es, -ing, -ed kən'vʌls, -iz,
 -iŋ, -t
convulsion, -s kən'vʌlʃən, -z
convulsionary kən'vʌlʃnəri [-ʃənə-]
convulsive, -ly, -ness kən'vʌlsiv, -li, -nis
Conway 'kɔnwei
con|y, -ies 'kəun|i, -iz
Conybeare 'kɔnibiə*, 'kʌn-
Conyngham 'kʌniŋəm
coo (s. v.), -es, -ing, -ed ku:, -z, -iŋ, -d
Cooch ku:tʃ
cooee (s. v.), -s, -ing, -d 'ku(:)i[-i:], -z,
 -iŋ, -d
cook (s. v.), -s, -ing, -ed kuk, -s, -iŋ, -t
Cook(e) kuk
cookery; -book/s 'kukəri; -buk/s
cook-hou|se, -ses 'kukhau|s, -ziz
cookie, -s 'kuki, -z
cook-room, -s 'kukrum [-ru:m], -z
cook-shop, -s 'kukʃɔp, -s
cool (s. adj. v.), -er, -est, -ly, -ness; -s,
 -ing, -ed, -er/s ku:l, -ə*, -ist, -li [-i],
 -nis; -z, -iŋ, -d, -ə*/z
coolant, -s 'ku:lənt, -s
cool-headed 'ku:l'hedid ['-,-- when at-
 tributive]
Coolidge 'ku:lidʒ
coolie, -s 'ku:li, -z
Cooling 'ku:liŋ
coom, -s ku:m, -z
coomb, -s ku:m, -z

Coomb(e) ku:m
Coomber 'ku:mbə*
Coombes ku:mz
coon, -s; -song/s ku:n, -z; -sɔŋ/z
coop (s. v.), -s, -ing, -ed ku:p, -s, -iŋ, -t
co-op, -s 'kəuɔp, -s
cooper (s. v.) (C.), -s, -ing, -ed 'ku:pə*,
 -z, -riŋ, -d
cooperage, -s 'ku:pəridʒ, -iz
co-operat|e, -es, -ing, -ed, -or/s kəu-
 'ɔpəreit, -s, -iŋ, -id, -ə*/z
co-operation, -s kəu,ɔpə'reiʃən [,---'--],
 -z
co-operative (s. adj.), -s kəu'ɔpərətiv, -z
coopery 'ku:pəri
Coopman 'ku:pmən
co-opt, -s, -ing, -ed kəu'ɔpt, -s, -iŋ, -id
co-optation ,kəuɔp'teiʃən
co-option kəu'ɔpʃən
co-ordinate (s. adj.), -s, -ly, -ness
 kəu'ɔ:dnit [-dinit, -dənit], -s, -li, -nis
co-ordinat|e (v.), -es, -ing, -ed kəu'ɔ:-
 dineit [-dŋeit], -s, -iŋ, -id
co-ordination kəu,ɔ:di'neiʃən [-dŋ'ei-]
co-ordinative kəu'ɔ:dinətiv [-dŋət-,
 -dineit-]
coot, -s ku:t, -s
Coote ku:t
co-ownership 'kəu'əunəʃip
cop (s. v.), -s, -ping, -ped kɔp, -s, -iŋ, -t
copaiba kɔ'paibə [kəu'p-]
copal 'kəupəl [kəu'pæl]
coparcener, -s 'kəu'pɑːsinə* [kəu'p-], -z
copartner, -s; -ship/s 'kəu'pɑːtnə*, -z;
 -ʃip/s
cop|e (s. v.) (C.), -es, -ing, -ed kəup, -s,
 -iŋ, -t
copeck, -s 'kəupek ['kɔp-], -s
Copeland 'kəuplənd
Copenhagen ,kəupn'heigən [-pən-]
coper, -s 'kəupə*, -z
Copernic|an, -us kəu'pə:nik|ən, -əs
Cophetua kəu'fetjuə [-tjwə]
coping (s.), -s 'kəupiŋ, -z
coping-stone, -s 'kəupiŋ-stəun, -z
copious, -ly, -ness 'kəupjəs [-piəs], -li,
 -nis
Copland 'kɔplənd, 'kəuplənd
Copleston 'kɔplstən
Copley 'kɔpli
Copp kɔp
Copped kɔpt
copper (s. v.), -s, -ing, -ed 'kɔpə*, -z,
 -riŋ, -d
copperas 'kɔpərəs
copper-bottomed 'kɔpə'bɔtəmd [also
 'kɔpə,b- when attributive]
Copperfield 'kɔpəfi:ld

copper-plate 'kɔpə-pleit
copper-smith, -s 'kɔpə-smiθ, -s
coppery 'kɔpəri
coppice, -s 'kɔpis, -iz
copra 'kɔprə
copse, -s kɔps, -iz
Copt, -s kɔpt, -s
Copthall 'kɔptɔ:l [-thɔ:l]
Coptic 'kɔptik
copul|a, -ae, -as 'kɔpjul|ə, -i:, -əz
copulat|e, -es, -ing, -ed 'kɔpjuleit, -s, -iŋ,
  -id
copulation, -s ˌkɔpju'leiʃən, -z
copulative 'kɔpjulətiv [-leit-]
cop|y (s. v.), -ies, -ying, -ied, -ier/s
  'kɔp|i, -iz, -iiŋ, -id, -iə*/z
copy-book, -s 'kɔpibuk, -s
copyhold, -s, -er/s 'kɔpihəuld, -z, -ə*/z
copyist, -s 'kɔpiist, -s
copyright (s. v.), -s, -ing, -ed 'kɔpirait,
  -s, -iŋ, -id
coquet (s. v.), -s, -ting, -ted kɔ'ket
  [kəu'k-], -s, -iŋ, -id
coquetr|y, -ies 'kɔkitr|i ['kəuk-], -iz
coquette (s.), -s kɔ'ket [kəu'k-], -s
coquettish, -ly, -ness kɔ'ketiʃ [kəu'k-],
  -li, -nis
cor, -s kɔ:*, -z
Cora 'kɔ:rə
coracle, -s 'kɔrəkl, -z
coral, -s 'kɔrəl, -z
corallaceous ˌkɔrə'leiʃəs
corall|ine, -ite 'kɔrəl|ain [-rḷ-], -ait
coral-reef, -s 'kɔrəlri:f, -s
Coram 'kɔ:rəm
Coran kɔ'rɑ:n [kɔ:'r-, ku'r-, kə'r-]
coranto, -s kɔ'ræntəu [kə'r-], -z
corban 'kɔ:bæn
corbel, -s 'kɔ:bəl, -z
Corbett 'kɔ:bit [-bet, -bət]
Corbyn 'kɔ:bin
Corcoran 'kɔ:kərən
Corcyra kɔ:'saiərə
cord (s. v.), -s, -ing, -ed; -age kɔ:d, -z,
  -iŋ, -id; -idʒ
Cordelia kɔ:'di:ljə [-liə]
cordelier (C.), -s ˌkɔ:di'liə*, -z
cordial (s. adj.), -s, -ly 'kɔ:djəl [-diəl],
  -z, -i
cordialit|y, -ies ˌkɔ:di'ælit|i, -iz
cordillera (C.) ˌkɔ:di'ljɛərə [-'lɛərə]
cording (s.) 'kɔ:diŋ
cordite 'kɔ:dait
cor|don (s. v.), -dons, -doning, -doned
  'kɔ:|dn [-dən], -dnz [-dənz], -dṇiŋ
  [-dəniŋ], -dnd [-dənd]
Cordova, -n/s 'kɔ:dəvə, -n/z
corduroy, -s 'kɔ:dərɔi [-djur-], -z

cor|e (s. v.), -es, -ing, -ed, -er/s kɔ:*
  [kɔə*], -z, -riŋ, -d, -rə*/z
Corea, -n/s kə'riə [kɔ'riə, kɔ:'riə], -n/z
co-regent, -s 'kəu'ri:dʒənt, -s
co-religionist, -s 'kəuri'lidʒənist [-dʒṇ-],
  -s
Corelli kə'reli [kɔ'r-]
co-respondent,   -s   'kəurisˌpɔndənt
  ['kəuris'p-], -s
corf, -s kɔ:f, -s
Corfe kɔ:f
Corfu kɔ:'fu: [-'fju:]
Corgi (dog), -s 'kɔ:gi, -z
coriaceous ˌkɔri'eiʃəs
coriander, -s ˌkɔri'ændə*, -z
Corin 'kɔrin
Corinth 'kɔrinθ
Corinthian, -s kə'rinθiən [ku'r-, -θjən],
  -z
Coriolanus ˌkɔriəu'leinəs
Corioles kə'raiəli:z [kɔ'r-]
cork (s. v.) (C.), -s, -ing, -ed; -age
  kɔ:k, -s, -iŋ, -t; -idʒ
corker (C.), -s 'kɔ:kə*, -z
Corkran 'kɔ:krən
cork-screw (s. v.), -s, -ing, -ed 'kɔ:k-
  skru:, -z, -iŋ [-skruiŋ], -d
corky 'kɔ:ki
Cormac (king in Irish mythology)
  'kə:mæk ['kɔ:m-]
Cormack 'kɔ:mæk
cormorant, -s 'kɔ:mərənt, -s
corn (s. v.), -s, -ing, -ed kɔ:n, -z, -iŋ, -d
Cornbury 'kɔ:nbəri
corn-chandler, -s 'kɔ:nˌtʃɑ:ndlə*, -z
corn-crake, -s 'kɔ:nkreik, -s
cornea, -s 'kɔ:niə, -z
Corneille kɔ:'nei [-neil] (kɔrnɛ:j)
Cornelia kɔ:'ni:ljə [-liə]
cornelian, -s kɔ:'ni:ljən [kə'n-, -liən], -z
Cornelius kɔ:'ni:ljəs [-liəs]
Cornell   kɔ:'nel   [also   'kɔ:nel   when
  attributive]
corner (s. v.), -s, -ing, -ed 'kɔ:nə*, -z,
  -riŋ, -d
corner-stone, -s 'kɔ:nə-stəun, -z
corner-wise 'kɔ:nəwaiz
cornet, -s 'kɔ:nit, -s
corn-field, -s 'kɔ:nfi:ld, -z
cornflour 'kɔ:nflauə*
corn-flower, -s 'kɔ:nflauə*, -z
Cornhill 'kɔ:n'hil [also '--, -'- according
  to sentence-stress]
cornice, -s 'kɔ:nis, -iz
Cornish, -man, -men 'kɔ:niʃ, -mən,
  -mən [-men]
cornopean, -s kə'nəupjən [kɔ:'n-, -piən],
  -z

cornucopia, -s ,kɔ:nju'kəupjə [-pĭə], -z
Cornwall 'kɔ:nwəl [*rarely* -wɔ:l]
Cornwallis kɔ:n'wɔlis
corolla, -s kə'rɔlə, -z
corollar|y, -ies kə'rɔlər|i, -iz
Coromandel ,kərəu'mændl
coron|a, -ae, -as kə'rəun|ə, -i:, -əz
Corona (*fem. name*) 'kɔrənə
coronach (C.), -s 'kɔrənək [-nəx, -næk], -s
coronal (*s.*), -s 'kɔrənl, -z
coronal (*adj.*) (*pertaining to the sun's corona*) kə'rəunl, (*medical, botanical and phonetic senses*) 'kɔrənl [kə'rəunl]
coronary 'kɔrənəri
coronation, -s ,kɔrə'neiʃən [-rn̩'ei-], -z
Coronel 'kɔrənel
coroner, -s 'kɔrənə* [-rn̩ə*], -z
coronet, -s 'kɔrənit [-rn̩it], -s
coronis, -es kə'rəunis, -iz
corpor|al (*s. adj.*), -als, -ally 'kɔ:pər|əl, -əlz, -əli
corporality ,kɔ:pə'ræliti
corporate, -ly, -ness 'kɔ:pərit, -li, -nis
corporation, -s ,kɔ:pə'reiʃən, -z
corporator, -s 'kɔ:pəreitə*, -z
corporeal, -ly kɔ:'pɔ:rĭəl, -i
corps (*sing.*) kɔ:*, (*plur.*) kɔ:z
corpse, -s kɔ:ps, -iz
corpulen|ce, -cy, -t 'kɔ:pjulən|s, -si, -t
corpus (C.) 'kɔ:pəs
corpuscle, -s 'kɔ:pʌsl [kɔ:'pʌsl], -z
corpuscular kɔ:'pʌskjulə*
corpuscule, -s kɔ:'pʌskju:l, -z
corral, -s kɔ:'rɑ:l, -z
correct (*adj. v.*), -est, -ly, -ness; -s, -ing, -ed, -or/s kə'rekt, -ist, -li, -nis; -s, -iŋ, -id, -ə*/z
correction, -s kə'rekʃən, -z
correctional kə'rekʃənl [-ʃnəl, -ʃn̩l, -ʃn̩l, -ʃənəl]
correctitude kə'rektitju:d
corrective, -s kə'rektiv, -z
correlat|e, -es, -ing, -ed 'kɔrileit [-rel-, -rəl-], -s, -iŋ, -id
correlation, -s ,kɔri'leiʃən [-re'l-, -rə'l-], [-z
correlative, -ly, -ness kɔ'relətiv [kə'r-, -'reɪt-], -li, -nis
correspond, -s, -ing/ly, -ed ,kɔris'pɔnd [-rəs-], -z, -iŋ/li, -id
corresponden|ce/s, -t/s, -tly ,kɔris-'pɔndən|s/iz [-rəs-], -t/s, -tli
corridor, -s; -train/s 'kɔridɔ:* [-də*], -z; -trein/z
Corrie 'kɔri
Corrientes ,kɔri'entes
corrigend|um, -a 'kɔri'dʒend|əm [-i'gen-], -ə

corrigible 'kɔridʒəbl [-dʒib-]
corroborant, -s kə'rɔbərənt, -s
corroborat|e, -es, -ing, -ed, -or/s kə'rɔbəreit, -s, -iŋ, -id, -ə*/z
corroboration, -s kə,rɔbə'reiʃən, -z
corroborative kə'rɔbərətiv [-bəreit-]
corroboree, -s kə'rɔbəri [kɔ'r-, -ri:], -z
corrod|e, -es, -ing, -ed kə'rəud, -z, -iŋ, -id
corrodible kə'rəudəbl [-dib-]
corrosion, -s kə'rəuʒən, -z
corrosive (*s. adj.*), -s, -ly, -ness kə-'rəusiv [-əuziv], -z, -li, -nis
corrugat|e, -es, -ing, -ed 'kɔrugeit [-rəg-], -s, -iŋ, -id
corrugation, -s ,kɔru'geiʃən [-rə'g-], -z
corrupt (*adj. v.*), -est, -ly, -ness; -s, -ing, -ed, -er/s kə'rʌpt, -ist, -li, -nis; -s, -iŋ, -id, -ə*/z
corruptibility kə,rʌptə'biliti [-ti'b-, -lət-]
corruptib|le, -ly, -leness kə'rʌptəb|l [-tib-], -li, -lnis
corruption, -s kə'rʌpʃən, -z
corruptive kə'rʌptiv
corsage, -s kɔ:'sɑ:ʒ ['kɔ:sɑ:ʒ] (kɔrsa:ʒ), -iz
corsair, -s 'kɔ:sɛə*, -z
corse, -s kɔ:s, -iz
corselet, -s 'kɔ:slit, -s
corset, -s 'kɔ:sit, -s
Corsica, -n/s 'kɔ:sikə, -n/z
corslet, -s 'kɔ:slit, -s
cortège, -s kɔ:'teiʒ (kɔrtɛ:ʒ), -iz
Cortes 'kɔ:tes [-tez] ('kortes)
cort|ex, -ices 'kɔ:t|eks, -isi:z
cortical 'kɔ:tikəl
cortisone 'kɔ:tizəun
corundum kə'rʌndəm
Corunna kɔ'rʌnə [kə'r-]
coruscat|e, -es, -ing, -ed 'kɔrəskeit, -s, -iŋ, -id
coruscation, -s ,kɔrəs'keiʃən, -z
corvée, -s 'kɔ:vei (kɔrve), -z
corvette, -s kɔ:'vet, -s
Corwen 'kɔ:win [-wen]
corybant, -s, corybantes 'kɔribænt, -s, ,kɔri'bænti:z
corybantic ,kɔri'bæntik
Corydon 'kɔridən [-dɔn]
coryphae|us, -i ,kɔri'fi:|əs, -ai
Coryton 'kɔritn
cos (C.) kɔs
cosaque, -s kɔ'zɑ:k [kə'z-], -s
cosec 'kəusek
cosecant, -s 'kəu'si:kənt, -s
Cosgrave 'kɔzgreiv
cosh (*instrument*), -es kɔʃ, -iz
cosh (*mathematical term*) kɔʃ

Cosham (in Hants) 'kɔsəm
cosher (feast, pamper), -s, -ing, -ed
'kɔʃə*, -z, -riŋ, -d
cosher (=kosher) 'kəuʃə* ['kɔʃ-]
    Note.—The Jewish pronunciation is
    with əu.
co-signator|y, -ies 'kəu'signətər|i, -iz
cosine, -s 'kəusain, -z
cos-lettuce, -s 'kɔs'letis ['kɔs,l-], -iz
cosmetic (s. adj.), -s, -al, -ally kɔz-
    'metik, -s, -əl, -əli
cosmic, -al, -ally 'kɔzmik, -əl, -əli
cosmi|sm, -st/s 'kɔzmi|zəm, -st/s
cosmogonic, -al, -ally ,kɔzməu'gɔnik,
    -əl, -əli
cosmogon|ist/s, -y kɔz'mɔgən|ist/s, -i
cosmograph|er/s, -y kɔz'mɔgrəf|ə*/z, -i
cosmographic, -al, -ally ,kɔzməu'græfik
    -əl, -əli
cosmological ,kɔzməu'lɔdʒikəl
cosmolog|ist/s, -y kɔz'mɔlədʒ|ist/s, -i
cosmonaut, -s 'kɔzmənɔ:t, -s
cosmopolitan (s. adj.), -s ,kɔzməu-
    'pɔlitən, -z
cosmopolitanism ,kɔzmə'pɔlitənizəm
    [-tɲi-]
cosmopolite, -s kɔz'mɔpəlait, -s
cosmos 'kɔzmɔs
Cossack, -s 'kɔsæk, -s
cosset (s. v.), -s, -ing, -ed 'kɔsit, -s, -iŋ,
    -id
cost (s. v.), -s, -ing kɔst [kɔ:st], -s, -iŋ
Costa 'kɔstə
costal 'kɔstl
costard (apple), -s 'kʌstəd ['kɔs-], -z
Costard (Shakespearian character)
    'kɔstəd [-tɑ:d]
Costello (surname) kɔs'teləu [kəs-],
    'kɔstələu
    Note.—J. A. Costello, the Irish states-
    man, pronounces 'kɔstələu.
coster, -s; -monger/s 'kɔstə*, -z;
    -,mʌŋgə*/z
costive, -ly, -ness 'kɔstiv, -li, -nis
costl|y, -ier, -iest, -iness 'kɔstl|i ['kɔ:s-],
    -iə* [-jə*], -iist [-jist], -inis
costmary 'kɔstmɛəri
costume (s.), -s 'kɔstju:m [kɔs'tju:m], -z
costum|e (v.), -es, -ing, -ed 'kɔstju:m
    [-'-], -z, -iŋ, -d
costumier, -s kɔs'tju:miə* [-miə*], -z
Cosway, -s 'kɔzwei, -z
cos|y (s. adj.), -ies; -ier, -iest, -ily,
    -iness 'kəuz|i, -iz; -iə* [-jə*], -iist
    [-jist], -ili, -inis
cot, -s kɔt, -s
cot (mathematical term) kɔt   [-s
cotangent, -s 'kəu'tændʒənt ['kəu,t-],

cot|e (s. v.), -es, -ing, -ed kəut, -s, -iŋ,
    -id
co-tenant, -s 'kəu'tenənt, -s
coterie, -s 'kəutəri, -z
coterminous 'kəu'tə:minəs [kəu't-]
Cotgrave 'kɔtgreiv
cotill(i)on, -s kə'tiljən [kɔ't-], -z
Coton 'kəutn
cotoneaster, -s kə,təuni'æstə* [kɔ,t-], -z
Cotopaxi ,kɔtəu'pæksi
co-trustee, -s 'kəu-trʌs'ti:, -z
Cotswold, -s 'kɔtswəuld [-wəld], -z
Cotsworth 'kɔtswə:θ
cottabus 'kɔtəbəs
cottage, -s; -r/s 'kɔtidʒ, -iz; -ə*/z
Cottam 'kɔtəm
Cottenham 'kɔtɲəm ['kɔtnəm]
cotter (C.), -s 'kɔtə*, -z
Cotterell 'kɔtrəl
Cottesloe 'kɔtsləu
Cottian 'kɔtiən [-tjən]
Cottingham 'kɔtiɲəm
cott|on (s. v.) (C.), -ons, -oning, -oned
    'kɔt|n, -nz, -ɲiŋ, -nd
cotton-grass 'kɔtngrɑ:s
cotton-plant, -s 'kɔtnplɑ:nt, -s
cotton-seed 'kɔtnsi:d
cotton-spinner, -s 'kɔtn,spinə*, -z
cotton-tail, -s 'kɔtnteil, -z
cotton-wool 'kɔtn'wul
cottony 'kɔtɲi
cotyled|on/s, -onous ,kɔti'li:d|ən/z,
    -ənəs [-ɲəs]
couch (s. v.), -es, -ing, -ed kautʃ, -iz,
    -iŋ, -t
Couch ku:tʃ
couchant 'kautʃənt
couchée, -s 'ku:ʃei (kuʃe), -z
couchette, -s ku:'ʃet, -s
Coué, -ism 'ku:ei, -izəm
cougar, -s 'ku:gə*, -z
cough (s. v.), -s, -ing, -ed, -er/s kɔf
    [kɔ:f], -s, -iŋ, -t, -ə*/z
Coughlan 'kɔglən, 'kɔklən ['kɔxlən]
Coughlin 'kɔglin, 'kɔklin ['kɔxlin]
could (from can) kud (strong form), kəd
    (weak form)
couldn't 'kudnt
couleur de rose 'ku:lə(:)də'rəuz (kulœr-
    dəro:z)
coulisse, -s ku:'li:s [ku'l-], -iz
couloir, -s 'ku:lwɑ:* [-wɔ:*], -z
coulomb, -s 'ku:lɔm, -z
Coulsdon (in Surrey) 'kəulzdən, 'ku:l-
    Note.—'kəul- is the traditional local
    pron. People unfamiliar with the
    place generally pron. 'ku:l-, as also
    do many new residents in the district.

Coulson 'kəulsn, 'ku:lsn
coulter, -s 'kəultə*, -z
Coulton 'kəultən
council, -s 'kaunsl [-sil], -z
council-chamber, -s 'kaunsl,tʃeimbə* [-sil-], -z
councillor, -s 'kaunsilə* [-sələ*, -s]ə*, -slə*], -z
couns|el (s. v.), -els, -elling, -elled, -ellor/s 'kauns|əl, -əlz, -liŋ [-əliŋ, -liŋ], -əld, -lə*/z [-ələ*/z, -lə*/z]
count (s. v.), -s, -ing, -ed kaunt, -s, -iŋ, -id
count-down 'kauntdaun
countenanc|e (s. v.), -es, -ing, -ed 'kauntinəns, -iz, -iŋ, -t
counter (s. adj. v. adv.), -s, -ing, -ed 'kauntə*, -z, -riŋ, -d
counteract, -s, -ing, -ed ,kauntə'rækt, [-tər'ækt], -s, -iŋ, -id
counteraction (counteracting), -s ,kauntə'rækʃən [-tər'æk-], -z
counter-action (action by way of reply), -s 'kauntər,ækʃən [-tə,æk-], -z
counteractive, -ly ,kauntə'ræktiv [-tər'æk-], -li
counter-attack, -s 'kauntərə,tæk [-təə,tæk], -s
counter-attraction, -s 'kauntərə,træk-ʃən [-təə,træk-], -z [-iz
counterbalance (s.), -s 'kauntə,bæləns,
counterbalanc|e (v.), -es, -ing, -ed ,kauntə'bæləns ['kauntə'b-], -iz, -iŋ, -t
counterblast, -s 'kauntə-blɑ:st, -s
counter-blow, -s 'kauntə-bləu, -z
counter-charg|e (s. v.), -es, -ing, -ed 'kauntə-tʃɑ:dʒ, -iz, -iŋ, -d
counter-claim (s. v.), -s, -ing, -ed 'kauntə-kleim, -z, -iŋ, -d
counter-clockwise 'kauntə'klɔkwaiz ['--,-- when in contrast with clockwise]
counterfeit (s. v.), -s, -ing, -ed 'kauntə-fit [-fi:t], -s, -iŋ, -id
counterfoil, -s 'kauntəfɔil, -z
counter-intelligence 'kauntərin,teli-dʒəns [-təin-]
countermand (s.v.), -s, -ing, -ed ,kauntə-'mɑ:nd ['kauntə'm-], -z, -iŋ, -id
counter-move, -s 'kauntəmu:v, -z
counterpane, -s 'kauntəpein [-pin], -z
counterpart, -s 'kauntəpɑ:t, -s
counter-plot, -s 'kauntə-plɔt, -s
counterpoint 'kauntəpoint
counterpois|e (s. v.), -es, -ing, -ed 'kauntəpoiz, -iz, -iŋ, -d
counter-revolution, -s 'kauntərevə,lu:-ʃən [-v],ʊ:-, -və,lju:-], -z

counterscarp, -s 'kauntə-skɑ:p, -s
countersign (s.), -s 'kauntəsain, -z
countersign(v.), -s, -ing, -ed 'kauntəsain ['kauntə's-], -z, -iŋ, -d
counterstroke, -s 'kauntə-strəuk, -s
counter-tenor, -s 'kauntə'tenə* ['--,--], -z
countervail, -s, -ing, -ed 'kauntəveil [,--'-], -z, -iŋ, -d
countess, -es 'kauntis, -iz
counting-hou|se, -ses 'kauntiŋhau|s, -ziz
countless 'kauntlis
countrified 'kʌntrifaid
countr|y, -ies 'kʌntr|i, -iz
country-folk, -s 'kʌntrifəuk, -s
country-hou|se, -ses 'kʌntri'hau|s, -ziz
country|man, -men 'kʌntri|mən, -mən
country-seat, -s 'kʌntri'si:t, -s
country-side 'kʌntrisaid ['--'-]
country|woman, -women 'kʌntri|-,wumən, -,wimin
count|y, -ies 'kaunt|i, -iz
coup, -s ku:, -z
coup d'état, -s 'ku:dei'tɑ: [-de't-] (kudeta), -z
coupé, -s 'ku:pei (kupe), -z
Couper 'ku:pə*
Coupland 'ku:plənd
coup|le (s. v.), -les, -ling, -led 'kʌp|l, -lz, -liŋ [-liŋ], -ld
coupler, -s 'kʌplə*, -z
couplet, -s 'kʌplit, -s
coupling (s.), -s 'kʌpliŋ, -z
coupon, -s 'ku:pɔn [rarely -pɔ̃:ŋ, -pɔ:ŋ, -pɔŋ] (kupɔ̃), -z
courage (C.) 'kʌridʒ
courageous, -ly, -ness kə'reidʒəs, -li, -nis
courant (newspaper), -s ku'rænt, -s
courante, -s ku'rɑ̃:nt [-'rɔ̃:nt, -'rɑ:nt, -'rɔ:nt, -'rænt] (kurɑ̃:t), -s
courier, -s 'kuriə*, -z
Courland 'kuələnd [-lænd]
cours|e (s. v.), -es, -ing, -ed, -er/s kɔ:s [kɔəs], -iz, -iŋ, -t, -ə*/z
court (s. v.), -s, -ing, -ed kɔ:t [kɔət], -s, -iŋ, -id
Courtauld 'kɔ:təuld, 'kɔ:təu
court-card, -s 'kɔ:tkɑ:d ['kɔət-], -z
court-dress, -es 'kɔ:t'dres ['kɔət-], -iz
Courtenay 'kɔ:tni ['kɔət-]
courteous, -ly, -ness 'kɔ:tjəs ['kɔ:t-, 'kɔət-, -tĭəs], -li, -nis
courtesan, -s ,kɔ:ti'zæn [,kɔət-], -z
courtes|y, -ies kə:tis|i ['kɔ:t-, 'kɔət-, -təs-], -iz
court-guide, -s 'kɔ:tgaid ['kɔət-], -z
Courthope 'kɔ:təp ['kɔət-], -thəup

court-hou|se, -ses 'kɔ:thau|s ['kɔət-, '-'-], -ziz
Courtice 'kɔ:tis
courtier, -s 'kɔ:tjə* ['kɔət-, -tĭə*, -tiə*], -z
courtl|y, -ier, -iest, -iness 'kɔ:tl|i ['kɔət-], -ĭə* [-jə*], -iist [-jist], -inis
court-marti|al (s. v.), -als, -alling, -alled 'kɔ:t'mɑ:ʃ|əl ['kɔət-], -əlz, -ļiŋ [-əliŋ], -əld
Courtneidge 'kɔ:tnidʒ ['kɔət-]
Courtney 'kɔ:tni ['kɔət-]
court-plaster 'kɔ:t'plɑ:stə* ['kɔət-, '-ˌ--]
courtship, -s 'kɔ:t-ʃip ['kɔət-], -s
courts-martial 'kɔ:ts'mɑ:ʃəl ['kɔəts-]
courtyard, -s 'kɔ:t-jɑ:d ['kɔ:t'jɑ:d, 'kɔət-], -z
cousin, -s 'kʌzn, -z
Cousins 'kʌznz
Coutts ku:ts
Couzens 'kʌznz
cove (C.), -s kəuv, -z
covenant (s. v.), -s, -ing, -ed, -er/s 'kʌvənənt [-vin-, -vņ-], -s, -iŋ, -id, -ə*/z
Covent 'kovənt [old-fashioned 'kʌv-]
Coventry 'kovəntri [rarely 'kʌv-]
cov|er (s.v.), -ers, -ering/s, -ered, -erage 'kʌv|ə*, -əz, -əriŋ/z, -əd, -əridʒ
Coverack 'kovəræk [locally also -rək]
Coverdale 'kʌvədeil
coverlet, -s 'kʌvəlit, -s
Coverley 'kʌvəli
Covernton 'kʌvə(:)ntən
cover-point, -s 'kʌvə'pɔint ['kʌvəp-], -s
covert (s.) (shelter, cloth), -s 'kʌvə*, -z ['kʌvət, -s]
Note.—See also wing-covert.
covert (adj.), -ly 'kʌvət, -li
covert-coat, -s 'kʌvət'kəut ['---, less freq. 'kʌvəkəut], -s
coverture 'kʌvətjuə* [-tʃuə*]
covet, -s, -ing, -ed 'kʌvit, -s, -iŋ, -id
covetous, -ly, -ness 'kʌvitəs, -li, -nis
covey (of birds), -s 'kʌvi, -z
covey (familiar diminutive of cove), -s 'kəuvi, -z
Covington 'kʌviŋtən
cow (s. v.), -s, -ing, -ed kau, -z, -iŋ, -d
Cowal 'kau-əl
Cowan 'kau-ən
coward (C.), -s 'kauəd ['kau-əd], -z
cowardice 'kauədis ['kau-ədis]
cowardl|y, -iness 'kauədl|i ['kau-əd-], -inis
cowbane 'kaubein
cowboy, -s 'kaubɔi, -z
cow-catcher, -s 'kauˌkætʃə*, -z

Cowden (in Kent) 'kauden [kau'den]
Cowdenbeath 'kaudn'bi:θ
Cowdray 'kaudrei [attributively also -dri]
Cowdrey 'kaudri
Cowen 'kauin ['kau-ən], 'kəuin ['kəuən]
cower, -s, -ing, -ed 'kauə* ['kau-ə*], -z, -riŋ, -d
Cowes kauz
cowherd, -s 'kauhə:d, -z
cowhide 'kauhaid
cow-hou|se, -ses 'kauhau|s, -ziz
Cowie 'kaui
cowl, -s kaul, -z
Cowley 'kauli
cowlike 'kaulaik
Cowper 'kaupə*, 'ku:pə*
Note.—The poet called himself 'ku:pə*. 'ku:pə* is also the pronunciation in Cowper Powys ('ku:pə 'pəuis) and Cowper-Black.
cow-pox 'kau-pɔks
cow-puncher, -s 'kauˌpʌntʃə*, -z
cowr|ie [-r|y], -ies 'kaur|i ['kauər-], -iz
cowshed, -s 'kau-ʃed, -z
cowslip, -s 'kauslip, -s
Cowt|an, -on 'kaut|n, -n
cox (C.), -es kɔks, -iz
coxcomb, -s 'kɔkskəum, -z
coxswain, -s 'kɔkswein [nautical pronunciation 'kɔksn], -z
Coxtie 'kɔksti
cox|y, -ier, -iest, -iness 'kɔks|i, -ĭə*, -iist, -inis
coy, -er, -est, -ly, -ness kɔi, -ə*, -ist, -li, -nis
coyish, -ly, -ness 'kɔiiʃ, -li, -nis
coyote, -s 'kɔiəut [kɔi'əut], -s [kɔi'əuti, -z]
coypu, -s 'kɔipu: [-pju:], -z
Coysh kɔiʃ
coz kʌz
coz|en, -ens, -ening, -ened, -ener/s 'kʌz|n, -nz, -ņiŋ, -nd, -ņə*/z
Cozens 'kʌznz
Coz|y (stove), -ies 'kəuz|i, -iz
crab, -s kræb, -z
crab-apple, -s 'kræbˌæpl, -z
Crabbe kræb
crabbed, -ly, -ness 'kræbid, -li, -nis
crabtree (C.), -s 'kræbtri:, -z
crack (s. v.), -s, -ing, -ed kræk, -s, -iŋ, -t
crack-brain, -ed 'krækbrein, -d
Crackenthorpe 'krækənθɔ:p
cracker, -s 'krækə*, -z
crack|le, -les, -ling, -led 'kræk|l, -lz, -ļiŋ [-liŋ], -ld
crackling (s.) 'krækliŋ
crackly 'kræk|i ['krækli]

cracknel, -s 'kræknḷ [-nəl], -z
Cracknell 'kræknḷ [-nəl]
Cracow 'krækəu ['krɑːk-, -kau]
crad|le (s. v.), -les, -ling, -led 'kreid|l,
-lz, -liŋ [-lịŋ], -ld
Cradley 'kreidli
craft, -s krɑːft, -s
crafts|man, -men, -manship 'krɑːfts|-
mən, -mən, -mənʃip
craft|y, -ier, -iest, -ily, -iness 'krɑːft|i,
-iə* [-jə*], -iist [-jist], -ili, -inis
crag, -s kræg, -z
Cragg kræg
cragg|y, -ier, -iest, -ily, -iness 'kræg|i,
-iə*, -iist, -ili, -inis
crags|man, -men 'krægz|mən, -mən
[-men]
Craig, -ie kreig, -i
Craigavon (Viscount) kreig'ævən
Craigenputtock ˌkreigən'pʌtək
Craik kreik
crak|e (s. v.), -es, -ing, -ed kreik, -s, -iŋ,
-t
cram (s. v.), -s, -ming, -med, -mer/s
kræm, -z, -iŋ, -d, -ə*/z
crambo 'kræmbəu
Cramer 'krɑːmə*
cram-full 'kræm'ful [also '-- when
followed by a stress]
Cramlington 'kræmliŋtən
cramoisy 'kræmɔizi
cramp (s. v.) (C.), -s, -ing, -ed kræmp,
-s, -iŋ, -t [kræmt]
cramp-iron, -s 'kræmpˌaiən, -z
crampon, -s 'kræmpən, -z
Crampton 'kræmᵖtən
cran, -s kræn, -z
cranage 'kreinidʒ
Cranage (surname) 'krænidʒ
cranberr|y, -ies 'krænbər|i, -iz
Cranborne 'krænbɔːn [-bɔən]
Cranbourn(e) 'krænbɔːn [-bɔən, -buən]
Cranbrook 'krænbruk
cran|e (s. v.) (C.), -es, -ing, -ed krein, -z,
-iŋ, -d
Cranford 'krænfəd
cranial 'kreinjəl [-nịəl]
craniolog|ist/s, -y ˌkreini'ɔlədʒ|ist/s, -i
crani|um, -ums, -a 'kreinj|əm [-nị|əm],
-əmz, -ə
crank, -s kræŋk, -s
Crankshaw 'kræŋkʃɔː
crank|y, -ier, -iest, -ily, -iness 'kræŋk|i,
-iə* [-jə*], -iist [-jist], -ili, -inis
Cran|leigh, -ley, -mer 'kræn|li, -li, -mə*
crann|y, -ies, -ied 'kræn|i, -iz, -id
Cran|ston, -worth 'kræn|stən, -wəːθ
crape, -s kreip, -s

crapulen|ce, -t/ly 'kræpjulən|s, -t/li
crapulous 'kræpjuləs
crash (s. v.), -es, -ing, -ed kræʃ, -iz, -iŋ,
-t
Crashaw 'kræʃɔː
crash-div|e (s. v.), -es, -ing, -ed 'kræʃ-
daiv, -z, -iŋ, -d
crash-helmet, -s 'kræʃˌhelmit, -s
crash-land, -s, -ing, -ed 'kræʃlænd, -z,
-iŋ, -id
crasis 'kreisis
crass, -er, -est, -ly, -ness kræs, -ə*, -ist,
-li, -nis
crassitude 'kræsitjuːd
cratch, -es krætʃ, -iz
Cratchit 'krætʃit
crate, -s kreit, -s
crater, -s 'kreitə*, -z
Crathie 'kræθi
cravat, -s, -ted krə'væt, -s, -id
crav|e, -es, -ing/s, -ed, -er/s kreiv, -z,
-iŋ/z, -d, -ə*/z
craven (C.), -s 'kreivən, -z
craw, -s krɔː, -z
Crawcour 'krɔːkə*
crawfish, -es 'krɔː-fiʃ, -iz
Crawford 'krɔːfəd
crawl (s. v.), -s, -ing, -ed, -er/s krɔːl, -z,
-iŋ, -d, -ə*/z
Crawley 'krɔːli
crawl|y, -ier, -iest, -iness 'krɔː|li, -iə*
[-jə*], -iist [-jist], -inis
crayfish, -es 'krei-fiʃ, -iz
crayon, -s 'kreiən ['kreiɔn], -z
craze, -s, -d kreiz, -iz, -d
craz|y, -ier, -iest, -ily, -iness 'kreiz|i,
-iə* [-jə*], -iist [-jist], -ili, -inis
Creagh krei
Creaghan 'kriːgən
creak (s. v.), -s, -ing, -ed kriːk, -s, -iŋ, -t
creak|y, -ier, -iest, -ily, -iness 'kriːk|i,
-iə* [-jə*], -iist [-jist], -ili, -inis
cream, -s kriːm, -z
cream-cheese, -s 'kriːm'tʃiːz, -iz
cream-coloured 'kriːmˌkʌləd
creamer|y, -ies 'kriːmər|i, -iz
cream-laid 'kriːm'leid
cream-wove 'kriːm'wəuv
cream|y, -ier, -iest, -ily, -iness 'kriːm|i,
-iə* [-jə*], -iist [-jist], -ili, -inis
creas|e (s. v.), -es, -ing, -ed kriːs, -iz, -iŋ,
-t
Creas(e)y 'kriːsi
creasy (adj.) 'kriːsi
creat|e, -es, -ing, -ed kri(ː)'eit, -s, -iŋ, -id
creation (C.), -s kri(ː)'eiʃən, -z
creationi|sm, -st/s kri(ː)'eiʃni|zəm
[-ʃəni-], -st/s

creative, -ly, -ness kri(:)'eitiv, -li, -nis
creator (C.), -s kri(:)'eitə*, -z
creature, -s 'kri:tʃə*, -z
crèche, -s kreiʃ, -iz
Crécy 'kresi
credence 'kri:dəns
credential, -s kri'denʃəl, -z
credibility ,kredi'biliti [-də'b-, -lət-]
credib|le, -ly, -leness 'kredəb|l [-dib-],
    -li, -lnis
credit (s. v.), -s, -ing, -ed, -or/s 'kredit,
    -s, -iŋ, -id, -ə*/z
creditab|le, -ly, -leness 'kreditəb|l, ,li-
Crediton 'kreditn   [-lnis
credo, -s 'kri:dəu ['kreid-], -z
credulity kri'dju:liti [kre'd-, krə'd-]
credulous, -ly, -ness 'kredjuləs, -li, -nis
creed (C.), -s kri:d, -z
creek, -s kri:k, -s
creel, -s kri:l, -z
creep, -s, -ing, crept kri:p, -s, -iŋ, krept
creeper, -s 'kri:pə*, -z
creep|y, -ier, -iest, -ily, -iness 'kri:p|i,
    -iə* [-jə*], -iist [-jist], -ili, -inis
Crees kri:s, kri:z
creese, -s kri:s, -iz
Creighton 'kraitn
cremat|e, -es, -ing, -ed, -or/s kri'meit
    [krə'm-], -s, -iŋ, -id, -ə*/z
cremation, -s kri'meiʃən [krə'm-], -z
crematori|al, -um/s ,kremə'tɔ:rĭ|əl,
    -əm/z
cremator|y, -ies 'kremətər|i, -iz
crème-de-menthe   'kreimdə'mɑ:nt
    [-'mɔ:nt, -'mɔnt] (krɛːmdəmã:t)
Cremona kri'məunə [krə'm-]
crenate 'kri:neit
crenel(l)at|e, -es, -ing, -ed 'krenileit
    [-nəl-], -s, -iŋ, -id
crenel(l)ation, -s ,kreni'leiʃən [-nə'l-], -z
Creole, -s 'kri:əul ['kriəul], -z
Creolian kri(:)'əuljən [-lĭən]
creosote 'kriəsəut ['kri:əs-]
crêpe, -s kreip, -s
crêpe de chine 'kreipdə'ʃi:n (krɛpdə-
    ʃin)
crepitat|e, -es, -ing, -ed 'krepiteit, -s,
    -iŋ, -id
crepitation, -s ,krepi'teiʃən, -z
crépon 'krepɔ̃:ŋ ['kreip-, -pɔ:ŋ, -pɔn]
    (krepɔ̃)
crept (from creep) krept
crepuscular kri'pʌskjulə* [kre'p-]
crepuscule 'krepəskju:l
Crerar 'kriərə*
crescendo, -s kri'ʃendəu [krə'ʃ], -z
crescent (moon, shape), -s 'kresnt
    [old-fashioned -eznt], -s

crescent (growing, when applied to
    objects other than the moon) 'kresnt
Crespigny (surname) 'krepini, 'krepni,
    'krespini, (in London streets) kres'pi:ni
cress, -es kres, -iz
Cressida 'kresidə
Cresswell 'krezwəl, -esw-
Cressy 'kresi
crest (s. v.), -s, -ing, -ed krest, -s, -iŋ, -id
crestfallen 'krest,fɔ:lən
Creswick 'krezik
cretaceous kri'teiʃəs [kre't-, -ʃjəs, -ʃĭəs]
Cretan, -s 'kri:tən, -z
Crete kri:t
Cretic, -s 'kri:tik, -s
cretin, -s 'kretin ['kri:t-], -z
cretinism 'kretinizəm ['kri:t-]
cretonne, -s kre'tɔn ['kretɔn], -z
Creusa kri'u:zə [kri'ju:-]
crevasse, -s, -d kri'væs [krə'v-], -iz, -t
crevice, -s 'krevis, -iz
crew, -s kru:, -z
crew (from crow) kru:
crew-cut 'kru:-kʌt
Crewe kru:
crewel, -s 'kru:il [kruil, -əl], -z
Crewkerne 'kru:kə:n ['krukən, rarely
    kru:'kə:n]
Crianlarich kriən'lærik [-ix]
crib (s. v.), -s, -bing, -bed, -ber/s krib,
    -z, -iŋ, -d, -ə*/z
cribbage 'kribidʒ
cribbage-board, -s 'kribidʒbɔ:d [-bɔəd],
    -z
Criccieth 'krikieθ [-kĭəθ, -kjəθ] (Welsh
    'krikjeθ)
Crichel 'kritʃəl
Crichton 'kraitn
crick (s. v.), -s, -ing, -ed krik, -s, -iŋ, -t
cricket, -s, -er/s 'krikit, -s, -ə*/z
cricket-match, -es 'krikitmætʃ, -iz
cricklite 'kriklait
cricoid 'kraikɔid
cried (from cry) kraid
Crieff kri:f
crier, -s 'krai-ə* ['kraiə*], -z
cries (from cry) kraiz
crime, -s kraim, -z
Crimea, -n krai'miə [kri'm-], -n
crimin|al/s, -ally 'krimin|l/z, -əli
criminality ,krimi'næliti
criminat|e, -es, -ing, -ed 'krimineit, -s,
    -iŋ, -id
crimination, -s ,krimi'neiʃən, -z
criminolog|ist/s, -y ,krimi'nɔlədʒ|ist/s,
    -i
crimp (adj. v.), -s, -ing, -ed krimp, -s,
    -iŋ, -t [krimt]

crims|on (s. v.), -ons, -oning, -oned
'krimz|n, -nz, -ŋiŋ [-niŋ], -nd
crinal 'krainl
cring|e (s. v.), -es, -ing, -ed, -er/s
krin dʒ, -iz, -iŋ, -d, -ə*/z
crink|le, -les, -ling, -led 'kriŋk|l, -lz,
-liŋ [-liŋ], -ld
crinkly 'kriŋkli
crinoid, -s 'krainɔid ['krin-], -z
crinoline (s.), -s 'krinəli:n [-lin, ˌkrinə-
'li:n], -z
crinoline (adj.) 'krinəlin
Crippen 'kripin
cripp|le (s. v.), -les, -ling, -led 'krip|l,
-lz, -ŋiŋ [-liŋ], -ld
Cripplegate 'kripl geit [-git]
Crisfield 'krisfi:ld
cris|is, -es 'krais|is, -i:z
crisp (C.), -er, -est, -ly, -ness krisp, -ə*,
-ist, -li, -nis
crisp-bread 'krispbred
Crispin 'krispin
criss-cross 'kriskrɔs [-krɔ:s]   [-ənz, -ə
criteri|on (C.), -ons, -a krai'tiəri|ən,
-ənz, -ə
critic, -s; -al, -ally, -alness 'kritik, -s;
-əl, -əli, -əlnis
criticism, -s 'kritisizəm, -z
criticizable [-isa-] 'kritisaizəbl [ˌkriti's-]
criticiz|e [-is|e], -es, -ing, -ed 'kritisaiz,
-iz, -iŋ, -d
critique, -s kri'ti:k, -s
Crittenden 'kritndən
croak (s. v.), -s, -ing/s, -ed, -er/s krəuk,
-s, -iŋ/z, -t, -ə*/z
croak|y, -ier, -iest, -ily, -iness 'krəuk|i,
-iə* [-jə*], -iist [-jist], -ili, -inis
Croat, -s 'krəuət [-æt], -s
Croatia krəu'eiʃ|ə [-ʃiə, -ʃə]
Croatian, -s krəu'eiʃ|ən [-ʃiən, -ʃən], -z
crochet (s. v.), -s, -ing, -ed 'krəuʃei [-ʃi],
-z, -iŋ, -d
crochet-hook, -s 'krəuʃihuk [-ʃeih-], -s
crock, -s krɔk, -s
Crocker 'krɔkə*
crockery 'krɔkəri
crocket, -s 'krɔkit, -s
Crockett 'krɔkit
crocodile, -s 'krɔkədail, -z
crocus, -es 'krəukəs, -iz
Croesus 'kri:səs
croft (C.), -s krɔft [krɔ:ft], -s
crofter, -s 'krɔftə* ['krɔ:f-], -z
Croker 'krəukə*
Cro-Magnon krəu'mænjɔ̃:ŋ (krɔmaɲɔ̃)
Cromarty 'krɔməti
Crombie 'krɔmbi, 'krʌm-
Crome krəum
Cromer 'krəumə*

cromlech, -s 'krɔmlek, -s
Crommelin 'krʌmlin, 'krɔm-
Crompton 'krʌmptən, 'krɔm-
Cromwell 'krɔmwəl ['krʌm-, -wel]
Cromwellian krɔm'welïən [krʌm-, -ljən]
crone, -s krəun, -z
Cronin 'krəunin
cron|y, -ies 'krəun|i, -iz
crook (s. v.) (C.), -s, -ing, -ed (p. part.)
kruk, -s, -iŋ, -t
Crookback 'krukbæk
crook-backed 'krukbækt
Crooke, -s kruk, -s
crooked (adj.) (not straight), -er, -est,
-ly, -ness 'krukid, -ə*, -ist, -li, -nis
crooked (adj.) (having a crook) krukt
Croome kru:m
croon (s. v.), -s, -ing, -ed, -er/s kru:n, -z,
-iŋ, -d, -ə*/z
crop (s. v.), -s, -ping, -ped krɔp, -s, -iŋ, -t
cropper, -s 'krɔpə*, -z
croquet (s. v.), -s, -ing, -ed 'krəukei
[-ki], -z, -iŋ, -id
croquette, -s krɔ'ket [krəu-], -s
crore, -s krɔ:* [krɔə*], -z
Crosby 'krɔzbi, 'krɔsbi ['krɔ:sbi]
Crosfield 'krɔsfi:ld ['krɔ:s-]
Croshaw 'krəuʃɔ:
crosier, -s 'krəuʒə*, -z
Crosier 'krəuʒjə* [-zïə*], 'krəuʒə*
cross (s. adj. v.) (C.), -es; -er, -est, -ly,
-ness; -ing, -ed krɔs [krɔ:s], -iz; -ə*,
-ist, -li, -nis; -iŋ, -t
cross-action, -s 'krɔsˌækʃən ['krɔ:s-], -z
cross-bar, -s 'krɔsbɑ:* ['krɔ:s-], -z
cross-beam, -s 'krɔsbi:m ['krɔ:s-], -z
cross-bench, -es 'krɔsbentʃ ['krɔ:s-], -iz
crossbill, -s 'krɔsbil ['krɔ:s-], -z
crossbones 'krɔsbəunz ['krɔ:s-]
crossbow, -s 'krɔsbəu ['krɔ:s-], -z
crossbred 'krɔsbred ['krɔ:s-]
crossbreed, -s 'krɔsbri:d ['krɔ:s-], -z
cross-bun, -s 'krɔs'bʌn ['krɔ:s-], -z
cross-country 'krɔs'kʌntri ['krɔ:s-, '-ˌ--
when followed by a stress]
crosscut, -s 'krɔskʌt ['krɔ:s-], -s
crosse, -s krɔs, -iz
Crosse krɔs [krɔ:s]
cross-examination, -s 'krɔsigˌzæmi-
'neiʃən ['krɔ:s-, -eg-], -z
cross-examin|e, -es, -ing, -ed, -er/s
'krɔsig'zæmin ['krɔ:s-, -eg-], -z, -iŋ, -d,
-ə*/z
cross|-eyed, -grained 'krɔs|aid ['krɔ:s-],
-greind
crossing (s.), -s 'krɔsiŋ ['krɔ:s-], -z
crossing-sweeper, -s 'krɔsiŋˌswi:pə*
['krɔ:s-], -z

cross-jack, -s 'krɔsdʒæk ['krɔ:s-], -s

cross-legged 'krɔslegd ['krɔ:s-]

Cross|ley, -man 'krɔs|li ['krɔ:s-], -mən

crosspatch, -es 'krɔspætʃ ['krɔ:s-], -iz

cross-purpose, -s 'krɔs'pə:pəs ['krɔ:s-], -iz

cross-questi|on, -ons, -oning, -oned 'krɔs'kwestʃ|ən ['krɔ:s-, -eʃtʃ-, -'--], -ənz, -əniŋ [-ʃiŋ], -ənd

cross-road, -s 'krɔsrəud ['krɔ:s-], -z

cross-row, -s 'krɔsrəu ['krɔ:s-], -z

cross-section, -s 'krɔs'sekʃən ['krɔ:s-], -z

cross-stitch 'krɔsstitʃ ['krɔ:s-]

crossway, -s 'krɔswei ['krɔ:s-wei], -z

cross-wise 'krɔswaiz ['krɔ:s-waiz]

cross-word, -s 'krɔswə:d ['krɔ:s-wə:d], -z

Crosthwaite 'krɔsθweit ['krɔ:s-]

crotal|um, -a 'krɔtəl|əm, -ə

crotch (C.), -es krɔtʃ, -iz

crotchet, -s, -y, -iness 'krɔtʃit, -s, -i, -inis

croton (C.) 'krəutən

crouch (C.), -es, -ing, -ed krautʃ, -iz, -iŋ, -t

croup, -s kru:p, -s

croupier, -s 'kru:piə* [-pĭə*, -pjə*, -piei] (krupje), -z

crow (s. v.), -s, -ing, -ed, crew krəu, -z, -iŋ, -d, kru:

crowbar, -s 'krəubɑ:*, -z

crowd (s. v.), -s, -ing, -ed kraud, -z, -iŋ, -id

Crowe krəu

crow-foot 'krəu-fut

Crow|hurst, -land, -ley 'krəu|hə:st, -lənd, -li

crown (s. v.), -s, -ing, -ed kraun, -z, -iŋ, -d

Crowndale 'kraundeil

crown-glass 'kraun'glɑ:s [in contrast '--]

crown-land, -s 'kraun'lænd [in contrast '--], -z

crown-prince, -s 'kraun'prins [also '-- when attributive], -iz

crow-quill, -s 'krəu-kwil, -z

crow's|-foot, -feet 'krəuz|fut, -fi:t

crow's-nest, -s 'krəuznest, -s

Crowte kraut

Crowther 'krauðə*

Croyd|en, -on 'krɔid|n, -n

crozier, -s 'krəuʒə*, -z

Crozier 'krəuzjə* [-zĭə*], 'krəuʒə*

crucial 'kru:ʃəl [-ʃĭəl, -ʃjəl]

crucible, -s 'kru:sibl, -z

crucifix, -es 'kru:sifiks, -iz

crucifixion (C.), -s ,kru:si'fikʃən, -z

cruciform 'kru:sifɔ:m

cruci|fy, -fies, -fying, -fied, -fier/s 'kru:si|fai, -faiz, -faiiŋ, -faid, -faiə*/z

crude, -r, -st, -ly, -ness kru:d, -ə*, -ist, -li, -nis

Cruden 'kru:dn [-dən]

crudit|y, -ies 'kru:dit|i, -iz

cruel, -ness kruəl ['kru:əl, kruil, 'kru:il, kru:l], -nis

cruel|ler, -lest, -ly 'kruəl|ə* ['kru:il-, 'kruil-, 'kru:əl-], -ist, -i

cruelt|y, -ies 'kruəlt|i ['kru:əl-, 'kruil-, 'kru:il-, 'kru:l-], -iz

cruet, -s; -stand/s 'kru(:)it, -s; -stænd/z

Crui(c)kshank 'krukʃæŋk

cruis|e (s. v.), -es, -ing, -ed, -er/s kru:z, -iz, -iŋ, -d, -ə*/z

crumb (s. v.), -s, -ing, -ed krʌm, -z, -iŋ, -d

crumb-brush, -es 'krʌm-brʌʃ, -iz

crumb|le, -les, -ling, -led 'krʌmb|l, -lz, -liŋ, -ld

crumby 'krʌmi

Crummock 'krʌmək

crummy 'krʌmi

crump, -s, -ing, -ed krʌmp, -s, -iŋ, -t [krʌmt]

crumpet, -s 'krʌmpit, -s

crump|le, -les, -ling, -led 'krʌmp|l, -lz, -liŋ [-ḷiŋ], -ld

crunch, -es, -ing, -ed krʌntʃ, -iz, -iŋ, -t

crupper, -s 'krʌpə*, -z

crusade, -s, -er/s kru:'seid, -z, -ə*/z

cruse, -s kru:z, -iz

crush (s. v.), -es, -ing, -ed, -er/s krʌʃ, -iz, -iŋ, -t, -ə*/z

crush-hat, -s 'krʌʃ'hæt, -s

crush-room, -s 'krʌʃrum [-ru:m], -z

Crusoe 'kru:səu ['kru:zəu]

crust, -s krʌst, -s

crusta|cea, -cean/s, -ceous krʌs'tei|ʃə [-ʃĭə, -ʃə], -ʃjən/z [-ʃĭən/z, -ʃən/z], -ʃjəs [-ʃĭəs, -ʃəs]

crustate 'krʌsteit

crustated krʌs'teitid

crustation, -s krʌs'teiʃən, -z

crusted 'krʌstid

crust|y, -ier, -iest, -ily, -iness 'krʌst|i, -iə* [-jə*], -iist [-jist], -ili, -inis

crutch, -es, -ed krʌtʃ, -iz, -t

Crutched Friars 'krʌtʃid'fraiəz ['krʌtʃt-]

Cruttwell 'krʌtwəl

crux, -es krʌks, -iz

cr|y (s. v.), -ies, -ying, -ied, -ier/s kr|ai, -aiz, -aiiŋ, -aid, -ai-ə*/z [-aiə*/z]

cry-bab|y, -ies 'krai,beib|i, -iz

crypt, -s kript, -s

cryptic, -al, -ally 'kriptik, -əl, -əli

crypto, -s 'kriptəu, -z
cryptogam, -s 'kriptəugæm, -z
cryptogram, -s 'kriptəugræm, -z
cryptograph, -s 'kriptəugrɑːf [-græf], -s
cryptograph|er/s, -y krip'tɔgrəf|ə*/z, -i
cryptology krip'tɔlədʒi
Crysell 'kraisl
crystal, -s 'kristl, -z
crystal-gaz|er/s, -ing 'kristl͵geiz|ə*/z, -iŋ
crystalline 'kristəlain [-tl͵ain]
crystallizable [-isa-] 'kristəlaziəbl [-tl͵ai-]
crystallization [-isa-], -s ͵kristəlai-'zeiʃən [-tl͵ai-], -z
crystalliz|e [-is|e], -es, -ing, -ed 'kristəlaiz [-tl͵aiz], -iz, -iŋ, -d
crystallograph|er/s, -y ͵kristə'lɔgrə-f|ə*/z, -i
crystalloid, -s 'kristəlɔid, -z
C-spring, -s 'siː-spriŋ ['siː'spriŋ], -z
cub (s. v.), -s, -bing, -bed kʌb, -z, -iŋ, -d
Cuba, -n/s 'kjuːbə, -n/z
cubage 'kjuːbidʒ
cubbish 'kʌbiʃ
cubb|y, -ies 'kʌb|i, -iz
cubby-hole, -s 'kʌbihəul, -z
cub|e (s. v.), -es, -ing, -ed kjuːb, -z, -iŋ, -d
cubic, -al, -ally 'kjuːbik, -əl, -əli
cubicle, -s 'kjuːbikl, -z
cub|ism, -ist/s 'kjuːb|izəm, -ist/s
cubistic kjuː'bistik
cubit, -s, -al 'kjuːbit, -s, -l
Cubitt 'kjuːbit
cuboid, -s 'kjuːbɔid, -z
Cuchulinn 'kuːkulin ['kuːxu-]
Cuckfield 'kukfiːld
cucking-stool, -s 'kʌkiŋstuːl, -z
Cuckmere 'kukmiə*
cuckold (s. v.), -s, -ing, -ed 'kʌkəuld [-kəld], -z, -iŋ, -id
cuck|oo (s. v.), -oos, -ooing, -ooed 'kuk|uː, -uːz, -u(ː)iŋ, -uːd
cuckoo (interj.) 'kuˈkuː ['kuku:]
cuckoo-clock, -s 'kukuː-klɔk, -s
cuckoo-flower, -s 'kukuː-͵flauə*, -z
cuckoo-pint, -s 'kukuː-pint, -s
cuckoo-spit, -s 'kukuː-spit, -s
cucumber, -s 'kjuːkʌmbə* ['kjukʌm-, 'kjuːkəm-], -z
cud, -s kʌd, -z
Cudahy 'kʌdəhi
cudd|le (s. v.), -les, -ling, -led 'kʌd|l, -lz, -l͵iŋ [-liŋ], -ld
cudd|y, -ies 'kʌd|i, -iz
cudg|el (s. v.), -els, -elling, -elled 'kʌdʒ|əl, -əlz, -l͵iŋ [-əliŋ], -əld
Cudworth 'kʌdwə(ː)θ

cue, -s kjuː, -z
Cufa 'kjuːfə
cuff (s. v.), -s, -ing, -ed kʌf, -s, -iŋ, -t
Cuffe kʌf
Cuffley 'kʌfli
Cufic 'kjuːfik
cui bono 'kwiː'bɔnəu ['kuːi'bɔnəu, 'kuːi'bəunəu, old-fashioned 'kai-'bəunəu]
cuirass, -es kwi'ræs, -iz
cuirassier, -s ͵kwirə'siə*, -z
cuisine kwi(ː)'ziːn (kɥizin)
cuisse, -s kwis, -iz
cul-de-sac, -s 'kuldə'sæk, 'kʌldəsæk (kyldəsak, pronounced as if French), -s
Note.—The actual French pronunciation is kydsak or kytsak.
Culebra ku(ː)'lebrə
Culham 'kʌləm
culinary 'kʌlinəri [old-fashioned 'kjuːl-]
cull, -s, -ing, -ed kʌl, -z, -iŋ, -d
Cull|en, -ey 'kʌl|in, -i
cullender, -s 'kʌlində*, -z
Cullinan 'kʌlinən [-næn]
Cullinnan kʌ'linən [kə'l-]
Culloden kə'lɔdn [kʌ'l-, -'ləudn]
Cullompton kə'lʌmptən
culm, -s kʌlm, -z
Culme kʌlm
culminat|e, -es, -ing, -ed 'kʌlmineit, -s, -iŋ, -id
culmination, -s ͵kʌlmi'neiʃən, -z
culotte, -s kju(ː)'lɔt (kylɔt), -s
culpability ͵kʌlpə'biliti [-lət-]
culpab|le, -ly, -leness 'kʌlpəb|l, -li, -lnis
culprit, -s 'kʌlprit, -s
Culross (place in Scotland) 'kuːrɔs [-rəs], (Scottish surname) 'kuːrɔs [-rəs], (English surname) 'kʌlrɔs, (street in London) 'kʌlrɔs [kʌl'rɔs]
cult, -s kʌlt, -s
Culter (in Scotland) 'kuːtə*
cultivable 'kʌltivəbl
cultivat|e, -es, -ing, -ed, -or/s; -able 'kʌltiveit, -s, -iŋ, -ə*/z; -əbl
cultivation ͵kʌlti'veiʃən
Cults kʌlts
cultur|able, -al 'kʌltʃər|əbl [-tʃur-], -əl
culture, -s, -d 'kʌltʃə*, -z, -d
culver, -s 'kʌlvə*, -z
culverin, -s 'kʌlvərin, -z
culvert, -s; -age 'kʌlvət, -s; -idʒ
Culzean (in Ayrshire) kə'lein
cum kʌm
cumbent 'kʌmbənt
cumb|er, -ers, -ering, -ered, -erer/s 'kʌmb|ə*, -əz, -əriŋ, -əd, -ərə*/z

Cumberland 'kʌmbələnd [-bḷənd]
cumbersome, -ly, -ness 'kʌmbəsəm, -li, -nis
Cumbrian, -s 'kʌmbriən, -z
cumbrous, -ly, -ness 'kʌmbrəs, -li, -nis
cumin 'kʌmin
cummerbund, -s 'kʌməbʌnd, -z
cummin 'kʌmin
Cumming, -s 'kʌmiŋ, -z
Cummuskey (surname) 'kʌmski
Cumnor 'kʌmnə*
cumulate (adj.) 'kju:mjulit [-mjəl-, -leit]
cumulat|e (v.), -es, -ing, -ed 'kju:mju-leit [-mjəl-], -s, -iŋ, -id
cumulation, -s ˌkju:mju'leiʃən [-mjə'l-], -z
cumulative, -ly, -ness 'kju:mjulətiv [-mjəl-, -leit-], -li, -nis
cumulus 'kju:mjuləs [-mjəl-]
Cunard, -er/s kju:'nɑːd [also '-- when attributive], -ə*/z
cunctation, -s kʌŋk'teiʃən, -z
cunctator, -s kʌŋk'teitə*, -z
Cund|all, -ell 'kʌnd|l, -l
cuneiform 'kju:niifɔ:m [-njif-, -nif-]
cuniform 'kju:nifɔ:m
Cunliffe 'kʌnlif
cunning (s. adj.), -est, -ly, -ness 'kʌniŋ, -ist, -li, -nis
Cunningham 'kʌniŋəm
cup (s. v.), -s, -ping, -ped kʌp, -s, -iŋ, -t
Cupar 'ku:pə*
cup-bearer, -s 'kʌpˌbeərə*, -z
cupboard, -s 'kʌbəd, -z
cupboard-love 'kʌbədlʌv ['kʌbəd'l-]
cupful, -s 'kʌpful, -z
cupid (C.), -s 'kju:pid, -z
cupidity kju(:)'piditi
cupola, -s 'kju:pələ, -z
cupping-glass, -es 'kʌpiŋglɑːs, -iz
cupr|eous, -ic, -ous 'kju:pr|iəs, -ik, -əs
cupriferous kju(:)'prifərəs
cur, -s kə:*, -z
curability ˌkjuərə'biliti [ˌkjɔər-, ˌkjɔː:r-, ˌkjə:r-, -lət-]
curable 'kjuərəbl ['kjɔər-, 'kjɔː:r-, 'kjə:r-]
curaç|ao (C.), -oa (C.) ˌkjuərə'səu [ˌkjɔər-, ˌkjɔː:r-], -əuə
curac|y, -ies 'kjuərəs|i ['kjɔər-, 'kjɔː:r-, 'kjə:r-], -iz
Curan 'kʌrən
curare kju'rɑːri [kjuə'r-]
curate, -s 'kjuərit ['kjɔər-, 'kjɔː:r-, 'kjə:r-], -s
curative 'kjuərətiv ['kjɔər-, 'kjɔː:r-, 'kjə:r-]
curator, -s; -ship/s kjuə'reitə* [kju'r-, kjɔə'r-, kjɔː:'r-, kjə(:)'r-], -z; -ʃip/s

curb (s. v.), -s, -ing, -ed kə:b, -z, -iŋ, -d
curbstone, -s 'kə:bstəun, -z
curd, -s kə:d, -z
curd|le, -les, -ling, -led 'kə:d|l, -lz, -liŋ [-ḷiŋ], -ld
curd|y, -ier, -iest, -iness 'kə:d|i, -iə* [-jə*], -iist [-jist], -inis
cur|e (s. v.), -es, -ing, -ed, -er/s kjuə* [kjɔə*, kjɔː:*], -z, -riŋ, -d, -rə*/z
curfew, -s 'kə:fju:, -z
cu|ria, -riae 'kjuə|riə ['kjɔər-, 'kjɔː:r-, 'kuər-], -rii: ['kuəriai]
curie, -s 'kjuəri, -z
curio, -s 'kjuəriəu ['kjɔər-, 'kjɔː:r-, 'kjə:r-], -z
curiosit|y, -ies ˌkjuəri'ɔsit|i [ˌkjɔər-, ˌkjɔː:r-, ˌkjə:r-], -iz
curious, -ly, -ness 'kjuəriəs ['kjɔər-, 'kjɔː:r-, 'kjə:r-], -li, -nis
curium 'kjuəriəm
curl (s. v.), -s, -ing, -ed, -er/s kə:l, -z, -iŋ, -d, -ə*/z
curlew, -s 'kə:lju: [-lu:], -z
curling (s.) 'kə:liŋ
curling-iron, -s 'kə:liŋˌaiən, -z
curling-stone, -s 'kə:liŋ-stəun, -z
curling-tongs 'kə:liŋ-tɔŋz
curl|y, -ier, -iest 'kə:l|i, -iə* [-jə*], -iist [-jist]
curmudgeon, -s kə:'mʌdʒən, -z
curr, -s, -ing, -ed kə:*, -z, -riŋ, -d
curragh (C.), -s 'kʌrə, -z
Curran 'kʌrən
currant, -s 'kʌrənt, -s
currenc|y, -ies 'kʌrəns|i, -iz
current (s. adj.), -s, -ly, -ness 'kʌrənt, -s, -li, -nis
Currer 'kʌrə*
curricul|um, -a kə'rikjul|əm [-kjəl-], -ə
Currie 'kʌri
currish, -ly, -ness 'kə:riʃ, -li, -nis
curr|y (s. v.) (C.), -ies, -ying, -ied, -ier/s 'kʌr|i, -iz, -iiŋ, -id, -iə*/z
curry-powder 'kʌriˌpaudə*
curs|e (s. v.), -es, -ing, -ed kə:s, -iz, -iŋ, -t
cursed (adj.), -ly, -ness 'kə:sid, -li, -nis
cursive, -ly, -ness 'kə:siv, -li, -nis
Cursor Mundi 'kə:sɔ:'mundi: [-'mʌndai]
cursor|y, -ily, -iness 'kə:sər|i, -ili, -inis
cursus 'kə:səs
curt, -er, -est, -ly, -ness kə:t, -ə*, -ist, -li, -nis
curtail, -s, -ing, -ed, -ment/s kə:'teil, -z, -iŋ, -d, -mənt/s
curtain, -s, -ed 'kə:tn [-tən, -tin], -z, -d
curtain-raiser, -s 'kə:tnˌreizə*, -z
curtesy 'kə:tisi [-təsi]
Curti|ce, -s(s) 'kə:ti|s, -s

curtsey (s. v.), -s, -ing, -ed 'kə:tsi, -z, -iŋ ['kə:tsjiŋ], -d
curts|y (s. v.), -ies, -ying, -ied 'kə:ts|i, -iz, -iiŋ [-jiŋ], -id
curvation, -s kə:'veiʃən, -z
curvature, -s 'kə:vətʃə*, [-tʃuə*, -tjuə*], -z
curv|e (s. v.), -es, -ing, -ed kə:v, -z, -iŋ, -d
curvet (s. v.), -s, -(t)ing, -(t)ed kə:'vet, -s, -iŋ, -id
curviline|a, -ar ,kə:vi'linǐ|əl [-nj|əl], -ə*
curvital 'kə:vitl
Curwen 'kə:win [-wən]
Curzon 'kə:zn
Cusack 'kju:sæk, 'kju:zək
cushat, -s 'kʌʃət [-ʃæt], -s
Cushing 'kuʃiŋ
cushi|on (s. v.), -ons, -oning, -oned 'kuʃ|ən [-in], -ənz [-inz], -ŋiŋ [-əniŋ, -iniŋ], -ənd [-ind]
Cushny 'kʌʃni
cushy 'kuʃi
Cusins 'kju:zinz
cusp, -s kʌsp, -s
cuspidor, -s 'kʌspidɔ:*, -z
cuss, -es kʌs, -iz
cussed, -ly, -ness 'kʌsid, -li, -nis
Custance 'kʌstəns
custard, -s 'kʌstəd, -z
custard-apple, -s 'kʌstəd,æpl, -z
custodial kʌs'təudjəl [-dǐəl]
custodian, -s kʌs'təudjən [-dǐən], -z
custody 'kʌstədi
custom, -s 'kʌstəm, -z
customar|y, -ily, -iness 'kʌstəmər|i, -ili, -inis
customer, -s 'kʌstəmə*, -z
custom-hou|se, -ses 'kʌstəmhau|s, -ziz
custos, custodes 'kʌstɔs, kʌs'təudi:z
cut (s. v.), -s, -ting, -ter/s kʌt, -s, -iŋ, ə*/z
cutaneous kju(:)'teinjəs [-nǐəs]
cut-away 'kʌtəwei
Cutch kʌtʃ (Hind. kəch)
cutcherr|y, -ies kʌ'tʃer|i [kə'tʃ-], -iz
cute, -r, -st, -ly, -ness kju:t, -ə*, -ist, -li, -nis
Cutforth 'kʌtfɔ:θ
Cuthbert, -son 'kʌθbət, -sn
cuticle, -s 'kju:tikl, -z
cuticular kju(:)'tikjulə*
cutis 'kju:tis
cutlass, -es 'kʌtləs, -iz
cutler, -s, -y 'kʌtlə*, -z, -ri
cutlet, -s 'kʌtlit, -s
cut-off, -s 'kʌtɔf [-ɔ:f], -s
cut-out, -s 'kʌtaut, -s

Cuttell kə'tel
cutter, -s 'kʌtə*, -z
cut-throat, -s 'kʌtθrəut, -s
cutting (s.), -s 'kʌtiŋ, -z
cuttle (C.), -s; -bone 'kʌtl, -z; -bəun
cuttle-fish, -es 'kʌtlfiʃ, -iz
cutt|y, -ies 'kʌt|i, -iz
cutwater, -s 'kʌt,wɔ:tə*, -z
cuvette, -s kju:'vet (kyvɛt), -s
Cuvier 'kju:viei ['ku:-] (kyvje)
Cuxhaven 'kuks,ha:vən (kuks'ha:fən)
Cuyp, -s kaip, -s
cwm, -s ku:m [kum] (Welsh kum), -z
cwt., cwts. 'hʌndrədweit [-drid-], -s
cyanate 'saiəneit
cyanic sai'ænik
cyanide, -s 'saiənaid, -z
cyanogen sai'ænədʒin [-dʒen]
cybernetic, -s ,saibə:'netik [-bə'n-], -s
Cyclades 'siklədi:z
cyclamen, -s 'sikləmən [-klim-], -z
cyc|le (s. v.), -les, -ling, -led 'saik|l, -lz, -liŋ, -ld
cyclic, -al, -ally 'saiklik ['sik-], -əl, -əli
cyclist, -s 'saiklist, -s
cyclograph, -s 'saikləugra:f [-græf], -s
cycloid, -s 'saiklɔid, -z
cycloidal sai'klɔidl
cyclometer, -s sai'klɔmitə*, -z
cyclone, -s 'saikləun, -z
cyclonic sai'klɔnik
cyclopaed|ia [-ped-], -ias, -ic ,saikləu-'pi:d|jə [-d|ǐə], -jəz [-ǐəz], -ik
cyclopean sai'kləupjən [-pǐən, ,saikləu-'pi:ən]
cyclops, cyclopes 'saiklɔps, sai'kləupi:z
cyclostyl|e (s. v.), -es, -ing, -ed 'saikləu-stail, -z, -iŋ, -d
cyclotron, -s 'saiklətrɔn, -z
cyder, -s 'saidə*, -z
cygnet, -s 'signit, -s
Cygnus 'signəs
cylinder, -s 'silində*, -z
cylindric, -al, -ally si'lindrik, -əl, -əli
cylindriform si'lindrifɔ:m
cylindroid, -s 'silindrɔid [si'l-], -z
cyli|x, -ces 'saili|ks, -si:z
cyma, -s, -ta 'saimə, -z, -tə
cymar, -s si'ma:*, -z
cymbal, -s 'simbəl, -z
cymbalo, -s 'simbələu, -z
Cymbeline 'simbili:n [-bəl-]
cyme, -s saim, -z
cymograph, -s 'saiməugra:f [-græf], -s
Cymr|ic, -y 'kimr|ik, -i
Cynewulf 'kiniwulf
cynic (s. adj.), -s, -al, -ally 'sinik, -s, -əl -əli

cynicism, -s 'sinisizəm, -z
cynocephalic ˌsainəuse'fælik
cynocephalous ˌsainəu'sefələs
cynosure, -s 'sinəzjuə* ['sain-, -əʒjuə*,
    -əʒuə*, -əsjuə*, -əʃuə*], -z
Cynthi|a, -us 'sinθi|ə [-θj|ə], -əs
cyph|er (s. v.), -ers, -ering, -ered
    'saif|ə*, -əz, -əriŋ, -əd
cy près 'si:'prei
cypress, -es 'saipris [-prəs], -iz
Cyprian, -s 'sipriən, -z
Cypriot, -s 'sipriət [-riɔt], -s
Cypriote, -s 'sipriəut, -s
Cyprus 'saiprəs
Cyrenaica ˌsaiərə'neiikə [-ri'n-]
Cyrene sai'ri:ni [ˌsaiə'r-]
Cyrenian sai'ri:njən [ˌsaiə'r-, si'r-,
    -niən]
Cyrenius sai'ri:njəs [ˌsaiə'r-, -niəs]

Cyril 'sirəl [-ril]
Cyrille 'siril, si'ri:l
Cyrillic si'rilik
Cyrus 'saiərəs
cyst, -s, -ic, -oid sist, -s, -ik, -ɔid
cystitis sis'taitis
Cythera si'θiərə
Cytherean ˌsiθə'ri(:)ən
cytology sai'tɔlədʒi
czar (C.), -s zɑ:*, -z
czardas, -es 'tʃɑ:dæʃ ['zɑ:dæs, -dəs], -iz
czarevitch (C.), -es 'zɑ:rəvitʃ [-riv-], -iz
czarevna (C.), -s zɑ:'revnə, -z
czarina, -s zɑ:'ri:nə, -z
Czech, -s tʃek, -s
Czechoslovak, -s 'tʃekəu'sləuvæk, -s
Czechoslovakia, -n 'tʃekəu-sləu'vækiə
    [-'vækjə, 'vɑ:kiə, -'vɑ:kjə], -n
Czerny 'tʃə:ni ['zə:-]

D

D (*the letter*), **-'s** di:, -z
dab (*s. v.*), **-s, -bing, -bed, -ber/s** dæb,
-z, -iŋ, -d, -ə*/z
dabb|le, -les, -ling, -led, -ler/s 'dæb|l,
-lz, -liŋ [-liŋ], -ld, -lə*/z [-lə*/z]
dabchick, -s 'dæbtʃik, -s
da capo dɑ:'kɑ:pəu
dace deis
dachshund, -s 'dækshund, -z
Da|cia, -cian/s 'dei|sjə [-sïə, -ʃjə, -ʃïə,
-ʃə], -sjən/z [-sïən/z, -ʃjən/z, -ʃïən/z,
-ʃən/z]
dacoit, -s, -age də'kɔit, -s, -idʒ
Dacre, -s 'deikə*, -z
dacron 'dækrɔn ['dei-]
dactyl, -s 'dæktil, -z
dactylic dæk'tilik
dactylogram, -s dæk'tiləugræm ['----],
-z
dactylography ˌdækti'lɔgrəfi
dad, -s dæd, -z
Daddo 'dædəu
dadd|y, -ies 'dæd|i, -iz
daddy-long-legs 'dædi'lɔŋlegz [ˌdæd-]
dado, -s 'deidəu, -z
Daedalus 'di:dələs
daemon, -s 'di:mən, -z
D'Aeth deiθ
daffadowndill|y, -ies 'dæfədaun'dil|i, -iz
daffodil, -s 'dæfədil, -z
daft, -er, -est, -ly, -ness dɑ:ft, -ə*, -ist,
-li, -nis
dag, -s dæg, -z
dagger, -s 'dægə*, -z
Daggett 'dægit
dago, -(e)s 'deigəu, -z
dagoba, -s 'dɑ:gəbə, -z
Dagobert 'dægəubə:t
Dagon 'deigɔn [-gən]
Dagonet 'dægənət [-nit]
daguerr(e)otype, -s də'gerəutaip, -s
D'Aguilar 'dægwilə*
dahlia, -s 'deiljə [-ïə], -z
Dahomey də'həumi
Daiches (*surname*) 'deiʃiz, 'deitʃiz
Dail Eireann dail'ɛərən [dɔil-, *rarely*
dɑ:l-, dɔ:l-]
dail|y (*s. adj. adv.*), **-ies** 'deil|i, -iz
Daimler (*car*) **-s** 'deimlə*, -z

Dain, -es dein, -z
Daintree 'deintri: [-tri]
daint|y (*s. adj.*), **-ies; -ier, -iest, -ily,
-iness** 'deint|i, -iz; -ïə* [-jə*], -iist
[-jist], -ili, -inis
Dairen dai'ren
dair|y, -ies 'dɛər|i, -iz
dairy-farm, -s 'dɛərifɑ:m, -z
dairymaid, -s 'dɛərimeid, -z
dairy|man, -men 'dɛəri|mən [-mæn],
mən [-men]
dais, -es 'deiis [deis], -iz
dais|y (**D.**), **-ies** 'deiz|i, -iz
daisy-chain, -s 'deizi-tʃein, -z
dak (*post in India*), **-s** dɑ:k [*old-
fashioned* dɔ:k], -s
Dakar 'dækə*, 'dækɑ:*
Dakota, -s də'kəutə, -z
Dalai Lama, -s 'dælai'lɑ:mə ['dɑ:lai-,
də'lai-], -z
Dalbeattie dæl'bi:ti
Dalbiac 'dɔ:lbiæk
Dalby 'dɔ:lbi, 'dælbi
Daldy 'dældi
dale (**D.**), **-s** deil, -z
D'Alembert 'dæləmbɛə* [-lɔm-]
(dalãbɛ:r)
dales|man, -men 'deilz|mən [-mæn],
-mən [-men]
Dalgleish dæl'gli:ʃ
Dalhousie dæl'hauzi
Dalila də'lailə
Dalkeith dæl'ki:θ
Dalkey (*suburb of Dublin*) 'dɔ:ki
Dallam 'dæləm
Dallas 'dæləs
dalliance 'dælïəns [-ljəns]
dall|y, -ies, -ying, -ied, -ier/s 'dæl|i, -iz,
-iiŋ, -id, -ïə*/z
Dalmanutha ˌdælmə'nu:θə [-'nju:-]
Dalma|tia, -tian/s dæl'mei|ʃjə [-ʃïə,
-ʃə], -ʃjən/z [-ʃïən/z, -ʃən/z]
Dalmeny dæl'meni
Dalnaspidal ˌdælnə'spidl
Dalny 'dælni
Dalry dæl'rai
Dalrymple dæl'rimpl [dəl'r-], 'dælrimpl
*Note.—The family name of the Earl
of Stair is* dæl'r- [dəl'r-].

Dalston 'dɔːlstən ['dɔl-]
Dalton 'dɔːltən ['dɔl-]
Dalua dæ'luːə [dəʹl-]
Dalwhinnie dæl'wini [-'hw-]
Daly 'deili
Dalyell 'dæljəl, diː'el
Dalzell dæl'zel, diː'el
Dalziel 'dælzïəl [-zjəl], 'dæljəl [-lïəl], diː'el
Note.—The form diː'el *is chiefly used in Scotland.*
dam (s. v.), -s, -ming, -med dæm, -z, -iŋ, -d
damag|e (s. v.), -es, -ing, -ed 'dæmidʒ, -iz, -iŋ, -d
Damaraland də'mɑːrəlænd ['dæmərə-]
Damaris 'dæməris
damascene, -s 'dæməsiːn [ˌdæmə's-], -z
Damascus də'mɑːskəs [-'mæs-]
damask, -s 'dæməsk, -s
dame, -s deim, -z
Damien 'deimjən [-mïən]
damn, -s, -ing, -ed dæm, -z, -iŋ, -d
damnab|le, -ly, -leness 'dæmnəb|l, -li, -lnis
damnation, -s dæm'neiʃən, -z
damnatory 'dæmnətəri
damni|fy, -fies, -fying, -fied 'dæmni|fai, -faiz, -faiiŋ, -faid
Damocles 'dæməkliːz
Damon 'deimən [-mɔn]
damosel, -s 'dæməuzel, -z
damp (s. adj. v.), -er, -est, -ly, -ness, -ish; -s, -ing, -ed dæmp, -ə*, -ist, -li, -nis, -iʃ; -s, -iŋ, -t [dæmt]
damp-course, -s 'dæmpkɔːs, -iz
damp|en, -ens, -ening, -ened 'dæmp|ən, -ənz, -niŋ [-əniŋ], -ənd
damper, -s 'dæmpə*, -z
Dampier 'dæmpjə* [-pïə*, -pïə*]
damp-proof 'dæmppruːf
damsel, -s 'dæmzəl, -z
damson, -s 'dæmzən, -z
dan (D.), -s dæn, -z
Dana (*personal name*) (*in U.S.A.*) 'deinə, (*in Canada*) 'dænə
Danaë 'dæneïi: [-niː:]
Danakil ˌdænə'kiːl
Danbury 'dænbəri
Danby 'dænbi
lanc|e (s. v.), -es, -ing, -er/s dɑːns, -iz, -iŋ, -t, -ə*/z
Dance dɑːns, dæns
lance-music 'dɑːnsˌmjuːzik
Dancer (*surname*) 'dɑːnsə*
lancing-girl, -s 'dɑːnsiŋgə:l [*rarely* -gəəl], -z
lancing-master, -s 'dɑːnsiŋˌmɑːstə*, -z

dancing-mistress, -es 'dɑːnsiŋˌmistris, -iz
Danckwerts 'dæŋkwəːts
dandelion, -s 'dændilaiən, -z
dandiacal dæn'daiəkəl
dandi|fy, -fies, -fying, -fied 'dændi|fai, -faiz, -faiiŋ, -faid
dand|le, -les, -ling, -led 'dænd|l, -lz, -liŋ [-l̩iŋ], -ld
dandr|iff, -uff 'dændr|if, -ʌf [-əf]
dand|y, -ies; -yish, -yism 'dænd|i, -iz; -iiʃ [-jiʃ], -iizəm
Dane, -s dein, -z
danegeld 'deingeld
Dane|lagh, -law 'dein|lɔ:, -lɔ:
danger, -s 'deindʒə*, -z
Dangerfield 'deindʒəfiːld
dangerous, -ly, -ness 'deindʒrəs, -li, -nis
danger-signal, -s 'deindʒə,signl [-nəl], -z
dang|le (D.), -les, -ling, -led, -ler/s 'dæŋg|l, -lz, -liŋ [-l̩iŋ], -ld, -lə*/z
Daniel(l), -s 'dænjəl, -z
Danish 'deiniʃ
Danite, -s 'dænait, -s
dank, -er, -est, -ly, -ness dæŋk, -ə*, -ist, -li, -nis
Dannatt 'dænət
Dannemora ˌdæni'mɔːrə
Dannreuther 'dænrɔitə*
danseuse, -s dɑːn'səːz [dɑ̃:n's-, dɔ̃:n's-, dɔːn's-] (dɑ̃sø:z), -iz
Dansville 'dænzvil
Dante 'dænti ['dɑːn-, -tei]
Dantzic 'dæntsik
Danube 'dænjuːb
Danubian dæ'njuːbjən [də'n-, -bïən]
Dan|vers, -ville 'dæn|və(:)z, -vil
Danzig 'dæntsig [-ik] ('dantsiç)
Daphn|e, -is 'dæfn|i, -is
dapper (D.), -est 'dæpə*, -rist
dappled 'dæpld
dapple-grey 'dæpl'grei
darbies 'dɑːbiz
Darbishire 'dɑːbiʃiə* [-ʃə*]
Darby 'dɑːbi
D'Arcy, Darcy 'dɑːsi
Dardanelles ˌdɑːdə'nelz [-dn'elz]
Dardani|a, -us dɑː'deinj|ə [-nï|ə], -əs
Dardanus 'dɑːdənəs
dar|e (D.), -es, -ing, -ed, durst dɛə*, -z, -riŋ, -d, də:st
dare-devil, -s 'dɛə,devl, -z
daren't dɛənt
Darenth 'dærənθ
Dares 'dɛəriːz
daresay 'dɛə'sei [*also* '--, -'- *according to sentence-stress*]

Daresbury (*Baron*) 'dɑ:zbəri
Darfield 'dɑ:fi:ld
Darfur 'dɑ:fə* [dɑ:'fə:*]
Dargue dɑ:g
Darien 'dɛəriən, 'dær-
daring (*adj.*), -ly 'dɛəriŋ, -li
Darius də'raiəs
Darjeeling dɑ:'dʒi:liŋ
dark, -er, -est, -ly, -ness dɑ:k, -ə*, -ist,
     -li, -nis
dark|en, -ens, -ening, -ened 'dɑ:k|ən,
     -ənz, -niŋ [-ɲiŋ, -əniŋ], -ənd
dark-haired 'dɑ:k'hɛəd ['-- *when attri-*
     butive]
darkish 'dɑ:kiʃ
darkling 'dɑ:kliŋ
dark-room, -s 'dɑ:krum [-ru:m], -z
dark-skinned 'dɑ:k-skind [also '-'- *when*
     not attributive]
darksome 'dɑ:ksəm
dark|y, -ies 'dɑ:k|i, -iz
Darlaston 'dɑ:ləstən
Darley 'dɑ:li
darling (D.), -s 'dɑ:liŋ, -z
Darlington 'dɑ:liŋtən
Darmady (*surname*) dɑ:'meidi
Darmstadt 'dɑ:mstæt ('dɑrmʃtat)
darn (*s. v.*), -s, -ing, -ed dɑ:n, -z, -iŋ, -d
darnel 'dɑ:nl
darning-needle, -s 'dɑ:niŋˌni:dl, -z
Darnley 'dɑ:nli
Darracq 'dærək
Darrell 'dærəl
Darsie 'dɑ:si
dart (*s. v.*) (D.), -s, -ing, -ed dɑ:t, -s, -iŋ,
     -id
darter, -s 'dɑ:tə*, -z
Dartford 'dɑ:tfəd
Dartie 'dɑ:ti
Dartle 'dɑ:tl
Dartmoor 'dɑ:tmuə* [-mɔə*, -mɔ:*]
Dartmouth 'dɑ:tməθ
Darton 'dɑ:tn
Darwen 'dɑ:win
Darwin, -ism 'dɑ:win, -izəm
Darwinian dɑ:'winiən [-njən]
Daryll 'dæril
Dasent 'deisənt
dash (*s. v.*) (D.), -es, -ing, -ed, -er/s
     dæʃ, -iz, -iŋ, -t, -ə*/z
dash-board, -s 'dæʃbɔ:d [-bɔəd], -z
dashing (*adj.*), -ly 'dæʃiŋ, -li
Dashwood 'dæʃwud
dastard, -s 'dæstəd, -z
dastardl|y (*adj.*), -iness 'dæstədl|i, -inis
data (*plur. of* datum) 'deitə ['dɑ:tə]
datar|y, -ies 'deitər|i, -iz
Datch|ery, -et 'dætʃ|əri, -it

dat|e (*s. v.*), -es, -ing, -ed deit, -s, -iŋ, -id
date-palm, -s 'deitpɑ:m ['deit'p-], -z
date-tree, -s 'deittri:, -z
Dathan 'deiθæn [-θən]
datival də'taivəl [dei't-]
dative (*s. adj.*), -s 'deitiv, -z
dat|um, -a 'deit|əm ['dɑ:t-], -ə
daub (*s. v.*), -s, -ing, -ed, -er/s dɔ:b,
     -z, -iŋ, -d, -ə*/z
Daubeney 'dɔ:bəni
Daudet 'dəudei (dodɛ)
daughter, -s 'dɔ:tə*, -z
daughter - in - law, daughters - in - law
     'dɔ:tərinlɔ: [-təin-], 'dɔ:təzinlɔ:
daughterl|y, -iness 'dɔ:təl|i, -inis
Daukes dɔ:ks
Daulis 'dɔ:lis
Daun dɔ:n
daunt (D.), -s, -ing, -ed dɔ:nt, -s, -iŋ, -id
dauntless, -ly, -ness 'dɔ:ntlis, -li, -nis
dauphin (D.), -s 'dɔ:fin, -z
Dauphine 'dɔ:fin [-fi:n]
Dauphiné 'dəufinei [-ni] (dofine)
dauphiness (D.), -es 'dɔ:finis [-nes], -iz
Davenant 'dævinənt
davenport (D.), -s 'dævnpɔ:t [-vmp-], -s
Daventry 'dævəntri [*old-fashioned local*
     pronunciation 'deintri]
Davey 'deivi
David, -s 'deivid, -z
Davidge 'dævidʒ
Davidson 'deividsn
Davies 'deivis
Davis 'deivis
Davison 'deivisn
davit, -s 'dævit, -s
Davos 'dɑ:vɔs [-vəus, dɑ:'vəus]
dav|y (D.), -ies 'deiv|i, -iz
davy-lamp, -s 'deivi'læmp ['deivil-], -s
daw (D.), -s dɔ:, -z
dawd|le, -les, -ling, -led, -ler/s 'dɔ:d|l,
     -lz, -liŋ [-liŋ], -ld, -lə*/z [-lə*/z]
Dawdon 'dɔ:dn
Dawe, -s dɔ:, -z
Dawk|es, -ins 'dɔ:k|s, -inz
Dawl|ey, -ish 'dɔ:l|i, -iʃ
dawn (*s. v.*) (D.), -s, -ing, -ed dɔ:n, -z,
     -iŋ, -d
Dawson 'dɔ:sn
day (D.), -s dei, -z
day-boarder, -s 'dei,bɔ:də* [-,bɔəd-], -z
day-book, -s 'deibuk, -s
day-boy, -s 'deibɔi, -z
daybreak, -s 'dei-breik, -s
day-dream, -s 'dei-dri:m, -z
day-labour, -er/s 'dei,leibə* ['dei'l-]
     -rə*/z
Daylesford 'deilzfəd [-lsf-]

daylight 'deilait
daylight-saving 'deilait,seiviŋ
day-lil|y, -ies 'dei,lil|i ['dei'l-], -iz
day-school, -s 'dei-sku:l, -z
dayspring 'dei-spriŋ
day-star, -s 'dei-stɑ:*, -z
day-time 'dei-taim
Dayton 'deitn
Daytona dei'təunə
daywork 'deiwə:k
daz|e, -es, -ing, -ed, -edly deiz, -iz, -iŋ, -d, -idli
dazz|le, -les, -ling/ly, -led 'dæz|l, -lz, -liŋ/li [-ḷiŋ/li], -ld
D-day 'di:-dei
D.D.T. 'di:di:'ti:
de (note in Tonic Sol-fa), -s di:, -z
deacon (D.), -s 'di:kən, -z
deaconess, -es 'di:kənis [-kṇis, -es], -iz
deacon|hood, -ry, -ries, -ship/s 'di:kən|-hud, -ri, -riz, -ʃip/s
dead ded
dead-alive 'dedə'laiv
dead-beat 'ded'bi:t
dead-drunk 'ded'drʌŋk
dead|en, -ens, -ening, -ened 'ded|n, -nz, -ṇiŋ [-niŋ], -nd
dead-eye (D.), -s 'dedai, -z
deadhead, -s 'dedhed, -z
dead-heat, -s 'ded'hi:t ['--], -s
dead-letter, -s 'ded'letə*, -z
deadline, -s 'dedlain, -z
deadlock, -s 'dedlɔk, -s
deadl|y, -ier, -iest, -iness 'dedl|i, -iə* [-jə*], -iist [-jist], -inis
dead-march, -es 'ded'mɑ:tʃ, -iz
dead-nettle, -s 'ded'netl [-,--], -z
dead-pan 'ded'pæn ['--]
dead-reckoning, -s 'ded'rekṇiŋ [-kəniŋ], -z
dead-set, -s 'ded'set ['dedset], -s
dead-wall, -s 'ded'wɔ:l, -z
dead-water, -s 'ded,wɔ:tə*, -z
dead-weight, -s 'dedweit ['ded'weit], -s
deaf, -er, -est, -ly, -ness def, -ə*, -ist, -li, -nis
deaf|en, -ens, -ening, -ened 'def|n, -nz, -ṇiŋ [-niŋ], -nd
deaf-mute, -s 'def'mju:t, -s
Deakin 'di:kin
deal (s. v.) (D.), -s, -ing/s, dealt, dealer/s di:l, -z, -iŋ/z, delt, 'di:lə*/z
Dealtry (surname) 'dɔ:ltri, 'diəltri, (road in London) 'deltri
dean, -s; -ship/s di:n, -z; -ʃip/s
Dean(e) di:n
deaner|y, -ies 'di:nər|i, -iz
Deans di:nz

dear (s. adj. interj.), -s; -er, -est, -ly, -ness diə*, -z; -rə*, -rist, -li, -nis
Dearmer 'diəmə*
dearth (D.), -s də:θ, -s
dear|y, -ies 'diər|i, -iz
Dease di:s
death, -s deθ, -s
Death (surname) deiθ, deθ, di:θ, di(:)'æθ
deathbed, -s 'deθbed, -z
death-bell, -s 'deθbel, -z
death-blow, -s 'deθbləu, -z
death|dut|y, -ies 'deθ,dju:t|i, -iz
death|less, -like 'deθ|lis, -laik
death|ly, -lier, -liest, -liness 'deθ|li, -liə* [-ljə*], -liist [-ljist], -linis
death-mask, -s 'deθmɑ:sk, -s
death-rate, -s 'deθreit, -s
death-rattle, -s 'deθ,rætl, -z
death's-head, -s 'deθshed, -z
death-trap, -s 'deθtræp, -s
death-warrant, -s 'deθ,wɔrənt, -s
death-watch 'deθwɔtʃ
débâcle, -s dei'bɑ:kl [de'b-, di'b-], -z
debar, -s, -ring, -red di'bɑ:*, -z, -riŋ, -d
debark, -s, -ing, -ed di'bɑ:k, -s, -iŋ, -t
debarkation, -s ,di:bɑ:'keiʃən, -z
debas|e, -es, -ing/ly, -ed, -ement di'beis, -iz, -iŋ/li, -t, -mənt
debatab|le, -ly di'beitəb|l, -li
debat|e (s. v.), -es, -ing, -ed, -er/s di'beit, -s, -iŋ, -id, -ə*/z
De Bathe də'bɑ:θ
debauch (s. v.), -es, -ing, -ed, -er/s di'bɔ:tʃ, -iz, -iŋ, -t, -ə*/z
debauchee, -s ,debɔ:'tʃi: [-ɔ:'ʃi:], -z
debaucher|y, -ies di'bɔ:tʃər|i, -iz
Debbitch 'debitʃ
Debeney 'debəni
Debenham 'debnəm [-bṇəm]
debenture, -s di'bentʃə* [də'b-], -z
debile 'di:bail
debilitat|e, -es, -ing, -ed di'biliteit, -s, -iŋ, -id
debilitation di,bili'teiʃən
debility di'biliti
debit (s. v.), -s, -ing, -ed 'debit, -s, -iŋ, -id
De Blaquiere də'blækiə*
debonair, -ly, -ness ,debə'nɛə* [-bɔ'n-], -li, -nis
Deborah 'debərə
debouch, -es, -ing, -ed, -ment di'bautʃ [-'bu:ʃ], -iz, -iŋ, -t, -mənt
De Bourgh də'bə:g
De Bow də'bəu
Debrett də'bret [di'b-]
debris 'deibri: ['deb-, -brĭ]
debt, -s det, -s

debtor, -s 'detə*, -z
debunk, -s, -ing, -ed 'di:'bʌŋk [-'-], -s, -iŋ, -t [-'bʌŋt]
De Bunsen də'bʌnsn
De Burgh də'bə:g
Debussy də'busi(:) [-'bu:s-, -'bju:s-] (dəbysi)
début, -s 'deibu: ['deb-, -bju:, -'-] (deby), -z
débutant, -s 'debju(:)tã:ŋ ['deib-, -tɔ̃:ŋ, -ta:ŋ, -tɔ:ŋ, -tɔŋ] (debytã), -z
débutante, -s 'debju(:)ta:nt ['deib-, -tɔ̃:nt, -tænt, -tã:nt, -tɔ:nt, -tɔnt] (debytã:t), -s
decachord, -s 'dekəkɔ:d, -z
decade, -s 'dekeid [-kəd, -kid, di'keid, de'keid], -z
decaden|ce, -cy, -t 'dekədən|s [di'keid-, de'keid-], -si, -t
decagon, -s 'dekəgən, -z
decagram(me), -s 'dekəgræm, -z
decalcification 'di:ˌkælsifi'keiʃən
decalci|fy, -fies, -fying, -fied di:'kælsi|-fai ['di:'k-], -faiz, -faiiŋ, -faid
decalitre, -s 'dekəˌli:tə*, -z
decalogue, -s 'dekəlɔg, -z
Decameron di'kæmərən [de'k-]
decametre, -s 'dekəˌmi:tə*, -z
decamp, -s, -ing, -ed di'kæmp, -s, -iŋ, -t [di'kæmt]
decanal di'keinl [de'k-]
decani di'keinai [de'k-]
decant, -s, -ing, -ed di'kænt, -s, -iŋ, -id
decantation, -s ˌdi:kæn'teiʃən, -z
decanter, -s di'kæntə*, -z
decapitat|e, -es, -ing, -ed di'kæpiteit [di:'k-], -s, -iŋ, -id
decapitation, -s diˌkæpi'teiʃən [di:ˌk-], -z
decapod, -s 'dekəpɔd, -z
Decapolis di'kæpəlis [de'k-]
decarbonization [-isa-] di:ˌkɑ:bənai'zeiʃən ['di:ˌkɑ:bənai'z-, -bəni'z-, -bŋai'z-, -bŋi'z-]
decarboniz|e [-is|e], -es, -ing, -ed di:-'kɑ:bənaiz ['di:'k-, -bŋaiz], -iz, -iŋ, -d
decarburiz|e [-is|e], -es, -ing, -ed di:'kɑ:bjuəraiz ['di:'k-], -iz, -iŋ, -d
decasyllabic 'dekəsi'læbik
decasyllable, -s 'dekəsiləbl, -z
decay (s. v.), -s, -ing, -ed di'kei, -z, -iŋ, -d
Decca 'dekə
Deccan 'dekən [-kæn] (Hind. dəkhən)
deceas|e (s. v.), -es, -ing, -ed di'si:s, -iz, -iŋ, -t
deceit, -s di'si:t, -s
deceit|ful, -fully, -fulness di'si:t|fᴜl, -fuli [-fəli], -fᴜlnis
deceivable, -ness di'si:vəbl, -nis

deceiv|e, -es, -ing, -ed -er/s di'si:v, -z, -iŋ, -d, -ə*/z
deceleration, -s 'di:ˌselə'reiʃən, -z
December, -s di'sembə* [di:'s-], -z
decemvir, -s di'semvə* [-və:*], -z
decemvirate, -s di'semvirit [-vər-], -s
decen|cy, -cies, -t/ly 'di:sn|si, -siz, -t/li
decennial di'senjəl [de's-, di:'s-, -nĭəl]
decentralization [-isa-] di:ˌsentrəlai-'zeiʃən ['di:ˌsentrəlai'z-, -trḷai'z-, -trəli'z-, -trḷi'z-]
decentraliz|e [-is|e], -es, -ing, -ed di:'sentrəlaiz ['di:'s-], -iz, -iŋ, -d
deception, -s di'sepʃən, -z
deceptive, -ly, -ness di'septiv, -li, -nis
decibel, -s 'desibel [-bəl, -bl], -z
decid|e, -es, -ing, -ed/ly, -er/s di'said, -z, -iŋ, -id/li, -ə*/z
deciduous, -ly, -ness di'sidjŭəs [-djwəs], -li, -nis
Decies 'di:ʃiz
decigram(me), -s 'desigræm, -z
decilitre, -s 'desiˌli:tə*, -z
decillion, -s di'siljən [di:'s-], -z
decim|al, -als, -ally 'desim|əl, -əlz, -əli
decimaliz|e [-is|e], -es, -ing, -ed 'desi-məlaiz, -iz, -iŋ, -d
decimat|e, -es, -ing, -ed, -or/s 'desi-meit, -s, -iŋ, -id, -ə*/z
decimation ˌdesi'meiʃən
decimetre, -s 'desiˌmi:tə*, -z
deciph|er, -ers, -ering, -ered di'saif|ə*, -əz, -əriŋ, -əd
decipherable di'saifərəbl
decision, -s di'siʒən, -z   [-nis
decisive, -ly, -ness di'saisiv [-aiziv], -li, -nis
Decius di'ʃjəs [-ʃĭəs, -sjəs, -sĭəs, 'dekĭəs, 'desĭəs]
deck (s. v.), -s, -ing, -ed, -er/s dek, -s, -iŋ, -t, -ə*/z
deck-cabin, -s 'dek'kæbin [also '-ᴗ,-- for contrast], -z
deck-chair, -s 'dektʃɛə* ['-'-], -z
deck-hand, -s 'dekhænd, -z
deck-hou|se, -ses 'dekhau|s, -ziz
deckle, -s 'dekl, -z
deckle-edge, -d 'dekl'edʒ ['dekḷedʒ], -d
deck-passenger, -s 'dekˌpæsindʒə*, -z
declaim, -s, -ing, -ed, -er/s; -ant/s di'kleim, -z, -iŋ, -d, -ə*/z; -ənt/s
declamation, -s ˌdeklə'meiʃən, -z
declamatory di'klæmətəri
declarable di'klɛərəbl
declaration, -s ˌdeklə'reiʃən, -z
declarat|ive/ly, -ory di'klærət|iv/li [-'klɛər-], -əri
declar|e, -es, -ing, -ed, -er/s di'klɛə*, -z, -riŋ, -d, -rə*/z

declass, -es, -ing, -ed 'di:'klɑ:s [-'-], -iz, -iŋ, -t

declension, -s di'klenʃən, -z

declination, -s ˌdekli'neiʃən, -z

declin|e (s. v.), -es, -ing, -ed; -able di'klain, -z, -iŋ, -d; -əbl

declinometer, -s ˌdekli'nɔmitə*, -z

declivitous, -ly, -ness di'klivitəs, -li, -nis

declivit|y, -ies di'klivit|i, -iz

declutch, -es, -ing, -ed 'di:'klʌtʃ ['di:-klʌtʃ, di:'klʌtʃ], -iz, -iŋ, -t

decoct, -s, -ing, -ed di'kɔkt, -s, -iŋ, -id

decoction, -s di'kɔkʃən, -z

decod|e, -es, -ing, -ed 'di:'kəud [di:'k-], -z, -iŋ, -id

décolleté(e) dei'kɔltei [de'k-, di'k-] (dekɔlte)

decolo(u)rization [-isa-] di:ˌkʌlərai-'zeiʃən ['di:ˌk-]

decolo(u)riz|e [-is|e], -es, -ing, -ed di:'kʌləraiz, -iz, -iŋ, -d

decompos|e, -es, -ing, -ed; -able ˌdi:-kəm'pəuz ['di:-kəm'p-], -iz, -iŋ, -d; -əbl

decomposition, -s ˌdi:-kɔmpə'ziʃən ['di:ˌkɔmpə'z-], -z

decompound, -s, -ing, -ed ˌdi:-kəm-'paund ['di:-kəm'p-], -z, -iŋ, -id

deconsecrat|e, -es, -ing, -ed di:'kɔn-sikreit ['di:'k-], -s, -iŋ, -id

deconsecration, -s 'di:ˌkɔnsi'kreiʃən, -z

decontaminat|e, -es, -ing, -ed 'di:-kən-'tæmineit [ˌdi:-], -s, -iŋ, -id

decontamination 'di:-kənˌtæmi'neiʃən [ˌdi:-kən-]

decontrol (s. v.), -s, -ling, -led 'di:-kən-'trəul [ˌdi:-kən-], -z, -iŋ, -d

decor, -s 'deikɔ:* ['dekɔ:*, di'kɔ:*], -z

decorat|e, -es, -ing, -ed -or/s 'dekəreit, -s, -iŋ, -id, -ə*/z

decoration, -s ˌdekə'reiʃən, -z

decorative, -ly, -ness 'dekərətiv, -li, -nis

decorous, -ly, -ness 'dekərəs [old-fashioned and poetical di'kɔ:rəs], -li, -nis

decorum di'kɔ:rəm

De Courcy də'kuəsi [-'kɔəs-, -'kɔ:s-], də'kə:si

decoy (v.), -s, -ing, -ed di'kɔi, -z, -iŋ, -d

decoy (s.), -s 'di:kɔi [di'kɔi], -z

decoy-duck, -s di'kɔidʌk [di'kɔi'd-], -s

decrease (s.), -s 'di:-kri:s [di:'kri:s, di'k-, -'-], -iz

decreas|e (v.), -es, -ing/ly, -ed di:'kri:s [di'k-, 'di:-k-], -iz, -iŋ/li, -t

decree (s. v.), -s, -ing, -d di'kri:, -z, -iŋ, -d

decrement, -s 'dekrimənt, -s

decrepit, -est, -ness; -ude di'krepit, -ist, -nis; -ju:d

decrepitation, -s diˌkrepi'teiʃən, -z

decrescendo, -s 'di:-kri'ʃendəu, -z

De Crespigny də'krepini, də'krespini

decrial, -s di'kraiəl, -z

decr|y, -ies, -ying, -ied, -ier/s di'kr|ai, -aiz, -aiŋ, -aid, -ai-ə*/z [-aiə*/z]

decumben|ce, -cy, -t/ly di'kʌmbən|s, -si, -t/li

decup|le (s. adj. v.), -les, -ling, -led 'dekjup|l, -lz, -liŋ, -ld

Dedan, -ite/s 'di:dən, -ait/s

Deddes 'dedis

Deddington 'dediŋtən

Dedham 'dedəm

dedicat|e, -es, -ing, -ed, -or/s 'dedikeit, -s, -iŋ, -id, -ə*/z

dedicatee, -s ˌdedikə'ti:, -z

dedication, -s ˌdedi'keiʃən, -z

dedicatory 'dedikətəri [-keitəri]

de Dion, -s də'di(:)ən [-'di:ɔ:ŋ, -'di:ɔ:ŋ, -'di:ɔŋ, -'di:ɔn] (dədjɔ̃), -z

Ded|lock, -man 'ded|lɔk, -mən

deduc|e, -es, -ing, -ed di'dju:s, -iz, -iŋ, -t

deducibility diˌdju:sə'biliti [-si'b-, -lət-]

deducible di'dju:səbl [-sib-]

deduct, -s, -ing, -ed; -ive/ly di'dʌkt, -s, -iŋ, -id; -iv/li

deduction, -s di'dʌkʃən, -z

Dee di:

deed, -s di:d, -z

Deedes di:dz

Deek(e)s di:ks

deem, -s, -ing, -ed di:m, -z, -iŋ, -d

Deems di:mz

deemster, -s 'di:mstə*, -z

deep (s. adj.), -s, -er, -est, -ly, -ness di:p, -s, -ə*, -ist, -li, -nis

deep-drawn 'di:p'drɔ:n ['-- when attributive]

deep|en, -ens, -ening, -ened 'di:p|ən, -ənz, -ŋiŋ [-əniŋ, -niŋ], -ənd

deep-laid 'di:p'leid [also 'di:p-leid when attributive]

deep-mouthed 'di:p'mauðd [-'mauθt, '-- when attributive]

deep-rooted 'di:p'ru:tid [also 'di:pˌru:tid when attributive]

deep-sea 'di:p'si: [also '-- when attributive]

deep-seated 'di:p'si:tid [also '-ˌ-- when attributive]

deer diə*

Deerfield 'diə-fi:ld

deer-forest, -s 'diəˌfɔrist, -s

deer-hound, -s 'diəhaund, -z

deer-park, -s 'diə-pɑ:k, -s

deer-skin 'diə-skin
deer-stalk|ing, -er/s 'diə‚stɔ:k|iŋ, -ə*/z
defac|e, -es, -ing, -ed, -er/s, -ement/s di'feis, -iz, -iŋ, -t, -ə*/z, -mənt/s
de facto di:'fæktəu [dei'f-]
defalcat|e, -es, -ing, -ed 'di:fælkeit [di:'fæl-, rarely 'di:fɔ:l-], -s, -iŋ, -id
defalcation, -s ‚di:fæl'keiʃən [-fɔ:l-], -z
defalcator, -s 'di:fælkeitə* [-fɔ:l-], -z
defamation, -s ‚defə'meiʃən [‚di:fə'm-], -z
defamatory di'fæmətəri
defam|e, -es, -ing, -ed, -er/s di'feim, -z, -iŋ, -d, -ə*/z
default (s. v.), -s, -ing, -ed, -er/s di'fɔ:lt [-'fɔlt], -s, -iŋ, -id, -ə*/z
defeasance di'fi:zəns
defeasib|le, -ly, -leness di'fi:zəb|l [-zib-], -li, -lnis
defeat (s. v.), -s, -ing, -ed di'fi:t, -s, -iŋ, -id
defeati|sm, -st/s di'fi:ti|zəm, -st/s
defect, -s di'fekt ['di:fekt], -s
defection, -s di'fekʃən, -z
defective, -ly, -ness di'fektiv, -li, -nis
defence, -s di'fens, -iz
defenceless, -ly, -ness di'fenslis, -li, -nis
defend, -s -ing, -ed, -er/s di'fend, -z, -iŋ, -id, -ə*/z
defendant, -s di'fendənt, -s
defensibility di‚fensi'biliti [-sə'b-, -lət-]
defensib|le, -ly di'fensəb|l [-sib-], -li
defensive, -ly, -ness di'fensiv, -li, -nis
defer, -s, -ring, -red, -rer/s di'fə:*, -z, -riŋ, -d, -rə*/z
deferen|ce, -t 'defərən|s, -t
deferenti|al, -ally ‚defə'renʃ|əl, -əli
defian|ce, -t/ly, -tness di'faiən|s, -t/li, -tnis
deficien|cy, -cies, -t/ly di'fiʃən|si, -siz, -t/li
deficit, -s 'defisit ['di:f-, di'fisit], -s
defilad|e (s. v.), -es, -ing, -ed ‚defi'leid, -z, -iŋ, -id
defile (s.), -s 'di:fail [di'fail, di:'f-], -z
defil|e (v.), -es, -ing, -ed, -er/s, -ement di'fail, -z, -iŋ, -d, -ə*/z, -mənt
definable di'fainəbl
defin|e, -es, -ing, -ed, -er/s di'fain, -z, -iŋ, -d, -ə*/z
definite, -ly, -ness 'definit [-fṇit, -fnit], -li, -nis
definition, -s ‚defi'niʃən [-fṇ'iʃ-], -z
definitive, -ly, -ness di'finitiv [de'f-], -li, -nis
deflagrat|e, -es, -ing, -ed, -or/s 'deflə‚greit ['di:f-], -s, -iŋ, -id, -ə*/z
deflagration, -s ‚deflə'greiʃən [‚di:f-], -z

deflat|e, -es, -ing, -ed di'fleit [di:'f-, 'di:'f-], -s, -iŋ, -id
deflation di'fleiʃən [di:'f-, 'di:'f-]
deflect, -s, -ing, -ed, -or/s di'flekt, -s, -iŋ, -id, -ə*/z
deflection [-exion], -s di'flekʃən, -z
defloration, -s ‚di:flɔ:'reiʃən [‚def-], -z
deflower, -s, -ing, -ed di:'flauə* [di'f-, 'di:'f-], -z, -iŋ, -d
Defoe di'fəu [də'f-]
De Forest də'fɔrist
deform, -s, -ing, -ed, -er/s di'fɔ:m, -z, -iŋ, -d, -ə*/z
deformation, -s ‚di:fɔ:'meiʃən, -z
deformit|y, -ies di'fɔ:mit|i, -iz
defraud, -s, -ing, -ed, -er/s di'frɔ:d, -z, -iŋ, -id, -ə*/z
defray, -s, -ing, -ed, -er/s, -ment di'frei, -z, -iŋ, -d, -ə*/z, -mənt
defrayal, -s di'freiəl, -z
De Freitas də'freitəs
defrock, -s, -ing, -ed 'di:'frɔk [di:'f-], -s -iŋ, -t [-nis
deft, -er, -est, -ly, -ness deft, -ə*, -ist -,li,
defunct (s. adj.), -s di'fʌŋkt, -s
def|y, -ies, -ying, -ied, -ier/s di'f|ai, -aiz, -aiiŋ, -aid, -aiə*/z
Degas də'gɑ: (dəgɑ)
De Gaulle də'gəul (dəgo:l)
degauss, -es, -ing, -ed 'di:'gaus [di:'g-], -iz, -iŋ, -t
degeneracy di'dʒenərəsi
degenerate (adj.), -ly, -ness di'dʒenərit, -li, -nis
degenerat|e (v.), -es, -ing, -ed di'dʒenəreit, -s, -iŋ, -id
degeneration di‚dʒenə'reiʃən
degenerative di'dʒenərətiv [-nəreit-]
deglutinat|e, -es, -ing, -ed di'glu:tineit, -s, -iŋ, -id
deglutition ‚di:glu:'tiʃən
degradation, -s ‚degrə'deiʃən, -z
degrad|e, -es, -ing/ly, -ed di'greid, -z, -iŋ/li, -id
degree, -s di'gri:, -z
dehisc|e, -es, -ing, -ed; -ence, -ent di'his [di:'h-], -iz, -iŋ, -t; -ns, -nt
Dehra Dun 'deiərə'du:n ['dɛər-] (Hind. dehradun)
dehumaniz|e [-is|e], -es, -ing, -ed di:'hju:mənaiz, -iz, -iŋ, -d
dehydrat|e, -es, -ing, -ed di:'haidreit, -s, -iŋ, -id
dehydration ‚di:hai'dreiʃən
dehypnotiz|e [-is|e], -es, -ing, -ed 'di:'hipnətaiz, -iz, -iŋ, -d
de-ic|e, -es, -ing, -ed, -er/s 'di:'ais, -iz -iŋ, -t, -ə*/z

deicide, -s 'di:isaid ['deiis-], -z
deictic 'daiktik
deification, -s ,di:ifi'keiʃən [,deiif-], -z
dei|fy, -fies, -fying, -fied 'di:i['deii-]|fai, -faiz, -faiiŋ, -faid
Deighton (surname) 'daitn, 'deitn, (place in Yorks.) 'di:tn
deign, -s, -ing, -ed dein, -z, -iŋ, -d
deipnosophist, -s daip'nɔsəfist, -s
Deirdre 'diədri [-drei]
dei|sm, -st/s 'di:i['deii-]|zəm, -st/s
deistic, -al di:'istik [dei'i-], -əl
deit|y (D.), -ies 'di:it|i ['di:ət-, 'diət-, 'deiit-], -iz
deject, -s, -ing, -ed/ly, -edness di'dʒekt, -s, -iŋ, -id/li, -idnis
dejection di'dʒekʃən
déjeuner, -s 'deizənei [-ʒə:n-] (deʒøne, -ʒœne), -z
de jure di:'dʒuəri [rarely dei'juəri]
Dekker 'dekə*
de la Bère (English surname) ,delə'biə*
Delagoa ,delə'gəuə [also 'deləg- in Delagoa Bay]
delaine də'lein [di'l-]
Delamain 'deləmein
De la Mare ,delə'mɛə*
Delamere 'deləmiə*
De Lancey də'lɑːnsi
Deland 'di:lənd
Delan|e, -y də'lein [di'l-], -i
De la Pasture də'læpətjə* [-tjuə*, -tʃə*]
De la Poer ,delə'puə* [-'pɔə*, -'pɔ:*]
De la Pole ,delə'pəul
De la Rue 'deləru: [,delə'r-]
De Laszlo də'læsləu
de la Torre (English surname) ,delə'tɔ:*
Delaware 'deləwɛə*
De la Warr 'deləwɛə*
delay (s. v.), -s, -ing, -ed, -er/s di'lei, -z, -iŋ, -d, -ə*/z
del credere del'kredəri
dele 'di:li(:)
delectab|le, -ly, -leness di'lektəb|l, -li, -lnis
delectation ,di:lek'teiʃən
delegac|y, -ies 'deligəs|i, -iz
delegate (s.), -s 'deligit [-geit], -s
delegat|e (v.), -es, -ing, -ed 'deligeit, -s, -iŋ, -id
delegation, -s ,deli'geiʃən, -z
delend|um, -a di'lend|əm [di:'l-], -ə
delet|e, -es, -ing, -ed di'li:t [di:'l-], -s, -iŋ, -id
deleterious, -ly, -ness ,deli'tiəriəs [dil-, ,di:l-], -li, -nis
deletion, -s di'li:ʃən [di:'l-], -z
delf delf

Delft, -ware delft, -wɛə*
Delham 'deləm
Delhi 'deli
Delia, -n/s 'di:ljə [-liə], -n/z
deliber|ate (adj.), -ately, -ateness di'libər|it, -itli [-ətli], -itnis
deliberat|e (v.), -es, -ing, -ed, -or/s di'libəreit, -s, -iŋ, -id, -ə*/z
deliberation, -s di,libə'reiʃən, -z
deliberative, -ly di'libərətiv, -li
delicac|y, -ies 'delikəs|i, -iz
delicate, -ly, -ness 'delikit, -li, -nis
delicatessen, -s ,delikə'tesn, -z
delicious, -ly, -ness di'liʃəs, -li, -nis
delict, -s 'di:likt, -s
delight (s. v.), -s, -ing, -ed/ly di'lait, -s, -iŋ, -id/li
delight|ful, -fully, -fulness di'lait|ful, -fəli [-fuli], -fulnis
delightsome di'laitsəm
Delilah di'lailə
delimit, -s, -ing, -ed di:'limit [di'l-], -s, -iŋ, -id
delimitation, -s di,limi'teiʃən [,di:-limi't-], -z
delineat|e, -es, -ing, -ed, -or/s di-'linieit, -s, -iŋ, -id, -ə*/z
delineation, -s di,lini'eiʃən, -z
delinquen|cy, -cies, -t/s di'liŋkwən|si, -siz, -t/s
deliquesc|e, -es, -ing, -ed ,deli'kwes, -iz, -iŋ, -t
deliquescen|ce, -t ,deli'kwesn|s, -t
delirious, -ly, -ness di'liriəs [-'liər-], -li, -nis
delirium, -tremens di'liriəm [-'liər-], -'tri:menz
De l'Isle (English name) də'lail
Delisle (French name) də'li:l (dəlil)
Delius 'di:ljəs [-liəs]
deliv|er, -ers, -ering, -ered, -erer/s di'liv|ə*, -əz, -əriŋ, -əd, -ərə*/z
deliverance, -s di'livərəns, -iz
deliver|y, -ies di'livər|i, -iz
dell, -s del, -z
Delmar 'delmɑ:*
Delos 'di:lɔs
de-lou|se, -ses, -sing, -sed 'di:'lau|s [-z] -siz [-ziz], -siŋ [-ziŋ], -st [-zd]
Delphi (in Greece) 'delfai [-fi], (city in U.S.A.) 'delfai
Note.—'delfai is the traditional pronunciation among those concerned with Greek history, and appears to be still the most usual form.
Delph|ian, -ic 'delf|iən [-jən], -ik
delphinium, -s del'finiəm [-njəm], -z
delta, -s 'deltə, -z

deltoid 'deltɔid
delud|e, -es, -ing, -ed, -er/s di'lu:d [-'lju:d], -z, -iŋ, -id, -ə*/z
delug|e (s. v.), **-es, -ing, -ed** 'delju:dʒ [-ljudʒ], -iz, -iŋ, -d
delusion, -s di'lu:ʒən [-'lju:-], -z
delusive, -ly, -ness di'lu:siv [-'lju:-], -li, -nis
delusory di'lu:səri [-'lju:-]
de luxe də'luks [-'lu:ks, -'lʌks]
delv|e, -es, -ing, -ed, -er/s delv, -z, -iŋ, -d, -ə*/z
Delville 'delvil
demagnetization [-isa-], **-s** 'di:,mæg-nitai'zeiʃən [di:,m-], -z
demagnetiz|e [-is|e], **-es, -ing, -ed** 'di:'mægnitaiz [di:'m-], -iz, -iŋ, -d
demagogic, -al ,demə'gɔgik [-'gɔdʒik], -əl
demagogue, -s 'deməgɔg, -z
demagogy 'deməgɔgi [-gɔdʒi]
demand (s. v.), **-s, -ing, -ed** di'ma:nd, -z, -iŋ, -id
Demant di'mænt [də'm-]
demarcat|e, -es, -ing, -ed 'di:ma:keit, -s, -iŋ, -id
demarcation ,di:ma:'keiʃən
démarche, -s 'deima:ʃ [-'-'-], -iz
Demas 'di:mæs
dematerializ|e [-is|e], **-es, -ing, -ed** 'di:mə'tiəriəlaiz, -iz, -iŋ, -d
De Mauley də'mɔ:li
demean, -s, -ing, -ed ; -our/s di'mi:n, -z, -iŋ, -d; -ə*/z
dement, -s, -ing, -ed di'ment, -s, -iŋ, -id
dementia di'menʃiə [-ʃjə, -ʃə]
Demerara (district in British Guiana) ,demə'ra:rə, (sugar from there) ,demə'reərə
demerit, -s di:'merit ['di:,m-], -s
demesne, -s di'mein [də'm-, -'mi:n], -z
Demeter di'mi:tə* [-tiə*]
Demetrius di'mi:triəs
demigod, -s 'demigɔd, -z
demijohn, -s 'demidʒɔn, -z
demilitariz|e [-is|e], **-es, -ing, -ed** 'di:'militəraiz [di:'m-], -iz, -iŋ, -d
,demilitarization [-isa-] 'di:,militərai-'zeiʃən [di:,m-, -ri'z-]
demi-monde 'demi'mɔ̃:nd [-'mɔ:nd, -'mɔnd] (dəmimɔ̃:d)
demis|e (s. v.), **-es, -ing, -ed** di'maiz, -iz, -iŋ, -d
demi-semiquaver, -s 'demisemi,kwei-və*, -z
demission, -s di'miʃən, -z
demiurge, -s 'di:miə:dʒ ['dem-], -iz
demivolt, -s 'demivɔlt, -s

demob, -s, -bing, -bed 'di:'mɔb [-'-'-], -z, -iŋ, -d
demobilization [-isa-], **-s** 'di:,məubilai-'zeiʃən [-li'z-, -b̦-], -z
demobiliz|e [-is|e], **-es, -ing, -ed,** di:-'məubilaiz ['di:m-, -b̦aiz], -iz, -iŋ, -d
democrac|y, -ies di'mɔkrəs|i, -iz
democrat, -s 'deməkræt [-muk-], -s
democratic, -al, -ally ,demə'krætik [-mu'k-], -əl, -əli
democratization [-isa-] di,mɔkrətai-'zeiʃən [-ti'z-]
democratiz|e [-is|e], **-es, -ing, -ed** di'mɔkrətaiz, -iz, -iŋ, -d
Democritus di'mɔkritəs
demogorgon, -s 'di:məu'gɔ:gən, -z
demography di:'mɔgrəfi
Demoivre də'mɔivə* [di'm-]
De Moleyns 'deməli:nz [-mul-]
demolish, -es, -ing, -ed, -er/s di'mɔliʃ, -iz, -iŋ, -t, -ə*/z
demolition, -s ,demə'liʃən [,di:m-, -mu'l-], -z
demon, -s 'di:mən, -z
demonetization [-isa-] di:,mʌnitai-'zeiʃən [-,mɔn-]
demonetiz|e [-is|e], **-es, -ing, -ed** di:'mʌnitaiz ['di:'m-, di'm-, -'mɔn-], -iz, -iŋ, -d
demoniac (s. adj.), **-s** di'məuniæk [-njæk], -s
demoniac|al, -ally ,di:məu'naiək|əl [-mu'n-], -əli
demonic di:'mɔnik [di'm-]
demoni|sm, -st/s 'di:məni|zəm, -st/s
demonology ,di:mə'nɔlədʒi
demonstrability ,demənstrə'biliti [di-,mɔns-, -lət-]
demonstrab|le, -ly 'demənstrəb|l [di'mɔn-], -li
demonstrat|e, -es, -ing, -ed, -or/s 'demənstreit, -s, -iŋ, -id, -ə*/z
demonstration, -s ,deməns'treiʃən, -z
demonstrative (s. adj.), **-s, -ly, -ness** di'mɔnstrətiv, -z, -li, -nis
demoralization [-isa-] di,mɔrəlai'zeiʃən [-r̦ai'z-, -rəli'z-, -r̦i'z-]
demoraliz|e [-is|e], **-es, -ing, -ed** di-'mɔrəlaiz [-r̦aiz], -iz, -iŋ, -d
De Morgan də'mɔ:gən
de mortuis 'dei 'mɔ:tjuis ['di:-, -tu:is]
Demos 'di:mɔs
Demosthenes di'mɔsθəni:z [də'm-, -θin-]
demotic di(:)'mɔtik
Dempster 'dempstə* [-riŋ, -d
demur (s. v.), **-s, -ring, -red** di'mə:*, -z, **demure, -r, -st, -ly, -ness** di'mjuə* [-'mjɔə*, -'mjɔ:*], -rə*, -rist, -li, -nis

demurrage di'mʌridʒ
demurrer (*one who demurs*), **-s** di-'məːrə*, -z
demurrer (*objection on ground of irrelevance*), **-s** di'mʌrə*, -z
Demuth də'muːθ
dem|y, -ies di'm|ai [də'm-], -aiz
demyship, -s di'mai-ʃip [də'm-], -s
den, -s den, -z
dena|rius, -rii di'nɛə|rïəs, -riai [de-'nɑːrïəs, de'nɑːriiː]
denary 'diːnəri
denationalization [-isa-] 'diːˌnæʃɳəlai-'zeiʃən [-ʃnəl-, -ʃɳ̩-, -ʃɳ̩-, -ʃənəl-, -li'z-]
denationaliz|e [-is|e], **-es, -ing, -ed** diː'næʃɳəlaiz ['diːʃn-, -ʃnəl-, -ʃɳ̩-, -ʃɳ̩-, -ʃənəl-], -iz, -iŋ, -d
denaturalization [-isa-] 'diːˌnætʃrəlai-'zeiʃən [-tʃur-, -tʃər-, -li'z-]
denaturaliz|e [-is|e], **-es, -ing, -ed** diː-'nætʃrəlaiz ['diːʃn-, -tʃur-, -tʃər-], -iz, -iŋ, -d
Denbigh, -shire 'denbi, -ʃiə* [-ʃə*]
Denby 'denbi
dendrology den'drɔlədʒi
dene (**D.**), **-s** diːn, -z
Deneb 'deneb
Denebola di'nebələ [de'n-, dəˌn-]
dengue 'deŋgi
Denham 'denəm
Denholm(e) 'denəm
Denia, -s 'diːnjə [-nïə], -z
deniable di'naiəbl
denial, -s di'naiəl, -z
denier (*coin*), **-s** di'niə* ['denïə*, 'denïə*], -z
denier (*thickness of yarn*) 'deniei ['denïə*, -njə*] (dənje)
denier (*one who denies*), **-s** di'nai-ə* [-'naïə*], -z
denigrat|e, -es, -ing, -ed 'denigreit, -s, -iŋ, -id
denigration ˌdeni'greiʃən
Denis 'denis
Denise də'niːz [de'n-]
Denison 'denisn
denizen, -s 'denizn, -z
Denman 'denmən
Denmark 'denmɑːk
Dennehy 'denəhi, -hiː
Dennis 'denis
Denny, -s 'deni, -s
denominat|e, -es, -ing, -ed di'nɔmineit, -s, -iŋ, -id
denomination, -s diˌnɔmi'neiʃən, -z
denominational diˌnɔmi'neiʃənl [-ʃnəl, -ʃɳ̩, -ʃn̩, -ʃənəl]

denominationalism diˌnɔmi'neiʃɳəl-izəm [-ʃnəl-, -ʃɳ̩-, -ʃn̩-, -ʃənəl-]
denominative di'nɔminətiv
denominator, -s di'nɔmineitə*, -z
denotation, -s ˌdiːnəu'teiʃən, -z
denot|e, -es, -ing, -ed di'nəut, -s, -iŋ, -id
dénouement, -s dei'nuːmãːŋ [-mɑːŋ, -mõː*ŋ̃*, -mɔːŋ, -mɔŋ] (denumã), -z
denounc|e, -es, -ing, -ed, -er/s, -ement/s di'nauns, -iz, -iŋ, -t, -ə*/z, -mənt/s
de novo diː'nəuvəu [dei-]
dense, -r, -st, -ly, -ness dens, -ə*, -ist, -li, -nis
densit|y, -ies 'densit|i, -iz
dent (*s. v.*) (**D.**), **-s, -ing, -ed** dent, -s, -iŋ, -id
dental (*s. adj.*), **-s** 'dentl, -z
dentaliz|e [-is|e], **-es, -ing, -ed** 'dentə-laiz, -iz, -iŋ, -d
dentate 'denteit
dentated 'denteitid [den't-]
denticle, -s 'dentikl, -z
dentifrice, -s 'dentifris, -iz
dentil, -s 'dentil, -z
dentilingual (*s. adj.*), **-s** 'denti'liŋgwəl, -z
dentine 'dentiːn
dentist, -s, -ry 'dentist, -s, -ri
dentition den'tiʃən
Denton 'dentən
denture, -s 'dentʃə*, -z
denudation, -s ˌdiːnju(ː)'deiʃən, -z
denud|e, -es, -ing, -ed di'njuːd, -z, -iŋ, -id
denunciat|e, -es, -ing, -ed, -or/s di'nʌn-sieit [-nsjeit, -nʃieit, -nʃjeit], -s, -iŋ, -id, -ə*/z
denunciation, -s diˌnʌnsi'eiʃən, -z
denunciatory di'nʌnsiətəri [-nʃïə-, -nsjə-, -nʃjə-, di'nʌnsieitəri, di'nʌnʃieitəri]
Denver 'denvə*
den|y, -ies, -ying, -ied, -ier/s di'n|ai, -aiz, -aiiŋ, -aid, -ai-ə*/z [-aïə*/z]
Denys 'denis
Denyse də'niːz [de'n-]
Denzil 'denzil
deodand, -s 'dïəudænd, -z
deodar, -s 'dïəudɑː*, -z
deodara, -s dïə'dɑːrə [diəu'd-, -'dɛərə], -z
deodorant, -s diː'əudərənt [di'əu-], -s
deodorization [-isa-], **-s** diːˌəudərai'zei-ʃən [diˌəu-, -ri'z-], -z
deodoriz|e [-is|e], **-es, -ing, -ed, -er/s** diː'əudəraiz [di'əu-], -iz, -iŋ, -d, -ə*/z
deoxidization [-isa-], **-s** diːˌɔksidai'zei-ʃən ['diːˌɔ-], -z
deoxidiz|e [-is|e], **-es, -ing, -ed, -er/s** diː'ɔksidaiz ['diːˌɔ-], -iz, -iŋ, -d, -ə*/z
depart, -s, -ing, -ed di'pɑːt, -s, -iŋ, -id

department, -s di'pɑːtmənt, -s
departmental ˌdiːpɑːt'mentl
departure, -s di'pɑːtʃə*, -z
depast|ure, -ures, -uring, -ured diː-
'pɑːstʃ|ə*, -əz, -əriŋ, -əd
depauperiz|e [-is|e], -es, -ing, -ed
'diː'pɔːpəraiz, -iz, -iŋ, -d
depend, -s, -ing, -ed di'pend, -z, -iŋ, -id
dependable, -ness di'pendəbl, -nis
dependant, -s di'pendənt, -s
dependen|ce, -cy, -cies, -t/s, -tly di-
'pendən|s, -si, -siz, -t/s, -tli
Depere di'piə* [də'p-]
Depew di'pju: [de'p-]
depict, -s, -ing, -ed di'pikt, -s, -iŋ, -id
depiction di'pikʃən
depilat|e, -es, -ing, -ed 'depileit, -s, -iŋ,
-id
depilatory di'pilətəri [de'p-]
deplet|e, -es, -ing, -ed di'pliːt [diː'p-], -s,
-iŋ, -id
depletion, -s di'pliːʃən [diː'p-], -z
deplet|ive, -ory di'pliːt|iv [diː'p-], -əri
deplorab|le, -ly, -leness di'plɔːrəb|l
[-'plɔər-], -li, -lnis
deplor|e, -es, -ing, -ed di'plɔː* [-'plɔə*],
-z, -riŋ, -d
deploy, -s, -ing, -ed; -ment di'plɔi, -z,
-iŋ, -d; -mənt
depolarization [-isa-] 'diːˌpəulərai'zeiʃən
[-ri'z-]
depolariz|e [-is|e], -es, -ing, -ed diː-
'pəuləraiz ['diː'p-], -iz, -iŋ, -d
deponent (s. adj.), -s di'pəunənt, -s
depopulat|e, -es, -ing, -ed, -or/s diː-
'pɔpjuleit, -s, -iŋ, -id, -ə*/z
depopulation diːˌpɔpju'leiʃən ['diːˌp-]
deport, -s, -ing, -ed di'pɔːt, -s, -iŋ, -id
deportation, -s ˌdiːpɔː'teiʃən, -z
deportment di'pɔːtmənt
deposal, -s di'pəuzəl, -z
depos|e, -es, -ing, -ed di'pəuz, -iz, -iŋ, -d
deposit (s. v.), -s, -ing, -ed, -or/s di-
'pɔzit, -s, -iŋ, -id, -ə*/z
depositar|y, -ies di'pɔzitər|i, -iz
deposition, -s ˌdepə'ziʃən [ˌdiːp-, -pu'z-],
-z
depositor|y, -ies di'pɔzitər|i, -iz
depot, -s 'depəu, -z
depravation ˌdeprə'veiʃən
deprav|e, -es, -ing, -ed, -edly, -edness
di'preiv, -z, -iŋ, -d, -dli [-idli], -dnis
[-idnis]
depravity di'præviti
deprecat|e, -es, -ing/ly, -ed, -or/s
'deprikeit, -s, -iŋ/li, -id, -ə*/z
deprecation, -s ˌdepri'keiʃən, -z
deprecatory 'deprikətəri [-keit-]

depreciat|e, -es, -ing/ly, -ed, -or/s
di'priːʃieit [-ʃjeit, -sieit, -sjeit], -s,
-iŋ/li, -id, -ə*/z
depreciation diˌpriːʃi'eiʃən [-si'ei-]
depreciatory di'priːʃjətəri [-ʃiət-, -ʃət-,
-ʃieitəri]
depredat|e, -es, -ing, -ed, -or/s 'de-
prideit [-prəd-], -s, -iŋ, -id, -ə*/z
depredation, -s ˌdepri'deiʃən [-prə'd-], -z
depredatory di'predətəri
depress, -es, -ing/ly, -ed, -or/s di'pres,
-iz, -iŋ/li, -t, -ə*/z
depression, -s di'preʃən, -z
deprivation, -s ˌdepri'veiʃən [ˌdiːprai'v-],
-z
depriv|e, -es, -ing, -ed di'praiv, -z, -iŋ,
-d
Deptford 'detfəd
depth, -s depθ, -s
depth-charge, -s 'depθtʃɑːdʒ, -iz
deputation, -s ˌdepju(ː)'teiʃən, -z
deput|e, -es, -ing, -ed di'pjuːt, -s, -iŋ, -id
deputiz|e [-is|e], -es, -ing, -ed 'de-
pjutaiz, -iz, -iŋ, -d
deput|y, -ies 'depjut|i, -iz
De Quincey də'kwinsi
derail, -s, -ing, -ed, -ment/s di'reil
[diː'r-, 'diː'r-], -z, -iŋ, -d, -mənt/s
derang|e, -es, -ing, -ed, -ement/s
di'reindʒ [də'r-], -iz, -iŋ, -d, -mənt/s
derat|e, -es, -ing, -ed diː'reit, -s, -iŋ, -id
de-ra|tion, -tions, -tioning, -tioned
'diː'ræ|ʃən, -ʃənz, -ʃəniŋ [-ʃŋiŋ, -ʃniŋ],
-ʃənd
Derbe 'dəːbi
Derby, -shire 'dɑːbi, -ʃə* [-ʃiə*]
    Note.—The form 'dəːbi is also heard,
    mainly from dialectal speakers.
Dereham 'diərəm
Derek 'derik
derelict (s. adj.), -s 'derilikt, -s
dereliction ˌderi'likʃən
derequisi|tion, -tions, -tioning, -tioned
'diːˌrekwi'zi|ʃən, -ʃənz, -ʃəniŋ [-ʃŋiŋ,
-ʃniŋ], -ʃənd
D'Eresby 'diəzbi
De Reszke də'reski
Derg(h) dəːg
Derham 'derəm
derid|e, -es, -ing/ly, -ed, -er/s di'raid
[də'r-], -z, -iŋ/li, -id, -ə*/z
de rigueur dəri'gəː* [dərigœːr]
Dering 'diəriŋ
derision di'riʒən [də'r-]
derisive, -ly, -ness di'raisiv [də'r-,
-'raiziv, -'riziv], -li, -nis
derisory di'raisəri [də'r-, -'raizəri]
derivation, -s ˌderi'veiʃən, -z

derivative (*s. adj.*), **-s**, **-ly** di'rivətiv [də'r-], -z, -li

deriv|e, **-es**, **-ing**, **-ed**; **-able** di'raiv [də'r-], -z, -iŋ, -d; -əbl

d'Erlanger (*Eng. surname*) 'dɛəlɑ:nʒei [-lɔ̃:n-]

derm, **-al** də:m,-əl

dermatitis ,də:mə'taitis

dermatolog|ist/s, **-y** ,də:mə'tɔlədʒ|ist/s, -i

derogat|e, **-es**, **-ing**, **-ed** 'derəuɡeit, -s, -iŋ, -id

derogation ,derəu'ɡeiʃən

derogator|y, **-ily**, **-iness** di'rɔɡətər|i [də'r-], -ili, -inis

De Rohan də'rəuən

Deronda də'rɔndə [di'r-]

De Ros də'ru:s

derrick (D.), **-s** 'derik, -s

derring-do 'deriŋ'du:

derringer (D.), **-s** 'derindʒə*, -z

Derry 'deri

De Rutzen də'rʌtsn

Derviche 'də:vitʃ

dervish (D.), **-es** 'də:viʃ, -iz

Derwent (*river*) 'də:wənt [-went, -wint], 'dɑ:w-

Note.—Viscount FitzAlan of Derwent pronounces 'dɑ:w-.

Derwentwater 'də:wənt,wɔ:tə* [-went-, -wint-]

De Salis də'sælis [di's-], -'sɑ:lis

Desart 'dezət

de Satgé də'sætdʒei

Desbarres dei'bɑ:*

Desborough 'dezbrə

descal|e, **-es**, **-ing**, **-ed** 'di:'skeil, -z, -iŋ, -d

descant (*s.*), **-s** 'deskænt, -s

descant (*v.*), **-s**, **-ing**, **-ed** dis'kænt [des-], -s, -iŋ, -id

Descartes dei'kɑ:t ['deikɑ:t] (dekart)

descend, **-s**, **-ing**, **-ed** di'send, -z, -iŋ, -id

descendant (*s. adj.*), **-s** di'sendənt, -s

descendent di'sendənt

descent, **-s** di'sent, -s

describ|e, **-es**, **-ing**, **-ed**, **-er/s**; **-able** dis'kraib, -z, -iŋ, -d, -ə*/z; -əbl

description, **-s** dis'kripʃən, -z

descriptive, **-ly**, **-ness** dis'kriptiv, -li, -nis

descr|y, **-ies**, **-ying**, **-ied** dis'kr|ai, -aiz, -aiiŋ, -aid

Desdemona ,dezdi'məunə

desecrat|e, **-es**, **-ing**, **-ed**, **-or/s** 'desikreit, -s, -iŋ, -id, -ə*/z

desecration, **-s** ,desi'kreiʃən, -z

de Selincourt də'selinkɔ:t [-liŋk-]

desensitiz|e [-is|e], **-es**, **-ing**, **-ed** 'di:-'sensitaiz, -iz, -iŋ, -d

desert (*s.*) (*what is deserved*), **-s** di'zə:t, -s

desert (*s. adj.*) (*wilderness, desolate*), **-s** 'dezət, -s

desert (*v.*), **-s**, **-ing**, **-ed**, **-er/s** di'zə:t, -s, -iŋ, -id, -ə*/z

desertion, **-s** di'zə:ʃən, -z

deserv|e, **-es**, **-ing/ly**, **-ed**, **-edly** di'zə:v, -z, -iŋ/li, -d, -idli

deshabille 'dezæbi:l [-zəb-]

déshabillé ,deizæ'bi:ei [,dez-, -zə'b-, -'bi:lei] (dezabije)

desiccat|e, **-es**, **-ing**, **-ed** 'desikeit, -s, -iŋ, -id

desiccation ,desi'keiʃən

desiccative de'sikətiv [di's-, 'desikətiv]

desiderat|e, **-es**, **-ing**, **-ed** di'zidəreit [di'si-], -s, -iŋ, -id

desideration, **-s** di,zidə'reiʃən [di,si-], -z

desiderative di'zidərətiv [di'si-]

desiderat|um, **-a** di,zidə'reit|əm [di,si-, -'rɑ:t-], -ə

design (*s. v.*), **-s**, **-ing**, **-ed**, **-edly**, **-er/s**; **-able** di'zain, -z, -iŋ, -d, -idli, -ə*/z; -əbl

designate (*adj.*) 'dezignit [-neit]

designat|e (*v.*), **-es**, **-ing**, **-ed**, **-or/s** 'dezigneit, -s, -iŋ, -id, -ə*/z

designation, **-s** ,dezig'neiʃən, -z

desilveriz|e [-is|e], **-es**, **-ing**, **-ed** di:-'silvəraiz ['di:'s-], -iz, -iŋ, -d

desinence, **-s** 'desinəns, -iz

desirability di,zaiərə'biliti [-lət-]

desirab|le, **-ly**, **-leness** di'zaiərəb|l, -li, -lnis

desir|e (*s. v.*), **-es**, **-ing**, **-ed**, **-er/s** di'zaiə*, -z, -riŋ, -d, -rə*/z

Désirée (*English name*) dei'ziərei [de'z-]

desirous, **-ly** di'zaiərəs, -li

desist, **-s**, **-ing**, **-ed** di'zist [di'sist], -s, -iŋ, -id

desistance di'zistəns [di'sis-]

desk, **-s** desk, -s

Deslys dei'li:s

Des Moines (*in U.S.A.*) di'mɔin [-'mɔinz]

Desmond 'dezmənd

desolate (*adj.*), **-ly**, **-ness** 'desəlit [-sl̩-], -li, -nis

desolat|e (*v.*), **-es**, **-ing**, **-ed**, **-or/s** 'desəleit, -s, -iŋ, -id, -ə*/z

desolation, **-s** ,desə'leiʃən, -z

despair (*s. v.*), **-s**, **-ing/ly**, **-ed** dis'pɛə*, -z, -riŋ/li, -d

Despard 'despəd [-pɑ:d]

despatch (*s. v.*), **-es**, **-ing**, **-ed**, **-er/s** dis'pætʃ, -iz, -iŋ, -t, -ə*/z

despatch-boat, -s dis'pætʃbəut, -s
despatch-box, -es dis'pætʃbɔks, -iz
despatch-rider, -s dis'pætʃ,raidə*, -z
desperado, -es ,despə'rɑːdəu [-'reid-], -z
desperate, -ly, -ness 'despərit, -li, -nis
desperation ,despə'reiʃən
despicability ,despikə'biliti [dis,pik-,
  -lət-]
despicab|le, -ly, -leness 'despikəb|l
  [dis'pik-], -li, -lnis
despis|e -es, -ing, -ed, -er/s dis'paiz,
  -iz, -iŋ, -d, -ə*/z
despite, -ful, -fully dis'pait, -ful, -fuli
  [-fəli]
despoil, -s, -ing, -ed, -er/s dis'pɔil, -z,
  -iŋ, -d, -ə*/z
despond (D.), -s, -ing/ly, -ed dis'pɔnd,
  -z, -iŋ/li, -id
desponden|ce, -cy, -t/ly dis'pɔndən|s,
  -si, -t/li
despot, -s 'despɔt [-pət], -s
despotic, -al, -ally, -alness des'pɔtik
  [dis-], -əl, -əli, -əlnis
despotism, -s 'despətizəm, -z
dessert, -s di'zəːt, -s
dessert-kni|fe, -ves di'zəːtnai|f, -vz
dessert-service, -s di'zəːt,səːvis, -iz
dessert-spoon, -s di'zəːt-spuːn, -z
destination, -s ,desti'neiʃən, -z
destin|e, -es, -ing, -ed 'destin, -z, -iŋ, -d
destin|y, -ies 'destin|i, -iz
destitute, -ly, -ness 'destitjuːt, -li, -nis
destitution ,desti'tjuːʃən
destroy, -s, -ing, -ed, -er/s dis'trɔi, -z,
  -iŋ, -d, -ə*/z
destructibility dis,trʌkti'biliti [-tə'b-,
  -lət-]
destructible dis'trʌktəbl [-tib-]
destruction, -s dis'trʌkʃən, -z
destructive, -ly, -ness dis'trʌktiv, -li,
  -nis
destructor, -s dis'trʌktə*, -z
desuetude di'sju(ː)itjuːd ['deswitjuːd,
  'diːswi-]   [-inis
desultor|y, -ily, -iness 'desəltər|i, -ili,
Desvaux 'deivəu, dei'vəu, də'vəu
Des Vœux dei'vəː:
detach, -es, -ing, -ed, -edly, -ment/s;
  -able di'tætʃ, -iz, -iŋ, -t, -tli [-idli],
  -mənt/s; -əbl
detail (s. v.), -s, -ing, -ed 'diːteil
  [di'teil], -z, -iŋ, -d
detain, -s, -ing, -ed, -er/s di'tein, -z, -iŋ,
  -d, -ə*/z
detainee, -s ,diːtei'niː [ditei'niː], -z
detainer (legal term) di'teinə*
detect, -s, -ing, -ed, -or/s; -able
  di'tekt, -s, -iŋ, -id, -ə*/z; -əbl

detection, -s di'tekʃən, -z
detective (s. adj.), -s di'tektiv, -z
detent, -s di'tent, -s
detention, -s di'tenʃən, -z
deter, -s, -ring, -red di'tə:*, -z, -riŋ, -d
Deterding 'detədiŋ
detergent (s. adj.), -s di'tə:dʒənt, -s
deteriorat|e, -es, -ing, -ed di'tiəriəreit,
  -s, -iŋ, -id
deterioration di,tiəriə'reiʃən
determinable di'tə:minəbl
determinant (s. adj.), -s di'tə:minənt, -s
determinate, -ly, -ness di'tə:minit, -li,
  -nis
determination, -s di,tə:mi'neiʃən, -z
determinative di'tə:minətiv
determin|e, -es, -ing, -ed/ly di'tə:min,
  -z, -iŋ, -d/li
determini|sm, -st/s di'tə:mini|zəm, -st/s
deterrent (s. adj.), -s di'terənt [in the
  army also 'detərənt], -s
detest, -s, -ing, -ed di'test, -s, -iŋ, -id
detestab|le, -ly, -leness di'testəb|l, -li,
  -lnis
detestation ,diː:tes'teiʃən [dites't-]
dethron|e, -es, -ing, -ed, -ement
  di'θrəun, -z, -iŋ, -d, -mənt
Detmold (surname) 'detməuld, (German
  town) 'detməuld ('dɛtmɔlt)
detonat|e, -es, -ing, -ed, -or/s 'detəu-
  neit ['diːt-], -s, -iŋ, -id, -ə*/z
detonation, -s ,detəu'neiʃən [,diːt-], -z
détour, -s 'diːtuə* ['dei-, dei'tuə*,
  di't-] (detuːr), -z
detract, -s, -ing/ly, -ed, -or/s di'trækt,
  -s, -iŋ/li, -id, -ə*/z
detraction, -s di'trækʃən, -z
detract|ive, -ory di'trækt|iv, -əri
detrain, -s, -ing, -ed diː'trein ['-'-], -z,
  -iŋ, -d
de Trey də'trei
detriment, -s 'detrimənt, -s
detrimental ,detri'mentl
detrition di'triʃən
detritus di'traitəs
Detroit də'trɔit [di't-]
de trop də'trəu (dətro)
detruncat|e, -es, -ing, -ed diː'trʌŋkeit
  ['diː:-t-], -s, -iŋ, -id
detruncation, -s ,diː:-trʌŋ'keiʃən, -z
Dettol 'detɔl [-təl]
Deucalion dju(ː)'keiljə˘ [-liən]
deuce, -s djuːs, -iz
deuc|ed, -edly djuːs|t ['djuːs|id], -idli
deuterium dju(ː)'tiəriəm
deuteronomic ,djuːtərə'nɔmik
Deuteronomy ,djuːtə'rɔnəmi ['djuːtər-
  ənəmi]

deutzia, -s 'dju:tsjə ['dɔits-, -sĭə], -z
deva, -s 'deivə ['di:və] (Hind. deva), -z
de Valera dəvə'leərə ['dev-]
devaluation, -s ˌdi:vælju'eiʃən, -z
deval|ue, -ues, -uing, -ued 'di:'væl|ju:
  [di:'v-, -ju], -ju:z [-juz], -juiŋ [-jwiŋ],
  -ju:d [-jud]
Devanagari ˌdeivə'nɑ:gəri [ˌdev-]
Devant də'vænt [di'v-]
devastat|e, -es, -ing, -ed 'devəsteit, -s,
  -iŋ, -id
devastation, -s ˌdevəs'teiʃən, -z
develop, -s, -ing, -ed, -er/s, -ment/s;
  -able di'veləp [də'v-], -s, -iŋ, -t, -ə*/z,
  -mənt/s; -əbl
Devenish 'devn̩iʃ [-vəniʃ]
Deventer 'devəntə*
Deventhaugh 'devənthɔ:
De Vere də'viə* [di'v-]
Devereux 'devəru:, -ru:ks
Deveron 'devərən
Devers (surname) 'di:vəz, 'devəz
Deverson 'devəsn
De Vesci də'vesi
deviat|e, -es, -ing, -ed, -or/s 'di:vieit
  [-vjeit], -s, -iŋ, -id, -ə*/z
deviation, -s ˌdi:vi'eiʃən, -z
deviation|ism, -ist/s ˌdi:vi'eiʃən|izəm
  [-ʃn̩-], -ist/s
device, -s di'vais, -iz
dev|il (s. v.), -ils, -illing, -illed 'dev|l,
  -lz, -liŋ [-liŋ], -ld
devil-fish, -es 'devlfiʃ, -iz
devilish, -ly, -ness 'devl̩iʃ [-vliʃ], -li, -nis
devil-may-care 'devlmei'kɛə*
devilment, -s 'devlmənt, -s
devilr|y, -ies 'devlr|i, -iz
devil-worship, -per/s 'devl̩wə:ʃip, -ə*/z
Devine də'vain [di'v-]
devious, -ly, -ness 'di:vjəs [-vĭəs], -li,
  -nis
devis|e, -es, -ing, -ed, -er/s; -able
  di'vaiz, -iz, -iŋ, -d, -ə*/z; -əbl
devisee, -s ˌdevi'zi: [divai'zi:], -z
devisor, -s ˌdevi'zɔ:* [divai'zɔ:*,
  di'vaizɔ:*], -z
devitalization [-isa-] di:ˌvaitəlai'zeiʃən
  ['di:ˌvai-, -tlai-]
devitaliz|e [-is|e], -es, -ing, -ed di:'vaitəl-
  aiz ['di:'v-, -tlai-], -iz, -iŋ, -d
Devizes di'vaiziz
devocalization [-isa-], -s di:ˌvəukəlai-
  'zeiʃən ['di:ˌvəukəlai'z-, -klai-], -z
devocaliz|e [-is|e], -es, -ing, -ed di:-
  'vəukəlaiz ['di:'v-, -klaiz], -iz, -iŋ, -d
devoic|e, -es, -ing, -ed 'di:'vɔis [di:'v-],
  -iz, -iŋ, -t
devoid di'vɔid

devolution, -s ˌdi:və'lu:ʃən [-vl̩'u:-,
  -və'lju:-], -z
devolv|e, -es, -ing, -ed di'vɔlv, -z, -iŋ, -d
Devon, -shire 'devn, -ʃiə* [-ʃə*]
Devonian, -s de'vəunjən [di'v-, -nĭən],
  -z
Devonport 'devnpɔ:t [-vmp-]
devot|e, -es, -ing, -ed/ly, -edness
  di'vəut, -s, -iŋ, -id/li, -idnis
devotee, -s ˌdevəu'ti:, -z
devotion, -s di'vəuʃən, -z
devo|tional, -tionally di'vəu|ʃənl [-ʃnəl,
  -ʃn̩l, -ʃn̩l, -ʃənəl], -ʃnəli [-ʃnəli, -ʃn̩li,
  -ʃnl̩i, -ʃənəli]
devour, -s, -ing, -ed, -er/s di'vauə*, -z,
  -riŋ, -d, -rə*/z
devout, -er, -est, -ly, -ness di'vaut, -ə*,
  -ist, -li, -nis
dew, -s dju:, -z
dewan, -s di'wɑ:n, -z
Dewar 'dju(:)ə*
dewberr|y, -ies 'dju:ber|i [-bər-], -iz
dew-claw, -s 'dju:-klɔ:, -z
dew-drop, -s 'dju:-drɔp, -s
D'Ewes dju:z
De Wet də'vet [də'wet]
Dewey 'dju(:)i
De Wiart (English name) də'waiət
dewlap, -s 'dju:læp, -s
dew-point, -s 'dju:-pɔint, -s
dew-pond, -s 'dju:-pɔnd, -s
Dewsbury 'dju:zbəri
dew|y, -iness 'dju:|i [dju|i], -inis
dexter 'dekstə*
dexterity deks'teriti
dexterous, -ly, -ness 'dekstərəs, -li, -nis
dextrose 'dekstrəus
dey, -s dei, -z
D'Eyncourt 'deinkə:t [-kɔ:t]
De Zoete də'zu:t
dhobi, -(e)s 'dəubi (Hind. dhobi), -z
dhow, -s dau, -z
diabetes ˌdaiə'bi:ti:z
diabetic, -s ˌdaiə'betik [-'bi:t-], -s
diabolic, -al, -ally ˌdaiə'bɔlik, -əl, -əli
diabolism dai'æbəlizəm
diaboliz|e [-is|e], -es, -ing, -ed dai-
  'æbəlaiz, -iz, -iŋ, -d
diabolo di'ɑ:bələu [-'æb-]
diachronic 'daiə'krɔnik [ˌdaiə-]
diaconal dai'ækənl
diaconate, -s dai'ækənit [-neit], -s
diacritic (s. adj.), -s, -al ˌdaiə'kritik, -s,
  -əl
diadem, -s 'daiədem [-dəm], -z   [-əl
diaeres|is, -es dai'iəris|is [dai'er-, -rəs-],
  -i:z
diagnos|e, -es, -ing, -ed 'daiəgnəuz
  [ˌdaiəg'n-], -iz, -iŋ, -d

diagnos|is, -es ˌdaiəg'nəus|is, -iːz
diagnostic (s. adj.), -s ˌdaiəg'nɔstik, -s
diagon|al (s. adj.), -als, -ally dai'ægən|l,
   -lz, -əli [-l̩i]
diagram, -s 'daiəgræm, -z
diagrammatic, -al, -ally ˌdaiəgrə'mætik,
   -əl, əli
dial (s. v.), -s, -ling, -led 'daiəl, -z,
   'daiəliŋ, 'daiəld
dialect, -s 'daiəlekt, -s
dialectal ˌdaiə'lektl   [-əli
dialectic, -s, -al, -ally ˌdaiə'lektik, -s, -əl
dialectician, -s ˌdaiəlek'tiʃən, -z
dialectolog|ist/s, -y ˌdaiəlek'tɔlədʒ|ist/s,
   -i
diallage (figure of speech) dai'æləgi
   [-lədʒi]
diallage (mineral) 'daiəlidʒ
dialogi|sm, -st/s dai'ælədʒi|zəm, -st/s
dialogue, -s 'daiəlɔg, -z
dial-plate, -s 'daiəlpleit, -s
dialys|is, -es dai'ælis|is [-ləs-], -iːz
diamagnetic (s. adj.), -s, -ally ˌdaiəmæg-
   'netik ['daiəmæg'n-, -məg-], -s, -əli
diamagnetism   ˌdaiə'mægnitizəm
   ['daiə'm-]
diameter, -s dai'æmitə*, -z
diametr|al, -ally dai'æmitr|əl, -əli
diametric|al, -ally ˌdaiə'metrik|əl, -əli
diamond, -s 'daiəmənd, -z   [[-l̩i]
diamond-field, -s 'daiəməndfiːld, -z
Diana dai'ænə
dianthus, -es dai'ænθəs, -iz
diapason, -s ˌdaiə'peisn [-'peizn], -z
diaper, -s 'daiəpə*, -z
diaphanous dai'æfənəs
diaphone, -s 'daiəfoun, -z
diaphonic ˌdaiə'fonik
diaphragm, -s 'daiəfræm [-frəm], -z
diaphragmatic ˌdaiəfræg'mætik [-frəg-]
diapositive, -s ˌdaiə'pozitiv [-zət-], -z
diarch|y, -ies 'daiɑːk|i, -iz
diarist, -s 'daiərist, -s
diarrhoea ˌdaiə'riə
diar|y, -ies 'daiər|i, -iz
Diaspora dai'æspərə
diastase 'daiəsteis
diastole, -s dai'æstəli, -z
diatherm|ic, -ous ˌdaiə'θəːm|ik, -əs
diatom, -s 'daiətəm [-tɔm], -z
diatonic, -ally ˌdaiə'tɔnik, -əli
diatribe, -s 'daiətraib, -z
dib (s. v.), -s, -bing, -bed, -ber/s dib, -z,
   -iŋ, -d, -ə*/z
Dibb dib
dibb|le (s. v.), -les, -ling, -led, -ler/s
   'dib|l, -lz, -liŋ [-l̩iŋ], -ld, -lə*/z
   [-lə*/z]

Dibdin 'dibdin
dicast, -s 'dikæst, -s
dice (plur. of die) dais
dic|e (v.), -es, -ing, -ed dais, -iz, -iŋ, -t
dice-box, -es 'daisbɔks, -iz
Dicey 'daisi
dichloride, -s dai'klɔːraid, -z
dichotom|y, -ies dai'kɔtəm|i [di-], -iz
Dick dik
dickens (D.) 'dikinz
Dickensian di'kenziən [-'kens-, -zjən]
Dicker 'dikə*
dickey, -s 'diki, -z
Dickins 'dikinz
Dickinson 'dikinsn
Dicksee 'diksi(ː)
Dickson 'diksn
dick|y (D.), -ies 'dik|i, -iz
dickybird, -s 'dikibəːd, -z
dicotyledon, -s 'dai,kɔti'liːdən [ˌdai-k-],
   [-z
dictaphone, -s 'diktəfoun, -z
dictate (s.), -s 'dikteit, -s
dictat|e (v.), -es, -ing, -ed, -or/s dik-
   'teit, -s, -iŋ, -id, -ə*/z
dictation, -s dik'teiʃən, -z
dictatorial, -ly ˌdiktə'tɔːriəl, -i
dictatorship, -s dik'teitəʃip, -s
diction 'dikʃən
dictionar|y, -ies 'dikʃənr|i [-ʃənər-], -iz
dict|um, -a, -ums 'dikt|əm, -ə, -əmz
did (from do) did
Didache 'didəki(ː)
didactic, -al, -ally di'dæktik [dai'd-], -əl,
   -əli
didacticism di'dæktisizəm, [dai'd-]
didapper, -s 'daidæpə*, -z
Didcot 'didkət
didd|le, -les, -ling, -led, -ler/s 'did|l, -lz,
   -liŋ [-l̩iŋ], -ld, -lə*/z [-lə*/z]
Diderot 'diːdərəu (didro)
didn't didnt [also 'didn when not final]
Dido 'daidəu
Didymus 'didiməs
die (s.) (stamp), -s dai, -z
die (s.) (cube), dice dai, dais
die (v.), -s, dying, died dai, -z, -iŋ, -d
dielectric (s. adj.), -s ˌdaii'lektrik, -s
Dieppe di(ː)'ep (djɛp)
dies (from die) daiz
Diesel, -s 'diːzəl, -z
die-sink, -er/s, -ing 'dai-siŋk, -ə*/z, -iŋ
dies irae 'diːeiz'iərai ['diːez-, 'diːes-,
   -'iərei, old-fashioned 'daiiz'aiəriː]
dies|is, -es 'daiis|is ['daiəs-], -iːz
dies non, -s 'daiiz'nɔn, -z
diet (s. v.), -s, -ing, -ed 'daiət, -s, -iŋ, -id
dietar|y (s. adj.), -ies 'daiətər|i ['daiit-],
   -iz

dietetic (*s. adj.*), **-s, -al, -ally** ˌdaii'tetik [ˌdaiə't-], -s, -əl, -əli

dietitian [-ician], **-s** ˌdaii'tiʃən [ˌdaiə't-], -z

differ, -s, -ing, -ed 'difə*, -z, -riŋ, -d

differen|ce, -ces, -t/ly 'difrən|s [-fərən-], -siz, -t/li

differenti|al, -als, -ally ˌdifə'renʃ|əl, -əlz, -əli

differentiat|e, -es, -ing, -ed ˌdifə'renʃieit [-ʃjeit], -s, -iŋ, -id

differentiation, -s ˌdifərenʃi'eiʃən [-nsi-], -z

difficile 'difisi:l

difficult 'difikəlt [-fək-]

difficult|y, -ies 'difikəlt|i [-fək-], -iz

diffiden|ce, -t/ly 'difidən|s, -t/li

diffract, -s, -ing, -ed di'frækt, -s, -iŋ, -id

diffraction di'frækʃən

diffuse (*adj.*), **-ly, -ness** di'fju:s, -li, -nis

diffus|e (*v.*), **-es, -ing, -ed, -edly, -edness, -er/s** di'fju:z, -iz, -iŋ, -d, -idli, -idnis, -ə*/z

diffusibility di,fju:zə'biliti [-zi'b-, -lət-]

diffusible di'fju:zəbl [-zib-]

diffusion di'fju:ʒən

diffusive, -ly, -ness di'fju:siv, -li, -nis

dig (*s. v.*), **-s, -ging, -ged, dug** dig, -z, -iŋ, -d, dʌg

dig. (*in phrase* **infra dig.**) dig

digamma, -s dai'gæmə ['daigæmə], -z

Digby 'digbi

digest (*s.*), **-s** 'daidʒest, -s

digest (*v.*), **-s, -ing, -ed** di'dʒest [dai'dʒ-], -s, -iŋ, -id

digestibility di,dʒestə'biliti [dai,dʒ-, -ti'b-, -lət-]

digestible di'dʒestəbl [dai'dʒ-, -tib-]

digestion, -s di'dʒestʃən [dai'dʒ-, -eʃtʃ-], -z

digestive (*s. adj.*), **-s, -ly, -ness** di'dʒestiv [dai'dʒ-], -z, -li, -nis

digger, -s 'digə*, -z

Digges digz

diggings 'digiŋz

Diggle, -s 'digl, -z

Diggory 'digəri

dight dait

Dighton 'daitn

digit, -s; -al/s 'didʒit, -s; -l/z

digitali|n, -s ˌdidʒi'teili|n, -s

digni|fy, -fies, -fying, -fied 'digni|fai, -faiz, -faiiŋ, -faid

dignitar|y, -ies 'dignitər|i, -iz

dignit|y, -ies 'dignit|i, -iz

digraph, -s 'daigrɑ:f [-græf], -s

digress, -es, -ing, -ed dai'gres [di'g-], -iz, -iŋ, -t

digression, -s dai'greʃən [di'g-], -z

digressive, -ly, -ness dai'gresiv [di'g-], -li, -nis

digs (*lodgings*) digz

Dijon 'di:ʒɔ̃:ŋ [-ʒɔːŋ, -ʒɔŋ, -ʒɔn] (diʒɔ̃)

dik|e (*s. v.*), **-es, -ing, -ed** daik, -s, -iŋ, -t

dilapidat|e, -es, -ing, -ed di'læpideit, -s, -iŋ, -id

dilapidation, -s di,læpi'deiʃən, -z

dilatability dai,leitə'biliti [di,l-, -'bilət-]

dilatation, -s ˌdailei'teiʃən [-lət-], -z

dilat|e, -es, -ing, -ed, -er/s; -able dai'leit [di'l-], -s, -iŋ, -id, -ə*/z; -əbl

dilation, -s dai'leiʃən [di'l-], -z

dilator|y, -ily, -iness 'dilətər|i, -ili, -inis

dilemma, -s di'lemə [dai'l-], -z

dilettante, -s ˌdili'tænti, -z

dilettantism ˌdili'tæntizəm

diligence (*industry*) 'dilidʒəns

diligence (*coach*), **-s** 'diliʒɑ̃:ns [-ʒɑ:ns, -ʒɔ̃:ns, -ʒɔ:ns, -dʒəns] (diliʒɑ̃:s), -iz

diligent, -ly 'dilidʒənt, -li

Dilke, -s dilk, -s

dill (**D.**), **-s** dil, -z

Dillon 'dilən

Dillwyn (*English surname*) 'dilin, 'dilwin

dilly-dall|y, -ies, -ying, -ied 'dilidæl|i, -iz, -iiŋ, -id

diluent (*s. adj.*), **-s** 'diljŭənt [-ljwənt], -s

dilut|e (*adj. v.*), **-eness; -es, -ing, -ed** dai'lju:t [di'l-, -'lu:t], -nis; -s, -iŋ, -id

dilutee, -s ˌdailju:'ti: [-lu:'t-], -z

dilution, -s dai'lu:ʃən [di'l-, -'lju:-], -z

diluvia|l, -n dai'lu:vjə|l [di'l-, -'lju:-, -viə-], -n

diluvi|um, -a dai'lu:vj|əm [di'l-, -'lju:-, -vi|əm], -ə

Dilwyn 'dilwin (*Welsh* 'dilwin)

Dilys 'dilis (*Welsh* 'dilis)

dim (*adj. v.*), **-mer, -mest, -ly, -ness; -s, -ming, -med** dim, -ə*, -ist, -li, -nis; -z, -iŋ, -d

Diman 'daimən

dime, -s daim, -z

dimension, -s di'menʃən [dai'm-], -z

dimensional di'menʃənl [dai'm-, -ʃnəl, ʃnl̩, -ʃnl̩, -ʃənəl]

dimeter, -s 'dimitə*, -z

dimidiate (*adj.*) di'midiit [-djit]

dimidiat|e (*v.*), **-es, -ing, -ed** di'midieit, -s, -iŋ, -id

dimidiation di,midi'eiʃən

diminish, -es, -ing, -ed; -able di'miniʃ, -iz, -iŋ, -t; -əbl

diminuendo, -s di,minju'endəu, -z

diminution, -s ˌdimi'nju:ʃən, -z

diminutive, -ly, -ness di'minjutiv, -li, -nis

dimity 'dimiti
Dimmesdale 'dimzdeil
dimmish 'dimiʃ
dim-out, -s 'dimaut, -s
dimp|le (s. v.), -les, -ling, -led 'dimp|l,
-lz, -liŋ [-l̩iŋ], -ld
dimply 'dimpli
Dimsdale 'dimzdeil
din (s. v.), -s, -ning, -ned din, -z, -iŋ, -d
Dinah 'dainə
dinar, -s (monetary unit in Yugoslavia)
'di:nɑ:*, (in Persia, Iraq, Jordan)
'di:nɑ:* [di:'nɑ:*], -z
Note.—Bankers usually say 'di:nɑ:*
for the dinar of Persia, Iraq, and
Jordan, but many people who have
been in the Middle East pronounce
di:'nɑ:*.
Dindigul 'dindigəl
din|e, -es, -ing, -ed dain, -z, -iŋ,
-d, -ə*/z
Dinely (surname) 'dinli
ding, -s, -ing, -ed diŋ, -z, -iŋ, -d
dingdong 'diŋ'dɔŋ [also '--, -'-' according
to sentence-stress]
dingey, -s 'diŋgi [-ɲi], -z
dingh|y, -ies 'diŋg|i, -iz
dingle (D.), -s 'diŋgl, -z
Dingley 'diŋli
dingo, -s 'diŋgəu, -z
Dingwall 'diŋwɔ:l [-wəl]
ding|y (s.) (boat), -ies 'diŋg|i, -iz
ding|y (adj.) (dirty, drab), -ier, -iest, -ily,
-iness 'dindʒ|i, -iə* [-jə*], -iist [-jist],
-ili, -inis
dining-car, -s 'dainiŋ-kɑ:*, -z
dining-room, -s 'dainiŋrum [-ru:m], -z
dining-table, -s 'dainiŋ,teibl, -z
dink|y, -ier, -iest, -iness 'diŋk|i, -iə*
[-jə*], -iist [-jist], -inis
Dinmont 'dinmont [-mənt]
Dinneford 'dinifəd
dinner, -s 'dinə*, -z
dinner-bell, -s 'dinəbel, -z   [-z
dinner-hour, -s 'dinər,auə* ['dinə,auə*],
dinner-jacket, -s 'dinə,dʒækit, -s
dinner-part|y, -ies 'dinə,pɑ:t|i, -iz
dinner-service, -s 'dinə,sə:vis, -iz
dinner-set, -s 'dinəset, -s
dinner-table, -s 'dinə,teibl, -z
dinner-time, -s 'dinətaim, -z
dinner-wagon, -s 'dinə,wægən, -z
Dinocrates dai'nɔkrəti:z
Dinorah di'nɔ:rə
dinosaur, -s 'dainəusɔ:*, -z
dinosaur|us, -i ,dainə'sɔ:r|əs ['--'--], -ai
dinotheri|um, -a ,dainəu'θiəri̇|əm, -ə
dint dint

Dinwiddie din'widi
diocesan dai'ɔsisən [-səs-]
diocese, -s 'daiəsis [-si:s, -si:z], -iz
Diocles 'daiəkli:z
Diocletian ,daiə'kli:ʃjən [-ʃi̇ən, -ʃən]
Diodorus ,daiə'dɔ:rəs
Diogenes dai'ɔdʒini:z [-dʒən-]
Diomed 'daiəmed
Diomede 'daiəmi:d
Diomedes ,daiə'mi:di:z
Dion (Greek) 'daiən, (French) 'di(:)ən
['di:ɔ:ŋ, 'di:ɔ:ŋ, 'di:ɔŋ, 'di:ɔn] (djɔ̃),
(in D. Boucicault) 'daiən
Dionysia, -n ,daiə'nizi̇ə [-zjə, -ʒiə,
-ʒjə, -siə, -sjə], -n
Dionysius ,daiə'nisiəs [-sjəs]
Dionysus ,daiə'naisəs
diopter, -s dai'ɔptə*, -z
dioptric dai'ɔptrik
Dior 'diɔ:* [di'ɔ:*] (djɔ:r)
diorama, -s ,daiə'rɑ:mə ['daiər-], -z
dioramic ,daiə'ræmik
Diosy di'əusi
dioxide, -s dai'ɔksaid ['dai'ɔ-], -z
dip (s. v.), -s, -ping, -ped, -per/s dip, -s,
-iŋ, -t, -ə*/z
diphtheria dif'θiəri̇ə [dip'θ-]
diphthong, -s 'difθɔŋ ['dipθ-], -z
diphthong|al, -ally dif'θɔŋg|əl [dip'θ-
-ɔŋ|əl], -əli
diphthongization [-isa-], -s ,difθɔŋ-
gai'zeiʃən [,dipθ-, -ɔŋai-], -z
diphthongiz|e [-is|e], -es, -ing, -ed
'difθɔŋgaiz ['dipθ-, -ɔŋai-], -iz, -iŋ, -d
diplodoc|us, -uses, -i di'plɔdək|əs, -əsiz,
diploma, -s di'pləumə, -z   [-ai
diplomacy di'pləuməsi
diplomat, -s 'dipləmæt [-pləum-,
-plum-], -s
diplomatic (s. adj.), -s, -al, -ally ,di-
plə'mætik [-pləu'm-, -plu'm-], -s, -əl
diplomatist, -s di'pləumətist, -s   [-əli
diplomatiz|e [-is|e], -es, -ing, -ed
di'pləumətaiz, -iz, -iŋ, -d
dipole, -s 'dai-pəul, -z
dipper, -s 'dipə*, -z
Diprose 'diprəuz
dipsomania ,dipsəu'meinjə [-ni̇ə]
dipsomaniac (s. adj.), -s ,dipsəu-
'meini̇æk [-njæk], -s
dipter|a, -al, -ous 'diptər|ə, -əl, -əs
diptych, -s 'diptik, -s
dire, -r, -st, -ness 'daiə*, -rə*, -rist, -nis
direct (adj. v.), -est, -ness; -s, -ing, -ed,
-or/s di'rekt [də'r-, dai'r-, occasionally
'dairekt when attributive adj.], -ist,
-nis; -s, -iŋ, -id, -ə*/z
direction, -s di'rekʃən [də'r-, dai'r-], -z

directional di'rekʃənl [də'r-, dai'r-,
-ʃnəl, -ʃn̩, -ʃn̩, -ʃənəl]
directive (s. adj.), -s di'rektiv [də'r-,
dai'r-], -z
directly di'rektli [də'r-, dai'r-, 'drekli]
*Note.—The form 'drekli is not used
in the sense of 'in a straight
manner'; it is, however, frequent
in the sense of 'at once', and still
more frequent in the sense of 'as
soon as'.*
directorate, -s di'rektərit [də'r-, dai'r-], -s
directorship, -s di'rektəʃip [də'r-,
dai'r-], -s
director|y, -ies di'rektər|i [də'r-], -iz
dire|ful, -fully, -fulness 'daiə|ful, -fuli
[-fəli], -fulnis
dirge, -s də:dʒ, -iz
dirigible (s. adj.), -s 'diridʒəbl [-dʒib-,
di'ridʒ-], -z
dirk (D.), -s də:k, -s
dirndl [-dle], -s 'də:ndl, -z
dirt də:t
dirt-cheap 'də:t'tʃi:p
dirt-track, -s 'də:ttræk, -s
dirt|y (adj. v.), -ier, -iest, -ily, -iness;
-ies, -ying, -ied 'də:t|i, -iə* [-jə*],
-iist [-jist], -ili, -inis; -iz, -iiŋ [-jiŋ], -id
Dis dis   [-iz
disabilit|y, -ies ,disə'bilit|i [,dizə-, -lət-],
disab|le, -les, -ling, -led, -lement dis-
'eib|l [di'zei-], -lz, -liŋ [-liŋ], -ld,
-lmənt
disabus|e, -es, -ing, -ed ,disə'bju:z
['disə'b-], -iz, -iŋ, -d
disaccustom, -s, -ing, -ed 'disə'kʌstəm
[,dis-], -z, -iŋ, -d
disadvantage, -s ,disəd'va:ntidʒ ['—'—'],
-iz
disadvantageous, -ly, -ness ,disæd-
va:n'teidʒəs ['dis,ædva:n't-, -vən-],
-li, -nis
disaffect, -s, -ing, -ed/ly, -edness ,dis-
ə'fekt ['disə'f-], -s, -iŋ, -id/li, -idnis
disaffection ,disə'fekʃən ['disə'f-]
disagree, -s, -ing, -d, -ment/s ,dis-
ə'gri: ['disə'g-], -z, -iŋ, -d, -mənt/s
disagreeab|le, -ly, -leness, -les ,dis-
ə'griəb|l, -li, -lnis, -lz
disallow, -s, -ing, -ed 'disə'lau [,dis-], -z,
-iŋ, -d
disallow|able, -ance ,disə'lau-|əbl
[-'lau|ə-], -əns
disappear, -s, -ing, -ed ,disə'piə*
['disə'p-], -z, -riŋ, -d
disappearance, -s ,disə'piərəns, -iz
disappoint, -s, -ing, -ed, -ment/s ,dis-
ə'pɔint ['disə'p-], -s, -iŋ, -id, -mənt/s

disapprobation ,disæprəu'beiʃən ['dis-
,æprəu'b-, -pru'b-]
disapproval ,disə'pru:vəl ['disə'p-]
disapprov|e, -es,-ing/ly, -ed 'disə'pru:v
[,dis-], -z, -iŋ/li, -d
disarm, -s, -ing, -ed dis'a:m [di'za:m],
-z, -iŋ, -d
disarmament dis'a:məmənt [di'za:m-]
disarrang|e, -es, -ing, -ed 'disə'reindʒ
[,dis-], -iz, -iŋ, -d
disarrangement, -s ,disə'reindʒmənt, -s
disarray (s. v.), -s, -ing, -ed 'disə'rei, -z,
-iŋ, -d
disarticulat|e, -es, -ing, -ed 'disa:-
'tikjuleit, [,dis-], -s, -iŋ, -id
disarticulation ,disa:,tikju'leiʃən ['dis-
a:,tikju'l-]
disaster, -s di'za:stə*, -z
disastrous, -ly, -ness di'za:strəs, -li, -nis
disavow, -s, -ing, -ed 'disə'vau [,dis-],
-z, -iŋ, -d
disband, -s, -ing, -ed, -ment dis'bænd,
-z, -iŋ, -id, -mənt [dis'bænmənt]
disbar, -s, -ring, -red dis'ba:*, -z, -riŋ, -d
disbark, -s, -ing, -ed dis'ba:k, -s, -iŋ, -t
disbelief 'disbi'li:f ['—]
disbeliev|e, -es, -ing, -ed, -er/s 'dis-
bi'li:v [,dis-], -z, -iŋ, -d, -ə*/z
disburs|e, -es, -ing, -ed, -ement/s dis-
'bə:s, -iz, -iŋ, -t, -mənt/s
disc, -s disk, -s
discard (s.), -s 'diska:d [dis'ka:d], -z
discard (v.), -s, -ing, -ed dis'ka:d, -z, -iŋ,
-id
discern, -s, -ing, -ed, -er/s, -ment di'sə:n
[di'zə:n], -z, -iŋ, -d, -ə*/z, -mənt
discernib|le, -ly, -leness di'sə:nəb|l
[di'zə:-, -nib-], -li, -lnis   [-iz
discharge (s.), -s dis'tʃa:dʒ ['distʃa:dʒ],
discharg|e (v.), -es, -ing, -ed, -er/s
dis'tʃa:dʒ, -iz, -iŋ, -d, -ə*/z
disciple, -s; -ship di'saipl, -z; -ʃip
disciplinarian, -s ,disipli'nɛəriən [-səp-],
-z
disciplin|e (s. v.), -es, -ing, -ed; -ary
'disiplin [-səp-], -z, -iŋ, -d; -əri
disc-jockey, -s 'disk,dʒɔki, -z
disclaim, -s, -ing, -ed, -er/s dis'kleim,
-z, -iŋ, -d, -ə*/z
disclaimer (denial), -s dis'kleimə*, -z
disclos|e, -es, -ing, -ed dis'kləuz, -iz, -iŋ,
-d
disclosure, -s dis'kləuʒə*, -z
discobol|us, -i dis'kɔbəl|əs [-b|l|-], -ai
discolo(u)ration, -s dis,kʌlə'reiʃən
[,disk-], -z
discolour, -s, -ing, -ed dis'kʌlə*, -z,
-riŋ, -d

discomfit, -s, -ing, -ed dis'kʌmfit, -s, -iŋ, -id
discomfiture dis'kʌmfitʃə*
discomfort (s. v.), -s, -ing, -ed dis-'kʌmfət, -s, -iŋ, -id
discompos|e, -es, -ing, -ed ‚diskəm-'pəuz ['diskəm'p-], -iz, -iŋ, -d
discomposure ‚diskəm'pəuʒə* ['dis-kəm'p-]
disconcert, -s, -ing, -ed ‚diskən'sə:t ['diskən's-], -s, -iŋ, -id
disconnect, -s, -ing, -ed 'diskə'nekt [‚dis-], -s, -iŋ, -id
disconnection ‚diskə'nekʃən ['diskə'n-]
disconsolate, -ly, -ness dis'kɔnsəlit, -li, -nis
discontent, -ed, -edly, -edness 'dis-kən'tent [‚dis-], -id, -idli, -idnis
discontinuance ‚diskən'tinjŭəns ['dis-kən't-, -njwəns]
discontin|ue, -ues, -uing, -ued 'diskən-'tin|ju(:) [‚dis-], -ju(:)z, -juiŋ [-jwiŋ], -ju(:)d
discontinuit|y, -ies 'dis‚kɔnti'nju(:)it|i [‚dis-], -iz
discontinuous, -ly 'diskən'tinjŭəs [‚dis-, -njwəs], -li
discord (s.), -s 'diskɔ:d, -z
discord (v.), -s, -ing, -ed dis'kɔ:d, -z, -iŋ, -id
discordan|ce, -cy, -t/ly dis'kɔ:dən|s, -si, -t/li
discothèque, -s 'diskəutek [-teik], -s (diskɔtɛk)
discount (s.), -s 'diskaunt, -s
discount (v.), -s, -ing, -ed, -er/s 'dis-kaunt, dis'kaunt, -s, -iŋ, -id, -ə*/z
discountenanc|e, -es, -ing, -ed dis'kaun-tinəns [-tən-], -iz, -iŋ, -t
discourag|e, -es, -ing/ly, -ed, -ement/s dis'kʌridʒ, -iz, -iŋ/li, -d, -mənt/s
discourse (s.), -s dis'kɔ:s ['diskɔ:s, -ɔəs], -iz
discours|e (v.), -es, -ing, -ed, -er/s dis'kɔ:s [-'kɔəs], -iz, -iŋ, -t, -ə*/z
discourteous, -ly, -ness dis'kə:tjəs [-'kɔ:t-, -'kɔət-, -tiəs], -li, -nis
discourtesy dis'kə:tisi [-'kɔ:t-, -'kɔət-]
discov|er, -ers, -ering, -ered, -erer/s dis'kʌv|ə*, -əz, -əriŋ, -əd, -ərə*/z
discoverable dis'kʌvərəbl
discovert dis'kʌvət
discover|y, -ies dis'kʌvər|i, -iz
discredit, -s, -ing, -ed dis'kredit ['dis'k-], -s, -iŋ, -id
discreditab|le, -ly, -leness dis'kredit-əb|l, -li, -lnis   [-nis
discreet, -est, -ly, -ness dis'kri:t, -ist, -li,

discrepan|cy, -cies, -t dis'krepən|si, -siz, -t
discrete, -ly, -ness dis'kri:t [also '-- when attributive], -li, -nis
discretion, -s dis'kreʃən, -z
discre|tional, -tionally dis'kre|ʃənl [-ʃnəl, -ʃn̩l, -ʃnl, -ʃənəl], -ʃnəli [-ʃnəli, -ʃn̩li, -ʃnli, -ʃənəli]
discretionar|y, -ily dis'kreʃnər|i [-ʃənər-], -ili
discriminate (adj.), -ly dis'kriminit, -li
discriminat|e (v.), -es, -ing/ly, -ed dis-'krimineit, -s, -iŋ/li, -id
discrimination, -s dis‚krimi'neiʃən, -z
discriminative, -ly dis'kriminətiv [-neit-], -li
discriminatory dis'kriminətəri [dis-‚krimi'neitəri]
discursion, -s dis'kə:ʃən, -z
discursive, -ly, -ness dis'kə:siv, -li, -nis
discursory dis'kə:səri
disc|us, -i 'disk|əs, -ai
discuss, -es, -ing, -ed; -able dis'kʌs, -iz, -iŋ, -t; -əbl
discussion, -s dis'kʌʃən, -z
disdain (s. v.), -s, -ing, -ed dis'dein [diz'd-], -z, -iŋ, -d
disdain|ful, -fully, -fulness dis'dein|ful [diz'd-], -fuli [-fəli], -fulnis
disease, -s, -d di'zi:z, -iz, -d
disembark, -s, -ing, -ed 'disim'ba:k [‚dis-, -sem-], -s, -iŋ, -t
disembarkation, -s ‚disemba:'keiʃən ['disemba:'k-, -sim-], -z
disembarkment, -s ‚disim'ba:kmənt ['disim'b-, -sem-], -s
disembarrass, -es, -ing, -ed 'disim-'bærəs [‚dis-, -sem-], -iz, -iŋ, -t
disembarrassment, -s ‚disim'bærəsmənt ['disim'b-, -sem-], -s
disembod|y, -ies, -ying, -ied 'disim-'bɔd|i [‚dis-, -sem-], -iz, -iiŋ [-jiŋ], -id
disemb|owel, -owels, -owelling, -owelled ‚disim'b|auəl [-sem-, -auil, -aul], -z, -auəliŋ [-auiliŋ], -auəld [-auild, -auld]
disenchant, -s, -ing, -ed 'disin'tʃɑ:nt [‚dis-, -sen-], -s, -iŋ, -id
disenchantment, -s ‚disin'tʃɑ:ntmənt ['disin'tʃ-, -sen-], -s
disencumb|er, -ers, -ering, -ered 'disin-'kʌmb|ə* [‚dis-, -sen-], -əz, -əriŋ, -əd
disendow, -s, -ing, -ed 'disin'dau [‚dis-, -sen-], -z, -iŋ, -d
disendowment, -s ‚disin'daumənt ['dis-in'd-, -sen-]
disenfranchis|e, -es, -ing, -ed 'disin-'fræntʃaiz [‚dis-, -sen-], -iz, -iŋ, -d

disenfranchisement ˌdisin'frænt∫izmənt ['disin'f-, -sen-]

disengag|e, -es, -ing, -ed 'disin'geidʒ [ˌdis-, -siŋ'g-, -sen'g-], -iz, -iŋ, -d

disentail (s. v.), -s, -ing, -ed 'disin'teil [ˌdis-, -sen-], -z, -iŋ, -d

disentang|le, -les, -ling, -led 'disin-'tæŋg|l [ˌdis-, -sen-], -lz, -liŋ [-liŋ], -ld

disentanglement ˌdisin'tæŋglmənt ['dis-in't-, -sen-]

disentit|le, -les, -ling, -led 'disin'tait|l [ˌdis-, -sen-], -lz, -liŋ [-liŋ], -ld

disequilibrium 'disekwi'libriəm

disestablish, -es, -ing, -ed 'disis'tæbli∫ [ˌdis-, -ses-], -iz, -iŋ, -t

disestablishment ˌdisis'tæbli∫mənt ['dis-is't, -ses-]

disfavour 'dis'feivə* [dis'f-]

disfiguration, -s dis,figjuə'rei∫ən [ˌdisf-], -z

disfigur|e, -es, -ing, -ed, -ement/s dis-'figə*, -z, -riŋ, -d, -mənt/s

disfranchis|e, -es, -ing, -ed 'dis'frænt∫aiz [dis'f-], -iz, -iŋ, -d

disfranchisement dis'frænt∫izmənt

disgorg|e, -es, -ing, -ed dis'gɔːdʒ, -iz, -iŋ, -d

disgrac|e (s. v.), -es, -ing, -ed dis'greis [diz-], -iz, -iŋ, -t

disgrace|ful, -fully, -fulness dis'greis-|ful [diz-], -fuli [-fəli], -fulnis

disgruntled dis'grʌntld

disguis|e (s. v.), -es, -ing, -ed, -er/s dis'gaiz [diz-], -iz, -iŋ, -d, -ə*/z

disgust (s. v.), -s, -ing/ly, -ed dis'gʌst [diz-], -s, -iŋ/li, -id

dish (s. v.), -es, -ing, -ed di∫, -iz, -iŋ, -t

dishabille ˌdisæ'biːl [-sə'b-]

disharmony 'dis'hɑːməni [dis'h-]

dish|cloth, -cloths 'di∫|klɔθ [-klɔː θ], -klɔθs [-klɔːðz, -klɔːθs]

dish-cover, -s 'di∫ˌkʌvə*, -z

disheart|en, -ens, -ening, -ened dis-'hɑːt|n, -nz, -niŋ [-ņiŋ], -nd

disherison dis'herizn [-isn]

dishev|el, -els, -elling, -elled di'∫ev|əl, -əlz, -liŋ [-liŋ], -əld

dishful, -s 'di∫ful, -z

dishonest, -ly dis'ɔnist [di'zɔ-], -li

dishonest|y, -ies dis'ɔnist|i [di'zɔ-], -iz

dishonour (s. v.), -s, -ing, -ed, -er/s dis'ɔnə* [di'zɔ-], -z, -riŋ, -d, -rə*/z

dishonourab|le, -ly, -leness dis'ɔnərəb|l [di'zɔ-], -li, -lnis

dishors|e, -es, -ing, -ed dis'hɔːs, -iz, -iŋ, -t

dishwasher, -s 'di∫ˌwɔ∫ə*, -z

dish-water 'di∫ˌwɔːtə*

disillusi|on (s. v.), -ons, -oning, -oned, -onment/s ˌdisi'luːʒ|ən ['dis-, -'ljuː-], -ənz, -ņiŋ [-əniŋ], -ənd, -ənmənt/s

disinclination ˌdisinkli'nei∫ən ['—'—, -iŋk-, -ntl-, -lə'n-]

disinclin|e, -es, -ing, -ed 'disin'klain [ˌdis-, -iŋ'kl-, -in'tl-], -z, -iŋ, -d

disinfect, -s, -ing, -ed ˌdisin'fekt, -s, -iŋ, -id

disinfectant (s. adj.), -s ˌdisin'fektənt, -s

disinfection, -s ˌdisin'fek∫ən, -z

disinfestation 'disinfes'tei∫ən

disinflation ˌdisin'flei∫ən

disingenuous, -ly, -ness ˌdisin'dʒen-jŭəs [-njwəs], -li, -nis

disinherit, -s, -ing, -ed 'disin'herit [ˌdis-], -s, -iŋ, -id

disinheritance ˌdisin'heritəns ['disin'h-]

disintegrable dis'intigrəbl

disintegrat|e, -es, -ing, -ed, -or/s dis-'intigreit, -s, -iŋ, -id, -ə*/z

disintegration, -s dis,inti'grei∫ən [ˌdisin-], -z

disinter, -s, -ring, -red 'disin'tə:* [ˌdis-], -z, -riŋ, -d

disinterested, -ly, -ness dis'intristid ['dis'in-, -'intərest-, -'intrəst-], -li, -nis [-s

disinterment, -s ˌdisin'tə:mənt ['—'—],

disjoin, -s, -ing, -ed dis'dʒɔin, -z, -iŋ, -d

disjoint, -s, -ing, -ed/ly, -edness dis-'dʒɔint, -s, -iŋ, -id/li, -idnis

disjunct, -s dis'dʒʌŋkt

disjunction, -s dis'dʒʌŋk∫ən, -z

disjunctive, -ly dis'dʒʌŋktiv ['dis'dʒ-], -li

disk, -s disk, -s

dislik|e (s. v.), -es, -ing, -ed dis'laik, -iŋ, -t

Note.—The stress '-- is, however, used in the expression likes and dislikes.

dislocat|e, -es, -ing, -ed 'disləukeit, -s, -iŋ, -id

dislocation, -s ˌdisləu'kei∫ən, -z

dislodg|e, -es, -ing, -ed, -(e)ment dis-'lɔdʒ, -iz, -iŋ, -d, -mənt

disloy|al, -ally, -alty 'dis'lɔi|əl [dis'l-], -əli, -əlti

dism|al, -ally, -alness 'dizm|əl, -əli, -əlnis

dismant|le, -les, -ling, -led dis'mænt|l, -lz, -liŋ, -ld [-id

dismast, -s, -ing, -ed 'dis'mɑːst, -s, -iŋ, -iŋ

dismay (s. v.), -s, -ing, -ed dis'mei [diz'm-], -z, -iŋ, -d

dismember, -s, -ing, -ed, -ment dis-'membə*, -z, -riŋ, -d, -mənt

dismiss, -es, -ing, -ed dis'mis, -iz, -iŋ, -t

dismissal, -s dis'misəl, -z

dismount, -s, -ing, -ed 'dis'maunt [dis'm-], -s, -iŋ, -id

Disney 'dizni

disobedien|ce, -t/ly ˌdisə'bi:djən|s ['--'—, -diən-], -t/li

disobey, -s, -ing, -ed 'disə'bei [ˌdis-], -z, -iŋ, -d

disoblig|e, -es, -ing/ly, -ingness, -ed 'disə'blaidʒ [ˌdis-], -iz, -iŋ/li, -iŋnis, -d

disord|er (s. v.), -ers, -ering, -ered dis-'ɔ:d|ə* [di'zɔ:-], -əz, -əriŋ, -əd

disorder|ly, -liness dis'ɔ:də|li [di'zɔ:-], -linis

disorganization [-isa-] dis,ɔ:gənai'zei-ʃən [di,zɔ:-, ˌdisɔ:-, -gŋai'z-, -gəni'z-, -gŋi'z-]

disorganiz|e [-is|e], -es, -ing, -ed dis-'ɔ:gənaiz [di'zɔ:-, 'dis'ɔ:-, -gŋaiz], -iz, -iŋ, -d

disown, -s, -ing, -ed dis'əun ['dis'əun], ⁺-z, -iŋ, -d

disparag|e, -es, -ing/ly, -ed, -er/s, -ement dis'pæridʒ, -iz, -iŋ/li, -d, -ə*/z, -mənt

disparate (s. adj.), -s 'dispərit [-reit], -s

disparity dis'pæriti

dispassionate, -ly, -ness dis'pæʃŋit [-ʃənit, -ʃnit], -li, -nis

dispatch (s. v.), -es, -ing, -ed, -er/s dis'pætʃ, -iz, -iŋ, -t, -ə*/z

dispatch-boat, -s dis'pætʃbəut, -s

dispatch-box, -es dis'pætʃbɔks, -iz

dispatch-rider, -s dis'pætʃˌraidə*, -z

dispel, -s, -ling, -led dis'pel, -z, -iŋ, -d

dispensable dis'pensəbl

dispensar|y, -ies dis'pensər|i, -iz   [-z

dispensation, -s ˌdispen'seiʃən [-pən-], dispensator|y (s. adj.), -ies dis'pensə-tər|i, -iz

dispens|e, -es, -ing, -ed, -er/s dis'pens, -iz, -iŋ, -t, -ə*/z

dispeop|le, -les, -ling, -led 'dis'pi:p|l [dis'p-], -lz, -liŋ [-liŋ], -ld

dispersal, -s dis'pə:səl, -z

dispers|e, -es, -ing, -ed, -er/s dis'pə:s, -iz, -iŋ, -t, -ə*/z

dispersion, -s dis'pə:ʃn, -z

dispersive dis'pə:siv

dispirit, -s, -ing, -ed/ly, -edness di'spirit, -s, -iŋ, -id/li, -idnis

displac|e, -es, -ing, -ed, -ement/s dis-'pleis, -iz, -iŋ, -t [also 'dis-pleist when attributive], -mənt/s

display (s. v.), -s, -ing, -ed, -er/s dis'plei, -z, -iŋ, -d, -ə*/z

displeas|e, -es, -ing/ly, -ingness, -ed dis'pli:z, -iz, -iŋ/li, -iŋnis, -d

displeasure dis'pleʒə*

disport, -s, -ing, -ed dis'pɔ:t, -s, -iŋ, -id

dispos|e, -es, -ing, -ed, -er/s; -able, -al/s dis'pəuz, -iz, -iŋ, -d, -ə*/z; -əbl, -əl/z

disposition, -s ˌdispə'ziʃən [-pu'z-], -z

dispossess, -es, -ing, -ed 'dispə'zes [ˌdis-, -pu'z-], -iz, -iŋ, -t

disproof 'dis'pru:f [-'-]

disproportion, -ed 'disprə'pɔ:ʃən [ˌdis-, -pru'p-], -d ['--,--]

dispropor|tional, -tionally ˌdisprə'pɔ:|-ʃənl ['disprə'p-, -pru'p-, -ʃnəl, -ʃŋl, -ʃnl, -ʃənəl], -ʃŋəli [-ʃnəli, -ʃŋli, -ʃnli, -ʃənəli]

disproportionate, -ly, -ness ˌdisprə-'pɔ:ʃnit ['disprə'p-, -pru'p-, -ʃŋit, -ʃənit], -li, -nis

disproval dis'pru:vəl ['dis'p-]

disprov|e, -es, -ing, -ed 'dis'pru:v [dis'p-], -z, -iŋ, -d

disputable dis'pju:təbl ['dispjutəbl]

disputableness dis'pju:təblnis

disputant (s. adj.), -s dis'pju:tənt ['dispjutənt], -s

disputation, -s ˌdispju(:)'teiʃən, -z

disputatious, -ly, -ness ˌdispju(:)'teiʃəs, -li, -nis

disputative dis'pju:tətiv

disput|e (s. v.), -es, -ing, -ed, -er/s dis-'pju:t, -s, -iŋ, -id, -ə*/z

Note.—The stress pattern '-- is increasingly used for the noun.

disqualification, -s dis,kwɔlifi'keiʃən [ˌdisk-], -z

disquali|fy, -fies, -fying, -fied dis'kwɔli|-fai ['dis'k-], -faiz, -faiiŋ, -faid

disquiet (s. v.), -s, -ing, -ed dis'kwaiət, -s, -iŋ, -id

disquietude dis'kwaiitju:d [-'kwaiət-]

disquisition, -s ˌdiskwi'ziʃən, -z

disquisitional ˌdiskwi'ziʃənl [-ʃnəl, -ʃŋl, -ʃnl, -ʃənəl]

disquisitive dis'kwizitiv

Disraeli dis'reili

disregard (s. v.), -s, -ing, -ed 'disri'gɑ:d [ˌdis-, -rə'g-], -z, -iŋ, -id

disregard|ful, -fully ˌdisri'gɑ:d|ful ['dis-ri'g-, -rə'g-], -fuli [-fəli]

disrepair 'disri'pɛə* [ˌdis-, -rə'p-]

disreputability dis,repjutə'biliti [-lət-]

disreputab|le, -ly, -leness dis'repju-təb|l [-pjət-], -li, -lnis

disrepute 'disri'pju:t [ˌdis-, -rə'p-]

disrespect 'disris'pekt [ˌdis-, -rəs-]

disrespect|ful, -fully, -fulness ˌdis-ris'pekt|ful ['disris'p-, -rəs-], -fuli [-fəli], -fulnis

disrob|e, -es, -ing, -ed 'dis'rəub [dis'r-],
-z, -iŋ, -d
disrupt, -s, -ing, -ed dis'rʌpt, -s, -iŋ, -id
disruption, -s dis'rʌpʃən, -z
disruptive dis'rʌptiv
Diss dis
dissatisfaction 'dis,sætis'fækʃən [,dis-
sæt-]
dissatisfactor|y, -ily, -iness 'dis,sætis-
'fæktər|i [,dissæt-], -ili, -inis
dissatis|fy, -fies, -fying, -fied 'dis'sætis|-
fai [dis's-], -faiz, -faiiŋ, -faid
dissect, -s, -ing, -ed, -or/s; -ible
di'sekt, -s, -iŋ, -id, -ə*/z; -əbl [-ibl]
dissecting-room, -s di'sektiŋrum
[-ru:m], -z
dissection, -s di'sekʃən, -z
disseis|e, -es, -ing, -ed; -in/s 'dis'si:z
[dis'si:z], -iz, -iŋ, -d; -in/z
dissemblance, -s di'sembləns, -iz
dissemb|le, -les, -ling, -led, -ler/s
di'semb|l, -lz, -liŋ, -ld, -lə*/z
disseminat|e, -es, -ing, -ed, -or/s di-
'semineit, -s, -iŋ, -id, -ə*/z
dissemination di,semi'neiʃən
dissension, -s di'senʃən, -z
dissent (s. v.), -s, -ing, -ed, -er/s
di'sent, -s, -iŋ, -id, -ə*/z
dissentient, -s di'senʃiənt [-fjənt, -ʃənt],
-s
dissertation, -s ,disə(:)'teiʃən, -z
disservice, -s 'dis'sə:vis [dis's-], -iz
dissev|er, -ers, -ering, -ered, -erment;
-erance dis'sev|ə*, -əz, -əriŋ, -əd,
-əmənt; -ərəns
dissiden|ce, -t/s 'disidən|s, -t/s
dissimilar, -ly 'di'similə* ['dis's-, di-
'sim-], -li
dissimilarit|y, -ies ,disimi'lærit|i [,diss-,
'dissimi'l-], -iz
dissimilat|e, -es, -ing, -ed di'simileit
['di's-], -s, -iŋ, -id
dissimilation, -s 'disimi'leiʃən [,dis-,
di,s-], -z
dissimilitude ,disi'militju:d [,diss-, 'dissi'm-]
dissimulat|e, -es, -ing, -ed, -or/s di-
'simjuleit, -s, -iŋ, -id, -ə*/z
dissimulation, -s di,simju'leiʃən, -z
dissipat|e, -es, -ing, -ed; -ive 'disipeit,
-s, -iŋ, -id; -iv
dissipation, -s ,disi'peiʃən, -z
dissociable (separable) di'səuʃjəbl
[-ʃiəbl], (unsociable) di'səuʃəbl
dissociat|e, -es, -ing, -ed di'səuʃieit
['di's-, -əuʃjeit, -əusieit, -əusjeit],
-s, -iŋ, -id
dissociation di,səusi'eiʃən [,dis-, -əuʃi-]

dissolubility di,sɔlju'biliti [-lət-]
dissolub|le, -ly, -leness di'sɔljub|l, -li,
-lnis
dissolute (s. adj.), -s, -ly, -ness 'disəlu:t
[-lju:t], -s, -li, -nis
dissolution, -s ,disə'lu:ʃən [-'lju:-], -z
dissolvability di,zɔlvə'biliti [-lət-]
dissolv|e, -es, -ing, -ed; -able di'zɔlv, -z,
-iŋ, -d; -əbl
dissolvent (s. adj.), -s di'zɔlvənt [di'sɔ-],
-s
dissonan|ce, -ces, -t/ly 'disənən|s [-sn̩-],
-siz, -t/li
dissuad|e, -es, -ing, -ed di'sweid, -z, -iŋ,
-id
dissuasion di'sweiʒən
dissuasive, -ly, -ness di'sweisiv, -li, -nis
dissyll- = disyll-
dissymmetric 'disi'metrik ['dissi'm-,
,diss-]
dissymmetry 'di'simitri ['dis's-, dis's-]
distaff, -s 'dista:f, -s
distan|ce (s. v.), -es, -ing, -ed 'distəns,
-iz, -iŋ, -t
distant, -ly 'distənt, -li
distaste, -s 'dis'teist [dis't-], -s
distaste|ful, -fully, -fulness dis'teist|-
ful ['dis't-], -fuli [-fəli], -fulnis
distemp|er (s. v.), -ers, -ering, -ered
dis'temp|ə*, -əz, -əriŋ, -əd
distend, -s, -ing, -ed dis'tend, -z, -iŋ, -id
distensible dis'tensəbl [-sib-]
distension dis'tenʃən
distich, -s, -ous 'distik, -s, -əs
distil, -s, -ling, -led, -ler/s dis'til, -z, -iŋ,
-d, -ə*/z
distillate, -s 'distilit [-leit], -s
distillation, -s ,disti'leiʃən, -z
distillatory dis'tilətəri
distiller|y, -ies dis'tilər|i, -iz
disti|nct, -nctest, -nctly, -nctness dis-
'tiŋ|kt, -ŋktist, -ŋktli [-ŋkli], -ŋktnis
[-ŋknis]
distinction, -s dis'tiŋkʃən, -z
distinctive, -ly, -ness dis'tiŋktiv, -li, -nis
distinguish, -es, -ing, -ed; -able, -ably
dis'tiŋgwiʃ, -iz, -iŋ, -t; -əbl, -əbli
distoma, -s 'distəumə, -z
distort, -s, -ing, -ed dis'tɔ:t, -s, -iŋ, -id
distortion, -s dis'tɔ:ʃən, -z
distract, -s, -ing, -ed/ly, -edness dis-
'trækt, -s, -iŋ, -id/li, -idnis
distraction, -s dis'trækʃən, -z
distrain, -s, -ing, -ed, -er/s; -able dis-
'trein, -z, -iŋ, -d, -ə*/z; -əbl
distrainee, -s ,distrei'ni:, -z
distrainor, -s ,distrei'nɔ:*, -z
distraint, -s dis'treint, -s

distrait, -e dis'trei ['distrei] (distrɛ), -t
distraught dis'trɔːt
distress (s. v.), -es, -ing/ly, -ed dis'tres, -iz, -iŋ/li, -t
distress|ful, -fully dis'tres|ful, -fuli [-fəli]
distributable dis'tribjutəbl
distribut|e, -es, -ing, -ed, -or/s dis'tribju(ː)t ['distribjuːt], -s, -dis'tribjutiŋ ['distribjuːtiŋ], dis'tribjutid ['distribjuːtid], dis'tribjutə*/z ['distribjuːtə*/z]
distribution, -s ˌdistri'bjuːʃən, -z
distributive, -ly dis'tribjutiv, -li
district, -s 'distrikt, -s
distringas dis'triŋgæs [-gəs]
distrust (s. v.), -s, -ing, -ed dis'trʌst ['dis't-], -s, -iŋ, -id
distrust|ful, -fully, -fulness dis'trʌst|-ful ['dis't-], -fuli [-fəli], -fulnis
disturb, -s, -ing, -ed, -er/s dis'təːb, -z, -iŋ, -d, -ə*/z
disturbance, -s dis'təːbəns, -iz
distyle, -s 'distail ['dai-stail], -z
disulphate, -s dai'sʌlfeit [-fit], -s
disulphide, -s dai'sʌlfaid, -z
disunion, -s 'dis'juːnjən [dis'j-, -nїən], -z
disunit|e, -es, -ing, -ed 'disjuː'nait [ˌdis-, -juː'n-], -s, -iŋ, -id
disuse (s.), 'dis'juːs [dis'j-]
disus|e (v.), -es, -ing, -ed 'dis'juːz [dis'j-], -iz, -iŋ, -d [also 'disjuːzd when attributive]
disyllabic 'disi'læbik [ˌdisi'l-, 'disil-, 'dai-]
disyllable, -s di'siləbl ['di's-, 'daiˌs-], -z
ditch (s. v.), -es, -ing, -ed, -er/s ditʃ, -iz, -iŋ, -t, -ə*/z
Ditchling 'ditʃliŋ
ditch-water 'ditʃˌwɔːtə*
dither, -s, -ing, -ed 'diðə*, -z, -riŋ, -d
dithyramb, -s 'diθiræmb, -z
dithyramb|us, -i, -ic/s ˌdiθi'ræmb|əs, -ai, -ik/s
ditto, -s 'ditəu, -z
Ditton 'ditn
ditt|y, -ies 'dit|i, -iz
diuretic (s. adj.), -s ˌdaijuə'retik [-ju'r-], -s
diurn|al (s. adj.), -als, -ally dai'əːn|l, -lz, -li
diva, -s 'diːvə, -z [-əli
divagat|e, -es, -ing, -ed 'daivəgeit, -s, -iŋ, -id
divagation, -s ˌdaivə'geiʃən, -z
divalent 'dai ˌveilənt ['dai'v-, dai'v-]
divan, -s di'væn [dai'v-, 'daivæn], -z
divaricat|e, -es, -ing, -ed dai'værikeit [di'v-], -s, -iŋ, -id

divarication, -s daiˌværi'keiʃən [diˌv-], -z
div|e (s. v.), -es, -ing, -ed, -er/s daiv, -z, -iŋ, -d, -ə*/z
dive-bomb, -s, -ing, -ed, -er/s 'daivbɔm, -z, -iŋ, -d, -ə*/z
Diver 'daivə*
diverg|e, -es, -ing, -ed dai'vəːdʒ [di'v-], -iz, -iŋ, -d
divergen|ce, -ces, -cy, -cies, -t/ly dai'vəːdʒən|s [di'v-], -siz, -si, -siz, -t/li
divers (adj.) 'daivə(ː)z
diverse, -ly dai'vəːs ['daivəːs], -li
diversification, -s daiˌvəːsifi'keiʃən, -z
diversi|fy, -fies, -fying, -fied dai'vəːsi|-fai, -faiz, -faiiŋ, -faid
diversion, -s dai'vəːʃən [di'v-], -z
diversit|y, -ies dai'vəːsit|i [di'v-], -iz
divert, -s, -ing/ly, -ed dai'vəːt [di'v-], -s, -iŋ/li, -id
Dives (rich man) 'daiviːz, (surname) daivz
divest, -s, -ing, -ed dai'vest [di'v-], -s, -iŋ, -id
divestiture dai'vestitʃə* [di'v-]
divid|e (s. v.), -es, -ing, -ed/ly, -er/s; -able di'vaid, -z, -iŋ, -id/li, -ə*/z; -əbl
dividend, -s 'dividend [-dənd], -z
dividend-warrant, -s 'dividendˌwɔrənt [-dənd-], -s
divination, -s ˌdivi'neiʃən, -z
divine (s. adj.), -s, -r, -st, -ly, -ness di'vain, -z, -ə*, -ist, -li, -nis
divin|e (v.), -es, -ing, -ed, -er/s di'vain, -z, -iŋ, -d, -ə*/z
diving-bell, -s 'daiviŋbel, -z
diving-dress, -es 'daiviŋdres, -iz
divining-rod, -s di'vainiŋrɔd, -z
divinit|y, -ies di'vinit|i, -iz
divisibility diˌvizi'biliti [-zə'b-, -lət-]
divisib|le, -ly di'vizəb|l [-zib-], -li
division, -s di'viʒən, -z
divisional di'viʒənl [-ʒn̩l, -ʒn̩l]
divisive, -ly, -ness di'vaisiv, -li, -nis
divisor, -s di'vaizə*, -z
divorc|e (s. v.), -es, -ing, -ed, -er/s, -ement di'vɔːs, -iz, -iŋ, -t, -ə*/z, -mənt
divorcée, -s di(ː)ˌvɔː'si: ['--'-, -'-, divɔː'sei] (divɔrse), -z
divot, -s 'divət, -s
divulg|e, -es, -ing, -ed dai'vʌldʒ [di'v-], -iz, -iŋ, -d
divulsion, -s dai'vʌlʃən [di'v-], -z
diwan, -s di'wɑːn, -z
Dix diks
Dixey 'diksi
Dixie 'diksi

Dixon 'diksn
Dixwell 'dikswəl [-wel]
diz|en, -ens, -ening, -ened 'daiz|n, -nz, -ɲiŋ, -nd
dizz|y (adj. v.), -ier, -iest, -ily, -iness; -ies, -ying, -ied 'diz|i, -iə*, -iist, -ili, -inis; -iz, -iiŋ, -id
Djakarta dʒə'kɑːtə
Dnie|per, -ster 'dni:|pə*, -stə*
do (s.) (musical note), -s dəu, -z
do (s.) (swindle, entertainment), -s du:, -z
do. 'ditəu
do (v.); dost; doth; doeth; does; doing, did, done, doer/s du: (strong form), du (weak form, also alternative strong form before vowels), də, d (weak forms); dʌst (strong form), dəst (weak form); dʌθ (strong form), dəθ (weak form); 'du(:)iθ; dʌz (strong form), dəz, dz (weak forms); 'du(:)iŋ, did, dʌn, 'du(:)ə*/z
Doane dəun
Dobb, -s dɔb, -z
dobbin (D.), -s 'dɔbin, -z
Dobell dəu'bel
Dobie 'dəubi
Dobrée 'dəubrei
Dobson 'dɔbsn
docent, -s dəu'sent ['dəusənt], -s
Docet|ism, -ist/s dəu'si:t|izəm, -ist/s
docile 'dəusail ['dɔs-]
docility dəu'siliti
dock (s. v.), -s, -ing, -ed, -er/s; -age dɔk, -s, -iŋ, -t, -ə*/z; -idʒ
Docker 'dɔkə*
docket (s. v.), -s, -ing, -ed 'dɔkit, -s, -iŋ, -id
dock-land 'dɔklænd
dockyard, -s 'dɔkjɑːd, -z
doct|or (s. v.), -ors, -oring, -ored; -orate/s, -orship/s 'dɔkt|ə*, -əz, -əriŋ, -əd; -ərit/s, -əʃip/s
doctrinaire, -s ˌdɔktri'nɛə*, -z
doctrin|al, -ally dɔk'train|l ['dɔktrin-], -əli
doctrinarian, -s ˌdɔktri'nɛərïən, -z
doctrine, -s 'dɔktrin, -z
document (s.), -s 'dɔkjumənt, -s
document (v.), -s, -ing, -ed 'dɔkjument, -s, -iŋ, -id
documental ˌdɔkju'mentl
documentar|y (s. adj.), -ies ˌdɔkju'men-tər|i, -iz
documentation ˌdɔkjumen'teiʃən [-mən-]
Docwra 'dɔkrə
Dod(d), -s dɔd, -z
dodder (s. v.), -s, -ing, -ed 'dɔdə*, -z, -riŋ, -d

Doddington 'dɔdiŋtən
Doddridge 'dɔdridʒ
dodecagon, -s dəu'dekəgən, -z
dodecahedr|on, -ons, -a; -al 'dəudikə-'hedr|ən [-'hi:d-, 'dəudikəˌh-, ˌdəudikə'h-], -ənz, -ə; -əl
Dodecanese ˌdəudikə'ni:z [-dek-]
dodg|e (s. v.) (D.), -es, -ing, -ed, -er/s dɔdʒ, -iz, -iŋ, -d, -ə*/z
Dodgson 'dɔdʒsn
Dodington 'dɔdiŋtən
dodo (D.), -s 'dəudəu, -z
Dodona dəu'dəunə
Dodsley 'dɔdzli
Dodson 'dɔdsn
Dodwell 'dɔdwəl [-wel]
doe (D.), -s dəu, -z
Doeg 'dəueg
doer, -s 'du(:)ə*, -z
does (from do) dʌz (strong form), dəz, dz (weak forms)
doeskin, -s 'dəu-skin, -z
doesn't 'dʌznt [also 'dʌzn when not final]
doeth (from do) 'du(:)iθ
doff, -s, -ing, -ed, -er/s dɔf, -s, -iŋ, -t, -ə*/z
Dofort 'dəufəːt
dog (s. v.), -s, -ging, -ged (p. tense, p. partic.) dɔg, -z, -iŋ, -d
dog-bane 'dɔgbein
Dogberry 'dɔgberi [-bəri]
dog-biscuit, -s 'dɔgˌbiskit, -s
dog-cart, -s 'dɔgkɑːt, -s
dog-collar, -s 'dɔgˌkɔlə*, -z
dog-days 'dɔgdeiz
doge, -s dəudʒ, -iz
dog-ear (s. v.), -s, -ing, -ed 'dɔgiə*, -z, -riŋ, -d
dog-faced 'dɔgfeist
dog-fancier, -s 'dɔgˌfænsïə* [-sjə*], -z
dog-fight, -s 'dɔgfait, -s
dog-fish, -es 'dɔgfiʃ, -iz
dogged (adj.), -ly, -ness 'dɔgid, -li, -nis
dogger (D.), -s 'dɔgə*, -z
doggerel 'dɔgərəl [-ril]
Doggett 'dɔgit
doggish, -ly, -ness 'dɔgiʃ, -li, -nis
doggo 'dɔgəu
doggrel 'dɔgrəl
dogg|y (s. adj.), -ies 'dɔg|i, -iz
dog-headed 'dɔgˌhedid
dog-kennel, -s 'dɔgˌkenl, -z
dog-Latin 'dɔg'lætin ['-ˌ--]
dogma, -s 'dɔgmə, -z
dogmatic (s. adj.), -s, -al, -ally dɔg-'mætik, -s, -əl, -əli
dogmati|sm, -st/s 'dɔgməti|zəm, -st/s

dogmatiz|e [-is|e], -es, -ing, -ed, -er/s 'dɔgmətaiz, -iz, -iŋ, -d, -ə*/z
dog-rose, -s 'dɔg-rəuz, -iz
dog's-ear (s. v.), -s, -ing, -ed 'dɔgz-iə*, -z, -riŋ, -d
dog-skin 'dɔgskin
dog-star 'dɔgstɑ:*
dog-tired 'dɔg'taiəd
dog|-tooth, -teeth 'dɔg|tu:θ, -ti:θ
dog-watch, -es 'dɔgwɔtʃ, -iz
dogwood 'dɔgwud
doh (note in Tonic Sol-fa), -s dəu, -z
Doherty 'dəuəti, dəu'hə:ti, 'dɔhəti ['dɔxə-]
Dohnanyi dɔk'nɑ:nji(:) [dɔx'n-]
Dohoo 'du:hu:
doil|y, -ies 'dɔil|i, -iz
doing, -s 'du(:)iŋ, -z
doit, -s dɔit, -s
dolce 'dɔltʃi ['dəul-] ('dɔltʃe)
doldrum, -s 'dɔldrəm, -z
dol|e (s. v.), -es, -ing, -ed dəul, -z, -iŋ, -d
dole|ful, -fully, -fulness 'dəul|fʊl, -fuli [-fəli], -fʊlnis
dolerite 'dɔlərait
Dolgellau dɔl'geθlai [-'gelai] (Welsh dɔl'geɫa, -ɫai)
dolichocephalic 'dɔlikəuse'fælik [-si'f-, -ke'f-, -ki'f-]
doll, -s dɔl, -z
dollar (D.), -s 'dɔlə*, -z
Dollond 'dɔlənd
dollop, -s 'dɔləp, -s
doll's-hou|se, -ses 'dɔlzhau|s, -ziz
doll|y (D.), -ies 'dɔl|i, -iz
dolman, -s 'dɔlmən, -z
dolmen, -s 'dɔlmen, -z
dolomite (D.), -s 'dɔləmait, -s
dolor 'dəulə*
dolorous, -ly, -ness 'dɔlərəs, -li, -nis
dolour 'dəulə*
dolphin, -s 'dɔlfin, -z
dolt, -s dəult, -s
doltish, -ly, -ness 'dəultiʃ, -li, -nis
Dolton 'dəultən
domain, -s dəu'mein, -z
Dombey 'dɔmbi
dome, -s, -d dəum, -z, -d
Domesday 'du:mzdei [-s, -əli
domestic (s. adj.), -s, -ally dəu'mestik,
domesticat|e, -es, -ing, -ed dəu'mesti-keit, -s, -iŋ, -id
domestication dəu,mesti'keiʃən
domesticity ,dəumes'tisiti [,dɔm-]
domett (material) dəu'met
Domett (surname) 'dɔmit
domicil|e (s. v.), -es, -ing, -ed 'dɔmisail [-sil], -z, -iŋ, -d

domiciliary ,dɔmi'siljər [-liiəri]
dominant (s. adj.), -s, -ly 'dɔminənt, -s, -li
dominat|e, -es, -ing, -ed, -or/s 'dɔmi-neit, -s, -iŋ, -id, -ə*/z
domination, -s ,dɔmi'neiʃən, -z
domineer, -s, -ing, -ed ,dɔmi'niə*, -z, -riŋ, -d
Domingo dəu'miŋgəu [dɔ'm-]
Dominic 'dɔminik
Dominica (in the Leeward Islands) ,dɔmi'ni:kə
dominical də'minikəl [dɔ'm-]
Dominican (republic, religious order), -s də'minikən [dɔ'm-], (of Dominica) ,dɔmi'ni:kən, -z
dominie, -s 'dɔmini, -z
dominion, -s də'minjən [-nïən], -z
domino, -es 'dɔminəu, -z
Domitian dəu'miʃïən [dɔ'm-, -ʃjən, -ʃən]
Domvil(l)e 'dʌmvil
don (s. v.) (D.), -s, -ning, -ned dɔn, -z, -iŋ, -d
dona(h), -s 'dəunə, -z
Donaghadee ,dɔnəkə'di: [-nəxə-]
Donalbain 'dɔnlbein
Donald, -son 'dɔnld, -sn
Donat 'dəunæt
donat|e, -es, -ing, -ed dəu'neit, -s, -iŋ, -id
Donatello ,dɔnə'teləu
donation, -s dəu'neiʃən, -z
Donatist, -s 'dəunətist, -s
donative, -s 'dəunətiv, -z
donator, -s dəu'neitə*, -z
donatory 'dəunətəri ['dɔn-]
Donatus dəu'neitəs
Don Carlos dɔn'kɑ:lɔs
Doncaster 'dɔŋkəstə*
done (from do) dʌn
Done dəun
donee, -s dəu'ni:, -z
Donegal (place) 'dɔnigɔ:l ['dʌn-, ,--'-]
Note.—,dʌni'gɔ:l appears to be the most usual pronunciation in Ireland.
Donegall (Marquess) 'dɔnigɔ:l
Donelson 'dɔnlsn
Doneraile 'dʌnəreil
Donetz dɔ'nets (da'njets)
donga, -s 'dɔŋgə, -z
Dongan 'dɔŋgən
Dönges (South African surname) 'də:njes
Don Giovanni ,dɔndʒiəu'vɑ:ni [-'væni] (dondʒo'vanni)
Dongola 'dɔŋgələ
Donington 'dʌniŋtən

Doniphan 'dɔnifən
Donizetti ˌdɔni'zeti [-i'dze-] (doni-'dzetti)
donjon, -s 'dɔndʒən ['dʌn-], -z
Don Juan dɔn'dʒu(:)ən
donkey, -s 'dɔŋki, -z
donkey-engine, -s 'dɔŋkiˌendʒin, -z
donna, -s 'dɔnə, -z
Donnan 'dɔnən
Donne dʌn, dɔn
Donnington 'dɔniŋtən
donnish 'dɔniʃ
Donnithorne 'dɔniθɔːn
Donnybrook 'dɔnibruk
Dono(g)hue 'dʌnəhuː, 'dɔn-
Donohoe 'dʌnəhuː, 'dɔn-
donor, -s 'dəunə* [-nɔː*], -z
do-nothing, -s 'duːˌnʌθiŋ, -z
Donough 'dɔnəu
Donoughmore 'dʌnəmɔː* [-mɔə*]
Donovan 'dɔnəvən
Don Pasquale ˌdɔnpæs'kwɑːli
Don Quixote dɔn'kwiksət [-səut, -sɔt]
donship, -s 'dɔn-ʃip, -s
don't dəunt [also dəun when not final, also dəump before the sounds p, b, m, and dəuŋk before k, g]
Note.—Weak forms dən, dn may sometimes be heard in the expression I don't know, and a weak form dəm in the expression I don't mind.
Doo duː
dood|le (s. v.), -les, -ling, -led 'duːd|l, -lz, -liŋ [-l̩iŋ], -ld
doodlebug, -s 'duːdlbʌg, -z
doom (s. v.), -s, -ing, -ed duːm, -z, -iŋ, -d
Doomsday 'duːmzdei
Doon(e) duːn
door, -s dɔː* [dɔə*], -z
door-bell, -s 'dɔːbel ['dɔə-], -z
Note.—Front door bell has stress '--'-.
door-keeper, -s 'dɔːˌkiːpə* ['dɔə-], -z
door-knocker, -s 'dɔːˌnɔkə* ['dɔə-], -z
Doorly 'duəli
door-mat, -s 'dɔːmæt ['dɔə-], -s
door-nail, -s 'dɔːneil ['dɔə-], -z
door-plate, -s 'dɔːpleit ['dɔə-], -s
door-post, -s 'dɔːpəust ['dɔə-], -s
doorstep, -s 'dɔːstep ['dɔə-], -s
doorway, -s 'dɔːwei ['dɔə-], -z
dop|e (s. v.), -es, -ing, -ed, -er/s dəup, -s, -iŋ, -t, -ə*/z
Dora 'dɔːrə
dorado, -s də'rɑːdəu [dɔ'r-], -z
Doran 'dɔːrən
Dorando də'rændəu [dɔ'r-]

Dorcas 'dɔːkəs [-kæs]
Dorchester 'dɔːtʃistə*
Dore dɔː* [dɔə*]
Doreen dɔː'riːn [dɔ'r-, də'r-, 'dɔːriːn]
Dorian (s. adj.), -s 'dɔːrïən, -z
Doric 'dɔrik
Doricism, -s 'dɔrisizəm, -z
Doris (modern Christian name) 'dɔris, (district and fem. name in Greek history) 'dɔːris
Dorking 'dɔːkiŋ
dorman|cy, -t 'dɔːmən|si, -t
dormer-window, -s 'dɔːməˈwindəu, -z
dormie 'dɔːmi
dormitor|y, -ies 'dɔːmitr|i, -iz
dor|mouse, -mice 'dɔː|maus, -mais
dormy 'dɔːmi
Dornoch 'dɔːnɔk [-nək, -nɔx, -nəx]
Dornton 'dɔːntən
Dorothea ˌdɔrə'θiə
Dorothy 'dɔrəθi
Dorr dɔː*
Dorrien 'dɔrïən
Dorriforth 'dɔrifɔːθ
Dorrit 'dɔrit
dors|al, -ally 'dɔːs|əl, -əli
Dors|et, -etshire 'dɔːs|it, -it-ʃiə* [-it-ʃə*]
dor|y, -ies 'dɔːr|i, -iz
dosage, -s 'dəusidʒ, -iz
dos|e (s. v.), -es, -ing, -ed dəus, -iz, -iŋ, -t
doss, -es dɔs, -iz
dossal, -s 'dɔsəl, -z
doss-hou|se, -ses 'dɔshau|s, -ziz
dossier, -s 'dɔsiei (dosje), -z
dost (from do) dʌst (strong form), dəst (weak form)
dot (s. v.), -s, -ting, -ted dɔt, -s, -iŋ, -id
dotage 'dəutidʒ
dotard, -s 'dəutəd, -z
dot|e, -es, -ing/ly, -ed, -er/s dəut, -s, -iŋ/li, -id, -ə*/z
doth (from do) dʌθ (strong form), dəθ (weak form)
Dothan 'dəuθæn [-θən]
Dotheboys Hall 'duːðəbɔiz'hɔːl
dott(e)rel, -s 'dɔtrəl, -z
dottle, -s 'dɔtl, -z
dott|y, -ier, -iest, -ily, -iness 'dɔt|i, -iə*, -iist, -ili, -inis
Douai (French town) 'duːei (dwe), (school near Reading) 'dauei ['dauiˌ, (version of Bible) 'dauei ['dauiˌ 'duːei]
douane, -s duː(ː)'ɑːn, -z
doub|le (s. adj. v.), -ly, -leness; -les, -ling, -led 'dʌb|l, -li, -lnis; -lz, -liŋ [-l̩iŋ], -ld

double-barrelled 'dʌbl‚bærəld ['--'--]
double-bass, -es 'dʌbl'beis, -iz
double-bedded 'dʌbl‚bedid
Doublebois 'dʌblbɔiz
double-breasted 'dʌbl'brestid ['dʌbl-‚brestid]
double-cross, -es -ing, -ed 'dʌbl'krɔs [-'krɔːs], -iz, -iŋ, -t
Doubleday 'dʌbldei
double-deal|er/s, -ing 'dʌbl'diːl|ə*/z ['dʌbl‚d-], -iŋ
double-decked 'dʌbldekt
double-decker, -s 'dʌbl'dekə* ['dʌbl‚d-], -z
double-dyed 'dʌbl'daid [also 'dʌbldaid when attributive]
double-edged 'dʌbl'edʒd ['---]
double entendre 'duːblãːnˈtãːndr [-ɔ̃ːn'tɔ̃ːndr, -ɑːn'tɑːndr, -ɔːn'tɔːndr, -ɔn'tɔndr] (dublãtãːdr, pronounced as if French)
double entente 'duːblãːnˈtãːnt [-ɔ̃ːn'tɔ̃ːnt, -ɑːn'tɑːnt, -ɔːn'tɔːnt, -ɔn'tɔnt] (dublãtãːt)
double-entry 'dʌbl'entri
double-faced 'dʌblfeist
double-first, -s 'dʌbl'fəːst, -s
double-headed 'dʌbl‚hedid
double-locked 'dʌbl'lɔkt
double-minded 'dʌbl'maindid ['--‚--]
double-quick 'dʌbl'kwik
double-stopping, -s 'dʌbl'stɔpiŋ, -z
double-stout 'dʌbl'staut
doublet, -s 'dʌblit, -s
double-tongued 'dʌbl'tʌŋd ['dʌbltʌŋd]
doubloon, -s dʌb'luːn, -z
doubt (s. v.), -s, -ing/ly, -ed, -er/s daut, -s, -iŋ/li, -id, -ə*/z
doubt|ful, -fullest, -fully, -fulness 'daut|fʊl, -fulist [-fəlist], -fuli [-fəli], -fulnis
Doubting 'dautiŋ
doubtless, -ly 'dautlis, -li
douch|e (s. v.), -es, -ing, -ed duːʃ, -iz, -iŋ, -t
Doudney 'daudni, 'duːdni, 'djuːdni
Dougal(l) 'duːgəl
Dougan 'duːgən
dough dəu
Dougherty 'dəuəti
doughfaced 'dəu-feist
dough-nut, -s 'dəunʌt ['dəu'nʌt], -s
dought|y (D.), -ier, -iest, -ily, -iness 'daut|i, -iə* [-jə*], -iist [-jist], -ili, -inis
dough|y, -ily, -iness 'dəu|i, -ili, -inis
Douglas(s) 'dʌgləs
Douie dui ['duːi], 'daui

Doukhobor, -s 'duːkəubɔː:*, -z
douloureux (in tic d.) ‚duːlə'rəː: [-lu(ː)'r-]
Doulton 'dəultən
dour duə*
Douro 'duərəu
Dousabel 'duːsəbel
dous|e, -es, -ing, -ed daus, -iz, -iŋ, -t
Doust daust
Dousterswivel 'duːstəswivl
dove, -s dʌv, -z
Dove (surname, tributary of River Trent) dʌv
dove-colour, -ed 'dʌv‚kʌlə*, -d
dove-cot, -s 'dʌvkɔt, -s
dovecote, -s 'dʌvkəut [-kɔt], -s
Dovedale 'dʌvdeil
dove-like 'dʌvlaik
Dover 'dəuvə*
dovetail (s. v.), -s, -ing, -ed 'dʌvteil, -z, -iŋ, -d
Dovey (in Wales) 'dʌvi (Welsh 'dəvi)
Dow dau
dowager, -s 'dauədʒə* ['dauidʒ-], -z
Dowden 'daudn
dow|dy (s. adj.), -ies, -ier, -iest, -ily, -iness 'daud|i, -iz, -iə* [-jə*], -iist [-jist], -ili, -inis
dowel (s. v.), -s, -ling, -led 'dauəl ['dauil, 'dauel], -z, -iŋ, -d
Dowell 'dauəl [-il, -el]
dower, -s; -less 'dauə*, -z; -lis
Dowgate 'daugit [-geit]
Dowie 'daui
Dowland 'daulənd
dowlas (D.) 'dauləs
Dowle daul
Dowler 'daulə*
down (s. adj. v. adv. prep. interj.), -s, -ing, -ed daun, -z, -iŋ, -d
Down, -shire daun, -ʃiə* [-ʃə*]
down-bed, -s 'daun'bed [in contrast '--], -z
downcast 'daunkɑːst ['-'-]
down-draught, -s 'daun'drɑːft ['--], -s
Downe, -s daun, -z
Downey 'dauni
downfall, -s 'daunfɔːl, -z
Downham 'daunəm
down-hearted 'daun'hɑːtid
downhill 'daun'hil [also '--, -'- according to sentence-stress]
Downing 'dauniŋ
downland (D.) 'daunlænd
Downpatrick daun'pætrik
downpour, -s 'daunpɔː* [-pɔə*], -z
down-quilt, -s 'daun'kwilt [in contrast '--], -s
downright, -ness 'daunrait, -nis

downrush, -es 'daunrʌʃ, -iz
Downs daunz
Downside 'daun-said
down-sitting 'daun'sitiŋ ['daun͵s-]
downstairs 'daun'stɛəz [also '—, -'—
  according to sentence-stress]
downstream 'daun'stri:m [in contrast '—]
Downton 'dauntən
downtrodden 'daun͵trɔdn
downward, -s 'daunwəd, -z
down|y, -ier, -iest 'daun|i, -iə* [-jə*],
  -iist [-jist]
dowr|y, -ies 'dauər|i ['daur-], -iz
dowsabel (D.), -s 'du:səbel ['daus-], -z
dows|e, -es, -ing, -ed, -er/s dauz [daus],
  -iz, 'dauziŋ ['dausiŋ], dauzd [daust],
  'dauzə*/z ['dausə*/z]
Dowse daus
dowsing-rod, -s 'dauziŋrɔd ['dausiŋ-], -z
Dowson 'dausn
Dowton 'dautn
doxolog|y, -ies dɔk'sɔlədʒ|i, -iz
doyen, -s 'dɔiən ['dɔien, 'dwaiɛ̃:ŋ]
  (dwajɛ̃), -z
Doyle dɔil
doyley, -s 'dɔili, -z
D'Oyl(e)y 'dɔili
doz|e (s. v.), -es, -ing, -ed, -er/s dəuz,
  -iz, -iŋ, -d, -ə*/z
dozen, -s, -th 'dʌzn, -z, -θ
doz|y, -ier, -iest, -ily, -iness 'dəuz|i, -iə*
  [-jə*], -iist [-jist], -ili, -inis
Dr. 'dɔktə*, 'detə*
drab (s. adj.), -s dræb, -z
drabb|le, -les, -ling, -led 'dræb|l, -lz,
  -liŋ [-liŋ], -ld
dracaena, -s drə'si:nə, -z
Drachenfels 'drækənfelz [-fels] ('draxən-
  fels)
drachm, -s dræm, -z
drachm|a, -as, -ae 'drækm|ə, -əz, -i:
Draco (Greek legislator) 'dreikəu, (English surname) 'dra:kəu
Draconian drei'kəunjən [drə'k-, -niən]
draff dræf
draft (s. v.), -s, -ing, -ed, -er/s dra:ft, -s,
  -iŋ, -id, -ə*/z
drafts|man, -men, -manship 'dra:fts|-
  mən, -mən [-men], -mənʃip
drag (s. v.), -s, -ging, -ged dræg, -z, -iŋ,
  -d
Drage dreidʒ
dragg|le, -les, -ling, -led 'dræg|l, -lz, -liŋ
  [-liŋ], -ld
draggle-tail, -s, -ed 'dræglteil, -z, -d
drag-net, -s 'drægnet, -s
drago|man, -mans, -men 'drægəʊ|mən
  [-mæn], -mənz [-mænz], -mən [men]

dragon, -s 'drægən, -z
dragonet, -s 'drægənit [-net], -s
dragon-fl|y, -ies 'drægənfl|ai, -aiz
dragon|ish, -like 'drægən|iʃ [-gŋ|-], -laik
dragonnade, -s ͵drægə'neid, -z
dragon's-blood 'drægənzblʌd
dragoon, -s drə'gu:n, -z
drain (s. v.), -s, -ing, -ed, -er/s; -able,
  -age drein, -z, -iŋ, -d, -ə*/z; -əbl, -idʒ
draining-board, -s 'dreiniŋbɔ:d [-bɔəd],
  -z
drain-pipe, -s 'dreinpaip, -s
drake (D.), -s dreik, -s
dram (s. v.), -s, -ming, -med dræm, -z,
  -iŋ, -d
drama, -s 'dra:mə, -z
dramatic, -al, -ally drə'mætik, -əl, -əli
dramatis personae 'dra:mətis-pə:'səunai
  ['dræmətis-pə:'səuni:]
dramatist, -s 'dræmətist. -s
dramatization [-isa-], -s ͵dræmətai-
  'zeiʃən [-ti'z-], -z
dramatiz|e [-is|e], -es, -ing, -ed; -able
  'dræmətaiz, -iz, -iŋ, -d; -əbl
dramaturge, -s 'dræmətə:dʒ, -iz
dramaturgic ͵dræmə'tə:dʒik
drambuie dræm'bju:i
drank (from drink) dræŋk
drap|e, -es, -ing, -ed dreip, -s, -iŋ, -t
draper (D.), -s 'dreipə*, -z
draper|y, -ies 'dreipər|i, -iz
Drapier 'dreipiə* [-pjə*]
drastic, -ally 'dræstik ['dra:s-], -əli
drat dræt
draught, -s dra:ft, -s
draught-board, -s 'dra:ftbɔ:d [-bɔəd], -z
draught-horse, -s 'dra:fthɔ:s, -iz
draught-net, -s 'dra:ftnet, -s
draughts|man (person who draws), -men
  'dra:fts|mən, -mən
draughts|man (piece used in game of
  draughts), -men 'dra:fts|mæn [-mən],
  -men [-mən]
draught|y, -ier, -iest, -ily, -iness
  'dra:ft|i, -iə* [-jə*], -iist [-jist], -ili,
  -inis
Dravidian, -s drə'vidiən [-djən], -z
draw (s. v.), -s, -ing, drew, drawn; draw-
  able drɔ:, -z, -iŋ, dru:, drɔ:n; 'drɔ:əbl
drawback, -s 'drɔ:bæk, -s
drawbridge, -s 'drɔ:bridʒ, -iz
Drawcansir 'drɔ:kænsə*
drawee, -s drɔ:'i:, -z
drawer (person who draws), -s 'drɔ:ə*
  [drɔə*], -z
drawer (sliding box), -s drɔ:* [drɔə*], -z
drawers (garment) drɔ:z [drɔəz]
drawing-board, -s 'drɔ:iŋbɔ:d [-bɔəd], -z

drawing-kni|fe, -ves 'drɔ:iŋnai|f, -vz
drawing-master, -s 'drɔ:iŋ,mɑ:stə*, -z
drawing-pen, -s 'drɔ:iŋpen, -z
drawing-pencil, -s 'drɔ:iŋ,pensl, -z
drawing-pin, -s 'drɔ:iŋpin, -z
drawing-room, -s (*room for drawing*)
  'drɔ:iŋrum [-ru:m], (*reception room*)
  'drɔiŋrum, -z
drawing-table, -s 'drɔ:iŋ,teibl, -z
drawl (*s. v.*), **-s, -ing, -ed, -er/s** drɔ:l,
  -z, -iŋ, -d, -ə*/z
drawn (*from* **draw**) drɔ:n
draw-well, -s 'drɔ:wel, -z
Drax dræks
dray, -s drei, -z
dray|man, -men 'drei|mən [-mæn],
  -mən [-men]
Drayton 'dreitn
dread (*s. v.*), **-s, -ing, -ed** dred, -z, -iŋ, -id
dread|ful, -fully, -fulness 'dred|ful, -fuli
  [-fəli], -fulnis
dreadnought (D.), -s 'drednɔ:t, -s
dream (*s. v.*), **-s, -ing/ly, -ed, -t, -er/s**
  dri:m, -z, -iŋ/li, dremt [drempt,
  rarely dri:md], dremt [-mpt],
  'dri:mə*/z
dreamland 'dri:mlænd
dreamless, -ly 'dri:mlis, -li
dream|y, -ier, -iest, -ily, -iness 'dri:m|i,
  -iə* [-jə*], -iist [-jist], -ili, -inis
drear driə*
drear|y, -ier, -iest, -ily, -iness, -isome
  'driər|i, -iə*, -iist, -ili, -inis, -isəm
dredg|e (*s. v.*), **-es, -ing, -ed, -er/s**
  dredʒ, -iz, -iŋ, -d, -ə*/z
dregg|y, -ily, -iness 'dreg|i, -ili, -inis
dregs dregz
drench (*s. v.*), **-es, -ing, -ed, -er/s**
  drenʃ, -iz, -iŋ, -t, -ə*/z
Dresden 'drezdən ('dre:sdən)
dress (*s. v.*), **-es, -ing, -ed, -er/s** dres, -iz,
  -iŋ, -t, -ə*/z
dressage 'dresɑ:ʒ [-ɑ:dʒ]
dress-circle, -s 'dres'sə:kl, -z
dress-coat, -s 'dres'kəut, -s
dresser (*piece of furniture*), **-s** 'dresə*, -z
dressing-case, -s 'dresiŋ-keis, -iz
dressing-gown, -s 'dresiŋgaun, -z
dressing-jacket, -s 'dresiŋ,dʒækit, -s
dressing-room, -s 'dresiŋrum [-ru:m], -z
dressing-table, -s 'dresiŋ,teibl, -z
dressmak|er/s, -ing 'dres,meik|ə*/z, -iŋ
dress-suit, -s 'dres'sju:t [-'su:t], -s
dress|y, -ier, -iest, -ily, -iness 'dres|i,
  -iə*, -iist, -ili, -inis
drew (*from* **draw**) dru:
Drew, -s dru:, -z
Dreyfus 'dreifəs, 'draif-

dribb|le (*s. v.*), **-les, -ling, -led, -ler/s**
  'drib|l, -lz, -liŋ, [-liŋ], -ld, -lə*/z
  [-lə*/z]
driblet, -s 'driblit, -s
dried (*from* **dry** *v.*) draid
drier (*s. adj.*), **-s** 'drai-ə* ['draiə*], -z
dries (*from* **dry** *v.*) draiz
driest 'draiist
Driffield 'drifi:ld
drift (*s. v.*), **-s, -ing, -ed** drift, -s, -iŋ, -id
drift-ice 'drift-ais
driftless 'driftlis
drift-wood 'drift-wud
drifty 'drifti
drill (*s. v.*), **-s, -ing, -ed** dril, -z, -iŋ, -d
drill-sergeant, -s 'dril,sɑ:dʒənt, -s
drily (=**dryly**) 'drai-li ['draili]
drink (*s. v.*), **-s, -ing, drank, drunk,**
  drinker/s driŋk, -s, -iŋ, dræŋk,
  drʌŋk, 'driŋkə*/z
drinkable 'driŋkəbl
drinking-bout, -s 'driŋkiŋbaut, -s [-z
drinking-fountain, -s 'driŋkiŋ,fauntin,
drinking-horn, -s 'driŋkiŋhɔ:n, -z
drinking-song, -s 'driŋkiŋsɔŋ, -z
drinking-water 'driŋkiŋ,wɔ:tə*
drink-offering, -s 'driŋk,ɔfəriŋ, -z
Drinkwater 'driŋk,wɔ:tə*
drip (*s. v.*), **-s, -ping/s, -ped, -per/s** drip,
  -s, -iŋ/z, -t, -ə*/z
drip-dry 'drip'drai
dripping (*melted fat*) 'dripiŋ
dripping-pan, -s 'dripiŋpæn, -z
drip-stone, -s 'drip-stəun, -z
drivable 'draivəbl
driv|e (*s. v.*), **-es, -ing, drove, driven,**
  driver/s draiv, -z, -iŋ, drəuv, 'drivn,
  'draivə*/z
driv|el (*s. v.*), **-els, -elling, -elled,**
  -eller/s 'driv|l, -lz, -liŋ [-liŋ], -ld,
  -lə*/z [-lə*/z]
Driver 'draivə*
driving-belt, -s 'draiviŋbelt, -s
driving-iron, -s 'draiviŋ,aiən, -z
driving-wheel, -s 'draiviŋwi:l [-ŋhw-], -z
drizz|le (*s. v.*), **-les, -ling, -led** 'driz|l, -lz,
  -liŋ [-liŋ], -ld
drizzly 'drizli [-zli]
Droeshout 'dru:shaut
Drogheda (*place*) 'drɔiidə ['drɔ:idə,
  'drɔ:ədə, 'drɔhədə], (*Earl*) 'drɔiidə
drogher, -s 'drəugə*, -z
Droitwich 'drɔit-witʃ [*rarely* 'drɔititʃ]
droll, -er, -est, -y drəul, -ə*, -ist, -li
  ['drəuli]
droller|y, -ies 'drəulər|i, -iz
dromedar|y, -ies 'drʌmədər|i ['drɔm-,
  -mid-], -iz

Dromio 'drəumiəu [-mjəu]
Dromore 'drəumɔ:* [-mɔə*]
dron|e (s. v.), -es, -ing, -ed drəun, -z, -iŋ, -d
Dronfield 'drɔnfi:ld
droop, -s, -ing/ly, -ed dru:p, -s, -iŋ/li, -t
drop (s. v.), -s, -ping/s, -ped, -per/s drɔp, -s, -iŋ/z, -t, -ə*/z
drop-curtain, -s 'drɔp,kə:tn [-tən, -tin], -z
drop-kick, -s 'drɔpkik, -s
drop-scene, -s 'drɔpsi:n, -z
dropsic|al, -ally, -alness 'drɔpsik|əl, -əli, -əlnis
dropsy 'drɔpsi
Dros drɔs
drosera 'drɔsərə
droshk|y, -ies 'drɔʃk|i, -iz
drosometer, -s drɔ'sɔmitə*, -z
dross, -y drɔs, -i
drought, -s, -y draut, -s, -i
drove (s.), -s drəuv, -z
drove (from drive) drəuv
drover, -s 'drəuvə*, -z
drow, -s drau, -z
Drower, 'drauə*
drown, -s, -ing, -ed draun, -z, -iŋ, -d
drows|e (s. v.), -es, -ing, -ed drauz, -iz, -iŋ, -d
drows|y, -ier, -iest, -ily, -iness 'drauz|i, -iə* [-jə*], -iist [-jist], -ili, -inis
Drs. 'dɔktəz
drub, -s, -bing, -bed drʌb, -z, -iŋ, -d
Druce dru:s
Drucker 'drukə*
drudg|e (s. v.), -es, -ing/ly, -ed drʌdʒ, -iz, -iŋ/li, -d
drudgery 'drʌdʒəri
drug (s. v.), -s, -ging, -ged drʌg, -z, -iŋ, -d
drugget, -s 'drʌgit, -s
druggist, -s 'drʌgist, -s
druid, -s, -ess/es, -ism 'dru(:)id, -z, -is/iz [-es/iz], -izəm
druidic, -al dru(:)'idik, -əl
drum (s. v.), -s, -ming, -med, -mer/s drʌm, -z, -iŋ, -d, -ə*/z
Drumclog drʌm'klɔg
drum-fire 'drʌm,faiə*
drumhead, -s 'drʌmhed, -z
drum-major, -s 'drʌm'meidʒə*, -z
Drummond 'drʌmənd
drumstick, -s 'drʌm-stik, -s
drunk (s. adj.), -s drʌŋk, -s
drunk (from drink) drʌŋk
drunkard, -s 'drʌŋkəd, -z
drunken, -ly, -ness 'drʌŋkən, -li, -nis
drupe, -s dru:p, -s

Drury 'druəri
druse (geological term), -s dru:z, -iz
Druse (surname) dru:z, dru:s
Druse (member of sect in Syria), -s dru:z, -iz
Drusilla dru(:)'silə
dr|y (adj. v.), -ier, -iest, -yly, -yness; -ies, -ying, -ied, -ier/s dr|ai, -ai-ə* [-aiə*], -aiist, -ai-li [-aili], -ai-nis [-ainis]; -aiz, -aiiŋ, -aid, -ai-ə*/z [-aiə*/z]
dryad, -s 'drai-əd ['draiəd, 'draiæd], -z
Dryasdust 'drai-əzdʌst ['draiəz-]
dry-bob, -s 'draibɔb, -z
Dryburgh 'draibərə
dry-clean, -s, -ing, -ed, -er/s 'drai'kli:n, -z, -iŋ, -d, -ə*/z
Dryden 'draidn
dry-dock (s. v.), -s, -ing, -ed 'drai'dɔk ['--], -s, -iŋ, -t
Dryfesdale 'draifsdeil
Dryhurst 'draihə:st
drying (from dry v.) 'draiiŋ
dryly 'drai-li ['draili]
dry-measure 'drai,meʒə*
dryness 'drai-nis ['drainis]
dry-nurs|e (s. v.), -es, -ing, -ed 'drai-'nə:s, -iz, -iŋ, -t
dry-plate, -s 'drai'pleit ['drai-pleit], -s
dry-point 'drai-pɔint
dry-rot 'drai'rɔt ['drairɔt]
drysalter, -s 'drai,sɔ:ltə* [-,sɔl-], -z
drysalter|y, -ies 'drai,sɔ:ltər|i [-,sɔl-], -iz
Drysdale 'draizdeil
dryshod 'drai'ʃɔd ['drai-ʃɔd]
dual 'dju(:)əl
duali|sm, -st/s 'dju(:)əli|zəm, -st/s
dualistic ,dju(:)ə'listik
dualit|y, -ies dju(:)'ælit|i, -iz
Duane du(:)'ein
dub (s. v.), -s, -bing, -bed dʌb, -z, -iŋ, -d
dubbin 'dʌbin
Dubhe 'dubei
dubiety dju(:)'baiəti [-aiiti]
dubious, -ly, -ness 'dju:bjəs [-bɪəs], -li, -nis
dubitat|e, -es, -ing, -ed 'dju:biteit, -s, -iŋ, -id
dubitation, -s ,dju:bi'teiʃən [djubi't-], -z
dubitative, -ly 'dju:bitətiv [-teit-], -li
Dublin 'dʌblin
Du Buisson (English name) 'dju:bisn
duc|al, -ally 'dju:k|əl, -əli
Du Cane dju'kein [dju:'k-]
ducat, -s 'dʌkət, -s
duce, -s 'du:tʃi, -z
Duchesne (English name) dju:'ʃein, du:'ʃein

duchess, -es 'dʌtʃis, -iz
duch|y, -ies 'dʌtʃ|i, -iz
Ducie 'djuːsi
duck (s. v.), -s, -ing, -ed dʌk, -s, -iŋ, -t
duck-bill, -s 'dʌkbil, -z
duck-board, -s 'dʌkbɔːd [-bəəd], -z
duckling, -s 'dʌkliŋ, -z
duck-pond, -s 'dʌkpɔnd, -z
duck's-egg, -s 'dʌks-eg, -z
duck-shot 'dʌkʃɔt
duckweed 'dʌk-wiːd
Duckworth 'dʌkwə(ː)θ
duck|y, -ies 'dʌk|i, -iz
Du Croz (English surname) dju'krəu
duct, -s dʌkt, -s   [[dju:'k-]
ductile 'dʌktail
ductility dʌk'tiliti
ductless 'dʌktlis
dud, -s dʌd, -z
Duddell dʌ'del, dju(ː)'del
Duddeston 'dʌdstən
Duddington 'dʌdiŋtən
Duddon 'dʌdn
dude, -s djuːd, -z
Dudeney (surname) 'duːdni, 'djuːdni
dudgeon, -s 'dʌdʒən, -z
Dudhope 'dʌdəp
Dudley 'dʌdli
Dudu 'duːduː
due (s. adj.), -s djuː, -z
duel (s. v.), -s, -ling, -led, -ler/s; -list/s
   'dju(ː)əl [-il], -z, -iŋ, -d, -ə*/z; -ist/s
duenna, -s dju(ː)'enə, -z
Duer 'dju(ː)ə*
duet, -s dju(ː)'et, -s
duettino, -s ,dju(ː)e'tiːnəu, -z
duettist, -s dju(ː)'etist, -s
duetto, -s dju(ː)'etəu, -z
Duff dʌf
duffel 'dʌfəl
duffer, -s 'dʌfə*, -z
Dufferin 'dʌfərin
Duffield 'dʌfiːld
duffle-coat, -s 'dʌflkəut, -s
Duffy 'dʌfi
dug (s.), -s dʌg, -z
dug (from dig) dʌg
Dugald 'duːgəld
Dugan 'duːgən
Dugdale 'dʌgdeil
dugong, -s 'duːgɔŋ ['djuː-], -z
dug-out (s.), -s 'dʌgaut, -s
dug-out (adj.) 'dʌg'aut
Duguid 'djuːgid, 'duːgid
duiker, -s 'daikə*, -z
duke (D.), -s djuːk, -s
dukedom, -s 'djuːkdəm, -z
duker|y, -ies 'djuːkər|i, -iz

Dukinfield 'dʌkinfiːld
Dukw, -s dʌk, -s
dulcamara ,dʌlkə'mɑːrə [-'mɛər-]
Dulce (Christian name) 'dʌlsi
dulcet 'dʌlsit
Dulcie 'dʌlsi
dulci|fy, -fies, -fying, -fied 'dʌlsi|fai,
   -faiz, -faiiŋ, -faid
dulcimer, -s 'dʌlsimə*, -z
Dulcinea ,dʌlsi'niə [dʌl'sinɪə]
dulia dju:'laiə
dull (adj. v.), -er, -est, -y, -ness; -s, -ing,
   -ed dʌl, -ə*, -ist, -i [-li], -nis; -z, -iŋ, -d
dullard, -s 'dʌləd, -z
dull|-brained, -eyed 'dʌl|breind, -aid
Dulles 'dʌlis [-ləs]
dullish 'dʌliʃ
dulness (=dullness) 'dʌlnis
Duluth dju:'luːθ [du'l-]
Dulwich 'dʌlidʒ [-itʃ]
duly 'djuːli
Duma 'duːmə ['djuː-]
Dumain dju(ː)'mein
Dumaresq du:'merik
Dumas 'djuːmɑ: ['duː-] (dymɑ)
Du Maurier (English surname) dju(ː)-
   'mɔːriei [du:-, -'mɔr-]
Dumayne dju(ː)'mein
dumb (adj. v.), -ly, -ness; -s, -ing, -ed
   dʌm, -li, -nis; -z, -iŋ, -d
Dumbarton dʌm'bɑːtn
dumb-bell, -s 'dʌmbel, -z
dumbfound, -s, -ing, -ed, -er/s dʌm-
   'faund, -z, -iŋ, -id, -ə*/z
Dumbiedikes 'dʌmbidaiks
dumb-show, -s 'dʌm'ʃəu, -z
dumb-waiter, -s 'dʌm'weitə*, -z
dumdum, -s 'dʌmdʌm, -z
Dumfries, -shire dʌm'friːs [dəm-], -ʃiə*
   [-ʃə*, dʌm'friːʃʃiə*]
dumky, -s 'dumki, -z
dumm|y (s. adj.), -ies 'dʌm|i, -iz
Dumnorix 'dʌmnəriks
dump, -s, -ing, -ed dʌmp, -s, -iŋ, -t
   [dʌmt]
Dumphreys 'dʌmfriz
dumpish, -ly, -ness 'dʌmpiʃ, -li, -nis
dumpling, -s 'dʌmpliŋ, -z
dumps dʌmps
dump|y, -ier, -iest 'dʌmp|i, -iə* [-jə*],
   -iist [-jist]
Dumville 'dʌmvil
dun (s. adj. v.), -s, -ning, -ned dʌn, -z,
   -iŋ, -d
Dunalley dʌ'næli
Dunbar (place, surname) dʌn'bɑː*,
   'dʌnbɑː*
   Note.—In Scotland always -'-.

Dunblane dʌn'blein
Duncan 'dʌŋkən ['dʌnk-]
Duncannon dʌn'kænən [dʌŋ'k-]
Duncansby 'dʌŋkənzbi ['dʌnk-]
dunce, -s dʌns, -iz
Dunciad 'dʌnsiæd
Duncombe 'dʌnkəm ['dʌŋk-]
Dundalk dʌn'dɔ:k [-'dɔ:lk, *also* '-- *when attributive*]
Dundas dʌn'dæs, 'dʌndæs
Dundee dʌn'di: ['dʌn'd-, *also* 'dʌnd- *when attributive*]
dunderhead, -s 'dʌndəhed, -z
Dundonald dʌn'dɔnl̩d
dundrear|y (**D.**), -ies dʌn'driər|i, -iz
Dundrennan dʌn'drenən
Dundrum dʌn'drʌm ['dʌndrəm]
dune, -s dju:n, -z ⌈[-dn]
Dunedin (*in New Zealand*) dʌ'ni:din
Dunell dju'nel [dju:'n-]
Dunfermline dʌn'fə:mlin [dʌm'f-]
dung dʌŋ
Dungannon dʌn'gænən [dʌŋ'g-]
dungaree, -s ˌdʌŋgə'ri: ['--'-], -z
Dungarvan dʌn'gɑ:vən [dʌŋ'g-]
Dungeness ˌdʌnaʒi'nes ['--'-, dʌndʒ'nes, ['-'-]
dungeon, -s 'dʌndʒən, -z
dung-hill, -s 'dʌŋhil, -z
Dunglison 'dʌŋglisn
dungy 'dʌŋi
Dunholme 'dʌnəm
Dunkeld dʌn'keld [dʌŋ'k-]
Dunker, -s 'dʌŋkə*, -z
Dunkirk dʌn'kə:k ['dʌn'kə:k, dʌŋ'k-, 'dʌŋ'k-]
Dun Laoghaire dʌn'liəri [*less usually* -'leərə]
Dunlap 'dʌnləp [-læp]
dunlin, -s 'dʌnlin, -z
Dunlop (*surname*) 'dʌnlɔp, dʌn'lɔp
Dunlop (*tyre*), -s 'dʌnlɔp, -s
Dunmail dʌn'meil
Dunmore dʌn'mɔ:* [-'mɔə*], *attributively also* '--, *as in* **D. Road**
Dunmow 'dʌnməu
Dunn(e) dʌn
Dunning 'dʌniŋ
dunnock, -s 'dʌnək, -s
Dunnottar dʌ'nɔtə* [də'n-]
Dunraven dʌn'reivn
Dunrobin dʌn'rɔbin
Dunsany dʌn'seini
Dunse dʌns
Dunsinane (*in Perthshire*) dʌn'sinən
Note.—This name has to be pronounced 'dʌnsinein *in Shakespeare's 'Macbeth'.*

Dunstable 'dʌnstəbl
Dunstaffnage dʌn'stæfnidʒ [-'stɑ:f-]
Dunst|an, -er, -on 'dʌnst|ən, -ə*, -ən
Dunton 'dʌntən
duo, -s 'dju(:)əu, -z
duodecennial ˌdju(:)əudi'senjəl [-nɪəl]
duodecimal, -s ˌdju(:)əu'desiməl [djüə'd-], -z
duodecimo, -s ˌdju(:)əu'desiməu [djüə'd-], -z
duodenal ˌdju(:)əu'di:nl [djüə'd-]
duodenary ˌdju(:)əu'di:nəri [djüəd-]
duoden|um, -ums, -a ˌdju(:)əu'di:n|əm [djüə'd-], -əmz, -ə
duologue, -s 'djuəlɔg ['dju:ə-], -z
Duparcq (*surname*) du:'pɑ:k
dup|le (s. v.), -es, -ing, -ed dju:p, -s, -iŋ, -t
dupery 'dju:pəri
Du Plat dju:'plɑ:
duple 'dju:pl
Dupleix (*governor in India*) dju:'pleiks (dypleks), (*historian*) dju:'plei (dyplɛ)
duplex 'dju:pleks
duplicate (s. adj.), -s 'dju:plikit, -s
duplicat|e (v.), -es, -ing, -ed, -or/s 'dju:-plikeit, -s, -iŋ, -id, -ə*/z
duplication, -s ˌdju:pli'keiʃən, -z
duplicature, -s 'dju:plikeitʃə* ['dju:plikətjuə*], -z
duplicity dju(:)'plisiti
dupl|y, -ies dju(:)'pl|ai, -aiz
Dupont (*American surname*) 'dju:pɔnt
Duquesne (*French naval commander*) dju(:)'kein (dykɛ:n), (*place in U.S.A.*) dju(:)'kein [du:'k-]
durability ˌdjuərə'biliti [ˌdjɔər-, ˌdjɔ:r-, -lət-]
durab|le, -ly, -leness 'djuərəb|l ['djɔər-, 'djɔ:r-], -li, -lnis
dural 'djuərəl ['djɔə-, 'djɔ:-]
duralumin djuə'ræljumin [djɔə'r-, djɔ:'r-]
duramen djuə'reimen
durance 'djuərəns
Durand djuə'rænd
Durant dju'rɑ:nt, dju'rænt
duration, -s djuə'reiʃən [djɔə'r-, djɔ:'r-], -z
durative 'djuərətiv ['djɔər-, 'djɔ:r-]
Durban 'də:bən
durbar, -s 'də:bɑ:*, -z
Durbin 'də:bin
Durden 'də:dn
durdle, -s 'də:dl, -z
Durell djuə'rel
Dürer, -s 'djuərə* ('dy:rər), -z
duress djuə'res ['djuəres, 'djuəris]
Durham 'dʌrəm

during 'djuəriŋ ['djɔər-, 'djɔːr-, 'djəːr-, 'dʒuər-, 'dʒɔːr-, 'dʒəːr-]
Durlacher də'læke*
Durnford 'dəːnfəd
Durran dʌ'ræn [də'r-]
Durrant 'dʌrənt
Durrell 'dʌrəl
durst (from dare), -n't dəːst, 'dəːsnt
Durward 'dəːwəd
Duse 'duːzi
dusk (s. adj. v.), -s, -ing, -ed dʌsk, -s, -iŋ, -t
dusk|y, -ier, -iest, -ily, -iness 'dʌsk|i, -ïə* [-jə*], -iist [-jist], -ili, -inis
dust (s. v.), -s, -ing, -ed dʌst, -s, -iŋ, -id
dustbin, -s 'dʌstbin, -z
dust-cart, -s 'dʌstkɑːt, -s
dust-coat, -s 'dʌstkəut, -s
dust-colour, -ed 'dʌst,kʌlə*, -d
duster, -s 'dʌstə*, -z
dusthole, -s 'dʌsthəul, -z
dust|man, -men 'dʌst|mən, -mən
dust-pan, -s 'dʌstpæn, -z
dustproof 'dʌstpruːf
dust|y, -ier, -iest, -ily, -iness 'dʌst|i, -ïə* [-jə*], -iist, [-jist], -ili, -inis
Dutch, -man, -men dʌtʃ, -mən, -mən
Dutch|woman, -women 'dʌtʃ|,wumən, -,wimin
duteous, -ly, -ness 'djuːtjəs [-tïəs], -li, -nis
Duthie 'dʌθi
Duthoit də'θɔit
dutiable 'djuːtjəbl [-tïəb-]
duti|ful, -fully, -fulness 'djuːti|ful, -fuli [-fəli], -fulnis
Dutton 'dʌtn
dut|y, -ies 'djuːt|i, -iz
duty-free 'djuːti'friː
duumvir, -s dju(ː)'ʌmvə* ['djuːəmv-, duː'um-], -z
duumvirate, -s dju(ː)'ʌmvirit [-vər-], -s
duumviri (alternative plur. of duumvir) duː'umviri: [dju(ː)'ʌmvirai, -vər-]
Duveen dju(ː)'viːn
dux, -es dʌks, -iz
Duxbury 'dʌksbəri
D.V. (deo volente) 'diː'viː
Dvorak [-řák] 'dvɔːʒɑːk [-ɔːrɑːk, -æk]
dwale dweil
dwarf (s. v.), -s, -ing, -ed dwɔːf, -s, -iŋ, -t
dwarfish, -ly, -ness 'dwɔːfiʃ, -li, -nis
dwell, -s, -ing/s, dwelt, dweller/s dwel, -z, -iŋ/z, dwelt, 'dwelə*/z

dwelling-hou|se, -ses 'dweliŋhau|s, -ziz
dwelling-place, -s 'dweliŋpleis, -iz
Dwight dwait
Dwina 'dviːnə ['dwiː-] (dvji'na)
dwind|le, -les, -ling, -led 'dwind|l, -lz, -liŋ, [-liŋ], -ld
dyad, -s 'daiæd ['dai-əd], -z
Dyak, -s 'daiæk ['dai-ək], -s
dyarch|y, -ies 'daiɑːk|i, -iz
Dyce dais
Dyche daitʃ
dye (s. v.), -s, -ing, -d, -r/s dai, -z, -iŋ, -d, 'dai-ə*/z ['daiə*/z]
Dyer 'dai-ə* ['daiə*]
dyestuff, -s 'dai-stʌf, -s
dye-wood 'daiwud
dye-works 'daiwəːks
Dyffryn 'dʌfrin (Welsh 'dəfrin)
dying (from die v.) 'daiiŋ
dyk|e (s. v.), -es, -ing, -ed daik, -s, -iŋ, -t
Dyke, -s daik, -s
Dylan 'dilən (Welsh 'dəlan)
Dym|ock, -oke 'dim|ək, -ək
Dymon|d, -t 'daimən|d, -t
dynameter, -s dai'næmitə* [di'n-], -z
dynamic, -al, -ally, -s dai'næmik [di'n-], -əl, -əli, -s
dynamism 'dainəmizəm
dynamit|e (s. v.), -es, -ing, -ed, -er/s 'dainəmait, -s, -iŋ, -id, -ə*/z
dynamo, -s 'dainəməu, -z
dynamometer, -s ,dainə'mɔmitə*, -z
dynamometric, -al ,dainəməu'metrik, -əl
dynast, -s 'dinəst ['dinæst, 'dainəst, 'dainæst], -s
dynastic di'næstik [dai'n-]
dynast|y, -ies 'dinəst|i ['dain-], -iz
dynatron, -s 'dainətrɔn, -z
dyne, -s dain, -s
Dynevor 'dinivə*
Dysart 'daisət [-sɑːt]
dysarthria dis'ɑːθrïə
dyscrasia dis'kreizjə [-zïə, -ʒjə, -ʒïə, -ʒə]
dysenteric ,disn'terik [-sən-, -sen-]
dysentery 'disntri [-sən-]
dyslalia dis'leilïə [-ljə]
dyslexia dis'leksïə [-ksjə]
Dyson 'daisn
dyspepsia dis'pepsïə [-sjə]
dyspeptic (s. adj.), -s dis'peptik, -s
dyspnoea dis'pni(ː)ə
dziggetai, -s 'dzigitai, -z

E

E (*the letter*), -'s i:, -z
each i:tʃ
Ead|ie, -y 'i:d|i, -i
eager, -ly, -ness 'i:gə*, -li, -nis
eagle, -s 'i:gl, -z
eagle-eyed 'i:gl'aid ['i:glaid]
Eaglefield 'i:glfi:ld
Eaglehawk 'i:glhɔ:k
eagle-owl, -s 'i:gl'aul [*in contrast* '---], -z
eaglet, -s 'i:glit, -s
eagre, -s 'eigə* ['i:gə*], -z
Ealing 'i:liŋ
Eames i:mz, eimz
Eamon 'eimən
ear, -s iə*, -z
ear-ache 'iəreik
Eardley 'ə:dli
ear-drum, -s 'iədrʌm, -z
eared iəd
earl, -s; -dom/s ə:l, -z; -dəm/z
Earl(e) ə:l
earl-marshal, -s 'ə:l'mɑ:ʃəl, -z
Earl's Court 'ə:lz'kɔ:t
earl|y, -ier, -iest, -iness 'ə:l|i, -iə* [-jə*], -iist [-jist], -inis
earmark (*s. v.*), -s, -ing, -ed 'iəmɑ:k, -s, -iŋ, -t   [[ə:nt]
earn (E.), -s, -ing, -ed ə:n, -z, -iŋ, -d
earnest (*s. adj.*), -s, -ly, -ness 'ə:nist, -s, -li, -nis
earnest-money, -s 'ə:nist,mʌni, -z
earnings 'ə:niŋz
Earp ə:p
earring, -s 'iəriŋ, -z
Earsdon 'iəzdən
earshot 'iə-ʃɒt
earth (*s.*), -s ə:θ, -s [ə:ðz]
earth (*v.*), -s, -ing, -ed ə:θ, -s, -iŋ, -t
earth-board, -s 'ə:θbɔ:d [-bɔəd], -z
earth-born 'ə:θbɔ:n
earthbound 'ə:θbaund
earth-bred 'ə:θbred
earth-closet, -s 'ə:θ,klɒzit, -s
earthen, -ware 'ə:θən, -wɛə*
earthiness 'ə:θinis
earthl|y, -ier, -iest, -iness 'ə:θl|i, -iə* [-jə*], -iist [-jist], -inis
earthly-minded, -ness 'ə:θli'maindid ['ə:θli,m-], -nis

earthquake, -s 'ə:θkweik, -s
earthward 'ə:θwəd
earthwork, -s 'ə:θ-wə:k, -s
earthworm, -s 'ə:θ-wə:m, -z
earthy 'ə:θi
ear-trumpet, -s 'iə,trʌmpit, -s
ear-wax 'iəwæks
earwig, -s 'iəwig, -z
ear-witness, -es 'iə'witnis [-,wit-], -iz
Easebourne 'i:zbɔ:n [-bɔən]
Easdale 'i:zdeil
eas|e (*s. v.*), -es, -ing, -ed i:z, -iz, -iŋ, -d
easel, -s 'i:zl, -z
easement, -s 'i:zmənt, -s
Easingwold 'i:ziŋwəuld
east (E.) i:st
Eastbourne 'i:stbɔ:n [-bɔən]
Eastcheap 'i:sttʃi:p
East-end, -er/s 'i:st'end, -ə*/z
Easter, -s 'i:stə*, -z
Easter-day, -s 'i:stə'dei ['---], -z
easterly 'i:stəli
eastern, -most 'i:stən [-tn], -məust [-məst]
East Ham 'i:st'hæm
Eastham 'i:sthəm
Easthampton 'i:st'hæmptən [i:st'h-]
easting 'i:stiŋ
Eastlake 'i:stleik
Eastleigh 'i:stli: ['i:st'li:]
Eastman 'i:stmən
east-north-east 'i:stnɔ:θ'i:st [*in nautical usage* -nɔ:r'i:st]
Easton 'i:stən
Eastport 'i:stpɔ:t
east-south-east 'i:stsauθ'i:st [*in nautical usage also* -sau'i:st]
eastward, -ly, -s 'i:stwəd, -li, -z
Eastwood 'i:stwud
eas|y, -ier, -iest, -ily, -iness 'i:z|i, -iə* [-jə*], -iist [-jist], -ili, -inis
easy-chair, -s 'i:zi'tʃɛə*, -z
easygoing 'i:zi,gəuiŋ ['--'--]
eat (*pres. tense*), -s, -ing, ate, eat|en, -er/s; -able/s i:t, -s, -iŋ, et [eit], 'i:t|n, -ə*/z; -əbl/z
eat (*old-fashioned spelling of* ate) et
eating-hou|se, -ses 'i:tiŋhau|s, -ziz
Eaton 'i:tn

eau-de-Cologne 'əudəkə'ləun [-dik-]
eau-de-vie 'əudə'vi: (odvi)
eau-forte, eaux-fortes 'əu'fɔ:t (ofɔrt), -s
eave, -s (E.) i:v, -z
eavesdrop, -s, -ping, -ped, -per/s
'i:vzdrɔp, -s, -iŋ, -t, -ə*/z
Ebal 'i:bæl [-bəl]
ebb (s. v.), -s, -ing, -ed eb, -z, -iŋ, -d
Ebbsfleet 'ɛbzfli:t
ebb-tide, -s 'eb'taid ['ebt-], -z
Ebbw 'ebu: (Welsh 'ebu)
Ebel e'bel, 'i:bl
Ebenezer ,ebi'ni:zə*
Ebionite, -s 'i:bjənait [-bïən-], -s
E-boat, -s 'i:bəut, -s
ebon, -ite 'ebən, -ait
ebony 'ebəni
Eboracum i(:)'bɔrəkəm
ebriate 'i:briit
ebriety i(:)'braiəti
Ebrington 'ebriŋtən
Ebro 'i:brəu ['eb-] ('ebro)
ebullien|ce, -cy, -t i'bʌljən|s [-'bul-,
-lïən-], -si, -t
ebullition, -s ,ebə'liʃən [-bu'l-], -z
Ebury 'i:bəri
E.C. 'i:'si:
écarté ei'kɑ:tei (ekarte)
Ecbatana ek'bætənə [,ekbə'tɑ:nə]
Ecce Homo 'eksi'həuməu [-'hɔməu]
eccentric (s. adj.), -s, -al, -ally ik'sen-
trik [ek-], -s, -əl, -əli
eccentricit|y, -ies ,eksen'trisit|i [-sən-],
-iz
Ecclefechan ,ekl'fekən [-'fexən]
Eccles, -field 'eklz, -fi:ld
eccles|ia, -iast/s i'kli:z|jə [-ïə], -iæst/s
Ecclesiastes i,kli:zi'æsti:z [-i'ɑ:s-]
ecclesiastic (s. adj.), -s, -al, -ally
i,kli:zi'æstik [-i'ɑ:s-], -s, -əl, -əli
ecclesiasticism i,kli:zi'æstisizəm [-i'ɑ:s-]
Ecclesiasticus i,kli:zi'æstikəs [-i'ɑ:s-]
Eccleston 'eklstən
echelon, -s, -ned 'eʃəlɔn ['eiʃ-], -z, -d
echidn|a, -ae e'kidn|ə [i'k-], -i:
echin|us, -i e'kain|əs [i'k-], -ai
echo (s. v.), -es, -ing, -ed 'ekəu, -z, -iŋ,
echoic e'kəuik [i'k-]   [-d
Echuca i'tʃu:kə
Eckersl(e)y 'ekəzli
Eck|ert, -ford 'ek|ə(:)t, -fəd
éclair, -s 'eiklɛə* [-'-, i'k-], -z
eclampsia i'klæmpsïə [e'k-, -sjə]
éclat, -s 'eiklɑ: (ekla), -z
eclectic (s. adj.), -s, -al, -ally ek'lektik
[i'klek-, i:'klek-], -s, -əl, -əli
eclecticism ek'lektisizəm [i'klek-,
i:'klek-]

eclips|e (s. v.), -es, -ing, -ed i'klips, -iz,
-iŋ, -t
ecliptic, -s i'kliptik, -s
eclogue, -s 'eklɔg, -z
economic, -al, -ally, -s ,i:kə'nɔmik
[,ek-], -əl, -əli, -s
economist, -s i(:)'kɔnəmist, -s
economiz|e [-is|e], -es, -ing, -ed, -er/s
i(:)'kɔnəmaiz, -iz, -iŋ, -d, -ə*/z
econom|y, -ies i(:)'kɔnəm|i, -iz
ecru 'eikru: [e'kru:]
ecstas|y, -ies 'ekstəs|i, -iz
ecstatic, -al, -ally eks'tætik [ik-], -əl, -əli
ectoplasm 'ektəuplæzəm
Ecuador ,ekwə'dɔ:* ['ekwəd-]
ecumenic, -al ,i:kju(:)'menik, -əl
eczema 'eksimə
eczematous ek'semətəs [ek'zem-, rarely
ek'si:m-, ek'zi:m-]
edacious i'deiʃəs [i:'d-, e'd-]
Edam (cheese) 'i:dæm
Edda -s 'edə, -z
Eddington 'ediŋtən
edd|y (s. v.) (E.), -ies, -ying, -ied 'ed|i,
-iz, -iiŋ, -id
Eddystone 'edistən
Ede i:d
edelweiss 'eidlvais
Eden, -bridge 'i:dn, -bridʒ
Edenfield (in Lancs.) 'i:dnfi:ld
Edessa i'desə
Edgar 'edgə*
Edgbaston 'edʒbəstən
Edgcumbe 'edʒkəm [-ku:m]
edg|e (s. v.) (E.), -es, -ing, -ed edʒ, -iz,
Edgecomb(e) 'edʒkəm   [-iŋ, -d
Edgecote 'edʒkəut [-kət]
Edgehill (name of a hill) 'edʒ'hil, (sur-
name) 'edʒhil
edgeless 'edʒlis
Edgerton 'edʒətn
edge|ways, -wise 'edʒ|weiz, -waiz
Edgeworth 'edʒwə:θ
edging, -s 'edʒiŋ, -z
Edgington 'edʒiŋtən
Edgley 'edʒli
Edgware (town) 'edʒwɛə*, (Road) 'edʒ-
wɛə* [-wə*]
edgy 'edʒi
edibility ,edi'biliti [-də'b-, -lət-]
edible (s. adj.), -s, -ness 'edibl [-dəb-],
-z, -nis
edict, -s 'i:dikt, -s
Edie 'i:di
edification ,edifi'keiʃən
edifice, -s 'edifis, -iz
edi|fy, -fies, -fying, -fied 'edi|fai, -faiz,
-faiiŋ, -faid

edile, -s 'i:dail, -z
Edina i'dainə [e'd-]
Edinburgh 'edinbərə ['edn-, -bʌrə]
Edington 'ediŋtən
Edison 'edisn
Ediss 'i:dis, 'edis
edit, -s -ing, -ed, -or/s 'edit, -s, -iŋ, -id, -ə*/z
Edith 'i:diθ
edition, -s i'diʃən, -z
editorial (s. adj.), -s, -ly ‚edi'tɔ:rïəl, -z, -i
editorship, -s 'editəʃip, -s
Edmond, -s 'edmənd, -z
Edmonton 'edməntən
Edmund, -s 'edmənd, -z
Edna 'ednə
Edom, -ite/s 'i:dəm, -ait/s
Edridge 'edridʒ
Edsall 'edsl
educability ‚edju(:)kə'biliti [-lət-]
educable 'edjukəbl
educat|e, -es, -ing, -ed, -or/s 'edju(:)-keit [-dʒu(:)-], -s, -iŋ, -id, -ə*/z
education ‚edju(:)'keiʃən [-dʒu(:)-]
educa|tional, -tionally ‚edju(:)'keiʃənl [-dʒu(:)-, -ʃnəl, -ʃn̩l, -ʃnl̩, -ʃənəl], -ʃŋəli [-ʃnəli, -ʃn̩li, -ʃnl̩i, -ʃənəli]
educationalist, -s ‚edju(:)'keiʃŋəlist [-dʒu(:)-, -ʃnəl-, -ʃn̩l-, -ʃnl̩-, -ʃənəl-], -s
educationist, -s ‚edju(:)'keiʃnist [-dʒu(:)-, -ʃn̩ist, -ʃənist], -s
educative 'edju(:)kətiv [-dʒu(:)-, -keit-]
educ|e, -es, -ing, -ed i(:)'dju:s, -iz, -iŋ, -t
eduction, -s i(:)'dʌkʃən, -z
Edward, -(e)s 'edwəd, -z
Edwardian (s. adj.), -s ed'wɔ:djən [-dïən], -z
Edwin, -stowe 'edwin, -stəu
eel, -s i:l, -z
e'en i:n
e'er ɛə*
eer|ie, -y, -ily, -iness 'iər|i, -i, -ili, -inis
effac|e, -es, -ing, -ed, -ement; -eable i'feis [e'f-], -iz, -iŋ, -t, -mənt; -əbl
effect (s. v.), -s, -ing, -ed i'fekt, -s, -iŋ, -id
effective, -s, -ly, -ness i'fektiv, -z, -li, -nis
effectual, -ly i'fektʃŭəl [-tʃwəl, -tʃul, -tjŭəl, -tjwəl, -tjul], -i
effectuality i‚fektju'æliti [-tʃu-]
effectuat|e, -es, -ing, -ed i'fektjueit [-tʃu-], -s, -iŋ, -id
effeminacy i'feminəsi [e'f-]
effeminate (adj.), -ly, -ness i'feminit [e'f-], -li, -nis
effeminat|e (v.), -es, -ing, -ed i'femi-neit [e'f-], -s, -iŋ, -id
Effendi e'fendi
efferent 'efərənt

effervesc|e, -es, -ing, -ed; -ence, -ent ‚efə'ves, -iz, -iŋ, -t; -ns, -nt
effete e'fi:t [i'f-]
efficacious, -ly, -ness ‚efi'keiʃəs, -li, -nis
efficacity ‚efi'kæsiti
efficacy 'efikəsi
efficien|cy, -t/ly i'fiʃən|si, -t/li
Effie 'efi
effig|y, -ies 'efidʒ|i, -iz
Effingham 'efiŋəm
effloresc|e, -es, -ing, -ed; -ence, -ent ‚eflɔ:'res [-flɔ'r-, -flə'r-], -iz, -iŋ, -t; -ns, -nt
effluen|ce, -t/s 'eflŭən|s [-flwən-], -t/s
effluvium e'flu:vjəm [i'f-, -vïəm]
efflux, -es 'eflʌks, -iz
effort, -s; -less 'efət, -s; -lis
effronter|y, -ies i'frʌntər|i [e'f-], -iz
effulg|e, -es, -ing, -ed e'fʌldʒ [i'f-], -iz, -iŋ, -d
effulgen|ce, -t/ly e'fʌldʒən|s [i'f-], -t/li
effuse (adj.) e'fju:s [i'f-]
effus|e (v.), -es, -ing, -ed e'fju:z [i'f-], -iz, -iŋ, -d
effusion, -s i'fju:ʒən [e'f-], -z
effusive, -ly, -ness i'fju:siv [e'f-], -li, -nis
Efik 'efik
eft, -s eft, -s
e.g. 'i:'dʒi: [fərig'za:mpl]
egad i'gæd
egalitarian i‚gæli'tɛərïən
Egan 'i:gən
Egbert 'egbə:t [-bət]
Egeria i(:)'dʒiərïə
Egerton 'edʒətn
Egeus (in Greek mythology) 'i:dʒju:s, (Shakespearian character) i(:)'dʒi:əs
egg (s. v.), -s, -ing, -ed, -er/s eg, -z, -iŋ, -d, -ə*/z
egg-cup, -s 'egkʌp, -s
Eggle|ton, -ston 'egl|tən, -stən
egg-plant, -s 'egplɑ:nt, -s
egg-shaped 'egʃeipt
eggshell, -s 'egʃel, -z
egg-spoon, -s 'eg-spu:n, -z
Egham 'egəm
Eglamore 'egləmɔ:* [-mɔə*]
eglantine (E.) 'egləntain
Eglingham (in Northumb.) 'eglindʒəm
Eglinton 'eglintən
Eglon 'eglɔn
Egmont 'egmɔnt [-mənt]
ego, -s 'egəu ['i:g-], -z
egoi|sm, -st/s 'egəui|zəm, -st/s
egoistic, -al, -ally ‚egəu'istik, -əl, -əli
Egon 'egən [-gɔn]
egoti|sm, -st/s 'egəuti|zəm, -st/s
egotistic, -al, -ally ‚egəu'tistik, -əl, -əli

egotiz|e [-is|e], -es, -ing, -ed 'egəutaiz, -iz, -iŋ, -d

egregious, -ly, -ness i'gri:dʒəs [-dʒjəs, -dʒiəs], -li, -nis

Egremont (in Cheshire, Cumberland) 'egrəmɔnt [-grim-]

egress, -es 'i:gres, -iz

egression, -s i(:)'greʃən, -z

egressive i(:)'gresiv

egret, -s 'i:gret ['eg-], -s

Egton 'egtən

Egypt 'i:dʒipt

Egyptian, -s i'dʒipʃən, -z

egyptolog|ist/s, -y ,i:dʒip'tɔlədʒ|ist/s, -i

eh ei

eider, -s 'aidə*, -z

eiderdown, -s 'aidədaun, -z

eider-duck, -s 'aidə'dʌk [in contrast '---], -s

eidograph, -s 'aidəugrɑ:f [-græf], -s

eidol|on, -ons, -a ai'dəul|ɔn, -ɔnz, -ə

Eifel 'aifəl

Eiffel Tower, -s 'aifəl'tauə*, -z

Eiger 'aigə*

eight, -s eit, -s

eighteen, -s, -th/s 'ei'ti:n [also 'eit-, ei't-, according to sentence-stress], -z, -θ/s

eightfold 'eitfəuld

eighth, -s, -ly eitθ, -s, -li

eightieth, -s 'eitiiθ [-tjiθ, -tïəθ, -tjəθ], -s

eightish 'eitiʃ

eight|pence, -penny 'eit|pəns, -pəni

eight|y, -ies 'eit|i, -iz

Note.—In the N. of England often 'eitti.

Eilean (near Inverness) 'i:lən

Eileen 'aili:n

Eiloart 'ailəuɑ:t

Einstein 'ainstain

Eire 'ɛərə

Eirene ai'ri:ni [,aiə'r-]

eirenicon, -s ai'ri:nikɔn [,aiə'r-, -'ren-], -z

Eisenhower 'aizən,hauə*

eisteddfod, -s [-au] ais'teðvɔd [-vəd] (Welsh əis'teðvɔd), -z [-ai] (-ai)

either 'aiðə* ['i:ðə*]

ejaculat|e, -es, -ing, -ed i'dʒækjuleit, -s, -iŋ, -id

ejaculation, -s i,dʒækju'leiʃən, -z

ejaculative i'dʒækjulətiv [-leit-]

ejaculatory i'dʒækjulətəri [-leitəri]

eject (s.), -s 'i:dʒekt, -s

eject (v.), -s, -ing, -ed, -or/s; -ment/s i(:)'dʒekt, -s, -iŋ, -id, -ə*/z; -mənt/s

ejection, -s i(:)'dʒekʃən, -z

ek|e (v. adv.), -es, -ing, -ed i:k, -s, -iŋ, -t

Ekron 'ekrɔn

elabor|ate (adj.), -ately, -ateness i'læbər|it, -itli [-ətli], -itnis

elaborat|e (v.), -es, -ing, -ed, -or/s i'læbəreit, -s, -iŋ, -id, -ə*/z

elaboration, -s i,læbə'reiʃən [-bɔ'r-], -z

elaborative i'læbərətiv [-reit-]

Elah 'i:lə

Elaine e'lein

Elam, -ite/s 'i:ləm, -ait/s

élan ei'lɑ̃:ŋ [-'lɔ̃:ŋ] (elɑ̃)

eland (E.), -s 'i:lənd, -z

elaps|e, -es, -ing, -ed i'læps, -iz, -iŋ, -t

elastic (s. adj.), -s, -ally i'læstik [-'lɑ:s-], -s, -əli

elasticity ,elæs'tisiti [il-, ,i:l-, -ləs-, -lɑ:s-]

elat|e (adj. v.), -es, -ing, -ed/ly i'leit, -s, -iŋ, -id/li

elation i'leiʃən

Elba 'elbə

Elbe elb

elbow (s. v.), -s, -ing, -ed 'elbəu, -z, -iŋ, -d

elbow-chair, -s 'elbəu'tʃɛə* ['---], -z

elbow-grease 'elbəugri:s

elbow-room 'elbəurum [-ru:m]

Elcho 'elkəu

elder (s. adj.), -s 'eldə*, -z

elder-berr|y, -ies 'eldə,ber|i ['eldəbər-], -iz

elderl|y, -iness 'eldəl|i, -inis [-iz

elder-wine 'eldə'wain ['---]

eldest 'eldist

Eldon 'eldən

El Dorado ,eldə'rɑ:dəu [-dɔ'r-]

Eldred 'eldrid [-red]

Eldridge 'eldridʒ

Eleanor 'elinə* [-lən-]

Eleanora ,eliə'nɔ:rə [-ljə-]

Eleazar ,eli'eizə*

elecampane, -s ,elikæm'pein, -z

elect (s. adj. v.), -s, -ing, -ed, -or/s; -ive/ly i'lekt, -s, -iŋ, -id, -ə*/z; -iv/li

election, -s i'lekʃən, -z

electioneer, -s, -ing, -ed, -er/s i,lek-ʃə'niə* [-ʃɲ'iə*], -z, -riŋ, -d, -rə*/z

electoral i'lektərəl

electorate, -s i'lektərit, -s

Electra i'lektrə

electric, -al, -ally i'lektrik [ə'lek-], -əl, -əli

electrician, -s ilek'triʃən [,elek-, ,i:lek-, ,elik-], -z

electricity ilek'trisiti [,elek-, ,i:lek-, ,elik-, -'trizi-, -'trizə-, -'trisə-]

electrification, -s i,lektrifi'keiʃən, -z

electri|fy, -fies, -fying, -fied; -fiable i'lektri|fai, -faiz, -faiiŋ, -faid; -faiəbl

electro-biology i'lektrəʊbai'ɔlədʒi
electro-chemistry i'lektrəʊ'kemistri
electrocut|e, -es, -ing, -ed i'lektrəkju:t, -s, -iŋ, -id
electrocution, -s i,lektrə'kju:ʃən, -z
electrode, -s i'lektrəud, -z
electro-dynamic, -s i'lektrəʊdai'næmik [di'n-], -s
electro-kinetics i'lektrəʊkai'netiks
electrolier, -s i,lektrəʊ'liə*, -z
electrolys|e, -es, -ing, -ed i'lektrəʊlaiz, -iz, -iŋ, -d
electrolys|is, -es ilek'trɔlis|is [,el-, ,i:l-, -ləs-], -i:z
electrolyte, -s i'lektrəʊlait, -s
electrolytic i,lektrəʊ'litik
electro-magnet, -s, -ism i'lektrəʊ'mægnit [i'lektrəʊ,m-], -s, -izəm
electro-magnetic i'lektrəʊmæg'netik [-məg-]
electrometer, -s ilek'trɔmitə* [,el-, ,i:l-], iz
electromotive i'lektrəʊ'məutiv
electro-motor, -s i'lektrəʊ'məutə* [i'lektrəʊ,m-], -z
electron, -s i'lektrɔn, -z
electronic, -s ilek'trɔnik [,el-, ,i:l-], -s
electrophone, -s i'lektrəfəun, -z
electrophorus, -es ilek'trɔfərəs [,el-, ,i:l-], -iz
electroplat|e (s. v.), -es, -ing, -ed, -er/s i'lektrəʊpleit [i'lektrəʊ'p-], -s, -iŋ, -id, -ə*/z
electro-polar i'lektrəʊ'pəʊlə*
electro-positive i'lektrəʊ'pozətiv [-zit-]
electroscope, -s i'lektrəskəup, -s
electrostatic, -s i'lektrəʊ'stætik, -s
electro-therapeutic, -s i'lektrəʊθerə'pju:tik, -s
electro-therapy i'lektrəʊ'θerəpi
electro-thermal i'lektrəʊ'θə:məl
electrotype, -s i'lektrəʊtaip, -s
electrum i'lektrəm
electuar|y, -ies i'lektjuər|i [-tjwər-], -iz
eleemosynary ,elii:'mɔsinəri [,eli:'m-, ,eli'm-, -'mɔzi-]
elegan|ce, -t/ly 'eligən|s, -t/li
elegiac (s. adj.), -s, -al ,eli'dʒaiək, -s, -əl
elegist, -s 'elidʒist, -s
elegit i'li:dʒit [e'l-]
elegiz|e [-is|e], -es, -ing, -ed 'elidʒaiz, -iz, -iŋ, -d
eleg|y, -ies 'elidʒ|i, -iz
element, -s 'elimənt, -s
element|al (s. adj.), -als-, -ally, ,eli-'ment|l, -lz, -əli
elementar|y, -ily, -iness ,eli'mentər|i, -ili, -inis

elemi 'elimi
elenchus i'leŋkəs
Eleonora ,eliə'nɔ:rə [-ljə-]
elephant, -s 'elifənt, -s
elephantiasis ,elifən'taiəsis [-fæn-]
elephantine ,eli'fæntain
Eleusinian ,elju(:)'siniən [-njən]
Eleusis e'lju:sis [i'l-]
elevat|e, -es, -ing, -ed, -or/s; -ory 'eliveit, -s, -iŋ, -id, -ə*/z; -əri
elevation, -s ,eli'veiʃən, -z
eleven, -s, -th/s i'levn, -z, -θ/s
elevenish i'levniʃ
eleven|pence, -penny i'levn|pəns [-vm|p-], -pəni
elevenses i'levnziz
elf, -ves elf, -vz
elfin (s. adj.), -s 'elfin, -z
elfish 'elfiʃ
elf|-land, -lock/s 'elf-|lænd, -lɔk/s
Elfrida el'fri:də
Elgar 'elgə* [-gɑ:*]
Elgie 'eldʒi, 'elgi
Elgin, -shire 'elgin, -ʃiə* [-ʃə*]
Elham (in Kent) 'i:ləm
Eli 'i:lai
Elia 'i:ljə [-liə]
Eliab i'laiæb [e'l-, -'lai-əb]
Eliakim i'laiəkim [e'l-]
Elias i'laiəs [e'l-, -aiæs]
Eliashow e'laiəʃəʊ
Elibank 'elibæŋk
elicit, -s, -ing, -ed i'lisit [e'l-], -s, -iŋ, -id
elicitation i,lisi'teiʃən [e,l-]
elid|e, -es, -ing, -ed; -able i'laid, -z, -iŋ, -id; -əbl
Elie 'i:li
Eliezer ,eli'i:zə*
eligibility ,elidʒə'biliti [-dʒi'b-, -lət-]
eligib|le, -ly, -leness 'elidʒəb|l [-dʒib-], -li, -lnis
Elihu i'laihju: [e'l-]
Elijah i'laidʒə
Eliman 'elimən
Elimelech i'liməlek [e'l-]
eliminat|e, -es, -ing, -ed i'limineit [e'l-], -s, -iŋ, -id
elimination, -s i,limi'neiʃən, [e,l-], -z
Elinor 'elinə*
Eliot(t) 'eljət [-liət]
Eliphaz 'elifæz
Elis 'i:lis
Elisabeth i'lizəbəθ
Elisha (prophet) i'laiʃə, (place in Northumb.) e'liʃə
elision, -s i'liʒən, -z
Elissa i'lisə
élite ei'li:t (elit)

elixir, -s i'liksə* [e'l-], -z
Eliza i'laizə
Elizabeth i'lizəbəθ
Elizabethan, -s iˌlizə'bi:θən, -z
Elizabethian, -s iˌlizə'bi:θjən [-θïən], -z
elk, -s elk, -s
Elkanah el'kɑ:nə [-'kein-]
Elkhart 'elkhɑ:t
Elkin 'elkin
Elkington 'elkiŋtən
Elkins 'elkinz
ell, -s el, -z
Ella 'elə
Ellaline 'eləli:n
Ellam 'eləm
Elland, -un 'elənd, -ən
Ellangowan ˌelən'gau-ən
Ellen, -borough 'elin, -bərə
Ellery 'eləri
Ellesmere 'elzmiə*
Ellet 'elit
Ellice 'elis
Ellicott 'elikət [-kɔt]
Elliman 'elimən
Ellingham (in Northumb.) 'elindʒəm,
 (surname) 'eliŋəm
Elliot(t), -son 'eljət [-lïət], -sn
ellipse, -s i'lips, -iz
ellips|is, -es i'lips|is, -i:z
ellipsoid, -s i'lipsoid, -z
ellipsoidal ˌelip'soidl [ilip's-]
elliptic, -al, -ally i'liptik, -əl, -əli
ellipticity ˌelip'tisiti [ilip't-]
Ellis, -on, -ton 'elis, -n, -tən
Ellsworth 'elzwə:θ
Ellwood 'elwud
elm (E.), -s elm, -z
Elmes elmz
Elmhurst 'elmhə:st
Elmina el'mi:nə
Elmo 'elməu
Elmore 'elmɔ:* [-mɔə*]
Elmsley 'elmzli
Elmwood 'elmwud
elocution ˌelə'kju:ʃən
elocutionary ˌeləu'kju:ʃnəri [-ʃnəri,
 -ʃnəri]
elocutionist, -s ˌeləu'kju:ʃŋist [-ʃənist,
 -ʃnist], -s
Elohim e'ləuhim
Eloi i:'ləuai ['i:ləuai, 'i:lɔi]
Eloisa ˌeləu'i:zə [-'i:sə]
elongat|e, -es, -ing, -ed 'i:lɔŋgeit, -s, -iŋ,
 -id
elongation, -s ˌi:lɔŋ'geiʃən, -z
elop|e, -es, -ing, -ed, -ement/s i'ləup,
 -s, -iŋ, -t, -mənt/s
eloquen|ce, -t/ly 'eləukwən|s, -t/li

Elphin, -ston(e) 'elfin, -stən
Elsa (English name) 'elsə, (German
 name) 'elzə ['ɛlza:]
else, -'s els, -iz
elsewhere 'els'wɛə* [-s'hw-]
Elsie 'elsi
Elsinore ˌelsi'nɔ:* [-'nɔə*, '---]
 Note.—The stressing ˌ-'-' has to be
 used in Shakespeare's 'Hamlet'.
Elsmere 'elzmiə*
Elspeth 'elspəθ [-peθ]
Elstree 'elstri: ['elz-, -tri]
Elswick 'elsik, 'elzik, 'elzwik
 Note.—Elswick in Northumb. is
 locally 'elsik or 'elzik.
Elsworthy 'elzˌwə:ði
Eltham (in Kent) 'eltəm [-lθəm]
Elton 'eltən
elucidat|e, -es, -ing, -ed, -or/s i'lu:sideit
 [-'lju:-], -s, -iŋ, -id, -ə*/z
elucidation, -s iˌlu:si'deiʃən [-ˌlju:-], -z
elucidative i'lu:sideitiv [-'lju:-, -dət-]
elucidatory i'lu:sideitəri [-'lju:-]
elud|e, -es, -ing, -ed i'lu:d [-'lju:d], -z,
 -iŋ, -id
elusion, -s i'lu:ʒən [-'lju:-], -z
elusive, -ly, -ness i'lu:siv [-'lju:-], -li,
 -nis
elusory i'lu:səri ['lju:-]
elvan 'elvən
Elvedon (in Suffolk) 'elvdən ['eldən]
elver, -s 'elvə*, -z
elves (plur. of elf) elvz
Elv|ey, -in 'elv|i, -in
Elvira el'vaiərə, el'viərə
elvish 'elviʃ
Elwes 'elwiz [-wez]
Ely 'i:li
Elyot 'eljət [-lïət]
Elysi|an, -um i'lizï|ən [-zj|-], -əm
elzevir (E.) 'elzivïə* [-zəv-]
em, -s em, -z
'em (weak form of them) əm [m]
emaciat|e, -es, -ing, -ed i'meiʃieit [e'm-,
 -'meiʃjeit, -'meisieit, -'meisjeit,
 -'mæsieit], -s, -iŋ, -id
emaciation iˌmeisi'eiʃən [e,m-, -ˌmeiʃi-,
 -ˌmæsi-]
emanat|e, -es, -ing, -ed; -ive 'eməneit
 [rarely 'i:m-], -s, -iŋ, -id; -iv
emanation, -s ˌemə'neiʃən [rarely
 ˌi:m-], -z
emancipat|e, -es, -ing, -ed, -or/s
 i'mænsipeit [e'm-], -s, -iŋ, -id, -ə*/z
emancipation, -s iˌmænsi'peiʃən [e,m-],
 -z
Emanuel i'mænjŭəl [e'm-, -njwəl,
 -njuel]

emasculate (*adj.*) i'mæskjulit [-'mɑ:s-]
emasculat|e (*v.*), -es, -ing, -ed, -or/s
i'mæskjuleit [-'mɑ:s-], -s, -iŋ, -id,
-ə*/z
emasculation, -s i͵mæskju'leiʃən
[-͵mɑ:s-], -z
Emaus 'emɔ:s
embalm, -s, -ing, -ed, -er/s, -ment/s
im'bɑ:m [em-], -z, -iŋ, -d, -ə*/z,
-mənt/s
embank, -s, -ing, -ed, -ment/s im-
'bæŋk [em-], -s, -iŋ, -t [-'bæŋt],
-mənt/s
embarcation, -s ͵embɑ:'keiʃən, -z
embargo (*s.*), -s em'bɑ:gəu [im-], -z
embargo (*v.*), -es, -ing, -ed em'bɑ:gəu
[im-], -z, -iŋ, -d
embark, -s, -ing, -ed im'bɑ:k [em-], -s,
-iŋ, -t
embarkation, -s ͵embɑ:'keiʃən, -z
embarrass, -es, -ing, -ed, -ment/s im-
'bærəs [em-], -iz, -iŋ, -t, -mənt/s
embass|y, -ies 'embəs|i, -iz
embatt|le, -les, -ling, -led im'bæt|l
[em-], -lz, -l̩iŋ [-liŋ], -ld
embay, -s, -ing, -ed im'bei [em-], -z, -iŋ,
-d
embed, -s, -ding, -ded, -ment im'bed
[em-], -z, -iŋ, -id, -mənt
embellish, -es, -ing, -ed, -er/s, -ment/s
im'beliʃ, -iz, -iŋ, -t, -ə*/z, -mənt/s
ember, -s 'embə*, -z
Ember|-day/s, -week/s 'embə|dei/z,
-wi:k/s
embezz|le, -les, -ling, -led, -ler/s,
-lement/s im'bez|l [em-], -lz, -l̩iŋ
[-liŋ], -ld, -l̩ə*/z [-lə*/z], -lmənt/s
embitter, -s, -ing, -ed, -er/s, -ment
im'bitə* [em-], -z, -riŋ, -d, -rə*/z,
-mənt
emblaz|on, -ons, -oning, -oned, -on-
ment/s; -onry im'bleiz|ən [em-],
-ənz, -n̩iŋ [-niŋ], -ənd, -ənmənt/s;
-ənri
emblem, -s 'embləm [-lem, -lim], -z
emblematic, -al, -ally ͵embli'mætik
[-lə'm-], -əl, -əli
emblematiz|e [-is|e], -es, -ing, -ed
em'blemətaiz ['emblem-], -iz, -iŋ,-d
emblement, -s 'emblmənt, -s
embod|y, -ies, -ying, -ied, -iment/s
im'bɒd|i [em-], -iz, -iiŋ, -id, -imənt/s
embold|en, -ens, -ening, -ened im-
'bəuld|ən [em-], -ənz, -n̩iŋ [-niŋ], -ənd
embolism, -s 'embəlizəm, -z
embonpoint ͵ɔ̃:mbɔ̃:m'pwɛ̃:ŋ [͵ɔ:m-
bɔ:m-, ͵ɔmbɔm-, -'pwɑ̃:ŋ, -'pwɑ:ŋ,
-'pwɔŋ, -'pwæŋ] (ãbɔ̃pwɛ̃)

embosom, -s, -ing, -ed im'buzəm
[em-], -z, -iŋ, -d
emboss, -es, -ing, -ed, -er/s, -ment/s
im'bɒs [em-], -iz, -iŋ, -t, -ə*/z,
-mənt/s
embouchure, -s ͵ɔmbu'ʃuə* [-'ʃjuə*]
(ãbuʃy:r), -z
emb|owel, -owels, -owelling, -elled
im'b|auəl [em-], -auil, -aul], -z,
-auəliŋ [-auiliŋ], -auəld [-auild, -auld]
embower, -s, -ing, -ed im'bauə* [em-],
-z, -riŋ, -d
embrac|e (*s. v.*), -es, -ing, -ed, -er/s,
-ement im'breis [em-], -iz, -iŋ, -t,
-ə*/z, -mənt
embranchment, -s im'brɑ:ntʃmənt
[em-], -s
embrasure, -s im'breiʒə* [em-, -ʒuə,
-ʒuə*], -z
embrocat|e, -es, -ing, -ed 'embrəukeit,
-s, -iŋ, -id
embrocation, -s ͵embrəu'keiʃən, -z
embroglio, -s em'brəuljəu [im-, -liəu], -z
embroid|er, -ers, -ering, -ered, -erer/s
im'brɔid|ə* [em-], -əz, -əriŋ, -əd,
-ərə*/z
embroider|y, -ies im'brɔidər|i [em-], -iz
embroil, -s, -ing, -ed, -ment/s im'brɔil
[em-], -z, -iŋ, -d, -mənt/s
embryo, -s 'embriəu, -z
embryolog|ist/s, -y ͵embri'ɔlədʒ|ist/s, -i
embry|on, -ons, -a 'embri|ɔn [-ən],
-ɔnz [-ənz], -ə
embryonic ͵embri'ɔnik
Embury 'embəri
Emeer, -s e'miə* [i'm-, 'emiə*], -z
Emeline 'emili:n
emend, -s, -ing, -ed; -able i(:)'mend, -z,
-iŋ, -id; -əbl
emendat|e, -es, -ing, -ed, -or/s 'i:men-
deit, -s, -iŋ, -id, -ə*/z
emendation, -s ͵i:men'deiʃən, -z
emendatory i(:)'mendətəri
emerald, -s 'emərəld ['emrəld], -z
emerg|e, -es, -ing, -ed i'mə:dʒ, -iz, -iŋ, -d
emergen|ce, -t/ly i'mə:dʒən|s, -t/li
emergenc|y, -ies i'mə:dʒəns|i, -iz
emeritus i(:)'meritəs
emerod, -s 'emərɔd, -z
emersion, -s i(:)'mə:ʃən, -z
Emerson 'eməsn
emery (E.), -paper/s, -powder, -wheel/s
'eməri, -͵peipə*/z, -͵paudə*, -wi:l/z
[-hw-]
emetic (*s. adj.*), -s, -al, -ally i'metik, -s,
-əl, -əli
émeute, -s ei'mə:t [*sometimes facetiously*
i:'mju:t] (emø:t), -s

emigrant (s. adj.), -s 'emigrənt, -s
emigrat|e, -es, -ing, -ed, -or/s 'emigreit,
 -s, -iŋ, -id, -ə*/z
emigratory 'emigrətəri [-greit-]
emigration, -s ˌemi'greiʃən, -z
émigré, -s 'emigrei, -z
Emilia i'miliə [-ljə]
Emily 'emili
eminen|ce, -ces, -cy, -t/ly 'eminən|s,
 -siz, -si, -t/li
Emir, -s e'miə* [i'm-, 'emiə*], -z   [-s
emirate ˌ-s e'miərit [i'm-, 'emiər-, -reit],
emissar|y (s. adj.), -ies 'emisər|i, -iz
emission, -s i'miʃən [i:'m-], -z
emissive i'misiv [i:'m-]
emit, -s, -ting, -ted, -ter/s i'mit [i:'m-],
 -s, -iŋ, -id, -ə*/z
emitter-valve, -s i'mitəvælv [i:'m-], -z
Emley 'emli
Emma 'emə
Emmanuel (biblical name) i'mænjŭəl
 [e'm, -jwəl, -juel], (Cambridge college)
 i'mænjŭəl [-njul]
Emmaus e'meiəs
Emmeline 'emili:n
emmet (E.), -s 'emit, -s
Emm|ie, -y 'em|i, -i
emollient (s. adj.), -s i'mɔliənt [e'm-,
 -ljənt], -s
emolument, -s i'mɔljumənt [e'm-], -s
Emory 'eməri
emotion, -s; -less i'məuʃən, -z; -lis
emo|tional, -tionally i'məuʃənl [-ʃnəl,
 -ʃn̩l, -ʃn̩l, -ʃənəl], -ʃn̩əli [-ʃnəli, ʃn̩li,
 -ʃnl̩i, -ʃənəli]
emotionalism i'məuʃn̩əlizəm[-ʃnəl-,-ʃn̩l-,
 -ʃnl-, -ʃənəl-]
emotive i'məutiv
empan|el, -els, -elling, -elled, -el-
 ment/s im'pæn|l [em-], -lz, -l̩iŋ, -ld,
 -lmənt/s
Empedocles em'pedəukli:z
emperor, -s 'empərə*, -z
emphasis 'emfəsis
emphasiz|e [-is|e], -es, -ing, -ed 'em-
 fəsaiz, -iz, -iŋ, -d
emphatic, -al, -ally, -alness im'fætik
 [em-], -əl, -əli, -əlnis
emphysema, -s ˌemfi'si:mə, -z
empire, -s 'empaiə*, -z
empiric (s. adj.), -s, -al, -ally em'pirik
 [im-], -s, -əl, -əli
empirici|sm, -st/s em'pirisi|zəm [im-],
 -st/s
emplacement, -s im'pleismənt [em-], -s
employ (s. v.), -s, -ing, -ed, -er/s,
 -ment/s; -able im'plɔi [em-], -z, -iŋ,
 -d, -ə*/z, -mənt/s; -əbl

employé, -s ɔm'plɔiei [ɔ̃:m-, ɔ:m-]
 (ãplwaje), -z
employee, -s ˌemplɔi'i : [em'plɔii:, im-
 'plɔii:], -z
emporium, -s em'pɔ:rïəm, -z
empower, -s, -ing, -ed im'pauə* [em-],
 -z, -riŋ, -d
empress, -es 'empris, -iz
Empson 'empsn
emption 'empʃən
empt|y (s. adj. v.), -ier, -iest, -ily,
 -iness; -ies, -ying, -ied 'empt|i, -ïə*
 [-jə*], -iist [-jist], -ili, -inis; -iz, -iiŋ
 [-jiŋ], -id
empty-handed 'empti'hændid
empyema ˌempai'i:mə
empyrea|l, -n ˌempai'ri(:)ə|l [-pi'r-, em-
 'pirïə-], -n
Emsworth 'emzwə(:)θ
emu, -s 'i:mju:, -z
emulat|e, -es, -ing, -ed, -or/s 'emjuleit,
 -s, -iŋ, -id, -ə*/z
emulation ˌemju'leiʃən
emulative 'emjulətiv [-leit-]
emulous, -ly 'emjuləs, -li
emulsi|fy, -fies, -fying, -fied i'mʌlsi|fai,
 -faiz, -faiiŋ, -faid
emulsion, -s i'mʌlʃən, -z
emunctor|y (s. adj.), -ies i'mʌŋktər|i, -iz
enab|le, -les, -ling, -led i'neib|l [e'n-],
 -lz, -liŋ [-l̩iŋ], -ld
enact, -s, -ing, -ed, -or/s, -ment/s;
 -ive i'nækt [e'n-], -s, -iŋ, -id, -ə*/z,
 -mənt/s; -iv
enam|el(s.v.),-els,-elling,-elled,-eller/s,
 -ellist/s i'næm|əl, -əlz, -l̩iŋ [-əliŋ],
 -əld, -lə*/z [-ələ*/z], -list/s [-əlist/s]
enamour, -s, -ing, -ed i'næmə* [e'n-], -z,
 -riŋ, -d
Encaenia en'si:njə [-nïə]
encag|e, -es, -ing, -ed in'keidʒ [en-],
 -iz, -iŋ, -d
encamp, -s, -ing, -ed, -ment/s in'kæmp
 [en-], -s, -iŋ, -t [-'kæmt], -mənt/s
encas|e, -es, -ing, -ed, -ement/s in'keis
 [en-], -iz, -iŋ, -t, -mənt/s
encaustic (s. adj.), -s, -ally en'kɔ:stik,
 -s, -əli
enceinte (s. adj.), -s ã:ŋ'sɛ̃:nt [ã:n'sɛ̃:nt,
 ɔ̃:ŋ'sɛ̃:nt,   ɔ̃:n'sɛ̃:nt,   ɑ:n'sænt,
 ɔ:ŋ'sænt, ɔn'sænt, ɔn'sænt] (ãsɛ̃:t), -s
Enceladus en'selədəs
encephalic ˌenkə'fælik [ˌenki'f-, ˌense'f-,
 ˌensi'f-]
encephalitis ˌenkefə'laitis [en ˌkef-,
 ˌensef-, en ˌsef-]
encephalogram, -s en'sefələugræm [in's-,
 en'k-, in'k-], -z

encephalograph, -s en'sefələugrɑːf [in's-, en'k-, in'k-, -græf], -s

enchain, -s, -ing, -ed, -ment in'tʃein [en-], -z, -iŋ, -d, -mənt

enchant, -s, -ing, -ed, -er/s, -ress/es, -ment/s in'tʃɑːnt [en-], -s, -iŋ, -id, -ə*/z, -ris/iz, -mənt/s

enchiridion, -s ,enkaiə'ridiən [,eŋk-, -diɔn], -z

encircle|le, -les, -ling, -led, -lement/s in'səːk|l [en-], -lz, -liŋ, -ld, -lmənt/s

Encke 'eŋkə

enclasp, -s, -ing, -ed in'klɑːsp [en-], -s, -iŋ, -t

enclave, -s 'enkleiv ['ɔŋ-klɑːv, 'ɔ̃ːη-k-, 'ɑːŋ-k-, 'ɑ̃ːη-k-, -'-] (ãklɑːv), -z

enclitic (s. adj.), -s, -ally in'klitik [iŋ-, en-, -n'tl-], -s, -əli

enclos|e, -es, -ing, -ed, -er/s in'kləuz [iŋ-, en-], -iz, -iŋ, -d, -ə*/z

enclosure, -s in'kləuʒə* [iŋ-, en-], -z

encom|iast/s, -ium/s en'kəum|iæst/s [eŋ-], -jəm/z [-ïəm/z]

encompass, -es, -ing, -ed in'kʌmpəs [iŋ-, en-], -iz, -iŋ, -t

encore (s. v.), -es, -ing, -ed ɔŋ'kɔː* [-'kɔə*, '—], -z, -riŋ, -d

encore (interj.) ɔŋ'kɔː* [-'kɔə*]

encount|er (s. v.), -ers, -ering, -ered in-'kaunt|ə* [iŋ-, en-], -əz, -əriŋ, -əd

encourag|e, -es, -ing/ly, -ed, -er/s, -ement/s in'kʌridʒ [iŋ-, en-], -iz, -iŋ/li, -d, -ə*/z, -mənt|s

encroach, -es, -ing/ly, -ed, -er/s, -ment/s in'krəutʃ [iŋ-, en-], -iz, -iŋ/li, -t, -ə*/z, -mənt/s

encrust, -s, -ing, -ed in'krʌst [iŋ-, en-], -s, -iŋ, -id

encumb|er, -ers, -ering, -ered in'kʌmb|ə* [iŋ-, en-], -əz, -əriŋ, -əd

encumbrance, -s in'kʌmbrəns [iŋ-, en-], -iz

encyclic, -s, -al/s en'siklik [in-], -s, -əl/z

encyclop(a)edia, -s, -n en,saikləu'piːdjə [in,saik-, ,ensaik-, -klu'p-, -diə], -z, -n

encyclop(a)edic, -al en,saikləu'piːdik [in,saik-, ,ensaik-, -klu'p-], -əl

encyclop(a)edi|sm, -st/s en,saikləu'piː-di|zəm [in,saik-, ,ensaik-, -klu'p-], -st/s

end (s. v.), -s, -ing, -ed end, -z, -iŋ, -id

endang|er, -ers, -ering, -ered, -erer/s, -erment in'deindʒ|ə* [en-], -əz, -əriŋ, -əd, -ərə*/z, -əmənt

endeav|our (s. v.), -ours, -ouring, -oured in'dev|ə*, -əz, -əriŋ, -əd

Endell 'endl

endemic (s. adj.), -s, -al, -ally, en-'demik, -s, -əl, -əli

Enderby 'endə(ː)bi

endermic, -al, -ally en'dəːmik, -əl, -əli

Endicott 'endikət [-kɔt]

ending (s.), -s 'endiŋ, -z

endive, -s 'endiv, -z

endless, -ly, -ness 'endlis, -li, -nis

endlong 'endlɔŋ

endmost 'endməust

endocrine 'endəukrain

endogamy en'dɔgəmi

Endor 'endɔː*

endors|e, -es, -ing, -ed, -er/s, ement/s in'dɔːs [en-], -iz, -iŋ, -t, -ə*/z, -mənt/s

endorsee, -s ,endɔː'siː, -z

endow, -s, -ing, -ed, -ment/s in'dau [en-], -z, -iŋ, -d, -mənt/s

endower, -s in'dau-ə* [en-], -z

endu|le, -es, -ing, -ed in'dju: [en-], -z, -iŋ [-'djuiŋ], -d

endurab|le, -ly, -leness in'djuərəb|l [en-, -'djoər-, -'djɔːr-, -'djəːr-], -li, -lnis

endur|e, -es, -ing, -ed, -er/s; -ance in'djuə* [en-, -'djoə*, -'djɔː*, -'djəː*], -z, -riŋ, -d, -rə*/z; -rəns

end|ways, -wise 'end|weiz, -waiz

Endymion en'dimiən [-mjən]

Eneas i(ː)'niːæs ['iːniæs]

Eneid 'iːniid [-njid]

enema, -s 'enimə [i'niːmə], -z

enem|y, -ies 'enim|i [-nəm-], -iz

energetic, -al, -ally ,enə'dʒetik [-nəː'dʒ-], -əl, -əli

energiz|e [-is|e], -es, -ing, -ed, -er/s 'enədʒaiz [-nəː'dʒ-], -iz, -iŋ, -d, -ə*/z

energumen, -s ,enəː'gjuːmen, -z

energ|y, -ies 'enədʒ|i, -iz

enervat|e, -es, -ing, -ed 'enəːveit [-nəv-], -s, -iŋ, -id

enervation ,enəː'veiʃən [-nə'v-]

enfeeb|le, -les, -ling, -led, -lement in-'fiːb|l [en-], -lz, -liŋ [-ļiŋ], -ld, -lmənt

enfeoff, -s, -ing, -ed, -ment/s in'fef [en-, -'fiːf], -s, -iŋ, -t, -mənt/s

Enfield 'enfiːld

enfilad|e (s. v.), -es, -ing, -ed ,enfi'leid, -z, -iŋ, -id

enfold, -s, -ing, -ed, -ment in'fəuld [en-], -z, -iŋ, -id, -mənt

enforc|e, -es, -ing, -ed, -edly, -ement in'fɔːs [en-], -iz, -iŋ, -t, -idli, -mənt

enfranchis|e, -es, -ing, -ed in'fræntʃaiz [en-], -iz, -iŋ, -d

enfranchisement, -s in'fræntʃizmənt [en-], -s

Engadine 'eŋgədi:n

engag|e, -es, -ing/ly, -ed, -er/s, -ement/s in'geidʒ [iŋ-, en-], -iz, -iŋ/li, -d, -ə*/z, -mənt/s

Engedi en'gi:di [eŋ'g-, -'ged-]

engend|er, -ers, -ering, -ered in'dʒend|ə* [en-], -əz, -əriŋ, -əd

engin|e (s. v.), **-es, -ing, -ed; -ery** 'endʒin, -z, -iŋ, -d; -əri

engine-driver, -s 'endʒin,draivə*, -z

engineer (s. v.), **-s, -ing, -ed** ,endʒi'niə*, -z, -riŋ, -d

engird, -s, -ing, -ed in'gə:d [iŋ-, en-], -z, -iŋ, -id

England, -er/s 'iŋglənd [-ŋl-, rarely 'eŋ-], -ə*/z

Engledow 'eŋgldau

Engle|field, -wood 'eŋgl|fi:ld, -wud

English 'iŋgliʃ [-ŋl-, rarely 'eŋ-]

english, -es, -ing, -ed 'iŋgliʃ [-ŋl-, rarely 'eŋ-], -iz, -iŋ, -t

English|man, -men 'iŋgliʃ|mən [-ŋl-, rarely 'eŋ-], -mən [-men]

Englishry 'iŋgliʃri [-ŋl-, rarely 'eŋ-]

English|woman, -women 'iŋgliʃ|-,wumən [-ŋl-, rarely 'eŋ-], -,wimin

engraft, -s, -ing, -ed, -ment in'grɑ:ft [iŋ-, en-], -s, -iŋ, -id, -mənt

engrail|ed in'greild [iŋ-, en-]

engrain, -s -ing, -ed in'grein [iŋ-, en-], -z, -iŋ, -d

engrav|e, -es, -ing/s, -ed, -er/s; -ery in'greiv [iŋ-, en-], -z, -iŋ/z, -d, -ə*/z; -əri

engross, -es, -ing, -ed, -er/s, -ment/s in'grəus [iŋ-, en-], -iz, -iŋ, -t, -ə*/z, -mənt/s

engulf, -s, -ing, -ed, -ment in'gʌlf [iŋ-, en-], -s, -iŋ, -t, -mənt

enhanc|e, -es, -ing, -ed, -ement/s in-'hɑ:ns [en-, -'hæns], -iz, -iŋ, -t, -mənt/s

enharmonic, -al, -ally ,enhɑ:'mɔnik ['enhɑ:'m-], -əl, -əli

Enid 'i:nid

enigma, -s i'nigmə [e'n-], -z

enigmatic, -al, -ally ,enig'mætik, -əl, -əli

enigmatist, -s i'nigmətist [e'n-], -s

enigmatiz|e [-is|e], -es, -ing, -ed i'nigmətaiz [e'n-], -iz, -iŋ, -d

Enim 'i:nim

enjambment, -s in'dʒæmmənt [en-], -s

enjoin, -s, -ing, -ed, -er/s in'dʒɔin [en-], -z, -iŋ, -d, -ə*/z

enjoy, -s, -ing, -ed, -er/s, -ment/s in'dʒɔi [en-], -z, -iŋ, -d, -ə*/z, -mənt/s

enjoyab|le, -ly, -leness in'dʒɔiəb|l [en-], -li, -lnis

enkind|le, -les, -ling, -led in'kind|l [en-], -lz, -liŋ, -ld

enlac|e, -es, -ing, -ed, -ement/s in'leis [en-], -iz, -iŋ, -t, -mənt/s

enlarg|e, -es, -ing, -ed, -er/s, -ement/s in'lɑ:dʒ [en-], -iz, -iŋ, -d, -ə*/z, -mənt/s

enlight|en, -ens, -ening, -ened, -enment in'lait|n [en-], -nz, -ŋiŋ [-niŋ], -nd, -nmənt

enlist, -s, -ing, -ed, -ment/s in'list [en-], -s, -iŋ, -id, -mənt/s

enliv|en, -ens, -ening, -ened, -ener/s in'laiv|n [en-], -nz, -ŋiŋ [-niŋ], -nd, -nə*/z [-nə*/z]

en masse ɑ̃:ŋ'mæs [ɔ̃:ŋ-, ɑ:ŋ-, ɔ:ŋ-, ɔŋ-] (ɑ̃mas)

enmesh, -es, -ing, -ed in'meʃ [en-], -iz, -iŋ, -t

enmit|y, -ies 'enmit|i, -iz

Ennis 'enis

Enniscorthy ,enis'kɔ:θi

Enniskillen ,enis'kilin

Ennius 'eniəs [-njəs]

ennob|le, -les, -ling, -led, -lement i'nəub|l [e'n-], -lz, -liŋ, -ld, -lmənt

ennui ɑ̃:'nwi: [ɔ̃:'n-, ɑ:'n-, ɔ:'n-, ɔ'n-'--] (ɑ̃nɥi)

Eno, -'s 'i:nəu, -z

Enoch 'i:nɔk

enormit|y, -ies i'nɔ:mit|i, -iz

enormous, -ly, -ness i'nɔ:məs, -li, -nis

Enos 'i:nɔs

enough i'nʌf [ə'nʌf, ŋ'ʌf]

enounc|e, -es, -ing, -ed i(:)'nauns, -iz, -iŋ, -t

enow i'nau

en passant ɑ̃:m'pæsɑ̃:ŋ [ɔ̃:m'pæsɔ̃:ŋ, ɑ:m'pæsɑ:ŋ, ɔ:m'pæsɔ:ŋ, ɔm'pæsɔŋ, -'pɑ:s-] (ɑ̃pɑsɑ̃)

enquir|e, -es, -ing, -ed, -er/s in'kwaiə* [iŋ-, en-], -z, -riŋ, -d, -rə*/z

enquir|y, -ies in'kwaiər|i [iŋ-, en-], -iz

enrag|e, -es, -ing, -ed in'reidʒ [en-], -iz, -iŋ, -d

enrapt in'ræpt [en-]

enrapt|ure, -ures, -uring, -ured in'ræp-tʃ|ə* [en-], -əz, -əriŋ, -əd

enregist|er, -ers, -ering, -ered in-'redʒist|ə* [en-], -əz, -əriŋ, -əd

enrich, -es, -ing, -ed, -ment in'ritʃ [en-], -iz, -iŋ, -t, -mənt

enrob|e, -es, -ing, -ed in'rəub [en-], -z, -iŋ, -d

enrol, -s, -ling, -led, -ment/s in'rəul [en-], -z, -iŋ, -d, -mənt/s en route ã:*n*'ru:t [ɔ̃:*n*'r-, ɑ:n'r-, ɔ:n'r-, ɔn'r-] (ãrut)

en|s, -tia en|z, -ʃïə [-ʃjə, -tïə, -tjə]

ensample, -s en'sɑ:mpl, -z

ensanguined in'sæŋgwind [en-]

ensconc|e, -es, -ing, -ed in'skɔns [en-], -iz, -iŋ, -t

ensemble, -s ã:*n*'sã:*m*bl [ɔ̃:*n*'sɔ̃:*m*bl, ɑ:n'sɑ:mbl, ɔ:n'sɔ:mbl, ɔn'sɔmbl] (ãsã:bl), -z

enshrin|e, -es, -ing, -ed, -ement in-'ʃrain [en-], -z, -iŋ, -d, -mənt

enshroud, -s, -ing, -ed in'ʃraud [en-], -z, -iŋ, -id

ensign (flag), -s 'ensain [in the navy 'ensn], -z

ensign (officer), -s; -cy, -cies, -ship/s 'ensain, -z; -si, -siz, -ʃip/s

ensign (v.), -s, -ing, -ed en'sain [in-], -z, -iŋ, -d

ensilage 'ensilidʒ

enslav|e, -es, -ing, -ed, -er/s, -ement in'sleiv [en-], -z, -iŋ, -d, -ə*/z, -mənt

ensnar|e, -es, -ing, -ed, -er/s in'snɛə* [en-], -z, -riŋ, -d, -rə*/z [-d

ensoul, -s, -ing, -ed in'səul [en-], -z, -iŋ,

ensu|e, -es, -ing, -ed in'sju: [en-, -'su:], -z, -iŋ [-'sjuiŋ, -'suiŋ], -d

ensur|e, -es, -ing, -ed in'ʃuə* [en-, -'ʃɔə*, -'ʃɔ:*], -z, -riŋ, -d

entablature, -s en'tæblətʃə* [in-, -blitʃ-, -tʃuə*, -tjuə*], -z

entail (s. v.), -s, -ing, -ed, -er/s, -ment in'teil [en-], -z, -iŋ, -d, -ə*/z, -mənt

entangl|le, -les, -ling, -led, -lement/s in'tæŋg|l [en-], -lz, -liŋ, -ld, -lmənt/s

entente, -s ã:*n*'tã:nt [ɔ̃:*n*'tɔ̃:nt, ɑ:n'tɑ:nt, ɔ:n'tɔ:nt, ɔn'tɔnt] (ãtã:t), -s

ent|er, -ers, -ering, -ered, -erer/s 'ent|ə*, -əz, -əriŋ, -əd, -ərə*/z

enteric en'terik

enteritis ,entə'raitis

enterology ,entə'rolədʒi

enterotomy ,entə'rotəmi

enterpris|e, -es, -ing/ly 'entəpraiz, -iz, -iŋ/li

entertain, -s, -ing/ly, -ed, -er/s, -ment/s ,entə'tein, -z, -iŋ/li, -d, -ə*/z, -mənt/s

enthral, -s, -ling, -led, -ment in'θrɔ:l [en-], -z, -iŋ, -d, -mənt

enthrall = enthral

enthron|e, -es, -ing, -ed, -ement/s in'θrəun [en-], -z, -iŋ, -d, -mənt/s

enthus|e, -es, -ing, -ed in'θju:z [en-], -iz, -iŋ, -d

enthusia|sm, -st/s in'θju:ziæ|zəm [en-, -'θu:-, -zjæ-], -st/s

enthusiastic, -al, -ally in,θju:zi'æstik [en-, -,θu:-, -i'ɑ:s-], -əl, -əli

entia (plur. of ens) 'enʃïə [-ʃjə, -tïə, -tjə]

entic|e, -es, -ing/ly, -ed, -er/s, -ement/s in'tais [en-], -iz, -iŋ/li, -t, -ə*/z, -mənt/s

entire, -ly, -ness in'taiə* [en-], -li, -nis

entiret|y, -ies in'taiətli [en-], -iz

Note.—There exists also a form in'taiərəti [en-], a recent innovation.

entit|le, -les, -ling, -led in'tait|l [en-], -lz, -liŋ [-liŋ], -ld

entit|y, -ies 'entit|i, -iz

entomb, -s, -ing, -ed, -ment/s in-'tu:m [en-], -z, -iŋ, -d, -mənt/s

entomologic|al, -ally ,entəmə'lodʒik|əl [-təuməu'l], -əli   [-i

entomolog|ist/s, -y ,entəu'molədʒ|ist/s,

entomologiz|e [-is|e], -es, -ing, -ed ,entəu'molədʒaiz, -iz, -iŋ, -d

entourage, -s ,ɔntu'rɑ:ʒ [,ɔ̃:nt-, ,ɔ:nt-, ,ã:nt-, ,ɑ:nt-, -tuə'r-] (ãtura:ʒ), -iz

entr'acte, -s 'ɔntrækt [ɔn'trækt, ɔ̃:*n*'t-, 'ɔ:n't-, ã:nt-, ɑ:n't-] (ãtrakt), -s

entrails 'entreilz

entrain, -s, -ing, -ed in'trein [en-], -z, -iŋ, -d

entramm|el, -els, -elling, -elled in-'træm|əl [en-], -əlz, -liŋ [-əliŋ], -əld

entrance (s.) (entry, place of entry, etc.), -s 'entrəns, -iz

entranc|e (v.) (put in state of trance, delight), -es, -ing/ly, -ed, -ement/s in'trɑ:ns [en-], -iz, -iŋ/li, -t, -mənt/s

entrant (s. adj.), -s 'entrənt, -s

entrap, -s, -ping, -ped, -per/s, -ment in'træp [en-], -s, -iŋ, -t, -ə*/z, -mənt

entreat, -s, -ing/ly, -ed, -ment in'tri:t [en-], -s, -iŋ/li, -id, -mənt

entreaty, -ies in'tri:t|i [en-], -iz

entrecôte, -s 'ɔntrəkəut ['ɔ̃:nt-, 'ɔ:nt-, 'ã:nt-, 'ɑ:nt-] (ãtrəko:t), -s

entrée, -s 'ɔntrei ['ɔ̃:nt-, 'ɔ:nt-, 'ã:nt-, 'ɑ:nt-] (ãtre), -z

entremets (sing.) 'ɔntrəmei ['ɔ̃:nt-, 'ɔ:nt-, 'ã:nt-, 'ɑ:nt-] (ãtrəmɛ), (plur.) -z

entrench, -es, -ing, -ed, -ment/s in-'trentʃ [en-], -iz, -iŋ, -t, -mənt/s

entrenching-tool, -s in'trentʃiŋtu:l [en-] -z

entrepôt, -s 'ɔntrəpəu ['ɔ̃:nt-, 'ɔ:nt-, 'ã:nt-, 'ɑ:nt-] (ãtrəpo), -z

entrepreneur, -s ,ɔntrəprə'nə:* [,ɔ̃:n-, ,ɔ:n-, ,ã:n-, ,ɑ:n-, -pre'n-] (ãtrəprənœ:r), -z

entresol, -s 'ɔntrəsol ['ɔ̃:n-, 'ɔ:n-, 'ã:n-, 'ɑ:n-] (ãtrəsɔl), -z

entropy 'entrəpi
entrust, -s, -ing, -ed in'trʌst [en-], -s, -iŋ, -id
entr|y, -ies 'entr|i, -iz
entwin|e, -es, -ing, -ed in'twain [en-], -z, -iŋ, -d
entwist, -s, -ing, -ed in'twist [en-], -s, -iŋ, -id
enumerable i'nju:mərəbl [i:'n-]
enumerat|e, -es, -ing, -ed, -or/s i'nju:-məreit, -s, -iŋ, -id, -ə*/z
enumeration, -s i,nju:mə'reiʃən, -z
enumerative i'nju:mərətiv [-reit-]
enunciable i'nʌnʃɪəbl [-nʃjə-, -nsɪə-, -nsjə-]
enunciat|e, -es, -ing, -ed, -or/s i'nʌn-sieit [-nsjeit, -nʃieit, -nʃjeit], -s, -iŋ, -id, -ə*/z
enunciation, -s i,nʌnsi'eiʃən, -z
enunciative i'nʌnʃɪətiv [-nʃjət-, -nsɪət-, -nsjət-, -nʃieit-, -ʃjeit-, -nsieit-, -nsjeit-]
enur|e, -es, -ing, -ed i'njuə*, -z, -riŋ, -d
envelop, -s, -ing, -ed, -ment/s in-'veləp [en-], -s, -iŋ, -t, -mənt/s
envelope, -s 'envələup ['ɔn-, -vil-], -s
envenom, -s, -ing, -ed in'venəm [en-], -z, -iŋ, -d
enviab|le, -ly, -leness 'envɪəb|l [-vjə-], -li, -lnis
envious, -ly, -ness 'envɪəs [-vjəs], -li, -nis
envir|on (v.), -ons, -oning, -oned, -onment/s in'vaiər|ən [en-], -ənz, -əniŋ [-ŋiŋ], -ənd, -ənmənt/s
environs (s.) in'vaiərənz ['environz, en'vaiər-]
envisag|e, -es, -ing, -ed in'vizidʒ [en-], -iz, -iŋ, -d
envoy, -s 'envɔi, -z
env|y (s. v.), -ies, -ying, -ied, -ier/s 'env|i, -iz, -iiŋ [-jiŋ], -id, -ɪə*/z [-jə*/z]
enwrap, -s, -ping, -ped in'ræp [en-], -s, -iŋ, -t
enwreath|e, -es, -ing, -ed in'ri:ð [en-], -z, -iŋ, -d
enzyme, -s 'enzaim, -z
eocene 'i(:)əusi:n
Eochaidh 'jɔkei ['jɔxei]
Eoli-=Aeoli-
eolith, -s 'i:əuliθ, -s
Eothen (title of book by Kinglake) i(:)'əuθen ['i(:)əuθen]
epact, -s 'i:pækt, -s
Epaminondas e,pæmi'nɔndæs [i,p-]
eparch, -s; -y, -ies 'epɑ:k, -s; -i, -iz
epaulement, -s e'pɔ:lmənt [i'p-], -s

epaulet, -s 'epəulet [-pɔ:l-, ,epə'let], -s
epenthes|is, -es e'penθis|is [-θəs-], -i:z
epenthetic ,epen'θetik
epergne, -s i'pə:n [e'pεən], -z
epexegesis e,peksi'dʒi:sis
epexegetic, -al, -ally e,peksi'dʒetik, -əl, -əli
ephah, -s 'i:fə, -z
ephemer|a, -as, -al i'femər|ə [e'f-, -'fi:m-], -əz, -əl
ephemeralit|y, -ies i,femə'rælit|i [e,f-, -,fi:m-], -iz
ephemeris, ephemerides i'feməris [e'f-, -'fi:m-], ,efi'meridi:z
ephemeron, -s i'femərɔn [e'f-, -'fi:m-, -rən], -z
ephemerous i'femərəs [e'f-, -'fi:m-]
Ephesian, -s i'fi:ʒjən [-i:ʒɪən, -i:ʒən, -i:zjən, -i:zɪən], -z
Ephesus 'efisəs
ephod, -s 'i:fɔd ['ef-], -z
Ephraim 'i:freiim [-frɪəm]
Ephrata 'efrətə
Ephron 'efrɔn ['i:f-]
epiblast, -s 'epiblæst, -s
epic (s. adj.), -s 'epik, -s
epicene (s. adj.), -s 'episi:n, -z
epicentre, -s 'episentə*, -z
Epicharmus ,epi'kɑ:məs
epici|sm, -st/s 'episi|zəm, -st/s
Epictetus ,epik'ti:təs
epicure, -s 'epikjuə* [-kjɔə*, -kjɔ:*], -z
Epicurean, -s ,epikjuə'ri(:)ən [-kjɔə'r-, -kjɔ:'r-], -z
epicurism 'epikjuərizəm [-kjɔər-, -kjɔ:r-]
Epicurus ,epi'kjuərəs [-'kjɔər-, -'kjɔ:r-]
epicycle, -s 'episaikl, -z
epicyclic ,epi'saiklik [-'sik-]
epicycloid, -s 'epi'saiklɔid [,epi's-], -z
Epidaurus ,epi'dɔ:rəs
epidemic (s. adj.), -s, -al, -ally ,epi-'demik, -s, -əl, -əli
epiderm|al, -ic, -is, -oid ,epi'də:m|əl, -ik, -is, -ɔid
epidiascope, -s ,epi'daiəskəup, -s
epigene 'epidʒi:n
epigenesis ,epi'dʒenisis
epiglott|al, -ic ,epi'glɔt|l ['epi'g-, 'epi,g-], -ik
epiglottis, -es ,epi'glɔtis ['epi'g-, 'epi,g-], -iz
epigone, -s 'epigəun, -z
Epigoni e'pigənai [-ni:]
epigram, -s 'epigræm, -z
epigrammatic, -al, -ally ,epigrə'mætik, -əl, -əli
epigrammatist, -s ,epi'græmətist, -s

epigrammatiz|e [-is|e], -es, -ing, -ed ‚epi'græmətaiz, -iz, -iŋ, -d

epigraph, -s 'epigrɑ:f [-græf], -s

epigrapher, -s e'pigrəfə* [i'p-], -z

epigraphic ‚epi'græfik

epigraph|ist/s, -y e'pigrəf|ist/s [i'p-], -i

epilepsy 'epilepsi

epileptic (s. adj.), -s, -al ‚epi'leptik, -s, -əl

epilogic ‚epi'lɔdʒik

epilogiz|e [-is|e], -es, -ing, -ed e'piləu-dʒaiz [i'p-], -iz, -iŋ, -d

epilogue, -s 'epilɔg, -z

Epimenides ‚epi'menidi:z

Epinal 'epinl (epinal)

epiphan|y (E.), -ies i'pifən|i [e'p-, -fŋ|i], -iz

Epipsychidion ‚episai'kidiɔn [-ipsai-, -diən]

Epirus e'paiərəs [i'p-]

episcopac|y, -ies i'piskəpəs|i [e'p-], -iz

episcop|al, -ally i'piskəp|əl [e'p-], -əli

episcopalian (s. adj.), -s, -ism i‚piskəu-'peiljən [e‚p-, -liən], -z, -izəm

episcopate, -s i'piskəupit [e'p-, -peit], -s

episcope, -s 'episkəup, -s

episcopiz|e [-is|e], -es, ing, -ed i'pis-kəupaiz [e'p-], -iz, -iŋ, -d

episode, -s 'episəud, -z

episodic, -al, -ally ‚epi'sɔdik, -əl, -əli

epistle, -s i'pisl, -z

epistler, -s i'pisⱡə*, -z

epistolary i'pistələri [e'p-, -tⱡəri]

epistoler, -s i'pistələ* [e'p-], -z

epistoliz|e [-is|e], -es, -ing, -ed i'pis-təlaiz [e'p-], -iz, -iŋ, -d

epistyle, -s 'epistail, -z

epitaph, -s 'epitɑ:f [-tæf], -s

epithalami|um, -a, -ums ‚epiθə'lei-mj|əm [-mĭ|-], -ə, -əmz

epithelium, -s ‚epi'θi:ljəm [-lĭəm], -z

epithet, -s 'epiθet [-θit], -s

epithetic ‚epi'θetik

epitome, -s i'pitəmi [e'p-], -z

epitomic, -al ‚epi'tɔmik, -əl

epitomist, -s i'pitəmist [e'p-], -s

epitomiz|e [-is|e], -es, -ing, -ed, -er/s i'pitəmaiz [e'p-], -iz, -iŋ, -d, -ə*/z

epoch, -s 'i:pɔk [rarely 'ep-], -s

epochal 'epɔkəl [i:'pɔk-]

epoch-making 'i:pɔk‚meikiŋ

epode, -s 'epəud, -z

eponym, -s 'epəunim, -z

eponymous i'pɔniməs [e'p-]

epopee, -s 'epəupi:, -z

epos, -es 'epɔs, -iz

Epping 'epiŋ

Epps eps

epsilon, -s ep'sailən [rarely 'epsilən], -z

Epsom 'epsəm

Epstein (sculptor) 'epstain

Epworth 'epwə:θ

equability ‚ekwə'biliti [‚i:k-, -lət-]

equab|le, -ly, -leness 'ekwəb|l ['i:k-], -li, -lnis

equ|al (s. adj. v.), -ally, -alness; -als, -alling, -alled 'i:kw|əl, -əli, -əlnis; -əlz, -əliŋ, -əld

equalit|y, -ies i(:)'kwɔlit|i, -iz

equalization [-isa-], -s ‚i:kwəlai'zeiʃən [-li'z-], -z

equaliz|e [-is|e], -es, -ing, -ed 'i:kwəlaiz, -iz, -iŋ, -d

equanimity ‚ekwə'nimiti [‚i:k-]

equanimous, -ly, -ness i(:)'kwæniməs [e'k-], -li, -nis

equat|e, -es, -ing, -ed i'kweit [i:'k-], -s, -iŋ, -id

equation, -s i'kweiʒən [-eiʃən], -z

equator, -s i'kweitə*, -z

equatorial (s. adj.), -s, -ly ‚ekwə'tɔ:rĭəl [‚i:k-], -z, -i

equerr|y, -ies 'ekwər|i [i'kwer|i], -iz
Note.—The pronunciation at court is i'kweri.

equestrian (s. adj.), -s, -ism i'kwes-trĭən [e'k-], -z, -izəm

equestrienne, -s i‚kwestri'en [e‚k-], -z

equiangular ‚i:kwi'æŋgjulə*

equidistant, -ly 'i:kwi'distənt [‚i:k-], -li

equilateral 'i:kwi'lætərəl [‚i:k-]

equilibrat|e, -es, -ing, -ed ‚i:kwi-'laibreit [-'lib-, i(:)'kwilib-], -s, -iŋ, -id

equilibration ‚i:kwilai'breiʃən [‚i:kwi-li'b-, i(:)‚kwili'b-]

equilibrist, -s i(:)'kwilibrist [‚i:kwi-'librist], -s

equilibrium ‚i:kwi'librĭəm

equimultiple, -s 'i:kwi'mʌltipl [‚i:k-], -z

equine 'ekwain ['i:k-]

equinoctial (s. adj.), -s ‚i:kwi'nɔkʃəl [‚ek-], -z

equinox, -es 'i:kwinɔks ['ek-], -iz

equip, -s, -ping, -ped, -ment/s i'kwip, -s, -iŋ, -t, -mənt/s

equipage, -s 'ekwipidʒ, -iz

equipois|e (s. v.), -es, -ing, -ed 'ekwi-pɔiz ['i:k-], -iz, -iŋ, -d

equitab|le, -ly, -leness 'ekwitəb|l, -li, -lnis

equitation ‚ekwi'teiʃən

equit|y, -ies 'ekwit|i, -iz

equivalen|ce, -t/s, -tly i'kwivələn|s [-v|ə-], -t/s, -tli

equivoc|al, -ally, -alness i'kwivək|əl [-vuk-], -əli, -əlnis

equivocat|e, -es, -ing, -ed, -or/s i'kwivəkeit [-vuk-], -s, -iŋ, -id, -ə*/z,
equivocation, -s i,kwivə'keiʃən [-vu'k-] -z
equivoke [-voque], -s 'ekwivəuk, -s
Equuleus e'kwuliəs
er (interj.) ʌ:, ə:
era, -s 'iərə, -z
eradiat|e, -es, -ing, -ed i'reidieit [i:'r-, -djeit], -s, -iŋ, -id
eradiation i,reidi'eiʃən [i:,r-]
eradicable i'rædikəbl
eradicat|e, -es, -ing, -ed i'rædikeit, -s, -iŋ, -id
eradication i,rædi'keiʃən
eradicative i'rædikətiv [-keit-]
Erard, -s 'erɑ:d (erɑ:r), -z
eras|e, -es, -ing, -ed, -er/s, -ement; -able i'reiz, -iz, -iŋ, -d, -ə*/z, -mənt; -əbl
erasion, -s i'reiʒən, -z
Erasmian, -s, -ism i'ræzmiən [e'r-, -mjən], -z, -izəm
Erasmus i'ræzməs [e'r-]
Erastian, -s, -ism i'ræstiən [e'r-, -tjən], -z, -izəm
Erastus i'ræstəs [e'r-]
erasure, -s i'reiʒə*, -z
Erath i'rɑ:θ [e'r-]
Erdington 'ə:diŋtən
ere ɛə*
Erebus 'eribəs
Erec 'iərek
Erechtheum ,erek'θi(:)əm
Erechtheus i'rekθju:s [e'r-, -θíəs, -θjəs]
erect (adj. v.), -ly, -ness; -s, -ing, -ed; -ile i'rekt, -li, -nis; -s, -iŋ, -id; -ail
erection, -s i'rekʃən, -z
eremite, -s 'erimait, -s
eremitic, -al ,eri'mitik, -əl
Eretria, -n/s i'retriə [e'r-], -n/z
erewhile ɛə'wail [-'hw-]
Erewhon 'eriwɔn [-wən, -ihw-]
erg, -s ə:g, -z
ergo 'ə:gəu
ergon, -s 'ə:gɔn, -z
ergonic, -s, -ally ə:'gɔnik, -s, -əli
ergosterol ə:'gɔstərɔl [-stiər-]
ergot, -ism 'ə:gət [-gɔt], -izəm
eric (E.), -s 'erik, -s
erica (E.) 'erikə
ericaceous ,eri'keiʃəs
Erie 'iəri
Erin 'iərin
Eris 'eris
eristic, -s e'ristik, -s
Erith 'iəriθ
Eritrea, -n/s ,eri'treiə [-'triə], -n/z
Erle ə:l

erl-king, -s 'ə:l-kiŋ ['ə:l'kiŋ], -z
Erlynne 'ə:lin
ermine, -s, -d 'ə:min, -z, -d
erne (E.), -s ə:n, -z
Ernest 'ə:nist
Ernle 'ə:nli
erod|e, -es, -ing, -ed i'rəud [e'r-], -z, -iŋ, -id
Eroica e'rəuikə [i'r-]
Eros 'iərɔs ['erɔs, also 'erəuz by Greek scholars]
erosion, -s i'rəuʒən [e'r-], -z
erosive i'rəusiv [e'r-]
erotic (s. adj.), -s i'rɔtik [e'r-], -s
erotica i'rɔtikə [e'r-]
eroticism i'rɔtisizəm [e'r-]
err, -s, -ing, -ed ə:*, -z, -riŋ, -d
errand, -s 'erənd, -z
errand-boy, -s 'erəndbɔi, -z
errant, -ly, -ry 'erənt, -li, -ri
erratic, -al, -ally i'rætik [e'r-], -əl, -əli
errat|um, -a e'rɑ:t|əm [i'r-, -'reit-], -ə
Erroll 'erəl
erroneous, -ly, -ness i'rəunjəs [e'r-, -niəs], -li, -nis
error, -s 'erə*, -z
ersatz 'əzæts (ɛr'zats)
Erse ə:s
Erskine 'ə:skin
erst ə:st
erstwhile 'ə:st-wail [-thw-]
erubescen|ce, -cy, -t ,eru(:)'besn|s, -si, -t
eruct, -s, -ing, -ed i'rʌkt [i:'r-], -s, -iŋ, -id
eructat|e, -es, -ing, -ed i'rʌkteit [i:'r-], -s, -iŋ, -id
eructation, -s ,i:rʌk'teiʃən, -z
erudite, -ly, -ness 'eru(:)dait [-rju(:)-], -li, -nis
erudition ,eru(:)'diʃən [-rju(:)-]
erupt, -s, -ing, -ed i'rʌpt [e'r-], -s, -iŋ, -id
eruption, -s i'rʌpʃən [e'r-], -z
eruptive, -ly, -ness i'rʌptiv [e'r-], -li, -nis
Ervine 'ə:vin
erysipelas ,eri'sipiləs [-pəl-, -lis]
erythema ,eri'θi:mə
Eryx 'eriks
Erzerum 'ɛəzəru:m
Esau 'i:sɔ:
escalad|e (s. v), -es, -ing, -ed ,eskə'leid ['---], -z, -iŋ, -id
escalat|e, -es, -ing, -ed 'eskəleit, -s, -iŋ, -id
escalation ,eskə'leiʃən
escalator, -s 'eskəleitə*, -z
escallop, -ed is'kɔləp [es-], -t
escapade, -s ,eskə'peid, -z

escap|e (s. v.), -es, -ing, -ed, -ement/s is'keip [es-], -s, -iŋ, -t, -mənt/s

escapi|sm, -st/s is'keipi|zəm [es-], -st/s

escarp (s. v.), -s, -ing, -ed, -ment/s is'kɑ:p [es-], -s, -iŋ, -t, -mənt/s

eschalot, -s 'eʃəlɔt [‚eʃə'l-], -s

eschar, -s 'eskɑ:*, -z

escharotic (s. adj.), -s ‚eskə'rɔtik, -s

eschatological ‚eskətə'lɔdʒikəl [-kæt-]

eschatolog|ist/s, -y ‚eskə'tɔlədʒ|ist/s, -i

escheat (s. v.), -s, -ing, -ed is'tʃi:t [es-], -s, -iŋ, -id

eschew, -s, -ing, -ed is'tʃu: [es-], -z, -iŋ [-'tʃuiŋ], -d

eschscholtzia, -s is'kɔlʃə [is'kɔltʃə, es-'kɔltsiə, es'kɔltsjə, e'ʃɔltsiə, e'ʃɔltsjə], -z

Escombe 'eskəm   ⌊-z

Escorial ‚eskɔri'ɑ:l [es'kɔ:riəl]

escort (s.), -s 'eskɔ:t, -s

escort (v.), -s, -ing, -ed is'kɔ:t [es-], -s, -iŋ, -id

Escow 'eskəu

escritoire, -s ‚eskri(:)'twɑ:* [-'twɔ:*, '---] (eskritwa:r), -z

escudo, -s es'ku:dəu, -z

esculent (s. adj.), -s 'eskjulənt, -s

Escurial es'kjuəriəl

escutcheon, -s is'kʌtʃən [es-], -z

Esdaile 'ezdeil

Esdraelon ‚ezdrei'i:lɔn [-drə'i:-]

Esdras 'ezdræs [-rəs]

Esher 'i:ʃə*

Esias i'zaiəs [e'z-, -æs]

Esk esk

Eskimo, -s 'eskiməu, -z

Esmé 'ezmi

Esmeralda ‚ezmə'rældə

Esmond(e) 'ezmənd

esophageal i(:)‚sɔfə'dʒi(:)əl

esopha|gus, -gi i(:)'sɔfə|gəs, -gai [-dʒai]

esoteric, -al, -ally ‚esəu'terik [‚i:s-], -əl, -əli

espalier (s. v.), -s, -ing, -ed is'pæljə* [es-, -liə*], -z, -riŋ, -d

esparto es'pɑ:təu

especi|al, -ally is'peʃ|əl [es-], -əli [-‚li]

Esperant|ist/s, -o ‚espə'rænt|ist/s [-pe'r-, -'rɑ:n-], -əu

Espeut es'pju:t

espial is'paiəl [es-]

espionage ‚espiə'nɑ:ʒ [‚espjə'nɑ:ʒ, 'espiənidʒ, es'paiənidʒ, is'paiənidʒ] (espjona:ʒ, pronounced as French espionnage)

esplanade, -s ‚esplə'neid [-'nɑ:d, rarely 'esplənɑ:d], -z

Esplanade (in Western Australia) 'esplənɑ:d

espous|e, -es, -ing, -ed, -er/s; -al/s is'pauz [es-], -iz, -iŋ, -d, -ə*/z; -əl/z

espressivo ‚espre'si:vəu

espresso e'spresəu [i's-]

esprit 'espri: (espri)

esprit-de-corps 'espri:də'kɔ:* (espridkɔ:r)

esp|ly, -ies, -ying, -ied is'p|ai [es-], -aiz, -aiiŋ, -aid

Espy 'espi

Esq. is'kwaiə* [es-]

Esquiline 'eskwilain

Esquimalt es'kwaimɔ:lt

Esquimau, -x 'eskiməu, -z

esquire, -s is'kwaiə* [es-], -z

ess, -es es, -iz

essay (s.), -s; -ist/s 'esei [-si], -z; -ist/s

essay (v.), -s, -ing, -ed, -er/s e'sei ['esei], -z, -iŋ, -d, -ə*/z

esse 'esi

Essen 'esn

essence, -s 'esns, -iz

Essene, -s 'esi:n [e'si:n], -z

essenti|al, -ally, -alness i'senʃ|əl [e's-], -əli [-‚li], -əlnis

essentiality i‚senʃi'æliti [e‚s-]

Essex 'esiks

establish, -es, -ing, -ed, -er/s, -ment/s is'tæbliʃ [es-], -iz, -iŋ, -t, -ə*/z, -mənt/s

estate, -s is'teit [es-], -s

estate-car, -s is'teitkɑ:*, -z

Estcourt 'estkɔ:t

Este 'esti

esteem (s. v.), -s, -ing, -ed is'ti:m [es-], -z, -iŋ, -d

Estey 'esti

Esther 'estə*, 'esθə* esp. in the N.

esthet-= aesthet-

Esthonia, -n/s es'təunjə [es'θəu-, -niə], -n/z

estimab|le, -ly, -leness 'estiməb|l, -li, -lnis

estimate (s.), -s 'estimit [-meit], -s

estimat|e (v.), -es, -ing, -ed, -or/s 'estimeit, -s, -iŋ, -id, -ə*/z

estimation ‚esti'meiʃən

estiv- = aestiv-

Estmere 'estmiə*

Estonia, -n/s es'təunjə [-niə], -n/z

estop, -s, -ping, -ped; -page, -pel/s is'tɔp [es-], -s, -iŋ, -t; -idʒ, -əl/z

estrade, -s es'trɑ:d, -z

estrang|e, -es, -ing, -ed, -edness, -ement/s is'treindʒ [es-], -iz, -iŋ, -d, -idnis, -mənt/s

estreat (s. v.), -s, -ing, -ed is'tri:t [es-], -s, -iŋ, -id

estuar|y, -ies 'estjŭər|i [-tjwər-, -tjuər-, -tʃŭər-, -tʃwər-, -tʃuər-, -tjur-, -tʃur-], -iz

esurien|ce, -cy, -t i'sjuərĭən|s, -si, -t

eta 'i:tə

etacism 'eitəsizm

Etah 'i:tə

Etain 'etein

Etamin 'etəmin

etc. it'setrə [et-, ət-]

etcetera, -s it'setrə [et-, ət-], -z

etch, -es, -ing/s, -ed, -er/s etʃ, -iz, -iŋ/z, -t, -ə*/z

etern|al, -ally i(:)'tə:n|l, -əli [-l̩i]

eternaliz|e [-is|e], -es, -ing, -ed i(:)'tə:nəlaiz, -iz, -iŋ, -d

eternit|y, -ies i(:)'tə:nit|i, -iz

eterniz|e [-is|e], -es, -ing, -ed i:'tə:naiz, -iz, -iŋ, -d

Etesian i'ti:ʒĭən [-ʒĭən, -ʒən]

Eteson 'i:tsn

Ethbaal eθ'beiəl [usual Jewish pronunciation eθ'bɑ:l]

Ethel, -bald, -bert 'eθəl, -bɔ:ld, -bə:t

Ethelberta ˌeθəl'bə:tə ['--,--]

Ethelburga ˌeθəl'bə:gə ['--,--]

Ethel|red, -wulf 'eθəl|red, -wulf

ether, -s 'i:θə*, -z

ethereal, -ly i(:)'θiərĭəl, -i

etherealiz|e [-is|e], -es, -ing, -ed i(:)'θiərĭəlaiz, -iz, -iŋ, -d

Etherege 'eθəridʒ

etheric, -s -ally i(:)'θerik, -s, -əli

Etherington 'eθəriŋtən

etheriz|e [-is|e], -es, -ing, -ed 'i:θəraiz, -iz, -iŋ, -d

ethic (s. adj.), -s, -al, -ally 'eθik, -s, -əl, -əli

Ethiop, -s 'i:θiɔp [-θjɔp], -s

Ethiopia, -n/s ˌi:θi'əupjə [-pĭə], -n/z

Ethiopic ˌi:θi'ɔpik [-i'əup-]

ethnic, -al, -ally 'eθnik, -əl, -əli

ethnographer, -s eθ'nɔgrəfə*, -z

ethnographic ˌeθnəu'græfik

ethnography eθ'nɔgrəfi

ethnologic, -al, -ally ˌeθnəu'lɔdʒik, -əl, -əli

ethnolog|ist/s, -y eθ'nɔlədʒ|ist/s, -i

etholog|ist/s, -y i(:)'θɔlədʒ|ist/s, -i

ethos 'i:θɔs

ethyl (commercial and general pronunciation) 'eθil, (chemists' pronunciation) 'i:θail

ethylene 'eθili:n

etiolat|e, -es, -ing, -ed 'i:tiəuleit [-tĭəl-], -s, -iŋ, -id

etiolog|ist/s, -y ˌi:ti'ɔlədʒ|ist/s, -i

etiquette 'etiket [ˌeti'ket]

Etna 'etnə

Eton 'i:tn

Etonian, -s i(:)'təunjən [-nĭən], -z

Etruria, -n/s i'truərĭə, -n/z

Etruscan, -s i'trʌskən, -z

Ettrick, 'etrik

Etty 'eti

etui, -s e'twi:, -z

etymologic, -al, -ally ˌetimə'lɔdʒik, -əl, -əli

etymolog|ist/s, -y, -ies ˌeti'mɔlədʒ|ist/s, -i, -iz

etymologiz|e [-is|e], -es, -ing, -ed ˌeti'mɔlədʒaiz, -iz, -iŋ, -d

etymon, -s 'etimɔn, -z

Euboea ju:'biə [ju'b-, -'bi:ə]

eucalyptus, -es ˌju:kə'liptəs [juk-], -iz

Eucharist, -s 'ju:kərist, -s

eucharistic, -al, -ally ˌju:kə'ristik [juk-], -əl, -əli

euchre (s. v.), -s, -ing, -d 'ju:kə*, -z, -riŋ, -d

Euclid, -s 'ju:klid, -z

Euclidean ju:'klidĭən [ju'k-, -djən]

eud(a)emoni|sm, -st/s ju:'di:məni|zəm [ju'd-], -st/s

eudiometer, -s ˌju:di'ɔmitə* [jud-], -z

Eudocia ju:'dəuʃjə [ju'd-, -ʃĭə, -sjə, -sĭə]

Eudora ju:'dɔ:rə [ju'd-]

Eudoxia ju:'dɔksĭə [ju'd-, -sjə]

Eudoxus ju:'dɔksəs [ju'd-]

Eugen (English name) 'ju:dʒen [-dʒin, -dʒən], (German name) 'ɔigən (ɔy'ge:n)

Eugene (English name) ju:'ʒein, 'ju:dʒi:n, ju:'dʒi:n

Note.—Eugene Goossens, the musician, pronounces ju:'ʒein.

Eugene Onegin 'ju:dʒi:n ɔ'njeigin (jiv'genji a'njegin)

Eugénia ju:'dʒi:njə [ju'dʒ-, -nĭə]

eugenic, -s ju:'dʒenik [ju'dʒ-], -s

Eugénie (as English name) ju:'ʒeini, ju:'ʒi:ni, ju:'dʒi:ni

Eugenius ju:'dʒi:njəs [ju'dʒ-, -nĭəs]

Eulalia ju:'leiljə [ju'l-, -lĭə]

Euler (English name) 'ju:lə*, (German name) 'ɔilə* ('ɔylər)

eulogist, -s 'ju:lədʒist, -s

eulogistic, -al, -ally ˌju:lə'dʒistik, -əl, -əli

eulogium, -s ju:'ləudʒəm [ju'l-, -dʒĭəm], -z

eulogiz|e [-is|e], -es, -ing, -ed 'ju:lədʒaiz, -iz, -iŋ, -d

eulog|y, -ies 'ju:lədʒ|i, -iz

Eunice (modern Christian name) 'ju:nis (biblical name) ju(:)'naisi

eunuch, -s, -ism 'ju:nək, -s, -izəm

euonymus, -es ju(:)'ɔnimǝs, -iz
eupepsia ju:'pepsiǝ [-sjǝ]
eupeptic ju:'peptik
Euphemia ju:'fi:mjǝ [ju'f-, -miǝ]
euphemism, -s 'ju:fimizǝm, -z
euphemistic, -al, -ally ,ju:fi'mistik, -ǝl, -ǝli
euphemiz|e [-is|e], -es, -ing, -ed 'ju:fi- maiz, -iz, -iŋ, -d
euphonic, -al, -ally ju:'fɔnik [ju'f-], -ǝl, -ǝli
euphonious, -ly ju:'fǝunjǝs [ju'f-, -niǝs], -li
euphonium, -s ju:'fǝunjǝm [ju'f-, -niǝm], -z
euphoniz|e [-is|e], -es, -ing, -ed 'ju:- fǝnaiz [-fǝun-, -fun-], -iz, -iŋ, -d
euphony 'ju:fǝni [-fun-]
euphoria ju(:)'fɔ:riǝ
euphrasy 'ju:frǝsi
Euphrates ju:'freiti:z [ju'f-]
Euphronius ju:'frǝunjǝs [ju'f-, -niǝs]
Euphrosyne ju:'frɔzini: [ju'f-]
Euphues 'ju:fju(:)i:z
euphui|sm/s, -st/s 'ju:fju(:)i|zǝm/z, -st/s
euphuistic ,ju:fju(:)'istik
Eurasian, -s juǝ'reiʒǝn [jɔǝ'r-, jɔ:'r-, -eiʒiǝn, -eiʒǝn, -eiʃǝn], -z
eureka juǝ'ri:kǝ
eurhythm|ic/s, -y ju:'riðm|ik/s [ju'r-, juǝ'r-, -'riθm-], -i
Euripides juǝ'ripidi:z
Euripus juǝ'raipǝs
Europa juǝ'rǝupǝ
Europe 'juǝrǝp ['jɔ:r-]
European, -s ,juǝrǝ'pi(:)ǝn [,jɔ:r-], -z
europeaniz|e [-is|e], -es, -ing, -ed ,juǝrǝ'pi(:)ǝnaiz [,jɔ:r-], -iz, -iŋ, -d
Eurus 'juǝrǝs
Eurydice juǝ'ridisi(:)
Eurylochus juǝ'rilǝkǝs
Eusebian, -s ju:'si:bjǝn [ju's-, -biǝn], -z
Eusebius ju:'si:bjǝs [ju's-, -biǝs]
Euskarian, -s ju:s'kɛǝriǝn, -z
Eustace 'ju:stǝs [-tis]
Eustachian ju:s'teifjǝn [-ʃiǝn, -ʃǝn, rarely -'teikjǝn, -'teikiǝn]
Eustachius ju:s'teikjǝs [-kiǝs]
Eustis 'ju:stis
Euston 'ju:stǝn
Eutaw 'ju:tɔ:
Euterpe ju:'tǝ:pi [ju't-]
euthanasia ,ju:θǝ'neizjǝ [-eiziǝ, -eiʒjǝ, -eiʒiǝ, -eiʒǝ]
Eutropius ju:'trǝupjǝs [ju't-, -piǝs]
Euxine 'ju:ksain

Eva 'i:vǝ
evacuant (s. adj.), -s i'vækjŭǝnt [i:'v-, -kjwǝnt], -s
evacuat|e, -es, -ing, -ed, -or/s i'væk- jueit [i:'v-], -s, -iŋ, -id, -ǝ*/z
evacuation, -s i,vækju'eiʃǝn [i:,v-], -z
evacuee, -s i,vækju(:)'i: [i:,v-], -z
evad|e, -es, -ing, -ed, -er/s i'veid, -z, -iŋ, -id, -ǝ*/z
evaluat|e, -es, -ing, -ed i'væljueit, -s, -iŋ, -id
evaluation, -s i,vælju'eiʃǝn, -z
Evan 'evǝn
Evander i'vændǝ*
evanesc|e, -es, -ing, -ed ,i:vǝ'nes [,ev-], -iz, -iŋ, -t   [-t/li
evanescen|ce, -t/ly ,i:vǝ'nesn|s [,ev-],
evangel, -s i'vændʒel [-dʒǝl], -z
evangelic (s. adj.), -s, -al/s, -ally, -alism ,i:væn'dʒelik [,ev-, -vǝn-], -s, -ǝl/z, -ǝli, -ǝlizǝm
Evangeline i'vændʒili:n [-dʒǝl-, -dʒl-]
evangelist, -s i'vændʒilist [-dʒǝl-, -dʒl-], -s
evangelistic i,vændʒi'listik [dʒǝ'l-, -dʒl'istik]
evangelization [-isa-] i,vændʒilai'zei- ʃǝn [-dʒel-, -dʒl-, -li'z-]
evangeliz|e [-is|e], -es, -ing, -ed i'vændʒilaiz [-dʒǝl-, -dʒl-], -iz, -iŋ, -d
Evans 'evǝnz
Evanson 'evǝnsn
Evanston 'evǝnstǝn
Evansville 'evǝnzvil
evaporable i'væpǝrǝbl
evaporat|e, -es, -ing, -ed, -or/s i'væ- pǝreit, -s, -iŋ, -id, -ǝ*/z
evaporation, -s i,væpǝ'reiʃǝn, -z
evasion, -s i'veiʒǝn, -z
evasive, -ly, -ness i'veisiv, -li, -nis
eve (E.), -s, i:v, -z
Evele(i)gh 'i:vli
Evelina ,evi'li:nǝ
Eveline 'i:vlin, 'evlin, 'evili:n
Evelyn 'i:vlin, 'evlin
ev|en (s. adj. v. adv.), -enly, -enness; -ens, -ening, -ened 'i:v|ǝn, -ǝnli, -ǝnnis; -ǝnz, -ǝniŋ [-ǝniŋ], -ǝnd
Evenden 'evǝndǝn
evening (s.) (close of day), -s 'i:vniŋ, -z
Evens 'evǝnz
evensong, -s 'i:vǝnsɔŋ, -z
event, -s; -ful i'vent, -s; -ful [-fǝl]
eventide, -s 'i:vǝntaid, -z
eventual, -ly i'ventʃŭǝl [-tjwǝl, -tjŭǝl, -tʃwǝl, -tjul, -tʃul], -i
eventualit|y, -ies i,ventju'ælit|i [-tʃu-], -iz

eventuat|e, -es, -ing, -ed i'ventjueit, -s, -iŋ, -id

ever 'evə*

Ever|ard, -est, -ett 'evər|ɑːd, -ist, -it

evergreen (s. adj.), -s 'evəgriːn, -z

Everitt 'evərit

everlasting, -ly, -ness ˌevə'lɑːstiŋ, -li, -nis

evermore 'evə'mɔː* [-'mɔː*, also sometimes '— when followed by a stress]

Evers 'evəz

Evershed 'evəʃed

eversion i'vəːʃən [iː'v-]

Eversley 'evəzli

evert, -s, -ing, -ed i'vəːt [iː'v-], -s, -iŋ, -id

every, -body 'evri, -ˌbɔdi [-bədi]

everyday (adj.) 'evridei ['—'-]

Everyman 'evrimæn

everyone 'evriwʌn

everything 'evriθiŋ

everywhere 'evriwɛə* [-ihw-]

Evesham 'iːvʃəm [locally also 'iːviʃəm]

Evett, -s 'evit, -s

evict, -s, -ing, -ed i(ː)'vikt, -s, -iŋ, -id

eviction, -s i(ː)'vikʃən, -z

evidenc|e (s. v.), -es, -ing, -ed 'evidəns, -iz, -iŋ, -t

evident, -ly 'evidənt, -li

evidenti|al, -ally ˌevi'denʃ|əl, -əli

evidentiary ˌevi'denʃəri

ev|il (s. adj.), -ils, -illy 'iːv|l [-il], -lz [-ilz], -ili

evil-doer, -s 'iːvl'du(ː)ə* ['iːvil-], -z

evil-eye, -s, -d 'iːvl'ai ['iːvil'ai], -z, -d

evil-minded, -ness 'iːvl'maindid ['iːvil-], '—ˌ—), -nis

evil-speaking 'iːvl'spiːkiŋ ['iːvil-]

evinc|e, -es, -ing, -ed; -ive i'vins, -iz, -iŋ, -t; -iv

evincib|le, -ly i'vinsəb|l [-sib-], -li

evirat|e, -es, -ing, -ed 'iːvireit ['ev-], -s, -iŋ, -id

eviscerat|e, -es, -ing, -ed i'visəreit [iː'v-], -s, -iŋ, -id

evisceration iˌvisə'reiʃən [iː'ˌv-]

evocat|e, -es, -ing, -ed 'evəukeit ['iːv-], -s, -iŋ, -id

evocation, -s ˌevəu'keiʃən [ˌiːv-], -z

evok|e, -es, -ing, -ed i'vəuk [iː'v-], -s, -iŋ, -t

evolute, -s 'iːvəluːt ['ev-, -ljuːt], -s

evolution, -s ˌiːvə'luːʃən [ˌev-, -'ljuː-], -z

evolutional ˌiːvə'luːʃənl [ˌev-, -'ljuː-, -ʃnəl, -ʃnl̩, -ʃnl̩, -ʃənəl]

evolutionary ˌiːvə'luːʃnəri [ˌev-, -'ljuː-, -ʃnəri, -ʃənəri]

evolutioni|sm, -st/s ˌiːvə'luːʃəni|zəm [ˌev-, -'ljuː-, -ʃn̩i-], -st/s

evolv|e, -es, -ing, -ed; -able i'vɔlv [iː'v-], -z, -iŋ, -d; -əbl

Evors 'iːvɔːz

evulsion, -s i'vʌlʃən [iː'v-], -z

Ewart 'juː(ː)ət

Ewbank 'juːbæŋk

ewe, -s; -lamb/s juː, -z; -læm/z

Ewell 'juː(ː)əl

Ewen 'juː(ː)in

ewe-neck, -s 'juːnek, -s

ewer, -s 'juː(ː)ə*, -z

Ewing 'juː(ː)iŋ

ex eks

exacerbat|e, -es, -ing, -ed eks'æsə(ː)-beit, -s, -iŋ, -id

exacerbation, -s eksˌæsə(ː)'beiʃən, -z

exact (adj. v.), -er, -est, -ly, -ness; -s, -ing, -ed, -er/s, -or/s ig'zækt [eg-], -ə*, -ist, -li [ig'zækli, 'gzækli], -nis [ig'zæknis]; -s, -iŋ, -id, -ə*/z, -ə*/z

exaction, -s ig'zækʃən [eg-], -z

exactitude ig'zæktitjuːd [eg-]

exaggerat|e, -es, -ing, -ed, -or/s ig-'zædʒəreit [eg-], -s, -iŋ, -id, -ə*/z

exaggeration, -s igˌzædʒə'reiʃən [eg-], -z

exaggerative ig'zædʒərətiv [eg-, -reit-]

exalt, -s, -ing, -ed/ly, -edness ig'zɔːlt [eg-, -'zɔlt], -s, -iŋ, -id/li, -idnis

exaltation, -s ˌegzɔːl'teiʃən [ˌeks-, -ɔl-], -z

exam, -s ig'zæm [eg-], -z   [-z

examen, -s eg'zeimen, -z

examination, -s igˌzæmi'neiʃən [eg-], -z

examin|e, -es, -ing, -ed, -er/s ig'zæmin [eg-], -z, -iŋ, -d, -ə*/z

examinee, -s igˌzæmi'niː [eg-], -z

examp|le (s. v.), -les, -ling, -led ig-'zɑːmp|l [eg-], -lz, -liŋ, -ld

exarch, -s; -ate/s 'eksɑːk, -s; -eit/s

exasperat|e, -es, -ing, -ed, -or/s ig-'zɑːspəreit [eg-, -'zæs-], -s, -iŋ, -id, -ə*/z

exasperation igˌzɑːspə'reiʃən [eg-, -ˌzæs-]

Excalibur eks'kælibə*

excavat|e, -es, -ing, -ed, -or/s 'ekskəveit, -s, -iŋ, -id, -ə*/z

excavation, -s ˌekskə'veiʃən, -z

exceed, -s, -ing, -ed ik'siːd [ek-], -z, -iŋ, -id

exceeding (adj.), -ly ik'siːdiŋ [ek-], -li

excel, -s, -ling, -led ik'sel [ek-], -z, -iŋ, -d

excellen|ce, -ces, -cy, -cies, -t/ly 'eksələn|s, -siz, -si, -siz, -t/li

excelsior ek'selsiɔː* [ik-, -siə*, -sjə*]

except (v. prep. conj.), -s, -ing, -ed ik'sept [ek-], -s, -iŋ, -id

exception, -s ik'sepʃən [ek-], -z
exceptionab|le, -ly, -leness ik'sepʃnəb|l [ek-, -ʃŋə-, -ʃənə-], -li, -lnis
excep|tional, -tionally ik'sep|ʃənl [ek-, -ʃnəl, -ʃŋl, -ʃŋl, -ʃənəl], -ʃŋəli [-ʃnəli, -ʃŋli, -ʃŋli, -ʃənəli]   [-s
excerpt (s.), -s 'eksə:pt [ik'sə:pt, ek's-], excerpt (v.), -s, -ing, -ed ek'sə:pt [ik-], -s, -iŋ, -id
excerption, -s ek'sə:pʃən [ik-], -z
excess (s. v.), -es, -ing, -ed ik'ses [ek-] (also 'ekses when noun is used attributively), -iz, -iŋ, -t
excessive, -ly, -ness ik'sesiv [ek-], -li, -nis
exchang|e (s. v.), -es, -ing, -ed, -er/s; -eable iks'tʃeindʒ [eks-], -iz, -iŋ, -d, -ə*/z; -əbl
exchangeability iks,tʃeindʒə'biliti [eks-, -lət-]
exchangee, -s ,ekstʃein'dʒi: [iks,tʃ-], -z
exchequer, -s iks'tʃekə* [eks-], -z
excisable ek'saizəbl [ik-]
excise (s.) (tax), -man, -men ek'saiz [ik's-, 'eksaiz], -mæn, -men
excis|e (v.) (cut out), -es, -ing, -ed ek'saiz [ik-], -iz, -iŋ, -d
excision, -s ek'siʒən [ik-], -z
excitability ik,saitə'biliti [ek-, -lət-]
excitant, -s 'eksitənt [ik'saitənt], -s
excitation, -s ,eksi'teiʃən, -z
excitat|ive, -ory ek'saitət|iv [ik-], -əri
excit|e, -es, -ing, -ed, -er/s, -ement/s; -able/ness ik'sait [ek-], -s, -iŋ, -id, -ə*/z, -mənt/s; -əbl/nis
exclaim, -s, -ing, -ed iks'kleim [eks-], -z, -iŋ, -d
exclamation, -s ,eksklə'meiʃən, -z
exclamatory eks'klæmətəri [iks-]
exclud|e, -es, -ing, -ed iks'klu:d [eks-], -z, -iŋ, -id
exclusion, -s iks'klu:ʒən [eks-], -z
exclusionist, -s iks'klu:ʒənist [eks-, -ʒŋist], -s
exclusive, -ly, -ness iks'klu:siv [eks-], -li, -nis
excogitat|e, -es, -ing, -ed eks'kɔdʒi-teit [iks-], -s, -iŋ, -id
excogitation, -s eks,kɔdʒi'teiʃən [iks,kɔdʒ-, ,ekskɔdʒ-], -z
excommunicat|e, -es, -ing, -ed ,ekskə-'mju:nikeit [-'mjun-], -s, -iŋ, -id
excommunication, -s 'ekskə,mju:ni-'keiʃən [-,mjun-], -z
excoriat|e, -es, -ing, -ed eks'kɔ:rieit [iks-, -'kɔr-], -s, -iŋ, -id
excoriation, -s eks,kɔ:ri'eiʃən [iks-, -,kɔr-], -z

excrement, -s 'ekskrimənt [-krəm-], -s
excremental ,ekskri'mentl [-krə'm-]
excrementitious ,ekskrimen'tiʃəs [-krəm-]
excrescen|ce, -ces, -t iks'kresn|s [eks-], -siz, -t
excret|e, -es, -ing, -ed; -ive, -ory eks'kri:t [iks-], -s, -iŋ, -id; -iv, -əri
excretion, -s eks'kri:ʃən [iks-], -z
excruciat|e, -es, -ing/ly, -ed iks'kru:-ʃieit [eks-, -ʃjeit], -s, -iŋ/li, -id
excruciation iks,kru:ʃi'eiʃən [eks-, -u:si-]
exculpat|e, -es, -ing, -ed 'ekskʌlpeit, -s, -iŋ, -id
exculpation ,ekskʌl'peiʃən
exculpatory eks'kʌlpətəri ['ekskʌl-peitəri]
excurs|e, -es, -ing, -ed iks'kə:s [eks-], -iz, -iŋ, -t
excursion, -s iks'kə:ʃən [eks-], -z
excursionist, -s iks'kə:ʃŋist [eks-, -ʃənist], -s
excursioniz|e [-is|e], -es, -ing, -ed iks'kə:ʃŋaiz [eks-, -ʃənaiz], -iz, -iŋ, -d
excursive, -ly, -ness eks'kə:siv [iks-], -li, -nis
excursus, -es eks'kə:səs [iks-], -iz
excusab|le, -ly, -leness iks'kju:zəb|l [eks-], -li, -lnis
excusatory iks'kju:zətəri [eks-]
excuse (s.), -s iks'kju:s [eks-], -iz
excus|e (v.), -es, -ing, -ed iks'kju:z [eks-], -iz, -iŋ, -d
Exe eks
exeat, -s 'eksiæt [-sjæt], -s
execrab|le, -ly, -leness 'eksikrəb|l, -li, -lnis
execrat|e, -es, -ing, -ed 'eksikreit, -s, -iŋ, -id
execration, -s ,eksi'kreiʃən, -z
execrat|ive, -ively, -ory 'eksikreit|iv, -ivli, -əri
executant, -s ig'zekjutənt [eg-], -s
execut|e, -es, -ing, -ed, -er/s; -able 'eksikju:t, -s, -iŋ, -id, -ə*/z; -əbl
execution, -s ,eksi'kju:ʃən, -z
executioner, -s ,eksi'kju:ʃnə* [-ʃŋə*, -ʃənə*], -z
executive (s. adj.), -s, -ly ig'zekjutiv [eg-], -z, -li
executor, -s; -ship/s ig'zekjutə* [eg-], -z; -ʃip/s
executory ig'zekjutəri [eg-]
executrix, -es ig'zekjutriks [eg-], -iz
exegesis ,eksi'dʒi:sis
exegetic, -al, -ally, -s ,eksi'dʒetik, -əl, -əli, -s
Exell 'eksl

exemplar, -s ig'zemplə* [eg-, -lɑ:*], -z
exemplarity ,egzem'plæriti
exemplar|y, -ily, -iness ig'zemplər|i [eg-], -ili, -inis
exemplification, -s ig,zemplifi'keiʃən [eg-], -z
exempli|fy, -fies, -fying, -fied ig'zempli|fai [eg-], -faiz, -faiiŋ, -faid
exempt (adj. v.), -s, -ing, -ed ig'zempt [eg-], -s, -iŋ, -id
exemption, -s ig'zempʃən [eg-], -z
exequatur, -s ,eksi'kweitə*, -z
exequies 'eksikwiz
exercis|e (s. v.), -es, -ing, -ed, -er/s 'eksəsaiz, -iz, -iŋ, -d, -ə*/z
exercitation eg,zə:si'teiʃən [ig-]
exergue, -s ek'sə:g ['eksə:g], -z
exert, -s, -ing, -ed; -ive ig'zə:t [eg-], -s, -iŋ, -id; -iv
exertion, -s ig'zə:ʃən [eg-], -z
exes 'eksiz
Exeter 'eksitə* [-sətə*]
exeunt 'eksiʌnt [-sjʌnt, -sïənt, -sjənt]
exfoliat|e, -es, -ing, -ed eks'fəulieit [-ljeit], -s, -iŋ, -id
exfoliation, -s eks,fəuli'eiʃən [,eksfəu-], -z
exhalant eks'heilənt [eg'zei-]
exhalation, -s ,ekshə'leiʃən [,egzə'l-], -z
exhal|e, -es, -ing, -ed eks'heil [eg'zeil], -z, -iŋ, -d
exhaust (s. v.), -s, -ing, -ed, -er/s; -ible, -less ig'zɔ:st [eg-], -s, -iŋ, -id, -ə*/z; -əbl [-ibl], -lis
exhaustion ig'zɔ:stʃən [eg-]
exhaustive, -ly, -ness ig'zɔ:stiv [eg-], -li, -nis
exhibit (s.), -s ig'zibit [eg'zib-, 'egzib-], -s
exhibit (v.), -s, -ing, -ed, -or/s; -ive, -ory ig'zibit [eg-], -s, -iŋ, -id, -ə*/z; -iv, -əri
exhibition, -s ,eksi'biʃən, -z
exhibitioner, -s ,eksi'biʃŋə* [-ʃənə*, -ʃnə*], -z
exhibitionism ,eksi'biʃŋizəm [-ʃəni-]
exhilarant, -s ig'zilərənt [eg'z-, ek's-], -s
exhilarat|e, -es, -ing, -ed ig'ziləreit [eg'z-, ek's-], -s, -iŋ, -id
exhilaration ig,zilə'reiʃən [eg,z-, ek,s-]
exhilarative ig'zilərətiv [eg'z-, ek's-, -reit-]
exhort, -s, -ing, -ed ig'zɔ:t [eg-], -s, -iŋ, -id
exhortation, -s ,egzɔ:'teiʃən [,eksɔ:-], -z
exhortat|ive, -ory ig'zɔ:tət|iv [eg-], -əri
exhumation, -s ,ekshju:'meiʃən, -z
exhum|e, -es, -ing, -ed, -er/s eks'hju:m [ig'zju:m], -z, -iŋ, -d, -ə*/z

exigen|ce, -ces, -t 'eksidʒən|s ['egzi-], -siz, -t
exigenc|y, -ies 'eksidʒəns|i ['egzidʒ-, ig'zidʒ-, eg'zidʒ-, ek'sidʒ-], -iz
Note.—In the speech of young people the stress is usually on the second syllable. The pronunciations with stress on the first syllable seem likely to become old-fashioned before long.
exiguity ,eksi'gju(:)iti
exiguous, -ness eg'zigjŭəs [ig'z-, ek's-, -gjwəs], -nis
exil|e (s. v.), -es, -ing, -ed 'eksail ['egz-], -z, -iŋ, -d
exilic eg'zilik [ek's-]
exility eg'ziliti [ek's-]
exist, -s, -ing, -ed ig'zist [eg-], -s, -iŋ, -id
existen|ce, -ces, -t ig'zistən|s [eg-], -siz, -t
existential ,egzis'tenʃəl
existentialism ,egzis'tenʃəlizəm [-ʃli-]
exit, -s 'eksit ['egzit], -s
ex libris eks'laibris [-'lib-]
Exmoor 'eksmuə* [-mɔə*, -mɔ:*]
Exmouth (in Devon) 'eksmauθ [-məθ], (in Australia) 'eksmauθ
Note.—Both pronunciations are heard locally at Exmouth in Devon.
exode, -s 'eksəud, -z
exodus (E.), -es 'eksədəs, -iz
ex officio ,eksə'fiʃiəu [-sɔ'f-, -ʃjəu, -isiəu, -isjəu]
exogam|ous, -y ek'sɔgəm|əs, -i
exon, -s 'eksɔn, -z
exonerat|e, -es, -ing, -ed ig'zɔnəreit [eg-], -s, -iŋ, -id
exoneration ig,zɔnə'reiʃən [eg-]
exonerative ig'zɔnərətiv [eg-, -reit-]
exorbitan|ce, -cy, -t/ly ig'zɔ:bitən|s [eg-], -si, -t/li
exorcis|e, -es, -ing, -ed 'eksɔ:saiz ['egz-], -iz, -iŋ, -d
exorci|sm, -st/s 'eksɔ:si|zəm ['egz-], -st/s
exordium, -s ek'sɔ:djəm [eg'z-, -dïəm], -z
exoteric (s. adj.), -s, -al, -ally ,eksəu-'terik, -s, -əl, -əli
exotic (s. adj.), -s ig'zɔtik [ek's-, eg'z-], -s
expand, -s, -ing, -ed, -er/s iks'pænd [eks-], -z, -iŋ, -id, -ə*/z
expanse, -s iks'pæns [eks-], -iz
expansibility iks,pænsə'biliti [eks-, -si'b-, -lət-]
expansib|le, -ly, -leness iks'pænsəb|l [eks-, -sib-], -li, -lnis
expansile iks'pænsail [eks-]
expansion, -s iks'pænʃən [eks-], -z

expansive, -ly, -ness iks'pænsiv [eks-], -li, -nis

ex parte 'eks'pɑːti [-'--]

expatiat|e, -es, -ing, -ed eks'peiʃieit [iks-, -ʃjeit], -s, -iŋ, -id

expatiation, -s eks,peiʃi'eiʃən [iks-], -z

expatiat|ive, -ory eks'peiʃjət|iv [iks-, -ʃiət-, -ʃieit-], -əri

expatriat|e, -es, -ing, -ed eks'pætrieit [iks-, -'peit-], -s, -iŋ, -id

expatriation eks,pætri'eiʃən [iks,pæt-, ,ekspeit-, ,ekspæt-]

expect, -s, -ing, -ed, -er/s iks'pekt [eks-], -s, -iŋ, -id, -ə*/z

expectan|ce, -cy, -cies, -t/ly iks'pektən|s [eks-], -si, -siz, -t/li

expectation, -s ,ekspek'teiʃən, -z

expectorant (s. adj.), -s eks'pektərənt [iks-], -s

expectorat|e, -es, -ing, -ed eks'pektəreit [iks-], -s, -iŋ, -id

expectoration eks,pektə'reiʃən [iks-]

expedien|ce, -cy, -t/s, -tly iks'piːdjən|s [eks-, -diən-], -si, -t/s, -tli

expedit|e, -es, -ing, -ed 'ekspidait [-ped-], -s, -iŋ, -id

expedition, -s ,ekspi'diʃən, -z　　　[-nis

expeditious, -ly, -ness ,ekspi'diʃəs, -li,

expel, -s, -ling, -led; -lable iks'pel [eks-], -z, -iŋ, -d; -əbl

expend, -s, -ing, -ed iks'pend [eks-], -z, -iŋ, -id

expendable (s. adj.), -s iks'pendəbl [eks-], -z

expenditure, -s iks'penditʃə* [eks-], -z

expense, -s iks'pens [eks-], -iz

expensive, -ly, -ness iks'pensiv [eks-], -li, -nis

experienc|e (s. v.), -es, -ing, -ed iks'piəriəns [eks-], -iz, -iŋ, -t　　　[-s

experiment (s.), -s iks'perimənt [eks-]

experiment (v.), -s, -ing, -ed iks'periment [eks-], -s, -iŋ, -id

experiment|al, -ally eks,peri'ment|l [iks,per-, ,eksper-], -əli [-l̩i]

experimentali|sm, -st/s eks,peri'mentəli|zəm [iks,per-, ,eksper-, -t|li-], -st/s

experimentaliz|e [-is|e], -es, -ing, -ed eks,peri'mentəlaiz [iks,per-, ,eksper-], -iz, -iŋ, -d

experimentation, -s eks,perimen'teiʃən [iks-], -z

expert (s.), -s 'ekspəːt, -s

expert (adj.), -est, -ly, -ness 'ekspəːt [also eks'pəːt, iks'pəːt, when not attributive], -ist, -li, -nis

expertise ,ekspəː'tiːz

xpiable 'ekspiəbl [-pjə-]

expiat|e, -es, -ing, -ed, -or/s 'ekspieit [-pjeit], -s, -iŋ, -id, -ə*/z

expiation, -s ,ekspi'eiʃən, -z

expiatory 'ekspiətəri [-pjət-, -pieit-]

expiration, -s ,ekspaiə'reiʃən [-pə'r-, -pi'r-], -z

expiratory iks'paiərətəri [eks-]

expir|e, -es, -ing, -ed iks'paiə* [eks-], -z, expiry iks'paiəri [eks-]　　　[-riŋ, -d

explain, -s, -ing, -ed, -er/s; -able iks'plein [eks-], -z, -iŋ, -d, -ə*/z; -əbl

explanation, -s ,eksplə'neiʃən, -z

explanator|y, -ily, -iness iks'plænətər|i [eks-, -nit-], -ili, -inis

expletive (s. adj.), -s, -ly eks'pliːtiv [iks-], -z, -li　　　　　　[iks'p-]

explicable 'eksplikəbl [eks'plikəbl, Note.—The pronunciations with stress on the second syllable are becoming common, and seem likely to supersede the other before long.

explicat|e, -es, -ing, -ed 'eksplikeit, -s, -iŋ, -id

explication, -s ,ekspli'keiʃən, -z

explicative eks'plikətiv [iks-, 'eksplikeitiv]

explicatory eks'plikətəri [iks-, 'eksplikeitəri]　　　　　　[-nis

explicit, -ly, -ness iks'plisit [eks-], -li,

explod|e, -es, -ing, -ed, -er/s iks'pləud [eks-], -z, -iŋ, -id, -ə*/z

exploit (s.), -s 'eksplɔit, -s

exploit (v.), -s, -ing, -ed iks'plɔit [eks-], -s, -iŋ, -id

exploitation ,eksplɔi'teiʃən

exploration, -s ,eksplɔː'reiʃən [-plə'r-], -z

explorat|ive, -ory eks'plɔːrət|iv [iks-, -'plɔər-, -'plɔr-], -əri

explor|e, -es, -ing, -ed, -er/s iks'plɔː* [eks-, -'plɔə*], -z, -riŋ, -d, -rə*/z

explosion, -s iks'pləuʒən [eks-], -z

explosive (s. adj.), -s, -ly, -ness iks'pləusiv [eks-, -əuziv], -z, -li, -nis

exponent, -s eks'pəunənt [iks-], -s

exponential ,ekspəu'nenʃəl

export (s.), -s 'ekspɔːt, -s

export (v.), -s, -ing, -ed, -er/s eks'pɔːt [iks-, 'ekspɔːt], -s, -iŋ, -id, -ə*/z

exportable eks'pɔːtəbl [iks-]

exportation ,ekspɔː'teiʃən

exposal, -s iks'pəuzəl [eks-], -z

expos|e, -es, -ing, -ed, -edness, -er/s iks'pəuz [eks-], -iz, -iŋ, -d, -dnis, -ə*/z

exposé, -s eks'pəuzei (ɛkspoze), -z

exposition, -s ,ekspəu'ziʃən [-pu'z-], -z

expositive eks'pɔzitiv [iks-, -zət-]

exposit|or/s, -ory eks'pɔzit|ə*/z [iks-], -əri

expostulat|e, -es, -ing, -ed, -or/s iks-'postjuleit [eks-, -tʃu-], -s, -iŋ, -id, -ə*/z

expostulation, -s iks,pɔstju'leiʃən [eks-, -tʃu-], -z

expostulative iks'pɔstjulətiv [eks-, -tʃu-, -leit-]

expostulatory iks'pɔstjulətəri [eks-, -tʃu-, -leitəri]

exposure, -s iks'pəuʒə* [eks-], -z

expound, -s, -ing, -ed, -er/s iks'paund [eks-], -z, -iŋ, -id, -ə*/z

express (s. adj. v.), -es; -ly, -ness; -ing, -ed iks'pres [eks-], -iz; -li, -nis; -iŋ, -t

expressible iks'presəbl [eks-, -sib-]

expression, -s iks'preʃən [eks-], -z

expressional iks'preʃənl [eks-, -ʃnl, -ʃnl̩]

expression|ism, -ist/s iks'preʃn|izəm [eks-, -ʃən-], -ist/s [-ʃn̩'is-]

expressionistic iks,preʃə'nistik [eks-,

expressionless iks'preʃənlis [eks-]

expressive, -ly, -ness iks'presiv [eks-], -li, -nis [-men

express|man, -men iks'pres|mæn [eks-],

expropriat|e, -es, -ing, -ed, -or/s eks-'prəuprieit, -s, -iŋ, -id, -ə*/z

expropriation, -s eks,prəupri'eiʃən [,eksprəu-], -z [-iŋ, -d

expugn, -s, -ing, -ed eks'pju:n [iks-], -z,

expugnable eks'pʌgnəbl [iks-]

expulsion, -s iks'pʌlʃən [eks-], -z

expulsive iks'pʌlsiv [eks-]

expung|e, -es, -ing, -ed eks'pʌndʒ [iks-], -iz, -iŋ, -d

expurgat|e, -es, -ing, -ed, -or/s 'eks-pə:geit, -s, -iŋ, -id, -ə*/z

expurgation, -s ,ekspə:'geiʃən, -z

expurgatorial eks,pə:gə'tɔ:riəl [,ekspə:-]

expurgatory eks'pə:gətəri

exquisite, -ly, -ness 'ekskwizit [eks-'kwizit, iks'kwizit], -li, -nis

Note.—*The forms* eks'kwizit *and* iks'kwizit *are becoming very common.*

exscind, -s, -ing, -ed ek'sind [ik-], -z, -iŋ, -id [-id

exsect, -s, -ing, -ed ek'sekt [ik-], -s, -iŋ,

exsection, -s ek'sekʃən [ik-], -z

ex-service 'eks'sə:vis ['eks,sə:vis]

exsiccat|e, -es, -ing, -ed, -or/s 'eksikeit ['ekssi-], -s, -iŋ, -id, -ə*/z

exsiccation ,eksi'keiʃən [,ekssi-]

extant eks'tænt [iks't-, 'ekstənt]

extemporaneous, -ly, -ness eks,tem-pə'reinjəs [,ekstem-, -pu'r-, -niəs], -li, -nis

extemporary iks'tempərəri [eks-]

extempore eks'tempəri [iks-]

extemporization [-isa-], -s eks,tem-pərai'zeiʃən [iks-, -pur-], -z

extemporiz|e [-is|e], -es, -ing, -ed, -er/s iks'tempəraiz [eks-, -pur-], -iz, -iŋ, -d, -ə*/z [-iŋ, -id

extend, -s, -ing, -ed iks'tend [eks-], -z,

extensibility iks,tensə'biliti [eks-, -si'b-, -lət-]

extensible iks'tensəbl [eks-, -sib-]

extensile eks'tensail [iks-]

extension, -s iks'tenʃən [eks-], -z

extensive, -ly, -ness iks'tensiv [eks-], -li, -nis

extensor, -s iks'tensə* [eks-], -z

extent, -s iks'tent [eks-], -s

extenuat|e, -es, -ing/ly, -ed eks'ten-jueit [iks-], -s, -iŋ/li, -id

extenuation, -s eks,tenju'eiʃən [iks-], -z

extenuative eks'tenjŭətiv [iks-, -jwət-, -jueit-]

extenuatory eks'tenjŭətəri [iks-, -jwət-, -jueitəri]

exterior (s. adj.), -s, -ly eks'tiəriə* ['eks't-, iks't-], -z, -li

exteriority eks,tiəri'ɔriti [,ekstiə-, iks,t-]

exterioriz|e [-is|e], -es, -ing, -ed eks'tiəriəraiz [iks-], -iz, -iŋ, -d

exterminable eks'tə:minəbl [iks-]

exterminat|e, -es, -ing, -ed, -or/s iks-'tə:mineit [eks-], -s, -iŋ, -id, -ə*/z

extermination, -s iks,tə:mi'neiʃən [eks-], -z

exterminative iks'tə:minətiv [eks-, -neit-] [-neit-]

exterminatory iks'tə:minətəri [eks-,

extern (s. adj.), -s eks'tə:n ['eks'tə:n], -z

extern|al (s. adj.), -als, -ally eks'tə:n|l ['eks't-, 'ekst-, iks't-], -lz, -əli [-li]

Note.—*The form* 'ekstə:nl *is chiefly used attributively, or when the word is in contrast with* internal.

externali|sm, -st/s eks'tə:nəli|zəm [-nli-, iks't-], -st/s

externality ,ekstə:'næliti

externalization [-isa-] eks,tə:nəlai'zei-ʃən [iks't-, -nlai-]

externaliz|e [-is|e], -es, -ing, -ed eks-'tə:nəlaiz [iks't-, -nlaiz], -iz, -iŋ, -d

exterritorial 'eks,teri'tɔ:riəl

extinct iks'tiŋkt [eks-]

extinction, -s iks'tiŋkʃən [eks-], -z

extinctive iks'tiŋktiv [eks-]

extinguish, -es, -ing, -ed, -er/s, -ment, -able iks'tiŋgwiʃ [eks-], -iz, -iŋ, -t -ə*/z, -mənt; -əbl

extirpat|e, -es, -ing, -ed, -or/s 'eks-tə:peit [-təp-], -s, -iŋ, -id, -ə*/z

extirpation, -s ,ekstə:'peiʃən, -z

extol, -s, -ling, -led iks'təul [eks-, -'tɔl], -z, -iŋ, -d
Exton 'ekstən
extort, -s, -ing, -ed, -er/s iks'tɔːt [eks-], -s, -iŋ, -id, -ə*/z
extortion, -s iks'tɔːʃən [eks-], -z
extortionate,   -ly   iks'tɔːʃn̩it [eks-, -ʃənit, -ʃnit], -li
extortioner, -s iks'tɔːʃn̩ə* [eks-, -ʃənə*, -ʃnə*], -z
extra (s. adj. adv.), -s 'ekstrə, -z
extract (s.), -s 'ekstrækt, -s
extract (v.), -s, -ing, -ed, -or/s; -able, -ive iks'trækt [eks-], -s, -iŋ, -id, -ə*/z; -əbl, -iv
extraction, -s iks'trækʃən [eks-], -z
extradit|e, -es, -ing, -ed; -able 'ekstrədait, -s, -iŋ, -id; -əbl
extradition, -s ˌekstrə'diʃən, -z
extrados, -es eks'treidɔs, -iz
extrajudici|al, -ally 'ekstrədʒu(ː)'diʃ|əl, -əli [-l̩i]
extramural 'ekstrə'mjuərəl [-'mjɔər-, -'mjɔːr-]
extraneous, -ly eks'treinjəs [-nɪəs], -li
extraordinar|y, -ily, -iness iks'trɔːdnr|i [eks'trɔː-, ˌekstrə'ɔː-, -dinəri, -dənəri], -ili, -inis
extrapolat|e, -es, -ing, -ed eks'træpəuleit [iks-], -s, -iŋ, -id
extrasensory 'ekstrə'sensəri
extraterritorial 'ekstrəˌteri'tɔːrɪəl
extravagan|ce, -ces, -t/ly iks'trævigən|s [eks-, -vəg-], -siz, -t/li
extravaganza,   -s   eksˌtrævə'gænzə [iksˌtræv-, ˌekstræv-], -z
extravasat|e, -es, -ing, -ed eks'trævəseit [iks-], -s, -iŋ, -id
extravasation,   -s   eksˌtrævə'seiʃən [ˌekstræv-], -z
extreme (s. adj.), -s, -st, -ly, -ness iks'triːm [eks-], -z, -ist, -li, -nis
Note.—Some Catholics pronounce 'ekstriːm in extreme unction.
extremi|sm, -st/s iks'triːmi|zəm [eks-], -st/s
extremit|y, -ies iks'tremit|i [eks-], -iz
extricable 'ekstrikəbl
extricat|e, -es, -ing, -ed 'ekstrikeit, -s, -iŋ, -id
extrication ˌekstri'keiʃən
extrinsic, -al, -ally eks'trinsik, -əl, -əli
extroversion ˌekstrəu'vəːʃən
extrovert, -s 'ekstrəuvəːt -s
extrud|e, -s, -ing, -ed eks'truːd [iks-], -z, -iŋ, -id
extrusion, -s eks'truːʒən [iks-], -z
extrus|ive, -ory eks'truːs|iv [iks-], -əri

exuberan|ce, -cy, -t/ly ig'zjuːbərən|s [eg-, -'zuː-], -si, -t/li
exuberat|e, -es, -ing, -ed ig'zjuːbəreit [eg-, -'zuː-], -s, -iŋ, -id
exudation, -s, eksjuː'deiʃən [ˌegz-], -z
exud|e, -es, -ing, -ed ig'zjuːd [eg'z-, ek's-], -z, -iŋ, -id
exult, -s, -ing/ly, -ed ig'zʌlt [eg-], -s, -iŋ/li, -id
exultan|ce, -cy, -t/ly ig'zʌltən|s [eg-], -si, -t/li
exultation ˌegzʌl'teiʃən [ˌeks-, -əl-]
exuviae ig'zjuːvii: [eg-, -'zuː-]
exuvial ig'zjuːvjəl [eg-, -'zuː-, -vɪəl]
exuviat|e, -es, -ing, -ed ig'zjuːvieit [eg-, -'zuː-, -vjeit], -s, -iŋ, -id
exuviation igˌzjuːvi'eiʃən [eg-, -ˌzuː-]
ex voto 'eks'vəutəu
Eyam i:əm
eyas, -es 'aiəs, -iz
Eyck aik
eye (s. v.), -s, -ing, -d ai, -z, -iŋ, -d
Eye (place) ai
eye-ball, -s 'ai-bɔːl, -z
eyebright 'ai-brait
eyebrow, -s 'ai-brau, -z
eyeglass, -es 'ai-glɑːs, -iz
eye-hole, -s 'aihəul, -z
eyelash, -es 'ai-læʃ, -iz
eyeless 'ailis
eyelet, -s 'ailit, -s
eye-lid, -s 'ailid, -z
eyemark, -s 'ai-mɑːk, -s
Eyemouth 'aiməθ
eye-opener, -s 'aiˌəupnə* [-pn̩ə*], -z
eye-piece, -s 'ai-piːs, -iz
eye-rhyme, -s 'airaim, -z
eyeshot 'ai-ʃɔt
eyesight, -s 'ai-sait, -s
eyesore, -s 'ai-sɔː* [-sɔə*], -z
eye|-tooth, -teeth 'ai|-tuːθ, -tiːθ
eyewash 'aiwɔʃ
eye-water 'aiˌwɔːtə*
eye-witness, -es 'ai'witnis [-ˌwit-], -iz
Eyles ailz
Eynsford 'einsfəd
Eynsham (in Oxfordshire) 'einʃəm [locally 'ensəm]
eyot, -s eit ['eiət], -s
Note.—The local pronunciation in the Thames valley is eit.
eyre (E.) ɛə*
eyr|ie, -y, -ies 'aiər|i ['ɛər-], -i, -iz
Eyton (in Shropshire) 'aitn, (in Herefordshire) 'eitn, (surname) 'aitn, 'i:tn
Ezekiel i'zi:kjəl [-kɪəl]
Eziongeber 'i:ziɔn'gi:bə* [-zɪən-, -zjən-]
Ezra 'ezrə

F

F (*the letter*), -'s ef, -s
fa (*musical note*), -s fɑ:, -z
Fabel 'feibəl
Faber (*English name*) 'feibə*, (*German name*) 'fɑ:bə* ('fɑ:bər)
Fabian, -s 'feibjən [-biən], -z
Fa|bius, -bii 'fei|bjəs [-biəs], -biai
fable, -s, -d 'feibl, -z, -d
fabric, -s 'fæbrik, -s
fabricat|e, -es, -ing, -ed, -or/s 'fæbri- keit, -s, -iŋ, -id, -ə*/z
fabrication, -s ˌfæbri'keiʃən, -z
Fabricius fə'briʃiəs [-fjəs, -ʃəs]
fabulist, -s 'fæbjulist, -s
fabulous, -ly, -ness 'fæbjuləs, -li, -nis
Fabyan 'feibjən [-biən]
façade, -s fə'sɑ:d [fæ's-], -z
fac|e (*s. v.*), -es, -ing, -ed feis, -iz, -iŋ, -t
face-ache 'feis-eik
face-lifting 'feisˌliftiŋ
facer, -s 'feisə*, -z
facet, -s, -ed 'fæsit [-set, 'feis-], -s, -id
facetiae fə'si:ʃii: [-ʃji:]
facetious, -ly, -ness fə'si:ʃəs, -li, -nis
facia, -s 'feiʃə, -z
faci|al, -ally 'feiʃ|əl [-ʃj|əl, -ʃi|əl], -əli
facile 'fæsail [-sil]
facilitat|e, -es, -ing, -ed fə'siliteit, -s, -iŋ, -id
facilitation fəˌsili'teiʃən
facilit|y, -ies fə'silit|i [-lət-], -iz
facing (*s.*), -s 'feisiŋ, -z
facsimile, -s fæk'simili, -z
fact, -s fækt, -s
fact-finding 'fæktˌfaindiŋ
faction, -s 'fækʃən, -z
factional 'fækʃənl [-ʃn̩l, -ʃn̩l]
factious, -ly, -ness 'fækʃəs, -li, -nis
factitious, -ly, -ness fæk'tiʃəs, -li, -nis
factitive 'fæktitiv
factor, -s; -age 'fæktə*, -z; -ridʒ
factorial fæk'tɔ:riəl
factor|y, -ies 'fæktər|i, -iz
factotum, -s fæk'təutəm, -z
factual 'fæktʃuəl [-tjwəl, -tjul, -tjŭəl, -tʃwəl, -tʃul]
facul|a, -ae 'fækjul|ə, -i:
facultative 'fækəltətiv [-teit-]
facult|y, -ies 'fækəlt|i, -iz

fad, -s fæd, -z
Faddiley 'fædili
faddi|sh, -sm, -st/s 'fædi|ʃ, -zəm, -st/s
Faddle 'fædl
fadd|y, -ier, -iest, -ily, -iness 'fæd|i, -iə*, -iist, -ili, -inis
fad|e, -es, -ing, -ed feid, -z, -iŋ, -id
Fadladeen ˌfædlə'di:n
faeces 'fi:si:z
Faed feid
faerie [-ry] (F.) 'feiəri ['fɛər-]
Faeroe, -s 'fɛərəu, -z
Faeroese ˌfɛərəu'i:z
Fafner 'fɑ:fnə* ['fæf-] ('fa:fnər)
fag (*s. v.*), -s, -ging, -ged fæg, -z, -iŋ, -d
Fagan 'feigən
fag-end, -s 'fæg'end ['fægend], -z
Fagg(e) fæg
Faggetter 'fægitə*
faggot, -s 'fægət, -s
Fagin 'feigin
fag-master, -s 'fægˌmɑ:stə*, -z
fagott|ist/s, -o/s fə'gɔt|ist/s, -əu/z
fah (*note in Tonic Sol-fa*), -s fɑ:, -z
Fah|ey, -ie 'fei|i, -i
Fahrenheit 'færənhait ['fɑ:r-]
Fahy 'fɑ:i
faience fai'ɑ̃:ns [fei-, -'ɔ̃:ns, -'ɑ:ns, -'ɔ:ns] (fajɑ̃:s)
fail (*s. v.*), -s, -ing/s, -ed feil, -z, -iŋ/z, -d
faille (*silk material*) feil
Failsworth 'feilzwə:θ
failure, -s 'feiljə*, -z
fain fein
Fainall 'feinɔ:l
faint (*s. adj. v.*), -s, -ly, -ness; -ing, -ed feint, -s, -li, -nis; -iŋ, -id
faint-heart, -s 'feinthɑ:t, -s
faint-hearted, -ly, -ness 'feint'hɑ:tid ['feintˌh-], -li, -nis
faintish 'feintiʃ
Fainwell 'feinwel [-wəl]
fair (*s. adj. adv.*) (F.), -s, -er, -est, -ly -ness fɛə*, -z, -rə*, -rist, -li, -nis
Fairbairn, -s 'fɛəbɛən, -z
Fairbank, -s 'fɛəbæŋk, -s
Fairbeard 'fɛəbiəd
Fairbrother 'fɛəˌbrʌðə*

Fairburn 'fɛəbə:n
Fairbury 'fɛəbəri
Fairchild 'fɛə-tʃaild
Fairclough 'fɛə-klʌf
fair-do 'fɛə'du:
fair-faced 'fɛə'feist
Fairfax 'fɛə-fæks
Fairfield 'fɛə-fi:ld
Fairford 'fɛəfəd
fair-haired 'fɛə'hɛəd ['fɛəh- *esp. when attributive*]
Fairhaven 'fɛə‚heivən
Fairholme 'fɛəhəum
Fairholt 'fɛəhəult
fairish 'fɛəriʃ
Fairlegh 'fɛəli
Fairleigh 'fɛəli, -li:
Fairlight 'fɛəlait
Fairman 'fɛəmən
fair-minded 'fɛə'maindid ['fɛə‚m-]
Fairmont 'fɛəmənt [-mɔnt]
Fairmount 'fɛəmaunt
Fairport 'fɛə-pɔ:t
Fairscribe 'fɛə-skraib
Fairservice 'fɛə‚sə:vis
fair-spoken 'fɛə'spəukən ['fɛə‚s-]
Fairview 'fɛəvju:
fairway, -s 'fɛəwei, -z
fair-weather 'fɛə‚weðə*
Fairweather 'fɛə‚weðə*
fair|y (*s. adj.*), -ies 'fɛər|i, -iz
fairy|land, -like 'fɛəri|lænd, -laik
fairy-ring, -s 'fɛəri'riŋ, -z
fairy-tale, -s 'fɛəriteil, -z
faith (F.), -s feiθ, -s
faith|ful (F.), -fully, -fulness 'feiθ|fʊl, -fuli [-fəli], -fʊlnis
Faithfull 'feiθfʊl
faith-heal|er/s, -ing 'feiθ‚hi:l|ə*/z, -iŋ
faithless, -ly, -ness 'feiθlis, -li, -nis
Faithorne 'fei-θɔ:n
fak|e (*s. v.*), -es, -ing, -ed, -er/s feik, -s, -iŋ, -t, -ə*/z
Fakenham 'feikṇəm [-knəm]
Fakes feiks
fakir, -s; -ism 'feikiə* ['fæ-, 'fɑ:-, fə'kiə*], -z; -rizəm
Fal fæl
fa-la, -s fɑ:'lɑ:, -z
Falaba ‚fælə'bɑ:
falcate, -d 'fælkeit, -id
falchion, -s 'fɔ:ltʃən, -z
falcon, -s, -er/s 'fɔ:lkən ['fɔlk-, 'fɔ:k-], -z, -ə*/z
Note.—'fɔ:k- *is the usual pronunciation among those who practise the sport of falconry.*
Falconbridge 'fɔ:kənbridʒ ['fɔ:lk-, 'fɔlk-]

Falconer 'fɔ:knə*, fɔ:lkənə* ['fɔlk-]
falconry 'fɔ:lkənri ['fɔlk-, 'fɔ:k-] (*see note to* falcon)
Falcy 'fælsi, 'fɔ:lsi
Falder 'fɔ:ldə* ['fɔl-]
falderal, -s 'fældə'ræl ['—], -z
faldstool, -s 'fɔ:ldstu:l, -z
Falerii fə'liəriai [fæ'l-, -rii:]
Falernian fə'lə:njən [-niən]
Falk fɔ:k
Falkenbridge 'fɔ:kənbridʒ ['fɔ:lk-, 'fɔlk-]
Falkirk 'fɔ:lkə:k ['fɔlk-]
Falkland (*Viscount*) 'fɔ:klənd, (*place in Scotland*) 'fɔ:lklənd ['fɔlk-], (*islands*) 'fɔ:lklənd ['fɔlk-, -'fɔ:k-]
Falkner 'fɔ:knə*
fall (*s. v.*), -s, -ing, fell, fallen fɔ:l, -z, -iŋ, fel, 'fɔ:lən
fallacious, -ly, -ness fə'leiʃəs, -li, -nis
fallac|y, -ies 'fæləs|i, -iz
fal-lal, -s 'fæ'læl ['fæl'læl, -'-], -z
Faller 'fælə*
fallibility ‚fæli'biliti [-lə'b-, -lət-]
fallib|le, -ly, -leness 'fæləb|l [-lib-], -li, -nis
Fallod|en, -on 'fæləud|ən, -ən
fall-out 'fɔ:laut
fallow (*s. adj. v.*), -s, -ness; -ing, -ed 'fæləu, -z, -nis; -iŋ, -d
fallow-deer 'fæləudiə* ['fæləu'd-]
Fallowfield 'fæləufi:ld
Fallows 'fæləuz
Falmouth 'fælməθ
false, -r, -st, -ly, -ness fɔ:ls [fɔls], -ə*, -ist, -li, -nis
falsehood, -s 'fɔ:lshud ['fɔls-, -sud], -z
falsetto, -s fɔ:l'setəu [fɔl-], -z
Falshaw 'fɔ:lʃɔ: ['fɔl-]
falsification, -s 'fɔ:lsifi'keiʃən ['fɔls-, ‚—'—], -z
falsi|fy -fies, -fying, -fied, -fier/s 'fɔ:lsi|fai ['fɔls-], -faiz, -faiiŋ, -faid, -faiə*/z [-fai-ə*/z]
falsit|y, -ies 'fɔ:lsit|i ['fɔls-], -iz
Falstaff 'fɔ:lstɑ:f ['fɔl-]
Falstaffian fɔ:ls'tɑ:fjən [fɔl-, -fiən]
falt|er (*s. v.*), -ers, -ering/ly, -ered, -erer/s 'fɔ:lt|ə* ['fɔl-], -əz, -əriŋ/li, -əd, -ərə*/z
Famagusta ‚fæmə'gustə [‚fɑ:m-]
fame, -d feim, -d
familiar (*s. adj.*), -s, -ly fə'miljə* [-liə*], -z, -li
familiarit|y, -ies fə‚mili'ærit|i, -iz
familiariz|e (-is|e), -es, -ing, -ed fə'miljəraiz [-liər-], -iz, -iŋ, -d
famil|y, -ies 'fæmil|i [-məl-], -iz
famine, -s 'fæmin, -z

famish, -es, -ing, -ed 'fæmiʃ, -iz, -iŋ, -t
famous, -ly, -ness 'feiməs, -li, -nis
fan (s. v.) (F.), **-s, -ning, -ned** fæn, -z, -iŋ, -d
fanatic (s. adj.), **-s, -al, -ally** fə'nætik [fn̩'æ-], -s, -əl, -əli
fanaticism fə'nætisizəm [fn̩'æ-]
fanaticiz|e (-is|e), -es, -ing, -ed fə'nætisaiz [fn̩'æ-], -iz, -iŋ, -d
fanci|ful, -fully, -fulness 'fænsi|ful, -fuli [-fəli], -fulnis
Fancourt 'fænkɔːt
fanc|y (s. adj. v.), **-ies, -ying, -ied, -er/s** 'fæns|i, -iz, -iiŋ [-jiŋ], -id, -iə*/z [-jə*/z]
fancy-ball, -s 'fænsi'bɔːl, -z
fancy-dress, -es 'fænsi'dres [also '— when attributive], -iz
fancy-free 'fænsi'friː
fancy-work 'fænsiwəːk
fandango, -s fæn'dæŋgəu, -z
fane (F.), **-s** fein, -z
Faneuil 'fænl
fanfare, -s 'fænfɛə*, -z
fanfaronade, -s ,fænfærə'nɑːd [-'neid], -z
fang (F.), **-s, -ed; -less** fæŋ, -z, -d; -lis
Faning 'feiniŋ
fanlight, -s 'fænlait, -s
fanner, -s 'fænə*, -z
Fann|ick, -ing, -y 'fæn|ik, -iŋ, -i
Fanshawe 'fænʃɔː
fantail, -s 'fæn-teil, -z
fantasia, -s fæn'teizjə [-'tɑːz-, -zïə, ,fæntə'ziə, ,fæntə'siə], -z
fantastic, -al, -ally, -alness fæn'tæstik [fən-], -əl, -əli, -əlnis
fantas|y, -ies 'fæntəs|i [-əz|i], -iz
fantod, -s 'fæntɒd, -z
far fɑː*
farad, -s 'færəd, -z
Faraday 'færədi [-dei]
far-away (adj.) 'fɑːrəwei
farce, -s fɑːs, -iz
farceur, -s fɑː'səː*, -z
farcic|al, -ally 'fɑːsik|əl, -əli
farcy 'fɑːsi
fardel, -s 'fɑːdəl, -z
Fardell 'fɑːdel
far|e (s. v.), **-es, -ing, -ed** fɛə*, -z, -riŋ,
Farebrother 'fɛə,brʌðə*   [-d
Fareham 'fɛərəm
farewell, -s 'fɛə'wel ['—, -'- according to sentence-stress], -z
Farewell 'fɛəwel [-wəl]
far-famed 'fɑː'feimd [also 'fɑː-feimd when attributive]
far-fetched 'fɑː'fetʃt [also 'fɑː-fetʃt when attributive]

far-flung 'fɑː'flʌŋ [also 'fɑː-flʌŋ when attributive]
Farg|o, -us 'fɑːg|əu, -əs
Faribault 'færibəu
Faridkot fə'riːdkəut (Hind. fəridkoṭ)
farina fə'rainə
Farina fə'riːnə
farinaceous ,færi'neiʃəs
Faring|don, -ton 'færiŋ|dən, -tən
farinose 'færinəus
Farjeon 'fɑːdʒən
Far|leigh, -ley 'fɑː|li, -li
farm (s. v.), **-s, -ing, -ed, -er/s** fɑːm, -z, -iŋ, -d, -ə*/z
Farm|an, -er 'fɑːm|ən, -ə*
farmhou|se, -ses 'fɑːmhau|s, -ziz
Farmington 'fɑːmiŋtən
farmstead, -s 'fɑːmsted, -z
farmyard, -s 'fɑːmjɑːd ['-'-], -z
Farnaby 'fɑːnəbi
Farnborough 'fɑːnbərə
Farn(e) fɑːn
Farn|ham, -worth 'fɑːn|əm, -wəːθ
faro 'fɛərəu
Faroe 'fɛərəu
faroese ,fɛərəu'iːz
farouche fə'ruːʃ [fɑː'r-, fæ'r-]
Farquhar 'fɑːkwə*, 'fɑːkə*
Farquharson 'fɑːkəsn, 'fɑːkwə-
Farr fɑː*
farrago, -(e)s fə'rɑːgəu [-'reig-], -z
Farragut 'færəgət
Farr|ant, -ar 'fær|ənt, -ə*
Farr|en, -er 'fær|ən, -ə*
far-reaching 'fɑː'riːtʃiŋ [also 'fɑː,r- when attributive]
farrier, -s; -y, -ies 'færïə*, -z; -ri, -riz
Farring|don, -ford, -ton 'færiŋ|dən, -fəd, -tən
farrow (s. v.) (F.), **-s, -ing, -ed** 'færəu, -z, -iŋ, -d
far-seeing 'fɑː'siːiŋ ['fɑː,siːiŋ]
far-sighted, -ness 'fɑː'saitid, -nis
Farsley 'fɑːzli
farth|er, -est 'fɑːð|ə*, -ist
farthing, -s 'fɑːðiŋ, -z
farthingale, -s 'fɑːðiŋgeil, -z
Farwell 'fɑːwel [-wəl]
fasces 'fæsiːz
fascia, -s (name-board, instrument board, belt on a planet) 'feiʃə [-ʃjə, -ʃïə], (strip of stone, wood, etc., in architecture) 'feiʃə [-ʃjə, -ʃïə, also when referring to classical architecture 'feisjə], (medical term) 'fæʃïə [-ʃjə, -ʃə], -z
fasciated 'fæʃieitid
fascicle, -s 'fæsikl, -z

fascicule, -s 'fæsikju:l, -z
fascinat|e, -es, -ing/ly, -ed, -or/s 'fæsineit, -s, -iŋ/li, -id, -ə*/z
fascination, -s ˌfæsi'neiʃən, -z
fascine, -s fæ'si:n [fə's-], -z
fascism 'fæʃizəm [-æsi-]
Fascist, -s 'fæʃist [-æsi-], -s
Fascisti fæ'ʃisti: [fə'ʃ-]
fash, -es, -ing, -ed fæʃ, -iz, -iŋ, -t
fashi|on (s. v.), -ons, -oning, -oned, -oner/s 'fæʃ|ən, -ənz, -ŋiŋ [-əniŋ], -ənd, -ŋə*/z [-ənə*/z]
fashionab|le, -ly, -leness 'fæʃnəb|l [-ʃnə-], -li, -lnis
fashion-plate, -s 'fæʃənpleit, -s
Fasolt 'fɑ:zɔlt ('fɑ:zɔlt)
fast (s. adj. v. adv.), -s, -er, -est, -ness; -ing, -ed, -er/s fɑ:st, -s, -ə*, -ist, -nis; -iŋ, -id, -ə*/z
fast-day, -s 'fɑ:stdei, -z
fast|en, -ens, -ening, -ened 'fɑ:s|n, -nz, -niŋ [-ŋiŋ], -nd
fastener, -s 'fɑ:snə*, -z
fastening (s.) (contrivance for fastening), -s 'fɑ:sniŋ, -z
fasti (F.) 'fæsti: [-tai]
fastidious, -ly, -ness fəs'tidiəs [fæs-, -djəs], -li, -nis
fastness, -es 'fɑ:stnis, -iz
Fastnet 'fɑ:stnet [-nit]
Fastolf 'fæstɔlf
fat (s. adj.), -ter, -test, -ness, -ted fæt, -ə*, -ist, -nis, -id
fat|al, -ally 'feit|l, -əli [tļi]
fatali|sm, -st/s 'feitəli|zəm [-tļi-], -st/s
fatalistic ˌfeitə'listik [-tļ'i-]
fatalit|y, -ies fə'tælit|i [fei't-], -iz
fate (F.), -s, -ed feit, -s, -id
fateful 'feitfʊl
fathead, -s 'fæthed, -z
fath|er (s. v.), -ers, -ering, -ered 'fɑ:ð|ə*, -əz, -əriŋ, -əd
fatherhood 'fɑ:ðəhud
father-in-law, fathers-in-law 'fɑ:ðərinlɔ: [-ðəin-], 'fɑ:ðəzinlɔ:
fatherland, -s 'fɑ:ðəlænd, -z
fatherless 'fɑ:ðəlis
fatherl|y, -iness 'fɑ:ðəl|i, -inis
fathom (s. v.), -s, -ing, -ed; -able, -less 'fæðəm, -z, -iŋ, -d; -əbl, -lis
fathom-line, -s 'fæðəmlain, -z
fatigu|e (s. v.), -es, -ing/ly, -ed fə'ti:g, -z, -iŋ/li, -d
Fatima 'fætimə
fatling, -s 'fætliŋ, -z
fatt|en, -ens, -ening, -ened, -ener/s 'fæt|n, -nz, -ŋiŋ, -nd, -ŋə*/z
fattish 'fætiʃ

fatt|y (s. adj.), -ies, -ier, -iest, -iness 'fæt|i, -iz, -iə*, -iist, -inis
fatuity fə'tju(:)iti [fæ't-]
fatuous, -ly, -ness 'fætjŭəs [-tjwəs], -li, -nis
faubourg, -s 'fəubuəg [-bə:g] (fobu:r), -z
faucal 'fɔ:kəl
fauces 'fɔ:si:z
faucet, -s 'fɔ:sit, -s
Fauc|ett, -it 'fɔ:s|it, -it
Faudel 'fɔ:dl
faugh pɸ: [fɔ:]
   Note.—This ɸ is often accompanied by vibration of the lips.
Faulconbridge 'fɔ:kənbridʒ ['fɔ:lk-]
Faulds fəuldz, fɔ:ldz
Faulhorn 'faulhɔ:n
Faulk fɔ:k
Faulkes fɔ:ks, fɔ:lks
Faulkland 'fɔ:klənd, ['fɔ:lk-]
Faulkner 'fɔ:knə*
Faulks fəuks
fault, -s fɔ:lt [fɔlt], -s
faultfind|er/s, -ing 'fɔ:lt,faind|ə*/z ['fɔlt-], -iŋ
faultless, -ly, -ness 'fɔ:ltlis ['fɔlt-], -li, -nis
fault|y, -ier, -iest, -ily, -iness 'fɔ:lt|i ['fɔlt-], -iə* [-jə*], -iist [-jist], -ili, -inis
faun, -s fɔ:n, -z
fauna 'fɔ:nə
Faunch fɔ:ntʃ
Fauntleroy 'fɔ:ntlərɔi ['fɔnt-]
Faust faust
Faustina fɔ:s'ti:nə
Faustus 'fɔ:stəs
fauteuil, -s 'fəutə:i [fəu'tə:i, -ə:l] (fotœ:j), -z
Faux fəu, fɔ:ks
faux pas (sing.) 'fəu'pɑ:, (plur.) 'fəu'pɑ:z
Favel (surname) 'feivəl
Faversham 'fævəʃəm
Favoni|an, -us fə'vəunj|ən [fei'v-, -ni|ən], -əs
fav|our (s. v.), -ours, -ouring, -oured, -ourer/s 'feiv|ə*, -əz, -əriŋ, -əd, -ərə*/z
favourab|le, -ly, -leness 'feivərəb|l, -li, -lnis
favourit|e, -es; -ism 'feivərit, -s; -izəm
favourless 'feivəlis
Fawcett 'fɔ:sit, 'fɔsit
Fawkes fɔ:ks
Fawkner 'fɔ:knə*
Fawley 'fɔ:li
fawn (s. adj. v.), -s, -ing/ly, -ed, -er/s fɔ:n, -z, -iŋ/li, -d, -ə*/z

Fawssett 'fɔ:sit
fay (F.), -s fei, -z
Fayette fei'et
Fayette City 'feiet'siti
Fayetteville 'feietvil
Faygate 'feigeit
Faza(c)kerley fə'zækəli
fe (name of note in Tonic Sol-fa), -(')s
fi:, -z
fe (syllable used in Tonic Sol-fa for
counting a short note off the beat)
generally fi, but the first fe in the
sequence ta fe tay fe is sometimes
sounded as fə. See ta.
Feaist fi:st
fealty 'fi:əlti
fear (s. v.), -s, -ing, -ed fiə*, -z, -riŋ, -d
Fearenside 'fə:nsaid, 'fiərənsaid
fear|ful, -fully, -fulness 'fiə|ful, -fəli
[-fuli], -fulnis
Feargus 'fə:gəs
fearless, -ness 'fiəlis, -li, -nis
Fearn(e) fə:n
Fearnside 'fə:nsaid
Fearon 'fiərən
fearsome, -ly, -ness 'fiəsəm, -li, -nis
feasibility ,fi:zə'biliti [-zi'b-, -lət-]
feasib|le, -ly, -leness 'fi:zəb|l [-zib-], -li,
-lnis
feast (s. v.), -s, -ing, -ed, -er/s fi:st, -s,
-iŋ, -id, -ə*/z
feat, -s fi:t, -s [-riŋ, -d
feather (s. v.), -s, -ing, -ed feðə*, -z,
feather-bed, -s 'feðəbed ['feðə'bed], -z
feather-brain, -s, -ed 'feðəbrein, -z, -d
feather-edge, -s 'feðəredʒ ['feðəedʒ,
'—'-], -iz
feather-head, -s 'feðəhed, -z
featherstitch (s. v.), -es, -ing, -ed
'feðəstitʃ, -iz, -iŋ, -t
Featherston 'feðəstən
Featherstone 'feðəstən [-stəun]
Featherstonehaugh 'feðəstənhɔ:
featherweight, -s 'feðəweit, -s
feather|y, -iness 'feðər|i, -inis
Featley 'fi:tli
featly 'fi:tli
featur|e (s. v.), -es, -ing, -ed; -eless
'fi:tʃə*, -z, -riŋ, -d; -lis
febrifuge, -s 'febrifju:dʒ, -iz
febrile 'fi:brail
February 'febrŭəri [-ruər-, -rər-, -rur-]
Note.—There exists also a fairly
common pronunciation 'febjuəri.
fecit 'fi:sit ['feikit]
Feckenham 'fekŋəm
feckless, -ly, -ness 'feklis, -li, -nis
feculen|ce, -t 'fekjulən|s, -t

fecund 'fi:kənd ['fek-, -kʌnd]
fecundat|e, -es, -ing, -ed 'fi:kəndeit
['fek-, -kʌn-], -s, -iŋ, -id
fecundation ,fi:kən'deiʃən [,fek-, -kʌn-]
fecundity fi'kʌnditi [fi:'k-, fe'k-]
fed (from feed) fed
federal 'fedərəl
federali|sm, -st/s 'fedərəli|zəm, -st/s
federate (s. adj.), -s 'fedərit [-reit], -s
federat|e (v.), -es, -ing, -ed 'fedəreit, -s,
-iŋ, -id
federation, -s ,fedə'reiʃən, -z
federative 'fedərətiv [-reit-]
fee (s. v.), -s, -ing, -d fi:, -z, -iŋ, -d
feeb|le, -ler, -lest, -ly, -leness 'fi:b|l, -lə*,
-list, -li, -lnis
feeble-minded, -ness 'fi:bl'maindid
['fi:bl,m-], -nis
feed (s. v.), -s, -ing, fed, feeder/s fi:d, -z,
-iŋ, fed, 'fi:də*/z
feed-back 'fi:dbæk
feeding-bottle, -s 'fi:diŋ,botl, -z
feeding-cup, -s 'fi:diŋ-kʌp, -s
feed-pipe, -s 'fi:dpaip, -s
feed-tank, -s 'fi:dtæŋk, -s
fee-faw-fum 'fi:'fɔ:'fʌm ['fi:-fɔ:'f-]
fee-fo-fum 'fi:'fəu'fʌm ['fi:-fəu'f-]
Feeheny 'fi:ni, 'fiəni
feel (s. v.), -s, -ing, felt fi:l, -z, -iŋ, felt
feeler, -s 'fi:lə*, -z
feeling (s. adj.), -s, -ly 'fi:liŋ, -z, -li
fee-simple, -s 'fi:'simpl, -z
feet (plur. of foot) fi:t
fee-tail 'fi:'teil
feign, -s, -ing, -ed, -edly, -edness fein,
-z, -iŋ, -d, -idli, -idnis
Feilden 'fi:ldən
Feilding 'fi:ldiŋ
Feiling 'failiŋ
Feiller 'failə*
feint (s. v.), -s, -ing, -ed feint, -s, -iŋ, -id
Feiron 'fiərən
Feisal 'faisəl ['feis-]
Feist fi:st
feldspar 'feldspɑ:* ['fel-spɑ:*]
Felicia fi'lisiə [fe'l-, -sjə, -ʃiə, -ʃjə]
felicitat|e, -es, -ing, -ed fi'lisiteit [fe'l-,
fə'l-], -s, -iŋ, -id
felicitation, -s fi,lisi'teiʃən [fe,l-, fə,l-], -z
felicitous, -ly, -ness fi'lisitəs [fe'l-, fə'l-],
-li, -nis
felicity (F.) fi'lisiti [fe'l-, fə'l-]
feline (s. adj.), -s 'fi:lain, -z
felinity fi'liniti [fi:'l-]
Felix, -stowe 'fi:liks, -təu
Felkin 'felkin
fell (s. adj. v.) (F.), -s, -ing, -ed, -er/s
fel, -z, -iŋ, -d, -ə*/z

fell (from fall) fel
fellah, -s, -een 'felə, -z, -hi:n [ˌfelə'hi:n]
Felling 'felin
felloe, -s 'feləu, -z
fellow, -s 'feləu [colloquially also 'felə in sense of 'person'], -z
fellow|-citizen/s, -creature/s 'feləu|-'sitizən/z, -'kri:tʃə*/z
Fellowes 'feləuz
fellow-feeling 'feləu'fi:lin
fellow|-man, -men 'feləu|'mæn, -'men
Fellows 'feləuz
fellowship, -s 'feləuʃip, -s
Felltham 'felθəm
fell|y, -ies 'fel|i, -iz
felo de se 'fi:ləudi:'si: [fe-, -'sei]
felon, -s 'felən,-z
felonious, -ly, -ness fi'ləunjəs [fe'l-, -niəs], -li, -nis
felon|y, -ies 'felən|i, -iz
Felpham 'felpəm
felspar 'fel-spɑ:*
Felste(a)d 'felstid [-ted]
felt (s.), -s felt, -s
felt (from feel) felt
Feltham (place) 'feltəm, (personal name) 'felθəm
felting, -s 'feltin, -z
Felton 'feltən
felucca, -s fe'lʌkə [fi'l-], -z
female (s. adj.), -s 'fi:meil, -z
feme, -s fi:m, -z
feminine, -ly, -ness 'feminin, -li, -nis
femininit|y, -ies ˌfemi'ninit|i, -iz
femini|sm, -st/s 'femini|zəm, -st/s
feminiz|e [-is|e], -es, -ing, -ed 'feminaiz, -iz, -in, -d
femora (alternative plur. of femur) 'femərə ['fi:m-]
femoral 'femərəl
femur, -s 'fi:mə*, -z
fen, -s (F.) fen, -z
fenc|e (s. v.), -es, -ing, -ed, -er/s; -eless fens, -iz, -in, -t, -ə*/z; -lis
Fenchurch 'fen-tʃə:tʃ
fend, -s, -ing, -ed fend, -z, -in, -id
fender, -s 'fendə*, -z
Fenella fi'nelə
fenestr|a, -al fi'nestr|ə [fə'n-], -əl
fenestrat|e, -es, -ing, -ed fi'nestreit [fə-], -s, -in, -id
fenestration, -s ˌfenis'treiʃən [-nəs-], -z
Fenham 'fenəm
Fenian, -s; -ism 'fi:njən [-niən], -z; -izəm
Fenimore 'fenimɔ:* [-mɔə*]
Fenn fen
fennel 'fenl

Fennell 'fenl
Fennessy 'fenisi [-nəs-]
Fennimore 'fenimɔ:* [-mɔə*]
fenny (F.) 'feni
Fenton 'fentən
Fenwick (English surname) 'fenik [-wik] (American surname) 'fenwik, (places in Great Britain) 'fenik
Feodor 'fi(:)əudɔ:*
Feodora ˌfi(:)əu'dɔ:rə
feoff (v.), -s, -ing, -ed, -er/s, -ment/s fef [fi:f], -s, -in, -t, -ə*/z, -mənt/s
feoffee, -s fe'fi: [fi:'fi:], -z
feoffor, -s fe'fɔ:* [fi:'fɔ:*], -z
ferae naturae 'fiəri:nə*tjuəri: [-'tjɔər-, -'tjɔ:r-]
feral 'fiərəl
Feramors 'ferəmɔ:z
Ferdinand 'fə:dinənd [-dnənd]
feretor|y, -ies 'feritər|i, -iz
Fergus, -(s)on 'fə:gəs, -n
ferial 'fiəriəl ['fer-]
ferine 'fiərain
Feringhee, -s fə'ringi, -z
Fermanagh fə(:)'mænə
ferment (s.), -s 'fə:ment, -s
ferment (v.), -s, -ing, -ed; -able fə(:)'ment, -s, -in, -id; -əbl
fermentation, -s ˌfə:men'teiʃən [-mən-], -z
fermentative, -ly, ness fə'mentətiv, -li, -nis
Fermor 'fə:mɔ:*
Fermoy (near Cork) fə:'mɔi, (street in London) 'fə:mɔi
fern (F.), -s fə:n, -z
Fernandez (Spanish navigator) fə:'nændez [fə'n-], see also Juan F.
ferner|y, -ies 'fə:nər|i, -iz
Fernhough 'fə:nhəu
Fernihough [-nyh-] 'fə:nihʌf, -həu
ferny 'fə:ni
ferocious, -ly, -ness fə'rəuʃəs [fi'r-, fe'r-], -li, -nis
ferocity fə'rɔsiti [fi'r-, fe'r-]
Ferrand 'ferənd
Ferranti fə'rænti [fi-, fe-]
Ferrar 'ferə*
ferrel (F.), -s 'ferəl, -z
ferreous 'feriəs
Ferrer, -s 'ferə*, -z
ferret (s. v.) (F.), -s, -ing, -ed 'ferit, -s, -in, -id
ferric 'ferik
Ferrier 'feriə*
Ferris, -burg 'feris, -bə:g
ferro-concrete 'ferəu'kɔnkri:t [-'kɔnk-]
ferrotype, -s 'ferəutaip, -s

ferrous 'ferəs
ferruginous fe'ru:dʒinəs [fə'r-]
ferrule, -s 'feru:l [-rəl], -z
 Note.—'ferəl is the pronunciation used
  by those connected with the umbrella
  trade.
ferr|y (s. v.) (F.), -ies, -ying, -ied 'fer|i,
 -iz, -iiŋ, -id
ferry-boat, -s 'feribəut, -s
ferry|man, -men 'feri|mən [-mæn],
 -mən [-men]
fertile, -ly 'fə:tail, -li
fertility fə(:)'tiliti
fertilization [-isa-] ˌfə:tilai'zeiʃən [-li'z-]
fertiliz|e [-is|e], -es, -ing, -ed, -er/s
 'fə:tilaiz, -iz, -iŋ, -d, -ə*/z
ferule, -s 'feru:l, -z
ferven|cy, -t/ly, -tness 'fə:vən|si, -t/li,
 -tnis
fervid, -ly, -ness 'fə:vid, -li, -nis
fervour 'fə:və*
fescue, -s 'feskju:, -z
fesse, -s fes, -iz
Fessenden 'fesndən
fest|al, -ally 'fest|l, -əli
fest|er (s. v.), -ers, -ering, -ered 'fest|ə*,
 -əz, -əriŋ, -əd
Festiniog fes'tiniog (Welsh fes'tinjog)
festival, -s 'festəvəl [-tiv-], -z
festive, -ly, -ness 'festiv, -li, -nis
festivit|y, -ies fes'tivit|i, -iz
festoon (s. v.), -s, -ing, -ed fes'tu:n, -z,
 -iŋ, -d
Festus 'festəs
fetch (s. v.), -es, -ing, -ed, -er/s fetʃ, -iz,
 -iŋ, -t, -ə*/z
fête, -s; -day/s feit, -s; -dei/z
fetid, -ly, -ness 'fetid ['fi:tid], -li, -nis
fetish, -es; -ism 'fi:tiʃ ['fetiʃ], -iz; -izəm
fetlock, -s, -ed 'fetlɔk, -s, -t
fetter (s. v.) (F.), -s, -ing, -ed 'fetə*, -z,
 -riŋ, -d
Fettes (place) 'fetis, (surname) 'fetis,
 'fetiz
Fettesian, -s fe'ti:zjən [-zɪən], -z
fett|le (s. v.), -les, -ling, -led 'fet|l, -lz,
 -liŋ, -ld
feu (s. v.), -s, -ing, -ed fju:, -z, -iŋ
 [fjuiŋ], -d
feud, -s; -al fju:d, -z; -l
feudali|sm, -st/s 'fju:dəli|zəm [-dḷi-],
 -st/s
feudality fju:'dæliti
feudalization [-isa-] ˌfju:dəlai'zeiʃən
 [-dḷai'z-, -dəli'z-, -dḷi'z-]
feudaliz|e [-is|e], -es, -ing, -ed 'fju:dəl-
 aiz [-dḷaiz], -iz, -iŋ, -d
feudatory 'fju:dətəri

feuilleton, -s 'fə:itɔ̃:ŋ ['fə:lt-, -tɔ:ŋ,
 -tɔŋ] (fœjtɔ̃), -z
fever, -s, -ed 'fi:və*, -z, -d
fever-heat 'fi:vəhi:t
feverish, -ly, -ness 'fi:vəriʃ, -li, -nis
Feversham 'fevəʃəm
few, -er, -est, -ness fju:, -ə* [fjuə*], -ist
 [fjuist], -nis
fey fei
fez (F.), -es fez, -iz
Fezzan fe'zɑ:n ['fezæn]
Ffitch fitʃ
Ffolliot 'fɔljət [-lɪət]
Ffoulkes fəuks, fəulks, fauks, fu:ks
Ffrangcon 'fræŋkən
fiancé(e), -s fi'ɑ:nsei [fi'ɔ̃:ns-, fi'ɑ:ns-,
 fi'ɔ:ns-, fi'ɔns-, fi'ɔ:ŋs-, fi'ɔŋs-] (fjɑ̃se),
 -z
fiasco, -s fi'æskəu, -z
fiat (decree), -s 'faiæt ['fai-ət], -s
Fiat (car), -s fiət ['fi:æt], -s
fib (s. v.), -s, -bing, -bed, -ber/s fib, -z,
 -iŋ, -d, -ə*/z
fibre, -s, -d; -less 'faibə*, -z, -d; -lis
fibreglass 'faibəglɑ:s
fibriform 'faibrifɔ:m
fibr|il/s, -in 'faibr|il/z, -in
fibrositis ˌfaibrəu'saitis
fibrous, -ly, -ness 'faibrəs, -li, -nis
fibul|a, -as, -ae 'fibjul|ə, -əz, -i:
fichu, -s 'fi:ʃu: ['fiʃ-, -ʃu:] (fiʃy), -z
fick|le, -ler, -lest, -leness 'fik|l, -lə*,
 -list, -lnis
fiction, -s 'fikʃən, -z
fictional 'fikʃənl [-ʃnəl, -ʃn̩l, -ʃn̩l, -ʃənəl]
fictionist, -s 'fikʃənist [-ʃnist], -s
fictitious, -ly, -ness fik'tiʃəs, -li, -nis
fictive 'fiktiv
fid, -s fid, -z
fidd|le (s. v.), -les, -ling, -led, -ler/s
 'fid|l, -lz, -liŋ [-liŋ], -ld, -lə*/z [-lə*/z]
fiddle-bow, -s 'fidlbəu, -z
fiddle-case, -s 'fidlkeis, -iz
fiddle-de-dee 'fidldi'di:
fiddle-fadd|le (s. v. interj.), -les, -ling,
 -led 'fidlˌfæd|l, -lz, -liŋ, -ld
fiddlestick, -s 'fidlstik, -s
Fidele fi'di:li
Fidelia fi'di:ljə [-lɪə]
Fidelio (opera) fi'deiliəu [-ljəu]
fidelity fi'deliti [fai'd-]
fidget (s. v.), -s, -ing, -ed 'fidʒit, -s, -iŋ,
 -id
fidget|y, -ier, -iest, -ily, -iness 'fidʒit|i,
 -iə*, -iist, -ili, -inis
Fido 'faidəu
fiducial, -ly fi'dju:ʃjəl [-u:ʃɪəl, -u:sjəl,
 -u:sɪəl], -i

fiduciar|y, -ies fi'dju:ʃjər|i [-u:ʃïə-, -u:ʃə-, -u:sjə-, -u:sïə-], -iz
fie fai
fief, -s fi:f, -s
field (s. v.) (F.), -s, -ing, -ed, -er/s fi:ld, -z, -iŋ, -id, -ə*/z
field-day, -s 'fi:lddei, -z
Field|en, -er 'fi:ld|ən, -ə*
fieldfare, -s 'fi:ldfɛə*, -z
field-glass, -es 'fi:ldglɑ:s, -iz
field-grey 'fi:ld'grei
field-gun, -s 'fi:ldgʌn, -z
field-hospital, -s 'fi:ld'hɔspitl,-z
field-ice 'fi:ld-ais
Fielding 'fi:ldiŋ
field-marshal, -s 'fi:ld'mɑ:ʃəl ['-,--], -z
field|-mouse, -mice 'fi:ld|maus, -mais
field-officer, -s 'fi:ld,ɔfisə*, -z
fields|man, -men 'fi:ldz|mən, -mən [-men] [-s
field-telegraph, -s 'fi:ld'teligrɑ:f [-græf],
field-telephone, -s 'fi:ld'telifəun, -z
field-work, -s 'fi:ld-wə:k, -s
Fieller 'failə*
fiend (F.), -s fi:nd, -z
fiendish, -ly, -ness 'fi:ndiʃ, -li, -nis
Fiennes fainz
fierce, -r, -st, -ly, -ness fiəs, -ə*, -ist, -li, -nis
fier|y, -ily, -iness 'faiər|i, -ili, -inis
fif|e (s. v.), -es, -ing, -ed, -er/s faif, -s, -iŋ, -t, -ə*/z
Fife, -shire faif, -ʃiə* [-ʃə*]
fife-major, -s 'faif'meidʒə*, -z
Fifield 'faifi:ld
fifteen, -s, -th/s 'fif'ti:n [also 'fift-, fif't- according to sentence-stress], -z, -θ/s
fifth, -s, -ly fifθ [-ftθ], -s, -li
fift|y, -ies, -ieth/s, -yfold 'fift|i, -iz, -iiθ/s [-jiθ/s, -iəθ/s, -jəθ/s], -ifəuld
fifty-fifty 'fifti'fifti
fig (s. v.), -s, -ging, -ged fig, -z, -iŋ, -d
Figaro 'figərəu (figaro)
Figg, -is fig, -is
fight (s. v.), -s, -ing, fought, fighter/s fait, -s, -iŋ, fɔ:t, 'faitə*/z
fighting-cock, -s 'faitiŋ-kɔk, -s
fig-lea|f, -ves figli:|f, -vz
figment, -s 'figmənt, -s
fig-tree, -s 'figtri:, -z
figurability ,figjurə'biliti [-gər-, -lət-]
figurable 'figjurəbl [-gər-]
figurant, -s 'figjurənt, -s
figurante (French fem. of figurant), -s ,figju'rɑ̃:nt [-'rɔ̃:nt, -'rɑ:nt, -'rɔ:nt] (figyrɑ̃:t), -s
figurant|e (Italian form of figurant), -i ,figju'rænt|i, -i:

figuration, -s ,figju'reiʃən, -z
figurative, -ly, -ness 'figjurətiv [-gjər-, -gər-], -li, -nis
figur|e (s. v.), -es, -ing, -ed 'figə*, -z, -riŋ, -d
figure-head, -s 'figəhed, -z
figurine, -s 'figjuri:n, -z
Fiji fi:'dʒi: ['-'-, also '-- when attributive]
Fijian, -s fi:'dʒi:ən, -z
filacer, -s 'filəsə*, -z
filament, -s 'filəmənt, -s
filamentous ,filə'mentəs
filature, -s 'filətʃə* [-tjuə*, -tjə*, -tʃuə*], -z
filbert, -s 'filbə(:)t, -s
filch, -es, -ing, -ed, -er/s filtʃ, -iz, -iŋ, -t, -ə*/z
Fildes faildz
fil|e (s. v.), -es, -ing, -ed fail, -z, -iŋ, -d
filemot 'filimɔt
Filey 'faili
filial, -ly, -ness 'filjəl [-lïəl], -i, -nis
filiation ,fili'eiʃən
filibeg, -s 'filibeg, -z
filibust|er (s. v.), -ers, -ering, -ered 'filibʌst|ə*, -əz, -əriŋ, -əd
filigr|ane, -ee 'filigr|ein, -i:
filings 'failiŋz
Filioque ,fi:li'əukwi [,fail-, ,fil-]
Filipino, -s ,fili'pi:nəu, -z
Filkin, -s 'filkin, -z
fill (s. v.), -s, -ing, -ed, -er/s fil, -z, -iŋ, -d, -ə*/z
fillet (s. v.), -s, -ing, -ed 'filit, -s, -iŋ, -id
fillip (s. v.), -s, -ing, -ed 'filip, -s, -iŋ, -t
Fillmore 'filmɔ:* [-mɔə*]
fill|y, -ies 'fil|i, -iz
film, -s film, -z
film-actor, -s 'film,æktə*, -z
filmland 'filmlænd
film-star, -s 'film-stɑ:*, -z
film|y, -ier, -iest, -ily, -iness 'film|i, -ïə* [-jə*], -iist [-jist], -ili, -inis
Filon (surname) 'failən
filt|er (s. v.), -ers, -ering, -ered 'filt|ə*, -əz, -əriŋ, -əd
filter-paper, -s 'filtə,peipə* ['filtə'p-], -z
filth filθ
filth|y, -ier, -iest, -ily, -iness 'filθ|i, -ïə* [-jə*], -iist [-jist], -ili, -inis
filtrate (s.), -s 'filtrit [-reit], -s
filtrat|e (v.), -es, -ing, -ed 'filtreit, -s, -iŋ, -id
filtration, -s fil'treiʃən, -z
fin, -s fin, -z
finable 'fainəbl
fin|al, -ally 'fain|l, -əli [-l̩i]
finale, -s fi'nɑ:li, -z

finalist, -s 'fainəlist [-nˌlist], -s
finality fai'næliti
finaliz|e [-is|e], -es, -ing, -ed 'fainəlaiz [-nˌlaiz], -iz, -iŋ, -d
financ|e (s. v.), -es, -ing, -ed fai'næns [fi'n-, 'fainæns], -iz, -iŋ, -t
financi|al, -ally fai'nænʃ|əl [fi'n-], -əli
financier (s.), -s fai'nænsiə* [fi'n-, -sjə*], -z
finch (F.), -es fintʃ, -iz
Finchale (Priory in Durham) 'fiŋkl
Finchampsted (in Berks.) 'fintʃəmsted [-tid]
Finchley 'fintʃli
find (s. v.), -s, -ing/s, found, finder/s faind, -z, -iŋ/z, faund, 'faində*/z
Findlater 'findlətə* [-leitə*]
Findlay 'findlei [-li]
fin|e (s. adj. v.), -es; -er, -est, -ely, -eness; -ing, -ed fain, -z; -ə*, -ist, -li, -nis; -iŋ, -d
fine-draw, -s, -ing, -n, fine-drew 'fain-'drɔː ['--], -z, -iŋ, -n, 'fain'druː ['--]
finery 'fainəri
fine-spun 'fain'spʌn ['fain-spʌn]
finess|e (s. v.), -es, -ing, -ed fi'nes, -iz, -iŋ, -t
Fingal (place) 'fiŋgəl
Fingall (Lord) fiŋ'gɔːl
fing|er (s. v.), -ers, -ering/s, -ered 'fiŋg|ə*, -əz, -əriŋ/z, -əd
finger-alphabet, -s 'fiŋgər,ælfəbit [-gə,æl-, -bet], -s
finger-board, -s 'fiŋgəbɔːd, [-bəəd], -z
finger-bowl, -s 'fiŋgəbəul, -z
finger-breadth, -s 'fiŋgəbredθ [-bretθ], -s
finger-glass, -es 'fiŋgəglɑːs, -iz
finger-mark, -s 'fiŋgəmɑːk, -s
finger-nail, -s 'fiŋgəneil, -z
finger-plate, -s 'fiŋgə-pleit, -s
finger-post, -s 'fiŋgəpəust, -s
finger-print, -s 'fiŋgə-print, -s
finger-stall, -s 'fiŋgə-stɔːl, -z
Fingest (in Bucks.) 'findʒist
finial, -s 'fainiəl ['fin-], -z
finic|al, -ally, -alness 'finik|əl, -əli, -əlnis
finicking 'finikiŋ
finick|y, -ier, -iest, -ily, -iness 'finik|i, -iə*, -iist, -ili, -inis
finikin 'finikin
finis 'finis ['fiːnis, 'fainis]
finish (s. v.), -es, -ing, -ed, -er/s 'finiʃ, -iz, -iŋ, -t, -ə*/z
Finisterre ,finis'teə* ['finisteə*]
finite, -ly, -ness 'fainait, -li, -nis
finitude 'fainitjuːd
Finlaison 'finlisn

Finland, -er/s 'finlənd, -ə*/z
Finlay 'finlei [-li]
Finlayson 'finlisn
Finley 'finli
Finn, -s fin, -z
Finnan 'finən
Finney 'fini
Finn|ic, -ish 'fin|ik, -iʃ
Finnon 'finən
Finno-Ugrian 'finəu'juːgriən
finny 'fini
Finsbury 'finzbəri
Finsteraarhorn ,finstər'ɑːhɔːn
Finzean 'fiŋən
Finzi 'finzi
Fiona fi'əunə
fiord, -s fjɔːd [fi'ɔːd], -z
fiorin 'faiərin
fir, -s fəː*, -z
Firbank 'fəːbæŋk
fir|e (s. v.), -es, -ing, -ed, -er/s 'faiə*, -z, -riŋ, -d, -rə*/z
fire-alarm, -s 'faiərə,lɑːm ['faiəə,l-], -z
fire-arm, -s 'faiərɑːm ['faiəɑːm], -z
fireball, -s 'faiəbɔːl, -z
fire-balloon, -s 'faiəbə,luːn, -z
fire-bomb, -s 'faiəbɔm, -z
fire-box, -es 'faiəbɔks, -iz
firebrand, -s 'faiəbrænd, -z
fire-brick, -s 'faiəbrik, -s
fire-brigade, -s 'faiəbri,geid, -z
fireclay 'faiə-klei
fire-control, -s 'faiə-kən,trəul, -z
firedamp 'faiədæmp
fire-dance, -s 'faiə-dɑːns, -iz
fire-drill, -s 'faiə-dril, -z
fire-eat|er/s, -ing 'faiər,iːt|ə*/z ['faiə,iːt-], -iŋ
fire-engine, -s 'faiər,endʒin ['faiə,en-], -z
fire-escape, -s 'faiəris,keip ['faiəis-], -s
fire-extinguisher, -s 'faiəriks,tiŋgwiʃə* ['faiəiks-, -eks-], -z
fire-fight|er/s, -ing 'faiə,fait|ə*/z, -iŋ
firefl|y, -ies 'faiə-fl|ai, -aiz
fire-guard, -s 'faiəgɑːd, -z
fire-hose, -s 'faiəhəuz, -iz
fire-insurance, -s 'faiərin,ʃuərəns ['faiəin-, -,ʃɔər-, -,ʃɔːr-], -iz
fire-iron, -s 'faiər,aiən ['faiə,aiən], -z
fire-light, -er/s 'faiəlait, -ə*/z
firelock, -s 'faiəlɔk, -s
fire|man, -men 'faiə|mən, -mən [-men]
fireplace, -s 'faiə-pleis, -iz
fire-plug, -s 'faiə-plʌg, -z
fire-power 'faiə,pauə*
fireproof 'faiə-pruːf
fire-screen, -s 'faiə-skriːn, -z
fire-ship, -s 'faiə-ʃip, -s

fireside, -s 'faiə-said, -z
fire-stick, -s 'faiə-stik, -s
firestone 'faiə-stəun
fire-trap, -s 'faiə-træp, -s
fire-watch, -es, -ing, -ed, -er/s 'faiəwɔtʃ,
-iz, -iŋ, -t, -ə*/z
fire-water 'faiə,wɔ:tə*
firewood 'faiəwud
fireworks 'faiəwə:ks
fire-worship, -per/s 'faiə,wə:ʃip, -ə*/z
firing, -line/s, -party, -parties, -point/s,
-squad/s 'faiəriŋ, -lain/z, -,pɑ:ti,
-,pɑ:tiz, -point/s, -skwɔd/z
firkin, -s 'fə:kin, -z
firm (s. adj.), -s, -er, -est, -ly, -ness
fə:m, -z, -ə*, -ist, -li, -nis
firmament, -s 'fə:məmənt, -s
firman, -s fə:'mɑ:n ['fə:mɑ:n, 'fə:mən], -z
firr|y, -iness 'fə:r|i, -inis
Firsby 'fə:zbi
first, -ly fə:st, -li
firstborn 'fə:sʔbɔ:n
first-class 'fə:sʔ'klɑ:s [also '— when
attributive]
first-fruit, -s 'fə:stfru:t, -s
first-hand 'fə:st'hænd [also '— when
attributive]
firstling, -s 'fə:stliŋ, -z
firstly 'fə:stli
first-rate 'fə:st'reit [also '— when
attributive]
firth (F.), -s fə:θ, -s
fisc fisk
fiscal (s. adj.), -s 'fiskəl, -z
fish (s. v.) (F.), -es, -ing, -ed, -er/s fiʃ,
-iz, -iŋ, -t, -ə*/z
fish-ball, -s 'fiʃbɔ:l, -z
fishbone, -s 'fiʃbəun, -z
fish-cake, -s 'fiʃkeik, -s
fish-carver, -s 'fiʃ,kɑ:və*, -z
fisher (F.), -s 'fiʃə*, -z
fisher|man, -men 'fiʃə|mən, -mən
[-men]
fisher|y, -ies 'fiʃər|i, -iz
Fishguard 'fiʃgɑ:d
fish-hook, -s 'fiʃhuk ['fiʃuk], -s
fishing-rod, -s 'fiʃiŋrɔd, -z
fishing-tackle 'fiʃiŋ,tækl
Fishkill 'fiʃkil
fish-kni|fe, -ves 'fiʃnai|f, -vz
fishmonger, -s 'fiʃ,mʌŋgə*, -z
fishplate, -s 'fiʃpleit, -s
fishpond, -s 'fiʃpɔnd, -z
fish-sauce 'fiʃ'sɔ:s
fish-slice, -s 'fiʃslais, -iz
fish-strainer, -s 'fiʃ,streinə*, -z
fishtail 'fiʃteil
fish-torpedo, -es 'fiʃtɔ:,pi:dəu, -z

Fishwick 'fiʃwik
fishwi|fe, -ves 'fiʃwai|f, -vz
fish|woman, -women 'fiʃ|,wumən,
-,wimin
fish|y, -ier, -iest, -ily, -iness 'fiʃ|i, -iə*,
-iist, -ili, -inis
Fisk(e) fisk
Fison 'faisn
fissile 'fisail
fission 'fiʃən
fissionable 'fiʃnəbl [-ʃənəbl]
fissiparous fi'sipərəs
fissure, -s, -d 'fiʃə* [-ʃuə*], -z, -d
fist, -s; -ic, -ical fist, -s; -ik, -ikəl
fisticuff, -s 'fistikʌf, -s
fistul|a, -as, -ar, -ous 'fistjul|ə, -əz, -ə*,   [-əs
-li, -nis; -iŋ/li, -id, -ə*/z
fit (s. adj. v.), -s, -ter, -test, -ly, -ness;
-ting/ly, -ted, -ter/s fit, -s, -ə*, -ist,
fitch (F.), -es fitʃ, -iz
Fitchburg 'fitʃbə:g
fitchew, -s 'fitʃu:, -z
fit|ful, -fully, -fulness 'fit|ful, -fuli
[-fəli], -fulnis
fitment, -s 'fitmənt, -s
fitting-out 'fitiŋ'aut
fitting-room, -s 'fitiŋrum [-ru:m], -z
fitting-shop, -s 'fitiŋ-ʃɔp, -s
Fitzalan fits'ælən
Fitzcharles fits'tʃɑ:lz
Fitzclarence fits'klærəns
Fitzdottrel fits'dɔtrəl
Fitzgeorge fits'dʒɔ:dʒ
Fitzgerald fits'dʒerəld
Fitzgibbon fits'gibən
Fitzhardinge fits'hɑ:diŋ
Fitzharris fits'hæris
Fitzherbert fits'hə:bət
Fitzhugh fits'hju:
Fitzjames fits'dʒeimz [in James Fitz-
james often 'fitsdʒ-]
Fitzjohn (surname) fits'dʒɔn
Fitzjohn's Avenue 'fitsdʒɔnz'ævinju:
Fitzmaurice fits'mɔris
Fitzpatrick fits'pætrik
Fitzroy (surname) fits'rɔi, (square and
street in London) 'fitsrɔi
Fitzsimmons fits'simənz
Fitzstephen fits'sti:vən
Fitzurse fits'ə:s
Fitzwalter fits'wɔ:ltə* [-'wɔl-]
Fitzwilliam fits'wiljəm
Fitzwygram fits'waigrəm
five, -s, -fold faiv, -z, -fəuld
five-ish 'faiviʃ
fivepen|ce, -ny 'faifpən|s ['faivp-], -i
five-ply 'faivplai ['-'-]
fiver, -s 'faivə*, -z

fix (*s. v.*), **-es, -ing, -ed, -edly, -edness,
-er/s; -able, -ative** fiks, -iz, -iŋ, -t,
-idli, -idnis, -ə*/z; -əbl, -ətiv
fixation fik'seiʃən
fixity 'fiksiti
fixture, -s 'fikstʃə*, -z
fizz (*s. v.*), **-es, -ing, -ed, -er/s** fiz, -iz,
-iŋ, -d, -ə*/z
fizz|le (*s. v.*), **-les, -ling, -led** 'fiz|l, -lz,
-liŋ [-liŋ], -ld
fizz|y, -ier, -iest, -iness 'fiz|i, -Iə*,
-iist, -inis
fjord, -s fjɔːd, -z
flab flæb
flabbergast, -s, -ing, -ed 'flæbəgɑːst, -s,
-iŋ, -id
flabb|y, -ier, -iest, -ily, -iness 'flæb|i,
-Iə*, -iist, -ili, -inis
flaccid, -ly, -ness 'flæksid, -li, -nis
flaccidity flæk'siditi
Flaccus 'flækəs
Fladgate 'flædgit [-geit]
flag (*s. v.*), **-s, -ging, -ged** flæg, -z, -iŋ, -d
flag-captain, -s 'flæg'kæptin ['-,--], -z
flag-day, -s 'flægdei, -z
flagellant, -s 'flædʒilənt [flə'dʒel-,
flæ'dʒel-], -s
flagellat|e, -es, -ing, -ed, -or/s 'flædʒe-
leit [-dʒil-, -dʒəl-], -s, -iŋ, -id, -ə*/z
flagellation, -s ,flædʒe'leiʃən [-dʒi'l-,
-dʒə'l-], -z
flagell|um, -a flə'dʒel|əm [flæ'dʒ-], -ə
flageolet, -s ,flædʒəu'let ['---], -s
Flagg flæg
flaggy 'flægi
flagitious, -ly, -ness flə'dʒiʃəs, -li, -nis
flag-lieutenan|t, -ts, -cy, -cies 'flægle-
'tenən|t [-lə't-, -lef't-, -ləf't-], -ts, -si,
-siz
Note.—*Until recently the usual pronunciation in the navy was
-luː'tenən- or -'luːtnən-. These
forms appear to be now nearly
obsolete.*
flag-officer, -s 'flæg,ɔfisə*, -z
flagon, -s 'flægən, -z
flagran|cy, -t/ly 'fleigrən|si, -t/li
flag|-ship/s, -staff/s 'flægʃip/s, -stɑːf/s
flagstone, -s 'flægstəun, -z
flag-wagging 'flæg,wægiŋ
flag-waving 'flæg,weiviŋ
Flaherty 'flɛəti, 'flɑːhəti, 'flæhəti
flail (*s. v.*), **-s, -ing, -ed** fleil, -z, -iŋ, -d
flair, -s flɛə*, -z
flak flæk
flak|e (*s. v.*), **-es, -ing, -ed** fleik, -s, -iŋ, -t
flake-white 'fleik'wait [-'hw-, *in contrast* 'fleik-wait, 'fleikhwait]

flak|y, -ily, -iness 'fleik|i, -ili, -inis
flam, -s flæm, -z
Flambard 'flæmbɑːd [-bəd]
flambeau (**F.**), -s 'flæmbəu, -z
Flamborough 'flæmbərə
flamboyant flæm'bɔiənt
flam|e (*s. v.*), **-es, -ing, -ed** fleim, -z,
-iŋ, -d
flame-colour, -ed 'fleim,kʌlə*, -d
flamen, -s 'fleimen, -z
flamingo, -(e)s flə'miŋgəu [flæ'm-], -z
Flaminius flə'miniəs [flæ'm-, -njəs]
Flammock 'flæmək
Flamstead 'flæmstid [-sted]
Flamsteed 'flæmstiːd
flamy 'fleimi
flan, -s flæn, -z
Flanders 'flɑːndəz
flange, -s, -d flænʤ, -iz, -d
flank (*s. v.*), **-s, -ing, -ed, -er/s** flæŋk,
-s, -iŋ, -t [flæŋt], -ə*/z
flannel, -s, -led 'flænl, -z, -d
flannelette ,flænl'et [-nə'let]
flannelly 'flænli
flap (*s. v.*), **-s, -ping, -ped** flæp, -s, -iŋ, -t
flapdoodle 'flæp,duːdl
flapjack, -s 'flæpdʒæk, -s
flapper, -s 'flæpə*, -z
flar|e (*s. v.*), **-es, -ing/ly, -ed** flɛə*, -z,
-riŋ/li, -d
flare-pa|th, -ths 'flɛə-pɑː|θ, -ðz
flare-up, -s 'flɛər'ʌp ['--], -s
flash (*s. adj. v.*) (**F.**), -es, -ing, -ed flæʃ,
-iz, -iŋ, -t
flashback, -s 'flæʃbæk, -s
flash-card, -s 'flæʃkɑːd, -z
flashlight, -s 'flæʃlait, -s
flash-point, -s 'flæʃpɔint, -s
flash|y, -ier, -iest, -ily, -iness 'flæʃ|i,
-Iə*, -iist, -ili, -inis
flask, -s flɑːsk, -s
flasket, -s 'flɑːskit, -s
flat (*s. adj.*), -s, -ter, -test, -ly, -ness
flæt, -s, -ə*, -ist, -li, -nis
Flatbush 'flætbuʃ
flatfish, -es 'flætfiʃ, -iz
flatfoot 'flætfut
flat-footed 'flæt'futid ['-,--]
flathead, -s 'flæthed, -z
flat-iron, -s 'flæt,aiən, -z
Flatland 'flætlænd
flatlet, -s 'flætlit, -s
flatt|en, -ens, -ening, -ened 'flæt|n,
-nz, -ɲiŋ [-niŋ], -nd
flatter, -s, -ing/ly, -ed, -er/s 'flætə*, -z,
-riŋ/li, -d, -rə*/z
flatter|y, -ies 'flætər|i, -iz
flattish 'flætiʃ

flatulen|ce, -cy, -t/ly 'flætjulən|s, -si, -t/li
flatus, -es 'fleitəs, -iz
flat|ways, -wise 'flæt|weiz, -waiz
flaunt, -s, -ing/ly, -ed, -er/s flɔ:nt, -s, -iŋ/li, -id, -ə*/z
flautist, -s 'flɔ:tist, -s
Flavel 'flævəl
Flavell flə'vel, 'fleivəl
Flavi|a, -an, -us 'fleivj|ə [-vǐ|ə], -ən, -əs
flavorous 'fleivərəs
flav|our (s. v.), -ours, -ouring/s, -oured; -ourless 'fleiv|ə*, -əz, -əriŋ/z, -əd; -əlis
flaw (s. v.), -s, -ing, -ed flɔ:, -z, -iŋ, -d
flawless, -ly, -ness 'flɔ:lis, -li, -nis
flax, -en flæks, -ən
Flaxman 'flæksmən
flaxy 'flæksi
flay, -s, -ing, -ed, -er/s flei, -z, -iŋ, -d, -ə*/z
flea, -s fli:, -z
fleabane 'fli:bein
flea-bite, -s 'fli:bait, -s
fleam, -s fli:m, -z
Fleance 'fli:əns [fliəns]
Fleay flei
flèche, -s fleiʃ, -iz
fleck (s. v.), -s, -ing, -ed flek, -s, -iŋ, -t
Flecknoe 'fleknəu
flection, -s 'flekʃən, -z
flectional 'flekʃənl [-ʃn̩l, -ʃnl, -ʃənəl]
fled (from flee) fled
fledg|e, -es, -ing, -ed; -(e)ling/s fledʒ, -iz, -iŋ, -d; -liŋ/z
flee, -s, -ing, fled, fleer/s fli:, -z, -iŋ, fled, 'fli:ə*/z
fleec|e (s. v.), -es, -ing, -ed, -er/s; -y, -iness fli:s, -iz, -iŋ, -t, -ə*/z; -i, -inis
Fleeming 'flemiŋ
fleer (sneer) (s. v.), -s, -ing, -ed fliə*, -z, -riŋ, -d
fleet (s. adj. v.) (F.), -s; -er, -est, -ly, -ness; -ing/ly, -ed fli:t, -s; -ə*, -ist, -li, -nis; -iŋ/li, -id
Fleetwood 'fli:t-wud
Fleming, -s, -ton 'flemiŋ, -z, -tən
Flemish 'flemiʃ
Flemming 'flemiŋ
flens|e, -es, -ing, -ed flenz, -iz, -iŋ, -d
flesh (s. v.), -es, -ing/s, -ed fleʃ, -iz, -iŋ/z, -t
flesh-colour, -ed 'fleʃ‚kʌlə*, -d
flesh-eat|er/s, -ing 'fleʃ‚i:t|ə*/z, -iŋ
flesh-hook, -s 'fleʃhuk ['fleʃuk], -s
fleshless 'fleʃlis
fleshl|y, -iness 'fleʃl|i, -inis
flesh-pot, -s 'fleʃpɔt, -s

flesh-tint 'fleʃtint
flesh-wound, -s 'fleʃwu:nd, -z
fiesh|y, -iness 'fleʃ|i, -inis
fletcher (F.), -s 'fletʃə*, -z
Flete fli:t
fleur-de-lis 'flə:də'li: [-'li:s] (flœrdəli)
Fleur de Lis (place in Mon.) ‚flə:də'li:
flew (from fly v.) flu:
flex, -es fleks, -iz
flexibility ‚fleksə'biliti [-si'b-, -lət-]
flexib|le, -ly, -leness 'fleksəb|l [-sib-], -li, -lnis
flexion, -s 'flekʃən, -z
flexor, -s 'fleksə*, -z
flexure, -s 'flekʃə*, -z
flibbertigibbet, -s 'flibəti'dʒibit, -s
flick (s. v.), -s, -ing, -ed flik, -s, -iŋ, -t
flicker (s. v.), -s, -ing, -ed 'flikə*, -z, -riŋ, -d
flick-kni|fe, -ves 'fliknai|f, -vz
flier, -s 'flai-ə* ['flaiə*], -z
flight (F.), -s flait, -s
flight-deck, -s 'flaitdek, -s
flight|y, -ier, -iest, -ily, -iness 'flait|i, -iə* [-jə*], -iist [-jist], -ili, -inis
flim-flam, -s 'flim-flæm, -z
Flimnap 'flimnæp
flims|y, -ier, -iest, -ily, -iness 'flimz|i, -iə* [-jə*], -iist [-jist], -ili, -inis
flinch, -es, -ing/ly, -ed, -er/s flintʃ, -iz, -iŋ/li, -t, -ə*/z
flinders (F.) 'flindəz
fling (s. v.), -s, -ing, flung fliŋ, -z, -iŋ, flʌŋ
flint (F.), -s flint, -s
flint-glass 'flint'glɑ:s ['flintg-]
flint-lock, -s 'flint-lɔk, -s
Flintshire 'flint-ʃiə* [-ʃə*]
flintstone 'flintstəun
Flintwinch 'flint-wintʃ
flint|y, -ier, -iest, -ily, -iness 'flint|i, -iə* [-jə*], -iist [-jist], -ili, -inis
flip (s. v.), -s, -ping, -ped flip, -s, -iŋ, -t
flip-flap (s. adv.), -s 'flipflæp, -s
flippan|cy, -t/ly, -tness 'flipən|si, t-/li, [-tnis
flipper, -s 'flipə*, -z
flirt (s. v.), -s, -ing/ly, -ed flə:t, -s, -iŋ/li, -id
flirtation, -s flə:'teiʃən, -z
flirtatious flə:'teiʃəs
flit, -s, -ting, -ted flit, -s, -iŋ, -id
flitch (F.), -es flitʃ, -iz
Flite flait
flitter, -s, -ing, -ed 'flitə*, -z, -riŋ, -d
flitter-mouse, -mice 'flitə|maus, -mais
Flixton 'flikstən
float (s. v.), -s, -ing, -ed, -er/s; -able, -age fləut, -s, -iŋ, -id, -ə*/z; -əbl, -idʒ

floatation flǝu'teiʃǝn

floating|-bridge/s, -dock/s 'flǝutiŋ|-'bridʒ/iz, -'dɔk/s

float-stone, -s 'flǝutstǝun, -z

floccule, -s 'flɔkjuːl, -z

flocculent 'flɔkjulǝnt

flock (s. v.), -s, -ing, -ed; -y flɔk, -s, -iŋ, -t; -i

Flockton 'flɔktǝn

Flodden 'flɔdn

floe, -s flǝu, -z

flog, -s, -ging/s, -ged flɔg, -z, -iŋ/z, -d

flood (s. v.) (F.), -s, -ing, -ed; -gate/s flʌd, -z, -iŋ, -id; -geit/s

floodtide 'flʌdtaid

Flook fluk

floor (s. v.), -s, -ing, -ed, -er/s flɔː* [flɔǝ*], -z, -riŋ, -d, -rǝ*/z

floor|-cloth, -cloths 'flɔː|klɔθ ['flɔǝ|-, -klɔːθ], -klɔθs [-klɔːðz, -klɔːθs]

flop (s. v. adv. interj.), -s, -ping, -ped, -per/s flɔp, -s, -iŋ, -t, -ǝ*/z

flopp|y, -ier, -iest, -ily, -iness 'flɔp|i, -iǝ*, -iist, -ili, -inis

flora (F.) 'flɔːrǝ

floral 'flɔːrǝl ['flɔr-]

Floren|ce, -tine 'flɔrǝn|s, -tain

Flores 'flɔːriz

florescen|ce, -t flɔː'resn|s [flɔ'r-], -t

floret, -s 'flɔːrit [-ret], -s

Florian 'flɔːriǝn

floriat|e, -es, -ing, -ed 'flɔːrieit, -s, -iŋ, -id

floricultur|al, -ist/s ˌflɔːri'kʌltʃǝr|ǝl [ˌflɔr-, -tʃur-], -ist/s

floriculture 'flɔːrikʌltʃǝ* ['flɔr-]

florid, -est, -ly, -ness 'flɔrid, -ist, -li, -nis

Florida 'flɔridǝ

floriferous flɔː'rifǝrǝs [flɔ'r-]

Florimel 'flɔrimel

florin, -s 'flɔrin, -z

Florinda flɔː'rindǝ [flɔ'r-, flǝ'r-]

Florio 'flɔːriǝu

florist, -s 'flɔrist, -s

Florizel 'flɔrizel

Florrie 'flɔri

floruit 'flɔːruit [-rjuit]

Florus 'flɔːrǝs

floss (F.), -y flɔs, -i

Flossie 'flɔsi

floss-silk 'flɔs'silk

flotation, -s flǝu'teiʃǝn, -z

flotilla, -s flǝu'tilǝ, -z

flotsam 'flɔtsǝm [-sæm]

Floud flʌd

floun|ce (s. v.), -es, -ing, -ed flauns, -iz, -iŋ, -t

flound|er (s. v.), -ers, -ering, -ered 'flaund|ǝ*, -ǝz, -ǝriŋ, -ǝd

flour (s. v.), -s, -ing, -ed 'flauǝ*, -z, -riŋ, -d

flourish (s. v.), -es, -ing/ly, -ed 'flʌriʃ, -iz, -iŋ/li, -t

flour-mill, -s 'flauǝmil, -z

floury 'flauǝri

flout (s. v.), -s, -ing/ly, -ed flaut, -s, -iŋ/li, -id

fl|ow (s. v.), -ows, -owing/ly, -owing-ness, -owed fl|ǝu, -ǝuz, -ǝuiŋ/li, -ǝuiŋnis, -ǝud

flower (s. v.) (F.), -s, -ing, -ed, -er/s 'flauǝ*, -z, -riŋ, -d, -rǝ*/z

flower-bearing 'flauǝˌbeǝriŋ

flower|-bed/s, -bud/s 'flauǝ|bed/z, -bʌd/z

floweret, -s 'flauǝrit [-ret], -s

flower|-garden/s, -girl/s, -head/s 'flauǝ|ˌgɑːdn/z, -gǝːl/z [rarely -geǝl/z], -hed/z

flowerless 'flauǝlis

flower|-pot/s, -service/s, -stalk/s 'flauǝ|pɔt/s, -ˌsǝːvis/iz, -stɔːk/s

flowery 'flauǝri

flown (from fly) flǝun

Floy|d, -er flɔi|d, -ǝ*

'flu fluː

fluctuat|e, -es, -ing, -ed 'flʌktjueit [-tʃueit], -s, -iŋ, -id

fluctuation, -s ˌflʌktju'eiʃǝn [-tʃu-], -z

Flud|d, -yer flʌd, -jǝ*

flue, -s fluː, -z

Fluellen flu(ː)'elin

fluen|cy, -t/ly, -tness 'flu(ː)ǝn|si, -t/li, -tnis

flue-pipe, -s 'fluː-paip, -s

flue-work 'fluːwǝːk

fluff (s. v.), -s, -ing, -ed; -y, -ier, -iest, -iness flʌf, -s, -iŋ, -t; -i, -iǝ*, -iist, -inis

fluid (s. adj.), -s 'flu(ː)id, -z

fluidity flu(ː)'iditi

fluk|e (s. v.), -es, -ing, -ed, -er/s; -y, -ier, -iest, -iness fluːk, -s, -iŋ, -t, -ǝ*/z; -i, -iǝ* [-jǝ*], -iist [-jist], -inis

flummery 'flʌmǝri

flummox, -es, -ing, -ed 'flʌmǝks, -iz, -iŋ, -t

flump (s. v.), -s, -ing, -ed flʌmp, -s, -iŋ, -t [flʌmt]

flung (from fling) flʌŋ

flunkey, -s; -ism 'flʌŋki, -z; -izǝm

fluor 'flu(ː)ɔ* ['flu(ː)ǝ*]

fluorescen|ce, -t fluǝ'resn|s [ˌfluːǝ'r-, ˌflu(ː)ɔː'r-, ˌflu(ː)ɔ'r-], -t

fluoric flu(ː)'ɔrik

fluoridation ˌfluǝrai'deiʃǝn [ˌflɔːr-]

fluoride 'fluǝraid ['flɔːr-]

fluor|ine, -ite 'fluǝr|iːn ['fluːǝr-], -ait

fluor-spar 'fluə-spɑ:* ['flu:ə-, 'flu:ɔ:-]
flurr|y (s. v.), -ies, -ying, -ied 'flʌr|i,
-iz, -iiŋ, -id
flush (s. v.), -es, -ing, -ed flʌʃ, -iz, -iŋ, -t
flushing (F.), -s 'flʌʃiŋ, -z
flust|er (s. v.), -ers, -ering, -ered 'flʌst-
t|ə*, -əz, -əriŋ, -əd
flut|e (s. v.) (F.), -es, -ing, -ed; -ist/s;
-y, -ier, -iest, -iness flu:t, -s, -iŋ, -id;
-ist/s; -i, -ɪə* [-jə*], -iist [-jist], -inis
flutter (s. v.) (F.), -s, -ing, -ed, -er/s
'flʌtə*, -z, -riŋ, -d, -rə*/z
fluvial 'flu:vjəl [-vɪəl]
flux, -es flʌks, -iz
fluxion, -s 'flʌkʃən, -z
fluxional 'flʌkʃənl [-ʃn̩l, -ʃnl]
fil|y (s. v.) (all senses) (F.), -ies, -ying,
flew, flown, flier/s fl|ai, -aiz, -aiiŋ,
flu:, fləun, 'flai-ə*/z ['flaiə*/z]
flyable 'flai-əbl ['flaiəbl]
fly-blow, -s, -n 'flai-bləu, -z, -n
fly-bomb, -s 'flaibɔm, -z
fly|-catcher/s, -fishing 'flai|ˌkætʃə*/z,
flyer, -s 'flai-ə* ['flaiə*], -z   [-ˌfiʃiŋ
flying|-man, -men 'flaiiŋ|mæn, -men
flying-officer, -s 'flaiiŋˌɔfisə*, -z
fly-lea|f, -ves 'flaili:|f, -vz
fly-line, -s 'flailain, -z
fly|man, -men 'flai|mən, -mən [-men]
Flyn|n, -t flin, -t
flyover, -s 'flai,əuvə*, -z
fly-paper, -s 'flai,peipə*, -z
fly-sheet, -s 'flai-ʃi:t, -s
fly-swatter, -s 'flai,swɔtə*, -z
flyway, -s 'flaiwei, -z
flywheel, -s 'flaiwi:l [-hwi:l], -z
Foakes fəuks
foal (s. v.), -s, -ing, -ed fəul, -z, -iŋ, -d
foam (s. v.), -s, -ing, -ed; -y, -iness
fəum, -z, -iŋ, -d; -i, -inis
Foard fɔ:d [fɔəd]
fob (s. v.), -s, -bing, -bed fɔb, -z, -iŋ, -d
focal 'fəukəl
Fochabers 'fɔxəbəz ['fɔxə-]
Focke (surname) fɔk
fo'c'sle, -s 'fəuksl, -z
fo|cus (s.), -ci 'fəu|kəs, -sai [-ki:]
focus (v.), -ses, -sing, -sed 'fəukəs, -iz,
fodder 'fɔdə*   [-iŋ, -t
foe, -s fəu, -z
foe|man, -men 'fəu|mən, -mən [-men]
foetal 'fi:tl
foetid, -ly, -ness 'fi:tid, -li, -nis
foetus, -es 'fi:təs, -iz
fog (s. v.), -s, -ging, -ged fɔg, -z, -iŋ, -d
fog-bank, -s 'fɔgbæŋk, -s
fog-bound 'fɔgbaund
Fogerty 'fəugəti

fogey, -s, -ish, -ism 'fəugi, -z, -iʃ, -izəm
Fogg fɔg
fogg|y, -ier, -iest, -ily, -iness 'fɔg|i,
-ɪə*, -iist, -ili, -inis
fog-horn, -s 'fɔghɔ:n, -z
fogram, -s 'fəugræm, -z
fog-signal, -s 'fɔgˌsignl̩ [-nəl], -z
fog|y, -ies 'fəug|i, -iz
fogyi|sh, -sm 'fəugii|ʃ, -zəm
foible, -s 'fɔibl, -z
foil (s. v.), -s, -ing, -ed fɔil, -z, -iŋ, -d
foison, -s 'fɔizn, -z
foist, -s, -ing, -ed fɔist, -s, -iŋ, -id
Foker 'fəukə*
fold (s. v.), -s, -ing, -ed, -er/s fəuld, -z,
-iŋ, -id, -ə*/z
Foley 'fəuli
Folgate 'fɔlgit [-geit]
Folger 'fəuldʒə*
foliage 'fəuliidʒ [-ljidʒ]
foliate (adj.) 'fəuliit [-ljit, -lieit, -ljeit]
foliat|e (v.), -es, -ing, -ed 'fəulieit
[-ljeit], -s, -iŋ, -id
foliation, -s ˌfəuli'eiʃən, -z
folio, -s 'fəuliəu [-ljəu], -z
Foliot 'fɔlɪət [-ljət]
Foljambe 'fuldʒəm
folk, -s fəuk, -s
folk-dance, -s 'fəukdɑ:ns, -iz
Folkes fəulks
Folkestone 'fəukstən
folklore 'fəuk-lɔ:* [-lɔə*]
folklorist, -s 'fəukˌlɔ:rist, -s
folk-song, -s 'fəuksɔŋ, -z
folk-tale, -s 'fəukteil, -z
Foll|en, -ett 'fɔl|in [-ən], -it
Follick 'fɔlik
follicle, -s 'fɔlikl, -z
Folliott 'fɔlɪət [-ljət]
foll|ow (s. v.), -ows, -owing/s, -owed,
-ower/s 'fɔl|əu, -əuz, -əuiŋ/z, -əud,
-əuə*/z
follow-my-leader 'fɔləumi'li:də*
follow-on, -s 'fɔləu'ɔn, -z
follow-through, -s 'fɔləu'θru:, -z
foll|y, -ies (F.) 'fɔl|i, -iz
Fomalhaut 'fəuməlɔut ['fɔməlhɔ:t]
foment, -s, -ing, -ed, -er/s fəu'ment,
-s, -iŋ, -id, -ə*/z
fomentation, -s ˌfəumen'teiʃən [-mən-], -z
fond, -er, -est, -ly, -ness fɔnd, -ə*, -ist,
-li, -nis ['fɔnnis]
fond|le, -les, -ling, -led, -ler/s 'fɔnd|l̩,
-lz, -liŋ, -ld, -lə*/z
font, -s, -al fɔnt, -s, -l
Fontenoy 'fɔntənɔi [-tin-]
Fonteyn fɔn'tein
Fonthill 'fɔnthil

Foochow fu:'tʃau ['-'-]
food, -s; -less fu:d, -z, -lis
food-stuff, -s 'fu:dstʌf, -s
fool (s. v.), -s, -ing, -ed fu:l, -z, -iŋ, -d
fooler|y, -ies 'fu:lər|i, -iz
fool-hard|y, -iest, -ily, -iness 'fu:l-
  ˌhɑ:d|i, -iist [-jist], -ili, -inis
foolish, -ly, -ness 'fu:liʃ, -li, -nis
fool-proof 'fu:l-pru:f
foolscap (cap), -s 'fu:lzkæp, -s
foolscap (paper size) 'fu:lskæp [-lzk-]
f|oot (s.), -eet f|ut, -i:t
foot (v.), -s, -ing, -ed fut, -s, -iŋ, -id
football, -s, -er/s 'futbɔ:l, -z, -ə*/z
foot-ba|th, -ths 'futbɑ:|θ, -ðz
footboard, -s 'futbɔ:d [-bɔəd], -z
foot-bridge, -s 'futbridʒ, -iz
Foote fut
footer 'futə*
foot|-fall/s, -guard/s 'fut|fɔ:l/z, -gɑ:d/z
foot-fault (s. v.), -s, -ing, -ed 'futfɔ:lt
  [-fɔlt], -s, -iŋ, -id
foothill, -s 'futhil, -z
foothold, -s 'futhəuld, -z
footing (s.), -s 'futiŋ, -z
foot|le, -les, -ling, -led 'fu:t|l, -lz, -liŋ, -ld
foot-light, -s 'futlait, -s
foot|man, -men 'fut|mən, -mən
footmark, -s 'futmɑ:k, -s
footnote, -s 'futnəut, -s
footpad, -s 'futpæd, -z
foot-passenger, -s 'futˌpæsindʒə*, -z
footpa|th, -ths 'futpɑ:|θ, -ðz
footplate, -s 'futpleit, -s
foot-pound, -s 'fut-paund, -z
foot-print, -s 'futprint, -s
foot-pump, -s 'futpʌmp, -s
foot-race, -s 'fut-reis, -iz
foot-rule, -s 'fut-ru:l, -z
Foots Cray 'futs'krei
foot-soldier, -s 'futˌsəuldʒə* [rarely
footsore 'futsɔ:* [-sɔə*]   [-djə*], -z
footstep, -s 'futstep, -s
footstool, -s 'futstu:l, -z
foot-warmer, -s 'fut,wɔ:mə*, -z
footwear 'futweə*
fooz|le (s. v.) (F.), -les, -ling, -led, -ler/s
  'fu:z|l, -lz, -ļiŋ [-liŋ], -ld, -ļə*/z
  [-lə*/z]
fop, -s fɔp, -s
fopper|y, -ies 'fɔpər|i, -iz
Foppington 'fɔpiŋtən
foppish, -ly, -ness 'fɔpiʃ, -li, -nis
for (prep. conj.) fɔ:* (strong form), fɔr
  (occasional strong form before vowels),
  fə* (weak form), f (alternative weak
  form before consonants), fr (alternative
  weak form before vowels).

forag|e (s. v.), -es, -ing, -ed, -er/s
  'fɔridʒ, -iz, -iŋ, -d, -ə*/z
forasmuch fərəz'mʌtʃ [ˌfɔ:r-, ˌfɔr-]
foray (s. v.), -s, -ing, -ed 'fɔrei, -z, -iŋ, -d
forbade (from forbid) fə'bæd [fɔ:'b-,
  -'beid]
forbear (s.) (ancestor), -s 'fɔ:bɛə*, -z
forbear (v.), -s, -ing/ly, forbore, for-
  borne fɔ:'bɛə*, -z, -riŋ/li, fɔ:'bɔ:*
  [-'bɔə*], fɔ:'bɔ:n
  Note.—The verb forbear is sometimes pronounced 'fɔ:bɛə* when
  contrasted with bear. This change
  of stress is not generally made in the
  inflected forms of the word.
forbearance fɔ:'bɛərəns
Forbes fɔ:bz, 'fɔ:bis
forbid, -s, -ding/ly, forbade, forbidden
  fə'bid [fɔ:'b-], -z, -iŋ/li, fə'bæd
  [fɔ:'b-, -'beid], fə'bidn [fɔ:'b-]
forbore (from forbear) fɔ:'bɔ:* [-'bɔə*]
forc|e (s. v.) (F.), -es, -ing, -ed, -edly,
  -edness, -er/s fɔ:s, -iz, -iŋ, -t, -idli,
  -idnis, -ə*/z
force|ful, -fully, -fulness 'fɔ:s|ful, -fuli
  [-fəli], -fulnis
force-meat 'fɔ:s-mi:t
forceps, -es 'fɔ:seps [-sips], -iz
force-pump, -s 'fɔ:s-pʌmp, -s
forcer, -s 'fɔ:sə*, -z
forcib|le, -ly, -leness 'fɔ:səb|l [-sib-], -li,
  -lnis
forcing-pit, -s 'fɔ:siŋpit, -s
ford (s. v.) (F.), -s, -ing, -ed; -able
  fɔ:d, -z, -iŋ, -id; -əbl
Fordcombe 'fɔ:dkəm
Ford|e, -er, -ham, -ingbridge fɔ:d, -ə*,
  -əm, -iŋbridʒ
fordone fɔ:'dʌn
Fordoun 'fɔ:dən [-dn]
Fordyce 'fɔ:dais
fore fɔ:* [fɔə*]
forearm (s.), -s 'fɔ:rɑ:m ['fɔərɑ:m,
  'fɔ:ɑ:m, 'fɔəɑ:m], -z
forearm (v.), -s, -ing, -ed fɔ:r'ɑ:m
  [fɔər'ɑ:m, fɔ:'ɑ:m, fɔə'ɑ:m, '-'-], -z,
  -iŋ, -d
forebod|e, -es, -ing/ly, -ed, -er/s
  fɔ:'bəud [fə'b-], -z, -iŋ/li, -id, -ə*/z
foreboding (s.), -s fɔ:'bəudiŋ [fə'b-], -z
forecabin, -s 'fɔ:ˌkæbin ['fɔəˌk-], -z
forecast (s.), -s 'fɔ:-kɑ:st ['fɔə-], -s
forecast (v.), -s, -ing, -ed, -er/s
  'fɔ:-kɑ:st   ['fɔə-kɑ:st,   fɔ:'kɑ:st,
  fɔə'kɑ:st], -s, -iŋ, -id, -ə*/z
forecastle, -s 'fəuksl, -z
foreclos|e, -es, -ing, -ed fɔ:'kləuz, -iz,
  -iŋ, -d

foreclosure, -s fɔː'kləuʒə*, -z
forecourt, -s 'fɔː-kɔːt ['fɔə-], -s
foredoom, -s, -ing, -ed fɔː'duːm, -z, -iŋ, -d
fore-end, -s 'fɔːrend ['fɔərend, 'fɔːend, 'fɔəend], -z
fore|father/s, -finger/s 'fɔː|ˌfɑːðə*/z ['fɔə|-], -ˌfiŋgə*/z
fore|-foot, -feet 'fɔː|-fut ['fɔə-], -fiːt
forefront 'fɔː-frʌnt ['fɔə-]
fore|go, -goes, -going, -went, -gone, -goer/s fɔː|'gəu, -'gəuz, -'gəuiŋ, -'went, -'gɒn [-'gɔːn, as adjective 'fɔːg-, 'fɔəg-], -'gəuə*/z
foreground, -s 'fɔːgraund ['fɔəg-], -z
forehand 'fɔːhænd ['fɔə-]
forehead, -s 'fɒrid [-red, 'fɔːhed, 'fɔəhed], -z
foreign, -er/s 'fɒrən [-rin], -ə*/z
forejudg|e, -es, -ing, -ed fɔː'dʒʌdʒ, -iz, -iŋ, -d
fore|know, -knows, -knowing, -knew, -known fɔː|'nəu, -'nəuz, 'nəuiŋ, -'njuː, -'nəun
foreknowledge 'fɔː'nɒlidʒ [fɔː'n-]
Note.—There is also a form '-nəul-.
forel 'fɒrəl
foreland (F.), -s 'fɔːlənd ['fɔəl-], -z
foreleg, -s 'fɔːleg ['fɔəl-], -z
forelock, -s 'fɔːlɒk ['fɔə-], -s
fore|man (F.), -men 'fɔː|mən, -mən
foremast, -s 'fɔːmɑːst ['fɔə-, nautical pronunciation -məst], -s
foremost 'fɔːməust ['fɔə-, -məst]
forenoon, -s 'fɔːnuːn ['fɔə-], -z
forensic fə'rensik [fɔ'r-]
fore-ordain, -s, -ing, -ed 'fɔːrɔː'dein ['fɔə-], -z, -iŋ, -d
forepart, -s 'fɔːpɑːt ['fɔə-], -s
fore|run, -runs, -running, -ran fɔː|'rʌn [fɔə-], -'rʌnz, -'rʌniŋ, -'ræn
forerunner, -s 'fɔːˌrʌnə* ['fɔə-, '-'--], -z
foresail, -s 'fɔːseil ['fɔə-, nautical pronunciation -sl], -z
fore|see, -sees, -seeing, -saw, -seen fɔː|'siː [fɔə|-], -'siːz, -'siːiŋ, -'sɔː, -'siːn
foreshad|ow, -ows, -owing, -owed, -ower/s fɔː'ʃæd|əu ['fɔə-], -əuz, -əuiŋ, -əud, -əuə*/z
foreshore, -s 'fɔː-ʃɔː* ['fɔː-ʃɔə*, 'fɔə-ʃɔə*], -z
foreshort|en, -ens, -ening, -ened fɔː-'ʃɔːt|n [fɔə-], -nz, -niŋ [-niŋ], -nd
foreshow, -s, -ing, -ed, -n fɔː'ʃəu [fɔə-], -z, -iŋ, -d, -n
foresight, -s 'fɔːsait ['fɔə-sait], -s
foreskin, -s 'fɔːskin ['fɔə-skin], -z
forest (F.), -s 'fɒrist, -s

forestall, -s, -ing, -ed, -er/s fɔː'stɔːl [fɔə-], -z, -iŋ, -d, -ə*/z
forester (F.), -s 'fɒristə*, -z
forest-land 'fɒristlænd
forestry 'fɒristri
foretaste (s.), -s 'fɔː-teist ['fɔə-], -s
foretast|e (v.), -es, -ing, -ed fɔː'teist [fɔə-], -s, -iŋ, -id
fore|tell, -tells, -telling, -told, -teller/s fɔː|'tel [fɔə-], -'telz, -'teliŋ, -'təuld, -'telə*/z
forethought 'fɔː-θɔːt ['fɔə-θɔːt]
foretop, -s; -mast/s 'fɔː-tɒp ['fɔə-t-, nautical pronunciation -təp], -s; -mɑːst/s
fore-topsail, -s 'fɔː-tɒpseil ['fɔə-t-, nautical pronunciation -sl], -z
forever fə'revə*
forewarn, -s, -ing, -ed fɔː'wɔːn [fɔə-], -z, -iŋ, -d
forewent (from forego) fɔː'went [fɔə-]
fore|woman, -women 'fɔː|ˌwumən ['fɔə-], -ˌwimin
foreword, -s 'fɔːwəːd ['fɔə-], -z
forfeit (s. v.), -s, -ing, -ed, -er/s; -able 'fɔːfit, -s, -iŋ, -id, -ə*/z; -əbl
forfeiture, -s 'fɔːfitʃə*, -z
forfend, -s, -ing, -ed fɔː'fend, -z, -iŋ, -id
forgat (archaic form of forgot) fɔː'gæt [fə'g-]
forgather, -s, -ing, -ed fɔː'gæðə*, -z, -riŋ, -d
forgave (from forgive) fə'geiv
forg|e (s. v.), -es, -ing, -ed, -er/s fɔːdʒ, -iz, -iŋ, -d, -ə*/z
forger|y, -ies 'fɔːdʒər|i, -iz
for|get, -gets, -getting, -got, -gotten fə|'get, -'gets, -'getiŋ, -'gɒt, -'gɒtn
forget|ful, -fully, -fulness fə'get|ful, -fuli [-fəli], -fulnis
forget-me-not, -s fə'getminɒt, -s
forgiv|e, -es, -ing, forgave, forgiv|en; -able, -eness fə'giv, -z, -iŋ, fə'geiv, fə'giv|n; -əbl, -nis
for|go, -goes, -going, -went, -gone fɔː|'gəu, -'gəuz, -'gəuiŋ, -'went, -'gɒn [-'gɔːn]
forgot (from forget) fə'gɒt
Forington 'fɒriŋtən
fork (s. v.), -s, -ing, -ed fɔːk, -s, -iŋ, -t
fork|y, -iness 'fɔːk|i, -inis
forlorn, -ness fə'lɔːn, -nis
form (s. v.), -s, -ing, -ed, -er/s fɔːm, -z, -iŋ, -d, -ə*/z
form|al, -ally 'fɔːm|əl, -əli
formaldehyde fɔː'mældihaid
formalin 'fɔːməlin
formali|sm, -st/s 'fɔːməli|zəm [-mli-], [-st/s]

formalit|y, -ies fɔ:'mælit|i, -iz
Forman 'fɔ:mən
formant, -s 'fɔ:mənt, -s
format, -s 'fɔ:mæt, -s [-mɑ:, -z]
formation, -s fɔ:'meiʃən, -z
formative 'fɔ:mətiv
forme, -s fɔ:m, -z
former (adj.), -ly 'fɔ:mə*, -li
formic 'fɔ:mik
formidab|le, -ly, -leness 'fɔ:mid̄əb|l
[fɔ:'mid-, fə'm-], -li, -lnis
Formidable (name of ship) fɔ:'mid̄əbl
['fɔ:mid-]
formless, -ness 'fɔ:mlis, -nis
Formorian, -s fɔ:'mɔ:riən, -z
Formos|a, -an/s fɔ:'məus|ə [-əuz|ə],
-ən/z
Formosus fɔ:'məusəs
formul|a, -ae, -as 'fɔ:mjul|ə, -i:, -əz
formular|y, -ies 'fɔ:mjulər|i, -iz
formulat|e, -es, -ing, -ed 'fɔ:mjuleit, -s,
-iŋ, -id
formulation, -s ˌfɔ:mju'leiʃən, -z
Forn|ax, -ey 'fɔ:n|æks, -i
fornicat|e, -es, -ing, -ed, -or/s 'fɔ:ni-
keit, -s, -iŋ, -id, -ə*/z
fornication ˌfɔ:ni'keiʃən
forrader 'fɔrədə*
Forres 'fɔris
Forrest, -er 'fɔrist, -ə*
for|sake, -sakes, -saking, -sook, -saken
fə|'seik [fɔ:'s-], -'seiks, -'seikiŋ, -'suk,
-'seikən
Forshaw 'fɔ:ʃɔ:
forsooth fə'su:θ [fɔ:'s-]
Forster 'fɔ:stə*
forswear, -s, -ing, forswore, forsworn
fɔ:'swɛə*, -z, -riŋ, fɔ:'swɔ:* [-əə*],
fɔ:'swɔ:n
Forsyte, -ism 'fɔ:sait, -izəm
Forsyth fɔ:'saiθ
forsythia, -s fɔ:'saiθjə [fə's-, -θɪə], -z
fort, -s fɔ:t, -s
fortalice, -s 'fɔ:təlis, -iz
forte (strong point), -s 'fɔ:tei [-ti, fɔ:t], -s
forte (in music), -s 'fɔ:ti, -z   [[fɔ:ts]
Fortescue 'fɔ:tiskju:
Forteviot 'fɔ:ti:vjət [-vɪət]
forth (F.) fɔ:θ
forthcoming fɔ:θ'kʌmiŋ [also '-,-- when
attributive]
forthwith 'fɔ:θ'wiθ ['-wið, fɔ:θ'w-]
Forties (area in the North Sea) 'fɔ:tiz
fortieth, -s 'fɔ:tiiθ [-tjiθ, -tɪəθ, -tjəθ], -s
fortification, -s ˌfɔ:tifi'keiʃən, -z
forti|fy, -fies, -fying, -fied, -fier/s;
-fiable 'fɔ:ti|fai, -faiz, -faiiŋ, -faid,
-faiə*/z; -faiəbl

Fortinbras 'fɔ:tinbræs
fort|is (phonetic term), -es 'fɔ:t|is, -i:z
[-eiz]
fortissimo, -s fɔ:'tisiməu, -z
fortitude 'fɔ:titju:d
fortnight, -s 'fɔ:tnait, -s
fortnightl|y (F.), -ies 'fɔ:t,naitl|i [fɔ:t'n-],
-iz
Fortnum 'fɔ:tnəm
fortress, -es 'fɔ:tris, -iz
fortuitous, -ly, -ness fɔ:'tju(:)itəs, -li,
-nis
fortuit|y, -ies fɔ:'tju(:)it|i, -iz
fortun|ate, -ately, -ateness 'fɔ:tʃn|it,
[-tʃn̩|it, -tʃən|it], -itli [-ətli], -itnis
Fortunatus ˌfɔ:tju(:)'neitəs
fortune, -s; -less 'fɔ:tʃən [-tʃu:n,
-tju:n], -z; -lis
Fortune (surname) 'fɔ:tju:n
fortune|-hunter/s, -teller/s fɔ:tʃən|-
ˌhʌntə*/z, -ˌtelə*/z
fort|y, -ies, -ieth/s, -yfold 'fɔ:t|i, -iz,
-iiθ/s [-jiθ/s, -ɪəθ/s, -jəθ/s], -ifəuld
forum, -s 'fɔ:rəm, -z
forward (s. adj. v. interj.), -s, -ly, -ness,
-er, -est; -ing, -ed, -er/s 'fɔ:wəd [in
nautical use 'fɔrəd], -z, -li, -nis, -ə*,
-ist; -iŋ, -id, -ə*/z
forwent (from forgo) fɔ:'went
Fos|bery, -broke, -bury 'fɔz|bəri, -bruk,
-bəri
Foss fɔs
fosse, -s fɔs, -iz
fossil, -s 'fɔsl [-sil], -z
fossiliferous ˌfɔsi'lifərəs
fossilization [-isa-] ˌfɔsilai'zeiʃən
[-li'z-]
fossiliz|e [-is|e], -es, -ing, -ed 'fɔsilaiz,
-iz, -iŋ, -d
fost|er (s. v.) (F.), -ers, -ering, -ered,
-erer/s; -erage 'fɔst|ə*, -əz, -əriŋ, -əd,
-ərə*/z; -əridʒ
foster|-brother/s, -child, -children,
-father/s, -mother/s, -sister/s 'fɔstə|-
ˌbrʌðə*/z, -tʃaild, -ˌtʃildrən [-ˌtʃuld-],
-ˌfɑ:ðə*/z, -ˌmʌðə*/z, -ˌsistə*/z
fother, -s 'fɔðə*, -z
Fothergill 'fɔðəgil
Fothering|ay, -ham 'fɔðəriŋ|gei, -əm
Fouberts 'fu:bə:ts
fought (from fight) fɔ:t
foul (s. adj. v.), -s; -er, -est, -ly, -ness;
-ing, -ed faul, -z; -ə*, -ist, -li ['fauli],
-nis; -iŋ, -d
Foulden 'fəuldən
Foulds fəuldz
Foulerton 'fulətn
Foulger 'fu:ldʒə*, 'fu:lgə*

Foulis faulz
Foulkes fəuks, fauks
foul-mouthed 'faulmauðd ['-'-]
foulness 'faulnis
Foulness 'faul'nes [*also* '— *and* -'- *according to sentence stress*]
foul-play 'faul'plei
Foulsham (*in Norfolk*) 'fəulʃəm
foul-spoken 'faul₁spəukən ['-'--]
found, -s, -ing, -ed, -er/s faund, -z, -iŋ, -id, -ə*/z
found (*from* find) faund
foundation, -s faun'deiʃən, -z
foundationer, -s faun'deiʃŋə* [-ʃənə*, -ʃnə*], -z
found|er, -ers, -ering, -ered 'faund|ə*, -əz, -əriŋ, -əd
foundling (F.), -s 'faundliŋ, -z
foundress, -es 'faundris [-res], -iz
foundr|y, -ies 'faundr|i, -iz
fount (*fountain, source*), -s faunt, -s
fount (*of type*), -s faunt [fɔnt], -s
Note.—*Those connected with the printing trade generally pronounce* fɔnt.
fountain (F.), -s 'fauntin, -z
fountain-head, -s 'fauntin'hed ['—], -z
fountain-pen, -s 'fauntinpen [-tən-], -z
four, -s, -th/s, -thly fɔ:* [fɔə*], -z, -θ/s, -θli
four-cornered 'fɔ:'kɔːnəd ['fɔə-, *also* '-₁-- *when attributive*]
four-dimensional 'fɔ:-di'menʃənl ['fɔə-, -dai'm-, -ʃnəl, -ʃn̩l, ʃn̩l, -ʃənəl]
fourfold 'fɔ:-fəuld ['fɔə-]
four-footed 'fɔ:'futid ['fɔə-, *also* '-₁-- *when attributive*]
Fourier ['furiei ['furiə*] (furje)
four-in-hand, -s 'fɔ:rin'hænd ['fɔərin-, 'fɔ:in-], -z
fourish 'fɔ:riʃ ['fɔər-]
four-legged 'fɔ:legd ['fɔə-, -'legid]
fourpence 'fɔ:pəns
fourpenny 'fɔ:pəni [-pn̩i, -pni]
four-ply 'fɔ:-plai ['fɔə-, '-'-]
four-poster, -s 'fɔ:'pəustə* ['fɔə-], -z
fourscore 'fɔ:'skɔ:* ['fɔə'skɔə*, *also* 'fɔ:-skɔ:*, 'fɔə-skɔə* *when immediately followed by a stress*]
four-sidedness 'fɔ:'saididnis ['fɔə's-]
foursome, -s 'fɔ:səm ['fɔə-], -z
foursquare 'fɔ:'skwɛə* ['fɔə'skwɛə*, 'fɔ:-skwɛə*, 'fɔə-skwɛə*]
fourteen, -s, -th/s 'fɔ:'ti:n ['fɔə-, *also* '—, -'- *according to sentence-stress*], -z, -θ/s
fourth, -s -ly fɔ:θ [fɔəθ], -s, -li
four-wheeler, -s 'fɔ:'wi:lə* ['fɔə-, -'hw-], -z

Fowey fɔi ['fəui]
Fowke fauk, fəuk
Fowkes fəuks
fowl (*s. v.*), -s, -ing, -ed, -er/s faul, -z, -iŋ, -d, -ə*/z
Fowler 'faulə*
Fowles faulz
fowl-hou|se, -ses 'faulhau|s, -ziz
fowling|-net/s, -piece/s 'fauliŋ|net/s, -pi:s/iz
fowl-run, -s 'faulrʌn, -z
Fownes faunz
fox (*s. v.*) (F.), -es, -ing, -ed fɔks, -iz, -iŋ, -t
Foxboro' 'fɔksbərə
fox-brush, -es 'fɔksbrʌʃ, -iz
Foxcraft 'fɔkskrɔft [-krɔ:ft]
Foxfield 'fɔksfi:ld
foxglove, -s 'fɔksglʌv, -z
foxhole, -s 'fɔkshəul, -z
foxhound, -s 'fɔkshaund, -z
foxhunt, -s 'fɔkshʌnt, -s
foxtrot, -s 'fɔkstrɔt, -s
Foxwell 'fɔkswəl [-wel]
fox|y, -ier, -iest, -ily, -iness 'fɔks|i, -iə* [-jə*], -iist [-jist], -ili, -nis
foyer, -s 'fɔiei (fwaje), -z
Foyers 'fɔiəz
Foyle fɔil
fracas (*sing.*) 'frækɑ:; (*plur.*) -z
Frackville 'frækvil
fraction, -s 'frækʃən, -z
fractional 'frækʃənl [-ʃnəl, -ʃn̩l, -ʃn̩l, -ʃənəl]
fractious, -ly, -ness 'frækʃəs, -li, -nis
frac|ture (*s. v.*), -tures, -turing, -tured 'fræk|tʃə*, -tʃəz, -tʃəriŋ, -tʃəd
Fradin 'freidin
fragile, -ly, -ness 'frædʒail [*rarely* -dʒil], -li, -nis
fragility frə'dʒiliti [fræ'dʒ-]
fragment, -s 'frægmənt, -s
fragmental fræg'mentl
fragmentar|y, -ily, -iness 'frægmən-tər|i [fræg'mentər|i], -ili, -inis
fragmentation ₁frægmen'teiʃən [-mən-]
fragran|ce, -cy, -t/ly, -tness 'freigrən|s, -si, -t/li, -tnis
frail, -er, -est, -ly, -ness freil, -ə*, -ist, -li, -nis
frailt|y, -ies 'freilt|i, -iz
Fram fræm
fram|e (*s. v.*), -es, -ing, -ed, -er/s freim, -z, -iŋ, -d, -ə*/z
frame-up, -s 'freimʌp ['-'-], -s
framework, -s 'freimwə:k, -s
Framingham 'freimiŋəm
Framlingham 'fræmliŋəm

Frampton 'fræmptən
franc, -s fræŋk, -s
France frɑːns
Frances 'frɑːnsis
Francesca fræn'seskə, fræn'tʃeskə
franchise, -s 'fræntʃaiz, -iz
Francie 'frɑːnsi
Francillon fræn'silən
Francis 'frɑːnsis
Franciscan, -s fræn'siskən, -z
Francisco (personal name) fræn'siskəu,
   (in San Francisco) frən'siskəu
Franck frɑ̃ːŋk [frɑːŋk, fræŋk] (frɑ̃ːk)
Franco-German 'fræŋkəu'dʒɔːmən
francolin, -s 'fræŋkəulin, -z
Franconia, -n fræŋ'kəunjə [-nɪə], -n
frangibility ˌfrændʒi'biliti [-dʒə'b-, -lət-]
frangible, -ness 'frændʒibl [-dʒəb-], -nis
frank (adj. v.), -er, -est, -ly, -ness; -s,
   -ing, -ed fræŋk, -ə*, -ist, -li, -nis; -s,
   -iŋ, -t [fræŋt]
Frank, -s fræŋk, -s
Frankau (English surname) 'fræŋkəu
Frankfort (-furt) 'fræŋkfət [-fɔːt]
frankincense 'fræŋkinˌsens
Frankish 'fræŋkiʃ
Frankland 'fræŋklənd
franklin (F.), -s 'fræŋklin, -z
Franklyn 'fræŋklin
frantic, -ally, -ness 'fræntik, -əli, -nis
Franz frænts
frap, -s, -ping, -ped fræp, -s, -iŋ, -t
Frascati fræs'kɑːti
Fraser, -burgh 'freizə*, -bərə [-bʌrə]
fratern|al, -ally frə'təːn|l, -əli
fraternit|y, -ies frə'təːnit|i, -iz
fraternization [-isa-] ˌfrætənai'zeiʃən
   [-təːn-, -ni'z-]
fraterniz|e [-is|e], -es, -ing, -ed, -er/s
   'frætənaiz [-təːn-], -iz, -iŋ, -d, -ə*/z
fratricidal ˌfrætri'saidl [ˌfreit-]
fratricide, -s 'frætrisaid ['freit-], -z
Fratton 'frætn
fraud, -s frɔːd, -z
fraudulen|ce, -t/ly 'frɔːdjulən|s, -t/li
fraught frɔːt
fray (s. v.), -s, -ing, -ed frei, -z, -iŋ,
   -d
Frazer 'freizə*
frazil 'freizil
frazz|le (s. v.), -les, -ling, -led 'fræz|l, -lz,
   -liŋ [-liŋ], -ld
freak, -s friːk, -s
Freake friːk
freakish, -ly, -ness 'friːkiʃ, -li, -nis
freak|y, -ier, -iest, -ily, -iness 'friːk|i,
   -iə* [-jə*], -iist [-jist], -ili, -inis
Frean friːn

freck|le (s. v.), -les, -ling, -led 'frek|l,
   -lz, -liŋ [-liŋ], -ld
freckly 'frekli [-li]
Frecknall 'freknɔːl [-nl]
Fred, -die, -dy fred, -i, -i
Frederic(k) 'fredrik
Frederica ˌfredə'riːkə
free (adj. v.), -r, -st, -ly; -s, -ing, -d,
   -r/s friː:, -ə* [friə*], -ist, -li; -z, -iŋ,
   -d, -ə*/z [friə*/z]
freebooter, -s 'friːˌbuːtə*, -z
free-born 'friː'bɔːn ['friːbɔːn esp. when
   attributive]
freed|man, -men 'friːd|mæn [-mən],
   -men [-mən]
freedom, -s 'friːdəm, -z
free-for-all 'friːfərˌɔːl [ˌ--'-]
free-hand (adj.) 'friːhænd   [-nis
free-hearted, -ly, -ness 'friː'hɑːtid, -li,
freehold, -s; -er/s 'friːhəuld ['friːəuld],
   -z; -ə*/z
free-lance, -s 'friː'lɑːns ['--], -iz
Freeling 'friːliŋ
free|man (of a city), -men 'friː|mən,
   -mən, (opposed to slave) 'friː|mæn
   [-mən], -men [-mən]
Freeman 'friːmən
freemason, -s 'friːˌmeisn, -z
freemasonry 'friːˌmeisnri   ['friː'm-,
   friː'm-]
Freeport 'friː-pɔːt
freesia, -s 'friːzjə [-zɪə, -ʒjə, -ʒɪə, -ʒə], -z
free-spoken 'friː'spəukən ['ˌ-'--]
freestone 'friː-stəun
freethinker, -s 'friː'θiŋkə*, -z
Freetown 'friː-taun
free-trade, -er/s 'friː'treid, -ə*/z
free-wheel (s. v.), -s, -ing, -ed 'friː'wiːl
   [-'hw-, '--], -z, -iŋ, -d
freewill 'friː'wil [also '--, -'- according to
   sentence-stress]
freez|e, -es, -ing, froze, frozen, freezer/s
   friːz, -iz, -iŋ, frəuz, 'frəuzn, 'friːzə*/z
freezing-machine, -s 'friːziŋməˌʃiːn, -z
freezing-mixture 'friːziŋˌmikstʃə*
freezing-point 'friːziŋpoint
Freiburg 'fraibəːg
freight (s. v.), -s, -ing, -ed, -er/s; -age
   freit, -s, -iŋ, -id, -ə*/z; -idʒ
Fremantle 'friːmæntl
fremitus 'fremitəs
Fremont fri'mɔnt
French frentʃ
frenchi|fy, -fies, -fying, -fied 'frentʃi|-
   fai, -faiz, -faiiŋ, -faid
French|man, -men 'frentʃ|mən, -mən
french-polish (s. v.), -es, -ing, -ed, -er/s
   'frentʃ'poliʃ, -iz, -iŋ, -t, -ə*/z

French|woman, -women 'frent∫|-,wumən, -,wimin

french|y, -ily, -iness 'frent∫|i, -ili, -inis

frenz|y, -ies, -ied/ly 'frenz|i, -iz, -id/li

frequen|ce,-cy, -cies 'fri:kwən|s, -si, -siz

frequent (adj.), -ly, -ness 'fri:kwənt, -li, -nis

frequent (v.), -s, -ing, -ed, -er/s fri-'kwent [fri:'k-], -s, -iŋ, -id, -ə*/z

frequentation ,fri:kwen'tei∫ən

frequentative (s. adj.), -s fri'kwentətiv, -z

Frere friə*

fresco, -(e)s 'freskəu, -z

fresh, -er, -est, -ly, -ness fre∫, -ə*, -ist, -li, -nis

fresh|en, -ens, -ening, -ened 'fre∫|n, -nz, -ṇiŋ [-niŋ], -nd

fresher (s.), -s 'fre∫ə*, -z

freshet, -s 'fre∫it, -s

fresh|man, -men 'fre∫|mən, -mən

freshwater (F.) 'fre∫,wɔ:tə*

Fresno 'freznəu

fret (s. v.), -s, -ting, -ted, -ter/s fret, -s, -iŋ, -id, -ə*/z

fret|ful, -fully, -fulness 'fret|fʊl, -fuli [-fəli], -fʊlnis

fret|saw/s, -work 'fret|sɔ:/z, -wə:k

Freud, -ian frɔid, -jən [-iən]

Frey (English surname) frei

Freyer friə*, 'fraiə*

friability ,fraiə'biliti [-lət-]

friable, -ness 'fraiəbl, -nis

friar, -s 'fraiə*, -z

friar|y, -ies 'fraiər|i, -iz

fribb|le (s. v.), -les, -ling, -led, -ler/s 'frib|l, -lz, -ḷiŋ [-liŋ], -ld, -ḷə*/z [-lə*/z]

fricandeau, -x 'frikəndəu [-kɑ:n-] (frikãdo), -z

fricassee (s.), -s ,frikə'si: ['frikəs-], -z

fricassee (v.), -s, -ing, -d ,frikə'si:, -z, -iŋ, -d

fricative (s. adj.), -s 'frikətiv, -z

friction, -s; -less 'frik∫ən, -z; -lis

frictional 'frik∫ənl [-∫ṇl, -∫nḷ, -∫ənəl]

Friday, -s 'fraidi [-dei], -z

fridge, -s frid3, -iz

fried (from fry) fraid

friend, -s frend, -z

friendless, -ness 'frendlis, -nis

friendl|y, -ier, -iest, -iness 'frendl|i, -iə* [-jə*], -iist [-jist], -inis

Friendl|y, -ies 'frendl|i, -iz

friendship, -s 'frend∫ip, -s

Friern 'fraiən

fries (from fry) fraiz

Fries fri:s [fri:z]

Friesian 'fri:zjən [-ziən, -3jən, -3iən, -3ən]

Friesic 'fri:zik

Friesland, -er/s 'fri:zlənd [-lænd], -ə*/z

frieze (F.), -s fri:z, -iz

frigate, -s 'frigit [-gət], -s

fright (s. v.), -s, -ing, -ed frait, -s, -iŋ, -id

fright|en, -ens, -ening, -ened 'frait|n, -nz, -niŋ [-ṇiŋ], -nd

fright|ful, -fully, -fulness 'frait|fʊl, -fli [-fəli, -fuli], -fʊlnis

frigid, -ly, -ness 'frid3id, -li, -nis

frigidity fri'd3iditi

Friis fri:s

frill (s. v.), -s, -ing, -ed fril, -z, -iŋ, -d

frill|y, -ier, -iest 'fril|i, -iə*, -iist

Frimley 'frimli

fring|e (s. v.), -es, -ing, -ed; -eless, -y frind3, -iz, -iŋ, -d; -lis, -i

fripper|y, -ies 'fripər|i, -iz

frisette, -s fri'zet, -s

Frisian, -s 'frizjən [-zjən, -3iən, -3jən, -3ən], -z

frisk (s. v.), -s, -ing, -ed, -er/s frisk, -s, -iŋ, -t, -ə*/z

frisket, -s 'friskit, -s

frisk|y, -ier, -iest, -ily, -ness 'frisk|i, -iə* [-jə*], -iist [-jist], -ili, -inis

Friswell 'frizwəl [-wel]

frit (s. v.), -s, -ting, -ted frit, -s, -iŋ, -id

frith (F.), -s friθ, -s

Frithsden (near Berkhamsted) 'fri:zdən ['friz-, 'friθsdən]

fritillar|y, -ies fri'tilər|i, -iz

fritter (s. v.), -s, -ing, -ed 'fritə*, -z, -riŋ, -d

Fritton 'fritn

Fritz frits

friv|ol, -ols, -ol(l)ing, -ol(l)ed 'friv|əl, -əlz, -ḷiŋ [-əliŋ], -əld

frivolit|y, -ies fri'vɔlit|i, -iz

frivolous, -ly, -ness 'frivələs [-vḷəs], -li, -nis

Frizell fri'zel

frizette, -s fri'zet, -s

Frizinghall 'fraiziŋhɔ:l

Frizington 'friziŋtən

friz(z), -es, -ing, -ed friz, -iz, -iŋ, -d

frizz|le, -les, -ling, -led 'friz|l, -lz, -ḷiŋ [-liŋ], -ld

frizzl|y, -iness 'friz|li [-zl|i], -inis

frizz|y, -ier, -iest, -iness 'friz|i, -iə*, -iist, -inis

fro frəu

Fröbel 'frə:bəl ('frø:bəl)

Frobisher 'frəubi∫ə*

frock, -s frɔk, -s

frock-coat, -s, -ed 'frɔk'kəut [also 'frɔkk- when followed by a stress], -s, -id

frog, -s frɔg, -z
frogg|y (s. adj.), -ies 'frɔg|i, -iz
frog|man, -men 'frɔg|mən, -mən
frog-march, -es, -ing, -ed 'frɔgmɑ:tʃ, -iz, -iŋ, -t
Frogmore 'frɔgmɔ:* [-mɔə*]
frolic (s. v.), -s, -king, -ked 'frɔlik, -s, -iŋ, -t
frolicsome, -ness 'frɔliksəm, -nis
from frɔm (strong form), frəm, frm (weak forms)
Frome (in Somerset) fru:m
frond, -s frɔnd, -z
front (s. adj. v.), -s, -ing, -ed frʌnt, -s, -iŋ, -id
frontage, -s 'frʌntidʒ, -iz
frontal (s.), -s 'frʌntl ['frɔn-], -z
frontal (adj.) 'frʌntl   [-z
frontier, -s 'frʌntiə* ['frɔn-, -tïə*, -tjə*],
frontispiece, -s 'frʌntispi:s ['frɔn-], -iz
front|less, -let/s 'frʌnt|lis, -lit/s
frost (s. v.) (F.), -s, -ing, -ed frɔst [frɔ:st], -s, -iŋ, -id
frost|bite/s, -bitten, -bound 'frɔst|-bait/s ['frɔ:st-], -ˌbitn, -baund
frostwork 'frɔst-wə:k ['frɔ:st-]
frost|y, -ier, -iest, -ily, -iness 'frɔst|i ['frɔ:st-], -ïə* [-jə*], -iist [-jist], -ili, -inis
froth (s. v.), -s, -ing, -ed frɔθ [frɔ:θ], -s, -iŋ, -t
Frothingham 'frɔðiŋəm
froth|y, -ier, -iest, -ily, -iness 'frɔθ|i ['frɔ:θ|i], -ïə*, -iist, -ili, -inis
Froud fru:d, fraud
Froude fru:d
frou-frou 'fru:-fru:
froward, -ly, -ness 'frəuəd, -li, -nis
Frowde fru:d, fraud
frown (s. v.), -s, -ing/ly, -ed fraun, -z, -iŋ/li, -d
frowst (s. v.), -s, -ing, -ed; -y, -iness fraust, -s, -iŋ, -id; -i, -inis
frowz|y, -iness 'frauz|i, -inis
froze, -n (from freeze) frəuz, -n
fructiferous frʌk'tifərəs
fructification ˌfrʌktifi'keiʃən
fructi|fy, -fies, -fying, -fied 'frʌkti|fai, -faiz, -faiiŋ, -faid
frug|al, -ally, -alness 'fru:g|əl, -əli, -əlnis
frugality fru(:)'gæliti
fruit (s. v.), -s, -ing, -ed; -age fru:t, -s, -iŋ, -id; -idʒ
fruitarian, -s fru:'tɛəriən, -z
fruiterer, -s 'fru:tərə*, -z
fruit|ful, -fully, -fulness 'fru:t|ful, -fuli [-fəli], -fulnis

fruition fru(:)'iʃən
fruitless, -ly, -ness 'fru:tlis, -li, -nis
fruit|y, -ier, -iest, -iness 'fru:t|i, -ïə*, -iist, -inis
frumenty 'fru:mənti
frump, -s; -ish frʌmp, -s; -iʃ
frustrat|e, -es, -ing, -ed frʌs'treit ['frʌstreit], -s, -iŋ, -id
frustration frʌs'treiʃən
frust|um, -a, -ums 'frʌst|əm, -ə, -əmz
fr|y (s. v.) (F.), -ies, -ying, -ied fr|ai, -aiz, -aiiŋ, -aid
Frye frai
Fuad 'fu(:)æd
fuchsia, -s 'fju:ʃə, -z
fuchsine 'fu:ksi:n
fu|cus, -ci 'fju:|kəs, -sai
fudd|le (s. v.), -les, -ling, -led, -ler/s 'fʌd|l, -lz, -liŋ, -ld, -lə*/z
fudg|e (s. v.), -es, -ing, -ed fʌdʒ, -iz, -iŋ, -id
Fudge fju:dʒ, fʌdʒ
fuel, -s fjuəl [fjuil, 'fju:əl, fju:l], -z
fug, -s fʌg, -z
fugacious, -ly, -ness fju(:)'geiʃəs, -li, -nis
fugacity fju(:)'gæsiti
fugal 'fju:gəl
fugg|y, -ier, -iest, -iness 'fʌg|i, -ïə*, -iist, -inis
fugitive (s. adj.), -s, -ly, -ness 'fju:dʒi-tiv [-dʒət-], -z, -li, -nis
fugle|man, -men 'fju:glmæn [-mən], -men [-mən]
fugue, -s fju:g, -z
Fuehrer, -s 'fjuərə* ['fjɔə-, 'fjɔ:-], -z
Fulcher 'fultʃə*
fulcr|um, -a, -ums 'fʌlkr|əm, ['ful-] -ə, -əmz
fulfil, -s, -ling, -led, -ler/s, -ment ful'fil, -z, -iŋ, -d, -ə*/z, -mənt
Fulford 'fulfəd
fulgent, -ly 'fʌldʒənt, -li
fulgurat|e, -es, -ing, -ed 'fʌlgjuəreit, -s, -iŋ, -id
Fulham 'fuləm
fuliginous, -ly fju:'lidʒinəs, -li
Fulke fulk
full, -er, -est, -y, -ness ful, -ə*, -ist, -i, -nis
full-blooded 'ful'blʌdid [also '-ˌ-- when attributive]
full-blown 'ful'bləun [also '-- when attributive]
full-bodied 'ful'bɔdid [also '-ˌ-- when attributive]
fuller (F.), -s 'fulə*, -z
Fullerton 'fulətn
full-face 'ful'feis ['ful-feis]

full-fledged 'ful'fledʒd [also 'ful-fledʒd when attributive]
full-grown 'ful'grəun [also '— when attributive]
full-length 'ful'leŋθ [also '— when attributive]
fulmar, -s 'fulmə*, -z
Fulmer (in Bucks.) 'fulmə*
fulminat|e, -es, -ing, -ed 'fʌlmineit, -s, -iŋ, -id
fulmination, -s ˌfʌlmi'neiʃən, -z
fulness 'fulnis
fulsome, -ly, -ness 'fulsəm, -li, -nis
Fulton 'fultən
Fulvia 'fʌlvĭə [-vjə]
fulvous 'fʌlvəs
Fulwood 'fulwud
fumb|le, -les, -ling, -led, -ler/s 'fʌmb|l, -lz, -liŋ, -ld, -lə*/z   [-d
fum|e (s. v.), -es, -ing, -ed fju:m, -z, -iŋ,
fumigat|e, -es, -ing, -ed, -or/s 'fju:mi- geit, -s, -iŋ, -id, -ə*/z
fumigation, -s ˌfju:mi'geiʃən, -z
fun fʌn
funambulist, -s fju(:)'næmbjulist, -s
Funchal fun'ʃɑ:l
functi|on (s. v.), -ons, -oning, -oned 'fʌŋkʃ|ən, -ənz, -ṇiŋ [-əniŋ], -ənd
func|tional, -tionally 'fʌŋk|ʃənl [-ʃnəl, -ʃṇl, -ʃnḷ, -ʃənəl], -ʃṇəli [-ʃnəli, -ʃṇḷi, -ʃṇḷi, -ʃənəli]
functionar|y, -ies 'fʌŋkʃṇər|i [-ʃənər-, -ʃnər-], -iz
fund (s. v.), -s, -ing, -ed fʌnd, -z, -iŋ, -id
fundament, -s 'fʌndəmənt, -s
fundament|al (s. adj.), -als, -ally ˌfʌndə'ment|l, -lz, -əli [-ḷi]
fundamentali|sm, -st/s ˌfʌndə'ment- əli|zəm [-tḷi-], -st/s
fundamentality ˌfʌndəmen'tæliti
fund-holder, -s 'fʌndˌhəuldə*, -z
fundless 'fʌndlis
Fundy 'fʌndi
funeral, -s 'fju:nərəl, -z
funereal fju(:)'niəriəl
fungible (s. adj.), -s 'fʌndʒibl, -z
fung|us, -i, -uses; -oid, -ous, -usy 'fʌŋg|əs, -ai ['fʌndʒi, 'fʌndʒai], -əsiz; -oid, -əs, -əsi
tunicle, -s 'fju:nikl, -z
tunicular (s. adj.), -s fju(:)'nikjulə* [fə'nik-, fṇ'ik-, -kjəl-], -z
tunicul|us, -i fju(:)'nikjul|əs, -ai
tunk (s. v.) (F.), -s, -ing, -ed fʌŋk, -s, -iŋ, -t [fʌŋt]
tunkia, -s 'fʌŋkjə [-kĭə], -z
tunk|y, -ier, -iest, -ily, -iness 'fʌŋk|i, -ĭə* [-jə*], -iist [-jist], -ili, -inis

funnel, -s 'fʌnl, -z
funn|y, -ier, -iest, -ily, -iness 'fʌn|i, -ĭə*, -iist, -ili, -inis
funnybone, -s 'fʌnibəun, -z
fur (s. v.), -s, -ring, -red fə:*, -z, -riŋ, -d
Furbear 'fə:beə*
furbelow, -s 'fə:biləu, -z
furbish, -es, -ing, -ed 'fə:biʃ, -iz, -iŋ, -t
furcate (adj.) 'fə:keit [-kit]
furcat|e (v.), -es, -ing, -ed 'fə:keit [fə:'k-], -s, -iŋ, -id
furcation, -s fə:'keiʃən, -z
furibund 'fjuəribʌnd ['fjɔər-, 'fjɔ:r-, -bənd]
furioso (F.) ˌfjuəri'əuzəu [ˌfjɔər-, ˌfjɔ:r-, -'əusəu]
furious, -ly, -ness 'fjuərĭəs ['fjɔər-, 'fjɔ:r-, 'fjɔ:r|-], -li, -nis
furl, -s, -ing, -ed fə:l, -z, -iŋ, -d
furlong, -s 'fə:lɔŋ, -z
furlough, -s 'fə:ləu, -z
furnace, -s 'fə:nis, -iz
Furneaux 'fə:nəu
Furness 'fə:nis [-nes]
Furneux (in Herts.) 'fə:niks [-nu:]
    Note.—'fə:niks is the more usual local pronunciation.
furnish, -es, -ing, -ed, -er/s 'fə:niʃ, -iz, -iŋ, -t, -ə*/z
furniture 'fə:nitʃə*
Furnival(l) 'fə:nivəl
furore (admiration, craze), -s fjuə'rɔ:ri ['fjuərɔ:*], -z
furore (musical term) fu'rɔ:ri
furrier (s.), -s 'fʌrĭə*, -z
furrier|y, -ies 'fʌrĭər|i, -iz
furr|ow (s. v.), -ows, -owing, -owed; -owy 'fʌr|əu, -əuz, -əuiŋ, -əud; -əui
furr|y, -ier, -iest, -iness 'fə:r|i [rarely 'fʌr-], -ĭə*, -iist, -inis
furth|er (adj. v. adv.), -ers, -ering, -ered, -erer/s 'fə:ð|ə*, -əz, -əriŋ, -əd, -ərə*/z
furtherance 'fə:ðərəns
furthermore 'fə:ðə'mɔ:* [-'mɔə*]
furthermost 'fə:ðəməust
furthest 'fə:ðist
furtive, -ly, -ness 'fə:tiv, -li, -nis
furuncle, -s 'fjuərʌŋkl, -z
fur|y (F.), -ies 'fjuər|i ['fjɔər-, 'fjɔ:r-, 'fjə:r-], -iz
furze; -bush/es fə:z; -buʃ/iz
Fusbos 'fʌzbɔs
fuscous 'fʌskəs   [-d
fus|e (s. v.), -es, -ing, -ed fju:z, -iz, -iŋ,
fusee, -s fju:'zi:, -z
fuselage, -s 'fju:zilɑ:ʒ [-lidʒ], -iz
fusel-oil 'fju:zl'oil
fusibility ˌfju:zə'biliti [-zi'b-, -lət-]

fusible 'fju:zəbl [-zib-]
fusil, -s 'fju:zil, -z
fusile 'fju:sail [-u:zail]
fusilier, -s ˌfju:zi'liə* [-zə'liə*, -zl̩'iə*], -z
fusillade, -s ˌfju:zi'leid, -z
fusion, -s 'fju:ʒən, -z
fuss (s. v.), -es, -ing, -ed, -er/s fʌs, -iz, -iŋ, -t, -ə*/z
fuss|y, -ier, -iest, -ily, -iness 'fʌs|i, -ɪə*, -iist, -ili, -inis
fustian 'fʌstɪən [-tjən]
fustic 'fʌstik [-iŋ, -id
fustigat|e, -es, -ing, -ed 'fʌstigeit, -s, fustigation, -s ˌfʌsti'geiʃən, -z
fust|y, -ier, -iest, -ily, -iness 'fʌst|i, -ɪə* [-jə*], -iist [-jist], -ili, -inis

futile, -ly, -ness 'fju:tail, -li, -nis
futilit|y, -ies fju(:)'tilit|i, -iz
futtock, -s 'fʌtək, -s
future (s. adj.), -s 'fju:tʃə*, -z
futurist, -s 'fju:tʃərist [-tʃur-], -s
futurit|y, -ies fju(:)'tjuərit|i [-'tjɔər-, -'tjɔ:r-], -iz
fuzz (s. v.), -es, -ing, -ed fʌz, -iz, -iŋ, -d
fuzzball, -s 'fʌzbɔ:l, -z
fuzzbuzz, -es 'fʌzbʌz, -iz
fuzz|y, -ier, -iest, -ily, -iness 'fʌz|i, -ɪə*, -iist, -ili, -inis
Fyf(f)e faif
Fyfield 'faifi:ld ['fai-fi:ld]
Fyne, -s fain, -z
Fyson 'faisn

G

G (*the letter*), **-'s** dʒiː, -z
gab (*s. v.*), **-s, -bing, -bed** gæb, -z, -iŋ, -d
Gabbatha 'gæbəθə
Gabbitas 'gæbitæs
gabb|le, -les, -ling, -led, -ler/s 'gæb|l̩,
  -lz, -liŋ [-liŋ], -ld, -lə*/z [-lə*/z]
gaberdine, -s 'gæbədiːn [ˌgæbə'diːn], -z
gaberlunzie, -s ˌgæbə'lʌnzi ['gæbəl-,
Gabii 'gæbiː [-biai] |-nji], -z
gabion, -s 'geibjən [-bǐən], -z
gable, -s, -d 'geibl, -z, -d
gablet, -s 'geiblit, -s
gable-window, -s 'geibl'windəu, -z
Gaboon gə'buːn
Gabriel 'geibrǐəl
gab|y, -ies 'geib|i, -iz
Gaby 'gɑːbi
Gacrux (*star*) 'gei-krʌks
gad (*s. v. interj.*) (**G.**), **-s, -ding, -ded**
  gæd, -z, -iŋ, -id
gadabout, -s 'gædəbaut, -s
Gadara 'gædərə
Gadarene, -s ˌgædə'riːn ['gædəriːn], -z
Gaddesdon 'gædzdən
Gade (*English river*) geid, (*Danish
  composer*) 'gɑːdə
Gades 'geidiːz
gadfl|y, -ies 'gædfl|ai, -aiz
gadget, -s, -ry 'gædʒit, -s, -ri
Gadhel, -s 'gædel, -z
Gadhelic gæ'delik [gə'd-]
Gadite, -s 'gædait, -s
gadroon, -s gə'druːn, -z
Gads|by, -den, -hill 'gædz|bi, -dən, -hil
gadwall, -s 'gædwɔːl, -z
gadzooks 'gæd'zuːks
Gaekwad 'gaikwɑːd (*Hind.* gaekvaʈ)
Gael, -s geil, -z
Gaelic 'geilik ['gælik]
Gaetulia giː'tjuːljə [dʒiː-, -lǐə]
gaff (*s. v.*), **-s, -ing, -ed** gæf, -s, -iŋ, -t
gaffe, -s gæf, -s
gaffer, -s 'gæfə*, -z
Gaffney 'gæfni
gag (*s. v.*), **-s, -ging, -ged** gæg, -z, -iŋ, -d
gaga (*s. adj.*), **-s** 'gɑːgɑː ['gæ-], -z
gag|e (*s. v.*) (**G.**), **-es, -ing, -ed** geidʒ, -iz,
  -iŋ, -d
gaiet|y (**G.**), **-ies** 'geiət|i ['geiit-], -iz

gaily 'geili
gain (*s. v.*), **-s, -ing/s, -ed, -er/s; -able,
  -less** gein, -z, -iŋ/z, -d, -ə*/z; -əbl, -lis
Gaines geinz
gain|ful, -fully, -fulness 'gein|ful, -fuli
  [-fəli], -fulnis
gain|say, -says, -saying, -sayed, -said,
  -sayer/s gein|'sei, -'seiz, -'seiiŋ, -'seid,
  -'seid [-'sed], -'seiə*/z
  *Note.—Also pronounced by some with
  stress on first syllable :* 'geinsei,
  'geinseiz, *etc.*
Gainsborough, -s 'geinzbərə, -z
Gairdner 'geədnə*, 'gɑː:d-
Gairloch 'geəlɔk [-lɔx]
Gaisberg 'gaizbəːg
Gaisford 'geisfəd
gait, -s geit, -s
gaiter, -s 'geitə*, -z
Gaitskell 'geitskəl
Gaius 'gaiəs
gala, -s 'gɑːlə ['geil-], -z
Gala (*river*) 'gɑːlə
galactic gə'læktik
Galahad 'gæləhæd
Galan (*surname*) 'geilən
galantine, -s 'gæləntiːn [ˌgælən'tiːn], -z
Galapagos gə'læpəgəs [-gɔs]
Galapas 'gæləpæs
Galashiels ˌgælə'ʃiːlz
Galata 'gælətə
Galatea ˌgælə'tiə
Galatia gə'leiʃə [-ʃĭə, -ʃə]
Galatian, -s gə'leiʃjən [-ʃĭən, -ʃən], -z
galax|y, -ies 'gæləks|i, -iz
Galba 'gælbə
galbanum 'gælbənəm
Galbraith gæl'breiθ
gale (**G.**), **-s** geil, -z
Galen 'geilin [-lən]
galena (**G.**) gə'liːnə
galenic, -al gə'lenik [gei'l-], -əl
Galerius gə'liərǐəs
Galesburg 'geilzbəːg
Galicia, -n gə'liʃĭə [-ʃjə-, -sĭə, -sjə], -n
Galilean, -s ˌgæli'li(ː)ən, -z
Galilee 'gælili:
Galileo ˌgæli'leiəu [-'liːəu]
galingale 'gæliŋgeil

Galion 'gælïən [-ljən]
galipot 'gælipɔt
gall (s. v.), -s, -ing, -ed gɔːl, -z, -iŋ, -d
Gallagher 'gæləhə* [-əxə*]
Gallaher 'gæləhə*
gallant (s.), -s 'gælənt [rarely gə'lænt],
gallant (adj.) (brave), -ly, -ness 'gælənt,
   -li, -nis   [-s
gallant (adj.) (amorous), -ly, -ness
   'gælənt [rarely gə'lænt], -li, -nis
gallantry 'gæləntri
Gallatin 'gælətin
gall-bladder, -s 'gɔːl,blædə*, -z
galleon, -s 'gælïən [-ljən], -z
galler|y, -ies, -ied 'gælər|i, -iz, -id
galley, -s 'gæli, -z
galley-proof, -s 'gæli-pruːf, -s
galley-slave, -s 'gæli-sleiv, -z
gall-fl|y, -ies 'gɔːl-fl|ai, -aiz
Gallia 'gælïə
galliambic (s. adj.), -s ,gæli'æmbik, -s
gallic (G.) 'gælik
Gallican (s. adj.), -s 'gælikən, -z
gallice 'gælisi(ː)
gallicism, -s 'gælisizəm, -z
galliciz|e [-is|e], -es, -ing, -ed 'gælisaiz,
   -iz, -iŋ, -d
gallinaceous ,gæli'neiʃəs [-ʃjəs, -ʃïəs]
Gallio 'gælïəu
galliot, -s 'gælïət, -s
Gallipoli gə'lipəli
Gallipolis (in America) ,gælipə'liːs
gallipot, -s 'gælipɔt, -s
gallivant, -s, -ing, -ed ,gæli'vænt ['---],
gall-nut, -s 'gɔːlnʌt, -s   [-s, -iŋ, -id
gallon, -s 'gælən, -z
galloon gə'luːn   [-s, -iŋ, -t, -ə*/z
gallop (s. v.), -s, -ing, -ed, -er/s 'gæləp,
gallopade, -s ,gælə'peid, -z
Gallovidian (s. adj.), -s ,gæləu'vidïən
   [-djən], -z
galloway (G.), -s 'gæləwei [-luw-], -z
gallows 'gæləuz
gallows-bird, -s 'gæləuzbəːd, -z
gall-stone, -s 'gɔːl-stəun, -z
Gallup 'gæləp
Gallus 'gæləs
galop, -s 'gæləp, -s
galore gə'lɔː* [-'lɔə*]
galosh, -es gə'lɔʃ, -iz
Galpin 'gælpin
Galsham 'gɔːlsəm ['gɔl-]
Galsworthy 'gɔːlzwəːði, 'gæl-
   Note.—John Galsworthy, the author,
   is commonly called 'gɔːlzwəːði. He
   pronounced so, but there are members
   of his family who call themselves
   'gælzwəːði.

Galt, -on gɔːlt [gɔlt], -ən
galumph, -s, -ing, -ed gə'lʌmf, -s, -iŋ, -t
Galvani gæl'vɑːni
galvanic gæl'vænik
galvanism 'gælvənizəm [-vṇi-]
galvaniz|e [-is|e], -es, -ing, -ed, -er/s
   'gælvənaiz [-vṇaiz], -iz, -iŋ, -d, -ə*/z
galvanometer,   -s   ,gælvə'nɔmitə*
   [-vṇ'ɔ-], -z
Galvestone 'gælvistən
Galway 'gɔːlwei
Gama 'gɑːmə
Gamage 'gæmidʒ
Gamaliel gə'meiljəl [-lïəl, in Jewish
   usage also gə'mɑːlïəl, ,gæmə'liːəl]
gamba, -s 'gæmbə, -z
gambado (jump), -(e)s gæm'beidəu
   [-'bɑːd-], -z
gambadoes (leggings) gæm'beidəuz
Gambetta gæm'betə
Gambia 'gæmbïə [-bjə]
gambier (substance used in dyeing)
   'gæmbïə*
Gambier (surname) 'gæmbïə* [-bïə*,
   -bjə*]
gambist, -s 'gæmbist, -s
gambit, -s 'gæmbit, -s
gamb|le (s. v.) (G.), -les, -ling, -led,
   -ler/s 'gæmb|l, -lz, -liŋ, -ld, -lə*/z
gambling-hou|se, -ses 'gæmbliŋhau|s,
gamboge gæm'buːʒ   [-ziz
gamb|ol (s. v.), -ols, -olling, -olled
   'gæmb|əl, -əlz, -ļiŋ [-əliŋ], -əld
gam|e (s. adj. v.), -es; -er, -est, -ely,
   -eness; -ing, -ed geim, -z; -ə*, -ist, -li,
   -nis; -iŋ, -d
game|-bag/s,   -cock/s,   -keeper/s,
   -law/s,   -licence/s   'geim|bæg/z,
   -kɔk/s, -,kiːpə*/z, -lɔː/z, -,laisəns/iz
Game|lyn, -lin 'gæmilin [-mlin]
games|-master/s, -mistress/es 'geimz|-
   ,mɑːstə*/z, -,mistris/iz
gamester, -s 'geimstə*, -z
gaming|-house, -houses, -table/s 'geim-
   -iŋ|haus, -,hauziz, -,teibl/z
gamma, -s 'gæmə, -z
Gammell 'gæməl
gammer, -s 'gæmə*, -z
gammon (s. v.), -s, -ing, -ed 'gæmən, -s,
   -iŋ, -d
gamp (G.), -s gæmp, -s
gamut, -s 'gæmət, -s
gam|y, -ier, -iest, -iness 'geim|i, -ïə*
   [-jə*], -iist [-jist], -inis
gander, -s 'gændə*, -z
Gandercleugh 'gændəkluː, -kluːx
gandharva, -s 'gʌndəvə ['gændhɑːvə]
   (Hind. gəndhərva), -z

Gandhi 'gændi: ['gɑ:n-, -di] (Hind.
  gãdhi)
Gandhi|ism, -ite/s 'gændi|izəm, -ait/s
gang, -s; -er/s gæŋ, -z; -ə*/z
Ganges 'gændʒi:z
gangli|on, -a, -ons 'gæŋgli|ən, -ə, -ənz
gangren|e (s. v.), -es, -ing, -ed 'gæŋ-
  gri:n, -z, -iŋ, -d
gangster, -s 'gæŋstə* [-ŋks-], -z
gangway, -s 'gæŋwei, -z
Gannel 'gænl
gannet, -s 'gænit, -s
Gannett 'gænit
gan(n)ister 'gænistə*
Gannon 'gænən
ganoid 'gænɔid
gantr|y, -ies 'gæntr|i, -iz
Ganymede 'gænimi:d
gaol (s. v.), -s, -ing, -ed, -er/s dʒeil, -z,
  -iŋ, -d, -ə*/z
gaolbird, -s 'dʒeilbə:d, -z
gap, -s gæp, -s
gap|e (s. v.), -es, -ing, -ed, -er/s geip,
  -s, -iŋ, -t, -ə*/z
garag|e (s. v.), -es, -ing, -ed 'gærɑ:dʒ
  [-ridʒ, -rɑ:ʒ], -iz, -iŋ, -d
garb, -s, -ed gɑ:b, -z, -d
garbage 'gɑ:bidʒ
garb|le, -les, -ling, -led 'gɑ:b|l, -lz, -l̩iŋ
  [-liŋ], -ld
Garbutt 'gɑ:bət
Garcia (English surname) 'gɑ:ʃjə [-ʃïə],
  'gɑ:sjə [-sïə]
gard|en (s. v.) (G.), -ens, -ening, -ened,
  -ener/s 'gɑ:d|n, -nz, -niŋ, -nd, -nə*/z
gardenia, -s gɑ:'di:njə [gə'd-, -nïə], -z
garden-part|y, -ies 'gɑ:dn̩pɑ:t|i, -iz
Gard(i)ner 'gɑ:dnə*
garefowl, -s 'geəfaul, -z
Gareth 'gæreθ [-riθ] (Welsh 'gareθ)
Garfield 'gɑ:fi:ld ['gɑ:-fi:ld]
garfish 'gɑ:-fiʃ
Gargantua gɑ:'gæntjŭə [-tjwə]
gargantuan gɑ:'gæntjŭən [-tjwən]
Gargery 'gɑ:dʒəri
garg|le (s. v.), -les, -ling/s, -led 'gɑ:g|l,
  -lz, -liŋ/z, -ld
gargoyle, -s 'gɑ:gɔil, -z
Garibaldi ˌgæri'bɔ:ldi [-'bæl-]
Garioch (district in Scotland, surname)
  'gæriɔk [-ɔx]
garish, -ly, -ness 'geəriʃ ['gær-], -li, -nis
garland (G.), -s 'gɑ:lənd, -z
garlic, -ky 'gɑ:lik, -i
Garlick 'gɑ:lik
garment, -s, -ed 'gɑ:mənt, -s, -id
garner (s. v.), -s, -ing, -ed 'gɑ:nə*, -z,
  -riŋ, -d

garnet, -s 'gɑ:nit, -s
Garn|et(t), -ham 'gɑ:n|it, -əm
garnish (s. v.), -es, -ing, -ed, -ment/s
  'gɑ:niʃ, -iz, -iŋ, -t, -mənt/s
garnishee (s. v.), -s, -ing, -d ˌgɑ:ni'ʃi:,
  -z, -iŋ, -d
garniture 'gɑ:nitʃə*
Garr|ard, -att 'gær|əd, -ət
Garraway 'gærəwei
garret, -s 'gærət [-rit], -s
Garr|et(t), -ick 'gær|ət [-it], -ik
Garrioch (district in Scotland) 'giəri,
  (surname) 'gæriɔk [-əx]
garris|on (s. v.) (G.), -ons, -oning, -oned
  'gæris|n, -nz, -n̩iŋ [-ən̩iŋ], -nd
Garr|od, -o(u)ld 'gær|əd, -əld
garrot, -s 'gærət, -s
garrott|e (s. v.), -es, -ing, -ed, -er/s
  gə'rɔt, -s, -iŋ, -id, -ə*/z
garrulity gæ'ru:liti [gə'r-, -'rju:-]
garrulous, -ly, -ness 'gæruləs [-rəl-,
  -rjul-], -li, -nis
Garston 'gɑ:stən
garter (s. v.), -s, -ing, -ed 'gɑ:tə*, -z,
  -riŋ, -d
garth (G.), -s gɑ:θ, -s
Garwood 'gɑ:wud
gas (s.), -es gæs, -iz
gas (v.), -ses, -sing, -sed gæs, -iz, -iŋ, -t
gas|-bag/s, -bracket/s, -burner/s 'gæs|-
  bæg/z, -ˌbrækit/s, -ˌbə:nə*/z
Gascoigne 'gæskɔin
Gascon, -s 'gæskən, -z
gasconnad|e (s. v.), -es, -ing, -ed ˌgæs-
  kə'neid, -z, -iŋ, -id
Gascony 'gæskəni
Gascoyne 'gæskɔin
Gaselee 'geizli(:)
gaselier, -s ˌgæsə'liə*, -z
gas-engine, -s 'gæsˌendʒin, -z
gaseous, -ness 'gæsjəs [-sïəs, -zjəs, -zïəs,
  -ʃjəs, -ʃïəs, 'geis-, 'geiz-], -nis
gas-fire, -s 'gæsfaiə* ['-'-], -z
gas|-fitter/s, -fixture/s 'gæsˌfitə*/z,
  -ˌfikstʃə*/z
gash (s. v.), -es, -ing, -ed gæʃ, -iz, -iŋ, -t
gas-helmet, -s 'gæsˌhelmit, -s
gasi|fy, -fies, -fying, -fied 'gæsi|fai
  ['geizi-], -faiz, -faiiŋ, -faid
gas-jet, -s 'gæsdʒet, -s
Gaskell 'gæskəl [-kel]
gasket, -s 'gæskit, -s
Gaskin (G.), -s 'gæskin, -z
gas-light 'gæslait
gas-main, -s 'gæsmein, -z
gas|-man, -men 'gæs|mæn, -men
gas|-mantle/s, -mask/s 'gæsˌmæntl/z,
  -mɑ:sk/s

gas-meter, -s 'gæs,miːtə*, -z
gasolene 'gæsəuliːn
gasometer, -s gæ'sɒmitə* [gə'sɒ-, gə'zɒ-], -z
gasp (s. v.), -s, -ing, -ed gɑːsp, -s, -iŋ, -t
gas|-pipe/s, -ring/s 'gæs|paip/s, -riŋ/z
gas-stove, -s 'gæsstəuv ['-'-], -z
gass|y, -ier, -iest, -iness 'gæs|i, -iə*, -iist, -inis
gasteropod, -s 'gæstərəpɒd, -z
gastric 'gæstrik
gastritis gæs'traitis
gastronomic, -al ,gæstrə'nɒmik, -əl
gastronom|ist/s, -y gæs'trɒnəm|ist/s, -i
gasworks 'gæswəːks
Gatacre 'gætəkə*
gat|e (s. v.), -es, -ing, -ed geit, -s, -iŋ, -id
gatecrash, -es, -ing, -ed, -er/s 'geit-kræʃ, -iz, -iŋ, -t, -ə*/z
gate|-fine/s, -keeper/s 'geit|fain/z, -,kiːpə*/z
gate-legged 'geit-legd
gateless 'geit-lis
gate|-money, -post/s 'geit|,mʌni, -pəust/s
Gatenby 'geitnbi
Gater 'geitə*
Gates geits
Gateshead 'geitshed
gateway, -s 'geit-wei, -z
Gath gæθ
gath|er (s. v.), -ers, -ering/s, -ered, -erer/s 'gæð|ə*, -əz, -əriŋ/z, -əd, -ərə*/z
Gathorne 'geiθɔːn
Gat|ley, -ling 'gæt|li, -liŋ
Gatti 'gæti
Gatty 'gæti
Gatwick 'gætwik
gauche gəuʃ
gaucherie, -s 'gəuʃəri(ː), -z
gaucho, -s 'gautʃəu ['gɔːtʃ-], -z
gaud, -s gɔːd, -z
Gauden 'gɔːdn
gaud|y, -ier, -iest, -ily, -iness 'gɔːd|i, -iə* [-jə*], -iist [-jist], -ili, -inis
gaug|e (s. v.), -es, -ing, -ed, -er/s, -eable geidʒ, -iz, -iŋ, -d, -ə*/z; -əbl
Gaul, -s, -ish gɔːl, -z, -iʃ
gauleiter, -s 'gau,laitə*, -z
gaum (s. v.), -s, -ing, -ed gɔːm, -z, -iŋ, -d
Gaumont 'gəumɒnt [-mənt]
gaunt (G.), -er, -est, -ly, -ness gɔːnt, -ə*, -ist, -li, -nis
gauntlet (G.), -s, -ed 'gɔːntlit, -s, -id
Gauntlett 'gɔːntlit, 'gɑːn-
Gauss gaus
Gautama 'gautəmə (Hind. gəwtəmə)

gauz|e, -es; -y, -iness gɔːz, -iz, -i, -inis
gave (from give) geiv
gavel, -s 'gævl, -z
gavelkind 'gævlkaind [-kind]
Gaveston 'gævistən
Gavey 'geivi
Gavin 'gævin
gavotte, -s gə'vɒt, -s
Gawain 'gɑːwein ['gæw-]
Gawith (surname) 'geiwiθ
gawk, -s gɔːk, -s
gawk|y, -ier, -iest, -iness 'gɔːk|i, -iə*, -iist, -inis
gay (G.), -er, -est, gaily, gayness gei, -ə* [geə*], -ist, 'gei-li ['geili], 'gei-nis ['geinis]
Gayn|ham, -or 'gein|əm, -ə*
Gaza (in Egypt, formerly in Palestine) 'gɑːzə [in biblical use also 'geizə]
Gaza (Greek scholar) 'gɑːzə
gaz|e (s. v.), -es, -ing, -ed, -er/s geiz, -iz, -iŋ, -d, -ə*/z
gazebo, -s gə'ziːbəu, -z
gazelle, -s gə'zel, -z
gazett|e (s. v.), -es, -ing, -ed gə'zet, -s, -iŋ, -id
gazetteer, -s ,gæzi'tiə* [-zə't-], -z
gazogene 'gæzəudʒiːn
Geall giːl
gear (s. v.), -s, -ing, -ed giə*, -z, -riŋ, -d
gear|-box/es, -case/s 'giə|bɒks/iz, -keis/iz
Geare giə*
Geary 'giəri
Gebal 'giːbəl [-bæl]
Gebir 'dʒiːbiə*
gecko, -s 'gekəu, -z
Ged ged
Geddes 'gedis
gee (s. v.) (G.), -s, -ing, -d dʒiː, -z, -iŋ, -d
geegee, -s 'dʒiːdʒiː, -z
Geelong dʒi'lɒŋ [dʒə'l-]
Geering 'giəriŋ
geese (plur. of goose) giːs
Geeson 'dʒiːsn
gee-up 'dʒiːʌp
geezer, -s 'giːzə*, -z
Gehazi gi'heizai [ge'h-, gə'h-, -'heizi, -'hɑːzi]
Gehenna gi'henə [gə'h-]
Geierstein 'gaiəstain
Geiger 'gaigə*
Geikie 'giːki
geisha, -s 'geiʃə, -z
gelatine ,dʒelə'tiːn ['dʒelət-]
gelatiniz|e [-is|e], -es, -ing, -ed dʒi'lætinaiz [dʒe'l-, dʒə'l-], -iz, -iŋ, -d
gelatinous dʒi'lætinəs [dʒe'l-, dʒə'l-]

geld (*adj. v.*), **-s, -ing, -ed** geld, -z, -iŋ, -id

gelding (*s.*), **-s** 'geldiŋ, -z

gelid, **-ly, -ness** 'dʒelid, -li, -nis

gelignite 'dʒelignait

Gell gel, dʒel

Gell|an, **-er** 'gel|ən, -ə*

Gellatl(e)y 'gelətli, ge'lætli

gem, **-s** dʒem, -z

Gemara ge'mɑːrə [gi'mˈ-]

geminat|e, **-es, -ing, -ed** 'dʒemineit, -s, -iŋ, -id

gemination ˌdʒemi'neiʃən

Gemini (*constellation*) 'dʒeminai [-niː, -ni], (*aircraft*) 'dʒemini

Gemistus dʒe'mistəs [dʒi'mˈ-]

Gemmi 'gemi

gemmiferous dʒe'mifərəs

gemot, **-s** gi'məut [gə'mˈ-], -s

gemsbok, **-s** 'gemzbɔk, -s

gemshorn, **-s** 'gemzhɔːn, -z

gen dʒen

gendarme, **-s** 'ʒɑ̃ːndɑːm ['ʒɔ̃ːnd-, 'ʒɑːnd-, 'ʒɔːnd-, 'ʒɔnd-] (ʒɑ̃darm), -z

gender (*s. v.*), **-s, -ing, -ed** 'dʒendə*, -z, -riŋ, -d

gene (**G.**), **-s** dʒiːn, -z

genealogic|al, **-ally** ˌdʒiːnjə'lɔdʒik|əl [ˌdʒen-, -nɪə-], -əli

genealog|ist/s, **-y, -ies** ˌdʒiːni'ælədʒ|ist/s [ˌdʒen-], -i, -iz

genera (*plur. of* genus) 'dʒenərə

gener|al (*s. adj.*), **-als, -ally** 'dʒenər|əl, -əlz, -əli

generalissimo, **-s** ˌdʒenərə'lisiməu, -z

generalit|y, **-ies** ˌdʒenə'rælit|i, -iz

generalization [-isa-], **-s** ˌdʒenərəlai'zeiʃən [-li'z-], -z

generaliz|e [-is|e-], **-es, -ing, -ed; -able** 'dʒenərəlaiz, -iz, -iŋ, -d; -əbl

generalship 'dʒenərəlʃip

generat|e, **-es, -ing, -ed, -or/s** 'dʒenəreit, -s, -iŋ, -id, -ə*/z

generation, **-s** ˌdʒenə'reiʃən, -z

generative 'dʒenərətiv [-reit-]

generator, **-s** 'dʒenəreitə*, -z

generatri|x, **-ces** 'dʒenəreitri|ks, -siːz

generic, **-ally** dʒi'nerik [dʒə'n-, dʒe'n-], -əli

generosity ˌdʒenə'rɔsiti [-əli

generous, **-ly, -ness** 'dʒenərəs, -li, -nis

genesis 'dʒenisis

Genesis (*book of the Bible*) 'dʒenisis [*old-fashioned* -siz]

Genesius dʒi'niːsjəs [dʒe'n-, dʒə'n-, -sɪəs]

Genesta dʒi'nestə [dʒe'n-, dʒə'n-]

genet, **-s** 'dʒenit, -s

genetic, **-s, -ally** dʒi'netik [dʒe'n-, dʒə'n-], -s, -əli

geneticist, **-s** dʒi'netisist [dʒe-, dʒə-,], -s

Geneva, **-n/s** dʒi'niːvə [dʒə'n-], -n/z

Genevieve (*in Coleridge's poem ' Love '*) ˌdʒenə'viːv, 'dʒenivi:v

Geneviève (*Saint*) ˌʒenvi'eiv (ʒənvjɛːv)

genial (*amiable*), **-ly, -ness** 'dʒiːnjəl [-nɪəl], -i, -nis

genial (*of the chin*) dʒi'naiəl

geniality ˌdʒiːni'æliti

genie, **-s** 'dʒiːni, -z

genista, **-s** dʒi'nistə [dʒe'n-, dʒə'n-], -s

genital, **-s** 'dʒenitl, -z

genitival ˌdʒeni'taivəl

genitive, **-s** 'dʒenitiv [-nət-], -z

ge|nius, **-nii, -niuses** 'dʒiː|njəs [-nɪəs], -niai, -njəsiz [-nɪəsiz]

Gennesare|t, **-th** gi'nezəri|t [ge'n-, gə'n-, -re|t], -θ

Genoa 'dʒenəuə [dʒə'nəuə]

genocide 'dʒenəusaid

Genoese ˌdʒenəu'iːz [*also* 'dʒenəuiːz *when attributive*]

genre ʒɑ̃ːŋr [ʒɔ̃ːŋr, ʒɑːŋr, ʒɔːŋr, ʒɔŋr] (ʒɑ̃ːr)

gen|s, **-tes** dʒen|z, -tiːz

Genseric 'gensərik ['dʒen-]

Gensing 'gensiŋ [-nsiŋ]

gent, **-s** dʒent, -s

genteel, **-ly, -ness** dʒen'tiːl [dʒən-], -li, -nis

gentes (*plur. of* gens) 'dʒenti:z

gentian, **-s** 'dʒenʃɪən [-ʃən, -ʃən], -z

gentile (**G.**), **-s** 'dʒentail, -z

gentility dʒen'tiliti [dʒən-]

gent|le, **-ler, -lest, -ly, -leness** 'dʒent|l, -lə*, -list, -li, -lnis

gentlefolk, **-s** 'dʒentlfəuk, -s

gentle|man, **-men** 'dʒentl|mən, -mən [-men]

gentle|man-at-arms, **-men-at-arms** 'dʒentl|mənət'ɑːmz, -mənət'ɑːmz [-men-]

gentlemanlike 'dʒentlmənlaik

gentlemanl|y, **-iness** 'dʒentlmənl|i, -inis

gentle|woman, **-women** 'dʒentl|ˌwumən, -ˌwimin

gentry (**G.**) 'dʒentri

genuflect, **-s, -ing, -ed** 'dʒenju(:)flekt, -s, -iŋ, -id

genuflection, **-s** ˌdʒenju(:)'flekʃən, -z

genuine, **-ly, -ness** 'dʒenjuin, -li, -nis

gen|us, **-era** 'dʒiːn|əs ['dʒen|əs], 'dʒenərə

Geo. dʒɔːdʒ

geocentric, **-al, -ally** ˌdʒi(:)əu'sentrik, -əl, -əli

geode, **-s** 'dʒi(:)əud, -z

geodesic, **-al** ˌdʒi(:)əu'desik [-'diːs-], -əl

geodesy dʒi(ː)'ɔdisi
Geoffr(e)y 'dʒefri
Geoghegan 'geigən, 'gəugən
geographer, -s dʒi'ɔgrəfə* ['dʒjɔg-], -z
geographic, -al, -ally dʒïə'græfik [dʒiəu'g-], -əl, -əli
geograph|y, -ies dʒi'ɔgrəf|i ['dʒjɔg-, 'dʒɔg-], -iz
geologic, -al, -ally dʒïə'lɔdʒik [dʒiəu'l-], -əl, -əli
geolog|ist/s, -y dʒi'ɔlədʒ|ist/s, -i
geologiz|e [-is|e], -es, -ing, -ed dʒi'ɔlədʒaiz, -iz, -iŋ, -d
geomancy 'dʒi:əumænsi
geometer, -s dʒi'ɔmitə*, -z
geometric, -al, -ally dʒïə'metrik [dʒiəu'm-], -əl, əli
geometrician, -s ,dʒiəumə'triʃən [dʒi,ɔm-, -mi't-], -z
geometr|y, -ies dʒi'ɔmitr|i ['dʒjɔm-, 'dʒɔm-], -iz
geophysic|al, -s 'dʒi(ː)əu'fizik|əl, -s
Geordie 'dʒɔːdi
George, -s dʒɔːdʒ, -iz
georgette dʒɔː'dʒet
Georgia, -n/s 'dʒɔːdʒjə [-dʒïə], -n/z
Georgiana ,dʒɔːdʒi'ɑːnə
georgic (G.), -s 'dʒɔːdʒik, -s
Georgina dʒɔː'dʒiːnə
Geraint 'geraint
Gerald 'dʒerəld
Geraldine 'dʒerəldiːn, -dain
Note.—'dʒerəldain in Coleridge's 'Christabel.'
geranium, -s dʒi'reinjəm [dʒə'r-, -nïəm], -z
Gerard (English name) 'dʒerɑːd ['dʒerəd], dʒe'rɑːd [dʒə'rɑːd]
Gérard (French name) dʒe'rɑːd (ʒerɑːr)
gerfalcon, -s 'dʒɔː,fɔːlkən [-,fɔːkən], -z
Note.—Those who practise the sport of falconry pronounce -,fɔːk-.
Gergesene, -s 'gəːgisiːn [-gəs-, -ges-, ,ᵎ—ᵎ-], -z
geriatric, -s ,dʒeri'ætrik, -s
geriatrician, -s ,dʒerïə'triʃən, -z
geriatry 'dʒerïətri
Gerizim ge'raizim [gəˈr-, -'riːzim, 'gerizim]
germ, -s dʒəːm, -z
Germain (street) 'dʒəːmən [-mein]
German, -s 'dʒəːmən, -z
germander dʒəː'mændə* [dʒə'm-]
germane dʒəː'mein ['—]
Germanic dʒəː'mænik [dʒə'm-]
germani|sm/s, -st/s 'dʒəːməni|zəm/z, -st/s
germanization [-isa-] ,dʒəː'mənai'zeiʃən

germaniz|e [-is|e], -es, -ing, -ed 'dʒəːmənaiz, -iz, -iŋ, -d
Germany 'dʒəːməni
germicide, -s 'dʒəːmisaid, -z
germinal 'dʒəːminl
germinat|e, -es, -ing, -ed 'dʒəːmineit, -s, -iŋ, -id
germination, -s ,dʒəːmi'neiʃən, -z
Gerontius gə'rɔntïəs [gi'r-, ge'r-, -ntjəs, -nʃïəs, -nʃjəs, -nʃəs]
gerontolog|ist/s, -y ,dʒerɔn'tɔlədʒ|ist/s [-rən-], -i
Gerrans 'gerənz
Gerrard 'dʒerəd [-rɑːd], dʒe'rɑːd [dʒə'rɑːd]
Note.—The telephone exchange in London is pronounced 'dʒerəd or 'dʒerɑːd
Gerrard's Cross 'dʒerədz'krɔs [-rɑːdz-, -'krɔːs]
Gerry 'geri
gerrymand|er (s. v.), -ers, -ering, -ered 'dʒerimænd|ə* [rarely 'ge-], -əz, -əriŋ, -əd
Gershwin 'gəːʃwin
Gert|ie, -y 'gəːt|i, -i
Gertrude 'gəːtruːd
gerund, -s 'dʒerənd [-rʌnd], -z
gerundive, -s dʒi'rʌndiv [dʒe'r-, dʒə'r-], -z
Gervase 'dʒəːvəs
Geryon 'gerïən
gesso 'dʒesəu
gest, -s dʒest, -s
gestalt gə'ʃtɑːlt [-'ʃtælt]
Gestapo ges'tɑːpəu
gestation dʒes'teiʃən
gestatorial ,dʒestə'tɔːrïəl
gesticulat|e, -es, -ing, -ed, -or/s dʒes'tikjuleit, -s, -iŋ, -id, -ə*/z
gesticulation, -s dʒes,tikju'leiʃən, -z
gesticulatory dʒes'tikjulətəri [-leit-]
gesture, -s 'dʒestʃə*, -z
get, -s, -ting, got get, -s, -iŋ, gɔt
Getae 'geitai [dʒiːtiː]
get-at-able get'ætəbl
get-away, -s 'getəwei, -z
Gethin 'geθin
Gethsemane geθ'seməni
get-rich-quick 'get-ritʃ'kwik
Getty 'geti
Gettysburg 'getizbəːg
get-up, -s 'getʌp ['get'ʌp, get'ʌp], -s
geum, -s 'dʒiːəm [dʒïəm], -z
gewgaw, -s 'gjuːgɔː, -z
geyser (hot spring), -s 'gaizə* ['giː z-], -z
Note.—In New Zealand the pronunciation is always 'gaizə*.

geyser (*apparatus for heating water*), **-s** 'giːzə* [*in New Zealand* 'gaizə*], -z

Ghana 'gɑːnə

Ghanaian, **-s** gɑːˈneiən, -z

ghastl|y, **-ier, -iest, -iness** 'gɑːstl|i, -iə* [-jə*], -iist [-jist], -inis

Ghat, **-s** gɔːt, -s

ghee giː

Ghent gent

gherkin, **-s** 'gəːkin, -z

ghetto, **-s** 'getəu, -z

Ghibelline, **-s** 'gibilain, -z

Ghoorka, **-s** 'guəkə, -z

ghost, **-s; -like** gəust, -s; -laik

ghostl|y, **-iness** 'gəustl|i, -inis

ghost-writer, **-s** 'gəust,raitə*, -z

ghoul, **-s; -ish** guːl [gaul], -z; -iʃ

Ghurka, **-s** 'guəkə ['gəːk-], -z

G.I., **-'s** 'dʒiːˈai [*attributively* 'dʒiːai], -z

giant, **-s; -like** 'dʒaiənt, -s; -laik

giantess, **-es** 'dʒaiəntis [-tes], -iz

Giaour 'dʒauə*

Gibb gib

gibber, **-s, -ing, -ed** 'dʒibə*, -z, -riŋ, -d

gibberish 'dʒibəriʃ ['gib-]

gibbet (*s. v.*), **-s, -ing, -ed** 'dʒibit, -s, -iŋ, -id

Gibbie 'dʒibi

gibbon (G.), **-s** 'gibən, -z

gibbosity giˈbɔsiti

gibbous, **-ly, -ness** 'gibəs, -li, -nis

Gibbs gibz

gib|e (*s. v.*), **-es, -ing/ly, -ed, -er/s** dʒaib, -z, -iŋ/li, -d, -ə*/z

Gibeah 'gibiə

Gibeon 'gibiən

giblet, **-s** 'dʒiblit, -s

Giblett 'giblit

Gibraltar dʒiˈbrɔːltə* [-rɔl-]

Gibraltarian, **-s** ,dʒibrɔːlˈtɛəriən [-rɔl-], -z

Gibson 'gibsn

gibus, **-es** 'dʒaibəs ['dʒib-], -iz

Gick dʒik

Gidding, **-s** 'gidiŋ, -z

gidd|y (G.), **-ier, -iest, -ily, -iness** 'gid|i, -iə*, -iist, -ili, -inis

giddy-headed 'gidi,hedid

Gidea 'gidiə

Gideon 'gidiən

Gielgud (*English name*) 'giːlgud ['gil-]

Gieve giːv

Giffard 'dʒifəd

Giffen 'gifin, 'dʒifin

Gifford (*place near Haddington*) 'gifəd, (*surname*) 'gifəd, 'dʒifəd

Note.—*The present Baron Gifford is* 'dʒifəd.

gift, **-s, -ed** gift, -s, -id

gig, **-s** gig, -z

Gigadibs 'gigədibz

gigant|ean, **-esque** ,dʒaigænˈt|i(ː)ən, -esk

gigantic, **-ally** dʒaiˈgæntik, -əli

gigg|le (*s. v.*), **-les, -ling, -led, -ler/s** 'gig|l, -lz, -liŋ [-liŋ], -ld, -lə*/z [-lə*/z]

Gight (*in Scotland*) gikt [gixt]

Gigli 'dʒiːli(ː) [-lji(ː)]

Giglio 'dʒiːliəu [-ljəu]

gigolo, **-s** 'ʒigələu, -z

gigot, **-s** 'dʒigət, -s

gigue, **-s** ʒiːg [ʒig], -z

Gihon 'gaihɔn [*in Jewish usage sometimes* 'giːhəun]

gila (*monster lizard*), **-s** 'hiːlə, -z

Gilbert 'gilbət

Gilbertian gilˈbəːtjən [-tiən]

Gilbey 'gilbi

Gilboa gilˈbəuə

Gilchrist 'gilkrist

gild, **-s, -ing, -ed, gilt, gilder/s** gild, -z, -iŋ, -id, gilt, 'gildə*/z

Gilder, **-sleeve, -some** 'gildə*, -sliːv, -səm

Gilding 'gildiŋ

Gildredge 'gil-dridʒ, ['gild-ridʒ, -redʒ]

Gilead 'giliæd

Giles dʒailz

Gilfil 'gilfil

Gilfillan gilˈfilən

Gilford 'gilfəd

Gilgal 'gilgæl [-gɔːl, *rarely* gilˈgɔːl]

Gilham 'giləm

Gilheney (*surname*) giˈliːni

Gilheny gilˈhiːni

Gilkes dʒilks

gill (*respiratory organ, ravine*), **-s** gil, -z

gill (*measure*), **-s** dʒil, -z

Gill gil

Note.—*But* dʒil *in* Jack and Gill (*now more usually written* Jack and Jill).

Gillam 'giləm

Gillard giˈlɑːd, 'gilɑːd, 'giləd

Gillen 'gilən

Gilleney (*surname*) 'giləni

Gillespie giˈlespi

Gillett 'gilit, 'gilet, giˈlet, dʒiˈlet

Gillette (*surname, razor*), **-s** dʒiˈlet, -s

Gilley 'gili

Gilliam 'giliəm

Gillian 'dʒiliən [-ljən], 'gil-

Gilliat 'giliət [-ljət]

Gillick 'gilik

gillie (G.), **-s** 'gili, -z

Gillies 'gilis

Gilling, -s 'gilin, -z
Gillingham (in Kent) 'dʒiliŋəm, (in Dorset and Norfolk) 'gil-, (surname) 'gil-, 'dʒil-
Gillison 'gilisn
Gillmore 'gilmɔ:* [-mɔə*]
Gillott 'dʒilət, 'gilət
Gill|ow, -ray 'gil|əu, -rei
Gills gilz
Gillson 'dʒilsn
gillyflower, -s 'dʒili,flauə*, -z
Gil|man, -mer, -more 'gil|mən, -mə*, -mɔ:* [-mɔə*]
Gilmour 'gilmə* [-mɔ:*, -mɔə*]
Gilpatrick gil'pætrik
Gilpin 'gilpin
Gilroy 'gilrɔi
Gilson 'dʒilsn, 'gilsn
gilt (s.) gilt
gilt-edged 'gilt-edʒd [also 'gilt'edʒd when not attributive]
Gilwhite 'gilwait ['gilhw-]
gimbal, -s 'dʒimbəl, -z
gimb|le, -les, -ling, -led 'gimb|l, -lz, -liŋ, -ld
Gimblett 'gimblit
gimcrack, -s 'dʒimkræk, -s
gimlet, -s 'gimlit, -s
gimmick, -s 'gimik, -s
gimp gimp
Gimson 'gimsn, 'dʒimsn
gin (s.) (all senses), -s dʒin, -z
Ginevra dʒi'nevrə
Gingell 'gindʒəl
ginger, -s 'dʒindʒə*, -z
ginger-ale 'dʒindʒər'eil [-dʒə'eil]
gingerbeer, -s 'dʒindʒə'biə*, -z
gingerbeer-bottle, -s ,dʒindʒə'biə,bɔtl, -z
gingerbread, -s 'dʒindʒəbred, -z
gingerly 'dʒindʒəli
ginger-wine 'dʒindʒə'wain
ginger|y, -iness 'dʒindʒər|i, -inis
gingham, -s 'giŋəm, -z
gingival dʒin'dʒaivəl
gingko, -s 'giŋkəu, -z
Ginkel(l) 'giŋkəl
Ginn gin
gin-palace, -s 'dʒin,pælis [-əs], -iz
Ginsberg 'ginzbə:g
ginseng 'dʒinseŋ
gin-shop, -s 'dʒin-ʃɔp, -s
gin-sling, -s 'dʒin'sliŋ, -z
Giovanni ,dʒiəu'vɑ:ni [dʒəu'v-, -'væni] (dʒo'vanni)
gip (gipsy), -s dʒip, -s
gip (to clean fish), -s, -ping, -ped gip, -s, -iŋ, -t
Gippsland 'gipslænd

gips|y, -ies 'dʒips|i, -iz
giraffe, -s dʒi'rɑ:f [-'ræf], -s
Giralda dʒi'rældə
girandole, -s 'dʒirəndəul, -z
gird (s. v.), -s, -ing, -ed, girt gə:d, -z, -iŋ, -id, gə:t
girder, -s 'gə:də*, -z
gird|le (s. v.), -les, -ling, -led 'gə:d|l, -lz, -liŋ [-liŋ], -ld
Girdlestone 'gə:dlstən
Girgashite, -s 'gə:gəʃait, -s
Girgasite, -s 'gə:gəsait, -s
girl, -s; -hood; -ish/ly, -ishness gə:l [rarely gɛəl], -z; -hud; -iʃ/li, -iʃnis
Girondist, -s dʒi'rɔndist, -s
girt (s.), -s gə:t, -s
girt (from gird) gə:t
girth, -s gə:θ, -s
Girtin 'gə:tin
Girton 'gə:tn
Girtonian, -s gə:'təunjən [-nɪən], -z
Gisbourne 'gizbɔ:n [-bɔən]
Gissing 'gisiŋ
gist, -s dʒist, -s
Gita 'gi:tə (Hind. gita)
gittern, -s 'gitə:n, -z
Giuseppe dʒu(:)'sepi (dʒu'seppe)
giv|e, -es, -ing, gave, giv|en, -er/s giv, -z, -iŋ, geiv, 'giv|n, -ə*/z
give-and-take 'givən'teik
Givenchy gi'ventʃi (ʒivãʃi)
Gizeh 'gi:zei [-zi]
gizzard, -s 'gizəd, -z
glacé 'glæsei
glacial 'gleisjəl [-sɪəl, -fjəl, -fɪəl, -fəl, 'glæsɪəl, 'glæsjəl]
glaciation ,glæsi'eifən [,gleis-]
glacier, -s 'glæsjə* ['gleis-, -sɪə*], -z
glacis (sing.) 'glæsis ['glæsi], (plur.) 'glæsiz
glacises (alternative plur. of glacis) 'glæsisiz
glad (adj.)·glad|der, -dest, -ly, -ness glæd; 'gl ed|ə*, -ist, -li, -nis
glad (v.), -s, -ding, -ded glæd, -z, -iŋ, -id
gladd|en, -ens, -ening, -ened 'glæd|n, -nz, -ṇiŋ [-niŋ], -nd
glade, -s gleid, -z
gladiator, -s 'glædieitə*, -z
gladiatorial ,glædɪə'tɔ:rɪəl [-djə-]
gladiole, -s 'glædiəul, -z
gladiol|us, -i ,glædi'əul|əs ['glædiəul-, 'glædɪəl-, rarely glə'daiəl-], -ai
gladsome, -ly, -ness 'glædsəm, -li, -nis
gladstone (G.), -s 'glædstən, -z
Gladstonian glæds'təunjən [-nɪən]
Glad|win, -ys 'glæd|win, -is
glagolitic ,glægəu'litik

glair, -eous, -y glɛə*, -rïəs, -ri

Glaisdale (in Yorks.) 'gleizdeil [locally -dl]

Glaisher 'gleiʃə*

glaive, -s gleiv, -z

Glamis glɑːmz

Glamorgan, -shire glə'mɔːgən, -ʃïə [-ʃə*]

glamorous, -ly 'glæmərəs, -li

glamour 'glæmə*

glanc|e (s. v.), -es, -ing/ly, -ed glɑːns, -iz, -iŋ/li, -t

gland, -s glænd, -z

glander|s, -ed 'glændə|z ['glɑː-n-], -d

glandiferous glæn'difərəs

glandul|ar, -ous 'glændjul|ə*, -əs

glandule, -s 'glændjuːl, -z

Glanvill(e) 'glænvil

Glapthorne 'glæpθɔːn

glar|e (s. v.), -es, -ing/ly, -ingness, -ed glɛə*, -z, -riŋ/li, -riŋnis, -d

Glarus 'glɑːrəs

Glasgow 'glɑːsgəu ['glɑːzg-, 'glɑːsk-, 'glæsg-, 'glæzg-, 'glæsk-]

glasier (G.), -s 'gleizjə* [-zïə*, -ʒjə*, -ʒïə*, -ʒə*], -z

Glasneven glɑːs'nevən

glass, -es glɑːs, -iz

glass-blow|er/s, -ing 'glɑːs,bləu|ə*/z, -iŋ

Glasscock (surname) 'glɑːskɔk, -kəu

glass-cutter, -s 'glɑːs,kʌtə*, -z

glassful, -s 'glɑːsful, -z

glass-hou|se, -ses 'glɑːshau|s, -ziz

glass-paper 'glɑːs,peipə*

glassware 'glɑːs-wɛə*

glass-work, -s 'glɑːs-wəːk, -s

glasswort 'glɑːs-wəːt

glass|y, -ier, -iest, -ily, -iness 'glɑːs|i, -ïə* [-jə*], -iist [-jist], -ili, -inis

Glastonbury 'glæstənbəri ['glæsn-, 'glɑːs-]

Glaswegian, -s glæs'wiːdʒjən [glɑː-s, glæz-, glɑːz-, glɑːïən, -dʒən], -z

glaucoma, -tous glɔː'kəumə, -təs

glaucous 'glɔːkəs

Glave gleiv

glaz|e (s. v.), -es, -ing, -ed, -er/s gleiz, -iz, -iŋ, -d, -ə*/z

Glazebrook 'gleizbruk

glazier, -s 'gleizjə* [-zïə, -ʒjə*, -ʒïə* -ʒə*], -z

Glazunov 'glæzu(ː)nɔf [-nɔv] (gləzu'nof)

gleam (s. v.), -s, -ing, -ed; -y gliːm, -z, -iŋ, -d; -i

glean, -s, -ing/s, -ed, -er/s gliːn, -z, -iŋ/z, -d, -ə*/z

glebe, -s gliːb, -z

glee, -s gliː, -z

glee|ful, -fully, -fulness 'gliː|ful, -fuli [-fəli], -fulnis

glee|man, -men 'gliː|mən [-mæn], -mən [-men]

glee-singer, -s 'gliː,siŋə*, -z

Glegg gleg

Gleichen (English surname) 'glaikən

Glemsford 'glemsfəd

glen (G.), -s glen, -z

Glenallan glen'ælən

Glenalmond glen'ɑːmənd

Glenavon (in N. Ireland) glen'ævən

Glenavy (in N. Ireland) glen'eivi

Glencairn glen'keən

Glencoe glen'kəu

Glendale glen'deil, 'glendeil

Glendin(n)ing glen'diniŋ

Glendower glen'dauə*

Glenelg glen'elg

Glenfinnan glen'finən

glengarr|y, -ies glen'gær|i, -iz

Glenlivet glen'livit

Glenmore glen'mɔː* [-mɔə*]

Glenrothes glen'rɔθis

Glenwood 'glenwud

glib, -ber, -best, -ly, -ness glib, -ə*, -ist, -li, -nis

glid|e (s. v.), -es, -ing/ly, -ed, -er/s glaid, -z, -iŋ/li, -id, -ə*/z

glimmer (s. v.), -s, -ing/s, -ingly, -ed 'glimə*, -z, -riŋ/z, -riŋli, -d

glimps|e (s. v.), -es, -ing, -ed glimps, -iz, -iŋ, -t

glint, -s, -ing, -ed glint, -s, -iŋ, -id

glissad|e (s. v.), -es, -ing, -ed gli'sɑːd [-'seid], -z, -iŋ, -id

Glisson 'glisn

glist|en, -ens, -ening, -ened 'glis|n, -nz, -niŋ [-niŋ], -nd

glitt|er (s. v.), -ers, -ering/ly, -ered 'glit|ə*, -əz, -əriŋ/li, -əd

Gloag (surname) gləug

gloaming 'gləumiŋ

gloat, -s, -ing, -ed gləut, -s, -iŋ, -id

global 'gləubəl

globe, -s gləub, -z

globe-trott|er/s, -ing 'gləub,trɔt|ə*/z, -iŋ

globose 'gləubəus [gləu'b-]

globous 'gləubəs

globosity gləu'bɔsiti

globular, -ly 'glɔbjulə*, -li

globule, -s 'glɔbjuːl, -z

glockenspiel, -s 'glɔkənspiːl, -z

gloom (s. v.), -s, -ing, -ed gluːm, -z, -iŋ, -d

gloom|y, -ier, -iest, -ily, -iness 'gluːm|i, -ïə* [-jə*], -iist [-jist], -ili, -inis

Gloria, -s 'glɔːrɪə, -z
Gloriana ˌglɔːri'ɑːnə
glorification ˌglɔːrifi'keiʃən
glori|fy, -fies, -fying, -fied, -fier/s 'glɔːri|fai, -faiz, -faiiŋ, -faid, -faiə*/z
glorious, -ly, -ness 'glɔːrɪəs, -li, -nis
glor|y (s. v.), -ies, -ying, -ied 'glɔːr|i, -iz, -iiŋ, -id
glory-hole, -s 'glɔːrihəul, -z
Glos. glɔs
gloss (s. v.), -es, -ing, -ed, -er/s glɔs, -iz, -iŋ, -t, -ə*/z
glossarial glɔ'sɛərɪəl
glossar|ist/s, -y, -ies 'glɔsər|ist/s, -i, -iz
glossematic, -s ˌglɔsi'mætik, -s
glossic 'glɔsik
glossograph|er/s, -y glɔ'sɔgrəf|ə*/z, -i
glossological ˌglɔsəu'lɔdʒikl
glossolog|ist/s, -y glɔ'sɔlədʒ|ist/s, -i
Glossop 'glɔsəp
gloss|y, -ier, -iest, -ily, -iness 'glɔs|i, -iə*, -iist, -ili, -inis
Gloster 'glɔstə*
glottal 'glɔtl [rarely 'gləutl]
glottic 'glɔtik
glottis, -es 'glɔtis, -iz
glottology glɔ'tɔlədʒi
Gloucester, -shire 'glɔstə* ['glɔː-s-], -ʃiə* [-ʃə*]
    Note.—Older members of county families usually pronounce 'glɔː-s-.
glove, -s, -d glʌv, -z, -d
glove-fight, -s 'glʌvfait, -s
glover (G.), -s 'glʌvə*, -z
glove-stretcher, -s 'glʌvˌstretʃə*, -z
gl|ow (s. v.), -ows, -owing/ly, -owed gl|əu, -əuz, -əuiŋ/li, -əud
glower, -s, -ing, -ed 'glauə*, -z, -riŋ, -d
glow-worm, -s 'gləuwəːm, -z
gloxinia, -s glɔk'sinjə [-niə], -z
gloz|e (s. v.), -es, -ing, -ed gləuz, -iz, -iŋ, -d
Glubbdubdrib ˌglʌbdʌb'drib
glucose 'gluːkəus [-əuz]
glu|e (s. v.), -es, -ing, -ed, -er/s gluː, -iŋ, [gluiŋ], -d, -ə*/z [gluə*/z]
glue-pot, -s 'gluː-pɔt, -s
gluey, -ness 'glu(ː)i, -nis
gluish 'glu(ː)iʃ
glum, -mer, -mest, -ly, -ness glʌm, -ə*, -ist, -li, -nis
glut (s. v.), -s, -ting, -ted glʌt, -s, -iŋ, -id
glut|en, -in 'gluːt|ən [-|in, -|n], -in
glutinous, -ly, -ness 'gluːtinəs, -li, -nis
glutton, -s 'glʌtn, -z
gluttoniz|e [-is|e], -es, -ing, -ed 'glʌtn̩-aiz [-tənaiz], -iz, -iŋ, -d
gluttonous, -ly 'glʌtnəs [-tənəs], -li

gluttony 'glʌtni [-təni]
glycerine ˌglisə'riːn ['glisəriːn, 'glisərin]
glycogen 'glikəudʒen ['glaik-]
glycol 'glaikɔl ['glik-, -kəl]
Glyn glin
Glynde (in Sussex) glaind
Glyndebourne 'glaindbɔːn [-bəən]
Glynne glin
glyph, -s glif, -s
glyptic 'gliptik
glyptography glip'tɔgrəfi
G|-man, -men 'dʒiː|mæn, -men
gnaphalium næ'feiljəm [nə'f-, -lɪəm]
gnar, -s, -ring, -red nɑː*, -z, -riŋ, -d
gnarl, -s, -ed nɑːl, -z, -d
gnash, -es, -ing, -ed næʃ, -iz, -iŋ, -t
gnat, -s næt, -s
gnathic 'næθik
gnaw, -s, -ing, -ed, -er/s nɔː, -z, -iŋ, -d, gneiss nais [gn-]   [-ə*/z
gnome (goblin), -s nəum, -z
gnome (maxim), -s 'nəumiː, -z
gnomic, -al 'nəumik, -əl
gnomish 'nəumiʃ
gnomon, -s 'nəumɔn [-mən], -z
gnomonic, -al, -ally nəu'mɔnik, -əl, -əli
gnos|is, -es 'nəus|is, -iːz
Gnossall (near Stafford) 'nəusl
gnostic (s. adj.), -s 'nɔstik, -s
gnosticism 'nɔstisizəm
gnu, -s nuː [njuː], -z
go (s. v.), -es, -ing, went, gone, goer/s gəu, -z, -iŋ, went, gɔn [gɔːn], 'gəuə*/z
Goa 'gəuə
Goad gəud, 'gəuəd
goad (s. v.), -s, -ing, -ed gəud, -z, -iŋ, -id
go-ahead 'gəuəhed
goal, -s; -keeper/s, -post/s gəul, -z; -ˌkiːpə*/z, -pəust/s
Goanese ˌgəuə'niːz
goat, -s gəut, -s
goatee, -s gəu'tiː: [also 'gəuti: in goatee beard], -z
goat-herd, -s 'gəuthəːd, -z
Goathland 'gəuθlənd
goatish 'gəutiʃ
goat's-beard, -s 'gəutsbiəd, -z
goat-sucker, -s 'gəutˌsʌkə*, -z
gob, -s gɔb, -z
gobang gəu'bæŋ ['gəub-]
gobbet, -s 'gɔbit, -s
gobb|le, -les, -ling, -led, -ler/s 'gɔb|l, -lz, -liŋ [-liŋ], -ld, -lə*/z [-lə*/z]
Gobbo 'gɔbəu
Gobelin 'gəubəlin ['gɔbəlin] (gɔblɛ̃)
go-between, -s 'gəu-biˌtwiːn, -z
Gobi 'gəubi
goblet, -s 'gɔblit, -s

goblin, -s 'gɔblin, -z
gob|y, -ies 'gəub|i, -iz
go-by 'gəubai
go-cart, -s 'gəu-kɑːt, -s
god, -s gɔd, -z
God gɔd [*rarely* gɔːd]
Godalming 'gɔdlmiŋ
god|child, -children 'gɔd|tʃaild, -ˌtʃil-drən [-ˌtʃuldrən, -ˌtʃldrən]
Goddard 'gɔdəd, -dɑːd
god-daughter, -s 'gɔdˌdɔːtə*, -z
goddess, -es 'gɔdis, -iz
Goderich 'gəudritʃ
godetia, -s gəu'diːʃə [-ʃjə, -ʃĭə], -z
godfather, -s 'gɔdˌfɑːðə*, -z
god-fearing 'gɔdˌfiəriŋ
god-forsaken 'gɔdfəˌseikn
God|free, -frey 'gɔd|fri, -fri
god-given 'gɔdˌgivən
godhead (G.), -s 'gɔdhed, -z
Godiva gəu'daivə
Godkin 'gɔdkin
godless, -ly, -ness 'gɔdlis, -li, -nis
godlike 'gɔdlaik
godl|y, -ier, -iest, -iness 'gɔdl|i, -ĭə* [-jə*], -iist [-jist], -inis
Godman (*surname*) 'gɔdmən
God-man (*Christ*) 'gɔd'mæn ['--]
Godmanchester 'gɔdmənˌtʃestə*
godmother, -s 'gɔdˌmʌðə*, -z
Godolphin gə'dɔlfin
godown, -s 'gəudaun, -z
godparent, -s 'gɔdˌpeərənt, -s
God's-acre, -s 'gɔdzˌeikə*, -z
godsend, -s 'gɔdsend, -z
godson, -s 'gɔdsʌn, -z
god-speed 'gɔd'spiːd [-'-]
godward (G.) 'gɔdwəd
Godwin 'gɔdwin
godwit, -s 'gɔdwit, -s
Goethe 'gəːtə [-ti] ('gøːtə)
Goff(e) gɔf
goffer, -s, -ing, -ed 'gəufə*, -z, -riŋ, -d
Gog, -s gɔg, -z
Gogarty 'gəugəti
gogg|le (*s. v.*), -les, -ling, -led 'gɔg|l, -lz, -liŋ [-liŋ], -ld
goggle-eyed 'gɔglaid
Gogmagog 'gɔgməgɔg
Gogo 'gəugəu
going|s, -s-on 'gəuiŋ|z, -z'ɔn
goitre, -s, -d 'gɔitə*, -z, -d
goitrous 'gɔitrəs
Golby 'gəulbi
Golconda gɔl'kɔndə
gold gəuld
gold-beater, -s 'gəuldˌbiːtə*, -z
gold-beater's skin gəuld'biːtəzskin

gold-digger, -s 'gəuldˌdigə*, -z
gold-dust 'gəulddʌst ['gəuld'd-]
golden 'gəuldən
goldfield, -s 'gəuldfiːld, -z
goldfinch, -es 'gəuldfintʃ, -iz
goldfish, -es 'gəuldfiʃ, -iz
Golding 'gəuldiŋ
gold-lace 'gəuld'leis
gold-leaf 'gəuldliːf
gold-mine, -s 'gəuldmain, -z
Goldsborough 'gəuldzbərə
Goldschmidt (*English name*) 'gəuldʃmit
goldsmith (G.), -s 'gəuldsmiθ, -s
goldstick, -s 'gəuldstik, -s
gold-wire 'gəuld'waiə*
golf (*s. v.*), -s, -ing, -ed, -er/s gɔlf [*rarely* gɔf], -s, -iŋ, -t, -ə*/z
golf|-club/s, -links 'gɔlf|klʌb/z [*rarely* 'gɔf-], -links
Golgotha 'gɔlgəθə
Goliath gəu'laiəθ
Golightly (*surname*) gəu'laitli
Gollancz gə'lænts, gɔ'lænts, 'gɔlənts
  Note.—*Those unfamiliar with the name sometimes use other pronunciations such as* 'gɔlæŋks *or* gɔ'læŋks.
  V. *Gollancz, of the publishing firm,* pronounced gə'lænts.
golliwog, -s 'gɔliwɔg, -z
golly 'gɔli
golosh, -es gə'lɔʃ, -iz
Golton 'gɔltən
Gomar, -ist/s 'gəumə*, -rist/s
Gomersal (*in Yorks.*) 'gɔməsəl
Gomes 'gəumez
Gomme gɔm
Gomorrah gə'mɔrə
Gomshall (*in Surrey*) 'gʌmʃəl ['gɔm-]
Gondibert 'gɔndibəːt
gondola, -s 'gɔndələ, -z
gondolier, -s ˌgɔndə'liə*, -z
gone (*from* go) gɔn [gɔːn]
Goneril 'gɔnəril
gonfalon, -s 'gɔnfələn, -z
gong, -s gɔŋ, -z
Gonin 'gəunin
goniometer, -s ˌgəuni'ɔmitə*, -z
gonorrhea ˌgɔnə'riə
Gonville 'gɔnvil
Gooch guːtʃ
good (*s. adj.*) (G.), -s, -ness gud, -z, -nis
good (*interj.*) gud
Good|ale, -all, -body 'gud|eil, -ɔːl, -ˌbodi
good-bye (*s.*), -s gud'bai, -z
good-bye (*interj.*) 'gud'bai [gud'b-]
Goodchild 'gudtʃaild
good day (*on meeting*) gud'dei ['-'-], (*on parting*) 'gud'dei [-'-]

Goode gud
Goodell gu'del
Good|enough, -eve 'gud|inʌf, -iːv
good evening (on meeting) gud'iːvniŋ,
  (on parting) 'gud'iːvniŋ
Goodfellow 'gud,feləu
good-for-nothing (s. adj.), -s 'gudfə-
  ,nʌθiŋ [-fŋ,ʌθiŋ, -f,nʌθiŋ], -z
Goodge gudʒ [guːdʒ]
Goodhart 'gudhɑːt
good-hearted 'gud'hɑːtid
good-humoured, -ly 'gud'hjuːməd
  [gud'hjuː-, old-fashioned -'juː-], -li
goodish 'gudiʃ
Goodliffe 'gudlif
good-looking 'gud'lukiŋ [also '-,--, -'--
  according to sentence stress]
goodl|y, -ier, -iest, -iness 'gudl|i, -ɪə*
  [-jə*], -iist [-jist], -inis
good|man, -men 'gud|mæn, -men
Goodman 'gudmən
good morning (on meeting) gud'mɔːniŋ
  ['-'--], (on parting) 'gud'mɔːniŋ [-'--]
good morrow gud'mɔrəu   [-li
good-natured, -ly 'gud'neitʃəd [gud'n-],
goodness 'gudnis
good-night 'gud'nait [gud'n-]
Good|rich, -sir, -son 'gud|ritʃ, -sə*, -sn
goods-train, -s 'gudztrein, -z
good-tempered,   -ly   'gud'tempəd
  [gud't- also '-,-- when attributive], -li
goodwi|fe, -ves 'gudwai|f, -vz
goodwill, -s 'gud'wil [-'-'], -z
Good|win, -wood 'gud|win, -wud
good|y (G.), -ier, -iest, -ily, -iness
  'gud|i, -ɪə*, -iist, -ili, -inis
Good|year, -yer 'gud|jə(ː)*, -jə*
goof|y, -ier, -iest, -ily, -iness 'guːf|i,
  -ɪə*, -iist, -ili, -inis
Googe gudʒ [guːdʒ]
Googie 'guːgi
googly 'guːgli
Goole guːl
goon, -s guːn, -z
Goonhilly 'guːn,hili
goop|y, -ier, -iest, -ily, -iness 'guːp|i,
  -ɪə*, -iist, -ili, -inis
goosander, -s guː'sændə*, -z
g|oose (bird), -eese g|uːs, -iːs
goose (tailor's iron), -s guːs, -iz
gooseberr|y, -ies; -y-fool 'guzbər|i, -iz;
  -i'fuːl
goose|-flesh, -grass 'guːs|fleʃ, -grɑːs
goose-note, -s 'guːs-nəut, -s
goose-quill, -s 'guːs-kwil, -z
goose-step 'guːsstep
goosey, -s 'guːsi, -z
gopher, -s 'gəufə*, -z

Gophir 'gəufə*
Gorboduc 'gɔːbədʌk
Gordi|an, -um 'gɔːdj|ən [-dɪ|ən], -əm
Gordon 'gɔːdn
Gordonstoun 'gɔːdənstən
gor|e (s. v.) (G.), -es, -ing, -ed gɔː*
  [gɔə*], -z, -riŋ, -d
Gorell 'gɔrəl   -iŋ, -d
gorg|le (s. v.), -es, -ing, -ed gɔːdʒ, -iz,
gorgeous, -ly, -ness 'gɔːdʒəs, -li, -nis
Gorges 'gɔːdʒiz
gorget, -s 'gɔːdʒit, -s
Gorgie 'gɔːgi
Gorgon, -s 'gɔːgən, -z
Gorgonzola, -s ,gɔːgən'zəulə, -z
Gorham 'gɔːrəm
gorilla, -s gə'rilə [gu'r-], -z
Goring 'gɔːriŋ
Gorizia gɔ'ritsɪə [gə'r-]
Gorleston 'gɔːlstən
gormandiz|e [-is|e], -es, -ing, -ed,
  -er/s 'gɔːməndaiz, -iz, -iŋ, -d, -ə*/z
Gornergrat 'gɔːnəgræt
Goronwy gə'rɔnwi (Welsh go'ronuɪ)
Gorringe 'gɔrindʒ
gorse gɔːs
Gorst gɔːst
Gorton 'gɔːtn
gor|y, -ier, -iest, -ily, -iness 'gɔːr|i, -ɪə*,
  -iist, -ili, -inis
gos, -es gɔs, -iz
Goschen 'gəuʃən
gosh gɔʃ
goshawk, -s 'gɔshɔːk, -s
Goshen 'gəuʃən
gosling (G.), -s 'gɔzliŋ, -z
go-slow 'gəu'sləu
gospel (G.), -s 'gɔspəl [-pel], -z
gospeller, -s 'gɔspələ*, -z
Gosport 'gɔspɔːt
gossamer 'gɔsəmə*
Gosschalk 'gɔstʃɔːk
Goss(e) gɔs
gossip (s. v.), -s, -ing, -ed; -y 'gɔsip, -s,
  -iŋ, -t; -i
got (from get) gɔt
Göteborg 'gəːtəbɔːg (Swed. jøːtə'bɔrj)
Goth, -s gɔθ, -s
Gotha (in Germany) 'gəuθə ['gəutə]
  ('gɔːtaː), (old-fashioned English
  spelling of Göta in Sweden) 'gəutə
Gotham (in Notts.) 'gəutəm, (in New
  York) 'gəuθəm, 'gɔθəm
Note.—In man of Gotham the usual
  pronunciation is 'gəutəm, but
  'gɔtəm may sometimes be heard
  from people unfamiliar with the
  place in Notts.

Gothenburg 'gɔθənbə:g ['gɔtn-]
Gothic 'gɔθik
gothicism, -s 'gɔθisizəm, -z
gothiciz|e [-is|e], -es, -ing, -ed 'gɔθisaiz, -iz, -iŋ, -d
Gothland 'gɔθlənd
gotten (*from* get) 'gɔtn
gouache gu'ɑ:ʃ [gwɑ:ʃ] (gwaʃ)
Gouda (*Dutch town, cheese*) 'gaudə
Goudie 'gaudi
goug|e (*s. v.*), -es, -ing, -ed gaudʒ [gu:dʒ], -iz, -iŋ, -d
Gough gɔf
goulash, -es 'gu:læʃ [-lɑ:ʃ], -iz
Goulburn (*place name*) 'gəulbə:n, (*surname*) 'gu:lbə:n
Gould gu:ld
Goulden 'gu:ldən
Goulding 'gu:ldiŋ
Gounod 'gu:nəu (guno)
gourd, -s guəd, -z
Gourl|ay, -ey 'guəl|i, -i
gourmand, -s 'guəmənd (gurmã), -z
gourmet, -s 'guəmei (gurmɛ), -z
gout, -y, -ily, -iness gaut, -i, -ili, -inis
Govan 'gʌvən
Gover 'gəuvə*
govern, -s, -ing, -ed; -able, -ance, -ess/es 'gʌvən, -z, -iŋ ['gʌvn̩iŋ], -d; -əbl ['gʌvn̩əbl], -əns ['gʌvn̩əns], -is/iz ['gʌvn̩is/iz]
government, -s 'gʌvnmənt [-vn̩mənt, -vənmənt, -vəmənt], -s
governmental ˌgʌvən'mentl
governor, -s 'gʌvənə* [-vn̩ə*, -vnə*], -z
governor-general, -s 'gʌvənə'dʒenərəl [-vn̩ə-, -vnə-], -z
governorship, -s 'gʌvənəʃip [-vn̩ə-, -vnə-], -s
Govey 'gəuvi
Govier 'gəuviə* [-viə*]
Gow gau
Gowan 'gau-ən
Gowen 'gau-ən ['gauin]
Gower 'gauə*, gɔ:* [gɔə*]
    Note.—'gauə* *is used in* Gower Street *and for the place in Wales.* gɔ:* [gɔə*] *is the family name of the Duke of Sutherland; this pronunciation is also used in* Leveson-Gower (*q.v.*).
Gowing 'gauiŋ
gowk, -s gauk, -s
gown, -s, -ed gaun, -z, -d
gowns|man, -men 'gaunz|mən, -mən [-men]
Gowrie 'gauəri
Gozo 'gəuzəu

G.P., -'s 'dʒi:'pi:, -z
grab (*s. v.*), -s, -bing, -bed, -ber/s græb, -z, -iŋ, -d, -ə*/z
grabb|le, -les, -ling, -led 'græb|l, -lz, -liŋ [-liŋ], -ld
Grabham 'græbəm
Gracch|us, -i 'græk|əs, -i: [-ai]
grac|e (*s. v.*) (G.), -es, -ing, -ed greis, -iz, -iŋ, -t
Gracechurch 'greis-tʃə:tʃ
grace|ful, -fully, -fulness 'greis|ful, -fuli [-fəli], -fulnis
graceless, -ly, -ness 'greislis, -li, -nis
grace-note, -s 'greis-nəut, -s
Gracie 'greisi
gracious, -ly, -ness 'greiʃəs, -li, -nis
grackle, -s 'grækl, -z
gradat|e, -es, -ing, -ed grə'deit, -s, -iŋ, -id
gradation, -s grə'deiʃən, -z
gradational grə'deiʃənl [-ʃn̩l, -ʃn̩l, -ʃənəl]
grad|e (*s. v.*), -es, -ing, -ed greid, -z, -iŋ, -id
Gradgrind 'grædgraind
gradient, -s 'greidjənt [-diənt], -s
gradin, -s 'greidin, -z
gradual (*s. adj.*), -s, -ly 'grædʒuəl [-dʒwəl, -dʒul, -djuəl, -djwəl, -djul], -z, -i
graduate (*s.*), -s 'grædʒuət [-djuət, -djuit, -djueit, -dʒuit], -s
graduat|e (*v.*), -es, -ing, -ed 'grædjueit [-dʒueit], -s, -iŋ, -id
graduation, -s ˌgrædju'eiʃən [-dʒu-], -z
graduator, -s 'grædjueitə*, -z
gradus, -es 'grædəs ['greid-], -iz
Grady 'greidi
Graeme greim
graft (*s. v.*), -s, -ing, -ed, -er/s grɑ:ft, -s, -iŋ, -id, -ə*/z
Grafton 'grɑ:ftən
Graham(e) 'greiəm [grɛəm]
Grahamston 'greiəmstən ['grɛəm-]
Grahamstown 'greiəmztaun ['grɛəm-]
grail (G.), -s greil, -z
grain (*s. v.*), -s, -ing, -ed, -er/s; -y grein, -z, -iŋ, -d, -ə*/z; -i
Grainger 'greindʒə*
gram, -s græm, -z
gramercy grə'mə:si
graminaceous ˌgreimi'neiʃəs [ˌgræm-]
gramineous grei'miniəs [græ'm-, -njəs]
graminivorous ˌgræmi'nivərəs
grammalogue, -s 'græmələg, -z
grammar, -s 'græmə*, -z
grammar-school, -s 'græmə-sku:l, -z
grammarian, -s grə'mɛəriən, -z
grammatic, -al, -ally grə'mætik, -əl, -əli

grammaticiz|e [-is|e], **-es, -ing, -ed** grə'mætisaiz, -iz, -iŋ, -d

gramme, -s græm, -z

gramophone, -s 'græməfəun, -z

Grampian, -s 'græmpjən [-pïən], -z

grampus, -es 'græmpəs, -iz

Granada grə'nɑːdə (grɑ'nada)

granar|y, -ies 'grænər|i, -iz

Granbury 'grænbəri

Granby 'grænbi

grand; grand|er, -est, -ly, -ness grænd; 'grænd|ə*, -ist, -li, -nis ['grænnis]

grandam, -s 'grændæm, -z

grand-aunt, -s 'grænd-ɑːnt, -s

grand|child, -children 'græn-|tʃaild, -,tʃildrən [-,tʃuldrən, -,tʃldrən]

granddad, -s 'grændæd [-ndd-], -z

granddaughter, -s 'græn,dɔːtə* [-nd,d-], -z

grand-duchess, -es 'grænd'dʌtʃis [*also* 'grænd,d-, *esp. when followed by a stress*], -iz

grand-duke, -s 'grænd'djuːk [*also* 'grændd- *esp. when followed by a stress*], -s

grandee, -s græn'diː, -z

grandeur 'grændʒə* [-djuə*, -djə*]

grandfather, -s 'grænd,fɑːðə*, -z

Grandgent 'grændʒent [-dʒənt]

grandiloquen|ce, -t/ly græn'diləkwən|s [-luk-], -t/li

grandiose, -ly 'grændiəus [-djəus, -diəuz, -djəuz], -li

grandiosity ,grændi'ɔsiti

Grandison 'grændisn

grandma, -s 'grænmɑː, -z

grandmamma, -s 'grænmə,mɑː, -z [-z 'grænmˌmɑː, -z]

grandmother, -s 'græn,mʌðə* [-nd,m-], -z

grand-nephew, -s 'græn,nevju: [-nd,n-, -,nefjuː, '-'--], -z

grand-niece, -s 'grænniːs [-ndn-, '-'-], -iz

grandpa, -s 'grænpɑː, -z

grandpapa, -s 'grænpə,pɑː, -z [-s 'grænpɑː,pɑː, -z]

grandparent, -s 'græn,peərənt [-nd,p-], -s

grandsire, -s 'græn,saiə* [-nd,s-], -z

grandson, -s 'grænsʌn [-nds-], -z

grand-stand, -s 'grændstænd ['-'-], -z

grand-uncle, -s 'grænd,ʌŋkl, -z

grange (G.), -s greindʒ, -iz

Grangemouth 'greindʒmaθ [-mauθ]

granger (G.), -s 'greindʒə*, -z

grangeriz|e [-is|e], **-es, -ing, -ed** 'greindʒəraiz, -iz, -iŋ, -d

Grange|town, -ville 'greindʒ|taun, -vil

granite (G.), -s 'grænit, -s

granitic græ'nitik

grann|y, -ies 'græn|i, -iz

granolithic ,grænəu'liθik

grant (s. v.) (G.), -s, -ing, -ed grɑːnt, -s, -iŋ, -id

grantee, -s grɑːn'tiː, -z

Grantham (*in Lincs.*) 'grænθəm [*rarely* 'græntəm], (*surname*) 'grænθəm

Grantie 'grɑːnti

Granton 'grɑːntən ['græn-]

grantor, -s grɑːn'tɔː*, -z

Grantown 'græntaun

granular, -y 'grænjulə*, -ri

granulat|e, -es, -ing, -ed 'grænjuleit [-njəl-], -s, -iŋ, -id

granulation, -s ,grænju'leiʃən, -z

granule, -s 'grænjuːl, -z

granul|ite, -ous 'grænjul|ait, -əs

Granville 'grænvil

grape (G.), -s greip, -s

grape-cure, -s 'greipkjuə* [-kjɔə*, -kjɔː*], -z

grape-fruit, -s 'greip-fruːt, -s

grape-shot 'greip-ʃɔt

grape|-stone/s, -sugar, -vine/s 'greip|-stəun/z, -,ʃugə*, -vain/z

graph, -s græf [grɑːf], -s

graphic (G.), -s, -al, -ally 'græfik, -s, -əl, -əli

graphite 'græfait ['greif-]

graphology græ'fɔlədʒi

graphometer, -s græ'fɔmitə*, -z

graphophone, -s 'græfəfəun, -z

grapnel, -s 'græpnəl [-nl], -z

grapp|le, -les, -ling, -led, -ler/s 'græp|l, -lz, -liŋ [-liŋ], -ld, -lə*/z [-lə*/z]

grappling-iron, -s 'græpliŋ,aiən [-pliŋ-], -z

grapy 'greipi

Grasmere 'grɑːs-miə*

grasp (s. v.), -s, -ing/ly, -ed, -er/s grɑːsp, -s, -iŋ/li, -t, -ə*/z

grass (s. v.), -es, -ing, -ed grɑːs, -iz, -iŋ

grass-cutter, -s 'grɑːs,kʌtə*, -z

grass-green 'grɑːs'griːn ['grɑːs-g-]

grasshopper, -s 'grɑːs,hɔpə*, -z

grass-land 'grɑːs-lænd

grass-plot, -s 'grɑːs'plɔt ['grɑːs-plɔt], -s

grass-wid|ow/s, -ower/s 'grɑːs-'wid|əu/z, -əuə*/z

grass|y, -ier, -iest 'grɑːs|i, -ïə* [-jə*], -iist [-jist]

grata (*in* **persona grata**) 'grɑːtə [*old-fashioned* 'greitə]

grat|e (s. v.), -es, -ing/ly, -ed, -er/s greit, -s, -iŋ/li, -id, -ə*/z

grate|ful, -fully, -fulness 'greit|fᴜl, -fuli [-fəli], -fᴜlnis

Gratian 'greiʃjən [-ʃïən]

Gratiano (*Shakespearian character*) ,grɑːʃi'ɑːnəu [,græ-]

gratification, -s ,grætifi'keiʃən, -z

grati|fy, -fies, -fying, -fied, -fier/s 'græti|fai, -faiz, -faiiŋ, -faid, -faiə*/z

gratin 'grætẽ:ŋ [-tæŋ] (gratẽ)

grating (s.), -s 'greitiŋ, -z

Gratiot (in U.S.A.) 'græʃiət [-ʃjət, 'greiʃ-]

gratis 'greitis ['grɑːtis, 'grætis]

gratitude 'grætitjuːd

Grattan 'grætn

gratuitous, -ly, -ness grə'tju(ː)itəs, -li, -nis

gratuit|y, -ies grə'tju(ː)it|i, -iz

gravam|en, -ina grə'veim|en, -inə

grave (accent above a letter) grɑːv

grav|e (s. adj. v.) (other senses), -es; -er, -est, -ely, -eness; -ing, -ed, -en, -er/s greiv, -z; -ə*, -ist, -li, -nis; -iŋ, -d, -ən, -ə*/z

grave|-clothes, -digger/s 'greiv|kləuðz [old-fashioned -kləuz,] -,digə*/z

grav|el (s. v.), -els, -elling, -elled, -elly 'græv|əl, -əlz, -liŋ [-əliŋ], -əld, -li [-əli]

gravel|-pit/s, -walk/s 'grævəl|pit/s, -'wɔːk/s

graven (from grave v.) 'greivən

Graves (surname) greivz, (wine) grɑːv

Gravesend greivz'end [-v'zend, -'-]

grave|-stone/s, -yard/s 'greiv|stəun/z, -jɑːd/z

graving-dock, -s 'greiviŋdɔk, -s

gravitat|e, -es, -ing, -ed 'græviteit, -s, -iŋ, -id

gravitation ,grævi'teiʃən

gravity 'græviti

gravure grə'vjuə* [-'vjɔə*, -'vjɔː*]

grav|y, -ies 'greiv|i, -iz

gravy-spoon, -s 'greivi-spuːn, -z

gray (s. adj.) (G.), -s, -er, -est, -ness grei, -z, -ə* [greə*], -ist, 'grei-nis ['greinis]

graybeard, -s 'greibiəd, -z

gray-eyed 'greiaid

gray-haired 'grei'hɛəd ['greih- when attributive]

gray-headed 'grei'hedid ['grei,h- when attributive]

grayish 'greiiʃ

grayling, -s 'greiliŋ, -z

Grayson 'greisn

graystone 'grei-stəun

graz|e, -es, -ing, -ed greiz, -iz, -iŋ, -d

grazier, -s 'greizjə* [-zїə*, -ʒjə*, -ʒїə*, -ʒə*], -z

grease (s.), -s, grіːs, -iz [-ʒə*], -z

greas|e (v.), -es, -ing, -ed, -er/s griːz [griːs], -iz ['griːsiz], -iŋ ['griːsiŋ], griːzd [griːst], -ə*/z

grease-box, -es 'griːsbɔks, -iz

grease-paint 'griːs-peint

grease-trap, -s 'griːs-træp, -s

greas|y, -ier, -iest, -ily, -iness 'griːz|i ['griːs|i], -їə* [-jə*], -iist [-jist], -ili, -inis

Note.—Some people use the forms 'griːsi and 'griːzi with a difference of meaning, 'griːsi having reference merely to the presence of grease and 'griːzi having reference to slipperiness caused by grease. Thus with such speakers a candlestick might be 'griːsi (i.e. covered with candlegrease) without necessarily being 'griːzi, while a road might be 'griːzi (i.e. slippery) without being exactly 'griːsi.

great, -er, -est, -ly, -ness greit, -ə*, -ist, -li, -nis

great-aunt, -s 'greit'ɑːnt ['--], -s

great-coat, -s 'greitkəut [also -'- when preceded by a stress], -s

great-grand|child, -children 'greit-'græn-|tʃaild, -,tʃildrən [-,tʃuldrən, -,tʃldrən]

great-granddaughter, -s 'greit'græn-,dɔːtə* [-nd,d-], -z

great-grandfather, -s 'greit'grænd-,fɑːðə*, -z

great-grandmother, -s 'greit'græn-,mʌðə* [-nd,m-], -z

great-grandparent, -s 'greit'grænd-,pɛərənt, -s

great-grandson, -s 'greit'grænsʌn [-nds-], -z

Greatham (in Durham) 'griːtəm, (in Northants. and Sussex) 'gretəm

Greathead 'greithed

Greatheart 'greithɑːt

great-hearted 'greit'hɑːtid [also 'greit,h-, esp. when attributive]

Greatorex 'greitəreks

greats greits

great-uncle, -s 'greit'ʌŋkl ['-,--], -z

greaves griːvz

Greaves griːvz, greivz

grebe, -s griːb, -z

Grecian, -s 'griːʃən, -z

Grec|ism, -ize 'griːs|izm, -aiz

Greco-Roman 'grekəu'rəumən ['griːk-]

Greece griːs

greed, -y, -ier, -iest, -ily, -iness griːd, -i, -їə* [-jə*], -iist [-jist], -ili, -inis

Greek, -s griːk, -s

Greel(e)y 'griːli

green (s. adj. v.), -s; -er, -est, -ly, -ness; -ing, -ed griːn, -z; -ə*, -ist, -li, -nis; -iŋ, -d

Green(e) griːn

Greenall 'griːnɔːl
Greenaway 'griːnəwei
greenery 'griːnəri
green-eyed 'griːnaid
Greenfield 'griːnfiːld
greenfinch, -es 'griːnfintʃ, -iz
greenfly 'griːnflai
Greenford 'griːnfəd
greengage, -s 'griːngeidʒ ['griːŋg-,
'-'-, also -'-, according to sentence-
stress], -iz
greengrocer, -s 'griːnˌgrəusə* [-iːŋˌg-],
-z
Greenhalgh 'griːnhælʃ, -hældʒ, -hɔː
Green|haulgh, -hill 'griːn|hɔː, -hil
Greenhithe 'griːnhaið
greenhou|se, -ses 'griːnhau|s, -ziz
greenish (G.), -ness 'griːniʃ, -nis
Greenland (country), -er/s 'griːnlənd
[-lænd], -ə*/z
Greenland (surname) 'griːnlənd
Greenleaf 'griːnliːf
Greenock 'griːnək ['grin-, 'gren-]
Greenore griː'nɔː* [-'nɔə*]
Greenough 'griːnəu
Green|point, -port 'griːn|pɔint, -pɔːt
green-room, -s 'griːnrum [-ruːm], -z
greensand 'griːn-sænd
Greenslade 'griːn-sleid
Greensleeves 'griːn-sliːvz
greenstone 'griːn-stəun
greensward 'griːn-swɔːd
Green|ville, -well 'griːn|vil, -wəl [-wel]
Greenwich 'grinidʒ ['gren-, -itʃ]
greenwood (G.), -s 'griːnwud, -z
greeny 'griːni
greet (G.), -s, -ing/s, -ed griːt, -s, -iŋ/z,
Greetland 'griːtlənd   [-id
Greg(g) greg
gregarious, -ly, -ness gri'gɛəriəs [grə'g-,
gre'g-], -li, -nis
Gregorian, -s gri'gɔːriən [grə'g-, gre'g-],
-z
Gregory, -powder 'gregəri, -ˌpaudə*
Greig greg
gremlin, -s 'gremlin, -z
Grenada gre'neidə [grə'n-]
grenade, -s gri'neid [gre'n-, grə'n-], -z
grenadier (G.), -s ˌgrenə'diə*, -z
grenadin, -s 'grenədin, -z
grenadine ˌgrenə'diːn ['grenədiːn]
Grenadines ˌgrenə'diːnz
Grendel 'grendl
Gren|fell, -ville 'gren|fel [-fəl], -vil
Gresham 'greʃəm
Gres|ley, -well 'grez|li, -wəl
Greta (English name) 'griːtə, 'gretə,
'greitə

Gretel (German name) 'gretl ('greːtəl)
Gretna 'gretnə
Greuze, -s grəːz (grøːz), -iz
Greville 'grevil [-vl]
grew (from grow) gruː
grey (s. adj.) (G.), -s, -er, -est, -ness
grei, -z, -ə* [greə*], -ist, 'grei-nis
['greinis]
greybeard, -s' greibiəd, -z
greycoat (G.), -s 'grei-kəut, -s
grey-eyed 'greiaid
grey-haired 'grei'hɛəd ['grei,h- when
attributive]
grey-headed 'grei'hedid ['grei,h- when
attributive]
greyhound, -s 'greihaund, -z
greyish 'greiiʃ
Grey|lock, -son 'grei|lɔk, -sn
Gribble 'gribl
Grice grais
grid, -s grid, -z
griddle, -s 'gridl, -z
gridiron, -s 'gridˌaiən, -z
Gridley 'gridli
grief, -s griːf, -s
Grieg (Norwegian composer) griːg
Grierson 'griəsn
grievance, -s 'griːvəns, -iz
griev|e, -es, -ing, -ed, -er/s griːv, -z,
-iŋ, -d, -ə*/z
grievous, -ly, -ness 'griːvəs, -li, -nis
griffin (G.), -s 'grifin, -z
Griffith, -s 'grifiθ, -s
grig, -s grig, -z
Grigg, -s grig, -z
Grildrig 'grildrig
grill (s. v.), -s, -ing, -ed, -er/s gril, -z,
-iŋ, -d, -ə*/z
grillage, -s 'grilidʒ, -iz
grille, -s gril, -z
grill-room, -s 'grilrum [-ruːm], -z
grilse grils
grim, -mer, -mest, -ly, -ness grim, -ə*,
-ist, -li, -nis
grimac|e (s. v.), -es, -ing, -ed gri'meis,
-iz, -iŋ, -t
Grimald 'griməld
grimalkin, -s gri'mælkin, -z
grim|e (s. v.), -es, -ing, -ed graim, -z,
-iŋ, -d
Grimes graimz
Grimm grim
Grimond 'grimənd
Grimsby 'grimzbi
Grimsel 'grimzl
Grim|shaw, -wig 'grim|ʃɔː, -wig
grim|y, -ier, -iest, -ily, -iness 'graim|i,
-iə* [-jə*], -iist [-jist], -ili, -inis

grin (s. v.), -s, -ning, -ned grin, -z, -iŋ, -d

grind (s. v.), -s, -ing, ground, grinder/s graind, -z, -iŋ, graund, 'graində*/z

Grindal 'grindəl

Grindelwald 'grindlvɑːld

grindery 'graindəri

Grindon 'grindən

grindstone, -s 'graindstəun, -z

Grinnell gri'nel

Grinstead 'grinstid [-sted]

grip (s. v.), -s, -ping, -ped grip, -s, -iŋ, -t

grip|e (s. v.), -es, -ing, -ed graip, -s, -iŋ, -t

gripes (s.) graips

grippe grip [griːp] (grip)

gripsack, -s 'gripsæk, -s

Griqua, -s, -land 'grikwə, -z, -lænd

grisaille gri'zeil [gri(ː)'zai, -'zail] (grizɑːj)

Griscom 'griskəm

Griselda gri'zeldə

grisette, -s gri'zet, -s

Grisewood 'graizwud

griskin 'griskin

grisl|y, -ier, -iest, -iness 'grizl|i, -ĭə*, -iist, -inis

Grisons 'griːzɔ̃ːŋ [-zɔːŋ, -zɔŋ] (grizɔ̃)

grist grist

gristle 'grisl

gristly 'grisl|i [-sli]

Griswold 'grizwəuld

grit, -s ; -stone grit, -s; -stəun

gritt|y, -ier, -iest, -ily, -iness 'grit|i, -ĭə*, -iist, -ili, -inis

Grizel gri'zel

grizzle, -d 'grizl, -d

grizzl|y (s. adj.), -ies 'grizl|i, -iz

groan (s. v.), -s, -ing/s, -ed grəun, -z, -iŋ/z, -d

groat (coin), -s grəut, -s

groats (grain) grəuts

Grobian, -s 'grəubjən [-bĭən], -z

grocer, -s 'grəusə*, -z

grocer|y, -ies 'grəusər|i, -iz

Grocott 'grɔkət

Grocyn 'grəusin

grog grɔg

grogg|y, -ier, -iest, -ily, -iness 'grɔg|i, -ĭə*, -iist, -ili, -inis

grogram 'grɔgrəm

grog-shop, -s 'grɔgʃɔp, -s

groin, -s grɔin, -z

gromwell 'grɔmwəl [-wel]

Grongar 'grɔŋgə*

groom (s. v.), -s, -ing, -ed grum [gruːm], -z, -iŋ, -d

grooms|man,   -men   'grumz|mən ['gruːmz-], -mən [-men]

groov|e (s. v.), -es, -ing, -ed gruːv, -z, -iŋ, -d

groov|y, -ier, -iest, -iness 'gruːv|i, -ĭə* [-jə*], -iist [-jist], -inis

grop|e, -es, -ing/ly, -ed, -er/s grəup, -s, -iŋ/li, -t, -ə*/z

Grosart 'grəuzɑːt

grosbeak, -s 'grəusbiːk, -s

groschen 'grəuʃən ['grɔʃ-]

Grose grəus, grəuz

Grosmont (in Yorks.) 'grəumənt [-mont, locally also 'grəusmənt], (in Mon.) 'grɔsmənt

gross (s. adj.), -er, -est, -ly, -ness grəus, -ə*, -ist, -li, -nis

Gross (surname) grɔs, grəus

Grossmith 'grəus-miθ

Grosvenor 'grəuvnə*

Grote grəut

grotesque, -ly, -ness grəu'tesk, -li, -nis

grotto, -s 'grɔtəu, -z

ground (s. v.) (all senses), -s, -ing, -ed, -er/s graund, -z, -iŋ, -id, -ə*/z

ground (from grind) graund

groundage 'graundidʒ

ground-ash 'graund'æʃ

ground-bass, -es 'graund'beis, -iz

ground-floor, -s 'graund'flɔː* [-'flɔə*, also '-- esp. when attributive], -z

ground-hog, -s 'graund'hɔg ['--], -z

ground-ivy 'graund'aivi

groundless, -ly, -ness 'graundlis, -li, -nis

groundling, -s 'graundliŋ, -z

ground|-man,   -men   'graund|mæn [-mən], -men [-mən]

ground-nut, -s 'graundnʌt, -s

ground-plan, -s 'graund'plæn ['--], -z

ground-rent, -s 'graund-rent, -s

groundsel 'graunsl

grounds|man,   -men   'graundz|mən [-mæn], -mən [-men]

ground-swell, -s 'graund'swel ['--], -z

groundwork 'graund-wəːk

group (s. v.), -s, -ing/s, -ed gruːp, -s, -iŋ/z, -t

grous|e (s. v.) (G.), -es, -ing, -ed, -er/s graus, -iz, -iŋ, -t, -ə*/z

grove (G.), -s grəuv, -z

grov|el, -els, -elling, -elled, -eller/s 'grɔv|l ['grʌv-], -lz, -liŋ [-liŋ], -ld, -lə*/z [-lə*/z]

Grover 'grəuvə*

gr|ow, -ows, -owing, grew, gr|own, -ower/s gr|əu, -əuz, -əuiŋ, gruː, gr|əun, -əuə*/z

growl (s. v.), -s, -ing, -ed, -er/s graul, -z, -iŋ, -d, -ə*/z

grown-up (s.), -s 'grəunʌp ['grəun'ʌp, grəun'ʌp], -s
grown-up (adj.) 'grəunʌp
growth, -s grəuθ, -s
groyne, -s grɔin, -z
grub (s. v.), -s, -bing, -bed, -ber/s grʌb, -z, -iŋ, -d, -ə*/z
grubb|y, -ier, -iest, -iness 'grʌb|i, -ɪə*, -iist, -inis
grudg|e (s. v.), -es, -ing/ly, -ed grʌdʒ, -iz, -iŋ/li, -d
gruel gruəl ['gru:əl, gruil]
gruelling (s. adj.), -s 'gruəliŋ ['gru:əl-], -z
Gruenther (American surname) 'grʌnθə*
gruesome, -ly, -ness 'gru:səm, -li, -nis
gruff, -er, -est, -ly, -ness grʌf, -ə*, -ist, -li, -nis
grumb|le, -les, -ling, -led, -ler/s 'grʌmb|l, -lz, -liŋ, -ld, -lə*/z
grump|y, -ier, -iest, -ily, -iness 'grʌmp|i, -ɪə* [-jə*], -iist [-jist], -ili, -inis
Grundig 'grundig
Grundtvig (English surname) 'gruntvig
Grundy 'grʌndi
grunt (s. v.), -s, -ing, -ed, -er/s grʌnt, -s, -iŋ, -id, -ə*/z
Gruyère 'gru:jɛə* (gryjɛ:r)
gryphon, -s 'grifən, -z
Guadalquivir ,gwɑ:dəl'kwivə* [,gwɑ:dəlki'viə*] (gwadalki'bir)
Guadeloupe ,gwɑ:də'lu:p
Guaira 'gwaiərə
guano, -s 'gwɑ:nəu [gju(:)'ɑ:nəu], -z
Guarani, -s ,gwɑ:rə'ni:, -z
guarantee (s. v.), -s, -ing, -d ,gærən'ti:, -z, -iŋ, -d
guarantor, -s ,gærən'tɔ:* [gə'ræntɔ:*], -z
guarant|y, -ies 'gærənt|i, -iz
guard (s. v.) (G.), -s, -ing, -ed/ly, -edness gɑ:d, -z, -iŋ, -id/li, -idnis
guardian (G.), -s; -ship 'gɑ:djən [-dɪən], -z; -ʃip
guardrail, -s 'gɑ:d-reil, -z
guard-room, -s 'gɑ:d-rum [-ru:m], -z
guard-ship, -s 'gɑ:dʃip, -s
guards|man, -men 'gɑ:dz|mən [-mæn], -mən [-men]
Guarner|i, -ius/es gwɑ:'niər|i, -ɪəs/iz
Guatemala, -n/s ,gwæti'mɑ:lə [,gwɑ:t-], -n/z
guava, -s 'gwɑ:və, -z
Guayaquil ,gwaiə'ki:l [-'kil]
Guayra (old-fashioned spelling of Guaira) 'gwaiərə
Gubbins 'gʌbinz
gudgeon, -s 'gʌdʒən, -z

Gudrun 'gudru:n [gu'd-]
Gue gju:
Guedalla gwi'dælə [gwe'd-, gwə'd-]
guelder-rose, -s 'geldə'rəuz, -iz
Guelph gwelf
guerdon, -s 'gə:dən, -z
guerilla gə'rilə
guernsey (G.), -s 'gə:nzi, -z
guerrilla, -s gə'rilə, -z
guess (s. v.), -es, -ing, -ed, -er/s; -able, -work ges, -iz, -iŋ, -t, -ə*/z; -əbl, -wə:k
guest (G.), -s gest, -s
guest-chamber, -s 'gest,tʃeimbə*, -z
guest-hou|se, -ses 'gesthau|s, -ziz
guest-night, -s 'gestnait, -s
guest-room, -s 'gest-rum [-ru:m], -z
guest-towel, -s 'gest,tauəl [-taul], -z
guffaw (s. v.), -s, -ing, -ed gʌ'fɔ: [gə'f-], -z, -iŋ, -d
Guggisberg (English surname) 'gʌgis-bə:g
Guiana gai'ænə [old-fashioned British pronunciation gi'ɑ:nə]
Note.—The local pronunciation is gai'ænə.
Guianese ,gaiə'ni:z
guid|e (s. v.), -es, -ing, -ed; -ance gaid, -z, -iŋ, -id; -əns
guide-book, -s 'gaidbuk, -s
guide-post, -s 'gaidpəust, -s
guide-rail, -s 'gaid-reil, -z
guide-rope, -s 'gaid-rəup, -s
Guido 'gwi:dəu
guidon, -s 'gaidən, -z
guild, -s gild, -z
Guildenstern 'gildənstə:n
guilder, -s 'gildə*, -z
Guildford 'gilfəd
guildhall (G.), -s 'gild'hɔ:l [also '— esp. when attributive], -z
Guilding 'gildiŋ
guile gail
guile|ful, -fully, -fulness 'gail|ful, -fuli [-fəli], -fulnis
guileless, -ly, -ness 'gaillis, -li, -nis
Guilford 'gilfəd
Guillamore 'giləmɔ:* [-mɔə*]
Guillebaud (English surname) 'gi:lbəu, 'gilibəu
guillemot, -s 'gilimɔt, -s
Guillim 'gwilim
guillotin|e (s. v.), -es, -ing, -ed ,gilə'ti:n ['gilət-], -z, -iŋ, -d
Note.—Some people use '—— for the noun and ,—'- for the verb.
guilt, -y, -ier, -iest, -ily, -iness gilt, -i, -ɪə* [-jə*], -iist [-jist], -ili, -inis

guiltless, -ly, -ness 'giltlis, -li, -nis
guinea (G.), -s 'gini, -z
guinea|-corn, -fowl/s, -pig/s 'gini|
 kɔ:n, -faul/z, -pig/z
Guinevere 'gwiniviə* ['gin-]
Guinness 'ginis, gi'nes
    Note.—Some members of the family
    of Lord Iveagh call themselves
    gi'nes; others call themselves 'ginis.
    The beer is called 'ginis.
Guisborough (in Yorks.) 'gizbərə
guise, -s gaiz, -iz
Guise gi:z [gwi:z] (gɥi:z, gi:z)
Guiseley 'gaizli
guitar, -s gi'tɑ:*, -z
guitarist, -s gi'tɑ:rist, -s
Guiver 'gaivə*
Gujarat ˌgu:dʒə'rɑ:t [ˌgudʒ-] (Hind.
    gwʝrat)
Gujarati ˌgu(:)dʒə'rɑ:ti (Hind. gwʝrati)
gulch (s. v.), -es gʌlʃ, -iz
gulden, -s 'guldən ['gu:l-], -z
gules gju:lz
gulf, -s; -y gʌlf, -s; -i
gull (s. v.) (G.), -s, -ing, -ed gʌl, -z, -iŋ,
    -d
gull-catcher, -s 'gʌlˌkætʃə*, -z
guller|y, -ies 'gʌlər|i, -iz
gullet, -s 'gʌlit, -s
gullibility ˌgʌli'biliti [-lə'b-, -lət-]
gullible 'gʌləbl [-lib-]
Gulliver 'gʌlivə*
gull|y (G.), -ies 'gʌl|i, -iz
gulp (s. v.), -s, -ing, -ed gʌlp, -s, -iŋ, -t
gum (s. v.) (all senses), -s, -ming, -med,
    -mer/s gʌm, -z, -iŋ, -d, -ə*/z
gumboil, -s 'gʌmbɔil, -z
Gummere 'gʌməri
Gummidge 'gʌmidʒ
gumm|y (s. adj.), -ies, -ier, -iest, -iness
    'gʌm|i, -iz, -iə*, -iist, -inis
gumption 'gʌmpʃən
gum-tree, -s 'gʌm-tri:, -z
gun (s. v.), -s, -ning, -ned, -ner/s gʌn,
    -z, -iŋ, -d, -ə*/z
gun|-barrel/s, -boat/s, -carriage/s,
    -case/s, -cotton 'gʌn|ˌbærəl/z,
    -bəut/s, -ˌkæridʒ/iz, -keis/iz, -ˌkɔtn
Gunby Hadath 'gʌnbi'hædəθ
gun-drill 'gʌn-dril
gun-fire 'gʌnˌfaiə*
gun|man, -men 'gʌn|mən [-mæn],
    -mən [-men]
gun-metal 'gʌnˌmetl
gunnel, -s 'gʌnl, -z
Gunner 'gʌnə*
Gunnersbury 'gʌnəzbəri
gunnery 'gʌnəri

Gunning 'gʌniŋ
Gunnison 'gʌnisn
gunny 'gʌni
gunpowder 'gʌnˌpaudə*
gun-room, -s 'gʌnrum [-ru:m], -z
gun-runn|er/s, -ing 'gʌnˌrʌn|ə*/z, -iŋ
gunshot, -s 'gʌn-ʃɔt, -s
gunsmith, -s 'gʌn-smiθ, -s
gun-stock, -s 'gʌn-stɔk, -s
Gunt|er, -ram 'gʌnt|ə*, -rəm
gunwale, -s 'gʌnl, -z
Gupta 'guptə (Hind. gwpta)
gurg|le (s. v.), -les, -ling, -led 'gə:g|l,
    -lz, -liŋ, -ld
Gurkha, -s 'guəkə ['gə:k-], -z
Gurley 'gə:li
Gurnall 'gə:nl
gurnard (G.), -s 'gə:nəd, -z
gurnet, -s 'gə:nit, -s
Gur|ney, -ton 'gə:|ni, -tn
guru, -s 'guru: ['gu:r-, 'guər-] (Hind.
    gwru), -z
Gus gʌs
gush (s. v.), -es, -ing/ly, -ed, -er/s gʌʃ;
    -iz, -iŋ/li, -t, -ə*/z
Gushington 'gʌʃiŋtən
gusset, -s 'gʌsit, -s
Guss|ie, -y 'gʌs|i, -i,
gust, -s gʌst, -s
gustation gʌs'teiʃən
gustatory 'gʌstətəri
Gustavus gus'tɑ:vəs [gʌs-]
gusto 'gʌstəu
gust|y, -ier, -iest, -ily, -iness 'gʌst|i,
    -iə* [-jə*], -iist [-jist], -ili, -inis
gut (s. v.), -s, -ting, -ted gʌt, -s, -iŋ, -id
Gutenberg 'gu:tnbə:g
Guthrie 'gʌθri
gutta-percha 'gʌtə'pə:tʃə [ˌ--'--]
gutter (s. v.), -s, -ing, -ed 'gʌtə*, -z,
    -riŋ, -d
guttersnipe, -s 'gʌtə-snaip, -s
guttur|al (s. adj.), -als, -ally 'gʌtər|əl,
    -əlz, -əli
guy (G.), -s gai, -z
Guyda (Christian name) 'gaidə
Guy Fawkes 'gai'fɔ:ks
Guysborough 'gaizbərə
Guzman (character in Kingsley's ' West-
    ward Ho!') 'gʌzmən ['guzm-, 'guθ-
    mɑ:n]
guzz|le, -les, -ling, -led, -ler/s 'gʌz|l, -lz,
    -liŋ [-liŋ], -ld, -lə*/z [-lə*/z]
Gwalia 'gwɑ:ljə [-liə]
Gwalior 'gwɑ:liɔ:* [-ljɔ:*] (Hind.
    gvalyər)
Gwatkin 'gwɔtkin
Gwen gwen

Gwendo|len, -line, -lyn 'gwendə|lin, -lin [-liːn], -lin
Gwinear 'gwiniə*
Gwinnett gwi'net
Gwladys 'glædis (Welsh 'gwladɨs)
Gwrych gu'riːk [-'riːx] (Welsh gwrɨːx)
Gwydyr 'gwidiə* [-də*] (Welsh 'gwɨdir)
gwyniad, -s 'gwiniæd, -z
Gwyn(ne) gwin
Gye dʒai, gai
Gyges 'gaidʒiːz
Gyle (surname) gail
gym dʒim
gymkhana, -s dʒim'kɑːnə, -z
gymnasium, -s dʒim'neizjəm [-zɨəm], -z
gymnast, -s 'dʒimnæst, -s
gymnastic, -s, -al, -ally dʒim'næstik, -s, -əl, -əli
gymnosophist, -s dʒim'nɔsəfist, -s
Gympie 'gimpi
gynaecological ˌgainikə'lɔdʒikəl [-niːk-]
gynaecolog|ist/s, -y ˌgaini'kɔlədʒ|ist/s [-niː'k-], -i
Gyngell 'gindʒə i

gyp, -s dʒip, -s
Gyp (nickname) dʒip, (French authoress) ʒip (ʒip)
gyps|eous, -ous 'dʒips|iəs [-jəs], -əs
gypsophila, -s dʒip'sɔfilə, -z
gypsum 'dʒipsəm
gyps|y, -ies 'dʒips|i, -iz
gyrate (adj.) 'dʒaiərit ['dʒaiəreit]
gyrat|e (v.), -es, -ing, -ed ˌdʒaiə'reit, -s, -iŋ, -id
gyration, -s ˌdʒaiə'reiʃən, -z
gyratory 'dʒaiərətəri [ˌdʒaiə'reitəri]
gyr|e (s. v.), -es, -ing, -ed 'dʒaiə*, -z, -riŋ, -d
gyrodine, -s 'dʒaiərəudain, -z
gyromancy 'dʒaiərəumænsi
gyron, -s 'dʒaiərən [-rɔn], -z
gyroscope, -s 'dʒaiərəskəup ['gaiə-], -s
gyroscopic ˌdʒaiərəs'kɔpik [ˌgaiə-]
gyrosin, -s 'dʒaiərəuzin, -z
gyrostat, -s 'dʒaiərəustæt ['gaiə-], -s
gyrostatic, -s ˌdʒaiərəus'tætik [ˌgaiə-], -s
gyv|e, -es, -ing, -ed dʒaiv, -z, -iŋ, -d

H

H (*the letter*), -'s eitʃ, -iz
ha hɑ:
Haakon 'hɔ:kɔn ['hɑ:k-, -kən]
Haarlem 'hɑ:lem [-ləm]
Habakkuk 'hæbəkək [-kʌk, hə'bækək]
Habberton 'hæbətən
habeas corpus 'heibjəs'kɔ:pəs [-bïəs-, -biæs-]
habendum hə'bendəm [hæ'b-]
haberdasher, -s, -y 'hæbədæʃə*, -z, ˌ-ri
habergeon, -s 'hæbədʒən, -z
Habershon 'hæbəʃən
habiliment, -s hə'bilimənt [hæ'b-, *also occasionally* ə'b- *when not initial*], -s
habilitat|e, -es, -ing, -ed, -or/s hə'biliteit [hæ'b-, *also occasionally* ə'b- *when not initial*], -s, -iŋ, -id, -ə*/z
habilitation həˌbili'teiʃən [hæˌb-, *also occasionally* əˌb- *when not initial*]
Habington 'hæbiŋtən
habit (*s. v.*), -s, -ing, -ed 'hæbit, -s, -iŋ, -id
habitab|le, -ly, -leness 'hæbitəb|l, -li, -lnis
habitant (*inhabitant*), -s 'hæbitənt, -s
habitant (*Canadian*), -s 'hæbitɔ̃:ŋ ['æb-, -tɔŋ] (abitɑ̃), -z
habitat, -s 'hæbitæt, -s
habitation, -s ˌhæbi'teiʃən, -z
habitual, -ly hə'bitjʊəl [hæ'b-, -tjwəl, -tjul, -tjüəl, -tʃwəl, -tʃul, *also occasionally* ə'b- *when not initial*], -i
habituat|e, -es, -ing, -ed hə'bitjueit [hæ'b-, -tʃueit, *also occasionally* ə'b- *when not initial*], -s, -iŋ, -id
habitude, -s 'hæbitju:d, -z
habitué, -s hə'bitjuei [hæ'b-, *also occasionally* ə'b- *when not initial*] (abitye), -z
Habsburg 'hæpsbə:g
hachures hæ'ʃjuə* [-'ʃuə*]
hacienda, -s ˌhæsi'endə, -z
hack (*s. v.*) (H.), -s, -ing, -ed, -er/s hæk, -s, -iŋ, -t, -ə*/z
hackberr|y, -ies 'hækber|i [-bər|i], -iz
hacker|y, -ies 'hækər|i, -iz
Hackett 'hækit
hack|le (*s. v.*), -les, -ling, -led 'hæk|l, -lz, -l̩iŋ [-liŋ], -ld

hackney (*s. v.*) (H.), -s, -ing, -ed 'hækni, -z, -iŋ ['hæknjiŋ], -d
hacksaw, -s 'hæksɔ:, -z
hackwork 'hækwə:k
had (*from* have) hæd (*strong form*), həd, əd, d (*weak forms*)
Hadad 'heidæd
Hadadezer ˌhædə'di:zə*
Hadar (*star*) 'heidɑ:*
Hadath 'hædəθ
Haddington 'hædiŋtən
haddock (H.), -s 'hædək, -s
Haddon 'hædn
had|e, -es, -ing, -ed heid, -z, -iŋ, -id
Haden 'heidn
Hades 'heidi:z
Hadfield 'hædfi:ld
hadji, -s 'hædʒi(:), -z
Had|leigh, -ley, -low 'hæd|li, -li, -ləu
hadn't 'hædnt [*also* 'hædn *when not final*]
Hadow 'hædəu
Hadrian 'heidrïən
hadst hædst (*strong form*), hədst, ədst (*weak forms*)
Hadubrand 'hædubrænd
haemal 'hi:məl
haematite 'hemətait
haemoglobin ˌhi:məu'gləubin ['--'--]
haemophilia ˌhi:məu'filïə
haemorrhage, -s 'heməridʒ, -iz
haemorrhoid, -s 'hemərɔid, -z
Haes (*English surname*) heiz
haft, -s hɑ:ft, -s
hag, -s hæg, -s
Hagar (*biblical name*) 'heigɑ:* [-gə*], (*modern personal name*) 'heigə*
Hagarene, -s 'hægəri:n [ˌ--'-, ˌheigɑ:-'ri:n], -z
hagberr|y, -ies 'hægber|i [-bər|i], -iz
Hagerstown 'heigəztaun
Haggai 'hægeiai [-giai, -gai, hæ'geiai]
haggard (H.), -est 'hægəd, -ist
Hagger, -ston 'hægə*, -stən
haggis, -es 'hægis, -iz
haggish, -ly, -ness 'hægiʃ, -li, -nis
hagg|le, -les, -ling, -led, -ler/s 'hæg|l, -lz, -l̩iŋ [-liŋ], -ld, -l̩ə*/z [-lə*/z]
hagio|grapher/s, -graphy ˌhægi'ɔ-|grəfə*/z, -grəfi

hagiolatry ˌhægi'ɔlətri
hagiolog|ist/s, -y ˌhægi'ɔlədʒ|ist/s, -i
hagioscope, -s 'hægiəskəup [-gjəs-], -s
hag-seed 'hægsi:d
Hague heig
hag-weed 'hægwi:d
ha-ha hɑ:'hɑ:
Haidarabad 'haidərəbæd ['haidərə'b-,
   ˌhaidərə'b-] (Hind. həydərabad)
Haidee hai'di:
Haifa 'haifə
Haig heig
Haigh heig, hei
hail (s. v. interj.), -s, -ing, -ed; -y heil,
   -z, -iŋ, -d; -i
Hailes heilz
Haile Selassie 'hailisi'læsi
Haileybury 'heilibəri
hail-fellow, -s 'heil,feləu, -z
hail-fellow-well-met 'heil,feləu'wel'met
Hailsham 'heilʃəm
hailstone, -s 'heil-stəun, -z
hailstorm, -s 'heil-stɔ:m, -z
Hainan hai'næn ['-'-]
Hainault (forest) 'heinɔ:t [-nɔ:lt, -nɔlt]
Hainhault 'heinɔ:lt
hair, -s hɛə*, -z
hair-breadth, -s 'hɛə-bredθ [-bretθ], -s
hairbrush, -es 'hɛə-brʌʃ, -iz
haircloth 'hɛə-klɔθ [-klɔ:θ]
haircut, -s 'hɛə-kʌt, -s
haircutt|er/s, -ing 'hɛə,kʌt|ə*/z, -iŋ
hair-do, -s 'hɛə-du:, -z
hairdresser, -s 'hɛə,dresə*, -z
hair-dye, -s 'hɛə-dai, -z
hairgrass 'hɛə-grɑ:s
hairless 'hɛəlis
hair-line, -s 'hɛəlain, -z
hair-net, -s 'hɛənet, -s
hair-oil 'hɛərɔil ['hɛəɔil]
hairpin, -s 'hɛəpin, -z
hair's-breadth, -s 'hɛəzbredθ [-bretθ],
   -s
hair-shirt, -s 'hɛə'ʃə:t ['--], -s
hair-slide, -s 'hɛə-slaid, -z
hair-space, -s 'hɛə-speis, -iz
hair-splitting 'hɛə,splitiŋ
hair-spring, -s 'hɛə-spriŋ, -z
hair-stroke, -s 'hɛə-strəuk, -s
hair|y, -ier, -iest, -ily, -iness 'hɛər|i,
   -iə*, -iist, -ili, -inis
Haiti 'heiti
Haitian, -s 'heiʃjən [-ʃiən, -ʃən, 'heitjən,
   -tiən], -z
hake, -s heik, -s
Hakluyt 'hæklu:t
Hakodate ˌhækəu'dɑ:ti
Hal hæl

halation, -s hə'leiʃən [hæ'l-], -z
halberd, -s 'hælbə(:)d ['hɔ:l-], -z
halberdier, -s ˌhælbə(:)'diə*, -z
halcyon, -s 'hælsiən [-sjən], -z
Halcyone hæl'saiəni
Hald|ane, -on 'hɔ:ld|ein ['hɔl-], -ən
hal|e (adj. v.) (H.), -er, -est; -es, -ing,
   -ed heil, -ə*, -ist; -z, -iŋ, -d
Hales, -worth heilz, -wə:θ
hal|f, -ves hɑ:|f, -vz
   Note 1.—Words not entered below
   which are formed by prefixing half-
   to a participle have double stress
   e.g. half-done 'hɑ:f'dʌn, half-
   ashamed 'hɑ:f-ə'ʃeimd, half-dressed
   'hɑ:f'drest.
   Note 2.—Half past, in half past ten,
   half past eleven, etc., is pronounced 'hɑ:pəs(t) by many:
   'hɑ:pəs 'ten, 'hɑ:pəst i'levn, etc.
half a crown 'hɑ:fə'kraun [also '—,
   ˌ-'- according to sentence-stress]
half a dozen 'hɑ:fə'dʌzn [also '—ˌ-,
   ˌ-'- according to sentence-stress]
half and half 'hɑ:fənd'hɑ:f
half-back, -s 'hɑ:f'bæk ['--], -s
half-baked 'hɑ:f'beikt ['--]
half-binding 'hɑ:f,baindiŋ
half-blood 'hɑ:fblʌd
half-bound 'hɑ:f'baund ['--]
half-bred 'hɑ:fbred
half|-breed/s, -brother/s, -caste/s 'hɑ:f|-
   bri:d/z, -ˌbrʌðə*/z, -kɑ:st/s
half-crown, -s 'hɑ:f'kraun [also -'-
   when preceded by a stress], -z
half-dozen, -s 'hɑ:f'dʌzn [also '-ˌ—, -'-—,
   according to sentence-stress], -z
half-hardy 'hɑ:f'hɑ:di [also '-ˌ— when
   attributive]
half-hearted 'hɑ:f'hɑ:tid ['hɑ:f,h-, esp.
   when attributive]
half-hearted|ly, -ness 'hɑ:f'hɑ:tid|li, -nis
half-holiday, -s 'hɑ:f'hɔlədi [-lid-, -dei],
   -z
half-hose 'hɑ:f'həuz ['--]
half-hour, -s 'hɑ:f'auə* [also '—, -'-
   according to sentence-stress], -z
half-hourly 'hɑ:f'auəli
half-length, -s 'hɑ:f'leŋθ [-ŋkθ, '--], -s
half-mast 'hɑ:f'mɑ:st
half-measure, -s 'hɑ:f'meʒə* ['-ˌ—], -z
half-moon, -s 'hɑ:f'mu:n [also -'- when
   preceded by a stress], -z
half-mourning 'hɑ:f'mɔ:niŋ [-'mɔən-]
half-nelson 'hɑ:f'nelsn
Halford 'hɔ:lfəd ['hɔl-], 'hæl-
half-pay 'hɑ:f'pei
halfpence 'heipəns

halfpenn|y, -ies; -yworth/s 'heipn|i [-pn̩|i, -pən|i], -iz; -iwə:θ/s ['heipəθ/s]
Halfpenny 'hɑːfpeni [-pəni]
half-plate, -s 'hɑːfpleit, -s
half-price 'hɑːf'prais [also '—, -'-, according to sentence-stress]
half-seas-over 'hɑːfsi:z'əuvə*
half-shift, -s 'hɑːf'ʃift ['—], -s
half-sister, -s 'hɑːf,sistə*, -z
half-size 'hɑːf'saiz [also '— when attributive]
half-sovereign, -s 'hɑːf'sovrin, -z
half-tide 'hɑːf'taid ['—]
half-time, -r/s 'hɑːf'taim, -ə*/z
half-tint, -s 'hɑːf'tint, -s
half-tone, -s 'hɑːf'təun, -z
half-tru|th, -ths 'hɑːf-tru:|θ, -ðz
half-volley, -s 'hɑːf'voli, -z
half-way 'hɑːf'wei [also '—, -'- according to sentence-stress]
half-witted 'hɑːf'witid [also '-,— when attributive]
half-year, -s 'hɑːf'jə:* [-'jiə*], -z
half-yearly 'hɑːf'jə:li [-'jiəli]
Haliburton 'hælibə:tn
halibut 'hælibət [-bʌt]
Halicarnassus ,hælikɑː'næsəs
halidom 'hælidəm
Halidon 'hælidən
Halifax 'hælifæks
Halkett 'hɔːlkit, 'hælkit, 'hækit
hall (H.), -s hɔːl, -z
Hallam 'hæləm
Hallé 'hælei [-li]
hallelujah (H.), -s ,hæli'lu:jə, -z
Haller 'hælə*
Halley 'hæli
halliard = halyard
Halli|day, -well 'hæli|dei, -wəl [-wel]
hall-mark (s. v.), -s, -ing, -ed 'hɔːl-mɑːk ['-'-], -s, -iŋ, -t
hallo(a) hə'ləu ['hʌ'ləu, rarely 'hæ'ləu, hæ'ləu]
halloo (s. v. interj.), -s, -ing, -ed hə'lu: [hæ'l-], -z, -iŋ, -d
hall|ow, -ows, -owing, -owed 'hæl|əu, -əuz, -əuiŋ, -əud
Hallowe'en 'hæləu'i:n [,hæ-]
Hallowmas, -es 'hæləumæs [-məs], -iz
Hallows 'hæləuz
hallucination, -s hə,lu:si'neiʃən [-,lju:-, also occasionally ə,l- when not initial], -z
hallucinatory hə'lu:sinətəri [-'lju:-, hə,lu:si'neitəri]
halm, -s hɑːm, -z
halma 'hælmə
halo (s.), -(e)s 'heiləu, -z

hall|o (v.), -oes, -oing, -oed 'heil|əu, -əuz, -əuiŋ, -əud
Halpine 'hælpin
Hals (Dutch artist), -es hæls [hælz], -iz
Halsbury 'hɔːlzbəri ['hɔl-]
Halsey 'hɔːlsi, 'hɔːlzi, 'hælzi
Halstead 'hɔːlsted ['hɔl-, -stid], 'hæl-
halt (s. adj. v.), -s, -ing/ly, -ed hɔːlt [hɔlt], -s, -iŋ/li, -id
halter, -s 'hɔːltə* ['hɔl-], -z
halv|e, -es, -ing, -ed hɑːv, -z, -iŋ, -d
halves (plur. of half) hɑːvz
halyard, -s 'hæljəd, -z
Halys 'heilis
ham (H.), -s hæm, -z   [-z
hamadryad, -s ,hæmə'drai-əd [-'draiæd],
Haman (biblical name) 'heimæn [-mən], (modern surname) 'heimən
Hamar 'heimɑː*
Hamath 'heimæθ
Hamble, -den, -don, -ton 'hæmbl, -dən, -dən, -tən
Hamblin 'hæmblin
Hambourg 'hæmbə:g [-buəg]
Hambro 'hæmbrə
Hamburg 'hæmbə:g
hamburger, -s 'hæmbə:gə*, -z
hamburg(h), -s 'hæmbərə, -z
Hamelin 'hæmilin
Hamerton 'hæmətən
ham-fisted 'hæm'fistid
ham-handed 'hæm,hændid ['-'-—]
Hamilcar hæ'milkɑː* [hə'm-, 'hæmil-]
Hamilton 'hæmiltən
Hamiltonian ,hæmil'təunjən [-niən]
Hamish 'heimiʃ
Hamite, -s 'hæmait, -s
Hamitic hæ'mitik [hə'm-]
hamlet (H.), -s 'hæmlit, -s
Haml|ey, -in 'hæml|i, -in
hammam, -s 'hæmæm [-məm, hə'mɑːm, 'hʌmʌm], -z
hammer (s. v.) (H.), -s, -ing, -ed 'hæmə*, -z, -riŋ, -d
hammer-blow, -s 'hæmə-bləu, -z
Hammerfest 'hæməfest
hammer-head, -s 'hæməhed, -z
Hammersmith 'hæməsmiθ
hammock, -s 'hæmək, -s
Ham(m)ond 'hæmənd
Hammurabi ,hæmu'rɑːbi
Hampden 'hæmpdən, 'hæmdən
hamper (s. v.), -s, -ing, -ed 'hæmpə*, -z, -riŋ, -d
Hampshire 'hæmpʃiə* [-ʃə*]
Hamp|stead, -ton 'hæmp|stid [-sted], [-tən
Hamshaw 'hæmʃɔː
hamster, -s 'hæmstə*, -z

hamstring (s. v.), -s, -ing, -ed, ham-
strung 'hæm-striŋ, -z, -iŋ, -d,
'hæm-strʌŋ
hamza, -s 'hæmzə, -z
Han (Chinese dynasty) hæn
Hanan 'hænən
Hananiah ˌhænə'naiə
Hanbury 'hænbəri
Hancock 'hænkɔk
hand (s. v.) (H.), -s; hand|ing, -ed, -er/s
hænd, -z; 'hænd|iŋ, -id, -ə*/z
hand|-bag/s, -barrow/s, -bell/s, -bill/s,
-book/s, -cart/s 'hænd|bæg/z,
-ˌbærəu/z, -bel/z, -bil/z, -buk/s,
-kɑ:t/s
Handcock 'hændkɔk
handcuff (s. v.), -s, -ing, -ed 'hændkʌf,
-s, -iŋ, -t
Handel 'hændl
Handelian hæn'di:ljən [-lïən]
handful, -s hændful, -z
hand-glass, -es 'hændglɑ:s, -iz
hand-grenade, -s 'hændgri,neid [-grə,n-,
-gre,n-, '--'-], -z
handgrip, -s 'hændgrip, -s
handhold, -s 'hændhəuld, -z
handicap (s. v.), -s, -ping, -ped, -per/s
'hændikæp, -s, -iŋ, -t, -ə*/z
handi|craft/s, -work 'hændi|krɑ:ft/s,
-wə:k
handkerchief, -s 'hæŋkətʃif, -s
Note.—There exists also a pronunciation 'hæŋkətʃi:f with a plural
-tʃi:fs or -tʃi:vz.
hand|le (s. v.), -les, -ling, -led, -ler/s
'hænd|l, -lz, -liŋ [-ˌliŋ], -ld, -lə*/z
[-ˌə*/z]
handle-bar, -s 'hændlbɑ:*, -z
handless 'hændlis
Handley 'hændli
hand|-line/s, -loom/s 'hænd|lain/z,
-lu:m/z
hand-made 'hænd'meid [also '-- when
attributive]
hand-maid, -s, -en/s 'hændmeid, -z, -n/z
hand-out, -s 'hændaut, -s
hand-rail, -s 'hænd-reil, -z
Hands hændz
hand-screen, -s 'hændskri:n, -z
handsel = hansel
handshake, -s 'hændʃeik, -s
handsome, -r, -st, -ly, -ness 'hænsəm,
-ə*, -ist, -li, -nis
handwork 'hænd-wə:k
hand-worked 'hænd'wə:kt['hænd-wə:kt]
handwriting, -s 'hænd,raitiŋ, -z
hand|y, -ier, -iest, -ily, -iness 'hænd|i,
-ïə* [-jə*], -iist [-jist], -ili, -inis

handy-man, -men 'hændimæn [-mən],
-men
hang, -s, -ing/s, -ed, hung, hanger/s
hæŋ, -z, -iŋ/z, -d, hʌŋ, 'hæŋə*/z
hangar, -s 'hæŋə* [-ŋgə*, -ŋgɑ:*], -z
hang-dog (s. adj.), -s 'hæŋdɔg, -z
Hanger 'hæŋə*
hanger-on, hangers-on 'hæŋər'ɔn,
'hæŋəz'ɔn
hang|man, -men 'hæŋ|mən, -mən
hang-nail, -s 'hæŋ,neil, -z
hang-over, -s 'hæŋˌəuvə*, -z
hank, -s hæŋk, -s
hank|er, -ers, -ering, -ered 'hæŋk|ə*,
-əz, -əriŋ, -əd
Hankow hæn'kau [hæŋ'k-, '-'-]
hank|y, -ies 'hæŋk|i, -iz
hanky-panky 'hæŋki'pæŋki ['--,--]
Hanley 'hænli
Hannah 'hænə
Hann|ay, -en 'hæn|ei, -ən
Hannibal 'hænibəl
Hannington 'hæniŋtən
Hanoi hæ'nɔi
Hanover 'hænəuvə* (ha'no:vər)
Hanoverian, -s ˌhænəu'viərïən, -z
Hansa 'hænsə [-nzə]
Hansard 'hænsɑ:d [-səd]
Hanse, -s hæns, -iz
Hanseatic ˌhænsi'ætik [-nzi-]
hans|el, -els, -elling, -elled 'hæns|əl,
-əlz, -əliŋ [-ˌliŋ], -əld
Hänsel (German name) 'hænsəl ('hɛnzəl)
Hans|ell, -on 'hæns|l, -n
hansom (H.), -s; -cab/s 'hænsəm, -z;
-'kæb/z
Hants hænts
Han|way, -well 'hæn|wei, -wəl [-wel]
hap (s. v.), -s, -ping, -ped hæp, -s, -iŋ, -t
haphazard 'hæp'hæzəd [hæp'h-]
hapless, -ly, -ness 'hæplis, -li, -nis
haply 'hæpli
hap'orth, -s 'heipəθ, -s
happ|en, -ens, -ening/s -ened 'hæp|ən,
-ənz, -ɲiŋ/z [-əniŋ/z, -niŋ/z], -ənd
Happisburgh (in Norfolk) 'heizbərə
happ|y, -ier, -iest, -ily, -iness 'hæp|i,
-ïə*, -iist, -ili, -inis
happy-go-lucky 'hæpigəu'lʌki ['--,--]
Hapsburg 'hæpsbə:g
hara-kiri 'hærə'kiri
harangu|e (s. v.), -es, -ing, -ed, -er/s
hə'ræŋ [also occasionally ə'r- when
not initial], -z, -iŋ, -d, -ə*/z
harass, -es, -ing, -ed, -er/s 'hærəs, -iz,
-iŋ, -t, -ə*/z
Harben 'hɑ:bən
Harberton 'hɑ:bətən
harbinger, -s 'hɑ:bindʒə*, -z

Harborough 'hɑ:bərə
harb|our (s. v.), -ours, -ouring, -oured,
-ourer/s; -ourage, -ourless 'hɑ:b|ə*,
-əz, -əriŋ, -əd, -ərə*/z; -əridʒ, -əlis
harbour-master, -s 'hɑ:bə,mɑ:stə*, -z
Harcourt 'hɑ:kət [-kɔ:t]
hard (H.), -er, -est, -ly, -ness hɑ:d, -ə*,
-ist, -li, -nis
hardbake (s.) 'hɑ:dbeik
hard-baked 'hɑ:d'beikt ['--]
hard-bitten 'hɑ:d'bitn ['--]
hardboard 'hɑ:dbɔ:d [-bəəd]
hard-boiled 'hɑ:d'bɔild ['-- when attri-
butive]
Hardcastle 'hɑ:d,kɑ:sl
hard-earned 'hɑ:d'ə:nd [also '-- when
attributive]
hard|en (H.), -ens, -ening, -ened
'hɑ:d|n, -nz, -niŋ [-niŋ], -nd
hard-featured 'hɑ:d'fi:tʃəd ['-,--]
hard-fought 'hɑ:d'fɔ:t ['--]
hard-grained 'hɑ:d'greind ['--]
hard-headed 'hɑ:d'hedid [also '-,--, -'--
according to sentence-stress]
hard-hearted, -ly, -ness 'hɑ:d'hɑ:tid
[also '-,--, -'-- according to sentence-
stress], -li, -nis
Hardicanute 'hɑ:dikənju:t ['hɑ:dikə'n-]
hardihood 'hɑ:dihud
Harding(e) 'hɑ:diŋ
hard|ish, -ly 'hɑ:d|iʃ, -li
Hardres hɑ:dz
Hardress 'hɑ:dres [-dris]
hardship, -s 'hɑ:dʃip, -s
hard-up 'hɑ:d'ʌp [-'-]
hardware 'hɑ:d-weə*
Hardwick(e) 'hɑ:d-wik
hardwood 'hɑ:d-wud
hard|y (H.), -ier, -iest, -ily, -iness,
-ihood 'hɑ:d|i, -iə* [-jə*], -iist [-jist],
-ili, -inis, -ihud
hare (H.), -s; -bell/s, -brained heə*,
-z; -bel/z, -breind
harelip, -s -ped 'heə'lip ['--], -s, -t
harem, -s 'heərəm [-rem, hə'ri:m,
hɑ:'ri:m, 'hɑ:ri:m], -z
Harenc (surname) 'hʌrəŋ
hare's-foot 'heəzfut
Harewood 'hɑ:wud, 'heəwud
   Note.—The Earl of Harewood pronounces 'hɑ:wud, and his house is
called 'hɑ:wud 'haus. The village
in Yorks. is now generally pronounced 'heəwud, though 'hɑ:wud
may sometimes be heard from very
old people there. Other people with
the surname Harewood pronounce
'heəwud.

Har|ford, -graves 'hɑ:|fəd, -greivz
Hargreaves 'hɑ:gri:vz, -greivz
haricot, -s 'hærikəu, -z
Harington 'hæriŋtən
hark (v. interj.), -s, -ing, -ed hɑ:k, -s,
-iŋ, -t
Harlaw 'hɑ:lɔ: [hɑ:'lɔ:]
Harlech 'hɑ:lek [-lex]
Harleian hɑ:'li(:)ən ['hɑ:liən, esp. when
attributive]
Harlem 'hɑ:ləm [-lem]
harlequin, -s 'hɑ:likwin, -z
harlequinade, -s ,hɑ:likwi'neid, -z
Harlesden 'hɑ:lzdən
Harley 'hɑ:li
Harlock 'hɑ:lɔk
harlot, -s, -ry 'hɑ:lət, -s, -ri
Harlow(e) 'hɑ:ləu
harm (s. v.), -s, -ing, -ed hɑ:m, -z, -iŋ, -d
Harman 'hɑ:mən
Harmer 'hɑ:mə*
harm|ful, -fully, -fulness 'hɑ:m|fʊl,
-fuli [-fəli], -fʊlnis
harmless, -ly, -ness 'hɑ:mlis, -li, -nis
Harmonia hɑ:'məunjə [-niə]
harmonic (s. adj.), -s, -al, -ally
hɑ:'mɔnik, -s, -əl, -əli
harmonic|a/s, -on/s hɑ:'mɔnik|ə/z,
-ən/z
harmonious, -ly, -ness hɑ:'məunjəs
[-niəs], -li, -nis
harmonist, -s 'hɑ:mənist, -s
harmonium, -s hɑ:'məunjəm [-niəm], -z
harmonization [-isa-], -s ,hɑ:mənai-
'zeiʃən, -z
harmoniz|e [-is|e], -es, -ing, -ed, -er/s
'hɑ:mənaiz, -iz, -iŋ, -d, -ə*/z
harmon|y, -ies 'hɑ:mən|i, -iz
Harmsworth 'hɑ:mzwə(:)θ
Harnack 'hɑ:næk
harness (s. v.) (H.), -es, -ing, -ed, -er/s
'hɑ:nis, -iz, -iŋ, -t, -ə*/z
Harold 'hærəld
Harosheth 'hærəuʃeθ
harp (s. v.), -s, -ing, -ed, -er/s hɑ:p, -s,
-iŋ, -t, -ə*/z
Harpenden 'hɑ:pəndən
Harper 'hɑ:pə*
Harpham 'hɑ:pəm
harpist, -s 'hɑ:pist, -s
Harpocration ,hɑ:pəu'kreiʃjən [-ʃiən]
harpoon (s. v.), -s, -ing, -ed, -er/s
hɑ:'pu:n, -z, -iŋ, -d, -ə*/z
harpsichord, -s 'hɑ:psikɔ:d, -z
harp|y, -ies 'hɑ:p|i, -iz
harquebus, -es 'hɑ:kwibəs, -iz
Harraden 'hærədən [-den]
Harrap 'hærəp

harridan, -s 'hæridən, -z
Harrie 'hæri
harrier, -s 'hæriə*, -z
Harr|ies, -iet 'hær|is, -iət
Harri|man, -ngton 'hæri|mən, -ŋtən
Harriot 'hæriət
Harris, -on 'hæris, -n
Harrisson 'hærisn
Harrod, -s 'hærəd, -z
Harrogate 'hærəʊgit [-geit]
Harrop 'hærəp ⌐-z
Harrovian, -s hə'rəuvjən [hæ'r-, -viən],
harr|ow (s. v.) (H.), -ows, -owing/ly,
-owed 'hær|əu, -əuz, -əuiŋ/li, -əud
Harrowby 'hærəʊbi
harr|y (H.), -ies, -ying, -ied 'hær|i, -iz,
-iiŋ, -id
Harsant 'hɑːsənt
harsh, -er, -est, -ly, -ness hɑːʃ, -ə*, -ist,
-li, -nis
hart (H.), -s hɑːt, -s
hartal, -s 'hɑːtɑːl [-təl] (Hind. hərtal), -z
Harte hɑːt
hartebeest, -s 'hɑːtibiːst, -s
Hartford 'hɑːtfəd
Harthan (surname) 'hɑːðən, 'hɑːθən
Hartington 'hɑːtiŋtən
Hartland 'hɑːtlənd
Hartlepool 'hɑːtlipuːl ['hɑːtlpuːl]
Hartley 'hɑːtli
harts|horn (H.), -tongue/s 'hɑːts|hɔːn,
-tʌŋ/z
Hartz hɑːts
harum-scarum 'hɛərəm'skɛərəm
Harun-al-Raschid   hæ'ruːnælræ'ʃiːd
[hɑːˈr-, '—'—, -'ræʃid]
haruspex, haruspices hə'rʌspeks ['hærə-
speks], hə'rʌspisiːz
Harvard 'hɑːvəd [-vɑːd]
Harverson 'hɑːvəsn
harvest (s. v.), -s, -ing, -ed, -er/s
'hɑːvist, -s, -iŋ, -id, -ə*/z
harvest-bug, -s 'hɑːvistbʌg, -z
harvest-festival, -s 'hɑːvist'festivl, -z
harvest-home 'hɑːvist'həum
harvest|-man, -men ; -moon/s 'hɑːvist|-
mæn, -men; -'muːn/z
Harvey 'hɑːvi
Harwich 'hæridʒ [rarely -itʃ]
Harwood 'hɑːwud
Harz hɑːts
has (from have) hæz (strong form), həz,
əz, z, s (weak forms)
    Note.—The form z is used only after
    words ending in a voiced sound
    other than z or ʒ; s is used only
    after words ending in a breathed
    consonant other than s or ʃ.

Hasdrubal 'hæzdrubəl [-bæl]
Haselden 'hæzldən
Hasemer 'heizmə*
hash (s. v.), -es, -ing, -ed, -er/s hæʃ,
-iz, -iŋ, -t, -ə*/z
hashish 'hæʃiːʃ [-ʃiʃ]
Haslam 'hæzləm
Haslemere 'heizlmiə*
haslet 'heizlit
Haslett 'heizlit [-lət], 'hæzlit
Haslingden 'hæzliŋdən
hasluck 'hæzlʌk [-lək]
hasn't 'hæznt [also 'hæzn when not final]
hasp (s. v.), -s, -ing, -ed hɑːsp [hæsp], -s,
-iŋ, -t
Hassall 'hæsl
Hassan (district in India) 'hʌsən
['hæs-], (Arabic name) hə'sɑːn ['hæsən,
'hʌsən]
hassock (H.), -s 'hæsək, -s
hast (from have) (H.) hæst (strong
form), həst, əst, st (weak forms)
hast|e (s. v.), -es, -ing, -ed, heist, -s, -iŋ,
-id
hast|en, -ens, -ening, -ened 'heis|n, -nz,
-niŋ [-niŋ], -nd
Hastings 'heistiŋz
hast|y, -ier, -iest, -ily, -iness 'heist|i,
-iə* [-jə*], -iist [-jist], -ili, -inis
hasty-pudding 'heisti,pudiŋ
hat, -s hæt, -s
hat-band, -s 'hætbænd, -z
hat-box, -es 'hætbɔks, -iz
hat-brush, -es 'hætbrʌʃ, -iz
hatch (s. v.) (H.), -es, -ing, -ed hætʃ, -iz,
-iŋ, -t
hatchet, -s 'hætʃit, -s
hatchment, -s 'hætʃmənt, -s
hatchway (H.), -s 'hætʃwei, -z
hat|e (s. v.), -es, -ing, -ed, -er/s heit, -s,
-iŋ, -id, -ə*/z
hate|ful, -fully, -fulness 'heit|ful, -fuli
[-fəli], -fulnis
Hatfield 'hætfiːld
hath (from have) hæθ (strong form),
həθ, əθ (weak forms)
Hathaway 'hæθəwei
Hather|ell, -leigh, -ley 'hæðə|rəl, -li
[-liː], -li
Hathersage 'hæðəsidʒ [-sedʒ]
Hatherton 'hæðətən [-tn]
Hathorn(e) 'hɔːθɔːn
Hathway 'hæθwei
hatless 'hætlis
hat-peg, -s 'hætpeg, -z
hat-pin, -s 'hætpin, -z
hat-rack, -s 'hæt-ræk, -s
hatred 'heitrid

hat-stand, -s 'hæt-stænd, -z
hatter, -s 'hætə*, -z
Hatteras 'hætərəs
Hatt|o, -on 'hæt|əu, -n
hauberk, -s 'hɔːbəːk, -s
haugh, -s hɔː, -z
Haughton 'hɔːtn
haught|y, -ier, -iest, -ily, -iness 'hɔːt|i,
    -iə* [-jə*], -iist [-jist], -ili, -inis
haul (s. v.), -s, -ing, -ed; -age hɔːl, -z,
    -iŋ, -d; -idʒ
haulier, -s 'hɔːljə* [-lĭə*], -z
haulm, -s hɔːm, -z
haunch, -es hɔːntʃ, -iz
haunt (s. v.), -s, -ing, -ed hɔːnt, -s, -iŋ,
    -id
Hausa, -s 'hausə ['hauzə], -z
hautboy, -s 'əubɔi ['həu-], -z
hauteur əu'təː* ['əutəː*] (otœːr)
Havana, -s hə'vænə [also occasionally
    ə'v- when not initial], -z
Havant 'hævənt
Havard 'hævɑːd [-vəd]
have (one who has), -s hæv, -z
have (v.); hast; has; having; had hæv
    (strong form), həv, əv, v (weak forms);
    hæst (strong form), həst, əst, st (weak
    forms); hæz (strong form), həz, əz, z, s
    (weak forms); hæviŋ; hæd (strong
    form), həd, əd, d (weak forms)
    Note.—The weak form z is used only
    after voiced sounds other than z and
    ʒ. The weak form s is used only
    after breathed consonants other than
    s and ʃ.
Havell 'hævəl
Havelo(c)k 'hævlɔk [-lək]
haven, -s 'heivn, -z
have-not, -s 'hævnɔt, -s
haven't 'hævnt [also 'hævn when not
    final]
haver (v.) (talk nonsense), -s, -ing, -ed
    'heivə*, -z, -riŋ, -d
Haverford, -west 'hævəfəd, -'west
Havergal 'hævəgəl
Haverhill 'heivəril
haversack, -s 'hævəsæk, -s
Haverstock 'hævəstɔk
Havil|ah, -and 'hævil|ə, -ənd
havoc 'hævək
Havre hɑːvrə [-və*]
haw (s. v.), -s, -ing, -ed hɔː, -z, -iŋ, -d
Hawaii hɑː'waĭi: [hə'w-, -'wɑːi:]
Hawaiian hɑː'waii-ən [hə'w-, -'waijən]
Haward 'heiwəd, 'hɔːəd, hɔːd
Hawarden (in Flintshire) 'hɑːdn ['hɔːdn],
    (Viscount) 'hei,wɔːdn, (town in U.S.A.)
    'hei,wɑːdn

Haweis 'hɔːis
Hawes hɔːz
hawfinch, -es 'hɔː-fintʃ, -iz
haw-haw (s.), -s 'hɔːhɔː, -z (interj.)
    'hɔː'hɔː:
Hawick 'hɔːik
hawk (s. v.), -s, -ing, -ed, -er/s hɔːk, -s,
    -iŋ, -t, -ə*/z
Hawke, -s hɔːk, -s
hawk-eyed 'hɔːk-aid
Hawkins 'hɔːkinz
hawkish 'hɔːkiʃ
Hawksley 'hɔːksli
hawkweed 'hɔːk-wiːd
Hawkwood 'hɔːk-wud
Hawley 'hɔːli
Haworth 'hɔːəθ, 'hɔːwə(ː)θ, 'hauəθ
hawse, -s; -hole/s, -pipe/s hɔːz, -iz;
    -həul/z, -paip/s
hawser, -s 'hɔːzə*, -z
hawthorn, -s 'hɔːθɔːn, -z
Hawthornden 'hɔːθɔːndən
Hawthorne 'hɔːθɔːn
hay (H.) hei
hay-box, -es 'hei-bɔks, -iz
hay-cart, -s 'hei-kɑːt, -s
haycock, -s 'hei-kɔk, -s
Haycock 'heikɔk ['hei-kɔk]
Hayd|en, -on 'heid|n, -n
Haydn (Eng. surname) 'heidn, (Austrian
    composer) 'haidn
Hayes, -ford heiz, -fəd
hay-fever 'hei,fiːvə* ['-'--]
hay-field, -s 'hei-fiːld, -z
hay-fork, -s 'hei-fɔːk, -s
hayhow 'heihau
Hayhurst 'haiəst, 'heihəːst
Hayles heilz
hay-loft 'hei-lɔft [-lɔːft], -s
hay-mak|er/s, -ing 'hei,meik|ə*/z, -iŋ
Haymarket 'hei,mɑːkit
Haynes heinz
hayrick, -s 'heirik, -s
Hays heiz
haystack, -s 'hei-stæk, -s
Hayt|er, -or 'heit|ə*, -ə*
hayward (H.), -s 'heiwəd, -z
Hazael 'hæzeiel ['heiz-, -zeiəl, hæ'z-,
    hə'z-]
hazard (s. v.) (H.), -s, -ing, -ed 'hæzəd,
    -z, -iŋ, -id
hazardous, -ly, -ness 'hæzədəs, -li, -nis
haz|e (s. v.), -es, -ing, -ed heiz, -iz, -iŋ,
    -d
hazel, -s; -nut/s 'heizl, -z; -nʌt/s
Hazelhurst 'heizlhəːst
Hazen 'heizn
Hazledean 'heizldiːn

Hazlerigg 'heizlrig
Hazlett 'heizlit [-lət], 'hæzlit [-lət]
Hazlitt 'heizlit, 'hæzlit
   *Note.—William Hazlitt, the essayist,
called himself* 'heizlit, *and the
present members of his family pronounce the name thus. He is, however, commonly referred to as*
'hæzlit. *In the* Hazlitt Gallery *in
London the pronunciation is* 'hæzlit.
Hazor 'heizɔ:*
haz|y, -ier, -iest, -ily, -iness 'heiz|i, -ɪə*
   [-jə*], -iist [-jist], -ili, -inis
H-bomb, -s 'eitʃbɔm, -z
he hi: (*normal form*), i:, hi, i (*frequent
weak forms*)
head (*s. v.*) (H.), -s, -ing, -ed hed, -z,
   -iŋ, -id
headach|e, -es, -y 'hedeik, -s, -i
headband, -s 'hedbænd, -z
head|-cloth, -cloths 'hed|klɔθ [-klɔ:θ],
   -klɔθs [-klɔ:ðz, -klɔ:θs]
head-dress, -es 'heddres, -iz
header, -s 'hedə*, -z
head-first 'hed'fə:st
head-gear, -s 'hedgiə*, -z
head-hunt|er/s, -ing 'hed,hʌnt|ə*/z, -iŋ
heading, -s 'hediŋ, -z
Headingl(e)y 'hediŋli
Headlam 'hedləm
headland, -s 'hedlənd, -z
headless 'hedlis
head-light, -s 'hedlait, -s
headline, -s 'hedlain, -z
headlong 'hedlɔŋ
head|man, -men (*of group of workers*)
   'hed|'mæn ['hedmæn], -'men ['--], (*of
tribe*) 'hed|mæn [-mən], -men [-mən]
head|-master/s, -mistress/es 'hed|-
   'mɑ:stə*/z, -'mistris/iz
head-note, -s 'hednəut, -s
head-on 'hed'ɔn ['--]
headphone, -s 'hedfəun, -z
headpiece, -s 'hedpi:s, -iz
headquarters   'hed'kwɔ:təz   [*also*
   'hed,k-, hed'k-, *according to sentence-
stress*]
head-rest, -s 'hed-rest, -s
head-room 'hed-rum [-ru:m]
headship, -s 'hedʃip, -s
heads|man, -men 'hedz|mən, -mən
headstone (H.), -s 'hedstəun, -z
headstrong 'hedstrɔŋ
head-water, -s 'hed,wɔ:tə*, -z
headway, -s 'hedwei, -z
head-wind, -s 'hedwind, -z
head-word, -s 'hedwə:d, -z
head-work 'hedwə:k

head|y, -ier, -iest, -ily, -iness 'hed|i, -ɪə*,
   -iist, -ili, -inis
Heagerty 'hegəti
heal (H.), -s, -ing, -ed, -er/s hi:l, -z, -iŋ,
   -d, -ə*/z
Healey 'hi:li
health, -s helθ, -s
health|ful, -fully, -fulness 'helθ|fuɭ,
   -fuli [-fəli], -fuɭnis
health-giving 'helθ,giviŋ
health|y, -ier, -iest, -ily, -iness 'helθ|i,
   -ɪə* [-jə*], -iist [-jist], -ili, -inis
Healy 'hi:li
Heanor (*near Derby*) 'hi:nə*
heap (*s. v.*), -s, -ing, -ed hi:p, -s, -iŋ, -t
hear, -s, -ing/s, heard, hearer/s hiə*,
   -z, -riŋ/z, hə:d, 'hiərə*/z
heard (*from* hear) (H.) hə:d
hear hear 'hiə'hiə* ['hjə:'hjə:*]
heark|en, -ens, -ening, -ened 'hɑ:k|ən,
   -ənz, -niŋ [-ṇiŋ, -əniŋ], -ənd
Hearn(e) hə:n
hearsay 'hiəsei
hearse, -s hə:s, -iz
hearse|-cloth, -cloths 'hə:s|klɔθ [-klɔ:θ],
   -klɔθs [-klɔ:ðz, -klɔ:θs]
Hearsey 'hə:si
Hearst hə:st
heart, -s hɑ:t, -s
heartache 'hɑ:t-eik
heart-beat, -s 'hɑ:tbi:t, -s
heart-blood 'hɑ:tblʌd
heartbreak, -ing 'hɑ:tbreik, -iŋ
heart-broken 'hɑ:t,brəukən
heartburn, -ing/s 'hɑ:tbə:n, -iŋ/z
heart|en, -ens, -ening, -ened 'hɑ:t|n, -nz,
   -ṇiŋ [-niŋ], -nd
heartfelt 'hɑ:tfelt
hearth, -s; -brush/es, -rug/s, -stone/s
   hɑ:θ, -s; -brʌʃ/iz, -rʌg/z, -stəun/z
heartless, -ly, -ness 'hɑ:tlis, -li, -nis
heart-rending 'hɑ:t,rendiŋ
heart-searching, -s 'hɑ:t,sə:tʃiŋ, -z
heart's-ease 'hɑ:ts-i:z
heart-service 'hɑ:t,sə:vis
heart-shaped 'hɑ:t-ʃeipt
heart-sick, -ness 'hɑ:t-sik, -nis
heartsore 'hɑ:t-sɔ:* [-sɔə*]
heart-string, -s 'hɑ:t-striŋ, -z
heart|y, -ier, -iest, -ily, -iness 'hɑ:t|i,
   -ɪə* [-jə*], -iist [-jist], -ili, -inis
heat (*s. v.*), -s, -ing, -ed, -er/s hi:t, -s,
   -iŋ, -id, -ə*/z
heath (H.), -s hi:θ, -s
Heathcoat 'hi:θkəut
Heathcote 'heθkət, 'hi:θkət
heathen (*s. adj.*), -s, -dom 'hi:ðən, -z,
   -dəm

heathenish, -ly, -ness 'hi:ðəniʃ [-ðŋiʃ], -li, -nis
heathenism 'hi:ðənizəm [-ðŋi-]
heatheniz|e [-is|e], **-es, -ing, -ed** 'hi:ðənaiz [-ðŋaiz], -iz, -iŋ, -d
heather (H.), -s, -y 'heðə*, -z, -ri
heather-bell, -s 'heðəbel, -z
Heath|field, -man 'hi:θ|fi:ld, -mən
heath|y, -ier, -iest, -ily, -iness 'hi:θ|i, -iə* [-jə*], -iist [-jist], -ili, -inis
Heaton 'hi:tn
heat-spot, -s 'hi:t-spɔt, -s
heat-stroke, -s 'hi:t-strəuk, -s
heat-wave, -s 'hi:t-weiv, -z
heav|e (s. v.), **-es, -ing, -ed, hove, heaver/s** hi:v, -z, -iŋ, -d, həuv, 'hi:və*/z
heaven, -s; -born 'hevn, -z; -bɔ:n
heavenl|y, -iness 'hevnl|i, -inis
heavenward, -s 'hevnwəd, -z
Heaviside 'hevisaid
heav|y, -ier, -iest, -ily, -iness 'hev|i, -iə* [-jə*], -iist [-jist], -ili, -inis
heavy-handed 'hevi'hændid ['--,--]
heavy-hearted 'hevi'hɑ:tid ['--,--]
heavy-laden 'hevi'leidn [also '--,-- when attributive]
heavy-weight, -s 'heviweit, -s
Heazell 'hi:zəl
Hebden 'hebdən
hebdomad|al, -ary heb'dɔməd|l, -əri
Hebe 'hi:bi(:)
Heber 'hi:bə*
Heberden 'hebədən
Hebraic, -al, -ally hi(:)'breiik [he'b-], -əl, -əli
Hebrai|sm/s, -st/s 'hi:breii|zəm/z, -st/s
hebraiz|e [-is|e], **-es, -ing, -ed** 'hi:breiaiz, -iz, -iŋ, -d
Hebrew, -s 'hi:bru:, -z
Hebrides 'hebridi:z [-brəd-]
Hebron (biblical place name) 'hebrɔn ['hi:b-], (modern surname) 'hebrən [-rɔn]
Hecate 'hekəti(:) [in Shakespeare sometimes 'hekət] [-z
hecatomb, -s 'hekətu:m [-təum, -təm],
heck|le, -les, -ling, -led, -ler/s 'hek|l, -lz, -l̩iŋ [-liŋ], -ld, -l̩ə*/z [-lə*/z]
Hecla 'heklə
hectare, -s 'hektɑ:* [-tɛə*, ek'tɑ:*] (ɛktɑ:r), -z
hectic 'hektik
hectogramme, -s 'hektəugræm, -z
hectograph (s. v.), **-s, -ing, -ed** 'hektəugrɑ:f [-græf], -s, -iŋ, -t
hectographic ,hektəu'græfik
hectolitre, -s 'hektəu,li:tə*, -z

hectometre, -s 'hektəu,mi:tə*, -z
hector (s. v.) **(H.), -s, -ing, -ed** 'hektə*, -z, -riŋ, -d
Hecuba 'hekjubə
Hecyra 'hekirə
hedera 'hedərə
Hedgcock 'hedʒkɔk
hedg|e (s. v.), **-es, -ing, -ed, -er/s** hedʒ, -iz, -iŋ, -d, -ə*/z
hedgehog, -s 'hedʒhɔg, -z
hedgehop, -s, -ping, -ped 'hedʒhɔp, -s, -iŋ, -t
Hedgeley 'hedʒli
Hedger, -ley 'hedʒə*, -li
hedgerow, -s 'hedʒrəu, -z
Hedges 'hedʒiz
hedge-sparrow, -s 'hedʒ,spærəu ['-'--], -z
Hedley 'hedli
hedoni|sm, -st/s 'hi:dəuni|zəm, -st/s
heed (s. v.), **-s, -ing, -ed** hi:d, -z, -iŋ, -id
heed|ful, -fully, -fulness 'hi:d|ful, -fuli [-fəli], -fulnis
heedless, -ly, -ness 'hi:dlis, -li, -nis
heehaw (s. v. interj.), **-s, -ing, -ed** 'hi:'hɔ: [-'-, '--], -z, -iŋ, -d
heel (s. v.), **-s, -ing, -ed** hi:l, -z, -iŋ, -d
Heelas 'hi:ləs
Heep hi:p
Heffer 'hefə*
heft|y, -ier, -iest, -ily, -iness 'heft|i, -iə* [-jə*], -iist [-jist], -ili, -inis
Hegarty 'hegəti
Hegel 'heigl ('he:gəl)
Hegelian hei'gi:ljən [he'g-, -lïən]
hegemony hi(:)'geməni ['hedʒim-, 'hegim-]
Hegira 'hedʒirə [hi'dʒaiərə, he'dʒaiərə]
he-goat, -s 'hi:gəut, -s
Heidelberg 'haidlbə:g
Heidsieck 'haidsi:k
heifer, -s 'hefə*, -z
heigh hei
heigh-ho 'hei'həu
Heigho 'heiəu, 'haiəu
height, -s hait, -s
height|en, -ens, -ening, -ened 'hait|n, -nz, -n̩iŋ [-niŋ], -nd
Heighton 'heitn
Heighway 'haiwei
Heinekey 'hainiki
Heinemann 'hainəmən [-mæn]
heinous, -ly, -ness 'heinəs, -li, -nis
Heinz haints
heir, -s; -dom, -less ɛə*, -z; -dəm, -lis
heir-apparent, heirs-apparent 'ɛərə-'pærənt ['ɛəə'p-, -'pɛər-], 'ɛəzə'p-
heir-at-law, heirs-at-law 'ɛərət'lɔ: ['ɛəət-], 'ɛəzət'lɔ:

heiress, -es 'ɛəris [-res], -iz
heirloom, -s 'ɛəlu:m, -z
heirship 'ɛəʃip
Hekla 'heklə
held (from hold) held
Helen 'helin
Helena 'helinə, he'li:nə [hi'l-, hə'l-, also
   occasionally i'l-, ə'l- when not initial]
   Note.—'helinə is the more usual
   pronunciation, except in the name
   of the island St. Helena (q.v.).
Helensburgh 'helinzbərə [-bʌrə]
Helenus 'helinəs
heliac 'hi:liæk
heliac|al, -ally hi(:)'laiək|əl [he'l-], -əli
Heliades he'laiədi:z
helianth|us, -i, -uses ˌhi:li'ænθ|əs [ˌhel-],
   -ai, -əsiz
helical 'helikəl
Helicon 'helikən [-kɔn]
helicopter, -s 'helikɔptə*, -z
Heligoland 'heligəʊlænd
heliocentric, -al, -ally ˌhi:liəʊ'sentrik
   [-ljəʊ-], -əl, -əli
Heliogabalus ˌhi:liəʊ'gæbələs [-ljəʊ-]
heliogram, -s 'hi:liəʊgræm [-ljəʊg-,
   -lïəg-], -z
heliograph, -s 'hi:liəʊgrɑ:f [-ljəʊg-,
   -lïəg-, -græf], -s
heliograph|er/s, -y ˌhi:li'ɔgrəf|ə*/z, -i
heliographic, -al ˌhi:liəʊ'græfik [-ljəʊ'g-,
   -lïə'g-], -əl
heliogravure, -s 'hi:liəʊgrə'vjuə*, -z
heliometer, -s ˌhi:li'ɔmitə*, -z
Heliopolis ˌhi:li'ɔpəlis
Helios 'hi:liɔs
helioscope, -s 'hi:ljəskəup [-lïəs-], -s
heliostat, -s 'hi:liəʊstæt [-ljəus-, -lïəs-],
   -s
heliotrope, -s 'heljətrəup [-lïə-, rarely
   'hi:l-], -s
helium 'hi:ljəm [-lïəm]
heli|x, -xes, helices 'hi:li|ks,   -ksiz,
   'helisi:z ['hi:l-]
hell (H.), -s hel, -z
he'll (= he will) hi:l
Hellas 'helæs
hellebore 'helibɔ:* [-bɔə*]
Hellene, -s 'heli:n, -z
Hellenic he'li:nik
helleni|sm/s, -st/s 'helini|zəm/z, -st/s
hellenistic, -al, -ally ˌheli'nistik, -əl, -əli
helleniz|e [-is|e], -es, -ing, -ed 'helinaiz,
   -iz, -iŋ, -d
Heller 'helə*
Hellespont 'helispɔnt
hell-fire 'hel'faiə*
hell-gate, -s 'hel'geit, -s

hell-hound, -s 'helhaund, -z
Hellingly (in Sussex) 'heliŋlai
hellish, -ly, -ness 'heliʃ, -li, -nis
hello 'he'ləu [-'-, hə'ləu]
hellward 'helwəd
helm, -s helm, -z
helmet, -s, -ed 'helmit, -s, -id
Helmholtz 'helmhəults ('hɛlmhɔlts)
helminth, -s 'helminθ, -s
Helmsley (in Yorks.) 'helmzli [locally
   'hemz-]
helms|man, -men 'helmz|mən, -mən
   [-men]
helot, -s; -age, -ism, -ry 'helət, -s; -idʒ,
   -izəm, -ri
help (s. v.), -s, -ing, -ed, -er/s help, -s,
   -iŋ, -t, -ə*/z
help|ful, -fully, -fulness 'help|fʊl, -fuli
   [-fəli], -fʊlnis
helpless, -ly, -ness 'helplis, -li, -nis
helpmate, -s 'helpmeit, -s
helpmeet, -s 'helpmi:t, -s
Helps helps
Helsingfors 'helsiŋfɔ:z
Helsinki 'helsiŋki [-'--]
Helston(e) 'helstən
helter-skelter 'heltə'skeltə*
helve, -s helv, -z
Helvellyn hel'velin
Helvetia, -n/s hel'vi:ʃjə [-ʃïə], -n/z
Helvetic hel'vetik
Helvetius hel'vi:ʃjəs [-ʃïəs] (ɛlvɛsjys)
Hely 'hi:li
hem (s. v.), -s, -ming, -med hem, -z, -iŋ,
   -d
hem (interj.) m̩m [hm]
hemal 'hi:məl [-ml]
he|-man, -men 'hi:|mæn, -men
Hemans 'hemənz
hematite 'hemətait
Hemel Hempstead 'heməl'hempstid
Heming 'hemiŋ
hemicycle, -s 'hemiˌsaikl, -z
hemisphere, -s 'hemisfiə*, -z
hemispheric, -al ˌhemi'sferik, -əl
hemistich, -s 'hemistik, -s
hemline, -s 'hemlain, -z
hemlock, -s 'hemlɔk, -s
hemoglobin ˌhi:məʊ'gləubin ['--'--]
hemorrhage, -s 'heməridʒ, -iz
hemorrhoid, -s 'hemərɔid, -z
hemp, -en; -seed hemp, -ən; -si:d
Hemp(e)l 'hempl
hem-stitch (s. v.), -es, -ing, -ed
   'hem-stitʃ, -iz, -iŋ, -t
Hemy 'hemi
hen, -s; -bane hen, -z; -bein
hence hens

hence|forth, -forward 'hens|'fɔ:θ, -'fɔ:wəd

hench|man, -men 'hentʃ|mən, -mən

hen-coop, -s 'henku:p, -s

hendecagon, -s hen'dekəgən, -z

hendecasyllabic, -s 'hendekəsi'læbik, -s

hendecasyllable, -s 'hendekə‚siləbl, -z

Henderson 'hendəsn

hendiadys hen'daiədis

Hendon 'hendən

Heneage 'henidʒ

Hengist 'heŋgist

Henley 'henli

Henlopen hen'ləupən

henna 'henə

henner|y, -ies 'henər|i, -iz

Henness(e)y 'henisi [-nəs-]

Henniker 'henikə*

Henning 'heniŋ

henpeck, -s, -ing, -ed 'henpek, -s, -iŋ, -t

Henrietta ‚henri'etə

Henriques (English surname) hen'ri:kiz

hen-roost, -s 'henru:st, -s

Henry 'henri

Hensen 'hensn

Hens|ley, -low(e) 'henz|li, -ləu

Henson 'hensn

Henty 'henti

hepatic hi'pætik [he'p-]

hepatica, -s hi'pætikə [he'p-], -z

hepatite 'hepətait

hepatitis ‚hepə'taitis

Hepburn 'hebə(:)n ['hepb-]

Hephaestus hi'fi:stəs [he'f-]

Hephzibah 'hefsibə ['heps-]

heptachord, -s 'heptəkɔ:d, -z

heptad, -s 'heptæd, -z

heptaglot 'heptəglɔt

heptagon, -s 'heptəgən, -z

heptagonal hep'tægənl

heptahedr|on, -ons, -a; -al 'heptə'hedr|ən [-'hi:d-, 'heptə‚h-, ‚heptə'h-], -ənz, -ə; -əl

heptameron hep'tæmərən

heptarch, -s; -y, -ies 'heptɑ:k, -s; -i, -iz

Heptateuch 'heptətju:k

Hepworth 'hepwə:θ

her hə:* (normal form), ə:*, hə*, ə* (frequent weak forms)

Heraclean ‚herə'kli(:)ən

Heracles 'herəkli:z ['hiər-]

Heraclitus ‚herə'klaitəs

herald (s. v.), -s, -ing, -ed; -ry 'herəld, -z, -iŋ, -id; -ri

heraldic, -ally he'rældik [hi'r-, hə'r-], -əli

Herapath (surname) 'herəpɑ:θ

Herat he'ræt [hi'r-, hə'r-, -'rɑ:t]

herb, -s; -age hə:b, -z; -idʒ

herbaceous hə:'beiʃəs [hə'b-]

herbal 'hə:bəl

herbalist, -s 'hə:bəlist [-b‚list], -s

herbarium, -s hə:'bɛərĭəm, -z

Herbert 'hə:bət

herbivorous hə:'bivərəs

herborist, -s 'hə:bərist, -s

herboriz|e [-is|e], -es, -ing, -ed 'hə:bəraiz, -iz, -iŋ, -d

Herculaneum ‚hə:kju'leinjəm [-nĭəm]

herculean ‚hə:kju'li(:)ən [hə:'kju:ljən, -'kju:lĭən]

Hercules 'hə:kjuli:z

herd (s. v.) (H.), -s, -ing, -ed hə:d, -z, -iŋ, -id

Herdener 'hə:dənə* [-din-]

herd-instinct 'hə:d'instiŋkt ['-‚--]

herds|man, -men 'hə:dz|mən, -mən

here hiə*

hereabouts 'hiərə‚bauts

hereafter hiər'ɑ:ftə*

hereby 'hiə'bai [also '--, -'- according to sentence-stress]

hereditable hi'reditəbl [he'r-, hə'r-]

hereditament, -s ‚heri'ditəmənt [-rə'd-, -tim-], -s

hereditar|y, -ily, -iness hi'reditər|i [he'r-, hə'r-, also occasionally i'r-, ə'r- when not initial], -ili, -inis

heredity hi'rediti [he'r-, hə'r-, also occasionally i'r-, ə'r- when not initial]

Hereford, -shire 'herifəd, -ʃiə* [-ʃə*]

herein 'hiər'in [-'-]

hereinafter 'hiərin'ɑ:ftə* [‚-'--]

hereof hiər'ɔv [-'ɔf]

hereon hiər'ɔn

Herero, -s 'hiərərəu [he'riərəu, hə'riərəu], -z

heresiarch, -s he'ri:ziɑ:k, -s

heres|y, -ies 'herəs|i [-ris-], -iz

heretic (s. adj.), -s 'herətik [-rit-], -s

heretic|al, -ly hi'retik|əl [hə'r-, also occasionally i'r-, ə'r- when not initial], -əli

hereto 'hiə'tu: [-'-]

heretofore 'hiətu'fɔ:* [-'fɔə*, ‚-'-]

hereunder hiər'ʌndə*

hereunto 'hiərʌn'tu: [‚-'-]

hereupon 'hiərə'pɔn ['---, ‚-'-]

Hereward 'heriwəd

herewith 'hiə'wiθ [-'wiθ, -'-]

Herford 'hə:fəd, 'hɑ:fəd

heriot, -s 'heriət, -s

herit|able, -age/s, -or/s 'herit|əbl, -idʒ/iz, -ə*/z

Herkomer, -s 'hə:kəmə*, -z

Herlichy 'hə:liki

Herlihy 'hə:lihi
Herman 'hə:mən
hermaphrodite, -s hə:'mæfrədait [-frud-], -s
Hermes 'hə:mi:z
hermetic, -al, -ally hə:'metik, -əl, -əli
Hermia 'hə:mjə [-mɪə]
Hermione hə:'maiəni
hermit, -s 'hə:mit, -s
hermitage (H.), -s 'hə:mitidʒ, -iz
hermit-crab, -s 'hə:mit'kræb ['---], -z
hermitical hə:'mitikəl
Hermocrates hə:'mɔkrəti:z
Hermogenes hə:'mɔdʒini:z
Hermon 'hə:mən
hern, -s hə:n, -z
Herne hə:n
hernia, -l 'hə:njə [-nɪə], -l
hero (H.), -es 'hiərəu, -z
Herod 'herəd
Herodian, -s he'rəudjən [hi'r-, hə'r-, -dɪən], -z
Herodias he'rəudiæs [hi'r-, hə'r-]
Herodotus he'rɔdətəs [hi'r-, hə'r-]
heroic, -s, -al, -ally hi'rəuik [he'r-, hə'r-], -s, -əl, -əli
heroin 'herəuin
heroi|ne, -nes, -sm 'herəui|n, -nz, -zəm
heron (H.), -s; -ry, -ries 'herən, -z; -ri, -riz
hero-worship 'hiərəu,wə:ʃip
herpes 'hə:pi:z
Herr (German title) hɛə* (hɛr)
Herr|ick, -ies 'her|ik, -is
herring (H.), -s; -bone/s, -pond/s 'heriŋ, -z; -bəun/z, -pɔnd/z
Herrnhuter, -s 'hɛən,hu:tə* ['hɛərən-], -z
hers hə:z
Hersant 'hə:snt
Herschel(l) 'hə:ʃəl
herself hə:'self [hə's-, also ə:'s-, ə's- when not initial]
Herstmonceux ,hə:stmən'sju: [-mɔn-, -'su:]
Hertford (in England), -shire 'hɑ:fəd ['hɑ:tf-], -ʃiə* [-ʃə*]
Hertford (in U.S.A.) 'hə:tfəd
Herts. hɑ:ts [hə:ts]
Hertslet 'hə:tslit
Hertz, -ian hə:ts[hɛə-], -ɪən [-jən]
Hervey 'hɑ:vi, 'hə:vi
Herzegovina ,hɛətsəgəu'vi:nə [,hə:ts-]
Herzog (English surname) 'hə:tsɔg
he's (= he is or he has) hi:z (strong form), hiz, iz (occasional weak forms)
Hesba 'hezbə
Hesiod 'hi:siɔd ['hes-, -jəd, -ɪəd]

hesitan|ce, -cy, -t/ly 'hezitən|s, -si, -t/li
hesitat|e, -es, -ing/ly, -ed 'heziteit, -s, -iŋ/li, -id
hesitation, -s ,hezi'teiʃən, -z
Hesketh 'heskiθ [-keθ, -kəθ]
Hesper 'hespə*
Hesperian hes'piərɪən
Hesperides hes'peridi:z
Hesperus 'hespərəs
Hess|e, -en 'hes|i, -n
hessian (H.), -s 'hesɪən [-sjən], -z
Hester 'hestə*
Hesychius he'sikɪəs
heteroclite (s. adj.), -s 'hetərəuklait, -s
heterodox, -y 'hetərəudɔks, -i
heterodyne 'hetərəudain
heterogeneity ,hetərəudʒi'ni:iti [-dʒə'n-, -'ni(:)əti]
heterogeneous, -ly, -ness 'hetərəu'dʒi:njəs [,het-, -'dʒen-, -nɪəs], -li, -nis
heterogenesis ,hetərəu'dʒenisis
heteronym|ous, -y ,hetə'rɔnim|əs, -i
hetero-sexual 'hetərəu'seksjŭəl [-sjwəl]
Hetherington 'heðəriŋtən
Hetton-le-Hole 'hetnli'həul
Hetty 'heti
Heugh (place) hju:f, (surname) hju:
heuristic hjuə'ristik
hew, -s, -ing, -ed, -n, -er/s hju:, -z, -iŋ [hjuiŋ], -d, -n, -ə*/z [hjuə*/z]
Hew|ard, -art, -etson, -ett, -itt 'hju(:)|əd, -ət, -itsn, -it, -it
Hewke hju:k
Hew|lett, -son 'hju:|lit, -sn
hexachord, -s 'heksəkɔ:d, -z
hexagon, -s 'heksəgən, -z
hexagon|al, -ally hek'sægən|l, -əli
hexahedr|on, -ons, -a; -al 'heksə'hedr|ən [-'hi:d-, ,heksə,h-, ,heksə'h-], -ənz, -ə; -əl
Hexam 'heksəm
hexameter, -s hek'sæmitə*, -z
Hexateuch 'heksətju:k
Hexham 'heksəm
hey hei
Heycock 'heikɔk ['hei-kɔk]
heyday 'heidei
Heyno 'heinəu
Heysham 'hi:ʃəm
Heytesbury 'heitsbəri
Heywood 'heiwud
Hezekiah ,hezi'kaiə
Hezlewood 'hezlwud
hi hai
hiatus, -es hai'eitəs, -iz
Hiawatha ,haiə'wɔθə
Hibbert 'hibə(:)t
hibernal hai'bə:nl

hibernat|e, -es, -ing, -ed 'haibəneit, -s, -iŋ, -id

hibernation, -s ˌhaibə'neiʃən, -z

Hibernia hai'bə:njə [-nïə]

Hibernian (s. adj.), -s (as ordinarily used) hai'bə:njən [-nïən], (in name of football club) hi'bə:njən [-nïən], -z

Hibernicism, -s hai'bə:nisizəm, -z

hibiscus hi'biskəs

hic hə̣ˀ [hik]

hiccup [-ough] (s. v.), -s, -ing, -ed 'hikʌp, -s, -iŋ, -t

Hichens 'hitʃinz

Hickinbotham 'hikinbɔtəm

hickory (H.) 'hikəri

Hick|s, -son hik|s, -sn

hid (from hide) hid

hidalgo, -s hi'dælgou, -z

hide (s.), -s haid, -z

hid|e (conceal), -es, -ing/s, hid, hidden haid, -z, -iŋ/z, hid, 'hidn

hid|e (beat), -es, -ing/s, -ed haid, -z, -iŋ/z, -id

hidebound 'haidbaund

hideous, -ly, -ness 'hidïəs [-djəs], -li, -nis

hiding-place, -s 'haidiŋpleis, -iz

hie, -s, -ing, -d hai, -z, -iŋ, -d

Hierapolis ˌhaiə'ræpəlis [-pul-]

hierarch, -s 'haiərɑ:k, -s

hierarchal ˌhaiə'rɑ:kəl

hierarchic, -al, -ally ˌhaiə'rɑ:kik, -əl, -əli

hierarch|y, -ies 'haiərɑ:k|i, -iz

hieratic ˌhaiə'rætik

hieroglyph, -s 'haiərəuglif, -s

hieroglyphic (s. adj.), -s, -al, -ally ˌhaiərəu'glifik, -s, -əl, -əli

Hieronymus ˌhaiə'rɔnïməs

hierophant, -s 'haiərəufænt, -s

hi-fi 'hai'fai

Higginbotham 'higinbɔtəm

Higgin|s, -son 'higin|z, -sn

higg|le, -les, -ling, -led, -ler/s 'hig|l, -lz, -liŋ [-liŋ], -ld, -lə*/z [-lə*/z]

higgledy-piggledy 'higldi'pigldi

high, -er, -est hai, 'hai-ə* ['haiə*], 'haiist

Higham, -s 'hai-əm, -z

highborn 'haibɔ:n

highbrow (s. adj.), -s 'hai-brau, -z

high-church, -man, -men 'hai'tʃə:tʃ, -mən, -mən [-men]

high-day, -s 'haidei, -z

high-falut|in, -ing 'hai-fə'lu:t|in, -iŋ

highflier [-flyer], -s 'hai'flai-ə* [-'flaiə*], -z

highflown 'hai-floun

Highflyer 'haiˌflai-ə*

high-frequency 'hai'fri:kwənsi

Highgate 'haigit [-geit]

high-handed 'hai'hændid [also 'haiˌh- when attributive]

highland (H.), -s; -er/s 'hailənd, -z; -ə*/z

high-level 'hai'levl

highlight (s. v.), -s, -ing, -ed 'hailait, -s, -iŋ, -id

highly (in a high manner) 'hai-li, ['haili], (very, very much) 'haili

highly-strung 'haili'strʌŋ

high-minded 'hai'maindid [also 'ˌ--, -'-- according to sentence-stress]

high-mindedness 'hai'maindidnis

high-necked 'hai'nekt [also '-- when attributive]

highness (quality of being high) 'hai-nis

Highness (title), -es 'hainis, -iz

high-pitched 'hai'pitʃt [also 'hai-pitʃt when attributive]

high-pressure 'hai'preʃə* [also '-,-- when attributive]

high-priced 'hai'praist [also 'hai-praist when attributive]

high-priest, -s, -hood 'hai'pri:st [also hai'p- when preceded by a stress], -s, -hud

high-principled 'hai'prinsəpld [-sip-]

high-rank|er/s, -ing 'haiˌræŋk|ə*/z, -iŋ

high-road, -s 'hairəud, -z

high-school, -s 'hai-sku:l, -z

high-sounding 'haiˌsaundiŋ [also 'hai's- when not attributive]

high-spirited 'hai'spiritid

high-stepper, -s 'hai'stepə* ['-,--], -z

high-stepping 'haiˌstepiŋ

High Street 'hai-stri:t

Highton 'haitn

high-toned 'hai'təund ['hai-təund]

high-up, -s 'haiʌp ['-'-], -s

high-water 'hai'wɔ:tə*

high-water-mark, -s 'hai'wɔ:təmɑ:k [hai'w-], -s

highway, -s 'haiwei, -z

highway-code 'haiwei'kəud ['--,-]

highway|man, -men 'haiwei|mən, -mən

hijacker, -s 'haiˌdʒækə*, -z

hik|e, -es, -ing, -ed, -er/s haik, -s, -iŋ, -t, -ə*/z

Hilaire (Belloc) 'hilɛə*

hilarious, -ly, -ness hi'lɛərïəs, -li, -nis

hilarity hi'læriti

Hilary 'hiləri

Hilda 'hildə

Hildebrand 'hildəbrænd

Hildegard(e) 'hildəgɑ:d

hill (H.), -s hil, -z

Hillary 'hiləri
Hillborn 'hilbɔːn
Hillel 'hilel [-ləl]
hill-folk 'hil-fəuk
Hillhead hil'hed ['hilhed]
Note.—The pronunciation in Scotland
is with -'-.
Hilliard 'hiliəd [-ljəd, -liɑːd, -ljɑːd]
Hillingdon 'hiliŋdən
hill|man, -men 'hil|mæn, -men
Hillman, -s 'hilmən, -z
hillock, -s 'hilək, -s
Hillsboro 'hilzbərə [-bʌrə]
Note.—The local pronunciation in
U.S.A. is with -ˌbʌrəu.
Hillsborough 'hilzbərə
hill-side, -s 'hil'said ['hil-said], -z
Hillside 'hil'said ['--]
hill-top 'hil'tɔp ['hil-tɔp], -s
Hilltop (name of road) 'hil-tɔp
hill|y, -ier, -iest, -iness 'hil|i, -iə*, -iist,
-inis
Hillyard 'hiljəd [-jɑːd]
hilt, -s, -ed hilt, -s, -id
Hilton 'hiltən
hilum, -s 'hailəm, -z
Hilversum 'hilvəsum [-səm]
him him (normal form), im (frequent
weak form)
Himalaya, -s, -n ˌhimə'leiə [rarely
hi'mɑːləjə, hi'mɑːljə, hi'mɑːliə],
(Hind. hymaləjə), -z, -n
himself him'self [also im- when not
initial]
Himyaritic ˌhimjə'ritik [-mïə-]
Hinchcliffe 'hintʃklif
Hinchliffe 'hintʃlif
Hinckley 'hiŋkli
hind (s. adj.) (H.), -s haind, -z
Hinde haind
hinder (adj.), -most 'haində*, -məust
hind|er (v.), -ers, -ering, -ered, -erer/s
'hind|ə*, -əz, -əriŋ, -əd, -ərə*/z
Hinderwell 'hindəwel [-wəl]
Hindi 'hindi: ['hin'd-, hin'd-] (Hind.
hyndi)
Hindle 'hindl
Hindley (surname) 'haindli, 'hindli,
(town in Lancs.) 'hindli
Hindlip 'hindlip
hindmost 'haindməust
hind-quarters 'haind'kwɔːtəz
hindrance, -s 'hindrəns, -iz
hindsight 'haindsait
Hindu [-doo], -s 'hin'du: [hin'du:, also
'hindu: when attributive], -z
Hinduism 'hindu(:)izəm
Hindu-Kush 'hindu:'ku:ʃ [-'kuʃ]

Hindustan ˌhindu'stɑːn [-'stæn]
Hindustani ˌhindu'stɑːni [-'stæni]
hing|e (s. v.), -es, -ing, -ed hindʒ, -iz,
-iŋ, -d
Hingston 'hiŋkstən
Hinkson 'hiŋksn
hint (s. v.), -s, -ing, -ed hint, -s, -iŋ, -id
hinterland 'hintələænd
Hinton 'hintən
Hiorns 'haiənz
hip (s. v.), -s, -ping, -ped hip, -s, -iŋ, -t
hip-ba|th, -ths 'hipbɑː|θ, -ðz
hip-bone, -s 'hipbəun, -z
hip-joint, -s 'hipdʒɔint, -s
Hipparchus hi'pɑːkəs
hipped hipt
hippety-hop, -pety 'hipəti'hɔp, -əti
Hippias 'hipiæs
hippish 'hipiʃ
hippo, -s 'hipəu, -z
Hippocrates hi'pɔkrəti:z
hippocratic ˌhipəu'krætik
Hippocrene ˌhipəu'kri:ni(:) [also in
poetry 'hipəukri:n]
Hippodamia ˌhipəudə'maiə
hippodrome (H.), -s 'hipədrəum, -z
Hippolyt|a, -e, -us hi'pɔlit|ə, -i:, -əs
hippopotam|us, -uses, -i ˌhipə'po-
təm|əs, -əsiz, -ai
Hiram (biblical name) 'haiərəm [-ræm],
(modern personal name) 'haiərəm,
(town in U.S.A.) 'haiərəm
hircine 'hə:sain
Hird hə:d
hir|e (s. v.), -es, -ing, -ed, -er/s;
-eling/s 'haiə*, -z, -riŋ, -d, -rə*/z;
-liŋ/z
Hiroshima hi'rɔʃimə [ˌhirɔ'ʃi:mə]
Hirst hə:st
hirsute 'hə:sjuːt
his hiz (normal form), iz (frequent weak
form)
hispanic his'pænik
hispanist, -s 'hispənist [-pæn-], -s
hiss (s. v.), -es, -ing, -ed, -er/s his, -iz,
-iŋ, -t, -ə*/z
hist s:t [hist]
histologic|al, -ally ˌhistə'lɔdʒik|əl, -əli
histolog|ist/s, -y his'tɔlədʒ|ist/s, -i
historian, -s his'tɔːriən [also occasionally
is- when not initial], -z
historic, -al, -ally his'tɔrik [also occasionally is- when not initial], -əl, -əli
historiograph|er/s, -y ˌhistɔ:ri'ɔ-
grəf|ə*/z [his,tɔ:r-, 'histɔr-, his,tɔr-],
-i
histor|y, -ies 'histər|i, -iz
Histriomastix 'histriəu'mæstiks

histrionic, -al, -ally ˌhistriˈɔnik, -əl, -əli
histrionism ˈhistriənizəm
hit (s. v.), -s, -ting, -ter/s hit, -s, -iŋ, -ə*/z
hitch (s. v.), -es, -ing, -ed hitʃ, -iz, -iŋ, -t
Hitch|cock, -ens ˈhitʃ|kɔk, -inz
hitch-hik|e, -es, -ing, -ed, -er/s ˈhitʃhaik, -s, -iŋ, -t, -ə*/z
Hitchin, -s ˈhitʃin, -z
hither (H.) ˈhiðə*
hitherto ˈhiðəˈtu: [also '---, ˌ--'- according to sentence-stress]
Hitler (German name) ˈhitlə* (ˈhitlər)
Hitlerian hitˈliəriən
Hitlerite, -p ˈhitlərait, -s
Hittite, -s ˈhitait, -s
hiv|e (s. v.), -es, -ing, -ed haiv, -z, -iŋ, -d
hives (disease) haivz
Hivite, -s ˈhaivait, -s
Hlakpa La ˈlɑ:kpəˈlɑ:
ho həu
Hoadl(e)y ˈhəudli
Hoangho ˈhəuæŋˈhəu
hoar (H.) hɔ:* [hɔə*]
hoard (s. v.), -s, -ing, -ed, -er/s hɔ:d [hɔəd], -z, -iŋ, -id, -ə*/z
hoarding (s.), -s ˈhɔ:diŋ [ˈhɔəd-], -z
Hoare hɔ:* [hɔə*]
hoar-frost, -s ˈhɔ:ˈfrɔst [ˈhɔəˈf-, -ˈfrɔ:st], -s
hoarse, -r, -st, -ly, -ness hɔ:s [hɔəs], -ə*, -ist, -li, -nis
hoar|y, -ier, -iest, -ily, -iness ˈhɔ:r|i [ˈhɔər-], -iə*, -iist, -ili, -inis
hoax (s. v.), -es, -ing, -ed, -er/s həuks, -iz, -iŋ, -t, -ə*/z
hob, -s hɔb, -z
Hobart ˈhəubɑ:t
hobbadehoy, -s ˈhɔbədiˈhɔi, -z
Hobbema, -s ˈhɔbimə, -z
Hobbes hɔbz
hobb|le (s. v.), -les, -ling, -led, -ler/s ˈhɔb|l, -lz, -l̩iŋ [-liŋ], -ld, -l̩ə*/z [-lə*/z]
hobbledehoy, -s ˈhɔbldiˈhɔi, -z
Hobbs hɔbz
hobb|y, -ies ˈhɔb|i, -iz
hobby-horse, -s ˈhɔbihɔ:s, -iz
Hobday ˈhɔbdei
hobgoblin, -s ˈhɔbgɔblin, -z
Hobhouse ˈhɔbhaus
hobnail, -s, -ed ˈhɔbneil, -z, -d
hobnob (s. v.), -s, -bing, -bed ˈhɔbnɔb [ˈ-ˈ-], -z, -iŋ, -d
hobo, -s ˈhəubəu, -z
Hoboken ˈhəuˌbəukən [-bək-]
Hobson ˈhɔbsn
Hoby ˈhəubi

Hoccleve ˈhɔkli:v
hochheimer ˈhɔkhaimə* [ˈhɔxh-]
hock, -s hɔk, -s
hockey ˈhɔki
hockey-stick, -s ˈhɔki-stik, -s
Hock|in, -ing ˈhɔk|in, -iŋ
hocus-pocus ˈhəukəsˈpəukəs
hod, -s hɔd, -z
Hodd|er, -esdon ˈhɔd|ə*, -zdən
hodge (H.), -s hɔdʒ, -iz
hodge-podge ˈhɔdʒpɔdʒ
Hodg|es, -kin/son ˈhɔdʒ|iz, -kin/sn
Hodgson ˈhɔdʒsn, in North also ˈhɔdʒən
hod|man, -men ˈhɔd|mən, -mən [-men]
hodograph, -s ˈhɔdəugrɑ:f [-græf], -s
hodometer, -s hɔˈdɔmitə*, -z
Hodson ˈhɔdsn
hoe (s. v.), -s, -ing, -d, -r/s həu, -z, -iŋ, -d, -ə*/z
Hoe həu
Hoey hɔi, ˈhəui
hog, -s hɔg, -z
Hogan ˈhəugən
Hogarth ˈhəugɑ:θ
Hogarthian həuˈgɑ:θjən [-θiən]
Hogben ˈhɔgbən [-ben]
Hogg hɔg
hogger|y, -ies ˈhɔgər|i, -iz
hogget (H.), -s ˈhɔgit, -s
hoggish, -ly, -ness ˈhɔgiʃ, -li, -nis
hogmanay ˈhɔgmənei [ˌ--'-]
hogshead, -s ˈhɔgzhed, -z
Hogue həug
Hohenlinden ˌhəuənˈlindən
Hohenzollern, -s ˌhəuənˈzɔlən [ˌhəuin-] (ˌhɔ:ənˈtsɔlərn), -z
hoik, -s, -ing, -ed hɔik, -s, -iŋ, -t
hoi polloi hɔiˈpɔlɔi [ˈ--'-]
hoist (s. v.), -s, -ing, -ed hɔist, -s, -iŋ, -id
hoity-toity ˈhɔitiˈtɔiti
hok(e)y-pok(e)y ˈhəukiˈpəuki
hokum ˈhəukəm
Holbech ˈhəulbi:tʃ
Holbeck ˈhɔlbek
Holbein, -s ˈhɔlbain, -z
Holborn (in London) ˈhəubən [ˈhəulb-]
Holbrook(e) ˈhəulbruk, ˈhɔl-
Holburn (near Aberdeen) ˈhɔlbə:n [ˈhəul-]
Holcroft ˈhəulkrɔft [-krɔ:ft]
hold (s. v.), -s, -ing, held, holder/s həuld, -z, -iŋ, held, ˈhəuldə*/z
hold-all, -s ˈhəuldɔ:l, -z
Holden ˈhəuldən
Holder ˈhəuldə*
Holdfast, -s ˈhəuldfɑ:st, -s
holding (s.), -s ˈhəuldiŋ, -z
Holdsworth ˈhəuldzwə:θ

hold-up, -s 'həuldʌp ['həuld'ʌp], -s
holl|e (s. v.) (H.), -es, -ing, -ed həul, -z, -iŋ, -d
hole-and-corner 'həulənd'kɔːnə*
Holford 'həulfəd
holiday, -s 'hɔlədi [-lid-, -dei], -z
Holiday 'hɔlidei
holiday - maker,   -s   'hɔlədi,meikə* [-lid-, -dei-], -z
Holies 'həuliz
Holifield 'hɔlifiːld
Holinshed 'hɔlinʃed
holism 'hɔlizm ['həu-]
Holkam 'həukəm
Holkar 'həulkə* (Hind. holkər)
holland (H.), -s 'hɔlənd, -z
hollandaise ,hɔlən'deiz [also '--- when attributive]
Hollander, -s 'hɔləndə*, -z
hollands 'hɔləndz
Holles 'hɔlis
Hollingsworth 'hɔliŋzwəːθ
Hollins 'hɔlinz
holl|o, -oes, -oing, -oed 'hɔl|əu, -əuz, -əuiŋ, -əud
Hollom 'hɔləm
holl|ow (s. adj. v.), -ows; -ower, -owest, -owly, -owness; -owing, -owed 'hɔl|əu, -əuz; -əuə*, -əuist, -əuli, -əunis; -əuiŋ, -əud
Holloway 'hɔləwei [-luw-]
hollow-eyed 'hɔləuaid
holl|y (H.), -ies 'hɔl|i, -iz
hollyhock, -s 'hɔlihɔk, -s
Hollywood 'hɔliwud
holm (H.), -s həum, -z
Holman 'həulmən
Holmby 'həumbi
Holmer 'həulmə*
Holmes, -dale həumz, -deil
holm-oak, -s 'həum'əuk, -s
holocaust, -s 'hɔləkɔːst, -s
Holofernes ,hɔləu'fəːniːz
holograph, -s 'hɔləugrɑːf [-græf], -s
holpen (archaic p. partic. of help) 'həulpən
Holroyd 'hɔlrɔid
Holst (Gustav H., musical composer) həulst
Holstein 'hɔlstain
holster, -s, -ed 'həulstə*, -z, -d
holt (H.), -s həult, -s
Holtby 'həultbi
Holtham (surname) 'həulθəm, 'hɔlθəm, 'həuθəm
holus-bolus 'həuləs'bəuləs
holl|y (H.), -ier, -iest, -iness 'həul|i, -iə* [-jə*], -iist [-jist], -inis

Holycross 'həuli-krɔs [-krɔːs]
Holyhead 'hɔlihed
Holyoake 'həuliəuk
Holyrood 'hɔliruːd
holyston|e (s. v.), -es, -ing, -ed 'həulistəun, -z, -iŋ, -d
Holy-week 'həuliwiːk
Holywell 'hɔliwəl [-wel]
homage; -r/s 'hɔmidʒ; -ə*/z
homburg (H.), -s 'hɔmbəːg, -z
home (s. adv.), -s həum, -z
Home həum, hjuːm
    Note.—hjuːm in Milne-Home, Douglas-Home, and the Earl of Home.
home-bred 'həum'bred [also '-- when attributive]
home-brewed 'həum'bruːd [also '-- when attributive]
home-coming, -s 'həum,kʌmiŋ, -z
home-grown 'həum'grəun [also '-- when attributive]
homeland (H.), -s 'həumlænd, -z
homeless, -ness 'həumlis, -nis
homelike 'həumlaik
homel|y, -ier, -iest, -iness 'həuml|i, -iə*, -iist, -inis
home-made 'həum'meid [also '-- when attributive]
Homer 'həumə*
Homeric (relating to Homer) həu'merik, (name of ship) 'həumərik
Homerton 'hɔmətən
homesick, -ness 'həum-sik, -nis
homespun, -s 'həum-spʌn, -z
homestead, -s 'həum-sted [-stid], -z
home-thrust, -s 'həum'θrʌst, -s
homeward, -s 'həumwəd, -z
Homfray 'hʌmfri
homicidal ,hɔmi'saidl ['---- esp. when attributive]
homicide, -s 'hɔmisaid, -z
Homildon 'hɔmildən
hominoid, -s 'hɔminɔid, -z
homil|y, -ies 'hɔmil|i, -iz
hominy 'hɔmini
homo 'həuməu
homoeopath, -s 'həumjəupæθ [-mïəp-], -s
homoeopathic, -al, -ally ,həumjəu-'pæθik [-miəu'p-, -miə'p-], -əl, -əli
homoeopath|ist/s, -y ,həumi'ɔpəθ|ist/s, -i
homogeneity ,hɔməudʒe'niːiti [,həum-, -dʒi'n-, -'ni(ː)əti]
homogeneous, -ly, -ness ,hɔməu'dʒiːnjəs [,həum-, -'dʒen-, -nïəs], -li, -nis
homogenize, -d hɔ'mɔdʒənaiz [hə-], -d

homograph, -s 'hɔməugrɑ:f [-məg-, -græf], -s
homographic ,hɔməu'græfik [,həum-]
homologous hɔ'mɔləgəs [həu'm-]
homologue, -s 'hɔmələg, -z
homology hɔ'mɔlədʒi [həu'm-]
homonym, -s 'hɔməunim, -z
homonymous, -ly hɔ'mɔniməs [həu'm-], -li
homonymy hɔ'mɔnimi [həu'm-]
homophone, -s 'hɔməufəun, -z
homophon|ous, -y hɔ'mɔfən|əs [həu'm-], -i
homorganic ,hɔmɔ:'gænik [,həu-]
homosexual, -ist/s 'həuməu'seksjŭəl ['hɔm-, -ksjwəl, -ksjul, -kʃŭəl, -kʃwəl, -kʃul], -ist/s
homosexuality 'həuməuseksju'æliti ['hɔm-, -kʃu-]
hon. (H.) (son of a peer, etc.) 'ɔnərəbl, (without salary) 'ɔnərəri
Hondur|as, -an/s hɔn'djuər|əs [-r|æs], -ən/z
hon|e (s. v.) (H.), -es, -ing, -ed həun, -z, -iŋ, -d
honest, -ly; -y 'ɔnist, -li; -i
honey, -ed 'hʌni, -d
honey-bag, -s 'hʌnibæg, -z
honey-bee, -s 'hʌnibi:, -z
Honeybourne 'hʌnibɔ:n [-bɔən, -buən]
honeycomb (H.), -s, -ed 'hʌnikəum, -z, -d
honeydew 'hʌnidju:
honey-guide, -s 'hʌnigaid, -z
honeymoon, -s 'hʌnimu:n, -z
honeysucker, -s 'hʌni,sʌkə*, -z
honeysuckle, -s 'hʌni,sʌkl, -z
Hong Kong hɔŋ'kɔŋ ['hɔŋ'k-]
Honiton 'hɔnitn [locally 'hʌn-]
Honolulu ,hɔnə'lu:lu:
Honor 'ɔnə*
honorarium, -s ,ɔnə'rɛəriəm [,hɔn-, -'rɑ:r-], -z
honorary 'ɔnərəri
honorific (s. adj.), -s ,ɔnə'rifik, -s
Honorius həu'nɔ:riəs [hɔ'n-]
honour (s. v.), -s, -ing, -ed 'ɔnə*, -z, -riŋ, -d
honourab|le, -ly, -leness 'ɔnərəb|l, -li, -lnis
honours|-man, -men 'ɔnəz|mæn, -men
Honyman 'hʌnimən
hood (s. v.) (H.), -s, -ing, -ed; -less hud, -z, -iŋ, -id; -lis
hoodwink, -s, -ing, -ed 'hudwiŋk, -s, -iŋ, -t [-wiŋt]
hoo|f (s.), -fs, -ves hu:|f, -fs, -vz
hoof (v.), -s, -ing, -ed hu:f, -s, -iŋ, -t

Hoog(h)ly 'hu:gli
hook (s. v.) (H.), -s, -ing, -ed, -er/s huk, -s, -iŋ, -t, -ə*/z
hookah, -s 'hukə [-kɑ:], -z
Hooke, -r huk, -ə*
hook-nosed 'huknəuzd
hook-up, -s 'hukʌp, -s
Hooley 'hu:li
hooligan (H.), -s 'hu:ligən, -z
hoop (s. v.), -s, -ing, -ed hu:p, -s, -iŋ, -t
hooper (H.), -s 'hu:pə*, -z
hooping-cough 'hu:piŋ-kɔf [-kɔ:f]
hoopoe, -s 'hu:pu:, -z
hooray hu'rei ['-'-]
hoot (s. v.), -s, -ing, -ed hu:t, -s, -iŋ, -id
hooter, -s 'hu:tə*, -z
hoover (s. v.) (H.), -s, -ing, -ed 'hu:və*, -z, -riŋ, -d
hooves (from hoof) hu:vz
hop (s. v.), -s, -ping, -ped, -per/s hɔp, -s, -iŋ, -t, -ə*/z
Hopcraft 'hɔpkrɑ:ft
hop|e (s. v.) (H.), -es, -ing, -ed həup, -s, -iŋ, -t
hope|ful (H.), -fully, -fulness 'həup|-ful, -fuli [-fəli], -tulnis
hopeless, -ly, -ness 'həuplis, -li, -nis
Hopetoun 'həuptən, -taun
hop-field, -s 'hɔpfi:ld, -z
Hopkin|s, -son 'hɔpkin|z, -sn
hoplite, -s 'hɔplait, -s
hop-manure 'hɔpmə,njuə* [-,njɔ:*, -,njə:*]
Hop-o'-my-thumb 'hɔpəmi'θʌm ['----]
hop-pick|er/s, -ing 'hɔp,pik|ə*/z, -iŋ
Hoppner, -s 'hɔpnə*, -z
hopscotch 'hɔpskɔtʃ
Hopton 'hɔptən
hop-vine, -s 'hɔpvain, -z
Hor hɔ:*
Horace 'hɔrəs [-ris]
Horatian hɔ'reiʃjən [hə'r-, -ʃiən, -ʃən]
Horatio hɔ'reiʃiəu [hə'r-, -ʃjəu]
Hora|tius, -tii hɔ'rei|ʃjəs [hə'r-, -ʃiəs, -ʃəs], -ʃiai
Horbury 'hɔ:bəri
horde, -s hɔ:d, -z
Horeb 'hɔ:reb
horehound 'hɔ:haund ['hɔəh-]
horizon, -s hə'raizn [hu'r-, also ə'r-, u'r- when not initial], -z
horizont|al, -ally ,hɔri'zɔnt|l, -əli [-ļi]
Horlick 'hɔ:lik
hormone, -s 'hɔ:məun, -z
horn (H.), -s hɔ:n, -z
hornbeam, -s 'hɔ:nbi:m, -z
hornbill, -s 'hɔ:nbil, -z
hornblende 'hɔ:nblend

hornbook, -s 'hɔːnbuk, -s
Horncastle 'hɔːn‚kɑːsl
Horne hɔːn
horned (poppy) 'hɔːnid [-nd], (of cattle,
  birds, etc.) hɔːnd, (poetically, as in
  horned moon) 'hɔːnid
-horned -hɔːnd
Hornell hɔː'nel
Horner 'hɔːnə*
hornet, -s 'hɔːnit, -s
Horniman 'hɔːnimən
hornpipe, -s 'hɔːnpaip, -s
Hornsey 'hɔːnzi
hornwork, -s 'hɔːn-wəːk, -s
horn|y, -ier, -iest, -iness 'hɔːn|i, -ïə*
  [-jə*], -iist [-jist], -inis
horny-handed 'hɔːni‚hændid
horography hɔ'rɔgrəfi [hɔː'r-]
horologe, -s 'hɔrələdʒ ['hɔːr-, -ləudʒ], -iz
horolog|er/s, -ist/s, -y hɔ'rɔlədʒ|ə*/z
  [hɔː'r-], -ist/s, -i
horological ‚hɔrə'lɔdʒikəl [‚hɔːr-]
horoscope, -s 'hɔrəskəup, -s
horoscopic ‚hɔrə'skɔpik
horoscop|ist/s, -y hɔ'rɔskəp|ist/s [hə'r-],
  -i
horrib|le, -ly, -leness 'hɔrəb|l [-rib-], -li,
  -lnis
horrid, -er, -est, -ly, -ness 'hɔrid, -ə*,
  -ist, -li, -nis
horrific hɔ'rifik
horri|fy, -fies, -fying, -fied 'hɔri|fai, -faiz,
  -faiiŋ, -faid
Horrocks, -es 'hɔrəks, -iz
horror, -s 'hɔrə*, -z
horror|-stricken, -struck 'hɔrə|‚strikən,
  -strʌk
Horsa 'hɔːsə
hors de combat 'hɔːdə'kɔ̃'mbɑ: [-'kɔːm-,
  -'kɔm-] (ɔrdəkɔ̃ba)
hors-d'œuvre, -s ɔː'dəːvr [hɔː'd-, '-'-,
  -və*, '-'--] (ɔrdœːvr), -z
horse, -s, -d hɔːs, -iz, -t
horseback 'hɔːsbæk
horse-block, -s 'hɔːsblɔk, -s
horse-box, -es 'hɔːsbɔks, -iz
horsebreaker, -s 'hɔːs‚breikə*, -z
horse-bus, -es 'hɔːsbʌs, -iz
horse-chestnut, -s 'hɔːs'tʃesnʌt [-nət,
  -stn-], -s
horse|-cloth, -cloths 'hɔːs|klɔθ [-klɔːθ],
  -klɔθs [-klɔːðz, -klɔːθs]
horse-dealer, -s 'hɔːs‚diːlə*, -z
horse-doctor, -s 'hɔːs‚dɔktə*, -z
horseflesh 'hɔːsfleʃ
horsefl|y, -ies 'hɔːsfl|ai, -aiz
Horse-guard, -s 'hɔːsgɑːd ['hɔːs'g-], -z
horse|-hair, -laugh/s 'hɔːs|hɛə*, -lɑːf/s

horse|man (H.), -men; -manship
  'hɔːs|mən, -mən [-men]; -mənʃip
horse-marine, -s 'hɔːsmə‚riːn, -z
horseplay 'hɔːs-plei
horse-pond, -s 'hɔːs-pɔnd, -z
horse-power 'hɔːs‚pauə*
horse-rac|e, -es, -ing 'hɔːs-reis, -iz, -iŋ
horse-radish, -es 'hɔːs‚rædiʃ ['-'--, '-'--],
  -iz
horse-sense 'hɔːssens
horse-shoe, -s 'hɔːʃʃuː ['hɔːsʃuː], -z
horse-show, -s 'hɔːʃʃəu ['hɔːs-], -z
horse-train|er/s, -ing 'hɔːs‚trein|ə*/z,
  -iŋ
horse-tram, -s 'hɔːs-træm ['hɔːs't-], -z
horse-truck, -s 'hɔːs-trʌk, -s
horse-whip (s. v.), -s, -ping, -ped
  'hɔːs-wip ['hɔːshw-], -s, -iŋ, -t
horse|-woman, -women 'hɔːs|‚wumən,
  -‚wimin
Horsfall 'hɔːs-fɔːl
Horsham 'hɔːʃəm
Horsley (surname, place name) 'hɔːsli,
  'hɔːzli
  Note.—The place in Surrey is pronounced both ways locally, the form
  with z being more frequent.
Horsmonden (in Kent) ‚hɔːsmən'den
  [old-fashioned local pronunciation
  ‚hɔːsn'den]
hors|y, -ier, -iest, -ily, -iness 'hɔːs|i, -ïə*
  [-jə*], -iist [-jist], -ili, -inis
hortat|ive, -ory 'hɔːtət|iv, -əri
Hortensi|a, -us hɔː'tensï|ə [-nsj|ə, -nʃï|ə,
  -nʃj|ə], -əs
horticultur|al, -ist/s ‚hɔːti'kʌltʃər|əl
  [-tʃur-], -ist/s
horticulture 'hɔːtikʌltʃə*
Horton 'hɔːtn
Horwich 'hɔridʒ
Hosack 'hɔsək
hosanna, -s həu'zænə, -z
hose, -s həuz, -iz
Hosea həu'ziə
hose-pipe, -s 'həuzpaip, -s
hosier, -s, -y 'həuzïə [-zjə*, -ʒə*, -ʒjə*,
  -ʒïə*], -z, -ri
Hosier (surname) 'həuzjə* [-zïə*]
Hosmer 'hɔzmə*
hospice, -s 'hɔspis, -iz
hospitab|le, -ly, -leness 'hɔspitəb|l
  [hɔs'pit-, həs-], -li, -lnis
hospital, -s 'hɔspitl, -z
hospitalit|y, -ies ‚hɔspi'tælit|i, -iz
hospital(l)er, -s 'hɔspitlə* [-tələ*], -z
host (H.), -s həust, -s
hostage, -s 'hɔstidʒ, -iz
hostel, -s; -ry, -ries 'hɔstəl, -z; -ri, -riz

hosteller, -s 'hɔstələ*, -z
hostess, -es 'həustis [-tes], -iz
hostile, -ly 'hɔstail, -li
hostilit|y, -ies hɔs'tilit|i [-lət-], -iz
hostler, -s 'ɔslə*, -z
hot (adj. v.), -ter, -test, -ly, -ness; -s,
  -ting, -ted hɔt, -ə*, -ist, -li, -nis; -s,
  -iŋ, -id
hotbed, -s 'hɔtbed, -z
hot-blooded 'hɔt'blʌdid ['hɔt,b-]
Hotchkiss 'hɔtʃkis
hotch|pot, -potch 'hɔtʃ|pɔt, -pɔtʃ
hot-dog, -s 'hɔt'dɔg, -z
hotel, -s həu'tel [əu't-], -z
  Note.—Some use the form əu'tel
  always; others use it occasionally
  when the word is not initial.
hotelier, -s həu'teliei [-lə*], -z
Hotham (surname) "hʌðəm
hothead, -s 'hɔthed, -z
hot-headed 'hɔt'hedid ['hɔt,h-]
hothou|se, -ses 'hɔthau|s, -ziz
hotpot, -s 'hɔtpɔt, -s
hotspur (H.), -s 'hɔtspə(:)*, -z
Hottentot, -s 'hɔtntɔt, -s
hot-water-bottle,   -s   hɔt'wɔːtə,bɔtl
  ['-'--,--], -z
hough (s. v.), -s, -ing, -ed hɔk, -s, -iŋ, -t
Hough hʌf, hɔf
Houghall (in Durham) 'hɔfl
Hougham (in Kent) 'hʌfəm
Houghton 'hɔːtn, 'hautn, 'həutn
  Note.—'hɔːtn, 'hautn seem more usual
  when the word is a surname; 'həutn
  seems more usual when the word is
  a place name.
Houghton - le - Spring   'həutnli'spriŋ
  [locally 'hautn-]
Houltby 'həultbi
hound (s. v.), -s, -ing, -ed haund, -z, -iŋ,
Houndsditch 'haundzditʃ   [-id
Hounslow 'haunzləu
hour, -s, -ly 'auə*, -z, -li
hourglass, -es 'auə-glɑːs, -iz
hour-hand, -s 'auəhænd, -z
houri, -s 'huəri, -z
hou|se (s.) (H.), -ses hau|s, -ziz
hous|e (v.), -es, -ing, -ed hauz, -iz, -iŋ, -d
house-agent/s,   -boat/s   'haus|,eidʒ-
  ənt/s, -bəut/s
house-break|er/s,   -ing   'haus,breik|-
  ə*/z, -iŋ
house-dog, -s 'hausdɔg, -z
house-dut|y, -ies 'haus,djuːt|i, -iz
house-fl|y, -ies 'hausfl|ai, -aiz
houseful, -s 'hausful, -z
household, -s; -er/s 'haushəuld, -z;
  -ə*/z

housekeep|er/s, -ing 'haus,kiːp|ə*/z, -iŋ
Housel 'hauzl
house-leek, -s 'haus-liːk, -s
houseless 'hauslis
housemaid, -s 'haus-meid, -z
housemaster, -s 'haus,mɑːstə*, -z
house-parlourmaid, -s 'haus'pɑːləmeid,
  -z
house-part|y, -ies 'haus,pɑːt|i, -iz
house-physician, -s 'hausfi,ziʃən, -z
house-room 'hausrum [-ruːm]
house-surgeon, -s 'haus,səːdʒən, -z
house-to-house 'haus-tə'haus
housetop, -s 'haus-tɔp, -s
house-warming, -s 'haus,wɔːmiŋ, -z
housewi|fe (woman), -ves 'haus-wai|f,
  -vz
housewi|fe (needle-case), -fes, -ves
  'hʌzi|f, -fs, -vz
housewifely 'haus,waifli
housewifery 'hauswifəri ['hʌzifri]
house-work 'haus-wəːk
Housman 'hausmən
Houston (English surname) 'huːstən,
  'haus-, (Scottish surname) 'huːstən,
  (city in U.S.A.) 'hjuːstən
Houyhnhnm, -s 'huiʰnəm [hu'inəm], -z
hove (from heave) (H.) həuv
hov|el (s. v.), -els, -elling, -elled, -eller/s
  'hɔv|əl ['hʌv-], -əlz, -liŋ [-əliŋ], -əld,
  -lə*/z [-ələ*/z]
Hovell (surname) 'həuvəl, 'hɔvəl,
  həu'vel
Hovenden 'hɔvndən
hov|er, -ers, -ering, -ered 'hɔv|ə*
  ['hʌv-], -əz, -əriŋ, -əd
hovercraft, -s 'hɔvə-krɑːft, -s
hover-fl|y, -ies 'hɔvə-fl|ai, -aiz
Hovis 'həuvis
how (H.) hau
Howard 'hau-əd ['hauəd]
howbeit 'hau'biːit [hau'b-]
howdah, -s 'haudə, -z
how do you do 'haudju'du: [-djə'd-,
  -di'd-, -dʒu'd-, -dʒə'd-]
howdy-do, -s 'haudi'du:, -z
Howe hau
Howell, -s 'hauəl, -z
however hau'evə*
  Note.—Variants 'hauevə*, 'hauəvə*
  are used by some people when the
  meaning is ' however that may be'.
Howick 'hauik
How|ie, -itt 'hau|i, -it
howitzer, -s 'hauitsə*, -z
howl (s. v.), -s, -ing, -ed haul, -z, -iŋ, -d
howler, -s 'haulə*, -z
Howley 'hauli

Howorth 'hauəθ
Howse hauz
howsoever ˌhausəu'evə*
Howson 'hausn
Howth (near Dublin) həuθ
Hoxton 'hɔkstən
hoy (s. interj.) (H.), -s hɔi, -z
hoyden (H.), -s 'hɔidn, -z
Hoylake 'hɔileik
hub, -s hʌb, -z
Huback 'hju:bæk
Hubback 'hʌbæk, -bək
Hubbard 'hʌbəd
hubble-bubble, -s 'hʌblˌbʌbl, -z
hubbub, -s 'hʌbʌb [-bəb], -z
hubbly, -ies 'hʌbli, -iz
Hubert 'hju:bə(:)t
huckaback, -s 'hʌkəbæk, -s
huckleberry|y, -ies 'hʌklbər|i [ˌber|i], -iz
Huckleberry 'hʌklbəri
Huckleberry 'hʌklbəri
Hucknall 'hʌknəl [-nl̩]
huckster, -s 'hʌkstə*, -z
Huddersfield 'hʌdəzfi:ld
hudd|le (s. v.), -les, -ling, -led 'hʌd|l, -lz,
  -l̩iŋ [-liŋ], -ld
Hud(d)leston 'hʌdlstən
Hudibras 'hju:dibræs
Hud|nott, -son 'hʌd|nɔt, -sn
hue, -s hju:, -z
hue and cry 'hju:ən'krai [-əŋ'k-]
Hueffer 'hefə*
huff (s. v.), -s, -ing, -ed hʌf, -s, -iŋ, -t
huffish, -ly, -ness 'hʌfiʃ, -li, -nis
huff|y, -ier, -iest, -ily, -iness 'hʌf|i, -iə*,
  -iist, -ili, -inis
hug (s. v.), -s, -ging, -ged hʌg, -z, -iŋ, -d
Hugall 'hju:gəl
huge, -r, -st, -ly, -ness hju:dʒ, -ə*, -ist,
  -li, -nis
Hugesson 'hju:gisn
hugger-mugger 'hʌgəˌmʌgə*
Huggin, -s 'hʌgin, -z
Hugh, -es hju:, -z
Hughenden 'hju:əndən
Hugo (Eng. name) 'hju:gəu
Hugon 'hju:gən [-gɔn]
Hugue|not, -nots 'hju:gə|nɔt [-nəu],
  -nɔts [-nəuz]
Huish 'hju:(:)iʃ
Hulbert 'hʌlbə(:)t
hulk, -s, -ing hʌlk, -s, -iŋ
hull (s. v.) (H.), -s, -ing, -ed hʌl, -z, -iŋ,
  -d
hullabaloo, -s ˌhʌləbə'lu:, -z
Hullah 'hʌlə
hullo 'hʌ'ləu [hʌ'l-]
Hulme hju:m, hu:m

Hulse hʌls
Hulsean hʌl'si(:)ən
hum (s. v.), -s, -ming, -med hʌm, -z,
  -iŋ, -d
human, -ly 'hju:mən, -li
humane, -r, -st, -ly, -ness hju(:)'mein,
  -ə*, -ist, -li, -nis
humani|sm, -st/s 'hju:məni|zəm, -st/s
humanistic ˌhju:mə'nistik
humanitarian, -s, -ism hju(:)ˌmæni-
  'tɛəriən [ˌhju:mæn-], -z, -izəm
humanit|y, -ies hju(:)'mænit|i, -iz
humanization [-isa-] ˌhju:mənai'zeiʃən
humaniz|e [-is|e], -es, -ing, -ed 'hju:-
  mənaiz, -iz, -iŋ, -d
humankind 'hju:mən'kaind
Humber, -s 'hʌmbə*, -z
Humbert 'hʌmbə(:)t
humb|le (adj. v.), -ler, -lest, -ly, -leness;
  -les, -ling, -led 'hʌmb|l, -lə*, -list, -li,
  -lnis; -lz, -liŋ, -ld
humble-bee, -s 'hʌmblbi:, -z
humble-pie 'hʌmbl'pai
Humboldt 'hʌmbəult ['hum-] ('humbɔlt)
humbug (s. v.), -s, -ging, -ged 'hʌmbʌg,
  -z, -iŋ, -d
humdrum 'hʌmdrʌm
Hume hju:m
humer|us, -i, -al 'hju:mər|əs, -ai, -əl
Humian 'hju:mjən [-miən]
humid, -ness 'hju:mid, -nis
humidity hju(:)'miditi
humiliat|e, -es, -ing, -ed hju(:)'milieit,
  -s, -iŋ, -id
humiliation, -s hju(:)ˌmili'eiʃən [ˌhju:-
  mil-], -z
humility hju(:)'militi [-lət-]
humming-bird, -s 'hʌmiŋbə:d, -z
humming-top, -s 'hʌmiŋ-tɔp, -s
hummock, -s, -ed; -y 'hʌmək, -s, -t; -i
humor|al, -alism, -alist/s 'hju:mər|əl,
  -əlizəm, -əlist/s
humoresque, -s ˌhju:mə'resk, -s
humorist, -s 'hju:mərist [old-fashioned
  'ju:-], -s
humoristic ˌhju:mə'ristik [old-fashioned
  ˌju:-]
humorous, -ly, -ness 'hju:mərəs [old-
  fashioned 'ju:-], -li, -nis
humour (s. v.), -s, -ing, -ed 'hju:mə*
  [old-fashioned 'ju:-], -z, -riŋ, -id
humoursome, -ly, -ness 'hju:məsəm
  [old-fashioned 'ju:-], -li, -nis
hump (s. v.), -s, -ing, -ed hʌmp, -s, -iŋ,
  -t [hʌmt]
humpback, -s, -ed 'hʌmpbæk, -s, -t
humph, m̩m, m̩m̩m, mm̩m, həh [hʌmf
Humphery 'hʌmfri

Humphr(e)y, -s 'hʌmfri, -z
Humpty-dumpty 'hʌmpti'dʌmpti
hump|y, -ier, -iest, -iness 'hʌmp|i, -iə* [-jə*], -iist [-jist], -inis
humus 'hju:məs
Hun, -s hʌn, -z
hunch (s. v.), -es, -ing, -ed hʌntʃ, -iz, -iŋ, -t
hunchback, -s, -ed 'hʌntʃbæk, -s, -t
hundred, -s 'hʌndrəd [-drid], -z
hundredfold 'hʌndrədfəuld [-drid-]
hundredth, -s 'hʌndrədθ [-dridθ, -drətθ, -dritθ], -s
hundredweight, -s 'hʌndrədweit [-drid-], -s
hung (from hang) hʌŋ
Hungarian, -s hʌŋ'gɛəriən, -z
Hungary 'hʌŋgəri
hunger (s. v.), -s, -ing, -ed, -er/s 'hʌŋ-gə*, -z, -riŋ, -d, -rə*/z
hunger-strik|e (s. v.), -es, -ing, hunger-struck, hunger-striker/s 'hʌŋgə-straik, -s, -iŋ, 'hʌŋgə-strʌk, 'hʌŋgə-ˌstraikə*/z
hungr|y, -ier, -iest, -ily, -iness 'hʌŋ-gr|i, -iə*, -iist, -ili, -inis
hunk, -s hʌŋk, -s
hunks, -es hʌŋks, -iz
Hunn|ic, -ish 'hʌn|ik, -iʃ
Hunstanton hʌn'stæntən [locally 'hʌnstən]
Hunsworth 'hʌnzwə(:)θ
hunt (s. v.) (H.), -s, -ing, -ed, -er/s hʌnt, -s, -iŋ, -id, -ə*/z
Hunter 'hʌntə*
Hunterian hʌn'tiəriən
hunting-box, -es 'hʌntiŋbɔks, -iz
hunting-cap, -s 'hʌntiŋ-kæp, -s
hunting-crop, -s 'hʌntiŋ-krɔp, -s
Huntingdon, -shire 'hʌntiŋdən, -ʃiə* [-ʃə*]
Huntingdonian, -s ˌhʌntiŋ'dəunjən [-niən], -z
hunting-field, -s 'hʌntiŋfi:ld, -z
Huntingford 'hʌntiŋfəd
hunting-ground, -s 'hʌntiŋgraund, -z
hunting-horn, -s 'hʌntiŋhɔ:n, -z
hunting-kni|fe, -ves 'hʌntiŋnai|f, -vz
hunting-song, -s 'hʌntiŋ-sɔŋ, -z
Huntington 'hʌntiŋtən
Huntl(e)y 'hʌntli
Hunton 'hʌntən
huntress, -es 'hʌntris, -iz
Hunts. hʌnts
hunts|man, -men, -manship 'hʌnts|-mən, -mən [-men], -mənʃip
Hunyadi 'hunjɑ:di ['hʌnj-, -'—]
Hurd hə:d

hurd|le (s. v.), -les, -ling, -led 'hə:d|l, -lz, -liŋ [-liŋ], -ld
hurdle-race, -s 'hə:dlreis, -iz
hurdy-gurd|y, -ies 'hə:di,gə:d|i, -iz
Hurford 'hə:fəd
hurl (s. v.), -s, -ing, -ed, -er/s hə:l, -z, -iŋ, -d, -ə*/z
hurley (H.), -s 'hə:li, -z
Hurlingham 'hə:liŋəm
Hurlstone 'hə:lstən
hurly-burly 'hə:li,bə:li
Huron 'hjuərən
hurrah (s. v.), -s, -ing, -ed hu'rɑ:, -z, -iŋ, -d
hurrah (interj.) hu'rɑ: ['hu'rɑ:]
hurray (s.), -s hu'rei, -z
hurray (interj.) hu'rei ['hu'rei]
hurricane, -s 'hʌrikən [-kin, -kein], -z
hurr|y (s. v.), -ies, -ying, -ied/ly, -ier/s 'hʌr|i, -iz, -iiŋ, -id/li, -iə*/z
hurry-scurry 'hʌri'skʌri
hurst, -s hə:st, -s
Hurstmonceux ˌhə:stmən'sju: [-mən-, -'su:]
Hurstpierpoint 'hə:stpiə'pɔint
hurt (s. v.) (H.), -s, -ing hə:t, -s, -iŋ
hurt|ful, -fully, -fulness 'hə:t|ful, -fuli [-fəli], -fulnis
hurt|le, -les, -ling, -led 'hə:t|l, -lz, -liŋ, -ld
husband (s. v.), -s, -ing, -ed 'hʌzbənd, -z, -iŋ, -id
husbandly 'hʌzbəndli
husband|man, -men 'hʌzbənd|mən, -mən [-men]
husbandry 'hʌzbəndri
hush (s. v.), -es, -ing, -ed hʌʃ, -iz, -iŋ, -t
hush (interj.) ʃ: [hʌʃ]
hushaby 'hʌʃəbai
Hushai 'hju:ʃeiai ['hu:-, -ʃai]
hush-hush 'hʌʃ'hʌʃ ['—]
hush-money 'hʌʃˌmʌni
husk, -s hʌsk, -s
Huskisson 'hʌskisn
husk|y, -ier, -iest, -ily, -iness 'hʌsk|i, -iə* [-jə*], -iist [-jist], -ili, -inis
hussar, -s hu'zɑ:*, -z
Hussey 'hʌsi
Hussite, -s 'hʌsait, -s
huss|y, -ies 'hʌs|i ['hʌz|i], -iz
Hussy 'hʌsi
hustings 'hʌstiŋz
hust|le, -les, -ling, -led, -ler/s 'hʌs|l, -lz, -liŋ [-liŋ], -ld, -lə*/z [-lə*/z]
hut, -s hʌt, -s
hutch, -es hʌtʃ, -iz
Hutch|eson, -ings 'hʌtʃ|isn, -iŋz
Hutchinson 'hʌtʃinsn

Hutchinsonian, -s 'hʌtʃin'səunjən [-niən], -z
Hutchison 'hʌtʃisn
Huth, -waite hu:θ, -weit
hutment, -s 'hʌtmənt, -s
Hutton 'hʌtn
Hux|ley, -table 'hʌks|li, -təbl
Huygens 'haigənz
huzza (s. interj.), **-s** hu'zɑ: [hʌ'z-], -z
Hwang-ho hwæŋ'həu ['-'-]
hyacinth (H.), -s 'haiəsinθ, -s
hyacinthine ,haiə'sinθain
Hyades 'haiədi:z
hyaena, -s hai'i:nə, -z
hyal|ine, -ite, -oid 'haiəl|in [-i:n, -ain], -ait, -ɔid
Hyam, -son 'haiəm, -sn
hybrid, -s; -ism 'haibrid, -z; -izəm
hybridity hai'briditi
hybridization [-isa-] ,haibridai'zeiʃən
hybridiz|e [-is|e], -es, -ing, -ed, -er/s 'haibridaiz, -iz, -iŋ, -d, -ə*/z
Hydaspes hai'dæspi:z
Hyde haid
Hyde Park 'haid'pɑ:k ['haidp-, haid'p- according to sentence-stress]
Hyderabad 'haidərəbæd ['haidərə'b-, ,haidərə'b-] (Hind. həydərabad)
hydra, -s 'haidrə, -z
Hydrabad 'haidrəbæd ['haidrə'b-, ,haidrə'b-]
hydrangea, -s hai'dreindʒə [-dʒjə, -dʒiə], -z
hydrant, -s 'haidrənt, -s
hydrargyrum hai'drɑ:dʒirəm
hydrate, -s 'haidreit [-rit], -s
hydraulic, -s hai'drɔ:lik [-'drɒl-], -s
hydro, -s 'haidrəu, -z [-z
hydrocarbon, -s 'haidrəu'kɑ:bən [-bɒn],
hydrocephalus 'haidrəu'sefələs [,hai-, -'kef-]
hydrochloric 'haidrəu'klɒrik [-'klɔ:r-, also '--,--, ,--'-- according to sentence-stress]
hydrodynamic, -al, -ally, -s 'haidrəudai'næmik [-di'n-], -əl, -əli, -s
hydrogen 'haidridʒən [-drədʒən, -drədʒin]
hydrogenous hai'drɒdʒinəs
hydrograph|er/s, -y hai'drɒgrəf|ə*/z, -i
hydrographic, -al, -ally ,haidrəu'græfik, -əl, -əli
hydro|logy, -lysis hai'drɒ|lədʒi, -lisis [-ləsis]
hydromechanics 'haidrəumi'kæniks
hydrometer, -s hai'drɒmitə*, -z
hydrometric, -al, -ally ,haidrəu'metrik, -əl, -əli

hydrometry hai'drɒmitri
hydropathic (s. adj.), **-s, -al, -ally** ,haidrəu'pæθik, -s, -əl, -əli
hydropath|ist/s, -y hai'drɒpəθ|ist/s, -i
hydrophobia ,haidrəu'fəubjə [-biə]
hydrophobic ,haidrəu'fəubik [-'fɒb-]
hydropic hai'drɒpik
hydroplane, -s 'haidrəuplein, -z
hydropsy 'haidrɒpsi
hydroquinone 'haidrəukwi'nəun [-'kwainəun, hai'drɒkinəun]
hydroscope, -s 'haidrəskəup, -s
hydrostat, -s 'haidrəustæt, -s
hydrostatic, -al, -ally, -s ,haidrəu'stætik, -əl, -əli, -s
hydrosulphuric 'haidrəusʌl'fjuərik [-'fjɔər-, -'fjɔ:r-]
hydrous 'haidrəs
hydrox|ide/s, -yl hai'drɒks|aid/z, -il
hyena, -s hai'i:nə, -z
Hygeia hai'dʒi(:)ə
hygiene 'haidʒi:n
hygienic, -ally hai'dʒi:nik, -əli
hygromet|er/s, -ry hai'grɔmit|ə*/z, -ri
hygrometric, -al, -ally ,haigrəu'metrik, -əl, -əli
hygroscope, -s 'haigrəskəup, -s
Hyksos 'hiksɒs
Hylas 'hailæs
Hylton 'hiltən [-tn]
Hyman haimən
hymen (H.), -s 'haimen, -z [-ən
hymene|al, -an ,haime'ni(:)|əl [-mə'n-],
Hymettus hai'metəs
hymn (s. v.), **-s, -ing, -ed** him, -z, -iŋ, -d
hymnal, -s 'himnəl [-nl̩], -z
hymnar|y, -ies 'himnər|i, -iz
hymn-book, -s 'himbuk, -s
hymnic 'himnik
hymnody 'himnəudi
hymnolog|ist/s, -y him'nɒlədʒ|ist/s, -i
Hyndley 'haindli
Hyndman 'haindmən
hyoid 'haiɔid
hypallage hai'pæləgi(:) [-lədʒi]
Hypatia hai'peiʃjə [-ʃiə, -ʃə]
hyperacute, -ness 'haipərə'kju:t, -nis
hyperbol|a, -ae, -as hai'pə:bəl|ə, -i:, -əz
hyperbole, -s hai'pə:bəli, -z
hyperbolic, -al, -ally ,haipə(:)'bɒlik, -əl, -əli
hyperboli|sm, -st/s hai'pə:bəli|zəm, -st/s
hyperboliz|e [-is|e], -es, -ing, -ed hai-'pə:bəlaiz, -iz, -iŋ, -d
hyperboloid, -s hai'pə:bələid, -z
hyperborean, -s ,haipə(:)bɔ:'ri(:)ən [-bɔ'ri(:)ən, -'bɔ:riən], -z

hypercritic|al, -ally 'haipə(:)'kritik|əl, -əli
hypercriticism 'haipə(:)'kritisizəm
hypercriticiz|e [-is|e], **-es**, **-ing**, **-ed** 'haipə(:)'kritisaiz, -iz, -iŋ, -d
Hyperides ˌhaipə'raidi:z
Hyperion hai'piəriən [-'per-]
hypersensitive 'haipə(:)'sensitiv [-sətiv]
hyper-space 'haipə(:)'speis
hypertroph|y, -ied hai'pə:trəuf|i, -id
hyph|en (*s. v.*), **-ens**, **-ening**, **-ened** 'haif|ən, -ənz, -ŋiŋ [-əniŋ], -ənd
hyphenat|e, **-es**, **-ing**, **-ed** 'haifəneit [-fin-], -s, -iŋ, -id
hypnosis hip'nəusis
hypnotic hip'nɔtik
hypnoti|sm, -st/s 'hipnəti|zəm, -st/s
hypnotization [-isa-] ˌhipnətai'zeiʃən
hypnotiz|e [-is|e], **-es**, **-ing**, **-ed**, **-er/s** 'hipnətaiz, -iz, -iŋ, -d, -ə*/z
hypo 'haipəu
hypocaust, -s 'haipəukɔ:st, -s
hypochond|ria, -riac/s ˌhaipəu'kɔnd|rĭə [ˌhip-], -riæk/s
hypochondriacal ˌhaipəukɔn'draiəkəl [ˌhip-, -kən-]
hypochondriasis ˌhaipəukɔn'draiəsis [ˌhip-, -kən-]
hypocris|y, -ies hi'pɔkrəs|i [-kris-], -iz
hypocrite, -s 'hipəkrit [-puk-], -s

hypocritic|al, -ally ˌhipəu'kritik|əl, -əli
hypocycloid, -s 'haipəu'saiklɔid, -z
hypoderm|a, -ic ˌhaipəu'də:m|ə, -ik
hypophosphate, -s ˌhaipəu'fɔsfeit [-fit], -s
hypostasis hai'pɔstəsis
hypostatiz|e [-is|e], **-es**, **-ing**, **-ed** hai'pɔstətaiz, -iz, -iŋ, -d
hypostyle 'haipəustail
hyposulphite ˌhaipəu'sʌlfait
hypotax|is, -es ˌhaipəu'tæks|is ['--,--], -i:z
hypotenuse, -s hai'pɔtinju:z [-nju:s, -tŋj-], -iz
hypothecat|e, **-es**, **-ing**, **-ed** hai'pɔθi-keit, -s, -iŋ, -id
hypothecation, -s hai,pɔθi'keiʃən, -z
hypothes|is, -es hai'pɔθis|is [-θəs-], -i:z
hypothetic, -al, -ally ˌhaipəu'θetik, -əl, -əli
hypsomet|er/s, -ry hip'sɔmit|ə*/z, -ri
hyrax, -es 'haiəræks, -iz
hyson (H.), 'haisn
hyssop 'hisəp
hysteria his'tiəriə
hysteric, -s, -al, -ally his'terik, -s, -əl, -əli
hysteron-proteron 'histərɔn'prɔtərɔn
hythe (H.), -s haið, -z

I

I (the letter, pron.), -'s ai, -z
Iacchus i'ækəs [ai'æk-]
Iachimo i'ækiməu [ai'æk-]
Iago i'ɑ:gəu
Iain iən ['i:ən]
iamb, -s 'aiæmb, -z
iamb|ic/s, -us/es ai'æmb|ik/s, -əs/iz
Ian iən ['i:ən]
I'Anson 'aiənsn
Ianthe ai'ænθi
Iason 'aiəsn
Ibadan (in Nigeria) i'bædən [-dn]
Ibbertson 'ibətsn [-bə:t-]
Ibbetson 'ibitsn
Iberia, -n/s ai'biərǐə, -n/z
Iberus ai'biərəs
ibex, -es 'aibeks, -iz
ibidem i'baidem ['ibidem]
ibis, -es 'aibis, -iz
Ibrahim 'ibrəhi:m [ˌibrə'hi:m]
Ibrox 'aibrɔks
Ibsen 'ibsn
Icaria, -n i'kɛərǐə [ai'k-], -n
Icarus 'aikərəs ['ik-]
ic|e (s. v.), -es, -ing, -ed ais, -iz, -iŋ, -t
ice-axe, -s 'ais-æks, -iz
iceberg, -s 'aisbə:g, -z
ice-boat, -s 'aisbəut, -s
icebound 'aisbaund
ice-breaker, -s 'aisˌbreikə*, -z
ice-cap, -s 'ais-kæp, -s
ice-cream, -s 'ais'kri:m [attributively 'ais-kri:m], -z
icedrome, -s 'aisdrəum, -z
icefall, -s 'aisfɔ:l, -z
ice|-field/s, -floe/s 'ais|fi:ld/z, -fləu/z
ice-hockey 'aisˌhɔki
ice-hou|se, -ses 'aishau|s, -ziz
Iceland 'aislənd
Icelander, -s 'aisləndə* [-lændə*], -z
Icelandic ais'lændik
ice|-man, -men 'ais|mæn [-mən], -men
ice-pack, -s 'ais-pæk, -s   [[-mən]
ice-pail, -s 'ais-peil, -z
ice-spar 'ais'spɑ:* ['aisspɑ:*]
Ichabod 'ikəbɔd ['ixə-]
ichneumon, -s ik'nju:mən, -z
ichnography ik'nɔgrəfi
ichor 'aikɔ:*

ichthyolog|ist/s, -y ˌikθi'ɔlədʒ|ist/s, -i
ichthyosaur|us, -i, -uses ˌikθǐə'sɔ:r|əs
[-θjə's-, -θiəu-], -ai, -əsiz
icicle, -s 'aisikl, -z
icing (s.) 'aisiŋ
Icknield 'ikni:ld
Ickornshaw 'ikɔ:nʃɔ:
Icolmkill 'i:kɔlm'kil
icon, -s 'aikɔn [-kən], -z
iconic ai'kɔnik
Iconium ai'kəunjəm [-nǐəm]   [-st/s
iconocla|sm, -st/s ai'kɔnəuklæ|zəm
iconoclastic aiˌkɔnəu'klæstik
iconograph|er/s, -y ˌaikɔ'nɔgrəf|ə*/z
[-kə'n-], -i
iconoscope, -s ai'kɔnəskəup, -s
icosahedr|on, -ons, -a; -al 'aikəsə-
'hedr|ən [-kɔs-, -'hi:d-, '---ˌ--, ˌ---'--],
-ənz, -ə; -əl
ictus, -es 'iktəs, -iz
ic|y, -ier, -iest, -ily, -iness 'ais|i, -ǐə*
[-jə*], -iist [-jist], -ili, -inis
id id
I'd (= I would, I should, or I had) aid
Ida 'aidə
Idaho 'aidəhəu
Idalia, -n ai'deiljə [-lǐə], -n
Iddesleigh 'idzli
Ide (in Devon) i:d
idea, -s ai'dǐə, -z
Note.—The pronunciation 'aidiə is
also sometimes heard, esp. when a
stress immediately follows.
ideal (s.), -s ai'diəl [-'di:əl, -'di:l], -z
ideal (adj.) ai'diəl [-'di:əl, -'di:l, '-- esp.
when attributive]
ideal|ism, -ist/s ai'diəl|izəm [ai'di:əl-,
'aidjəl-, 'aidǐəl-], -ist/s
idealistic aiˌdiə'listik [ai,di:ə'l-, ˌaidjə'l-,
ideality ˌaidi'æliti   [ˌaidǐə'l-]
idealization [-isa-], -s aiˌdiəlai'zeiʃən
[-,di:əl-, -li'z-], -z
idealiz|e [-is|e], -es, -ing, -ed ai'diəlaiz
[-'di:əl-], -iz, -iŋ, -d
ideally ai'diəli [-'di:əli]
idem 'aidem ['idem]
Note.—Some pronounce 'aid- when
referring to a person but 'id- when
referring to a thing.

Iden 'aidn
identic|al, -ally, -alness ai'dentik|əl
  [rarely i'd-], -əli, -əlnis
identification, -s ai,dentifi'keiʃən [rarely
  i,d-], -z
identi|fy, -fies, -fying, -fied, -fier/s;
  -fiable ai'denti|fai [rarely i'd-], -faiz,
  -faiiŋ, -faid, -faiə*/z; -faiəbl
identit|y, -ies ai'dentit|i [rarely i'd-], -iz
ideogram, -s 'idiəugræm ['aid-, -diəg-],
  -z
ideograph, -s 'idiəugrɑːf ['aid-, -diəg-,
  -græf], -s
ideographic, -al, -ally ,idiəu'græfik
  [,aid-, -diə'g-], -əl, -əli
ideography ,idi'ɔgrəfi [,aid-]
ideological ,aidɪə'lɔdʒikəl [,id-]
ideolog|ist/s, -y, -ies ,aidi'ɔlədʒ|ist/s
  [,id-], -i, -iz
Ides aidz
idioc|y, -ies 'idɪəs|i ['idjəs-], -iz
idiolect, -s 'idiəulekt, -s
idiom, -s 'idɪəm ['idjəm], -z
idiomatic, -al, -ally ,idɪə'mætik
  [,idjəu'm-, ,idiu'm-, ,idju'm-,
  ,idiəu'm-], -əl, -əli
idiosyncras|y, -ies ,idɪə'siŋkrəs|i [-djə's-,
  -diu's-, -dju's-, -diəu's-, -djəu's-], -iz
idiosyncratic, -ally ,idɪəsiŋ'krætik
  [,idiəu-, ,idjəu-], -əli
idiot, -s 'idɪət ['idjət], -s
idiotic, -al, -ally ,idi'ɔtik, -əl, -əli
idiotism, -s 'idɪətizəm ['idjət-], -z
Idist, -s 'i:dist, -s
id|le (adj. v.), -ly, -leness; -les, -ling,
  -led, -ler/s 'aid|l, -li, -lnis; -lz, -liŋ,
  -ld, -lə*/z
Ido 'i:dəu
idol, -s 'aidl, -z
idolater, -s ai'dɔlətə*, -z
idolatress, -es ai'dɔlətris [-tres], -iz
idolatrous, -ly ai'dɔlətrəs, -li
idolatr|y, -ies ai'dɔlətr|i, -iz
idoli|sm, -st/s 'aidəli|zəm, -st/s
idolization [-isa-] ,aidəulai'zeiʃən
idoliz|e [-is|e], -es, -ing, -ed, -er/s
  'aidəlaiz, -iz, -iŋ, -d, -ə*/z
Idomeneus ai'dɔminju:s [i'd-]
Idris 'idris
Idumea ,aidju(:)'mi(:)ə [,id-]
idyll, -s 'idil ['aid-], -z
idyllic ai'dilik [i'd-]
idyllist, -s 'aidilist, -s
i.e. 'ai'i: ['ðæt'iz]
if if
Ife (surname) aif
Iffley 'ifli
Ifor 'aivə*

Iggulden 'igldən
Ightham 'aitəm
igloo, -s 'iglu:, -z
Igna|tian, -tius ig'nei|ʃjən [-ʃiən, -ʃən],
  -ʃjəs [-ʃiəs, -ʃəs]
igneous 'ignɪəs [-njəs]
ignis-fatuus 'ignis'fætjŭəs [-tjwəs]
ignit|e, -es, -ing, -ed; -able ig'nait, -s,
  -iŋ, -id; -əbl
ignition ig'niʃən
ignobility ,ignəu'biliti
ignob|le, -ly, -leness ig'nəub|l, -li, -lnis
ignominious, -ly, -ness ,ignəu'minɪəs
  [-njəs], -li, -nis
ignominy 'ignəmini [-nɔm-]
ignoramus, -es ,ignə'reiməs [-nu'r-], -iz
ignoran|ce, -t/ly 'ignərən|s [-nur-], -t/li
ignor|e, -es, -ing, -ed ig'nɔ:* [-'nɔə*], -z,
  -riŋ, -d
Igoe (surname) 'aigəu
Igor 'i:gɔ:*
iguana, -s i'gwɑ:nə [,igju'ɑ:nə], -z
iguanodon, -s i'gwɑ:nədɔn [,igju'ɑ:-,
  -dən], -z
ike (I.), -s aik, -s
Ikey 'aiki
ikon, -s 'aikɔn, [-kən], -z
Ilchester 'iltʃistə*
ilex, -es 'aileks, -iz
Ilford 'ilfəd
Ilfracombe 'ilfrəku:m ['ilfrə'k-, ,ilfrə'k-]
iliac 'iliæk
Iliad 'ilɪəd ['iljəd, 'iliæd, 'iljæd]
Iliffe 'ailif
ili|um, -a 'ili|əm ['ilj|əm], -ə
Ilium 'ailɪəm ['il-, -ljəm]
ilk ilk
Ilkeston 'ilkistən
Ilkley 'ilkli
ill, -ness/es il, -nis/iz
I'll (= I will) ail
ill-advised 'iləd'vaizd
illative i'leitiv
ill-boding 'il'bəudiŋ
ill-bred 'il'bred [also '— when attributive]
ill-breeding 'il'bri:diŋ
ill-conditioned 'il-kən'diʃənd [also '—,—
  when attributive]
illeg|al, -ally i'li:g|əl ['i'l-], -əli
illegalit|y, -ies ,ili(:)'gælit|i ['ili(:)'g-],
  -iz
illegibility i,ledʒi'biliti ['iledʒi'b-,
  -dʒə'b-, ,-lət-]
illegib|le, -ly, -leness i'ledʒəb|l ['i'l-,
  -dʒib-], -li, -lnis
illegitimacy ,ili'dʒitiməsi ['ili'dʒ-]
illegitimate, -ly ,ili'dʒitimit ['ili'dʒ-,
  -təm-], -li

ill-fated 'il'feitid
ill-favoured, -ly, -ness 'il'feivəd [*also* '-,-- *when attributive*], -li, -nis
ill-feeling 'il'fi:liŋ
ill-gotten 'il'gɔtn [*also* '-,-- *when attributive*]
illiber|al, -ally i'libər|əl ['i'l-], -əli
illiberality i,libə'ræliti ['ilibə'r-]
illicit, -ly, -ness i'lisit ['i'l-], -li, -nis
illimitab|le, -ly, -leness i'limitəb|l ['i'l-], -li, -lnis
Illingworth 'iliŋwə(:)θ
Illinois ,ili'nɔi [*rarely* -'nɔiz]
illiteracy i'litərəsi ['i'l-]
illiterate (*s. adj.*), -s, -ly, -ness i'litərit ['i'l-], -s, -li, -nis
ill-judged 'il'dʒʌdʒd [*also* '-- *when attributive*]
ill-looking 'il,lukiŋ
ill-mannered 'il'mænəd
ill-nature 'il'neitʃə*
ill-natured, -ly 'il'neitʃəd [*also* '-,-- when attributive*], -li
illness, -es 'ilnis, -iz
Illogan i'ləugən
illogic|al, -ally, -alness i'lɔdʒik|əl ['i'l-], -əli, -əlnis
illogicalit|y, -ies 'ilɔdʒi'kælit|i [i,l-], -iz
ill-omened 'il'əumend [-mənd, -mind]
ill-starred 'il'stɑ:d [*also* 'il-stɑ:d *when attributive*]
ill-tempered 'il'tempəd [*also* '-,-- *when attributive*]
ill-timed 'il'taimd [*also* 'il-taimd *when attributive*]
ill-treat, -s, -ing, -ed, -ment 'il'tri:t [il't-], -s, -iŋ, -id, -mənt
illum|e, -es, -ing, -ed i'lju:m [i'lu:m], -z, -iŋ, -d
illuminat|e, -es, -ing, -ed, -or/s i'lju:-mineit [i'lu:-], -s, -iŋ, -id, -ə*/z
Illuminati i,lu:mi'nɑ:ti [*old-fashioned* -'neitai]
illumination, -s i,lju:mi'neiʃən, [i,lu:-]-z
illuminative i'lju:minətiv [i'lu:-, -neit-]
illumin|e, -es, -ing, -ed i'lju:min [i'lu:-], -z, -iŋ, -d
ill-usage 'il'ju:zidʒ [-'ju:s-]
ill-used 'il'ju:zd [*also* 'ilj-, il'j- *according to sentence-stress*]
illusion, -s i'lu:ʒən [i'lju:-], -z
illusioni|sm, -st/s i'lu:ʒəni|zəm [i'lju:-, -ʒn̩i-], -st/s
illusive, -ly, -ness i'lu:siv [i'lju:-], -li, -nis
illusor|y, -ily, -iness i'lu:sər|i [i'lju:-], -ili, -inis

illustrat|e, -es, -ing, -ed, -or/s 'iləs-treit, -s, -iŋ, -id, -ə*/z
illustration, -s ,iləs'treiʃən, -z
illustrative, -ly 'iləstreitiv [-strət-, *rarely* i'lʌstrətiv], -li
illustrious, -ly, -ness i'lʌstrɪəs, -li, -nis
ill-will 'il'wil
ill-wisher, -s 'il'wiʃə*, -z
Illyria, -n/s i'lirɪə, -n/z
Illyricum i'lirikəm
Ilminster 'ilminstə*
I'm (=I am) aim
imag|e (*s. v.*) (I.), -es, -ing, -ed 'imidʒ, -iz, -iŋ, -d
imagery 'imidʒəri
image-worship 'imidʒ,wə:ʃip
imaginab|le, -ly, -leness i'mædʒinəb|l, -li, -lnis
imaginar|y, -ily, -iness i'mædʒinər|i [-dʒnər-], -ili, -inis
imagination, -s i,mædʒi'neiʃən, -z
imaginative, -ly, -ness i'mædʒinətiv, -li, -nis
imagin|e, -es, -ing/s, -ed, -er/s i'mæ-dʒin, -z, -iŋ/z, -d, -ə*/z
imago, -s, imagines (*plur. of* imago) i'meigəu [i'mɑ:g-], -z, i'meidʒini:z [i'mɑ:gineiz]
imam, -s i'mɑ:m, -z
imbalance im'bæləns
imbecile, -s 'imbisi:l [-bəs-, -sail], -z
imbecilit|y, -ies ,imbi'silit|i [-bə's-], -iz
imbib|e, -es, -ing, -ed, -er/s im'baib, -z, -iŋ, -d, -ə*/z
imbroglio, -s im'brəuliəu [-ljəu], -z
imbru|e, -es, -ing, -ed im'bru:, -z, -iŋ [im'bruiŋ], -d
imbu|e, -es, -ing, -ed im'bju:, -z, -iŋ [im'bjuiŋ], -d
Imeson 'aimisn
imitability ,imitə'biliti [-lət-]
imitable 'imitəbl
imitat|e, -es, -ing, -ed, -or/s 'imiteit, -s, -iŋ, -id, -ə*/z
imitation, -s ,imi'teiʃən, -z
imitative, -ly, -ness 'imitətiv [-teit-], -li, -nis
immaculate, -ly, -ness i'mækjulit, -li, -nis
immanen|ce, -t 'imənən|s, -t
Immanuel i'mænjuəl [-njwəl, -njul]
immaterial, -ly ,imə'tiərɪəl ['imə't-], -i
immateriali|sm, -st/s ,imə'tiərɪəli|zəm ['imə't-], -st/s
immateriality ,imə,tiəri'æliti
immaterializ|e [-is|e], -es, -ing, -ed ,imə'tiərɪəlaiz ['imə't-], -iz, -iŋ, -d

immature, -ly, -ness ‚imə'tjuə* ['imə't-, -'tjɔə*, -'tjɔ:*, -'tʃuə*, -'tʃɔ:*], -li, -nis
immaturity ‚imə'tjuəriti ['imə't-, -'tjɔər-, -'tjɔ:r-, -'tʃuər-, -'tʃɔ:r-]
immeasurable i'meʒərəbl ['i'm-]
immeasurab|ly, -leness i'meʒərəb|li, -lnis
immediate, -ly i'mi:djət [-dʒət, -dïət, -diit, djit], -li
immemorial, -ly ‚imi'mɔ:rïəl, -li
immense, -ly, -ness i'mens, -li, -nis
immensit|y, -ies i'mensit|i, -iz
immers|e, -es, -ing, -ed i'mə:s, -iz, -iŋ, -t
immersion, -s i'mə:ʃən, -z
immersion-heater, -s i'mə:ʃən‚hi:tə*, -z
immigrant, -s 'imigrənt, -s
immigrat|e, -es, -ing, -ed 'imigreit, -s, -iŋ, -id
immigration, -s ‚imi'greiʃən, -z
imminen|ce, -t/ly 'iminən|s, -t/li
immobile i'məubail [-bi:l]
immobility ‚iməu'biliti ['iməu'b-, -lət-]
immobilization [-isa-] i‚məubilai'zeiʃən [-li'z-]
immobiliz|e [-is|e], -es, -ing, -ed i'məubilaiz, -iz, -iŋ, -d
immoderate, -ness i'mɔdərit ['i'm-], -nis
immoderately i'mɔdəritli [-rət-]
immoderation i‚mɔdə'reiʃən
immodest, -ly i'mɔdist ['i'm-], -li
immodesty i'mɔdisti ['i'm-]
immolat|e, -es, -ing, -ed, -or/s 'iməuleit, -s, -iŋ, -id, -ə*/z
immolation, -s ‚iməu'leiʃən, -z
immor|al, -ally i'mɔr|əl ['i'm-], -əli [-l̩i]
immoralit|y, -ies i'mɔr'ælit|i [-mɔ'r-], -iz
immort|al (s. adj.), -als, -ally i'mɔ:t|l ['i'm-], -lz, -əli [-li]
immortality ‚imɔ:'tæliti
immortaliz|e [-is|e], -es, -ing, -ed i'mɔ:təlaiz [-tl̩aiz], -iz, -iŋ, -d
immortelle, -s ‚imɔ:'tel, -z
immovability i‚mu:və'biliti ['imu:v-, -lət-]
immovab|le, -leness i'mu:vəb|l ['i'm-], -lnis
immovably i'mu:vəbli
immune i'mju:n
immunit|y, -ies i'mju:nit|i, -iz
immunization [-isa-] ‚imju(:)nai'zeiʃən [-ni'z-]
immuniz|e [-is|e], -es, -ing, -ed 'imju(:)naiz, -iz, -iŋ, -d
immur|e, -es, -ing, -ed, -ement i'mjuə* [-'mjɔə*, -'mjɔ:*], -z, -riŋ, -d, -mənt
immutability i‚mju:tə'biliti ['i‚m-, -lət-]
immutab|le, -ly, -leness i'mju:təb|l, -li, -lnis

Imogen 'iməudʒən [-dʒen]
imp (s. v.), -s, -ing, -ed imp, -s, -iŋ, -t [imt]
impact (s.), -s 'impækt, -s
impact (v.), -s, -ing, -ed im'pækt, -s, -iŋ, -id
impair, -s, -ing, -ed im'pɛə*, -z, -riŋ, -d
impairment im'pɛəmənt
impal|e, -es, -ing, -ed, -ement im'peil, -z, -iŋ, -d, -mənt
impalpab|le, -ly im'pælpəb|l ['im'p-], -li
imparisyllabic 'im‚pærisi'læbik
impart, -s, -ing, -ed im'pɑ:t, -s, -iŋ, -id
impartation ‚impɑ:'teiʃən
imparti|al, -ally, -alness im'pɑ:ʃ|əl ['im'p-], -əli, -əlnis
impartiality 'im‚pɑ:ʃi'æliti [‚impɑ:-, im‚pɑ:-]
impassability 'im‚pɑ:sə'biliti [-lət-]
impassable im'pɑ:səbl ['im'p-]
impasse, -s æm'pɑ:s (ɛ̃pɑ:s), -iz
impassible im'pæsibl [-səbl]
impassioned im'pæʃənd
impassive, -ly, -ness im'pæsiv, -li, -nis
impassivity ‚impæ'siviti ['impæ's-]
impatien|ce, -t/ly im'peiʃən|s, -t/li
impeach, -es, -ing, -ed, -er/s, -ment/s; -able im'pi:tʃ, -iz, -iŋ, -t, -ə*/z, -mənt/s; -əbl
impeccability im‚pekə'biliti [‚impek-, -lət-]
impeccable im'pekəbl
impecunious, -ness ‚im-pi'kju:njəs ['im-pi'k-, -nïəs], -nis
impedance im'pi:dəns
imped|e, -es, -ing, -ed im'pi:d, -z, -iŋ, -id
impediment, -s im'pedimənt, -s
impedimenta im‚pedi'mentə [‚imped-]
impel, -s, -ling, -led, -ler/s; -lent im'pel, -z, -iŋ, -d, -ə*/z; -ənt
impend, -s, -ing, -ed im'pend, -z, -iŋ, -id
impenetrability im‚penitrə'biliti ['im‚p-, -lət-]
impenetrab|le, -ly, -leness im'penitrəb|l, -li, -lnis
impeniten|ce, -t/ly im'penitən|s ['im'p-], -t/li
imperative (s. adj.), -s, -ly, -ness im'perətiv, -z, -li, -nis
imperator, -s ‚impə'rɑ:tɔ:* [-'reitɔ:*, -tə*], -z
imperatorial im‚perə'tɔ:rïəl [‚imper-]
imperceptibility 'im-pə‚septə'biliti [-pə:‚s-, -ti'b-, -lət-]
imperceptib|le, -ly, -leness ‚im-pə'septəb|l ['im-pə's-, -pə:'s-, -tib-], -li, -lnis

imperfect (s. adj.), **-s, -ly, -ness** im-
'pə:fikt ['im'p-], -s, -li, -nis
imperfection, **-s** ,im-pə'fekʃən ['im-pə'f-,
-pə:'f-], -z
imperforate im'pə:fərit ['im'p-]
imperial (s. adj.), **-s, -ly** im'piəriəl, -z, -i
imperiali|sm, **-st/s** im'piəriəli|zəm,
-st/s
imper|il,**-ils, -illing, -illed** im'per|il [-əl],
-ilz [-əlz], -iliŋ [-əliŋ, -|iŋ], -ild [-əld]
imperious, **-ly, -ness** im'piəriəs -li, -nis
imperishability im,periʃə'biliti ['im,p-,
-lət-]
imperishab|le, **-ly, -leness** im'periʃəb|l
['im'p-], -li, -lnis
impermeability im,pə:mjə'biliti ['im,p-,
-miə-, -lət-]
impermeab|le, **-ly, -leness** im'pə:mjəb|l
['im'p-, -miə-], -li, -lnis
impers|onal, **-onally** im'pə:s|nļ ['im'p-,
-ņļ, -ənl], -nəli [-ŋəļi, -ņļi, -nļi, -ənļi]
impersonality im,pə:sə'næliti ['im,p-,
-sņ'æ-]
impersonat|e, **-es, -ing, -ed, -or/s** im-
'pə:səneit [-sņeit], -s, -iŋ, -id, -ə*/z
impersonation, **-s** im,pə:sə'neiʃən
[-sņ'ei-], -z
impertinen|ce (insolence, etc.), **-t/ly**
im'pə:tinən|s [-tņən-], -t/li
impertinen|ce (irrelevance, etc.), **-t/ly**
im'pə:tinən|s ['im'p-], -t/li
imperturbability 'im-pə(:),tə:bə'biliti
[-lət-]
imperturbab|le, **-ly, -leness** ,im-pə(:)-
'tə:bəb|l ['im-pə(:)'t-], -li, -lnis
impervious, **-ly, -ness** im'pə:vjəs ['im'p-,
-vïəs], -li, -nis
impetigo ,impi'taigəu [-pe't-]
impetuosity im,petju'ɔsiti
impetuous, **-ly, -ness** im'petjŭəs [-tjwəs],
-li, -nis
impetus 'impitəs [-pət-]
Impey 'impi
impiet|y, **-ies** im'paiət|i ['im'p-, -aiit-],
-iz
imping|e, **-es, -ing, -ed, -ement/s** im-
'pindʒ, -iz, -iŋ, -d, -mənt/s
impious, **-ly, -ness** 'impïəs [-pjəs], -li,
-nis
impish, **-ly, -ness** 'impiʃ, -li, -nis
implacability im,plækə'biliti ['im,plæk-,
-,pleik-, -lət-]
implacab|le, **-ly, -leness** im'plækəb|l
[-'pleik-], -li, -lnis
implant (s.), **-s** 'im-plɑ:nt, -s
implant (v.), **-s, -ing, -er/s** im'plɑ:nt,
-s, -iŋ, -id, -ə*/z
implantation ,im-plɑ:n'teiʃən [-plæn-]

implement (s.), **-s** 'implimənt, -s
implement (v.), **-s, -ing, -ed** 'impliment
-s, -iŋ, -id
implementation ,implimen'teiʃən
implicate (s.) 'implikit [-keit]
implicat|e (v.), **-es, -ing, -ed** 'implikeit,
-s, -iŋ, -id
implication, **-s** ,impli'keiʃən, -z
implicative, **-ly** im'plikətiv ['implikei-
tiv], -li
implicit, **-ly, -ness** im'plisit, -li, -nis
implod|e, **-es, -ing, -ed** im'pləud, -z, -iŋ,
-id
implor|e, **-es, -ing/ly, -ed, -er/s** im-
'plɔ:* [-'pləə*], -z, -riŋ/li, -d, -rə*/z
implosion, **-s** im'pləuʒən, -z
implosive (s. adj.), **-s** im'pləusiv
['im'p-, -əuzi-], -z
impl|y, **-ies, -ying, -ied, -iedly** im'pl|ai,
-aiz, -aiiŋ, -aid, -aiidli
impolicy im'pɔlisi ['im'p-, -ləs-]
impolite, **-ly, -ness** ,im-pə'lait ['im-pə'l-,
-pəu'l-, -pu'l-], -li, -nis
impolitic im'pɔlitik ['im'p-, -lət-]
imponderable (s. adj.), **-s** im'pɔndərəbl,
-z
import (s.), **-s** 'impɔ:t, -s
import (v.), **-s, -ing, -ed, -er/s** im'pɔ:t
[rarely 'impɔ:t], -s, -iŋ, -id, -ə*/z
importable im'pɔ:təbl
importan|ce, **-t/ly** im'pɔ:tən|s, -t/li
importation, **-s** ,impɔ:'teiʃən, -z
importunate, **-ly, -ness** im'pɔ:tjunit, -li,
-nis
importun|e, **-es, -ing, -ed** im'pɔ:tju:n
[-tʃu:n, ,impɔ:'tju:n], -z, im'pɔ:tjuniŋ
[,impɔ:'tju:niŋ], im'pɔ:tju:nd [,im-
pɔ:'tju:nd]
importunit|y, **-ies** ,impɔ:'tju:nit|i, -iz
impos|e, **-es, -ing, -ed, -er/s; -able**
im'pəuz, -iz, -iŋ, -d, -ə*/z; -əbl
imposing (adj.), **-ly, -ness** im'pəuziŋ, -li,
-nis
imposition, **-s** ,impə'ziʃən [-pu'z-], -z
impossibilit|y, **-ies** im,pɔsə'bilit|i
[,impɔs-, -si'b-, -lət-], -iz
impossib|le, **-ly** im'pɔsəb|l [-sib-], -li
impost, **-s** 'impəust, -s
impos|tor/s, **-ture/s** im'pɔs|tə*/z,
-tʃə*/z
impoten|ce, **-cy, -t/ly** 'impətən|s [-put-],
-si, -t/li
impound, **-s, -ing, -ed** im'paund, -z,
-iŋ, -id
impoverish, **-es, -ing, -ed, -ment** im-
'pɔvəriʃ, -iz, -iŋ, -t, -mənt
impracticability, **-ies** im,præktikə-
'bilit|i ['im,præktikə'b-, -lət-], -iz

impracticab|le, -ly, -leness im'præktik-
  əb|l ['im'p-], -li, -lnis
imprecat|e, -es, -ing, -ed, or/s 'im-
  prikeit, -s, -iŋ, -id, -ə*/z
imprecation, -s ˌimpri'keiʃən [-pre'k-], -z
imprecatory 'imprikeitəri [im'prekə-
  təri]
impregn, -s, -ing, -ed im'pri:n, -z, -iŋ, -d
impregnability imˌpregnə'biliti [-lət-]
impregnab|le, -ly im'pregnəb|l, -li
impregnate (adj.) im'pregnit [-neit]
impregnat|e (v.), -es, -ing, -ed 'im-
  pregneit [im'pregneit], -s, -iŋ, -id
impregnation, -s ˌimpreg'neiʃən, -z
impresario, -s ˌimpre'sɑːriəu [-pri's-,
  -'zɑː-], -z
impress (s.), -es 'impres, -iz
impress (v.), -es, -ing, -ed im'pres, -iz,
  -iŋ, -t
impressibility imˌpresi'biliti [-sə'b-, -lət-]
impressib|le, -ly, -leness im'presəb|l
  [-sib-], -li, -lnis
impression, -s im'preʃən, -z
impressionability imˌpreʃnə'biliti [-ʃənə-,
  -ʃnə, -lət-]
impressionable im'preʃnəbl [-ʃənə-,
  -ʃnə-]
impressioni|sm, -st/s im'preʃni|zəm
  [-ʃəni-], -st/s
impressionistic imˌpreʃə'nistik [-ʃɲ'i-]
impressive, -ly, -ness im'presiv, -li, -nis
impressment, -s im'presmənt, -s
imprest, -s 'imprest, -s
imprimatur, -s ˌimpri'meitə* [-prai'm-],
  -z
imprimis im'praimis
imprint (s.), -s 'im-print, -s
imprint (v.), -s, -ing, -ed im'print, -s,
  -iŋ, -id
impris|on, -ons, -oning, -oned,
  -onment/s im'priz|n, -nz, -ɲiŋ, -nd,
  -nmənt/s
improbabilit|y, -ies imˌprɔbə'bilit|i
  ['imˌprɔbə'b-, -lət-], -iz
improbab|le, -ly im'prɔbəb|l ['im'p-], -li
improbity im'prəubiti ['im'p-, -'prɔb-]
impromptu, -s im'prɔmƥtjuː, -z
improper, -ly im'prɔpə* ['im'p-], -li
impropriat|e, -es, -ing, -ed, -or/s im-
  'prəuprieit, -s, -iŋ, -id, -ə*/z
impropriation, -s imˌprəupri'eiʃən, -z
impropriet|y, -ies ˌim-prə'praiət|i
  [-pru'p-], -iz
improvability imˌpruːvə'biliti [-lət-]
improvab|le, -ly, -leness im'pruːvəb|l,
  -li, -lnis
improv|e, -es, -ing, -ed, -er/s, -ement/s
  im'pruːv, -z, -iŋ, -d, -ə*/z, -mənt/s

improviden|ce, -t/ly im'prɔvidən|s, -t/li
improvisation, -s 'imprəvai'zeiʃən
  [-pruv-, ˌimprɔvi'z-], -z
improvis|e, -es, -ing, -ed, -er/s 'im-
  prəvaiz [-pruv-], -iz, -iŋ, -d, -ə*/z
impruden|ce, -t/ly im'pruːdən|s['im'p-],
  -t/li
impuden|ce, -t/ly 'impjudən|s, -t/li
impugn, -s, -ing, -ed, -er/s im'pjuːn, -z,
  -iŋ, -d, -ə*/*z
impuissan|ce, -t im'pju(ː)isn|s, -t
impulse, -s 'impʌls, -iz
impulsion, -s im'pʌlʃən, -z
impulsive, -ly, -ness im'pʌlsiv, -li, -nis
impunity im'pjuːniti
impur|e, -ely, -eness; -ity, -ities
  im'pjuə* ['im'p-, -'pjɔə*, -'pjɔː*], -li,
  -nis; -riti, -ritiz
imputability imˌpjuːtə'biliti [ˌimpjuːt-,
  -lət-]
imputation, -s ˌimpju(ː)'teiʃən, -z
imput|e, -es, -ing, -ed, -er/s; -able
  im'pjuːt, -s, -iŋ, -id, -ə*/z; -əbl
Imr|ay, -e, -ie 'imr|ei, -i, -i
in in
Ina 'ainə
inability ˌinə'biliti ['inə'b-, -lət-]
inaccessibility 'inæk,sesə'biliti [-nək-,
  -si'b-, -lət-]
inaccessib|le, -ly, -leness ˌinæk'sesəb|l
  ['inæk's-, -nək-, -sib-], -li, -lnis
inaccurac|y, -ies in'ækjurəs|i ['in'æ-,
  -kjər-, -ris-], -iz
inaccur|ate, -ately in'ækjur|it ['in'æ-,
  -kjər-], -itli [-ətli]
inaction in'ækʃən ['in'æ-]
inactive, -ly in'æktiv ['in'æ-], -li
inactivity ˌinæk'tiviti ['inæk't-]
inadequacy in'ædikwəsi ['in'æ-]
inadequate, -ly, -ness in'ædikwit
  ['in'æ-], -li, -nis
inadmissibility 'inədˌmisə'biliti [-si'b-,
  -lət-]
inadmissib|le, -ly ˌinəd'misəb|l ['in-
  əd'm-, -sib-], -li
inadverten|ce, -cy, -t/ly ˌinəd'və:-
  tən|s ['inəd'v-], -si, -t/li
inadvisable ˌinəd'vaizəbl ['inəd'v-]
inalienability inˌeiljənə'biliti ['inˌei-,
  -lïən-, -lət-]
inalienable in'eiljənəbl ['in'ei-, -lïən-]
inalienab|ly, -leness in'eiljənəb|li [-lïən-]
  -lnis
inamorata, -s inˌæmə'rɑːtə [ˌinæ-,
  -mɔ'r-], -z
inane, -ly, -ness i'nein, -li, -nis
inanimate, -ly, -ness in'ænimit ['in'æ-],
  -li, -nis

inanition ˌinəˈniʃən [-næˈn-]

inanit|y, -ies iˈnænit|i [-ˈnein-], -iz

inappeasable ˌinəˈpiːzəbl [ˈinəˈp-]

inapplicability ˈin͵æplikəˈbiliti [ˈin-ə͵plik-, -lət-]

inapplicable, -ness inˈæplikəbl [ˈinˈæ-, ˌinəˈplik-, ˈinəˈplik-], -nis   [-li

inapposite, -ly inˈæpəzit [ˈinˈæ-, -puz-],

inappreciab|le, -ly ˌinəˈpriːʃəb|l [ˈinəˈp-, -ʃjə-, -ʃiə-], -li

inapproachab|le, -ly ˌinəˈprəutʃəb|l [ˈinəˈp-], -li

inappropri|ate, -ately, -ateness ˌinə-ˈprəupri|it [ˈinəˈp-], -itli [-ətli], -itnis

inapt, -ly, -ness inˈæpt [ˈinˈæpt], -li, -nis

inaptitude inˈæptitjuːd [ˈinˈæ-]

inarticulate, -ly, -ness ˌinɑːˈtikjulit [ˈinɑːˈt-], -li, -nis

inartistic, -al, -ally ˌinɑːˈtistik [ˈinɑːˈt-], -əl, -əli

inasmuch inəzˈmʌtʃ

inattention ˌinəˈtenʃən [ˈinəˈt-]

inattentive, -ly, -ness ˌinəˈtentiv [ˈinəˈt-], -li, -nis

inaudibility in͵ɔːdəˈbiliti [ˈin͵ɔːdəˈb-, -diˈb-, -lət-]

inaudib|le, -ly, -leness inˈɔːdəb|l [ˈinˈɔː-, -dib-], -li, -lnis

inaugural iˈnɔːgjurəl [-gjər-]

inaugurat|e, -es, -ing, -ed, -or/s iˈnɔː-gjureit [-gjər-], -s, -iŋ, -id, -ə*/z

inauguration, -s i͵nɔːgjuˈreiʃən [-gjəˈr-], -z

inauspicious, -ly, -ness ˌinɔːsˈpiʃəs [ˈinɔːsˈp-, -nɔs-], -li, -nis

inborn ˈinˈbɔːn [also ˈinb- when attributive]

inbreath|e, -es, -ing, -ed ˈinˈbriːð, -z, -iŋ, -d [also ˈinbriːðd when attributive]

inbreed, -s, -ing, inbred ˈinˈbriːd, -z, -iŋ, ˈinˈbred [also ˈinbred when attributive]

Inca, -s ˈiŋkə, -z

incalculability in͵kælkjuləˈbiliti [ˈin-͵kælkjuləˈb-, (ˈ)iŋ͵k-, -kjəl-, -lət-]

incalculable, -ness inˈkælkjuləbl [ˈinˈk-, (ˈ)iŋˈk-, -kjəl-], -nis

incalculably inˈkælkjuləbli [iŋˈk-, -kjəl-]

incandescen|ce, -t ˈinkænˈdesn|s [ˌiŋ͵k-, -kən-], -t

incantation, -s ˌinkænˈteiʃən [ˌiŋ͵k-], -z

incapabilit|y, -ies in͵keipəˈbilit|i [ˈin͵keipəˈb-, (ˈ)iŋ͵k-, -lət-], -iz

incapable, -ness inˈkeipəbl [ˈinˈk-, (ˈ)iŋˈk-], -nis

incapacitat|e, -es, -ing, -ed ˌinkəˈpæsi-teit [ˈinkəˈp-, ˌiŋ͵k-, ˈiŋˈk-], -s, -iŋ, -id

incapacitation ˈinkə͵pæsiˈteiʃən [ˈiŋˈk-]

incapacit|y, -ies ˌinkəˈpæsit|i [ˈinkəˈp-, ˌiŋˈk-, ˈiŋˈk-], -iz

incarcerat|e, -es, -ing, -ed inˈkɑːsə-reit [iŋˈk-], -s, -iŋ, -id

incarceration, -s in͵kɑːsəˈreiʃən [ˌinkɑː-, iŋ͵k-, ͵iŋˈk-], -z

incarnadine inˈkɑːnədain [iŋˈk-]

incarnate (adj.) inˈkɑːnit [iŋˈk-, -neit]

incarnat|e (v.), -es, -ing, -ed ˈinkɑːneit [inˈkɑːneit, ˈiŋˈk-, iŋˈk-], -s, -iŋ, -id

incarnation (I.), -s ˌinkɑːˈneiʃən [ˌ͵iŋ͵k-], -z

incaution inˈkɔːʃən [ˈinˈk-]

incautious, -ly, -ness inˈkɔːʃəs [ˈinˈk-], -li, -nis

Ince ins

incendiar|ism, -y, -ies inˈsendjər|izəm [-diə-], -i, -iz

incense (s.) ˈinsens

incens|e (v.) (enrage), -es, -ing, -ed inˈsens, -iz, -iŋ, -t

incens|e (v.) (burn incense), -es, -ing, -ed ˈinsens, -iz, -iŋ, -t

incentive, -s inˈsentiv, -z

incept, -s, -ing, -ed, -or/s; -ive inˈsept, -s, -iŋ, -id, -ə*/z; -iv

inception, -s inˈsepʃən, -z

incertititude inˈsəːtitjuːd [ˈinˈs-]

incessant, -ly inˈsesnt, -li

incest ˈinsest

incestuous, -ly, -ness inˈsestjŭəs [-tjwəs], -li, -nis

inch (s. v.) (I.), -es, -ing, -ed intʃ, -iz, -iŋ, -t

Inch|bald, -cape, -colm, -iquin, -keith ˈintʃ|bɔːld, -keip, -kəm, -ikwin, -kiːθ

inchoate (adj.), -ly ˈinkəueit [ˈiŋˈk-, -kəuit, -ˈ--], -li

inchoat|e (v.), -es, -ing, -ed ˈinkəueit [ˈiŋˈk-], -s, -iŋ, -id

inchoation ˌinkəuˈeiʃən [ˌiŋˈk-]

inchoative ˈinkəueitiv [ˈiŋˈk-, inˈkəuə-tiv, iŋˈkəuətiv]

Inchrye intʃˈrai

inciden|ce, -t/s ˈinsidən|s, -t/s

incident|al, -ally, -alness ˌinsiˈdent|l, -|i [-əli], -lnis

incinerat|e, -es‘ -ing, -ed, -or/s in-ˈsinəreit, -s, -iŋ, -id, -ə*/z

incineration in͵sinəˈreiʃən

incipien|ce, -cy, -t/ly inˈsipiən|s [-pjən-], -si, -t/li

incis|e, -es, -ing, -ed, -or/s inˈsaiz, -iz, -iŋ, -d, -ə*/z

incision, -s inˈsiʒən, -z

incisive, -ly, -ness inˈsaisiv, -li, -nis

incitation, -s ˌinsaiˈteiʃən [-siˈt-], -z

incit|e, -es, -ing/ly, -ed, -er/s, -ement/s in'sait, -s, -iŋ/li, -id, -ə*/z, -mənt/s
incivilit|y, -ies ˌinsi'vilit|i ['insi'v-], -iz
Incledon 'iŋkldən
inclemen|cy, -t/ly in'klemən|si ['in'k-, (')iŋ'k-], -t/li
inclination, -s ˌinkli'neiʃən [ˌiŋkl- ˌˌintl-, -lə'n-], -z
incline (s.), -s in'klain [iŋ'kl-, in'tl-, 'inklain, 'iŋ-klain], -z
inclin|e (v.), -es, -ing, -ed; -able in'klain [iŋ'kl-, in'tl-], -z, -iŋ, -d; -əbl
inclos|e, -es, -ing, -ed in'kləuz [iŋ'kl-, in'tl-], -iz, -iŋ, -d
inclosure, -s in'kləuʒə* [iŋ'kl-, in'tl-], -z
includ|e, -es, -ing, -ed in'klu:d [iŋ'kl-, in'tl-], -z, -iŋ, -id
inclusion, -s in'klu:ʒən [iŋ'kl-, in'tl-], -z
inclusive, -ly in'klu:siv [iŋ'kl-, in'tl-, '-'--], -li
incog. in'kɔg ['in'k-, iŋ'k-, 'iŋ'k-]
incognito (s. adj. adv.), -s in'kɔgnitəu [iŋ'k-, ˌinkɔg'ni:təu], -z
incoheren|ce, -t/ly ˌinkəu'hiərən|s ['inkəu'h-, ˌiŋ-k-, 'iŋ-k-,] -t/li
incombustibility 'inkəmˌbʌstə'biliti ['iŋ-k-, -ti'b-, -lət-]
incombustible, -ness ˌinkəm'bʌstəbl ['inkəm'b-, ˌiŋ-k-, 'iŋ-k-, -tib-], -nis
income, -s 'inkʌm ['iŋk-, -kəm], -z
incomer, -s 'inˌkʌmə*, -z
income-tax, -es 'inkəmtæks ['iŋk-, -kʌm-], -iz
incoming (s. adj.), -s 'inˌkʌmiŋ, -z
incommensurability 'inkəˌmenʃərə'biliti ['iŋ-k-, -ʃur-, -lət-]
incommensurab|le (s. adj.), -les, -ly, -leness ˌinkə'menʃərəb|l ['inkə'm-, ˌiŋ-k-, 'iŋ-k-, -ʃur-], -lz, -li, -lnis
incommensurate, -ly, -ness ˌinkə'menʃərit ['inkə'm-, ˌiŋ-k-, 'iŋ-k-, -ʃur-], -li, -nis
incommod|e, -es, -ing, -ed ˌinkə'məud ['inkə'm-, ˌiŋ-k-, iŋ-k-], -z, -iŋ, -id
incommodious, -ly, -ness ˌinkə'məudjəs ['inkə'm-, ˌiŋ-k-, 'iŋ-k-, -dïəs], -li, -nis
incommunicab|le, -ly, -leness ˌin-kə'mju:nikəb|l ['inkə'm-, ˌiŋ-k-, 'iŋ-k-, -'mjun-], -li, -lnis
incommutab|le, -ly, -leness ˌinkə'mju:-təb|l ['inkə'm-, ˌiŋ-k-, 'iŋ-k-], -li, -lnis
incomparability inˌkɔmpərə'biliti [iŋˌk-, -lət-]
incomparab|le, -ly, -leness in'kɔmpər-əb|l [iŋ'k-], -li ˌ-lnis
incompatibility 'inkəmˌpætə'biliti [ˌiŋ-k-, 'iŋ-k-, -ti'b-, -lət-]

incompatib|le, -ly, -leness ˌinkəm-'pætəb|l ['inkəm'p-, ˌiŋ-k-, 'iŋ-k-, -tib-], -li, -lnis
incompeten|ce, -cy, -t/ly in'kɔmpi-tən|s ['in'k-, (')iŋ'k-], -si, -t/li
incomplete, -ly, -ness ˌinkəm'pli:t ['inkəm'p-, ˌiŋ-k-, 'iŋ-k-], -li, -nis
incompletion ˌinkəm'pli:ʃən ['inkəm'p-, ˌiŋ-k-, 'iŋ-k-]
incomprehensibility inˌkɔmprihensə-'biliti ['inˌkɔmprihensə'b-, iŋˌk-, 'iŋˌk-, -si'b-, -lət-]
incomprehensib|le, -ly, -leness in'kɔm-pri'hensəb|l ['inˌkɔmpri'h-, iŋˌk-, 'iŋˌk-, -sib-], -li, -lnis
incompressibility 'inkəmˌpresə'biliti ['iŋ-k-, -si'b-, -lət-]
incompressible, -ness ˌinkəm'presəbl ['inkəm'p-, ˌiŋ-k-, 'iŋ-k-, -sib-], -nis
incomputable ˌinkəm'pju:təbl ['in-kəm'p-, ˌiŋ-kəm'p-, 'iŋ-kəm'p-, in'kɔmpjutəbl, 'in'kɔmpjut-, iŋ'kɔm-pjut-, 'iŋ'kɔmpjut-]
inconceivability 'inkənˌsi:və'biliti ['iŋ-k-, -lət-]
inconceivable, -ness ˌinkən'si:vəbl ['inkən's-, ˌiŋ-k-, 'iŋ-k-], -nis
inconceivably ˌinkən'si:vəbli [ˌiŋ-k-]
inconclusive, -ly, -ness ˌinkən'klu:siv ['inkən'k-, ˌiŋ-k-, 'iŋ-k-, -n'tl-, -kən'k-], -li, -nis
incongruit|y, -ies ˌinkəŋ'gru(:)it|i [ˌiŋ-k-], -iz
incongruous, -ly, -ness in'kɔŋgrüəs [iŋ'k-, -grwəs], -li, -nis
inconsequen|ce, -ces, -t/ly in'kɔnsi-kwən|s [iŋ'k-], -siz, -t/li
inconsiderab|le, -ly, -leness ˌinkən-'sidərəb|l ['inkən's-, ˌiŋ-k-, 'iŋ-k-], -li, -lnis
inconsiderate, -ly, -ness ˌinkən'sidərit ['inkən's-, ˌiŋ-k-, 'iŋ-k-], -li, -nis
inconsideration 'inkənˌsidə'reiʃən ['iŋ-k-]
inconsisten|cy, -cies, -t/ly ˌinkən'sis-tən|si ['inkən's-, ˌiŋ-k-, 'iŋ-k-], -siz, -t/li
inconsolab|le, -ly, -leness ˌinkən'səul-əb|l ['inkən's-, ˌiŋ-k-, 'iŋ-k-], -li, -lnis
inconspicuous, -ly, -ness ˌinkən'spik-jüəs ['inkən's-, ˌiŋ-k-, 'iŋ-k-, -kjwəs], -li, -nis
inconstan|cy, -t/ly in'kɔnstən|si ['in'k-, iŋ'k-, 'iŋ'k-], -t/li
incontestability 'inkənˌtestə'biliti ['iŋ-k-, -lət-]
incontestab|le, -ly ˌinkən'testəb|l ['in-kən't-, ˌiŋ-k-, 'iŋ-k-], -li

incontinen|ce,   -t/ly   in'kɔntinən|s
['in'k-, iŋ'k-, 'iŋ'k-], -t/li
incontrollab|le,   -ly   ,inkən'trəuləb|l
['inkən't-, ,iŋ-k-, 'iŋ-k-], -li
incontrovertibility   in,kɔntrəvə:tə'biliti
['in,kɔntrəvə:tə'b-,   iŋ,k-,   'iŋ,k-,
-truv-, -ti'b-, -lət-]
incontrovertib|le,   -ly   'inkɔntrə'və:təb|l
['iŋ-k-,   -truv-,   -tib-,   -,--'---,   iŋ,k-,
-'-----, iŋ'k-], -li
inconvenienc|e   (s. v.),   -es,   -ing,   -ed
,inkən'vi:njəns   ['inkən'v-,   ,iŋ-k-,
'iŋ-k-, -niəns], -iz, -iŋ, -t
inconvenient,   -ly   ,inkən'vi:njənt   ['inkən'v-, ,iŋ-k-, 'iŋ-k-, -niənt], -li
inconvertibility   'inkən,və:tə'biliti
['iŋ-k-, -ti'b-, -lət-]
inconvertib|le,   -ly   ,inkən'və:təb|l
['inkən'v-, ,iŋ-k-, 'iŋ-k-, -tib-], -li
incorporate (adj.) in'kɔ:pərit [iŋ'k-]
incorporat|e   (v.),   -es,   -ing,   -ed   in-
'kɔ:pəreit [iŋ'k-], -s, -iŋ, -id
incorporation,   -s   in,kɔ:pə'reiʃən [iŋ,k-],
-z
incorporeal,   -ly   ,inkɔ:'pɔ:riəl   ['inkɔ:'p-,
,iŋ-k-, 'iŋ-k-], -i
incorrect, -ly, -ness ,inkə'rekt ['inkə'r-,
,iŋ-k-, 'iŋ-k-], -li, -nis
incorrigibility   in,kɔridʒə'biliti [iŋ,k-,
-dʒi'b-, -lət-]
incorrigib|le,   -ly,   -leness   in'kɔridʒəb|l
[iŋ'k-, -dʒib-], -li, -lnis
incorruptibility   'inkə,rʌptə'biliti ['iŋ-k-,
-ti'b-, -lət-]
incorruptib|le,   -ly,   -leness   ,inkə'rʌpt-
əb|l ['inkə'r-, ,iŋ-k-, 'iŋ-k-, -tib-], -li,
-lnis
incorruption   (when   contrasted   with
corruption,   as   is   usually   the   case)
'inkə,rʌpʃən   ['iŋ-k-],   (when   not   so
contrasted)   ,inkə'r-   ['inkə'r-,   ,iŋ-k-,
'iŋ-k-]
increase   (s.),   -s   'inkri:s   ['iŋ-kri:s,
in'kri:s, iŋ'kri:s], -iz
increas|e   (v.),   -es,   -ing/ly,   -ed   in-
'kri:s [iŋ'k-, 'inkri:s, 'iŋ-kri:s], -iz,
-iŋ/li, -t
incredibility   in,kredi'biliti [iŋ,k-, -də'b-,
-lət-]
incredib|le,   -ly,   -leness   in'kredəb|l
[iŋ'k-, -dib-], -li, -lnis
incredulity   ,inkri'dju:liti   [,iŋ-kri'd-,
-kre'd-, -krə'd-]
incredulous,   -ly,   -ness   in'kredjuləs
[iŋ'k-], -li, -nis   [-s
increment, -al, -s 'inkrimənt ['iŋk-], -l,
incriminat|e,   -es,   -ing,   -ed   in'krimineit
[iŋ'k-], -s, -iŋ, -id

incrimination in,krimi'neiʃən
incriminatory   in'kriminətəri   [iŋ'k-,
-neitəri]
incrust,   -s,   -ing,   -ed   in'krʌst   [iŋ'k-],
-s, -iŋ, -id
incrustation, -s ,inkrʌs'teiʃən [,iŋ-k-], -z
incubat|e,   -es,   -ing,   -ed,   -or/s;   -ive,
-ory   'inkjubeit   ['iŋk-],   -s,   -iŋ,   -id,
ə*/z; -iv, -əri
incubation ,inkju'beiʃən [,iŋk-]
incubus,   -es   'iŋkjubəs   ['ink-],   -iz
inculcat|e,   -es,   -ing,   -ed,   -or/s   'inkʌl-
keit ['iŋ-k-, -kəl-, in'kʌlkeit, iŋ'kʌl-],
-s, -iŋ, -id, -ə*/z
inculcation ,inkʌl'keiʃən [,iŋ-k-]
inculpat|e,   -es,   -ing,   -ed   'inkʌlpeit
['iŋ-k-, in'kʌlpeit, iŋ'k-], -s, -iŋ, -id
inculpation ,inkʌl'peiʃən [,iŋ-k-]
inculpatory in'kʌlpətəri [iŋ'k-, 'inkʌl-
peitəri, 'iŋ-kʌlpeitəri]
incumben|cy,   -cies,   -t/s,   -tly   in'kʌm-
bən|si [iŋ'k-], -siz, -t/s, -tli
incunabula ,inkju(:)'næbjulə [,iŋ-k-]
incur,   -s,   -ring,   -red   in'kə:*   [iŋ'k-],   -z,
-riŋ, -d
incurability in,kjuərə'biliti ['in,kjuər-
ə'b-,   iŋ,k-,   'iŋ,k-,   -jɔər-,   -jɔ:r-,
-,kjə:r-, -lət-]
incurable,   -ness   in'kjuərəbl   ['in'k-,
iŋ'k-, 'iŋ'k-, -'kjɔər-, -'kjɔ:r-, -'kjə:r-],
-nis
incurious in'kjuəriəs ['in'k-, iŋ'k-, 'iŋ'k-,
-'kjɔər-, -'kjɔ:r-, -'kjə:r-]
incursion, -s in'kə:ʃən [iŋ'k-], -z
incursive in'kə:siv [iŋ'k-]
incurvat|e,   -es,   -ing,   -ed   'inkə:veit
['iŋ-k-], -s, -iŋ, -id
incurvation ,inkə:'veiʃən [,iŋ-k-]
incurv|e,   -es,   -ing,   -ed   'in'kə:v   [in'k-,
iŋ'k-],   -z,   -iŋ,   -d   [also   'inkə:vd,
'iŋ-kə:vd, esp. when attributive]
incus|e (s. adj. v.),   -es,   -ing,   -ed   in-
'kju:z [iŋ'k-], -iz, -iŋ, -d
Ind (surname) ind, (India) ind [aind]
Indaur in'dɔ:* (Hind. yndəwr)
indebted, -ness in'detid, -nis
indecen|cy,   -cies,   -t/ly   in'di:sn|si   ['in'd-,
-siz, -t/li
indecipherable ,indi'saifərəbl ['indi's-]
indecision ,indi'siʒən ['indi's-]
indecisive,   -ly,   -ness   ,indi'saisiv
['indi's-], -li, -nis
indeclinable (s. adj.),   -s   ,indi'klainəbl
['indi'k-], -z
indecomposable 'in,di:kəm'pəuzəbl
indecorous,   -ly,   -ness   in'dekərəs   ['in'd-],
-li, -nis
indecorum ,indi'kɔ:rəm ['indi'k-]

indeed (*adv.*) in'di:d, (*interj.*) in'di:d
['in'd-]
indefatigable, -ness ,indi'fætigəbl, -nis
indefatigably ,indi'fætigəbli
indefeasibility 'indi,fi:zə'biliti [-zi'b-,
-lət-]
indefeasible ,indi'fi:zəbl ['indi'f-, -zib-]
indefeasibly ,indi'fi:zəbli [-zib-]
indefensibility 'indi,fensə'biliti [-si'b-,
-lət-]
indefensible ,indi'fensəbl ['indi'f-, -sib-]
indefensibly ,indi'fensəbli [-sib-]
indefinable ,indi'fainəbl ['indi'f-]
indefinably ,indi'fainəbli
indefinite, -ly, -ness in'definit ['in'd-,
-fnit, -fnit], -li, -nis
indelibility in,deli'biliti ['in,deli'b-,
-lə'b-, -lət-]
indelible in'delibl ['in'd-, -ləb-]
indelibly in'delibli [-ləb-]
indelicac|y, -ies in'delikəs|i ['in'd-], -iz
indelicate, -ly in'delikit ['in'd-], -li
indemnification, -s in,demnifi'keiʃən, -z
indemni|fy, -fies, -fying, -fied in'dem-
ni|fai, -faiz, -faiiŋ, -faid
indemnit|y, -ies in'demnit|i, -iz
indemonstrable in'demənstrəbl ['in'd-,
,indi'mons-, 'indi'mons-]
indent (*s.*), -s indent [-'-], -s
indent (*v.*), -s, -ing, -ed in'dent, -s, -iŋ,
-id
indentation, -s ,inden'teiʃən, -z
indenture, -s in'dentʃə*, -z
independen|ce, -cy ,indi'pendən|s, -si
independent (*s. adj.*), -s, -ly ,indi-
'pendənt ['indi'p-], -s, -li
Inderwick 'ində(:)wik
indescribable ,indis'kraibəbl ['indis'k-]
indescribably ,indis'kraibəbli
indestructibility 'indis,trʌktə'biliti
[-ti'b-, -lət-]
indestructible, -ness ,indis'trʌktəbl
['indis't-, -tib-], -nis
indestructibly ,indis'trʌktəbli [-tib-]
indeterminable, -ness ,indi'tə:mínəbl
['indi't-], -nis
indeterminate, -ly, -ness ,indi'tə:mínit
['indi't-], -li, -nis
indetermination 'indi,tə:mi'meiʃən
ind|ex, -exes, -ices 'ind|eks, -eksiz, -isi:z
India, -n/s 'indjə [-diə], -n/z
Indiana ,indi'ænə [-'ɑ:n-]
Indianapolis 'indiə'næpəlis [-djə-, -pul-]
india-rubber, -s 'indjə'rʌbə* [-dʒə-, *also*
'--,--, ,--'--, *according to sentence-
stress*], -z
indicat|e, -es, -ing, -ed, -or/s 'indikeit,
-s, -iŋ, -id, -ə*/z

indication, -s ,indi'keiʃən, -z
indicative (*s. adj.*) (*in grammar*), -s, -ly
in'dikətiv, -z, -li
indicative (*adj.*) (*pointing out*), -ly in-
'dikətiv ['indikeitiv], -li
indicatory in'dikətəri ['indikeitəri]
indict, -s, -ing, -ed, -er/s, -ment/s;
-able in'dait, -s, -iŋ, -id, -ə*/z,
-mənt/s; -əbl
indiction, -s in'dikʃən, -z
Indies 'indiz
indifferen|ce, -cy, -t/ly in'difrən|s
[-fərən-], -si, -t/li
indigen|ce, -t/ly 'indidʒən|s, -t/li
indigene, -s 'indidʒi:n, -z
indigenous in'didʒinəs [-dʒŋəs]
indigestibility 'indi,dʒestə'biliti [-ti'b-,
-lət-]
indigestible, -ness ,indi'dʒestəbl ['indi'dʒ-, -tib-], -nis
indigestion ,indi'dʒestʃən ['indi'dʒ-,
-eʃtʃ-]
indignant, -ly in'dignənt, -li
indignation ,indig'neiʃən
indignit|y, -ies in'dignit|i, -iz
indigo, -s 'indigəu, -z
indirect, -ly, -ness ,indi'rekt ['indi'r-,
-dai'r-, -də'r-], -li, -nis
indiscernible ,indi'sə:nəbl ['indi's-,
-di'zə:-, -nib-]
indisciplin|e,-able in'disiplin ['in'd-], -əbl
indiscreet, -ly, -ness ,indis'kri:t
['indis'k-], -li, -nis [-z
indiscretion, -s ,indis'kreʃən ['indis'k-],
indiscriminate, -ly ,indis'kriminit
['indis'k-], -li
indiscrimination 'indis,krimi'neiʃən
indispensability 'indis,pensə'biliti [-lət-]
indispensable, -ness ,indis'pensəbl
['indis'p-], -nis
indispos|e, -es, -ing, -ed ,indis'pəuz ['in-
dis'p-], -iz, -iŋ, -d
indisposition, -s ,indispə'ziʃən ['in-
,dispə'z-, -pu'z-], -z
indisputability 'indispju:tə'biliti [in-
'dispjutə'b-, -lət-]
indisputable, -ness 'indis'pju:təbl [,in-
dis'pju:t-, in'dispjutəbl], -nis
indisputably ,indis'pju:təbli [in'dis-
pjut-]
indissociable ,indi'səuʃjəbl ['indi's-,
-ʃə-, -ʃə-]
indissolubility 'indi,sɔlju'biliti [-lət-]
indissoluble, -ness ,indi'sɔljubl ['indi's-,
in'disəl-, 'in'disəl-], -nis
indissolubly ,indi'sɔljubli [in'disəl-]
indistinct, -ly, -ness ,indis'tiŋkt
['indis't-], -li, -nis

indistinctive, -ly, -ness ,indis'tiŋktiv ['indis't-], -li, -nis
indistinguishab|le, -ly, -leness ,indis-'tiŋgwiʃəb|l ['indis't-], -li, -lnis
indit|e, -es, -ing, -ed, -er/s in'dait, -s, -iŋ, -id, -ə*/z
individual (s. adj.), -s, -ly ,indi'vidjŭəl [-djwəl, -djul, -dʒŭəl, -dʒwəl, -dʒul], -z, -i
individuali|sm, -st/s ,indi'vidjŭəli|zəm [-djwəl-, -djul-, -dʒŭəl-, -dʒwəl-, -dʒul-], -st/s
individualistic ,indi,vidjŭə'listik ['indi-,vidjŭə'l-, -djwə'l-, -dju'l-, -dʒŭə'l-, -dʒwə'l-, -dʒu'l-]
individualit|y, -ies ,indi,vidju'ælit|i ['indi,vidju'æ-, -,vidʒu-], -iz
individualization [-isa-] ,indi,vidjŭəlai-'zeiʃən ['indi,v-, -djwəl-, -djul-, -dʒŭəl-, -dʒwəl-, -dʒul-, -li'z-]
individualiz|e [-is|e], -es, -ing, -ed ,indi'vidjŭəlaiz [-djwəl-, -djul-, -dʒŭəl-, -dʒwəl-, -dʒul-], -iz, -iŋ, -d
individu|um, -ums, -a ,indi'vidjŭ|əm [-djw|əm], -əmz, -ə
indivisïbility 'indi,vizi'biliti [-zə'b-, -lət-]
indivisib|le, -ly, -leness ,indi'vizəb|l ['indi'v-, -zib-], -li, -lnis
Indo-China 'indəu'tʃainə
Indo-Chinese 'indəu-tʃai'ni:z
indocile in'dəusail ['in'd-, -'dɔs-]
indocility ,indəu'siliti ['indəu's-]
indoctrinat|e, -es, -ing, -ed in'dɔk-trineit, -s, -iŋ, -id
indoctrination in,dɔktri'neiʃən
Indo-European, -s 'indəu,juərə'pi(:)ən [-,jɔər-, -,jɔ:r-], -z
Indo-Germanic 'indəudʒə(:)'mænik
indolen|ce, -t/ly 'indələn|s [-dul-], -t/li
indomitab|le, -ly in'dɔmitəb|l, -li
Indone|sia, -sian/s ,indəu'ni:|zjə [-zïə, -ʒə, -sjə, -sïə, -ʃə], -zjən/z [-zïən/z, -ʒən/z, -sjən/z, -sïən/z, -ʃən/z]
indoor 'indɔ:* [-dɔə*]
indoors 'in'dɔ:z [-'dɔəz, also in'd- when preceded by a stress]
Indore (former spelling of Indaur, q.v.) in'dɔ:* [-'dɔə*]
indors|e, -es, -ing, -ed, -ement/s in'dɔ:s, -iz, -iŋ, -t, -mənt/s
Indra 'indrə
indraught, -s 'in-drɑ:ft, -s [butive]
indrawn 'in'drɔ:n ['in-drɔ:n when attri-
indubitable, -ness in'dju:bitəbl, -nis
indubitably in'dju:bitəbli
induc|e, -es, -ing, -ed, -er/s, -ement/s in'dju:s, -iz, -iŋ, -t, -ə*/z, -mənt/s

induct, -s, -ing, -ed, -or/s in'dʌkt, -s, -iŋ, -id, -ə*/z
inductile in'dʌktail ['in'd-]
inductility ,indʌk'tiliti ['indʌk't-]
induction, -s in'dʌkʃən, -z
induction-coil, -s in'dʌkʃənkɔil, -z
inductive, -ly in'dʌktiv, -li
indulg|e, -es, -ing, -ed, -er/s in'dʌldʒ, -iz, -iŋ, -d, -ə*/z
indulgen|ce, -ces, -t/ly in'dʌldʒən|s, -siz, -t/li
indurat|e, -es, -ing, -ed 'indjuəreit [-jur-], -s, -iŋ, -id
Indus 'indəs
industrial, -ly in'dʌstrïəl, -i
industriali|sm, -st/s in'dʌstrïəli|zəm, -st/s
industrialization in,dʌstrïəlai'zeiʃən
industrializ|e, -es, -ing, -ed in'dʌs-trïəlaiz, -iz, -iŋ, -d
industrious, -ly in'dʌstrïəs, -li
industr|y, -ies 'indəstr|i, -iz
indwel|l, -ls, -ling, -t 'in'dwel [-'-], -z, -iŋ, -t
indweller, -s 'in,dwelə*, -z
inebriate (s. adj.), -s i'ni:briit [-brïət, -brieit], -s
inebriat|e (v.), -es, -ing, -ed i'ni:brieit, -s, -iŋ, -id
inebriation i,ni:bri'eiʃən
inebriety ,ini(:)'braiəti
inedible in'edibl ['in'e-, -dəb-]
inedited in'editid ['in'e-]
ineducable in'edjukəbl [-dʒu-]
ineffab|le, -ly, -leness in'efəb|l, -li, -lnis
ineffaceable ,ini'feisəbl ['ini'f-]
ineffaceably ,ini'feisəbli
ineffective, -ly ,ini'fektiv ['ini'f-], -li
ineffectual, -ly, -ness ini'fektʃŭəl ['ini'f-, -tʃwəl, -tʃul, -tjŭəl, -tjwəl, -tjul], -i, -nis
inefficacious, -ly ,inefi'keiʃəs ['inefi'k-], -li
inefficacy in'efikəsi ['in'e-]
inefficien|cy, -t/ly ,ini'fiʃən|si ['ini'f-], -t/li
inelastic ,ini'læstik ['ini'l-, '-lɑ:s-]
inelasticity ,inilæs'tisiti ['inilæs't-, 'ini:læs't-, -lɑ:s-]
inelegan|ce, -t/ly in'eligən|s ['in'e-], -t/li
ineligibility in,elidʒə'biliti ['in,elidʒə'b-, -lət-]
ineligib|le, -ly in'elidʒəb|l ['in'e-, -dʒib-], -li
ineluctable ,ini'lʌktəbl
inept, -ly, -ness i'nept [in'ept], -li, -nis
ineptitude i'neptitju:d [in'ep-]

inequalit|y,   -ies   ,ini(:)'kwɔlit|i ['ini(:)'k-], -iz

inequitab|le, -ly in'ekwitəb|l ['in'e-], -li

inequit|y, -ies in'ekwit|i ['in'e-], -iz

ineradicable ,ini'rædikəbl ['ini'r-]

ineradicably ,ini'rædikəbli

inert, -ly, -ness i'nə:t, -li, -nis

inertia i'nə:ʃjə [-ʃiə, -ʃə]

inescapable ,inis'keipəbl ['inis'k-]

inessential 'ini'senʃəl

inestimable in'estiməbl ['in'e-]

inestimably in'estiməbli

inevitability in,evitə'biliti [i,ne-, -lət-]

inevitable, -ness in'evitəbl ['in'e-, i'ne-, 'i'ne-], -nis

inevitably in'evitəbli [i'ne-]

inexact, -ly, -ness ,inig'zækt ['inig'z-, -eg-], -li, -nis

inexactitude, -s ,inig'zæktitju:d ['in-ig'z-, -eg-], -z

inexcusable,   -ness   ,iniks'kju:zəbl ['iniks'k-, -ek-], -nis

inexcusably ,iniks'kju:zəbli [-ek-]

inexhaustibility 'inig,zɔ:stə'biliti [-eg-, -ti'b-]

inexhaustible ,inig'zɔ:stəbl ['inig'z-, -eg-, -tib-]

inexhaustibly ,inig'zɔ:stəbli [-eg-, -tib-]

inexorability in,eksərə'biliti [-lət-]

inexorab|le, -ly, -leness in'eksərəb|l, -li, -lnis

inexpedien|cy,   -t/ly   ,iniks'pi:djən|si ['iniks'p-, -ek-, -dɪən-], -t/li

inexpensive   ,iniks'pensiv ['iniks'p-, -ek-]

inexperience,   -d   ,iniks'piəriəns ['iniks'p-, -ek-], -t

inexpert,   -ness   in'ekspə:t ['ineks'p-, -niks'p-, ,ineks'p-, 'in'eksp-], -nis

inexpiable, -ness in'ekspɪəbl ['in'e-, -pjə-], -nis

inexplicability in,eksplikə'biliti ['in,eks-plikə'b-, 'iniks,plikə'b-, 'ineks-,plikə'b-, -lət-]

inexplicable,   -ness   in'eksplikəbl ['in'e-, ,iniks'p-, 'iniks'p-], -nis

inexplicably in'eksplikəbli [,iniks'plik-, ,ineks'p-]

inexplicit ,iniks'plisit ['iniks'p-,-ek-]

inexplorable ,iniks'plɔ:rəbl ['iniks'p-, -ek-]

inexpressible ,iniks'presəbl ['iniks'p-, -ek-, -sib-]

inexpressibly ,iniks'presəbli [-sib-, -ek-]

inexpressive,   -ness   ,iniks'presiv ['iniks'p-, -ek-], -nis

inexpugnable ,iniks'pʌgnəbl ['iniks'p-, -ek-]

inextensible   ,iniks'tensəbl ['iniks't--ek-, -sib-]

inextinguishable   ,iniks'tiŋgwiʃəbl ['iniks't-, -ek-]

inextinguishably   ,iniks'tiŋgwiʃəbli [-ek-]

inextricable in'ekstrikəbl ['in'e-, ,iniks-'trik-, ,ineks'trik-]

inextricably in'ekstrikəbli [,iniks'trik-, ,ineks'trik-]

Inez 'i:nez

infallibility in,fælə'biliti [-li'b-, -lət-]

infallib|le, -ly in'fæləb|l [-lib-], -li

infamous, -ly, -ness 'infəməs [-fməs], infamy 'infəmi [-fmi]   [-li, -nis

infancy 'infənsi

infant, -s 'infənt, -s

infanta, -s in'fæntə, -z

infante, -s in'fænti, -z

infanticide, -s in'fæntisaid, -z

infant|ile, -ine 'infənt|ail, -ain

infantry, -man, -men 'infəntri, -mən [-mæn], -mən [-men]

infatuat|e, -es, -ing, -ed in'fætjueit [-'fætʃu-], -s, -iŋ, -id   [-z

infatuation, -s in,fætju'eiʃən [-,fætʃu-], infect, -s, -ing, -ed in'fekt, -s, -iŋ, -id

infection, -s in'fekʃən, -z

infectious, -ly, -ness in'fekʃəs, -li, -nis

infecundity ,infi'kʌnditi ['infi'k-, -fi:'k-, -fe'k-]

infelicit|ous,   -y   ,infi'lisit|əs ['infi'l-, -fe'l-], -i

infer, -s, -ring, -red; -able in'fə:*, -z, -riŋ, -d; -rəbl

inference, -s 'infərəns, -iz

inferenti|al, -ally ,infə'renʃ|əl, -əli

inferior (s. adj.), -s in'fiəriə* ['in'f-], -z

inferiority in,fiəri'ɔriti [,infiəri'ɔ-]

infern|al (s. adj.), -als, -ally in'fə:n|l, -lz, -əli [-li]

inferno, -s in'fə:nəu, -z

Inferno in'fə:nəu [-'fɛən-]

infertile in'fə:tail ['in'f-]

infest, -s, -ing, -ed in'fest, -s, -iŋ, -id

infestation ,infes'teiʃən

infidel, -s 'infidəl, -z

infidelit|y, -ies ,infi'delit|i [-fai'd-], -iz

infiltrat|e, -es, -ing, -ed 'infiltreit [-'--], -s, -iŋ, -id

infiltration, -s infil'treiʃən, -z

in fine in'faini [-'fi:n-]

infinite (in non-technical sense), -ly, -ness 'infinit [-fnit], -li, -nis

Note.—In church music it is customary to pronounce this word 'infinait or 'infainait, but these forms are not heard in ordinary speech.

infinite (*technical senses in mathematics and grammar, opposed to* finite) 'infinit [-fnit, 'in,fainait]
infinitesim|al, -ally ,infini'tesim|əl, -əli
infinitival in,fini'taivəl [,infini't-]
infinitive, -s, -ly in'finitiv, -z, -li
infinitude, -s in'finitju:d, -z
infinit|y, -ies in'finit|i, -iz
infirm, -ly in'fə:m ['in'fə:m], -li
infirmar|y, -ies in'fə:mər|i [-mr|i], -iz
infirmit|y, -ies in'fə:mit|i, -iz
infix (*s.*), -es 'infiks, -iz
infix (*v.*), -es, -ing, -ed in'fiks, -iz, -iŋ, -t
inflam|e, -es, -ing, -ed in'fleim, -z, -iŋ, -d
inflammability in,flæmə'biliti [-lət-]
inflammable, -ness in'flæməbl, -nis
inflammation, -s ,inflə'meiʃən, -z
inflammatory in'flæmətəri
inflat|e, -es, -ing, -ed, -or/s in'fleit, -s, -iŋ, -id, -ə*/z
inflation, -s in'fleiʃən, -z
inflationary in'fleiʃŋəri [-ʃnəri, -ʃŋri, -ʃənəri]
inflect, -s, -ing, -ed in'flekt, -s, -iŋ, -id
inflection, -s in'flekʃən, -z
inflectional in'flekʃənl [-ʃnəl, -ʃŋl, -ʃŋl, -ʃənəl]
inflective in'flektiv [-ʃənəl]
inflexibility in,fleksə'biliti ['in,fleksə'b-, -si'b-, -lət-]
inflexib|le, -ly, -leness in'fleksəb|l [-sib-], -li, -lnis
inflexion, -s in'flekʃən, -z
inflexional in'flekʃənl [-ʃnəl, -ʃŋl, -ʃŋl, -ʃənəl]
inflict, -s, -ing, -ed in'flikt, -s, -iŋ, -id
infliction, -s in'flikʃən, -z
inflow, -s 'in-fləu, -z
influenc|e (*s. v.*), -es, -ing, -ed 'inflüəns [-flwəns], -iz, -iŋ, -t
influent, -s 'inflüənt [-flwənt], -s
influenti|al, -ally ,influ'enʃ|əl, -əli
influenza ,influ'enzə
influx, -es 'inflʌks, -iz
influxion in'flʌkʃən
inform, -s, -ing, -ed, -er/s in'fɔ:m, -z, -iŋ, -d, -ə*/z
inform|al, -ally in'fɔ:m|l ['in'f-, -əl], -əli
informalit|y, -ies ,infɔ:'mælit|i ['in-fɔ:'m-], -iz
informant, -s in'fɔ:mənt, -s
information, -s ,infə'meiʃən [-fɔ:'m-], -z
informat|ive, -ory in'fɔ:mət|iv, -əri
infra 'infrə
infract, -s, -ing, -ed in'frækt, -s, -iŋ, -id
infraction, -s in'frækʃən, -z
infralapsarian, -s 'infrəlæp'seəriən, -z
infrangibility in,frændʒi'biliti ['in-,frændʒi'b-, -dʒə'b-, -lət-]

infrangible in'frændʒibl ['in'f-, -dʒəb-]
infra-red 'infrə'red
infra-structure, -s 'infrə,strʌktʃə*, -z
infrequen|cy, -t in'fri:kwən|si ['in'f-], -t
infrequently in'fri:kwəntli
infring|e, -es, -ing, -ed, -er/s, -ement/s in'frindʒ, -iz, -iŋ, -d, -ə*/z, -mənt/s
infuriat|e, -es, -ing, -ed in'fjuərieit [-'fjɔər-, -'fjɔ:r-, -'fjə:r-], -s, -iŋ, -id
infus|e, -es, -ing, -ed, -er/s in'fju:z, -iz, -iŋ, -d, -ə*/z
infusible (*capable of being infused*) in'fju:zəbl [-zib-]
infusible (*not fusible*) in'fju:zəbl ['in'f-, -zib-]
infusion, -s in'fju:ʒən, -z
infusoria, -l, -n ,infju:'zɔ:rɪə [-'sɔ:-], -l, -n
infusory in'fju:zəri [-u:sə-]
Ingall 'iŋgɔ:l
Ingatestone 'ingeitstəun ['iŋg-]
ingathering, -s 'in,gæðəriŋ, -z
Inge iŋ, indʒ
  Note.—*The late Dean of St. Paul's was* iŋ.
Ingelow 'indʒiləu
ingenious, -ly, -ness in'dʒi:njəs [-nɪəs], -li, -nis
ingénue, -s ,ɛ̃:nʒei'nju: [,ænʒ-, '—] (ɛ̃ʒeny), -z
ingenuity ,indʒi'nju(:)iti [-dʒə'n-]
ingenuous, -ly, -ness in'dʒenjüəs [-njwəs], -li, -nis
Ingersoll, -s 'iŋgəsɔl, -z
Ingestre 'iŋgestri
Ingham 'iŋəm
ingle (I.), -s 'iŋgl, -z
Ingle|borough, -by 'iŋgl|bərə, -bi
ingle-nook, -s 'iŋglnuk, -s
Inglewood 'iŋglwud
Inglis 'iŋglz, 'iŋglis
inglorious, -ly, -ness in'glɔ:rɪəs ['in'g-, iŋ'g-, 'iŋ'g-], -li, -nis
ingoing 'in,gəuiŋ
Ingold 'iŋgəuld
Ingoldsby 'iŋgəldzbi
ingot, -s 'iŋgət [-gɔt], -s
Ingpen 'iŋpen
Ingraham 'iŋgrəhəm [-grɪəm]
ingrain, -ed 'in'grein [*also* '—, -'- *according to sentence-stress*], -d
Ingram 'iŋgrəm
ingrate, -s in'greit, -s
ingratiat|e, -es, -ing, -ed in'greiʃieit [-ʃjeit], -s, -iŋ, -id
ingratitude in'grætitju:d ['in'g-, iŋ'g-, 'iŋ'g-]
Ingrebourne 'iŋgribɔ:n [-bɔən]

ingredient, -s in'gri:djənt [iŋ'g-, -dïənt],
ingress 'ingres ['iŋg-]   [-s
ingressive in'gresiv
in|growing, -growth 'in|ˌgrəuiŋ, -grəuθ
inguinal 'iŋgwinl
inhabit, -s, -ing, -ed, -er/s; -able,
    -ant/s in'hæbit, -s, -iŋ, -id, -ə*/z;
    -əbl, -ənt/s
inhabitation inˌhæbi'teiʃən
inhalation, -s ˌinhə'leiʃən, -z
inhal|e, -es, -ing, -ed, -er/s in'heil, -z,
    -iŋ, -d, -ə*/z
inharmonious, -ly, -ness ˌinhɑ:'məunjəs
    ['inhɑ:'m-, -nïəs], -li, -nis
inher|e, -es, -ing, -ed in'hiə*, -z, -riŋ, -d
inheren|ce,   -cy,   -t/ly   in'hiərən|s
    [-'her-], -si, -t/li
inherit, -s, -ing, -ed, -or/s; -able,
    -ance/s in'herit, -s, -iŋ, -id, -ə*/z;
    -əbl, -əns/iz
inheritrix, -es in'heritriks, -iz
inhibit, -s, -ing, -ed; -ory in'hibit, -s, -iŋ,
    -id; -əri
inhibition, -s ˌinhi'biʃən, -z
inhospitab|le, -ly, -leness in'hɔspitəb|l
    ['in'h-, ˌinhɔs'p-, 'inhɔs'p-], -li, -lnis
inhospitality 'inˌhɔspi'tæliti
inhuman, -ly in'hju:mən ['in'h-], -li
inhumane,   -ly   ˌinhju(:)'mein   ['in-
    hju(:)'m-], -li
inhumanit|y, -ies ˌinhju(:)'mænit|i ['in-
    hju(:)'m-], -iz
inhumation, -s ˌinhju(:)'meiʃən, -z
inhum|e, -es, -ing, -ed in'hju:m, -z, -iŋ,
    -d
Inigo 'inigəu
inimic|al, -ally i'nimik|əl, -əli
inimitability iˌnimitə'biliti [-lət-]
inimitab|le, -ly, -leness i'nimitəb|l, -li,
    -lnis
iniquitous, -ly i'nikwitəs, -li
iniquit|y, -ies i'nikwit|i, -iz
initi|al (s. adj. v.), -als, -ally; -al(l)ing,
    -al(l)ed i'niʃ|əl, -əlz, -əli [-ḷi]; -əliŋ
    [-ḷiŋ], -əld
initiate (s.), -s i'niʃiit [-ʃjit, -ʃieit,
    -ʃjeit, -ʃïət, -ʃjət], -s
initiat|e (v.), -es, -ing, -ed, -or/s
    i'niʃieit [-ʃjeit], -s, -iŋ, -id, -ə*/z
initiation, -s iˌniʃi'eiʃən, -z
initiative i'niʃïətiv [-ʃjət-, -ʃət-]
initiatory i'niʃïətəri [-ʃjət-, -ʃieitəri]
initio (in ab initio) i'niʃiəu [-'nitiəu, -si-]
inject, -s, -ing, -ed, -or/s in'dʒekt, -s,
    -iŋ, -id, -ə*/z
injection, -s in'dʒekʃən, -z
injudicious, -ly, -ness ˌindʒu(:)'diʃəs
    ['indʒu(:)'d-], -li, -nis

injunction, -s in'dʒʌŋkʃən, -z
injurant, -s 'indʒurənt [-dʒər-], -s
inj|ure, -ures, -uring, -ured, -urer/s
    'indʒ|ə*, -əz, -əriŋ, -əd, -ərə*/z
injurious, -ly, -ness in'dʒuərïəs
    [-'dʒɔər-, -'dʒɔ:r-, -'dʒə:r-], -li, -nis
injur|y, -ies 'indʒər|i, -iz
injustice in'dʒʌstis ['in'dʒ-]
ink (s. v.), -s, -ing, -ed, -er/s iŋk, -s, -iŋ,
    -t [iŋt], -ə*/z
ink-bottle, -s 'iŋkˌbɔtl, -z
Inkerman 'iŋkəmən
ink-horn, -s 'iŋk-hɔ:n, -z
inking-roller, -s 'iŋkiŋˌrəulə*, -z
inkling, -s 'iŋkliŋ, -z
ink-pot, -s 'iŋkpɔt, -s
ink-stain, -s 'iŋk-stein, -z
inkstand, -s 'iŋkstænd, -z
ink|y, -ier, -iest, -iness 'iŋk|i, -ïə*
    [-jə*], -iist [-jist], -inis
inland (s. adj.), -s 'inlənd [-lænd], -z
inland (adv.) in'lænd ['-'-]
inlander, -s 'inləndə*, -z
inlay (s.) 'inlei
inlay (v.), -s, -ing, inlaid 'in'lei [in'l-],
    -z, -iŋ, 'in'leid [also 'inleid when
    attributive]
inlet, -s 'inlet [-lit], -s
inly 'inli
Inman 'inmən
inmate, -s 'inmeit, -s
inmost 'inməust [-məst]
inn, -s in, -z
innate, -ly, -ness 'i'neit ['-, -'-], -li, -nis
innavigable i'nævigəbl ['in'næ-]
inner, -most 'inə*, -məust
innervat|e, -es, -ing, -ed 'inə:veit
    [i'nə:v-], -s, -iŋ, -id
innervation ˌinə:'veiʃən
Innes(s) 'inis
innings, -es 'iniŋz, -iz
Innisfail ˌinis'feil
Innisfree ˌinis'fri:
innkeeper, -s 'inˌki:pə*, -z
innocen|ce, -cy 'inəsən|s [-nus-], -si
innocent (s. adj.) (L.), -s, -ly 'inəsnt
    [-nus-, -nəus-], -s, -li
innocuous, -ly, -ness i'nɔkjŭəs ['i'nɔ-,
    -kjwəs], -li, -nis
innominate i'nɔminit [-neit]
Innous 'inəs
innovat|e, -es, -ing, -ed, -or/s 'inəuveit,
    -s, -iŋ, -id, -ə*/z
innovation, -s ˌinəu'veiʃən, -z
innoxious, -ly, -ness i'nɔkʃəs ['i'nɔ-], -li,
    -nis
Innsbruck 'inzbruk (insbruk)
innuendo, -es ˌinju(:)'endəu, -z

innumerability i,nju:mərə'biliti [-lət-]

innumerab|le, -ly, -leness i'nju:mər-əb|l, -li, -lnis

innutriti|on, -ous ,inju(:)'triʃ|ən ['inju(:)'t-], -əs [-t

inobservan|ce,-t ,inəb'zə:vən|s ['inəb'z-],

inoccupation 'in,ɔkju'peiʃən

inoculat|e, -es, -ing, -ed, -or/s i'nɔkju-leit, -s, -iŋ, -id, -ə*/z

inoculation, -s i,nɔkju'leiʃən, -z

inodorous in'əudərəs ['in'əu-]

inoffensive, -ly, -ness ,inə'fensiv ['inə'f-, -nu'f-], -li, -nis

inofficious ,inə'fiʃəs ['inə'f-, -nu'f-]

inoperative in'ɔpərətiv ['in'ɔ-]

inopportune, -ly in'ɔpətju:n ['in'ɔpət-, ,inɔpə't-, 'inɔpə't-], -li

inordinate, -ly, -ness i'nɔ:dinit [-dn̩it], -li, -nis

inorganic, -ally ,inɔ:'gænik ['inɔ:'g-], -əli

inosculat|e, -es, -ing, -ed i'nɔskjuleit, -s, -iŋ, -id

inosculation i,nɔskju'leiʃən

in-patient, -s 'in,peiʃənt, -s

input, -s 'in-put, -s

inquest, -s 'inkwest ['iŋk-], -s

inquietude in'kwaiitju:d [iŋ'k-, -aiət-]

inquir|e, -es, -ing/ly, -ed, -er/s in-'kwaiə* [iŋ'k-], -z, -riŋ/li, -d, -rə*/z

inquir|y, -ies in'kwaiər|i [iŋ'k-], -iz

inquisition (I.), -s ,inkwi'ziʃən [,iŋk-], -z

inquisitional ,inkwi'ziʃənl [,iŋk-, -ʃnəl, -ʃn̩|, -ʃn|, -ʃənəl]

inquisitive, -ly, -ness in'kwizitiv [iŋ'k-, -zət-], -li, -nis

inquisitor, -s in'kwizitə* [iŋ'k-], -z

inquisitorial, -ly in,kwizi'tɔ:rɪəl [iŋ,k-, ,inkwizi't-, ,iŋkwizi't-], -i

inroad, -s 'inrəud, -z

inrush, -es 'inrʌʃ, -iz

insalubr|ious, -ity ,in-sə'lu:br|ɪəs ['in-sə'l-, -'lju:-], -iti

insane, -ly, -ness in'sein ['in'sein], -li, -nis

insanitar|y, -ily, -iness in'sænitər|i ['in's-], -ili, -inis

insanity in'sæniti

insatiability in,seiʃjə'biliti [-ʃɪə-, -ʃə-, -lət-]

insatiable, -ness in'seiʃjəbl [-ʃɪə-, -ʃə-], -nis

insatiate in'seiʃiit [-ʃjit, -ʃjət, -ʃɪət]

inscrib|e, -es, -ing, -ed, -er/s in'skraib, -z, -iŋ, -d, -ə*/z

inscription, -s in'skripʃən, -z

inscrutability in,skru:tə'biliti [,inskru:-, -lət-]

inscrutab|le, -ly, -leness in'skru:təb|l, -li, -lnis

insect, -s 'insekt, -s

insectarium, -s ,insek'tɛərɪəm, -z

insecticide, -s in'sektisaid, -z

insectivorous ,insek'tivərəs

insecur|e, -ely, -ity ,in-si'kjuə* ['in-si'k-, -'kjɔə*, -'kjɔ:*, -'kjə:*], -li, -riti

inseminat|e, -es, -ing, -ed in'semineit, -s, -iŋ, -id

insemination in,semi'neiʃən [,insem-]

insensate, -ly, -ness in'senseit [-sit], -li, -nis

insensibility in,sensə'biliti [,insen-, -si'b-, -lət-]

insensib|le, -ly, -leness in'sensəb|l [-sib-], -li, -lnis

insensitive, -ness in'sensitiv ['in's-, -sət-], -nis

inseparability in,sepərə'biliti ['in-,sepərə'b-, -lət-]

inseparable in'sepərəbl ['in's-]

inseparab|ly, -leness in'sepərəb|li, -lnis

insert, -s, -ing, -ed in'sə:t, -s, -iŋ, -id

insertion, -s in'sə:ʃən, -z

inset (s.), -s 'in-set ['inset], -s

inset (v.), -s, -ting in'set [in'set], -s, -iŋ

inseverable in'sevərəbl ['in's-]

inshore 'in'ʃɔ:* [-'ʃɔə*, also 'in-ʃ-, in'ʃ-according to sentence-stress]

inside (s. adj. adv. prep.), -s 'in'said [also 'ins-, in's- according to sentence-stress], -z

insider, -s 'in'saidə* [also in's- when preceded by a stress], -z

insidious, -ly, -ness in'sidɪəs [-djəs], -li, -nis

insight 'insait

insignia in'signɪə [-njə]

insignifican|ce, -cy, -t/ly ,insig'nifi-kən|s ['insig'n-], -si, -t/li

insincere, -ly ,insin'sɪə* ['insin's-, -sn's-], -li

insincerit|y, -ies ,insin'serit|i ['insin's-, -sn's-], -iz

insinuat|e, -es, -ing/ly, -ed, -or/s in-'sinjueit, -s, -iŋ/li, -id, -ə*/z

insinuation, -s in,sinju'eiʃən, -z

insipid, -ly, -ness in'sipid, -li, -nis

insipidity ,insi'piditi

insipien|ce, -t in'sipɪən|s [-pjə-], -t

insist, -s, -ing, -ed in'sist, -s, -iŋ, -id

insisten|ce, -cy, -t/ly in'sistən|s, -si, Inskip 'inskip [-t/li

insobriety ,insəu'braiəti ['insəu'b-, -aiiti]

insolation ,insəu'leiʃən

insolen|ce, -t/ly 'insələn|s [-sul-], -t/li
insolubility in,sɔlju'biliti ['in,sɔlju'b-, -lət-]
insoluble, -ness in'sɔljubl ['in's-], -nis
insolvable in'sɔlvəbl ['in's-]
insolven|cy, -t in'sɔlvən|si ['in's-], -t
insomnia in'sɔmniə [-njə]
insomuch ,insəu'mʌtʃ
insouciance in'su:sjəns [-sïəns] (ẽsusjã:s)
insouciant in'su:sjənt [-sïənt] (ẽsusjã)
inspect, -s, -ing, -ed, -or/s in'spekt, -s, -iŋ, -id, -ə*/z
inspection, -s in'spekʃən, -z
inspectorate, -s in'spektərit, -s
inspectorship, -s in'spektəʃip, -s
inspectress, -es in'spektris, -iz
inspiration, -s ,inspə'reiʃən [-spi'r-], -z
inspirational ,inspə'reiʃənl [-spi'r-, -ʃnəl, -ʃn̩l, -ʃnl, -ʃənəl]
inspirator, -s 'inspəreitə* [-spir-], -z
inspiratory in'spaiərətəri
inspir|e, -es, -ing/ly, -ed, -er/s in-'spaiə*, -z, -riŋ/li, -d, -rə*/z
inspirit, -s, -ing, -ed in'spirit, -s, -iŋ, -id
inspissate in'spiseit
inst. 'instənt
instability ,instə'biliti ['instə'b-, -lət-]
install, -s, -ing, -ed in'stɔ:l, -z, -iŋ, -d
installation, -s ,instə'leiʃən [-stɔ:'l-], -z
instalment, -s in'stɔ:lmənt, -s
instance (s. v.), -es, -ing, -ed 'instəns, -iz, -iŋ, -t
instant (s. adj.), -s, -ly 'instənt, -s, -li
instantaneous, -ly, -ness ,instən'teinjəs [-nïəs], -li, -nis
instanter in'stæntə*
instead in'sted
instep, -s 'in-step, -s
instigat|e, -es, -ing, -ed, -or/s 'instigeit, -s, -iŋ, -id, -ə*/z
instigation, -s ,insti'geiʃən, -z
instil, -s, -ling, -led, -ment in'stil, -z, -iŋ, -d, -mənt
instillation ,insti'leiʃən
instinct (s.), -s 'instiŋkt, -s
instinct (adj.) in'stiŋkt
instinctive, -ly in'stiŋktiv, -li
institut|e (s. v.), -es, -ing, -ed, -or/s 'institju:t, -s, -iŋ, -id, -ə*/z
institution, -s ,insti'tju:ʃən, -z
institutional ,insti'tju:ʃənl [-ʃnəl, -ʃn̩l, -ʃnl, -ʃənəl]
instruct, -s, -ing, -ed, -or/s, -ress/es in'strʌkt, -s, -iŋ, -id, -ə*/z, -ris/iz
instruction, -s in'strʌkʃən, -z
instructional in'strʌkʃənl [-ʃnəl, -ʃn̩l, -ʃnl, -ʃənəl]

instructive, -ly, -ness in'strʌktiv, -li, -nis
instrument, -s 'instrumənt [-trəm-], -s
instrument|al, -ally; -alist/s ,instru-'ment|l [-trə'm-], -əli; -əlist/s [-list/s]
instrumentality ,instrumen'tæliti [-trəm-, -mən-]
instrumentation ,instrumen'teiʃən [-trəm-, -mən-]
insubordinate ,insə'bɔ:dn̩it [-dənit, -dinit]
insubordination 'insə,bɔ:di'neiʃən
insubstantial ,in-səb'stænʃəl ['in-səb'st-, -bz't-]
insufferable in'sʌfərəbl
insufferably in'sʌfərəbli
insufficien|cy, -t/ly ,insə'fiʃən|si ['insə'f-, ,in-s'fiʃ-, 'in-s'fiʃ-], -t/li
insular, -ly, -ism 'insjulə* [-sjəl-], -li, -rizəm
insularity ,insju'læriti [-sjə'l-]
insulat|e, -es, -ing, -ed, -or/s 'insju-leit [-sjəl-], -s, -iŋ, -id, -ə*/z
insulation ,insju'leiʃən [-sjə'l-]
insulin 'insjulin
insult (s.), -s 'insʌlt, -s
insult (v.), -s, -ing/ly, -ed, -er/s in'sʌlt, -s, -iŋ/li, -id, -ə*/z
insuperability in,sju:pərə'biliti ['in-,sju:pərə'b-, -,su:-, -lət-]
insuperable in'sju:pərəbl ['in's-, -'su:-]
insuperably in'sju:pərəbli [-'su:-]
insupportable, -ness ,in-sə'pɔ:təbl ['in-sə'p-, ,insə'p-, 'insə'p-], -nis
insupportably ,in-sə'pɔ:təbli [,insə'p-]
insuppressible ,in-sə'presəbl ['in-sə'p-, ,insə'p-, 'insə'p-, -sib-]
insur|e, -es, -ing, -ed, -er/s; -able, -ance/s in'ʃuə* [-'ʃɔə*, -'ʃɔ:*, -'ʃə:*], -z, -riŋ, -d, -rə*/z; -rəbl, -rəns/iz
insurgent, -s in'sə:dʒənt, -s
insurmountability 'insə(:),mauntə'biliti [-lət-]
insurmountable ,insə(:)'mauntəbl ['in-sə(:)'m-]
insurrection, -s ,insə'rekʃən, -z
insurrectional ,insə'rekʃənl [-ʃnəl, -ʃn̩l, -ʃnl, -ʃənəl]
insurrectionar|y (s. adj.), -ies ,insə'rek-ʃnər|i [-ʃnə-, -ʃənə-], -iz
insurrectioni|sm, -st/s ,insə'rekʃn̩i|zəm [-ʃəni-, -st/s
insusceptibility 'in-sə,septə'biliti [-ti'b-, -lət-]
insusceptible ,in-sə'septəbl ['in-sə's-, -tib-]
intact, -ness in'tækt ['in't-], -nis

intaglio, -s in'tɑːliəu [-'tæl-, -ljəu], -z
intake 'in-teik
intangibility in,tændʒə'biliti ['in,tæn-dʒə'b-, -dʒi'b-, -lət-]
intangible, -ness in'tændʒəbl ['in't-, -dʒib-], -nis
intangibly in'tændʒəbli [-dʒib-]
integer, -s 'intidʒə*, -z
integral (s.), -s 'intigrəl, -z
integral (adj.), -ly 'intigrəl [in'tegrəl], -i
  Note.—As a mathematical term always 'intigrəl.
integrat|e, -es, -ing, -ed 'intigreit, -s, -iŋ, -id
integration, -s ,inti'greiʃən, -z
integrity in'tegriti
integument, -s in'tegjumənt, -s
intellect, -s 'intilekt, -s
intellection ,inti'lekʃən
intellective ,inti'lektiv
intellectual, -ly ,inti'lektjŭəl [-tjwəl, -tjul, -tʃŭəl, -tʃwəl, -tʃul], -i
intellectuali|sm, -st/s ,inti'lektjŭəli|zəm [-tjwəl-, -tjul-, -tʃŭəl-, -tʃwəl-, -tʃul-], -st/s
intellectuality 'inti,lektju'æliti [-tʃu-]
intellectualiz|e [-is|e], -es, -ing, -ed ,inti'lektjŭəlaiz [-tjwəl-, -tjul-, -tʃŭəl-, -tʃwəl-, -tʃul-], -iz, -iŋ, -d
intelligen|ce, -ces, -t/ly, -cer/s in'telidʒən|s, -siz, -t/li, -sə*/z
intelligentsia in,teli'dʒentsïə [,inteli'dʒ-, -'gen-, -tsjə]
intelligibility in,telidʒə'biliti [-dʒi'b-, -lət-]
intelligib|le, -ly, -leness in'telidʒəb|l [-dʒib-], -li, -lnis
intemperance in'tempərəns ['in't-]
intemperate, -ly, -ness in'tempərit ['in't-], -li, -nis
intend, -s, -ing, -ed in'tend, -z, -iŋ, -id
intendan|ce, -cy, -t/s in'tendən|s, -si, -t/s
intense, -r, -st, -ly, -ness in'tens, -ə*, -ist, -li, -nis
intensification, -s in,tensifi'keiʃən, -z
intensi|fy, -fies, -fying, -fied, -fier/s in'tensi|fai, -faiz, -faiiŋ, -faid, -faiə*/z
intension in'tenʃən
intensit|y, -ies in'tensit|i [-sət-], -iz
intensive, -ly, -ness in'tensiv, -li, -nis
intent (s. adj.), -s, -er, -est, -ly, -ness in'tent, -s, -ə*, -ist, -li, -nis
intention, -s, -ed in'tenʃən, -z, -d
inten|tional, -tionally in'ten|ʃənl [-ʃnəl, -ʃŋl, -ʃnl, -ʃənəl], -ʃŋəli [-ʃnəli, -ʃŋli, -ʃnli, -ʃənəli]
inter (v.), -s, -ring, -red in'tə:*, -z, -riŋ, -d

inter (Latin prep., in such phrases as inter alia, inter se) 'intə(:)*
interact (s.), -s 'intərækt, -s
interact (v.), -s, -ing, -ed ,intər'ækt [-tə'ækt, '—'-], -s, -iŋ, -id
interaction ,intər'ækʃən [-tə'æ-, '—'—]
interactive ,intər'æktiv [-tə'æ-, '—'—]
interblend, -s, -ing, -ed 'intə(:)'blend [,in-], -z, -iŋ, -id
inter|breed, -breeds, -breeding, -bred 'intə(:)'|bri:d [,in-], -'bri:dz, -'bri:diŋ, -'bred
intercalary in'tə:kələri [,intə'kæləri]
intercalat|e, -es, -ing, -ed in'tə:kəleit, -s, -iŋ, -id
intercalation, -s in,tə:kə'leiʃən, -z
interced|e, -es, -ing, -ed, -er/s ,intə(:)-'si:d, -z, -iŋ, -id, -ə*/z
intercept (s.), -s 'intə(:)sept, -s
intercept (v.), -s, -ing, -ed, -er/s ,intə(:)-'sept, -s, -iŋ, -id, -ə*/z
interception, -s ,intə(:)'sepʃən, -z
interceptive ,intə(:)'septiv
interceptor, -s ,intə(:)'septə*, -z
intercession, -s ,intə'seʃən, -z
intercessional ,intə'seʃənl [-ʃnəl, -ʃŋl, -ʃnl, -ʃənəl]
intercessor, -s ,intə'sesə* ['intəsesə*], -z
intercessory ,intə'sesəri
interchange (s.), -s 'intə(:)'tʃeindʒ ['intə(:)tʃ-, ,intə(:)'tʃ-], -iz
interchang|e (v.), -es, -ing, -ed ,intə(:)-'tʃeindʒ ['intə(:)'tʃ-], -iz, -iŋ, -d
interchangeability 'intə(:),tʃeindʒə'biliti [-lət-]
interchangeable, -ness ,intə(:)'tʃeindʒ-əbl ['intə(:)'tʃ-], -nis
interchangeably ,intə(:)'tʃeindʒəbli
intercollegiate 'intə(:)kə'li:dʒiit [,in-, -kə'l-, -dʒiit, -dʒjət, -dʒïət, -dʒət]
intercolonial 'intə(:)kə'ləunjəl [,intə(:)-kə'l-, -nïəl]
intercommunicat|e, -es, -ing, -ed ,intə(:)kə'mju:nikeit ['intə(:)kə'm-, -'mjun-], -s, -iŋ, -id
intercommunication 'intə(:)kə,mju:ni-'keiʃən [-,mjun-]
intercommunion ,intə(:)kə'mju:njən ['—'—, -nïən]
intercommunity ,intə(:)kə'mju:niti ['—'—]
interconnect, -s, -ing, -ed 'intə(:)-kə'nekt [,in-], -s, -iŋ, -id
intercostal ,intə(:)'kɔstl ['intə(:)'k-]
intercourse 'intə(:)kɔːs [-kɔəs]
intercurren|ce, -t ,intə(:)'kʌrən|s ['intə(:)'k-], -t
interdental 'intə(:)'dentl [,intə(:)'d-]

interdependen|ce, -t ˌintə(:)di'pendən|s ['intə(:)di'p-], -t

interdict (s.), -s 'intə(:)dikt, -s

interdict (v.), -s, -ing, -ed ˌintə(:)'dikt, -s, -iŋ, -id

interdiction, -s ˌintə(:)'dikʃən, -z

interest (s. v.), -s, -ing, -ed/ly 'intrist [-tərest, -trəst], -s, -iŋ, -id/li

interesting (adj.), -ly 'intristiŋ [-tərest-, -trəst-, ˌintə'restiŋ], -li

interfer|e, -es, -ing, -ed, -er/s; -ence/s ˌintə'fiə*, -z, -riŋ, -d, -rə*/z; -rəns/iz

interfus|e, -es, -ing, -ed ˌintə(:)'fjuːz ['intə(:)'f-], -iz, -iŋ, -d

interfusion ˌintə(:)'fjuːʒn ['intə(:)'f-]

interglacial 'intə(:)'gleisjəl [-siəl, -ʃjəl, -ʃiəl, -ʃəl, -'glæsiəl, -'glæsjəl]

interim 'intərim

interior (s. adj.), -s, -ly in'tiəriə* ['in't], -z, -li

interject, -s, -ing, -ed, -or/s ˌintə(:)-'dʒekt, -s, -iŋ, -id, -ə*/z

interjection, -s ˌintə(:)'dʒekʃən, -z

interjec|tional, -tionally ˌintə(:)'dʒek|-ʃənl [-ʃnəl, -ʃn̩l, -ʃn̩l, -ʃənəl], -ʃnəli [-ʃnəli, -ʃn̩li, -ʃn̩li, -ʃənəli]

interknit, -s, -ting, -ted ˌintə(:)'nit ['intə(:)'n-], -s, -iŋ, -id

interlac|e, -es, -ing, -ed, -ement ˌintə(:)-'leis, -iz, -iŋ, -t, -mənt

Interlaken 'intə(:)lɑːkən

interlard, -s, -ing, -ed ˌintə(:)'lɑːd ['intə(:)'l-], -z, -iŋ, -id

interlea|f, -ves 'intəli:|f, -vz

interleav|e, -es, -ing, -ed ˌintə(:)'liːv ['intə(:)'l-], -z, -iŋ, -d

interlin|e, -es, -ing, -ed ˌintə(:)'lain ['intə(:)'l-], -z, -iŋ, -d   [-njə*]

interlinear ˌintə(:)'liniə* ['intə(:)'l-,

interlineation, -s 'intə(:)ˌlini'eiʃən, -z

interlink, -s, -ing, -ed ˌintə(:)'liŋk ['intə(:)'l-], -s, -iŋ, -t [-'liŋt]

interlock, -s, -ing, -ed ˌintə(:)'lɔk ['intə(:)'l-], -s, -iŋ, -t

interlocution, -s ˌintə(:)ləu'kjuːʃən ['intə(:)ləu'k-, -lɔ'k-], -z   [-ri

interlocutor, -s, -y ˌintə(:)'lɔkjutə*, -z,

interlop|e, -es, -ing, -ed ˌintə(:)'ləup ['intə(:)'l-], -s, -iŋ, -t

interloper, -s 'intə(:)ləupə* [ˌintə'l-], -z

interlude, -s 'intə(:)luːd [-ljuːd], -z

intermarriage -s ˌintə(:)'mæridʒ ['intə(:)'m··], -iz

intermarr|y, -ies, -ying, -ied 'intə(:)-'mær|i [ˌin-], -iz, -iiŋ, -id

intermedd|le, -les, -ling, -led, -ler/s ˌintə(:)'med|l ['intə(:)'m-], -lz, -liŋ [-liŋ], -ld, -lə*/z [-lə*/z]

intermediar|y, -ies ˌintə(:)'miːdjər|i [-diər-], -iz

intermediate (s. adj.), -s, -ly ˌintə(:)-'miːdjət [-diət, -djit, -diit], -s, -li

interment, -s in'tə:mənt, -s

intermezzo, -s ˌintə(:)'metsəu [-'medzəu] (inter'meddzo), -z

interminable in'tə:minəbl ['in't-]

interminab|ly, -leness in'tə:minəb|li, -lnis

interming|le, -les, -ling, -led ˌintə(:)-'miŋg|l ['intə(:)'m-], -lz, -liŋ, -ld

intermission ˌintə(:)'miʃən

intermit, -s, -ting/ly, -ted; -tent/ly ˌintə(:)'mit, -s, -iŋ/li, -id; -ənt/li

intermix, -es, -ing, -ed ˌintə(:)'miks ['intə(:)'m-], -iz, -iŋ, -t

intermixture, -s ˌintə(:)'mikstʃə* ['intə(:)'m-], -z

intern (s.), -s 'intə:n [-'-], -z

intern (v.), -s, -ing, -ed, -ment/s in'tə:n, -z, -iŋ, -d, -mənt/s

intern|al, -ally in'tə:n|l ['in't-], -əli [-l̩i]

interna|tional, -tionally ˌintə(:)'næ|ʃənl ['intə(:)'n-, -ʃnəl, -ʃn̩l, -ʃn̩l, -ʃənəl], -ʃnəli [-ʃnəli, -ʃn̩li, -ʃn̩li, -ʃənəli]

Internationale ˌintənæʃə'nɑːl [-ʃiə'n-, -ʃjə'n-]

internationali|sm, -st/s ˌintə(:)'næʃnəl-i|zəm [-ʃnəl-, -ʃn̩l-, -ʃn̩l-, -ʃənəl-], -st/s

internationalization [-isa-] 'intə(:)ˌnæʃ-nəlai'zeiʃən [ˌintə(:)ˌn-, -ʃnəl-, -ʃn̩l-, -ʃn̩l-, -ʃənəl-, -li'z-]

internationaliz|e [-is|e], -es, -ing, -ed ˌintə(:)'næʃnəlaiz [-ʃnəl-, -ʃn̩l-, -ʃn̩l-, -ʃənəl-], -iz, -iŋ, -d

internecine ˌintə(:)'niːsain ['intə(:)'n-]

internee, -s ˌintə:'niː, -z

interoceanic 'intə(:)r,əuʃi'ænik [-tə(:)ˌəu-]

interpellant, -s ˌintə(:)'pelənt, -s

interpellat|e, -es, -ing, -ed in'tə:peleit [-pil-], -s, -iŋ, -id

interpellation, -s in,tə:pe'leiʃən [-pi'l-], -z

interpenetrat|e, -es, -ing, -ed ˌintə(:)-'penitreit ['intə(:)'p-], -s, -iŋ, -id

interpenetration 'intə(:)ˌpeni'treiʃən

interplanetary ˌintə(:)'plænitəri ['intə(:)'p-]

interplay 'intə(:)'plei ['---]

interpolat|e, -es, -ing, -ed, -or/s in-'tə:pəuleit [-pul-], -s, -iŋ, -id, -ə*/z

interpolation, -s in,tə:pəu'leiʃən [-pu'l-], -z

interposal, -s ˌintə(:)'pəuzl, -z

interpos|e, -es, -ing, -ed, -er/s ˌintə(:)-'pəuz, -iz, -iŋ, -d, -ə*/z

interposition, -s in‚tə:pə'ziʃən [‚intə(:)-, -pu'z-], -z

interpret, -s, -ing, -ed, -er/s; -able in'tə:prit, -s, -iŋ, -id, -ə*/z; -əbl

interpretation, -s in‚tə:pri'teiʃən, -z

interpretative, -ly in'tə:pritətiv [-teit-], -li

interracial ‚intə(:)'reiʃjəl ['intə(:)'r-, -ʃiəl, -ʃəl]

interregnum, -s ‚intə'regnəm, -z

interrelation, -s 'intə(:)ri'leiʃən [‚in-], -z

interrogat|e, -es, -ing, -ed, -or/s in-'terəugeit [-rug-], -s, -iŋ, -id, -ə*/z

interrogation, -s in‚terəu'geiʃən [-ru'g-], -z

interrogative (s. adj.), **-s, -ly** ‚intə'rɔgətiv, -z, -li

interrogator|y (s. adj.), **-ies** ‚intə'rɔgətər|i, -iz

interrupt, -s, -ing, -ed, -er/s ‚intə'rʌpt, -s, -iŋ, -id, -ə*/z

interruption, -s ‚intə'rʌpʃən, -z

intersect, -s, -ing, -ed, -or/s ‚intə(:)-'sekt, -s, -iŋ, -id, -ə*/z

intersection, -s ‚intə(:)'sekʃən, -z

interspac|e (s. v.), **-es, -ing, -ed** 'intə(:)-'speis, -iz, -iŋ, -t

interspers|e, -es, -ing, -ed ‚intə(:)'spə:s, -iz, -iŋ, -t

interspersion ‚intə(:)'spə:ʃən

interstellar 'intə(:)'stelə* [‚in-, also 'intə‚s- when attributive]

interstice, -s in'tə:stis, -iz

intertribal ‚intə(:)'traibəl ['intə(:)'t-]

intertwin|e, -es, -ing, -ed ‚intə(:)'twain ['intə(:)'t-], -z, -iŋ, -id

intertwist, -s, -ing, -ed ‚intə(:)'twist ['intə(:)'t-], -s, -iŋ, -id

interval, -s 'intəvəl, -z

interven|e, -es, -ing, -ed, -er/s ‚intə(:)-'vi:n, -z, -iŋ, -d, -ə*/z

intervention, -s ‚intə(:)'venʃən, -z

interview (s. v.), **-s, -ing, -ed, -er/s** 'intəvju:, -z, -iŋ [-vjuiŋ], -d, -ə*/z [-vjuə*/z]

intervocalic ‚intə(:)vəu'kælik ['intə(:)-vəu'k-, -vu'k-]

interweav|e, -es, -ing, -ed, interwove, -n ‚intə(:)'wi:v ['intə(:)'w-], -z, -iŋ, -d, ‚intə'wəuv ['intə(:)'w-], -ən

intestac|y, -ies in'testəs|i, -iz

intestate (s. adj.), **-s** in'testit [-teit], -s

intestine (s. adj.), **-s** in'testin, -z

intestinal in'testinl [‚intes'tainl]

intimac|y, -ies 'intiməs|i, -iz

intimate (s. adj.), **-s, -ly** 'intimit, -s, -li

intimat|e (v.), **-es, -ing, -ed** 'intimeit, -s, -iŋ, -id

intimation, -s ‚inti'meiʃən, -z

intimidat|e, -es, -ing, -ed, -or/s in'timideit, -s, -iŋ, -id, -ə*/z

intimidation in‚timi'deiʃən

intimity in'timiti

intituled in'titju:ld

into 'intu ['intu:], 'intə

Note.—The variant 'intu: occurs chiefly at the ends of sentences; many people do not use this variant. The form 'intə is used only before words beginning with a consonant.

intolerab|le, -ly, -leness in'tɔlərəb|l, -li, -lnis

intoleran|ce, -t/ly in'tɔlərən|s ['in't-], -t/li

intonat|e, -es, -ing, -ed 'intəuneit, -s, -iŋ, -id

intonation, -s ‚intəu'neiʃən, -z

intonational ‚intəu'neiʃənl [-ʃnəl, -ʃn̩l, -ʃnl̩, -ʃənəl]

inton|e, -es, -ing, -ed, -er/s in'təun, -z, -iŋ, -d, -ə*/z

intoxicant (s. adj.), **-s** in'tɔksikənt, -s

intoxicat|e, -es, -ing, -ed in'tɔksikeit, -s, -iŋ, -id

intoxication in‚tɔksi'keiʃən

intractability in‚træktə'biliti ['in‚trækt-, -lət-]

intractab|le, -ly, -leness in'træktəb|l, -li, -lnis

intrados, -es in'treidɔs, -iz

intramural 'intrə'mjuərəl [-'mjɔər-, -'mjɔ:r-, -'mjə:r-]

intransigent in'trænsidʒənt [-'trɑ:nsi-, -'trænzi-, -'trɑ:nzi-]

intransitive, -ly in'trænsitiv ['in't-, -'trɑ:ns-], -li

intrench, -es, -ing, -ed, -ment/s in-'trentʃ, -iz, -iŋ, -t, -mənt/s

intrepid, -ly in'trepid, -li

intrepidity ‚intri'piditi [-tre'p-]

intricac|y, -ies 'intrikəs|i [in'trik-], -iz

intricate, -ly, -ness 'intrikit [in'trik-], -li, -nis

intrigu|e (s. v.), **-es, -ing, -ed, -er/s** in-'tri:g, -z, -iŋ, -d, -ə*/z

intrinsic, -ally in'trinsik [-nzik], -əli

introduc|e, -es, -ing, -ed, -er/s ‚intrə'dju:s [-tru'd-], -iz, -iŋ, -t, -ə*/z

introduction, -s ‚intrə'dʌkʃən [-tru'd-], -z

introduct|ive, -ory, -orily ‚intrə'dʌkt|iv [-tru'd-], -əri, -ərili

introit, -s 'intrɔit ['intrəuit, in'trəuit], -s

intromission ‚intrəu'miʃən

intromit, -s, -ting, -ted ‚intrəu'mit, -s, -iŋ, -id

introspect, -s, -ing, -ed ,intrəu'spekt, -s, -iŋ, -id

introspection ,intrəu'spekʃən

introspective ,intrəu'spektiv

introversion ,intrəu'və:ʃən

introvert (s.), -s 'intrəuvə:t, -s

introvert (v.), -s, -ing, -ed ,intrəu'və:t, -s, -iŋ, -id

intrud|e, -es, -ing, -ed, -er/s in'tru:d, -z, -iŋ, -id, -ə*/z

intrusion, -s in'tru:ʒən, -z

intrusive, -ly, -ness in'tru:siv, -li, -nis

intuit, -s, -ing, -ed in'tju(:)it ['intju(:)it], -s, in'tju(:)itiŋ, in'tju(:)itid

intuition ,intju(:)'iʃən

intuitional ,intju(:)'iʃənl [-ʃnəl, -ʃn̩l, -ʃnl̩, -ʃənəl]

intuitive, -ly, -ness in'tju(:)itiv, -li, -nis

intumescen|ce, -t ,intju(:)'mesn|s, -t

inundat|e, -es, -ing, -ed 'inʌndeit [-nən-], -s, -iŋ, -id

inundation, -s ,inʌn'deiʃən [-nən-], -z

inur|e, -es, -ing, -ed, -ement i'njuə* [-jɔə*, -jɔ:*], -z, -riŋ, -d, -mənt

inutility ,inju(:)'tiliti ['inju(:)'t-]

invad|e, -es, -ing, -ed, -er/s in'veid, -z, -iŋ, -id, -ə*/z

invalid (s. adj.) (infirm through illness, etc.), -s 'invəlid [-li:d], -z

invalid (adj.) (not valid) in'vælid ['in'v-]

invalid (v.), -s, -ing, -ed ,invə'li:d ['---], -z, -iŋ, -id

invalidat|e, -es, -ing, -ed in'vælideit, -s,

invalidation in,væli'deiʃən

invalidity ,invə'liditi

invaluable in'væljŭəbl [-ljwəb-, -ljub-]

invar in'vɑ:*

invariability in,vɛərĭə'biliti ['in,vɛə-rĭə'b-, -lət-]

invariable in'vɛərĭəbl ['in'v-]

invariab|ly, -leness in'vɛərĭəb|li, -lnis

invasion, -s in'veiʒən, -z

invasive in'veisiv

invective, -s in'vektiv, -z

inveigh, -s, -ing, -ed in'vei, -z, -iŋ, -d

inveig|le, -les, -ling, -led, -lement/s in'vi:g|l, [-'veig-], -lz, -liŋ [-liŋ], -ld, -lmənt/s

invent, -s, -ing, -ed, -er/s, -or/s in'vent, -s, -iŋ, -id, -ə*/z, -ɔ*/z

invention, -s in'venʃən, -z

inventive, -ly, -ness in'ventiv, -li, -nis

inventor|y, -ies 'inventr|i, -iz

Inver|ary, -arity ,invə'r|ɛəri, -æriti

Invercargill (in Scotland) ,invəkɑ:'gil [-'kɑ:gil], (in New Zealand) ,invə'kɑ:-gil

Invergordon ,invə'gɔ:dn

Inverkeithing ,invə'ki:ðiŋ

Inverlochy ,invə'lɔki [-'lɔxi]

inverness (I.), -es ,invə'nes ['— when attributive], -iz

Inverness-shire ,invə'nesʃiə* [-'nesʃə*, -'neʃʃiə*, -'neʃʃə*]

inverse (s. adj.), -s, -ly 'in'və:s [in'v-, also '— when attributive], -iz, -li

inversion, -s in'və:ʃən, -z

invert (s. adj.), -s 'invə:t, -s

invert (v.), -s, -ing, -ed in'və:t, -s, -iŋ, -id

invertebrata in,və:ti'brɑ:tə [-'breitə, 'in,və:ti'b-]

invertebrate, -s in'və:tibrit ['in'v-, -breit], -s

Inverurie ,invə'ruəri

invest, -s, -ing, -ed, -or/s in'vest, -s, -iŋ, -id, -ə*/z

investigat|e, -es, -ing, -ed, -or/s; -ive, -ory in'vestigeit, -s, -iŋ, -id, -ə*/z; -iv, -əri

investigation, -s in,vesti'geiʃən, -z

investiture, -s in'vestitʃə* [-tjuə*], -z

investment, -s in'vestmənt, -s

inveteracy in'vetərəsi

inveterate, -ly, -ness in'vetərit, -li, -nis

invidious, -ly, -ness in'vidiəs [-djəs], -li, -nis

invigilat|e, -es, -ing, -ed, -or/s in'vidʒi-leit, -s, -iŋ, -id, -ə*/z

invigilation, -s in,vidʒi'leiʃən, -z

invigorat|e, -es, -ing, -ed, -or/s in'vigəreit, -s, -iŋ, -id, -ə*/z

invigoration in,vigə'reiʃən

invincibility in,vinsi'biliti [-sə'b-, -lət-]

invincib|le, -ly, -leness in'vinsəb|l [-sib-], -li, -lnis

inviolability in,vaiələ'biliti ['in,vaiəl-ə'b-, -lət-]

inviolab|le, -ly, -leness in'vaiələb|l, -li, -lnis

inviolate, -ness in'vaiəlit [-leit], -li, -nis

invisibility in,vizə'biliti ['in,vizə'b-, -zi'b-, -lət-]

invisible in'vizəbl ['in'v-, -zib-]

invisib|ly, -leness in'vizəb|li [-zib-], -lnis

invitation, -s ,invi'teiʃən, -z

invit|e, -es, -ing/ly, -ingness, -ed, -er/s in'vait, -s, -iŋ/li, -iŋnis, -id, -ə*/z

invocate, -s, -ing, -ed 'invəukeit, -s, -iŋ, -id

invocation, -s ,invəu'keiʃən [-vu'k-], -z

invoic|e (s. v.), -es, -ing, -ed 'invɔis, -iz, -iŋ, -t

invok|e, -es, -ing, -ed in'vəuk, -s, -iŋ, -t

involucre, -s 'invəlu:kə* [-lju:-], -z

involuntar|y, -ily, -iness in'vɔləntər|i
['in'v-, -oln̩t-], -ili, -inis
involute, -s, -d 'invəlu:t [-lju:t], -s, -id
involution, -s ˌinvə'lu:ʃən [-'lju:-], -z
involv|e, -es, -ing, -ed in'vɔlv, -z, -iŋ, -d
involvement in'vɔlvmənt
invulnerability inˌvʌlnərə'biliti ['in-
ˌvʌlnərə'b-, -lət-]
invulnerable in'vʌlnərəbl ['in'v-]
invulnerab|ly, -leness in'vʌlnərəb|li,
-lnis
inward, -s, -ly, -ness 'inwəd, -z, -li, -nis
Inwards 'inwədz
inweav|e, -es, -ing, -ed, inwove, -n
'in'wi:v [in'w-], -z, -iŋ, -d, 'in'wəuv
[in'w-], -ən
Inwood 'inwud
inwrought 'in'rɔ:t [also 'inr- when
attributive]
io (I.), -s 'aiəu, -z
iodate, -s, -d 'aiəudeit, -s, -id
iodic ai'ɔdik
iodide, -s 'aiəudaid, -z
iodine 'aiəudi:n ['aiədain)
iodiz|e [-is|e], -es, -ing, -ed 'aiəudaiz,
-iz, -iŋ, -d
iodoform ai'ɔdəfɔ:m
Iolanthe ˌaiəu'lænθi
Iolcus i'ɔlkəs [ai'ɔl-]
iolite 'aiəulait
Iolo (Welsh Christian name) 'jəuləu
(Welsh 'jolo)
ion (I.), -s 'aiən ['aiɔn], -z
Iona ai'əunə
Ionesco jɔ'neskəu [ˌiɔ-, -sku:]
Ionia, -n/s ai'əunjə [-nïə], -n/z
Ionic ai'ɔnik
ionization [-isa-] ˌaiənai'zeiʃən
ioniz|e [-is|e], -es, -ing, -ed 'aiənaiz, -iz,
-iŋ, -d
ionosphere, -s ai'ɔnəsfiə*, -z
iota, -s; -cism/s ai'əutə, -z; -sizəm/z
I O U, -'s 'aiəu'ju:, -z
Iowa 'aiəuə ['aiəwə]
IPA 'ai-pi:'ei
ipecacuanha ˌipikækju'ænə ['ipi-
ˌkækju'æ-]
Iphicrates i'fikrəti:z
Iphigenia iˌfidʒi'naiə [ˌifidʒ-]
Ipoh 'i:pəu
ipso facto 'ipsəu'fæktəu
Ipswich 'ipswitʃ
Iquique i'ki:ki
Ira 'aiərə
Irak, -i/s i'rɑ:k, -i/z
Iran i'rɑ:n [iə'rɑ:n]
Iranian, -s i'reinjən [ai'r-, ˌaiə'r-,
-nïən], -z

Iraq, -i/s i'rɑ:k, -i/z
irascibility iˌræsi'biliti [aiəˌr-, -lət-]
irascib|le, -ly, -leness i'ræsib|l [ˌaiə'r-],
-li, -lnis
irate ai'reit [ˌaiə'r-]
Irawadi ˌirə'wɔdi ['irə'w-]
ire 'aiə*
Ire|dale, -dell 'aiə|deil, -del
ire|ful, -fully, -fulness 'aiə|ful, -fuli
[-fəli], -fulnis
Ireland 'aiələnd
Iremonger 'aiəˌmʌŋgə*
Irene ai'ri:ni [ˌaiə'r-], in modern use
also 'airi:n ['aiər-]
irenic, -al ai'ri:nik [ˌaiə'r-, -'ren-], -əl
irenicon, -s ai'ri:nikən [ˌaiə'r-, -'ren-,
-kɔn], -z
Ireton 'aiətn
irian (pertaining to the iris) 'aiərïən
Irian (New Guinea) 'irïən
iridescen|ce, -t ˌiri'desn|s, -t
iridium ai'ridïəm [ˌaiə'r-, i'rid-, -djəm]
Irion 'irïən
iris (I.), -es 'aiəris, -iz
Irish; -ism/s 'aiəriʃ; -izəm/z
Irish|man, -men 'aiəriʃ|mən, -mən
[-men]
Irishry 'aiəriʃri
Irish|woman, -women 'aiəriʃ|ˌwumən,
-ˌwimin
irk, -s, -ing, -ed ə:k, -s, -iŋ, -t
irksome, -ly, -ness 'ə:ksəm, -li, -nis
Irkutsk ə:'kutsk [iə'k-] (ir'kutsk)
iron (s. v.) (I.), -s, -ing, -ed 'aiən, -z, -iŋ,
ironbound 'aiənbaund   [-d
ironclad, -s 'aiənklæd, -z
iron-found|er/s, -ry, -ries 'aiən-
ˌfaund|ə*/z, -ri, -riz
irongray [-grey] 'aiən'grei [also 'aiəng-
when attributive]
ironic, -al, -ally ai'rɔnik [ˌaiə'r-], -əl,
-əli
ironing-board, -s 'aiəniŋbɔ:d [-bɔəd], -z
ironmonger, -s 'aiənˌmʌŋgə*, -z
ironmongery 'aiənˌmʌŋgəri
ironmould 'aiənməuld
ironside (I.), -s 'aiən-said, -z
iron-stone 'aiən-stəun
Ironton 'aiəntən
ironware 'aiənwɛə*
ironwood (I.) 'aiənwud
ironwork, -s 'aiənwə:k, -s
iron|y (s.) (sarcasm, etc.), -ies 'aiərən|i
[-rn̩-], -iz
irony (adj.) (like iron) 'aiəni
Iroquoian ˌirəu'kwɔiən
Iroquois (sing.) 'irəkwɔi [-kwɔiz], (plur.)
'irəkwɔiz

irradian|ce, -cy, -t i'reidjən|s [-diən-], -si, -t [-id
irradiat|e, -es, -ing, -ed i'reidieit, -s, -iŋ,
irradiation, -s i,reidi'eiʃən [,irei-], -z
irra|tional, -tionally i'ræ|ʃənl ['i'r-, -ʃnəl, -ʃn̩l, -ʃn̩l, -ʃənəl], -ʃnəli [-ʃnəli, -ʃn̩li, -ʃn̩li, -ʃənəli] [-ʃn̩'æ-]
irrationality i,ræʃə'næliti ['i,ræʃə'n-,
irrebuttable ,iri'bʌtəbl ['iri'b-]
irreceptive ,iri'septiv ['iri's-]
irreclaimable ,iri'kleiməbl ['iri'k-]
irreclaimably ,iri'kleiməbli
irrecognizable [-isa-] i'rekəgnaizəbl ['i'r-, 'i,rekəg'n-]
irreconcilability i,rekənsailə'biliti ['i,rekənsailə'b-, -lət-]
irreconcilable, -ness i'rekənsailəbl ['i'r-, 'i,rekən's-], -nis
irreconcilably i'rekənsailəbli [,irekən's-]
irrecoverable, -ness ,iri'kʌvərəbl ['iri'k-], -nis
irrecoverably ,iri'kʌvərəbli
irredeemable, -ness ,iri'di:məbl ['iri'd-], -nis
irredeemably ,iri'di:məbli
irredenti|sm, -st/s ,iri'denti|zəm, -st/s
irreducible, -ness ,iri'dju:səbl ['iri'd-, -sib-], -nis
irreducibly ,iri'dju:səbli [-sib-]
irreformable ,iri'fɔ:məbl ['iri'f-]
irrefragability i,refrəgə'biliti [-lət-]
irrefragab|le, -ly, -leness i'refrəgəb|l, -li, -lnis
irrefutability i,refjutə'biliti ['i,refjutə'b-, 'iri,fju:tə'b-, -lət-]
irrefutable i'refjutəbl ['i'r-, ,iri'fju:t-, 'iri'fju:t-]
irrefutably i'refjutəbli [,iri'fju:t-]
irregular, -ly i'regjulə* ['i'r-, -gjəl-], -li
irregularit|y, -ies i,regju'lærit|i ['i,regju'l-, -gjə'l-], -iz
irrelevan|ce, -cy, -cies, -t/ly i'relivən|s ['i'r-], -si, -siz, -t/li
irreligion ,iri'lidʒən ['iri'l-] [-nis
irreligious, -ly,-ness ,iri'lidʒəs ['iri'l-], -li,
irremediable ,iri'mi:djəbl ['iri'm-, -diə-]
irremediably ,iri'mi:djəbli [-diə-]
irremovability 'iri,mu:və'biliti [-lət-]
irremovable ,iri'mu:vəbl ['iri'm-]
irrepairable ,iri'pɛərəbl ['iri'p-] [-lət-]
irreparability i,repərə'biliti ['i,repərə'b-,
irreparable, -ness i'repərəbl ['i'r-], -nis
irreparably i'repərəbli
irrepatriable ,iri'pætriəbl ['iri'p-]
irreplaceable ,iri'pleisəbl ['iri'p-]
irrepressible, -ness ,iri'presəbl ['iri'p-, -sib-], -nis
irrepressibly ,iri'presəbli [-sib-]

irreproachability 'iri,prəutʃə'biliti [-lət-]
irreproachable, -ness ,iri'prəutʃəbl ['iri'p-], -nis
irreproachably ,iri'prəutʃəbli
irresistibility 'iri,zistə'biliti [-ti'b-, -lət-]
irresistible, -ness ,iri'zistəbl ['iri'z-, -tib-], -nis
irresistibly ,iri'zistəbli [-tib-]
irresoluble i'rezəljubl ['i'r-]
irresolute, -ly, -ness i'rezəlu:t ['i'r-, -zḷu:t, -zəlju:t], -li, -nis
irresolution 'i,rezə'lu:ʃən [-zḷ'u:-, -zə'lju:-]
irresolvability 'iri,zɔlvə'biliti [-lət-]
irresolvable, -ness ,iri'zɔlvəbl ['iri'z-], -nis
irrespective, -ly ,iris'pektiv ['iris'p-], -li
irresponsibility 'iris,pɔnsə'biliti [-si'b-, -lət-] [-sib-], -li
irresponsib|le, -ly ,iris'pɔnsəb|l ['iris'p-, -sib-], -li
irresponsive, -ly, -ness ,iris'pɔnsiv ['iris'p-], -li, -nis
irrestrainable ,iris'treinəbl ['iris't-]
irretentive ,iri'tentiv ['iri't-]
irretrievability 'iri,tri:və'biliti [-lət-]
irretrievable ,iri'tri:vəbl ['iri't-]
irretrievably ,iri'tri:vəbli [-t/li
irreveren|ce, -t/ly i'revərən|s ['i'r-],
irreversibility 'iri,və:sə'biliti [-si'b-, -lət-]
irreversible, -ness ,iri'və:səbl ['iri'v-, -sib-], -nis [-lət-]
irrevocability i,revəkə'biliti [-vuk-]
irrevocable i'revəkəbl [-vuk-], (when applied to letters of credit) ,iri'vəukəbl
irrevocably i'revəkəbli [-vuk-]
irrigable 'irigəbl
irrigat|e, -es, -ing, -ed, -or/s 'irigeit, -s, -iŋ, -id, -ə*/z
irrigation, -s ,iri'geiʃən, -z
irritability ,iritə'biliti [-lət-]
irritab|le, -ly, -leness 'iritəb|l, -li, -lnis
irritant (s. adj.), -s 'iritənt, -s
irritat|e, -es, -ing/ly, -ed ; -ive 'iriteit, -s, -iŋ/li, -id ; -iv
irritation, -s ,iri'teiʃən, -z
irruption, -s i'rʌpʃən, -z
irruptive, -ly i'rʌptiv, -li
Irv|ine, -ing 'ə:v|in, -iŋ
Irving|ism, -ite/s 'ə:viŋ|izəm, -ait/s
Irwin 'ə:win
is (from be) iz (strong form), z, s (weak forms)
    Note.—z is used only when the preceding word ends in a vowel or a voiced consonant other than z or ʒ. s is used only when the preceding word ends in a breathed consonant other than s or ʃ.

Isaac, -s 'aizək [-zik], -s
Isabel 'izəbel
Isabella ,izə'belə
Isaiah ai'zaiə [old-fashioned -'zeiə]
Isambard 'izəmbɑːd
Isard 'izɑːd
Iscariot is'kærïət
Ischia 'iskïə [-kjə]
Iseult iː'zuːlt [iˈzˈ, -ˈsuːlt]
Isham (surname) 'aiʃəm
Ishbosheth 'iʃbəʃeθ [-bɔʃ-, iʃ'bɔʃeθ, iʃ'bəuʃeθ]
Isherwood 'iʃə(ː)wud
Ishmael 'iʃmeiəl [-miəl, -mïəl]
Ishmaelit|e, -es, -ish 'iʃmiəlait [-miəl-, -mjəl-, -meiəl-, -məl-], -s, -iʃ
Ishtar 'iʃtɑ:*
Isidore 'izidɔ:* [-dɔə*]
Isidorian ,izi'dɔːrïən
isinglass 'aiziŋglɑːs
Isis 'aisis
Isla 'ailə
Islam 'izlɑːm [-læm, -ləm, iz'lɑːm, is'l-]
islamic iz'læmik [is'l-]
Islam|ism, -ite/s 'izləm|izəm, -ait/s
island, -s, -er/s 'ailənd, -z, -ə*/z
Islay 'ailei [locally 'ailə]
isle, -s ail, -z
islet, -s 'ailit [-let], -s
Isleworth 'aizlwə(ː)θ
Islington 'izliŋtən
Islip (archbishop) 'izlip, (in Oxfordshire) 'aislip
ism, -s 'izəm, -z
Ismail ,izmɑː'iːl [,ismɑː-, 'izmail, 'izmeil]
Ismailia ,izmai'liːə [,ismai-, -'liə]
Ismay 'izmei
isn't 'iznt [also occasionally 'izn when not final]
isobar, -s 'aisəubɑː*, -z
Isobel 'izəbel [-zəub-]
isochromatic ,aisəukrəu'mætik
isochron|al, -ism, -ous ai'sɔkrən|l, -izəm, -əs
Isocrates ai'sɔkrəti:z
isogloss, -es 'aisəuglɔs, -iz
isolate (s.), -s 'aisəuleit, -s
isolat|e (v.), -es, -ing, -ed 'aisəleit [-səul-, rarely 'aizəl-, 'aizəul-], -s, -iŋ, -id
isolation ,aisəu'leiʃən [-st/s
isolationi|sm, -st/s ,aisəu'leiʃŋi|zəm, -st/s
isolative 'aisəl/ətiv [-səuleit-]
Isolda i'zɔldə
Isolde i'zɔldə (iː'zɔldə)
isomeric ,aisəu'merik
isomer|ism, -ous ai'sɔmər|izəm, -əs
isometric, -al, -ally ,aisəu'metrik, -əl, -əli

isomorph|ic, -ism, -ous ,aisəu'mɔːf|ik, -izəm, -əs
isophone, -s 'aisəufəun, -z
isosceles ai'sɔsiliːz [-səl-, -s|-]
isotherm, -s 'aisəuθəːm, -z
isothermal ,aisəu'θəːməl
isotope, -s 'aisəutəup, -s
isotopic ,aisəu'tɔpik
isotype, -s 'aisəutaip, -s
Ispahan ,ispə'hɑːn [-'hæn]
Israel 'izreiəl [-riəl, -rïəl, in formal reading also -reiel]
Israeli, -s iz'reili, -z
Israelit|e, -es, -ish 'izriəlait [-rïəl-, -rəl-, -reiəl-], -s, -iʃ
Issachar 'isəkə* [-kɑ:*]
iss|ue (s. v.), -ues, -uing, -ued, -uer/s; -uable, -uance 'iʃ|uː ['isj|uː, 'iʃj|uː], -uːz, -u(ː)iŋ, -uːd, -u(ː)ə*/z; -u(ː)əbl, -u(ː)əns
Istanbul ,istæn'buːl [-tɑːn-]
isthmian (I.) 'isθmïən [-stm-, -sm-, -mjən]
isthmus, -es 'isməs [-sθm-, -stm-], -iz
istle 'istli
Istria 'istrïə
it it
itacism 'iːtəsizəm
Italian (s. adj.), -s i'tæljən, -z
italianate i'tæljəneit [-nət, -nit]
italianism, -s i'tæljənizəm, -z
italianiz|e [-is|e], -es, -ing, -ed i'tæljən-aiz, -iz, -iŋ, -d
italic (I.), -s i'tælik, -s
italicization i,tælisai'zeiʃən
italiciz|e [-is|e], -es, -ing, -ed i'tælisaiz, -iz, -iŋ, -d
Italy 'itəli ['itḷi]
itch (s. v.), -es, -ing, -ed itʃ, -iz, -iŋ, -t
Itchen 'itʃin
itch|y, -iness 'itʃ|i, -inis
item, -s 'aitəm [-tem, -tim], -z
iterat|e, -es, -ing, -ed 'itəreit, -s, -iŋ, -id
iteration ,itə'reiʃən
iterative 'itərətiv [-reit-]
Ithaca 'iθəkə
Ithamar 'iθəmɑ:* [-mə*]
Ithuriel i'θjuərïəl
itineran|cy, -t/s i'tinərən|si [ai't-], -t/s
itinerar|y, -ies ai'tinərər|i [i't-], -iz
itinerat|e, -es, -ing, -ed i'tinəreit [ai't-], -s, -iŋ, -id
its its
it's (= it is) its
itself it'self
Iuca ai'juːkə
Ivan 'aivən
Ivanhoe 'aivənhəu

Ivanoff i(:)'vɑːnəf [-nɔf] (i'vanəf)
Ivatt, -s 'aivət [-væt], -s
I've (= I have) aiv
Iveagh 'aivə
Ivens 'aivənz
Iver 'aivə*
Ives (*surname, and towns* **St. Ives** *in Cornwall and Hunts.*) aivz, (*in Stevenson's 'St. Ives'*) iːvz
Ivey 'aivi
Ivimey 'aivimi
Ivone 'aivən
Ivor 'aivə*

ivor|y (*s. adj.*) (**I.**), **-ies** 'aivər|i, -iz
ivory-black 'aivəri'blæk
iv|y (**I.**), **-ies, -ied** 'aiv|i, -iz, -id
Ivybridge 'aivibridʒ
ixia, -s 'iksiə [-sjə], -z
Ixion ik'saiən
Iza 'aizə
Izaby (*surname*) 'izəbi
izal 'aizəl
izard, -s 'izəd, -z
Izard 'aizɑːd, 'aizəd, 'izəd
Izod 'aizəd
Izzard 'izəd

J

J (*the letter*), **-'s** dʒei, -z
jab (*s. v.*), **-s, -bing, -bed** dʒæb, -z, -iŋ, -d
Jabalpur 'dʒʌbəl'puə* ['dʒæb-, -'pɔə*, -'pɔ:*] (*Hind.* ɟəbəlpwr)
jabber (*s. v.*), **-s, -ing, -ed, -er/s** 'dʒæbə*, -z, -riŋ, -d, -rə*/z
Jabberwock, -y 'dʒæbəwɔk, -i
Jabesh-gilead 'dʒeibeʃ'giliæd [-lĭəd, -ljəd]
Jabez 'dʒeibez [-biz]
Jabin 'dʒeibin
jabiru -s 'dʒæbiru:, -z
jaborandi ,dʒæbə'rændi [-bɔ:'r-]
jabot, -s 'ʒæbəu (ʒabo), -z
Jachin 'dʒeikin
jacinth, -s 'dʒæsinθ ['dʒeis-], -s
jack (J.), -s dʒæk, -s
jackal, -s 'dʒækɔ:l, -z
jackanapes, -es 'dʒækəneips, -iz
jackass, -es 'dʒækæs [-kɑ:s], -iz
Note.—'dʒækæs *is more usual for the animal and bird, but* 'dʒækɑ:s *is commoner when the word is used colloquially as a term of contempt.*
jack-boot, -s 'dʒækbu:t ['dʒæk'b-], -s
jackdaw, -s 'dʒækdɔ:, -z
jacket, -s, -ed 'dʒækit, -s, -id
jack-in-office, jacks-in-office 'dʒæk-in,ɔfis, 'dʒæks-in,ɔfis
jack-in-the-box, -es 'ʒækinðəbɔks, -iz
jack-in-the-green, -s 'dʒækinðəgri:n ['dʒækinðə'g-], -z
jack-kni|fe, -ves 'dʒæknai|f, -vz
Jackman 'dʒækmən
jack-of-all-trades 'dʒækəv'ɔ:l-treidz [,dʒæk-]
jack-o'-lantern, -s 'dʒækəu,læntən ['--'--], -z
jack-place, -s 'dʒækplein, -z
jackpot, -s 'dʒækpɔt, -s
jack-pudding, -s 'dʒæk'pudiŋ, -z
Jackson 'dʒæksn
jack-tar, -s 'dʒæk'tɑ:*, -z
Jacob 'dʒeikəb
Jacobean ,dʒækəu'bi(:)ən
Jacobi dʒə'kəubi
jacobian (J.), -s dʒə'kəubjən [-bĭən], -z

Jacobin, -s, -ism 'dʒækəubin [-kub-], -z, -izəm
Jacobit|e, -es, -ism 'dʒækəubait [-kub-], -s, -izəm
Jacob|s, -son 'dʒeikəb|z, -sn
jacob's-ladder, -s 'dʒeikəbz'lædə*, -z
jacobus (J.), -es dʒə'kəubəs, -iz
Jacoby dʒə'kəubi, 'dʒækəbi [-kub-]
Jacomb 'dʒeikəm
Jacqueline 'dʒækli:n ['ʒæ-]
jactitation ,dʒækti'teiʃən
jad|e (s. v.), -es, -ing, -ed dʒeid, -z, -iŋ, -id
jaeger (J.), -s 'jeigə*, -z
Jael 'dʒeiəl [dʒeil, 'dʒeiel]
Jaffa, -s 'dʒæfə, -z
jag (s. v.), -s, -ging, -ged dʒæg, -z, -iŋ, -d
Jagan (*Guyanese politician*) 'dʒægən
Jaggard 'dʒægəd
jagged (*adj.*), **-ly, -ness** 'dʒægid, -li, -nis
jagger (J.), -s 'dʒægə*, -z
jagg|y, -ier, -iest, -iness 'dʒæg|i, -ĭə*, -iist, -inis
Jago 'dʒeigəu
jaguar (J.), -s 'dʒægjŭə* [-gwə*], -z
Jah dʒɑ: [jɑ:]
Jahaz 'dʒeihæz
Jahveh 'jɑ:vei ['jɑ:'vei, 'dʒɑ:vei,' jɑ:və]
jail, -s dʒeil, -z
jailbird, -s 'dʒeilbə:d, -z
jailer, -s 'dʒeilə*, -z
Jaipur dʒai'puə* ['dʒai'p-, -'pɔə*, -'pɔ:*] (*Hind.* ɟəypwr)
Jairus dʒei'aiərəs ['dʒaiərəs]
Jalalabad dʒə,lɑ:lə'bɑ:d (*Hind.* ɟəlalabad)
jalap 'dʒæləp
jalousie, -s 'ʒælu(:)zi: [,ʒælu(:)'z-], -z
jam (s.), -s dʒæm, -z
jam (v.) (wedge, spread with jam), -s, -ming, -med dʒæm, -z, -iŋ, -d
Jam (Indian title), -s dʒɑ:m (*Hind.* ɟam), -z
Jamaica, -n/s dʒə'meikə, -n/z
jamb, -s dʒæm, -z
jamboree, -s ,dʒæmbə'ri: ['---], -z
James dʒeimz

Jameson (*surname*) 'dʒeimsn, 'dʒim-, 'dʒem-, -misn
James's 'dʒeimziz
Jamia 'dʒʌmɪə ['dʒæm-] (*Hind.* ɟəmya)
Jamieson (*surname*) 'dʒeimisn, 'dʒæm-, 'dʒem-, 'dʒim-
jam-jar, -s 'dʒæmdʒɑ:*, -z
jamm|y, -ier, -iest, -iness 'dʒæm|i, -ɪə*, -iist, -inis
jam-pot, -s 'dʒæm-pɔt, -s
Jamrach 'dʒæmræk
Jamy 'dʒeimi
Jan dʒæn
Jane dʒein
Janeiro dʒə'niərəu
Janet 'dʒænit
jang|le, -les, -ling, -led, -ler/s 'dʒæŋg|l, -lz, -liŋ [-liŋ], -ld, -lə*/z [-lə*/z]
Janiculum dʒæ'nikjuləm [dʒə'n-]
janissar|y, -ies 'dʒænisər|i, -iz
janitor, -s 'dʒænitə*, -z
Jan(n)ette dʒə'net
Jansen 'dʒænsn
Janseni|sm, -st/s 'dʒænsn̩i|zəm [-sən̩i-], -st/s
Jantzen 'jæntsən ['dʒæn-]
Januarius ˌdʒænju'ɛərɪəs
Januar|y, -ies 'dʒænjŭər|i [-njuər-, -njwər-, -njur-], -iz
Janus 'dʒeinəs
Jap, -s dʒæp, -s
japan (*s. v.*) (**J.**), -s, -ning, -ned, -ner/s dʒə'pæn, -z, -iŋ, -d, -ə*/z
Japanese ˌdʒæpə'ni:z ['dʒæpə'ni:z, -pn̩'i:z]
Jap|e (*s. v.*), -es, -ing, -ed dʒeip, -s, -iŋ, -t
japhet 'dʒeifet
Japhetic dʒei'fetik [dʒə'f-]
japonica, -s dʒə'pɔnikə, -z
Jaques (*surname*) dʒeiks, dʒæks, (*Shakespearian character*) 'dʒeikwiz
jar (*s. v.*), -s, -ring/ly, -red dʒɑ:*, -z, -riŋ/li, -d
Jardine 'dʒɑ:di:n
jardinière, -s ˌʒɑ:di'njɛə* [-ini'ɛə*] (ʒardinjɛ:r), -z
jarful, -s 'dʒɑ:-ful, -z
jargon, -s 'dʒɑ:gən, -z
jargonelle, -s ˌdʒɑ:gə'nel, -z
Jar|ley, -man 'dʒɑ:|li, -mən
Jarr|att, -ett 'dʒær|ət, -ət [-it]
Jarr|old, -ow 'dʒær|əld, -əu
jarvey, -s 'dʒɑ:vi, -z
Jarv|ie, -is 'dʒɑ:v|i, -is
Jas. dʒeimz [dʒæs]
jasey, -s 'dʒeizi, -z
Jasher 'dʒæʃə*
jasmine 'dʒæsmin [-æzm-]

Jason 'dʒeisn
jasper (**J.**), -s 'dʒæspə* [*rarely* 'dʒɑ:s-], -z
Jassy 'dʒæsi
jaundice, -d 'dʒɔ:ndis [*rarely* 'dʒɑ:n-], -t
jaunt (*s. v.*), -s, -ing, -ed dʒɔ:nt, -s, -iŋ, -id
jaunt|y, -ier, -iest, -ily, -iness 'dʒɔ:nt|i, -ɪə* [-jə*], -iist [-jist], -ili, -inis
Java 'dʒɑ:və
Javan (*of Java*) 'dʒɑ:vən, (*biblical name*) 'dʒeivæn
Javanese ˌdʒɑ:və'ni:z [*also* '— *when attributive*]
javelin (*spear*), -s 'dʒævlin [-vəlin], (**J.**) (*car, aeroplane*) 'dʒævəlin ['dʒævlin], -z
jaw (*s. v.*), -s, -ing, -ed dʒɔ:, -z, -iŋ, -d
jaw-bone, -s 'dʒɔ:bəun, -z
jaw-break|er/s, -ing 'dʒɔ:ˌbreik|ə*/z, -iŋ
Jaxartes dʒæk'sɑ:ti:z
jay (**J.**), -s dʒei, -z
jazz dʒæz
jazz-band, -s 'dʒæzbænd, -z
Jeaffreson 'dʒefəsn
Jeakes dʒeiks
jealous, -ly, -ness 'dʒeləs, -li, -nis
jealous|y, -ies 'dʒeləs|i, -iz
Jeames dʒi:mz
jean (*cotton fabric*) dʒein
Jean dʒi:n
Jeaner 'dʒenə*
Jeanette dʒi'net [dʒə'n-]
jeans (*trousers*) (**J.**) dʒi:nz
Jebb dʒeb
Jebus 'dʒi:bəs
Jebusite, -s 'dʒebjuzait [-bju:z-], -s
Jedburgh 'dʒedbərə
Jeddah 'dʒedə
Jedediah ˌdʒedi'daiə
jeep, -s dʒi:p, -s
jeer (*s. v.*), -s, -ing/ly, -ed, -er/s dʒiə*, -z, -riŋ/li, -d, -rə*/z
Jefferies 'dʒefriz
Jefferson 'dʒefəsn
Jeffery 'dʒefri
Jeffrey, -s 'dʒefri, -z
Jehan dʒi'hɑ:n [dʒə'h-] (*Hind.* ɟəhan)
Jehangir dʒi'hɑ:ŋgiə* [dʒə'h-] (*Hind.* ɟəhaŋgir)
Jehoahaz dʒi'həuəhæz [dʒə'h-]
Jehoash dʒi'həuæʃ [dʒə'h-]
Jehoiachin dʒi'hɔiəkin [dʒə'h-]
Jehoiada dʒi'hɔiədə [dʒə'h-]
Jehoiakim dʒi'hɔiəkim [dʒə'h-]
Jehonadab dʒi'hɔnədæb [dʒə'h-]
Jehoram dʒi'hɔ:rəm [dʒə'h-, -ræm]

Jehoshaphat dʒi'hɔʃəfæt [dʒə'h-]
Jehovah dʒi'həuvə [dʒə'h-]
jehu (J.), -s 'dʒi:hju:, -z
jejune, -ly, -ness dʒi'dʒu:n, -li, -nis
jejunum, -s dʒi'dʒu:nəm, -z
Jekyll (surname) 'dʒi:kil, 'dʒekil
  Note.—In Jekyll and Hyde frequently
  pronounced 'dʒekil.
Jelalabad, former spelling of Jalalabad,
  q.v.
Jelf dʒelf
jell, -s, -ing, -ed dʒel, -z, -iŋ, -d
Jellicoe 'dʒelikəu
jell|y (s. v.), -ies, -ying, -ied 'dʒel|i, -iz,
  -iiŋ [-jiŋ], -id
jelly-bag, -s 'dʒelibæg, -z
jelly-bag-stand, -s 'dʒelibæg‚stænd, -z
Jellyby 'dʒelibi
jelly-fish, -es 'dʒelifiʃ, -iz
jellygraph (s. v.), -s, -ing, -ed 'dʒeli-
  grɑ:f [-græf], -s, -iŋ, -t
Jemima dʒi'maimə [dʒə'm-]
jemm|y, -ies 'dʒem|i, -iz
Jena 'jeinə ('je:nɑ:)
Jenkin, -s, -son 'dʒeŋkin ['dʒenk-], -z,
  -sn
Jenner 'dʒenə*
jennet, -s 'dʒenit, -s
Jennifer 'dʒenifə*
Jennings 'dʒeniŋz
jenn|y (in machinery), -ies 'dʒen|i, -iz
jenn|y (in billiards), -ies 'dʒin|i ['dʒen-],
  -iz
Jenny 'dʒeni, 'dʒini
Jensen (car), -s 'dʒensn, -z
jeopardiz|e [-is|e], -es, -ing, -ed 'dʒepə-
  daiz, -iz, -iŋ, -d
jeopardy 'dʒepədi
Jephthah 'dʒefθə
jerboa, -s dʒə:'bəuə, -z
jeremiad, -s ‚dʒeri'maiəd [-'maiæd], -z
Jeremiah ‚dʒeri'maiə [-rə'm-]
Jeremy 'dʒerimi [-rəmi]
Jericho 'dʒerikəu
jerk (s. v.), -s, -ing, -ed dʒə:k, -s, -iŋ, -t
jerkin, -s 'dʒə:kin, -z
jerk|y, -ier, -iest, -ily, -iness 'dʒə:k|i,
  -iə* [-jə*], -iist [-jist], -ili, -inis
Jermyn 'dʒə:min
jeroboam (J.), -s ‚dʒerə'bəuəm, -z
Jerome (Saint) dʒə'rəum [dʒe'r-, dʒi'r-,
  rarely 'dʒerəm], (surname) dʒə'rəum
  [dʒe'r-, dʒi'r-], 'dʒerəm
  Note.—Jerome K. Jerome, the author,
  pronounced dʒə'rəum.
Jerram 'dʒerəm
Jerrold 'dʒerəld
jerr|y (J.), -ies 'dʒer|i, -iz

jerry-build|er/s, -ing 'dʒeri‚bild|ə*/z,
  -iŋ
jerry-built 'dʒeribilt
jersey (J.), -s 'dʒə:zi, -z
Jerubbaal 'dʒerəb'beiəl [Jewish pronunciation 'dʒerə'bɑ:l]
Jerusalem dʒə'ru:sələm [dʒi'r-]
Jervaulx (in Yorks.) 'dʒə:vəu ['dʒɑ:vəu]
Jervis 'dʒɑ:vis, 'dʒə:vis
Jervois 'dʒə:vis
Jespersen 'jespəsn
jess (s. v.) (J.), -es, -ing, -ed dʒes, -iz,
  -iŋ, -t
jessamine (J.) 'dʒesəmin
Jess|e, -el, -ica, -ie, -op 'dʒes|i, -l, -ikə,
  -i, -əp
jest (s. v.), -s, -ing/ly, -ed, -er/s dʒest,
  -s, -iŋ/li, -id, -ə*/z
Jeston 'dʒestən
Jesu 'dʒi:zju:
Jesuit, -s, -ism 'dʒezjuit [-zuit], -s,
  -izəm
jesuitic, -al, -ally ‚dʒezju'itik [-zu'it-],
  -əl, -əli
Jesus 'dʒi:zəs
jet (s. v.), -s, -ting, -ted dʒet, -s, -iŋ, -id
jet-black 'dʒet'blæk ['dʒetb- when
  attributive]
Jethro 'dʒeθrəu
jetsam 'dʒetsəm [-sæm]
jettis|on (s. v.), -ons, -oning, -oned
  'dʒetis|n [-tiz|n], -nz, -niŋ [-əniŋ], -nd
jett|y (s. adj.), -ies 'dʒet|i, -iz
jeu, -s ʒə: (ʒø), -z
Jeune dʒu:n
Jevons 'dʒevənz
Jew, -s dʒu:, -z
jewel (s. v.) (J.), -s, -led, jewelling
  'dʒu:əl [dʒuəl, dʒu:l, 'dʒu(:)il], -z, -d,
  'dʒu:əliŋ ['dʒuəliŋ, 'dʒu(:)iliŋ]
jewel-box, -es 'dʒu:əlbɔks ['dʒuəl-,
  'dʒu:l-, 'dʒu(:)il-], -iz
jewel-case, -s 'dʒu:əl-keis ['dʒuəl-
  'dʒu:l-, 'dʒu(:)il-], -iz
jeweller, -s 'dʒu:ələ* ['dʒuələ*,
  'dʒu(:)ilə*], -z
jewellery 'dʒu:əlri ['dʒuəl-, 'dʒu:l-,
  'dʒu(:)il-]
Jewess, -es 'dʒu(:)is ['dʒu(:)es], -iz
Jewin 'dʒu(:)in
Jewish, -ly, -ness 'dʒu(:)iʃ, -li, -nis
Jewry 'dʒuəri
Jewsbury 'dʒu:zbəri
jew's-harp, -s 'dʒu:z'hɑ:p, -s
Jeyes dʒeiz
jezail dʒe'zeil
Jezebel 'dʒezəbl [-zib-]
Jezreel dʒez'ri:l

Jhelum 'dʒiːləm (*Hind.* ɟehləm)
jib (*s. v.*), -s, -bing, -bed dʒib, -z, -iŋ, -d
jib-boom, -s 'dʒib'buːm, -z
jib|e (*s. v.*), -es, -ing, -ed dʒaib, -z, -iŋ, -d
jiff|y, -ies 'dʒif|i, -iz
jig (*s. v.*), -s, -ging, -ged dʒig, -z, -iŋ, -d
jigger, -s 'dʒigə*, -z
jiggered 'dʒigəd
jiggery-pokery 'dʒigəri'pəukəri
jigg|le (*v.*), -les, -ling, -led 'dʒig|l, -lz, -liŋ [-liŋ], -ld
jigot, -s 'dʒigət, -s
jigsaw, -s 'dʒigsɔː, -z
Jill dʒil
jilt (*s. v.*), -s, -ing, -ed dʒilt, -s, -iŋ, -id
Jim, -my dʒim, -i
jimjams 'dʒimdʒæmz
jimp, -s dʒimp, -s
jing|le (*s. v.*) (**J.**), -les, -ling, -led 'dʒiŋg|l, -lz, -liŋ, -ld
jingo (**J.**), -es 'dʒiŋgəu, -z
jingoism 'dʒiŋgəuizəm
jink, -s dʒiŋk, -s
jinn, -s dʒin, -z
jinnee, -s dʒi'niː, -z
jinrick|sha/s, -shaw/s dʒin'rik|ʃə/z, -ʃɔː/z
jitterbug, -s 'dʒitəbʌg, -z
jitters 'dʒitəz
jitter|y, -iness 'dʒitər|i, -inis
jiujitsu dʒjuː'dʒitsu: [dʒuː-]
jiv|e (*s. v.*), -es, -ing, -ed dʒaiv, -z, -iŋ, -d
Jno. dʒon
jo, -es dʒəu, -z
Joab 'dʒəuæb
Joachim (*violinist*) 'jəuəkim ('joːaxim)
Joan dʒəun
Joanna dʒəu'ænə
Joash 'dʒəuæʃ
job (*s. v.*), -s, -bing, -bed, -ber/s; -bery dʒob, -z, -iŋ, -d, -ə*/z; -əri
Job dʒəub
jobation dʒəu'beiʃən
jobmaster, -s 'dʒob,mɑːstə*, -z
Jobson 'dʒobsn, 'dʒəubsn
Jocasta dʒəu'kæstə
Jocelyn 'dʒoslin
Jochebed 'dʒokəbed
Jock dʒok
jockey (*s. v.*), -s, -ing, -ed; -ship 'dʒoki, -z, -iŋ, -d; -ʃip
Jockey Club 'dʒoki-klʌb
jocose, -ly, -ness dʒəu'kəus, -li, -nis
jocosity dʒəu'kositi
jocular, -ly 'dʒokjulə*, -li
jocularity ,dʒokju'læriti

jocund, -ly, -ness 'dʒokənd ['dʒəuk-, -kʌnd], -li, -nis
jocundity dʒəu'kʌnditi [dʒɔ'k-]
jod, -s jod, -z
jod|el, -els, -elling, -elled 'jəud|l ['jod-], -lz, -liŋ [-əliŋ], -ld
jodhpurs 'dʒodpuəz [-pəːz]
Jodrell 'dʒodrəl
Joe dʒəu
Joel 'dʒəuel ['dʒəuəl, dʒəul]
Joey 'dʒəui
jog (*s. v.*), -s, -ging, -ged, -ger/s dʒog, -z, -iŋ, -d, -ə*/z
jogg|le (*s. v.*), -les, -ling, -led 'dʒog|l, -lz, -liŋ [-liŋ], -ld
jog-trot 'dʒog'trot
johannes (*coin*), -es dʒəu'ænis, -iz
Johannes (*personal name*) jəu'hænis
Johannesburg dʒəu'hænisbəːg [-izb-]
Note.—*There exists also a local pro-nunciation dʒə'hɔnisbəːg, which is used by many English-speaking South Africans.*
Johannisburger jəu'hænisbəːgə*
John dʒon
john-dor|y, -ies 'dʒon'dɔːr|i [*also* dʒon'd- *when preceded by a stress*], -iz
Johnes dʒəunz, dʒonz
Johnian, -s 'dʒəunjən [-nɪən], -z
johnn|y (**J.**), -ies 'dʒon|i, -iz
John o' Groat's 'dʒonə'grəuts
John|s, -son dʒon|z, -sn
Johnsonese ,dʒonsə'niːz [-sŋ'iːz, '—'-]
Johnsonian dʒon'səunjən [-nɪən]
Johnston(e) 'dʒonstən, 'dʒonsn
Johore dʒəu'hɔː*
join (*s. v.*), -s, -ing, -ed, -er/s; -ery dʒɔin, -z, -iŋ, -d, -ə*/z; -əri
joint (*s. adj. v.*), -s, -ly; -ing, -ed, -er/s dʒɔint, -s, -li; -iŋ, -id, -ə*/z
joint-stock 'dʒɔint-stɔk
joint-tenan|cy, -cies, -t/s 'dʒɔint-'tenən|si, -siz, -t/s
jointure, -s 'dʒɔintʃə*, -z
joist, -s dʒɔist, -s
jok|e (*s. v.*), -es, -ing/ly, -ed, -er/s dʒəuk, -s, -iŋ/li, -t, -ə*/z
Jolland 'dʒolənd
Jolliffe 'dʒolif
jollification, -s ,dʒolifi'keiʃən, -z
jolli|fy, -fies, -fying, -fied 'dʒoli|fai, -faiz, -faiiŋ, -faid
jollit|y, -ies 'dʒolit|i, -iz
joll|y (**J.**), -ier, -iest, -ily, -iness 'dʒol|i, -iə*, -iist, -ili, -inis
jollyboat, -s 'dʒolibəut, -s
jolt (*s. v.*), -s, -ing/ly, -ed dʒəult, -s, -iŋ/li, -id

jolt|y, -ier, -iest, -ily, -iness 'dʒəult|i, -iə* [-jə*], -iist [-jist], -ili, -inis
Jolyon 'dʒɔljən
Jon dʒɔn
Jonadab 'dʒɔnədæb
Jonah 'dʒəunə
Jonas 'dʒəunəs [-næs]
Jonathan 'dʒɔnəθən
Jones dʒəunz
jongleur, -s ʒɔ̃:ŋ'glə:* [ʒɔ:ŋ-, ʒɔŋ-] (ʒɔ̃-glœ:r), -z
jonian 'dʒəunjən [-niən]
jonquil, -s 'dʒɔŋkwil, -z
Jonson 'dʒɔnsn
Joppa 'dʒɔpə
Jopson 'dʒɔpsn
Joram 'dʒɔ:rəm [-ræm]
Jordan, -s 'dʒɔ:dn, -z
jorum, -s 'dʒɔ:rəm, -z
joseph (J.), 'dʒəuzif [-zəf], -s
Josephine 'dʒəuzifi:n [-zəf-]
Josephus dʒəu'si:fəs
Josh dʒɔʃ
Joshua 'dʒɔʃwə [-ʃŭə, -ʃjŭə, -ʃjwə]
Josiah dʒəu'saiə [-'zaiə]
Josias dʒəu'saiəs [-'zaiəs]
joss, -es dʒɔs, -iz
joss-hou|se, -ses 'dʒɔshau|s, -ziz
joss-stick, -s 'dʒɔsstik, -s
Jost jəust
jost|le, -les, -ling, -led 'dʒɔs|l, -lz, -l̩iŋ [-liŋ], -ld
jot (s. v.), -s, -ting/s, -ted dʒɔt, -s, -iŋ/z, -id
jotation, -s jəu'teiʃən, -z
joule, -s dʒu:l [dʒaul], -z
Joule (English surname) dʒu:l, dʒəul, dʒaul
  Note.—Dr. J. P. Joule, the scientist, whose name was given to the unit of energy, pronounced dʒu:l. His near relatives also pronounce in this way. There are other people of this name who call themselves dʒəul and dʒaul.
journal, -s 'dʒə:nl, -z
journalese 'dʒə:nə'li:z [ˌ-'-']
journali|sm, -st/s 'dʒə:nəli|zəm [-nļi-], -st/s
journalistic ˌdʒə:nə'listik [-nļ'i-]
journaliz|e [-is|e], -es, -ing, -ed 'dʒə:nəlaiz [-nļaiz], -iz, -iŋ, -d
journ|ey (s. v.), -eys, -eying/s, -eyed 'dʒə:n|i, -iz, -iiŋ/z [-jiŋ/z], -id
journey|man, -men 'dʒə:ni|mən, -mən
joust, -s dʒaust [dʒu:st], -s
Jove dʒəuv
jovial, -ly, -ness 'dʒəuvjəl [-vĭəl], -i, -nis

joviality ˌdʒəuvi'æliti
Jowett 'dʒauit, 'dʒəuit
  Note.—'dʒauit appears to be the commoner pronunciation. Jowett cars are called 'dʒauits.
Jowitt 'dʒauit, 'dʒəuit
  Note.—Lord Jowitt (Lord Chancellor, 1945–51) pronounced 'dʒəuit.
jowl, -s dʒaul, -z
joy (s. v.) (J.), -s, -ing, -ed dʒɔi, -z, -iŋ, -d
Joyce dʒɔis
joy|ful, -fullest, -fully, -fulness 'dʒɔi|-ful, -fulist [-fəlist], -fuli [-fəli], -fulnis
joyless, -ly, -ness 'dʒɔilis, -li, -nis
joyous, -ly, -ness 'dʒɔiəs, -li, -nis
joy-ride, -s 'dʒɔiraid, -z
joy-stick, -s 'dʒɔi-stik, -s
jr. 'dʒu:njə* [-nĭə*]
Juan 'dʒu(:)ən
Juan Fernandez (island) 'dʒu(:)ən-fə'nændez
Juanita (as English Christian name) dʒŭə'ni:tə [ˌdʒu:ə'n-], also wə'ni:tə [hwə-] (approximations to the Spanish pronunciation xwa'nita)
Jubal 'dʒu:bəl [-bæl]
jubilant, -ly 'dʒu:bilənt, -li
Jubilate (s.), -s ˌdʒu:bi'lɑ:ti [ˌju:bi'lɑ:ti, old-fashioned ˌdʒu:bi'leiti], -z
jubilat|e (v.), -es, -ing, -ed 'dʒu:bileit, -s, -iŋ, -id
jubilation, -s ˌdʒu:bi'leiʃən, -z
jubilee, -s 'dʒu:bili [-li], -z
Judaea, -n/s dʒu:'diə [-'di:ə], -n/z
Judaeo- dʒu(:)'di:əu- (following element also stressed)
Juda(h) 'dʒu:də
Judaic, -al, -ally dʒu:(:)'deiik, -əl, -əli
Judai|sm, -st/s 'dʒu:deii|zəm, -st/s
judaiz|e [-is|e], -es, -ing, -ed, -er/s 'dʒu:deiaiz, -iz, -iŋ, -d, -ə*/z
Judas, -es 'dʒu:dəs, -iz
Judd dʒʌd
Jude dʒu:d
Judea, -n/s dʒu:'diə [-'di:ə], -n/z
judg|e (s. v.) (J.), -es, -ing, -ed dʒʌdʒ, -iz, -iŋ, -d
judg(e)ment, -s; -day/s, -hall/s, -seat/s 'dʒʌdʒmənt, -s; -dei/z, -hɔ:l/z, -si:t/s
judgeship, -s 'dʒʌdʒʃip [-dʃʃip, -dʃip], -s
judicature dʒu:dikətʃə* [dʒu(:)'dik-, -tjuə*]
judi|cial, -cially dʒu:(:)'diʃəl, -ʃəli [-ʃli]
judiciary dʒu:(:)'diʃiəri [-ʃjə-, -ʃə-]
judicious, -ly, -ness dʒu:(:)'diʃəs, -li, -nis
Judith 'dʒu:diθ

judo 'dʒuːdəu
Judson 'dʒʌdsn
Judy 'dʒuːdi
jug (s. v.), -s, -ging, -ged dʒʌg, -z, -iŋ, -d
jugful, -s 'dʒʌgful, -z
Juggernaut 'dʒʌgənɔːt
juggins (J.), -es 'dʒʌginz, -iz
jugg|le (s. v.), -les, -ling, -led, -ler/s
   'dʒʌg|l, -lz, -liŋ [-l̩iŋ], -ld, -lə*/z
   [-lə*/z]
jugglery 'dʒʌgləri
jug-jug 'dʒʌgdʒʌg
Jugoslav, -s 'juːgəu'slɑːv [-'slæv, also
   'juːgəu-sl- esp. when attributive], -z
Jugoslavia, -n 'juːgəu'slɑːvjə [-viə], -n
jugular 'dʒʌgjulə* [rarely 'dʒuːg-]
Jugurtha dʒuː'gəːθə
juice, -s; -less dʒuːs, -iz; -lis
juic|y, -ier, -iest, -ily, -iness 'dʒuːs|i,
   -iə* [-jə*], -iist [-jist], -ili, -inis
jujitsu dʒuː'dʒitsu:
jujube, -s 'dʒuːdʒu(ː)b, -z
juke-box, -es 'dʒuːkbɒks, -iz
Jukes dʒuːks
julep, -s 'dʒuːlep [-lip], -s
Julia, -n 'dʒuːljə [-liə], -n
Juliana ˌdʒuːli'ɑːnə, -'ænə
julienne ˌdʒuːli'en [ˌʒuː-] (ʒyljɛn)
Juliet 'dʒuːljət [-liət, -ljet]
Julius 'dʒuːljəs [-liəs]
Jul|y, -ies dʒuː(ː)'l|ai, -aiz
Julyan 'dʒuːljən
jumb|le (s. v.), -les,-ling,-led; -le-sale/s
   'dʒʌmb|l, -lz, -liŋ, -ld; -lseil/z
Jumbl|y, -ies 'dʒʌmbl|i, -iz
jumbo (J.), -s 'dʒʌmbəu, -z
Jumna 'dʒʌmnə (Hind. ʤəmna)
jump (s. v.), -s, -ing, -ed, -er/s dʒʌmp,
   -s, -iŋ, -t [dʒʌmt], -ə*/z
jun. 'dʒuːnjə* [-niə*]
junction, -s 'dʒʌŋkʃən, -z
juncture, -s 'dʒʌŋktʃə* , -z
June, -s dʒuːn, -z
Jungfrau 'juŋfrau
jungle, -s 'dʒʌŋgl, -z
jungle-fowl, -s 'dʒʌŋglfaul, -z
jungly 'dʒʌŋgli
junior, -s 'dʒuːnjə* [-niə*], -z
juniority ˌdʒuːni'ɔriti
juniper, -s 'dʒuːnipə* ['dʒun-], -z
Junius 'dʒuːnjəs [-niəs]
junk, -s dʒʌŋk, -s
junker (J.), -s 'juŋkə*, -z
junket, -s, -ing 'dʒʌŋkit, -s, -iŋ
junkie, -s 'dʒʌŋki, -z
Juno 'dʒuːnəu
Junoesque ˌdʒuːnəu'esk
Junonian dʒuː(ː)'nəunjən [-niən]

junt|a/s, -o/s 'dʒʌnt|ə/z, -əu/z
jupe, -s ʒuːp (ʒyp), -s
Jupiter 'dʒuːpitə* ['dʒup-]
jupon, -s 'ʒuːpɒn ['dʒuː-, -pɔ̃ː, -pɔːŋ,
   -pɒŋ] (ʒypɔ̃), -z
Jura 'dʒuərə
jurat, -s 'dʒuəræt, -s
juridic|al, -ally dʒuə'ridik|əl [dʒu'r-],
   -əli
jurisconsult, -s 'dʒuəriskən,sʌlt, -s
jurisdiction, -s ˌdʒuəris'dikʃən, -z
jurisdictional ˌdʒuəris'dikʃənl [-ʃnəl,
   -ʃn̩l, -ʃnl, -ʃənəl]
jurisprudence 'dʒuəris,pruːdəns
   [ˌdʒuəris'p-]
jurist, -s 'dʒuərist, -s
juror, -s 'dʒuərə*, -z
jur|y, -ies 'dʒuər|i, -iz
jury-box, -es 'dʒuəriboks, -iz
jury|man, -men 'dʒuəri|mən, -mən
   [-men]
jury-mast, -s 'dʒuərimɑːst [nautical
   pronunciation -məst], -s
jus dʒʌs
just (adj.) (J.), -er, -est, -ly, -ness
   dʒʌst, -ə*, -ist, -li, -nis
just (adv.) dʒʌst [rarely dʒest], with
   some dʒəst even when stressed
justice, -s 'dʒʌstis, -iz
justiciable dʒʌs'tiʃiəbl [-ʃjə-, -ʃə-]
justiciar, -s dʒʌs'tiʃiɑː* [-isi-], -z
justiciar|y, -ies dʒʌs'tiʃiər|i [-iʃjə-, -iʃə-,
   -isiə-, -isjə-], -iz
justifiab|le, -ly, -leness 'dʒʌstifaiəb|l
   [ˌdʒʌsti'f-], -li, -lnis
justification, -s ˌdʒʌstifi'keiʃən, -z
justificat|ive, -ory dʒʌs'tifikeit|iv, -əri
justi|fy, -fies, -fying, -fied, -fier/s
   'dʒʌsti|fai, -faiz, -faiiŋ, -faid, -faiə*/z
Justin 'dʒʌstin
Justinian dʒʌs'tiniən [-njən]
Justus 'dʒʌstəs
jut, -s, -ting, -ted dʒʌt, -s, -iŋ, -id
Juta (surname) 'dʒuːtə
jute (J.), -s dʒuːt, -s
Jutland 'dʒʌtlənd
Juvenal 'dʒuːvinl [-vənl]
juvenescen|ce, -t ˌdʒuːvi'nesn|s [-və'n-],
   -t
juvenile (s. adj.), -s 'dʒuːvinail [-vən-],
   -z
juvenility ˌdʒuːvi'niliti [-və'n-]
juxtapos|e, -es, -ing, -ed 'dʒʌkstəpəuz
   [ˌdʒʌkstə'p-], -iz, -iŋ, -d
juxtaposition, -s ˌdʒʌkstəpə'ziʃən
   [-pu'z-], -z
juxtapositional ˌdʒʌkstəpə'ziʃənl [-pu'z-,
   -ʃnəl, -ʃn̩l, -ʃnl, -ʃənəl]

K

K (the¹ letter), -'s kei, -z
Kaaba 'kɑ:bə ['kɑ:əbɑ:]
Kabaka, -s kə'bɑ:kə, -z
Kab(b)ala kə'bɑ:lə [kæ'b-]
Kabul 'kɔ:bl [-bul]
Kabyle, -s kə'bail [kæ'b-, 'kæbi:l], -z
Kabylia kæ'biliə [kə'b-, -ljə]
Kadesh 'keideʃ
Kadesh-barnea 'keideʃbɑ:'niə [-'bɑ:niə]
Kadmonite, -s 'kædmənait [-mɔn-], -s
Kaffir, -s 'kæfə*, -z
Kafka 'kæfkə
Kahn kɑ:n
kailyard, -s 'keiljɑ:d, -z
Kaiser, -s 'kaizə*, -z
kakemono, -s ˌkæki'məunəu, -z
Kalat kə'lɑ:t
kale keil
kaleidoscope, -s kə'laidəskəup, -s
kaleidoscopic kəˌlaidə'skɔpik
Kalends 'kælendz [-lindz, -ləndz]
Kalgoorlie kæl'guəli
Kaliningrad kə'li:ningrɑ:d [-græd]
Kalundborg 'kælənbɔ:g
kam|a, -ic 'kɑ:m|ə, -ik
Kamba Dzong 'kʌmbə'dʒɔŋ ['kæm-,
-'dzɔŋ]
Kamchatka kæm'tʃætkə
Kamel 'kæml
Kampala kæm'pɑ:lə
Kamerun 'kæməru:n [ˌ-'-, '--'-]
Kampong kæm'pɔŋ
kana (Japanese syllabic writing) 'kɑ:nə
Kanarese ˌkænə'ri:z ['--'-]
Kandahar ˌkændə'hɑ:* ['--'-]
Kandy 'kændi
Kane kein
kangaroo, -s ˌkæŋgə'ru: ['--'-, some-
times in Australia '---], -z
Kangchenjunga ˌkæntʃen'dʒʌŋgə [-tʃin-]
Kanpur (Cawnpore) kɑ:n'puə* (Hind.
kanpwr)
Kansas 'kænzəs [-nsəs]
Kant kænt
Kantian 'kæntiən [-tjən]
Kanti|sm, -st/s 'kænti|zəm, -st/s
kaolin 'keiəlin
kapok 'keipok
kappa 'kæpə

Karachi kə'rɑ:tʃi (Hind. kəraci)
Karakoram 'kærəkɔrəm [ˌkærə'kɔ:r-]
karate kə'rɑ:ti [kæ'r-]
Karen, -s kə'ren, -z
Karl kɑ:l
Karlsbad 'kɑ:lzbæd ('karlsba:t)
karm|a, -ik 'kɑ:m|ə, -ik
Note.—Some theosophists pronounce
'kɔ:mə, 'kɔ:mik, thus distinguishing
these words from kama, kamic.
'kɔ:mə is an attempt at the Hind.
pronunciation kərma.
Karnak 'kɑ:næk
karroo, -s kə'ru:, -z
Kars kɑ:z
Kashgar 'kæʃgɑ:*
Kashmir kæʃ'miə* ['-'-, also '-- when
attributive]
Kaspar 'kæspə* [-pɑ:*]
Katakana 'kætə'kɑ:nə
Kate keit
Kater 'keitə*
Katharina ˌkæθə'ri:nə
Katharine 'kæθərin
Katherine 'kæθərin
Kathleen 'kæθli:n
Kathie 'kæθi
Katie 'keiti
Katin (surname) 'keitin
Katisha 'kætiʃə [-ʃə]
Katmandu 'kɑ:tmɑ:n'du: ['kætmæn-]
(Hind. kaθhmɑ̃du)
Katrine 'kætrin
Kattegat ˌkæti'gæt ['--'-]
Katty 'kæti
Kaunda kɑ:'u(:)ndə
katydid, -s 'keitidid, -z
Kavanagh 'kævənə, kə'vænə
Note.—In Ireland always 'kævənə.
Kay kei
kayak, -s 'kaiæk, -s
Kaye, -s kei, -z
kea (parrot), -s 'keiə, -z
Kean(e) ki:n
Kearny 'kɔ:ni, 'kɑ:ni
Kearsarge 'kiəsɑ:dʒ
Kearsley 'kiəzli [locally 'kə:zli]
Kearsney (in Kent) 'kə:zni
Kearton 'kiətn, 'kə:tn

Keary 'kiəri
Keating(e) 'ki:tiŋ
Keats ki:ts
Keble 'ki:bl
Kedah (in Malaya) 'kedə
Kedar 'ki:dɑ:* [-də*]
Kedesh 'ki:deʃ
kedg|e (s. v.), -es, -ing, -ed kedʒ, -iz, -iŋ, -d
kedgeree, -s ,kedʒə'ri: ['—'-, '—], -z
Kedleston 'kedlstən
Kedron 'kedrɔn ['ki:d-]
Keeble 'ki:bl
keel (s. v.), -s, -ing, -ed ki:l, -z, -iŋ, -d
keelhaul, -s ,-ing, -ed 'ki:lhɔ:l, -z, -iŋ, -d
keelson, -s 'kelsn ['ki:l-], -z
keen, -er, -est, -ly, -ness ki:n, -ə*, -ist, -li, -nis
Keen(e) ki:n
keep (s. v.), -s, -ing, kept, keeper/s ki:p, -s, -iŋ, kept, 'ki:pə*/z
keepsake, -s 'ki:pseik, -s
Kefauver 'ki:,fəuvə* [-,fɔ:və*]
keg, -s keg, -z
Kegan 'ki:gən
Kehoe kjəu, 'ki(:)əu
Keig ki:g
Keighley (place in Yorks.) 'ki:θli, (surname) 'ki:θli, 'ki:li, 'kaili
Keightley 'ki:tli, 'kaitli
Keigwin 'kegwin
Keiller 'ki:lə*
Keir kiə*
Keith ki:θ
Kekewich 'kekwitʃ [-widʒ], 'kekiwitʃ
Kelantan ke'læntən [kə'l-]
Kelat ki'læt
Kelland 'kelənd
Kellas 'kelæs
Kell(e)y 'keli
Kellogg 'kelɔg
kelp kelp
kelpie, -s 'kelpi, -z
Kelsey 'kelsi, 'kelzi
Kelso 'kelsəu
kelson, -s 'kelsn, -z
Kelt, -s -ic kelt, -s, -ik
Kelvin 'kelvin
Kelway 'kelwi, -wei
Kemal (Pasha) ke'mɑ:l [kə'm-]
Kemble 'kembl
kemp (K.) kemp
Kempenfelt 'kempənfelt
Kempis 'kempis
ken (s. v.) (K.), -s, -ning, -ned ken, -z, -iŋ, -d
Kend|al(l), -rick 'kend|l, -rik
Kenealy ki'ni:li [kə'n-, ke'n-]

Kenelm 'kenelm
Kenilworth 'keni̇lwə:θ [-wəθ]
Kenite, -s 'ki:nait, -s
Kenmare ken'mɛə*
Kenmore 'kenmɔ:* [-mɔə*]
Kennaird ke'nɛəd [kə'n-]
Kennan 'kenən
Kennard ke'nɑ:d [kə'n-]
Kennedy 'kenidi
kenn|el (K.) (s. v.), -els, -elling, -elled 'ken|l, -lz, -liŋ, -ld
Kennerley 'kenəli
Kenn|et, -eth, -ey 'ken|it, -iθ, -i
Kenni|cot, -ington 'ken|ikət, -iŋtən
Kennish 'keniʃ
Kenny 'keni
Kenrick 'kenrik
Kensal 'kensl
Kensington 'kenziŋtən
Kensit 'kenzit [-nsit]
Kent, -s, -ish kent, -s, -iʃ
Kentucky ken'tʌki
Kenwood 'kenwud
Kenya 'kenjə ['ki:n-]
Note.—Both pronunciations are heard locally.
Kenyatta ken'jætə
Kenyon 'kenjən [-nïən]
Keogh kjəu, 'ki(:)əu
Kepler 'keplə*
Keppel 'kepəl
kept (from keep) kept
Ker kɑ:*, keə*, kɔ:* (in Scotland kɛr)
Kerala (in S. India) 'kerələ
Kerans 'kerənz
kerb, -s kə:b, -z
kerbstone, -s 'kə:bstəun, -z
kerchief, -s -ed 'kə:-tʃif, -s, -t
Kerenhappuch 'kiərenˈhæpuk ['ker-, -rən-, -pək]
Kergenwen kə'genwən
Kerguelen 'kə:gilin [-gəl-]
Kerioth 'kiəriɔθ ['ker-]
Kerith 'kiəriθ ['ker-]
kermes 'kə:miz [-mi:z]
Kermit 'kə:mit
kern (s. v.), -s, -ing, -ed kə:n, -z, -iŋ, -d
Kernahan 'kə:nəhən [-nïən]
kernel, -s 'kə:nl, -z
kerosene 'kerəsi:n [also '—'-, ,—'-, when not attributive]
Kerr kɑ:*, kə:*
Kerry 'keri
Kerse kə:s
kersey (K.), -s; -mere 'kə:zi, -z; -miə*
Kesteven kes'ti:vən
kestrel, -s 'kestrəl, -z
Keswick 'kezik

ketch (K.), -es ketʃ, -iz
ketchup, -s 'ketʃəp, -s
Kettering 'ketəriŋ
kettle (K.), -s 'ketl, -z
kettledrum, -s 'ketldrʌm, -z
Keturah ke'tjuərə [ki't-, kə'tuərə]
Keux kju:
Kew kju:
key (s. v.) (K.), -s, -ing, -ed ki:, -z, -iŋ, -d
keyboard, -s 'ki:bɔ:d [-bɔəd], -z
Keyes ki:z, kaiz
    Note.—Mrs Parkinson Keyes, the
    American novelist, pronounces kaiz.
key-hole, -s 'ki:həul, -z
Keymour 'ki:mə*
Keyne ki:n
Keynes (surname, place near Swindon)
    keinz
key-note, -s 'ki:nəut ['ki:'nəut], -s
key-ring, -s 'ki:riŋ, -z
Keyser 'ki:zə*, 'kaizə*
keystone, -s 'ki:-stəun, -z
Keyte (surname) ki:t
Kezia ki'zaiə [ke'z-]
khaki, -s 'kɑ:ki [-ki:], -z
Khalif, -s kɑ:'li:f [kə'li:f, 'kɑ:lif], -s
Khalifa, -s kɑ:'li:fə [kə'l-], -z
Khan kɑ:n
Khanpur   kɑ:n'puə*   ['--]   (Hind.
    khanpwr)
Khartum kɑ:'tu:m
Khatmandu, incorrect spelling of Kat-
    mandu, q.v.
Khayyam kai'ɑ:m [kai'jɑ:m]
khedival ki'di:vəl [ke'd-, kə'd-]
Khedive, -s ki'di:v [ke'd-, kə'd-], -z
khedivial ki'di:vjəl [ke'd-, kə'd-, -viəl]
Khelat (former spelling of Kalat)
    kə'lɑ:t [ki'l-, ke'l-]
khidmatgar, -s   'kidmətgɑ:*   (Hind.
    xydmətgar), -z
Khyber 'kaibə*
Kia Ora kiə'ɔ:rə
kibbutz ki(:)'bu:ts
kibe, -s kaib, -z
kibosh 'kaibɔʃ
kick (s. v.), -s, -ing, -ed, -er/s kik, -s, -iŋ,
    -t, -ə*/z
kick-off, -s 'kik'ɔf [-'ɔ:f, '--, also -'-
    when preceded by a stress], -s
kickshaw, -s 'kikʃɔ:, -z
kick-up, -s 'kik'ʌp [also kik'ʌp when
    preceded by a stress], -s
kid (s. v.), -s, -ding, -ded kid, -z, -iŋ, -id
Kidd kid
Kidderminster 'kidəminstə*
kiddle (K.), -s 'kidl, -z
kidd|y, -ies 'kid|i, -iz

kid-glove (adj.) 'kidglʌv ['kid'glʌv]
kidling, -s 'kidliŋ, -z
kidnap, -s, -ping, -ped, -per/s 'kidnæp,
    -s, -iŋ, -t, -ə*/z
kidney, -s; -bean/s 'kidni, -z; -'bi:n/z
Kidron 'kaidrɔn ['kid-]
Kieff 'ki:ef ('kijif)
Kiel ki:l
kier (K.), -s kiə*, -z
Kiev 'ki:ev [-ef] ('kijif)
Kikuyu ki'ku:ju:
Kilbowie kil'bəui
Kilburn 'kilbə(:)n
Kilchurn kil'hə:n [-'xə:n]
Kildale 'kildeil
Kildare kil'dɛə*
kilderkin, -s 'kildəkin, -z
Kilham 'kiləm
Kilimanjaro ,kilimən'dʒɑ:rəu
Kilkenny kil'keni
kill (s. v.), -s, -ing, -ed, -er/s kil, -z, -iŋ,
    -d, -ə*/z
Killaloe ,kilə'lu:
Killarney ki'lɑ:ni
Killearn ki'lə:n
Killick 'kilik
Killiecrankie ,kili'kræŋki
Killigrew 'kiligru:
Killin ki'lin
killjoy, -s 'kildʒɔi, -z
Killwick 'kilwik
Kilmacolm ,kilmə'kəum
Kilmainham kil'meinəm
Kilmansegg 'kilmənseg
Kilmarnock kil'mɑ:nək [-nɔk]
kiln, -s kiln [kil], -z
    Note.—The pronunciation kil appears
    to be used only by those concerned
    with the working of kilns.
kilo, -s 'ki:ləu, -z
kilocycle, -s 'kiləu,saikl, -z
kilogramme, -s 'kiləugræm, -z
kilolitre, -s 'kiləu,li:tə*, -z
kilometre [-meter], -s 'kiləu,mi:tə*
    [ki'lɔmitə*], -z
kiloton, -s 'kiləutʌn, -z
kilowatt, -s 'kiləuwɔt, -s
Kilpatrick kil'pætrik
Kilrush kil'rʌʃ
Kilsyth kil'saiθ
kilt (s. v.), -s, -ing, -ed kilt, -s ,-iŋ, -id
Kilwarden kil'wɔ:dn
Kim kim
Kimb|all, -erley 'kimb|l, -əli
Kimbolton kim'bəultən
Kimmeridge 'kiməridʒ
Kimmins 'kiminz
kimono, -s ki'məunəu , -z

kin kin
kinaesthetic, kaini(ː)s'θetik [ˌkin-]
Kincardine kin'kɑːdin [kiŋ'k-, -dn]
Kinchinjunga ˌkintʃin'dʒʌŋgə
kincob 'kiŋkəb
kind (s. adj.), -s, -er, -est, -ly, -ness
    kaind, -z, -ə*, -ist, -li, -nis ['kainnis]
kindergarten, -s 'kində,gɑːtn, -z
kind-hearted, -ly, -ness 'kaind'hɑːtid
    [also 'kaind,h- when attributive], -li,
    -nis
kind|le, -les, -ling, -led, -ler/s 'kind|l,
    -lz, -liŋ [-liŋ], -ld, -lə*/z [-lə*/z]
kindl|y, -ier, -iest, -iness 'kaindl|i, -iə*
    [-jə*], -iist [-jist], -inis
kindred 'kindrid
kine kain
kinema, -s 'kinimə, -z
kinematic, -al, -s ˌkaini'mætik [ˌkin-],
    -əl, -s
kinematograph, -s ˌkaini'mætəugrɑːf
    [ˌkin-, -græf], -s
kinesis kai'niːsis [ki'n-]
kinesthetic ˌkaini(ː)s'θetik [ˌkin-]
kinetic (s. adj.), -s kai'netik [ki'n], -s
king (K.), -s kiŋ, -z
king-at-arms, kings-at-arms 'kiŋət-
    'ɑːmz, 'kiŋzət'ɑːmz
kingcraft 'kiŋ-krɑːft
kingcup, -s 'kiŋ-kʌp ['kiŋkʌp], -s
kingdom (K.), -s 'kiŋdəm, -z
Kingdon 'kiŋdən
kingfisher, -s 'kiŋ,fiʃə*, -z
King|horn, -lake 'kiŋ|hɔːn, -leik
kingless 'kiŋlis
kinglet, -s 'kiŋlit, -s
kinglike 'kiŋlaik
kingl|y, -ier, -iest, -iness 'kiŋl|i, -iə*
    [-jə*], -iist [-jist], -inis
king-maker (K.), -s 'kiŋ,meikə*, -z
kingpin, -s 'kiŋ-pin ['-'-], -z
King's Bench 'kiŋz'bentʃ
Kings|borough, -bury, cote 'kiŋz|-
    bərə, -bəri, -kət [-kəut]
King's Counsel 'kiŋz'kaunsəl
kingship 'kiŋʃip
Kingsley 'kiŋzli
Kings|man (member of King's College,
    Cambridge), -men 'kiŋz|mən [-mæn],
    -mən [-men]
Kingston(e) 'kiŋstən [-ŋks-]
Kingstown 'kiŋstən [-ŋks-, 'kiŋztaun]
Kingsway 'kiŋzwei
Kingussie kiŋ'juːsi
kink (s. v.), -s, -ing, -ed kiŋk, -s, -iŋ, -t
    [kiŋt]
kinkajou, -s 'kiŋkədʒuː, -z
kinless 'kinlis

Kinn|aird, -ear, -oull ki'n|ɛəd, -iə*, -uːl
kino 'kiːnəu
Kinross kin'rɔs
Kinsale kin'seil
kinsfolk 'kinzfəuk
kinship 'kinʃip
kins|man, -men 'kinz|mən, -mən [-men]
kins|woman, -women 'kinz|,wumən,
    -,wimin
Kintore kin'tɔː* [-'tɔə*]
Kintyre kin'taiə*
Kinvig 'kinvig
kiosk, -s 'ki(ː)ɔsk [kjɔsk, ki'ɔsk], -s
Kioto ki'əutəu ['kjəutəu]
kip, -s kip, -s
Kipling 'kipliŋ
kipper (s. v.), -s, -ing, -ed 'kipə*, -z, -riŋ,
    -d
Kirby 'kəːbi
Kircaldie (surname) kə:'kɔːldi
Kirghiz 'kəːgiz
Kirjathjearim   'kəːdʒæθ'dʒiərim
    ['kiriæθ-, -dʒi'ɑːrim]
    Note.—The pronunciation 'kəːdʒæθ-
    is usual in the Church of England.
    'kiriæθ- is a form used by some Jews.
kirk, -s kəːk, -s
Kirk(e) kəːk
Kirkby (surname) 'kəːbi, 'kəːkbi, (place)
    'kəːbi
Kirkcaldy (place) kə:'kɔːdi [-'kɔːldi],
    (surname) kə:'kɔːdi
    Note.—The forms kə:'kædi and
    kə:'kɑːdi may be heard occasionally
    from Southern English people.
    They are probably imitations of
    a local Scottish pronunciation
    kər'kadɪ.
Kirkcudbright kə:'kuːbri [kə'k-]
Kirk|dale, -ham 'kəːk|deil, -əm
Kirkland 'kəːklənd
Kirkman 'kəːkmən
Kirkness kəːk'nes
Kirkpatrick kə:k'pætrik
Kirkstall (in Yorks.) 'kəːk-stɔːl
Kirkwall 'kəːk-wɔːl
Kirriemuir ˌkiri'mjuə*   [-'mjɔə*,
    -'mjɔː*]
kirsch, -wasser kiəʃ, -,vɑːsə* [-,væsə*]
kirtle, -s 'kəːtl, -z
Kishon 'kaiʃon [with some Jews 'kiːʃon]
kismet 'kismet ['kizmet]
kiss (s. v.), -es, -ing, -ed kis, -iz, -iŋ, -t
kissing-crust, -s 'kisiŋ-krʌst, -s
kit, -s kit, -s
kit-bag, -s 'kitbæg, -z
kitcat (K.), -s 'kitkæt, -s
kitchen (K.), -s 'kitʃin [-tʃən], -z

kitchener (K.), -s 'kitʃinə* [-tʃən-], -z
kitchenette, -s ˌkitʃi'net, -s
kitchen - garden,   - s   'kitʃin'gɑːdn
 ['kitʃin‚g-, -tʃən-], -z
kitchen-maid, -s 'kitʃinmeid [-tʃən-], -z
kitchen-midden, -s 'kitʃin'midn [-tʃən-],
 -z
Kitch|in, -ing 'kitʃ|in, -iŋ
kite, -s; -flying kait, -s; -‚flaiiŋ
kite-balloon, -s 'kaitbə‚luːn, -z
kith kiθ
Kitson 'kitsn
kitten, -s 'kitn, -z
kittenish 'kitŋiʃ
kittiwake, -s 'kitiweik, -s
kittle 'kitl
Kitto 'kitəu
Kittredge 'kitridʒ
Kitts kits
Kittson 'kitsn
Kitty 'kiti
kiwi, -s 'kiːwi(ː), -z
Klaipeda 'klaipidə [-pedə]
klaxon, -s 'klæksn, -z
kleptoma|nia, -niac/s ‚kleptəu'mei|njə
 [-niə], -niæk/s [-njæk/s]
Klondike 'klɔndaik
Kluge (English name) kluːdʒ
knack, -s næk, -s
knacker, -s 'nækə*, -z
knacker|y, -ies 'nækər|i, -iz
knag, -s; -gy næg, -z; -i
knap, -s, -ping, -ped, -per/s næp, -s, -iŋ,
 -t, -ə*/z
knapsack, -s 'næpsæk, -s
knar, -s nɑː*, -z
Knaresborough 'nɛəzbərə
knave, -s neiv, -z
knaver|y, -ies 'neivər|i, -iz
knavish, -ly, -ness 'neiviʃ, -li, -nis
knead, -s, -ing, -ed, -er/s niːd, -z, -iŋ,
 -id, -ə*/z
kneading-trough, -s 'niːdiŋtrɔf [-trɔːf],
 -s
 Note.—Some bakers pronounce -trau
 (plur. -trauz).
knee (s. v.), -s, -ing, -d niː, -z, -iŋ, -d
knee-breeches 'niː‚britʃiz
knee-cap, -s 'niː-kæp, -s
knee-deep 'niː'diːp ['niːdiːp]
knee-joint, -s 'niː-dʒɔint, -s
kneel, -s, -ing, -ed, knelt niːl, -z, -iŋ, -d,
 nelt
knell (s. v.), -s, -ing, -ed nel, -z, -iŋ, -d
Kneller, -s 'nelə*, -z
knelt (from kneel) nelt
Knesset 'kneset
knew (from know) njuː

knickerbocker (K.), -s 'nikəbokə*, -z
knickers 'nikəz
knick-knack, -s; -ery 'niknæk, -s; -əri
kni|fe (s.), -ves nai|f, -vz
knif|e (v.), -es, -ing, -ed naif, -s, -iŋ, -t
knife-board, -s 'naifbɔːd [-bɔəd], -z
knife-edge, -s, -d 'naif-edʒ, -iz, -d
knife-grind|er/s, -ing 'naif‚graind|ə*/z‚
knife-rest, -s 'naif-rest, -s   [-iŋ
knife-tray, -s 'naif-trei, -z
knight (s. v.) (K.), -s, -ing, -ed nait, -s,
 -iŋ, -id
knightage 'naitidʒ
knight-bachelor,   knights-bachelor
 'nait'bætʃələ* [-tʃilə*], 'naits'b-
knight-errant,   knights-errant   'nait-
 'erənt, 'naits'erənt
knighthood, -s 'naithud, -z
knightl|y, -ier, -iest, -iness 'naitl|i, -Iə*
 [-jə*], -iist [-jist], -inis
Knighton 'naitn
Knightsbridge 'naitsbridʒ
knight-service 'nait‚səːvis
knit, -s, -ting, -ted, -ter/s nit, -s, -iŋ,
 -id, -ə*/z
knitting-machine, -s 'nitiŋmə‚ʃiːn, -z
knitting-needle, -s 'nitiŋ‚niːdl, -z
knitwear 'nitwɛə*
knob, -s nɔb, -z
knobbly 'nɔbḷi [-bli]
knobb|y, -ier, -iest, -iness 'nɔb|i, -Iə*,
 -iist, -inis
knock (s. v.), -s, -ing/s, -ed, -er/s nɔk,
 -s, -iŋ/z, -t, -ə*/z
knockabout, -s 'nɔkəbaut, -s
Knockbreda nɔk'briːdə
knock-down 'nɔk'daun ['--]
knock-kneed 'nɔk'niːd ['--]
knock-out, -s 'nɔkaut ['-'-], -s
knock-up, -s 'nɔk'ʌp, -s
knoll, -s nəul, -z
Knoll|es, -ys nəul|z, -z
knop, -s nɔp, -s
Knossos 'knəusɔs ['knɔs-]
knot (s. v.), -s, -ting, -ted nɔt, -s, -iŋ, -id
knot-grass 'nɔtgrɑːs
knott|y, -ier, -iest, -ily, -iness 'nɔt|i,
 -Iə*, -iist, -ili, -inis
knout (s. v.), -s, -ing, -ed naut, -s, -iŋ,
 -id
know (s. v.), -s, -ing, knew, know|n,
 -er/s; -able nəu, -z, -iŋ, njuː, nəu|n,
 -ə*/z; -əbl
know-how 'nəuhau
knowing (adj.), -ly, -ness 'nəuiŋ, -li, -nis
knowledge, -s 'nɔlidʒ, -iz
 Note.—There is also a rare form
 'nəul-.

Knowles nəulz
know-nothing, -s 'nəu,nʌθiŋ, -z
Knox nɔks
knuck|le (s. v.), -les, -ling, -led 'nʌk|l,
-lz, -liŋ [-liŋ], -ld
knuckle-bone, -s 'nʌklbəun, -z
knuckleduster, -s 'nʌkl,dʌstə*, -z
knuckle-joint, -s 'nʌkldʒɔint, -s
knur(r), -s nə:*, -z
Knutsford 'nʌtsfəd
Knyvett 'nivit
koala, -s kəu'ɑ:lə, -z
Kobe 'kəubi
kobold, -s 'kɔbəuld ['kəub-, -bld], -z
kodak, -s 'kəudæk, -s
Kohathite, -s 'kəuəθait ['kəuhə-], -s
Koh-i-noor 'kəuinuə* [-nɔə*, -nɔ:*]
kohl kəul
kohl-rabi 'kəul'rɑ:bi
koine 'kɔini:
Koko 'kəu'kəu ['--]
kola (K.) 'kəulə
Kolaba kə'lɑ:bə [kɔ'l-]
Kolnai (surname) 'kɔlnai
Kongo 'kɔŋgəu
Königsberg 'kə:nigzbɛəg [-bə:g]
('kø:niçsbɛrk, -bɛrç)
Konrad 'kɔnræd
koodoo, -s 'ku:du:, -z
kookaburra, -s 'kukə,bʌrə, -z
kopeck, -s 'kəupek ['kɔp-], -s
kopje, -s 'kɔpi, -z
Kops kɔps
Korah 'kɔ:rə
Koran kɔ'rɑ:n [kɔ:'r-, ku'r-, kə'r-]
koranic kɔ'rænik [kɔ:'r-, ku'r-, kə'r-]
Korea, -n/s kə'riə [kɔ'r-, kɔ:'r-], -n/z
Koreish 'kɔ:raiʃ
kosher 'kəuʃə* [occasionally 'kɔʃə* by
non-Jews]
kotow (s. v.), -s, -ing, -ed 'kəu'tau [-'-],
-z, -iŋ, -d
Kough kjəu, kəu
koumiss 'ku:mis
Kowloon kau'lu:n ['-'-]
kowtow, -s, -ing, -ed 'kau'tau [-'-], -z,
-iŋ, -d
kraal, -s krɑ:l [krɔ:l], -z
Note.—Usually pronounced krɑ:l in
England, but krɔ:l in South Africa.
krait, -s krait, -s

Krakatoa ,krækə'təuə
kraken, -s 'krɑ:kən, -z
kremlin (K.), -s 'kremlin, -z
Kresge 'kresgi
kreutzer (K.), -s 'krɔitsə*, -z
kris, -es kri:s, -iz
Krishna 'kriʃnə
krone, -s 'krəunə, -z
Kronin 'krəunin
Kronshtadt 'krɔnʃtæt
Kruger 'kru:gə*
Krupp krup [krʌp]
Kuala Kangsar 'kwɑ:lə'kʌŋsə* ['kwɔl-,
-'kæŋ-]
Kuala Lumpur 'kwɑ:lə'lumpuə* ['kwɔl-,
-'lʌm-, -pə*]
Note.—In the City, Kuala Lumpur
shares are commonly referred to as
'kwɔlə'lʌmpəz.
Kublai Khan 'kublai'kɑ:n
kudos 'kju:dɔs
Kuibyshev 'kwibiʃev [-ʃef] ('kujbiʃif)
Ku-Klux-Klan 'kju:-klʌks'klæn
kultur kul'tuə* (kul'tu:r)
Kumassie ku(:)'mæsi
kümmel 'kuməl ['kim-] ('kyməl)
Kuomintang 'kwəumin'tæŋ
Kup (surname) kʌp
Kurath (American surname) 'kjuəræθ
Kurd, -s kə:d, -z
Kurdistan ,kə:dis'tɑ:n [-'tæn]
Kuril, -s ku'ri:l, -z   [-z
Kurile (old spelling of Kuril), -s ku'ri:l,
kursaal, -s 'kuəzɑ:l ['kuəsɑ:l, 'kə:sɑ:l], -z
Kuwait ku'weit
Kuyper 'kaipə*
Kwantung kwæn'tʌŋ ['-'-]
Kwoyu 'kwəu'ju: ⎣kwəu'ju:]
Kyd kid
Kyffin 'kʌfin
kyle (K.), -s kail, -z
kylin, -s 'kailin, -z
Kyllachy 'kailəki [-əxi]
kyloe, -s 'kailəu, -z
kymograph, -s 'kaiməugrɑ:f [-græf], -s
kymographic ,kaiməu'græfik
Kynance 'kainæns
Kynaston 'kinəstən
kyrie, -s 'kirii ['kaiəri, 'kiərii], -z
Kyrle kə:l
Kythe 'kaiθi

L

L (*the letter*), -'s el, -z
la (*musical note*), -s lɑː, -z
la (*meaningless syllable used for singing
    a melody*) lɑː (*length of vowel is de-
    termined by the note sung*)
la (*interj.*) lɔː
laager, -s 'lɑːgə*, -z
Laban 'leibən [-bæn]
lab|el, -els, -elling, -elled 'leib|l, -lz,
    -lɪŋ [-lɪŋ], -ld
labial (*s. adj.*), -s, -ly 'leibjəl [-biəl], -z, -i
labialization [-isa-] ˌleibiəlaiˈzeiʃən
    ['leibiəlaiˈz-, -bjəl-, -liˈz-]
labializ|e [-is|e], -es, -ing, -ed 'leibiəl-
    aiz [-bjəl-], -iz, -iŋ, -d
Labienus ˌlæbiˈiːnəs
labiodental (*s. adj.*), -s 'leibiəuˈdentl
    [-bjəu-], -z
laborator|y, -ies ləˈbɔrətər|i ['læbərə-],
    -iz
laborious, -ly, -ness ləˈbɔːrɪəs, -li, -nis
Labouchere ˌlæbu(ː)ˈʃɛə* ['læbu(ː)ʃɛə*]
lab|our, -ours, -ouring, -oured, -ourer/s
    'leib|ə*, -əz, -ərɪŋ, -əd, -ərə*/z
labourite, -s 'leibərait, -s
labour-saving 'leibəˌseivɪŋ
Labrador 'læbrədɔː*
Labuan ləˈbuːən [-ˈbuən, 'læbjŭən]
    *Note.—The pronunciation of those
    familiar with the place is* ləˈbuːən *or*
    ləˈbuən
laburnum, -s ləˈbəːnəm, -z
labyrinth, -s 'læbərɪnθ [-bir-], -s
labyrinth|ian, -ine ˌlæbəˈrɪnθ|iən [-biˈr-,
    -jən], -ain
lac, -s læk, -s
Laccadive, -s 'lækədiv, -z
lac|e (*s. v.*), -es, -ing, -ed leis, -iz, -iŋ, -t
Lacedaemon ˌlæsiˈdiːmən
Lacedaemonian, -s ˌlæsidiˈməunjən
    [-ˈniən], -z
lacerat|e (*v.*), -es, -ing, -ed 'læsəreit, -s,
    -iŋ, -id
laceration, -s ˌlæsəˈreiʃən, -z
Lacert|a (*constellation*), -ae ləˈsəːt|ə, -iː
Lacey 'leisi
laches 'leitʃiz ['lætʃiz]
Lachesis 'lækisis
Lachish 'leikiʃ

Lachlan 'læklən, 'lɔklən
lachrymal 'lækriməl
lachrymatory 'lækrimətəri [-meitəri]
lachrymose, -ly 'lækriməus, -li
lack (*s. v.*), -s, -ing, -ed læk, -s, -iŋ, -t
lackadaisical ˌlækəˈdeizikəl
lackaday 'lækədei ['--'-]
lackey (*s. v.*), -s, -ing, -ed 'læki, -z, -iŋ,
    -d
lack-lustre 'lækˌlʌstə*
Lacon 'leikən
Laconia, -n/s ləˈkəunjə [-niə], -n/z
laconic (L.), -al, -ally ləˈkɔnik, -əl, -əli
lacquer (*s. v.*), -s, -ing, -ed, -er/s
    'lækə*, -z, -riŋ, -d, -rə*/z
lacquey (*s. v.*), -s, -ing, -ed 'læki, -z, -iŋ,
    -d
lacrosse ləˈkrɔs [lɑːˈk-]
lactat|e, -es, -ing, -ed 'lækteit, -s, -iŋ, -id
lactation lækˈteiʃən
lacteal 'læktiəl [-tjəl]
lactic 'læktik
lactometer, -s lækˈtɔmitə*, -z
lacun|a, -ae, -as ləˈkjuːn|ə [ˈlæ'k-], -iː,
    -əz
lacustrine ləˈkʌstrain [ˈlæ'k-, -trin]
Lacy 'leisi
lad, -s læd, -z
Ladakh (*in Kashmir*) ləˈdɑːk [*old-
    fashioned* ləˈdɔːk]
Ladbroke 'lædbruk
ladder, -s 'lædə*, -z
laddie, -s 'lædi, -z
lad|le, -les, -ling, -led, -en leid, -z, -iŋ, -id,
    -n
Ladefoged (*English surname*) 'lædifəugid
ladida 'lɑːdiˈdɑː
ladies'|-man, -men 'leidiz|mæn, -men
Ladislaus 'lædislɔːs
Ladislaw 'lædislɔː
lad|le (*s. v.*), -les, -ling, -led 'leid|l, -lz,
    -lɪŋ [-lɪŋ], -ld
ladleful, -s 'leidlful, -z
Ladoga 'lædəugə ['lɑː-d-, *old-fashioned*
    ləˈdəugə] ('lædəgə)
ladrone (*Scottish term of reproach*), -s
    'lædrən, -z
ladrone (*highwayman in Spain, etc.*), -s
    ləˈdrəun, -z

Ladrone (*Islands*) lə'drəun
lad|y (**L.**), **-ies** 'leid|i, -iz
ladybird, -s 'leidibə:d, -z
lady-chapel, -s 'leidi,tʃæpəl, -z
Ladyday, -s 'leididei, -z
lady-help, -s 'leidi'help, -s
lady - in - waiting, ladies - in - waiting
'leidiin'weitiŋ [-djin-], 'leidizin-
'weitiŋ
lady-killer, -s 'leidi,kilə*, -z
lady|like, -love/s, -ship/s 'leidi|laik,
-lʌv/z, -ʃip/s
lady's-maid, -s 'leidizmeid, -z
Ladysmith 'leidi-smiθ
laendler, -s 'lendlə*, -z
Laertes lei'ə:ti:z
Laestrygones li:s'traigəni:z
Laetitia li'tiʃiə [li:'t-, -ʃjə, -ʃə]
Lafayette (*French name*) ˌlɑ:fai'et
(lafajɛt), (*in U.S.A.*) ˌlɑ:fei'et
Lafcadio læf'kɑ:diəu
Laffan 'læfən, lə'fæn
Laf(f)itte lɑ:'fi:t [læ'f-, lə'f-] (lafit)
lag (*s. v.*), **-s, -ging, -ged, -ger/s** læg, -z,
-iŋ, -d, -ə*/z
lager (*beer*), **-s** 'lɑ:gə*, -z
Lager (*English surname*) 'leigə*
laggard, -s 'lægəd, -z
lagoon, -s lə'gu:n, -z
Lagos 'leigɔs
lah (*note in Tonic Sol-fa*), **-s** lɑ:, -z
Lahore lə'hɔ:* [lɑ:'h-, -'hɔə*]
laic, -al 'leiik, -əl
laid (*from* **lay**) leid
Laidlaw 'leidlɔ:
lain (*from* **lie**) lein
Laing læŋ, leiŋ
lair, -s lɛə*, -z
laird (**L.**), **-s; -ship** lɛəd, -z; -ʃip
laissez-faire 'leisei'fɛə* (lɛsefɛ:r)
Laius 'laiəs ['leiəs]
laity 'leiiti ['leiəti]
lake (**L.**), **-s** leik, -s
Lakeland 'leik-lænd [-lənd]
lakeside (**L.**) 'leiksaid
lakh, -s lɑ:k [læk] (*Hind.* lakh)
lak|y, -ier, -iest 'leik|i, -iə*, -iist
Lalage 'læləgi(:) [-ədʒi]
Lalla Rookh 'lælə'ruk
L'Allegro læ'leigrəu
lam, -s, -ming, -med læm, -z, -iŋ, -d
lama (**L.**), **-s** 'lɑ:mə, -z
lamaser|y, -ies 'lɑ:məsər|i ['læməs-,
lə'mæs-], -iz
lamb (*s. v.*) (**L.**), **-s, -ing, -ed** læm, -z,
-iŋ, -d
lambast|e, -es, -ing, -ed læm'beist, -s,
-iŋ, -id

lambda, -s 'læmdə, -z
lambdacism, -s 'læmdəsizəm, -z
lamben|cy, -t 'læmbən|si, -t
Lambert 'læmbə(:)t
Lambeth 'læmbəθ [-beθ]
lambkin, -s 'læmkin [-mpk-], -z
lamblike 'læmlaik
lambrequin, -s 'læmbəkin [-brək-], -z
Lambretta læm'bretə
lambskin 'læm-skin
lamb's-wool 'læmzwul
Lambton 'læmtən [-mpt-]
lam|e (*adj. v.*), **-er, -est, -ely, -ness;
-es, -ing, -ed** leim, -ə*, -ist, -li, -nis;
-z, -iŋ, -d
Lamech 'leimek ['lɑ:mek, 'lɑ:mex]
lamell|a, -ae, -ar lə'mel|ə, -i:, -ə*
lament (*s. v.*), **-s, -ing, -ed** lə'ment, -s,
-iŋ, -id
lamentab|le, -ly 'læməntəb|l [-min-], -li
lamentation, -s (**L.**) ˌlæmen'teiʃən
[-mən-, -min-], -z
lamin|a, -ae, -as, -ar 'læmin|ə, -i:, -əz
laminat|e, -es, -ing, -ed 'læmineit, -s,
-iŋ, -id
Lamington (*Baron*) 'læmiŋtən
Lammas, -tide 'læməs, -taid
lammergeier, -s 'læməgaiə*, -z
Lammermoor ˌlæmə'muə* [-'mɔə*,
-'mɔ*, '---]
Lamond 'læmənd
Lamont 'læmənt, (*in U.S.A.*) lə'mɔnt
lamp, -s læmp, -s
lampas (*silk material*) 'læmpəs
lampas (*swelling in horse's mouth*)
'læmpəz
lampblack 'læmpblæk ['læmp'b-]
Lampet 'læmpit
Lampeter 'læmpitə*
Lampetie læm'petii:
lampion, -s 'læmpiən [-pjən], -z
lamplight, -er/s 'læmp-lait, -ə*/z
Lamplough 'læmplu:, -lʌf
Lamplugh 'læmplu:
lamp-oil 'læmp-ɔil
lampoon (*s. v.*), **-s, -ing, -ed, -er/s**
læm'pu:n, -z, -iŋ, -d, -ə*/z
lamp-post, -s 'læmppəust, -s
lamprey, -s 'læmpri, -z
lamp-shade, -s 'læmpʃeid, -z
Lampson 'læmpsn
Lanagan 'lænəgən
Lanark, -shire 'lænək [-nɑ:k], -ʃiə*
[-ʃə*]
Lancashire 'læŋkəʃiə* [-kiʃ-, -ʃə*]
Lancaster 'læŋkəstə* [-kis-]
Lancasterian, -s ˌlæŋkæs'tiəriən
[-kəs-], -z

Lancastrian, -s læŋ'kæstrɪən, -z
lanc|e (s. v.) (L.), -es, -ing, -ed lɑːns, -iz, -iŋ, -t
lance-corporal, -s 'lɑːns'kɔːpərəl ['lɑːns‚k-], -z
Lancelot 'lɑːnslət
lancer, -s 'lɑːnsə*, -z
lancet (L.), -s 'lɑːnsit, -s
Lancing 'lɑːnsiŋ
Lancs. læŋks
land (s. v.), -s, -ing, -ed lænd, -z, -iŋ, -id
landau, -s 'lændɔː, -z
land-breeze, -s 'lændbriːz, -iz
Lander 'lændə*
land-force, -s 'lændfɔːs, -iz
landgrabb|er/s, -ing 'lænd‚græb|ə*/z, -iŋ
landgrave, -s 'lændgreiv, -z
landgravine, -s 'lændgrəviːn, -z
landholder, -s 'lænd‚həuldə*, -z
landing (s.), -s; -net/s, -place/s, -stage/s 'lændiŋ, -z; -net/s, -pleis/iz, -steidʒ/iz
landlad|y, -ies 'læn‚leid|i [-nd‚l-], -iz
landless 'lændlis
landlocked 'lændlɔkt
landlord, -s, -ism 'lænlɔːd [-ndl-], -z, -izəm
land-lubber, -s 'lænd‚lʌbə*, -z
landmark, -s 'lændmɑːk, -s
land-mine, -s 'lændmain, -z
Land|on, -or 'lænd|ən, -ɔː* [-ə*]
land-own|er/s, -ing 'lænd‚əun|ə*/z, -iŋ
landrail, -s 'lænd-reil ['lændreil], -z
land-rover, -s 'lænd‚rəuvə*, -z
landscape, -s 'lænskeip [-nds-, old-fashioned -skip], -s
landscaper, -s 'læn‚skeipə* [-nd‚s-], -z
Landseer, -s 'lænsiə* [-nds-, -sjə*], -z
Land's End 'lændz'end
land|slide/s, -slip/s 'lænd|slaid/z, -slip/s
lands|man, -men 'lændz|mən, -mən
land-tax, -es 'lændtæks, -iz
land|ward, -wind/s 'lænd|wəd, -wind/z
landwehr 'lændveiə* [-vɛə*]
lane (L.), -s lein, -z
Lanfranc 'lænfræŋk
Lang læŋ
Lang|baine, -bourne, -dale 'læŋ|bein, -bɔːn [-bəən], -deil
Langbarugh 'læŋbɑːf
Lange (German name) 'læŋə ('laŋə)
Lang|ham, -holm 'læŋ|əm, -əm
Langhorne 'læŋhɔːn
Lang|land, -ley 'læŋ|lənd, -li
Langmere 'læŋmiə*
Lang|ridge, -rish(e) 'læŋg|ridʒ, -riʃ

Langside 'læŋ'said ['læŋ-said]
lang-syne 'læŋ'sain
Lang|ton, -try 'læŋ|tən, -tri
language, -s 'læŋgwidʒ, -iz
languid, -ly, -ness 'læŋgwid, -li, -nis
languish (L.), -es, -ing/ly, -ed, -ment 'læŋgwiʃ, -iz, -iŋ/li, -t, -mənt
languor, -ous 'læŋgə*, -rəs
Lanigan 'lænigən
lank, -er, -est, -ly, -ness læŋk, -ə*, -ist, -li, -nis
Lankester 'læŋkistə* [-kəs-]
lank|y, -ier, -iest, -ily, -iness 'læŋk|i, -iə* [-jə*], -iist [-jist], -ili, -inis
lanoline 'lænəuliːn [-lin]
Lansbury 'lænzbəri
Lansdown(e) 'lænzdaun
Lansing (in U.S.A.) 'lænsiŋ
lantern, -s 'læntən, -z
lanyard, -s 'lænjəd [-jɑːd], -z
Laocoön lei'ɔkəuɔn [-əuən]
Laodamia ‚leiəudə'maiə
Laodicea, -n/s ‚leiəudi'siə, -n/z
Laoighis (Irish county = Leix) liːʃ
Laoighise (Irish town) 'liːʃə
Laomedon lei'ɔmidən
Laos lauz [laus, 'lɑːɔs]
Laotian 'lauʃiən [-ʃjən]
Lao-tsze 'lɑːəu'tsei ['lau-, -'tsiː]
lap (s. v.), -s, -ping, -ped, -per/s læp, -s, -iŋ, -t, -ə*/z
La Paz lɑː'pæz (la'pas)
lap-dog, -s 'læpdɔg, -z
lapel, -s lə'pel [læ'pel], -z
lapful, -s 'læpful, -z
lapidar|y (s. adj.), -ies 'læpidər|i, -iz
lapis lazuli ‚læpis'læzjulai
Lapithae 'læpiθiː
Lapland 'læplænd
Laplander, -s 'læplændə* [-lən-], -z
Lapp, -s, -ish læp, -s, -iʃ
lappet, -s, -ed 'læpit, -s, -id
laps|e (s. v.), -es, -ing, -ed læps, -iz, -iŋ, -t
lapsus linguae 'læpsəs'liŋgwai [old-fashioned -gwi(ː)]
Laput|a, -an/s lə'pjuːt|ə, -ən/z
lapwing, -s 'læpwiŋ, -z
lar, lares lɑː*, 'lɛəriːz
Larbert 'lɑːbət
larboard 'lɑːbəd [-bɔːd, -bəəd]
larcenous, -ly 'lɑːsinəs [-sən-, -sn-], -li
larcen|y, -ies 'lɑːsən|i [-sni, -sn̩i], -iz
larch, -es lɑːtʃ, -iz
lard (s. v.), -s, -ing, -ed lɑːd, -z, -iŋ, -id
larder, -s 'lɑːdə*, -z
lares 'lɛəriːz
large, -r, -st, -ly, -ness lɑːdʒ, -ə*, -ist, -li, -nis

large-hearted, -ness 'lɑːdʒ'hɑːtid ['lɑːdʒ,h-], -nis
large-minded, -ness 'lɑːdʒ'maindid ['lɑːdʒ,m-], -nis
Largen 'lɑːdʒən
largess, -es lɑː'dʒes [-'ʒes, 'lɑː:-, -dʒis], -iz
larghetto (s. adv.), -s lɑː'getəu, -z
largish 'lɑːdʒiʃ
largo (s. adv.), -s 'lɑːgəu, -z
lariat (s. v.), -s, -ing, -ed 'lærïət, -s, -iŋ, -id
lark (s. v.), -s, -ing, -ed lɑːk, -s, -iŋ, -t
Larkin, -s 'lɑːkin, -z
larkspur, -s 'lɑːk-spə:* [-spə*], -z
lark|y, -ier, -iest, -iness 'lɑːk|i, -ïə* [-jə*], -iist [-jist], -inis
Larmor 'lɑːmɔː*
larrikin, -s 'lærikin, -z
Lars Porsena 'lɑːz'pɔːsinə
larum, -s 'lærəm, -z
larv|a, -ae, -al 'lɑːv|ə, -iː, -əl
laryngal lə'riŋgəl [læ'r-, leə'r-]
laryngeal ,lærin'dʒi(:)əl [,leərin'dʒ-, lə'rindʒïəl, lə'rindʒjəl]
laryngectom|y, -ies ,lærin'dʒektəm|i [,leər-, -ŋ'gek-], -iz
laryngitis ,lærin'dʒaitis [,leər-]
laryngolog|ist/s, -y ,læriŋ'gɔlədʒ|ist/s [,leər-], -i
laryngoscope, -s lə'riŋgəskəup [læ'r-, leə'r-, 'læriŋg-, 'leəriŋg-], -s
laryngoscopic lə,riŋgəs'kɔpik [læ,r-, leə,r-, ,læriŋg-, ,leəriŋg-]
laryngoscop|ist/s, -y ,læriŋ'gɔskəp|-ist/s [,leər-], -i
larynx, -es 'læriŋks ['leər-], -iz
Lascar, -s 'læskə*, -z
Lascelles 'læsəlz
lascivious, -ly, -ness lə'sivïəs [-vjəs], -li, -nis
laser, -s leizə*, -z
lash (s. v.), -es, -ing/s, -ed, -er/s læʃ, -iz, -iŋ/z, -t, -ə*/z
Lasham (in Herts.) 'læʃəm (locally 'læsəm)
Las Palmas læs'pælməs
lass, -es læs, -iz
Lassell læ'sel [lə's-]
lassie, -s 'læsi, -z
lassitude 'læsitjuːd
lasso (s.), -s læ'suː ['læsəu], -z
lass|o (v.), -oes, -oing, -oed læ's|uː, -uːz, -u(ː)iŋ, -uːd ['læs|əu, -əuz, -əuiŋ, -əud]
last (s. adj. v.), -s, -ly, -ing/ly, -ed lɑːst, -s, -li, -iŋ/li, -id
Las Vegas 'læs'veigəs ['lɑː:s-]

Latakia ,lætə'ki(:)ə
latch (s. v.), -es, -ing, -ed lætʃ, -iz, -iŋ, -t
latchet, -s 'lætʃit, -s
latchkey, -s 'lætʃkiː, -z
late, -r, -st, -ly, -ness leit, -ə*, -ist, -li, -nis
lateen lə'tiːn
laten|cy, -t/ly 'leitən|si, -t/li
later|al (s. v.), -als, -ally 'lætər|əl, -əlz, -əli
Lateran 'lætərən
latex 'leiteks
lath, -s lɑːθ, -s [lɑːðz]
Latham 'leiθəm, 'leiðəm
    Note.—Generally 'leiðəm in S. of England; always 'leiðəm in N.
Lathbury 'læθbəri
lathe, -s leið, -z
lather (s. v.), -s, -ing, -ed 'lɑːðə* ['læð-], -z, -riŋ, -d
Lathom 'leiθəm, 'leiðəm
Lathrop 'leiθrəp
lathy 'lɑːθi
Latimer 'lætimə*
Latin 'lætin
latini|sm/s, -st/s 'lætini|zəm/z, -st/s
latinity lə'tiniti [læ't-]
latiniz|e [-is|e], -es, -ing, -ed 'lætinaiz, -iz, -iŋ, -d
Latinus lə'tainəs
latish 'leitiʃ
latitude, -s 'lætitjuːd, -z
latitudinal ,læti'tjuːdinl
latitudinarian, -s, -ism 'læti,tjuːdi-'neəriən, -z, -izəm
Latium 'leiʃjəm [-ʃïəm]
latria lə'traiə
latrine, -s lə'triːn, -z
latter, -ly 'lætə*, -li
lattice, -s, -d 'lætis, -iz, -t
lattice-work 'lætis-wəːk
Latvia, -n/s 'lætvïə [-vjə], -n/z
laud (s. v.) (L.), -s, -ing, -ed lɔːd, -z, -iŋ, -id
laudab|le, -ly, -leness 'lɔːdəb|l, -li, -lnis
laudanum 'lɔdnəm ['lɔː-]
laudatory 'lɔːdətəri
Lauder, -dale 'lɔːdə*, -deil
laugh (s. v.), -s, -ing/ly, -ed, -er/s lɑːf, -s, -iŋ/li, -t, -ə*/z
Laughland 'lɔklənd [in Scotland 'lɔxlənd]
laughab|le, -ly, -leness 'lɑːfəb|l, -li, -lnis
laughing-gas 'lɑːfiŋ'gæs ['---]
laughing-stock, -s 'lɑːfiŋ-stɔk, -s
Laughlin 'lɔklin ['lɔxlin], 'lɔflin, 'lɑːflin
laughter 'lɑːftə*
Laughton 'lɔːtn
launce, -s lɑːns, -iz

Launce lɑːns, lɔːns
Launcelot 'lɑːnslət, 'lɔːns-
Launceston (in Cornwall) 'lɔːnstən
[locally 'lɑːn-], (in Tasmania)
'lɔːnsəstən [locally 'lɒnsəstən]
launch (s. v.), -es, -ing, -ed lɔːntʃ
[lɑːntʃ], -iz, -iŋ, -t
launder, -s, -ing, -ed 'lɔːndə* ['lɑːn-] -z,
-riŋ, -d
laundress, -es 'lɔːndris ['lɑːn-], -iz
laundr|y, -ies 'lɔːndr|i ['lɑːn-], -iz
laundry-|maid/s, -man, -men 'lɔːndri|-
meid/z ['lɑːn-], -mən [-mæn], -mən
[-men]
Laundy 'lɔːndi
Laura 'lɔːrə
laureate (s. adj.), -s, -ship/s 'lɔːriit ['lɔr-,
-riət], -s, -ʃip/s
laureat|e (v.), -es, -ing, -ed 'lɔːrieit
['lɔr-], -s, -iŋ, -id
laurel, -s, -led 'lɔrəl, -z, -d
Laurence 'lɔrəns
Laurie 'lɔːri, 'lɔri
Laurier (English name) 'lɔriə*,
(Canadian) 'lɔriei, 'lɔriə*
Lauriston 'lɔristən
laurustinus, -es ˌlɔrəs'tainəs, -iz
Lausanne ləu'zæn (lɔzan, lozan)
Lauterbrunnen 'lautəbrunən
lava 'lɑːvə
lavabo, -s (ritual) lə'veibəu, (basin)
lə'veibəu ['lævəbəu], -z
lavage, -s læ'vɑːʒ [-ɑːdʒ], -iz
Lavater lɑː'vɑːtə* ['lɑːvɑːtə*]
lavator|y, -ies 'lævətər|i, -iz
lav|e, -es, -ing, -ed leiv, -z, -iŋ, -d
lavender 'lævində* [-vən-]
Lavengro lə'veŋgrəu
lavor, -s 'leivə*, -z
Lavery 'leivəri, 'læv-
Lavington 'læviŋtən
Lavinia, -n lə'vinəi [-njə], -n
lavish (adj. v.), -ly, -ness; -es, -ing, -ed
'læviʃ, -li, -nis; -iz, -iŋ, -t
law (L.), -s lɔː, -z
law|-abiding, -book/s 'lɔː|ə,baidiŋ,
-buk/s
law-break|er/s, -ing 'lɔːˌbreik|ə*/z, -iŋ
Law|es, -ford lɔː|z, -fəd
law|ful, -fully, -fulness 'lɔː|ful, -fuli
[-fəli], -fulnis
law-giv|er/s, -ing 'lɔːˌgiv|ə*/z, -iŋ
lawks lɔːks
lawless (L.), -ly, -ness 'lɔːlis, -li, -nis
law|-list/s, -lord/s 'lɔː|list/s, -lɔːd/z
law-mak|er/s, -ing 'lɔːˌmeik|ə*/z, -iŋ
lawn, -s lɔːn, -z
lawn-mower, -s 'lɔːnˌməuə*, -z

lawn-tennis 'lɔːn'tenis [also lɔːn't- when
preceded by a stress]
Lawr|ance, -ence 'lɔr|əns [rarely 'lɔːr-],
-əns
Lawrenson 'lɔrənsn
Lawson 'lɔːsn
law-suit, -s 'lɔː-sjuːt [-suːt], -s
Lawton 'lɔːtn
lawyer, -s 'lɔːjə* ['lɔiə*], -z
lax, -er, -est, -ly, -ness læks, -ə*, -ist, -li,
-nis
laxative (s. adj.), -s 'læksətiv, -z
laxity 'læksiti
lay (s. adj. v.), -s, -ing, laid lei, -z, -iŋ,
leid
Layamon 'laiəmən [-mɔn] (Middle Eng.
'lɑːɣəmɔn)
Layard lɛəd
lay-brother, -s 'lei'brʌðə*, -z
lay-by, -s 'leibai, -z
Laycock 'leikɔk ['lei-kɔk]
layer (s.) (one who lays), -s 'leiə*, -z
layer (s.) (stratum, of plants), -s 'leiə*
[lɛə*], -z
layer (v.), -s, -ing, -ed 'lɛə* ['leiə*], -z,
-riŋ, -d
layette, -s lei'et, -s
lay-figure, -s 'lei'figə*, -z
lay|man, -men 'lei|mən, -mən
lay-out, -s 'leiaut ['-'-, -'-], -s
lay-reader, -s 'lei'riːdə*, -z
Layton 'leitn
lazar, -s 'læzə*, -z
lazaretto, -s ˌlæzə'retəu, -z
Lazarus 'læzərəs
laz|e, -es, -ing, -ed leiz, -iz, -iŋ, -d
Lazenby 'leiznbi
lazul|i, -ite 'læzjul|ai, -ait
laz|y, -ier, -iest, -ily, -iness 'leiz|i, -iə*
[-jə*], -iist [-jist], -ili, -inis
lazy-bones 'leiziˌbəunz
lb., lbs., paund, paundz
le (note in Tonic Sol-fa), -s liː, -z
lea (L.), -s liː, -z
leach (s. v.) (L.), -es, -ing, -ed liːtʃ, -iz,
-iŋ, -t
Leachman 'liːtʃmən
Leacock 'liːkɔk
lead (s. v.) (metal), -s, -ing, -ed led, -z,
-iŋ, -id
lead (s. v.) (to conduct, etc.), -s, -ing, led
liːd, -z, -iŋ, led
Lead (surname) liːd
leaden 'ledn
Leadenhall 'lednhɔːl
leader, -s; -ship 'liːdə*, -z; -ʃip
leaderette, -s ˌliːdə'ret, -s
lead-in, -s 'liːd'in, -z

leading-rein, -s 'li:diŋrein, -z
leading-strings 'li:diŋ-striŋz
lead-off, -s 'li:d'ɔf [-'ɔ:f], -s
lead-pencil, -s 'led'pensl [-sil], -z
leads (s.) (roofing) ledz
leady (like lead) 'ledi
lea|f (s.), **-ves** li:|f, -vz
leaf (v.), **-s, -ing, -ed** li:f, -s, -iŋ, -t
leafless 'li:f-lis
leaflet, -s 'li:f-lit, -s
leaf-mould 'li:fməuld
leaf|y, -ier, -iest, -iness 'li:f|i, -ɪə* [-jə*], -iist [-jist], -inis
leagu|e (s. v.), **-es, -ing, -ed** li:g, -z, -iŋ, -d
leaguer (L.), -s 'li:gə*, -z
Leah liə
Leahy 'li:i
leak (s. v.), **-s, -ing, -ed; -age/s** li:k, -s, -iŋ, -t; -idʒ/iz
Leake li:k
Leakey 'li:ki
leak|y, -ier, -iest, -iness 'li:k|i, -ɪə* [-jə*], -iist [-jist], -inis
leal li:l
Leamington 'lemiŋtən
lean (s. adj. v.), **-er, -est, -ly, -ness; -s, -ing, -ed, leant** li:n, -ə*, -ist, -li, -nis; -z, -iŋ, lent [li:nd], lent
Leander li(:)'ændə*
lean-to, -s 'li:ntu: ['li:n'tu:], -z
leap (s. v.), **-s, -ing, -ed, leapt** li:p [applied to horses by horsy people also lep], -s, -iŋ, lept [li:pt], lept
leaper, -s 'li:pə* [of horses also 'lepə*], -z
leap-frog 'li:pfrɔg
leap-year, -s 'li:p-jə:* [-jiə*], -z
Lear liə*
learn, -s, -ing, -ed, -t, -er/s lə:n, -z, -iŋ, -t [-d], -t, -ə*/z
learned (adj.), **-ly, -ness** 'lə:nid, -li, -nis
Learney (in Aberdeenshire) 'lɛəni
leas|e (s. v.), **-es, -ing, -ed** li:s, -iz, -iŋ, -t
leasehold (s. adj.), **-s; -er/s** 'li:shəuld, -z; -ə*/z
lease-|lend (s. v.), **-lends, -lending, -lent** 'li:s|'lend, -'lendz, -'lendiŋ, -'lent
leash (s. v.), **-es, -ing, -ed** li:ʃ, -iz, -iŋ, -t
leasing (telling lies) 'li:siŋ ['li:ziŋ]
Note.—'li:siŋ appears to be now superseding the older form 'li:ziŋ.
least, -ways, -wise li:st, -weiz, -waiz
leat, -s li:t, -s
Leatham 'li:θəm
Leathart 'li:θɑ:t
leather (s. v.), **-s, -ing, -ed** 'leðə*, -z, -riŋ, -d
leatherette ˌleðə'ret

Leatherhead 'leðəhed
leathern 'leðə(:)n
leath|ery, -eriness 'leð|əri, -ərinis
Leathes li:ðz   [li:f, -s]
leave (s.), **-s** li:v, -z [in the army also
leav|e (v.), **-es, -ing/s, left** li:v, -z, -iŋ/z, leaved li:vd   [left
leav|en, -ens, -ening, -ened 'lev|n, -nz, -niŋ [-nin], -nd
Leavenworth 'levnwə:θ
leaves (plur. of **leaf**) li:vz
Leavitt 'levit
Lebanese ˌlebə'ni:z
Lebanon 'lebənən
Le Beau lə'bəu
Leburn 'li:bə:n
lecherous, -ly, -ness 'letʃərəs, -li, -nis
lechery 'letʃəri
Lechlade 'letʃleid
Lechmere 'leʃmiə*, 'letʃ-
Leckhampton 'lekˌhæmptən
Lecky 'leki
Leconfield 'lekənfi:ld
lectern, -s 'lektə(:)n, -z
lection, -s 'lekʃən, -z
lectionar|y, -ies 'lekʃŋər|i [-ʃənər-, -ʃnər-], -iz
lector, -s 'lektɔ:*, -z
lect|ure (s. v.), **-ures, -uring, -ured, -urer/s; -ureship/s** 'lektʃ|ə*, -əz, -əriŋ, -əd, -ərə*/z; -əʃip/s
led (from **lead** li:d) led
Leda 'li:də
Ledbury 'ledbəri
ledge, -s ledʒ, -iz
ledger, -s 'ledʒə*, -z
ledger-line, -s 'ledʒəlain, -z
Ledi 'ledi
Lediard 'lediəd [-diɑ:d, -djəd]
Ledward 'ledwəd
Ledyard 'ledjəd
lee (L.), -s li:, -z
leech (L.), -es li:tʃ, -iz
Leeds li:dz
leek (L.), -s li:k, -s
leer (s. v.), **-s, -ing/ly, -ed** liə*, -z, -riŋ/li, -d
Lees li:z
leet, -s li:t, -s
leetle 'li:tl
leeward 'li:wəd [nautical pronunciation 'lu(:)əd, 'lju(:)əd]
Leeward (Islands) 'li:wəd
leeway 'li:wei
Lefanu 'lefənju:
Lefevre lə'fi:və*, lə'feivə*
Note.—lə'fi:və* in Sterne's 'Sentimental Journey'.

Lefroy lə'frɔi
left left
left-hand (adj.) 'lefthænd
left-hand|ed, -edness, -er/s 'left-
  'hænd|id, -idnis, -ə*/z
leftist, -s 'leftist, -s
left-off, -s 'left'ɔf [-'ɔːf, also '— when
  attributive], -s
leftward, -s 'leftwəd, -z
leg (s. v.), -s, -ging, -ged leg, -z, -iŋ, -d
legac|y, -ies 'legəs|i, -iz
leg|al, -ally 'li:g|əl, -əli
legali|sm, -st/s 'li:gəli|zəm [-g]i-], -st/s
legality li(:)'gæliti
legalization [-isa-] ,li:gəlai'zeiʃən [-g]ai-]
legaliz|e [-is|e], -es, -ing, -ed 'li:gəlaiz
  [-g]aiz], -iz, -iŋ, -d
legate, -s 'legit [-geit], -s
legatee, -s ,legə'ti:, -z
legatine 'legətain
legation, -s li'geiʃən [le'g-], -z
legatissimo ,legɑ:'tisiməu [-gə't-]
legato lə'gɑ:təu [li'g-]
leg-bail, -s 'leg'beil ['— when in contrast
  with off-bail], -z
leg-bye, -s 'leg'bai ['— when in contrast
  with off-bye], -z
legend, -s 'ledʒənd, -z
legendary 'ledʒəndəri [-dʒin-]
Leger 'ledʒə*, see also St. Leger
legerdemain 'ledʒədə'mein
Leggatt 'legət
Legge leg
-legged -legd [-'legid]
Leggett, -er 'legit, -ə*
legging, -s 'legiŋ, -z
leggy 'legi
Legh li:
leghorn (fowl), -s le'gɔ:n [li'g-, lə'g-], -z
leghorn (straw hat), -s 'leghɔ:n [le'gɔ:n,
  li'gɔ:n, lə'gɔ:n], -z
Leghorn (place) 'leg'hɔ:n [also '—, -'-,
  according to sentence-stress]
legibility ,ledʒi'biliti [-dʒə'b-, -lət-]
legib|le, -ly, -leness 'ledʒəb|l [-dʒib-],
  -li, -lnis
legion (L.), -s 'li:dʒən, -z
legionar|y (s. adj.), -ies 'li:dʒənər|i
  [-dʒnə-], -iz
legislat|e, -es, -ing, -ed, -or/s 'ledʒis-
  leit, -s, -iŋ, -id, -ə*/z
legislation ,ledʒis'leiʃən
legislative 'ledʒislətiv [-leit-]
legislature, -s 'ledʒisleitʃə* [-lətʃə*,
  -tjuə*, -tʃuə*], -z
legist, -s 'li:dʒist, -s
legitimacy li'dʒitiməsi   [-li, -nis
legitimate (adj.), -ly, -ness li'dʒitimit,

legitimat|e (v.), -es, -ing, -ed li'dʒiti-
  meit, -s, -iŋ, -id
legitimation li,dʒiti'meiʃən
legitimatiz|e [-is|e], -es, -ing, -ed
  li'dʒitimətaiz, -iz, -iŋ, -d
legitimist, -s li'dʒitimist, -s
legitimiz|e [-is|e], -es, -ing, -ed li'dʒiti-
  maiz, -iz, -iŋ, -d
leg-pull, -s, -ing, -ed 'legpul, -z, -iŋ, -d
Legros (English surname) lə'grəu
legume, -s 'legju:m, -z
leguminous le'gju:minəs [li'g-]
Lehigh 'li:hai
Lehmann 'leimən
lei 'leii:
Leicester, -shire 'lestə*, -ʃiə* [-ʃə*]
Leics. (always said in full) 'lestəʃiə*
  [-ʃə*]
Leiden (Dutch city) 'laidn
Leigh (surname) li:
Leigh (place name) li:, lai
  Note.—The places in Essex and
  Lancs. are li:; those in Surrey,
  Kent and Dorset are lai.
Leighton 'leitn
Leila 'li:lə
Leinster (Irish province) 'lenstə*, (Duke
  of) 'linstə*, (square in London)
  'lenstə*
Leipzig 'laipzig ('laiptsiç)
Leishman 'li:ʃmən, 'liʃ-
leister, -s 'li:stə*, -z
Leister 'lestə*
Leiston (in Suffolk) 'leistən
leisure, -d, -ly, -liness 'leʒə*, -d, -li,
  -linis
Leitch li:tʃ
Leith li:θ
leitmotif, -s 'laitməu,ti:f, -s
Leitrim 'li:trim
Leix (Irish county) li:ʃ
Le Lacheur lə'læʃə*
Leland 'li:lənd
Lelean lə'li:n
Lely (portraitist) 'li:li ['lili]
leman, -s 'lemən, -z
Leman (lake) 'lemən ['li:mən, li'mæn,
  lə'mæn], (surname) 'lemən, 'li:mən,
  (street in London) 'lemən [formerly
  li'mæn]
Le Marchant lə'mɑ:tʃənt
Lemare lə'meə*
Le May lə'mei
Lemberg 'lembə:g
Lemesurier lə'meʒərə*
lemma, -s 'lemə, -z
lemming, -s 'lemiŋ, -z
Lemnos 'lemnɔs

Lemoine lə'mɔin
lemon (L.), -s 'lemən, -z
lemonade, -s ,lemə'neid ['lemə'neid], -z
lemon-coloured 'lemən,kʌləd
lemon-drop, -s 'lemən-drɔp, -s
lemon-juice 'lemən-dʒuːs
lemon-squash, -es 'lemən'skwɔʃ, -iz
lemon-squeezer, -s 'lemən,skwiːzə*, -z
lemon-yellow 'lemən'jeləu
Lemuel 'lemjŭəl [-juel]
lemur, -s 'liːmə*, -z
Lena (personal name) 'liːnə, (Siberian river) 'leinə ('ljenə)
lend, -s, -ing, lent, lender/s lend, -z, -iŋ, lent, 'lendə*/z
lending-librar|y, -ies 'lendiŋ,laibrər|i [-bɹɾl-], -iz
Le Neve lə'niːv
length, -s leŋθ [-ŋkθ], -s
length|en, -ens, -ening, -ened 'leŋθ|ən [-ŋkθ-], -ənz, -əniŋ [-ŋiŋ, -niŋ], -ənd
length|ways, -wise 'leŋθ|weiz [-ŋkθ-], -waiz
length|y, -ier, -iest, -ily, -iness 'leŋθ|i [-ŋkθ-], -ïə* [-jə*], -iist [-jist], -ili, -inis
lenien|ce, -cy, -t/ly 'liːnjən|s [-nïən-], -si, -t/li
Lenin 'lenin ['leinin] ('ljenjin)
Leningrad 'leningræd [-grɑːd] (ljinjin-'grat)
lenis, lenes 'leinis ['liːnis], 'leineiz ['liːniːz]
lenitive (s. adj.), -s 'lenitiv, -z
lenity 'leniti ['liːn-]
Lennox 'lenəks
leno (L.) 'liːnəu
Lenoir (surname) lə'nwɑ:*, (town in U.S.A.) lə'nɔː*
Lenore lə'nɔː* [li'n-, -'nɔə*]
Lenox 'lenəks
lens, -es lenz, -iz
lent (from lend) lent
Lent, -en lent, -ən
Lenthall (surname) 'lentɔːl, (place in Yorks) 'lenθɔːl [-θəl]
lenticular len'tikjulə*
lentil, -s 'lentil [-tl], -z
Lentulus 'lentjuləs
Leo (constellation, name of popes) 'liː(ː)əu
Leofric 'leiəufrik
Leominster 'lemstə* ['leminstə*]
Leon 'liː(ː)ən
Léon (as English name) 'leiɔn ['leiən]
Leonard, -s 'lenəd, -z
Leonardo, -s ,liː(ː)əu'nɑːdəu, -z
Leonid, -s 'liː(ː)əunid, -z
Leonidas liː(ː)'ɔnidæs

leonine 'liː(ː)əunain
Leonora ,liː(ː)ə'nɔːrə
Leontes liː(ː)'ɔntiːz
leopard, -s; -ess/es 'lepəd, -z; -is/iz
Leopold 'liəpəuld
Lepanto li'pæntəu
Le Patourel lə'pæturəl [-tər-]
Lepel lə'pel
leper, -s 'lepə*, -z
lepidoptera ,lepi'dɔptərə
Lepidus 'lepidəs
Le Play lə'plei
Le Poer lə'pɔ:* [-'pɔə*]
Lepontine li'pɔntain [le'p-]
Leporis 'lepəris
leprechaun, -s 'leprəkɔːn [-prikɔːn, -prəhɔːn, -prihɔːn], -z
leprosy 'leprəsi
leprous, -ly, -ness 'leprəs, -li, -nis
Lepsius 'lepsiəs [-sjəs]
lept|on, -a 'lept|ɔn [-t|ən], -ə
Lepus (constellation) 'liːpəs ['lep-]
Le Queux lə'kjuː
Lereculey ,leri'kjuːli
Lermontoff 'lɛəmɔntɔf ['lɛəməntəf] ('ljerməntəf)
Lerwick 'lə:wik [locally 'lɛrwïk]
Lesbia, -n 'lezbïə [-bjə], -n
Lesbos 'lezbɔs
Le Seelleur lə'seilə*
lèse-majesté 'leiz'mæʒestei [-'mædʒ-, -ʒis-, -ʒəs-] (lɛːzmaʒɛste)
lese-majesty 'liː:z'mædʒisti [-dʒəs-]
lesion, -s 'liː:ʒən, -z
Leslie, -ley 'lezli, in U.S.A. 'lesli
Lesmahagow ,lesmə'heigəu
Lesotho lə'səutəu [-'suː-]
less, -er les, -ə*
lessee, -s le'siː: ['le'siː:], -z
less|en, -ens, -ening, -ened 'les|n, -nz, -niŋ [-niŋ], -nd
Lesseps le'seps ['leseps]
Lessing 'lesiŋ
lesson, -s 'lesn, -z
lessor, -s le'sɔ:* ['le'sɔ:*], -z
lest lest
Lestrade les'treid, -'trɑːd
L'Estrange ləs'treindʒ [les-]
let (s. v.), -s, -ting let, -s, -iŋ
Letchworth 'letʃwə(ː)θ
let-down, -s 'letdaun [-'-], -z
Lethaby 'leθəbi
lethal 'liː:θəl
lethargic, -al, -ally, -alness le'θɑːdʒik [li'θ-], -əl, -əli, -əlnis
lethargy 'leθədʒi
Lethe 'liː:θiː(ː)
Letheby 'leθəbi

Lethem 'leθəm
Letitia li'tiʃɪə [-ʃjə, -ʃə]
Lett, -s let, -s
letter (s. v.), -s, -ing, -ed 'letə*, -z, -riŋ, -d
letter-balance, -s 'letə,bæləns, -iz
letter-box, -es 'letəbɔks, -iz
letter-card, -s 'letəkɑːd, -z
letter-case, -s 'letəkeis, -iz
letter-perfect 'letə'pəːfikt
letterpress 'letə-pres
letter-weight, -s 'letəweit, -s
letter-writer, -s 'letə,raitə*, -z
Lettic 'letik
Lettice 'letis
Lettish 'letiʃ
Lettonian, -s le'təunjən [-nɪən], -z
Letts lets
lettuce, -s 'letis, -iz
Letty 'leti
Leuchars (place in Scotland) 'luːkəz ['ljuː-, -uːxəz] (Scottish 'luxərz), (southern surname) 'luːʃɑːz ['ljuː-]
leucocyte, -s 'ljuːkəusait ['luː-], -s
leucopathy lju:'kɔpəθi [luː-]
leucotomy lju:'kɔtəmi [luː-]
Leuctra 'ljuːktrə
leukaemia lju(ː)'kiːmɪə [lu(ː)-, lə-, -mjə]
Levant (s.) (E. Mediterranean, leather) li'vænt [lə'v-]
levant (adj.) (opp. couchant) 'levənt
levant (v.) (abscond), -s, -ing, -ed li'vænt [lə'v-], -s, -iŋ, -id
levanter (L.), -s li'væntə* [lə'v-], -z
Levantine 'levəntain [-vn-, -tiːn]
levee (royal reception), -s 'levi [-vei], -z
levee (embankment), -s 'levi [lə'viː], -z
lev|el (s. adj. v.), -els, -elness; -elling, -elled, -eller/s 'lev|l, -lz, -lnis; -ļiŋ [-əliŋ], -ld, -ļə*/z [-ələ*/z]
level-crossing, -s 'levl'krɔsiŋ [-'krɔːs-], -z
level-headed 'levl'hedid [also '--,-- when attributive]
Leven (loch) 'liːvən, (Earl of) 'liːvən, (surname) 'levən, 'liːvən
lev|er (s. v.) (L.), -ers, -ering, -ered; -erage 'liːv|ə*, -əz, -əriŋ, -əd; -əridʒ
leveret, -s 'levərit, -s
Leverett 'levərit
Leverhulme 'liːvəhjuːm
Leverkes (surname) 'levəkəs
Leveson (surname) 'levisn
Leveson-Gower 'luːsn'gɔː* ['ljuː-, -'gɔə*]
Levett 'levit
Levey 'liːvi, 'levi
Levi 'liːvai
leviable 'levɪəbl

leviathan (L.), -s li'vaɪəθən [lə'v-], -z
Levine lə'viːn
levirate 'liːvirit
Levis (in Quebec) 'levi
levitat|e, -es, -ing, -ed 'leviteit, -s, -iŋ, -id
levitation, -s ,levi'teiʃən, -z
Levite, -s 'liːvait, -s
levitic, -al, -ally li'vitik, -əl, -əli
Leviticus li'vitikəs
levit|y, -ies 'levit|i, -iz
lev|y (s. v.), -ies, -ying, -ied, -ier/s 'lev|i, -iz, -iiŋ [-jiŋ], -id, -ɪə*/z [-jə*/z]
Levy (surname) 'liːvi, 'levi, (American town) 'liːvai
lewd, -er, -est, -ly, -ness luːd [ljuːd], -ə*, -ist, -li, -nis
Lew|es, -in 'luː(ː)|is ['lju(ː)-], -in
lewis (L.), -es 'lu(ː)is ['lju(ː)is], -iz
Lewisham 'lu(ː)iʃəm ['lju(ː)-, -isəm]
   Note.—Former pronunciations 'lu(ː)isəm and 'luːsəm are probably now obsolete or nearly so.
Lewison 'lu(ː)isn ['lju(ː)-]
Lewsey 'ljuːsi
lexic|al, -ally 'leksik|əl, -əli
lexicograph|er/s, -y ,leksi'kɔgrəf|ə*/z, -i
lexicographic, -al ,leksikəu'græfik, -əl
lexicon, -s 'leksikən, -z
Lexington 'leksiŋtən
ley (land under grass) lei
Ley li:
Leybourne (in Kent) 'leibɔːn [-bɔən]
Leyburn (in Yorks.) 'leibəːn
Leycester 'lestə*
Leyden (old-fashioned spelling of Leiden, q.v.)
Leyden jar, -s 'leidn'dʒɑː:*, -z
Leyland 'leilənd
Leys liːz
Leyshon 'leiʃn
Leyton 'leitn
Lhasa 'lɑːsə ['læs-]
Lhuyd lɔid
li (Chinese measure of length) liː
liabilit|y, -ies ,laiə'bilit|i [-lət-], -iz
liable, -ness 'laiəbl, -nis
liaison, -s li(ː)'eizɔ̃:ŋ [-zɔn], -zən (ljɛzɔ̃), -z
   Note.—In military use always -zən.
liais|e, -es, -ing, -ed li'eiz, -iz, -iŋ, -d
Liam liəm
liang, -s li'æŋ, -z
liar, -s 'laiə*, -z
lias 'laiəs
liassic lai'æsik
Libanus 'libənəs
libat|e, -es, -ing, -ed lai'beit, -s, -iŋ, -id

libation, -s lai'beiʃən [li'b-], -z
lib|el, -els, -elling, -elled, -eller/s
'laib|əl, -əlz, -ļiŋ [-əliŋ], -əld, -ļə*/z
[-ələ*/z]
libellous, -ly 'laib|əs [-bələs], -li
Liber 'laibə*
liber|al (s. adj.), -als, -ally 'libər|əl, -əlz,
-əli
liberalism 'libərəlizəm
liberality ,libə'ræliti
liberaliz|e [-is|e], -es, -ing, -ed 'libərəl-
aiz, -iz, -iŋ, -d
liberat|e, -es, -ing, -ed, -or/s 'libəreit,
-s, -iŋ, -id, -ə*/z
liberation ,libə'reiʃən
Liberia, -n/s lai'biəriə, -n/z
libertin|age, -ism 'libətin|idʒ, -izəm
libertine, -s 'libə(:)tain [-ti:n, -tin], -z
Liberton 'libətn
libert|y (L.), -ies 'libət|i, -iz
libidinous, -ly, -ness li'bidinəs, -li, -nis
libido li'bi:dəu [-'baid-, 'libidəu]
libr|a (pound), -ae 'laibr|ə, -i: ['li:br|ə,
-ei, -ai]
Libra (constellation) 'laibrə ['li:b-, 'lib-]
librarian, -s; -ship lai'brɛəriən, -z; -ʃip
librar|y, -ies 'laibrər|i [-bŗr|i], -iz
libration, -s lai'breiʃən, -z
librettist, -s li'bretist, -s
librett|o, -os, -i li'bret|əu, -əuz, -i(:)
Libya, -n/s 'libiə [-bjə], -n/z
lice (plur. of louse) lais
licence, -s, -d 'laisəns, -iz, -t
licens|e, -es, -ing, -ed, -er/s 'laisəns, -iz,
-iŋ, -t, -ə*/z
licensee, -s ,laisən'si: ['laisən's-], -z
licentiate, -s lai'senʃiit [li's-, -ʃjit, -ʃiət,
-ʃjət], -s
licentious, -ly, -ness lai'senʃəs, -li, -nis
lichen, -s, -ed 'laikən [-kin, -ken,
'litʃin], -z, -d
lichenous 'laikinəs ['litʃ-]
Lichfield 'litʃfi:ld
lichgate, -s 'litʃgeit, -s
Licini|an, -us lai'sinï|ən [li's-, nj|-], -əs
licit 'lisit
lick (s. v.) (L.), -s, -ing/s, -ed, -er/s lik,
-s, -iŋ/z, -t, -ə*/z
licorice 'likəris
lictor, -s 'liktə* [-tɔ:*], -z
lid, -s lid, -z
Liddell 'lidl, li'del
Lidd|esdale, -on 'lid|zdeil, -n
Lidell li'del
Lido, -s 'li:dəu, -z
lie (s. v.) (falsehood, etc.), lies, lying/ly,
lied, liar/s lai, laiz, 'laiiŋ/li, laid,
'lai-ə*/z ['laiə*/z]

lie (v.) (recline, etc.), lies, lying, lay, lain,
lier/s lai, laiz, 'laiiŋ, lei, lein, 'lai-ə*/z
lie-abed, -s 'lai-əbed, -z
Liebig 'li:big
lief, -er li:f, -ə*
liege, -s li:dʒ, -iz
Liége li'eiʒ (ljɛ:ʒ)   [-men [-mən]
liege|man, -men 'li:dʒmæn [-mən],
lien, -s liən ['li:ən], -z
lieu lju: [lu:]
lieutenanc|y, -ies (army) lef'tenəns|i
[ləf-], (navy) le'tenəns|i [lə't-, lef't-,
ləf't-], -iz
    Note.—Until recently the usual pro-
    nunciation in the navy was lu:'tenən-
    or 'lu:tnən-. These forms appear to
    be now nearly obsolete in British
    English.
lieutenant, -s (army) lef'tenənt [ləf-],
(navy) le'tenənt [lə't-, lef't-, ləf't-], -s
(see note under lieutenancy)
lieutenant-colonel, -s lef'tenənt'kə:nl
[ləf-], -z
lieutenant-commander, -s le'tenənt-
kə'mɑ:ndə* [lə't-, lef't-, ləf't-], -z (see
note under lieutenancy)
lieutenant-general, -s lef'tenənt-
'dʒenərəl [ləf-], -z
lieutenant-governor, -s lef'tenənt-
'gʌvənə* [ləf-, -vŋə*, -vnə*], -z
li|fe, -ves lai|f, -vz
life-assurance, -s 'laif-ə,ʃuərəns [-,ʃɔər-,
-,ʃɔ:r-, -,ʃə:r-], -iz
life|-belt/s, -blood 'laif|belt/s, -blʌd
life-boat, -s 'laifbəut, -s
life-buoy, -s 'laifbɔi, -z
life-estate, -s 'laif-i'steit ['laif-i,steit], -s
life-giving 'laif,giviŋ
life-guard, -s 'laifgɑ:d, -z
life-interest, -s 'laif'intrist [-'intərest], -s
life-jacket, -s 'laif,dʒækit, -s
lifeless, -ly, -ness 'laif-lis, -li, -nis
lifelike 'laif-laik
life-line, -s 'laif-lain, -z
lifelong 'laif-lɔŋ
life-preserver, -s 'laifpri,zə:və*, -z
life-rent, -s 'laif-rent, -s
life-saving 'laif,seiviŋ
life-sentence, -s 'laif,sentəns, -iz
life-size 'laif'saiz [also '--, -'- according
to sentence-stress]
life-tenan|cy, -cies, -t/s 'laif'tenən|si,
-siz, -t/s
lifetime, -s 'laiftaim, -z
life-work, -s 'laif'wə:k ['--], -s
Liff|ey, -ord 'lif|i, -əd
lift (s. v.), -s, -ing, -ed, -er/s lift, -s, -iŋ,
-id, -ə*/z

lift-boy, -s 'liftbɔi, -z
lift|-man, -men 'lift|mæn, -men
ligament, -s 'ligəmənt, -s
ligament|al, -ous ‚ligə'ment|l, -əs
ligature, -s, -d 'ligətʃuə* [-tʃə*, -tjuə*],
-z, -d
liger, -s 'laigə*, -z
Ligertwood 'lidʒə(:)t-wud
light (s. adj. v.), -s; -er, -est, -ly, -ness;
-ing, -ed, lit lait, -s; -ə*, -ist, -li, -nis;
-iŋ, -id, lit
light|en, -ens, -ening, -ened 'lait|n, -nz,
-ŋiŋ [-niŋ], -nd
lighter, -s 'laitə*, -z
lighterage 'laitəridʒ
lighter|man, -men 'laitə|mən, -mən
light-fingered 'lait‚fiŋgəd ['-'--]
lightfoot (L.) 'laitfut
light-handed 'lait‚hændid ['-'--]
light-headed, -ly, -ness 'lait'hedid [also
'-‚-- when attributive], -li, -nis
light-hearted, -ly, -ness 'lait'hɑːtid
[also '-‚-- when attributive], -li, -nis
light-horse|man, -men 'lait'hɔːs|mən,
-mən
lighthou|se, -ses 'laithau|s, -ziz
lighthousekeeper, -s 'laithaus‚kiːpə*, -z
lightminded, -ly, -ness 'lait'maindid
[also '-‚-- when attributive], -li, -nis
lightning, -s 'laitniŋ, -z
lightning-conductor, -s 'laitniŋ-kən-
‚dʌktə*, -z
lightship, -s 'lait-ʃip, -s
lightsome, -ly, -ness 'laitsəm, -li, -nis
light-spirited 'lait'spiritid
light-wave, -s 'lait-weiv, -z
light-weight, -s 'lait-weit, -s
ligneous 'ligniəs [-njəs]
lignite 'lignait
lignum 'lignəm
Liguria, -n/s li'gjuəriə [-'gjɔər-,
-'gjɔːr-], -n/z
Li Hung Chang 'liːhuŋ'tʃæŋ [old-
fashioned 'laihʌŋ'tʃæŋ]
likable 'laikəbl
lik|e (s. adj. v.), -es, -ing, -ed laik, -s,
-iŋ, -t
likel|y, -ier, -iest, -iness, -ihood 'laikl|i,
-iə* [-jə*], -iist [-jist], -inis, -ihud
likeminded 'laik'maindid ['-‚--]
lik|en, -ens, -ening, -ened 'laik|ən,
-ənz, -ŋiŋ [-niŋ, -əniŋ], -ənd
likeness, -es 'laiknis, -iz
likewise 'laik-waiz
liking, -s 'laikiŋ, -z
lilac, -s 'lailək, -s
liliaceous ‚lili'eiʃəs
Lilia|n, -s 'liliə|n [-ljə-], -s

Lilith 'liliθ
Lill|a, -ey 'lil|ə, -i
Lilliput 'lilipʌt [-put, -pət]
lilliputian (L.), -s ‚lili'pjuːʃjən [-ʃïən,
-ʃən], -z
Lilly, -white 'lili, -wait [-hwait]
lilt (s. v.), -s, -ing, -ed lilt, -s, -iŋ, -id
lil|y (L.), -ies 'lil|i, -iz
lily-white 'lili'wait [-i'hw-, '--- when
attributive]
Lima (in Peru) 'liːmə [old-fashioned
'laimə], (in U.S.A.) 'laimə
limb, -s, -ed lim, -z, -d
limber (s. adj.), -s 'limbə*, -z
limbo (L.) 'limbəu
lim|e (s. v.), -es, -ing, -ed laim, -z, -iŋ, -d
Limehouse 'laimhaus
lime-juice 'laimdʒuːs
limekiln, -s 'laimkiln [-kil], -z
Note.—The pronunciation -kil appears
to be used only by those concerned
with the working of kilns.
lime-light, -s 'laimlait, -s
limen 'laimen
limerick (L.), -s 'limərik, -s
lime|stone, -tree/s 'laim|stəun, -triː/z
limewash (s. v.), -es, -ing, -ed 'laimwɔʃ,
-iz, -iŋ, -t
limewater 'laim‚wɔːtə*
liminal 'liminl
limit (s. v.), -s, -ing, -ed/ness; -able
'limit, -s, -iŋ, -id/nis; -əbl
limitation, -s ‚limi'teiʃən, -z
limitless 'limitlis
limitrophe 'limitrəuf
limn, -s, -ing, -ed, -er/s lim, -z, -iŋ
[-niŋ], -d, -nə*/z
Limoges li'məuʒ (limoːʒ)
limousine, -s 'limu(ː)ziːn [-məz-], -z
limp (s. adj. v.), -s; -er, -est, -ly, -ness;
-ing/ly, -ed limp, -s; -ə*, -ist, -li,
-nis; -iŋ/li, -t [limt]
limpet, -s 'limpit, -s
limpid, -est, -ly, -ness 'limpid, -ist, -li,
-nis
limpidity lim'piditi
Limpopo lim'pəupəu
limy 'laimi
Linacre 'linəkə*
linage, -s 'lainidʒ, -iz
linchpin, -s 'lintʃpin, -z
Lincoln, -shire 'liŋkən, -ʃiə* [-ʃə*]
Lincs. liŋks
Lind lind
Lindbergh 'lindbəːg
linden (L.), -s 'lindən, -z
Lindisfarne 'lindisfɑːn
Lindley 'lindli

Lindon 'lindən
Lind|say, -sey 'lind|zi, -zi
lin|e (s. v.) (L.), -es, -ing, -ed lain, -z, -iŋ, -d
lineage, -s 'liniidʒ [-njidʒ], -iz
lineal, -ly 'liniəl [-njəl], -i
lineament, -s 'liniəmənt [-njə-], -s
linear, -ly 'liniə [-njə*], -li
lineation, -s ‚lini'eiʃən, -z
line-engraving, -s 'lainin‚greiviŋ, -z
linen, -s 'linin, -z
linen-draper, -s, -y 'linin‚dreipə*, -z, -ri
liner, -s 'lainə*, -z
lines|man, -men 'lainz|mən, -mən [-men]
ling (L.), -s liŋ, -z
Ling|ay, -en 'liŋg|i, -ən
ling|er, -ers, -ering/ly, -ered, -erer/s 'liŋg|ə*, -əz, -əriŋ/li, -əd, -ərə*/z
lingerie 'læːnʒəri(ː) ['læŋʒ-] (lɛ̃ʒri)
lingo, -s 'liŋgəu, -z
lingua franca 'liŋgwə'fræŋkə
lingu|al (s. adj.), -als, -ally 'liŋgw|əl, -əlz, -əli
linguaphone (L.) 'liŋgwəfəun
linguist, -s 'liŋgwist, -s
linguistic, -s, -al, -ally liŋ'gwistik, -s, -əl, -əli
linguistician, -s ‚liŋgwis'tiʃən, -z
linguo-dental 'liŋgwəu'dentl
liniment, -s 'linimənt, -s
lining (s.), -s 'lainiŋ, -z
link (s. v.), -s, -ing, -ed liŋk, -s, -iŋ, -t [liŋt]
Linklater 'liŋk‚leitə*
links (s.) liŋks
Linley 'linli
Linlithgow lin'liθgəu
Linlithgowshire lin'liθgəuʃiə* [-ʃə*]
Linnae|an [-ne|-], -us li'ni(ː)|ən, -əs
linnet (L.), -s 'linit, -s
lino, -s 'lainəu, -z
lino-cut, -s 'lainəukʌt, -s
linoleum, -s li'nəuljəm [lai'n-, -liəm], -z
linotype, -s 'lainəutaip, -s
linseed, -oil 'linsiːd, -'ɔil
linsey, -woolsey 'linzi, -'wulzi
lint lint
lintel, -s 'lintl, -z
Linthwaite 'linθwət
Lint|on, -ot(t) 'lint|ən, -ot
lion, -s; -ess/es 'laiən, -z; -is/iz
Lionel 'laiənl
Lion-heart 'laiənhɑːt
lion-hearted 'laiən‚hɑːtid
lion-hunter, -s 'laiən‚hʌntə*, -z
lioniz|e [-is|e], -es, -ing, -ed 'laiənaiz, -iz, -iŋ, -d

lion-like 'laiənlaik
lion-tamer, -s 'laiən‚teimə*, -z
lip (s. v.), -s, -ping, -ped lip, -s, -iŋ, -t
Lipari 'lipəri ('liːpari)
lipogram, -s 'lipəugræm, -z
Lippincott 'lipiŋkət [-kɔt]
lip-reading 'lip‚riːdiŋ
lip-salve, -s 'lipsɑːv [rarely -sælv], -z
Lipscomb(e) 'lipskəm
lip-service 'lip‚səːvis
lip-stick, -s 'lip-stik, -s
Lipton 'liptən
liquefaction ‚likwi'fækʃən
lique|fy, -fies, -fying, -fied, -fier/s; -fiable 'likwi|fai, -faiz, -faiiŋ, -faid, -faiə*/z; -faiəbl
liqueur, -s; -glass/es li'kjuə* [-'kjɔə*, -'kjɔː*, -'kjə:*], -z; -glɑːs/iz
liquid (s. adj.), -s, -est, -ly, -ness 'likwid, -z, -ist, -li, -nis
liquidat|e, -es, -ing, -ed, -or/s 'likwideit, -s, -iŋ, -id, -ə*/z
liquidation, -s ‚likwi'deiʃən, -z
liquidity li'kwiditi
liquor (s. v.), -s, -ing, -ed 'likə*, -z, -riŋ, -d
liquorice 'likəris
lir|a, -as, -e 'liər|ə, -əz, -i
Lisa 'liːzə, 'laizə
Lisb|et, -eth 'lizb|it [-et], -əθ [-eθ, -iθ]
Lis|bon, -burn 'liz|bən, -bəːn
Liskeard lis'kɑːd
lisle (thread) lail
Lisle lail, liːl
Note.—Baron Lisle pronounces lail.
Lismore (in Scotland and Ireland) liz'mɔː* [-'mɔə*], (in Australia) 'lizmɔː* [-mɔə*]
lisp (s. v.), -s, -ing/ly, -ed, -er/s lisp, -s, -iŋ/li, -t, -ə*/z
lissome, -ness 'lisəm, -nis
Lisson 'lisn
list (s. v.), -s, -ing, -ed list, -s, -iŋ, -id
list|en, -ens, -ening, -ened, -ener/s 'lis|n, -nz, -niŋ [-niŋ], -nd, -nə*/z [-nə*/z]
Lister 'listə*
listerine 'listəriːn
listless, -ly, -ness 'listlis, -li, -nis
Liston 'listən
Listowel lis'təuəl
Liszt list
lit (from light) lit
litan|y, -ies 'litən|i [-tn̩|i], -iz
Litchfield 'litʃfiːld
literacy 'litərəsi
liter|al, -ally, -alness 'litər|əl, -əli, -əlnis
literali|sm, -st/s 'litərəli|zəm, -st/s

literality ˌlitəˈræliti
literar|y, -ily, -iness 'litərər|i [-tr̩r|i], -ili, -inis
literate (s. adj.), -s 'litərit, -s
literati ˌlitəˈrɑːti: [old-fashioned -'reitai]
literatim ˌlitəˈrɑːtim [-'reitim]
literature, -s 'litəritʃə* [-rətʃə*, -tjuə*], -z
litharge 'liθɑːdʒ
lithe, -r, -st, -ly, -ness laið, -ə*, -ist, -li, -nis
Litheby 'liðibi [-ðəb-]
lither (supple) 'liðə*
lithesome, -ness 'laiðsəm, -nis
Lithgow 'liθgəu
lithia 'liθiə [-θjə]
lithic 'liθik
lithium 'liθiəm [-θjəm]
litho, -s 'laiθəu, -z
lithochromatic, -s ˌliθəukrəu'mætik, -s
lithograph (s. v.), -s, -ing, -ed 'liθəu-grɑːf [-græf], -s, -iŋ, -t
Note.—In printers' usage 'laiθ-. So also with derived words (litho-grapher, etc.).
lithographer, -s li'θɔgrəfə*, -z
lithographic, -al, -ally ˌliθəu'græfik, -əl, -əli
lithography li'θɔgrəfi
lithoprint (s. v.), -s, -ing, -ed 'liθəu-print, -s, -iŋ, -id
lithosphere, -s 'liθəusfiə*, -z
lithotyp|e (s. v.), -es, -ing, -ed, -er/s 'liθəutaip, -s, -iŋ, -t, -ə*/z
Lithuania, -n/s ˌliθjuː(ː)'einjə [-θu(ː)-, -nïə], -n/z
litigant, -s 'litigənt, -s
litigat|e, -es, -ing, -ed 'litigeit, -s, -iŋ, -id
litigation, -s ˌliti'geiʃən, -z
litigious, -ly, -ness li'tidʒəs, -li, -nis
litmus 'litməs
litotes 'laitəuti:z
litre, -s 'li:tə*, -z
Littell li'tel
litter (s. v.), -s, -ing, -ed 'litə*, -z, -riŋ, -d
litt|le (L.), -ler, -lest, -leness 'lit|l, -lə*, -list, -lnis
Littlechild 'litl-tʃaild
little-englander, -s 'litl̩'iŋgləndə* [rarely -'eŋg-], -z
little-go, -es 'litlgəu, -z
Littlehampton 'litl̩hæmp͟tən ['--'--]
Littlejohn 'litldʒɔn
Littler 'litlə*
Littleton 'litltən
Litton 'litn
littoral, -s 'litərəl, -z

liturgic, -al, -ally li'tə:dʒik, -əl, -əli
liturgist, -s 'litə(ː)dʒist, -s
liturg|y, -ies 'litə(ː)dʒ|i, -iz
lituus, -es 'litjŭəs [-tjwəs], -iz
livable 'livəbl
live (adj.) laiv
liv|e (v.), -es, -ing, -ed, -er/s liv, -z, -iŋ, -d, -ə*/z
live-circuit, -s 'laiv'sə:kit, -s
livelihood, -s 'laivlihud, -z
livelong 'livlɔŋ ['laiv-]
livel|y, -ier, -iest, -iness 'laivl|i, -iə* [-jə*], -iist [-jist], -inis
liv|en, -ens, -ening, -ened 'laiv|n [-ən], -nz [-ənz], -n̩iŋ [-niŋ, -əniŋ], -nd [-ənd]
Livens 'livənz
liver, -s, -ish 'livə*, -z, -riʃ
live-rail, -s 'laiv'reil, -z
Livermore 'livəmɔ:* [-mɔə*]
Liverpool 'livəpu:l
Liverpudlian (s. adj.), -s ˌlivə'pʌdliən [-ljən], -z
liver|y, -ies, -ied 'livər|i, -iz, -id
livery|man, -men 'livəri|mən, -mən [-men]
livery-stable, -s 'livəri,steibl, -z
lives (plur. of life) laivz, (from live v.) livz
Livesey 'livsi, 'livzi
live-stock 'laivstɔk
Livia 'livïə [-vjə]
livid, -est, -ly, -ness 'livid, -ist, -li, -nis
lividity li'viditi
living (s.), -s 'liviŋ, -z
living-room, -s 'liviŋrum [-ru:m], -z
living-space 'liviŋ-speis
Livingston(e) 'liviŋstən
Livonia, -n/s li'vəunjə [-nïə], -n/z
Livy 'livi
lixiviat|e, -es, -ing, -ed lik'sivieit, -s, [-iŋ, -id
Liza 'laizə
lizard (L.), -s 'lizəd, -z
Lizzie 'lizi
llama (L.), -s 'lɑ:mə, -z
Llanberis læn'beris [θlæn-] (Welsh ɫan'beris)
Llandaff 'lændəf (Welsh ɫan'da:v)
Llandilo læn'dailəu [θlæn-] (Welsh ɫan'dəilo)
Llandovery læn'dʌvəri [θlæn-] (Welsh ɫan'dəvri)
Llandrindod Wells læn'drindɔd'welz [θlæn-] (Welsh ɫan'drindɔd'wels)
Llandudno læn'didnəu [θlæn-, -'dʌd-] (Welsh ɫan'didno)
Llanelly læ'neθli [lə'n-, θlæ'n-, θlə'n-] (Welsh ɫan'eɬi)

Llanfair 'lænfɛə* ['θlæn-, -nvaiə*]
(Welsh 'ḷanvair)
Llanfairfechan ˌlænfɛə'fekən [ˌθlæn-,
-nvaiə've-, -exən] (Welsh ḷanvair-
'vexan)
Llangattock læn'gætək [θlæn-] (Welsh
ḷan'gatok)
Llangollen læn'gɔθlən [θlæn-, -'gɔθlen]
(Welsh ḷan'goḷen)
Llanrwst læn'ru:st [θlæn-] (Welsh
ḷan'ru:st)
Llanuwchllyn læ'nju:klin [θlæ'n-,
-u:xlin] (Welsh ḷan'iuxḷin)
Llewellyn (English name) lu(:)'elin,
(Welsh name) lu(:)'elin [θlu(:)-]
(Welsh ḷe'welin)
Llewelyn lu(:)'elin [θlu(:)-] (Welsh
'ḷwelin, ḷe'welin)
Lloyd ləid
Llywelyn lə'welin [θlə-] (Welsh ḷə'welin)
lo ləu
load (s. v.), -s, -ing, -ed ləud, -z, -iŋ, -id
load-shedding 'ləudˌʃediŋ
loadstone, -s 'ləudstəun, -z
loa|f (s.), -ves ləu|f, -vz
loaf (v.), -s, -ing, -ed, -er/s ləuf, -s, -iŋ,
-t, -ə*/z
loaf-sugar 'ləufˌʃugə*
loam ləum
loam|y, -ier, -iest, -iness 'ləum|i, -iə*
[-jə*], -iist [-jist], -inis
loan (s. v.), -s, -ing, -ed ləun, -z, -iŋ, -d
loan-office, -s 'ləunˌɔfis, -iz
loan-collection, -s 'ləun-kəˌlekʃən, -z
loanword, -s 'ləun-wə:d, -z
loath (adj.), -ness ləuθ, -nis
loath|e (v.), -es, -ing/ly, -ed ləuð, -z,
-iŋ/li, -d
loathl|y, -iness 'ləuðl|i, -inis
loathsome, -ly, -ness 'ləuðsəm ['ləuθs-],
-li, -nis
loaves (plur. of loaf) ləuvz
lob (s. v.) (L.), -s, -bing, -bed, -ber/s lɔb,
-z, -iŋ, -d, -ə*/z
lobb|y (s. v.), -ies, -ying, -ied 'lɔb|i, -iz,
-iiŋ [-jiŋ], -id
lobe, -s, -d ləub, -z, -d
lobelia, -s ləu'bi:ljə [-liə], -z
Lobengula ˌləubən'gju:lə [-bəŋ'g-,
-ben'g-, -beŋ'g-, -'gu:lə]
lobotomy ləu'bɔtəmi
lobster, -s 'lɔbstə*, -z
lobular 'lɔbjulə*
lobule, -s 'lɔbju:l, -z
loc|al, -als, -ally 'ləuk|əl, -əlz, -əli [-ḷi]
locale, -s ləu'kɑ:l, -z
locali|sm, -st/s 'ləukəli|zəm [-kḷi-], -st/s
localit|y, -ies ləu'kælit|i, -iz

localization [-isa-] ˌləukəlai'zeiʃən
[-kḷai'z-, -kəli'z-, -kḷi'z-]
localiz|e [-is|e], -es, -ing, -ed 'ləukəlaiz
[-kḷaiz], -iz, -iŋ, -d
Locarno ləu'kɑ:nəu [lɔ'k-] (lo'karno)
locat|e, -es, -ing, -ed ləu'keit, -s, -iŋ, -id
location, -s ləu'keiʃən, -z
locative (s. adj.), -s 'lɔkətiv, -z
loc. cit. 'lɔk'sit ['lɔkəusi'tɑ:təu, old-
fashioned 'ləukəusi'teitəu]
loch (L.), -s lɔk [lɔx], -s
Lochaber lɔ'kɑ:bə* [-'kæb-, lɔ'x-]
Lochhead 'lɔkhed [in Scotland lɔx'hɛd]
Lochiel lɔ'ki:l [lɔ'xi:l]
Lochinvar ˌlɔkin'vɑ:* [ˌlɔxin-]
Lochleven lɔk'li:vən [lɔx-]
Lochnagar ˌlɔknə'gɑ:* [ˌlɔxn-]
lock (s. v.) (L.), -s, -ing, -ed lɔk, -s, -iŋ, -t
Locke lɔk
locker (L.), -s 'lɔkə*, -z
Lockerbie 'lɔkə(:)bi
locket, -s 'lɔkit, -s
lockgate, -s 'lɔk'geit ['--], -s
Lockhart 'lɔkət, 'lɔkhɑ:t
    Note.—The Bruce-Lockhart family
    pronounce 'lɔkət (or in the Scottish
    manner 'lɔkərt).
Lockie 'lɔki
lock-jaw 'lɔkdʒɔ:
lock-keeper, -s 'lɔkˌki:pə*, -z
lockout, -s 'lɔkaut ['-'-, also -'- when
preceded by a stress], -s
Locksley 'lɔksli
locksmith, -s 'lɔk-smiθ, -s
lockstitch, -es 'lɔk-stitʃ, -iz
lock-up, -s 'lɔkʌp, -s
Lock|wood, -yer 'lɔk|wud, -jə*
locomotion ˌləukə'məuʃən
locomotive (s. adj.), -s 'ləukəˌməutiv
[ˌləukə'm-], -z
locomotor (s.), -s 'ləukəˌməutə*, -z
locomotor (adj.) ˌləukə'məutə* ['--ˌ--]
locoum, -s 'ləukəm [-kum], -z
Locria, -n/s 'ləukriə, -n/z
Locris 'ləukris
locum, -s 'ləukəm, -z
locum-tenens 'ləukəm'ti:nenz [-'ten-]
locus, loci 'ləukəs ['lɔkəs], 'ləusai
['ləukai, 'lɔki:]
locust, -s 'ləukəst, -s
locution, -s ləu'kju:ʃən [lɔ'k-], -z
locutor|y, -ies 'lɔkjutə|ri, -iz
lode, -s; -star/s, -stone/s ləud, -z;
-stɑ:*/z, -stəun/z
lodg|e (s. v.) (L.), -es, -ing/s, -ed, -er/s
lɔdʒ, -iz, -iŋ/z, -d, -ə*/z
lodg(e)ment, -s 'lɔdʒmənt, -s
lodginghou|se, -ses 'lɔdʒiŋhau|s, -ziz

Lodore ləu'dɔ:* [-'dɔə*]
Lodovico ˌlɔdəu'vi:kəu
Lodowick 'lɔdəwik [-dəuik]
Loe lu:
Loeb lə:b [ləub]
  Note.—W. Heinemann Ltd., the publishers of the Loeb Classical Library,
  prefer lə:b.
loess 'ləuis [lə:s]
Loewe (English surname) 'ləui
Lofoten ləu'fəutən ['ləuˌfəutən]
loft (s. v.), -s, -ing, -ed, -er/s lɔft
  [lɔ:ft], -s, -iŋ, -id, -ə*/z
Lofthouse 'lɔftəs [-thaus]
Loftus 'lɔftəs
loft|y, -ier, -iest, -ily, -iness 'lɔft|i
  ['lɔ:f-] -ïə* [-jə*], -iist [-jist], -ili,
  -inis
log, -s lɔg, -z
Logan (personal name) 'ləugən
logan (L.) (rocking-stone), -s 'lɔgən, -z
loganberr|y, -ies 'ləugənbər|i [-ˌber-], -iz
logarithm, -s 'lɔgəriðəm [-iθəm], -z
logarithmic, -al, -ally ˌlɔgə'riðmik
  [-iθm-], -əl, -əli
log-book, -s 'lɔgbuk, -s
log-cabin, -s 'lɔgˌkæbin, -z
loggerhead, -s 'lɔgəhed, -z
loggia, -s 'lɔdʒə ['ləu-, -dʒïə, -dʒjə], -z
logging 'lɔgiŋ
Logia 'lɔgïə
logic, -al, -ally 'lɔdʒik, -əl, -əli
logician, -s ləu'dʒiʃən [lɔ'dʒ-], -z
Logie 'ləugi
logistic, -al, -s ləu'dʒistik [lɔ'dʒ-], -əl, -s
logogram, -s 'lɔgəugræm, -z
logograph, -s 'lɔgəugrɑ:f [-græf], -s
logomach|ist/s, -y, -ies lɔ'gɔmək|ist/s,
  -i, -iz
logopaedic, -s ˌlɔgəu'pi:dik ['--'--], -s
Log|os, -oi 'lɔg|ɔs, -ɔi
logotype, -s 'lɔgəutaip, -s
log-roll, -s, -ing, -ed, -er/s 'lɔg-rəul, -z,
  -iŋ, -d, -ə*/z
Logue ləug
log-wood 'lɔgwud
Lohengrin 'ləuingrin ['ləuən-, -ŋg-]
  ('lo:əngri:n)
loin, -s lɔin, -z
loin|-cloth, -cloths 'lɔin|klɔθ [-klɔ:θ],
  -klɔθs [-klɔ:ðz, -klɔ:θs]
Lois 'ləuis
loit|er, -ers, -ering, -ered, -erer/s
  'lɔit|ə*, -əz, -əriŋ, -əd, -ərə*/z
loll, -s, -ing, -ed, -er/s lɔl, -z, -iŋ, -d,
  -ə*/z
Lollard, -s 'lɔləd, -z
lollipop, -s 'lɔlipɔp, -s

lollop, -s, -ing, -ed 'lɔləp, -s, -iŋ, -t
Lomax 'ləumæks [-məks]
Lombard, -s 'lɔmbəd [-bɑ:d, old-
  fashioned 'lʌmbəd], -z
Lombardic lɔm'bɑ:dik
Lombardy 'lɔmbədi [old-fashioned
  'lʌm-]
Lomond 'ləumənd
Londesborough 'lɔnzbərə
London, -er/s, -ism/s 'lʌndən, -ə*/z,
  -izəm/z
Londonderry (place) ˌlʌndən'deri
  ['--'--, when attributive '--ˌ--]
Londonderry (Lord) 'lʌndəndəri [-deri]
lone ləun
lonel|y, -ier, -iest, -iness 'ləunl|i, -ïə*
  [-jə*], -iist [-jist], -inis
lonesome, -ly, -ness 'ləunsəm, -li, -nis
long (s. adj.) (L.), -s, -er, -est lɔŋ, -z,
  -gə*, -gist
long (v.), -s, -ing/ly, -ed, -er/s lɔŋ, -z,
  -iŋ/li, -d, -ə*/z
longboat, -s 'lɔŋbəut, -s
long-bow (L.), -s 'lɔŋbəu, -z
long-drawn 'lɔŋ'drɔ:n [also '-- when
  attributive]
long-drawn-out 'lɔŋdrɔ:n'aut
longeron, -s 'lɔndʒərən, -z
longeval lɔn'dʒi:vəl
longevity lɔn'dʒeviti
Longfellow 'lɔŋˌfeləu
Longford 'lɔŋfəd
longhand 'lɔŋhænd
long-headed 'lɔŋ'hedid ['-ˌ--, esp. when
  attributive]
longing (s.), -s 'lɔŋiŋ, -z
Longinus lɔn'dʒainəs [lɔŋ'gi:nəs]
longish 'lɔŋiʃ
longitude, -s 'lɔndʒitju:d [-ŋgi-], -z
longitudin|al, -ally ˌlɔndʒi'tju:din|l
  [-ŋgi-], -əli [-|i]
Longland 'lɔŋlənd
Longleat 'lɔŋli:t
long-leg|ged, -s 'lɔŋleg|d [-'legid], -z
long-lived 'lɔŋ'livd [-'laivd, also '--
  when attributive]
Longman, -s 'lɔŋmən, -z
long-off, -s 'lɔŋ'ɔf [-'ɔ:f], -s
long-on, -s 'lɔŋ'ɔn, -s
long-range 'lɔŋ'reindʒ [also '-- when
  attributive]
Longridge 'lɔŋgridʒ
Long|sdon, -shanks 'lɔŋ|zdən, -ʃæŋks
long-shore, -man, -men 'lɔŋʃɔ:* [-ʃɔə*],
  -mən, -mən [-men]
long-sighted, -ness 'lɔŋ'saitid ['lɔŋˌs-],
  -nis
Longstaff 'lɔŋ-stɑ:f

long-stop, -s 'lɔŋ-stɔp, -s
long-suffering 'lɔŋ'sʌfərɪŋ ['-ˌ---]
long-tailed 'lɔŋ-teild
Longton 'lɔŋtən
Longus 'lɔŋgəs
long|ways, -wise 'lɔŋ|weiz, -waiz
long-winded, -ness 'lɔŋ'windid, -nis
Lonsdale 'lɔnzdeil
loo (s. v.) (L.), -es, -ing, -ed luː, -z, -ɪŋ, -d
loob|y, -ies 'luːb|i, -iz
Looe luː
loofah, -s 'luːfɑ: [-fə], -z
look (s. v.), -s, -ing, -ed, -er/s luk, -s, -ɪŋ, -t, -ə*/z
looker - on,   lookers - on   'lukər'ɔn, 'lukəz'ɔn
looking-glass, -es 'lukɪŋglɑːs, -iz
look-out 'luk'aut [luk'aut when pre- ceded by a stress; in nautical usage 'lukaut]
loom, -s, -ing, -ed luːm, -z, -ɪŋ, -d
loon, -s luːn, -z
loon|y, -ies 'luːn|i, -iz
loop (s. v.), -s, -ing, -ed luːp, -s, -ɪŋ, -t
loophole, -s, -d 'luːphəul, -z, -d
Loos (battlefield) ləus [luːs]
loos|e (s. adj. v.), -es; -er, -est, -ely, -eness; -ing, -ed luːs, -iz; -ə*, -ist, -li, -nis; -ɪŋ, -t
loos|en, -ens, -ening, -ened 'luːs|n, -nz, -nɪŋ [-nɪŋ], -nd
loot (s. v.), -s, -ing, -ed, -er/s luːt, -s, -ɪŋ, -id, -ə*/z
lop (s. v.), -s, -ping, -ped, -per/s lɔp, -s, -ɪŋ, -t, -ə*/z
lop|e (s. v.), -es, -ing, -ed ləup, -s, -ɪŋ, -t
lop-eared 'lɔpiəd
Lopez 'ləupez
lopping (s.), -s 'lɔpɪŋ, -z
lop-sided, -ness 'lɔp'saidid [lɔp's-], -nis
loquacious, -ly, -ness ləu'kweiʃəs [lɔ'k-], -li, -nis
loquacity ləu'kwæsiti [lɔ'k-]
lor lɔː*
Loraine lɔ'rein [lə'r-]
Loram 'lɔːrəm
lorcha, -s 'lɔːtʃə, -z
lord (s. v.) (L.), -s, -ing, -ed lɔːd, -z, -ɪŋ, -id
    Note.—Lawyers addressing a judge in court sometimes pronounce my lord as mi'lʌd instead of the normal mi'lɔːd.
lordling, -s 'lɔːdlɪŋ, -z
lordl|y, -ier, -iest, -iness 'lɔːdl|i, -iə* [-jə*], -iist [-jist], -inis
Lord's-day, -s 'lɔːdz'dei ['--], -z
lordship (L.), -s 'lɔːdʃip, -s

lore lɔː* [lɔə*]
Loreburn 'lɔːbəːn ['lɔəb-]
Lorelei 'lɔːrəlai ['lɔr-] ('lɔːrəlai)
Lorenzo lɔ'renzəu [lə'r-]
Loretto (school) lə'retəu [lɔ'r-]
lorgnette, -s lɔː'njet (lɔrɲɛt), -s
Lorie 'lɔri
lorimer (L.), -s 'lɔrimə*, -z
loris, -es 'lɔːris, -iz
lorn lɔːn
Lorna 'lɔːnə
Lorne lɔːn
Lorraine lɔ'rein [lə'r-]
lorr|y, -ies 'lɔr|i, -iz
lor|y, -ies 'lɔːr|i, -iz
losable 'luːzəbl
Los Angeles lɔs'ændʒiliːz [-'æŋgi-, -liz, -lis]
los|e, -es, -ing, lost, loser/s luːz, -iz, -ɪŋ, lɔst [lɔːst], 'luːzə*/z
loss, -es lɔs [lɔːs], -iz
lost (from lose) lɔst [lɔːst]
Lostwithiel lɔst'wiθiəl [-θjəl]
lot (s. v.) (L.), -s, -ting, -ted lɔt, -s, -ɪŋ, -id
loth ləuθ
Lothair ləu'θɛə*
Lothario ləu'θɑːriəu [-'θɛər-]
Lothbury 'ləuθbəri ['lɔθ-]
Lothian 'ləuðjən [-ðiən]
lotion, -s 'ləuʃən, -z
lotter|y, -ies 'lɔtər|i, -iz
Lottie 'lɔti
lotto 'lɔtəu
lotus, -es; -eater/s 'ləutəs, -iz; -ˌiːtə*/z
Lou luː
loud, -er, -est, -ly, -ness laud, -ə*, -ist, -li, -nis
Loud|on, -oun 'laud|n, -n
loud-speaker, -s 'laud'spiːkə*, -z
Loudwater 'laud,wɔːtə*
lough (lake), -s lɔk [lɔx], -s
Lough (surname) lʌf
Loughborough 'lʌfbərə
Loughlin 'lɔklin
Loughman 'lʌfmən
Loughrea lɔk'rei [lɔx'r-]
Loughton 'lautn
Louie 'luː(ː)i
louis 'luː(ː)i, (plur.) -z
Louis (English name) 'luː(ː)i, 'luː(ː)is, (French name) 'luː(ː)i, 'luː(ː)i: (lwi)
Louisa luː(ː)'iːzə
Louisburg 'luː(ː)isbəːg
louis-d'or, -s 'luː(ː)i'dɔː*, -z
Louise (English name) luː(ː)'iːz
Louisiana luː(ː),iːzi'ænə [-'ɑːnə]
Louisville 'luː(ː)ivil

loung|e (s. v.), -es, -ing, -ed, -er/s 'laundʒ, -iz, -iŋ, -d, -ə*/z
lounge-lizard, -s 'laundʒ,lizəd, -z
Lounsbury 'launzbəri
lour (s. v.), -s, -ing, -ed 'lauə*, -z, -riŋ, -d
Lourdes luəd (lurd)
Lourenço Marques lə'rensəu'mɑ:k
louse (s.), lice laus, lais
lous|e (v.), -es, -ing, -ed lauz [laus], -iz, -iŋ, -d [laust]
lous|y, -ier, -iest, -ily, -iness 'lauz|i, -iə* [-jə*], -iist [-jist], -ili, -inis
lout (s. v.), -s, -ing, -ed laut, -s, -iŋ, -id
Louth (in Ireland) lauð, (in Lincs.) lauθ
loutish, -ly, -ness 'lautiʃ, -li, -nis
Louvain 'lu:vẽ:ŋ [-vein, -væŋ] (luvẽ)
louver, -s 'lu:və*, -z
Louvre lu:vr ['lu:və*] (lu:vr)
lovable, -ness 'lʌvəbl, -nis
Lovat 'lʌvət
lov|e (s. v.) (L.), -es, -ing/ly, -ed, -er/s lʌv, -z, -iŋ/li, -d, -ə*/z
loveable, -ness 'lʌvəbl, -nis
love-affair, -s 'lʌvə,fɛə*, -z
lovebird, -s 'lʌvbə:d, -z
love|-child,-children 'lʌv|tʃaild,-,tʃildrən [-,tʃuldrən]
Loveday 'lʌvdei
love-feast, -s 'lʌvfi:st, -s
Lovejoy 'lʌvdʒɔi
love-knot, -s 'lʌvnɔt, -s
Lovel(l) 'lʌvəl
Lovelace 'lʌvleis
loveless 'lʌvlis
love-letter, -s 'lʌv,letə*, -z
Lovell 'lʌvəl
lovelorn 'lʌvlɔːn
lovel|y (s. adj.), -ies, -ier, -iest, -iness 'lʌvl|i, -iz, -iə* [-jə*], -iist [-jist], -inis
love-making 'lʌv,meikiŋ
love-match, -es 'lʌvmætʃ, -iz
love-potion, -s 'lʌv,pəuʃən, -z
love-shaft, -s 'lʌvʃɑ:ft, -s
lovesick 'lʌvsik
love-song, -s 'lʌvsɔŋ, -z
love-stor|y, -ies 'lʌv,stɔːr|i, -iz
Lovett 'lʌvit
Loveys 'lʌvis
Lovibond 'lʌvibɔnd
Lovick 'lʌvik
loving-cup, -s 'lʌviŋkʌp ['–'-], -s
loving-kindness, -es 'lʌviŋ'kaindnis [,lʌviŋ'k-], -iz
low (adj. v. adv.) (L.), -er, -est, -ness; -s, -ing, -ed ləu, -ə*, -ist, 'ləu-nis; -z, -iŋ, -d

low-born 'ləu'bɔːn [also 'ləu-bɔːn when attributive]
low-bred 'ləu'bred [also 'ləu-bred when attributive]
low-brow 'ləu-brau
low-church, -man, -men 'ləu'tʃə:tʃ, -mən, -mən
low-down (s. adj.) 'ləu-daun
Lowe ləu
Lowein (surname) 'ləuin
Lowell 'ləuəl ['ləuel]
lower (compar. of low) 'ləuə*
lower (v.) (cause to descend), -s, -ing, -ed 'ləuə*, -z, -riŋ, -d
lower (v.) (look threatening), -s, -ing/ly, -ed 'lauə*, -z, -riŋ/li, -d
lower-case 'ləuəkeis
lowermost 'ləuəməust [-məst]
Lowery 'lauəri
Lowes ləuz
Lowestoft 'ləustɔft ['ləuis-, -təft, locally 'ləustəf]
Lowick 'ləuik
Lowis 'lauis
lowland (L.), -s, -er/s 'ləulənd, -z, -ə*/z
low-lived 'ləu-livd
lowl|y, -ier, -iest, -iness 'ləul|i, -iə* [-jə*], -iist [-jist], -inis
low-lying 'ləu'laiiŋ ['-,-- when attributive]
Lowndes laundz
low-necked 'ləu'nekt [also '– when attributive]
Lowood 'ləuwud
low-pressure 'ləu'preʃə* [also '-,-- when attributive]
Lowries 'lauəriz ['laur-]
Lowry 'lauəri ['lauri]
Lowsley 'ləuzli
Lowson 'ləusn, 'lausn
low-spirited, -ly, -ness 'ləu'spiritid, -li, -nis
Lowth lauθ
Lowther 'lauðə*
Lowton 'ləutn
Lowville (in U.S.A.) 'lauvil
Loxley 'lɔksli
loy|al, -ally 'lɔi|əl, -əli
loyalist -s 'lɔiəlist, -s
loyalt|y, -ies 'lɔiəlt|i, -iz
Loyd lɔid
Loyola lɔi'əulə ['lɔiclə, 'lɔiəulə]
lozenge, -s; -shaped 'lɔzindʒ, -iz; -ʃeipt
L. s. d. eles'di:
Ltd. 'limitid
lubber, -s 'lʌbə*, -z
lubberly 'lʌbəli

Lubbock 'lʌbək
lube lu:b [lju:b]
Lübeck 'lu:bek ['lju:-] ('ly:bɛk)
Lubin 'lu:bin
lubricant, -s 'lu:brikənt ['lju:-], -s
lubricat|e, -es, -ing, -ed, -or/s 'lu:bri-
keit ['lju:-], -s, -iŋ, -id, -ə*/z
lubrication, -s ˌlu:bri'keiʃən [ˌlju:-], -z
lubricity lu:'brisiti [lju:-]
Lucan 'lu:kən ['lju:-]
Lucania lu:'keinjə [lju:-, -nïə]
lucarne, -s lu:'kɑ:n [lju:-], -z
Lucas 'lu:kəs ['lju:-]
lucen|cy, -t 'lu:sn|si ['lju:-], -t
Lucentio lu:'senʃiəu [lju:-]
lucern(e) lu:'sə:n [lju:'s-, lu's- 'lu:sə:n]
Lucerne lu:'sə:n [lju:'s-, lu's-]
Lucia 'lu:sjə [-sïə]
Lucian 'lu:sjən [-sïən, -ʃjən, -ʃïən]
Luciana ˌlu:si'ɑ:nə
Lucianus ˌlu:si'ɑ:nəs [ˌlju:-, -si'ein-]
lucid, -est, -ly, -ness 'lu:sid ['lju:-], -ist,
-li, -nis
lucidity lu:'siditi [lju:-]
Lucie 'lu:si ['lju:-]
lucifer (L.), -s 'lu:sifə* ['lju:-], -z
Lucilius lu:'silïəs [-ljəs]
Lucina lu:'sainə [lju:-, lu:'ki:nə]
Lucius 'lu:sjəs [-sïəs, -ʃjəs, -ʃïəs]
luck (L.), -s lʌk, -s
luckless, -ly, -ness 'lʌklis, -li, -nis
Lucknow 'lʌknau ['lʌk'n-, ˌlʌk'n-]
(Hind. ləkhnəw)
luck|y, -ier, -iest, -ily, -iness 'lʌk|i, -ïə*,
-iist, -ili, -inis
Lucock 'lʌkɔk
lucrative, -ly 'lu:krətiv ['lju:-], -li
lucre 'lu:kə* ['lju:-]
Lucrece lu:'kri:s [lju:-]
Lucreti|a, -us lu:'kri:ʃj|ə [lju:'k-, lu'k-,
lju'k-, -ʃï|ə, -ʃ|ə], -əs
lucubrat|e, -es, -ing, -ed 'lu:kju(:)breit
['lju:-], -s, -iŋ, -id
lucubration, -s ˌlu:kju(:)'breiʃən [ˌlju:-],
-z
Lucullian lu:'kʌlïən [lju:'k-, lu'k-, lju'k-,
-ljən]
Lucullus lu:'kʌləs [lju:'k-, lu'k-, lju'k-]
Lucy 'lu:si
Lud lʌd
Ludgate 'lʌdgit [-geit]
ludicrous, -ly, -ness 'lu:dikrəs ['lju:-],
-li, -nis
Ludlow 'lʌdləu
ludo 'lu:dəu
luff (s. v.) (L.), -s, -ing, -ed lʌf, -s, -iŋ, -t
lug (s. v.), -s, -ging, -ged lʌg, -z, -iŋ, -d
Lugano lu:'gɑ:nəu (lu'ga:no)

Lugard lu:'gɑ:d
luggage 'lʌgidʒ
lugger, -s 'lʌgə*, -z
lugsail, -s 'lʌgseil [nautical pronunciation -sl], -z
lugubrious, -ly, -ness lu:'gu:brïəs
[lju:'g-, lu'g-, lə'g-, -'gju:-], -li, -nis
lug-worm, -s 'lʌgwə:m, -z
Luia 'lu:jə ['lu:ïə]
Luke lu:k [lju:k]
lukewarm, -ly, -ness 'lu:k-wɔ:m
['lju:k-], -li, -nis
lull (s. v.), -s, -ing, -ed lʌl, -z, -iŋ, -d
lullab|y, -ies 'lʌləb|ai, -aiz
lumbago lʌm'beigəu
lumbar 'lʌmbə*
lumb|er (s. v.), -ers, -ering, -ered,
-erer/s 'lʌmb|ə*, -əz, -əriŋ, -əd,
-ərə*/z
lumber-room, -s 'lʌmbərum [-ru:m], -z
luminar|y, -ies 'lu:minər|i ['lju:-], -iz
luminiferous ˌlu:mi'nifərəs [ˌlju:-]
luminosity ˌlu:mi'nɔsiti [ˌlju:-]
luminous, -ly, -ness 'lu:minəs ['lju:-], -li,
-nis
Lumley 'lʌmli
lummy 'lʌmi
lump (s. v.), -s, -ing, -ed lʌmp, -s, -iŋ, -t
[lʌmt]
Lumphanan lʌm'fænən
lumpish, -ly, -ness 'lʌmpiʃ, -li, -nis
lump|y, -ier, -iest, -iness 'lʌmp|i, -ïə*
[-jə*], -iist [-jist], -inis
lunacy 'lu:nəsi ['lju:-]
lunar 'lu:nə* ['lju:-]
lunate 'lu:neit ['lju:-, -nit]
lunated 'lu:neitid ['lju:-]
lunatic (s. adj.), -s 'lu:nətik ['lu:ɳtik], -s
lunation, -s lu:'neiʃən [lju:'n-, lu'n-,
lju'n-], -z
Luncarty 'lʌŋkəti
lunch (s. v.), -es, -ing, -ed lʌntʃ, -iz,
-iŋ, -t
luncheon, -s 'lʌntʃən, -z
Lund lund
Lundy 'lʌndi
lune, -s lu:n [lju:n], -z
lunette, -s lu:'net [lju:'n-, lu'n-, lju'n-],
-s
lung, -s lʌŋ, -z
lung|e (s. v.), -es, -ing, -ed lʌndʒ, -iz
-iŋ, -d
lunged (furnished with lungs) lʌŋd,
(from lunge) lʌndʒd
lung-fish, -es 'lʌŋ-fiʃ, -iz
lunul|a, -ae 'lu:njul|ə ['lju:-], -i:
lunule, -s 'lu:nju:l ['lju:-], -z
Lupercal 'lu:pə(:)kæl ['lju:-]

Lupercalia ˌluːpəːˈkeiljə [ˌljuː-, -pəˈk-, -liə]

lupin(e) (*flower*), -s ˈluːpin [ˈljuː-], -z

lupine (*adj.*) (*wolfish*) ˈluːpain [ˈljuː-]

lupulin ˈluːpjulin [ˈljuː-]

lupus ˈluːpəs [ˈljuː-]

lurch (*s. v.*), -es, -ing, -ed ləːtʃ, -iz, -iŋ, -t

lur|e (*s. v.*), -es, -ing, -ed ljuə* [luə*, ljɔə*, ljɔː*, ljəː*], -z, -riŋ, -d

lurid, -ly, -ness ˈljuərid [ˈluər-, ˈljɔər-, ˈljɔːr-, ˈljəːr-], -li, -nis

lurk, -s, -ing, -ed, -er/s ləːk, -s, -iŋ, -t, -ə*/z

lurking-place, -s ˈləːkiŋpleis, -iz

Lusaka lu(ː)ˈsɑːkə

Lusa|tia, -tian/s luːˈsei|ʃjə [-ʃiə, -ʃə], -ʃjən/z [-ʃiən/z, -ʃən/z]

luscious, -ly, -ness ˈlʌʃəs, -li, -nis

lush (L.) lʌʃ

Lushington ˈlʌʃiŋtən

Lusiad, -s ˈluːsiæd [ˈljuː-], -z

Lusitania ˌluːsiˈteinjə [ˌljuː-, -niə]

lust (*s. v.*), -s, -ing, -ed lʌst, -s, -iŋ, -id

lust|ful, -fully, -fulness ˈlʌst|ful, -fuli [-fəli], -fulnis

lustration, -s lʌsˈtreiʃən, -z

lustre, -s; -less ˈlʌstə*, -z; -lis

lustrel ˈlʌstrəl

lustrous, -ly, -ness ˈlʌstrəs, -li, -nis

lustr|um, -ums, -a ˈlʌstr|əm, -əmz, -ə

lust|y, -ier, -iest, -ily, -iness ˈlʌst|i, -iə* [-jə*], -iist [-jist], -ili, -inis

lute, -s; -string/s luːt [ljuːt], -s; -striŋ/z

Luth|er, -eran/s, -eranism, -erism ˈluːθ|ə* [ˈljuː-], -ərən/z, -ərənizəm, -ərizəm

Lutine (*bell at Lloyd's*) luːˈtiːn

lutist, -s ˈluːtist [ˈljuː-], -s

Luton ˈluːtn

Lutterworth ˈlʌtəwə(ː)θ

Luttrell ˈlʌtrəl

Lutwyche ˈlʌtwitʃ

Lutyens (*English surname*) ˈlʌtʃənz [-tjənz]

lux lʌks

luxe luks [luːks, lʌks] (lyks)

Luxemburg ˈlʌksəmbəːg

Luxor ˈlʌksɔː*

Luxulyan lʌkˈsiljən [-ˈsʌl-, -liən]

luxurian|ce, -t/ly lʌgˈzjuəriən|s [ləgˈzj-, lʌkˈsj-, ləkˈsj-, -jəːr-, -jɔər-, -jɔːr-, lʌgˈʒuə-, lʌgˈʒəː-, ləgˈʒ-], -t/li

luxuriat|e, -es, -ing, -ed lʌgˈzjuərieit [ləgˈzj-, lʌkˈsj-, ləkˈsj-, -jəːr-, -jɔər-, -jɔːr-, lʌgˈʒuə-, lʌgˈʒəː-, ləgˈʒ-], -s, -iŋ, -id

luxurious, -ly, -ness lʌgˈzjuəriəs [ləgˈzj-, lʌkˈsj-, ləkˈsj-, -jəːr-, -jɔər-, -jɔːr-, lʌgˈʒuə-, lʌgˈʒəː-, ləgˈʒ-], -li, -nis

luxur|y, -ies ˈlʌkʃər|i [-kʃur-], -iz

Luzon luːˈzɒn

Lyall ˈlaiəl

lycée, -s ˈliːsei (lise), -z

Lycett ˈlaisit [-set]

lyceum (L.), -s laiˈsiəm [-ˈsiːəm], -z

lychee, -s ˈlaiˈtʃiː [-ˈ-, ˈlitʃiː], -z

lychgate, -s ˈlitʃgeit, -s

lychnis ˈliknis

Lycia, -n/s ˈlisiə [-sjə, -ʃiə, -ʃjə], -n/z

Lycidas ˈlisidæs

Lycoming laiˈkɒmiŋ

lycopodium, -s ˌlaikəˈpəudjəm [-diəm], -z

Lycurgus laiˈkəːgəs

Lydall ˈlaidl

Lydd lid

lyddite ˈlidait

Lydekker laiˈdekə*

Lydgate (*fifteenth-century poet, place near Newmarket*) ˈlidgeit [-git], (*lane in Sheffield*) ˈlidʒit

Lydia, -n/s ˈlidiə [-djə], -n/z

Lydon ˈlaidn

lye (L.) lai

Lyell ˈlaiəl

Lyghe lai

Lygon ˈligən

lying (*from* lie), -ly ˈlaiiŋ, -li

lying-in ˈlaiiŋˈin [ˈ--- *when attributive*]

Lyly ˈlili

Lyme Regis ˈlaimˈriːdʒis

Lymington ˈlimiŋtən

Lympany (*surname*) ˈlimpəni

lymph, -s; -ous limf, -s; -əs

lymphatic, -s limˈfætik, -s

Lympne lim

Lynam ˈlainəm [-iŋ, -t; -lɒ-

lynch (L.), -es, -ing, -ed; -law lintʃ, -iz, -lɔː

Lynd|hurst, -on ˈlind|həːst, -ən

Lynmouth ˈlinməθ

Lynn lin

Lynton ˈlintən

lynx, -es liŋks, -iz

lynx-eyed ˈliŋks-aid

Lyon (*surname*) ˈlaiən

Lyonesse ˌlaiəˈnes [ˌlaiəˈn-]

Lyons (*English surname*) ˈlaiənz, (*French city*) ˈlaiənz [ˈliːɔ̃ːŋ] (*or as French* ljɔ̃)

Lyr|a (*constellation*), -ae ˈlaiər|ə, -iː

lyrate ˈlaiərit [-reit]

lyre, -s; -bird/s ˈlaiə*, -z; -bəːd/z

lyric (L.), -s, -al, -ally ˈlirik, -s, -əl, -əli

lyricism ˈlirisizəm

lyrist (*player on the lyre*), **-s** 'laiərist ['lir-], -s
lyrist (*lyric poet*), **-s** 'lirist, -s
Lysaght 'laisət, 'laisɑ:t
   Note.—Baron Lisle pronounces 'laisət.
Lysander lai'sændə*
Lysias 'lisiæs
Lysicrates lai'sikrəti:z
Lysippus lai'sipəs

Lysistrata lai'sistrətə
lysol 'laisɔl
Lystra 'listrə
Lyte lait
Lytham 'liðəm
Lythe laið
Lyttelton 'litltən [-tn]
Lytton 'litn
Lyveden 'livden

M

M (*the letter*), **-'s** em, -z
ma (*mother*), **-s** mɑː, -z
ma (*note in Tonic Sol-fa*), **-s** mɔː, -z
ma'am mæm [mɑːm, məm, m]
   Note.—mæm, *or alternatively* mɑːm,
   is used in addressing members of the
   royal family; servants addressing
   non-titled mistresses say məm *or* m.
Maas (*English surname*) mɑːz, (*river in*
   Holland) mɑːs
Mab mæb
Mabel 'meibəl
Mablethorpe 'meiblθɔːp
Mabley 'mæbli
Mabs mæbz
Mac mæk
macabre mə'kɑːbr [mæ'k-, -bə*]
macadam mə'kædəm
MacAdam mə'kædəm, mək'ædəm
macadamization [-isa-] mə,kædəmai-
   'zeiʃən
macadamiz|e [-is|e], **-es**, **-ing**, **-ed**
   mə'kædəmaiz, -iz, -iŋ, -d
MacAdoo ,mækə'duː, 'mækədu:
Macalister mə'kælistə*
McAll mə'kɔːl
McAllister mə'kælistə*
McAloren ,mækə'lɔːrən
McAlpine mə'kælpin, mə'kælpain
Macan mə'kæn
MacAnnaly ,mækə'næli
Macao mə'kau
McAra mə'kɑːrə
macaroni ,mækə'rəuni
macaroon, **-s** ,mækə'ru:n ['mækər-
   when attributive], -z
MacArthur mə'kɑːθə*, mək'ɑːθə*
macassar (M.); -oil mə'kæsə*; -r'ɔil
   [-'ɔil]
Macaulay mə'kɔːli
macaw, **-s** mə'kɔː, -z
Mc|Bain, -Bean mək|'bein, -'bein
Macbeth mək'beθ [mæk-]
   Note.—*In Scotland always* mək-.
McBride mək'braid
Maccabees ,mækəbi:z
Maccabeus ,mækə'bi(:)əs
McCall [MacC-] mə'kɔːl
McCallie mə'kɔːli

McCallum [MacC-] mə'kæləm
McCann mə'kæn
MacCarthy mə'kɑːθi
McClellan mə'klelən
Macclesfield 'mæklzfi:ld [-lsf-]
McClintock mə'klintək [-tɔk]
McClure [M'Clure] mə'kluə*
McConochie mə'kɔnəki [-əxi]
McCormick mə'kɔːmik
McCorquodale mə'kɔːkədeil
Mc|Crae, -Crea mə|'krei, -'krei
McCulloch mə'kʌlək [-ləx]
MacCumhail mə'ku:l
MacCunn mə'kʌn
MacDaire mək'dɑːrə
MacDonald [Macd-] mək'dɔnəld [mæk-]
McDonald mək'dɔnəld
MacDonnell [Macd-] ,mækdə'nel, (*in*
   Ireland) mək'dɔnl
McDonough mək'dʌnə
MacDougal [Macd-] mək'du:gəl [mæk-]
McDougall mək'du:gəl
McDowell mək'dauəl [-el, -il]
MacDuff mək'dʌf [mæk-]
   Note.—*In Scotland always* mək-.
mace, **-s** meis, -iz
McEachran mə'kekrən [-exr-]
Macedon 'mæsidən
Macedonia, **-n/s** ,mæsi'dəunjə [-nîə],
   -n/z
McElderry 'mæklderi
McEldowney 'mækldauni
MacElwain mə'kelwein, mək'el-
MacElwin mə'kelwin, mək'el-
macerat|e, **-es**, **-ing**, **-ed** 'mæsəreit, -s,
   -iŋ, -id
McErlain 'mækəlein
MacFarlane mək'fɑːlin [-lən]
Macfarren mək'færən
Macfie mək'fi: [mæk-]
McGahey mə'gæhi [-'gæxi], mə'geii
McGee mə'gi:
MacGillicuddy (*Reeks*) mə'gilikʌdi,
   (*family name*) 'mæglikʌdi
McGillivray mə'glivrei
McGrath mə'grɑː
McGregor mə'gregə*
MacGregor [Macg-, M'G-] mə'gregə*
mach mæk [mɑːk, mɔk]

Machen 'meitʃən [-tʃin], 'mækin
machete, -s mə'tʃeiti, -z
Machiavelli ˌmækiə'veli [-kjə-]
machiavellian ˌmækiə'veliən [-kjə-, -ljən]
machicolat|e, -es, -ing, -ed mæ'tʃikəu-leit [mə'tʃ-], -s, -iŋ, -id
Machin 'meitʃin
machinat|e, -es, -ing, -ed, -or/s 'mæki-neit, -s, -iŋ, -id, -ə*/z
machination, -s ˌmæki'neiʃən, -z
machin|e (s. v.), -es, -ing, -ed ; -e-gun/s mə'ʃi:n, -z, -iŋ, -d; -gʌn/z
machine-made mə'ʃi:nmeid
machinery mə'ʃi:nəri
machinist, -s mə'ʃi:nist, -s
McIlrath 'mæklrɑ:θ
MacIlwain 'mæklwein
MacIlwraith [McI-] 'mæklreiθ
Macindoe 'mækindu:
MacInn|es, -is mə'kin|is, -is
McIntosh 'mækintoʃ
MacIntyre 'mækintaiə*
Macirone ˌmætʃi'rəuni
MacIvor mə'ki:və*, mə'kaivə*
Mack mæk
Mackay mə'kai, mə'kei
    Note.—mə'kei mainly in U.S.A.
McKeag mə'ki:g
McKee mə'ki:
McKenna mə'kenə
Mackenzie mə'kenzi
mackerel, -s 'mækrəl, -z
Mackerras mə'kerəs
McKichan mə'kikən [-'kixən]
Mackie 'mæki
McKie mə'kai, mə'ki:
Mackin 'mækin
Mackin|lay, -ley mə'kin|li, -li
McKinley mə'kinli
mackintosh (M.), -es 'mækintoʃ, -iz
Mackmurdo mæk'mə:dəu [mək-]
Mackowie [MacK-] mə'kaui
MacLachlan mə'kloklən [-'kloxlən], mə'klæklən [-'klæxlən]
MacLaglan mək'læglən
MacL|aren, -aurin mə'kl|ærən, -ɔ:rin
McLaughlin mə'kloklin [-ɔxlin]
McLay mə'klei
MacL|ean(e) (surname), -ear mə'kl|ein [-'kl|i:n], -iə*
McLean mə'klein
MacLehose 'mæklhəuz
Macleod mə'klaud
McLeod mə'klaud
MacLiammoir mək'liəmɔ:*
Maclise mə'kli:s
Macmahon mək'mɑ:ən

MacManus mək'mænəs, -'mɑ:nəs, -'meinəs
McMaster mək'mɑ:stə*
Macmillan mək'milən [mæk-]
Macmorran mək'morən [mæk-]
MacNab mək'næb
Macnaghten [McN-] mək'nɔ:tn
Macnamara ˌmæknə'mɑ:rə
MacNaught, -on mək'nɔ:t [mæk-], -n
MacNeice mək'ni:s
Mâcon (in France, wine) 'mɑ:kɔ:ŋ ['mæ-, -kɔn, -kən] (mɑkɔ̃)
Macon (in U.S.A.) 'meikən
Maconchy mə'koŋki
Maconochie mə'konəki [-əxi]
MacOuart mə'kju(:)ət
McOutra mə'ku:trə
Macpelah mæk'pi:lə
MacPherson [Macph-] mək'fə:sn [mæk-]
Macquarie mə'kwori
Macquoid mə'kwoid
Macready mə'kri:di
macrocosm, -s 'mækrəukozəm, -z
macron, -s 'mækrɔn, -z
Macrow mə'krəu
McShea mək'ʃei
MacSwiney mək'swi:ni [mæk-]
MacTavish mək'tæviʃ
macul|a, -ae 'mækjul|ə, -i:
McVeagh mək'vei
McVean mək'vein
McVit(t)ie mək'viti
mad; mad|der, -dest, -ly, -ness mæd; 'mæd|ə*, -ist, -li, -nis
Madagascar ˌmædə'gæskə*
madam 'mædəm
madame (M.) 'mædəm (madam)
Madan 'mædən, 'meidn
madcap, -s 'mædkæp, -s
Maddalo 'mædələu
madd|en (M.), -ens, -ening, -ened 'mæd|n, -nz, -niŋ [-niŋ], -nd
madder (plant, colour), -s 'mædə*, -z
madding 'mædiŋ
Maddox 'mædəks
made (from make) meid
Madeira, -s mə'diərə, -z
Madeleine (English name) 'mædlin [-dəlin, -ein]
Madeley (in Shropshire) 'meidli
mademoiselle, -s ˌmædəm(w)ə'zel [ˌmæmwə'zel] (madmwazɛl), -z
Madge mædʒ
madhou|se, -ses 'mædhau|s, -ziz
Madingley 'mædiŋli
Madison 'mædisn
mad|man, -men 'mæd|mən, -mən [-men]

Madoc 'mædək
Madonna, -s mə'dɔnə, -z
Madras mə'drɑːs [-'dræs]
madrepore, -s ˌmædri'pɔː [-'pɔə*], -z
Madrid mə'drid
madrigal, -s 'mædrigəl, -z
madrigalist, -s 'mædrigəlist, -s
Madura (in S. India) 'mædjurə [-dʒu-]
Maecenas mi(ː)'siːnæs [mai's-, -nəs]
maelstrom 'meilstrəum
maenad, -s 'miːnæd, -z
maestoso ˌmɑːes'təuzəu [mais-, -əusəu]
maestro, -s mɑː'estrəu ['maistrəu], -z
Maeterlinck 'meitəliŋk ['mɑːt-]
Mae West, -s 'mei'west, -s
Mafeking 'mæfikiŋ
maffick, -s, -ing, -ed 'mæfik, -s, -iŋ, -t
mag (M.), -s mæg, -z
Magan 'meigən, mə'gæn
magazine, -s ˌmægə'ziːn [rarely '---].
  Note.—The stressing '--- is usual in
  the N. of England, but uncommon
  in the S.
Magdala 'mægdələ
magdalen, -s 'mægdəlin, -z
Magdalen (biblical name, modern Christian name, Canadian islands) 'mægdəlin, (Oxford college and street)
  'mɔːdlin
Magdalene (biblical name) ˌmægdə'liːni
  ['mægdəliːn, -lin], (modern Christian
  name) 'mægdəlin, (Cambridge college and street) 'mɔːdlin
Magdalenian ˌmægdə'liːnjən [-nïən]
Magdeburg 'mægdəbəːg [-dib-] ('mak-
  dəburk, -burç)
mage, -s meidʒ, -iz
Magee mə'giː
Magellan mə'gelən
magenta (M.) mə'dʒentə
Maggersfontein 'mɑːgəzˌfontein ['---ˌ-]
Maggie 'mægi
Maggiore ˌmædʒi'ɔːri [mæ'dʒɔːri,
  mə'dʒɔːri] (mad'dʒɔːre)
maggot, -s, -y 'mægət, -s, -i
Maghull (near Liverpool) mə'gʌl
Magi 'meidʒai [-gai]
magic (s. adj.), -al, -ally 'mædʒik, -əl,
  -əli
magician, -s mə'dʒiʃən, -z
magic-lantern, -s 'mædʒik'læntən
  [ˌmæ-], -z
magilp mə'gilp
Maginot 'mæʒinəu ['mædʒi-] (maʒino)
magisterial, -ly ˌmædʒis'tiəriəl, -i
magistrac|y, -ies 'mædʒistrəs|i, -iz
magistral mə'dʒistrəl [mæ'dʒ-]
magistrate, -s 'mædʒistreit [-trit], -s

magistrature, -s 'mædʒistrətjuə*
  [-tʃuə*, -tʃə*], -z
Magna Carta 'mægnə'kɑːtə
magnanimity ˌmægnə'nimiti
magnanimous, -ly mæg'næniməs [məg-],
  -li
magnate, -s 'mægneit [-nit], -s
magnesia (substance) mæg'niːʃə [məg-,
  -ʃjə, -ʃïə, -zjə, -zïə, -ʒə]
Magnesia (city) mæg'niːzjə [-zïə, -ʒjə,
  -ʒïə, -ʃjə, -ʃïə]
magnesium mæg'niːzjəm [məg-, -zïəm,
  -sjəm, -sïəm, -ʃjəm, -ʃïəm]
magnet, -s 'mægnit, -s
magnetic, -al, -ally mæg'netik [məg-],
  -əl, -əli
magnetism 'mægnitizəm
magnetiz|e [-is|e], -es, -ing, -ed, -er/s
  'mægnitaiz, -iz, -iŋ, -d, -ə*/z
magneto, -s mæg'niːtəu [məg-], -z
magnetron, -s 'mægnitron, -z
Magnificat, -s mæg'nifikæt [məg-], -s
magnification, -s ˌmægnifi'keiʃən, -z
magnificen|ce, -t/ly mæg'nifisn|s
  [məg-], -t/li
magnifico, -s mæg'nifikəu, -z
magni|fy, -fies, -fying, -fied, -fier/s;
  -fiable 'mægni|fai, -faiz, -faiiŋ, -faid,
  -faiə*/z; -faiəbl
magniloquen|ce, -t mæg'niləukwən|s,
  -t
Magnitogorsk mægˌniːtəu'gɔːsk (mag-
  ˌnjita'gorsk)
magnitude, -s 'mægnitjuːd, -z
magnolia, -s mæg'nəuljə [məg-, -lïə], -z
magnum, -s 'mægnəm, -z
magnum bonum, -s 'mægnəm'bəunəm
  [-'bon-], -z
Magnus 'mægnəs
Magog 'meigog
magpie, -s 'mægpai, -z
Magrath mə'grɑː
Magruder mə'gruːdə*
Maguire mə'gwaiə*
Ma|gus, -gi 'mei|gəs, -dʒai [-gai]
Magyar, -s 'mægjɑː* [-giɑː*], -z
Mahaffy mə'hæfi
Mahan mə'hæn, mɑːn
Mahanaim ˌmeiə'neiim [usual Jewish
  pronunciation ˌmɑːhɑː'nɑːim]
Mahany 'mɑːni
maharajah, -s ˌmɑːhə'rɑːdʒə (Hind.
  məharɑja), -z
maharanee, -s ˌmɑːhə'rɑːni: (Hind.
  məharani), -z
mahatma, -s mə'hɑːtmə [-'hæt-] (Hind.
  məhatma), -z
Mahdi, -s 'mɑːdi(ː), -z

mah-jong(g) 'mɑ:'dʒɔŋ
mahl-stick, -s 'mɔ:l-stik, -s
Mahmud mɑ:'mu:d
mahogany mə'hɔgəni [-gn̩i]
Mahomet (*prophet*) mə'hɔmit ['meiə-met, 'meiəmit, 'mɛəm-], (*English surname*) 'meiəmet ['mɛə-, -mit]
Mahometan, -s mə'hɔmitən, -z
Mahommed mə'hɔmid [-med]
Mahommedan, -s mə'hɔmidən, -z
Mahon mɑ:n, mə'hu:n, mə'həun
Mahon(e)y 'mɑ:əni ['mɑ:ni]
mahout, -s mə'haut, -s
Mahratta, -s mə'rætə, -z
maia 'maiə
maid, -s meid, -z
Maida 'meidə
maidan (M.), -s mai'dɑ:n, -z
maiden (*s. adj.*), -s, -ly; -hair/s 'meidn, -z, -li; -hɛə*/z
Maidenhead 'meidnhed
maidenhood 'meidnhud
maiden-name, -s 'meidnneim, -z
maid-servant, -s 'meid,sə:vənt, -s
Maidstone 'meidstən [-stəun]
maieutic mei'ju:tik [mai'j-]
mail (*s. v.*), -s, -ing, -ed meil, -z, -iŋ, -d
mail-bag, -s 'meilbæg, -z
mail-cart, -s 'meil-kɑ:t, -s
mail-coach, -es 'meil'kəutʃ ['meil-kəutʃ], -iz
Maillard (*surname*) 'meiləd
mail-order 'meil,ɔ:də*
mail-train, -s 'meil-trein, -z
maim, -s, -ing, -ed meim, -z, -iŋ, -d
main (*s. adj.*), -s, -ly mein, -z, -li
Main (*German river*) main [mein]
mainbrace, -s 'meinbreis, -iz
Maine mein
mainland 'meinlənd [-lænd]
mainmast, -s 'meinmɑ:st [*nautical pronunciation* -məst], -s
mainsail, -s 'meinseil [*nautical pronunciation* -sl], -z
mainspring, -s 'mein-spriŋ, -z
mainstay, -s 'mein-stei, -z
maintain, -s, -ing, -ed, -er/s; -able mein'tein [mən-, men-], -z, -iŋ, -d, -ə*/z; -əbl
maintenance 'meintənəns [-tin-, -tn̩əns, -tnəns]
Mainwaring 'mænəriŋ, (*in Wales* 'meinwəriŋ)
Mainz maints
Mais meiz
Maisie 'meizi
maison(n)ette, -s ,meizə'net, -s

Maitland 'meitlənd
maître(s) d'hôtel 'metrə dəu'tel ['meit-] (mɛ:trə dɔtel)
maize meiz
Majendie 'mædʒəndi
majestic (M.), -al, -ally mə'dʒestik, -əl, -əli
majest|y (M.), -ies 'mædʒist|i [-dʒəs-], -iz
majolica mə'jɔlikə [mə'dʒɔl-]
major (*s. adj. v.*) (M.), -s, -ing, -ed 'meidʒə*, -z, -riŋ, -d
Majorca mə'dʒɔ:kə [mə'jɔ:-]
major-domo, -s 'meidʒə'dəuməu, -z
major-general, -s 'meidʒə'dʒenərəl, -z
majorit|y, -ies mə'dʒɔrit|i [-rət-], -iz
Majuba mə'dʒu:bə
majuscule, -s 'mædʒəskju:l, -z
mak|e (*s. v.*), -es, -ing, made, mak|er, -ers meik, -s, -iŋ, meid, 'meik|ə*, -əz
make-believe 'meikbi,li:v [-bə,l-]
Makeham 'meikəm
Makepeace 'meikpi:s
Makerere mə'kerəri
makeshift, -s 'meikʃift, -s
make-up, -s 'meikʌp, -s
makeweight, -s 'meik-weit, -s
Makins 'meikinz
Makower mə'kauə*
Malabar ,mælə'bɑ:* ['mælə'b-, *also* 'mæləb- *when attributive*]
Malacca mə'lækə
Malachi 'mæləkai
malachite 'mæləkait
maladjusted 'mælə'dʒʌstid [*also* '--,-- *when attributive*]
maladjustment, -s 'mælə'dʒʌstmənt, -s
maladministration 'mæləd,minis'treiʃən
maladroit, -ly, -ness 'mælə'drɔit [,--'-, '---], -li, -nis
malad|y, -ies 'mæləd|i, -iz
mala fide 'meilə'faidi ['mælə'fidi, -'fidei]
Malaga 'mæləgə
Malagasy ,mælə'gæsi ['--'--]
malaise mæ'leiz
Malan (*English surname*) 'mælən, (*South African name*) mə'læn, mə'lɑ:n
Malaprop 'mæləprɔp
malapropism, -s 'mæləprɔpizəm, -z
malapropos 'mæl'æprəpəu ['---'-]
malaria, -l, -n mə'lɛəriə, -l, -n
Malawi mə'lɑ:wi
Malay (*s. adj.*), -s mə'lei, -z
Malaya, -n/s mə'leiə, -n/z
Malayalam ,mæli'ɑ:ləm [-lei'ɑ:-, -lə'jɑ:-]
Malaysia mə'leiziə [-zjə]
Malchus 'mælkəs

Malcolm 'mælkəm
malcontent, -s 'mælkən,tent, -s
Malden 'mɔːldən ['mɔl-]
Maldive, -s 'mɔːldiv ['mɔl-], -z
Maldivian, -s mɔːl'diviən [mɔl-, -vjən], -z
Maldon 'mɔːldən ['mɔl-]
male, -s meil, -z
malediction, -s ,mæli'dikʃən, -z
maledictory ,mæli'diktəri
malefaction, -s ,mæli'fækʃən, -z
malefactor, -s 'mælifæktə*, -z
malefic mə'lefik
maleficent mə'lefisnt [mæ'l-]
Malet 'mælit
malevolen|ce, -t/ly mə'levələn|s [mæ'l-, -vlə-], -t/li
malfeasance mæl'fiːzəns
Malfi 'mælfi
malformation, -s 'mælfɔː'meiʃən [-fə'm-], -z
Mali 'mɑːli
malic 'mælik ['meil-]
malice 'mælis
malicious, -ly, -ness mə'liʃəs, -li, -nis
malign (adj. v.), -ly; -s, -ing, -ed, -er/s mə'lain, -li; -z, -iŋ, -d, -ə*/z
malignan|cy, -t/ly mə'lignən|si, -t/li
malignity mə'ligniti
Malin (region of sea) 'mælin
Malines mæ'liːn (malin)
malinger, -s, -ing, -ed, -er/s mə'liŋgə*, -z, -riŋ, -d, -rə*/z
Malins 'meilinz
malkin, -s 'mɔːkin ['mɔːlk-], -z
Malkin 'mælkin
mall, -s mɔːl, -z
Mall (in The Mall, Chiswick Mall) mæl, (in Pall Mall) mæl [mel]
Note.—Members of West End clubs generally pronounce Pall Mall as 'pel'mel. With other Londoners the pronunciation 'pæl'mæl is common.
mallard, -s 'mæləd, -z
malleability ,mæliə'biliti [-ljə'b-, -lə'b-, -lət-]
malleable, -ness 'mæliəbl [-ljə-, -lə-], -nis
mallet (M.), -s 'mælit, -s
Malling (in Kent) 'mɔːliŋ
Mallorca mə'ljɔːkə [mə'lɔː-]
Mallory 'mæləri
mallow (M.), -s 'mæləu, -z
Malmaison, -s mæl'meizɔ̃ːŋ (malmɛzɔ̃), -z
Malmesbury 'mɑːmzbəri
malmsey (M.) 'mɑːmzi
malnutrition 'mælnju(ː)'triʃən

malodorant (s. adj.), -s mæ'ləudərənt, -s
malodorous mæ'ləudərəs
Malone mə'ləun
Malory 'mæləri
Malpas (near Truro) 'məupəs, (in Cheshire) 'mɔːlpəs ['mɔːpəs, 'mælpəs]
Malplaquet 'mælpləkei
malpractice, -s 'mæl'præktis [-'--], -iz
malt (s. v.), -s, -ing, -ed mɔːlt [mɔlt], -s, -iŋ, -id
Malta 'mɔːltə ['mɔl-]
Maltese 'mɔːl'tiːz [-ɔl-, also '--, -'-- according to sentence-stress]
Malthus 'mælθəs
Malthusian, -s, -ism mæl'θjuːzjən [-'θuː-, -ziən], -z, -izəm
Malton (in Yorks.) 'mɔːltən ['mɔl-]
Maltravers mæl'trævə(ː)z
maltreat, -s, -ing, -ed, -ment mæl'triːt, -s, -iŋ, -id, -mənt
maltster, -s 'mɔːltstə* ['mɔl-], -z
Malvern 'mɔːlvə(ː)n ['mɔl-, locally also 'mɔːvən]
malversation ,mælvə:'seiʃən
Malvolio mæl'vəuljəu [-liəu]
Malyon 'mæljən [-liən]
Mameluke, -s 'mæmiluːk [-ljuːk], -s
Mamie 'meimi
Mamilius mə'miliəs [mæ'm-, -ljəs]
mamma (mother), -s mə'mɑː:, -z
mamm|a (milk-secreting organ) -ae 'mæm|ə, -iː
mammal, -s 'mæməl, -z
mammalia,-n mæ'meiljə [mə'm-, -liə],-n
mammaliferous ,mæmə'lifərəs
mammary 'mæməri
mammon (M.) 'mæmən
mammoth, -s 'mæməθ, -s
mamm|y, -ies 'mæm|i, -iz
man (s.) (M.), men mæn, men
man (v.), -s, -ning, -ned mæn, -z, -iŋ, -d
manac|le, -les, -ling, -led 'mænək|l, -lz, -liŋ, -ld
manag|e, -es, -ing, -ed, -er/s, -ement/s 'mænidʒ, -iz, -iŋ, -d, -ə*/z, -mənt/s
manageability ,mænidʒə'biliti [-lət-]
manageab|le, -ly, -leness 'mænidʒəb|l, -li, -lnis
manageress, -es 'mænidʒə'res ['mænidʒəres, -ris], -iz
managerial ,mænə'dʒiəriəl
Manasseh mə'næsi [-sə]
Manasses mə'næsiz [-siːz]
man-at-arms, men-at-arms 'mænət-'ɑːmz, 'menət'ɑːmz
manatee (M.), -s ,mænə'tiː, -z
Manchester 'mæntʃistə* [-tʃestə*, -tʃəstə*]

Manchu, -s mæn'tʃuː ['mæn'tʃ-, *also* 'mæntʃu: *when attributive*], -z
Manchukuo 'mæntʃu:'kwəu
Manchuria, -n/s mæn'tʃuəriə [-'tʃɔər-, -'tʃɔːr-], -n/z
manciple, -s 'mænsipl, -z
Mancunian, -s mæŋ'kjuːnjən [-niən], -z
Mandalay ˌmændə'lei ['mændə'l-]
mandamus, -es mæn'deiməs, -iz
mandarin, -s 'mændərin, -z
mandate (*s.*), **-s** 'mændeit [-dit], -s
mandat|e (*v.*), **-es, -ing, -ed** 'mændeit [-'-], -s, -iŋ, -id
mandator|y (*s. adj.*), **-ies** 'mændətər|i, -iz
Mander (*surname*) 'mɑːndə*, 'mændə*
Mandeville 'mændəvil [-div-]
mandible, -s 'mændibl, -z
mandolin, -s 'mændəlin, -z
mandoline, -s ˌmændə'liːn ['mændəli:n, 'mændəlin], -z
mandragora mæn'drægərə [mən-]
mandrake, -s 'mændreik, -s
mandrill, -s 'mændril, -z
mane, -s, -d mein, -z, -d
man-eater, -s 'mænˌiːtə*, -z
manège, -s mæ'neiʒ ['mæneiʒ], -iz
manes (*ghosts*) (**M.**) 'mɑːneiz ['meini:z]
manet 'mænet [*old-fashioned* 'meinet]
Manfred 'mænfred [-frid]
man|ful, -fully, -fulness 'mæn|ful, -fuli [-fəli], -fulnis
manganese ˌmæŋgə'ni:z ['mæŋgən-]
manganic mæŋ'gænik
mange meindʒ
mangel-wurzel, -s 'mæŋgl'wəːzl ['--ˌ--],
manger, -s 'meindʒə*, -z [-z
mang|le, -les, -ling, -led 'mæŋg|l, -lz, -liŋ [-ˌliŋ], -ld
mango, -es 'mæŋgəu, -z
mangold, -s 'mæŋgəld, -z
mangosteen, -s 'mæŋgəusti:n, -z
mangrove, -s 'mæŋgrəuv, -z
mang|y, -ier, -iest, -ily, -iness 'meindʒ|i, -iə* [-jə*], -iist [-jist], -ili, -inis
man-hand|le, -les, -ling, -led 'mænˌhænd|l, -lz, -liŋ [-ˌliŋ], -ld
Manhattan mæn'hætən
manhole, -s 'mænhəul, -z
manhood (**M.**) 'mænhud
mania, -s 'meinjə [-niə], -z
maniac, -s 'meiniæk [-njæk], -s
maniac|al, -ally mə'naiək|əl, -əli
manic-depressive 'mænikdi'presiv
Manichean, -s ˌmæni'ki(ː)ən, -z
manicur|e (*s. v.*), **-es, -ing, -ed; -ist/s** 'mænikjuə* [-kjɔə*, -kjɔ:*, -kjə:*], -z, -riŋ, -d; -rist/s

manifest (*s. adj. v.*), **-ly; -s, -ing, -ed** 'mænifest, -li; -s, -iŋ, -id
manifestation, -s ˌmænifes'teiʃən [-fəs-], -z
manifesto, -s ˌmæni'festəu, -z
manifold, -ness 'mænifəuld [*rarely* 'men-], -nis
manikin, -s 'mænikin, -z
manil(l)a (**M.**), **-s** mə'nilə, -z
manioc 'mæniɔk
maniple, -s 'mænipl, -z
manipulat|e, -es, -ing, ed, -or/s mə'nipjuleit, -s, -iŋ, -id, -ə*/z
manipulation, -s məˌnipju'leiʃən, -z
Manitoba ˌmæni'təubə
mankind (*in general*) mæn'kaind, (*when opposed to* **womankind**) 'mænkaind
Manley 'mænli
manlike 'mænlaik
Manlius 'mænliəs [-ljəs]
man|ly, -lier, -liest, -liness 'mæn|li, -liə* [-ljə*], -liist [-ljist], -linis
Mann mæn
manna 'mænə
mannequin, -s 'mænikin, -z
manner, -s, -ed; -ism/s 'mænə*, -z, -d; -rizəm/z
manner|ly, -liness 'mænə|li, -linis
Manners 'mænəz
Mannheim 'mænhaim ('manhaim)
mannikin, -s 'mænikin, -z
Manning 'mæniŋ
mannish 'mæniʃ
Manns mænz
manny 'mæni
Manoah mə'nəuə
manoeuvrability məˌnuːvrə'biliti [-vər-, -lət-]
manoeuvrable mə'nuːvrəbl [-vər-]
manoeuv|re, -res, -ring, -red, -rer/s mə'nuːv|ə*, -əz, -əriŋ, -əd, -ərə*/z
man-of-war, men-of-war 'mænəv'wɔ:*, 'menəv'wɔ:*
manometer, -s mə'nɔmitə*, -z
manometric ˌmænəu'metrik
manor, -s 'mænə*, -z
manor-hou|se, -ses 'mænəhau|s, -ziz
manorial mə'nɔːriəl [mæ'n-]
manostat, -s 'mænəustæt, -s
Manresa (*town in Spain*) mæn'reisə [-'reizə] (man'resa), (*in names of streets, etc.*) mæn'riːzə [-'riːsə]
Mansa 'mænsə
manse, -s mæns, -iz
Mansel(l) 'mænsl
Mansergh 'mænsə*
Mansfield 'mænsfi:ld
mansion (**M.**), **-s** 'mænʃən, -z

mansion-hou|se (M.), -ses 'mænʃən-hau|s, -ziz
manslaughter 'mæn,slɔ:tə*
man-slayer, -s 'mæn,sleiə*, -z
mansuetude 'mænswitju:d
mantel, -s 'mæntl, -z
mantel-board, -s 'mæntlbɔ:d [-bɔəd], -z
mantelpiece, -s 'mæntlpi:s, -iz
mantelshel|f, -ves 'mæntlʃel|f, -vz
mantilla, -s mæn'tilə, -z
Mantinea ,mænti'niə [-'ni:ə]
mantis, -es 'mæntis, -iz
mant|le, -les, -ling, -led 'mænt|l, -lz, -liŋ [-l̩iŋ], -ld
mantra, -s 'mæntrə, -z
mantramistic ,mæntrə'mistik
mantrap, -s 'mæn-træp, -s
mantua (M.), -s 'mæntjŭə [-tjwə, 'mæntŭə], -z
manual (s. adj.), -s, -ly 'mænjŭəl [-njwəl, njul], -z, -i
Manuel 'mænjuel [-njŭəl, -njwəl]
manufactor|y, -ies ,mænju'fæktər|i, -iz
manufact|ure (s. v.), -ures, -uring, -ured, -urer/s ,mænju'fæktʃ|ə*, -əz, -əriŋ, -əd, -ərə*/z
manumission, -s ,mænju'miʃən, -z
manumit, -s, -ting, -ted ,mænju'mit, -s, -iŋ, -id
manur|e (s. v.), -es, -ing, -ed mə'njuə* [-'njɔə*, -'njɔ:*, -'njə:*], -z, -riŋ, -d
manuscript, -s 'mænjuskript [-njəs-], -s
Manutius mə'nju:ʃjəs [-ʃiəs, -ʃəs]
Manwaring 'mænəriŋ
Manx, -man, -men mæŋks, -mən [-mæn], -mən [-men]
many 'meni
manysided 'meni'saidid [-,saidid]
manysidedness 'meni'saididnis
Manyuema ,mænju(:)'eimə
maoism 'mauizəm
Maori, -s 'mauri ['mɑ:ər-], -z
Mao Tse-tung 'mau-tse'tuŋ
map (s. v.), -s, -ping, -ped mæp, -s, -iŋ, -t
maple (M.), -s 'meipl, -z
Mapother 'meipɔðə*
Mappin 'mæpin
maquillage ,mæki:'ɑ:ʒ [-ki'ɑ:ʒ] (maki-ja:ʒ)
maquis 'mæki: ['mɑ:k-] (maki)
mar (M.), -s, -ring, -red mɑ:*, -z, -riŋ, -d
marabou, -s 'mærəbu:, -z
maraschino (M.) ,mærəs'ki:nəu
Marathi, -s mə'rɑ:ti (Hind. məraṭhi), -z
Marathon 'mærəθən
maraud, -s, -ing, -ed, -er/s mə'rɔ:d, -z, -iŋ, -id, -ə*/z

Marazion ,mærə'zaiən
marble, -s, -d 'mɑ:bl, -z, -d
Marburg (German town) 'mɑ:buəg [-bə:g] ('marburk, -burç)
marcasite 'mɑ:kəsait
Marcel(le) mɑ:'sel [also '-- when attributive]
Marcella mɑ:'selə
Marcellus mɑ:'seləs
march (s. v.) (M.), -es, -ing, -ed mɑ:tʃ, -iz, -iŋ, -t
Marchant 'mɑ:tʃənt
Marchbank, -s 'mɑ:tʃbæŋk, -s
Marchmont 'mɑ:tʃmənt
Marchesi mɑ:'keizi
marchioness, -es 'mɑ:ʃənis [,mɑ:ʃə'nes], -iz
marchpane 'mɑ:tʃpein
Marco 'mɑ:kəu
Marconi mɑ:'kəuni
marconigram, -s mɑ:'kəunigræm, -z
Marcus 'mɑ:kəs
Marden (in Kent) 'mɑ:dən [old-fashioned mɑ:'den]
mare, -s mɛə*, -z
Marengo mə'reŋgəu
mare's-nest, -s 'mɛəznest, -s
mare's-tail, -s 'mɛəzteil, -z
Margaret 'mɑ:gərit
margarine ,mɑ:dʒə'ri:n [,mɑ:gə-, '---]
Margarita ,mɑ:gə'ri:tə
Margate 'mɑ:git [locally -geit]
marge mɑ:dʒ
Margerison mɑ:'dʒerisn, 'mɑ:dʒərisn
Margery 'mɑ:dʒəri
Margetson 'mɑ:dʒitsn, 'mɑ:gitsn
Margetts 'mɑ:gits
margin, -s 'mɑ:dʒin, -z
margin|al, -ally 'mɑ:dʒin|əl, -əli
marginalia ,mɑ:dʒi'neiljə [-liə]
Margoliouth 'mɑ:gəlju:θ
Margot 'mɑ:gəu
margrave (M.), -s 'mɑ:greiv, -z
margravine, -s 'mɑ:grəvi:n, -z
marguerite (M.), -s ,mɑ:gə'ri:t, -s
Margulies 'mɑ:gulis
Marham (in Norfolk) 'mærəm ['mɑ:r-]
Note.—The pronunciation of the local residents is 'mærəm. 'mɑ:rəm is used by those connected with the airfield there.
Marhamchurch 'mærəmtʃə:tʃ
Maria (English name) mə'raiə, mə'riə, (Latin name) mə'ri(:)ə
Marian 'mɛəriən, 'mær-
Mariana (English name) ,mɛəri'ænə [,mær-], -'ɑ:nə, (Spanish historian) ,mɑ:ri'ɑ:nə (mari'ana)

Marie (*Christian name*) 'mɑːri [-riː], mə'riː:, (*biscuits*) 'mɑːri [-riː]
Marienbad   mə'ri(ː)ənbɑːd   [mɑː'r-] (maː'riːənbaːt)
marigold (M.), -s 'mærigəuld, -z
marihuana (-juana) ˌmæri'hwɑːnə, -'dʒwɑːnə [-dʒuˈɑːnə]
Marilyn 'mærilin
Marina mə'riːnə
marinade ˌmæri'neid
marine (*s. adj.*), -s mə'riːn, -z
mariner, -s 'mærinə*, -z
mariolatry ˌmɛəri'ɔlətri [ˌmær-]
Marion 'mɛəriən, 'mær-
marionette, -s ˌmæriə'net, -s
Marischal (*college at Aberdeen*) 'mɑːʃəl
marish (*s. adj.*) (*marsh, marshy*), -es 'mæriʃ, -iz
marish (*adj.*) (*like a mare*) 'mɛəriʃ
Marishes 'mæriʃiz
marital 'mæritl [mə'raitl]
maritime (M.) 'mæritaim
Marius 'mɛəriəs, 'mæriəs
marj [marge] mɑːdʒ
marjoram 'mɑːdʒərəm
Marjoribanks 'mɑːtʃbæŋks, 'mɑːʃb-
Marjorǀie, -y 'mɑːdʒərǀi, -i
mark (*s. v.*) (M.), -s, -ing/s, -ed, -edly, -er/s mɑːk, -s, -iŋ/z, -t, -idli, -ə*/z
Markby 'mɑːkbi
market (*s. v.*) (M.), -s, -ing, -ed; -able 'mɑːkit, -s, -iŋ, -id; -əbl
market-day, -s 'mɑːkitdei, -z
market-garden, -s 'mɑːkitˌgɑːdn, -z
market-place, -s 'mɑːkitpleis, -iz
market-price, -s 'mɑːkit'prais, -iz
market-town, -s 'mɑːkittaun, -z
Markham 'mɑːkəm
Marks mɑːks
marksǀman, -men 'mɑːksǀmən, -mən [-men]
marl mɑːl
Marlborough 'mɔːlbərə ['mɑːl-]
   Note.—'mɔːlbərə *is the usual pronunciation of the name of the town in Wilts. and of the family name.* 'mɑːl- *is not infrequently heard in names of London streets.* 'mɑːl- *is also the form used for the name of the town in U.S.A. and the district in New Zealand.*
Marlene (*English name*) 'mɑːliːn, mɑː'liːn (*German name*) mɑː'leinə (mar'leːnə)
Marler 'mɑːlə*
Marlǀey, -ing 'mɑːlǀi, -iŋ
Marlow(e) 'mɑːləu
Marmaduke 'mɑːmədjuːk

marmalade, -s 'mɑːmələid [-mǀeid], -z
Marmion 'mɑːmjən [-mǀən]
marmite 'mɑːmait [-miːt]
Marmora 'mɑːmərə
marmoset, -s 'mɑːməuzet, -s
marmot, -s 'mɑːmət, -s
Marne mɑːn
Marner 'mɑːnə*
marocain 'mærəkein
maroon (*s. v.*), -s, -ing, -ed mə'ruːn, -z, -iŋ, -d
Marquand 'mɑːkwənd
marque mɑːk
marquee, -s mɑː'kiː:, -z
Marquesas mɑː'keisæs [-eizæs, -əs]
marquess [-quis], -es 'mɑːkwis, -iz
marquessate, -s 'mɑːkwisit, -s
marquet(e)ry 'mɑːkitri
marquisate, -s 'mɑːkwizit, -s
Marrakesh mə'rækeʃ [ˌmærə'keʃ]
marram 'mærəm
marriage, -s; -able 'mæridʒ, -iz; -əbl
marrow, -s, -y 'mærəu, -z, -i
marrowbone, -s 'mærəubəun, -z
marrowfat, -s 'mærəufæt, -s
marrǀy (*v. interj.*), -ies, -ying, -ied 'mærǀi, -iz, -iiŋ, -id
Marryat 'mæriət
Mars mɑːz
Marsala mɑː'sɑːlə
Marsden 'mɑːzdən
Marseillaise ˌmɑːsə'leiz [-sǀ'eiz, -sei'eiz] (marsεjε:z)
Marseilles mɑː'seilz
marsh (M.), -es mɑːʃ, -iz
marshǀal (*s. v.*), -als, -alling, -alled 'mɑːʃǀəl, -əlz, -liŋ [-əliŋ], -əld
Marshall 'mɑːʃəl
marshalsea (M.) 'mɑːʃəlsi: [-si]
marshǀy, -ier, -iest, -iness 'mɑːʃǀi, -iə* [-jə*], -iist [-jist], -inis
Marsland 'mɑːzlənd
Marston 'mɑːstən
marsupial (*s. adj.*), -s mɑː'sjuːpjəl [-'suː:-, -piəl], -z
mart, -s mɑːt, -s
Martel(l) mɑː'tel
martello mɑː'teləu
marten, -s 'mɑːtin, -z
Martha 'mɑːθə
martiǀal (M.), -ally 'mɑːʃǀəl, -əli
Martian, -s 'mɑːʃjən [-ʃiən], -z
martin (M.), -s 'mɑːtin, -z
Martineau 'mɑːtinəu
martinet, -s ˌmɑːti'net, -s
martini (M.), -s mɑː'tiːni, -z
Martinique ˌmɑːti'niːk
Martinmas ˌmɑːtinməs [-mæs]

martyr (s. v.) (M.), -s, -ing, -ed 'mɑ:tə*, -z, -riŋ, -d

martyrdom, -s 'mɑ:tədəm, -z

martyriz|e [-is|e], -es, -ing, -ed 'mɑ:-təraiz [-tir-], -iz, -iŋ, -d

marv|el (s. v.), -els, -elling, -elled 'mɑ:v|əl, -əlz, -ḷiŋ [-əliŋ], -əld

marvellous, -ly, -ness 'mɑ:vələs [-viləs],

Marx mɑ:ks   [-li, -nis

marxian 'mɑ:ksjən [-ïən]

marxi|sm, -st/s 'mɑ:ksi|zəm, -st/s

Mary 'meəri

Maryborough 'meəribərə [-bʌrə]

Maryculter ˌmeəri'ku:tə*

Maryland 'meərilænd [-lənd, also 'meri-lənd in imitation of American pronunciation]

Marylebone (road, district (without St.)) 'mærələbən [-bəun, 'mærəbən, 'mæri-bən, 'mɑ:libən]

Mary-le-Bone (preceded by St. as in the expressions Church of, Borough of St. M.) 'meərilə'bəun

Maryport 'meəripɔ:t

Marzials 'mɑ:zjəlz [-zïəlz]

marzipan ˌmɑ:zi'pæn ['--- -]

Masai (African people, language) 'mɑ:sai

Masaryk 'mæsərik

Mascagni mæs'kɑ:nji(:)

mascara mæs'kɑ:rə

mascot, -s 'mæskət [-skɔt], -s

masculine (s. adj.), -s 'mæskjulin ['mɑ:s-], -z

masculinity ˌmæskju'liniti [ˌmɑ:s-]

maser, -s 'meizə*, -z

Masefield 'meisfi:ld ['meiz-]

mash (s. v.) (M.), -es, -ing, -ed mæʃ, -iz, -iŋ, -t

Masham (in Yorks.) 'mæsəm, (surname) 'mæsəm, 'mæʃəm

masher, -s 'mæʃə*, -z

mash|ie [-sh|y], -ies 'mæʃ|i, -iz

Mashona, -land mə'ʃɔnə [old-fashioned -'ʃəun-], -lænd

Masie 'meizi

mask (s. v.), -s, -ing, -ed mɑ:sk, -s, -iŋ, -t

Maskell 'mɑ:skəl ['mæs-]

Maskelyne 'mæskilin [-kəl-]

Maslin 'mæzlin

masochism 'mæsəukizm

masochistic 'mæsəu'kistik

mason (M.), -s 'meisn, -z

masonic mə'sɔnik

masonry 'meisnri

masque, -s mɑ:sk [mæsk], -s

masquerad|e (s. v.), -es, -ing, -ed, -er/s ˌmæskə'reid [ˌmɑ:s-], -z, -iŋ, -id, -ə*/z

mass (s.) (quantity of matter), -es mæs, -iz

mass (s.) (celebration of Eucharist) (M.), -es mæs [mɑ:s], -iz

mass (v.), -es, -ing, -ed mæs, -iz, -iŋ, -t

Massachusetts ˌmæsə'tʃu:sits [-səts]

massac|re (s. v.), -res, -ring, -red 'mæsək|ə* [-sik-], -əz, -əriŋ, -əd

massag|e (s. v.), -es, -ing, -ed 'mæsɑ:ʒ [-ɑ:dʒ], -iz, -iŋ, -d

mass-book, -s 'mæsbuk ['mɑ:s-], -s

Massenet 'mæsənei (masnɛ)

masseur, -s   mæ'sə:*   ['mæ'sə:*] (masœ:r), -z

masseuse, -s   mæ'sə:z   ['mæ'sə:z] (masø:z), -iz

massif, -s 'mæsi:f [-'-], -s

Massinger 'mæsindʒə*

massive, -ly, -ness 'mæsiv, -li, -nis

mass-meeting, -s 'mæs'mi:tiŋ ['-ˌ--], -z

Masson 'mæsn

Massowa mə'səuə

mass-produc|e (v.), -es, -ing, -ed 'mæs-prəˌdju:s [-pruˌd-, '--'-], -iz, -iŋ, -t

mass - production   'mæsprəˌdʌkʃən [-pruˌd-, '--'--]

mass|y, -iness 'mæs|i, -inis

mast (all senses), -s mɑ:st, -s

mast|er (s. v.), -ers, -ering, -ered 'mɑ:st|ə*, -əz, -əriŋ, -əd

master|ful, -fully, -fulness 'mɑ:stə|ful, -fuli [-fəli], -fulnis

master-hand, -s 'mɑ:stəhænd, -z

master-key, -s 'mɑ:stəki:, -z

masterl|y, -iness 'mɑ:stəl|i, -inis

Masterman 'mɑ:stəmən

masterpiece, -s 'mɑ:stəpi:s, -iz

mastership, -s 'mɑ:stəʃip, -s

master-stroke, -s 'mɑ:stə-strəuk, -s

mastery 'mɑ:stəri

mast-head, -s 'mɑ:sthed, -z

mastic 'mæstik

masticat|e, -es, -ing, -ed, -or/s 'mæsti-keit, -s, -iŋ, -id, -ə*/z

mastication ˌmæsti'keiʃən

mastiff, -s 'mæstif ['mɑ:s-], -s

mastodon, -s 'mæstədɔn [-dən], -z

mastoid, -s 'mæstɔid, -z

mastoidal mæs'tɔidl

Masurian mə'sjuərïən

mat (s. v.), -s, -ting, -ted mæt, -s, -iŋ, -id

Matabele, -land ˌmætə'bi:li, -lænd

matador, -s 'mætədɔ:*, -z

match (s. v.), -es, -ing, -ed mætʃ, -iz, -iŋ, -t

match-board 'mætʃbɔ:d [-bəəd]

match-box, -es 'mætʃbɔks, -iz

matchless, -ly, -ness 'mætʃlis, -li, -nis

match-maker, -s 'mætʃˌmeikə*, -z
matchwood 'mætʃwud
mat|e (s. v.), -es, -ing, -ed meit, -s, -iŋ, -id
mater, -s 'meitə*, -z
material (s. adj.), -s, -ly mə'tiəriəl, -z, -i
materiali|sm, -st/s mə'tiəriəli|zəm, -st/s
materialistic məˌtiəriə'listik
materialization [-isa-], -s məˌtiəriəlai-'zeiʃən [-li'z-], -z
materializ|e [-is|e], -es, -ing, -ed mə'tiəriəlaiz, -iz, -iŋ, -d
materiel məˌtiəri'el [mæˌt-] (materjɛl)
matern|al, -ally mə'tə:n|l, -əli
maternity mə'tə:niti
mathematician, -s ˌmæθimə'tiʃən [-θəm-], -z
mathematic|s, -al, -ally ˌmæθi'mætik|s [-θəˈm-], -əl, -əli
Mather, -s 'meiðə*, 'mæðə*, -z
Matheson 'mæθisn [-θəs-]
Mathew, -s 'mæθju:, 'meiθ-, -z
Mathias mə'θaiəs
Mat(h)ilda mə'tildə
maths mæθs
matin, -s 'mætin, -z
matinée, -s 'mætinei, -z
Matlock 'mætlɔk
Maton 'meitn
Matravers mə'trævəz
matriarch, -y 'meitriɑ:k, -i
matric mə'trik
matricide, -s 'meitrisaid, -z
matriculat|e, -es, -ing, -ed mə'trikju-leit, -s, -iŋ, -id
matriculation, -s məˌtrikju'leiʃən, -z
matrimonial, -ly ˌmætri'məunjəl [-niəl], -i
matrimony 'mætriməni
matri|x, -xes, -ces 'meitri|ks ['mæt-], -ksiz, -si:z
Note.—Doctors generally pronounce 'meit-. Those connected with the printing trade pronounce 'mæt-. In the gramophone trade usage varies.
matron, -s; -hood, -ly 'meitrən, -z; -hud, -li
matt mæt
matter (s. v.), -s, -ing, -ed 'mætə*, -z -riŋ, -d
Matterhorn 'mætəhɔ:n
matter-of-fact 'mætərəv'fækt
Matthes 'mæθəs
Matthew, -s 'mæθju:, -z
Matthias mə'θaiəs
Matthiessen 'mæθisn
matting (s.) 'mætiŋ
mattins 'mætinz

mattock, -s 'mætək, -s
mattress, -es 'mætris, -iz
matur|e (adj. v.), -ely, -eness; -es, -ing, -ed; -ity mə'tjuə* [-'tjɔə*, -'tjɔ:*, -'tjə:*, -'tʃuə*, -'tʃɔə*, -'tʃɔ:*], -li -nis; -z, -riŋ, -d; -riti
Maturin (surname) 'mætjurin [-tʃur-, -tʃər-]
matutinal ˌmætju(:)'tainl [mə'tju:tinl]
maud (M.), -s mɔ:d, -z
Maude mɔ:d
maudlin 'mɔ:dlin
Mauger 'meidʒə*
Maugha|m, -n mɔ:|m, -n
maugre 'mɔ:gə*
maul (s. v.), -s, -ing, -ed mɔ:l, -z, -iŋ, -d
Mauleverer mɔ:'levərə*
maulstick, -s 'mɔ:l-stik, -s
Mau-Mau 'maumau [ˌ-'-]
maunder, -s, -ing, -ed 'mɔ:ndə*, -z, -riŋ, -d
maundy (M.) 'mɔ:ndi
Maunsell 'mænsəl
Maureen 'mɔ:ri:n [mɔ:'ri:n]
Mauretania ˌmɔri'teinjə [ˌmɔ:r-, -niə]
Maurice 'mɔris
Mauritius mə'riʃəs [mu'r-, mɔ:'r-, mɔ'r-, -ʃjəs]
Mauser, -s 'mauzə*, -z
mausoleum, -s ˌmɔ:sə'liəm [-'li:əm], -z
mauve, -s məuv, -z
mavis (M.) 'meivis
Mavourneen mə'vuəni:n [-'vɔən-, -'vɔ:n-]
maw, -s mɔ:, -z
Mawer 'mɔ:ə*
Mawhinny mə'wini [-'hw-]
mawkish, -ly, -ness 'mɔ:kiʃ, -li, -nis
Max mæks
maxill|a, -ae, -as, -ary mæk'sil|ə, -i:, -əz, -əri
maxim (M.), -s 'mæksim, -z
Maximilian ˌmæksi'miljən [-liən]
maxim|um, -a 'mæksim|əm, -ə
Maximus 'mæksiməs
Maxse 'mæksi
Maxwell 'mækswəl [-wel]
may (auxil. verb) mei (normal form), me (occasional strong form before vowels), mi, mə (occasional weak forms)
May mei
Mayall 'meiɔ:l
maybe 'meibi: [-bi]
may-bug, -s 'meibʌg, -z
may-day (M.), -s 'meidei, -z
Mayfair 'mei-fɛə* ['meifɛə*]
may-flower (M.), -s 'meiˌflauə*, -z

may-fl|y, -ies 'mei-fl|ai, -aiz
mayhap 'meihæp
Mayhew 'meihju:
maying 'meiiŋ
Maynard 'meinəd [-nɑ:d]
Maynooth mə'nu:θ
mayn't meint
Maynwaring 'mænəriŋ
Mayo, -s (in Ireland, surname) 'meiəu,
    (American Indian) 'maiəu, -z
mayonnaise, -s ˌmeiə'neiz [rarely
    ˌmaiə'n-, also '— when followed by a
    stress], -iz
mayor (M.), -s; -ess/es mɛə*, -z; -ris/iz
mayoralty 'mɛərəlti   [[-res/iz]
Mayou 'meiu:
maypole, -s 'mei-pəul, -z
may-queen, -s 'mei'kwi:n ['mei-kwi:n],
mazda (M.), -s 'mæzdə, -z   [-z
maze, -s meiz, -iz
Mazenod 'meiznɔd
Mazin (surname) 'meizin
Mazo de la Roche 'meizəu dəlɑ:'rɔ ʃ
mazurka, -s mə'zə:kə, -z
maz|y, -ier, -iest, -ily, -iness 'meiz|i,
    -iə* [-jə], -iist [-jist], -ili, -inis
me (note in Tonic Sol-fa), -s mi:, -z
me (pronoun) mi: (normal form), mi
    (frequent weak form)
mead (M.), -s mi:d, -z
Meaden 'mi:dn
meadow, -s, -y 'medəu, -z, -i
meadow-grass 'medəugrɑ:s
meadowsweet 'medəu-swi:t
Meagher mɑ:*
meagre, -r, -st, -ly, -ness 'mi:gə*, -rə*,
    -rist, -li, -nis
Meaker 'mi:kə*
meal, -s mi:l, -z
mealie, -s 'mi:li, -z
mealtime, -s 'mi:l-taim, -z
meal|y, -ier, -iest, -iness 'mi:l|i, -iə*
    [-jə*], -iist [-jist], -inis
mealy-bug 'mi:li-bʌg
mealy-mouthed 'mi:limauðd
mean (s. adj. v.), -s; -er, -est, -ly, -ness;
    -ing, meant mi:n, -z; -ə*, -ist, -li, -nis;
    -iŋ, ment
meander (s. v.) (M.), -s, -ing, -ed
    mi'ændə* [mi:'æ-], -z, -riŋ, -d
meaning (s. adj.), -s, -ly 'mi:niŋ, -z, -li
meaningless 'mi:niŋlis
means (s.) mi:nz
meant (from mean) ment
meantime 'mi:n'taim ['mi:n-taim]
meanwhile 'mi:n'wail [-'hw-, '—, also
    occasionally -'- when preceded by a
    stress]

Mearns mə:nz
Mears miəz
meas|les, -ly 'mi:z|lz, -li
measurab|le, -ly, -leness 'meʒərəb|l, -li,
    -lnis
measur|e (s. v.), -es, -ing, -ed, -er/s;
    -ement/s; -eless 'meʒə*, -z, -riŋ, -d,
    -rə*/z; -mənt/s; -lis
meat, -s mi:t, -s
Meates mi:ts
Meath (Irish county) mi:ð [often pro-
    nounced mi:θ by English people]
meatless 'mi:tlis
meat-offering, -s 'mi:tˌɔfəriŋ, -z
meat-pie, -s 'mi:t'pai, -z
meat-safe, -s 'mi:t-seif, -s
meatus, -es mi'eitəs [mi:'ei-], -iz
meat|y, -ier, -iest, -iness 'mi:t|i, -iə*,
    -iist, -inis
Mecca 'mekə
meccano (M.), -s mi'kɑ:nəu [me-, mə-],
    -z
mechanic, -s, -al, -ally mi'kænik, -s, -əl,
    -əli
mechanician, -s ˌmekə'niʃən, -z
mechanism, -s 'mekənizəm [-kn̩i-], -z
mechanization [-isa-] ˌmekənai'zeiʃən
    [-ni'z-]
mechaniz|e [-is|e], -es, -ing, -ed
    'mekənaiz, -iz, -iŋ, -d
Mechlin 'meklin
Mecklenburg 'meklinbə:g [-lən-]
medal, -s 'medl, -z
medallion, -s mi'dæljən [me'd-, mə'd-],
medallist, -s 'medlist [-dəl-], -s   [-z
medd|le, -les, -ling, -led, -ler/s 'medl|l,
    -lz, -liŋ [-liŋ], -ld, -lə*/z [-lə*/z]
meddlesome, -ness 'medlsəm, -nis
Mede, -s mi:d, -z
Medea mi'diə [mə'd-, -'di:ə]
me|dia (phonetic term), -diae 'me|diə,
    -dii: [-diai]
media (plur. of medium) 'mi:djə [-diə]
mediaeval=medieval
medial 'mi:djəl [-diəl]
median, -s 'mi:djən [-diən], -z
mediant, -s 'mi:djənt [-diənt], -z
mediate (adj.), -ly, -ness 'mi:diit [-djit,
    -djət, -diət], -li, -nis
mediat|e (v.), -es, -ing, -ed 'mi:dieit, -s,
    -iŋ, -id
mediation, -s ˌmi:di'eiʃən, -z
mediator (M.), -s 'mi:dieitə*, -z
mediatorial ˌmi:diə'tɔ:riəl [-djə-]
medic|al (s. adj.), -als, -ally 'medik|əl,
    -əlz, -əli
medicament, -s me'dikəmənt [mi'd-,
    mə'd-, 'medik-], -s

medicat|e, -es, -ing, -ed 'medikeit, -s, -iŋ, -id

medication ˌmedi'keiʃən

Medicean ˌmedi'tʃi(:)ən [-'si(:)ən]

Medici 'meditʃi(:) ('mɛ:ditʃi)

medicin|al, -ally me'disin|l [mi'd-, mə'd-, -sn̩|l], -əli [-l̩i]

medicine, -s; -chest/s; -man, -men 'medsin [-disin], -z; -tʃest/s; -mæn, -men

Note.—Some people distinguish between the 'science' ('medisin) and the 'substance' ('medsin); others make no such distinction but use the one form or the other for both senses.

medico, -s' medikəu, -z

mediev|al, -alism ˌmedi'i:v|əl [ˌmi:d-], -əlizəm [-l̩izəm]

Medill mə'dil

Medina (in Arabia) me'di:nə [mi'd-], (in U.S.A.) me'dainə [mi'd-]

medinal 'medinl

mediocre ˌmi:di'əukə* ['---, 'med-]

mediocrity ˌmi:di'ɔkriti [ˌmed-]

meditat|e, -es, -ing, -ed 'mediteit, -s, -iŋ, -id

meditation, -s ˌmedi'teiʃən, -z

meditative, -ly, -ness 'meditətiv [-teit-], -li, -nis

Mediterranean ˌmeditə'reinjən [-nïən]

medi|um (s. adj.), -a, -ums 'mi:dj|əm [-dï|-], -ə, -əmz

mediumistic ˌmi:djə'mistik [-dïə-]

medlar, -s 'medlə*, -z

medley (M.), -s 'medli, -z

Medlock 'medlɔk

Médoc, -s 'medɔk['meid-, me'dɔk], -s

medulla, -s me'dʌlə [mi'd-], -z

Medusa mi'dju:zə [me'd-, mə'd-]

Medway 'medwei

Mee mi:

meed, -s mi:d, -z

meek (M.), -er, -est, -ly, -ness mi:k, -ə*, -ist, -li, -nis

meerschaum, -s 'miəʃəm, -z

Meerut 'miərət (Hind. merəᵗh)

meet (s. adj. v.), -s, -ly, -ness; -ing/s, met mi:t, -s, -li, -nis; -iŋ/z, met

meeting-hou|se, -ses 'mi:tiŋhau|s, -ziz

meeting-place, -s ' mi:tiŋpleis, -iz

Meg meg

megacycle, -s 'megə,saikl, -z

megalithic ˌmegə'liθik

megalomania 'megələu'meinjə [ˌmeg-, -nïə]

megalomaniac, -s 'megələu'meiniæk [ˌmeg-, -njæk], -s

Megan 'megən

megaphone, -s 'megəfəun ,-z

megatheri|um, -a ˌmegə'θiəri|əm, -ə

megaton, -s 'megətʌn, -z

megilp mə'gilp

megrim, -s 'mi:grim, - z

Meier 'maiə*

Meighen (Canadian name) 'mi:ən

Meigs megz

Meikle 'mi:kl

Meiklejohn 'mikldʒɔn

meiosis mai'əusis

Meistersinger, -s 'maistə,siŋə*, -z

melancholia ˌmelən'kəuljə [-lən'k-, -lïə]

melancholic ˌmelən'kɔlik [-lən'k-]

melancholy (s. adj.) 'melənkəli [-ləŋk-, -,kɔli]

Melanchthon me'læŋkθɔn [mi'l-, -θən]

Melane|sia, -sian/s ˌmelə'ni:zjə [-zïə, -ʒjə, -ʒïə, -ʒə, -sjə, -sïə], -zjən/z [-zïən/z , -ʒjən/z, -ʒïən/z, -ʒən/z, -sjən/z, -sïən/z, -ʃjən/z, -ʃïən/z, -ʃən/z]

mélange, -s mei'lɑ̃:nʒ [-'lɔ̃:nʒ] (melɑ̃:ʒ), -iz

melanism 'melənizəm

Melanthios me'lænθïəs [-θïɔs]

Melba 'melbə

Melbourne 'melbən [-bɔ:n]

Note.—In Australia always 'melbən.

Melchett 'meltʃit

Melchizedek mel'kizədek

Melcombe 'melkəm

Meleager ˌmeli'eigə*

mêlée, -s 'melei ['meil-] (mɛle), -z

Melhuish 'meliʃ, 'melhjuiʃ [-ljuiʃ]

melinite 'melinait

Melita 'melitə

mellifluous me'lifluəs [-flwəs]

Mellin 'melin

Mellor 'melə* [-lɔ:*]

mellow (adj. v.), -er, -est, -ness; -s, -ing, -ed 'meləu, -ə*, -ist, -nis; -z, -iŋ, -d

melodic mi'lɔdik [me'l-, mə'l-]

melodious, -ly, -ness mi'ləudjəs [me'l-, mə'l-, -dïəs], -li, -nis

melodrama, -s 'meləu,drɑ:mə [ˌ--'--], -z

melodramatic ˌmeləudrə'mætik

melodramatist, -s ˌmeləu'dræmətist, -s

melod|y, -ies 'melədi [-lud-], -iz

melon, -s 'melən, -z

Melos (island) 'mi:lɔs ['mel-]

Melpomene mel'pɔmini(:)

Melrose 'melrəuz

melt, -s, -ing/ly, -ed melt, -s, -iŋ/li, -id

Mel|ton, -ville 'mel|tən, -vil

member, -s; -ship/s 'membə*, -z; -ʃip/s

membrane, -s 'membrein, -z
membran|eous, -ous mem'brein|jəs [-ïəs], -əs
Memel 'meiməl
memento, -s mi'mentəu [me'm-, mə'm-], -z
Memnon 'memnɔn
memo, -s 'meməu ['mi:məu], -z
memoir, -s 'memwɑ:* [-wɔ:*], -z
memorab|le, -ly 'memərəb|l, -li
memorand|um, -a, -ums ‚memə'rænd|əm [-mu'r-, -mɽ'æ-], -ə, -əmz
memorial (s. adj.), -s mi'mɔ:rïəl [me'm-, mə'm-], -z
memorializ|e [-is|e], -es, -ing, -ed mi'mɔ:rïəlaiz [me'm-, mə'm-], -iz, -iŋ, -d
memoriter mi'mɔritə* [me'm-, mə'm-]
memoriz|e [-is|e], -es, -ing, -ed 'meməraiz [-mur-, -mɽ-], -iz, -iŋ, -d
memor|y, -ies 'memər|i [-mur-, -mɽ-], -iz
Memphis 'memfis
memsahib, -s 'mem‚sɑ:hib [-sɑ:b], -z
men (plur. of man) men
menac|e (s. v.), -es, -ing/ly, -ed 'menəs [-nis], -iz, -iŋ/li, -t
ménage, -s me'nɑ:ʒ [mei'n-] (mena:ʒ), -iz
menagerie, -s mi'nædʒəri [me'n-, mə'n-, -'nɑ:dʒəri], -z
Menai (strait) 'menai (Welsh 'menai)
Menander mi'nændə* [me'n-, mə'n-]
mend, -s, -ing, -ed, -er/s mend, -z, -iŋ, -id, -ə*/z
mendacious, -ly men'deiʃəs, -li
mendacity men'dæsiti
Mendel 'mendl
Mendeli men'di:li
Mendelian men'di:ljən [-lïən]
Mendelssohn (English surname) 'mendlsn, (German composer) 'mendlsn [-səun]
mendican|cy, -t/s 'mendikən|si, -t/s
mendicity men'disiti
Mendip, -s 'mendip, -s
Mendoza men'dəuzə
mene 'mi:ni
Menelaus ‚meni'leïəs
menhir, -s 'menhïə*, -z
menial (s. adj.), -s, -ly 'mi:njəl [-nïəl], -z, -i
meningitis ‚menin'dʒaitis
Meno 'mi:nəu
men-of-war (plur. of man-of-war) 'menəv'wɔ:*
menopause 'menəupɔ:z
Menpes 'mempis ['menp-, -iz]
menses 'mensi:z

Menshevik, -s 'menʃəvik [-ʃiv-], -s
menstrual 'menstrŭəl [-trwəl]
menstruation ‚menstru'eiʃən
mensurability ‚menʃurə'biliti [-ʃər-, -nsjur-, -lət-]
mensurable 'menʃurəbl [-ʃər-]
mensuration ‚mensjuə'reiʃən [-sju'r-]
ment|al, -ally 'ment|l, -əli [-li]
mentalistic, -ally ‚mentə'listik [-tḷ'is-], -əli [-li]
mentalit|y, -ies men'tælit|i, -iz
Menteith men'ti:θ
menthol 'menθɔl [-θəl]
menti|on (s. v.), -ons, -oning, -oned; -onable 'menʃ|ən, -ənz, -ŋiŋ [-niŋ, -əniŋ], -ənd; -nəbl [-nəbl, -ənəbl]
Mentone men'təuni
mentor, -s 'mentɔ:*, - z
menu, -s 'menju:, -z
Menuhin (American violinist) 'menjuin [-nuhin, -nuin]
Menzies 'menziz, 'meṇis, 'miṇis
 Note.—The former Prime Minister of Australia is 'menziz.
Meolse mels
Meopham 'mepəm
Mepham 'mefəm
Mephibosheth me'fibəʃeθ [mi'f-, -buʃ-, among Jews also ‚mefi'bəuʃeθ, -'bɔʃeθ]
Mephistophelean [-lian] ‚mefistə'fi:ljən [-tɔ'f-, -lïən]
Mephistopheles ‚mefis'tɔfili:z [-fəl-, -fḷ-]
mephitic me'fitik
mephitis me'faitis
Mercadi mə:'kɑ:di
mercantile 'mə:kəntail
mercantilism 'mə:kəntilizm [-tail-]
Mercator mə:'keitɔ:* [-tə*]
Mercedes (English fem. name) 'mə:sidi:z, (car) mə:'seidi:z
mercenar|y (s. adj.), -ies 'mə:sinər|i [-snə-, -snə-], -iz
mercer (M.), -s 'mə:sə*, -z
merceriz|e [-is|e], -es, -ing, -ed 'mə:səraiz, -iz, -iŋ, -d
merchandise 'mə:tʃəndaiz
merchant, -s; -man, -men 'mə:tʃənt, -s; -mən, -mən [-men]
merchant-ship, -s 'mə:tʃənt-ʃip, -s
Merchison 'mə:kisn
Merchiston 'mə:kistən
Mercia, -n 'mə:ʃjə [-ʃïə], -n
merci|ful, -fully, -fulness 'mə:si|fuḷ, -fuli [-fəli], -fuḷnis
merciless, -ly, -ness 'mə:silis, -li, -nis
mercurial, -ly mə:'kjuərïəl [-'kjɔər-, -'kjɔ:r-, -'kjə:r-], -i
mercuric mə:'kjuərik

mercurous 'mə:kjurəs
mercury (M.) 'mə:kjuri [-kjər-]
Mercutio mə:'kju:ʃjəu [-ʃiəu]
merc|y (M.), -ies 'mə:s|i, -iz
mercy-seat, -s 'mə:sisi:t, -s
mere (s. adj.), -s, -st, -ly miə*, -z, -rist, -li
Meredith 'merədiθ [-rid-], in Wales me'rediθ
meretricious, -ly, -ness ,meri'triʃəs, -li, -nis
merganser, -s mə:'gænsə*, -z
merg|e, -es, -ing, -ed mə:dʒ, -iz, -iŋ, -d
merger, -s 'mə:dʒə*, -z
meridian, -s mə'ridiən [mi'r-, -djən], -z
meridional mə'ridiənl [mi'r-, -djən-]
meringue, -s mə'ræŋ, -z
merino mə'ri:nəu
Merioneth, -shire ,meri'oniθ [-neθ, -nəθ] (Welsh meri'oneθ), -ʃiə* [-ʃ-*]
merit (s. v.), -s, -ing, -ed 'merit, -s, -iŋ, -id
meritocrac|y, -ies, meri'tɔkrəs|i, -iz
meritorious, -ly, -ness ,meri'tɔ:riəs, -li, -nis
Merivale 'meriveil
merlin (M.), -s 'mə:lin, -z
mermaid, -s 'mə:meid, -z
mer|man, -men 'mə:|mæn, -men
Meroe 'merəui
Merope 'merəpi [-pi:]
Merovingian ,merəu'vindʒiən [-dʒjən]
Merrilies 'meriliz
Merrimac 'merimæk
Merriman 'merimən
merriment 'merimənt
Merrivale 'meriveil
merr|y (M.), -ier, -iest, -ily, -iness 'mer|i, -iə*, -iist, -ili, -inis
merry-andrew, -s 'meri'ændru:, -z
merry-go-round, -s 'merigəu,raund, -z
merrymak|er/s, -ing 'meri,meik|ə*/z, -iŋ
merrythought, -s 'meriθɔ:t, -s
Merryweather 'meri,weðə*
Mersey 'mə:zi
Merthyr 'mə:θə* (Welsh 'merθir)
Merthyr Tydfil 'mə:θə'tidvil (Welsh 'merθir'tidvil)
Merton 'mə:tn
mésalliance, -s me'zæliəns [mei'z-, -ljəns, -liɑ:ns, -liɔ:ns, -liɑ:ns, -liɔ:ns] (mezaljɑ̃:s), -iz
mesdames 'meidæm (medam)
meseems mi'si:mz
mesembryanthemum, -s mi,zembri'ænθiməm [mə,z-, -θəm-], -z
mesh (s. v.), -es, -ing, -ed meʃ, -iz, -iŋ, -t

Meshach [-ak] 'mi:ʃæk
Meshed 'meʃed
mesial 'mi:zjəl [-ziəl]
Mesmer 'mezmə*
mesmeric mez'merik
mesmeri|sm, -st/s 'mezməri|zəm, -st/s
mesmeriz|e [-is/e], -es, -ing, -ed, -er/s 'mezməraiz, -iz, -iŋ, -d, -ə*/z
mesne mi:n
meson, -s 'mi:zɔn ['mesɔn, 'mi:sɔn], -z
Mesopotamia ,mesəpə'teimjə [-miə]
mesotron, -s 'mesəutrɔn, -z
mesozoic ,mesəu'zəuik
mess (s. v.), -es, -ing, -ed mes, -iz, -iŋ, -t
message, -s 'mesidʒ, -iz
Messala me'sɑ:lə
messenger, -s 'mesindʒə* [-sn̩-], -z
Messiah, -s mi'saiə [me's-, mə's-], -z
messianic ,mesi'ænik
Messina me'si:nə [mə's-, mi's-]
messmate, -s 'mesmeit, -s
Messrs. 'mesəz
messuage, -s 'meswidʒ [-sjuidʒ], -iz
mess|y, -ier, -iest, -ily, -iness 'mes|i, -iə*, -iist, -ili, -inis
Mestre 'mestri
met (from meet) met
meta (solidified spirit) 'mi:tə
met|a, -ae (column in Roman circus) 'mi:t|ə, -i: ['meit|ə, -ai]
meta- (Greek prefix) 'metə-, ,metə-
Meta (Christian name) 'mi:tə
metabolism me'tæbəlizəm [-bul-]
metacentre, -s 'metə,sentə*, -z
metagalax|y, -ies 'metə,gæləks|i, -iz
met|al (s. v.), -als, -alling, -alled 'met|l, -lz, -liŋ, -ld
metallic mi'tælik [me't-, mə't-]
metalliferous ,metə'lifərəs
metallography ,metə'lɔgrəfi
metalloid 'metəloid
metallurg|ist/s, -y me'tælədʒ|ist/s [mi't-, 'metələ:dʒ-, 'metlə:dʒ-], -i
metamorphos|e, -es, -ing, -ed ,metə-'mɔ:fəuz, -iz, -iŋ, -d
metamorphos|is, -es (plur.) ,metə'mɔ:-fəs|is [,metəmɔ:'fəus-], -i:z
metaphor, -s 'metəfə*, -z
metaphoric, -al, -ally ,metə'fɔrik, -əl, -əli
metaphysician, -s ,metəfi'ziʃən, -z
metaphysic|s, -al, -ally ,metə'fizik|s ['metə'f-], -əl, -əli
metaplasm 'metəplæzəm
metathes|is, -es me'tæθəs|is [mi't-, mə't-, -θis-], -i:z
Metayers mi'teiəz [mə't-]
Metcalfe (surname) 'metkɑ:f [-kəf]

met|e, -es, -ing, -ed mi:t, -s, -iŋ, -id
Metellus mi'teləs [me't-]
metempsychosis ˌmetempsi'kəusis [me-ˌtem-, -psai'k-]
meteor, -s 'mi:tjə* [-tīə*, -tiɔ:*], -z
meteoric ˌmi:ti'ɔrik
meteorite, -s 'mi:tjərait [-tīə-], -s
meteorologic, -al ˌmi:tjərə'lɔdʒik [-tīə-], -əl
meteorolog|ist/s, -y ˌmi:tjə'rɔlədʒ|ist/s [-tīə], -i
meter, -s 'mi:tə*, -z
meth, -s meθ, -s
methane 'mi:θein
metheglin me'θeglin [mi'θ-, mə'θ-]
methinks mi'θiŋks
method, -s 'meθəd, -z
methodic, -al, -ally mi'θɔdik [me'θ-, mə'θ-], -əl, -əli
methodi|sm, -st/s 'meθədi|zəm, -st/s
methodological ˌmeθədə'lɔdʒikl
methodolog|y, -ies ˌmeθə'dɔlədʒ|i, -iz
methought mi'θɔ:t
Methuen (surname) 'meθjuin [-θjŭən, -θjwən], (American town) mi'θjuin [mə'θ-]
Methuselah mi'θju:zələ [mə'θ-, -'θu:-]
Methven 'meθvən [-ven]
methyl (commercial and general pronunciation) 'meθil, (chemists' pronunciation) 'mi:θail
methylated 'meθileitid [-θ|ei-]
meticulous, -ly mi'tikjuləs [me't-], -li
metonymy mi'tɔnimi [me't-]
metope, -s 'metəup, -s
metre, -s 'mi:tə*, -z
metric, -al, -ally 'metrik, -əl, -əli
metrics 'metriks
metrist, -s 'metrist, -s
Metroland 'metrəulænd
metronome, -s 'metrənəum [-tr‚əum], -z
metronomic ˌmetrə'nɔmik
Metropole 'metrəpəul
metropolis, -es mi'trɔpəlis [me't-, mə't-, -p‚is], -iz
metropolitan (s. adj.), -s ˌmetrə'pɔlitən, -z
mettle 'metl
Metz mets
meuse (track of hare), -s mju:z, -iz
Meux mju:z, mju:ks, mju:
mew (s. v.), -s, -ing, -ed mju:, -z, -iŋ [mjuiŋ], -d
mewl, -s, -ing, -ed mju:l, -z, -iŋ, -d
mews (s.) mju:z
Mexborough 'meksbərə
Mexic|an/s, -o 'meksik|ən/z, -əu
Meyer 'maiə*

Meyerbeer (composer) 'maiəbiə*
Meynell 'menl, 'meinl
Meyrick 'merik, 'meirik
mezzanine, -s 'metsəni:n ['mez-], -z
mezzo-soprano, -s 'medzəusə'prɑ:nəu ['metsəu-], -z
mezzotint, -s 'medzəutint [-metsəu-], -s
Mgr., Mgrs. mɔn'si:njə*, -z
mi (musical note), -s mi:, -z
Miami mai'æmi [-'ɑ:mi]
miaow, -s, -ing, -ed mi(:)'au [mjau], -z, -iŋ, -d
miasm|a, -as, -ata, -al mi'æzm|ə [mai'æ-], -əz, -ətə, -əl
miasmatic mīəz'mætik [ˌmaiæz-, ˌmaiəz-]
mica 'maikə
micaceous mai'keiʃəs
Micah 'maikə
Micaiah mai'kaiə [mi'k-]
Micawber mi'kɔ:bə*
mice (plur. of mouse) mais
Michael 'maikl
Michaelmas, -es 'miklməs, -iz
Michelangelo ˌmaikəl'ændʒiləu [-k]-, -dʒəl-]
Micheldever 'mitʃəldevə*
Michelin, -s 'miʃlin ['mitʃəlin], -z
Michelle mi:'ʃel [mi'ʃ-]
Michelmore 'mitʃəlmɔ:*
Michelson 'mitʃəlsn, 'mikəlsn
Michie 'miki, in Scotland also 'mixi
Michigan 'miʃigən
Michmash 'mikmæʃ
microbe, -s 'maikrəub, -z
microcephalic 'maikrəuke'fælik [ˌmai--əuki'f-, -əuse'f-, -əusi'f-]
microcephalous 'maikrəu'kefələs [ˌmai-, -əu'sef-]
microcop|y, -ies 'maikrəuˌkɔp|i, -iz
microcosm, -s 'maikrəuˌkɔzəm [-kruk-], -z
microfilm, -s 'maikrəufilm, -z [-z
micro-groove, -s 'maikrəugru:v, -z
micrometer, -s mai'krɔmitə*, -z
micron, -s 'maikrɔn [-rən], -z
micro-organism, -s 'maikrəu'ɔ:gənizəm [-gṇi-], -z
microphone, -s 'maikrəfəun, -z
microphonic ˌmaikrə'fɔnik
microscope, -s 'maikrəskəup [-krus-], -z
microscopic, -al, -ally ˌmaikrəs'kɔpik [-krus-], -əl, -əli
microscop|ist/s, -y mai'krɔskəp|ist/s, -i
microwatt, -s 'maikrəuwɔt, -s
mid mid
Midas 'maidæs [-dəs]
midday, -s 'middei [also 'mid'd- when not attributive], -z

midden, -s 'midn, -z
middle, -s 'midl, -z
middle-aged 'midl'eidʒd [also '---, esp.
  when attributive]
middlebrow 'midlbrau
middle-class 'midl'klɑːs [also '---, esp.
  when attributive]
middle|man, -men 'midl|mæn, -men
Middlemarch 'midlmɑːtʃ
Middlemast 'midlmɑːst, -mæst
middlemost 'midlməust
Middlesbrough 'midlzbrə
Middlesex 'midlseks
Middleton 'midltən
middling 'midlɪŋ [-dlɪŋ]
midd|y, -ies 'mid|i, -iz
midge, -s midʒ, -iz
midget, -s 'midʒit, -s
Midhurst 'midhəst
Midian, -ite/s 'midɪən [-djən], -ait/s
midland (M.), -s 'midlənd, -z
Midlothian mid'ləuðjən [-ðɪən]
midnight 'midnait
mid-off, -s 'mid'ɔf [-'ɔːf], -s
mid-on 'mid'ɔn, -z
midriff, -s 'midrif, -s
midship|man, -men 'midʃip|mən, -mən
midst midst [mitst]
midsummer (M.) 'mid,sʌmə*
midway 'mid'wei ['midw-]
Midway (Island) 'midwei
midwi|fe, -ves 'midwai|f, -vz
midwifery 'midwifəri
midwinter 'mid'wintə*
mien, -s miːn, -z
Miers 'maiəz
mig, -s mig, -z
might (s. v.) mait
mightn't 'maitnt
might|y, -ier, -iest, -ily, -iness 'mait|i,
  -ɪə* [-jə*], -iist [-jist], -ili, -inis
mignonette ,minjə'net ['---]
migraine, -s 'miːgrein ['mig-, 'mai-], -z
migrant (s. adj.), -s 'maigrənt, -s
migrat|e, -es, -ing, -ed, -or/s mai'greit
  ['maigreit], -s, -iŋ, -id, -ə*/z
migration, -s mai'greiʃən, -z
migratory 'maigrətəri [mai'greitəri]
Mikado, -s mi'kɑːdəu, -z
Mikardo mi'kɑːdəu
mike (M.), -s maik, -s
milady mi'leidi
Milan (in Italy) mi'læn [old-fashioned
  'milən]
  Note.—'milən is necessary for rhythm
  in Shakespeare's 'The Tempest'.
Milan (in U.S.A.) 'mailən, (Serabin
  king) 'miːlən

Milanese ,milə'niːz ['milə'n-]
milch miltʃ [milʃ]
mild, -er, -est, -ly, -ness maild, -ə*,
  -ist, -li, -nis
Mildenhall 'mildənhɔːl
mild|ew (s. v.), -ews, -ewing, -ewed
  'mild|juː, -juːz, -ju(ː)iŋ, -juːd
Mildmay 'maildmei
Mildred 'mildrid [-red]
mile (M.), -s mail, -z
mileage, -s 'mailidʒ, -iz
Miles mailz
Milesian, -s mai'liːzjən [mi'l-, -zɪən,
  -ʒən, -ʒɪən, -ʒən], -z
milestone, -s 'mail-stəun, -z
Miletus mi'liːtəs [mai'l-]
milfoil, -s 'milfɔil, -z
Milford 'milfəd
Milhaud 'miːjəu (mijo)
milieu, -s 'miːljə: (miljø), -z
militan|cy, -t/ly 'militən|si, -t/li
militari|sm, -st/s 'militəri|zəm, -st/s
militarization [-isa-] 'militərai'zeiʃən
  [,mil-, -ri'z-]
militariz|e [-is|e], -es, -ing, -ed 'mili-
  təraiz, -iz, -iŋ, -d
military 'militəri
militat|e, -es, -ing, -ed 'militeit, -s, -iŋ,
  -id
militia, -man, -men mi'liʃə, -mən, -mən
  [-men]
milk (s. v.), -s, -ing, -ed, -er/s milk, -s,
  -iŋ, -t, -ə*/z
milkmaid, -s 'milkmeid, -z
milk|man, -men 'milk|mən, -mən
  [-men]
milk-shake, -s 'milk'ʃeik ['--], -s
milksop, -s 'milksɔp, -s
milk-|tooth, -teeth 'milk|tuːθ, -tiːθ
milk-white 'milk-wait [-khw-]
milkwort, -s 'milk-wɔːt, -s
milk|y, -ier, -iest, -ily, -iness 'milk|i,
  -ɪə* [-jə*], -iist [-jist], -ili, -inis
mill (s. v.) (M.), -s, -ing, -ed mil, -z, -iŋ, -d
Millais (sing.) 'milei, (plur.) -z
Millard 'miləd, -lɑːd
Millbank 'milbæŋk
mill-board, -s 'milbɔːd [-bəəd]
millenary mi'lenəri ['milinəri]
millennium, -s mi'leniəm [-njəm], -z
millepede, -s 'milipiːd, -z
miller (M.), -s 'milə*, -z
millesimal mi'lesiməl
millet 'milit
mill-hand, -s 'milhænd, -z
milliard, -s 'miljɑːd [-liɑːd], -z
millibar, -s 'milibɑː:*, -z
Millicent 'milisnt

milligram(me), -s 'miligræm ,-z
millimeter, -s 'mili,mi:tə*, -z
milliner, -s 'milinə*, -z
millinery 'milinəri
million, -s 'miljən, -z
millionaire, -s ,miljə'nɛə*, -z
millionairess, -es ,miljə'nɛəris [-res], -iz
millionfold 'miljənfəuld
millionth, -s 'miljənθ, -s
Millom 'miləm
mill-pond, -s 'mil-pɔnd, -z
Mills milz
mill-stone, -s 'mil-stəun, -z
Milltimber 'mil,timbə*
mill-wheel, -s 'milwi:l ['milhw-], -z
Miln mil
Milne miln, mil
Milne-Home 'miln'hju:m
Milner 'milnə*
Milnes milz, milnz
Milngavie mil'gai
Milo 'mailəu ['mi:-]
milord, -s mi'lɔ:d [-'lɔ:*], -z
milreis (sing.) 'milreis, (plur.) 'milreis
  [-reiz]
Milton 'miltən
Miltonic mil'tɔnik
Milwaukee mil'wɔ:ki(:)
mime, -s maim, -z
mimeograph (s. v.), -s, -ing, -ed
  'mimɪəgrɑ:f [-miəug-, -græf], -s, -iŋ, -t
mimetic mi'metik
mimic (s. adj. v.) , -s, -king, -ked
  'mimik, -s, -iŋ, -t
mimicry 'mimikri
mimosa, -s mi'məuzə, -z
mimulus, -es 'mimjuləs, -iz
mina, -s 'mainə, -z
minaret, -s 'minəret, -s
minatory 'minətəri ['main-]
mince|e (s. v.), -es, -ing/ly, -ed mins, -iz,
  -iŋ/li, -t
mincemeat 'mins-mi:t
mince-pie, -s 'mins'pai, -z
Minch, -es, -in mintʃ, -iz, -in
mind (s. v.), -s, -ing, -ed maind, -z, -iŋ,
  -id
mind|ful, -fully, -fulness 'maind|ful,
  -fuli [-fəli], -fulnis
min|e (s. v.), -es, -ing, -ed, -er/s main,
  -z, -iŋ, -d, -ə*/z
mine (pron.) main
  Note.—On the stage, in serious drama,
  this word is sometimes pronounced
  min when attributive and unstressed.
minefield, -s 'main-fi:ld, -z
Minehead 'mainhed ['main'hed]
mine-layer, -s 'main,leiə*, -z

mine-laying 'main,leiiŋ
mineral (s. adj.), -s 'minərəl, -z
mineraliz|e[-is|e], -es, -ing, -ed 'minərəl-
  aiz, -iz, -iŋ, -d
mineralogic|al, -ally ,minərə'lɔdʒik|əl,
  -əli
mineralog|ist/s, -y ,minə'rælədʒ|ist/s, -i
Minerva mi'nə:və
mine-sweep|er/s, -ing 'main,swi:p|ə*/z,
  -iŋ
Minety 'mainti
minever 'minivə*
Ming miŋ
ming|le, -les, -ling, -led 'miŋg|l, -lz,
  -liŋ [-ļiŋ], -ld
mingogram, -s 'miŋgəugræm ['miŋəu-],
  -z
mingograph, -s 'miŋgəugrɑ:f ['miŋəu-,
  -græf], -s
ming|ly, -ier, -iest 'mindʒ|i, -iə* [-jə*],
  -iist [-jist]
miniature, -s 'minjətʃə* [-nɪətʃ-, -nitʃ-],
  -z
miniaturist, -s 'minjətjuərist [-nɪət-,
  -tʃər-, 'minitʃərist], -s
mini-bus, -es 'minibʌs, -iz
mini-car, -s 'minikɑ:*, -z
minikin (s. adj.), -s 'minikin, -z
minim (M.), -s 'minim, -z
minimal 'miniml [-məl]
minimiz|e [-is|e], -es, -ing, -ed 'mini-
  maiz, -iz, -iŋ, -d
minim|um, -a 'minim|əm, -ə
mining 'mainiŋ
minion, -s 'minjən [-nɪən], -z
minish, -es, -ing, -ed 'miniʃ, -iz, -iŋ, -t
mini-skirt, -s 'miniskə:t, -s
minist|er (s. v.), -ers, -ering, -ered
  'minist|ə*, -əz, -əriŋ, -əd
ministerial, -ly, -ist/s ,minis'tiərɪəl, -i,
  -ist/s
ministration, -s ,minis'treiʃən, -z
ministr|y, -ies 'ministr|i, -iz
miniver (M.) 'minivə*
mink miŋk
Minneapolis ,mini'æpəlis
Minne|haha, -sota ,mini|'hɑ:hɑ:, -'səutə
Minnesinger, -s 'mini,siŋə*, -z
Minnie 'mini
minnow, -s 'minəu, -z
minol 'mainɔl
minor (s. adj.), -s 'mainə*, -z
Minorca mi'nɔ:kə
Minories 'minəriz
minorit|y, -ies mai'nɔrit|i [mi'n-, mə'n-],
  -iz
Minos 'mainɔs
Minotaur, -s 'mainətɔ:*, -z

minster (M.), -s 'minstə*, -z
minstrel, -s; -sy 'minstrəl, -z; -si
mint (s. v.), -s, -ing, -ed; -age, mint, -s,
-iŋ, -id; -idʒ
Minto 'mintəu
mint-sauce 'mint'sɔːs
minuet, -s ˌminju'et ['minju'et], -s
minus (s. adj. prep.), -es 'mainəs, -iz
minuscule, -s 'minəskjuːl [-nis-,
mi'nʌskjuːl], -z
minute (very small), -st, -ly, -ness
mai'njuːt [mi'n-], -ist, -li, -nis
minute (s.) (division of time, angle), -s
'minit, -s
minute (s.) (memorandum), -s 'minit
[rarely -njuːt], -s
minut|e (v.), -es, -ing, -ed 'minit, -s,
-iŋ, -id
minute-book, -s 'minitbuk [rarely
-njuːt-], -s
minute-glass, -es 'minitglɑːs, -iz
minute-gun, -s 'minitgʌn, -z
minute-hand, -s 'minithænd, -z
minutiae mai'njuːʃiː [mi'n-, -ʃjiː]
minx, -es miŋks, -iz
miocene 'maiəusiːn
miracle, -s 'mirəkl [-rikl], -z
miraculous, -ly, -ness mi'rækjuləs
[mə'r-, -kjəl-], -li, -nis
mirage, -s 'mirɑːʒ [mi'rɑːʒ], -iz
Miranda mi'rændə
mire 'maiə*
Miriam 'miriəm
mirror, -s, -ed 'mirə*, -z, -d
mirth mə:θ
mirth|ful, -fully, -fulness 'mə:θ|ful,
-fuli [-fəli], -fulnis
mir|y, -ier, -iest, -iness 'maiər|i, -iə*,
-iist, -inis
Mirza 'mə:zə   [-z
misadventure, -s 'misəd'ventʃə* [ˌmis-],
misalliance, -s 'misə'laiəns [ˌmisə'l-], -iz
misanthrope, -s 'mizənθrəup ['misən-],
-s
misanthropic, -al, -ally ˌmizən'θrɔpik
[ˌmisən-], -əl, -əli
misanthrop|ist/s, -y mi'zænθrəp|ist/s
[mi'sæ-, -θrup-], -i
misapplication, -s 'misˌæpli'keiʃən, -z
misappl|y, -ies, -ying, -ied 'misə'pl|ai,
-aiz, -aiiŋ, -aid
misapprehend, -s, -ing, -ed 'misˌæpri-
'hend, -z, -iŋ, -id
misapprehension, -s 'misˌæpri'henʃən, -z
misappropriat|e, -es, -ing, -ed 'misə-
'prəuprieit, -s, -iŋ, -id
misappropriation, -s 'misəˌprəupri'eiʃən, -z

misbecoming 'misbi'kʌmiŋ, [-bə'k-]
misbegotten 'misbiˌgɔtn ['--'--]
misbehav|e, -es, -ing, -ed; -iour 'mis-
bi'heiv [-bə'h-], -z, -iŋ, -d; -jə*
misbelief 'misbi'liːf [-bə'l-, '---, ˌ-'-]
misbeliev|e, -es, -ing, -ed, -er/s 'mis-
bi'liːv [-bə'l-, '---, ˌ-'-], -z, -iŋ, -d,
-ə*/z
miscalculat|e, -es, -ing, -ed 'mis'kæl-
kjuleit [ˌmis-, -kjəl-], -s, -iŋ, -id
miscalculation, -s 'misˌkælkju'leiʃən
[-kjə'l-], -z
miscall, -s, -ing, -ed 'mis'kɔːl, -z, -iŋ, -d
miscarr|y, -ies, -ying, -ied; -iage/s 'mis-
'kær|i ['mis'k-], -iz, -iiŋ, -id; -idʒ/iz
miscegenation ˌmisidʒi'neiʃən
miscellaneous, -ly, -ness ˌmisi'leinjəs
[-sə'l-, -niəs], -li, -nis
miscellan|y, -ies mi'selən|i ['misil-], -iz
mischance, -s mis'tʃɑːns ['mis-tʃɑːns],
-iz
mischief, -s 'mis-tʃif, -s
mischief-mak|er/s, -ing 'mis-tʃif„meik|-
ə*/z, -iŋ
mischievous, -ly, -ness 'mis-tʃivəs, -li,
-nis
misconception, -s 'miskən'sepʃən, -z
misconduct (s.) mis'kɔndʌkt [-dəkt]
misconduct (v.), -s, -ing, -ed 'miskən-
'dʌkt [ˌmiskən'd-], -s, -iŋ, -id
misconstruction, -s 'miskəns'trʌkʃən
[ˌmiskəns't-], -z
misconstr|ue, -ues, -uing, -ued 'mis-
kən'str|uː [-'kɔnst-], -uːz, -u(ː)iŋ, -uːd
miscount (s. v.), -s, -ing, -ed 'mis'kaunt,
-s, -iŋ, -id
miscreant, -s 'miskriənt, -s
miscu|e (s. v.), -es, -ing, -ed 'mis'kjuː,
-z, -iŋ, [-'kjuiŋ], -d
misdeal, -s, -ing, misdealt 'mis-
'diːl, -z, -iŋ, 'mis'delt
misdeed, -s 'mis'diːd [mis'd-], -z
misdemean|ant/s, -our/s ˌmisdi'miːn|-
ənt/s, -ə*/z
misdirect, -s, -ing, -ed 'misdi'rekt
[-də'r-, -dai'r-], -s, -iŋ, -id
misdirection 'misdi'rekʃən   [-də'r-,
-dai'r-]
misdoing, -s 'mis'du(ː)iŋ, -z
mise-en-scène 'miːzɑ̃ː'n'sein [-zɔ̃ː'n's-,
-zɔn's-] (mizɑ̃sɛːn)
miser, -s 'maizə*, -z
miserab|le, -ly, -leness 'mizərəb|l, -li, -lnis
miserere, -s ˌmizə'riəri, -z
misericord, -s mi'zerikɔːd ['mizəri-], -z
miserl|y, -iness 'maizəl|i, -inis
miser|y, -ies 'mizər|i [-zr̩-], -iz
misfeasance mis'fiːzəns

misfir|e (s. v.), -es, -ing, -ed 'mis'faiə*, -z, -riŋ, -d
misfit, -s 'misfit ['mis'f-], -s
misfortune, -s mis'fɔ:tʃən [-tʃu:n, -tju:n], -z
misgiving, -s mis'giviŋ, -z
misgovern, -s, -ing, -ed, -ment 'mis-'gʌvən, -z, -iŋ, -d, -mənt
misguided, -ly 'mis'gaidid [mis'g-], -li
mishand|le, -les, -ling, -led 'mis'hænd|l [mis'h-], -lz, -liŋ [-]iŋ], -ld
mishap, -s 'mishæp [mis'h-], -s
misinform, -s, -ing, -ed 'misin'fɔ:m, -z, -iŋ, -d
misinterpret, -s, -ing, -ed 'misin'tə:prit, -s, -iŋ, -id
misinterpretation, -s 'misin,tə:pri'teiʃən, -z
misjudg|e, -es, -ing, -ed 'mis'dʒʌdʒ [mis-], -iz, -iŋ, -d
mis|lay, -lays, -laying, -laid mis|'lei, -'leiz, -'leiiŋ, -'leid
mis|lead, -leads, -leading, -led mis|'li:d, -'li:dz, -'li:diŋ, -'led
mismanag|e, -es, -ing, -ed, -ement 'mis'mænidʒ [mis'm-], -iz, -iŋ, -d, -mənt
misnomer, -s 'mis'nəumə* [mis'n-], -z
misogam|ist/s, -y mi'sɔgəm|ist/s [mai's-], -i
misogyn|ist/s, -y mai'sɔdʒin|ist/s [mi's-, -ɔgi-], -i
misplac|e, -es, -ing, -ed, -ement 'mis-'pleis, -iz, -iŋ, -t [also 'mispleist when attributive], -mənt
misprint (s.), -s 'mis'print ['misprint, also mis'p- when preceded by a stress], -s
misprint (v.), -s, -ing, -ed mis'print ['-'-], -s, -iŋ, -id
misprision mis'priʒən
mispronounc|e, -es, -ing, -ed 'mis-prə'nauns [-pru'n-, -prŋ'auns], -iz, -iŋ, -t
mispronunciation, -s 'misprə,nʌnsi-'eiʃən [-pru,n-, -prŋ,ʌn-], -z
misquotation, -s 'miskwəu'teiʃən, -z
misquot|e, -es, -ing, -ed 'mis'kwəut, -s, -iŋ, -id
mis|read (present), -reads, -reading, -read (past) 'mis|'ri:d, -'ri:dz, -'ri:diŋ, -'red
misreport, -s, -ing, -ed 'misri'pɔ:t, -s, -iŋ, -id
misrepresent, -s, -ing, -ed 'mis,repri-'zent, -s, -iŋ, -id
misrepresentation, -s 'mis,reprizen-'teiʃən [-zən-], -z

misrule 'mis'ru:l
miss (s. v.) (M.), -es, -ing, -ed mis, -iz, -iŋ, -t
missal, -s 'misəl, -z
missel 'mizəl ['misəl]
Missenden 'misndən
misshapen 'mis'ʃeipən ['miʃ'ʃ-]
missile, -s 'misail, -z
missing (adj.) 'misiŋ
mission, -s 'miʃən, -z
missionar|y, -ies 'miʃŋər|i [-ʃnər-, -ʃŋr-, -ʃənər-], -iz
missioner, -s 'miʃŋə* [-ʃənə*], -z
missis 'misiz
Mississippi ,misi'sipi
missive (s. adj.), -s 'misiv, -z
Missouri mi'zuəri [mi's-]
    Note.—American pron. has -z-.
misspel|l, -ls, -ling/s, -led, -t 'mis'spel, -z, -iŋ/z, -t [-d], -t
misspen|d, -ds, -ding, -t 'mis'spen|d, -dz, -diŋ, -t ['-- when attributive]
misstat|e, -es, -ing, -ed, -ement/s 'mis'steit, -s, -iŋ, -id, -mənt/s
missuit, -s, -ing, -ed 'mis'sju:t [-'su:t], -s, -iŋ, -id
miss|y, -ies 'mis|i, -iz
mist, -s mist, -s
mistakable mis'teikəbl
mis|take (s. v.), -takes, -taking, -took, -taken/ly mis|'teik, -'teiks, -'teikiŋ, -'tuk, -'teikən/li
mister 'mistə*
mistim|e, -es, -ing, -ed 'mis'taim, -z, -iŋ, -d
mistletoe 'misltəu ['mizl-]
mistral, -s 'mistrəl [mis'trɑ:l] (mistral), -z
mistranslat|e, -es, -ing, -ed 'mistræns-'leit [-trɑ:ns-, -trænz-, -trɑ:nz-, -træns-, -trənz-], -s, -iŋ, -id
mistranslation, -s 'mistræns'leiʃən [-trɑ:ns-, -trænz-, -trɑ:nz-, -træns-, -trənz-], -z
mistress, -es 'mistris, -iz
mistrust (s. v.), -s, -ing, -ed 'mis-'trʌst [mis't-], -s, -iŋ, -id
mist|y, -ier, -iest, -ily, -iness 'mist|i, -iə* [-jə*], -iist [-jist], -ili, -inis
misunderst|and, -ands, -anding/s, -ood 'misʌndə'st|ænd [,mis-], -ændz, -ændiŋ/z, -ud
misuse (s.) 'mis'ju:s [also 'mis-ju:s when followed by a stress]
misus|e (v.), -es, -ing, -ed 'mis'ju:z, -iz, -iŋ, -d
Mitch|am, -ell 'mitʃ|əm, -əl
mite, -s mait, -s

Mitford 'mitfəd
Mithr|a, -as 'miθr|ə, -æs
Mithridates ˌmiθri'deiti:z
mitigable 'mitigəbl
mitigat|e, -es, -ing, -ed 'mitigeit, -s, -iŋ, -id
mitigation ˌmiti'geiʃən
mitrailleuse, -s ˌmitrai'ə:z (mitrajø:z), -iz
mit|re (s. v.), -res, -ring, -red 'mait|ə*, -əz, -ˀriŋ, -əd
mitten, -s 'mitn, -z
mity 'maiti
Mitylene ˌmiti'li:ni
Mivart 'maivət [-vɑ:t]
mix (s. v.), -es, -ing, -ed, -er/s miks, -iz, -iŋ, -t, -ə*/z
mixture, -s 'mikstʃə*, -z
mix-up, -s 'miks'ʌp ['--], -s
Mizar (star) 'maizɑ:* [-zə*]
Mizen 'mizn
mizmaze, -s 'mizmeiz, -iz
Mizpah 'mizpə
mizzen, -s 'mizn, -z
mizzen-mast, -s 'miznmɑ:st [nautical pronunciation -məst], -s
mizz|le, -les, -ling, -led 'miz|l, -lz, -ˀiŋ [-liŋ], -ld
mnemonic (s. adj.), -s ni(:)'mɔnik [mn-], -s
Mnemosyne ni:'mɔzini: [mni:'m-, mni'm-, -ɔsi-]
Moab 'məuæb
Moabite, -s 'məuəbait, -s
moan (s. v.), -s, -ing/s, -ed məun, -z, -iŋ/z, -d
Moase məuz
moat (s. v.) (M.), -s, -ing, -ed məut, -s, -iŋ, -id
mob (s. v.), -s, -bing, -bed mɔb, -z, -iŋ, -d
Moberly 'məubə(:)li
mobile 'məubail [-bi:l, -bil]
mobility məu'biliti [-lət-]
mobilization [-isa-], -s ˌməubilai'zeiʃən [-bḷai'z-, -bili'z-, -bḷi'z-], -z
mobiliz|e [-is|e], -es, -ing, -ed 'məubilaiz [-bḷaiz], -iz, -iŋ, -d
moccasin, -s 'mɔkəsin, -z
mocha (coffee, leather, etc., from Mocha) 'mɔkə ['məukə]
Mocha (Arabian seaport) 'məukə ['mɔkə]
mock (adj. v.), -s, -ing/ly, -ed, -er/s mɔk, -s, -iŋ/li, -t, -ə*/z
mocker|y, -ies 'mɔkər|i, -iz
Mockett 'mɔkit
mocking-bird, -s 'mɔkiŋbə:d, -z

mock-turtle 'mɔk'tə:tl [mɔk't-]
mod|al, -ally 'məud|l, -əli
modality məu'dæliti
mode, -s məud, -z
mod|el (s. v.), -els, -elling, -elled, -eller/s 'mɔd|l, -lz, -ḷiŋ, -ld, -ḷə*/z
modena (colour) 'mɔdinə
Modena 'mɔdinə [mɔ'deinə, mə'd-, old-fashioned -'di:nə] ('mɔ:dena)
moderate (s. adj.), -s, -ly, -ness 'mɔdərit, -s, -li, -nis
moderat|e (v.), -es, -ing, -ed, -or/s 'mɔdəreit, -s, -iŋ, -id, -ə*/z
moderation, -s ˌmɔdə'reiʃən, -z
moderato, -s ˌmɔdə'rɑ:təu, -z
modern (s. adj.), -s, -ly, -ness 'mɔdən, -z, -li, -nis
moderni|sm, -st/s 'mɔdəni|zəm, -st/s
modernity mɔ'də:niti [məu'd-]
modernization [-isa-] ˌmɔdənai'zeiʃən [-ni'z-]
moderniz|e [-is|e], -es, -ing, -ed 'mɔdənaiz, -iz, -iŋ, -d
modest, -ly, -y 'mɔdist, -li, -i
modicum, -s 'mɔdikəm, -z
modification, -s ˌmɔdifi'keiʃən, -z
modi|fy, -fies, -fying, -fied, -fier/s; -fiable 'mɔdi|fai, -faiz, -faiiŋ, -faid, -faiə*/z; -faiəbl
modish, -ly, -ness 'məudiʃ, -li, -nis
modiste, -s məu'di:st, -s
modulat|e, -es, -ing, -ed, -or/s 'mɔdjuleit, -s, -iŋ, -id, -ə*/z
modulation, -s ˌmɔdju'leiʃən, -z
modul|us, -uses, -i 'mɔdjul|əs, -əsiz, -ai
modus 'məudəs
modus operandi 'mɔdəsˌɔpə'rændi: ['məudəsˌɔpə'rændai]
modus vivendi 'mɔdəsvi(:)'vendi: ['məudəsvi'vendai]
Moeran 'mɔ:rən
Moesia 'mi:sjə [-sïə, -ʃjə, -ʃïə, -zjə, -zïə, -ʒjə, -ʒïə]
Moeso-gothic 'mi:səu'gɔθik ['mi:zəu-]
Moffat 'mɔfət
mofussil məu'fʌsil
Mogador ˌmɔgə'dɔ:*
Moggach 'mɔgək [-əx]
Mogul, -s məu'gʌl ['məugʌl], -z
mohair 'məuhɛə*
Mohammed məu'hæmed [-mid]
Mohammedan, -s məu'hæmidən, -z
Mohave məu'hɑ:vi
Mohawk, -s 'məuhɔ:k, -s
Mohican, -s 'məuikən, -z
Mohun 'məuən ['məuhən], mu:n, mə'hʌn

moidore, -s 'mɔidɔ:* ['məuid-, -dɔə*, mɔi'd-], -z
Note.—The stressing -'- has to be used in J. Masefield's poem 'Cargoes'.
moiet|y, -ies 'mɔiət|i ['mɔiit-], -iz
moil (s. v.), -s, -ing, -ed mɔil, -z, -iŋ, -d
Moir 'mɔiə*
Moira 'mɔiərə
moire, -s mwɑ:* [mwɔ:*] (mwa:r), -z
moiré 'mwɑ:rei ['mwɔ:r-] (mware)
moist, -er, -est, -ness mɔist, -ə*, -ist, -nis
moist|en, -ens, -ening, -ened 'mɔis|n, -nz, -ɳiŋ [-niŋ], -nd
moisture 'mɔistʃə*
Moivre 'mɔivə*
Mojave (=Mohave) məu'hɑ:vi
moke, -s məuk, -s
molar (s. adj.), -s 'məulə*, -z
molasses məu'læsiz
molassine 'mɔləsi:n ['məul-]
mold=mould
Mold məuld
Moldavia, -n mɔl'deivjə [-vïə], -n
molder, moldy=mould-
mole, -s məul, -z
molecular məu'lekjulə* [mɔ'l-]
molecule, -s 'mɔlikju:l ['məul-], -z
mole-hill, -s 'məulhil, -z
Molesey 'məulzi
mole-skin, -s 'məul-skin, -z
molest, -s, -ing, -ed məu'lest, -s, -iŋ, -id
molestation, -s ˌməules'teiʃən, -z
Molesworth 'məulzwə(:)θ
Moleyns 'mʌlinz
Molière 'mɔliɛə* ['məul-, -ljɛə*] (mɔljɛ:r)
mollification ˌmɔlifi'keiʃən
molli|fy, -fies, -fying, -fied; -fiable 'mɔli|fai, -faiz, -faiiŋ, -faid; -faiəbl
mollusc, -s 'mɔləsk [-lʌsk], -s
mollusc|an, -oid, -ous mɔ'lʌsk|ən [mə'l-], -ɔid, -əs
moll|y (M.), -ies 'mɔl|i, -iz
mollycodd|le, -les, -ling, -led 'mɔli-kɔd|l, -lz, -liŋ [-liŋ], -ld
Moloch 'məulɔk
Molony mə'ləuni
molten 'məultən
molto 'mɔltəu ('molto)
Molton 'məultən
moly 'məuli
molybdenum mɔ'libdinəm [məu'l-, ˌmɔlib'di:nəm]
Molyneux 'mɔlinju:ks, 'mʌlinju:ks, 'mɔlinju:, 'mʌlinju:
Mombasa mɔm'bæsə [-'bɑ:sə]
moment, -s 'məumənt, -s

momentar|y, -ily -iness 'məuməntər|i, -ili, -inis
momentous, -ly, -ness məu'mentəs, -li, -nis
moment|um, -ums, -a məu'ment|əm, -əmz, -ə
Momerie 'mʌməri
Mon (language) məun
Mon. (abbrev. of Monmouthshire) mɔn
mona (M.), -s 'məunə, -z
Monaco 'mɔnəkəu [-nik-]
monad, -s 'mɔnæd ['məun-], -z
monadic mɔ'nædik [məu'n-]
Monaghan 'mɔnəhən [-nəxən, -nəkən]
monarch, -s 'mɔnək, -s
monarch|al, -ic, -ical mɔ'nɑ:k|əl [mə'n-], -ik, -ikəl
monarchi|sm, -st/s 'mɔnəki|zəm, -st/s
monarchiz|e [-is|e], -es, -ing, -ed 'mɔn-əkaiz, -iz, -iŋ, -d
monarch|y, -ies 'mɔnək|i, -iz
monaster|y, -ies 'mɔnəstər|i, -iz
monastic, -al, -ally mə'næstik [mɔ'n-], -əl, -əli
monasticism mə'næstisizəm [mɔ'n-]
monaural 'mɔn'ɔ:rəl
Monck mʌŋk
Monckton 'mʌŋktən
Moncrieff mən'kri:f [mɔn-]
Mond (English name) mɔnd
Monday, -s 'mʌndi [-dei], -z
monetary 'mʌnitəri
monetiz|e [-is|e], -es, -ing, -ed 'mʌni-taiz, -iz, -iŋ, -d
money (M.), -s, -ed 'mʌni, -z, -d
money-bill, -s 'mʌnibil, -z
money-box, -es 'mʌnibɔks, -iz
money-changer, -s 'mʌni,tʃeindʒə*, -z
money-grubb|er/s,-ing'mʌni,grʌb|ə*/z, -iŋ
money-lend|er/s, -ing 'mʌni,lend|ə*/z, -iŋ
money-market, -s 'mʌni,mɑ:kit, -s
money-order, -s 'mʌni,ɔ:də*, -z
Moneypenny 'mʌni,peni
money-spinner, -s 'mʌni,spinə*, -z
monger, -s 'mʌŋgə*, -z
Mongol, -s 'mɔŋgɔl [-gəl], -z
Mongolia, -n/s mɔŋ'gəuljə [-lïə], -n/z
mongoose, -s 'mɔŋgu:s ['mʌŋ-], -iz
mongrel, -s 'mʌŋgrəl, -z
Monica 'mɔnikə
Monier 'mʌnïə* ['mɔn-, -njə*]
moni|sm, -st/s 'mɔni|zəm, -st/s
monistic mɔ'nistik
monition, -s məu'niʃən [mɔ'n-], -z
monitor, -s; -ship/s 'mɔnitə*, -z; -ʃip/s
monitorial ˌmɔni'tɔ:rïəl

monitory 'mɔnitəri
monk (M.), -s, -ish mʌŋk, -s, -iʃ
monkey, -s 'mʌŋki, -z
monkey-engine, -s 'mʌŋki,endʒin, -z
monkey-puzzle, -s 'mʌŋki,pʌzl, -z
Monkhouse 'mʌŋkhaus
Monkton 'mʌŋktən
Monkwearmouth mʌŋk'wiəmauθ
Monmouth, -shire 'mɔnməθ [rarely
'mʌn-], -ʃiə* [-ʃə*]
Monna Lisa 'mɔnə'li:zə
mono (monotype), -s 'məunəu ['mɔnəu],
(of gramophone records, opp. stereo)
'mɔnəu, -z
Monoceros mə'nɔsərɔs [mɔ'n-]
monochord, -s 'mɔnəukɔːd, -z
monochrome, -s 'mɔnəkrəum, -z
monocle, -s 'mɔnɔkl [-nək-], -z
monocotyledon, -s 'mɔnəu,kɔti'li:dən, -z
monod|y, -ies 'mɔnəd|i, -iz
monogam|ist/s, -ous, -y mɔ'nɔgəm|-
ist/s [mə'n-], -əs, -i
monoglot 'mɔnəglɔt
monogram, -s 'mɔnəgræm, -z
monograph, -s 'mɔnəgrɑːf [-græf], -s
monolith, -s 'mɔnəuliθ, -s
monolithic ,mɔnəu'liθik
monologist, -s mɔ'nɔlədʒist, -s
monologiz|e [-is|e], -es, -ing, -ed, -er/s
mɔ'nɔlədʒaiz, -iz, -iŋ, -d, -ə*/z
monologue, -s 'mɔnəlɔg [rarely -ləug], -z
monoma|nia, -niac/s 'mɔnəu'mei|njə
[,mɔn-, -niə], -niæk/s
monophthong, -s 'mɔnəfθɔŋ, -z
monophthong|al, -ic ,mɔnəf'θɔŋg|əl, -ik
monophthongiz|e [-is|e], -es, -ing, -ed
'mɔnəfθɔŋgaiz, -iz, -iŋ, -d
monoplane, -s 'mɔnəuplein, -z
Monopole 'mɔnəpəul
monopolism mə'nɔpəlizəm [-pļizəm]
monopolist, -s mə'nɔpəlist [-pļist], -s
monopolistic mə,nɔpə'listik [-pļ'istik]
monopoliz|e [-is|e], -es, -ing, -ed, -er/s
mə'nɔpəlaiz [-pļaiz], -iz, -iŋ, -d, -ə*/z
monopol|y, -ies mə'nɔpəl|i [-pļ|i], -iz
monorail, -s 'mɔnəureil, -z
monosyllabic 'mɔnəusi'læbik [,mɔn-]
monosyllable, -s 'mɔnə,siləbl, -z
monothei|sm, -st/s 'mɔnəuθi:,i|zəm
['mɔnəu,θi:i-], -st/s
monoton|e (s. v.), -es, -ing, -ed 'mɔnə-
təun, -z, -iŋ, -d
monotonic ,mɔnə'tɔnik
monotonous, -ly mə'nɔtnəs [-tənəs], -li
monotony mə'nɔtni [-təni]
monotype, -s 'mɔnəutaip, -s
monovalen|ce, -t 'mɔnəu,veilən|s
['-'--, ,--'--], -t

monoxide, -s mɔ'nɔksaid [mə'n-], -z
Monro(e) mən'rəu [mʌn'rəu], 'mʌnrəu
Mons mɔnz [mɔ̃:ns] (mɔ̃:s)
Monsarrat (surname) ,mɔnsə'ræt
monseigneur, -s ,mɔnsen'jə:*
(mɔ̃sɛɲœ:r), -z
Monserrat (Spanish general) ,mɔnse'rɑːt
[-sə'r-]
monsieur (M.) mə'sjə:* (strong form)
(məsjø), məsjə* (weak form)
Monsignor mɔn'si:njə*
Monson 'mʌnsn
monsoon, -s mɔn'su:n [mən-], -z
monster, -s 'mɔnstə*, -z
monstrance, -s 'mɔnstrəns, -iz
monstrosit|y, -ies mɔns'trɔsit|i [mən-],
-iz
monstrous, -ly, -ness 'mɔnstrəs, -li,
-nis
montage, -s mɔn'tɑːʒ ['mɔntɑːʒ, mɔn-
tidʒ], -iz
Montagu(e) 'mɔntəgju: [-tig-], 'mʌn-
Montaigne mɔn'tein
Montana (state of U.S.A.) mɔn'tænə
[-'tɑːn-]
Mont Blanc mɔ̃:m'blɑ̃:ŋ [-blɔ̃:ŋ, mɔ:m-
'blɑːŋ, mɔm'blɔŋ, mɔn'blɔŋ,
mɔŋ'blɔŋ] (mɔ̃blɑ̃)
montbretia, -s mɔn'bri:ʃjə [mɔm'b-,
-ʃiə, -ʃə], -z
Mont Cenis ,mɔ̃:nsə'ni: [,mɔ:n-, ,mɔnt-]
(mɔ̃sni)
monte (M.) 'mɔnti
Monte Carlo ,mɔnti'kɑːləu
Montefiore ,mɔntifi'ɔːri [-'fjɔːri]
monteith, -s mɔn'ti:θ, -s
Monteith mən'ti:θ [mɔn-]
Montenegr|o, -ian/s, -in/s ,mɔnti'ni:-
gr|əu [-'neig-], -iən/z, -in/z
Monte Rosa ,mɔnti'rəuzə
Montesquieu ,mɔntes'kju: [-'kjə:]
(mɔ̃tɛskjø)
Montessori ,mɔnte'sɔːri [-ti's-]
Montevideo ,mɔntivi'deiəu [old-
fashioned -'vidiəu]
Montezuma ,mɔnti'zu:mə
Montfort (Simon de M.) 'mɔntfət [-fɔːt]
Montgolfier mɔnt'gɔlfiə* [mɔ̃:ŋ'gɔlfiei,
mɔ:ŋ'g-, mɔŋ'g-] (mɔ̃gɔlfje)
Montgomerie mənt'gʌməri [mɔnt'gɔm-,
mənt'gɔm-]
Montgomery, -shire mənt'gʌməri [mɔnt-
'gɔm-, mənt'gɔm-] (Welsh mɔnt'gəm-
ri), -ʃiə* [-ʃə*]
month, -s -ly mʌnθ, -s, -li
Montmorency ,mɔntmə'rensi
Montpelier (in U.S.A.) mɔnt'pi:ljə*
[-liə*]

Montpellier (in France) mɔ̃:m'peliei [mɔ:m'p-, mɔnt'p-] (m̃ɔpəlje, -pɛljə), (in names of streets, etc.) mɔnt'peliə* [mənt-, -ljə*]
Montreal ,mɔntri'ɔ:l
Montreux mɔn'trə: [-'tru:] (m̃ɔtrø)
Montrose mɔn'trəuz
Montserrat (island in West Indies) ,mɔntse'ræt [-sə'r-], (monastery in Spain) -'rɑ:t
Monty 'mɔnti
monument, -s 'mɔnjumənt [-jəm-], -s
monument|al, -ally ,mɔnju'ment|l [-jə'm-], -əli
Monzie (in Perthshire) mə'ni:
moo, -s, -ing, -ed mu:, -z, -iŋ, -d
mooch, -es, -ing, -ed mu:tʃ, -iz, -iŋ, -t
moo-cow, -s 'mu:-kau, -z
mood, -s mu:d, -z
mood|y (M.), -ier, -iest, -ily, -iness 'mu:d|i, -iə* [-jə*], -iist [-jist], -ili, -inis
moon (s. v.) (M.), -s, -ing, -ed; -beam/s mu:n, -z, -iŋ, -d; -bi:m/z
moon-cal|f, -ves 'mu:nkɑ:|f, -vz
moon|less, -light, -lit 'mu:n|lis, -lait, -lit
moonshine 'mu:n-ʃain
moonstruck 'mu:n-strʌk
moonstone, -s 'mu:n-stəun, -z
moony 'mu:ni
moor (s. v.) (M.), -s, -ing/s, -ed muə* [mɔə*, mɔ:*], -z, -riŋ/z, -d
moor-cock, -s 'muə-kɔk ['mɔə-, 'mɔ:-], -z
Moore muə*
Moorgate 'muəgit ['mɔə-, 'mɔ:-, -geit]
moorhen, -s 'muəhen ['mɔə-, 'mɔ:-], -z
mooring-mast, -s 'muəriŋmɑ:st ['mɔər-, 'mɔ:r-], -s
Moorish 'muəriʃ ['mɔər-, 'mɔ:r-]
moorland, -s 'muələnd ['mɔəl-, 'mɔ:l-, -lænd], -z
Note.—The variant -lænd is not used when the word is attributive.
moose, -s mu:s, -iz
moot (s. adj. v.), -s, -ing, -ed mu:t, -s, -iŋ, -id
mop (s. v.), -s, -ping, -ped mɔp, -s, -iŋ, -t
mop|e, -es, -ing/ly, -ed məup, -s, -iŋ/li, -t
moped (s.), -s 'məu-ped, -z
mopish, -ly, -ness 'məupiʃ, -li, -nis
mor|a, -ae, -as 'mɔ:r|ə, -i: [-ai], -əz
Morag 'mɔ:ræg
moraine, -s mɔ'rein [mə'r-], -z
mor|al (s. adj.), -als, -ally 'mɔr|əl, -əlz, -əli [-l̩i]

morale mɔ'rɑ:l [mə'r-]
moralist, -s 'mɔrəlist [-r̩list], -s
morality mə'ræliti [mɔ'r-]
moraliz|e (-is|e), -es, -ing, -ed, -er/s 'mɔrəlaiz [-r̩aiz], -iz, -iŋ, -d, -ə*/z
Moran 'mɔ:rən, 'mɔrən, mə'ræn [mɔ'ræn]
Morant mə'rænt [mɔ'r-]
morass, -es mə'ræs [mɔ'r-], -iz
moratorium, -s ,mɔrə'tɔ:riəm [,mɔ:r-], -z
Moravia, -n/s mə'reivjə [mɔ'r-, -viə], -n/z
Moray, -shire 'mʌri, -ʃiə* [-ʃə*]
morbid, -est, -ly, -ness 'mɔ:bid, -ist, -li, -nis
morbidity mɔ:'biditi
mordant (s. adj.), -s 'mɔ:dənt, -s
Mordecai ,mɔ:di'keiai
mordent, -s 'mɔ:dənt, -s
more (M.) mɔ:* [mɔə*]
Morea mɔ'riə [mə'r-, mɔ:'r-]
Morecambe 'mɔ:kəm
Moreen mɔ:'ri:n ['--]
morel (M.) mɔ'rel [mə'r-]
morello, -s mə'reləu [mɔ'r-], -z
moreover mɔ:'rəuvə* [mə'r-]
Moreton 'mɔ:tn
Morgan 'mɔ:gən
morganatic, -ally ,mɔ:gə'nætik, -əli
morgue, -s mɔ:g, -z
Moriah mɔ'raiə [mɔ:'r-, mə'r-]
Moriarty ,mɔri'ɑ:ti
moribund 'mɔribʌnd ['mɔ:r-, -bənd]
Morison 'mɔrisn
Morley 'mɔ:li
Mormon, -s, -ism 'mɔ:mən, -z, -izəm
morn, -s mɔ:n, -z
morning, -s 'mɔ:niŋ, -z
morning-coat, -s 'mɔ:niŋ'kəut ['mɔ:niŋkəut], -s
morning-dress 'mɔ:niŋ'dres -z
morning-room, -s 'mɔ:niŋrum [-ru:m]
morning-star, -s 'mɔ:niŋ'stɑ:* ['mɔ:niŋstɑ:*], -z
Mornington 'mɔ:niŋtən
morning-watch, -es 'mɔ:niŋ'wɔtʃ, -iz
Moroccan, -s mə'rɔkən, -z
morocco (M.), -s mə'rɔkəu, -z
moron, -s 'mɔ:rɔn [-rən], -z
morose, -ly, -ness mə'rəus [mɔ'r-], -li, -nis
Morpeth 'mɔ:peθ [-pəθ]
Morpheus 'mɔ:fju:s [-fjəs, -fiəs]
morpheme, -s 'mɔ:fi:m, -z
morphemic 'mɔ:'fi:mik
morph|ia, -ine 'mɔ:f|jə [-iə], -i:n
morphologic, -al, -ally ,mɔ:fə'lɔdʒik, -əl, -əli

morpholog|ist/s, -y mɔ:'fɔlədʒ|ist/s, -i
morphophonemic 'mɔ:fəʊfəʊ'ni:mik
morphophonology 'mɔ:fəʊfəʊ'nɔlədʒi
Morphy 'mɔ:fi
Morrell 'mʌrəl, mə'rel
morris (M.), -es 'mɔris, -iz
morris-dance, -s 'mɔris'dɑ:ns ['---], -iz
Morrison 'mɔrisn
morrow (M.), -s 'mɔrəu, -z
morse (M.), -s mɔ:s, -iz
morsel, -s 'mɔ:səl, -z
Morshead 'mɔ:zhed
mort, -s mɔ:t, -s
mort|al, -als, -ally 'mɔ:t|l, -lz, -əli [-l̩i]
mortalit|y (M.), -ies mɔ:'tælit|i, -iz
mortar, -s 'mɔ:tə*, -z
mortarboard, -s 'mɔ:təbɔ:d [-bɔəd], -z
mortgag|e (s. v.), -es, -ing, -ed 'mɔ:gidʒ, -iz, -iŋ, -d
mortgagee, -s ,mɔ:gə'dʒi:, -z
mortgagor, -s ,mɔ:gə'dʒɔ:*, -z
mortice, -s 'mɔ:tis, -iz
mortification ,mɔ:tifi'keiʃən
morti|fy, -fies, -fying, -fied 'mɔ:ti|fai, -faiz, -faiiŋ, -faid
Mortimer 'mɔ:timə*
mortis|e (s. v.), -es, -ing, -ed 'mɔ:tis, -iz, -iŋ, -t
Mort|lake, -lock 'mɔ:t|leik, -lɔk
mortmain 'mɔ:tmein
Morton 'mɔ:tn
mortuar|y, -ies 'mɔ:tjʊər|i [-tjwər-, -tjur-], -iz
mosaic (s. adj.) (M.), -s məʊ'zeiik, -s
Mosby 'mɔzbi
Moscheles 'mɔʃli(:)z ('mɔʃələs)
Moscow 'mɔskəʊ
Moseley 'məʊzli
moselle (M.), -s məʊ'zel, -z
Moses 'məʊziz
Moslem, -s 'mɔzlem [-ləm], -z
Mosley 'mɔzli, 'məʊzli
mosque, -s mɔsk, -s
mosquit|o (M.), -oes, -oey; -o-net/s məs'ki:t|əʊ [mɔs-], -əʊz, -əʊi; -əʊnet/s
moss (M.), -es mɔs, -iz
moss-grown 'mɔsgrəʊn
moss-rose, -s 'mɔs'rəuz ['--], -iz
moss|y, -ier, -iest, -iness 'mɔs|i, -ɨə*, -iist, -inis
mos|t, -tly məʊs|t, -t̬li
Mostyn 'mɔstin
Mosul 'məʊsəl
mot, -s məʊ, -z
mote, -s məʊt, -s
motel, -s məʊ'tel ['məʊtel], -z
motet, -s məʊ'tet, -s

moth, -s mɔθ, -s
moth-eaten 'mɔθ,i:tn
mother (s. v.), -s, -ing, -ed; -hood; -less 'mʌðə*, -z, -riŋ, -d; -hud, -lis
mother-countr|y, -ies 'mʌðə,kʌntr|i ['mʌðə'k-], -iz
mother-in-law, -s 'mʌðərinlɔ:, -z
motherl|y, -iness 'mʌðəl|i, -inis
mother-of-pearl 'mʌðərəv'pə:l
mothersill 'mʌðəsil
mothers-in-law (alternative plur. of **mother-in-law**) 'mʌðəzinlɔ:
motif, -s məʊ'ti:f ['məʊti:f], -s
moti|on (s. v.), -ons, -oning, -oned; -onless 'məʊʃ|ən, -ənz, -ŋiŋ [-əniŋ], -ənd; -ənlis
motivat|e, -es, -ing, -ed 'məʊtiveit, -s, -iŋ, -id
motivation ,məʊti'veiʃən
motive (s. adj.), -s 'məʊtiv, -z
motley (M.) 'mɔtli
Motopo məʊ'təʊpəʊ
motor (s. adj. v.), -s, -ing, -ed 'məʊtə*, -z, -riŋ, -d
motor-bicycle, -s 'məʊtə,baisikl, -z
motor-bike, -s 'məʊtəbaik, -s
motor-boat, -s 'məʊtəbəut, -s
motor-car, -s 'məʊtəkɑ:*, -z
motor-cycle, -s 'məʊtə,saikl ['--'--], -z
motorist, -s 'məʊtərist, -s
motor-ship, -s 'məʊtəʃip, -s
motor-spirit 'məʊtə'spirit ['--,--]
motorway, -s 'məʊtəwei, -z
motory 'məʊtəri
Mott mɔt
Mottistone 'mɔtistən [-stəun]
mottle, -s, -d 'mɔtl, -z, -d
motto, -s 'mɔtəu, -z
Mottram 'mɔtrəm
Mouat 'məʊət
mouch, -es, -ing, -ed mu:tʃ, -iz, -iŋ, -t
mouf(f)lon, -s 'mu:flɔn, -z
Moughton 'məʊtn
moujik, -s 'mu:ʒik [-dʒik], -s
Mouland (surname) mu(:)'lænd
mould (s. v.), -s, -ing/s, -ed məʊld, -z, -iŋ/z, -id
mould|er, -ers, -ering, -ered 'məʊld|ə*, -əz, -əriŋ, -əd
mould|y, -ier, -iest, -iness 'məʊld|i, -ɨə* [-jə*], -iist [-jist], -inis
Moule məʊl, mu:l
Moulmein maul'mein
moulsford 'məʊlsfəd [-lzf-]
moult (s. v.), -s, -ing, -ed məʊlt, -s, -iŋ, -id
Moulton 'məʊltən
Moultrie 'mɔ:ltri, 'mu:tri

mound (M.), -s maund, -z
Mounsey 'maunzi
mount (s. v.) (M.), -s, -ing, -ed maunt,
-s, -iŋ, -id
mountain, -s 'mauntin, -z
mountain-ash, -es 'mauntin'æʃ, -iz
mountaineer, -s, -ing ,maunti'niə*, -z,
-riŋ
mountainous 'mauntinəs
mountant, -s 'mauntənt, -s
Mountbatten maunt'bætn
mountebank, -s 'mauntibæŋk, -s
Mountjoy maunt'dʒɔi, 'mauntdʒɔi
Moura 'muərə
mourn, -s, -ing, -ed, -er/s mɔːn [mɔən,
rarely muən], -z, -iŋ, -d, -ə*/z
mourn|ful, -fully, -fulness 'mɔːn|ful
['mɔən-, rarely 'muən-], -fuli [-fəli],
-fulnis
mouse (s.), mice maus, mais
mous|e (v.), -es, -ing, -ed mauz, -iz, -iŋ,
-d [maus, -iz, -iŋ, -t]
mouse-hole, -s 'maushəul, -z
Mousehole (near Penzance) 'mauzl
mouser, -s 'mauzə* ['mausə*], -z
mouse-trap, -s 'maus-træp, -s
Mousir mu(:)'siə*
mousseline 'muːsliːn [muːs'liːn]
moustache, -s məs'taːʃ [mus-], -iz
mousy 'mausi
mou|th (s.), -ths mau|θ, -ðz
mouth (v.), -s, -ing, -ed mauð, -z, -iŋ, -d
mouthful, -s 'mauθful, -z
mouth-organ, -s 'mauθ,ɔːgən, -z
mouthpiece, -s 'mauθpiːs, -iz
mouth|y, -ier, -iest 'mauð|i, -iə* [-jə*],
-iist [-jist]
movability ,muːvə'biliti [-lət-]
movable, -s, -ness 'muːvəbl, -z, -nis
mov|e (s. v.), -es, -ing/ly, -ed, -er/s,
-ement/s muːv, -z, -iŋ/li, -d, -ə*/z,
-mənt/s
movie, -s; -tone 'muːvi, -z; -təun
mow (s.) (stack), -s məu, -z
mow (s.) (grimace), -s mau, -z
mow (v.) (cut down), -s, -ing, -ed, -n,
-er/s məu, -z, -iŋ, -d, -n, -ə*/z
Mowatt 'mauət, 'məuət
Mowbray 'məubrei, -bri
Mowgli 'maugli
mowing-machine, -s 'məuiŋmə,ʃiːn, -z
Mowll məul, muːl
Moxon 'mɔksn
moya (M.), -s 'mɔiə, -z
Moyes mɔiz
Moygashel (place) mɔi'gæʃəl, (linen)
'mɔigəʃəl
Moynihan 'mɔinjən [-nïən]

Mozambique ,məuzəm'biːk [-zæm-]
Mozart 'məutsaːt [old-fashioned
məu'zaːt]
M.P. (member of Parliament) 'em'piː:
Mr. 'mistə*
Mrs. 'misiz
MS 'em'es [em'es, 'mænjuskript, -jəs-]
MSS 'emes'es ['mænjuskripts, -jəs-]
mu mjuː
much, -ly, -ness mʌtʃ, -li, -nis
Muchalls 'mʌkəlz ['mʌxəlz]
mucilage, -s 'mjuːsilidʒ, -iz
mucilaginous ,mjuːsi'lædʒinəs
muck (s. v.), -s, -ing, -ed mʌk, -s, -iŋ, -t
mucker (s. v.), -s, -ing, -ed 'mʌkə*, -z,
-riŋ, -d
muckrake, -s 'mʌk-reik, -s
muck|y, -ier, -iest, -iness 'mʌk|i, -iə*,
-iist, -inis
muc|ous, -us 'mjuːk|əs, -əs
mud, -s mʌd, -z
mud-ba|th, -ths 'mʌdbaː|θ ['mʌd'b-], -ðz
mudd|le (s. v.), -les, -ling, -led, -ler/s
'mʌd|l, -lz, -lïŋ [-liŋ], -ld, -lə*/z
[-lə*/z]
muddleheaded 'mʌdl,hedid
mudd|y (adj. v.), -ier, -iest, -ily, -iness;
-ies, -ying, -ied 'mʌd|i, -iə*, -iist, -ili,
-inis; -iz, -iiŋ, -id
Mud(d)eford 'mʌdifəd
mud-guard, -s 'mʌdgaːd, -z
Mudie 'mjuːdi
mudlark, -s 'mʌdlaːk, -s
muezzin, -s mu(:)'ezin, -z
muff (s. v.), -s, -ing, -ed mʌf, -s, -iŋ, -t
muffin, -s 'mʌfin, -z
muffineer, -s ,mʌfi'niə*, -z
muff|le (s. v.), -les, -ling, -led 'mʌf|l, -lz, -lïŋ
[-liŋ], -ld
muffler, -s 'mʌflə*, -z
mufti 'mʌfti
mug (s. v.), -s, -ging, -ged mʌg, -z, -iŋ,
-d
mugger, -s 'mʌgə*, -z
muggins, -es 'mʌginz, -iz
Muggins 'mʌginz, 'mjuːginz
Muggleton 'mʌgltən
mugg|y, -ier, -iest, -iness 'mʌg|i, -iə*,
-iist, -inis
mugwump, -s 'mʌgwʌmp, -s
Muir, -head mjuə* [mjɔə*, mjɔ:*], -hed
Mukden 'mukdən
Mukle 'mjuːkli
mulatto, -s mju(:)'lætəu, -z
mulberr|y, -ies 'mʌlbər|i, -iz
Mulcaster 'mʌlkæstə*
mulch (s. v.), -es, -ing, -ed mʌlʧ, -iz, -iŋ,
-t

mulct (s. v.), -s, -ing, -ed mʌlkt, -s, -iŋ, -id

mule, -s mjuːl, -z

muleteer, -s ˌmjuːliˈtiə*, -z

Mulgrave 'mʌlgreiv

mulish, -ly, -ness 'mjuːliʃ, -li, -nis

mull (s. v.) (M.), -s, -ing, -ed mʌl, -z, -iŋ, -d

Mullah, -s 'mʌlə, -z

mullein 'mʌlin

mullet (M.), -s 'mʌlit, -s

mulligatawny ˌmʌligəˈtɔːni ['mʌligə't-]

Mullin|ar, -er 'mʌlin|ə*, -ə*

Mullinger 'mʌlindʒə*

mullion (M.), -s, -ed 'mʌliən [-ljən], -z, -d

mullock 'mʌlək

Mulready mʌl'redi

multifarious, -ly, -ness ˌmʌlti'fɛərïəs, -li, -nis

multiform 'mʌltifɔːm

multilateral 'mʌlti'lætərəl

multiliter|al, -ally 'mʌlti'litər|əl, -əli

multi-millionaire, -s 'mʌltimiljə'nɛə*, -z

multiple (s. adj.), -s 'mʌltipl, -z

multiplex 'mʌltipleks

multiplicand, -s ˌmʌltipli'kænd, -z

multiplication, -s ˌmʌltipli'keiʃən, -z

multiplicative ˌmʌlti'plikətiv ['mʌltiplikeitiv]

multiplicator, -s 'mʌltiplikeitə*, -z

multiplicity ˌmʌlti'plisiti

multipl|y, -ies, -ying, -ied, -ier/s 'mʌltipl|ai, -aiz, -aiiŋ, -aid, -aiə*/z

multi-purpose 'mʌlti'pə:pəs

multitude, -s 'mʌltitjuːd, -z

multitudinous, -ly, -ness ˌmʌlti'tjuːdinəs [-dŋəs], -li, -nis

multum in parvo 'multəmin'paːvəu ['mʌl-]

mum mʌm

mumb|le, -les, -ling/ly, -led, -ler/s 'mʌmb|l, -lz, -liŋ/li, -ld, -lə*/z

Mumbles 'mʌmblz

Mumm mʌm

mummer, -s, -y 'mʌmə*, -z, -ri

mummification ˌmʌmifi'keiʃən

mummi|fy, -fies, -fying, -fied 'mʌmi|fai, -faiz, -faiiŋ, -faid

mumm|y, -ies 'mʌm|i, -iz

mump, -s, -ing, -ed mʌmp, -s, -iŋ, -t [mʌmt]

mumpish, -ly, -ness 'mʌmpiʃ, -li, -nis

mumps (s.) mʌmps

munch, -es, -ing, -ed mʌntʃ, -iz, -iŋ, -t

Munchausen mʌn'tʃɔːzn [mun'tʃauzn] (also as German Münchhausen 'mynç-ˌhauzən)

mundane, -ly 'mʌndein ['-'-], -li

Munich 'mjuːnik

municipal mju(ː)'nisipəl

municipalit|y, -ies mjuː(ː)ˌnisi'pælit|i [ˌmjuː:nisi'p-], -iz

municipaliz|e [-is|e], -es, -ing, -ed mjuː(ː)'nisipəlaiz, -iz, -iŋ, -d

munificen|ce, -t/ly mjuː(ː)'nifisn|s, -t/li

muniment, -s 'mjuːnimənt, -s

munition, -s mju(ː)'niʃən, -z

Munro mʌn'rəu [mən-], 'mʌnrəu

Munsey 'mʌnzi

Munster 'mʌnstə*

muntjak, -s 'mʌntdʒæk, -s

mural, -s 'mjuərəl ['mjɔər-, 'mjɔːr-, 'mjəːr-], -z

Murchie 'məːki, in S. England also 'məːtʃi

Murchison 'məːtʃisn, 'məːkisn

Murcott 'məːkət

murd|er (s. v.), -ers, -ering, -ered, -erer/s 'məːd|ə*, -əz, -əriŋ, -əd, -ərə*/z

murderess, -es 'məːdəris [-res], -iz

murderous, -ly 'məːdərəs, -li

Murdoch 'məːdɔk

Mure mjuə* [mjɔə*, mjɔː*]

muriate 'mjuəriit ['mjɔər-, 'mjɔːr-, -rieit]

muriatic ˌmjuəri'ætik [ˌmjɔər-, ˌmjɔːr-, '----]

Muriel 'mjuəriəl ['mjɔər-, 'mjɔːr-, 'mjəːr-]

Murillo, -s mjuə'riləu [mju'r-, -ljəu], -z

Murison 'mjuərisn ['mjɔər-, 'mjɔːr-]

murk|y, -ier, -iest, -ily, -iness 'məːk|i, -iə* [-jə*], -iist [-jist], -ili, -inis

murm|ur (s. v.), -urs, -uring/ly, -ured, -urer/s 'məːm|ə*, -əz, -əriŋ/li, -əd, -ərə*/z

murph|y (M.), -ies 'məːf|i, -iz

murrain 'mʌrin [-rein]

Murray 'mʌri

Murree 'mʌri

Murrell 'mʌrəl, mʌ'rel [mə'rel]

Murrie (surname) 'mjuəri

Murry 'mʌri

Murtagh 'məːtə

Murtle 'məːtl

Mus. Bac., -'s 'mʌz'bæk, -s

muscat (M.), -s 'mʌskət, -s

muscatel, -s ˌmʌskə'tel ['--'-], -z

Muschamp 'mʌskəm

muscle, -s 'mʌsl, -z

muscle-bound 'mʌslbaund

Muscovite, -s 'mʌskəuvait, -s

Muscovy 'mʌskəuvi

muscular, -ly 'mʌskjulə* [-jəl-], -li

muscularity ,mʌskju'læriti

Mus.D., -'s 'mʌz'di:, -z

mus|e (s. v.) (M.), -es, -ing/ly, -ed mju:z, -iz, -iŋ/li, -d

musette, -s mju(:)'zet, -s

museum, -s mju(:)'ziəm, -z

Musgrave 'mʌzgreiv

mush (s. v.), -es, -ing, -ed mʌʃ, -iz, -iŋ, -t

mushroom, -s 'mʌʃrum, -z

mush|y, -ier, -iest, -iness 'mʌʃ|i, -iə*, -iist, -inis

music 'mju:zik

musical (s.), -s 'mju:zikəl [,mju:zi'kæl, -'kɑ:l], -z

music|al (adj.), -ally, -alness 'mju:zik|əl, -əli, -əlnis

musical-box, -es 'mju:zikəlbɔks, -iz

musicale, -s ,mju:zi'kæl [-'kɑ:l], -z

music-hall, -s 'mju:zikhɔ:l, -z

musician, -s, -ly mju(:)'ziʃən, -z, -li

musicolog|ist/s, -y ,mju:zi'kɔlədʒ|ist/s, -i

music-stand, -s 'mju:zik-stænd, -z

music-stool, -s 'mju:zik-stu:l, -z

Musidor|a, -us ,mju:si'dɔ:r|ə, -əs

musk, -y mʌsk, -i

musk-deer 'mʌsk'diə* ['--]

musket, -s; -ry 'mʌskit, -s; -ri

musketeer, -s ,mʌski'tiə*, -z

Muskett 'mʌskit

musk-ox, -en 'mʌsk-ɔks ['mʌsk'ɔks], -ən

musk-rat, -s 'mʌsk-ræt ['mʌsk'ræt], -s

musk-rose, -s 'mʌsk-rəuz ['-'-], -iz

Muslim, -s 'muslim ['muzlim, 'mʌzlim],

muslin, -s 'mʌzlin, -z [-z

musquash 'mʌs-kwɔʃ

mussel, -s 'mʌsl, -z

Musselburgh 'mʌslbərə [-bʌrə]

Mussolini ,musə'li:ni(:)

Mussorgsky mu'sɔ:gski (mu'sorkskij, 'musərkskij)

Mussulman, -s 'mʌslmən, -z

must (s. adj.) mʌst

must (v.) mʌst (strong form), məst, məs, mst, ms (weak forms)

mustang, -s 'mʌstæŋ, -z

Mustapha (Turkish) 'mustəfə, (Egyptian) mus'tɑ:fə

Mustapha Kemal 'mustəfəke'mɑ:l [-ki'm-]

mustard (M.) 'mʌstəd

mustardseed 'mʌstədsi:d

Mustel 'mʌstəl [-tl]

must|er (s. v.), -ers, -ering, -ered 'mʌst|ə*, -əz, -əriŋ, -əd

mustn't 'mʌsnt [also occasionally 'mʌsn when not final]

must|y, -ier, -iest, -ily, -iness 'mʌst|i, -iə* [-jə*], -iist [-jist], -ili, -inis

mutability ,mju:tə'biliti [-lət-]

mutable 'mju:təbl

mutat|e, -es, -ing, -ed mju:'teit, -s, -iŋ, -id

mutation, -s mju(:)'teiʃən, -z

mutatis mutandis mu:'tɑ:tis-mu:'tændis [mju(:)'teitis-mju(:)-]

mut|e (s. adj. v.), -es; -ely, -eness; -ing, -ed mju:t, -s; -li, -nis; -iŋ, -id

mutilat|e, -es, -ing, -ed, -or/s 'mju:ti-leit, -s, -iŋ, -id, -ə*/z

mutilation, -s ,mju:ti'leiʃən, -z

mutineer, -s ,mju:ti'niə*, -z

mutinous, -ly, -ness 'mju:tinəs [-tɳəs], -li, -nis

mutin|y (s. v.), -ies, -ying, -ied 'mju:-tin|i [-tɳ|-, -tən|-], -iz, -iiŋ, -id

mutism 'mju:tizəm

mutt|er (s. v.), -ers, -ering/ly, -ered, -erer/s 'mʌt|ə*, -əz, -əriŋ/li, -əd, -ərə*/z

mutton (M.); -chop/s 'mʌtn; -'tʃɔp/s

muttony 'mʌtɳi

mutual, -ly 'mju:tʃuəl [-tʃwəl, -tʃul, -tjuəl, -tjwəl, -tjul], -i

mutuality ,mju:tju'æliti [-tʃu-]

muzz|le (s. v.), -les, -ling, -led 'mʌz|l, -lz, -liŋ [-liŋ], -ld

muzzle-load|er/s, -ing 'mʌzl,ləud|ə*/z, -iŋ

muzz|y, -ier, -iest, -iness 'mʌz|i, -iə*, -iist, -inis

my mai (normal form), mi (frequent weak form)

Note.—Many people confine the use of mi to the special expression my lord (see lord) and (at Eton College) to the expressions my tutor and my dame. Some use mi in common idioms, such as never in my life, but not elsewhere. On the stage, in serious drama, there is a tradition still followed by many actors to pronounce mi whenever the word is unstressed.

Mycenae mai'si:ni(:)

mycolog|ist/s, -y mai'kɔlədʒ|ist/s, -i

Myers 'maiəz

Myerscough (in Lancs.) 'maiəskəu

Myfanwy mə'vænwi (Welsh mə'vanwi)

mynheer, -s main'hiə* [-'heə*], -z

Mynheer (form of address in S. Africa) mə'niə* (Afrikaans mə'ne:r)

Mynott 'mainət

myope, -s 'maiəup, -s

myopia mai'əupjə [-piə]

myopic mai'ɔpik

myosis mai'əusis
myosotis ˌmaiəu'səutis
Myra 'maiərə
myriad, -s 'mirïəd, -z
myrmidon (M.), -s 'mə:midən [-dn, -dɔn], -z
myrrh mə:*
Myrrha 'mirə
myrrhic ['mə:rik ['mir-]
myrrhine 'mə:rain ['mir-]
myrrhite 'mə:rait ['mir-]
myrrhy 'mə:ri
myrtle (M.), -s 'mə:tl, -z
myself mai'self [mi's-, mə's-]
Mysia 'misïə [-sjə, -ʃïə, -ʃjə]
Mysore mai'sɔ:* [-'sɔə*]
mysterious, -ly, -ness mis'tiərïəs, -li, -nis
myster|y, -ies 'mistər|i, -iz

mystic (s. adj.), -s 'mistik, -s
mystic|al, -ally, -alness 'mistik|əl, -əli, -əlnis
mysticism 'mistisizəm
mystification ˌmistifi'keiʃən
mysti|fy, -fies, -fying, -fied 'misti|fai, -faiz, -faiiŋ, -faid
mystique mis'ti:k
myth, -s miθ [rarely maiθ], -s
mythic, -al, -ally 'miθik, -əl, -əli
Mytholmroyd (in Yorks.) 'miðəmrɔid
mythologic, -al, -ally ˌmiθə'lɔdʒik [ˌmaiθ-], -əl, -əli
mytholog|ist/s, -y, -ies mi'θɔlədʒ|ist/s [mai'θ-], -i, -iz
mythologiz|e [-is|e], -es, -ing, -ed mi'θɔlədʒaiz [mai'θ-], -iz, -iŋ, -d
Mytilene ˌmiti'li:ni(:)
myxomatosis ˌmiksəumə'təusis

N

N *(the letter),* **-'s** en, -z
N.A.A.F.I. 'næfi
Naaman 'neɪəmən
Naas *(in Ireland)* neis
nab *(s. v.),* **-s, -bing, -bed** næb, -z, -iŋ, -d
Nabarro *(English surname)* nə'bɑːrəu
Nabha 'nɑːbə *(Hind.* nabha)
Nablus 'nɑːbləs
nabob, -s 'neibɔb, -z
Naboth 'neibɔθ
nacelle, -s næ'sel, -z
nacre 'neikə*
nacreous 'neikrɪəs
nacrite 'neikrait
nadir, -s 'neidiə* [-də*, 'nædiə*], -z
nag *(s. v.)* **(N.), -s, -ging, -ged, -ger/s** næg, -z, -iŋ, -d, -ə*/z
Naga, -s; -**land** 'nɑːgə, -z; -lænd
Nagaina nə'gainə
Nagari 'nɑːgəri
Nagasaki ˌnægə'sɑːki
Nahum *(prophet)* 'neihəm [-hʌm], *(modern surname)* 'neiəm
naiad, -s 'naiæd, -z
nail *(s. v.),* **-s, -ing, -ed** neil, -z, -iŋ, -d
nail-brush, -es 'neilbrʌʃ, -iz
nail-scissors 'neilˌsizəz
Nain 'neiin [nein]
Nairn(e) neən
Nairnshire 'neənʃiə* [-ʃə*]
Nairobi ˌnaiə'rəubi
Naish næʃ
naïve -ly nɑː'iːv [nai'iːv], -li
naive, -ly neiv, -li
naïveté, nɑː'iːvtei [nai'iːv-] (naifte)
naked -ly, -ness 'neikid, -li, -nis
Naldera nʌl'dɛərə [næl-, -'diər-] *(Hind.* nəldʒera)
namby-pamby 'næmbi 'pæmbi
nam|e *(s. v.),* **-es, -ing, -ed; -eless** neim, -z, -iŋ, -d; -lis
namely 'neimli
name-plate, -s 'neim-pleit, -s
namesake, -s 'neim-seik, -s
Namier 'neimiə* [-mjə*, -mɪə*]
Nanaimo næ'naiməu [nə'n-]
Nancy 'nænsi
nankeen næŋ'kiːn [næn'k-]

Nanki|n, -ng næn'ki|n ['næn'k-, (')næŋ'k-, *also* '-- *when followed by a stress*], -ŋ
Nannie 'næni
nann|y (N.), -ies 'næn|i, -iz
Nansen 'nænsn
Nantucket næn'tʌkit
Nantwich *(in Cheshire)* 'næntwitʃ *[locally also* -waitʃ]
Naomi 'neiəmi ['neiəum-]
nap *(s. v.),* **-s, -ping, -ped** næp, -s, -iŋ, -t
napalm 'neipɑːm ['næp-]
nape, -s neip, -s
napery 'neipəri
Naphtali 'næftəlai
naphtha, -lene 'næfθə ['næpθ-], -liːn
naphthol 'næfθɔl ['næpθ-]
Napier 'neipiə* [-pɪə*, -pjə*], nə'piə*
napierian nə'piəriən [nei'p-]
napkin, -s; -ring/s 'næpkin, -z; -riŋ/z
Naples 'neiplz
napoleon (N.), -s nə'pəuljən [-lɪən], -z
napoleonic nəˌpəuli'ɔnik
Narbonne nɑː'bɔn (narbɔn)
narcissism 'nɑː'sisizm
narcissistic ˌnɑːsi'sistik
narciss|us (N.), -uses, -i nɑː'sis|əs, -əsiz, -ai
narcosis nɑː'kəusis
narcotic *(s. adj.),* **-s** nɑː'kɔtik, -s
narcoti|sm, -st/s 'nɑːkəti|zəm, -st/s
nard nɑːd
Nares nɛəz
narghile, -s 'nɑːgili, -z
Narkunda nɑː'kʌndə *(Hind.* nərkwnɖə)
narrat|e, -es, -ing, -ed, -or/s nə'reit [næ'r-], -s, -iŋ, -id, -ə*/z
narration, -s nə'reiʃən [næ'r-], -z
narrative *(s. adj.),* **-s** 'nærətiv, -z
narr|ow *(s. adj. v.),* **-ows, -ower, -owest, -owly, -owness; -owing, -owed** 'nær|əu, -əuz, -əuə*, -əuist, -əuli, -əunis; -əuiŋ, -əud
narrow-gauge 'nærəugeidʒ
narrow-minded, -ly, -ness 'nærəu-'maindid ['--,--], -li, -nis
narwhal, -s 'nɑːwəl, -z
nas|al *(s. adj.),* **-als, -ally** 'neiz|əl, -əlz, -əli

nasalism 'neizəlizəm [-zļi-]

nasality nei'zæliti [nə'z-]

nasalization [-isa-], -s ˌneizəlai'zeiʃən [-zļai'z-, -zəli'z-, -zļi'z-], -z

nasaliz|e [-is|e], -es, -ing, -ed 'neizəl-aiz [-zļ-], -iz, -iŋ, -d

nascent 'næsnt

Naseby 'neizbi

Nash, -ville næʃ, -vil

Nasmyth 'neizmiθ [-eism-], 'næzmiθ

Nassau (German province) 'næsau ('nasau), (princely family) 'næsɔː [-sau], (in Bahamas and U.S.A.) 'næsɔː:

nasturtium, -s nəs'tə:ʃəm [-ʃm], -z

nast|y, -ier, -iest, -ily, -iness 'nɑ:st|i, -iə* [-jə*], -iist [-jist], -ili, -inis

natal (adj.) 'neitl

Natal nə'tæl

natation nə'teiʃən [nei-]

Nathan 'neiθən [-θæn]

Nathaniel nə'θænjəl

nation, -s 'neiʃən, -z

na|tional, -tionally 'næ|ʃənl [-ʃnəl, -ʃnļ, -ʃnļ, -ʃənəl], -ʃnəli [-ʃnəli, -ʃnļi, -ʃnļi, -ʃənəli]

nationali|sm, -st/s 'næʃnəli|zəm [-ʃnəl-, -ʃnļ-, -ʃnļ-, -ʃənəl-], -st/s

nationalistic ˌnæʃnə'listik [-ʃnə'li-, -ʃnļ'i-, -ʃnļ'i-, -ʃənə'li-]

nationalit|y, -ies ˌnæʃə'nælit|i [-ʃņ'æ-], -iz

nationalization [-isa-] ˌnæʃnəlai'zei-ʃən [-ʃnəl-, -ʃnļ-, -ʃnļ-, -ʃənəl-, -li'z-]

nationaliz|e [-is|e], -es, -ing, -ed 'næʃnəlaiz [-ʃnəl-, -ʃnļ-, -ʃnļ-, -ʃənəl-], -iz, -iŋ, -d

native (s. adj.), -s, -ly 'neitiv, -z, -li

nativit|y (N.), -ies nə'tivit|i, -iz

N.A.T.O. 'neitəu

natron 'neitrən [-rɔn]

natter (s. v.), -s, -ing, -ed 'nætə*, -z, -riŋ, -d

natt|y, -ier, -iest, -ily, -iness 'næt|i, -iə*, -iist, -ili, -inis

natur|al (s. adj.), -als, -ally, -alness 'nætʃr|əl [-tʃur-, -tʃər-], -əlz, -əli, -əlnis

naturali|sm, -st/s 'nætʃrəli|zəm [-tʃur-, -tʃər-], -st/s

naturalistic ˌnætʃrə'listik [-tʃur-, -tʃər-]

naturalization [-isa-] ˌnætʃrəlai'zeiʃən [-tʃur-, -tʃər-, -li'z-]

naturaliz|e [-is|e], -es, -ing, -ed 'nætʃrəlaiz [-tʃur-, -tʃər-], -iz, -iŋ, -d

nature, -s, -d 'neitʃə*, -z, -d

naturi|sm, -st/s 'neitʃəri|zəm, -st/s

naught, -s nɔ:t, -s

naught|y, -ier, -iest, -ily, -iness 'nɔ:t|i, -iə* [-jə*], -iist [-jist], -ili, -inis

nausea 'nɔ:sjə [-sïə, -ʃjə, -ʃïə]

nauseat|e, -es, -ing, -ed 'nɔ:sieit [-sjeit, -ʃieit, -ʃjeit], -s, -iŋ, -id

nauseous, -ly, -ness 'nɔ:sjəs [-sïəs, -ʃjəs, -ʃïəs], -li, -nis

Nausicaa nɔ:'sikïə [-keiə]

nautch, -es nɔ:tʃ, -iz

nautic|al, -ally 'nɔ:tik|əl, -əli

nautilus, -es 'nɔ:tiləs, -iz

naval 'neivəl

Navarino ˌnævə'ri:nəu

Navarre nə'vɑ:* (nava:r)

nave, -s neiv, -z

navel, -s 'neivəl, -z

navicert, -s 'nævisə:t, -s

navigability ˌnævigə'biliti [-lət-]

navigable, -ness 'nævigəbl, -nis

navigat|e, -es, -ing, -ed, -or/s 'nævi-geit, -s, -iŋ, -id, -ə*/z

navigation ˌnævi'geiʃən

navv|y, -ies 'næv|i, -iz

nav|y, -ies 'neiv|i, -iz

nawab, -s nə'wɑ:b, -z

Nawanagar nə'wɑ:nəgə* (Hind. nəvanəgər)

nay nei

Naylor 'neilə*

Nazarene, -s ˌnæzə'ri:n, -z

Nazareth 'næzəriθ [-rəθ]

Nazarite, -s 'næzərait, -s

naze (N.), -s neiz, -iz

Nazeing 'neiziŋ

Nazi, -s 'nɑ:tsi ['nɑ:zi], -z

nazism 'nɑ:tsizəm ['nɑ:zi-]

N.B. 'en'bi: ['nəutə'bi:ni, -'beni]

N.E. 'en'i: ['nɔ:θ'i:st]

ne (in ne plus ultra) nei [ni:]

Neaera ni(:)'iərə

Neagh nei

Neal(e) ni:l

Neanderthal ni'ændətɑ:l

neap (s. adj.), -s ni:p, -s

Neapolis ni'æpəlis

Neapolitan, -s niə'pɔlitən [ˌni:ə-], -z

near (adj. v. adv. prep.), -er, -est, -ly, -ness; -s, -ing, -ed niə*, -rə*, -rist, -li, -nis; -z, -riŋ, -d

nearby (adj.) 'niəbai

nearside 'niə-said

near-sighted, -ness 'niə'saitid, -nis

Neasden 'ni:zdən

neat, -er, -est, -ly, -ness ni:t, -ə*, -ist, -li, -nis

'neath ni:θ

Neath (river in Wales) ni:θ

Neb|at, -o 'ni:b|æt, -əu

Nebraska ni'bræskə [ne'b-, nə'b-]
Nebuchadnezzar ‚nebjukəd'nezə*
nebul|a, -ae, -as, -ar, -ous 'nebjul|ə, -i:,
-əz, -ə*, -əs
nebulosity ‚nebju'lɔsiti
necessarily 'nesisərili [-səs-, -ser-,
‚nesi'serili, ‚nesə'serili]
necessar|y (s. adj.), -ies; -iness 'nesi-
sər|i [-səs-, -ser-], -iz; -inis
necessitat|e, -es, -ing, -ed ni'sesiteit
[ne's-, nə's-], -s, -iŋ, -id
necessitous, -ly, -ness ni'sesitəs [ne's-,
nə's-], -li, -nis
necessit|y, -ies ni'sesit|i [ne's-, nə's-], -iz
neck, -s nek, -s
neckband, -s 'nekbænd, -z
neck|-cloth, -cloths 'nek|klɔθ [-klɔ:θ],
-klɔθs [-klɔ:ðz, -klɔ:θs]
neckerchief, -s 'nekətʃif [-tʃi:f], -s
necklace, -s 'neklis, -iz
necklet, -s 'neklit, -s
neck-line, -s 'nek-lain, -z
neck-tie, -s 'nek-tai, -z
neckwear 'nek-wɛə*
necrolog|ist/s, -y, -ies ne'krɔlədʒ|ist/s,
-i, -iz
necromanc|er/s,-y 'nekrəumæns|ə*/z, -i
necropolis, -es ne'krɔpəlis [ni'k-], -iz
necrosis ne'krəusis [ni'k-]
nectar 'nektə* [-ta:*]
nectarine, -s 'nektərin, -z
Nedd|y, -ies 'ned|i, -iz
Neden 'ni:dn
née nei
need (s. v.), -s, -ing, -ed ni:d, -z, -iŋ, -id
need|ful, -fully, -fulness 'ni:d|ful, -fuli
[-fəli], -fulnis
Needham 'ni:dəm
needle (N.), -s; -case/s, -ful/s, -shaped
'ni:dl, -z; -keis/iz, -ful/z, -ʃeipt
needless, -ly, -ness 'ni:dlis, -li, -nis
needle|woman, -women 'ni:dl|‚wumən,
-‚wimin
needlework 'ni:dlwə:k
needn't 'ni:dnt ['ni:tnt, also occasionally
'ni:dn, 'ni:tn when not final]
needs (adv.) ni:dz
need|y, -ier, -iest, -ily, -iness 'ni:d|i,
-iə* [-jə*], -iist [-jist], -ili, -inis
ne'er nɛə*
ne'er-do-well, -s 'nɛədu(:)‚wel, -z
nefarious, -ly, -ness ni'fɛəriəs [ne'f-,
nə'f-], -li, -nis
negation, -s ni'geiʃən [ne'g-], -z
negativ|e (s. adj. v.), -es; -ely, -eness;
-ing, -ed 'negətiv, -z; -li, -nis; -iŋ, -d
neglect (s. v.), -s, -ing, -ed, -er/s
ni'glekt, -s, -iŋ, -id, -ə*/z

neglect|ful, -fully, -fulness ni'glekt|ful,
-fuli [-fəli], -fulnis
négligé 'negli:ʒei [-liʒ-] (negliʒe)
negligen|ce, -ces, -t/ly 'neglidʒən|s,
-siz, -t/li
negligible 'neglidʒəbl [-dʒib-]
negotiability ni‚gəuʃjə'biliti [-ʃiə-, -ʃə-,
-lət-]
negotiable ni'gəuʃjəbl [-ʃiə, -ʃə-]
negotiat|e, -es, -ing, -ed, -or/s ni'gəuʃi-
eit [-ʃjeit, -sieit, -sjeit], -s, -iŋ, -id,
-ə*/z
negotiation, -s ni‚gəuʃi'eiʃən [-əusi-], -z
negress, -es 'ni:gris [-gres], -iz
negrillo, -s ne'griləu [ni'g-], -z
Negri Sembilan 'negrisem'bi:lən [-səm-]
negrito, -s ne'gri:təu [ni'g-], -z
negro (N.), -es 'ni:grəu, -z
negroid 'ni:grɔid
negus (N.) 'ni:gəs
Nehemiah ‚ni:i'maiə [‚ni:hi'm-,
‚ni:hə'm-, niə'm-]
Nehru 'neəru: (Hind. nehru)
neigh (s. v.), -s, -ing, -ed nei, -z, -iŋ, -d
neighb|our, -ours, -ouring, -ourly, -our-
liness 'neib|ə*, -əz, -əriŋ, -əli, -əlinis
neighbourhood, -s 'neibəhud [old-
fashioned -bərud], -z
Neil(l) ni:l
Neilson 'ni:lsn
neither 'naiðə* ['ni:ðə*]
Nellie [-ly] 'neli
Nelson 'nelsn
nem. con. 'nem'kɔn
Nemesis 'nemisis
Nemo 'ni:məu
nemophila, -s ni'mɔfilə*, -z
Nen (river) nen
Nene (river) nen [ni:n], (name of ship)
ni:n, (aero-engine) ni:n
nenuphar, -s 'nenjufa:*, -z
neo-latin 'ni(:)əu'lætin
neolithic ‚ni(:)əu'liθik
neolog|ism/s, -ist/s, -y ni(:)'ɔlədʒ|-
izəm/z, -ist/s, -i
neologiz|e [-is|e], -es, -ing, -ed ni(:)-
'ɔlədʒaiz, -iz, -iŋ, -id
neon 'ni:ən ['ni:ɔn, niən]
neophyte, -s 'ni(:)əufait, -s
Nepal ni'pɔ:l [ne'p-, -'pɑ:l]
Nepalese ‚nepɔ:'li:z
nepenthe ne'penθi [ni'p-]
neper, -s 'ni:pə*, -z
nephew, -s 'nevju(:) ['nefj-], -z
nephritis ne'fraitis
ne plus ultra 'nei-plus'ultra: [-trə,
'ni:-plʌs'ʌltrə]
Nepos 'ni:pɔs ['nep-]

nepotism 'nepətizəm [-pɔt-]
Neptune 'neptjuːn [-tʃuːn]
neptunian (N.) nep'tjuːnjən [-nïən]
neptunium nep'tjuːnjəm [-nïəm]
Nereid, -s 'niəriid, -z
Nereus 'niərjuːs [-riuːs, -rïəs]
Neri 'niəri
Nerissa ni'risə [ne'r-, nə'r-]
Nero 'niərəu
nerv|e (s. v.), -es, -ing, -ed; -eless
    nəːv, -z, -iŋ, -d; -lis
nerve-cell, -s 'nəːvsel, -z
nerve-centre, -s 'nəːv₁sentə*, -z
nervine 'nəːviːn
nervous, -ly, -ness 'nəːvəs, -li, -nis
nerve-racking 'nəːv₁rækiŋ
nerv|y, -ier, -iest, -ily, -iness 'nəːv|i,
    -ïə* [-jə*], -iist [-jist], -ili, -inis
Nesbit(t) 'nezbit
nescience 'nesïəns [-sjəns]
Nesfield 'nesfiːld
ness (N.), -es nes, -iz
nest (s. v.), -s, -ing, -ed nest, -s, -iŋ, -id
Nesta 'nestə
nest-egg, -s 'nesteg, -z
nest|le, -les, -ling, -led 'nes|l, -lz, -liŋ
    [-liŋ], -ld
Nestlé 'nesli ['nesl]
nestling (s.) (young bird), -s 'nestliŋ, -z
Nestor 'nestɔ:* [-tə*]
Nestorian, -s nes'tɔːrïən, -z
net (s. v.), -s, -ting, -ted net, -s, -iŋ, -id
nether, -most 'neðə*, -məust [-məst]
Netherland, -s, -er/s 'neðələnd [-ðḷənd],
    -z, -ə*/z
Netley 'netli
Nettie 'neti
nett|le (s. v.), -les, -ling, -led 'net|l, -lz,
    -liŋ [-liŋ], -ld
Nettle|fold, -ship 'netl|fəuld, -ʃip
nettlerash 'netlræʃ
net-work, -s 'net-wəːk, -s
Neuchâtel ₁nəːʃæ'tel [-ʃə't-, 'nəːʃətel]
    (nœʃatɛl)
neume, -s njuːm, -z
neural 'njuərəl
neuralg|ia, -ic njuə'rældʒ|ə [njə'r-,
    nju'r-], -ik
neurasthenia ₁njuərəs'θiːnjə [₁njəːr-,
    -nïə]
neurasthenic (s. adj.), -s ₁njuərəs-
    'θenik [₁njəːr-], -s
neuritis njuə'raitis [njə'r-, nju'r-]
neurological ₁njuərə'lɔdʒikl [₁njəːr-]
neurolog|ist/s, -y njuə'rɔlədʒ|ist/s
    [njə'r-, nju'r-], -i
neuros|is, -es njuə'rəus|is [njə'r-,
    nju'r-], -iːz

neurotic (s. adj.), -s njuə'rɔtik [njə'r-,
    nju'r-], -s
neuter (s. adj.), -s 'njuːtə*, -z
neutr|al (s. adj.), -als, -ally 'njuːtr|əl,
    -əlz, -əli
neutrality nju(:)'træliti
neutralization [-isa-] ₁njuːtrəlai'zeiʃən
    [-trḷai'z-, -trəli'z-, -trḷi'z-]
neutraliz|e [-is|e], -es, -ing, -ed 'njuː-
    trəlaiz [-trḷaiz], -iŋ, -iz, -d
neutron, -s 'njuːtrɔn [-trən], -z
Neva 'neivə [old-fashioned 'niːvə]
    (nji'va)
Nevada ne'vɑːdə [ni'v-, nə'v-]
Neve niːv
névé 'nevei
never, -more 'nevə*, -'mɔː* [-'mɔə*]
nevertheless ₁nevəðə'les ['nev-]
Nevey 'nevi
Nevil 'nevil
Nevill(e) 'nevil
Nevin, -son 'nevin, -sn
Nevis (in Scotland) 'nevis, (in West
    Indies) 'niːvis
new, -er, -est, -ly, -ness njuː, -ə*
    [njuə*], -ist [njuist], -li, -nis
Newark (in Notts.) 'nju(:)ək
Newbiggin (place) 'njuː₁bigin, (surname)
    'njuː₁bigin, njuː'bigin
Newbol|d, -t 'njuːbəul|d, -t
newborn 'njuːbɔːn
New|burgh, -bury 'njuː|bərə, -bəri
Newcastle 'njuː₁kɑːsl
    Note.—Newcastle in Northumb. is
    locally nju'kæsl.
Newcome, -s 'njuːkəm, -z
newcomer, -s 'njuː'kʌmə* ['njuː₁k-], -z
Newdigate 'njuːdigit [-geit]
Newe njuː:
newel, -s 'njuːəl [njuːl], -z
new-fangled 'njuː₁fæŋgld ['njuː'f-]
new-fashioned 'njuː'fæʃənd [also 'njuː₁f-
    when attributive]
Newfoundland (place) ₁njuːfənd'lænd
    ['njuːfəndlənd, 'njuːfəndlænd, nju(:)-
    'faundlənd]
    Note.—₁njuːfənd'lænd is the local
    form; it is also the nautical pro-
    nunciation in England.
Newfoundland (dog), -s nju(:)'faund-
    lənd, -z
Newgate 'njuːgit [-geit]
Newhaven nju(:)'heivn ['njuː'h-,
    'njuː₁h-]
Newington 'nju(:)iŋtən
new-laid (when attributive) 'njuːleid,
    (otherwise) 'njuːleid
New|man, -market 'njuː|mən, -₁mɑːkit

Newn|es, -ham nju:n|z, -əm
New Orleans nju:'ɔ:liənz [-ljənz, ˌnju:-ɔ:'li:nz]
New|port, -quay 'nju:|pɔ:t, -ki(:)
New Quay 'nju:'ki:
news nju:z
news-agent, -s 'nju:zˌeidʒənt, -s
news-boy, -s 'nju:zbɔi, -z
news-letter, -s 'nju:zˌletə* ['-'--], -z
newsmonger, -s 'nju:zˌmʌŋgə*, -z
New South Wales 'nju:sauθ'weilz
newspaper, -s 'nju:sˌpeipə* [rarely 'nju:zˌp-], -z
news-print 'nju:zprint
newsreel, -s 'nju:zri:l, -z
news-sheet, -s 'nju:zʃi:t [-u:ʒʃ-], -z
Newstead 'nju:stid [-sted]
newsvendor, -s 'nju:zˌvendə* [-dɔ:*], -z
newsy 'nju:zi
newt, -s nju:t, -s
Newton 'nju:tn
Newtonian nju(:)'təunjən [-nɪən]
Newtown 'nju:taun
New York, -er/s 'nju:'jɔ:k [nju:'j-, nju'j-], -ə*/z
New Zealand, -er/s nju:'zi:lənd [nju'z-], -ə*/z
next nekst [often also neks when followed by a word beginning with a consonant]
nexus, -es 'neksəs, -iz
Ngaio (authoress, suburb of Wellington, N.Z.) 'naiəu
Ngami ŋ'gɑ:mi ['ŋɑ:mi]
Niagara nai'ægərə [-grə]
nib, -s nib, -z
nibb|le (s. v.), -les, -ling, -led 'nib|l, -lz, -lɪŋ [-lɪŋ], -ld
Nibelung, -s, -en 'ni:bəluŋ [-bil-], -z, -ən
niblick, -s 'niblik, -s
Nicaea nai'si(:)ə
Nicaragua, -n/s ˌnikə'rægjŭə [-'rægjwə, -'rɑ:gwə], -n/z
nice, -r, -st, -ly, -ness nais, -ə*, -ist, -li, -nis
Nice (in France) ni:s (nis)
Nicene nai'si:n ['nai's-, sometimes also 'nais- when attributive]
nicet|y, -ies 'naisit|i [-sət-], -iz
niche, -s, -d nitʃ [ni:ʃ], -iz, -t
Nichol, -(l)s, -son 'nikəl, -z, -sn
Nicholas 'nikələs [-k]əs]
nick (s. v.) (N.), -s, -ing, -ed nik, -s, -iŋ, -t
nick|el (s. v.), -els, -elling, -elled 'nik|l, -lz, -lɪŋ [-əlɪŋ], -ld
Nickleby 'niklbi
nick-nack, -s 'niknæk, -s

nicknam|e (s. v.), -es, -ing, -ed 'nik-neim, -z, -iŋ, -d
Nicobar 'nikəubɑ:*
Nicodemus ˌnikəu'di:məs
Nicolas 'nikələs [-k]əs]
Nicol(l), -s 'nikəl, -z
Nicomachean ˌnaikɔmə'ki(:)ən [nai-ˌkɔm-]
Nicomachus nai'kɔməkəs
Nicosia ˌnikəu'si(:)ə
nicotine 'nikəti:n ['nikə't-, ˌnikə't-]
nicotinism 'nikəti:nizəm [-tin-]
niece, -s ni:s, -iz
Niersteiner 'niəstainə*
Nietzsche 'ni:tʃə ('ni:tʃə)
Nigel 'naidʒəl
Niger (river) 'naidʒə*
Nigeria, -n nai'dʒiərɪə, -n
niggard, -s 'nigəd, -z
niggard||y, -iness 'nigədl|i, -inis
nigger, -s 'nigə*, -z
nigg|le, -les, -ling, -led 'nig|l, -lz, -lɪŋ [-lɪŋ], -ld
niggl|y, -iness 'nigl|i, -inis
nigh nai
night, -s nait, -s
night-bell, -s 'naitbel, -z
night-bird, -s 'naitbə:d, -z
nightcap, -s 'naitkæp, -s
nightdress, -es 'naitdres, -iz
nightfall 'naitfɔ:l
nightgown, -s 'naitgaun, -z
nightie, -s 'naiti, -z
nightingale (N.), -s 'naitiŋgeil, -z
nightjar, -s 'naitdʒɑ:*, -z
night|-light/s, -long 'nait|lait/s, -lɔŋ
nightly 'naitli
nightmar|e, -es, -ish 'naitmɛə*, -z, -riʃ
night-porter, -s 'naitˌpɔ:tə* ['-'--], -z
night-school, -s 'nait-sku:l, -z
night-season 'nait'si:zən ['nait,s-]
nightshade 'nait-ʃeid
nightshirt, -s 'nait-ʃə:t, -s
night-time 'naittaim
night-walk|er/s, -ing 'naitˌwɔ:k|ə*/z, -iŋ
nightwatch, -es 'nait'wɔtʃ ['nait-wɔtʃ], -iz
night-watch|man, -men 'nait'wɔtʃ|-mən, -mən
night-work 'nait-wə:k
nihili|sm, -st/s 'naiili|zəm ['naihil-, 'naiəl-], -st/s
Nijmegen 'naimeigən
Nike 'naiki:
nil nil
nil desperandum 'nil despə'rændəm
Nile nail
Nilgiri, -s 'nilgiri, -z

nilometer, -s nai'lɔmitə*, -z
Nilotic nai'lɔtik
nimb|le, -ler, -lest, -ly, -leness 'nimb|l,
 -lə*, -list, -li, -lnis
nimb|us, -uses, -i 'nimb|əs, -əsiz, -ai
Nimeguen 'naimeigən
nimini-piminy 'nimini'pimini
Nimrod 'nimrɔd
Nina (Christian name) 'ni:nə, 'nainə,
 (goddess) 'ni:nə
nincompoop, -s 'ninkəmpu:p ['niŋk-], -s
nine, -s, -fold nain, -z, -fəuld
ninepence, -s 'nainpəns ['naimp-], -iz
ninepenny 'nainpəni ['naimp-]
ninepin, -s 'nain-pin, -z
nineteen, -s, -th/s 'nain'ti:n [also
 '--, -'- according to sentence-stress], -z,
 -θ/s
ninetieth, -s 'naintiiθ [-tjiθ, -tïəθ,
 -tjəθ], -s
ninet|y-ies 'naint|i, -iz
Nineveh 'ninivi [-və]
ninish 'nainiʃ
ninn|y, -ies 'nin|i, -iz
ninth, -s, -ly nainθ, -s, -li
Ninus 'nainəs
Niobe 'naiəubi
nip (s. v.), -s, -ping, -ped nip, -s, -iŋ, -t
nipper, -s 'nipə*, -z
nipple, -s 'nipl, -z
Nippon 'nipɔn
nipp|y, -ier, -iest, -iness 'nip|i, -ïə*, -iist,
 -inis
Nirvana niə'vɑ:nə [nə:'v-] (Hind.
 nyrvaɳa)
Nisan 'naisæn [Jewish pronunciation
 'nisɑ:n]
Nisbet 'nizbit
Nish niʃ
nisi 'naisai
nitrate, -s 'naitreit [-trit], -s
nitre 'naitə*
nitr|ic, -ite/s 'naitr|ik, -ait/s
nitrogen 'naitrədʒən [-tridʒ-]
nitrogenous nai'trɔdʒinəs [-dʒən-,
 -dʒɳ-]
nitro - glycerine 'naitrəu-glisə'ri:n
 [-'glisəri:n, -'glisərin]
nitrous 'naitrəs
nitwit, -s 'nitwit, -s
Niven 'nivən
nix, -es niks, -iz
Nixey 'niksi
nixie, -s 'niksi, -z
Nixon 'niksn
Nizam, -s nai'zæm [nai'zɑ:m, ni'zɑ:m],
 -z
Nkrumah n'kru:mə, əŋ'kru:mə

no (s. interj.), -es nəu, -z
 Note.—The interjection, when spoken
 abruptly, is sometimes pronounced
 nəupº.
no (adj.) nəu (normal form), nə (in the
 expression no more do I (we, etc.))
no. (N.), nos. (N.) 'nʌmbə*, -z
Noah 'nəuə [nɔə, nɔ:]
Noakes nəuks
nob, -s nɔb, -z
no-ball (s. v.), -s, -ing, -ed 'nəu'bɔ:l, -z,
 -iŋ, -d
nobb|le, -les, -ling, -led 'nɔb|l, -lz, -ḷiŋ
 [-liŋ], -ld
nobb|y, -ier, -iest, -ily, -iness 'nɔb|i,
 -ïə*, -iist, -ili, -inis
Nobel (Swedish chemist) nəu'bel [also
 'nəubel in Nobel prize]
nobilit|y, -ies nəu'bilit|i [-lət-], -iz
nob|le (s. adj.) (N.), -les, -ler, -lest, -ly,
 -leness 'nəub|l, -z, -lə*, -list, -li, -lnis
noble|man, -men 'nəubl|mən, -mən
noble-minded, -ness 'nəubl'maindid
 [also 'nəubl‚m- when attributive], -nis
noblesse nəu'bles
nobod|y, -ies 'nəubəd|i [-‚bɔd|i], -iz
noctambul|ant, -ism, -ist/s nɔk'tæm-
 bjul|ənt, -izəm, -ist/s
nocturn|al, -ally nɔk'tɔ:n|l, -əli
nocturn(e), -s 'nɔktə:n ['nɔk't-, nɔk't-],
 -z
nod (s. v.) (N.), -s, -ding, -ded nɔd, -z,
 -iŋ, -id
nodal 'nəudl
noddle, -s 'nɔdl, -z
nodd|y, -ies 'nɔd|i, -iz
node, -s nəud, -z
nodul|ar, -ous 'nɔdjul|ə*, -əs
nodule, -s 'nɔdju:l, -z
Noel (personal name) 'nəuəl [-el, -il],
 (Christmas) nəu'el
noggin, -s 'nɔgin, -z
nohow 'nəuhau
nois|e (s. v.), -es, -ing, -ed nɔiz, -iz, -iŋ, -d
noiseless, -ly, -ness 'nɔizlis, -li, -nis
noisette, -s nwɑ:'zet [nwɔ:'z-], -s
noisome, -ly, -ness 'nɔisəm, -li, -nis
nois|y, -ier, -iest, -ily, -iness 'nɔiz|i,
 -ïə* [-jə*], -iist [-jist], -ili, -inis
Nokes nəuks
Nokomis nəu'kəumis
nolens volens 'nəulenz'vəulenz
Noll nɔl
nomad, -s 'nəumæd [-məd, 'nɔmæd], -z
nomadic, -ally nəu'mædik [nɔ'm-], -əli
no-man's-land 'nəumænzlænd
nom de plume, -s 'nɔ̃:mdə'plu:m ['nɔm-]
 (nɔ̃dplym), -z

nomenclature, -s nəu'menklətʃə*
['nəumenkleitʃə*, 'nəumənklei-], -z
nomic 'nəumik ['nɔmik]
nomin|al, -ally 'nɔmin|l, -əli
nominat|e, -es, -ing, -ed, -or/s 'nɔmi-
neit, -s, -iŋ, -id, -ə*/z
nomination, -s ,nɔmi'neiʃən, -z
nominative (s. adj.), -s 'nɔminətiv, -z
nominee, -s ,nɔmi'ni:, -z
non nɔn
non-acceptance 'nɔnək'septəns [-næk-]
nonage 'nəunidʒ ['nɔn-]
nonagenarian, -s ,nəunədʒi'nɛərɪən
[,nɔn-], -z
non-appearance 'nɔnə'piərəns
nonary 'nəunəri
non-attendance 'nɔnə'tendəns
non-belligeren|cy, -t/s 'nɔnbi'lidʒərən|si
[-be'l-, -bə'l-, -dʒrən-], -t/s
nonce, -word/s nɔns, -wə:d/z
non-certifiable 'nɔn'sə:tifaiəbl ['nɔn-
,sə:ti'fai-]
nonchalan|ce, -t/ly 'nɔnʃələn|s, -t/li
non-collegiate, -s 'nɔnkə'li:dʒiit [-kɔ'l-,
-dʒit, -dʒjət-, -dʒiət], -s
non-combatant, -s 'nɔn'kɔmbətænt
[-'kʌm-], -s
non-commissioned 'nɔnkə'miʃənd [also
'--,-- when attributive]
non-committal 'nɔnkə'mitl
non-compliance 'nɔnkəm'plaiəns
non-conducting 'nɔnkən'dʌktiŋ ['--,--]
non-conductor, -s 'nɔnkən,dʌktə*
['--'--], -z
nonconformist, -s 'nɔnkən'fɔ:mist
['nɔŋ-k-], -s
nonconformity 'nɔnkən'fɔ:miti ['nɔŋ-k-]
non-contentious 'nɔnkən'tenʃəs
non-delivery 'nɔndi'livəri
nondescript (s. adj.), -s 'nɔndiskript, -s
none (s.) (church service), -s nəun, -z
none (adj. pron. adv.) nʌn
nonentit|y, -ies nɔ'nentit|i [nə'n-], -iz
nones nəunz
non-essential, -s 'nɔni'senʃəl, -z
non-existen|ce, -t 'nɔnig'zistən|s [-eg-],
-t
non-feasance 'nɔn'fi: zəns
nonillion, -s nəu'niljən, -z
non-intervention 'nɔn,intə(:)'venʃən
nonjuror, -s 'nɔn'dʒuərə* ['-,--], -z
non-member, -s 'nɔn,membə* ['nɔn'm-],
-z
non-observance 'nɔnəb'zə:vəns
nonpareil 'nɔnpərəl ['nɔnpə'reil,
'nɔm-prəl]
non-payment 'nɔn'peimənt
non-performance 'nɔnpə'fɔ:məns

nonplus, -ses, -sing, -sed 'nɔn'plʌs [-'-'-],
-iz, -iŋ, -t
non-resident, -s 'nɔn'rezidənt, -s
nonsense 'nɔnsəns [occasionally also
'nɔn'sens when used interjectionally]
nonsensic|al, -ally, -alness nɔn'sensi-
k|əl, -əli, -əlnis
non sequitur, -s 'nɔn'sekwitə*, -z
non-stop, -s -ping 'nɔn'stɔp, -s, -iŋ
nonsuch, -es 'nʌn-sʌtʃ, -iz
nonsuit (s. v.), -s, -ing, -ed 'nɔn'sju:t
[-'su:t], -s, -iŋ, -id
non-user 'nɔn'ju:zə*
noodle, -s 'nu:dl, -z
nook, -s nuk, -s
noon, -s nu:n, -z
Noonan 'nu:nən
noonday 'nu:ndei
no one 'nəuwʌn
noontide 'nu:n-taid
noo|se (s. v.), -ses, -sing, -sed nu:|s
[nu:|z], -siz [-ziz], -siŋ [-ziŋ], -st [-zd]
nor nɔ:* (normal form), nə* (occasional
weak form)
Nora(h) 'nɔ:rə
Nordenfelt 'nɔ:dnfelt
Nordic 'nɔ:dik
Nore nɔ:* [nɔə*]
Norfolk 'nɔ:fək
Norgate 'nɔ:geit [-git]
Norham 'nɔrəm ['nɔ:r-]
Norland 'nɔ:lənd
norm, -s nɔ:m, -z
norm|al, -ally 'nɔ:m|əl, -əli [-l̩i]
normalcy 'nɔ:məlsi
normality nɔ:'mæliti
normalization [-isa-] ,nɔ:məlai'zeiʃən
[-m̩ai'z-, -məli'z-, -m̩li'z-]
normaliz|e [-is|e], -es, -ing, -ed 'nɔ:mə-
laiz [-m̩aiz], -iz, -iŋ, -d
Norman, -s 'nɔ:mən, -z
Normanby 'nɔ:mənbi
Normandy (in France) 'nɔ:məndi, (in
Surrey) 'nɔ:məndi [also locally
nɔ:'mændi]
Normanton 'nɔ:məntən
Norn, -s nɔ:n, -z
Norris 'nɔris
Norroy, -s 'nɔrɔi, -z
Norse, -man, -men nɔ:s, -mən, -mən
[-men]
north (N.) nɔ:θ
Northallerton nɔ:'θælətn
Northampton, -shire nɔ:'θæmptən
[nɔ:θ'hæm-, locally nə'θæm-], -ʃiə*
[-ʃə*]
Northanger nɔ:'θæŋgə*
Northants. nɔ:'θænts

North|brook, -cliffe, -cote 'nɔːθ|bruk, -klif, -kət [-kəut]
north-east 'nɔːθ'iːst (nautical pronunciation nɔːr'iːst, also '--,-'-, according to sentence-stress]
north-easter, -s 'nɔːθ'iːstə* [in nautical usage also nɔːr'iːstə*], -z
north-easterly 'nɔːθ'iːstəli [in nautical usage also nɔːr'iːstəli]
north-eastern 'nɔːθ'iːstən
north-eastward, -s 'nɔːθ'iːstwəd, -z
Northen 'nɔːðən
northerly 'nɔːðəli
northern, -most 'nɔːðən, -məust [-məst]
northerner, -s 'nɔːðənə*, -z
North|field, -fleet 'nɔːθ|fiːld, -fliːt
northing 'nɔːθiŋ
Northland 'nɔːθlənd
North|man, -men 'nɔːθ|mən, -mən [-men]
north-north-east 'nɔːθnɔːθ'iːst [nautical pronunciation 'nɔːnɔːr'iːst]
north-north-west 'nɔːθnɔːθ'west [nautical pronunciation 'nɔːnɔː'west]
north-polar 'nɔːθ'pəulə*
Northumberland nɔː'θʌmbələnd [nə'θ-, -blənd]
Northumbria, -n/s nɔː'θʌmbrïə, -n/z
northward, -s, -ly 'nɔːθwəd, -z, -li
north-west, -er/s, -erly 'nɔːθ'west [nautical pronunciation nɔː'west, also '--, -'- according to sentence-stress], -ə*/z, -əli
north-west|ern, -ward 'nɔːθ'west|ən, -wəd
North|wich, -wood 'nɔːθ|witʃ, -wud
Norton 'nɔːtn
Norway 'nɔːwei
Norwegian, -s nɔː'wiːdʒən, -z
Norwich (in England) 'nɔridʒ [-itʃ], (in U.S.A.) 'nɔːwitʃ
Norwood 'nɔːwud
nos. (N.) 'nʌmbəz
nos|e (s. v.), -es, -ing, -ed nəuz, -iz, -iŋ, -d
nose-bag, -s 'nəuzbæg, -z
nose-div|e (s. v.), -es, -ing, -ed 'nəuzdaiv, -z, -iŋ, -d
nosegay, -s 'nəuzgei, -z
nose-ring, -s 'nəuzriŋ, -z
nosey 'nəuzi
nostalg|ia, -ic, -ically nɔst'ældʒ|ïə [-|jə, -|ə], -ik, -ikəli
Nostradamus ,nɔstrə'deiməs
nostril, -s 'nɔstril, -z
nostrum, -s 'nɔstrəm, -z
nosy 'nəuzi
not nɔt (normal form), nt, n (weak forms used after auxiliary verbs only)

nota bene 'nəutə'biːni [-'beni]
notabilit|y, -ies ,nəutə'bilit|i [lət-], -iz
notab|le, -ly, -leness 'nəutəb|l, -li, -lnis
notarial, -ly nəu'tɛərïəl, -i
notar|y, -ies 'nəutər|i, -iz
notation, -s nəu'teiʃən, -z
notch (s. v.), -es, -ing, -ed nɔtʃ, -iz, -iŋ, -t
not|e (s. v.), -es, -ing, -ed nəut, -s, -iŋ, -id
note|-book/s, -paper, -worthy 'nəut|-buk/s, -,peipə*, -,wəːði
nothing, -s, -ness 'nʌθiŋ, -z, -nis
notic|e (s. v.), -es, -ing, -ed 'nəutis, -iz, -iŋ, -t
noticeab|le, -ly 'nəutisəb|l, -li
notice-board, -s 'nəutisbɔːd [-bɔəd], -z
notifiable 'nəutifaiəbl [,nəuti'fai-]
notification, -s ,nəutifi'keiʃən, -z
noti|fy, -fies, -fying, -fied 'nəuti|fai, -faiz, -faiiŋ, -faid
notion, -s 'nəuʃən, -z
notional 'nəuʃənl [-ʃnəl, -ʃn̩l, -ʃn̩l, -ʃənəl]
notoriety ,nəutə'raiəti
notorious, -ly, -ness nəu'tɔːrïəs, -li, -nis
Notre Dame (English Catholic pronunciation) ,nəutrə'daːm [,nɔt-] (notrədam) (Amer. ,noutɪ'deim)
Nottingham, -shire 'nɔtiŋəm, -ʃïə* [-ʃə*]
Notting Hill 'nɔtiŋ'hil
Notts. nɔts
notwithstanding ,nɔtwiθ'stændiŋ [-wið'-]
nougat, -s 'nuːgaː ['nʌgət], 'nuːgaːz ['nʌgəts]
nought, -s nɔːt, -s
noun, -s naun, -z
nourish, -es, -ing, -ed; -ment 'nʌriʃ, -iz, -iŋ, -t; -mənt
nous naus
nouveau riche 'nuː'vəu'riːʃ
Nova Scotia 'nəuvə'skəuʃə [,nəu-]
novel (s. adj.), -s 'nɔvəl, -z
novelette, -s ,nɔvə'let [-vi'let, -vl̩'et], -s
novelist, -s 'nɔvəlist [-vl̩ist], -s
Novello nə'veləu
novelt|y, -ies 'nɔvəlt|i, -iz
November, -s nəu'vembə*, -z
Novial (language) 'nəuvjəl [-vïəl]
novice, -s 'nɔvis, -iz
noviciate [-itiate], -s nəu'viʃiit [nɔ'v-, -ʃieit], -s
now, -adays nau, -ədeiz
Nowell (personal name) 'nəuəl [-el], (Christmas) nəu'el
nowhere 'nəuwɛə* ['nəuhw-]
nowise 'nəuwaiz

Nox nɔks
noxious, -ly, -ness 'nɔkʃəs, -li, -nis
noyau, -s 'nwaiəu ['nwɔiəu, 'nɔiəu]
(nwajo), -z
Noyes nɔiz
nozzle, -s 'nɔzl, -z
-n't (=not) -nt
nu nju:
nuance, -s nju(:)'ɑ̃:ns [-'ɔ̃:ns, -'ɑ:ns,
-'ɔ:ns, '--] (nɥɑ̃:s), -iz
nubble, -s 'nʌbl, -z
nubbly 'nʌbḷi
Nubia, -n/s 'nju:bjə [-bɪə], -n/z
nucl|eus, -ei, -eal, -ear, -eic 'nju:kl|ɪəs
[-jəs], -iai, -ɪəl [-jəl], -ɪə* [-jə*], -iik
nude (s. adj.), -s nju:d, -z
nudg|e (s. v.), -es, -ing, -ed nʌdʒ, -iz,
-iŋ, -d
nudi|sm, -st/s 'nju:di|zəm, -st/s
nudit|y, -ies 'nju:dit|i, -iz
nugatory 'nju:gətəri
Nugent 'nju:dʒənt
nugget, -s 'nʌgit, -s
nuisance, -s 'nju:sns, -iz
null nʌl
nullah 'nʌlə, -z
nullification ˌnʌlifi'keiʃən
nulli|fy, -fies, -fying, -fied 'nʌli|fai,
-faiz, -faiiŋ, -faid
nullit|y, -ies 'nʌlit|i, -iz
Numantia nju(:)'mæntɪə [-tjə, -ʃɪə, -ʃjə]
Numa Pomp.lius 'nju:mə-pɔm'pilɪəs
[-ljəs]
numb (adj. v.), -ly, -ness; -s, -ing, -ed
nʌm, -li, -nis; -z, -iŋ, -d
numb|er (s. v.), -ers (N.), -ering, -ered;
-erless 'nʌmb|ə*, -əz, -əriŋ, -əd; -əlis
numerable 'nju:mərəbl
numeral (s. adj.), -s 'nju:mərəl, -z
numeration ˌnju:mə'reiʃən
numerative, -s 'nju:mərətiv, -z
numerator, -s 'nju:məreitə*, -z
numeric|al, -ally nju(:)'merik|əl, -əli
numerous, -ly, -ness 'nju:mərəs, -li, -nis
Numidia, -n/s nju(:)'midɪə [-djə], -n/z
numismatic, -s, -ally ˌnju:miz'mætik, -s,
-əli
numismatist, -s nju(:)'mizmətist, -s
numskull, -s 'nʌmskʌl, -z
nun (N.), -s nʌn, -z
Nunc Dimittis, -es 'nʌŋkdi'mitis
[-dai'm-], -iz
nuncio, -s 'nʌnʃiəu [-ʃjəu, -siəu, -sjəu], -z

Nuneaton nʌ'ni:tn
Nuneham 'nju:nəm
nunkey, -s 'nʌŋki, -z
Nunn nʌn
nunner|y, -ies 'nʌnər|i, -iz
nuptial, -s 'nʌpʃəl, -z
Nuremberg 'njuərəmbəːg ['njɔər-,
'njɔːr-, -rim-]
nurs|e (s. v.), -es, -ing, -ed nəːs, -iz, -iŋ,
-t
nurs(e)ling, -s 'nəːs-liŋ, -z
nurse-maid, -s 'nəːs-meid, -z
nurser|y, -ies 'nəːsər|i, -iz
nursery-maid, -s 'nəːsrimeid, -z
nursery|man, -men 'nəːsri|mən, -mən
nurtur|e (s. v.), -es, -ing, -ed 'nəːtʃə*, -z,
-riŋ, -d
nut, -s nʌt, -s
nutat|e, -es, -ing, -ed nju:'teit, -s, -iŋ,
-id
nutation, -s nju:'teiʃən, -z
nut-brown 'nʌtbraun
nutcracker, -s 'nʌtˌkrækə*, -z
nuthatch, -es 'nʌthætʃ, -iz
nutmeg, -s 'nʌtmeg, -z
nutria 'nju:trɪə
nutrient 'nju:trɪənt
nutriment 'nju:trimənt
nutrition nju(:)'triʃən
nutritious, -ly, -ness nju(:)'triʃəs, -li,
-nis
nutritive 'nju:tritiv [-trət-]
nutshell, -s 'nʌt-ʃel, -z
Nuttall 'nʌtɔːl
Nutter 'nʌtə*
nutty 'nʌti
Nuwara Eliya (in Ceylon) nju:'reiljə
[njuə'r-, nju'r-, -lɪə]
nux vomica 'nʌks'vɔmikə
N.W. 'en'dʌblju(:) ['nɔː'θ'west]
Nyanja (people, language) 'njændʒə
[ni'æn-]
Nyanza (lake) 'njænzə [ni'æn-, nai'æn-]
Nyasa (lake) 'njæsə [ni'æs-, nai'æs-]
Nyasaland 'njæsəlænd [ni'æs-, nai'æs-]
Nyerere nje'rɛəri [nji-, njə-, niə-, -'reri]
nylon 'nailən [-lɔn]
nymph, -s, -al nimf, -s, -əl
nymphet nim'fet
nymph-like 'nimf-laik
nymphoman|ia, -iac/s ˌnimfəu'mein|ɪə
[-jə], -iæk [-jæk]/s
nystagmus nis'tægməs

O

O (*the letter*), -'s [-es] əu, -z
O (*interj.*) əu
o' (*abbreviation of* of) ə (*weak form only*)
oaf, -s, -ish əuf, -s; -iʃ
oak, -s əuk, -s
oak-apple, -s 'əuk͵æpl, -z
oak-bark 'əukbɑːk
Oakeley 'əukli
oaken 'əukən
Oak|es, -ey əuk|s, -i
oak-gall, -s 'əukgɔːl, -z
Oakham 'əukəm
Oakhampton 'əuk'hæmptən [əuk'h-]
Oakland, -s 'əuk-lənd, -z
Oak|leigh, -ley 'əuk|li, -li
oakling, -s 'əuk-liŋ, -z
Oaks əuks
oakum, -picking 'əukəm, -͵pikiŋ
Oakworth 'əuk-wə(ː)θ
oar (*s. v.*), -s, -ing, -ed ɔː* [ɔə*], -z, -riŋ, -d
oars|man, -men 'ɔːz|mən ['ɔəz-], -mən
oas|is, -es əu'eis|is, -iːz
oast, -s əust, -s
oast-hou|se, -ses 'əusthau|s, -ziz
oat, -s əut, -s
oatcake, -s 'əut'keik ['əutk-], -s
oaten 'əutn
Oates əuts
oa|th, -ths əu|θ, -ðz [-θs]
oath-break|er/s, -ing 'əuθ͵breik|ə*/z, -iŋ
Oatlands 'əutləndz
oatmeal 'əutmiːl
Ob (*river in Siberia*) ɔb (opj)
Obadiah ͵əubə'daiə
Oban 'əubən
obbligato, -s ͵ɔbli'gɑːtəu, -z
obduracy 'ɔbdjurəsi
obdurate, -ly, -ness 'ɔbdjurit [-reit, ɔb'djuərit, ɔb'djəːrit], -li, -nis
obduration ͵ɔbdjuə'reiʃən [-djə'r-, -djɔə'r-, -djɔː'r-]
obeah 'əubiə [-bïə]
Obed 'əubed
Obededom ͵əubed'iːdəm ['--'--]
obedien|ce, -t/ly ə'biːdjən|s [əu'b-, -dïən-], -t/li
O'Beirne əu'bɛən
obeisance, -s əu'beisəns, -iz

obelisk, -s 'ɔbilisk [-bəl-], -s
obelus, -es 'ɔbiləs, -iz
Ober - Ammergau ͵əubər'æməgau [-bə'æm-] (͵oːbər'amərgau)
Oberland 'əubələænd
Oberlin (*in U.S.A.*) 'əubə(ː)lin
Oberon 'əubərən [-rɔn]
obes|e, -eness, -ity əu'biːs, -nis, -iti
obey, -s, -ing, -ed, -er/s ə'bei [əu'b-], -z, -iŋ, -d, -ə*/z [-'beə*/z]
obfuscat|e, -es, -ing, -ed 'ɔbfʌskeit [-fəs-], -s, -iŋ, -id
obfuscation, -s ͵ɔbfʌs'keiʃən [-fəs-], -z
obi, -s 'əubi, -z
Obi (*river in Siberia*) 'əubi (opj)
Obion əu'baiən
obit, -s 'ɔbit ['əubit], -s
obiter 'ɔbitə*
obituarist, -s ə'bitjŭərist [ɔ'b-, -tjwər-, -tjuər-, -tjər-, -tjur-], -s
obituar|y, -ies ə'bitjŭər|i [ɔ'b-, -tjwər-, -tjuər-, -tjər-, -tjur-], -iz
object (*s.*), -s 'ɔbdʒikt [-dʒekt], -s
object (*v.*), -s, -ing, -ed, -or/s əb'dʒekt, -s, -iŋ, -id, -ə*/z
object-glass, -es 'ɔbdʒiktglɑːs [-dʒekt-], -iz
objecti|fy, -fies, -fying, -fied ɔb'dʒekti|fai [əb-], -faiz, -faiiŋ, -faid
objection, -s əb'dʒekʃən, -z
objectionab|le, -ly əb'dʒekʃnəb|l [-ʃnəb-, -ʃənəb-], -li
objective (*s.*), -s əb'dʒektiv [ɔb-], -z
objective (*adj.*), -ly, -ness əb'dʒektiv [ɔb'dʒ-, 'ɔb'dʒ-], -li, -nis
objectivism əb'dʒektivizəm [ɔb-]
objectivity ͵ɔbdʒek'tiviti
objectless 'ɔbdʒiktlis [-dʒekt-]
object-lesson, -s 'ɔbdʒikt͵lesn [-dʒekt-], -z
objurgat|e, -es, -ing, -ed 'ɔbdʒəːgeit, -s, -iŋ, -id
objurgation, -s ͵ɔbdʒəː'geiʃən, -z
objurgatory ɔb'dʒəːgətəri [əb'dʒ-, 'ɔbdʒəːgeitəri]
oblate (*s.*), -s 'ɔbleit, -s
oblate (*adj.*) 'ɔbleit [ɔ'bleit, əu'b-]
oblation, -s əu'bleiʃən [ɔ'b-], -z
obligant, -s 'ɔbligənt, -s

obligation, -s ˌɔbli'geiʃən, -z
obligato (s. adj.), -s ˌɔbli'gɑːtəu, -z
obligator|y, -ily, -iness ɔ'bligətər|i
[ə'b-, 'ɔbligətər-, 'ɔbligeitər-], -ili,
-inis
oblig|e, -es, -ing/ly, -ingness, -ed
ə'blaidʒ, -iz, -iŋ/li, -iŋnis, -d
obligee, -s ˌɔbli'dʒiː, -z
obligor, -s ˌɔbli'gɔː*, -z
oblique, -ly, -ness ə'bliːk [ɔ'b-, əu'b-],
-li, -nis
obliquit|y, -ies ə'blikwit|i [ɔ'b-, əu'b-],
-iz
obliterat|e, -es, -ing, -ed ə'blitəreit
[ɔ'b-], -s, -iŋ, -id
obliteration, -s əˌblitə'reiʃən [ɔˌb-], -z
oblivion ə'bliviən [ɔ'b-, -vjən]
oblivious, -ly, -ness ə'bliviəs [ɔ'b-,
-vjəs], -li, -nis
oblong (s. adj.), -s 'ɔblɔŋ, -z
obloquy 'ɔbləkwi
obnoxious, -ly, -ness əb'nɔkʃəs [ɔb-], -li,
-nis
Obock əu'bɔk ['əubɔk]
oboe, -s 'əubəu [old-fashioned 'əubɔi], -z
oboist, -s 'əubəuist, -s
obol, -s 'ɔbɔl [-bəl], -z
obole, -s 'ɔbəul, -z
O'Br|ien, -yan əu'br|aiən, -aiən
obscene, -ly, -ness əb'siːn [ɔb-], -li, -nis
obscenit|y, -ies əb'siːnit|i [ɔb-, -'sen-] -iz
obscurant (s. adj.) ɔb'skjuərənt [əb-,
-bz'k-]
obscurant|ism, -ist/s ˌɔbskjuə'rænt|izəm
[-bzk-, -kju'r-, ɔb'skjuərənt-, əb-
'skjuərənt-, -bz'k-], -ist/s
obscuration, -s ˌɔbskjuə'reiʃən [-bzk-,
-kju'r-, -kjə'r-], -z
obscur|e (adj. v.), -er, -est, -ely,
-eness; -es, -ing, -ed əb'skjuə* [ɔb-,
-bz'k-, -jəə*, -jɔː*, -jə:*], -rə*, -rist,
-li, -nis; -z, -riŋ, -d
obscurit|y, -ies əb'skjuərit|i [ɔb-, -bz'k-,
-jəər-, -jɔːr-, -jə:r-], -iz
obsecration, -s ˌɔbsi'kreiʃən [-se'k-], -z
obsequial ɔb'siːkwiəl [əb-, -kwjəl]
obsequies 'ɔbsikwiz
obsequious, -ly, -ness əb'siːkwiəs [ɔb-,
-kwjəs], -li, -nis
observab|le, -ly, -leness əb'zəːvəb|l, -li,
-lnis
observan|ce, -ces, -cy əb'zəːvən|s, -siz,
-si
observant, -ly əb'zəːvənt, -li
observation, -s ˌɔbzə(ː)'veiʃən, -z
observa|tional, -tionally ˌɔbzə(ː)'vei|ʃənl
[-ʃnəl, -ʃn̩l, -ʃn̩l, -ʃənəl], -ʃnəli [-ʃnəli,
-ʃn̩li, -ʃn̩li, -ʃənəli]

observator|y, -ies əb'zəːvətr|i [-tər-], -iz
observ|e, -es, -ing/ly, -ed, -er/s əb'zəːv,
-z, -iŋ/li, -d, -ə*/z
obsess, -es, -ing, -ed əb'ses [ɔb-], -iz,
-iŋ, -t
obsession, -s əb'seʃən [ɔb-], -z
obsidian ɔb'sidiən [-djən]
obsolescen|ce, -t ˌɔbsəu'lesn|s, -t
obsolete, -ly, -ness 'ɔbsəliːt [-sli̩t, -sliːt],
-li, -nis
obstacle, -s 'ɔbstəkl [-bzt-, -tikl], -z
obstetric, -al, -s ɔb'stetrik [-bz't-], -əl, -s
obstetrician, -s ˌɔbste'triʃən [-bzt-], -z
obstinac|y, -ies 'ɔbstinəs|i [-bzt-, -tənə-],
-iz
obstinate, -ly, -ness 'ɔbstinit [-bzt-,
-tənit], -li, -nis
obstreperous, -ly, -ness əb'strepərəs
[ɔb-, -bz't-], -li, -nis
obstruct, -s, -ing, -ed, -or/s əb'strʌkt
[-bz't-], -s, -iŋ, -id, -ə*/z
obstruction, -s əb'strʌkʃən [-bz't-], -z
obstructionism əb'strʌkʃənizəm [-bz't-,
-ʃni-]
obstructionist, -s əb'strʌkʃənist [-bz't-,
-ʃni-], -s
obstructive, -ly, -ness əb'strʌktiv
[-bz't-], -li, -nis
obstruent (s. adj.), -s 'ɔbstrŭənt, -s
obtain, -s, -ing, -ed, -er/s; -able
əb'tein, -z, -iŋ, -d, -ə*/z; -əbl
obtrud|e, -es, -ing, -ed, -er/s əb'truːd
[ɔb-], -z, -iŋ, -id, -ə*/z
obtrusion, -s əb'truːʒən [ɔb-], -z
obtrusive, -ly, -ness əb'truːsiv [ɔb-], -li,
-nis
obturat|e, -es, -ing, -ed, -or/s 'ɔbtjuə-
reit [-tjur-], -s, -iŋ, -id, -ə*/z
obturation, -s ˌɔbtjuə'reiʃən [tju'r-], -z
obtuse, -ly, -ness əb'tjuːs [ɔb-], -li, -nis
obverse (s. adj.), -s 'ɔbvəːs, -iz
obversely ɔb'vəːsli
obvert, -s, -ing, -ed ɔb'vəːt, -s, -iŋ, -id
obviat|e, -es, -ing, -ed 'ɔbvieit [-vjeit],
-s, -iŋ, -id
obvious, -ly, -ness 'ɔbviəs [-vjəs], -li, -nis
O'Byrne əu'bəːn
O'Callaghan əu'kæləhən [-gən]
ocarina, -s ˌɔkə'riːnə, -z
O'Casey əu'keisi
Occam' ɔkəm
occasi|on (s. v.), -ons, -oning, -oned
ə'keiʒ|ən, -ənz, -ṇiŋ [-əniŋ, -niŋ], -ənd
occa|sional, -sionally ə'kei|ʒənl [-ʒnəl,
-ʒn̩l, -ʒn̩l, -ʒənəl], -ʒnəli, [-ʒnəli, -ʒn̩li,
-ʒn̩li, -ʒənəli]
occasionali|sm -st/s ə'keiʒnəli|zəm
[-ʒnəl-, -ʒn̩l-, -ʒn̩l-, -ʒənəl-], -st/s

occident (O.) 'ɔksidənt
occidental (s. adj.) (O.), -s ˌɔksi'dentl,
-z
occidentali|sm, -st/s ˌɔksi'dentəli|zəm
[-t|i-], -st/s
occidentaliz|e [-is|e], -es, -ing, -ed
ˌɔksi'dentəlaiz [-t|aiz], -iz, -iŋ, -d
occipit|al, -ally ɔk'sipit|l, -əli
occiput, -s 'ɔksipʌt [-pət], -s
Occleve 'ɔkli:v
occlud|e, -es, -ing, -ed ɔ'klu:d [ə'k-], -z,
-iŋ, -id
occlusion, -s ɔ'klu:ʒən [ə'k-], -z
occlusive (s. adj.), -s ɔ'klu:siv [ə'k-], -z
occult (adj.), -ly, -ness ɔ'kʌlt [ə'k-,
'ɔkʌlt], -li, -nis
occult (v.), -s, -ing, -ed ɔ'kʌlt [ə'k-], -s,
-iŋ, -id
occultation, -s ˌɔkəl'teiʃən [-kʌl-], -z
occulti|sm, -st/s 'ɔkəlti|zəm ['ɔkʌl-,
ɔ'kʌl-], -st/s
occupan|cy, -t/s 'ɔkjupən|si, -t/s
occupation, -s ˌɔkju'peiʃən, -z
occupational ˌɔkju(:)'peiʃənl [-ʃnəl, -ʃŋḷ,
-ʃn̩ḷ, -ʃənəl]
occup|y, -ies, -ying, -ied, -ier/s 'ɔkju-
p|ai, -aiz, -aiiŋ, -aid, -aiə*/z
occur, -s, -ring, -red ə'kə:*, -z, -riŋ, -d
occurrence, -s ə'kʌrəns, -iz
ocean, -s 'əuʃən, -z
Oceania, -n/s ˌəuʃi'einjə [-nĭə], -n/z
oceanic (O.) ˌəuʃi'ænik [ˌəusi-]
Oceanica ˌəuʃi'ænikə
oceanograph|er/s, -y ˌəuʃjə'nɔgrəf|ə*/z
[-ʃĭə-], -i
oceanographic ˌəuʃjənəu'græfik [-ʃĭə-]
Oceanus əu'siənəs [əu'ʃĭə-]
ocell|us, -i əu'sel|əs, -ai [-i:]
ocelot, -s 'əusilɔt [-lət], -s
ochery 'əukəri
Ochill 'əukil ['əuxil]
Ochiltree (in Scott's 'Antiquary')
'əuki̇ltri: ['əuxi̇l-], (in U.S.A.)
'əuki̇tri:
och|re (s. v.), -res, -reing, -red 'əuk|ə*,
-əz, -əriŋ, -əd
ochreous 'əukriəs ['əukərəs]
ochry 'əukəri ['əukri]
Ochterlony ˌɔktə'ləuni [ˌɔxt-]
Ock|ham, -ley 'ɔk|əm, -li
Ocklynge 'ɔklindʒ
O'Clery əu'kliəri
o'clock ə'klɔk
Ocmulgee əuk'mʌlgi
O'Con|nell, -(n)or əu'kɔn|ḷ, -ə*
Ocracoke 'əukrəkəuk
octagon, -s 'ɔktəgən, -z
octagonal ɔk'tægənl

octahedr|on, -ons, -a; -al 'ɔktə'hedr|ən
[-'hi:d-, 'ɔktə,h-, ˌɔktə'h-], -ənz, -ə;
-əl
octane 'ɔktein
octant, -s 'ɔktənt, -s
Octateuch 'ɔktətju:k
octave (musical term), -s 'ɔktiv [rarely
-teiv], -z
octave (ecclesiastical term), -s 'ɔkteiv
[-tiv], -z
Octavia, -n ɔk'teivjə [-vĭə], -n
Octavius ɔk'teivjəs [-vĭəs]
octavo, -s ɔk'teivəu, -z
octennial ɔk'tenjəl [-nĭəl]
octet(te), -s ɔk'tet, -s
octillion, -s ɔk'tiljən, -z
October, -s ɔk'təubə*, -z
octodecimo, -s 'ɔktəu'desiməu [ˌɔk-], -z
octogenarian, -s ˌɔktəudʒi'nɛərĭən, -z
octopus, -es 'ɔktəpəs, -iz
octoroon, -s ˌɔktə'ru:n, -z
octosyllabic 'ɔktəusi'læbik [-təs-]
octosyllable, -s 'ɔktəu,siləbl [-tə,s-], -z
octroi, -s 'ɔktrwɑː [-trwɔ:] (ɔktrwɑ), -z
octuple 'ɔktju(:)pl
ocular, -ly 'ɔkjulə*, -li
oculist, -s 'ɔkjulist, -s
O'Curry əu'kʌri
od (O.), -s ɔd, -z
odalisque, -s 'əudəlisk, -s
O'Daly əu'deili
Odam 'əudəm
odd, -er, -est, -ly, -ness ɔd, -ə*, -ist, -li,
-nis
Oddfellow, -s 'ɔd,feləu, -z
Oddie 'ɔdi
oddish 'ɔdiʃ
oddit|y, -ies 'ɔdit|i, -iz
odd-looking 'ɔd,lukiŋ
oddment, -s 'ɔdmənt, -s
odds ɔdz
Oddy 'ɔdi
ode, -s əud, -z
O'Dea əu'dei
Odell əu'del
Odeon 'əudjən [-dĭən]
Oder 'əudə* ('o:dər)
Odessa əu'desə
Ode|um, -a, -ums əu'di(:)|əm ['əudj|əm,
'əudĭ|əm], -ə, -əmz
Odgers 'ɔdʒəz
Odham 'ɔdəm
Odiham 'əudihəm
Odin 'əudin
odious, -ly, -ness 'əudjəs [-dĭəs], -li, -nis
odium 'əudjəm [-dĭəm]
Odling 'ɔdliŋ
Odlum 'ɔdləm

Odo 'əudəu
Odoacer ‚odəu'eisə* [‚əud-]
O'Doherty əu'dəuəti, -'dɔhəti [-'dɔxə-]
odol 'əudɔl
O'Donnell əu'dɔnl
odontolog|ist/s, -y ‚odɔn'tɔlədʒ|ist/s, -i
odoriferous, -ly, -ness ‚əudə'rifərəs
[‚ɔd-], -li, -nis
odorous, -ly, -ness 'əudərəs, -li, -nis
odour, -s, -ed, -less 'əudə*, -z, -d, -lis
O'Dowd əu'daud
odsbodikins 'ɔdz'bɔdikinz [ɔdz'b-]
O'Dwyer əu'dwaiə*
Ody 'əudi
Odysseus ə'disju:s [ɔ'd-, əu'd-, -siəs,
-sjəs]
Odyssey 'ɔdisi
oecumenic, -al ‚i:kju(:)'menik, -əl
oedema i(:)'di:mə
oedematous i(:)'demətəs
Oedipus 'i:dipəs
œillade, -s ə:'jɑ:d (œjad), -z
Oeneus 'i:nju:s [-njəs, -niəs]
Oenomaus ‚i:nəu'meiəs
Oenone i(:)'nəuni(:)
o'er (contracted form of over) 'əuə* [ɔə*,
ɔ:*]
oes (plur. of O) əuz
oesophageal i(:)‚sɔfə'dʒi(:)əl
oesipha|gus, -gi, -guses i(:)sɔfə|gəs, -gai
[-dʒai], -gəsiz
oestrus, -es 'i:strəs, -iz
Oettle 'ə:tli
Oetzmann 'əutsmən
of ɔv (strong form), əv, v, f (weak forms)
Note.—The form f occurs only before
breathed consonants.
off ɔf [ɔ:f]
Offa 'ɔfə
offal 'ɔfəl
Offaly 'ɔfəli
off-bail, -s 'ɔf'beil ['ɔ:f-, '— when in contrast with leg-bail], -z
off-bye, -s 'ɔf'bai ['ɔ:f-, '— when in contrast with leg-bye], -z
off-drive, -s 'ɔfdraiv ['ɔ:f-], -z
Offenbach 'ɔfənbɑ:k
offence, -s, -less ə'fens [ɔ'f-], -iz, -lis
offend, -s, -ing, -ed, -er/s ə'fend [ɔ'f-],
-z, -iŋ, -id, -ə*/z
offensive (s. adj.), -s, -ly, -ness ə'fensiv
[ɔ'f-], -z, -li, -nis
off|er (s. v.), -ers, -ering/s, -ered,
-erer/s; -erable 'ɔf|ə*, -əz, -əriŋ/z,
-əd, -ərə*/z; -ərəbl
offertor|y, -ies 'ɔfətər|i, -iz
off-hand 'ɔf'hænd ['ɔ:f'h-, also '—, -'-
according to sentence-stress]

off-handed 'ɔf'hændid ['ɔ:f-]
office, -s 'ɔfis, -iz
office-bearer, -s 'ɔfis‚bɛərə*, -z
office-boy, -s 'ɔfisbɔi, -z
officer, -s 'ɔfisə* ['ɔfsə*], -z
offici|al (s. adj.), -als, -ally, -alism
ə'fiʃ|əl [ɔ'f-], -əlz, -əli [-ḷi], -əlizəm
[-ḷizəm]
officialdom ə'fiʃəldəm [ɔ'f-]
officialese ə‚fiʃə'li:z [ə'fiʃəli:z, ə'fiʃḷi:z]
officiat|e, -es, -ing, -ed ə'fiʃieit [ɔ'f-], -s,
-iŋ, -id
officinal ‚ɔfi'sainl [ɔ'fisinl]
officious, -ly, -ness ə'fiʃəs [ɔ'f-], -li, -nis
offing, -s 'ɔfiŋ [ɔ:f-], -z
offish 'ɔfiʃ ['ɔ:f-]
Offor 'ɔfə*
off-print, -s 'ɔfprint ['ɔ:f-], -s
offset (s. v.), -s, -ting 'ɔfset ['ɔ:f-], -s, -iŋ
offshoot, -s 'ɔfʃu:t ['ɔ:f-], -s
offside 'ɔf'said ['ɔ:f's-, -'-]
offspring, -s 'ɔfspriŋ ['ɔ:f-], -z
off-the-record 'ɔfðə'rekɔ:d ['ɔ:f-]
off-time 'ɔftaim ['ɔ:f-, '-'-]   [-'flɑ:t-]
O'Flaherty əu'fleəti [-'flæhəti, -'flɑ:ət-,
O'Flynn əu'flin
oft ɔft [ɔ:ft]   [-taimz
often, -times 'ɔfn ['ɔ:f-, -fən, -ftən],
often|er, -est 'ɔfn|ə* ['ɔ:f-, -fn|ə*,
-fən|ə*, -ftən|ə*, -ftŋ|ə*, -ftn|ə*], -ist
ofttimes 'ɔfttaimz ['ɔ:f-]
Og, -den ɔg, -dən
ogee, -s 'əudʒi: [əu'dʒi:], -z
Ogemaw 'əugimɔ:
og(h)am, -s 'ɔgəm, -z
og(h)amic ɔ'gæmik
Ogil|by, -vie, -vy 'əugl|bi, -vi, -vi
ogival əu'dʒaivəl
ogive, -s 'əudʒaiv [əu'dʒ-], -z
og|le (O.), -les, -ling, -led, -ler/s 'əug|l,
-lz, -liŋ [-ḷiŋ], -ld, -lə*/z [-ḷə*/z]
Ogle|by, -thorpe 'əugl|bi, -θɔ:p
Ogpu 'ɔgpu
O'Grady əu'greidi
ogr|e, -es, -ish 'əugə*, -z, -riʃ
ogress, -es 'əugris [-res], -iz
o'Groat ə'grəut
oh əu
O'Hagan əu'heigən
O'Halloran əu'hælərən
O'Hara əu'hɑ:rə
O'Hare əu'hɛə*
O'Hea əu'hei
Ohio əu'haiəu
ohm (O.), -s əum, -z
oho əu'həu
oil (s. v.), -s, -ing, -ed, -er/s ɔil, -z, -iŋ,
-d, -ə*/z

oil-bag, -s 'ɔilbæg, -z
oil-box, -es 'ɔilbɔks, -iz
oil-burner, -s 'ɔil,bə:nə*, -z
oil-cake, -s 'ɔil-keik, -s
oil-can, -s 'ɔil-kæn, -z
oil|cloth, -cloths 'ɔil-|klɔθ [-klɔ:θ],
  -klɔθs [-klɔ:ðz, -klɔ:θs]
oil-colour, -s 'ɔil,kʌlə*, -z
oil-field, -s 'ɔil-fi:ld, -z
oil-fuel 'ɔil-fjuəl [-fjuil, -,fju:əl, -fju:l]
oil|man, -men 'ɔil|mən [-mæn], -mən
  [-men]
oil-paint, -s; -ing/s 'ɔil'peint ['— when
  in contrast with other kinds of paint],
  -s; -iŋ/z
oil-silk 'ɔil-silk ['-'-]
oil-skin 'ɔil-skin, -z
oil-stone, -s 'ɔil-stəun, -z
oil-stove, -s 'ɔil-stəuv, -z
oil-well, -s 'ɔil-wel, -z
oil|y, -ier, -iest, -iness 'ɔil|i, -ɪə*
  [-jə*], -iist [-jist], -inis
ointment, -s 'ɔintmənt, -s
Oisin 'ɔizin
Oistrakh 'ɔistrɑ:k [-ɑ:x]
Ojai (in California) 'əuhai
Ojibway, -s əu'dʒibwei [ɔ'dʒ-], -z
O.K. 'əu'kei [əu'kei]
okapi, -s əu'kɑ:pi, -z
okay, -s, -ing, -ed 'əu'kei [əu'kei], -z,
  -iŋ, -d
O'Keeffe əu'ki:f
Okehampton 'əuk'hæmptən [əuk'h-]
O'Kelly əu'keli
Okhotsk əu'kɔtsk [ɔ'k-] (a'xotsk)
Okinawa ,ɔki'nɑ:wə
Oklahoma ,əuklə'həumə
Olav (Norwegian name) 'əuləv [-læv]
Olave 'ɔliv [-ləv, -leiv]
Olcott 'ɔlkət
old, -er, -est, -ness əuld, -ə*, -ist, -nis
Oldbuck 'əuldbʌk
Oldbury 'əuldbəri
Oldcastle 'əuld,kɑ:sl
old-clothes|man, -men 'əuld'kləuðə|-
  mæn [əuld'k-, -mən, old-fashioned
  -'kləuz-], -men [-mən]
olden 'əuldən
Oldenburg 'əuldənbə:g ('ɔldənburk,
  -burç)
old-fashioned 'əuld'fæʃənd [also '-,—,
  -'— according to sentence-stress]
Oldfield 'əuldfi:ld
old-fog(e)yish 'əuld'fəugiiʃ [-gjiʃ, also
  əuld'f- when preceded by a stress]
old-gentlemanly 'əuld'dʒentlmənli [also
  əuld'dʒ- when preceded by a stress]
Oldham 'əuldəm

oldish 'əuldiʃ
old-maidish 'əuld'meidiʃ [also əuld'm-
  when preceded by a stress]
Oldrey 'əuldri
old-time 'əuldtaim
old-womanish 'əuld'wuməniʃ [also
  əuld'w- when preceded by a stress]
old-world 'əuld-wə:ld ['əuld'w-]
oleaginous, -ness ,əuli'ædʒinəs, -nis
oleander (O.), -s ,əuli'ændə*, -z
O'Leary əu'liəri
oleaster, -s ,əuli'æstə*, -z
olefiant 'əulifaiənt [əu'li:fiənt, -'lef-]
oleograph, -s 'əuliəugrɑ:f [-liəg-, -ljəug-,
  -græf], -s
oleography ,əuli'ɔgrəfi
oleomargarine 'əuliəu,mɑ:dʒə'ri:n
  [-,mɑ:gə'r-, -'mɑ:dʒər-, -'mɑ:gər-]
olfactory ɔl'fæktəri
Olga 'ɔlgə
olibanum ɔ'libənəm [əu'l-]
Olifa(u)nt 'ɔlifənt
Oliffe 'ɔlif
oligarch, -s 'ɔligɑ:k, -s
oligarchal 'ɔligɑ:kəl [,ɔli'g-]
oligarchic ,ɔli'gɑ:kik
oligarch|y, -ies 'ɔligɑ:k|i, -iz
oligocene ɔ'ligəusi:n ['—]
olio, -s 'əuliəu [-ljəu], -z
Oliphant 'ɔlifənt
olivaceous ,ɔli'veiʃəs
olive (O.), -s; -branch/es, -coloured
  'ɔliv, -z; -brɑ:ntʃ/iz, -,kʌləd
olive oil 'ɔliv'ɔil
oliver (O.), -s 'ɔlivə*, -z
Oliverian ,ɔli'viəriən
Olivet 'ɔlivet [-vit]
olive|-tree/s, -wood 'ɔliv|tri:/z, -wud
Olivia ɔ'liviə [ə'l-, əu'l-, -vjə]
Olivier (Sir Laurence) ə'liviei [ɔ'l-]
olivine, -s ,ɔli'vi:n ['ɔliv-], -z
olla podrida, -s 'ɔləpɔ'dri:də ['ɔljə-,
  -pə'd-], -z
Ollendorf 'ɔləndɔ:f [-lin-] ('ɔləndɔrf)
Ollerton 'ɔlətn
Olley 'ɔli
Olliffe 'ɔlif
Ollivant 'ɔlivənt
Olmstead 'ɔmsted
Olney (in Bucks.) 'əulni ['əuni]
-olog|y, -ies -'ɔlədʒ|i, -iz
Olver 'ɔlvə*
Olymp|ia, -iad/s, -ian, -ic/s, -us əu'lim-
  p|iə [-jə], -iæd/z [-jæd/z], -iən [-jən],
  -ik/s, -əs
Olynth|iac/s, -us əu'linθ|iæk/s [-jæk/s],
  -əs
Omagh 'əumə

Omaha 'əuməhɑ:
O'Malley əu'mæli, -'meili
Oman əu'mɑ:n
Omar 'əumɑ:*
ombre 'ɔmbə*
ombudsman 'ɔmbudzmən [-mæn]
Omdurman ,ɔmdə:'mɑ:n
O'Meara əu'mɑ:rə, -'miərə
omega (O.), -s 'əumigə [-meg-], -z
omelet(te), -s 'ɔmlit [-let], -s
omen, -s, -ed 'əumen [-mən], -z, -d
omer (O.), -s əumə*, -z
omicron, -s əu'maikrən, -z   [-nis
ominous, -ly, -ness 'ɔminəs ['əum-], -li,
omissible əu'misibl [-səb-]
omission, -s ə'miʃən [əu'm-], -z
omit, -s, -ting, -ted ə'mit [əu'm-], -s, -iŋ,
Ommaney 'ɔməni   [-id
omnibus, -es 'ɔmnibəs, -iz
omnifarious ,ɔmni'fɛəriəs
omnipoten|ce, -t/ly ɔm'nipətən|s, -t/li
omnipresen|ce, -t 'ɔmni'prezən|s [,ɔm-],
   -t
omniscien|ce, -t/ly ɔm'nisiən|s [-sjən-,
   -ʃiən-, -fjən-, -ʃən-], -t/li
omnium, -s 'ɔmnïəm [-njəm], -z
omnium gatherum, -s 'ɔmnïəm'gæðə-
   rəm [-njəm-], -z
omnivorous, -ly ɔm'nivərəs, -li
Omond 'əumənd
O'Morchoe əu'mʌrəu
omphalos 'ɔmfələs
Omri 'ɔmrai
Omsk ɔmsk
on (s. adj. adv. prep.) ɔn (normal form,
   strong and weak), ən, n (rare weak
   forms).
onager, -s 'ɔnəgə*, -z
Onan 'əunæn [-nən]
once wʌns
once-over 'wʌns,əuvə*
oncer, -s 'wʌnsə*, -z
oncoming (s. adj.), -s 'ɔn,kʌmiŋ, -z
on-drive, -s 'ɔn-draiv, -z
one, -s wʌn, -z
O'Neal əu'ni:l
one-eyed 'wʌn'aid [also '-- when attri-
   butive]
Onega ɔ'njegə [ɔ'negə, əu'neigə, old-
   fashioned 'əunigə] (a'njegə)
one-horse (adj.) 'wʌn'hɔ:s ['wʌnh-]
O'Neil(l) əu'ni:l
oneiromancy əu'naiərəumænsi
one-ish 'wʌniʃ
one-legged 'wʌn'legd [-'legid, 'wʌnlegd,
   'wʌn,legid]
oneness 'wʌnnis
oner, -s 'wʌnə*, -z

onerous, -ly, -ness 'ɔnərəs ['əun-], -li,
   -nis
oneself wʌn'self
onesided, -ly, -ness 'wʌn'saidid [wʌn's-],
   -li, -nis
Onesimus əu'nesiməs
ongoing, -s 'ɔn,gəuiŋ, -z
Onians ə'naiənz [əu'n-]
Onich (near Fort William) 'əunik [-nix]
onion, -s, -y 'ʌnjən, -z, -i
Onions 'ʌnjənz
on-licence, -s 'ɔn,laisəns, -iz
onlook|er/s, -ing 'ɔn,luk|ə*/z, -iŋ
only 'əunli
onomastic ,ɔnəu'mæstik
onomasticon, -s ,ɔnəu'mæstikən [-kɔn],
   -z
onomatolog|ist/s, -y ,ɔnəumə'tɔlədʒ|-
   ist/s, -i
onomato|poeia, -poeias, -poeic ,ɔnəu-
   mætəu'pi(:)ə [ɔ,nɔmət-, ə,nɔmət-],
   -'pi(:)əz, -'pi:ik
Onoto, -s əu'nəutəu [ɔ'n-], -z
on|rush/es, -set/s, -slaught/s 'ɔn|-
   rʌʃ/iz, -set/s, -slɔ:t/s
Onslow 'ɔnzləu
Ontario ɔn'tɛəriəu
onto 'ɔntu, 'ɔntə
   Note.—The form 'ɔntə is used only
   before words beginning with a
   consonant.
ontologic, -al, -ally ,ɔntəu'lɔdʒik, -əl, -əli
ontolog|ist/s, -y ɔn'tɔlədʒ|ist/s, -i
onus 'əunəs
onward, -s 'ɔnwəd, -z
onyx, -es 'ɔniks ['əun-], -iz
oof u:f
oolite, -s 'əuəlait ['əuəul-], -s
oolitic ,əuə'litik [,əuəu'l-]
oolog|ist/s, -y əu'ɔlədʒ|ist/s, -i
Oolong 'u:lɔŋ ['u:'lɔŋ]
ooze (s. v.), -es, -ing, -ed u:z, -iz, -iŋ, -d
ooz|y, -ier, -iest, -ily, -iness 'u:z|i, -ïə*
   [-jə*], -iist [-jist], -ili, -inis
opacity əu'pæsiti
opal, -s 'əupəl, -z
opalescen|ce, -t ,əupə'lesn|s, -t
opaline (s.), -s 'əupəli:n [-lain], -z
opaline (adj.) 'əupəlain
opaque, -ly, -ness əu'peik, -li, -nis
op. cit. 'ɔp'sit
op|e, -es, -ing, -ed əup, -s, -iŋ, -t
op|en (adj. v.), -ener, -enest, -enly,
   -enness; -ens, -ening, -ened, -ener/s
   'əup|ən ['əup|m], -ṇə* [-ənə*, -nə*],
   -ṇist [-ənist, -nist], -ṇli [-ənli, -ṇli],
   -ṇnis [-ənnis, -ṃnis]; -ənz [-mz], -niŋ
   [-ṇiŋ], -ənd [-md], -nə*/z [-ṇə*/z]

open-air 'əupn̩'ɛə* ['əupən'ɛə*, '---]
opencast 'əupənkɑ:st [-pn-]
open-eyed 'əupn̩'aid ['əupən'aid, '---]
open-handed 'əupn̩'hændid [-pən-, '--,--]
open - handedness   'əupn̩'hændidnis [-pən-]
open-hearted, -ly, -ness 'əupən,hɑ:tid, -li, -nis
opening (s.), -s 'əupniŋ, -z
open-minded, -ly, -ness 'əupn̩'maindid ['əupən'm-, 'əupm̩'m-, '--,--], -li, -nis
open-mouthed 'əupn̩'mauðd [-pən'm-, -pm̩'m-, '---]
Openshaw 'əupənʃɔ:
open-work 'əupn̩wə:k [-pənw-, -pm̩w-]
opera, -s; -bouffe, -cloak/s, -glass/es, -hat/s, -house, -houses 'ɔpərə, -z; -'bu:f, -kləuk/s, -glɑ:s/iz, -hæt/s, -haus, -,hauziz
operant (s. adj.), -s 'ɔpərənt, -s
operat|e, -es, -ing, -ed, -or/s 'ɔpəreit, -s, -iŋ, -id, -ə*/z
operatic ,ɔpə'rætik
operation, -s ,ɔpə'reiʃən, -z
operational ,ɔpə'reiʃənl [-ʃnəl, -ʃn̩l, -ʃnl, -ʃənəl]
operative (s.), -s 'ɔpərətiv, -z
operative (adj.), -ly, -ness 'ɔpərətiv ['ɔpəreitiv], -li, -nis
operetta, -s ,ɔpə'retə, -z
Ophelia ɔ'fi:ljə [əu'f-, -liə]
ophicleide, -s 'ɔfiklaid, -z
ophidia, -n ɔ'fidiə [əu'f-], -n
Ophir 'əufə* [rarely -fiə*]
Ophiuchus ɔ'fju:kəs
ophthalm|ia, -ic ɔf'θælm|iə [ɔp'θ-, -m|jə], -ik
ophthalmolog|ist/s, -y ,ɔfθæl'mɔlədʒ|ist/s [,ɔpθ-], -i
opiate, -s 'əupiit [-pjit, -pieit, -pjeit], -s
opiated 'əupieitid
Opie 'əupi
opin|e, -es, -ing, -ed əu'pain, -z, -iŋ, -d
opinion, -s; -ated ə'pinjən, -z; -eitid
opium; -den/s 'əupjəm [-pïəm]; -den/z
opium-eater, -s 'əupjəm,i:tə* [-pïəm-], -z
opodeldoc ,ɔpəu'deldɔk [-dək]
opopanax əu'pɔpənæks
Oporto əu'pɔ:tou (Port. u'portu)
opossum, -s ə'pɔsəm, -z
Oppenheim, -er 'ɔpənhaim, -ə*
oppidan (s. adj.), -s 'ɔpidən, -z
opponent, -s ə'pəunənt [ɔ'p-], -s
opportune, -ly, -ness 'ɔpətju:n [,ɔpə-'tju:n], -li, -nis
opportuni|sm, -st/s 'ɔpətju:ni|zəm [-tjun-, ,ɔpə'tju:n-], -st/s

opportunit|y, -ies ,ɔpə'tju:nit|i [-'tjun-, -nət-, -'tju:n̩t|i], -iz
oppos|e, -es, -ing, -ed, -er/s; -able ə'pəuz [ɔ'p-], -iz, -iŋ, -d, -ə*/z; -əbl
opposite, -ly, -ness 'ɔpəzit [-əsit], -li, -nis
opposition, -s ,ɔpə'ziʃən [-pəu'z-], -z
oppress, -es, -ing, -ed, -or/s ə'pres [ɔ'p-], -iz, -iŋ, -t, -ə*/z
oppression, -s ə'preʃən [ɔ'p-], -z
oppressive, -ly, -ness ə'presiv [ɔ'p-], -li, -nis
opprobrious, -ly, -ness ə'prəubriəs [ɔ'p-], -li, -nis
opprobrium ə'prəubriəm [ɔ'p-]
oppugn, -s, -ing, -ed, -er/s ɔ'pju:n, -z, -iŋ, -d, -ə*/z
oppugnan|cy, -s ɔ'pʌgnən|si, -t
optative (s. adj.), -s 'ɔptətiv [ɔp'teitiv], -z
optic (s. v.), -s, -al, -ally 'ɔptik, -s, -əl, -əli
optician, -s ɔp'tiʃən, -z
optimate 'ɔptimit [-meit]
optimates ,ɔpti'meiti:z
optime, -s 'ɔptimi, -z
optimi|sm, -st/s 'ɔptimi|zəm, -st/s
optimistic, -al, -ally ,ɔpti'mistik, -əl, -əli
optimum 'ɔptiməm
option, -s 'ɔpʃən, -z
op|tional, -tionally 'ɔp|ʃənl [-ʃnəl, -ʃn̩l, -ʃn̩l, -ʃənəl], -ʃn̩əli [-ʃnəli, -ʃn̩li, -ʃn̩li, -ʃənəli]
opulen|ce, -t 'ɔpjulən|s, -t
opus 'əupəs ['ɔpəs]
opuscule, -s ɔ'pʌskju:l [əu'p-], -z
or (s.) ɔ:*
or (conj.) ɔ:* (normal form) ə* (occasional weak form)
    Note.—The weak form is chiefly used in common phrases, such as two or three minutes.
orach|(e), -es 'ɔritʃ, -iz
oracle, -s 'ɔrəkl [-rik-], -z
oracular, -ly, -ness ɔ'rækjulə* [ɔ:'r-, ə'r-], -li, -nis
or|al (s. adj.), -als, -ally 'ɔ:r|əl, -əlz, -əli [-li]
Oran ɔ:'rɑ:n [ɔ'r-, -'ræn]
orang, -s 'ɔ:rəŋ [-ræŋ, old-fashioned ɔ:'ræŋ, ɔ'ræŋ, ə'ræŋ], -z
orange (s. adj.) (O.), -s 'ɔrindʒ, -iz
orangeade 'ɔrindʒ'eid [,ɔr-]
orange-blossom, -s 'ɔrindʒ,blɔsəm, -z
orange-coloured 'ɔrindʒ,kʌləd
orange-juice 'ɔrindʒdʒu:s
Orange|man, -men 'ɔrindʒ|mən [-mæn], -mən [-men]
orange-peel 'ɔrindʒpi:l

oranger|y, -ies 'ɔrindʒər|i, -iz
orange-tree, -s 'ɔrindʒtri:, -z
orange-yellow 'ɔrindʒ'jeləu
orang-outa|n/s, -ng/s 'ɔ:rəŋ'u:tæ|n/z
[-ræŋ-, -tɑ:|n/z, old-fashioned ɔ:'ræŋ-
u(:)'tæ|n/z, ɔ'ræŋ-, ə'ræŋ-], -ŋ/z
orat|e, -es, -ing, -ed ɔ:'reit [ɔ'r-], -s, -iŋ,
-id
oration, -s ɔ:'reiʃən [ɔ'r-, ə'r-], -z
oratio obliqua ɔ'rɑ:tiəu ɔ'bli:kwə [ɔ:'r-,
ə'r-,   ə'b-,   old-fashioned   ə'reiʃiəu
ə'blaikwə]
orator, -s 'ɔrətə* [-rit-], -z
oratoric|al, -ally ,ɔrə'tɔrik|əl, -əli
oratorio, -s ,ɔrə'tɔ:riəu, -z
orator|y (O.), -ies 'ɔrətər|i, -iz
orb (s. v.), -s, -ing, -ed ɔ:b, -z, -iŋ, -d
orbed (adj.) ɔ:bd [in poetry generally
'ɔ:bid]
orbicular, -ness ɔ:'bikjulə*, -nis
orbit, -s, -al 'ɔ:bit, -s, -l
orc, -s ɔ:k, -s
Orcadian, -s ɔ:'keidjən [-diən], -z
orchard (O.), -s 'ɔ:tʃəd, -z
Orchardson 'ɔ:tʃədsn
Orchehill 'ɔ:tʃil
orchestra, -s 'ɔ:kistrə [-kes-, -kəs-], -z
orchestral ɔ:'kestrəl
orchestrat|e, -es, -ing, -ed 'ɔ:kistreit
[-kes-, -kəs-], -s, -iŋ, -id
orchestration, -s ,ɔ:kes'treiʃən [-kis-,
-kəs-], -z
orchestrion, -s ɔ:'kestriən, -z
orchid, -s 'ɔ:kid, -z
orchidaceous ,ɔ:ki'deiʃəs
orchideous ɔ:'kidiəs
orchil 'ɔ:tʃil
orchis, -es 'ɔ:kis, -iz
Orchy 'ɔ:ki ['ɔ:xi] (Scottish 'ɔrxɨ)
Orczy 'ɔ:tsi ['ɔ:ksi]
Ord ɔ:d
ordain, -s, -ing, -ed, -er/s ɔ:'dein, -z, -iŋ,
-d, -ə*/z
Orde ɔ:d
ordeal, -s ɔ:'di:l [-'di:əl, -'diəl], -z
ord|er (s. v.), -ers, -ering, -ered; -erless
'ɔ:d|ə*, -əz, -əriŋ, -əd; -əlis
orderl|y (s. adj.), -ies, -iness 'ɔ:dəl|i, -iz,
-inis
ordinaire ,ɔ:di'nɛə* ['ɔ:dinɛə*] (ordinɛ:r)
ordinal (s. adj.), -s 'ɔ:dinl, -z
ordinance, -s 'ɔ:dinəns [-dŋəns], -iz
ordinand, -s ,ɔ:di'nænd, -z
ordinar|y (s. adj.), -ies, -ily, 'ɔ:dŋr|i
[-dinər-, -dənər-, -dŋər-], -iz, -ili
ordinate, -s 'ɔ:dŋit [-dɨnit], -s
ordination, -s ,ɔ:di'neiʃən, -z
ordnance 'ɔ:dnəns

ordure 'ɔ:djuə*
ore (O.), -s ɔ:* [ɔə*], -z
oread, -s 'ɔ:riæd, -z
Oreb 'ɔ:reb
O'Regan əu'ri:gən
Oregon 'ɔrigən [-gɔn]
O'|Reilly, -Rell əu|'raili, -'rel
Orellana ,ɔre'lɑ:nə [-ri'l-]
Orestes ɔ'resti:z [ɔ:'r-]
Orford 'ɔ:fəd
organ, -s; -blower/s, -builder/s, -case/s
'ɔ:gən,   -z;   -,bləuə*/z,   -,bildə*/z,
-keis/iz
organd|y [-ie], -ies 'ɔ:gənd|i [ɔ:'gæn-],
-iz
organ-grinder, -s 'ɔ:gən,graində*, -z
organic, -al, -ally ɔ:'gænik, -əl, -əli
organism, -s 'ɔ:gənizəm [-gŋizəm], -z
organist, -s 'ɔ:gənist [-gŋist], -s
organizability [-isa-] 'ɔ:gə,naizə'biliti
[,ɔ:g-, -gŋ,ai-, -lət-]
organization [-isa-], -s ,ɔ:gənai'zeiʃən
[-gŋai'z-, -gəni'z-, -gŋi'z-], -z
organiz|e [-is|e], -es, -ing, -ed, -er/s;
-able 'ɔ:gənaiz [-gŋaiz], -iz, -iŋ, -d,
-ə*/z; -əbl
organ-loft, -s 'ɔ:gənlɔft [-lɔ:ft], -s
organon, -s 'ɔ:gənɔn, -z
organ-pipe, -s 'ɔ:gənpaip, -s
organ-screen, -s 'ɔ:gən-skri:n, -z
organum, -s 'ɔ:gənəm, -z
orgasm, -s 'ɔ:gæzəm, -s
org|y, -ies 'ɔ:dʒ|i, -iz
Oriana ,ɔri'ɑ:nə [,ɔ:r-]
oriel (O.), -s 'ɔ:riəl, -z
orient (s. adj.) (O.) 'ɔ:riənt ['ɔr-]
orient (v.), -s, -ing, -ed 'ɔ:rient ['ɔr-], -s,
-iŋ, -id
oriental (s. adj.) (O.), -s ,ɔ:ri'entl [,ɔr-],
-z
orientali|sm,   -st/s   ,ɔ:ri'entəli|zəm
[,ɔr-, -tʃi-], -st/s
orientaliz|e [-is|e], -es, -ing, -ed ,ɔ:ri'en-
təlaiz [,ɔr-], -iz, -iŋ, -d
orientat|e, -es, -ing, -ed 'ɔ:rienteit
['ɔr-, -riən-, ,ɔ:ri'enteit, ,ɔri'en-], -s,
-iŋ, -id
orientation, -s ,ɔ:rien'teiʃən [,ɔr-, -riən-],
-z
orifice, -s 'ɔrifis, -iz
oriflamme, -s 'ɔriflæm, -z
Origen 'ɔridʒen
origin, -s 'ɔridʒin, -z
original (s. adj.), -s; -ness ə'ridʒənl
[ɔ'r-, -dʒinl, -dʒŋl, -dʒnl, -dʒənəl], -z;
-nis
originally ə'ridʒŋəli [ɔ'r-, -dʒinəli,
-dʒnəli, -dʒŋli, -dʒli, -dʒənəli]

originalit|y, -ies ə,ridʒi'nælit|i [ɔ,r-], -iz
originat|e, -es, -ing, -ed, -or/s; -ive
  ə'ridʒineit [ɔ'r-], -s, -iŋ, -id, -ə*/z; -iv
origination ə,ridʒi'neiʃən [ɔ,r-]
Orinoco ,ori'nəukəu
oriole, -s 'ɔ:riəul, -z
Orion ə'raiən [ɔ'r-, ɔ:'r-]
O'Riordan əu'raiədən, -'riəd-
orison, -s 'ɔrizən, -z
Orissa ɔ'risə [ɔ:'r-, ə'r-]
Orkney, -s 'ɔ:kni, -z
Orlando ɔ:'lændəu
Orleanist, -s ɔ:'liənist, -s
Orleans (in France) ɔ:'liənz ['ɔ:liənz,
  'ɔ:ljənz] (orleã), (in U.S.A.) 'ɔ:liənz
  [-ljənz, ɔ:'li:nz]
Orlon 'ɔ:lɔn
Orm(e) ɔ:m
Ormelie 'ɔ:mili
ormer, -s 'ɔ:mə*, -z
Ormes, -by ɔ:mz, -bi
Ormiston 'ɔ:mistən
ormolu 'ɔ:məulu: (ɔrmɔly, pronounced
  as if French)
Ormond(e) 'ɔ:mənd
Orms|by, -kirk 'ɔ:mz|bi, -kə:k
Ormulum 'ɔ:mjuləm
Ormuz 'ɔ:mʌz
ornament (s.), -s 'ɔ:nəmənt, -s
ornament (v.), -s, -ing, -ed 'ɔ:nəment,
  -s, -iŋ, -id
ornament|al, -ally ,ɔ:nə'ment|l, -əli [-|i]
ornamentation, -s ,ɔ:nəmen'teiʃən, -z
Ornan 'ɔ:næn
ornate, -ly, -ness ɔ:'neit ['ɔ:neit], -li, -nis
ornithologic|al, -ally ,ɔ:niθə'lɔdʒik|l, -əli
ornitholog|ist/s, -y ,ɔ:ni'θɔlədʒ|ist/s, -i
orographic, -al ,ɔrəu'græfik [,ɔ:r-], -əl
orography ɔ'rɔgrəfi [ɔ:'r-]
orological ,ɔrə'lɔdʒikəl [,ɔ:r-]
orology ɔ'rɔlədʒi [ɔ:'r-]
Oronsay 'ɔrənsei [-nzei]
Orontes ɔ'rɔnti:z [ə'r-]
Oroonoko ,ɔru:'nəukəu
Orosius ə'rəusjəs [ɔ'r-, -siəs]
orotund 'ɔrəutʌnd ['ɔ:r-]
O'Rourke əu'rɔ:k
Orpah 'ɔ:pə
orphan, -s 'ɔ:fən, -z
orphanage, -s 'ɔ:fənidʒ [-fɲi-], -iz
Orphean ɔ:'fi(:)ən
Orpheus 'ɔ:fju:s
orpiment 'ɔ:pimənt
Orpington, -s 'ɔ:piŋtən, -z
Orr ɔ:*
Orrell 'ɔrəl
orrer|y (O.), -ies 'ɔrər|i, -iz
orris 'ɔris

Orrm, -in ɔ:m, -in
Orrock 'ɔrək
Orsino ɔ:'si:nəu
Orson 'ɔ:sn
Orth ɔ:θ
orthochromatic 'ɔ:θəukrəu'mætik [,ɔ:θ-]
orthodonti|cs, -st/s ,ɔ:θəu'dɔnti|ks,
  -st/s
orthodox, -ly 'ɔ:θədɔks, -li
orthodox|y, -ies 'ɔ:θədɔks|i, -iz
orthoepical ,ɔ:θəu'epikəl
orthoep|ist/s, -y 'ɔ:θəuep|ist/s [ɔ:'θəuip-,
  ,ɔ:θəu'ep-], -i
orthogonal ɔ:'θɔgənl
othographer, -s ɔ:'θɔgrəfə*, -z
orthographic, -al, -ally ,ɔ:θəu'græfik,
  -əl, -əli
orthograph|ist/s, -y ɔ:'θɔgrəf|ist/s, -i
orthopaedic [-ped-], -s ,ɔ:θəu'pi:dik, -s
orthopaedy [-ped-] 'ɔ:θəupi:di
orthophonic, -s ,ɔ:θəu'fəunik [-'fɔ-], -s
orthophony ɔ:'θɔfəni
Ortler 'ɔ:tlə*
ortolan, -s 'ɔ:tələn, -z
Orton 'ɔ:tn
Orville 'ɔ:vil
Orwell 'ɔ:wəl [-wel]
oryx, -es 'ɔriks, -iz
Osage əu'seidʒ ['əuseidʒ]
Osaka 'ɔ:səkə [əu'sɑ:kə]
Osbaldiston(e) ,ɔzbəl'distən
Osbert 'ɔzbə:t [-bət]
Osborn(e) 'ɔzbən [-bɔ:n]
Osbourne 'ɔzbən [-bɔ:n]
Oscan, -s 'ɔskən, -z
Oscar, -s 'ɔskə*, -z
oscillat|e, -es, -ing, -ed, -or/s 'ɔsileit, -s,
  -iŋ, -id, -ə*/z
oscillation, -s ,ɔsi'leiʃən, -z
oscillatory 'ɔsilətəri [-leitəri]
oscillogram, -s ɔ'siləugræm [ə's-], -z
oscillograph, -s ɔ'siləugrɑ:f [ə's-, -græf],
osculant 'ɔskjulənt |-s
osculat|e, -es, -ing, -ed 'ɔskjuleit, -s, -iŋ,
  -id
osculation, -s ,ɔskju'leiʃən, -z
osculator|y (s.), -ies 'ɔskjulətər|i, -iz
osculatory (adj.) 'ɔskjulətəri [-leitəri]
Osgood 'ɔzgud
O'Shaughnessy əu'ʃɔ:nisi [-nəsi]
O'Shea əu'ʃei
osier, -s 'əuʒə* ['əuʒjə*, -ʒiə*, 'əuzjə*,
  -ziə*], -z
Osirian, -s əu'saiəriən [ɔ's-], -z
Osiris əu'saiəris [ɔ's-]
Osler 'əuzlə*, 'əuslə*
Oslo 'ɔzləu ['ɔsləu]
Osman ɔz'mɑ:n [ɔs'mɑ:n]

Osmanli, -s ɔz'mænli [ɔs'm-, -'mɑ:n-], -z
osmium 'ɔzmiəm [-mjəm]
Osmond 'ɔzmənd
osmosis ɔz'məusis
osmotic ɔz'mɔtik
osmund (O.), -s 'ɔzmənd, -z
osmunda, -s ɔz'mʌndə, -z
Osnaburg(h) 'ɔznəbə:g
osprey, -s 'ɔspri ['ɔsprei], -z
Ospringe 'ɔsprindʒ
Ossa 'ɔsə
osseous 'ɔsïəs [-sjəs]
Ossett 'ɔsit
Ossian 'ɔsïən [-sjən]
Ossianic ,ɔsi'ænik
ossicle, -s 'ɔsikl, -z
ossification ,ɔsifi'keiʃən
ossifrage, -s 'ɔsifridʒ, -iz
ossi|fy, -fies, -fying, -fied 'ɔsi|fai, -faiz, -faiiŋ, -faid
Ossory 'ɔsəri
ossuar|y, -ies 'ɔsjüər|i [-sjwə-], -iz
Ostend ɔs'tend
ostensibility ɔs,tensi'biliti [-sə'b-, -lət-]
ostensib|le, -ly ɔs'tensəb|l [-sib-], -li
ostentation ,ɔsten'teiʃən [-tən-]
ostentatious, -ly, -ness ,ɔsten'teiʃəs [-tən-], -li, -nis
osteologic|al, -ally,ɔstïə'lɔdʒik|əl [-tjə'l-, -tiəu'l-], -əli
osteolog|ist/s, -y ,ɔsti'ɔlədʒ|ist/s, -i
osteopath, -s 'ɔstïəpæθ [-tjəup-, -tiəup-], -s
osteopathic ,ɔstïə'pæθik [-tjəu'p-, -tiəu'p-]
osteopath|ist/s, -y ,ɔsti'ɔpəθ|ist/s, -i
Osterley 'ɔstəli
Ostia 'ɔstïə [-tjə]
ostiar|y, -ies 'ɔstïər|i [-tjə-], -iz
osti|um (O.), -a 'ɔstï|əm [-tj|əm], -ə
ostler, -s 'ɔslə*, -z
ostracism 'ɔstrəsizəm
ostraciz|e [-is|e], -es, -ing, -ed 'ɔstrə-saiz, -iz, -iŋ, -d
ostrich, -es; -feather/s 'ɔstritʃ [-idʒ], -iz; -,feðə*/z
Ostrogoth, -s 'ɔstrəugɔθ, -s
O'Sullivan əu'sʌlivən
Oswald 'ɔzwəld
Oswaldtwistle 'ɔzwəldtwisl
Oswego, -s ɔz'wi:gəu, -z
Oswestry 'ɔzwəstri [-wis-, -wes-]
Otago (in New Zealand) əu'tɑ:gəu [ɔ't-]
Otaheite ,əutɑ:'heiti [-tə'h-]
otar|y, -ies 'əutər|i, -iz
Ot|ford, -fried 'ɔt|fəd, -fri:d
Othello əu'θeləu [ɔ'θ-]
other, -s; -wise 'ʌðə*, -z; -waiz

Othman ɔθ'mɑ:n
Othniel 'ɔθnïəl [-njəl]
Otho 'əuθəu
otiose, -ly, -ness 'əuʃiəus [-ʃjəus, 'əutiəus, -tjəus], -li, -nis
otiosity ,əuʃi'ɔsiti
Otis 'əutis
otitis əu'taitis
Otley 'ɔtli
otolog|ist/s, -y əu'tɔlədʒ|ist/s, -i
otoscope, -s 'əutəskəup, -s
Otranto ɔ'træntəu ['ɔtrəntəu] ('ɔ:tranto)
Otsego ɔt'si:gəu
Ottaw|a, -ay 'ɔtəw|ə, -ei
otter, -s 'ɔtə*, -z
Otterburn 'ɔtəbə:n
otter-hound, -s 'ɔtəhaund, -z
Ott|ery, -ley 'ɔt|əri, -li
otto (O.) 'ɔtəu
ottoman (O.), -s 'ɔtəumən, -z
Ottoway 'ɔtəwei
Otway 'ɔtwei
oubliette, -s ,u:bli'et, -s
Oubridge 'u:bridʒ
Oude aud
Oudenarde 'u:dənɑ:d [-din-]
Oudh aud
Ough əu
Ougham 'əukəm
ought, -n't ɔ:t, -nt [occasionally also 'ɔ:tn when not final]
Oughter (Lough) 'u:ktə*
Oughterard ,u:tə'rɑ:d
Oughton 'autn, 'ɔ:tn
Oughtred 'ɔ:tred [-rid], 'u:t-, 'aut-
Ouida 'wi:də
ouija 'wi:dʒɑ: [-dʒə]
Ouin (surname) 'əuin
Ould əuld
Ouless 'u:lis [-les]
ounce, -s auns, -iz
Oundle 'aundl
our, -s 'auə* [ɑ:*], -z
oursel|f, -ves ,auə'sel|f [ɑ:-], -vz
Oury 'auəri
Ouse u:z
ousel, -s 'u:zl, -z
Ouseley 'u:zli
Ousey 'u:zi
Ousley (in U.S.A.) 'ausli
oust, -s, -ing, -ed, -er/s aust, -s, -iŋ, -id, -ə*/z
Ouston 'austən
out aut
out-and-out 'autnd'aut ['autn̩'aut]
outbalanc|e, -es, -ing, -ed aut'bæləns ['aut'b-], -iz, -iŋ, -t   [-iŋ
outbid, -s, -ding aut'bid ['aut'bid], -z,

outboard 'autbɔ:d [-bɔəd]

outbound 'autbaund

outbrav|e, -es, -ing, -ed aut'breiv ['aut'b-], -z, -iŋ, -d

out|break/s, -building/s, -burst/s 'aut|breik/s, -,bildiŋ/z, -bə:st/s

outcast, -s 'autkɑ:st, -s

outcast|e (s. adj. v.), -es, -ing, -ed 'aut-kɑ:st, -s, -iŋ, -id

outclass, -es, -ing, -ed aut'klɑ:s ['aut'k-], -iz, -iŋ, -t

out|come/s, -crop/s, -cry, -cries 'aut|-kʌm/z, -krɔp/s, -krai, -kraiz

outdar|e, -es, -ing, -ed aut'dɛə* ['aut-'dɛə*], -z, -riŋ, -d

outdistanc|e, -es, -ing, -ed aut'distəns ['aut'd-], -iz, -iŋ, -t

out|do, -does, -doing, -did, -done aut|'du: ['aut|'d-], -'dʌz, -'du(:)iŋ, -'did, -'dʌn

outdoor 'autdɔ:* [-dɔə*]

outdoors 'aut'dɔ:z [-'dɔəz, also -'- when preceded by a stress]

outer, -most 'autə*, -məust [-məst]

outerwear 'autə-wɛə*

outfac|e, -es, -ing, -ed aut'feis ['aut'f-], -iz, -iŋ, -t

outfall, -s 'autfɔ:l, -z

outfield, -s, -er/s 'autfi:ld, -z, -ə*/z

outfit (s. v.), -s, -ting, -ted, -ter/s 'aut-fit, -s, -iŋ, -id, -ə*/z

outflank, -s, -ing, -ed aut'flæŋk ['aut'f-], -s, -iŋ, -t [-'flæŋt]

outflow (s.), -s 'autfləu, -z

outfl|ow (v.), -ows, -owing, -owed aut-'fl|əu, -əuz, -əuiŋ, -əud

outgener|al, -als, -alling, -alled aut-'dʒenər|əl ['aut'dʒ-], -əlz, -əliŋ, -əld

outgo (s.), -es 'autgəu, -z

out|go (v.), -goes, -going, -went, -gone aut|'gəu ['aut|'g-], -'gəuz, -'gəuiŋ, -'went, -'gɔn [-'gɔ:n]

outgoer, -s 'aut,gəuə*, -z

outgoing (s. adj.), -s 'aut,gəuiŋ, -z

outgrow (s.), -s 'autgrəu, -z

out|grow (v.), -grows, -growing, -grew, -grown aut|'grəu ['aut|'grəu], -'grəuz, -'grəuiŋ, -'gru:, -'grəun

outgrowth, -s 'autgrəuθ, -s

outguard, -s 'autgɑ:d, -z

out-herod, -s, -ing, -ed aut'herəd ['aut'h-], -z, -iŋ, -id

outhou|se, -ses 'authau|s, -ziz

Outhwaite 'u:θweit, 'əuθweit, 'auθweit Note.—More commonly 'u:θ-.

outing, -s 'autiŋ, -z

Outis 'autis

Outlander, -s 'aut,lændə*, -z

outlandish, -ly, -ness aut'lændiʃ, -li, -nis

outlast, -s, -ing, -ed aut'lɑ:st ['aut'lɑ:st], -s, -iŋ, -id

outlaw (s. v.), -s, -ing, -ed; -ry 'aut-lɔ:, -z, -iŋ, -d; -ri

outlay (s.), -s 'aut-lei, -z

outlay (v.), -s, -ing, outlaid aut'lei, -z, -iŋ, aut'leid

outlet, -s 'aut-let [-lit], -s

outlier, -s 'aut,laiə*, -z

outlin|e (s. v.), -es, -ing, -ed 'aut-lain, -z, -iŋ, -d

outliv|e, -es, -ing, -ed aut'liv ['aut'liv], -z, -iŋ, -d

outlook, -s 'aut-luk, -s

outlying 'aut,laiiŋ

outmanœuv|re, -res, -ring, -red ,aut-mə'nu:v|ə* ['autmə'n-], -əz, -əriŋ, -əd

outmarch, -es, -ing, -ed 'aut'mɑ:tʃ, -iz, -iŋ, -t

outmatch, -es, -ing, -ed aut'mætʃ ['aut'm-], -iz, -iŋ, -t

outmost 'autməust

outnumb|er, -ers, -ering, -ered aut-'nʌmb|ə* ['aut'n-], -əz, -əriŋ, -əd

out-of-doors 'autəv'dɔ:z [-'dɔəz, also ,-'- when preceded by a stress]

out-of-the-way 'autəvðə'wei [-təð-]

outpac|e, -es, -ing, -ed aut'peis ['aut-'peis], -iz, -iŋ, -t

outpatient, -s 'aut,peiʃənt, -s

out-pensioner, -s 'aut,penʃənə* [-ʃŋə*, -ʃnə*], -z

outplay, -s, -ing, -ed aut'plei ['aut'p-], -z, -iŋ, -d

outport, -s 'autpɔ:t, -s

outpost, -s 'autpəust, -s

outpour (s.), -s 'autpɔ:* [-pɔə*], -z

outpour (v.), -s, -ing, -ed aut'pɔ:* ['aut'p-, -'pɔə*], -z, -riŋ, -d

outpouring (s.), -s 'aut,pɔ:riŋ [-,pɔər-], -z

output, -s 'autput, -s

outrag|e (s. v.), -es, -ing, -ed 'aut-reidʒ [-ridʒ], -iz, -iŋ, -d

outrageous, -ly, -ness aut'reidʒəs, -li, -nis

Outram 'u:trəm

outrang|e, -es, -ing, -ed aut'reindʒ ['aut'r-], -iz, -iŋ, -d

outré 'u:trei (utre)

outreach, -es, -ing, -ed aut'ri:tʃ ['aut'r-], -iz, -iŋ, -t

Outred 'u:trid [-red]

out-relief 'aut-ri,li:f

out|ride, -rides, -riding, -rode, -ridden aut'raid ['aut'r-], -'raidz, -'raidiŋ, -'rəud, -'ridn

outrider, -s 'aut‚raidə*, -z
outrigger, -s 'aut‚rigə*, -z
outright (adj.) 'aut-rait, (adv.) aut'rait
outriv|al, -als, -alling, -alled aut-
 'raiv|əl ['aut'r-], -əlz, -ḷiŋ [-əliŋ], -əld
out|run, -runs, -running, -ran aut|'rʌn
 ['aut|'r-], -'rʌnz, -'rʌniŋ, -'ræn
outrush, -es 'aut-rʌʃ, -iz
out|sell, -sells, -selling, -sold aut|'sel
 ['aut|'s-], -'selz, -'seliŋ, -'səuld
outset, -s 'aut-set, -s
out|shine, -shines, -shining, -shined,
 -shone aut|'ʃain ['aut|'ʃ-], -'ʃainz,
 -'ʃainiŋ, -'ʃaind, -'ʃon
outside (s. adj. adv. prep.), -s 'aut'said
 ['--, -'- according to sentence-stress],
 -z
outsider, -s 'aut'saidə* [aut's-], -z
outsize, -s, -d 'aut-saiz, -iz, -d
outskirt, -s 'aut-skɔ:t, -s
Outspan, -s 'aut-spæn, -z
outspan (v.), -s, -ning, -ned aut'spæn
 ['aut's-], -z, -iŋ, -d
outspok|en, -enly, -enness aut'spəuk|ən
 ['aut's-], -ənli [-ṇli], -ənnis [-ṇnis]
outspread 'aut'spred ['--, -'- according
 to sentence-stress]
outstanding (conspicuous, undone, remaining due) aut'stændiŋ ['aut's-],
 (sticking out (ears)) 'aut‚stændiŋ
outstar|e, -es, -ing, -ed aut'stɛə*
 ['aut's-], -z, -riŋ, -d
outstay, -s, -ing, -ed aut'stei ['aut's-],
 -z, -iŋ, -d
outstretch, -es, -ing, -ed aut'stretʃ
 ['aut's-], -iz, -iŋ, -t ['aut-stretʃt when
 attributive]
outstrip, -s, -ping, -ped aut'strip
 ['aut's-], -s, -iŋ, -t
outtop, -s, -ping, -ped aut'tɔp ['aut-
 'tɔp], -s, -iŋ, -t
outv|ie, -ies, -ying, -ied aut'v|ai
 ['aut'v-], -aiz, -aiiŋ, -aid
outvot|e, -es, -ing, -ed aut'vəut ['aut-
 'vəut], -s, -iŋ, -id
out-voter (non-resident voter), -s 'aut-
 ‚vəutə*, -z
outwalk, -s, -ing, -ed aut'wɔ:k ['aut'w-],
 -s, -iŋ, -t
outward, -s, -ly, -ness 'aut-wəd, -z, -li,
 -nis
outwear, -s, -ing, outworn aut'wɛə*,
 ['aut'w-], -z, -riŋ, aut'wɔ:n ['aut'w-,
 when attributive 'aut-wɔ:n]
outweigh, -s, -ing, -ed aut'wei ['aut-
 'wei], -z, -iŋ, -d
outwent (from outgo) aut'went ['aut-
 'went]

outwit, -s, -ting, -ted aut'wit, -s, -iŋ, -id
outwork (s.), -s 'aut-wə:k, -s
outwork (v.), -s, -ing, -ed aut'wə:k
 ['aut'wə:k], -s, -iŋ, -t
out-worker, -s 'aut‚wə:kə*, -z
outworn (when attributive) 'aut-wɔ:n,
 (when not attributive) aut'wɔ:n['aut'w-]
ouzel, -s 'u:zl, -z
ova (plur. of ovum) 'əuvə
ov|al (s. adj.), -als, -ally 'əuv|əl, -əlz, -əli
ovarial əu'veəriəl
ovariotomy əu‚veəri'ɔtəmi [‚əuvɛə-]
ovar|y, -ies 'əuvər|i, -iz
ovate (s.) (Welsh title), -s 'ɔvit, -s
ovate (adj.) (egg-shaped) 'əuveit [-vit]
ovation, -s əu'veiʃən, -z
oven, -s; -bird/s 'ʌvn, -z; -bə:d/z
over (s. adj. prep.), -s 'əuvə*, -z
 Note.—Compounds with over- not
  entered below have double stress, and
  their pronunciation may be ascertained by referring to the simple
  words. Thus over-cautious, over-
  peopled are pronounced 'əuvə-
  'kɔ:ʃəs, 'əuvə'pi:pld.
over-abundan|ce, -t 'əuvərə'bʌndən|s, -t
overact, -s, -ing, -ed 'əuvər'ækt
 ['əuvə'ækt], -s, -iŋ, -id
overall (s. adj.) (O.), -s 'əuvərɔ:l, -z
overall (adv.) ‚əuvər'ɔ:l
over-anxiety 'əuvəræŋ'zaiəti ['əuvææŋ-]
over-anxious, -ly 'əuvər'æŋkʃəs
 ['əuvə'æ-], -li
overarm 'əuvərɑ:m
overaw|e, -es, -ing, -ed ‚əuvər'ɔ:
 [‚əuvə'ɔ:], -z, -iŋ, -d
overbalanc|e, -es, -ing, -ed ‚əuvə-
 'bæləns, -iz, -iŋ, -t
overbear, -s, -ing, overbore, overborne
 ‚əuvə'bɛə*, -z, -riŋ, ‚əuvə'bɔ:*
 [-'bɔə*], ‚əuvə'bɔ:n
overbearing (adj.), -ly, -ness ‚əuvə-
 'bɛəriŋ, -li, -nis
over|blow, -blows, -blowing, -blew,
 -blown 'əuvə|'bləu, -'bləuz, -'bləuiŋ,
 -'blu:, -'bləun
overboard 'əuvəbɔ:d [‚əuvə'bɔ:d, -əd]
overboil, -s, -ing, -ed 'əuvə'bɔil, -z, -iŋ,
 -d
overbold, -ly 'əuvə'bəuld, -li
overbrim, -s, -ming, -med 'əuvə'brim,
 -z, -iŋ, -d
overbuil|d, -ds, -ding, -t 'əuvə'bil|d, -dz,
 -diŋ, -t
overburd|en, -ens, -ening, -ened ‚əuvə-
 'bə:d|n, -nz, -ṇiŋ [-niŋ], -nd
Overbury 'əuvəbəri
over-busy 'əuvə'bizi

over-care|ful, -fully, -fulness 'əuvə-
'kɛə|fʊl, -fuli [-fəli], -fʊlnis
overcast 'əuvə-kɑːst [,əuvə'kɑːst]
overcharge (s.), -s 'əuvə'tʃɑːdʒ
['əuvə-tʃ-], -iz
overcharg|e (v.), -es, -ing, -ed
'əuvə'tʃɑːdʒ [,əu-], -iz, -iŋ, -d
overcloud, -s, -ing, -ed ,əuvə'klaud, -z,
-iŋ, -id
overcoat, -s 'əuvəkəut, -s
over-colour (s.), -s 'əuvə,kʌlə*, -z
over-colour (v.), -s, -ing, -ed 'əuvə'kʌlə*,
-z, -riŋ, -d
over|come, -comes, -coming, -came
,əuvə'|kʌm, -'kʌmz, -'kʌmiŋ, -'keim
Note.—The stress '--- is occasionally
used by some when a stress follows,
e.g. in the expression to vanquish
and overcome all her enemies occurring in the Church service.
over-confiden|ce, -t/ly 'əuvə'kɔnfidən|s,
-t/li
over-cooked 'əuvə'kukt [also 'əuvə-
kukt, ,əuvə'kukt according to sentence stress]
over-credulous 'əuvə'kredjuləs
overcrowd, -s, -ing, -ed ,əuvə'kraud
['əuvə'k-], -z, -iŋ, -id
over-develop, -s, -ing, -ed, -ment
'əuvədi'veləp, -s, -iŋ, -t, -mənt
over|do, -does, -doing, -did, -done
,əuvə'|du: ['əuvə'|d-], -'dʌz, -'du(:)iŋ,
-'did, -'dʌn
overdone (over-cooked) 'əuvə'dʌn ['---]
Overdone 'əuvədʌn   [-iz
overdose (s.), -s 'əuvədəus ['əuvə'dəus]
overdos|e (v.), -es, -ing, -ed 'əuvə'dəus,
-iz, -iŋ, -t
overdraft, -s 'əuvədrɑːft, -s
overdraught, -s 'əuvədrɑːft, -s
over|draw, -draws, -drawing, -drew,
-drawn 'əuvə'|drɔ:, -'drɔ:z, -'drɔːiŋ,
'dru:, -'drɔːn
overdress, -es, -ing, -ed 'əuvə'dres, -iz,
-iŋ, -t
overdrive (s.) 'əuvədraiv
over|drive (v.), -drives, -driving, -drove,
-driven 'əuvə'|draiv, -'draivz,
-'draiviŋ, -'drəuv, -'drivn
overdue 'əuvə'dju: [also '---, ,--'- according to sentence stress]
overeat, -s, -ing, -en, overate 'əuvər'iːt
[-'iːt], -s, -iŋ, -n, 'əuvər'et [-və'et,
-vər'eit, -və'eit]
overestimate (s.), -s 'əuvər'estimit
['əuvə'es-], -s
overestimat|e (v.), -es, -ing, -ed 'əuvər-
'estimeit [,əu-, -və'es-], -s, -iŋ, -id

over - estimation 'əuvər,esti'meiʃən
[-və,es-]
overexcit|e, -es, -ing, -ed, -ement
'əuvərik'sait [-vəik-, -ek-], -s, -iŋ, -id,
-mənt
overexert, -s, -ing, -ed 'əuvərig'zəːt
[-vəig-, -eg-], -s, -iŋ, -id
overexertion 'əuvərig'zəːʃən [-vəig-,
-eg-]
overexpos|e, -es, -ing, -ed 'əuvəriks-
'pəuz [-vəik-, -ek-], -iz, -iŋ, -d
over-exposure 'əuvəriks'pəuʒə* [-vəik-,
-ek-]
overfatigu|e (s. v.), -es, -ing, -ed
'əuvəfə'tiːg, -z, -iŋ, -d
overfeed, -s, -ing, overfed 'əuvə'fiːd, -z,
-iŋ, 'əuvə'fed
overflow (s.), -s 'əuvə-fləu, -z
overfl|ow (v.), -ows, -owing, -owed
,əuvə'fl|əu, -əuz, -əuiŋ, -əud
over|-fond, -full 'əuvə|'fɔnd, -'ful
over|go, -goes, -going, -went, -gone
,əuvə|'gəu, -'gəuz, -'gəuiŋ, -'went,
-'gɔn [-'gɔːn]
overground 'əuvəgraund ['əuvə'g-]
over|grow, -grows, -growing, -grew,
-grown 'əuvə|'grəu [,əu-], -'grəuz,
-'grəuiŋ, -'gru:, -'grəun ['əuvəgrəun
when attributive]
overgrowth, -s 'əuvəgrəuθ, -s
overhand (s. adj.), -s 'əuvəhænd, -z
overhang (s.), -s 'əuvəhæŋ, -z
over|hang (v.), -hangs, -hanging, -hung
'əuvə'|hæŋ [,əu-], -'hæŋz, -'hæŋiŋ
[also 'əuvə,h- when attributive], -'hʌŋ
[also 'əuvəhʌŋ when attributive]
over|-happy, -hasty 'əuvə|'hæpi, -'heisti
overhaul (s.), -s, 'əuvəhɔːl [,--'-], -z
overhaul (v.), -s, -ing, -ed 'əuvə'hɔːl, -z,
-iŋ, -d
overhead (s. adj.), -s 'əuvəhed, -z
overhead (adv.) 'əuvə'hed [,--'-]
overhear, -s, -ing, overheard ,əuvə-
'hiə*, -z, -riŋ, ,əuvə'həːd
overheat, -s, -ing, -ed 'əuvə'hiːt, -s, -iŋ,
-id
over-indulg|e, -es, -ing, -ed; -ence
'əuvərin'dʌldʒ [-vəin-], -iz, -iŋ, -d;
-əns
overjoy, -s, -ing, -ed ,əuvə'dʒɔi, -z, -iŋ, -d
over-kind 'əuvə'kaind
overlad|e, -es, -ing, -ed, -en 'əuvə'leid,
-z, -iŋ, -id, -n
overlaid ,əuvə'leid [also 'əuvəl- when
attributive]
overland (adj.) 'əuvəlænd
overland (adv.), ,əuvə'lænd
overlap (s.), -s 'əuvəlæp, -s

overlap (v.), -s, -ping, -ped ˌəuvəˈlæp, -s, -iŋ, -t

overlay (s.), -s ˈəuvəlei, -z

overlay (v.), -s, -ing, overlaid ˌəuvəˈlei, -z, -iŋ, ˌəuvəˈleid [also ˈəuvəl- when attributive]

overleaf ˈəuvəˈliːf [ˌ--ˈ-]

over|leap (leap over), -leaps, -leaping, -leaped, -leapt ˌəuvəˈliːp, -ˈliːps, -ˈliːpiŋ, -ˈlept [-ˈliːpt], -ˈlept

over-leap (leap too far), -leaps, -leaping, -leaped, -leapt ˈəuvəˈliːp, -ˈliːps, -ˈliːpiŋ, -ˈlept [-ˈliːpt], -ˈlept

overload (s.), -s ˈəuvələud, -z

overload (v.), -s, -ing, -ed ˈəuvəˈləud [ˌəu-], -z, -iŋ, -id

overlook, -s, -ing, -ed ˌəuvəˈluk, -s, -iŋ, -t

overlord, -s ˈəuvələːd, -z

overlying ˌəuvəˈlaiiŋ [ˈəuvəˈl-]

over|man, -men ˈəuvə|mæn, -men

overmantel, -s ˈəuvəˈmæntl, -z

overmast|er, -ers, -ering, -ered ˌəuvəˈmɑːst|ə*, -əz, -əriŋ, -əd

overmatch, -es, -ing, -ed ˌəuvəˈmætʃ, -iz, -iŋ, -t

overmuch ˈəuvəˈmʌtʃ [ˈəuvəm-]

over-nice ˈəuvəˈnais

overnight ˈəuvəˈnait [also ˈ---, ˌ--ˈ- according to sentence-stress]

overpass, -es, -ing, -ed ˌəuvəˈpɑːs, -iz, -iŋ, -t

overpast (adj.) ˈəuvəˈpɑːst [ˌəuvəˈp-]

over|pay, -pays, -paying, -paid, -payment/s ˈəuvə|ˈpei, -ˈpeiz, -ˈpeiiŋ, -ˈpeid, -ˈpeimənt/s

overplus, -es ˈəuvə-plʌs, -iz

overpower, -s, -ing/ly, -ed ˌəuvəˈpauə*, -z, -riŋ/li, -d

overprint (s.), -s ˈəuvə-print, -s

overprint (v.), -s, -ing, -ed ˈəuvəˈprint [ˈəuvə-print], -s, -iŋ, -id

overproduc|e, -es, -ing, -ed ˈəuvə-prəˈdjuːs [-pruˈd-], -iz, -iŋ, -t

overproduction ˈəuvə-prəˈdʌkʃən

overproud ˈəuvəˈpraud [[-pruˈd-]

overrat|e, -es, -ing, -ed ˈəuvəˈreit [ˌəu-], -s, -iŋ, -id

overreach (s.), -es ˈəuvə-riːtʃ, -iz

overreach (v.), -es, -ing, -ed ˌəuvəˈriːtʃ, -iz, -iŋ, -t

overread (pres. tense), -s, -ing, overread (past) ˈəuvəˈriːd, -z, -iŋ, ˈəuvəˈred

overrefin|e, -es, -ing, -ed, -ement/s ˈəuvə-riˈfain, -z, -iŋ, -d, -mənt/s

over|ride, -rides, -riding, -rode, -ridden ˌəuvə|ˈraid, -ˈraidz, -ˈraidiŋ, -ˈrəud, -ˈridn

overripe, -ness ˈəuvəˈraip, -nis

overrip|en, -ens, -ening, -ened ˈəuvəˈraip|n, -nz, -niŋ [-ṇiŋ], -nd

overrul|e, -es, -ing, -ed, -er/s ˌəuvəˈruːl, -z, -iŋ, -d, -ə*/z

overrun, -s, -ning, overran ˌəuvəˈrʌn, -z, -iŋ, ˌəuvəˈræn

over-scrupulous, -ly, -ness ˈəuvəˈskruː-pjuləs [-pjəl-], -li, -nis

oversea, -s ˈəuvəˈsiː [also ˈ---, ˌ--ˈ- according to sentence-stress], -z

over|see, -sees, -seeing, -saw, -seen ˈəuvə|ˈsiː [ˌəu-], -ˈsiːz, -ˈsiːiŋ, -ˈsɔː, -ˈsiːn

overseer, -s ˈəuvəsiə* [-ˌsiːə*], -z

overshad|ow, -ows, -owing, -owed ˌəuvəˈʃæd|əu, -əuz, -əuiŋ, -əud

over-shoot, -shoots, -shooting, -shot ˈəuvəˈʃuːt [ˌəu-], -ˈʃuːts, -ˈʃuːtiŋ, -ˈʃɔt

oversight, -s ˈəuvəsait, -s

oversize (s.), -s, -d ˈəuvəsaiz, -iz, -d

overslaugh, -s ˈəuvə-slɔː, -z

over|sleep, -sleeps, -sleeping, -slept ˈəuvə|ˈsliːp [ˌəu-], -ˈsliːps, -ˈsliːpiŋ, -ˈslept

oversoon ˌəuvəˈsuːn [ˈəuvəˈs-]

overspen|d, -ds, -ding, -t ˈəuvəˈspen|d, -dz, -diŋ, -t

overspread, -s, -ing ˌəuvəˈspred, -z, -iŋ

overstat|e, -es, -ing, -ed ˈəuvəˈsteit, [ˈəuvə-steit], -s, -iŋ, -id

overstatement, -s ˈəuvəˈsteitmənt, [ˈ--,--], -s

overstay, -s, -ing, -ed ˈəuvəˈstei [ˈəuvə-stei], -z, -iŋ, -d

overstep, -s, -ping, -ped ˈəuvəˈstep [ˌəu-], -s, -iŋ, -t

overstock, -s, -ing, -ed ˈəuvəˈstɔk, -s, -iŋ, -t

overstrain (s.) ˈəuvə-strein [ˈəuvəˈstrein, ˌəuvəˈstrein]

overstrain (v.), -s, -ing, -ed ˈəuvəˈstrein [ˌəu-], -z, -iŋ, -d

Overstrand ˈəuvə-strænd

overstretch, -es, -ing, -ed ˈəuvəˈstretʃ, -iz, -iŋ, -t

overstrung (in state of nervous tension) ˈəuvəˈstrʌŋ

overstrung (piano) ˈəuvə-strʌŋ

oversubscrib|e, -es, -ing, -ed ˈəuvəsəb-ˈskraib [-bzˈk-], -z, -iŋ, -d

oversupp|ly, -ies ˈəuvəsəˈpl|ai, -aiz

overt, -ly ˈəuvəːt [əuˈvəːt], -li

over|take, -takes, -taking, -took, -taken ˈəuvə|ˈteik, -ˈteiks, -ˈteikiŋ, -ˈtuk, -ˈteikən [-ˈteikŋ]

overtask, -s, -ing, -ed ˈəuvəˈtɑːsk, -s, -iŋ, -t

overtax, -es, -ing, -ed 'əuvə'tæks [ˌəu-],
-iz, -iŋ, -t
overthrow (s.), -s 'əuvə-θrəu, -z
over|throw (v.), -throws, -throwing,
-threw, -thrown ˌəuvə|'θrəu, -'θrəuz,
-'θrəuiŋ, -'θru:, -'θrəun
overthrust, -s 'əuvə-θrʌst, -s
overtilt, -s, -ing, -ed ˌəuvə'tilt, -s, -iŋ, -id
overtime 'əuvətaim
overtir|e, -es, -ing, -ed 'əuvə'taiə* [ˌəu-],
-z, -riŋ, -d
Overton 'əuvətn
overtone, -s 'əuvətəun, -z
overtop, -s, -ping, -ped 'əuvə'tɔp [ˌəu-],
-s, -iŋ, -t
Overtoun 'əuvətn
over-trump, -s, -ing, -ed 'əuvə-trʌmp
['əuvə'trʌmp], -s, -iŋ, -t [-ʌmt]
overture, -s 'əuvətjuə* [-tjə*, -tʃuə*,
-tʃə*], -z
overturn (s.), -s 'əuvətə:n, -z
overturn (v.), -s, -ing, -ed ˌəuvə'tə:n, -z,
-iŋ, -d
overval|ue, -ues, -uing, -ued 'əuvə-
'væl|ju: [-ju], -ju:z [-juz], -juiŋ
[-jwiŋ], -ju:d [-jud]
overview, -s 'əuvəvju:, -z
overwear 'əuvəwɛə*
overweening ˌəuvə'wi:niŋ
overweight (s.), -s 'əuvəweit, -s
overweight (v.), -s, -ing, -ed 'əuvə'weit
[ˌ‒'-'], -s, -iŋ, -id
overwhelm, -s, -ing/ly, -ed ˌəuvə-
'welm [-'hwelm], -z, -iŋ/li, -d
overwork (s.) (extra work) 'əuvəwə:k
overwork (s.) (excessive work) 'əuvə-
'wə:k
overwork (v.), -s, -ing, -ed, -er/s
'əuvə'wə:k [ˌəu-], -s, -iŋ, -t, -ə*/z
overwrought 'əuvə'rɔ:t [ˌəu-]
Ovid (Latin poet) 'ɔvid, (American surname) 'əuvid
Ovidian ɔ'vidiən [əu'v-, -djən]
Oviedo ˌɔvi'eidəu (o'bjedo)
oviform 'əuvifɔ:m
ovine 'əuvain
Ovingdean 'ɔviŋdi:n
Ovingham (in Northumb.) 'ɔvindʒəm
Ovington (in Yorks., street in London)
'ɔviŋtən, (in Norfolk, surname)
'əuviŋtən
oviparous əu'vipərəs
Ovoca əu'vəukə
ovoid (s. adj.), -s 'əuvɔid, -z
ovular 'əuvjulə*
ovule, -s 'əuvju:l, -z
ov|um, -a 'əuv|əm, -ə
Owbridge 'əubridʒ

ow|e, -es, -ing, -ed əu, -z, -iŋ, -d
Owego əu'wi:gəu
Owen, -s; -ite/s 'əuin, -z; -ait/s
Ower 'auə*
Owers 'auəz
owing (from owe) 'əuiŋ
owl, -s aul, -z
owler|y, -ies 'aulər|i, -iz
Owles əulz
owlet, -s 'aulit [-let], -s
Owlett 'aulit [-let]
owlish, -ly, -ness 'auliʃ, -li, -nis
own, -s, -ing, -ed, -er/s əun, -z, -iŋ, -d,
ə-*/z
ownership 'əunəʃip
Owsley 'auzli
Owyhe əu'waihi:
ox, -en ɔks, -ən
oxalate, -s 'ɔksəleit [-lit], -s
oxalic ɔk'sælik
oxalis 'ɔksəlis
Oxbrow 'ɔksbrau
oxen (plur. of ox) 'ɔksən
Oxen|den, -ford 'ɔksn|dən, -fəd [-fɔ:d]
Oxenham 'ɔksŋəm [-snəm]
Oxenhope 'ɔksnhəup
ox-eye, -s, -d 'ɔksai ['ɔks-ai], -z, -d
Oxford, -shire 'ɔksfəd, -ʃiə* [-ʃə*]
ox-hide, -s 'ɔkshaid, -z
oxidat|e, -es, -ing, -ed 'ɔksideit, -s, -iŋ,
-id
oxidation ˌɔksi'deiʃən
oxide, -s 'ɔksaid, -z
oxidization [-isa-] ˌɔksidai'zeiʃən
oxidiz|e [-is|e], -es, -ing, -ed, -er/s;
-able 'ɔksidaiz, -iz, -iŋ, -d, -ə*/z; -əbl
Oxley 'ɔksli
oxlip, -s 'ɔkslip, -s
oxo 'ɔksəu
Oxon. 'ɔksɔn [-sən]
Oxonian, -s ɔk'səunjən [-nĭən], -z
Oxshott 'ɔkʃɔt
ox-tail, -s 'ɔks-teil, -s
ox-tongue, -s 'ɔks-tʌŋ, -z
Oxus 'ɔksəs
oxy-acetylene 'ɔksĭə'setili:n [-siæ's-]
oxychloride, -s 'ɔksi'klɔ:raid, -z
oxygen 'ɔksidʒən
oxygenat|e, -es, -ing, -ed ɔk'sidʒineit
['ɔksi-, -dʒən-], -s, -iŋ, -id
oxygenation ˌɔksidʒi'neiʃən [ɔkˌsidʒ-,
-dʒə'n-]
oxygenous ɔk'sidʒinəs [-dʒən-]
oxyhydrogen 'ɔksi'haidridʒən [-drədʒ-]
oxymel 'ɔksimel
oxymoron, -s ˌɔksi'mɔ:rɔn [-'mɔər-,
-rən], -z
oxytone (s. adj.), -s 'ɔksitəun, -z

oyer 'ɔiə*
oyes əu'jes
oyez əu'jes ['əujes, 'əujez]
oyster (O.), -s; -bed/s, -bar/s 'ɔistə*,
-z; -bed/z, -bɑ:*/z
oyster-catcher, -s 'ɔistə,kætʃə*, -z
oyster-fisher|y, -ies 'ɔistə,fiʃər|i, -iz
Oystermouth 'ɔistəmauθ

oyster-patt|y, -ies 'ɔistə'pæt|i, -iz
oyster-shell, -s 'ɔistəʃel, -z
oz., ozs. auns, 'aunsiz
Ozanne əu'zæn
ozokerit(e) əu'zəukərit [ɔ'z-, ə'z-]
ozone 'əuzəun [əu'zəun]
ozonic əu'zɔnik
ozoniferous ,əuzəu'nifərəs

P

P (*the letter*), -'s piː, -z
pa, -s pɑː, -z
pabulum 'pæbjuləm
pac|e (*s. v.*), -es, -ing, -ed, -er/s peis, -iz, -iŋ, -t, -ə*/z
pace (*prep.*) 'peisi
pace-maker, -s 'peis,meikə*, -z
Pachmann (*famous pianist*) 'pɑːkmən [-mɑːn]
pachyderm, -s 'pækidəːm, -z
pachydermat|a, -ous ,pæki'dəːmət|ə, -əs
pacific (P.), -ally pə'sifik, -əli
pacification, -s ,pæsifi'keiʃən, -z
pacificatory pə'sifikətəri [pæ's-, -keitəri, 'pæsifikeitəri]
pacificist, -s pə'sifisist, -s
pacifism 'pæsifizəm
pacifist, -s 'pæsifist, -s
paci|fy, -fies, -fying, -fied, -fier/s 'pæsi|fai, -faiz, -faiiŋ, -faid, -faiə*/z
pack, -s, -ing, -ed, -er/s pæk, -s, -iŋ, -t, -ə*/z
package, -s 'pækidʒ, -iz
pack-animal, -s 'pæk,æniməl, -z
Packard 'pækɑːd
Packer 'pækə*
packet, -s 'pækit, -s
packet-boat, -s 'pækitbəut, -s
packhorse, -s 'pækhɔːs, -iz
pack-ice 'pækais
packing-|case/s, -needle/s, -paper, -sheet/s 'pækiŋ|keis/iz, -,niːdl/z, -,peipə*, -ʃiːt/s
pack|man, -men 'pæk|mən, -mən
pack|-saddle/s, -thread 'pæk|,sædl/z, -θred
pact, -s pækt, -s
pad (*s. v.*), -s, -ding, -ded pæd, -z, -iŋ, -id
Padanaram ,peidən'ɛəræm [-dæn-, -rəm, *rarely* ,pæd-, -'ær-, -'ɑːr-]
Paddington 'pædiŋtən
padd|le (*s. v.*), -les, -ling, -led, -ler/s 'pæd|l, -lz, -liŋ [-liŋ], -ld, -lə*/z [-lə*/z]
paddle-board, -s 'pædlbɔːd [-bɔəd], -z
paddle-box, -es 'pædlbɒks, -iz
paddle-wheel, -s 'pædlwiːl [-hwiːl], -z
paddock (P.), -s 'pædək, -s
padd|y (P.), -ies 'pæd|i, -iz

Padella pə'delə
Paderewski (*famous pianist*) ,pædə'revski [-'refski]
padlock (*s. v.*), -s, -ing, -ed 'pædlɒk, -s, -iŋ, -t
Padraic Colum 'pɑːdrik'kɒləm
padre, -s 'pɑːdri, -z
padrone, -s pə'drəuni [pæ'd-], -z
Padstow 'pædstəu
Padua, -n/s 'pædjŭə ['pɑːdŭə], -n/z
paean, -s 'piːən, -z
paediatri- *see* pediatri-
paeon, -s 'piːən, -z
paeonic piː'ɒnik
paeony = peony
Paflagonia, -n/s ,pæflə'gəunjə [-nĭə], -n/z
pagan (*s. adj.*), -s 'peigən, -z
Pagani pə'gɑːni
Paganini ,pægə'niːni(ː)
paganism 'peigənizəm [-gnizəm]
paganiz|e [-is|e], -es, -ing, -ed 'peigənaiz, -iz, -iŋ, -d
pag|e (*s. v.*) (P.), -es, -ing, -ed peidʒ, -iz, -iŋ, -d
pageant, -s 'pædʒənt, -s
pageantry 'pædʒəntri
Paget 'pædʒit
paginal 'pædʒinl ['peidʒ-]
paginat|e, -es, -ing, -ed 'pædʒineit ['peidʒ-], -s, -iŋ, -id
pagination, -s ,pædʒi'neiʃən [,peidʒ-], -z
paging (*s.*) 'peidʒiŋ
Pagliacci ,pæli'ɑːtʃi [-'ætʃi]
pagoda, -s pə'gəudə, -z
pah pɑː [pɑːh, pʌh, phɑː, pɸː]
Pahang pə'hʌŋ [-'hæŋ]
Note.—Usually pronounced pə'hʌŋ *in Malaya.*
paid (*from* pay) peid
Paignton 'peintən
pail, -s; -ful/s peil, -z; -ful/z
paillasse, -s 'pæliæs ['pæljæs, ,pæli'æs, pæl'jæs], -iz
paillette, -s pæl'jet [,pæli'et] (pajɛt), -s
pain (*s. v.*), -s, -ing, -ed pein, -z, -iŋ, -d
Pain(e) pein
pain|ful, -fully, -fulness 'pein|ful, -fuli [-fəli], -fulnis

painless, -ly, -ness 'peinlis, -li, -nis
painstak|er/s, -ing 'peinz,teik|ə*/z, -iŋ
Painswick 'peinzwik
paint (s. v.), -s, -ing/s, -ed, -er/s;
-able peint, -s, -iŋ/z, -id, -ə*/z; -əbl
paint-|box/es, -brush/es 'peint|bɔks/iz,
-brʌʃ/iz
Painter 'peintə*
paint|y, -ier, -iest 'peint|i, -ïə*, -iist
pair (s. v.), -s, -ing, -ed pɛə*, -z, -riŋ,
-d
pair-horse 'pɛəhɔ:s
pairing-time, -s 'pɛəriŋ-taim, -z
Paisley 'peizli
pajamas pə'dʒɑːməz
Pakeman 'peikmən
Pakenham 'pæknəm [-kənəm]
Pakistan ,pɑːkis'tɑːn [-'tæn, '--'-]
Pakistani, -s ,pɑːkis'tɑːni, -z
pal, -s pæl, -z
palace, -s 'pælis [-ləs], -iz
paladin, -s 'pælədin, -z
palaeobotany 'pæliəu'bɔtəni ['peil-, -tni]
palaeograph|er/s, -y ,pæli'ɔgrəf|ə*/z
[,peil-], -i
palaeographic ,pæliəu'græfik [,peil-,
-lïə'g-]
palaeolithic ,pæliəu'liθik [,peil-, -lïə'l-]
palaeontological 'pæliɔntə'lɔdʒikəl
[,pæl-, 'peil-, ,peil-]
palaeontolog|ist/s, -y ,pæliɔn'tɔlədʒ|-
ist/s [,peil-], -i
palaeotype 'pæliəutaip [-lïət-]
palaeozoic ,pæliəu'zəuik [,peil-]
Palairet 'pælərit [-ret]
Palamedes ,pælə'miːdiːz
Palamon 'pæləmən [-mɔn]
palanquin [-nkeen], -s ,pælən'kiːn
[-əŋ'k-], -z
palatab|le, -ly, -leness 'pælətəb|l [-lit-],
-li, -lnis
palatal (s. adj.), -s 'pælətl [pə'leitl], -z
palatalization [-isa-], -s 'pælətəlai-
'zeiʃən [pə,læt-, pə,leit-, -tḷai'z-,
-təli'z-, -tḷi'z-], -z
palataliz|e [-is|e], -es, -ing, -ed 'pælə-
təlaiz [pə'læt-, pə'leit-, -tḷaiz], -iz, -iŋ,
-d
palate, -s 'pælit [-lət], -s
palatial pə'leiʃəl [-ʃjəl, -ʃïəl]
palatinate (P.), -s pə'lætinit [-tṇit], -s
palatine (P.) 'pælətain
palatogram, -s 'pælətəugræm [pə'læt-],
-z
palatography ,pælə'tɔgrəfi
palav|er (s. v.), -ers, -ering, -ered,
-erer/s pə'lɑːv|ə*, -əz, -ərïŋ, -əd,
-ərə*/z

pal|e (s. adj. v.), -er, -est, -ely, -eness;
-es, -ing, -ed peil, -ə*, -ist, -li, -nis;
-z, -iŋ, -d
pale-face, -s 'peil-feis, -iz
paleo- see palaeo-
Palermo pə'lɛːməu [-'lɛəm-] (pa'lɛrmo)
Palestine 'pælistain [-ləs-, -les-]
Palestinian, -s ,pæles'tinïən [-lis-, -ləs-,
-njən], -z
Palestrina ,pæles'triːnə [-lis-, -ləs-]
paletot, -s 'pæltəu, -z
palette, -s; -knife, -knives 'pælit [-let],
-s; -naif, -naivz
Paley 'peili
Palfery 'pɔːlfəri ['pɔl-]
palfrey (P.), -s 'pɔːlfri ['pɔl-], -z
Palgrave 'pɔːlgreiv, 'pæl-
Pali 'pɑːli
palimpsest, -s 'pælimpsest, -s
Palin 'peilin
palindrome, -s 'pælindrəum, -z
paling (s.), -s 'peiliŋ, -z
palingenesis ,pælin'dʒenisis
palinode, -s 'pælinəud, -z
palisad|e (s. v.), -es, -ing, -ed ,pæli'seid,
-z, -iŋ, -id
palish 'peiliʃ
Palk pɔːlk [pɔlk]
pall (s. v.), -s, -ing, -ed pɔːl, -z, -iŋ, -d
palladi|an (P.), -um/s pə'leidj|ən
[-dï|ən], -əm/z
Pallas 'pæləs [-ləs]
pall-bearer, -s 'pɔːl,bɛərə*, -z
pallet, -s 'pælit, -s
palliasse, -s 'pæliæs ['pæljæs, ,pæli'æs,
pæl'jæs], -iz
palliat|e, -es, -ing, -ed 'pælieit, -s, -iŋ,
-id
palliation ,pæli'eiʃən
palliative (s. adj.), -s 'pælïətiv [-ljət-], -z
pallid, -est, -ly, -ness 'pælid, -ist, -li, -nis
Palliser 'pælisə*
pallium, -s 'pæliəm, -z
Pall Mall 'pæl'mæl ['pel'mel, also
'--, -'- according to sentence-stress]
Note.—The pronunciation with e is
generally employed by members of
West End clubs. With other Londoners the pronunciation with æ
is common.
pallor 'pælə*
palm (s. v.), -s, -ing, -ed pɑːm, -z, -iŋ, -d
palm|a (P.), -ar 'pɑːlm|ə, -ə*
palmaceous pæl'meiʃəs [-ʃjəs, -ʃïəs]
palmate 'pælmit [-meit]
palmer (P.), -s 'pɑːmə*, -z
Palmerston 'pɑːməstən
palmhou|se, -ses 'pɑːmhau|s, -ziz

palmist, -s 'pɑːmist, -s
palmistry 'pɑːmistri
palmitine, -s 'pælmitiːn [ˌpælmi't-], -z
palm-oil 'pɑːmɔil ['pɑːm'ɔil]
Palm Sunday, -s 'pɑːm'sʌndi [-dei], -z
palm|y, -ier, -iest 'pɑːm|i, -ɪə* [-jə*],
   -iist [-jist]
palmyra (P.), -s pæl'maiərə, -z
Palomar 'pæləʊmɑː*
palpability ˌpælpə'biliti [-lət-]
palpab|le, -ly, -leness 'pælpəb|l, -li, -lnis
palpat|e, -es, -ing, -ed 'pælpeit, -s, -iŋ, -id
palpation pæl'peiʃən
palpitat|e, -es, -ing, -ed 'pælpiteit, -s,
   -iŋ, -id
palpitation, -s ˌpælpi'teiʃən, -z
palsgrave, -s 'pɔːlzgreiv, -z
Palsgrave 'pɔːlzgreiv, 'pælzgreiv
pals|y, -ies, -ied 'pɔːlz|i ['pɔl-], -iz, -id
palt|er, -ers, -ering, -ered, -erer/s
   'pɔːlt|ə* ['pɔl-], -əz, -əriŋ, -əd, -ərə*/z
paltr|y, -ier, -iest, -ily, -iness 'pɔːltr|i
   ['pɔl-], -ɪə*, -iist, -ili, -inis
pam (P.), -s pæm, -z
Pamela 'pæmilə [-məl-]
Pamir, -s pə'miə*, -z
Pampa (territory in South America), -s
   'pæmpə, -z
pampas (grass) 'pæmpəs
pamp|er, -ers, -ering, -ered, -erer/s
   'pæmp|ə*, -əz, -əriŋ, -əd, -ərə*/z
pamphlet, -s 'pæmflit, -s
pamphleteer, -s, -ing ˌpæmfli'tiə*, -z,
   -riŋ
Pamphylia, -n/s pæm'filiə [-ljə], -n/z
pan (P.), -s, -ning, -ned pæn, -z, -iŋ, -d
panacea, -s ˌpænə'siə [-'siːə], -z
panache, -s pə'næʃ [pæ'n-, -'nɑːʃ], -iz
panama (P.), -s ˌpænə'mɑː ['pænə'm-,
   also 'pænəm- when followed by a stress],
   -z
Panamanian, -s ˌpænə'meinjən [-nɪən],
   -z
pan-american 'pæn-ə'merikən
pan-anglican 'pæn'æŋglikən
pancake, -s 'pænkeik ['pæŋ-keik], -s
panchayat, -s pʌn'tʃaiət [pæn-, pən-,
   -'tʃɑːjət], -s
panchromatic 'pænkrəʊ'mætik ['pæŋ-k-]
Pancras 'pæŋkrəs
pancreas, -es 'pæŋkrɪəs, -iz
pancreatic ˌpæŋkri'ætik
panda, -s 'pændə, -z
Pandean pæn'diːən [-'diən]
pandect, -s 'pændekt, -s
pandemic (s. adj.), -s pæn'demik, -s
pandemonium, -s ˌpændi'məʊnjəm
   [-nɪəm], -z

pander (s. v.), -s, -ing, -ed 'pændə*, -z,
   -riŋ, -d
pandora (P.), -s pæn'dɔːrə, -z
pan|e (s. v.), -es, -ing, -ed pein, -z, -iŋ, -d
panegyric (s. adj.), -s, -al ˌpæni'dʒirik
   [-nə'dʒ-], -s, -əl
panegyrist, -s ˌpæni'dʒirist ['--ˌ--, '---ˌ-],
   -s
panegyriz|e [-is|e], -es, -ing, -ed
   'pænidʒiraiz, -iz, -iŋ, -d
pan|el, -els, -elling/s, -elled 'pæn|l, -lz,
   -liŋ/z [-əliŋ/z], -ld
panful, -s 'pæn-ful, -z
pang, -s pæŋ, -z
Pangbourne 'pæŋbɔːn [-buən, -bɔən,
   -bən]
pan-german 'pæn'dʒəːmən
pan-germanic 'pændʒəː'mænik[-dʒə'm-]
Pangloss 'pæŋglɒs
panic, -s, -ky; -monger/s, -stricken
   'pænik, -s, -i; -ˌmʌŋgə*/z, -ˌstrikən
pan-indian 'pæn'indjən [-diən]
Panini 'pɑːnini(ː) (Hind. pəŋyni)
panjandrum, -s pən'dʒændrəm [pæn-], -z
Pankhurst 'pæŋkhəːst
pannage 'pænidʒ
pannier, -s 'pænɪə* [-njə*], -z
pannikin, -s 'pænikin, -s
Pannill 'pænil
panopl|y, -ies, -ied 'pænəpl|i, -iz, -id
panoram, -s 'pænəræm, -z
panorama, -s ˌpænə'rɑːmə, -z
panoramic ˌpænə'ræmik [-'rɑːm-]
pan-pipe, -s 'pæn-paip, -s
pan-slavism 'pæn'slɑːvizəm [-'slæv-]
pans|y (s. v.), -ies, -ying, -ied 'pænz|i,
   -iz, -iiŋ, -id
pant (s. v.), -s, -ing/ly, -ed pænt, -s,
   -iŋ/li, -id
pantagraph, -s 'pæntəgrɑːf [-græf], -s
pantaloon, -s ˌpæntə'luːn, -z
pantechnicon, -s pæn'teknikən, -z
panthei|sm, -st/s 'pænθi(ː)i|zəm, -st/s
pantheistic, -al ˌpænθi(ː)'istik, -əl
pantheon (P.), -s 'pænθɪən [pæn'θi(ː)ən],
   -z
panther, -s 'pænθə*, -z
panties 'pæntiz
pantile, -s 'pæntail, -z
pantisocrac|y, -ies ˌpænti'sɒkrəs|i, -iz
pantograph, -s 'pæntəʊgrɑːf [-græf-], -s
pantographic, -al ˌpæntəʊ'græfik, -əl
pantomime, -s; -ist/s 'pæntəmaim, -z;
   -ist/s
pantomimic, -al, -ally ˌpæntəʊ'mimik,
   -əl, -əli
pantr|y, -ies 'pæntr|i, -iz
pants (s.) pænts

Panza 'pænzə
panzer, -s 'pæntsə* ['pænzə*], -z
pap, -s pæp, -s
papa, -s pə'pɑ:, -z
papacy|y, -ies 'peipəs|i, -iz
papal 'peipəl
papali|sm, -st/s 'peipəli|zəm [-pḷi-], -st/s
papalize|e [-is|e], -es, -ing, -ed 'peipəl-
aiz [-pḷaiz], -iz, -iŋ, -d
papaverous pə'peivərəs
papaw, -s pə'pɔ:, -z
papaya, -s pə'paiə, -z
pap|er (s. v.), -ers, -ering, -ered, -erer/s
'peip|ə*, -əz, -əriŋ, -əd, -ərə*/z
paper-back, -s 'peipəbæk, -s
paper-case, -s 'peipəkeis, -iz
paper-chase, -s 'peipə-tʃeis, -iz
paper-clip, -s 'peipə-klip, -s
paper-cutter, -s 'peipəˌkʌtə*, -z
paper-file, -s 'peipəfail, -z
paper-hang|er/s, -ing 'peipəˌhæŋ|ə*/z,
-iŋ
paper-kni|fe, -ves 'peipənai|f, -vz
paper-maker, -s 'peipəˌmeikə*, -z
paper-mill, -s 'peipəmil, -z
paper-money 'peipəˌmʌni
paper-nautilus, -es 'peipə'nɔ:tiləs, -iz
paper-office, -s 'peipərˌɔfis [-pəˌɔf-], -iz
paper-weight, -s 'peipəweit, -s
Paphlagonia, -n/s ˌpæflə'gəunjə [-niə],
-n/z
Paphos (in Cyprus) (ancient city) 'peifɔs,
(modern town) 'pæfɔs
papier-mâché 'pæpjei'mɑ:ʃei [-piei-,
-'mæʃei] (papjemaʃe)
papill|a, -ae, -ar, -ary pə'pil|ə, -i:, -ə*,
-əri
papist, -s 'peipist, -s
papistic, -al, -ally pə'pistik [pei'p-],
-əl, -əli
papistry 'peipistri
papoose, -s pə'pu:s, -iz
pappus (P.), -es 'pæpəs, -iz
Papua, -n/s 'pæpjüə ['pɑ:-, -puə], -n/z
papyr|us, -i, -uses pə'paiər|əs, -ai, -əsiz
Papyrus (as name of a horse) 'pæpirəs
par (P.) pɑ:*
para (P.), -s 'pɑ:rə, -z
parabas|is, -es pə'ræbəs|is, -i:z
parable, -s 'pærəbl, -z
parabola, -s pə'ræbələ, -z
parabolic, -al, -ally ˌpærə'bɔlik, -əl, -əli
paraboloid, -s pə'ræbəlɔid, -z
Paracelsus ˌpærə'selsəs
parachut|e (s. v.), -es, -ing, -ed, -er/s
'pærəʃu:t ['--'-, ˌ--'-], -s, -iŋ, -id, -ə*/z
parachutist, -s 'pærəʃu:tist ['--'--, ˌ--'--],
-s

Paraclete 'pærəkli:t
parad|e (s. v.), -es, -ing, -ed pə'reid, -z,
-iŋ, -id
parade-ground, -s pə'reidgraund, -z
paradigm, -s 'pærədaim, -z
paradigmatic, -al, -ally ˌpærədig-
'mætik, -əl, -əli
paradise (P.), -s 'pærədais, -iz
paradisiac ˌpærə'disiæk [-'dizi-]
paradisiacal ˌpærədi'saiəkəl [-di'zai-]
paradisic, -al ˌpærə'dizik, -əl
parados, -es 'pærədɔs, -iz
paradox, -es 'pærədɔks, -iz
paradoxic|al, -ally, -alness ˌpærə'dɔksi-
k|əl, -əli, -əlnis
paraffin 'pærəfin [-fi:n, ˌ--'-]
paraffine 'pærəfi:n
paragoge, -s ˌpærə'gəudʒi, -z
paragogic ˌpærə'gɔdʒik
paragon, -s 'pærəgən, -z
paragraph (s. v.), -s, -ing, -ed 'pærə-
grɑ:f [-græf], -s, -iŋ, -t
Paraguay 'pærəgwai [-gwei, ˌpærə'gwai]
Paraguayan ˌpærə'gwaiən [-'gweiən]
parakeet, -s 'pærəki:t [ˌ--'-], -s
paraldehyde pə'rældihaid [-dəh-]
paralexia ˌpærə'leksiə [-sjə]
parallax, -es 'pærəlæks [-rḷæks], -iz
parallel (s. v.), -s, -ing, -ed; -ism
'pærəlel [-rḷel, -rələl, -rḷəl], -z, -iŋ, -d;
-izəm
parallelepiped, -s ˌpærələ'lepiped [-rḷe'l-
-rələ'l-, -rḷə'l-, 'pærəˌlelə'paiped,
'pærḷˌelə'paip-], -z
parallelogram, -s ˌpærə'leləugræm
[-rḷ'el-], -z
paralysant, -s 'pærəlaizənt [-rḷai-,
pə'rælizənt], -s
paralys|e, -es, -ing, -ed 'pærəlaiz
[-rḷaiz], -iz, -iŋ, -d
paralys|is, -es pə'rælis|is [-ləs-], -i:z
paralytic (s. adj.), -s ˌpærə'litik [-rḷ'it-],
-s
parameter, -s pə'ræmitə*, -z
paramount, -ly 'pærəmaunt, -li
paramour, -s 'pærəmuə* [-mɔə*, -mɔ:*],
-z
parapet, -s, -ed 'pærəpit [-pet], -s, -id
paraphernalia ˌpærəfə'neiljə [-liə]
paraphras|e (s. v.), -es, -ing, -ed 'pærə-
freiz, -iz, -iŋ, -d
paraphrastic, -ally ˌpærə'fræstik, -əli
parapleg|ia, -ic ˌpærə'pli:dʒ|ə, -ik
parapsychologic, -al, -ally 'pærəˌsaikə-
'lɔdʒik ['pærəˌpsai-], -əl, -əli
parapsycholog|ist/s, -y pærəsai'kɔlədʒ|-
ist/s ['pærəpsai-], -i
parasang, -s 'pærəsæŋ, -z

parasite, -s 'pærəsait, -s
parasitic, -al, -ally, -alness ˌpærə'sitik,
  -əl, -əli, -əlnis
parasol, -s 'pærəsɔl [ˌ--'-], -z
parataxis ˌpærə'tæksis
paratroop, -s, -er/s 'pærətruːp, -s, -ə*/z
paratyphoid 'pærə'taifɔid ['--ˌ--]
paravane, -s 'pærəvein, -z
parboil, -s, -ing, -ed 'paːbɔil, -z, -iŋ, -d
parc|el (s. v. adv.), -els, -elling, -elled
  'paːs|l, -lz, -ḷiŋ [-əliŋ], -ld
parch, -es, -ing, -ed, -edness paːtʃ, -iz,
  -iŋ, -t, -idnis [-tnis]
parchment (P.), -s 'paːtʃmənt, -s
pard, -s paːd, -z
Pardoe 'paːdəu
pard|on (s. v.), -ons, -oning, -oned,
  -oner/s 'paːd|n, -nz, -ṇiŋ [-niŋ],
  -nd, -ṇə*/z [-nə*/z]
pardonab|le, -ly, -leness 'paːdṇəb|l
  [-dnə-], -li, -lnis
par|e, -es, -ing, -ed pɛə*, -z, -riŋ, -d
paregoric ˌpærə'gɔrik [-ri'g-]
parent, -s; -age 'pɛərənt, -s; -idʒ
parent|al, -ally pə'rent|l, -əli
parenthes|is, -es pə'renθis|is [-θəs-], -iːz
parenthetic, -al, -ally ˌpærən'θetik,
  -əl, -əli
parenthood 'pɛərənthud
parentless 'pɛərəntlis
parerg|on, -a pæ'rəːg|ɔn, -ə
par excellence paːr'eksəlãːns [-sel-,
  -lɔ̃ːns, -laːns, -lɔːns] (parɛksəlãːs)
parget (s. v.), -s, -ing, -ed 'paːdʒit, -s,
  -iŋ, -id
Pargiter 'paːdʒitə*
parhe|lion, -lia paː'hiː|ljən [-ljɔn, -lïən,
  -liɔn], -ljə [-lïə]
pariah, -s 'pærïə, -z
Parian, -s 'pɛərïən, -z
parietal pə'raiitl
paring (s.), -s 'pɛəriŋ, -z
Paris (French capital, Trojan prince)
  'pæris
parish (P.), -es 'pæriʃ, -iz
parishioner, -s pə'riʃənə* [-ʃṇ*, -ʃnə*],
  -z
Parisian, -s pə'rizjən [-zïən, -ʒjən,
  -ʒïən, -ʒən], -z
parisyllabic 'pærisi'læbik [ˌpær-]
parity 'pæriti
park (s. v.) (P.), -s, -ing, -ed paːk, -s,
  -iŋ, -t
Parke, -r paːk, -ə*
Parkestone 'paːkstən
Parkinson 'paːkinsn
Parkstone 'paːkstən
parlance 'paːləns

parley (s. v.) (P.), -s, -ing, -ed 'paːli,
  -z, -iŋ, -d
parliament, -s 'paːləmənt [-lim-, -ljə-],
  -s
parliamentarian, -s ˌpaːləmen'tɛərïən
  [-lim-, -ljə-, -mən-], -z
parliamentary ˌpaːlə'mentəri [-li'm-,
  -ljə-]
parlour, -s 'paːlə*, -z
parlour-car, -s 'paːlə-kaː:*, -z
parlour-maid, -s 'paːləmeid, -z
parlous, -ly 'paːləs, -li
Parma 'paːmə
Parmenter 'paːmintə*
Parmesan ˌpaːmi'zæn ['--- when attribu-
  tive]
Parminter 'paːmintə*
Parmiter 'paːmitə*
Parnassian paː'næsïən [-sjən]
Parnassus paː'næsəs
Parnell paː'nel, 'paːnl ['paːnəl]
parnellism 'paːnelizəm [-nəl-]
parnellite, -s 'paːnelait [-nəl-], -s
parochial, -ly; -ism pə'rəukjəl [-kïəl],
  -i; -izəm
parodist, -s 'pærədist, -s
parod|y (s. v.), -ies, -ying, -ied 'pærəd|i,
  -iz, -iiŋ, -id
parole pə'rəul
Parolles (Shakespearian character)
  pə'rɔliz [-lis, -liːz, -les, -lez]
Paros 'pɛərɔs
parotid, -s pə'rɔtid, -z
paroxysm, -s 'pærəksizəm, -z
paroxysmal ˌpærək'sizməl [-ml]
paroxytone, -s pə'rɔksitəun [pæ'r-], -z
parozone 'pærəzəun
parquet, -s 'paːkei [-ki], -z ['paːkit, -s]
parr (P.) paː:*
Parratt 'pærət
parricidal ˌpæri'saidl
parricide, -s 'pærisaid, -z
Parrish 'pæriʃ
parrot (P.), -s 'pærət, -s
parr|y (s. v.) (P.), -ies, -ying, -ied
  'pær|i, -iz, -iiŋ, -id
pars|e, -es, -ing, -ed paːz, -iz, -iŋ, -d
Parsee, -s paː'siː: ['paː'siː:], -z
Parsifal 'paːsifəl [-faː:l, -fæl]
parsimonious, -ly, -ness ˌpaːsi'məunjəs
  [-nïəs], -li, -nis
parsimony 'paːsiməni
parsley 'paːsli
parsnip, -s 'paːsnip, -z
parson, -s 'paːsn, -z
parsonage, -s 'paːsṇidʒ [-sni-], -iz
Parsons 'paːsnz
part (s. v.), -s, -ing, -ed paːt, -s, -iŋ, -id

partake|e, -es, -ing, partook, partak|en,
-er/s pɑː'teik, -s, -iŋ, pɑː'tuk,
pɑː'teik|ən, -ə*/z
parterre, -s pɑː'tɛə* (partɛːr), -z
Parthenia pɑː'θiːnjə [-nɪə]
parthenogenesis   'pɑːθinəu'dʒenisis
[,pɑː-θ-]
Parthenon, -s 'pɑːθinən [-θən-, -θn̩-], -z
Parthenope pɑː'θenəpi
Parthia, -n/s 'pɑːθjə [-θɪə], -n/z
parti|al, -ally 'pɑːʃ|əl, -əli
partiality ,pɑːʃi'æliti
participant, -s pɑː'tisipənt, -s
participat|e, -es, -ing, -ed , -or/s
pɑː'tisipeit, -s, -iŋ, -id, -ə*/z
participation, -s pɑː,tisi'peiʃən [,pɑː-tis-],
-z
participial, -ly ,pɑː'tisipɪəl [-pjəl], -i
participle, -s 'pɑːtisipl [-ts-], -z
particle, -s 'pɑːtikl, -z
particoloured 'pɑːti,kʌləd
particular (s. adj.), -s, -ly pə'tikjulə*
[-kjəl-], -z, -li
particularit|y, -ies pə,tikju'lærit|i, -iz
particulariz|e [-is|e], -es, -ing, -ed
pə'tikjuləraiz [-kjəl-], -iz, -iŋ, -d
parting (s.), -s 'pɑːtiŋ, -z
Partington 'pɑːtiŋtən
partisan, -s; -ship/s ,pɑːti'zæn ['--'-],
-z; -ʃip/s
partite 'pɑːtait
partiti|on (s. v.), -ons, -oning, -oned
pɑː'tiʃ|ən [pə't-], -ənz, -n̩iŋ [-əniŋ],
-ənd
partitive, -ly 'pɑːtitiv, -li
partly 'pɑːtli
partner (s. v.), -s, -ing, -ed; -ship/s
'pɑːtnə*, -z, -riŋ, -d; -ʃip/s
Parton 'pɑːtn
partook (from partake) pɑː'tuk
partridge (P.), -s 'pɑːtridʒ, -iz
part-singing 'pɑːt,siŋiŋ
part-song, -s 'pɑːt-sɒŋ, -z
parturition, -s ,pɑːtjuə'riʃən [-tjə'r-], -z
part|y, -ies 'pɑːt|i, -iz
party|-man, -men 'pɑːti|mæn, -men
party-spirit 'pɑːti'spirit
party-wall, -s 'pɑːti'wɔːl, -z
parvenu, -s 'pɑːvənjuː (parvəny), -z
pas (sing.) pɑː, (plur.) -z
Pasadena ,pæsə'diːnə
paschal 'pɑːskəl ['pæs-]
pasha (P.), -s 'pɑːʃə [rarely 'pæʃə,
pə'ʃɑː], -z
paspalum 'pæspələm
pasquinade, -s ,pæskwi'neid, -z
pass (s. v.), -es, -ing, -ed, -er/s pɑːs, -iz,
-iŋ, -t, -ə*/z

passab|le, -ly, -leness 'pɑːsəb|l, -li, -lnis
passacaglia, -s ,pæsə'kɑːljə [-lɪə], -z
passag|e (s. v.), -es, -ing, -ed 'pæsidʒ,
-iz, -iŋ, -d
passant (in heraldry) 'pæsənt, (in chess)
'pæsɑ̃ː[ŋ ['pɑːs-, -sɔ̃ːŋ, -sɑːŋ, -sɔːŋ,
-sɒŋ] (pɑsɑ̃)
pass-book, -s 'pɑːsbuk, -s
Passe (surname) pæs
passé(e) 'pɑːsei ['pæs-] (pɑse)
passenger, -s 'pæsindʒə*, -z
passe-partout, -s 'pæspɑːtuː ['pɑːs-,
-pətuː] (pɑspartu)
passer (one who passes), -s 'pɑːsə*, -z
passer (sparrow), -es 'pæsə*, -riːz
passer-by, passers-by 'pɑːsə'bai, 'pɑːsəz-
'bai
passerine 'pæsərain
Passfield 'pæsfiːld ['pɑːs-]
passibility ,pæsi'biliti [-lət-]
passible 'pæsibl
passim 'pæsim
passing-note, -s 'pɑːsiŋnəut, -s
passion (P.), -s 'pæʃən, -z
passionate, -ly, -ness 'pæʃənit [-ʃn̩it,
-ʃnit], -li, -nis
passion-flower, -s 'pæʃən,flauə*, -z
passive, -ly, -ness 'pæsiv, -li, -nis
passivity pæ'siviti [pə's-]
pass-key, -s 'pɑːs-kiː, -z
pass|man, -men 'pɑːs-|mæn [-mən],
-men [-mən]
Passmore 'pɑːs-mɔː* ['pæs-, -mɔə*]
Passover, -s 'pɑːs,əuvə*, -z
passport, -s 'pɑːs-pɔːt, -s
pass-word, -s 'pɑːs-wəːd, -z
past pɑːst
past|e (s. v.), -es, -ing, -ed peist, -s, -iŋ,
-id
paste-board 'peistbɔːd [-bɔəd]
pastel (coloured crayon, drawing made
with this), -s pæs'tel ['pæstel, -təl,
-tl], -z
pastel (attributive, as in p. shade) 'pæstl
[-təl, -tel, rarely pæs'tel]
pastelist, -s 'pæstəlist, -s
pastellist, -s pæs'telist ['pæstəlist], -s
pastern, -s 'pæstəːn, -z
Pasteur pæs'təː* [pɑːs-] (pɑstœːr)
pasteurization [-isa-] ,pæstərai'zeiʃən
[,pɑːs-, -stjə-, -stʃə-]
pasteuriz|e [-is|e], -es, -ing, -ed 'pæs-
təraiz ['pɑːs-, -stjə-, -stʃə-], -iz, -iŋ, -d
pastiche, -s pæs'tiːʃ ['pæstiːʃ], -iz
pastille, -s 'pæstəl [-stil, -stiːl, pæs'tiːl]
pastime, -s 'pɑːs-taim ['pæs-], -z
past-master, -s 'pɑːst'mɑːstə* ['-,--], -z
Paston 'pæstən

pastor, -s 'pɑ:stə*, -z
pastoral (s. adj.), -s 'pɑ:stərəl ['pæs-], -z
pastorale, -s ,pæstə'rɑ:li, -z
pastoralism 'pɑ:stərəlizəm ['pæs-]
pastorate, -s 'pɑ:stərit, -s
pastr|y, -ies 'peistr|i, -iz
pastrycook, -s 'peistrikuk, -s
pasturage 'pɑ:stjuridʒ [-tjər-, -tʃər-]
pastur|e (s. v.), -es, -ing, -ed 'pɑ:stʃə*
  [-tjuə*, -tjə*], -z, -riŋ [-tjuriŋ], -d
past|y (s.), -ies 'pæst|i [for the Cornish
  kind also 'pɑ:s-], -iz
past|y (adj.), -ier, -iest, -ily, -iness
  'peist|i, -iə* [-iə*], -iist [-jist], -ili, -inis
pat (s. v. adv.) (P.), -s, -ting, -ted pæt,
  -s, -iŋ, -id
pat-a-cake, -s 'pætəkeik, -s
Patagonia, -n/s ,pætə'gəunjə [-niə],
  -n/z
Patanjali pə'tʌndʒəli(:) [-'tæn-] (Hind.
Patara 'pætərə   [pətənɟəli)
patch, -es, -ing, -ed ; -able, -work pætʃ,
  -iz, -iŋ, -t; -əbl, -wə:k
patchouli 'pætʃuli(:)
patch|y, -ier, -iest, -ily, -iness 'pætʃ|i,
  -iə*, -iist, -ili, -inis
pate, -s peit, -s
pâté 'pɑ:tei ['pæ-, -ti] (pate)
Pateley 'peitli
patell|a, -as, -ae, -ar pə'tel|ə, -əz, -i:, -ə*
paten, -s 'pætən, -z
patent (s. adj. v.), -s, -ing, -ed ; -able
  'peitənt ['pæt-], -s, -iŋ, -id; -əbl
  Note.—'pætənt seems the more usual
  in letters patent and Patent Office.
  In patent leather, boots, etc.,
  'peitənt is practically universal;
  'peitənt seems the more usual, though
  by no means universal, in all other
  connexions.
patentee, -s ,peitən'ti: [,pæt-], -z
patent leather   'peitənt'leðə*   [also
  'peitənt,l- when attributive]
pater (P.), -s 'peitə*, -z
paterfamilias, -es 'peitəfə'miliæs [-ljæs,
  -liəs, -ljəs], -iz
patern|al, -ally pə'tə:n|l, -əli
paternity pə'tə:niti
Paternoster (Lord's Prayer), -s 'pætə-
  'nɔstə*, -z
Paternoster (Row) 'pætə,nɔstə*
Paterson 'pætəsn
Pateshall 'pætəʃəl [-tiʃ-]
Patey 'peiti
pa|th, -ths pɑ:|θ, -ðz
Pathan, -s pə'tɑ:n (Hind. pəthan), -z
pathetic, -ally, -alness pə'θetik, -əli,
  -əlnis

pathfinder (P.), -s 'pɑ:θ,faində*, -z
pathless 'pɑ:θlis
pathologic, -al, -ally ,pæθə'lɔdʒik, -əl,
  -əli
patholog|ist/s, -y pə'θɔlədʒ|ist/s [pæ'θ-],
  -i
pathos 'peiθɔs
pathway, -s 'pɑ:θ-wei, -z
Patiala ,pɑti'ɑ:lə [,pæt-, '--,--] (Hind.
  pətiala)
patience (P.), -s 'peiʃəns, -iz
patient (s. adj.), -s, -ly 'peiʃənt, -s, -li
patina 'pætinə
patio, -s 'pætiəu ['pɑ:tiəu, 'peiʃiəu], -z
pâtisserie, -s pə'ti:səri [pæ-], -z (pɑtisri)
Pat|man, -mos 'pæt|mən, -mɔs
Patmore 'pætmɔ:* [-mɔə*]
Patna 'pætnə (Hind. pətna)
patois (sing.) 'pætwɑ: [-wɔ:] (patwa),
  (plur.) -z
Paton 'peitn
Patras pə'træs
patriarch, -s 'peitriɑ:k
patriarchal ,peitri'ɑ:kəl
patriarchate, -s 'peitriɑ:kit [-keit], -s
Patricia pə'triʃə [-ʃiə, -ʃjə]
patrician, -s pə'triʃən, -z
patriciate pə'triʃiit [-ʃjit, -ʃieit, -ʃjeit]
Patrick 'pætrik
patrimonial, -ly ,pætri'məunjəl [-niəl],
  -i
patrimon|y, -ies 'pætrimən|i, -iz
patriot, -s 'peitriət ['pæt-], -s
patriotic, -ally ,pætri'ɔtik [,peit-], -əli
patriotism 'pætriətizəm ['peit-]
patristic pə'tristik
Patroclus pə'trɔkləs
patrol (s. v.), -s, -ling, -led ; -man, -men
  pə'trəul, -z, -iŋ, -d ; -mæn, -men
patron, -s 'peitrən ['pæt-], -z
patronage 'pætrənidʒ [-trŋidʒ, rarely
  'peit-]
patronal pə'trəunl [pæ't-]
patroness, -s 'peitrənis ['pæt-, -nes,
  -trŋ-], -iz
patroniz|e [-is|e], -es, -ing/ly, -ed, -er/s
  'pætrənaiz [-trŋaiz], -iz, -iŋ/li, -d,
  -ə*/z
patronymic (s. adj.), -s ,pætrə'nimik
  [-trŋ'im-], -s
patroon, -s pə'tru:n, -z
patten, -s 'pætn, -z
patter (s. v.), -s, -ing, -ed, -er/s 'pætə*,
  -z, -riŋ, -d, -rə*/z
Patterdale 'pætədeil
pattern, -s 'pætən [-tn], -z
Patterson 'pætəsn
patter-song, -s 'pætəsɔŋ, -z

Patteson 'pætisn
Pattison 'pætisn
Pattreiouex 'pætriəu
patt|y, -ies 'pæt|i, -z
paucity 'pɔːsiti
Paul, -'s pɔːl, -z
Pauline (scholar of St. Paul's school), -s
'pɔːlain, -z
Pauline (fem. name) pɔː'liːn, 'pɔːliːn
Pauline (adj.) (of St. Paul) 'pɔːlain
Paulinus pɔː'lainəs
Paulus 'pɔːləs
Pauncefote 'pɔːnsfut [-fət]
paunch, -es pɔːntʃ, -iz
pauper, -s 'pɔːpə*, -z
pauperism 'pɔːpərizəm
pauperization [-isa-] ˌpɔːpərai'zeiʃən
[-ri'z-]
pauperiz|e [-is|e], -es, -ing, -ed 'pɔːpər-
aiz, -iz, -iŋ, -d
Pausanias pɔː'seiniæs [-njæs, -njəs,
-niəs]
paus|e (s. v.), -es, -ing, -ed pɔːz, -iz, -iŋ,
-d
pavan(e), -s 'pævən [pə'væn], -z
pav|e, -es, -ing, -ed, -er/s peiv, -z, -iŋ,
-d, -ə*/z
pavé, -s 'pævei (pave), -z
pavement, -s 'peivmənt, -s
Pavia pə'viːə [pɑː'v-, -'viə] (pa'viːa)
pavilion (s. v.), -s, -ing, -ed pə'viljən
[-liən], -z, -iŋ, -d
paving-stone, -s 'peiviŋ-stəun, -z
paviour, -s 'peivjə* [-viə*], -s
Pavitt 'pævit
Pavlov 'pævlɔv [-lɔf] ('pavləf)
Pavlova 'pævləvə [pæv'ləuvə] ('pavləvə)
paw (s. v.), -s, -ing, -ed pɔː, -z, -iŋ, -d
pawk|y, -ier, -iest, -iness 'pɔːk|i, -iə*
[-jə*], -iist [-jist], -ili, -inis
pawl (s. v.), -s, -ing, -ed pɔːl, -z, -iŋ, -d
pawn (s. v.), -s, -ing, -ed, -er/s pɔːn, -z,
-iŋ, -d, -ə*/z
pawnbrok|er/s, -ing 'pɔːn,brəuk|ə*/z, -iŋ
pawnee, -s pɔː'ni: ['pɔː'ni:], -z
pawnshop, -s 'pɔːn-ʃɔp, -s
pawn-ticket, -s 'pɔːn,tikit, -s
pax (s. interj.), -es pæks, -iz
Paxton 'pækstən
pay (s. v.), -s, -ing, paid, payer/s,
payment/s pei, -z, -iŋ, peid, 'peiə*/z,
'peimənt/s
payable 'peiəbl
P.A.Y.E. 'pi:eiwai'i:
payee, -s pei'i:, -z
Payen-Payne 'pein'pein [pein'p-]
paymaster, -s 'pei,mɑːstə*, -z
paynim 'peinim

Paynter 'peintə*
pay-roll, -s 'peirəul, -z
Paysandu, -s ˌpeizən'dju:, -z
pay-sheet, -s 'pei-ʃiːt, -s
pea, -s pi:, -z
Peabody 'pi:ˌbɔdi
peace (P.), -s pi:s, -iz
peaceab|le, -ly, -leness 'pi:səb|l, -li, -lnis
peace|ful, -fully, -fulness 'pi:s|ful, -fuli
[-fəli], -fulnis
peacemaker, -s 'pi:s,meikə*, -z
peace-offering, -s 'pi:s,ɔfəriŋ, -z
Peacey 'pi:si
peach (s. v.), -es, -ing, -ed, -er/s pi:tʃ,
-iz, -iŋ, -t, -ə*/z
peach-colour, -ed 'pi:tʃ,kʌlə*, -d
Peachey 'pi:tʃi
pea-chick, -s 'pi:-tʃik, -s
peachy 'pi:tʃi
peacock (P.), -s 'pi:kɔk, -s
pea-fowl 'pi:-faul
pea-green 'pi:'gri:n ['pi:-gri:n, esp.
when attributive]
peahen, -s 'pi:'hen ['pi:-hen], -z
pea-jacket, -s 'pi:,dʒækit, -s
peak (s. v.) (P.), -s, -ing, -ed pi:k, -s, -iŋ,
-t
peal (s. v.), -s, -ing, -ed pi:l, -z, -iŋ, -d
Peall pi:l
pean (fur) pi:n
pean (=paean), -s 'pi:ən, -z
peanut, -s 'pi:-nʌt, -s
pear, -s pɛə*, -z
Pear (surname) piə*
Pearce piəs
Peard piəd
pearl (s. v.) (P.), -s, -ing, -ed; -barley,
-button/s pəːl, -z, -iŋ, -d; -'bɑːli,
-'bʌtn/z
pearl-diver, -s 'pəːl,daivə*, -z
pearl-fisher|y, -ies 'pəːl,fiʃər|i, -iz
pearlies 'pəːliz
pearly 'pəːli
pearmain 'pəːmein, 'pɛəmein
Pearman 'piəmən
Pears piəz, pɛəz
Note.—pɛəz in Pears' soap.
Pearsall 'piəsɔːl [-səl]
pear-shaped 'pɛə-ʃeipt
Pearson 'piəsn
Peart piət
Peary 'piəri
peasant, -s 'pezənt, -s
peasantry 'pezəntri
peas(e)cod, -s 'pi:zkɔd, -z
Peascod (road at Windsor) 'peskəd
pease (P.) pi:z
Peaseblossom 'pi:z,blɔsəm

pea-shooter, -s 'piː,ʃuːtə*, -z
pea-soup, -y 'piː'suːp, -i
peat; -bog/s piːt; -'bɔg/z
peat-moss 'piːt'mɔs ['--]
peat|y, -ier, -iest, -iness 'piːt|i, -ïə*
[-jə*], -iist [-jist], -inis
pebble, -s 'pebl, -z
pebbly 'peb|i [-bli]
pecan, -s pi'kæn, -z
peccability ,pekə'biliti [-lət-]
peccable 'pekəbl
peccadillo, -(e)s ,pekə'diləu, -z
peccant, -ly 'pekənt, -li
peccar|y, -ies 'pekər|i, -iz
peccavi   pe'kɑːviː: [old-fashioned
-'keivai]
Pechey 'piːtʃi
Pechili 'petʃili
peck (s. v.) (P.), -s, -ing, -ed, -er/s
pek, -s, -iŋ, -t, -ə*/z
Peckham 'pekəm
peckish, -ly, -ness 'pekiʃ, -li, -nis
Peckitt 'pekit
Pecksniff 'pek-snif
pectoral (s. adj.), -s 'pektərəl, -z
peculat|e, -es, -ing, -ed, -or/s 'pekju-
leit, -s, -iŋ, -id, -ə*/z
peculation, -s ,pekju'leiʃən, -z
peculiar (s. adj.), -s, -ly pi'kjuːljə*
[-lïə*], -z, -li
peculiarit|y, -ies pi,kjuːli'ærit|i, -iz
peculium, -s pi'kjuːljəm [pə'k-, -lïəm], -z
pecuniar|y, -ily pi'kjuːnjər|i [-nïə-], -ili
pedagogic, -al ,pedə'gɔdʒik [-'gɔgi-,
-'gəudʒi-], -əl
pedagogue, -s 'pedəgɔg, -z
pedagogy 'pedəgɔdʒi [-gɔgi, -gəudʒi]
ped|al (s. v.), -als, -alling, -alled 'ped|l,
-lz, -liŋ, -ld
pedal (adj.) (pertaining to the foot) 'pedl
['piːdl], (in geometry) 'pedl
pedant, -s 'pedənt, -s
pedantic, -al, -ally pi'dæntik [pe'd-], -əl,
-əli
pedantism 'pedəntizəm [-dn-, pi'dænt-,
pe'dænt-]
pedantr|y, -ies 'pedəntr|i, -iz
pedd|le, -les, -ling, -led 'ped|l, -lz, -liŋ
[-liŋ], -ld
pederast, -s, -y 'pedəræst ['piː-], -s, -i
pedestal, -s 'pedistl, -z
pedestrian (s. adj.), -s, -ism pi'destrïən
[pə'd-], -z, -izəm
pedestrianiz|e [-is|e], -es, -ing, -ed
pi'destrïənaiz [-iz], -iz, -iŋ, -d
pediatric, -s ,piːdi'ætrik, -s
pediatrician, -s ,piːdïə'triʃən, -z
pedicle, -s 'pedikl, -z

pedicure, -s 'pedikjuə* [-kjɔə*, -kjɔː:*],
-z
pedigree, -s, -d 'pedigriː:, -z, -d
pediment, -s 'pedimənt, -s
pedimental ,pedi'mentl
pedimented 'pedimentid [-mənt-]
pedlar, -s 'pedlə*, -z
pedometer, -s pi'dɔmitə* [pe'd-], -z
Pedro 'peidrəu ['ped-, 'piːd-]
Note.—The pronunciation 'piːdrəu
is generally used in Shakespeare's
'Much Ado.'
peduncle, -s pi'dʌŋkl, -z
Peeb|les,   -lesshire   'piːb|lz,   -lzʃïə*
[-lʒïə*, -lʃïə*, -ʃə*]
Peek piːk
peek|y, -ier, -iest 'piːk|i, -ïə*, -iist
peel (s. v.) (P.), -s, -ing/s, -ed piːl, -z,
-iŋ/z, -d
peeler, -s 'piːlə*, -z
peep (s. v.) (P.), -s, -ing, -ed, -er/s piːp,
-s, -iŋ, -t, -ə*/z
peep-bo 'piːp'bəu
peep-hole, -s 'piːp-həul, -z
peepshow, -s 'piːpʃəu, -z
peer (s. v.), -s, -ing, -ed pïə*, -z, -riŋ, -d
peerage, -s 'pïəridʒ, -iz
peeress, -es 'pïəris [-res], -iz
peerless (P.), -ly, -ness 'pïəlis, -li, -nis
peeved piːvd
peevish, -ly, -ness 'piːviʃ, -li, -nis
peewit, -s 'piːwit, -s
peg (s. v.) (P.), -s, -ging, -ged peg, -z,
-iŋ, -d
pegamoid 'pegəmɔid
Pegasus 'pegəsəs
Pegeen pe'giːn
Pegge peg
Peggotty 'pegəti
Peggy 'pegi
Pegr|am, -um 'piːgr|əm, -əm
peg-top, -s 'pegtɔp ['peg't-], -s
peignoir, -s 'peinwɑː* [-wɔː:*] (pɛɲwaːr),
-z
Peile piːl
Peiping pei'piŋ ['-'-]
pejorative 'piːdʒərətiv, pi'dʒɔrətiv [pə-]
Pek|in, -ing piː'k|in ['piː'k-], -iŋ
Pekinese ,piː'kiː'niːz ['piː:kiː'niːz]
Pekingese ,piː:kiŋ'iːz ['piː:kiŋ'iːz]
pekoe 'piːkəu
pelagic pe'lædʒik [pi'l-]
pelargonium, -s ,pelə'gəunjəm [-nïəm],
-z
Pelasgian, -s pe'læzgïən [pi'l-, -gjən], -z
pelasgic pe'læzgik [pi'l-, -zdʒik]
Peleg 'piːleg [rarely 'pel-]
pelerine, -s 'peləriːn, -z

Peleus 'pi:lju:s [-ljəs, -lïəs]
pelf pelf
Pelham 'peləm
Pelias 'pi:liæs [-lïəs, 'peliæs]
pelican, -s 'pelikən, -z
pelisse, -s pe'li:s [pi'l-], -iz
pellet, -s 'pelit, -s
Pelley 'peli
pellicle, -s 'pelikl, -z
Pellisier pə'lisiei [pe'l-, -sïə*, -sjə*]
pell-mell 'pel'mel
pellucid, -ly, -ness pe'lju:sid [pi'l-, -'lu:-], -li, -nis
Pelly 'peli
Pelman, -ism 'pelmən, -izəm
pelmet, -s 'pelmit, -s
Peloponnese 'peləpəni:s
Peloponnesian, -s ‚peləpə'ni:ʃən [-ʃjən, -ʃïən], -z
Peloponnesus ‚peləpə'ni:səs
Pelops 'pi:lɔps
pelt (s. v.), -s, -ing, -ed pelt, -s, -iŋ, -id
pelure pə'ljuə* [pi'l-]
pelv|is, -ises, -es, -ic 'pelv|is, -isiz, -i:z, -ik
Pemberton 'pembətən
Pembridge 'pembridʒ
Pembroke, -shire 'pembruk, -ʃïə* [-ʃə*]
Pemigewasset ‚pemigə'wɔsit
pemmican 'pemikən
pen (s. v.) (P.), -s, -ning, -ned pen, -z, -iŋ, -d
pen|al, -ally 'pi:n|l, -əli
penaliz|e [-is|e], -es, -ing, -ed 'pi:nəlaiz [-nḷaiz], -iz, -iŋ, -d
penalt|y, -ies 'penlt|i, -iz
penance, -s 'penəns, -iz
pen-and-ink 'penənd'iŋk
Penang pi'næŋ [pə'n-]
Penarth pe'nɑ:θ [pə'n-] (Welsh pen'arθ)
penates pe'nɑ:teis [pe'neiti:z, pi'n-, pə'n-]
Penberthy 'penbəθi, 'pen‚bə:θi, 'pen‚bə:ði
Note.—The shop in Oxford Street, London, is generally called 'penbəθi.
pence (plur. of penny) pens
penchant, -s 'pɑ̃:ŋʃɑ̃:ŋ ['pɔ̃:ŋʃɔ̃:ŋ, 'pɑ:ŋʃɑ:ŋ, 'pɔ:ŋʃɔ:ŋ, 'pɔŋʃɔŋ, 'pɑ:nʃɑ:ŋ, 'pɔ:nʃɔ:ŋ, 'pɔnʃɔŋ] (pɑ̃ʃɑ̃), -z
penc|il (s. v.), -ils, -illing, -illed 'pens|l, -lz, -ḷiŋ [-əliŋ], -ld
pencil-case, -s 'penslkeis, -iz
pendant, -s 'pendənt, -s
Pendeen pen'di:n
penden|cy, -t 'pendən|si, -t
Pendennis pen'denis

Pender 'pendə*
Pendine (in Wales) pen'dain (Welsh pen'dəin)
pending 'pendiŋ
Pendle|bury, -ton 'pendl|bəri, -tən
pendragon (P.), -s pen'drægən, -z
pendulous, -ly, -ness 'pendjuləs, -li, -nis
pendulum, -s 'pendjuləm [-djəl-], -z
Pendyce pen'dais
Penelope pi'neləpi [pə'n-]
penetrability ‚penitrə'biliti [-lət-]
penetrab|le, -ly, -leness 'penitrəb|l, -li, -lnis
penetralia ‚peni'treiljə [-lïə]
penetrat|e, -es, -ing/ly, -ed 'penitreit, -s, -iŋ/li, -id
penetration, -s ‚peni'treiʃən, -z
penetrative, -ly, -ness 'penitrətiv [-treit-], -li, -nis
Penfold 'penfould
penful, -s 'pen-ful, -z
Penge pendʒ
penguin, -s 'peŋgwin, -z
pen-holder, -s 'pen‚həuldə*, -z
penicillin ‚peni'silin [pe'nis-]
Penicuik 'penikuk
peninsul|a, -as, -ar pi'ninsjul|ə [pə'n-, pe'n-, -inʃu-], -əz, -ə*
penis, -es 'pi:nis, -iz
penitence 'penitəns
penitent (s. adj.), -s, -ly 'penitənt, -s, -li
penitenti|al, -ally ‚peni'tenʃ|əl, -əli
penitentiar|y, -ies ‚peni'tenʃər|i, -iz
penkni|fe, -ves 'pennai|f, -vz
Penmaenmaur ‚penmən'mauə* [-'mɔ:*, -'mɔə*] (Welsh penmaen'maur, -mən-)
pen|man, -men 'pen|mən, -mən
penmanship 'penmənʃip
Penn pen
pen-name, -s 'penneim, -z
pennant (P.), -s 'penənt, -s
Pennefather 'peni‚fɑ:ðə*, -‚feðə*
penniless 'penilis
Pennine, -s 'penain, -z
Pennington 'peniŋtən
pennon, -s 'penən, -z
Pennsylvania ‚pensil'veinjə [-sḷ-, -nïə]
penn|y (P.), -ies, pence 'pen|i, -iz, pens
penny-a-liner, -s 'peniə'lainə* [-njə-], -z
penny-royal 'peni'rɔiəl
pennyweight, -s 'peniweit, -s
pennyworth, -s 'penəθ ['peniwə(:)θ], -s
Penobscot pe'nɔbskɔt [pə'n-]
penological ‚pi:nə'lɔdʒikəl
penology pi:'nɔlədʒi
Penrhyn 'penrin (Welsh 'penhrin, 'pendrin)

Penrith (town in Cumberland) 'penriθ [pen'r-], (surname) 'penriθ

Penrose (surname) 'penrəuz, pen'r-, (place in Cornwall) pen'rəuz

Pensarn pen'sɑːn

penseroso ˌpensə'rəuzəu

Penshurst 'penzhəːst

pensi|on (s. v.) (monetary allowance etc.), -ons, -oning, -oned 'penʃ|ən, -ənz, -əniŋ [-ŋiŋ], -ənd

pension (s.) (boarding-house, board), -s 'pɑːŋsiɔ̃ː|ŋ ['pɔ̃ː|ŋ-, 'pɑːŋsiɔːŋ, 'pɔːŋ-siɔːŋ, 'pɑːns-, 'pɔːns-, 'pɔns-, -sjɔ̃ːŋ, -siɔːŋ] (pɑ̃sjɔ̃), -z

pensioner, -s 'penʃənə* [-ʃŋə*, -ʃnə*], -z

pensionnaire, -s ˌpɑːŋsiɔ̃'nɛə* [ˌpɔ̃ːŋs-, ˌpɑːns-, ˌpɔːns-, ˌpɔns-, -sjə-] (pɑ̃sjɔ-nɛːr), -z

pensive, -ly, -ness 'pensiv, -li, -nis

pent pent

pentad, -s 'pentæd, -z

pentagon (P.), -s 'pentəgən, -z

pentagon|al, -ally pen'tægən|l, -əli

pentagram, -s 'pentəgræm, -z

pentamerous pen'tæmərəs

pentameter, -s pen'tæmitə*, -z

Pentateuch 'pentətjuːk

pentatol 'pentətɔl

Pentecost, -s 'pentikɔst [rarely -kɔːst], -s

pentecostal ˌpenti'kɔstl [rarely -'kɔːs-]

Penthesilea ˌpenθesi'liː(ː)ə

penthou|se, -ses 'penthau|s, -ziz

Pentland, -s 'pentlənd, -z

Pentonville 'pentənvil

pentstemon, -s pent'stemən [-'stiːm-, 'pentstimən], -z

penult, -s pi'nʌlt [pe'n-, pə'n-], -s

penultimate (s. adj.), -s pi'nʌltimit [pe'n-, pə'n-], -s

penumbr|a, -as, -ae, -al pi'nʌmbr|ə [pe'n-, pə'n-], -əz, -iː, -əl

penurious, -ly, -ness pi'njuərïəs [pe'n-, pə'n-], -li, -nis

penury 'penjuri [-juəri]

pen-wiper, -s 'penˌwaipə*, -z

Penzance pen'zæns [pən-, locally pən'zɑːns]

peon, -s (Indian servant) pjuːn ['piːən], (in America) 'piːən, -z

peon|y, -ies 'piən|i, -iz

peop|le (s. v.), -les, -ling, -led 'piːp|l, -lz, -liŋ [-liŋ], -ld

pep, -talk pep, -tɔːk

Pepin 'pepin

pepper (s. v.) (P.), -s, -ing, -ed, -er/s 'pepə*, -z, -riŋ, -d, -rə*/z

pepper-box, -es 'pepəbɔks, -iz

pepper-caster [-tor], -s 'pepəˌkɑːstə*, -z

pepper-corn, -s 'pepəkɔːn, -z

peppermint, -s 'pepəmint [-mənt, 'pepmint, 'pepmənt], -s

pepper-pot, -s 'pepəpɔt, -s

pepper|y, -ily, -iness 'pepər|i, -ili, -inis

pep|sin, -tic 'pep|sin, -tik

Pepsu (Indian district) 'pepsu:

peptone, -s 'peptəun, -z

peptoniz|e [-is|e], -es, -ing, -ed 'peptənaiz, -iz, -iŋ, -d

Pepys 'pepis, piːps, peps
    Note.—The pronunciation in the family of the present Lord Cotten-ham is 'pepis. Samuel Pepys is generally referred to as piːps.

per pə:* (strong form), pə* (weak form)

Pera 'piərə

peradventure pərəd'ventʃə* [ˌpəː'rəd'v-, ˌperə-]

Perak 'pɛərə ['piərə, pə'ræk, pi'r-, pe'r-]
    Note.—Those who have lived in Malaya pronounce 'pɛərə or 'piərə.

perambulat|e, -es, -ing, -ed pə'ræmbju-leit, -s, -iŋ, -id

perambulation, -s pəˌræmbju'leiʃən, -z

perambulator, -s 'præmbjuleitə* [pə'ræm-], -z

per annum pər'ænəm

perceivab|le, -ly pə'siːvəb|l [pə:'s-], -li

perceiv|e, -es, -ing, -ed, -er/s pə'siːv [pə:'s-], -z, -iŋ, -d, -ə*/z

per cent pə'sent

percentage, -s pə'sentidʒ [pə:'s-], -iz

percept, -s 'pə:sept, -s

perceptibility pəˌseptə'biliti [pə:'s-, -ti'b-, -ʃət-]

perceptib|le, -ly, -leness pə'septəb|l [pə:'s-, -tib-], -li, -lnis

perception, -s pə'sepʃən [pə:'s-], -z

perceptive, -ly, -ness pə'septiv [pə:'s-], -li, -nis

Perceval 'pə:sivəl

perch (s. v.), -es, -ing, -ed, -er/s pə:tʃ, -iz, -iŋ, -t, -ə*/z

perchance pə'tʃɑːns [pə:'tʃ-]

Percheron, -s 'pə:ʃərɔn (perʃərɔ̃), -z

percipien|ce, -t/s pə(ː)'sipïən|s [-pjən-], -t/s

Percival 'pə:sivəl

percolat|e, -es, -ing, -ed, -or/s 'pə:-kəleit, -s, -iŋ, -id, -ə*/z

percolation, -s ˌpə:kə'leiʃən, -z

per contra pə:'kɔntrə

percuss, -es, -ing, -ed pə:'kʌs, -iz, -iŋ, -t

percussion, -s; -cap/s pə'kʌʃən [pə:ˌk-], -z; -kæp/s

percussive pə'kʌsiv [pə:'k-]

percutaneous, -ly ˌpə:kju(:)'teinjəs [-nĭəs], -li
Percy 'pə:si
per diem pə:'daiem [-'di:em]
Perdita 'pə:ditə
perdition pə:'diʃən
perdu(e) pə:'dju:
peregrin (s. adj.), -s 'perigrin, -z
peregrinat|e, -es, -ing, -ed, -or/s 'perigrineit, -s, -iŋ, -id, -ə*/z
peregrination, -s ˌperigri'neiʃən, -z
peregrine (s. adj.), -s 'perigrin [-gri:n], -z
Peregrine (personal name) 'perigrin
peremptor|y, -ily, -iness pə'remptər|i [pi'rem-, 'perəm-], -ili, -inis
Note.—'perəm- is more usual when the word is used as a legal term. Otherwise pə'rem- and pi'rem- are probably commoner.
perennial (s. adj.), -s, -ly pə'renjəl [pi'r-, -nĭəl], -z, -i
perez 'piərez
perfec|t (s. adj.), -ts, -tly, -tness 'pə:fik|t, -ts, -tli, -tnis
perfect (v.), -s, -ing, -ed pə'fekt [pə:'f-, 'pə:fikt], -s, -iŋ, -id
perfectibility pəˌfekti'biliti [pə:ˌf-, -tə'b-, -lət-]
perfectible pə'fektəbl [pə:'f-, -tib-]
perfection, -s pə'fekʃən, -z
perfervid pə:'fə:vid
perfidious, -ly, -ness pə:'fidĭəs [pə'f-, -djəs], -li, -nis
perfid|y, -ies 'pə:fid|i, -iz
perforable 'pə:fərəbl
perforate (adj.) 'pə:fərit
perforat|e (v.), -es, -ing, -ed, -or/s 'pə:fəreit, -s, -iŋ, -id, -ə*/z
perforation, -s ˌpə:fə'reiʃən, -z
perforce pə'fɔ:s [pə:'f-]
perform, -s, -ing, -ed, -er/s; -able, -ance/s pə'fɔ:m, -z, -iŋ, -d, -ə*/z; -əbl, -əns/iz
perfume (s.), -s 'pə:fju:m, -z
perfum|e (v.), -es, -ing, -ed pə'fju:m [pə:'f-, 'pə:f-], -z, -iŋ, -d
perfumed (adj.) 'pə:fju:md
perfumer, -s; -y pə'fju:mə* [pə:'f-], -z; -ri
perfunctor|y, -ily, -iness pə'fʌŋktər|i [pə:'f-], -ili, -inis
Perga, -mos 'pə:gə, -mɔs
Pergam|um, -us 'pə:gəm|əm, -əs
pergola, -s 'pə:gələ, -z
Pergolese ˌpə:gəʊ'leizi [ˌpɛəg-]
Perham 'perəm

perhaps pə'hæps, præps
Note.—pə'hæps is more usual in formal speech, and in colloquial when the word is said in isolation or used parenthetically (as in You know, perhaps, . . .). præps is common in other situations, esp. initially (e.g. in Perhaps we shall, Perhaps it is a mistake).
peri, -s 'piəri, -z
pericarditis ˌperikɑ:'daitis
pericardium, -s ˌperi'kɑ:djəm [-dĭəm], -z
pericarp, -s 'perikɑ:p, -s
Pericles 'perikli:z
peridot, -s 'peridɔt, -s
perigee, -s 'peridʒi:, -z
periheli|on, -a ˌperi'hi:lj|ən [-lĭ|ən], -ə
peril, -s 'peril [-rl], -z
perilous, -ly, -ness 'periləs [-rļəs], -li, -nis
Perim 'perim
perimeter, -s pə'rimitə* [pi'r-, pe'r-], -z
period, -s 'piərĭəd, -z
periodic ˌpiəri'ɔdik
periodic|al (s. adj.), -als, -ally ˌpiəri'ɔd-ik|əl, -əlz, -əli
periodicit|y, -ies ˌpiərĭə'disit|i [-rĭɔ'd-],
peripatetic, -ally ˌperipə'tetik, -əli
peripher|y, -ies, -al pə'rifər|i [pi'r-, pe'r-], -iz, -əl
periphras|is, -es pə'rifrəs|is [pi'r-, pe'r-], -i:z
periphrastic, -al, -ally ˌperi'fræstik, -əl, -əli
periscope, -s 'periskəup, -s
perish, -es, -ing/ly, -ed 'periʃ, -iz, -iŋ/li, -t
perishability ˌperiʃə'biliti [-lət-]
perishab|le, -ly, -leness 'periʃəb|l, -li, -lnis
perispomenon ˌperi'spəuminən [-nɔn]
peristalsis ˌperi'stælsis
peristaltic ˌperi'stæltik
peristyle, -s 'peristail, -z
peritoneum, -s ˌperitəu'ni:əm [-'niəm], -z
peritonitis ˌperitəu'naitis
Perivale 'periveil
periwig, -s 'periwig, -z
periwinkle, -s 'periˌwiŋkl, -z
Perizzite, -s 'perizait, -s
perj|ure, -ures, -uring, -ured, -urer/s 'pə:dʒ|ə*, -əz, -əriŋ, -əd, -ərə*/z
perjur|y, -ies 'pə:dʒər|i, -iz
perk, -s, -ing, -ed pə:k, -s, -iŋ, -t
Perkin, -s 'pə:kin, -z
perk|y, -ier, -iest, -ily, -iness 'pə:k|i, -ĭə* [-jə*], -iist [-jist], -ili, -inis

Perlis 'pə:lis
perm, -s pə:m, -z
permanenc|e, -es, -y, -ies 'pə:mənəns
 [-mɪn-], -iz, -i, -iz
permanent, -ly 'pə:mənənt [-mɪn-], -li
permanganate pə:'mæŋgənit [pə'm-,
 -neit]
permeability ˌpə:mjə'biliti [-mɪ̈ə-, -lət-]
permeable 'pə:mjəbl [-mɪ̈ə-]
permeat|e, -es, -ing, -ed 'pə:mieit
 [-mjeit], -s, -iŋ, -id
permeation ˌpə:mi'eiʃən
permissib|le, -ly, -leness pə'misəb|l
 [pə:'m-, -sib-], -li, -lnis
permission, -s pə'miʃən [pə:'m-], -z
permissive, -ly pə'misiv [pə:'m-], -li
permit (s.), -s 'pə:mit, -s
permit (v.), -s, -ting, -ted pə'mit [pə:'m-],
 -s, -iŋ, -id
permutation, -s ˌpə:mju(:)'teiʃən, -z
permut|e, -es, -ing, -ed; -able pə'mju:t
 [pə:'m-], -s, -iŋ, -id; -əbl
Pernambuco ˌpə:næm'bu:kəu [-nəm-]
pernicious, -ly, -ness pə:'niʃəs [pə'n-],
 -li, -nis
pernicket|y, -iness pə'nikit|i, -inis
perorat|e, -es, -ing, -ed 'perəreit [-rɔr-],
 -s, -iŋ, -id
peroration, -s ˌperə'reiʃən [-rɔ'r-], -z
Perouse pə'ru:z [pi'r-, pe'r-]
Perowne pə'rəun [pi'r-, pe'r-]
peroxide, -s pə'rɔksaid [pə:'r-], -z
perpend, -s, -ing, -ed pə'pend, -z, -iŋ,
 -id
perpendicular (s. adj.), -s, -ly ˌpə:pən-
 'dikjulə* [ˌpə:pm'd-], -z, -li
perpendicularity 'pə:pənˌdikju'læriti
 ['pə:pm,d-]
perpetrat|e, -es, -ing, -ed, -or/s 'pə:pi-
 treit, -s, -iŋ, -id, -ə*/z
perpetration, -s ˌpə:pi'treiʃən, -z
perpetual, -ly pə'petʃŭəl [-tʃwəl, -tʃul,
 -tjŭəl, -tjwəl, -tjul], -i
perpetuat|e, -es, -ing, -ed pə'petʃueit
 [pə:'p-, -'petʃu-], -s, -iŋ, -id
perpetuation, -s pəˌpetʃu'eiʃən [pə:ˌp-,
 -ˌpetju-], -z
perpetuit|y, -ies ˌpə:pi'tju(:)it|i [-pə't-],
 -iz
perpetuum mobile pə'petʃuum'məubilei
 [pə:'p-, -'petju-, -li]
perplex, -es, -ing/ly, -ed, -edly, -edness
 pə'pleks, -iz, -iŋ/li, -t, -idli [-tli],
 -idnis [-tnis]
perplexit|y, -ies pə'pleksit|i, -iz
perquisite, -s 'pə:kwizit, -s
Perrault 'perəu (pɛro)
Perrett 'perit

Perrier 'periei [-rɪ̈ə*] (pɛrje)
Perrin 'perin
perr|y (P.), -ies 'per|i, -iz
Perse pə:s
per se pə:'sei [-'si:]
persecut|e, -es, -ing, -ed, -or/s 'pə:si-
 kju:t, -s, -iŋ, -id, -ə*/z
persecution, -s ˌpə:si'kju:ʃən, -z
Persephone pə:'sefəni [-fɲi]
Persepolis pə:'sepəlis
Perseus 'pə:sju:s [-sjəs, -sɪ̈əs]
perseveration pə(:)ˌsevə'reiʃən
persever|e, -es, -ing/ly, -ed; -ance
 ˌpə:si'viə*, -z, -riŋ/li, -d; -rəns
Pershing 'pə:ʃiŋ
Persi|a, -an/s 'pə:ʃ|ə [rarely 'pə:ʒ|ə],
 -ən/z
persiflage ˌpɛəsi'flɑ:ʒ [ˌpə:s-, '---] (pɛrsi-
 flɑ:ʒ)
persimmon (P.), -s pə:'simən, -z
persist, -s, -ing/ly, -ed pə'sist [pə:'s-], -s,
 -iŋ/li, -id
persisten|ce, -cy pə'sistən|s [pə:'s-], -si
persistent, -ly pə'sistənt [pə:'s-], -li
person, -s 'pə:sn, -z
person|a, -ae pə:'səun|ə, -i: [-ai]
personable 'pə:sɲəbl [-sənə-, -snə-]
personage, -s 'pə:sɲidʒ [-sənidʒ, -snidʒ],
 -iz
pers|onal, -onally 'pə:s|n̩| [-ɲ̩, -ən|],
 -nəli [-ɲəli, -ɲ̩li, -n̩li, -ənl̩i]
personalit|y, -ies ˌpə:sə'nælit|i [-sɲ'æ-],
 -iz
personaliz|e [-is|e], -es, -ing, -ed
 'pə:sɲəlaiz [-snəl-, -sɲ̩l-, -snl̩-,
 -sənəl-], -iz, -iŋ, -d
personalt|y, -ies 'pə:snl̩t|i [-snəl-, -sən]-,
 -sɲl-], -iz
personat|e, -es, -ing, -ed, -or/s 'pə:sən-
 eit [-sɲeit], -s, -iŋ, -id, -ə*/z
personation, -s ˌpə:sə'neiʃən [-sɲ'ei-], -s
personification, -s pə:ˌsɔnifi'keiʃən
 [pəˌs-], -z
personi|fy, -fies, -fying, -fied pə:'sɔni|-
 fai [pə's-], -faiz, -faiiŋ, -faid
personnel, -s ˌpə:sə'nel [-sɲ'el], -z
perspective (s. adj.), -s, -ly pə'spektiv
 [pə:'s-], -z, -li
perspex 'pə:speks
perspicacious, -ly, -ness ˌpə:spi'keiʃəs,
 -li, -nis
perspicacity ˌpə:spi'kæsiti
perspicuity ˌpə:spi'kju(:)iti
perspicuous, -ly, -ness pə'spikjŭəs
 [pə:'s-, -kjwəs], -li, -nis
perspiration ˌpə:spə'reiʃən
perspir|e, -es, -ing, -ed pəs'paiə*, -z,
 -riŋ, -d

persuad|e, -es, -ing, -ed, -er/s pə'sweid [pə:'s-], -z, -iŋ, -id, -ə*/z

persuasion, -s pə'sweiȝən [pə:'s-], -z

persuasive, -ly, -ness pə'sweisiv [pə:'s-, -eiziv], -li, -nis

pert, -est, -ly, -ness pə:t, -ist, -li, -nis

pertain, -s, -ing, -ed pə:'tein [pə't-], -z, -iŋ, -d

Perth, -shire pə:θ, -ʃiə* [-ʃə*]

pertinacious, -ly, -ness ,pə:ti'neiʃəs, -li, -nis

pertinacity ,pə:ti'næsiti

pertinen|ce, -cy, -t/ly 'pə:tinən|s, -si, -t/li

perturb, -s, -ing, -ed, -er/s; -able pə'tə:b [pə:'t-], -z, -iŋ, -d, -ə*/z; -əbl

perturbation, -s ,pə:tə(:)'beiʃən, -z

Pertwee 'pə:twi(:)

Peru pə'ru: [pi'r-]

Perugia pə'ru:dȝə [pi'r-, pe'r-, -dȝiə, -dȝə] (pe'ru:dȝa)

Perugino ,peru(:)'dȝi:nəu (peru'dȝi:no)

peruke, -s pə'ru:k [pi'r-, pe'r-], -s

perusal, -s pə'ru:zəl [pi'r-, pe'r-], -z

perus|e, -es, -ing, -ed, -er/s pə'ru:z [pi'r-, pe'r-], -iz, -iŋ, -d, -ə*/z

Peruvian, -s pə'ru:vjən [pi'r-, pe'r-, -viən], -z

pervad|e, -es, -ing, -ed pə:'veid [pə'v-], -z, -iŋ, -id

pervasion pə:'veiȝən [pə'v-]

pervasive pə:'veisiv [pə'v-]

perverse, -ly, -ness pə'və:s [pə:'v-], -li, -nis

perversion, -s pə'və:ʃən [pə:'v-], -z

perversity pə'və:siti [pə:'v-]

pervert (s.), -s 'pə:və:t, -s

pervert (v.), -s, -ing, -ed, -er/s pə'və:t [pə:'v-], -s, -iŋ, -id, -ə*/z

pervious, -ly, -ness 'pə:vjəs [-viəs], -li, -nis

Pescadores ,peskə'dɔ:riz

peseta, -s pə'setə [pi's-, -'seitə] (pe'seta), -z

Peshawar pə'ʃɔ:ə* [pe'ʃ-, -'ʃauə*]

pesk|y, -ier, -iest, -ily, -iness 'pesk|i, iə* [-jə*], -iist [-jist], -ili, -inis

peso, -s 'peisəu, -z

pessar|y, -ies 'pesər|i, -iz

pessimi|sm, -st/s 'pesimi|zəm, -st/s

pessimistic, -al, -ally ,pesi'mistik, -əl, -əli

pest (P.), -s pest, -s

Pestalozzi ,pestə'lɔtsi (pesta'lɔttsi)

pest|er, -ers, -ering/ly, -ered, -erer/s 'pest|ə*, -əz, -əriŋ/li, -əd, -ərə*/z

Pest(h) pest

pesticide, -s 'pestisaid, -z

pestiferous, -ly pes'tifərəs, -li

pestilence, -s 'pestiləns, -iz

pestilent, -ly 'pestilənt, -li

pestilenti|al, -ally ,pesti'lenʃ|əl, -əli

pe|stle (s. v.), -stles, -stling, -stled 'pe|sl [-stl], -slz [-stlz], -sliŋ [-sliŋ, -stliŋ, -stliŋ], -sld [-stld]

Note.—The form 'pesl is usual among those accustomed to make frequent use of a pestle and mortar.

pestolog|ist/s, -y pes'tɔlədȝ|ist/s, -i

pet (s. v.), -s, -ting, -ted pet, -s, -iŋ, -id

petal, -s, -(l)ed 'petl, -z, -d

petaline 'petəlain

petard, -s pe'ta:d [pi't-], -z

Pete pi:t

Peter 'pi:tə*

Peterborough [-boro'] 'pi:təbrə [-bərə, -bʌrə]

Peterculter 'pi:tə,ku:tə*

Peterhead ,pi:tə'hed

Peters (English name) 'pi:təz, (German music publisher) 'pi:təz ['peit-] ('pe:tərs)

Petersburg 'pi:təzbə:g

Petersfield 'pi:təzfi:ld

petersham (P.), -s 'pi:təʃəm, -z

Pethick 'peθik

petite pə'ti:t

petiti|on (s. v.), -ons, -oning, -oned, -oner/s pi'tiʃ|ən [pə't-], -ənz, -ŋiŋ [-əniŋ, -niŋ], -ənd, -ŋə*/z [-ənə*/z, -nə*/z]

Peto 'pi:təu

Petrarch 'petra:k [old-fashioned 'pi:t-]

Petre 'pi:tə*

petrel, -s 'petrəl, -z

Petrie 'pi:tri

petrifaction ,petri'fækʃən

petri|fy, -fies, -fying, -fied 'petri|fai, -faiz, -faiiŋ, -faid

Petrograd 'petrəugræd [-gra:d]

petr|ol (s. v.), -ols, -oling, -oled 'petr|əl [-r|ɔl], -əlz [-ɔlz], -əliŋ [-liŋ, -ɔliŋ], -əld [-ɔld]

petroleum pi'trəuljəm [pə't-, -liəm]

Petruchio pi'tru:kiəu [pə't-, pe't-, -kjəu, -tʃiəu, -tʃjəu]

Pett pet

petticoat, -s, -ed 'petikəut, -s, -id

pettifogg|er/s, -ery, -ing 'petifɔg|ə*/z, -əri, -iŋ

Pettigrew 'petigru:

pettish, -ly, -ness 'petiʃ, -li, -nis

Pettit 'petit

pettitoes 'petitəuz

pett|y, -ier, -iest, -ily, -iness/es 'pet|i, -iə*, -iist, -ili, -inis/iz

Petula pə'tju:lə [pi't-, pe't-]

petulan|ce, -cy 'petjulən|s, -si

petulant, -ly 'petjulənt, -li
Petulengro ˌpetju'leŋgrəu [-tə'l-]
petunia, -s pi'tju:njə [pə't-, -nɪə], -z
Peugeot (car), -s 'pə:ʒəu (pøʒo), -z
Pevensey 'pevənzi
Peveril 'pevəril
pew, -s pju:, -z
pew-holder, -s 'pju:ˌhəuldə*, -z
pewit, -s 'pi:wit, -s
pew|-opener/s, -rent/s 'pju:ˌəupnə*/z,
   -rent/s
pewter, -s 'pju:tə*, -z
Peynell 'peinl [-nel]
pfennig, -s 'ᵽfenig ('pfɛniç), -z
Phaedo 'fi:dəu
Phaedr|a, -us 'fi:dr|ə, -əs
Phaer 'feiə*
Phaethon 'feiəθən ['feiiθ-]
phaeton, -s 'feitn, -z
phagocyte, -s 'fægəusait, -s
phalange, -s 'fælændʒ, -iz
phalanges (alternative plur. of phalanx)
   fæ'lændʒi:z [fə'l-]
phalanster|y, -ies 'fælənstər|i, -iz
phalanx, -es 'fælæŋks [rarely 'feil-],
   -iz
Phalaris 'fæləris
phalarope, -s 'fælərəup, -s
phallic 'fæ'ik
phallicism 'fælisizəm
phallus, -es 'fæləs, -iz
phanerogam, -s 'fænərəugæm, -z
phanerogamic ˌfænərəu'gæmik
phanerogamous ˌfænə'rogəməs
phantasm, -s 'fæntæzəm, -z
phantasmagoria ˌfæntæzmə'gorɪə [-təz-,
   -'go:r-]
phantasmagoric ˌfæntæzmə'gorik [-təz-]
phantasm|al, -ally, -ic fæn'tæzm|əl,
   -əli, -ik
phantom, -s 'fæntəm, -s
Pharamond 'færəmənd [-mond]
Pharaoh, -s 'fɛərəu, -z
pharisaic, -al, -ally, -alness ˌfæri'seiik
   [-'zeiik], -əl, -əli, -əlnis
pharisaism 'færiseiizəm
pharisee (P.), -s 'færisi:, -z
pharmaceutic, -al, -ally, -s ˌfɑ:mə-
   'sju:tik [-'su:-, -'kju:-], -əl, -əli, -s
pharmac|ist/s, -y, -ies 'fɑ:məs|ist/s, -i,
   -iz
pharmacolog|ist/s, -y ˌfɑ:mə'kolədʒ|-
   -ist/s, -i
pharmacopoeia, -s, -l ˌfɑ:məkə'pi:ə
   [-kəu'p-, -'piə], -z, -l
Pharos 'fɛəros
Pharsalia fɑ:'seiljə [-lɪə]
pharyngal fə'riŋgəl [fæ'r-, fɛə'r-]

pharyngeal ˌfærin'dʒi:əl [ˌfɛər-, -'dʒiəl,
   fə'rindʒiəl, fæ'rindʒ-, fɛə'rindʒ-,
   -'rindʒjəl]
pharyngitis ˌfærin'dʒaitis [ˌfɛər-]
pharynx, -es 'færiŋks ['fɛər-], -iz
phase, -s feiz, -iz
phas|is, -es 'feis|is, -i:z
phatic 'fætik
Phayre (fem. Christian name) fɛə*
Ph.D., -'s 'pi:eitʃ'di:, -z
Phear fɛə*
pheasant, -s 'feznt, -s
Phebe 'fi:bi
Phelps felps
phenacetin fi'næsitin [fe'n-, fə'n-, -sət-]
Phenice fi'naisi [fi:'n-, -si:]
Pheni|cia, -cian/s fi'ni|ʃɪə [fi:'n-, -ʃjə,
   -ʃə, -sɪə, -sjə], -ʃɪən/z [-ʃjən/z, -ʃən/z,
   -sɪən/z, -sjən/z]
phenobarbitone 'fi:nəu'bɑ:bitəun
phenol 'fi:nol
phenolphthalein ˌfi:nol'fθæliin
phenomen|on, -a, -al, -ally fi'nomin|ən,
   -ə, -l, -əli
phew ɸ:, ʸ:, pʸ:, ʸu:, ʸụ: [fju:]
phi, -s fai, -z
phial, -s 'faiəl, -z
Phidias 'fidiæs ['faid-]
Philadelphia, -n/s ˌfilə'delfjə [-fɪə], -n/z
philander, -s, -ing, -ed, -er/s fi'lændə*,
   -z, -riŋ, -d, -rə*/z
philanthrope, -s 'filənθrəup, -s
philanthropic, -al, -ally ˌfilən'θropik, -əl,
   -əli
philanthrop|ist/s, -y fi'lænθrəp|ist/s, -i
philatelic ˌfilə'telik [ˌfail-]
philatel|ist/s, -y fi'lætəl|ist/s, -i
Philbrick 'filbrik
Philemon fi'li:mon [fai'l-, -mən]
philharmonic (s. adj.), -s ˌfilɑ:'monik
   [-lə'm-, -lhɑ:'m-], -s
philhellene, -s 'fil,heli:n ['-'--], -z
philhellenic ˌfilhe'li:nik
philhellenism fil'helinizəm
philibeg, -s 'filibeg, -z
Philip, -pa 'filip, -ə
Philippi fi'lipai ['filipai]
Philippian, -s fi'lipɪən [-pjən], -z
Philippic, -s fi'lipik, -s
Philippine, -s 'filipi:n [old-fashioned
   -pain], -z
Philip(p)s 'filips
Philistia fi'listjə [-tɪə]
philistine (P.), -s 'filistain [rarely -tin],
   -z
philistinism 'filistinizəm
Phillimore 'filimo:* [-moə*]
Phillip(p)s 'filips

Phillpot, -s 'filpɔt, -s
Philoctetes ˌfiləkˈtiːtiːz [-lɔk-]
philologic, -al, -ally ˌfiləˈlɔdʒik, -əl, -əli
philologˈist/s, -y fiˈlɔlədʒˈist/s, -i
Philomel, -s 'filəmel [-ləum-], -z
Philomela ˌfiləuˈmiːlə
Philonous 'filəunaus
philosopher, -s fiˈlɔsəfə* [-ɔzə-], -z
philosophic, -al, -ally ˌfiləˈsɔfik [-əˈzɔ-],
   -əl, -əli
philosophiˈsm, -st/s fiˈlɔsəfiˈzəm [-ɔzə-],
   -st/s
philosophizˈe [-isˈe], -es, -ing, -ed
   fiˈlɔsəfaiz [-ɔzə-], -iz, -iŋ, -d
philosophˈy, -ies fiˈlɔsəfˈi [-ɔzə-], -iz
Philostratus fiˈlɔstrətəs
Philpot, -ts 'filpɔt, -s
philtre [-ter], -s 'filtə*, -z
Phineas 'finiæs [-niəs]
Phinees 'finiəs [-nies]
Phinehas 'finiæs [-niəs]
Phipˈps, -son 'fipˈs, -sn
phiz (P.) fiz
Phizackerley fiˈzækəli
phlebitic fliˈbitik [fliːˈb-, fleˈb-]
phlebitis fliˈbaitis [fliːˈb-, fleˈb-]
phlebotomy fliˈbɔtəmi [fliːˈb-, fleˈb-]
Phlegethon 'flegiθɔn [-θən]
phlegm, -s flem, -z
phlegmatic, -al, -ally fleg'mætik, -əl, -əli
phlogistic flɔˈdʒistik [-ɔˈgi-]
phlogiston flɔˈdʒistən [-ɔˈgi-, -tɔn]
phlox, -es flɔks, -iz
Phocian, -s 'fəuʃjən [-ʃiən, -sjən, -siən],
   -z
Phocion 'fəusjən [-siən, -siɔn, -sjɔn]
Phocis 'fəusis
Phoebˈe, -us 'fiːbˈi, -əs
Phoeniˈcia, -cian/s fiˈniˈʃiə [fiːˈn-, -ʃjə,
   -ʃə, -siə, -sjə], -ʃiən/z [-ʃjən/z, -ʃən/z,
   -siən/z, -sjən/z]
phoenix (P.), -es 'fiːniks, -iz
phon, -s fɔn, -z
phonatˈe, -es, -ing, -ed fəuˈneit, -s, -iŋ,
   -id
phonation fəuˈneiʃən
phonatory 'fəunətəri [fəuˈneitəri]
phonautograph,   -s   fəuˈnɔːtəgrɑːf
   [-græf], -s
phonˈe (s. v.), -es, -ing, -ed fəun, -z, -iŋ,
   -d
phonemathic ˌfəuni(ː)ˈmæθik
phonematic, -s ˌfəuni(ː)ˈmætik, -s
phoneme, -s 'fəuniːm, -z
phonemic, -s fəuˈniːmik, -s
phonemicist, -s fəuˈniːmisist, -s
phonetic, -al, -ally, -s fəuˈnetik, -əl, -əli,
   -s

phonetician, -s ˌfəuniˈtiʃən [ˌfɔn-, -neˈt-],
   -z
phoneticist, -s fəuˈnetisist, -s
phoneticizˈe [-isˈe], -es, -ing, -ed
   fəuˈnetisaiz, -iz, -iŋ, -d
phonetist, -s 'fəunitist [-net-], -s
phoney 'fəuni
phonic, -s 'fəunik ['fɔn-], -s
phonogram, -s 'fəunəgræm, -z
phonograph, -s 'fəunəgrɑːf [-græf], -s
phonographer, -s fəuˈnɔgrəfə*, -z
phonographist, -s fəuˈnɔgrəfist, -s
phonography fəuˈnɔgrəfi
phonographic, -al, -ally ˌfəunəˈgræfik,
   -əl, -əli
phonologicˈal, -ally ˌfəunəˈlɔdʒikˈəl, -əli
phonologist, -s fəuˈnɔlədʒist, -s
phonologˈy, -ies fəuˈnɔlədʒˈi, -iz
phonotype, -s 'fəunəutaip, -s
phonotypy 'fəunəutaipi
phosgene 'fɔzdʒiːn ['fɔs-]
phosphate, -s 'fɔsfeit [-fit], -s
phosphite, -s 'fɔsfait, -s
phosphorescˈe, -es, -ing, -ed; -ence,
   -ent ˌfɔsfəˈres, -iz, -iŋ, -t; -ns, -nt
phosphoric fɔsˈfɔrik
phosphorˈous, -us 'fɔsfərˈəs, -əs
phossy 'fɔsi
photo, -s 'fəutəu, -z
photochrome, -s 'fəutəkrəum, -z
photo-copˈy, -ies 'fəutəuˌkɔpˈi, -iz
photogenic ˌfəutəuˈdʒenik [-ˈdʒiːn-]
photograph (s. v.), -s, -ing, -ed 'fəutə-
   grɑːf [-græf], -s, -iŋ, -t
photographer, -s fəˈtɔgrəfə*, -z
photographic, -al, -ally ˌfəutəˈgræfik,
   -əl, -əli
photography fəˈtɔgrəfi
photogravure,   -s   ˌfəutəgrəˈvjuə*,
   [-təug-, -ˈvjɔə*, -ˈvjɔː*], -z
photosphere, -s 'fəutəusfiə*, -z
photostat (s. v.), -s, -ting, -ted 'fəutəu-
   stæt, -s, -iŋ, -id
photostatic ˌfəutəuˈstætik
phrasal 'freizəl
phrasˈe (s. v.), -es, -ing, -ed freiz, -iz,
   -iŋ, -d
phrase-book, -s 'freizbuk, -s
phrase-monger, -s 'freizˌmʌŋgə*, -z
phraseologic, -al, -ally ˌfreiziəˈlɔdʒik
   [-zjə-], -əl, -əli
phraseologˈy, -ies ˌfreiziˈɔlədʒˈi, -iz
phrenetic, -al friˈnetik [freˈn-], -əl
phrenic 'frenik
phrenologicˈal,   -ally   ˌfrenəˈlɔdʒikˈəl,
   -əli
phrenologˈist/s,   -y   friˈnɔlədʒˈist/s
   [freˈn-], -i

Phrygia, -n/s 'fridʒɪə [-dʒjə], -n/z
Phryne 'fraini(:)
phthisic 'θaisik ['fθai-, 'tai-, old-fashioned 'tizik]
phthisis 'θaisis ['fθai-, 'tai-]
phut fʌt
phylacter|y, -ies fi'læktər|i, -iz
Phyllis 'filis
phylloxer|a, -ae, -as ,filɔk'siər|ə [fi'lɔk-sər|ə], -i:, -əz
physic (s. v.), -s, -king, -ked 'fizik, -s, -iŋ, -t
physic|al, -ally 'fizik|əl, -əli
physician, -s fi'ziʃən, -z
physicist, -s 'fizisist, -s
physiognomic, -al, -ally ,fizɪə'nɔmik [-zjə-], -əl, -əli
physiognomist, -s ,fizi'ɔnəmist, -s
physiognom|y, -ies ,fizi'ɔnəm|i, -iz
physiography ,fizi'ɔgrəfi
physiologic, -al, -ally ,fizɪə'lɔdʒik [-zjə-], -əl, -əli
physiolog|ist/s, -y ,fizi'ɔlədʒ|ist/s, -i
physiophonic 'fizɪəu'fəunik [-'fɔn-]
physique fi'zi:k [fi:'z-]
pi (s. adj.), -s pai, -z
piacere pɪə'tʃiəri [,pi:ə-]
piaff|e (s. v.), -es, -ing, -ed pi'æf [pjæf], -s, -iŋ, -t
pianissimo, -s pjæ'nisiməu [,piæ'n-, pjɑ:'n, ,piɑ:'n-, pɪə'n-, pjə'n-], -z
Note.—Among professional musicians pjɑ:'n-, ,piɑ:'n-, pɪə'n- appear to be the most frequently used forms.
pianist, -s 'piənist ['pjænist, pi'æn-], -s
Note.—Professional musicians generally pronounce 'piənist.
piano (instrument), -s pi'ænəu ['pjæn-, 'pjɑ:n-, pi'ɑ:n-], -z
Note.—The forms 'pjɑ:n-, pi'ɑ:n-, are frequent among professional musicians.
piano (softly), -s 'pjɑ:nəu [pi'ɑ:-], -z
pianoforte, -s ,pjænəu'fɔ:ti [,pjɑ:n-, pi,ɑ:n-, '--,--], -z
pianola, -s pɪə'nəulə [pjæ'n-, ,piæ'n-], -z
piano-organ, -s pi'ænəu,ɔ:gən ['pjæn-, 'pjɑ:n-, pi'ɑ:n-], -z
piano-player, -s pi'ænəu,pleɪə* ['pjæn-, 'pjɑ:n-, pi'ɑ:n-], -z
piano-school, -s pi'ænəu-sku:l ['pjæn-, 'pjɑ:n-, pi'ɑ:n-], -z
piastre, -s pi'æstə* [pi'ɑ:s-], -z
piazza, -s pi'ætsə [pi'ɑ:tsə] ('pjattsa), -z
pibroch, -s 'pi:brɔk [-ɔx], -s
pica 'paikə
picaninn|y, -ies 'pikənin|i, -iz
Picardy 'pikədi [-kɑ:di]

picaresque ,pikə'resk
picaroon (s. v.), -s, -ing, -ed ,pikə'ru:n, -z, -iŋ, -d
Picasso pi'kæsəu
Piccadilly ,pikə'dili ['pikə'd-, also 'pikəd- when followed by a stress]
piccalilli 'pikəlili
piccaninn|y, -ies 'pikənin|i, -iz
piccolo, -s 'pikələu, -z
pice pais
pick (s. v.), -s, -ing, -ed, -er/s pik, -s, -iŋ, -t, -ə*/z
pickaback 'pikəbæk
pickaxe, -s 'pikæks, -iz
pickerel, -s 'pikərəl, -z
Pickering 'pikəriŋ
picket (s. v.), -s, -ing, -ed 'pikit, -s, -iŋ, -id
Pickford 'pikfəd
picking (s.), -s 'pikiŋ, -z
pick|le (s. v.), -les (P.), -ling, -led 'pik|l, -lz, -liŋ [-liŋ], -ld
picklock, -s 'piklɔk, -s
pick-me-up, -s 'pikmi(:)ʌp, -s
pickpocket, -s 'pik,pɔkit, -s
pick-up (electric), -s 'pikʌp, -s
Pickwick 'pikwik
Pickwickian pik'wikɪən [-kjən]
picnic (s. v.), -s, -king, -ked, -ker/s 'piknik, -s, -iŋ, -t, -ə*/z
picotee, -s ,pikə'ti:, -z
picquet (military term), -s 'pikit, -s
picric 'pikrik
Pict, -s pikt, -s
Pictish 'piktiʃ
pictograph, -s 'piktəugrɑ:f [-græf], -s
Picton 'piktən
pictorial, -ly pik'tɔ:rɪəl, -i
pict|ure (s. v.), -ures, -uring, -ured 'piktʃ|ə*, -əz, -əriŋ, -əd
picture|-book/s, -card/s 'piktʃə|buk/s, -kɑ:d/z
picture-galler|y, -ies 'piktʃə,gælər|i, -iz
picture-hat, -s 'piktʃəhæt, -s
picturesque, -ly, -ness ,piktʃə'resk, -li, -nis
picture-writing 'piktʃə,raitiŋ
pidgin 'pidʒin
Pidsley 'pidzli
pie, -s pai, -z
Piears pɪəz
piebald 'paibɔ:ld
piec|e (s. v.), -es, -ing, -ed, -er/s pi:s, -iz, -iŋ, -t, -ə*/z
piece-goods 'pi:sgudz
piecemeal 'pi:s-mi:l
piece-work 'pi:s-wə:k
pie-crust, -s 'pai-krʌst, -s

pied, -ness paid, -nis
pied-à-terre 'pjeita:'tɛə* (pjetatɛ:r)
Piedmont 'pi:dmənt [-mont]
Piedmontese ˌpi:dmən'ti:z [-mon-]
pie|man, -men 'pai|mən, -mən [-men]
pier, -s piə*, -z
pierc|e (P.), -es, -ing, -ed, -er/s; -eable
   piəs, -iz, -iŋ, -t, -ə*/z; -əbl
pierglass, -es 'piəglɑ:s, -iz
Pierian pai'eriən [pai'iər-, pi-]
Pier|point, -pont 'piə|point, -pont [-pənt]
Pierrepoint (English surname) 'piəpont
   [-pənt]
pierrot, -s 'piərəu ['pjər-, 'pjiər-], -z
Pier|s, -son piə|z, -sn
pietà, -s ˌpie'ta:, -z
Pietermaritzburg ˌpi:tə'mæritsbə:g
pieti|sm, -st/s 'paiəti|zəm ['paiit-], -st/s
piety 'paiəti ['paiiti]
piff|le (s. v.), -les, -ling, -led, -ler/s
   'pif|l, -lz, -liŋ [-liŋ], -ld, -lə*/z
   [-lə*/z]
pig (s. v.), -s, -ging, -ged pig, -z, -iŋ, -d
pigeon, -s 'pidʒin [-dʒən], -z
pigeon-hol|e (s. v.), -es, -ing, -ed
   'pidʒinhəul [-dʒən-], -z, -iŋ, -d
pigger|y, -ies 'pigər|i, -iz
piggish, -ly, -ness 'pigiʃ, -li, -nis
Piggott 'pigət
piggyback 'pigibæk
piggywig, -s 'pigiwig, -z
pigheaded, -ly, -ness 'pig'hedid [also
   'pigˌh- when attributive], -li, -nis
pig-iron 'pigˌaiən
piglet, -s 'piglit, -s
pigment, -s 'pigmənt, -s
pigm|y, -ies 'pigm|i, -iz
pignut, -s 'pignʌt, -s
Pig|ott, -ou 'pig|ət, -u:
pigskin, -s 'pigskin, -z
pig-sticking 'pigˌstikiŋ
pigst|y, -ies 'pigst|ai, -aiz
pigtail, -s 'pigteil, -z
pigwash 'pigwoʃ
pik|e (s. v.) (P.), -es, -ing, -ed paik, -s,
   -iŋ, -t
pike-keeper, -s 'paikˌki:pə*, -z
pikestaff, -s 'paikstɑ:f, -s
pilaf(f), -s 'pilæf [-'-], -s
pilaster, -s pi'læstə*, -z
Pilate 'pailət
Pilatus pi'lɑ:təs
pilau, -s pi'lau, -z
Pilbrow 'pilbrəu
pilch (P.), -es piltʃ, -iz
pilchard, -s 'piltʃəd, -z
pil|e (s. v.), -es, -ing, -ed pail, -z, -iŋ, -d
pileated 'pailieitid

pile-driv|er/s, -ing 'pailˌdraiv|ə*/z, -iŋ
pill|eus, -ei 'pail|iəs, -iai
pilf|er, -ers, -ering, -ered, -erer/s
   'pilf|ə*, -əz, -əriŋ, -əd, -ərə*/z
pilferage 'pilfəridʒ
pilgrim, -s; -age/s 'pilgrim, -z; -idʒ/iz
piling (s.), -s 'pailiŋ, -z
pill (s. v.), -s, -ing, -ed; -box/es pil, -z,
   -iŋ, -d; -boks/iz
pillag|e (s. v.), -es, -ing, -ed, -er/s
   'pilidʒ, -iz, -iŋ, -d, -ə*/z
pillar, -s, -ed 'pilə*, -z, -d
pillar-box, -es 'piləboks, -iz
pillion, -s 'piljən [-liən], -z
pillor|y (s. v.), -ies, -ying, -ied 'pilər|i,
   -iz, -iiŋ, -id
pillow, -s, -y 'piləu, -z, -i
pillow-case, -s 'piləukeis, -iz
pillow-slip, -s 'piləu-slip, -s
Pillsbury 'pilzbəri
pilocarpine ˌpailəu'kɑ:pin [-pain]
pilot (s. v.), -s, -ing, -ed; -age 'pailət, -s,
   -iŋ, -id; -idʒ
pilot|-boat/s, -engine/s 'pailət|bəut/s,
   -ˌendʒin/z
Pilsener 'pilznə* [-lsn-]
Piltdown 'piltdaun
pilule, -s 'pilju:l, -z
pimento pi'mentəu
Pimlico 'pimlikəu
pimp (s. v.), -s, -ing, -ed pimp, -s, -iŋ, -t
   [pimt]
pimpernel, -s 'pimpənel [-nl], -z
pimple, -s, -d 'pimpl, -z, -d
pimpl|y, -iness 'pimpl|i, -inis
Pimpo 'pimpəu
pin (s. v.), -s, -ning, -ned pin, -z, -iŋ, -d
pinafore (P.), -s 'pinəfɔ:* [-fɔə*], -z
pince-nez (sing.) 'pɛ̃:nsnei ['pæns-,
   'pins-, '-'-] (pɛ̃sne), (plur.) -z
pincers 'pinsəz
pinch (s. v.), -es, -ing, -ed, -er/s pintʃ,
   -iz, -iŋ, -t, -ə*/z
pinchbeck, -s 'pintʃbek, -s
Pinches 'pintʃiz
Pinckney 'piŋkni
pincushion, -s 'pinˌkuʃən ['piŋˌk-, -ʃin],
   -z
Pindar 'pində*
Pindaric (s. adj.), -s pin'dærik, -s
Pindus 'pindəs
pin|e (s. v.), -es, -ing, -ed pain, -z, -iŋ,
   -d
pineapple, -s 'painˌæpl, -z
pine-clad 'pain-klæd
Pinel pi'nel
Pinero pi'niərəu
piner|y, -ies 'painər|i, -iz

ping (*s. v. interj.*), **-s, -ing, -ed** piŋ, -z, -iŋ, -d

pingpong 'piŋpɔŋ

pinguid 'piŋgwid

pinhole, **-s** 'pinhəul, -z

pinion (*s. v.*), **-s, -ing, -ed** 'pinjən [-nɪən], -z, -iŋ, -d

pink (*s. adj. v.*) (**P.**), **-s, -ing, -ed** piŋk, -s, -iŋ, -t [piŋt]

Pinkerton 'piŋkətən

pink-eye, **-d** 'piŋk-ai, -d

pinkish 'piŋkiʃ

pink|y, **-iness** 'piŋk|i, -inis

pin-money 'pin,mʌni

pinnace, **-s** 'pinis [-nəs], -iz

pinnac|le (*s. v.*), **-les, -ling, -led** 'pinək|l, -lz, -liŋ [-liŋ], -ld

pinnate 'pinit [-neit]

pinner (**P.**), **-s** 'pinə*, -z

Pinocchio pi'nɔkiəu [-kjəu] (pi'nɔkkjo)

pin-point, **-s, -ing, -ed** 'pin-point, -s, -iŋ, -id

pin-prick, **-s** 'pin-prik, -s

pint, **-s** paint, -s

pintado, **-s** pin'tɑːdəu, -z

pintail, **-s** 'pin-teil, -z

Pinter 'pintə*

pint-pot, **-s** 'paint'pɔt ['paintp-], -s

pin-up, **-s** 'pinʌp, -s

pinxit 'piŋksit

pioneer (*s. v.*) (**P.**), **-s, -ing, -ed** ,paiə'niə*, -z, -riŋ, -d

pious, **-ly, -ness** 'paiəs, -li, -nis

pip (*s. v.*) (**P.**), **-s, -ping, -ped** pip, -s, -iŋ, -t

pip|e (*s. v.*) (**P.**), **-es, -ing, -ed, -er/s** paip, -s, -iŋ, -t, -ə*/z

pipeclay 'paipklei

pipe-line, **-s** 'paip-lain, -z

Piper 'paipə*

pipette, **-s** pi'pet, -s

piping (*s. adj.*) 'paipiŋ

pipit, **-s** 'pipit, -s

Pippa 'pipə

pippin, **-s** 'pipin, -z

pip-pip 'pip'pip

pipp|y, **-iness** 'pip|i, -inis

pipsqueak, **-s** 'pip-skwiːk, -s

piquancy 'piːkənsi

piquant, **-ly** 'piːkənt [-kɑːnt], -li

piqu|e (*s. v.*), **-es, -ing, -ed** piːk, -s, -iŋ, -t

piqué (*s. v.*), **-s, -ing, -d** 'piːkei (pike), -z, -iŋ, -d

piquet (*group of men*), **-s** 'pikit, -s

piquet (*card game*) pi'ket

pirac|y, **-ies** 'paiərəs|i ['pir-], -iz

Piraeus pai'ri(:)əs

pirat|e (*s. v.*), **-es, -ing, -ed** 'paiərit [-rət], -s, -iŋ, -id

piratic|al, **-ally** pai'rætik|əl [,paiə'r-], -əli

Piratin pi'rætin

Pirbright 'pə:brait

Pirie 'piri

pirouett|e (*s. v.*), **-es, -ing, -ed** ,piru'et, -s, -iŋ, -id

Pisa 'piːzə

pis aller, **-s** 'pi:z'ælei (pizale), -z

piscatorial ,piskə'tɔːriəl

piscatory 'piskətəri

piscean pi'siːən ['pisɪən, 'pisjən, 'piskɪən, 'piskjən, *by astrologers* 'pais-]

Pisces (*constellation*) 'pisiːz ['piski:z, *by astrologers* 'paisi:z]

pisciculture 'pisikʌltʃə*

piscina, **-s** pi'siːnə [-'sain-], -z

piscine (*s., bathing pool*), **-s** 'pisi:n [-'-], -z

piscine (*adj., of fish*) 'pisain

Piscis Austrinus 'pisis-ɔs'trainəs ['piskis-, -ɔːs-]

Pisgah 'pizgə [-gɑː]

pish piʃ [pʃ]

Pisidia pai'sidɪə [-djə]

Pisistratus pai'sistrətəs [pi's-]

pismire, **-s** 'pismaiə*, -z

pistachio, **-s** pis'tɑːʃiəu [-'tɑːʃjəu, -'tæʃ-, -'tætʃ-], -z

pistil, **-s** 'pistil, -z

pistol, **-s** 'pistl, -z

pistole, **-s** pis'təul ['--], -z

piston, **-s; -rod/s** 'pistən [-tn, -tin], -z; -rɔd/z

pit (*s. v.*), **-s, -ting, -ted** pit, -s, -iŋ, -id

pitapat 'pitə'pæt ['pitəp-]

Pitcairn (*surname*) pit'kɛən, (*island*) pit'kɛən ['pitk-]

pitch (*s. v.*), **-es, -ing, -ed** pitʃ, -iz, -iŋ, -t

pitch-black 'pitʃ'blæk

pitchblende 'pitʃblend

pitch-dark 'pitʃ'dɑːk

pitcher (**P.**), **-s** 'pitʃə*, -z

pitchfork (*s. v.*), **-s, -ing, -ed** 'pitʃfɔːk, -s, -iŋ, -t

pitchpine, **-s** 'pitʃpain, -z

pitch-pipe, **-s** 'pitʃpaip, -s

pitchy 'pitʃi

piteous, **-ly, -ness** 'pitɪəs [-tjəs], -li, -nis

pitfall, **-s** 'pitfɔːl, -z

Pitfodels pit'fɔdəlz

pith, **-s -less** piθ, -s, -lis

pithecanthrop|us, **-i** ,piθikæn'θrəup|əs [,--'---], -ai

Pither 'paiθə*, 'paiðə*

pith|y, **-ier, -iest, -ily, -iness** 'piθ|i, -ɪə*, -iist, -ili, -inis pitiab|le, -ly, -leness 'pitɪəb|l [-tjə-], -li, -lnis

piti|ful, -fully, -fulness 'piti|fʊl, -fuli [-fəli], -fulnis

pitiless, -ly, -ness 'pitilis, -li, -nis

Pitlochry pit'lɔkri [-'lɔxri]

pit|man (P.), -men 'pit|mən, -mən [-men]

Pitt pit

pittance, -s 'pitəns, -iz

Pitts, -burg(h) pits, -bəːg

pituitary pi'tju(ː)itəri

pit|y (s. v.), -ies, -ying/ly, -ied 'pit|i, -iz, -iiŋ/li, -id

Pius 'paiəs

pivot (s. v.), -s, -ing, -ed 'pivət, -s, -iŋ, -id

pivotal 'pivətl

pix|ie [-|y], -ies 'piks|i, -iz

pizzicato, -s ˌpitsi'kɑːtəu, -z

placability ˌplækə'biliti [ˌpleik-, -lət-]

placab|le, -ly, -leness 'plækəb|l ['pleik-], -li, -lnis

placard (s. v.), -s, -ing, -ed 'plækɑːd, -z, -iŋ, -id

placat|e, -es, -ing, -ed plə'keit [plei'k-], -s, -iŋ, -id

plac|e (s. v.), -es, -ing, -ed, -er/s pleis, -iz, -iŋ, -t, -ə/*z

placebo, -s plə'siːbəu [plæ's-], -z

place-kick, -s 'pleis-kik, -s

place|man, -men 'pleis|mən, -mən

placenta plə'sentə

placet, -s 'pleiset [-sit], -s

placid, -est, -ly, -ness 'plæsid, -ist, -li, -nis

placidity plæ'siditi [plə's-]

placket, -s; -hole/s 'plækit, -s; -həul/z

plagal 'pleigəl

plage, -s plɑːʒ, -iz

plagiari|sm/s, -st/s 'pleidʒjəri|zəm/z [-dʒɪə-, -dʒə-], -st/s

plagiariz|e [-is|e], -es, -ing, -ed 'pleidʒjəraiz [-dʒɪə-, -dʒə-], -iz, -iŋ, -d

plagiar|y, -ies 'pleidʒjər|i [-dʒɪə-, -dʒə-], -iz

plagu|e (s. v.), -es, -ing, -ed, -er/s pleig, -z, -iŋ, -d, -ə*/z

plague-spot, -s 'pleig-spɔt, -s

plagu|y, -ily, -iness 'pleig|i, -ili, -inis

plaice pleis

plaid, -s, -ed plæd, -z, -id

plain (s. adj.), -s, -er, -est, -ly, -ness plein, -z, -ə*, -ist, -li, -nis

plainsong 'plein-sɔŋ

plain-spoken 'plein'spəukən ['-,--]

plaint, -s pleint, -s

plaintiff, -s 'pleintif, -s

plaintive, -ly, -ness 'pleintiv, -li, -nis

plaister, -s 'plɑːstə*, -z

Plaistow (in E. London) 'plæstəu ['plɑː-s-]

Note.—The local pronunciation is 'plɑːstəu.

plait (s. v.), -s, -ing, -ed plæt, -s, -iŋ, -id

plan (s. v.), -s, -ning, -ned, -ner/s plæn, -z, -iŋ, -d, -ə*/z

planch, -es plɑːnʃ, -iz

planchette, -s plɑːn'ʃet [plɑ̃:n-, plɔ̃:n-, plɔ:n-, plɒn-] (plɑ̃ʃɛt), -s

plan|e (s. v.), -es, -ing, -ed plein, -z, -iŋ, -d

planet, -s 'plænit, -s

planetarium, -s ˌplæni'tɛərɪəm, -z

planetary 'plænitəri

plane-tree, -s 'plein-triː, -z

planimeter, -s plæ'nimitə* [plə'n-], -z

plank (s. v.), -s, -ing, -ed plæŋk, -s, -iŋ, -t [plæŋt]

plant (s. v.), -s, -ing, -ed, -er/s plɑːnt, -s, -iŋ, -id, -ə*/z

Plant (surname) plɑːnt

Plantagenet plæn'tædʒinit [-dʒən-, -net]

plantain, -s 'plæntin ['plɑː-n-], -z

plantation, -s plæn'teiʃən [plɑː-n-], -z

Plantin (type face) 'plæntin ['plɑːnt-]

plaque, -s plɑːk [plæk], -s

plaquette, -s plæ'ket [plɑː-'k-], -s

plash (s. v.), -es, -ing, -ed; -y plæʃ, -iz, -iŋ, -t; -i

plasm 'plæzəm

plasm|a, -ic 'plæzm|ə, -ik

Plassey 'plæsi

plast|er (s. v.), -ers, -ering, -ered, -erer/s 'plɑːst|ə*, -əz, -əriŋ, -əd, -ərə*/z

plastic, -s 'plæstik ['plɑː-s-], -s

plasticine 'plæstisiːn ['plɑː-s-]

plasticity plæs'tisiti [plɑː-s-]

plastographic ˌplæstəu'græfik [ˌplɑː-st-]

plat, -s plɑ: (pla), -z

Plata 'plɑːtə

Plataea plə'tiː(ː)ə

platan, -s 'plætən, -z

plat|e (s. v.), -es, -ing, -ed pleit, -s, -iŋ, -id

Plate (river in South America) pleit

plateau, -s [-x] 'plætəu [plæ'təu], -z

plate-basket, -s 'pleit,bɑːskit, -s

plateful, -s 'pleitful, -z

plate-glass 'pleit'glɑːs ['--]

plate-layer, -s 'pleit,leiə*, -z

platen, -s 'plætən, -z

plate-powder 'pleit,paudə*

plate-rack, -s 'pleit-ræk, -s

platform (s. v.), -s, -ing, -ed 'plætfɔːm, -z, -iŋ, -d

platiniz|e [-is|e], -es, -ing, -ed 'plæti-
naiz [-tŋaiz], -iz, -iŋ, -d
platinotype, -s 'plætinəʊtaip [-tŋəʊt-],
-s
platinum 'plætinəm [-tŋəm]
platitude, -s 'plætitju:d, -z
platitudinarian, -s 'plæti,tju:di'nɛərïən,
-z
platitudinous ,plæti'tju:dinəs
Plato 'pleitəu
platonic, -al, -ally plə'tɔnik [plei't-],
-əl, -əli
platoni|sm/s, -st/s 'pleitəʊni|zəm/z,
-st/s
platoon, -s plə'tu:n, -z
Platt, -s plæt, -s
platter, -s 'plætə*, -z
platypus, -es 'plætipəs, -iz
plaudit, -s 'plɔ:dit, -s
plausibility ,plɔ:zə'biliti [-zi'b-, -lət-]
plausib|le, -ly, -leness 'plɔ:zəb|l [-zib-],
-li, -lnis
Plautus 'plɔ:təs
play (s. v.), -s, -ing, -ed, -er/s plei, -z,
-iŋ, -d, -ə*/z [pleə*/z]
playable 'pleiəbl
play-actor, -s 'plei,æktə*, -z
play-bill, -s 'pleibil, -z
play-box, -es 'pleibɔks, -iz
Player, -'s 'pleiə*, -z
Playfair 'plei-fɛə* ['pleifɛə*]
playfellow, -s 'plei,feləu, -z
play|ful, -fully, -fulness 'plei|fʊl, -fuli
[-fəli], -fʊlnis
playgoer, -s 'plei,gəuə*, -z
playground, -s 'plei-graund, -z
playhou|se, -ses 'pleihau|s, -ziz
playing-field, -s 'pleiiŋfi:ld, -z
playmate, -s 'pleimeit, -s
plaything, -s 'plei-θiŋ, -z
playtime, -s 'plei-taim, -z
play-track, -s 'plei-træk, -s
playwright, -s 'pleirait, -s
plaza (P.), -s 'plɑ:zə ['plæzə], -z
plea, -s pli:, -z
plead, -s, -ing/ly, -ed, -er/s pli:d, -z,
-iŋ/li, -id, -ə*/z
pleading (s.), -s 'pli:diŋ, -z
pleasa(u)nce 'plezəns
pleasant, -er, -est, -ly, -ness 'pleznt,
-ə*, -ist, -li, -nis
pleasantr|y, -ies 'plezntr|i, -iz
pleas|e, -es, -ing/ly, -ed pli:z, -iz,
-iŋ/li, -d
pleasurab|le, -ly, -leness 'pleʒərəb|l, -li,
-lnis
pleasure, -s 'pleʒə*, -z
pleasure-boat, -s 'pleʒəbəut, -s

pleasure-ground, -s 'pleʒəgraund, -z
pleat (s. v.), -s, -ing, -ed pli:t, -s, -iŋ, -id
plebeian (s. adj.), -s pli'bi(:)ən, -z
plebiscite, -s 'plebisit [-sait, -si:t], -s
plebs plebz
plectrum, -s 'plektrəm, -z
pledg|e (s. v.), -es, -ing, -ed, -er/s
pledʒ, -iz, -iŋ, -d, -ə*/z
Pleiad, -s, -es 'plaiəd [old-fashioned
'pli:əd, pliəd, 'pleiæd], -z, -i:z
pleistocene 'plaistəusi:n
plenar|y, -ily 'pli:nər|i, -ili
plenipotentiar|y (s. adj.), -ies ,pleni-
pəʊ'tenʃər|i [-ʃïər-, -ʃjər-], -iz
plenitude 'plenitju:d
plenteous, -ly, -ness 'plentjəs [-tïəs],
-li, -nis
plenti|ful, -fully, -fulness 'plenti|fʊl,
-fuli [-fəli], -fʊlnis
plenty 'plenti [also often plentj in the
expression plenty of]
plenum, -s 'pli:nəm, -z
pleonasm, -s 'pli(:)ənæzəm [-i(:)əun-], -z
pleonastic, -al, -ally pliə'næstik [,pli:ə'n-,
-i(:)əu'n-], -əl, -əli
plesiosaur|us, -i, -uses 'pli:sïə'sɔ:r|əs
[-sjə's-, -siəu's-, '----, ,-'--], -ai, -əsiz
plethora 'pleθərə
plethoric ple'θɔrik [pli'θ-]
pleur|a, -ae, -as, -al 'pluər|ə, -i:, -əz, -əl
pleurisy 'pluərisi [-rəs-]
pleuritic pluə'ritik
pleuro - pneumonia 'pluərəunju(:) -
'məunjə [-nïə]
plexus, -es 'pleksəs, -iz
Pleyel, -s 'pleiəl [-el], -z
pliability ,plai-ə'biliti [-lət-]
pliab|le, -ly, -leness 'plai-əb|l, -li, -lnis
pliancy 'plai-ənsi
pliant, -ly, -ness 'plai-ənt, -li, -nis
pliers 'plaiəz
plight (s. v.), -s, -ing, -ed plait, -s, -iŋ,
-id
plimsoll (P.), -s 'plimsəl [-sɔl], -z
Plinlimmon plin'limən
plinth, -s plinθ, -s
Pliny 'plini
pliocene 'plai-əusi:n
plod (s. v.), -s, -ding, -ded, -der/s plɔd,
-z, -iŋ, -id, -ə*/z
Plomer (surname) 'plu:mə* ['plʌmə*]
Plomley 'plʌmli
plop (s. v. interj.), -s, -ping, -ped plɔp,
-s, -iŋ, -t
plosion, -s 'pləuʒən, -z
plosive (s. adj.), -s 'pləusiv [-əuzi-], -z
plot (s. v.), -s, -ting, -ted, -ter/s plɔt, -s,
-iŋ, -id, -ə*/z

plough (s. v.), -s, -ing, -ed, -er/s; -able;
-boy/s, -man, -men plau, -z, -iŋ, -d,
'plau-ə*/z, 'plau-əbl; -bɔi/z, -mən,
-mən [-men]
ploughshare, -s 'plau-ʃɛə*, -z
plover, -s 'plʌvə*, -z
Plow|den, -man 'plau|dn, -mən
Plowright 'plaurait
pluck (s. v.), -s, -ing, -ed plʌk, -s, -iŋ, -t
Pluckley 'plʌkli
pluck|y, -ier, -iest, -ily, -iness 'plʌk|i,
-ĭə*, -iist, -ili, -inis
plug (s. v.), -s, -ging, -ged plʌg, -z, -iŋ,
-d
plum, -s plʌm, -z
plumage, -s 'plu:midʒ, -iz
plumb (s. v.), -s, -ing, -ed, -er/s plʌm,
-z, -iŋ, -d, -ə*/z
plumbago, -s plʌm'beigəu, -z
Plumbe plʌm
plumb-line, -s 'plʌmlain, -z
plum|e (s. v.), -es, -ing, -ed plu:m, -z,
-iŋ, -d
Plummer 'plʌmə*
plummet, -s 'plʌmit, -s
plummy 'plʌmi
plump (s. adj. v. adv. interj.), -s; -er,
-est, -ly, -ness; -ing, -ed plʌmp, -s;
-ə*, -ist, -li, -nis; -iŋ, -t [plʌmt]
Plump|ton, -tre 'plʌmp|tən, -tri
plum-pudding, -s 'plʌm'pudiŋ [also
-'— when preceded by a stress], -z
Plumridge 'plʌmridʒ
Plumstead 'plʌmstid [-ted]
plumy 'plu:mi
plund|er (s. v.), -ers, -ering, -ered,
-erer/s; -erous 'plʌnd|ə*, -əz, -əriŋ,
-əd, -ərə*/z, -ərəs
plung|e (s. v.), -es, -ing, -ed, -er/s
plʌndʒ, -iz, -iŋ, -d, -ə*/z
Plunket(t) 'plʌŋkit
pluperfect, -s 'plu:'pə:fikt ['plu:‚p-], -s
plural (s. adj.), -s, -ly 'pluərəl ['plɔər-,
'plɔ:r-], -z, -i
plurali|sm, -st/s 'pluərəli|zm ['plɔər-,
'plɔ:r-, -rļi-], -st/s
pluralit|y, -ies pluə'rælit|i, -iz
pluraliz|e [-is|e], -es, -ing, -ed 'pluərəlaiz
['plɔər-, 'plɔ:r-, -rļaiz], -iz, -iŋ, -d
plus, -(s)es plʌs, -iz
plus-fours 'plʌs'fɔ:z [-'fɔəz]
plush, -es, -y plʌʃ, -iz, -i
Plutarch 'plu:ta:k
Pluto 'plu:təu
plutocracy plu:'tɔkrəsi
plutocrat, -s 'plu:təukræt, -s
plutocratic ‚plu:təu'krætik
Plutonian plu:'təunjən [-nĭən]

Plutonic plu:'tɔnik
plutonium plu:'təunjəm [-nĭəm]
pluvi|al, -ous 'plu:vj|əl [-vĭəl], -əs
pl|y (s. v.), -ies, -ying, -ied pl|ai, -aiz,
-aiiŋ, -aid
Plymouth 'pliməθ
plywood 'plaiwud
p.m. 'pi:'em [also pi:'em when preceded
by a stress]
pneumatic, -s, -al, -ally nju(:)'mætik, -s,
-əl, -əli
pneumatolog|ist/s, -y ‚nju:mə'tɔlədʒ|-
ist/s, -i
pneumonia nju(:)'məunjə [-nĭə]
pneumonic nju(:)'mɔnik
Pnompenh nɔm'pen ['-'-]
Pnyx ƥniks
po, -es pəu, -z
Po (Italian river) pəu
poach, -es, -ing, -ed, -er/s pəutʃ, -iz,
-iŋ, -t, -ə*/z
pochard, -s 'pəutʃəd, -z
pock, -s, -ed pɔk, -s, -t
pocket (s. v.), -s, -ing, -ed; -able, -ful/s
'pɔkit, -s, -iŋ, -id; -əbl, -ful/z
pocket-book, -s 'pɔkitbuk, -s
pocket - handkerchief,   -s   ‚pɔkit-
'hæŋkətʃif, -s (see note to handkerchief)
pocket-knif|e, -ves 'pɔkitnai|f, -vz
pocket-money 'pɔkit‚mʌni
Pocklington 'pɔkliŋtən
pockmark, -s, -ed 'pɔkma:k, -s, -t
poco 'pəukəu
Pocock 'pəukɔk
pococurante,   -s   'pəukəukjuə'rænti,
-z
pod (s. v.), -s, -ding, -ded pɔd, -z, -iŋ, -id
podagra pəu'dægrə [pɔ'd-, 'pɔdəgrə]
podg|y, -ier, -iest, -ily, -iness 'pɔdʒ|i,
-ĭə*, -iist, -ili, -inis
Poe pəu
Poel 'pəuel [-il, -əl]
poem, -s 'pəuim [-em], -z
poesy 'pəuizi ['pəuezi]
poet, -s 'pəuit [-et], -s
poetaster, -s ‚pəui'tæstə* [‚pəue't-], -z
poetess, -es 'pəuitis ['pəuet-, -tes], -iz
poetic, -al, -ally pəu'etik, -əl, -əli
poetiz|e [-is|e], -es, -ing, -ed, -er/s
'pəuitaiz ['pəuet-], -iz, -iŋ, -d, -ə*/z
poetry 'pəuitri ['pəuət-, rarely 'pɔit-]
Pogner (in Wagner's 'Die Meistersinger ') 'pəugnə* ('pɔ:gnər)
pogrom, -s 'pɔgrəm [-grɔm, pə'grɔm],
-z
poignan|cy, -t/ly 'pɔinən|si ['pɔinjə-,
'pɔignə-], -t/li

point (s. v.), -s, -ing, -ed, -er/s pɔint, -s, -iŋ, -id, -ə*/z
point-blank 'pɔint'blæŋk [also 'pɔintb- when attributive]
point-duty 'pɔint,dju:ti
pointed (adj.), -ly, -ness 'pɔintid, -li, -nis
point-lace 'pɔint'leis ['pɔint-leis]
pointless, -ness 'pɔintlis, -nis
points|man, -men 'pɔints|mən, -mən [-men]
pois|e (s. v.), -es, -ing, -ed pɔiz, -iz, -iŋ, -d
pois|on (s. v.), -ons, -oning, -oned, -oner/s 'pɔiz|n, -nz, -ŋiŋ [-niŋ], -nd, -ŋə*/z [-nə*/z]
poisonous, -ly, -ness 'pɔiznəs [-zŋəs], -li, -nis
Poitiers 'pwɑ:tjei [pwɑ:'tjei, old-fashioned pɔi'tiəz] (pwatje)
pok|e (s. v.), -es, -ing, -ed pəuk, -s, -iŋ, -t
poker, -s 'pəukə*, -z
pok|y, -ier, -iest, -ily, -iness 'pəuk|i, -iə* [-jə*], -iist [-jist], -ili, -inis
polacca, -s pəu'lækə, -z
Poland 'pəulənd
polar (s. adj.), -s 'pəulə*, -z
Polaris (star) pəu'læris [-'lɑ:r-, -'lɛər-; the rocket and submarine are usually pronounced with -'lɑ:r-]
polariscope, -s pəu'læriskəup, -s
polarity pəu'læriti
polarization [-isa-] ,pəulərai'zeiʃən [-ri'z-]
polariz|e [-is|e], -es, -ing, -ed, -er/s 'pəuləraiz, -iz, -iŋ, -d, -ə*/z
polder, -s 'pɔldə*, -z
Poldhu 'pɔldju:
pole, -s pəul, -z
Pole (inhabitant of Poland), -s pəul, -z
Pole (surname) pəul, pu:l
Note.—pu:l in Pole Carew (q.v.) and Chandos Pole ('ʃændɔs'pu:l).
pole|axe/s, -cat/s 'pəul|æks/iz, -kæt/s
Pole Carew 'pu:l'kɛəri [pu:l'k-]
polemic (s. adj.), -s, -al, -ally pɔ'lemik [pəu'l-], -s, -əl, -əli
pole-star, -s 'pəul-stɑ:*, -z
Polhill 'pəulhil
polic|e (s. v.), -es, -ing, -ed pə'li:s [pu'l-], -iz, -iŋ, -t
police|man, -men pə'li:smən [pl̩'i:s-, -pli:s-, pu'l-], -mən
polic|y, -ies 'pɔlis|i [-ləs-], -iz
policy-holder, -s 'pɔlisi,həuldə* [-ləs-], -z
polio 'pəuliəu [-ljəu]
poliomyelitis 'pəuliəʊmaiə'laitis [-ljəʊ-, -maii'l-, -maie'l-]

polish (s. v.), -es, -ing, -ed, -er/s 'pɔliʃ, -iz, -iŋ, -t, -ə*/z
Polish (adj.) (of Poland) 'pəuliʃ
polite, -st, -ly, -ness pə'lait [pu'l-], -ist, -li, -nis
politic, -s 'pɔlitik [-lət-], -s
politic|al, -ally pə'litik|əl [pu'l-], -əli
politician, -s ,pɔli'tiʃən [-lə'l't-], -z
polity 'pɔliti
Polixenes pɔ'liksəni:z [pə'l-, -sin-]
Polk pəuk
polka, -s 'pɔlkə ['pəul-], -z
poll (s. v.) (at elections), -s, -ing, -ed pəul, -z, -iŋ, -d
poll (s.) (parrot, student taking pass degree at Cambridge) (P.), -s pɔl, -z
poll (adj.) (hornless, cut, executed by one party) pəul
pollard (s. v.) (P.), -s, -ing, -ed 'pɔləd, -z, -iŋ, -id
pollen (P.), -s, -ing, -ed 'pɔlin [-lən], -z, -iŋ, -d
pollinat|e, -es, -ing, -ed 'pɔlineit, -s, -iŋ, -id
pollination ,pɔli'neiʃən
poll|-man, -men 'pɔl|mæn, -men
Pollock 'pɔlək
pollster, -s 'pəulstə*, -z
poll-tax, -es 'pəul-tæks, -iz
pollut|e, -es, -ing, -ed, -er/s pə'lu:t [-'lju:t], -s, -iŋ, -id, -ə*/z
pollution, -s pə'lu:ʃən [-'lju:-], -z
Pollux 'pɔləks
Polly 'pɔli
Polmont 'pəulmənt
polo 'pəuləu
polonaise, -s ,pɔlə'neiz, -iz
Polonius pə'ləunjəs [pɔ'l-, -nïəs]
polon|y, -ies pə'ləun|i, -iz
Polson 'pəulsn
poltergeist, -s 'pɔltəgaist, -s
poltroon, -s; -ery pɔl'tru:n, -z; -əri
Polwarth (in Berwickshire) 'pəulwəθ, (surname) 'pɔlwəθ
polyandrous ,pɔli'ændrəs
polyandry 'pɔliændri [,pɔli'æ-]
polyanthus, -es ,pɔli'ænθəs, -iz
Polybius pɔ'libiəs [pə'l-, -bjəs]
Polycarp 'pɔlikɑ:p
Polycrates pɔ'likrəti:z [pə'l-]
polygam|ist/s, -y, -ous pɔ'ligəm|ist/s [pə'l-], -i, -əs
polyglot (s. adj.), -s 'pɔliglɔt, -s
polygon, -s 'pɔligən, -z
polygonal pɔ'ligənl [pə'l-]
polyhedr|on, -ons, -a, -al ,pɔli'hedr|ən [-'hi:d-, 'pɔli,h-, ,pɔli'h-], -ənz, -ə, -əl
polylogue, -s 'pɔlilɔg, -z

Polyne|sia, -sian/s ˌpɔli'ni:|zjə [-zɪ̈ə, -ʒə, -ʒɪ̈ə, -ʒə, -sjə, -sɪ̈ə, -ʃjə, -ʃɪ̈ə, -ʃə], -zjən/z [-zɪ̈ən/z, -ʒjən/z, -ʒɪ̈ən/z, -ʒən/z, -sjən/z, -sɪ̈ən/z, -ʃjən/z, -ʃɪ̈ən/z, -ʃən/z]

polynomial (s. adj.), -s ˌpɔli'nəumjəl [-mɪ̈əl], -z

polyp, -s, -ous 'pɔlip, -s, -əs

Polyphemus ˌpɔli'fi:məs

polyphonic ˌpɔli'fɔnik

polyphony pə'lifəni [pɔ'l-]

polypodium, -s ˌpɔli'pəudjəm [-dɪ̈əm], -z

polypody 'pɔlipədi

polyp|us, -uses, -i 'pɔlip|əs, -əsiz, -ai

polysyllabic, -ally 'pɔlisi'læbik, -əli

polysyllable, -s 'pɔliˌsiləbl, -z

polysynthesis ˌpɔli'sinθisis [-θəs-]

polysynthetic ˌpɔlisin'θetik

polytechnic (s. adj.), -s ˌpɔli'teknik, -s

polythei|sm, -st/s 'pɔliθi(:)i|zəm, -st/s

polytheistic ˌpɔliθi(:)'istik

polythene 'pɔliθi:n

Polyxen|a, -us pɔ'liksin|ə [pə'l-, -sən-], -əs

Polzeath pɔl'zeθ [-'zi:θ]
  Note.—The local pronunciation is pɔl'zɛ:θ.

pomace 'pʌmis

pomade, -s pə'mɑ:d [pɔ'm-], -z

pomander, -s pəu'mændə*, -z

pomatum, -s pəu'meitəm, -z

pome, -s pəum, -z

pomegranate, -s 'pɔmiˌgrænit ['pɔməˌg-, 'pɔmˌg-], -s

pomelo, -s 'pɔmiləu, -z

Pomerania, -n/s ˌpɔmə'reinjə [-nɪ̈ə], -n/z

pomfret (fish), -s 'pɔmfrit, -s

Pomfret ['pʌmfrit ['pɔm-]

pomfret cake, -s 'pʌmfrit'keik ['pɔm-, '---], -s

pomm|el (s. v.), -els, -elling, -elled 'pʌm|l, -lz, -liŋ [-əliŋ], -ld

Pomona pəu'məunə

pomp, -s pɔmp, -s

pompadour (P.), -s 'pɔmpəduə* ['pɔ̃:mp-, 'pɔːmp-, -dɔə*, -dɔː*] (pɔ̃padu:r), -z

Pompeian pɔm'pi(:)ən

Pompeii pɔm'pi:ai ['pɔmpiai, pɔm'peii:, -'peii]

Pompey 'pɔmpi

pompom, -s 'pɔmpɔm, -z

pompon, -s 'pɔ̃:mpɔ̃:ŋ ['pɔːmpɔːŋ, 'pɔmpɔn] (pɔ̃pɔ̃), -z

pomposity pɔm'pɔsiti

pompous, -ly, -ness 'pɔmpəs, -li, -nis

ponce, -s pɔns, -iz

pond (s. v.) (P.), -s, -ing, -ed pɔnd, -z, -iŋ, -id

pond|er, -ers, -ering/ly, -ered 'pɔnd|ə*, -əz, -əriŋ/li, -əd

ponderability ˌpɔndərə'biliti [-lət-]

ponderable, -ness 'pɔndərəbl, -nis

ponderous, -ly, -ness 'pɔndərəs, -li, -nis

Ponders 'pɔndəz

Pondicherry ˌpɔndi'tʃeri [-i'ʃe-]

pongee pɔn'dʒi: [pʌn-]

poniard (s. v.), -s, -ing, -ed 'pɔnjəd [-jɑ:d], -z, -iŋ, -id

Pons asinorum 'pɔnz-æsi'nɔ:rəm

Ponsonby 'pʌnsnbi

Pontefract (in Yorks.) 'pɔntifrækt
  Note.—An old local pronunciation 'pʌmfrit is now obsolete. The pronunciation survives in pomfret cake (q. v.).

pontifex (P.), pontifices 'pɔntifeks, pɔn'tifisi:z

pontiff, -s 'pɔntif, -s

pontific, -al/s, -ally; -ate/s pɔn'tifik, -əl/z, -əli; -it/s [-eit/s]

Pontine 'pɔntain

Pontius 'pɔntjəs [-ntɪ̈əs, -ntʃjəs, -ntʃəs, -nʃjəs, -nʃəs]

pontoon, -s pɔn'tu:n, -z

Pontresina ˌpɔntri'si:nə [-trə's-]

Pontus 'pɔntəs

Pontypool ˌpɔnti'pu:l (Welsh ˌpɔntə'pu:l)

Pontypridd ˌpɔnti'pri:ð (Welsh ˌpɔntə'pri:ð)

pon|y, -ies 'pəun|i, -iz

pood, -s pu:d, -z

poodle, -s 'pu:dl, -z

pooh pỹ [phu:, pu:]

Pooh-Bah 'pu:'bɑ:

pooh-pooh, -s, -ing, -ed pu:'pu: ['pu:'p-], -z, -iŋ [-'puiŋ], -d

pool (s. v.), -s, -ing, -ed pu:l, -z, -iŋ, -d

Poole pu:l

Pooley 'pu:li

poon, -s pu:n, -z

Poona 'pu:nə [-nɑ:] (Hind. puna)

poop (s. v.), -s, -ing, -ed pu:p, -s, -iŋ, -t

poor, -er, -est, -ly, -ness puə* [pɔə*, pɔ:*], -rə*, -rist, -li, -nis

poor-box, -es 'puəbɔks ['pɔə-, 'pɔ:-], -iz

Poore puə*

poor-hou|se, -ses 'puəhau|s ['pɔə-, 'pɔ:-], -ziz

poor-law 'puələ: ['pɔə-, 'pɔ:-]

poorly 'puəli ['pɔə-, 'pɔ:-]

pop (s. v. interj.), -s, -ping, -ped, -per/s pɔp, -s, -iŋ, -t, -ə*/z

pop-corn 'pɔpkɔ:n

pope (P.), -s; -dom/s pəup, -s; -dəm/z

popery 'pəupəri
pop-gun, -s 'pɔpgʌn, -z
Popham 'pɔpəm
popinjay, -s 'pɔpindʒei, -z
popish, -ly, -ness 'pəupiʃ, -li, -nis
poplar (P.), -s 'pɔplə*, -z
poplin, -s 'pɔplin, -z
Popocatepetl 'pɔpəu,kæti'petl ['pəup-,
  -tə'p-] (Aztec po,poka'tepetḷ)
popp|le, -les, -ling, -led 'pɔp|l, -lz, -ḷiŋ
  [-liŋ], -ld
popp|y (P.), -ies 'pɔp|i, -iz
poppy-head, -s 'pɔpihed, -z
pop-shop, -s 'pɔpʃɔp, -s
populace 'pɔpjuləs [-lis]
popular, -ly 'pɔpjulə* [-pjəl-], -li
popularity ,pɔpju'læriti [-pjə'l-]
populariz|e [-is|e], -es, -ing, -ed 'pɔpju-
  ləraiz [-pjəl-], -iz, -iŋ, -d
populat|e, -es, -ing, -ed 'pɔpjuleit
  [-pjəl-], -s, -iŋ, -id
population, -s ,pɔpju'leiʃən, -z
populous, -ly, -ness 'pɔpjuləs [-pjəl-],
  -li, -nis
porage 'pɔridʒ
porcelain, -s 'pɔːsəlin [-lein], -z
porch, -es pɔːtʃ, -iz
Porchester 'pɔːtʃistə* [-tʃəs-]
porcine 'pɔːsain
porcupine, -s 'pɔːkjupain, -z
por|e (s. v.), -es, -ing, -ed pɔː* [pɔə*], -z,
  -riŋ, -d
porgy (fish) 'pɔːdʒi
Porgy (name) 'pɔːgi
pork, -er/s, -y pɔːk, -ə*/z, -i
pornographic ,pɔːnəu'græfik
pornography 'pɔːnɔgrəfi
porosity pɔː'rɔsiti
porous, -ly, -ness 'pɔːrəs, -li, -nis
porphyry (P.) 'pɔːfiri [-fəri]
porpoise, -s 'pɔːpəs, -iz
porridge 'pɔridʒ
porringer, -s 'pɔrindʒə*, -z
Porsena 'pɔːsinə [-sən-]
Porson 'pɔːsn
port (s. v.), -s, -ing, -ed pɔːt, -s, -iŋ, -id
portability ,pɔːtə'biliti [-lət-]
portable, -ness 'pɔːtəbl, -nis
Portadown ,pɔːtə'daun
portage 'pɔːtidʒ
portal (P.), -s 'pɔːtl, -z
portamento, -s ,pɔːtə'mentəu, -z
portcullis, -es pɔːt'kʌlis, -iz
Porte pɔːt
portend, -s, -ing, -ed pɔː'tend, -z, -iŋ, -id
portent, -s 'pɔːtent [-tənt], -s
portentous, -ly pɔː'tentəs, -li
porter (P.), -s; -age 'pɔːtə*, -z; -ridʒ

Porteus 'pɔːtjəs [-tïəs]
portfolio, -s pɔːt'fəuljəu [-liəu], -z
porthole, -s 'pɔːthəul, -z
Portia 'pɔːʃjə [-ʃïə]
portico, -s 'pɔːtikəu, -z
porti|on (s. v.), -ons, -oning, -oned
  'pɔːʃ|ən, -ənz, -ṇiŋ [-əniŋ], -ənd
Portishead 'pɔːtished
Portland 'pɔːtlənd
Portlaw pɔːt'lɔː
portl|y, -ier, -iest, -iness 'pɔːtl|i, -ïə*
  [-jə*], -iist [-jist], -inis
Portmadoc pɔːt'mædək (Welsh port-
  'madok)
Portman 'pɔːtmən
portmanteau, -s pɔːt'mæntəu, -z
Portobello ,pɔːtəu'beləu
Porto Rico ,pɔːtəu'riːkəu   [-ist/s
portrait, -s; -ist/s 'pɔːtrit [-treit], -s;
portraiture 'pɔːtritʃə [-trətʃ-, -tjuə*]
portray, -s, -ing, -ed, -er/s pɔː'trei, -z,
  -iŋ, -d, -ə*/z [pɔː'treə*/z]
portrayal, -s pɔː'treiəl [also -'treil when
  not immediately followed by a vowel],
  -z
portreeve, -s 'pɔːt-riːv, -z
Portrush pɔːt'rʌʃ
Port Said pɔːt'said [old-fashioned -'seid]
Port Salut ,pɔː-sə'luː (pɔrsaly)
Portsea 'pɔːtsi [-siː]
Portsmouth 'pɔːtsməθ
Portsoy pɔːt'sɔi
Portugal 'pɔːtjugəl [-tʃu-]
Portuguese ,pɔːtju'giːz [-tʃu-, '--'-]
posaune, -s pə'zɔːn, -z
pos|e (s. v.), -es, -ing, -ed, -er/s pəuz,
  -iz, -iŋ, -d, -ə*/z
Poseidon pɔ'saidən [pə's-]
poser (problem), -s 'pəuzə*, -z
poseur, -s pəu'zə:* (pozœːr), -z
posh pɔʃ
posit, -s, -ing, -ed 'pɔzit, -s, -iŋ, -id
position, -s pə'ziʃən [pu'z-], -z
positional pə'ziʃənl [pu'z-, -ʃnəl, -ʃṇl,
  -ʃnḷ, -ʃənəl]
positive (s. adj.), -s, -ly, -ness 'pɔzətiv
  [-zit-], -z, -li, -nis
positivi|sm, -st/s 'pɔzitivi|zəm [-zət-],
  -st/s
positron, -s 'pɔzitrɔn [-trən], -z
posse, -s 'pɔsi, -z
possess, -es, -ing, -ed, -or/s pə'zes
  [pu'z-], -iz, -iŋ, -t, -ə*/z
possession, -s pə'zeʃən [pu'z-], -z
possessive (s. adj.), -s, -ly, -ness
  pə'zesiv [pu'z-], -z, -li, -nis
possessory pə'zesəri [pu'z-]
posset 'pɔsit

possibilit|y, -ies ˌpɔsə'bilit|i [-si'b-, -lət-], -iz

possib|le, -ly 'pɔsəb|l [-sib-], -li

possum, -s 'pɔsəm, -z

post (s. v.), -s, -ing, -ed pəust, -s, -iŋ, -id

postage, -s 'pəustidʒ, -iz

postal 'pəustəl

postal-order (P.O.), -s 'pəustl,ɔ:də* ('pi:'əu), -z

post-bag, -s 'pəustbæg, -z

postcard, -s 'pəustka:d, -z

post-chaise, -s 'pəust-ʃeiz, -iz

postdat|e, -es, -ing, -ed 'pəust'deit ['--], -s, -iŋ, -id

post-diluvian 'pəustdai'lu:vjən [-di'l-, -'lju:-, -viən]

poster, -s 'pəustə*, -z

poste restante 'pəust'restɑ:nt [-tõ:nt, -tɑ:nt, -tɔ:nt, -tɔnt] (postrestɑ̃:t)

posterior, -ly pɔs'tiəriə*, -li

posteriority pɔs,tiəri'ɔriti [ˌpɔstiər-]

posterit|y, -ies pɔs'terit|i, -iz

postern, -s 'pəustə:n [-tən], -z

post-free 'pəust'fri:

Postgate 'pəustʰgeit [-git]

post-graduate 'pəustʰ'grædjuit [-djuət, -dʒuit]

post|haste, -horn/s, -horse/s 'pəust|-'heist, -hɔ:n/z, -hɔ:s/iz

posthumous, -ly 'pɔstjuməs, -li

postiche, -s pɔs'ti:ʃ ['--], -iz

postil, -s 'pɔstil, -z

postillion, -s pəs'tiljən [pɔs-, -liən], -z

post-impressioni|sm, -st/s 'pəust-im-'preʃni|zəm [-ʃəni-], -st/s

Postlethwaite 'pɔslθweit

post|man, -men 'pəust|mən, -mən

postmark (s. v.), -s, -ing, -ed 'pəust-mɑ:k, -s, -iŋ, -t

postmaster, -s 'pəust,mɑ:stə*, -z

post-meridian 'pəustmə'ridiən [-djən]

post-mistress, -es 'pəust,mistris, -iz

post-mortem, -s 'pəust'mɔ:tem [-təm, -'--], -z

post-natal 'pəust'neitl

post-office, -s 'pəust,ɔfis, -iz

postpon|e (s. v.), -es, -ing, -ed, -ement/s pəust'pəun [pəs'p-], -z, -iŋ, -d, -mənt/s

postposition, -s 'pəustpə'ziʃən [-pu'z-, '--,--], -z

postscript, -s 'pəusskript ['pəus-kript], -s

post-town, -s 'pəusttaun, -z

postulant, -s 'pɔstjulənt, -s

postulate (s.), -s 'pɔstjulit [-leit], -s

postulat|e (v.), -es, -ing, -ed 'pɔstju-leit, -s, -iŋ, -id

postulation, -s ˌpɔstju'leiʃən, -z

postum 'pəustəm

postur|e (s. v.), -es, -ing, -ed 'pɔstʃə* [-tjuə*], -z, -riŋ, -d

post-war 'pəust'wɔ:* [also 'pəust-wɔ:* when attributive]

pos|y -ies 'pəuz|i, -iz

pot (s. v.), -s, -ting, -ted, -er/s pɔt, -s, -iŋ, -id, -ə*/z

potable, -ness, -s 'pəutəbl, -nis, -z

potage, -s pɔ'tɑ:ʒ ['pɔtɑ:ʒ] (pɔta:ʒ), -iz

potash, -water 'pɔtæʃ, -,wɔ:tə*

potassium pə'tæsjəm [-siəm]

potation, -s pəu'teiʃən, -z

potato, -es pə'teitəu, -z

pot-bellied 'pɔt,belid ['-'--]

pot-boiler, -s 'pɔt,bɔilə*, -z

poteen pɔ'ti:n [pəu-, -'tʃi:n]

poten|cy, -t/ly 'pəutən|si, -t/li

potentate, -s 'pəutənteit [-tit], -s

potenti|al (s. adj.), -als, -ally pəu'tenʃ|əl [pu't-], -əlz, -əli

potentialit|y, -ies pəu,tenʃi'ælit|i [pu,t-], -iz

potentilla, -s ˌpəutən'tilə, -z

pot-hat, -s 'pɔt'hæt, -s

pother (s. v.), -s, -ing, -ed 'pɔðə*, -z, -riŋ, -d

pot-herb, -s 'pɔthə:b, -z

pot-hole, -s, -er/s 'pɔthəul, -z, -ə*/z

pothook, -s 'pɔthuk, -s

pothou|se, -ses 'pɔthau|s, -ziz

pot-hunter, -s 'pɔt,hʌntə*, -z

potion, -s 'pəuʃən, -z

Potiphar 'pɔtifə* [-fɑ:*]

pot-luck 'pɔt'lʌk

Potomac pə'təumək

Potosi (in Bolivia) ˌpɔtəu'si:, (in U.S.A.) pə'təusi

pot-pourri, -s pəu'puri(:) (popuri), -z

Potsdam 'pɔtsdæm

potsherd, -s 'pɔt-ʃə:d, -z

pot-shot, -s 'pɔt'ʃɔt ['pɔt-ʃɔt], -s

Pott pɔt

pottage 'pɔtidʒ

pott|er (s. v.) (P.), -ers, -ering, -ered, -erer/s 'pɔt|ə*, -əz, -əriŋ, -əd, -ərə*/z

potter|y, -ies (P.) 'pɔtər|i, -iz

pottle, -s 'pɔtl, -z

pott|y, -ier, -iest, -iness 'pɔt|i, -iə*, -iist, -inis

Pou (French-Canadian name) pju:

pouch (s.), -es pautʃ [in the army also pu:tʃ], -iz

pouch (v.), -es, -ing, -ed pautʃ, -iz, -iŋ, -t

pouf(fe), -s pu:f, -s

Poughill 'pɔfil

Poulett 'pɔ:lit [-let]

poulpe, -s puːlp, -s
poult (chicken), -s pəult, -s
poult (silk material) puːlt
poulter, -s 'pəultə*, -z
poulterer, -s 'pəultərə*, -z
poultic|e (s. v.), -es, -ing, -ed 'pəultis,
-iz, -iŋ, -t
Poultney 'pəultni
Poulton 'pəultən
poultry 'pəultri
poultry-farm, -s, -ing, -er/s 'pəultri-
faːm, -z, -iŋ, -ə*/z
poultry-yard, -s 'pəultrijaːd, -z
pounc|e (s. v.), -es, -ing, -ed pauns, -iz,
-iŋ, -t
Pouncefoot 'paunsfut
pound (s. v.) (P.), -s, -ing, -ed, -er/s
paund, -z, -iŋ, -id, -ə*/z
poundage, -s 'paundidʒ, -iz
Pounds paundz
Pount(e)ney 'pauntni
Poupart (surname) 'pəupaːt, 'puːpaːt
Pouparts (junction near Clapham Junction) 'puːpaːts
pour (s. v.), -s, -ing, -ed, -er/s pɔː*
[pɔə*], -z, -riŋ, -d, -rə*/z
pourboire, -s 'puəbwaː* [-bwɔː*] (pur-
bwaːr), -z
pourparler, -s puə'paːlei ['-'-—] (pur-
parle), -z
pout (s. v.), -s, -ing, -ed, -er/s paut, -s,
-iŋ, -id, -ə*/z
poverty 'pɔvəti
poverty-stricken 'pɔvəti,strikn [-kən]
Pow pau
P.O.W., -'s 'piːəu'dʌb|ju(ː), -z
powd|er (s. v.), -ers, -ering, -ered
'paud|ə*, -əz, -əriŋ, -əd
powder-magazine, -s 'paudəmægə,ziːn,
-z
powder-puff, -s 'paudəpʌf, -s
powder|y, -iness 'paudər|i, -inis
Powell 'pəuəl [-il, -əl], 'pau-
power (P.), -s 'pauə*, -z
power-cut, -s 'pauəkʌt, -s
power|ful, -fully, -fulness 'pauə|ful,
-fuli [-fəli, -fli], -fulnis
power-hou|se, -ses 'pauəhau|s, -ziz
powerless, -ly, -ness 'pauəlis, -li, -nis
Powerscourt (family name) 'pɔːzkɔːt
power-station, -s 'pauə,steiʃən, -z
Powicke 'pəuik
Powis (in Scotland) 'pəuis, (surname)
'pəuis, 'pauis, (square in London)
'pauis
Powles pəulz
Powlett 'pɔːlit
Pownall 'paunl

Pownceby 'paunsbi
pow-wow (s. v.), -s, -ing, -ed 'pau-
wau, -z, -iŋ, -d
Powyke 'pəuik
Powys (district in Wales, family name
of Viscount Lilford) 'pəuis
pox pɔks
Poynings 'pɔiniŋz
Poynt|er, -on 'pɔint|ə*, -ən
practicability ,præktikə'biliti [-lət-]
practicab|le, -ly, -leness 'præktikəb|l,
-li, -lnis
practic|al, -alness 'præktik|əl, -lnis
practicality ,prækti'kæliti
practically (in a practical manner)
'præktikəli [-kli], (very nearly) 'præk-
tikli [-kəli]
practice, -s 'præktis, -iz
practician, -s præk'tiʃən, -z
practis|e, -es, -ing, -ed, -er/s 'præktis,
-iz, -iŋ, -t, -ə*/z
practitioner, -s præk'tiʃŋə* [prək-,
-ʃənə*], -z
Praed preid
praenomen, -s priː'nəumen ['priː'n-], -z
praepostor, -s priː'pɔstə*, -z
praesidium, -s priː'sidiəm [priː'zid-,
-djəm], -z
praetor, -s; -ship/s 'priːtə* [-tɔː*], -z;
-ʃip/s
praetori|al, -an, -um/s, -a priː(ː)'tɔːri|əl,
-ən, -əm/z, -ə
pragmatic, -al, -ally præg'mætik, -əl,
-əli
pragmati|sm, -st/s 'prægməti|zəm, -st/s
Prague praːg
Note.—There existed until recently a
pronunciation preig which is now
probably obsolete.
Prai (in Malaya) prai
prairie (P.), -s; -land 'preəri, -z; -lænd
prais|e (s. v.), -es, -ing, -ed, -er/s
preiz, -iz, -iŋ, -d, -ə*/z
praiseworth|y, -iness 'preiz,wə:ð|i, -inis
Prakrit 'praːkrit
praline, -s 'praːliːn, -z
Prall prɔːl
pram (perambulator), -s præm, -z
pram (flat-bottomed boat), -s praːm, -z
pranc|e (P.), -es, -ing, -ed, -er/s praːns,
-iz, -iŋ, -t, -ə*/z
prandial 'prændiəl [-djəl]
prang (s. v.), -s, -ing, -ed præŋ, -z, -iŋ, -d
prank (s. v.), -s, -ing, -ed præŋk, -s, -iŋ,
-t [præŋt]
prank|ish, -some 'præŋk|iʃ, -səm
prat|e (s. v.), -es, -ing, -ed, -er/s preit,
-s, -iŋ, -id, -ə*/z

pratique, -s 'præti:k [-tik, præ'ti:k], -s
Pratt præt
pratt|le (s. v.), -les, -ling, -led, -ler/s
'præt|l, -lz, -liŋ [-liŋ], -ld, -lə*/z
[-lə*/z]
prawn, -s prɔ:n, -z
prax|is, -es 'præks|is, -i:z
Praxiteles præk'sitəli:z [-til-]
pray (P.), -s, -ing, -ed prei, -z, -iŋ, -d
prayer (one who prays), -s 'preiə*, -z
prayer (supplication), -s prɛə*, -z
prayer-book, -s 'prɛəbuk, -s
prayer|ful, -fully, -fulness 'prɛə|ful,
-fuli [-fəli], -fulnis
prayerless, -ly, -ness 'prɛəlis, -li, -nis
prayer-meeting, -s 'prɛə,mi:tiŋ, -z
prayer-rug, -s 'prɛə-rʌg, -z
prayer-wheel, -s 'prɛəwi:l ['prɛəhw-], -z
preach (s. v.), -es, -ing, -ed, -er/s
pri:tʃ, -iz, -iŋ, -t, -ə*/z
preachi|fy, -fies, -fying, -fied 'pri:tʃi|fai,
-faiz, -faiiŋ, -faid
pre-adamite 'pri:'ædəmait [-'---]
Preager 'preigə*
preamble, -s pri:'æmbl [pri'æ-], -z
prearrang|e, -es, -ing, -ed 'pri:ə'reindʒ,
-iz, -iŋ, -d
Prebble 'prebl
prebend, -s 'prebənd, -z
prebendar|y, -ies 'prebəndəri [-bmd-],
-iz
precarious, -ly, -ness pri'kɛərɪəs, -li, -nis
precatory 'prekətəri
precaution, -s pri'kɔ:ʃən [prə'k-], -z
precautionary　　pri'kɔ:ʃŋəri　　[prə'k-,
-ʃnə-, -ʃənə-]
preced|e, -es, -ing, -ed pri(:)'si:d, -z, -iŋ,
-id
preceden|ce, -cy pri(:)'si:dən|s ['presid-],
-si
precedent (s.), -s, -ed 'presidənt [rarely
'pri:s-], -s, -id　　　　　　　　　　[-li
precedent (adj.), -ly pri'si:dənt ['presid-],
precentor, -s pri(:)'sentə*, -z
precept, -s 'pri:sept, -s
preceptor, -s pri'septə*, -z
preceptor|y, -ies pri'septər|i, -iz
preces 'pri:si:z
precession, -s pri'seʃən, -z
precinct, -s 'pri:siŋkt, -s
preciosity ,preʃi'ɒsiti [-esi-]
precious, -ly, -ness 'preʃəs, -li, -nis
precipice, -s 'presipis, -iz
precipitan|ce, -cy pri'sipitən|s, -si
precipitate (s.), -s pri'sipitit [prə's-,
-teit], -s
precipitate (adj.), -ly pri'sipitit [prə's-],
-li

precipitat|e (v.), -es, -ing, -ed pri'si-pi
teit [prə's-], -s, -iŋ, -id
precipitation pri,sipi'teiʃən [prə,s-]
precipitous, -ly, -ness pri'sipitəs [prə's-],
-li, -nis
précis (sing.) 'preisi: ['pres-], (plur.) -z
precise, -ly, -ness pri'sais [prə's-], -li,
-nis
precisian, -s pri'siʒən [prə's-], -z
precision pri'siʒən [prə's-]
preclud|e, -es, -ing, -ed pri'klu:d, -z, -iŋ,
-d
preclu|sion, -sive pri'klu:|ʒən, -siv
precocious, -ly, -ness pri'kəuʃəs [prə'k-],
-li, -nis
precocity pri'kɒsiti [prə'k-]
preconceiv|e, -es, -ing, -ed 'pri:kən'si:v
[,pri:-], -z, -iŋ, -d [also 'pri:kənsi:vd
when attributive]
preconception,　　-s　　'pri:kən'sepʃən
[,pri:-], -z
preconcert, -s, -ing, -ed 'pri:kən'sə:t
[,pri:-], -s, -iŋ, -id
precursor, -s; -y pri(:)'kə:sə*, -z, -ri
predation, -s pri'deiʃən [pre'd-], -z
predator|y, -ily, -iness 'predətər|i, -ili,
-inis
predeceas|e, -es, -ing, -ed 'pri:di'si:s, -iz,
-iŋ, -t
predecessor, -s 'pri:disesə* [,pri:di's-], -z
predestinat|e, -es, -ing, -ed pri(:)-
'destineit, -s, -iŋ, -id
predestination pri(:),desti'neiʃən ['pri:-
,desti'neiʃən]
predestin|e, -es, -ing, -ed pri(:)'destin, -z,
-iŋ, -d
predetermination 'pri:di,tə:mi'neiʃən
predetermin|e, -es, -ing, -ed 'pri:di-
'tə:min [,pri:-], -z, -iŋ, -d
predicability ,predikə'biliti [-lət-]
predicable 'predikəbl
predicament, -s pri'dikəmənt [prə'd-], -s
predicate (s.), -s 'predikit [-keit,
'pri:dikit], -s
predicat|e (v.), -es, -ing, -ed 'predikeit,
-s, -iŋ, -id
predication, -s ,predi'keiʃən, -z
predicative, -ly pri'dikətiv [prə'd-], -li
predict, -s, -ing, -ed, -or/s; -able
pri'dikt [prə'd-], -s, -iŋ, -id, -ə*/z;
-əbl
prediction, -s pri'dikʃən [prə'd-], -z
predilection, -s ,pri:di'lekʃən, -z
predispos|e, -es, -ing, -ed 'pri:dis'pəuz
[,pri:-], -iz, -iŋ, -d
predisposition,　　-s　　'pri:,dispə'ziʃən
[,pri:dis-], -z
predominan|ce, -t/ly pri'dɒminən|s, -t/li

predominat|e, -es, -ing, -ed pri'dɔmi-
neit, -s, -iŋ, -id
predomination pri,dɔmi'neiʃən
predorsal 'pri:'dɔ:sl
Preece pri:s
pre-eminen|ce, -t/ly pri(:)'eminən|s,
-t/li
pre-empt, -s, -ing, -ed pri(:)'empt, -s,
-iŋ, -id
pre-emption pri(:)'empʃən
pre-emptive pri(:)'emptiv
preen, -s, -ing, -ed pri:n, -z, -iŋ, -d
pre-exist, -s, -ing, -ed; -ence, -ent
'pri:ig'zist, -s, -iŋ, -id; -əns, -ənt
prefab, -s 'pri:fæb ['-'-], -z
prefabricat|e,-es,-ing,-ed 'pri:'fæbrikeit
[-'---], -s, -iŋ, -id
pre-fabrication 'pri:,fæbri'keiʃən [,---'-,
-,-'--]
prefac|e (s. v.), -es, -ing, -ed 'prefis
[-fəs], -iz, -iŋ, -t
prefatorial ,prefə'tɔ:riəl
prefatory 'prefətəri
prefect, -s 'pri:fekt, -s
prefecture, -s 'pri:fektjuə* [-tʃuə*,
-tʃə*], -z [-riŋ, -d
prefer, -s, -ring, -red pri'fə:* [prə'f-], -z,
preferability ,prefərə'biliti [-lət-]
preferab|le, -ly, -leness 'prefərəb|l [rarely
pri'fə:r-, prə'fə:r-], -li, -lnis
preference, -s 'prefərəns, -iz
preferential ,prefə'renʃəl
preferment, -s pri'fə:mənt [prə'f-], -s
prefix (s.), -es 'pri:fiks, -iz
prefix (v.), -es, -ing, -ed pri:'fiks
['pri:fiks], -iz, -iŋ, -t
pregnable 'pregnəbl
pregnan|cy, -t/ly 'pregnən|si, -t/li
prehensible pri'hensəbl [-sib-]
prehensile pri'hensail
prehistoric, -ally 'pri:his'tɔrik [,pri:-],
-əli [-ḷi]
pre-history 'pri:'histəri
prejudg|e, -es, -ing, -ed 'pri:'dʒʌdʒ
[-'-], -iz, -iŋ, -d
prejudic|e (s. v.), -es, -ing, -ed 'pre-
dʒudis [-dʒəd-], -iz, -iŋ, -t
prejudici|al,-ally ,predʒu'diʃ|əl [-dʒə'd-],
-əli [-ḷi]
prelac|y, -ies 'preləs|i, -iz
prelate, -s 'prelit [-lət], -s
preliminar|y, -ies, -ily pri'liminər|i
[prə'l-, -'liminr-], -iz, -ili
prelud|e (s. v.), -es, -ing, -ed 'prelju:d,
-z, -iŋ, ['preljudiŋ], -id ['preljudid]
premature, -ly, -ness 'premə'tjuə*
[,pri:m-, -'tjə:*, -'tjɔə*, -'tjɔ:*, -'tʃə:*,
-'tʃuə*, '---, '--'-], -li, -nis

premeditat|e, -es, -ing, -ed/ly pri(:)-
'mediteit, -s, -iŋ, -id/li
premeditation pri(:),medi'teiʃən
premier (s. adj.), -s; -ship/s 'premjə*
[-miə*], -z; -ʃip/s
première, -s 'premiɛə*, -z
premise (s.), -s 'premis, -iz
premis|e (v.), -es, -ing, -ed pri'maiz
['premis], -iz, -iŋ, pri'maizd
['premist]
premium, -s 'pri:mjəm [-miəm], -z
premonition, -s ,pri:mə'niʃən [-məu'n-],
-z
premonitor|y, -ily pri'mɔnitər|i, -ili
pre-natal 'pri:'neitl
Prendergast 'prendəgæst [-gɑ:st]
prentice, -s 'prentis, -iz
Prenti|ce, -ss 'prenti|s, -s
preoccupation, -s pri(:),ɔkju'peiʃən
[,pri:ɔk-], -z
preoccup|y, -ies, -ying, -ied pri(:)-
'ɔkjup|ai, -aiz, -aiiŋ, -aid
preordain, -s, -ing, -ed 'pri:ɔ:'dein
[,pri:-], -z, -iŋ, -d
prep (s. adj.), -s prep, -s
prepaid (from prepay) 'pri:'peid [also
'pri:-peid when attributive]
preparation, -s ,prepə'reiʃən, -z
preparative, -ly pri'pærətiv [prə'p-], -li
preparator|y, -ily pri'pærətər|i [prə'p-],
-ili
prepar|e, -es, -ing, -ed, -edly, -edness,
-er/s pri'pɛə* [prə'p-], -z, -riŋ, -d,
-dli [-ridli], -dnis [-ridnis], -rə*/z
prepay, -s, -ing, prepaid, prepayment/s
'pri:'pei, -z, -iŋ, 'pri:'peid [also 'pri:-
peid when attributive], 'pri:'peimənt/s
prepense, -ly pri'pens, -li
preponderan|ce, -t/ly pri'pɔndərən|s
[prə'p-], -t/li
preponderat|e, -es, -ing/ly, -ed pri-
'pɔndəreit [prə'p-], -s, -iŋ/li, -id
preponderation pri,pɔndə'reiʃən [prə,p-]
prepos|e, -es, -ing, -ed pri:'pəuz, -iz,
-iŋ, -d
preposition, -s ,prepə'ziʃən, -z
preposi|tional, -tionally ,prepə'zi|ʃənl
[-pu'z-, -ʃnəl, -ʃnḷ, -ʃnḷ, -ʃənəl], -ʃnəli
[-ʃnəli, -ʃnḷi, -ʃnḷi, -ʃənəli]
prepositive pri'pɔzitiv
prepossess, -es, -ing/ly, -ed ,pri:-
pə'zes, -iz, -iŋ/li, -t
prepossession, -s ,pri:pə'zeʃən, -z
preposterous, -ly, -ness pri'pɔstərəs
[prə'p-], -li, -nis
prepuce, -s 'pri:pju:s, -iz
Pre-Raphaelite (s. adj.), -s 'pri:'ræfəl-
ait [pri:-, -fil-, -fḷ-, -fiəl-, -feiəl-],-s

prerequisite, -s 'pri:'rekwizit [pri:-], -s
prerogative (s. adj.), -s pri'rɔgətiv [prə'r-], -z
presage (s.), -s 'presidʒ, -iz
presag|e (v.), -es, -ing, -ed 'presidʒ [pri'seidʒ], -iz, -iŋ, -d
presbyopia ,prezbi'əupjə [-pɪə]
presbyter, -s 'prezbitə*, -z
presbyterian, -s, -ism ,prezbi'tiərɪən, -z, -izəm
presbyter|y, -ies 'prezbitər|i, -iz
prescien|ce, -t/ly 'presɪən|s [-sjə-, -ʃɪə-, -ʃjə-], -t/li
Prescot(t) 'preskət
prescrib|e, -es, -ing, -ed, -er/s pris-'kraib [prəs-], -z, -iŋ, -d, -ə*/z
prescript, -s 'pri:skript, -s
prescription, -s pris'kripʃən [prəs-], -z
prescriptive pris'kriptiv [prəs-]
presence, -s 'prezns, -iz
present (s.) (ordinary senses), -s 'preznt [-zənt], -s
present (s.) (military term), -s pri'zent [prə'z-], -s
present (adj.), -ly 'preznt [-zənt], -li
present (v.), -s, -ing, -ed, -ment pri'zent [prə'z-], -s, -iŋ, -id, -mənt
presentable, -ness pri'zentəbl [prə'z-], -nis
presentation, -s ,prezen'teiʃən [-zən-], -z
presentient pri'senʃɪənt [-ʃjənt, -ʃənt]
presentiment, -s pri'zentimənt [-i'se-], -s
presently 'prezntli [-zənt-]
preservation, -s ,prezə(:)'veiʃən, -z
preservative (s. adj.), -s pri'zə:vətiv, -z
preserv|e (s. v.), -es, -ing, -ed, -er/s; -able pri'zə:v, -z, -iŋ, -d, -ə*/z; -əbl
presid|e, -es, -ing, -ed pri'zaid, -z, -iŋ, -id
presidenc|y, -ies 'prezidəns|i, -iz
president, -s 'prezidənt, -s
presidential ,prezi'denʃəl
presidium, -s pri'sidɪəm [pri'zid-, -djəm], -z
press (s. v.), -es, -ing/ly, -ed, -er/s pres, -iz, -iŋ/li, -t, -ə*/z
press-agent, -s 'pres,eidʒənt, -s
press-conference, -s 'pres,kɔnfərəns, -iz
press-cutting, -s 'pres,kʌtiŋ, -z
pressgang, -s 'presgæŋ, -z
pression 'preʃən
press|man, -men 'pres|mən [-mæn], -mən [-men]
pressure, -s 'preʃə*, -z
pressure-cooker, -s 'preʃə,kukə*, -z
pressuriz|e [-is|e], -es, -ing, -ed 'preʃəraiz, -iz, -iŋ, -d
Prestage 'prestidʒ
Prestatyn pres'tætin (Welsh pres'tatin)

Presteign pres'ti:n
prestidigitation 'presti,didʒi'teiʃən
prestidigitator, -s ,presti'didʒiteitə*, -z
prestige pres'ti:ʒ
Prestige (surname) 'prestidʒ
prestissimo pres'tisiməu
presto (P.), -s 'prestəu, -z
Preston 'prestən
Prestonpans 'prestən'pænz
Prestwich 'prest-witʃ
presum|e, -es, -ing/ly, -ed; -able, -ably pri'zju:m [prə'z-, -'zu:m], -z, -iŋ/li, -d; -əbl, -əbli
presumption, -s pri'zʌmpʃən [prə'z-], -z
presumptive, -ly pri'zʌmptiv [prə'z-], -li
presumptuous, -ly, -ness pri'zʌmp-tjʊəs [prə'z-, -tjwəs, -tʃʊəs, -tʃwəs], -li, -nis
presuppos|e, -es, -ing, -ed ,pri:sə'pəuz ['--'-], -iz, -iŋ, -d
presupposition, -s ,pri:sʌpə'ziʃən, -z
pretence, -s pri'tens, -iz
pretend, -s, -ing, -ed, -er/s pri'tend, -z, -iŋ, -id, -ə*/z
pretension, -s pri'tenʃən, -z
pretentious, -ly, -ness pri'tenʃəs, -li, -nis
preterite, -s 'pretərit, -s
preterito-present, -s pri(:)'teritəu-'preznt [-zənt], -s
pretermission ,pri:tə'miʃən [-tə:'m-]
pretermit, -s, -ting, -ted ,pri:tə'mit [-tə:'m-], -s, -iŋ, -id
preternatur|al, -ally, -alness ,pri:tə-'nætʃr|əl [-tə:'n-, -tʃur-, -tʃər-], -əli, -əlnis
pretext, -s 'pri:tekst, -s
pre-tonic 'pri:'tɔnik
Pretori|a, -us pri'tɔ:rɪ|ə [prə't-], -əs
prett|y (adj. adv.), -ier, -iest, -ily, -iness 'prit|i [rarely 'prut-], -ɪə*, -iist, -ili, -inis
Pretty (surname) 'priti, 'preti
Pret(t)yman 'pritimən
pretty-pretty 'priti,priti
prevail, -s, -ing, -ed pri'veil [prə'v-], -z, -iŋ, -d
prevalen|ce, -t/ly 'prevələn|s [-vl̩-], -t/li
prevaricat|e, -es, -ing, -ed, -or/s pri-'værikeit, -s, -iŋ, -id, -ə*/z
prevarication, -s pri,væri'keiʃən, -z
prevent (hinder), -s, -ing, -ed, -er/s; -able pri'vent [prə'v-], -s, -iŋ, -id, -ə*/z; -əbl
prevent (go before), -s, -ing, -ed pri:-'vent [pri'v-], -s, -iŋ, -id
preventability pri,ventə'biliti [prə,v-, -lət-]

preventative (s. adj.), -s pri'ventətiv [prə'v-], -z
prevention pri'venʃən [prə'v-]
preventive, -ly, -ness pri'ventiv [prə'v-], -li, -nis
pre-view, -s 'pri:'vju: ['--], -z
previous, -ly, -ness 'pri:vjəs [-vɪəs], -li, -nis
prevision pri(:)'viʒən
Prevost (English surname) 'prevəu, 'prevəust, pre'vəu
pre-war 'pri:'wɔ:* ['-- when attributive]
prey (s. v.), -s, -ing, -ed prei, -z, -iŋ, -d
Priam 'praiəm [-æm]
priapism 'praiəpizəm
priapus (P.), -es prai'eipəs, -iz
pric|e (s. v.) (P.), -es, -ing, -ed prais, -iz, -iŋ, -t
priceless, -ness 'praislis, -nis
prick (s. v.), -s, -ing/s, -ed, -er/s prik, -s, -iŋ/z, -t, -ə*/z
prick|le (s. v.), -les, -ling, -led 'prik|l, -lz, -liŋ [-lịŋ], -ld
prickl|y, -iest, -iness 'prikl|i [-kḷ|i], -iist, -inis
pride (P.) praid
Prideaux 'pridəu, 'pri:d-
Pridham 'pridəm
prie-Dieu, -s 'pri:dʒə: (pridjø), -z
priest (P.), -s; -craft, -hood, -like pri:st, -s; -krɑ:ft, -hud, -laik
priestess, -es 'pri:stis [-tes], -iz
Priestley 'pri:stli
priestl|y, -iness 'pri:stl|i, -inis
priest-ridden 'pri:st,ridn
prig (s. v.), -s, -ging, -ged, -ger/s; -gery prig, -z, -iŋ, -d, -ə*/z; -əri
priggish, -ly, -ness 'prigiʃ, -li, -nis
prim (adj. v.) (P.), -mer, -mest, -ly, -ness; -s, -ming, -med prim, -ə*, -ist, -li, -nis; -z, -iŋ, -d
primac|y, -ies 'praiməs|i, -iz
prima-donna, -s 'pri:mə'dɔnə [,pri:-], -z
primaeval = primeval
prima facie 'praimə'feiʃi(:) [-si(:), -ʃii:, -sii:]
primage 'praimidʒ
primal 'praiməl
prim|ary (s. adj.), -aries, -arily, -ariness 'praim|əri, -əriz, -ərili, -ərinis
primate (archbishop), -s 'praimit [-meit], -s
primate (higher mammal), -s 'praimeit, prai'meiti:z ['praimeits]
primateship, -s 'praimit-ʃip, -s
prim|e (s. adj. v.), -es, -ing, -ed praim, -z, -iŋ, -d

primer (he who or that which primes), -s 'praimə*, -z
primer (elementary book), -s 'praimə* ['prim-], -z
primer (printing type) 'primə*
primeval prai'mi:vəl
primitive, -ly, -ness 'primitiv, -li, -nis
primogeniture ,praiməu'dʒenitʃə* [-tʃuə*, -tjuə*]
primordial prai'mɔ:djəl [-dɪəl]
primrose (P.), -s 'primrəuz, -iz
primula, -s 'primjulə, -z
primus, -es 'praiməs, -iz
prince (P.), -s; -dom/s, -like prins, -iz; -dəm/z, -laik
princel|y, -ier, -iest, -iness 'prinsl|i, -ɪə* [-jə*], -iist [-jist], -inis
princess, princesses prin'ses [but '-- when used attributively, also '-'-], prin'sesiz
Prince|ton, -town 'prins|tən, -taun
princip|al (s. adj.), -als, -ally, -alness 'prinsəp|əl [-sip-], -əlz, -li [-əli], -əlnis
principalit|y, -ies ,prinsi'pælit|i, -iz
principalship, -s 'prinsəpəlʃip [-sip-], -s
principate (s.), -s 'prinsipit [-peit], -s
Principia prin'sipɪə [-pjə]
principle, -s, -d 'prinsəpl [-sip-], -z, -d
Pring priŋ
Pringle 'priŋgl
Prinsep 'prinsep
print (s. v.), -s, -ing/s, -ed, -er/s print, -s, -iŋ/z, -id, -ə*/z
printable 'printəbl
printing-machine, -s 'printiŋmə,ʃi:n, -z
printing-office, -s 'printiŋ,ɔfis, -iz
printing-press, -es 'printiŋ,pres, -iz
print-seller, -s 'print,selə*, -z
print-shop, -s 'print-ʃɔp, -s
prior (s. adj.) (P.), -s 'praiə*, -z
prioress, -es 'praiəris [-res], -iz
priorit|y, -ies prai'ɔrit|i, -iz
prior|y, -ies 'praiər|i, -iz
Priscian 'priʃɪən [-ʃjən]
Priscilla pri'silə
pris|e (s. v.), -es, -ing, -ed praiz, -iz, -iŋ, -d
prism, -s 'prizəm, -z
prismatic, -al, -ally priz'mætik, -əl, -əli
prison, -s 'prizn, -z
prisoner, -s 'prizŋə* [-znə*], -z
prison-hou|se, -ses 'priznhau|s, -ziz
pristine 'pristain
Pritchard 'pritʃəd, -tʃɑ:d
prithee 'priði(:)
privacy 'privəsi ['praiv-]
private (s. adj.), -s, -ly, -ness 'praivit, -s, -li, -nis

privateer, -s ˌpraivəˈtiə* [-viˈt-], -z
privation, -s praiˈveiʃən, -z
privative, -ly ˈprivətiv, -li
privet, -s ˈprivit, -s
privilege, -s, -d ˈprivilidʒ, -iz, -d
privity ˈpriviti
priv|y (s. adj.), -ies, -ily ˈpriv|i, -iz, -ili
priz|e (s. v.), -es, -ing, -ed praiz, -iz, -iŋ, -d
prize-fight, -s, -er/s ˈpraizfait, -s, -ə*/z
prize|man, -men ˈpraiz|mən, -mən [-men]
P.R.O. (public relations officer) ˈpiːˈɑːrˈəu
pro (s. prep.), -s prəu, -z
probabilit|y, -ies ˌprobəˈbilit|i [-lət-], -iz
probab|le, -ly ˈprobəb|l, -li
probate, -s ˈprəubit [-beit], -s [-ˈbeit]
probation,-s prəˈbeiʃən [prəuˈb-, pruˈb-],
probationary prəˈbeiʃŋəri [prəuˈb-, pruˈb-, -ʃnə-, -ʃənə-]
probationer, -s prəˈbeiʃnə* [prəuˈb-, pruˈb-, -ʃŋ*, -ʃənə*], -z
probative ˈprəubətiv [-d
prob|e (s. v.), -es, -ing, -ed prəub, -z, -iŋ, -d
probity ˈprəubiti [ˈprob-]
problem, -s ˈprobləm [-lem, -lim], -z
problematic, -al, -ally ˌprobliˈmætik [-bləˈm-, -bleˈm-], -əl, -əli
proboscis, -es prəuˈbosis [pruˈb-], -iːz
Prob|us, -yn ˈprəub|əs, -in
procedure, -s prəˈsiːdʒə* [prəuˈs-, pruˈs-, -djuə*], -z
procedural prəˈsiːdʒərəl [prəuˈs-, pruˈs-, -djur-, -djər-]
proceed (v.), -s, -ing/s, -ed prəˈsiːd [prəuˈs-, pruˈs-], -z, -iŋ/z, -id
proceeds (s.) ˈprəusiːdz
proc|ess (s.), -esses ˈprəus|es [rarely ˈpros-, also sometimes -|is, esp. when followed by of], -esiz [-isiz]
process (v.) (go in a procession), -es, -ing, -ed prəˈses [prəuˈs-, pruˈs-], -iz, -iŋ, -t
process (v.) (treat by a process), -es, -ing, -ed ˈprəuses, -iz [ˈprəusisiz], -iŋ [ˈprəusisiŋ], -t
process-block, -s ˈprəusesblok [-sis-], -s
procession, -s prəˈseʃən [pruˈs-], -z
processional (s. adj.), -s prəˈseʃənl [pruˈs-, -ʃnəl, -ʃŋl, -ʃnl, -ʃənəl], -z
proclaim, -s, -ing, -ed, -er/s prəˈkleim [prəuˈk-, pruˈk-], -z, -iŋ, -d, -ə*/z
proclamation, -s ˌprokləˈmeiʃən, -z
proclitic (s. adj.), -s prəuˈklitik, -s
proclivit|y, -ies prəˈklivit|i [prəuˈk-, pruˈk-], -iz
proconsul, -s prəuˈkonsəl [ˈprəuˈk-], -z
proconsul|ar, -ate/s prəuˈkonsjul|ə* [ˈprəuˈk-, -sjəl-], -it/s [-eit/s]

proconsulship, -s prəuˈkonsəlʃip [ˈprəuˈk-], -s
procrastinat|e, -es, -ing, -ed, -or/s prəuˈkræstineit [pruˈk-], -s, -iŋ, -id, -ə*/z
procrastination, -s prəuˌkræstiˈneiʃən [pruˌk-], -z
procreant ˈprəukriənt
procreat|e, -es, -ing, -ed ˈprəukrieit, -s, -iŋ, -id
procreation ˌprəukriˈeiʃən
procreative ˈprəukrieitiv
Procter ˈproktə*
proctor (P.), -s ˈproktə*, -z
proctorial prokˈtɔːriəl
procumbent prəuˈkʌmbənt
procuration, -s ˌprokjuəˈreiʃən, -z
procurator, -s ˈprokjuəreitə*, -z
procur|e, -es, -ing, -ed, -er/s, -ess/es; -able prəˈkjuə* [pruˈk-, -ˈkjɔə*, -ˈkjɔː*, -ˈkjə:*], -z, -riŋ, -d, -rə*/z, -ris/iz [-res/iz]; -rəbl
Procyon (star) ˈprəusjən [-siən]
prod (s. v.), -s, -ding, -ded prod, -z, -iŋ, -id
prodig|al (s. adj.), -als, -ally, -alness ˈprodig|əl, -əlz, -əli, -əlnis
prodigality ˌprodiˈgæliti
prodigaliz|e [-is|e], -es, -ing, -ed ˈprodigəlaiz, -iz, -iŋ, -d
prodigious, -ly, -ness prəˈdidʒəs [pruˈd-], -li, -nis
prodig|y, -ies ˈprodidʒ|i, -iz
produce (s.) ˈprodjuːs
produc|e (v.), -es, -ing, -ed, -er/s prəˈdjuːs [pruˈd-], -iz, -iŋ, -t, -ə*/z
producible prəˈdjuːsəbl [pruˈd-, -sib-]
product, -s ˈprodʌkt [-dəkt], -s
production, -s prəˈdʌkʃən [pruˈd-], -z
productional prəˈdʌkʃənl [pruˈd-, -ʃnəl, -ʃŋl, -ʃnl, -ʃənəl]
productive, -ly, -ness prəˈdʌktiv [pruˈd-, -dək-], -li, -nis
productivity ˌprodʌkˈtiviti [ˌprəud-, proem, -s ˈprəuem, -z
profanation, -s ˌprofəˈneiʃən, -z
profan|e (adj. v.), -er, -est, -ely, -eness; -es, -ing, -ed, -er/s prəˈfein [pruˈf-], -ə*, -ist, -li, -nis; -z, -iŋ, -d, -ə*/z
profanit|y, -ies prəˈfænit|i [pruˈf-], -iz
profess, -es, -ing, -ed, -edly, -er/s, -or/s prəˈfes [pruˈf-], -iz, -iŋ, -t, -idli, -ə*/z, -ə*/z
profession, -s prəˈfeʃən [pruˈf-], -z
professional (s. adj.), -s prəˈfeʃənl [pruˈf-, -ʃnəl, -ʃŋl, -ʃnl, -ʃənəl], -z
professionalism prəˈfeʃŋəlizm [pruˈf-, -ʃnəl-, -ʃŋl-, -ʃnl-, -ʃənəl-]

professionally prə'feʃŋəli [pru'f-, -ʃnəli, -ʃŋli, -ʃnli, -ʃənəli]

professor, -s; -ate/s, -ship/s prə'fesə* [pru'f-], -z; -rit/s, -ʃip/s

professorial, -ly ˌprɔfe'sɔːriəl [-fi's-, -fə's-], -i

professoriate ˌprɔfe'sɔːriit [-fi's-, -fə's-]

proffer, -s, -ing, -ed, -er/s 'prɔfə*, -z, -riŋ, -d, -rə*/z

proficien|cy, -t/ly prə'fiʃən|si [pru'f-], -t/li

profil|e (s. v.), -es, -ing, -ed 'prəufail [old-fashioned -fiːl], -z, -iŋ, -d

profit (s. v.), -s, -ing, -ed, -er/s 'prɔfit, -s, -iŋ, -id, -ə*/z

profitab|le, -ly, -leness 'prɔfitəb|l, -li, -lnis

profiteer (s. v.), -s, -ing, -ed ˌprɔfi'tiə*, -z, -riŋ, -d

profitless 'prɔfitlis

profit-sharing 'prɔfitˌʃɛəriŋ

profligacy 'prɔfligəsi

profligate (s. adj.), -s, -ly, -ness 'prɔfligit, -s, -li, -nis

pro forma prəu'fɔːmə

profoun|d, -der, -dest, -dly, -dness prə'faun|d [pru'f-], -də*, -dist, -dli, -dnis

profundit|y, -ies prə'fʌndit|i [pru'f-], -iz

profuse, -st, -ly, -ness prə'fjuːs [pru'f-], -ist, -li, -nis

profusion, -s prə'fjuːʒən [pru'f-], -z

prog (s. v.), -s, -ging, -ged prɔg, -z, -iŋ, -d

progenitor, -s prəu'dʒenitə*, -z

progeniture prəu'dʒenitʃə* [-tjuə*, -tʃə*]

progen|y, -ies 'prɔdʒin|i [-dʒən-], -iz

prognathic prɔg'næθik

prognathism 'prɔgnəθizəm [prɔg-'næθ-]

prognathous prɔg'neiθəs ['prɔgnəθəs]

prognos|is, -es prɔg'nəus|is, -iːz

prognosticat|e, -es, -ing, -ed, -or/s prəg'nɔstikeit [prɔg-], -s, -iŋ, -d, -ə*/z

prognostication, -s prəgˌnɔsti'keiʃən [prɔg-], -z

program(me), -s 'prəugræm, -z

progress (s.), -es 'prəugres [rarely 'prɔg-], -iz

progress (v.), -es, -ing, -ed prəu'gres [pru'g-], -iz, -iŋ, -t

progression, -s prəu'greʃən [pru'g-], -z

progressional prəu'greʃənl [pru'g-, -ʃnəl, -ʃŋl, -ʃnl, -ʃənəl]

progressionist, -s prəu'greʃŋist [pru'g-, -ʃənist], -s

progressist, -s prəu'gresist [pru'g-], -s

progressive (s. adj.), -s, -ly, -ness prəu'gresiv [pru'g-], -z, -li, -nis

prohibit, -s, -ing, -ed, -or/s prə'hibit [prəu'h-, pru'h-], -s, -iŋ, -id, -ə*/z

prohibition, -s ˌprəui'biʃən [ˌprəuhi-], -z

prohibitioni|sm, -st/s ˌprəui'biʃŋi|zəm [ˌprəuhi-, -ʃəni-], -st/s

prohibitive, -ly prə'hibitiv [prəu'h-, pru'h-], -li

prohibitory prə'hibitəri [prəu'h-, pru'h-]

project (s.), -s 'prɔdʒekt [-dʒikt], -s

project (v.), -s, -ing, -ed, -or/s prə-'dʒekt [prəu'dʒ-, pru'dʒ-], -s, -iŋ, -id, -ə*/z

projectile (s.), -s 'prɔdʒiktail [-dʒek-, prəu'dʒektail, pru'dʒek-], -z

projectile (adj.) prəu'dʒektail [pru'dʒ-]

projection, -s prə'dʒekʃən [prəu'dʒ-, pru'dʒ-], -z

projective, -ly prə'dʒektiv [prəu'dʒ-, pru'dʒ-], -li

prolapse, -s 'prəulæps, -iz

prolate 'prəuleit [prəu'leit]

prolegomen|on, -a ˌprəule'gɔmin|ən [-li'g-, -|ɔn], -ə

proleps|is, -es prəu'leps|is [-'liːp-], -iːz

proleptic, -ally prəu'leptik [-'liːp-], -əli

proletarian (s. adj.), -s, -ism ˌprəuli-'tɛəriən [-le't-, -lə't-], -z, -izəm

proletariat ˌprəuli'tɛəriət [-le't-, -lə't-, -iæt]

proliferat|e, -es, -ing, -ed prəu'lifəreit, -s, -iŋ, -id

proliferation prəuˌlifə'reiʃən

prolific, -ness prəu'lifik [pru'l-], -nis

prolix 'prəuliks [prəu'liks]

prolixity prəu'liksiti

prolix|ly, -ness prəu'liks|li ['prəuliks-], -nis

prolocutor, -s prəu'lɔkjutə*, -z

prologu|e (s. v.), -es, -ing, -ed 'prəulɔg [rarely -ləug], -z, -iŋ, -d

prolong, -s, -ing, -ed prəu'lɔŋ [pru'l-], -z, -iŋ, -d

prolongation, -s ˌprəulɔŋ'geiʃən [ˌprɔl-], -z

promenad|e (s. v.), -es, -ing, -ed, -er/s ˌprɔmi'nɑːd [-mə'n-], -z, -iŋ, -id, -ə*/z

Note.—Also '— when attributive, as in p. concert. There exists also a pronunciation ˌprɔmi'neid [-mə'n-] used chiefly in square dancing.

Promethean prə'miːθjən [prəu'm-, pru'm-, -θiən]

Prometheus prə'miːθjuːs [prəu'm-, pru'm-, -θjəs, -θiəs]

prominence, -s 'prɔminəns, -iz

prominent, -ly 'prɔminǝnt, -li
promiscuity ˌprɔmis'kju(:)iti
promiscuous, -ly, -ness prǝ'miskjŭǝs [pru'm-, -kjwǝs], -li, -nis
promis|e (s. v.), -es, -ing/ly, -ed, -er/s 'prɔmis, -iz, -iŋ/li, -t, -ǝ*/z
promissory 'prɔmisǝri [prǝ'mis-, pru'mis-]
promontor|y, -ies 'prɔmǝntr|i [-tǝr-], -iz
promot|e, -es, -ing, -ed, -er/s prǝ'mǝut [pru'm-], -s, -iŋ, -id, -ǝ*/z
promotion, -s prǝ'mǝuʃǝn [pru'm-], -z
promotive prǝ'mǝutiv [pru'm-]
prompt (s. adj. v.), -s; -er, -est, -ly, -ness; -ing/s, -ed, -er/s prɔmpt, -s; -ǝ*, -ist, -li, -nis; -iŋ/z, -id, -ǝ*/z
promptitude 'prɔmptitju:d
promulgat|e, -es, -ing, -ed, -or/s 'prɔmǝlgeit [-mʌl-], -s, -iŋ, -id, -ǝ*/z
promulgation, -s ˌprɔmǝl'geiʃǝn [-mʌl-], -z
prone, -r, -st, -ly, -ness prǝun, -ǝ*, -ist, -li, -nis
prong (s. v.), -s, -ing, -ed prɔŋ, -z, -iŋ, -d
pronomin|al, -ally prǝu'nɔmin|l [pru'n-], -ǝli [-li]
pronoun, -s 'prǝunaun, -z
pronounc|e, -es, -ing, -ed, -edly, -er/s, -ement/s; -eable/ness prǝ'nauns [pru'n-, prn̩'auns], -iz, -iŋ, -t, -tli [-idli], -ǝ*/z, -mǝnt/s; -ǝbl/nis
pronunciamento, -s prǝˌnʌnsĭǝ'mentǝu [prǝu̩n-, pruˌn-, -sjǝ-, -ʃĭǝ-, -ʃjǝ-], -z
pronunciation, -s prǝˌnʌnsi'eiʃǝn [pruˌn-, prn̩ˌʌn-], -z
proof, -s; -less pru:f, -s; -lis
proof-read|er/s, -ing 'pru:f,ri:d|ǝ*/z, -iŋ
prop (s. v.), -s, -ping, -ped prɔp, -s, -iŋ, -t
propaedeutic, -al, -s ˌprǝupi:'dju:tik, -ǝl, -s
propagand|a, -ist/s ˌprɔpǝ'gænd|ǝ, -ist/s
propagandism ˌprɔpǝ'gændizǝm
propagat|e, -es, -ing, -ed, -or/s 'prɔpǝgeit, -s, -iŋ, -id, -ǝ*/z
propagation ˌprɔpǝ'geiʃǝn
proparoxytone (s. adj.), -s ˌprǝu-pǝ-'rɔksitǝun [-tn], -z
propel, -s, -ling, -led, -ler/s; -lent/s prǝ'pel [prǝu'p-, pru'p-], -z, -iŋ, -d, -ǝ*/z; -ǝnt/s
propensit|y, -ies prǝ'pensit|i [prǝu'p-, pru'p-], -iz
proper, -ly 'prɔpǝ*, -li ['prɔpl̩i]
properispomen|on, -a 'prǝuˌperi'spǝu-min|ǝn [-ɔn], -ǝ
Propertius prǝu'pǝ:ʃjǝs [pru'p-, -ʃĭǝs, -ʃǝs]
propert|y, -ies, -ied 'prɔpǝt|i, -iz, -id

prophec|y, -ies 'prɔfis|i [-s|ai], -iz [-aiz]
prophes|y, -ies, -ying, -ied, -ier/s 'prɔfis|ai, -aiz, -aiiŋ, -aid, -aiǝ*/z
prophet, -s 'prɔfit, -s
prophetess, -es 'prɔfitis [-tes], -iz
prophetic, -al, -ally prǝ'fetik [prǝu'f-, pru'f-], -ǝl, -ǝli
Prophit 'prɔfit
prophylactic (s. adj.), -s ˌprɔfi'læktik, -s
prophylaxis ˌprɔfi'læksis
propinquity prǝ'piŋkwiti [prǝu'p-, pru'p-, prɔ'p-]
propitiat|e, -es, -ing, -ed, -or/s prǝ-'piʃieit [pru'p-], -s, -iŋ, -id, -ǝ*/z
propitiation, -s prǝˌpiʃi'eiʃǝn [pruˌp-], -z
propitiatory prǝ'piʃĭǝtǝri [pru'p-, -ʃjǝ-tǝri, -ʃǝtǝri, -ʃieitǝri]
propitious, -ly, -ness prǝ'piʃǝs [pru'p-], -li, -nis
proporti|on (s. v.), -ons, -oning, -oned prǝ'pɔ:ʃ|ǝn [pru'p-, -ǝnz, -n̩iŋ [-niŋ, -ǝniŋ], -ǝnd
proportionab|le, -ly prǝ'pɔ:ʃn̩ǝb|l [pru'p-, -ʃnǝ-, -ʃǝnǝ-], -li
propor|tional, -tionally prǝ'pɔ:ʃǝnl [pru'p-, -ʃnǝl, -ʃn̩l̩, -ʃnl̩, -ʃǝnǝl], -ʃn̩ǝli [-ʃnǝli, -ʃn̩li, -ʃnli, -ʃǝnǝli]
proportionality prǝˌpɔ:ʃǝ'næliti [pruˌp-, -ʃn̩'æ-]
proportionate, -ly, -ness prǝ'pɔ:ʃnit [pru'p-, -ʃn̩it, -ʃǝnit], -li, -nis
propos|e, -es, -ing, -ed, -er/s; -al/s prǝ'pǝuz [pru'p-], -iz, -iŋ, -d, -ǝ*/z; -ǝl/z
proposition, -s ˌprɔpǝ'ziʃǝn, -z
propound, -s, -ing, -ed, -er/s prǝ-'paund [pru'p-], -z, -iŋ, -id, -ǝ*/z
proprietary prǝ'praiǝtǝri [pru'p-]
proprietor, -s; -ship/s prǝ'praiǝtǝ* [pru'p-], -z; -ʃip/s
proprietress, -es prǝ'praiǝtris [pru'p-, -tres], -iz
propriet|y, -ies prǝ'praiǝt|i [pru'p-], -iz
propriocep|tion, -tive 'prǝupriǝu'sep|ʃǝn, -tiv [-siv
propul|sion, -sive prǝ'pʌl|ʃǝn [pru'p-], -siv
propylae|um (P.), -a ˌprɔpi'li(:)|ǝm, -ǝ
pro rata prǝu'rɑ:tǝ ['prǝu'r-, -'reitǝ]
prorogation, -s ˌprǝurǝ'geiʃǝn [ˌprɔr-, -rǝu'g-], -z
prorogu|e, -es, -ing, -ed prǝ'rǝug [prǝu'r-, pru'r-], -z, -iŋ, -d
prosaic, -al, -ally, -ness prǝu'zeiik, -ǝl, -ǝli, -nis
proscheni|um, -ums, -a prǝu'si:nj|ǝm [-nĭ|ǝm], -ǝmz, -ǝ
proscrib|e, -es, -ing, -ed, -er/s prǝus-'kraib, -z, -iŋ, -d, -ǝ*/z

proscription, -s prəus'kripʃən, -z
proscriptive prəus'kriptiv
pros|e (s. v.), **-es, -ing, -ed, -er/s** prəuz, -iz, -iŋ, -d, -ə*/z
prosecut|e, -es, -ing, -ed, -or/s 'prɔsikju:t, -s, -iŋ, -id, -ə*/z
prosecution, -s ˌprɔsi'kju:ʃən, -z
prosecutrix, -es 'prɔsiˌkju:triks, -iz
proselyte, -s 'prɔsilait [-səl-], -s
proselytism 'prɔsilitizəm [-səl-]
proselytiz|e [-is|e], **-es, -ing, -ed** 'prɔsilitaiz [-səl-], -iz, -iŋ, -d
Proserpina prɔ'sə:pinə [prɔ's-]
Proserpine 'prɔsəpain
prosit 'prəusit
prosodic, -al prə'sɔdik [prəu's-], -əl
prosodist, -s 'prɔsədist, -s
prosod|y, -ies 'prɔsəd|i, -iz
prospect (s.) (P.), **-s** 'prɔspekt, -s
prospect (v.), **-s, -ing, -ed** prəs'pekt [prus-, prɔs-, 'prɔspekt], -s, -iŋ, -id
prospective, -ly, -ness prəs'pektiv [prus-, prɔs-], -li, -nis
prospector, -s prəs'pektə* [prus-, prɔs-], -z
prospectus, -es prəs'pektəs [prus-], -iz
prosp|er, -ers, -ering, -ered 'prɔsp|ə*, -əz, -əriŋ, -əd
prosperity prɔs'periti [prəs-]
Prospero 'prɔspərəu
prosperous, -ly, -ness 'prɔspərəs, -li, -nis
prostate, -s 'prɔsteit [-tit], -s
prostatic prɔ'stætik
prosthesis 'prɔsθisis [-θəs-]
prosthetic, -s prɔs'θetik, -s
prosthetist, -s prɔs'θi:tist [prəs-], -s
prostitut|e (s. v.), **-es, -ing, -ed** 'prɔstitju:t, -s, -iŋ, -id
prostitution, -s ˌprɔsti'tju:ʃən, -z
prostrate (adj.) 'prɔstreit [-rit]
prostrat|e (v.), **-es, -ing, -ed** prɔs'treit [prəs-], -s, -iŋ, -id
prostration, -s prɔs'treiʃən [prəs-], -z
pros|y, -ier, -iest, -ily, -iness 'prəuz|i, -iə* [-jə*], -iist [-jist], -ili, -inis
protagonist, -s prəu'tægənist, -s
Protagoras prəu'tægəræs [-gɔr-, -rəs]
protas|is, -es 'prɔtəs|is, -i:z
protean prəu'ti:ən ['prəutjən, 'prəu-tiən]
protect, -s, -ing/ly, -ed, -or/s prə'tekt [pru't-], -s, -iŋ/li, -id, -ə*/z
protection, -s prə'tekʃən [pru't-], -z
protectioni|sm, -st/s prə'tekʃəni|zəm [pru't-, -ʃɲi-], -st/s
protective, -ly, -ness prə'tektiv [pru't-], -li, -nis

protectorate, -s prə'tektərit [pru't-], -s
protectress, -es prə'tektris [pru't-], -iz
protégé(e), -s 'prəuteʒei ['prɔt-, -teiʒ-] (prɔteʒe), -z
proteid, -s 'prəuti:d [-ti:id, -tiid], -z
protein 'prəuti:n [-ti:in, -tiin]
pro tem prəu'tem
protest (s.), **-s** 'prəutest [rarely 'prɔtest], -s
protest (v.), **-s, -ing/ly, -ed, -er/s** prə'test [prəu't-, pru't-], -s, -iŋ/li, -id, -ə*/z
protestant (P.), **-s, -ism** 'prɔtistənt [-təs-], -s, -izəm
protestantiz|e [-is|e], **-es, -ing, -ed** 'prɔtistəntaiz [-təs-], -iz, -iŋ, -d
protestation, -s ˌprəutes'teiʃən [ˌprɔt-, -tis-, -təs-], -z
Proteus 'prəutju:s [-tjəs, -tiəs]
Protheroe 'prɔðərəu
prothes|is, -es 'prɔθis|is [-θəs-], -i:z
protium 'prəutjəm [-tiəm]
protocol, -s 'prəutəkɔl [-təuk-], -z
proton, -s 'prəutɔn, -z
protoplasm 'prəutəuplæzəm
prototype, -s 'prəutəutaip, -s
protozo|ic, -on, -a ˌprəutəu'zəu|ik, -ən [-ɔn], -ə
protract, -s, -ing, -ed/ly; -ile prə-'trækt [pru't-], -s, -iŋ, -id/li; -ail
protraction, -s prə'trækʃən [pru't-], -z
protractor, -s prə'træktə* [pru't-], -z
protrud|e, -es, -ing, -ed prə'tru:d [pru't-], -z, -iŋ, -id
protrusion, -s prə'tru:ʒən [pru't-], -z
protrusive, -ly, -ness prə'tru:siv [pru't-], -li, -nis
protuberan|ce/s, -t/ly prə'tju:bər-ən|s/iz [pru't-], -t/li
proud, -er, -est, -ly, -ness praud, -ə*, -ist, -li, -nis
Proust (French author) pru:st (prust)
proustian 'pru:stjən [-tiən]
Prout praut
provab|le, -ly, -leness 'pru:vəb|l, -li, -lnis
prov|e, -es, -ing, -ed, -en, -er/s pru:v, -z, -iŋ, -d, -ən, -ə*/z
provenance 'prɔvinəns [-vən-]
Provençal ˌprɔvã:n'sɑ:l [-võ:n's-, -vɑ:n's-, -vɔ:n's-, -vən's-] (prɔvɑ̃sal)
Provence prɔ'vã:ns [prəu'v-, -'võ:ns, -'vɑ:ns, -'vɔ:ns] (prɔvɑ̃:s)
provender 'prɔvində*
proverb, -s (P.) 'prɔvə:b [-vəb], -z
proverbial, -ly prə'və:bjəl [pru'v-, -biəl], -i

provid|e, -es, -ing, -ed, -er/s prə'vaid [pru'v-], -z, -iŋ, -id, -ə*/z
providen|ce (P.), -t/ly 'prɔvidən|s, -t/li
providenti|al, -ally ˌprɔvi'denʃ|əl, -əli
province, -s 'prɔvins, -iz
provinci|al (s. adj.), -als, -ally prə-'vinʃ|əl [pru'v-], -əlz, -əli
provincialism, -s prə'vinʃəlizəm [pru'v-, -ʃli-], -z
provinciality prəˌvinʃi'æliti [pru͵v-]
provincializ|e [-is|e], -es, -ing, -ed prə-'vinʃəlaiz [pru'v-, -ʃlaiz], -iz, -iŋ, -d
provisi|on, -ons, -oning, -oned prə-'viʒ|ən [pru'v-], -ənz, -ŋiŋ [-əniŋ], -ənd
provi|sional, -sionally prə'viʒ|ənl [pru'v-, -ʒnəl, -ʒn̩l, -ʒn̩l̩, -ʒənəl], -ʒnəli [-ʒnəli, -ʒn̩li, -ʒnli, -ʒənəli]
proviso, -(e)s prə'vaizəu [prəu'v-, pru'v-], -z
provisor, -s prə'vaizə* [pru'v-], -z
provisor|y, -ily prə'vaizər|i [pru'v-], -ili
provocation, -s ˌprɔvə'keiʃən [-vəu'k-], -z
provocative prə'vɔkətiv [prəu'v-, pru'v-], -z
provok|e, -es, -ing/ly, -ed, -er/s prə-'vəuk [pru'v-], -s, -iŋ/li, -t, -ə*/z
provost (civil and academic), -s 'prɔvəst, -s
provost-marshal (military), -s prə-'vəu'mɑ:ʃəl, -z
provostship, -s 'prɔvəst-ʃip, -s
prow, -s prau, -z
prowess 'prauis [-es]
prowl (s. v.), -s, -ing, -ed, -er/s praul, -z, -iŋ, -d, -ə*/z
Prowse praus, prauz
prox. prɔks ['prɔksiməu]
proxim|al, -ally 'prɔksim|əl, -əli
proximate, -ly 'prɔksimit, -li
proxime accessit, -s 'prɔksimiæk'sesit [-mïək-], -s
proximit|y, -ies prɔk'simit|i, -iz
proximo 'prɔksiməu
prox|y, -ies 'prɔks|i, -iz
prude, -s ; -ry pru:d, -z; -əri
pruden|ce (P.), -t/ly 'pru:dən|s, -t/li
prudenti|al, -ally pru(:)'denʃ|əl, -əli
prudish, -ly 'pru:diʃ, -li
prun|e (s. v.), -es, -ing, -ed pru:n, -z, -iŋ, -d
prunella (P.), -s pru(:)'nelə, -z
pruning-kni|fe, -ves 'pru:niŋnai|f, -vz
prurien|ce, -t/ly 'pruəriən|s, -t/li
Prussi|a, -an/s 'prʌʃ|ə, -ən/z
prussiate, -s 'prʌʃiit [-ʃjit, -ʃit], -s
prussic 'prʌsik
Prust prʌst

Pruth (tributary of the Danube) pru:t
pr|y, -ies, -ying/ly, -ied, -yer/s pr|ai, -aiz, -aiiŋ/li, -aid, 'prai-ə*/z
Prynne prin
Przemsyl 'pʃemisl
psalm (P.), -s ; -ist/s sɑ:m, -z; -ist/s
psalmodic sæl'mɔdik
psalmod|ist/s, -y 'sælməd|ist/s ['sɑ:m-, -mud-], -i
psalter, -s 'sɔ:ltə* ['sɔl-], -z
psalter|y, -ies 'sɔ:ltər|i ['sɔl-], -iz
psepholog|ist/s, -y pse'fɔlədʒ|ist/s, -i
pseudo- 'psju:dəu- ['psu:dəu-]
Note.—Compounds with pseudo- have double stress. Their pronunciation may be ascertained by referring to the simple words. Thus pseudo-classic is pronounced 'psju:dəu-'klæsik ['psu:-].
pseudonym, -s 'psju:dənim ['psu:-], -z
pseudonymity ˌpsju:də'nimiti [ˌpsu:-]
pseudonymous psju:'dɔniməs [psu:-]
pshaw (v.), -s, -ing, -ed pʃɔ: [ʃɔ:], -z, -iŋ, -d
pshaw (interj.) pɸ: [pʃɔ:]
psi psai
psittacosis ˌpsitə'kəusis
psoriasis psɔ'rai-əsis [psɔ:'r-, psu'r-, psə'r-]
Psyche 'saiki(:)
psychedelic ˌsaiki'delik
psychiatric, -al ˌsaiki'ætrik, -əl
psychiatr|ist/s, -y sai'kai-ətr|ist/s [si'k-, sə'k-], -i
psychic, -al, -ally 'saikik ['psaik-], -əl, -əli [-l̩i]
psychoanalys|e, -es, -ing, -ed ˌsaikəu-'ænəlaiz [ˌpsai-], -iz, -iŋ, -d
psychoanalysis ˌsaikəuə'næləsis [ˌpsai-, -lis-]
psychoanalyst, -s ˌsaikəu'ænəlist [ˌpsai-], -s
psychologic, -al, -ally ˌsaikə'lɔdʒik [ˌpsai-], -əl, -əli
psycholog|ist/s, -y sai'kɔlədʒ|ist/s [psai-], -i
psychologiz|e [-is|e], -es, -ing, -ed sai'kɔlədʒaiz [psai-], -iz, -iŋ, -d
psychometric ˌsaikəu'metrik [ˌpsai-]
psychometr|ist/s, -y sai'kɔmitr|ist/s [psai-, -mət-], -i
psychopathic ˌsaikəu'pæθik [ˌpsai-]
psychophonic 'saikəu'fəunik ['psai-, -'fɔn-]
psychophysical 'saikəu'fizikəl ['psai-]
psychos|is, -es sai'kəus|is [psai-], -i:z
psychosomatic ˌsaikəusəu'mætik [ˌpsai-]
psychotherapy 'saikəu'θerəpi ['psai-]

psychotic sai'kɔtik [psai-]
ptarmigan 'tɑːˌmigən [-məg-]
pterodactyl, -s ˌpterəu'dæktil, -z
pterosaur, -s 'pterəusɔː*, -z
ptisan, -s ti'zæn ['tizn], -z
Ptolemai|c, -s ˌtɔli'meii|k [-lə'm-], -s
Ptolem|y, -ies 'tɔlim|i [-ləm-], -iz
ptomaine 'təumein [təu'mein]
pub, -s; -by pʌb, -z, -i
puberty 'pjuːbəti [-bəːt-]
pubescen|ce, -t pjuː(:)'besn|s, -t
public, -ly 'pʌblik, -li
publican, -s 'pʌblikən, -z
publication, -s ˌpʌbli'keiʃən, -z
public-hou|se, -ses 'pʌblik'hau|s, -ziz
publicist, -s 'pʌblisist, -s
publicity pʌb'lisiti [pə'blis-]
public-spirited 'pʌblik'spiritid
publish, -es, -ing, -ed, -er/s 'pʌbliʃ, -iz,
-iŋ, -t, -ə*/z
Publius 'pʌblïəs [-ljəs]
puce pjuːs
puck (P.), -s pʌk, -s
pucker (s. v.), -s, -ing, -ed 'pʌkə*, -z,
-riŋ, -d
pudding, -s 'pudiŋ, -z
pudd|le (s. v.), -les, -ling, -led, -ler/s
'pʌd|l, -lz, -łiŋ [-liŋ], -ld, -łə*/z
[-lə*/z]
pudg|y, -ier, -iest 'pʌdʒ|i, -ïə*, -iist
Pudsey 'pʌdzi [locally 'pʌdsi]
pueblo, -s pu'ebləu ['pwe-], -z
puerile, -ly 'pjuərail ['pjɔər-, 'pjɔːr-,
'pjəːr-], -li
puerilit|y, -ies pjüə'rilit|i [pjuə'r-,
pjɔə'r-, pjɔː'r-, pjəː'r-], -iz
puerperal pjuː(:)'əːpərəl
Puerto Rico 'pwəːtəu'riːkəu
puff (s. v.), -s, -ing, -ed, -er/s pʌf, -s,
-iŋ, -t, -ə*/z
puff-ball, -s 'pʌfbɔːl, -z
puffin, -s 'pʌfin, -z
puff|y, -ier, -iest, -ily, -iness 'pʌf|i,
-ïə*, -iist, -ili, -inis
pug, -s pʌg, -z
puggaree, -s 'pʌgəri, -z
Pugh pjuː
pugili|sm, -st/s 'pjuːdʒili|zəm, -st/s
pugilistic, -ally ˌpjuːdʒi'listik, -əli
Pugin 'pjuːdʒin
pugnacious, -ly pʌg'neiʃəs, -li
pugnacity pʌg'næsiti
pug-nose, -s, -d 'pʌgnəuz, -iz, -d
puisne 'pjuːni
puissan|ce, -t 'pjuː(:)isn|s ['pwis-, some-
times in poetry pjuː(:)'is-, in show-
jumping 'pwiːsɑ̃ːns, -sɑːns, -sɔ̃ːns,
-sɔːns, -'-], -t

puk|e, -es, -ing, -ed pjuːk, -s, -iŋ, -t
pukka 'pʌkə
pulau, -s 'puːlau, -z
pul|e, -es, -ing, -ed pjuːl, -z, -iŋ, -d
Puleston (in Shropshire) 'pulistən
[locally also 'pilsn]
Pulitzer (Amer. publisher) 'pulitsə*,
(prize at Columbia Univ.) 'pjuːlitsə*
pull (s. v.), -s, -ing, -ed, -er/s pul, -z,
-iŋ, -d, -ə*/z
pullet, -s 'pulit, -s
pulley, -s 'puli, -z
pullman (P.), -s; -car/s 'pulmən, -z;
-kɑː*/z
pull-over, -s 'pulˌəuvə*, -z
pullulat|e, -es, -ing, -ed 'pʌljuleit, -s,
-iŋ, -id
pullulation ˌpʌlju'leiʃən
pull-up, -s 'pulʌp ['pul'ʌp], -s
pulmonary 'pʌlmənəri
pulmonic pʌl'mɔnik
pulp (s. v.), -s, -ing, -ed pʌlp, -s, -iŋ, -t
pulpi|fy, -fies, -fying, -fied 'pʌlpi|fai,
-faiz, -faiiŋ, -faid
pulpit, -s 'pulpit, -s
pulp|y, -ier, -iest, -iness 'pʌlp|i, -ïə*
[-jə*], -iist [jist], -inis
pulsat|e, -es, -ing, -ed pʌl'seit ['pʌlseit],
-s, -iŋ, -id
pulsatile 'pʌlsətail
pulsation, -s pʌl'seiʃən, -z
pulsative 'pʌlsətiv
pulsatory 'pʌlsətəri
puls|e (s. v.), -es, -ing, -ed pʌls, -iz, -iŋ, -t
Pulteney 'pʌltni, 'pəultni
pulverization [-isa-], -s ˌpʌlvərai'zeiʃən [-ri'z-], -z
pulveriz|e [-is|e], -es, -ing, -ed 'pʌlvər-
aiz, -iz, -iŋ, -d
puma, -s 'pjuːmə, -z
Pumblechook 'pʌmbl-tʃuk
pumic|e (s. v.), -es, -ing, -ed 'pʌmis,
-iz, -iŋ, -t
pumice-ston|e (s. v.), -es, -ing, -ed
'pʌmisstəun ['pʌmis-təun], -z, -iŋ, -d
pumm|el, -els, -elling, -elled 'pʌm|l, -lz,
-łiŋ [-əliŋ], -ld
pump (s. v.), -s, -ing, -ed, -er/s pʌmp,
-s, -iŋ, -t [pʌmt], -ə*/z
pumpernickel 'pumpənikl
pumpkin, -s 'pʌmpkin, -z
pun (s. v.), -s, -ning, -ned, -ner/s pʌn, -z,
-iŋ, -d, -ə*/z
Puna 'puːnə [-nɑː] (Hind. puna)
punch (s. v.) (P.), -es, -ing, -ed, -er/s
pʌntʃ, -iz, -iŋ, -t, -ə*/z
punchbowl, -s 'pʌntʃbəul, -z
puncheon, -s 'pʌntʃən, -z

Punchinello ˌpʌntʃiˈneləu
punch-ladle, -s 'pʌntʃˌleidl, -z
punctilio, -s pʌŋkˈtiliəu, -z
punctilious, -ly, -ness pʌŋkˈtiliəs [-ljəs],
-li, -nis
punctual, -ly 'pʌŋktjŭəl [-tjwəl, -tjul,
-tʃŭəl, -tʃwəl, -tʃul], -i
punctuality ˌpʌnktjuˈæliti [-tʃu-]
punctuat|e, -es, -ing, -ed, -or/s 'pʌŋk-
tjueit [-tʃu-], -s, -iŋ, -id, -ə*/z
punctuation, -s ˌpʌŋktʃtjuˈeiʃən [-tʃu-], -z
punct|ure (s. v.), -ures, -uring, -ured
'pʌŋktʃ|ə*, -əz, -əriŋ, -əd
pundit, -s 'pʌndit (Hind. pəndʒyt), -s
pungen|cy, -t/ly 'pʌndʒən|si, -t/li
Punic 'pju:nik
puniness 'pju:ninis
punish, -es, -ing, -ed, -er/s, -ment/s;
-able/ness 'pʌniʃ, -iz, -iŋ, -t, -ə*/z,
-mənt/s; -əbl/nis
punit|ive, -ory 'pju:nit|iv, -əri
Punjab pʌnˈdʒɑ:b ['-'-, '--]
punka(h), -s 'pʌŋkə, -z
punnet, -s 'pʌnit, -s
Punshon 'pʌnʃən
punster, -s 'pʌnstə*, -z
punt (s. v.), -s, -ing, -ed, -er/s pʌnt, -s,
-iŋ, -id, -ə*/z
pun|y, -ier, -iest, -iness 'pju:n|i, -iə*
[-jə*], -iist [-jist], -inis
pup (s. v.), -s, -ping, -ped pʌp, -s, -iŋ,
-t
pup|a, -ae, -al 'pju:p|ə, -i:, -əl
pupil, -s 'pju:pl [-pil], -z
pupil(l)|age, -ary 'pju:pil|idʒ, -əri
puppet, -s 'pʌpit, -s
pupp|y, -ies 'pʌp|i, -iz
Purbeck 'pə:bek
purblin|d, -dness 'pə:blain|d, -dnis
Purcell 'pə:sl [-sel, -səl]
purchas|e (s. v.), -es, -ing, -ed, -er/s;
-able 'pə:tʃəs [-tʃis], -iz, -iŋ, -t, -ə*/z;
-əbl
purdah 'pə:dɑ: [-də] (Hind. pərda)
Purd|ie, -ye 'pə:d|i, -i
pure, -r, -st, -ly, -ness pjuə* [pjɔə*,
pjɔ:*, pjə:*], -rə*, -rist, -li, -nis
purée, -s 'pjuərei ['pjɔər-, 'pjɔ:r-,
-'puər-] (pyre), -z
purf|le, -les, -ling, -led 'pə:f|l, -lz, -liŋ
[-liŋ], -ld
purfing (s.), -s 'pə:fliŋ, -z
purgation, -s pə:ˈgeiʃən, -z
purgative (s. adj.), -s 'pə:gətiv, -z
purgatorial ˌpə:gəˈtɔ:riəl
purgator|y (P.), -ies 'pə:gətər|i, -iz
purg|e (s. v.), -es, -ing, -ed pə:dʒ, -iz,
-iŋ, -d

purification (P.), -s ˌpjuərifiˈkeiʃən
[ˌpjɔər-, ˌpjɔ:r-, ˌpjə:r-], -z
purificatory 'pjuərifikeitəri ['pjɔər-,
'pjɔ:r-, 'pjə:r-, -kət-, ˌpjuərifiˈkeitəri,
ˌpjɔər-, ˌpjɔ:r-, ˌpjə:r-]
puri|fy, -fies, -fying, -fied, -fier/s
'pjuəri|fai ['pjɔər-, 'pjɔ:r-, 'pjə:r-],
-faiz, -faiiŋ, -faid, -fai-ə*/z
Purim 'pjuərim ['puə-]
puri|sm, -st/s 'pjuəri|zəm ['pjɔər-,
'pjɔ:r-, 'pjə:r-], -st/s
puristic, -al pjuəˈristik [pjɔəˈr-, pjɔ:ˈr-,
pjə:ˈr-], -əl
purit|an (P.), -ans, -anism 'pjuərit|ən
['pjɔər-, 'pjɔ:r-, 'pjə:r-], -ənz, -ənizəm
[-ŋizəm]
puritanic, -al, -ally ˌpjuəriˈtænik
[ˌpjɔər-, ˌpjɔ:r-, ˌpjə:r-], -əl, -əli
purity 'pjuəriti ['pjɔər-, 'pjɔ:r-, 'pjə:r-]
purl (s. v.), -s, -ing, -ed pə:l, -z, -iŋ, -d
Purley 'pə:li
purlieu, -s 'pə:lju:, -z
purloin, -s, -ing, -ed pə:ˈlɔin ['pə:lɔin],
-z, -iŋ, -d
purloiner, -s pə:ˈlɔinə*, -z
purp|le (s. adj. v.), -ler, -lest; -les,
-ling, -led 'pə:p|l, -lə* [-lə*], -list
[-list]; -lz, -liŋ [-liŋ], -ld
purplish 'pə:pliʃ [-pliʃ]
purport (s. v.), -s, -ing, -ed 'pə:pət
['pə:pɔ:t, pə:ˈpɔ:t, pə'pɔ:t], -s, -iŋ, -id
purp|ose (s. v.), -oses, -osing, -osed
'pə:p|əs, -əsiz, -əsiŋ, -əst
purpose|ful, -fully, -fulness 'pə:pəs|ful,
-fuli [-fəli], -fulnis
purposeless, -ly, -ness 'pə:pəslis, -li, -nis
purposely 'pə:pəsli
purposive 'pə:pəsiv
purr, -s, -ing, -ed pə:*, -z, -riŋ, -d
purs|e (s. v.), -es, -ing, -ed pə:s, -iz, -iŋ,
-t
purseful, -s 'pə:sful, -z
purse-proud 'pə:s-praud
purser, -s 'pə:sə*, -z
purse-string, -s 'pə:s-striŋ, -z
purslane 'pə:slin
pursuan|ce, -t/ly pə'sju(:)ən|s [-'su(:)-],
-t/li
purs|ue, -ues, -uing, -ued, -uer/s
pə'sj|u: [-'s|u:], -u:z, -u(:)iŋ, -u:d,
-u(:)ə*/z
pursuit, -s pə'sju:t [-'su:t], -s
pursuivant, -s 'pə:sivənt [old-fashioned
'pə:swi-], -s
purs|y, -iness 'pə:s|i, -inis
Purton 'pə:tn
purulen|cy, -t/ly 'pjuərulən|si [-rju-],
-t/li

Purv|er, -es 'pə:v|ə*, -is
purvey, -s, -ing, -ed pə:'vei [pə'v-], -z,
 -iŋ, -d
purvey|ance, -or/s pə:'vei|əns [pə'v-],
 -ə*/z
purview, -s 'pə:vju:, -z
pus, -es pʌs, -iz
Pusey, -ite/s 'pju:zi, -ait/s
push (s. v.), -es, -ing/ly, -ed, -er/s puʃ,
 -iz, -iŋ/li, -t, -ə*/z
pushball 'puʃbɔ:l
push-bike, -s 'puʃbaik, -s
push-button, -s 'puʃ,bʌtn, -z
push-car, -s 'puʃkɑ:*, -z
push-cart, -s 'puʃkɑ:t, -s
pushful, -ness 'puʃful [-fl], -nis
Pushkin 'puʃkin
Pushtu 'pʌʃtu: ['pʌʃ'tu:]
pusillanimity ,pju:silə'nimiti [-ju:zi-,
 -læ'n-]
pusillanimous, -ly, -ness ,pju:si'læni-
 məs [-ju:zi-], -li, -nis
puss, -es pus, -iz
puss|y (cat), -ies 'pus|i, -iz
pussyfoot, -s 'pusifut, -s
pustular 'pʌstjulə*
pustulat|e, -es, -ing, -ed 'pʌstjuleit, -s,
 -iŋ, -id
pustulation, -s ,pʌstju'leiʃən, -z
pustule, -s 'pʌstju:l, -z
pustulous 'pʌstjuləs
put (s.), (act of throwing a weight), -s
 put, -s
put (v.) (place, move, throw), -s, -ting
 put, -s, -iŋ
put(t) (s. v.) (at golf), -s, -ting, -ted,
 -ter/s pʌt, -s, -iŋ, -id, -ə*/z
putative 'pju:tətiv
Puteoli pju:'tiəli [-'tiəuli]
Putn|am, -ey 'pʌtn|əm [-æm], -i
putrefaction ,pju:tri'fækʃən
putre|fy, -fies, -fying, -fied 'pju:tri|fai,
 -faiz, -faiiŋ, -faid
putrescenc|e, -t pju:'tresn|s, -t
putrid, -ly, -ness 'pju:trid, -li, -nis
putridity pju:'triditi
putsch, -es putʃ, -iz
putt (s. v.) (P.), -s, -ing, -ed, -er/s pʌt, -s,
 -iŋ, -id, -ə*/z
puttee, -s 'pʌti, -z
Puttenham 'pʌtnəm
putter, -s 'pʌtə*, -z

Puttick 'pʌtik
putting-green, -s 'pʌtiŋgri:n, -z
putt|y (s. v.), -ies, -ying, -ied 'pʌt|i
 -iz, -iiŋ, -id
put-up 'put'ʌp ['putʌp]
puzz|le, -les, -ling/ly, -led 'pʌz|l, -lz,
 -liŋ/li [-liŋ/li], -ld
puzzler, -s 'pʌzlə* [-z|ə*], -z
Pwllheli puθ'leli [pul'heli]   (Welsh
 pu:ɬ'heli)
pyaemia pai'i:mjə [-mïə]
Pybus 'paibəs
Pyddoke 'pidək
Pye pai
pygmaean pig'mi:ən [-'miən]
Pygmalion pig'meiljən [-lïən]
pygm|y, -ies 'pigm|i, -iz
pyjama, -s pə'dʒɑ:mə [pi'dʒ-, old-
 fashioned pai'dʒ-], -z
Pyke paik
Pylades 'pilədi:z
pylon, -s 'pailən, -z
pyorrhoea ,paiə'riə
pyramid (P.), -s 'pirəmid, -z
pyramid|al, -ally pi'ræmid|l, -əli [-ḷi]
Pyramus 'pirəməs
pyre, -s 'paiə*, -z
Pyrene pai'ri:ni [,paiə'r-]
Pyren|ean, -ees ,pirə'n|i:ən [-ri'n-], -i:z
pyrethrum, -s pai'ri:θrəm [,paiə'r-], -z
pyretic pai'retik [,paiə'r-, pi'r-]
pyriform (pear-shaped) 'pirifɔ:m
pyrites pai'raiti:z [,paiə'r-, pi'r-, pə'r-]
pyritic pai'ritik [,paiə'r-]
pyro 'paiərəu ['pairəu]
pyrogallic ,pairəu'gælik [,paiər-]
pyromet|er/s,   -ry   pai'rɔmit|ə*/z
 [,paiə'r-], -ri   [-əl
pyrometric, -al ,pairəu'metrik [,paiər-],
pyrotechnic, -al, -ally, -s ,pairəu-
 'teknik [,paiər-], -əl, -əli, -s
Pyrrh|a, -ic/s, -us 'pir|ə, -ik/s, -əs
Pytchley .paitʃli
Pythagoras pai'θægəræs [-gɔr-, -rəs]
Pythagorean (s. adj.), -s pai,θægə'ri(:)ən
 [,paiθæg-, -gɔ'r-], -z
Pythian 'piθïən [-θjən]
Pythias 'piθiæs
python, -s 'paiθən, -z
pythoness, -es 'paiθənes [-nis], -iz
pythonic pai'θɔnik
pyx, -es piks, -iz

Q

Q (*the letter*), **-'s** kjuː, -z
Qantas 'kwɔntæs [-təs]
Q.C., -'s 'kjuː'siː, -z
q.e.d. 'kjuːiː'diː:
q.e.f. 'kjuːiː'ef
qua kwei
quack (*s. v.*), **-s, -ing, -ed; -ery, -ish** kwæk, -s, -iŋ, -t; -əri, -iʃ
quad, -s kwɔd, -z
Quadragesima ˌkwɔdrə'dʒesimə
quadragesimal ˌkwɔdrə'dʒesiməl
quadrangle, -s 'kwɔdræŋgl [kwɔ'dræŋ-, kwə'dræŋ-], -z
quadrangular kwɔ'dræŋgjulə* [kwə'd-]
quadrant, -s 'kwɔdrənt, -s
quadrate (*s. adj.*), **-s,** 'kwɔdrit [-reit], -s
quadrat|e (*v.*), **-es, -ing, -ed** kwɔ'dreit [kwə'd-], -s, -iŋ, -id
quadratic (*s. adj.*), **-s** kwə'drætik [kwɔ'd-], -s
quadrature 'kwɔdrətʃə* [-ritʃ-, -tjuə*]
quadric (*s. adj.*), **-s** 'kwɔdrik, -s
quadriga, -s kwə'driːgə [kwɔ'd-, -'draigə], -z
quadrilateral (*s. adj.*), **-s** ˌkwɔdri-'lætərəl, -z
quadrilingual 'kwɔdri'liŋgwəl [ˌ--'--]
quadrille, -s kwə'dril [*rarely* kə-], -z
quadrillion, -s kwɔ'driljən [kwə'd-], -z
quadrisyllabic 'kwɔdrisi'læbik ['---,--]
quadroon, -s kwɔ'druːn [kwə'd-], -z
quadrumanous kwɔ'druːmənəs [kwə'd-]
quadruped, -s 'kwɔdruped [-pid], -z
quadrup|le (*s. adj. v.*), **-les, -ly; -ling, -led** 'kwɔdrup|l [-druː'p-], -lz, -li; -liŋ, -ld
quadruplet, -s 'kwɔdruplit [-plet, kwə'druːplit], -s
quadruplicate (*s. adj.*), **-s** kwɔ'druː-plikit [kwə'd-, -keit], -s
quadruplicat|e (*v.*), **-es, -ing, -ed** kwɔ-'druːplikeit [kwə'd-], -s, -iŋ, -id
quaere 'kwiəri
quaestor, -s 'kwiːstə* [-tɔ:*], -z
quaff, -s, -ing, -ed, -er/s kwɑːf [kwɔf], -s, -iŋ, -t, -ə*/z
quag, -s kwæg [kwɔg], -z
quagga, -s 'kwægə, -z
quagmire, -s 'kwægmaiə* ['kwɔg-], -z

quail (*s. v.*) (**Q.**), **-s, -ing, -ed** kweil, -z, -iŋ, -d
Quaile kweil
Quain kwein
quaint, -er, -est, -ly, -ness kweint, -ə*, -ist, -li, -nis
quak|e (*s. v.*), **-es, -ing, -ed** kweik, -s, -iŋ, -t
Quaker, -s 'kweikə*, -z
qualification, -s ˌkwɔlifi'keiʃən, -z
qualificative (*s. adj.*), **-s** 'kwɔlifikətiv, -z
qualificatory 'kwɔlifikətəri [-keitəri]
quali|fy, -fies, -fying, -fied, -fier/s 'kwɔli|fai, -faiz, -faiiŋ, -faid, -fai-ə*/z [-faiə*/z]
qualitative, -ly 'kwɔlitətiv [-teit-], -li
qualit|y, -ies 'kwɔlit|i, -iz
qualm, -s kwɑːm [kwɔːm], -z
qualmish, -ly, -ness 'kwɑːmiʃ ['kwɔːm-], -li, -nis
Qualtrough 'kwɔltrəu
quandar|y, -ies 'kwɔndər|i [*rarely* kwɔn-'dɛər-], -iz
Quandary (*Peak*) 'kwɔndəri
quantic, -s 'kwɔntik, -s
quanti|fy, -fies, -fying, -fied, -fier/s, -fiable 'kwɔnti|fai, -faiz, -faiiŋ, -faid, -faiə*/z, -faiəbl
quantitative, -ly 'kwɔntitətiv [-teit-], -li
quantity, -ies 'kwɔntit|i, -iz
Quantock (*in Somerset*) 'kwɔntək, (*in names of streets, etc., in London*) 'kwɔntək [-tɔk]
quantum (*amount*) 'kwɔntəm, (*in Latin phrases*) 'kwæntəm ['kwɔn-]
quarantin|e (*s. v.*), **-es, -ing, -ed** 'kwɔrəntiːn [ˌ--'-], -z, -iŋ, -d
Quaritch 'kwɔritʃ
Quarles kwɔːlz
Quarmby 'kwɔːmbi
Quarr kwɔː*
quarr|el (*s. v.*), **-els, -elling, -elled, -eller/s** 'kwɔr|əl, -əlz, -əliŋ [-ɬiŋ], -əld, -ələ*/z [-ɬə*/z]
quarrelsome, -ly, -ness 'kwɔrəlsəm, -li, -nis
quarr|y (*s. v.*), **-ies, -ying, -ied** 'kwɔr|i, -iz, -iiŋ, -id

quarry|man, -men 'kwɔri|mən [-mæn], -mən [-men]
quart (*measure of capacity*), **-s** kwɔːt, -s
quart (*s. v.*) (*in card games, fencing*), **-s, -ing, -ed** kɑːt, -s, -iŋ, -id
quartan 'kwɔːtn [-tən]
quarter (*s. v.*), **-s, -ing/s, -ed; -age** 'kwɔːtə*, -z, -riŋ/z, -d; -ridʒ
quarter-day, -s 'kwɔːtədei, -z
quarter-deck, -s 'kwɔːtədek, -s
quarterl|y (*s. adv.*), **-ies** 'kwɔːtəl|i, -iz
Quartermaine 'kwɔːtəmein
quartermaster, -s 'kwɔːtə,mɑːstə*, -z
quartern, -s 'kwɔːtən [-tn], -z
quarter-plate, -s 'kwɔːtə-pleit, -s
quarter-tone, -s 'kwɔːtətəun, -z
quartet(te), -s kwɔː'tet, -s
quartic (*s. adj.*), **-s** 'kwɔːtik, -s
quartile, -s 'kwɔːtail, -z
quarto, -s 'kwɔːtəu, -z
quartus (**Q.**) 'kwɔːtəs
quartz kwɔːts
quash, -es, -ing, -ed kwɔʃ, -iz, -iŋ, -t
quashee (**Q.**), **-s** 'kwɔʃi, -z
quasi 'kwɑːzi(ː) ['kweisai]
quassia 'kwɔʃə
quatercentenar|y, -ies ,kwætəsen'tiːnər|i ['kwæt-, 'kwɔːt-, 'kwɔt-, 'kweit-, -'ten-, -'sentin-], -iz
Quatermain 'kwɔːtəmein
quaternar|y (*s. adj.*), **-ies** kwə'tɜːnər|i, -iz
quaternion, -s kwə'tɜːnjən [-nɪən], -z
quatorzain, -s kə'tɔːzein [kæ'tɔː-, 'kætəzein], -z
quatorze, -s kə'tɔːz, -iz
quatrain, -s 'kwɔtrein, -z
quatre-foil, -s 'kætrəfɔil [-təf-], -z
quatrillion, -s kwɔ'triljən [kwə't-], -z
quav|er (*s. v.*), **-ers, -ering/ly, -ered** 'kweiv|ə*, -əz, -əriŋ/li, -əd
quay, -s; -age kiː, -z; -idʒ
Quay (*place-name*) kiː, (*surname*) kwei
Quayle kweil
quean, -s kwiːn, -z
queas|y, -iness 'kwiːz|i, -inis
Quebec kwi'bek [kwə'b-]
queen (*s. v.*), **-s, -ing, -ed** kwiːn, -z, -iŋ, -d
Queenborough 'kwiːnbərə
Queenie 'kwiːni
queenlike 'kwiːnlaik
queenl|y, -ier, -iest, -iness 'kwiːnl|i, -ɪə* [-jə*], -iist [-jist], -inis
Queens|berry, -bury, -ferry, -land, -town 'kwiːnz|bəri, -bəri, -,feri, -lənd [-lænd], -taun
queer, -er, -est, -ly, -ness; -ish kwiə*, -rə*, -rist, -li, -nis; -riʃ

queerit|y, -ies 'kwiərit|i, -iz
quell, -s, -ing, -ed, -er/s kwel, -z, -iŋ, -d, -ə*/z
quench, -es, -ing, -ed, -er/s; -able kwentʃ, -iz, -iŋ, -t, -ə*/z; -əbl
Quen(n)ell kwi'nel, 'kwenl
quenelle, -s kə'nel [ki'n-], -z
Quentin 'kwentin
querist, -s 'kwiərist, -s
quern, -s kwɜːn, -z
querulous, -ly, -ness 'kweruləs [-rjul-, -rəl-], -li, -nis
quer|y (*s. v.*), **-ies, -ying, -ied** 'kwiər|i, -iz, -iiŋ, -id
Quesnel 'keinl
quest (*s. v.*), **-s, -ing, -ed** kwest, -s, -iŋ, -id
questi|on (*s. v.*), **-ons, -oning/ly, -oned, -oner/s** 'kwestʃ|ən [-eʃtʃ-], -ənz, -əniŋ/li [-ņiŋ/li, -niŋ/li], -ənd, -ənə*/z [-ņə*/z, -nə*/z]
questionab|le, -ly, -leness 'kwestʃənəb|l [-eʃtʃ-, -tʃnə-, -tʃnə-], -li, -lnis
questionar|y (*s. adj.*), **-ies** 'kwestʃənər|i [-tʃnər-], -iz
question-mark, -s 'kwestʃənmɑːk [-eʃtʃ-], -s
questionnaire, -s ,kwestiə'nɛə* [,kwestjə-, ,kwestʃə-, ,kes-, '---], -z
Quetta 'kwetə
queue (*s. v.*), **-s, -ing, -d** kjuː, -z, -iŋ [kjuiŋ], -d
queue-minded 'kjuː,maindid ['-'--]
Queux kjuː:
Quex kweks
quibbl|e (*s. v.*), **-les, -ling, -led, -ler/s** 'kwib|l, -lz, -liŋ [-liŋ], -ld, -lə*/z [-lə*/z]
Quibell 'kwaibəl, 'kwibəl, kwi'bel
   Note.—Baron Quibell of Scunthorpe pronounces 'kwai-.
quick (*s. adj.*) (**Q.**), **-s, -er, -est, -ly, -ness** kwik, -s, -ə*, -ist, -li, -nis
quick-change (*adj.*) 'kwik-tʃeindʒ
Quicke kwik
quick|en, -ens, -ening, -ened 'kwik|ən, -ənz, -ņiŋ [-əniŋ], -ənd
quick-fir|er/s, -ing 'kwik,faiər|ə*/z, -iŋ
quick|-freeze, -freezes, -freezing, -froze, -frozen, -freezer/s 'kwik|friːz, -,friːziz, -,friːziŋ, -frəuz, -,frəuzən, -,friːzə*/z
quicklime 'kwik-laim
Quickly 'kwikli
quickmarch 'kwik'mɑːtʃ
quick|sand/s, -set 'kwik|sænd/z, -set
quicksilv|er (*s. v.*), **-ers, -ering, -ered** 'kwik,silv|ə*, -əz, -əriŋ, -əd
quick-tempered 'kwik'tempəd ['kwik,t-]

quick-witted, -ness 'kwik'witid, -nis
quid, -s kwid, -z
quidnunc, -s 'kwidnʌŋk, -s
quid pro quo, -s 'kwidprəu'kwəu, -z
quiescen|ce, -t/ly kwai'esn|s, -t/li
quiet (s. adj. v.), -er, -est, -ly, -ness; -s, -ing, -ed 'kwaiət, -ə*, -ist, -li, -nis; -s, -iŋ, -id
quiet|en, -ens, -ening, -ened 'kwaiət|n, -nz, -ŋiŋ [-niŋ], -nd
quieti|sm, -st/s 'kwaiiti|zəm [-aiət-], -st/s
quietude 'kwaiitju:d [-aiət-]
quietus kwai'i:təs
Quiggin 'kwigin
quill (s. v.), -s, -ing, -ed kwil, -z, -iŋ, -d
Quilleash 'kwili:ʃ
Quiller-Couch 'kwilə'ku:tʃ
Quilliam 'kwiljəm [-lɪəm]
Quilp kwilp
quilt (s. v.), -s, -ing, -ed kwilt, -s, -iŋ, -id
Quilter 'kwiltə*
quin (Q.), -s kwin, -z
Quinault (surname) 'kwinlt [-nəlt, -nɔ:lt]
quince (Q.), -s kwins, -iz
quincentenar|y, -ies ˌkwinsen'ti:nər|i ['kwinsen't-, -'ten-, kwin'sentin-],-iz
Quinc(e)y 'kwinsi
quincunx,-es 'kwinkʌŋks ['kwiŋ-kʌŋks], -iz
quindecagon, -s kwin'dekəgən, -z
quingentenar|y, -ies 'kwindʒen'ti:nər|i [-'ten-], -iz
quinine kwi'ni:n ['kwini:n]
Quinney 'kwini
quinquagenarian, -s ˌkwiŋkwədʒi-'neəriən, -z
Quinquagesima ˌkwiŋkwə'dʒesimə
quinquennial kwiŋ'kwenɪəl [-njəl]
quinquennium, -s kwiŋ'kwenɪəm [-njəm], -z
quinquereme, -s 'kwiŋkwiri:m [-kwər-], -z
quinquina kwiŋ'kwainə
quinsy 'kwinzi
quint, -s (organ stop) kwint, (in piquet) kint [kwint, old-fashioned kent], -s
quintain, -s 'kwintin, -z
quintal, -s 'kwintl, -z
quintessence kwin'tesns
quintet(te), -s kwin'tet, -s
quintic (s. adj.), -s 'kwintik, -s
Quintilian kwin'tiljən [-lɪən]
quintillion, -s kwin'tiljən, -z

Quintin 'kwintin
Quinton 'kwintən
quintup|le, -les, -ling, -led 'kwintjup|l [-tju:p-], -lz, -liŋ, -ld
quintuplet, -s 'kwintjuplit [-plet, kwin'tju:plit], -s
quintus (Q.) 'kwintəs
quip, -s kwip, -s
quire, -s 'kwaiə*, -z
Quirey (surname) (in England) 'kwaiəri, (in Ireland) 'kwiəri
Quirinal 'kwirinəl
Quirinus kwi'rainəs
quirk (Q.), -s kwə:k, -s
quisling, -s 'kwizliŋ, -z
quit (adj. v.), -s, -ting, -ted kwit, -s, -iŋ, -id
quite kwait
Quito 'ki:təu
quit-rent, -s 'kwit-rent, -s
quits kwits
quittance, -s 'kwitəns, -iz
quiv|er (s. v.), -ers, -ering/ly, -ered 'kwiv|ə*, -əz, -əriŋ/li, -əd
qui vive ki:'vi:v
Quixote 'kwiksət [-səut] (ki'xote)
quixotic, -ally kwik'sɔtik, -əli
quiz (s. v.), -zes, -zing, -zed kwiz, -iz, -iŋ, -d
quizmaster, -s 'kwiz,mɑ:stə*, -z
quizzic|al, -ally 'kwizik|əl, -əli
quoad 'kwəuæd
quod (s. v.), -s, -ding, -ded kwɔd, -z, -iŋ, -id
quodlibet, -s 'kwɔdlibet, -s
quoin (s. v.), -s, -ing, -ed kɔin [kwɔin], -z, -iŋ, -d
quoit, -s kɔit [kwɔit], -s
quondam 'kwɔndæm [-dəm]
Quorn kwɔ:n
quorum, -s 'kwɔ:rəm, -z
quota (s. v.), -s, -ing, -ed 'kwəutə, -z, -iŋ [-əriŋ], -d
quotable 'kwəutəbl
quotation, -s kwəu'teiʃən, -z
quot|e (s. v.), -es, -ing, -ed kwəut, -s, -iŋ, -id
quoth, -a kwəuθ, -ə
quotidian kwɔ'tidɪən [kwəu't-, -djən]
quotient, -s 'kwəuʃənt, -s
quousque tandem kwəu'uskwi'tændem [-'ʌs-, -dəm]
Quy (in Cambs., surname) kwai
q.v. 'kju:'vi: ['witʃ'si:, 'kwɔd'videi, old fashioned 'kwɔd'vaidi]

R

R (*the letter*), **-'s** ɑ:*, -z
ra (*note in Tonic Sol-fa*), **-s** rɔ:, -z
Rabat (*in Morocco*) rə'bɑ:t
rabbet, -s 'ræbit, -s
rabbi, -s 'ræbai, -z
rabbinic, -al, -ally ræ'binik [rə'b-], -əl,
　-əli
rabbit, -s; -hole/s, -hutch/es 'ræbit, -s;
　-həul/z, -hʌtʃ/iz
rabbit-warren, -s 'ræbit,wɔrən [-rin], -z
rabble, -s 'ræbl, -z
rabid, -est, -ly, -ness 'ræbid, -ist, -li, -nis
rabies 'reibi:z [-biz, -bii:z, 'ræb-]
Rabin (*surname*) 'reibin
Rabindranath Tagore rə'bindrənɑ:t-
　tə'gɔ:* [-'gɔə*] (*Bengali* robindrɔ-
　nath ṭhakur, *Hind.* rəbindrənath
　ṭhakwr)
Rabshakeh 'ræbʃɑ:ki [-ʃəki, -ʃəkə]
Raby 'reibi
raca 'rɑ:kə
rac|e, -es, -ing, -ed, -er/s reis, -iz, -iŋ, -t,
　-ə*/z
race-course, -s 'reis-kɔ:s [-kɔəs], -iz
race-horse, -s 'reishɔ:s, -iz
race-meeting, -s 'reis,mi:tiŋ, -z
Racheil 'reiʃəl
Rachel 'reitʃəl
rachitis ræ'kaitis [rə'k-]
Rachmaninoff ræk'mæninɔf (rax'ma-
　njinəf)
raci|al, -ally 'reiʃ|əl [-ʃĭ|əl, -ʃj|əl], -əli
racialism 'reiʃəlizəm [-ʃĭəl-, -ʃjəl-]
Racine (*English personal name*) rə'si:n,
　(*French author*) ræ'si:n (rasin)
racism 'reisizəm
rack (*s. v.*), **-s, -ing, -ed** ræk, -s, -iŋ, -t
racket (*s. v.*), **-s, -ing, -ed; -y** 'rækit, -s,
　-iŋ, -id; -i
racketeer, -s ,ræki'tiə*, -z
rack-rail, -s 'ræk-reil ['ræk'r-], -z
rack-rent, -s 'ræk-rent, -s
raconteur, -s ,rækɔn'tə:* [-kɔ̃n-, -kɔːn-]
　(rakɔ̃tœːr), -z
racoon, -s rə'ku:n, -z
racquet, -s 'rækit, -s
rac|y, -ier, -iest, -ily, -iness 'reis|i, -ĭə*
　[-jə*], -iist [-jist], -ili, -inis
rad (**R.**), **-s** ræd, -z

radar 'reidə* [-dɑ:*]
Rad|cliffe, -ford 'ræd|klif, -fəd
radial, -ly 'reidjəl [-dĭəl], -i
radian, -s 'reidjən [-dĭən], -z
radiance, -s 'reidjəns [-dĭəns], -iz
radiant (*s. adj*], **-s, -ly** 'reidjənt [-dĭənt],
　-s, -li
radiat|e (*v.*), **-es, -ing, -ed** 'reidieit
　[-djeit], -s, -iŋ, -id
radiation, -s ,reidi'eiʃən, -z
radiator, -s 'reidieitə*, -z
radic|al (*s. adj.*), **-als, -ally, -alness;**
　-alism 'rædik|əl, -əlz, -əli [-ḷi], -əlnis;
　-əlizəm [-ḷizəm]
radio (*s.*), **-s** 'reidiəu [-djəu], -z
radi|o (*v.*), **-o(e)s, -oing, -oed** 'reidi|əu
　[-dj|əu], -əuz, -əuiŋ, -əud
radio-active ,reidiəu'æktiv [-djəu-]
radioactivity 'reidiəuæk'tiviti [-djəu-]
radiogenic 'reidiəu'dʒenik [-djəu-]
radiogram, -s 'reidiəuɡræm [-djəuɡ-], -z
radiograph, -s 'reidiəuɡrɑ:f [-djəuɡ-,
　-ɡræf], -s
radiography ,reidi'ɔɡrəfi
radiolocat|e, -es, -ing, -ed 'reidiəu-
　ləu'keit [-djəu-], -s, -iŋ, -id
radio-location 'reidiəuləu'keiʃən [-djəu-]
radiolog|ist/s, -y ,reidi'ɔlədʒ|ist/s, -i
radiometer, -s ,reidi'ɔmitə*, -z
radiotelegram, -s 'reidiəu'teligræm
　[-djəu-], -z
radiotelephone, -s 'reidiəu'telifəun
　[-djəu-], -z
radiotherapy 'reidiəu'θerəpi [-djəu-]
radish, -es 'rædiʃ, -iz
radium 'reidjəm [-dĭəm]
ra|dius, -dii 'rei|djəs [-dĭəs], -diai
radix, -es, radices 'reidiks, -iz, 'reidisi:z
Radleian, -s ræd'li(:)ən, -z
Radley 'rædli
Radmall 'rædmɔ:l
Radnor, -shire 'rædnə* [-nɔ:*], -ʃiə*
　[-ʃə*]
Rae rei
Raeburn, -s 'reibə:n, -z
Raemakers 'rɑ:mɑ:kəz
Raf ræf
R.A.F. 'ɑ:rei'ef
raffia 'ræfĭə [-fjə]

raff|le (s. v.), -les (R.), -ling, -led 'ræf|l, -lz, -lịŋ [-liŋ], -ld

raft (s. v.), -s, -ing, -ed rɑ:ft, -s, -iŋ, -id

rafter, -s, -ed 'rɑ:ftə*, -z, -d

rag (s. v.), -s, -ging, -ged ræg, -z, -iŋ, -d

ragamuffin, -s 'rægə,mʌfin, -z

rag-and-bone|-man, -men ,rægən'bəun|-mæn, -men

rag|e (s. v.), -es, -ing/ly, -ed reidʒ, -iz, -iŋ/li, -d

ragged (adj.), -er, -est, -ly, -ness 'rægid, -ə*, -ist, -li, -nis

Raglan 'ræglən

ragout, -s 'rægu:, -z

ragtag 'rægtæg

ragtime 'rægtaim

Rahab 'reihæb

Rahere rə'hiə*

raid (s. v.), -s, -ing, -ed, -er/s reid, -z, -iŋ, -id, -ə*/z

Raikes reiks

rail (s. v.), -s, -ing, -ed reil, -z, -iŋ, -d

railhead, -s 'reilhed, -z

railing, -s 'reiliŋ, -z

railler|y, -ies 'reilər|i, -iz

rail|road/s, -way/s 'reil|rəud/z, -wei/z

railway|man,-men 'reilwei|mən [-mæn], -mən [-men]

raiment 'reimənt

rain (s. v.), -s, -ing, -ed; -less rein, -z, -iŋ, -d; -lis

rainbow, -s 'reinbəu, -z

raincoat, -s 'reinkəut, -s

raindrop, -s 'rein-drɔp, -s

rainfall 'reinfɔ:l

rain-gauge, -s 'reingeidʒ, -iz

rainless 'reinlis

rainmak|er/s, -ing 'rein,meik|ə*/z, -iŋ

rainproof 'reinpru:f

rainstorm, -s 'rein-stɔ:m, -z

rainwater 'rein,wɔ:tə*

rain|y, -ier, -iest, -iness 'rein|i, -ĭə* [-jə*], -iist [-jist], -inis

rais|e, -es, -ing, -ed reiz, -iz, -iŋ, -d

raisin, -s 'reizn, -z

raison d'être 'reizõ:n'deitrə [-'detrə, -zɔ:n'd-, -zɔn'd-, -'deitə*] (rɛzõdɛ:tr̩)

raj rɑ:dʒ

rajah (R.), -s 'rɑ:dʒə, -z

Rajasthani ,rɑ:dʒəs'tɑ:ni (Hind. rajəs-thani)

Rajput 'rɑ:dʒput (Hind. rajpwt)

Rajputana ,rɑ:dʒpu'tɑ:nə (Hind. rajpwtana)

rak|e (s. v.), -es, -ing, -ed reik, -s, -iŋ, -t

rakish, -ly, -ness 'reikiʃ, -li, -nis

rale, -s rɑ:l, -z

Rale(i)gh 'rɔ:li, 'rɑ:li, 'ræli
Note.—The family of the late Sir Walter Raleigh pronounces 'rɔ:li. Raleigh bicycles are generally called 'ræli. When used as the name of a ship, the pronunciation is 'ræli.

rallentando, -s ,rælen'tændəu [-lən-, -lin-], -z

rall|y (s. v.), -ies, -ying, -ied 'ræl|i, -iz, -iiŋ, -id

Ralph (Christian name) reif, rælf

Ralph Cross (in Yorks.) 'rɑ:lf'krɔs ['rælf-, -'krɔ:s]

Ralston 'rɔ:lstən

ram (s. v.), -s, -ming, -med, -mer/s ræm, -z, -iŋ, -d, -ə*/z

Ramah 'rɑ:mə

Ramayana rɑ:'maiənə [-'mɑ:jənə] (Hind. ramajənə)

ramb|le (s. v.), -les, -ling, -led 'ræmb|l, -lz, -liŋ [-liŋ], -ld

rambler (R.), -s 'ræmblə*, -z

rambling (adj.), -ly 'ræmbliŋ, -li

ramekin [-quin], -s 'ræmkin, -z

Rameses 'ræmisi:z

ramification, -s ,ræmifi'keiʃən, -z

rami|fy, -fies, -fying, -fied 'ræmi|fai, -faiz, -faiiŋ, -faid

Ramillies 'ræmiliz

Ramoth-Gilead 'reimɔθ'giliæd [-məθ-, -ljæd]

ramp (s. v.), -s, -ing, -ed ræmp, -s, -iŋ, -t [ræmt]

rampag|e (s. v.), -es, -ing, -ed ræm'peidʒ, -iz, -iŋ, -d

rampageous, -ly, -ness ræm'peidʒəs, -li, -nis

rampan|cy, -t/ly 'ræmpən|si, -t/li

rampart, -s 'ræmpa:t [-pət], -s

rampion, -s 'ræmpjən [-pĭən], -z

ramrod, -s 'ræmrɔd, -z

Ramsay 'ræmzi

Ramsden 'ræmzdən

Ramsey 'ræmzi

Ramsgate 'ræmzgit [locally -geit]

ramshackle 'ræm,ʃækl ['ræm'ʃ-]

ran (from run) ræn

rance ræns

Rance (surname) rɑ:ns

ranch (s. v.), -es, -ing, -ed, -er/s rɑ:ntʃ [ræntʃ], -iz, -iŋ, -t, -ə*/z

rancid, -ness 'rænsid, -nis

rancidity ræn'siditi

rancorous, -ly 'ræŋkərəs, -li

rancour 'ræŋkə*

rand, -s rænd, -z

Rand (*usual pronunciation in England*) rænd, (*pronunciation of English-speaking South Africans*) rɑːnd, rɑːnt, rɔnt (*Afrikaans* rɑnt)
Rand|all, -ell 'rænd|l, -l
Randolph 'rændɔlf [-dəlf]
random 'rændəm
randomiz|e [-is|e], -es, -ing, -ed 'rændə-maiz, -iz, -iŋ, -d
randy 'rændi
Ranee, -s rɑːˈniː: [ˈ-ˈ-], -z
Ranelagh 'rænilə, 'rænələ
rang (*from* ring) ræŋ
rang|e (*s. v.*), -es, -ing, -ed reindʒ, -iz, -iŋ, -d
range-finder, -s 'reindʒˌfaində*, -z
ranger (R.), -s 'reindʒə*, -z
Rangoon ræŋˈguːn
rank (*s. adj. v.*) (R.), -s; -er, -est, -ly, -ness; -ing, -ed ræŋk, -s; -ə*, -ist, -li, -nis; -iŋ, -t [rænt]
Rankeillour ræŋˈkiːlə*
Rankin(e) 'ræŋkin
rank|le, -les, -ling, -led 'ræŋk|l, -lz, -liŋ, [-liŋ], -ld
Rannoch 'rænək [-əx]
Rann of Cutch 'rʌnəvˈkʌtʃ [ˈræn-]
Ranoe 'rɑːnəu
ransack, -s, -ing, -ed, -er/s 'rænsæk, -s, -iŋ, -t, -ə*/z
ransom (*s. v.*) (R.), -s, -ing, -ed, -er/s 'rænsəm, -z, -iŋ, -d, -ə*/z
Ransome 'rænsəm
rant (*s. v.*), -s, -ing/ly, -ed, -er/s rænt, -s, -iŋ/li, -id, -ə*/z
ranuncul|us, -uses, -i rəˈnʌŋkjul|əs, -əsiz, -ai
Ranworth 'rænwə:θ
rap (*s. v.*), -s, -ping, -ped ræp, -s, -iŋ, -t
rapacious, -ly, -ness rəˈpeiʃəs, -li, -nis
rapacity rəˈpæsiti
rap|e (*s. v.*), -es, -ing, -ed reip, -s, -iŋ, -t
Raphael (*angel*) 'ræfeiəl [ˈræfɑːel, 'ræfeil, 'reifiəl, *and in Jewish usage* 'reifl, 'ræfəel], (*modern surname*) 'reifl, 'ræfeil, (*Italian artist*) 'ræfeiəl [-fiəl, -feil]
rapid, -est, -ly, -ness 'ræpid, -ist, -li, -nis
rapidity rəˈpiditi [ræˈp-]
rapier, -s 'reipjə* [-piə*, -piə*], -z
rapine 'ræpain [-pin]
rapparee, -s ˌræpəˈriː:, -z
rapping, -s 'ræpiŋ, -z
rapport ræˈpɔ: (rapoːr)
rapporteur, -s ˌræpɔːˈtəː* (rapɔrtœːr), -z
rapprochement, -s ræˈprɔʃmɑ̃ːŋ [-mɔ̃ːŋ, -mɑːŋ, -mɔːŋ, -mɔŋ] (raprɔʃmɑ̃), -z
rapscallion, -s ræpˈskæljən [-liən] , -z

rapt ræpt
rapture, -d 'ræptjə*, -d
rapturous, -ly 'ræptʃərəs, -li
raptus, -es 'ræptəs, -iz
rara avis 'rɑːrəˈævis [ˈrɛərəˈeivis]
rare, -r, -st, -ly, -ness rɛə*, -rə*, -rist, -li, -nis
rarebit, -s 'rɛəbit [ˈræbit], -s
rarefaction ˌrɛəriˈfækʃən
rare|fy, -fies, -fying, -fied 'rɛəri|fai, -faiz, -faiiŋ, -faid
rarit|y, -ies 'rɛərit|i, -iz
rascal, -s 'rɑːskəl, -z
rascalit|y, -ies rɑːˈskælit|i, -iz
rascally 'rɑːskəli [-k|i]
ras|e, -es, -ing, -ed reiz, -iz, -iŋ, -d
rash (*s. adj.*), -es; -er, -est, -ly, -ness ræʃ, -iz; -ə*, -ist, -li, -nis
rasher (*s.*), -s 'ræʃə*, -z
rasp (*s. v.*), -s, -ing, -ed rɑːsp, -s, -iŋ, -t
raspberr|y, -ies 'rɑːzbər|i [ˈrɑːsb-], -iz
rasp|y, -iness 'rɑːsp|i, -inis
Rasselas 'ræsiləs [-læs]
rat, -s, -ting, -ted ræt, -s, -iŋ, -id
rata (*tree*), -s 'reitə, -z
rata (*in pro rata*) 'rɑːtə [ˈreitə]
ratability ˌreitəˈbiliti [-lət-]
ratab|le, -ly 'reitəb|l, -li
ratafia, -s ˌrætəˈfiə, -z
ratan, -s rəˈtæn [ræ't-], -z
rataplan ˌrætəˈplæn
ratatat 'rætəˈtæt
rat-catcher, -s 'rætˌkætʃə*, -z
ratchet, -s 'rætʃit, -s
Ratcliff(e) 'rætklif
rat|e (*s. v.*), -es, -ing, -ed reit, -s, -iŋ, -id
rateab|le, -ly 'reitəb|l, -li
ratel, -s 'reitel [-təl, -tl], -z
rate-payer, -s 'reitˌpeiə*, -z
Rath ræθ
Rathbone 'ræθbəun [-bən]
rather 'rɑːðə* [*as interj. also* 'rɑːˈðəː*]
Rathfarnham ræθˈfɑːnəm
rat-hole, -s 'ræthəul, -z
ratification, -s ˌrætifiˈkeiʃən, -z
rati|fy, -fies, -fying, -fied, -fier/s 'ræti|fai, -faiz, -faiiŋ, -faid, -faiə*/z
rating, -s 'reitiŋ, -z
ratio -s 'reiʃiəu [-ʃəu], -z
ratiocinat|e, -es, -ing, -ed ˌrætiˈɔsineit, -s, -iŋ, -id
ratiocination, -s ˌrætiɔsiˈneiʃən [-tiəus-], -z
rati|on (*s. v.*), -ons, -oning, -oned 'ræʃ|ən, -ənz, -niŋ [-əniŋ, -niŋ], -ənd
ra|tional, -tionally 'ræ|ʃənl [-ʃnəl, -ʃn̩l, -ʃn̩l, -ʃnəl], -ʃn̩əli [-ʃnəli -ʃn̩li, -ʃn̩li, -ʃənəli]

rationale, -s ˌræʃəˈnɑːl [-ʃiəuˈn-, -ʃjəˈn-, -ˈnɑːli], -z

rationali|sm, -st/s ˈræʃnəli|zəm [-ʃnəl-, -ʃn̩l-, -ʃn̩l-, -ʃənəl-], -st/s

rationalistic ˌræʃnəˈlistik [-ʃnəˈli-, -ʃn̩lˈi-, -ʃn̩lˈi-, -ʃənəˈli-]

rationality ˌræʃəˈnæliti [-ʃn̩ˈæ-]

rationalization [-isa-] ˌræʃnəlaiˈzeiʃən [-ʃnəl-, -ʃn̩l-, -ʃn̩l-, -ʃənəl-, -liˈz-]

rationaliz|e [-is|e], **-es**, **-ing**, **-ed** ˈræʃnəlaiz [-ʃnəl-, -ʃn̩l-, -ʃn̩l-, -ʃənəl-], iz, -iŋ, -d

Ratisbon ˈrætizbɔn [-isb-]

ratlin(e), -s ˈrætlin, -z

rat-race ˈræt-reis

rat-tail, -ed ˈrætteil, -d

rattan, -s rəˈtæn [ræˈt-], -z

ratt|le (s. v.), **-les**, **-ling**, **-led**, **-ler/s** ˈræt|l, -lz, -l̩iŋ, [-liŋ], -ld, -lə*/z [-lə*/z]

rattlesnake, -s ˈrætlsneik, -s

rat-trap, -s ˈrættræp, -s

raucous, -ly ˈrɔːkəs, -li

ravag|e (s. v.), **-es**, **-ing**, **-ed**, **-er/s** ˈrævidʒ, -iz, -iŋ, -d, -ə*/z

rav|e, -es, -ing/s, -ed reiv, -z, -iŋ/z, -d

rav|el, -els, -elling, -elled ˈræv|əl, -əlz, -l̩iŋ [-əliŋ], -əld

Ravel (French composer) ræˈvel (ravɛl)

ravelin, -s ˈrævlin [-vəlin], -z

raven (s.) (R.), **-s** ˈreivn [-vən], -z

raven (v.), **-s**, **-ing**, **-ed** ˈrævn, -nz, -n̩iŋ [-əniŋ], -nd

Ravening ˈreivn̩iŋ

Ravenna rəˈvenə

ravenous, -ly, -ness ˈrævənəs [-vinəs, -vn̩əs], -li, -nis

Ravensbourne ˈreivnzbɔːn [-bəən]

ravin(e) (plunder) ˈrævin

ravine (deep valley), **-s** rəˈviːn, -z

raving (s. adj. adv.), **-s** ˈreiviŋ, -z

ravish, -es, -ing/ly, -ed, -er/s, -ment ˈræviʃ, -iz, -iŋ/li, -t, -ə*/z, -mənt

raw, -er, -est, -ly, -ness rɔː, -ə*, -ist, ˈrɔː-li, ˈrɔː-nis

Raw|don, -lings, -lins, -linson ˈrɔː|dn, -liŋz, -linz, -linsn

ray (R.), **-s; -less** rei, -z; -lis

Ray|leigh, -ment, -mond, -ner, -nes ˈrei|li, -mənt, -mənd, -nə*, -nz

rayon ˈreiɔn [ˈreiən]

raz|e, -es, -ing, -ed reiz, -iz, -iŋ, -d

razor, -s ˈreizə*, -z

razorbill, -s ˈreizəbil, -z

razor-blade, -s ˈreizə-bleid, -z

razor-edge, -s ˈreizərˈedʒ [-zəˈedʒ, ˈ---], -iz

razor-shell, -s ˈreizəʃel, -z

Razzell rəˈzel

razzia, -s ˈræziə [-zjə], -z

razzle-dazzle ˈræzlˌdæzl

re (note in Tonic Sol-fa), **-s** rei [riː], -z

re (prep.) riː

re- (prefix denoting repetition) ˈriː-
  Note.—Compounds with this prefix not entered below have double stress. Thus **restamp** is ˈriːˈstæmp.

Rea rei, riə, riː
  Note.—Baron Rea pronounces riː.

reach (s. v.), **-es, -ing, -ed** riːtʃ, -iz, -iŋ, -t

react, -s, -ing, -ed ri(ː)ˈækt, -s, -iŋ, -id

reaction, -s ri(ː)ˈækʃən, -z

reactionar|y (s. adj.), **-ies** ri(ː)ˈækʃn̩-ər|i [-ʃənə-, -ʃnə-], -iz

reactive, -ly ri(ː)ˈæktiv, -li

reactor, -s ri(ː)ˈæktə*, -z

read (pres. tense) (R.), **-s, -ing** riːd, -z, -iŋ

read (past tense) red

readability ˌriːdəˈbiliti [-lət-]

readab|le, -ly, -leness ˈriːdəb|l, -li, -lnis

re-address, -es, -ing, -ed ˈriːəˈdres, -iz, -iŋ, -t

Reade riːd

reader, -s; -ship/s ˈriːdə*, -z; -ʃip/s

reading (s.), **-s** ˈriːdiŋ, -z

Reading ˈrediŋ

reading-desk, -s ˈriːdiŋdesk, -s

reading-glass, -es ˈriːdiŋglɑːs, -iz

reading-lamp, -s ˈriːdiŋlæmp, -s

reading-room, -s ˈriːdiŋrum [-ruːm], -z

readjus|t, -ts, -ting, -ted, -tment/s ˈriːəˈdʒʌs|t, -ts, -tiŋ, -tid, -tmənt/s

readmission, -s ˈriːədˈmiʃən, -z

readmit, -s, -ting, -ted; -tance ˈriːədˈmit, -s, -iŋ, -id; -əns

read|y, -ier, -iest, -ily, -iness ˈred|i, -iə* [-jə*], -iist [-jist], -ili, -inis

ready-made ˈrediˈmeid [ˈ--- when attributive]

reaffirm, -s, -ing, -ed ˈriːəˈfəːm, -z, -iŋ, -d

reagent, -s ri(ː)ˈeidʒənt, -s

real (monetary unit), **-s** reiˈɑːl, -z

real (adj.), **really** riəl [ˈriːəl], ˈriəli

reali|sm, -st/s ˈriəli|zəm [ˈriːəl-], -st/s

realistic, -ally riəˈlistik [ˌriːəˈl-, riəˈl-], -əli [-li]

realit|y, -ies ri(ː)ˈælit|i, -iz

realization [-isa-], **-s** ˌriəlaiˈzeiʃən [-liˈz-], -z

realiz|e [-is|e], **-es, -ing, -ed; -able** ˈriəlaiz, -iz, -iŋ, -d; -əbl

really ˈriəli

realm, -s relm, -z

realty ˈriəlti [ˈriːəl-]

ream (s. v.), -s, -ing, -ed ri:m, -z, -iŋ, -d

reamer, -s 'ri:mə*, -z

Rean 'ri:ən

reap, -s, -ing, -ed, -er/s ri:p, -s, -iŋ, -t, -ə*/z

reappear, -s, -ing, -ed; -ance/s 'ri:-ə'piə* ['riə'p-, rĭə'p-], -z, -riŋ, -d; -rəns/iz

reapplication, -s 'ri:,æpli'keiʃən, -z

reappl|y, -ies, -ying, -ied 'ri:ə'pl|ai, -aiz, -aiiŋ, -aid

reappoint, -s, -ing, -ed, -ment/s 'ri:-ə'pɔint ['riə'p-, rĭə'p-], -s, -iŋ, -id, -mənt/s

rear (s. v.), -s, -ing, -ed riə*, -z, -riŋ, -d

rear-admiral, -s 'riə'ædmərəl ['riər'æd-], -z

rear-guard, -s 'riəga:d, -z

re-arm, -s, -ing, -ed 'ri:'ɑ:m, -z, -iŋ, -d

rearrang|e, -es, -ing, -ed, -ement/s 'ri:ə'reindʒ ['riə'r-, rĭə'r-], -iz, -iŋ, -d, -mənt/s

reas|on, -ons, -oning/s, -oned, -oner/s 'ri:z|n, -nz, -ṇiŋ/z [-əniŋ/z], -nd, -ṇə*/z [-ənə*/z]

reasonab|le, -ly, -leness 'ri:zṇəb|l [-znə-], -li, -lnis

reassemb|le, -les, -ling, -led 'ri:ə'semb|l ['riə's-, rĭə's-], -lz, -liŋ, -ld

reassert, -s, -ing, -ed 'ri:ə'sə:t ['riə's-], -s, -iŋ, -id

reassur|e, -es, -ing/ly, -ed; -ance ,ri:ə'ʃuə* [riə-, rĭə-, -'ʃɔə*, -'ʃo:*, -'ʃə:*], -z, -riŋ/li, -d; -rəns

Réaumur 'reiəmjuə* [-mə*] (reomy:r)

Reay rei

rebarbative ri'ba:bətiv [rə'b-]

rebate (s.) (discount), -s 'ri:beit [ri'beit], -s

rebat|e (v.) (heraldic term), -es, -ing, -ed 'ræbit, -s, -iŋ, -ed

Rebecca ri'bekə [rə'b-]

rebec(k), -s 'ri:bek, -s

rebel (s.), -s 'rebl [-bəl], -z

rebel (v.), -s, -ling, -led ri'bel [rə'b-], -z, -iŋ, -d

rebellion, -s ri'beljən [rə'b-], -z

rebellious, -ly, -ness ri'beljəs [rə'b-], -li, -nis

re-bind, -s, -ing, re-bound 'ri:'baind, -z, -iŋ, 'ri:'baund

rebirth, -s 'ri:'bə:θ, -s

reborn 'ri:'bɔ:n

rebound (s.), -s ri'baund ['ri:baund], -z

rebound (adj.) 'ri:'baund

rebound (v.), -s, -ing, -ed ri'baund [ri:'b-], -z, -iŋ, -id

rebuff (s. v.), -s, -ing, -ed ri'bʌf, -s, -iŋ, -t

rebuil|d, -ds, -ding, -t 'ri:'bil|d, -dz, -diŋ, -t

rebuk|e (s. v.), -es, -ing/ly, -ed ri'bju:k [rə'b-], -s, -iŋ/li, -t

rebus, -es 'ri:bəs, -iz

rebut, -s, -ting, -ted ri'bʌt, -s, -iŋ, -id

rebutt|able, -al/s, -er/s ri'bʌt|əbl, -l/z, -ə*/z

recalcitrant (s. adj.), -s ri'kælsitrənt [rə'k-], -s

recall (s. v.), -s, -ing, -ed ri'kɔ:l [rə'k-], -z, -iŋ, -d

recant, -s, -ing, -ed ri'kænt, -s, -iŋ, -id

recantation, -s ,ri:kæn'teiʃən, -z

recapitulat|e, -es, -ing, -ed ,ri:kə'pitjuleit, -s, -iŋ, -id

recapitulation, -s 'ri:-kə,pitju'leiʃən [,ri:-], -z

recapitulatory ,ri:-kə'pitjulətəri [-leitəri]

recapt|ure (s. v.), -ures, -uring, -ured 'ri:'kæptʃ|ə*, -əz, -əriŋ, -əd

recast, -s, -ing 'ri:'ka:st, -s, -iŋ

recce (R.) 'reki

reced|e, -es, -ing, -ed ri(:)'si:d, -z, -iŋ, -id

receipt (s. v.), -s, -ing, -ed ri'si:t [rə's-], -s, -iŋ, -id

receiv|e, -es, -ing, -ed, -er/s; -able ri'si:v [rə's-], -z, -iŋ, -d, -ə*/z; -əbl

recency 'ri:snsi

recension, -s ri'senʃən [rə's-], -z

recent, -ly 'ri:snt, -li

receptacle, -s ri'septəkl [rə's-], -z

reception, -s ri'sepʃən [rə's-], -z

receptionist, -s ri'sepʃənist [rə's-, -ʃnist, -ʃnist]

receptive, -ness ri'septiv [rə's-], -nis

receptivity risep'tiviti [,ri:s-, ,res-]

recess, -es ri'ses [rə's-, 'ri:ses], -iz

recession, -s ri'seʃən [rə's-], -z

recessional, -s ri'seʃənl [rə's-, -ʃṇl, -ʃnl, -ʃənəl], -z

Rechab 'ri:kæb

recherché rə'ʃɛəʃei (rəʃɛrʃe)

re-christ|en, -ens, -ening, -ened 'ri:'krisn, -nz, -ṇiŋ [-niŋ], -nd

recidivist, -s ri'sidivist, -s

recipe, -s 'resipi, -z

recipient, -s ri'sipiənt [rə's-, -pjənt], -s

reciproc|al (s. adj.), -als, -ally, -alness ri'siprək|əl [rə's-, -pruk-], -əlz, -əli, -əlnis

reciprocat|e, -es, -ing, -ed ri'siprəkeit [rə's-, -pruk-], -s, -iŋ, -id

reciprocation ri,siprə'keiʃən [rə,s-, -pru'k-]

reciprocity ,resi'prɔsiti

recital, -s ri'saitl [rə's-], -z

recitation, -s ,resi'teiʃən, -z

recitative, -s ˌresitə'tiːv, -z
recit|e, -es, -ing, -ed, -er/s ri'sait [rə's-], -s, -iŋ, -id, -ə*/z
reck, -s, -ing, -ed rek, -s, -iŋ, -t
reckless, -ly, -ness 'reklis, -li, -nis
reck|on, -ons, -oning/s, -oned, -oner/s 'rek|ən, -ənz, -niŋ/z [-niŋ/z, -əniŋ/z], -ənd, -nə*/z [-ənə*/z]
reclaim, -s, -ing, -ed ri'kleim, -z, -iŋ, -d
reclaimable ri'kleiməbl
reclamation, -s ˌreklə'meiʃən, -z
reclin|e, -es, -ing, -ed ri'klain [rə'k-], -z, -iŋ, -d
recluse, -s ri'kluːs, -iz
recognition, -s ˌrekəg'niʃən [-kig-], -z
recognizab|le [-isa-], -ly 'rekəgnaizəb|l [ˌrekəg'n-, -kig-], -li
recognizance [-isa-], -s ri'kɔgnizəns [rə'k-, -'kɔni-], -iz
recogniz|e [-is|e], -es, -ing, -ed 'rekəgnaiz [-kig-], -iz, -iŋ, -d
recoil (s.), -s ri'kɔil ['riːkɔil], -z
recoil (v.), -s, -ing, -ed ri'kɔil [rə'k-], -z, -iŋ, -d
recollect (remember), -s, -ing, -ed ˌrekə'lekt [-k|'ekt, '--'-, '---], -s, -iŋ, -id
recollect (regain (one's composure, etc.)), -s, -ing, -ed ˌrekə'lekt [-k|'ekt, 'riː-kə'lekt], -s, -iŋ, -id
re-collect (collect over again), -s, -ing, -ed 'riː-kə'lekt, -s, -iŋ, -id
recollection, -s ˌrekə'lekʃən [-k|'ek-], -z
recommenc|e, -es, -ing, -ed 'riːkə'mens [ˌrekə'm-], -iz, -iŋ, -t
recommend, -s, -ing, -ed; -able ˌrekə-'mend, -z, -iŋ, -id; -əbl
recommendation, -s ˌrekəmen'deiʃən [-km-, -mən-], -z
recompens|e (s. v.), -es, -ing, -ed 'rekəmpens [-km-], -iz, -iŋ, -t
recompos|e, -es, -ing, -ed 'riːkəm'pəuz, -iz, -iŋ, -d
reconcilab|le, -ly 'rekənsailəb|l [ˌre-kən's-, -kn-], -li
reconcil|e, -es, -ing, -ed, -er/s 'rekən-sail [-kn-], -z, -iŋ, -d, -ə*/z [-z
reconciliation, -s ˌrekənsili'eiʃən [-kn-], -z
recondite ri'kɔndait [rə'k-, 'rekənd-]
reconduct, -s, -ing, -ed 'riː-kən'dʌkt, -s, -iŋ, -id
reconnaissance, -s ri'kɔnisəns [rə'k-], -iz
reconnoit|re, -res, -ring, -red ˌrekə-'nɔit|ə*, -əz, -əriŋ, -əd
reconqu|er, -ers, -ering, -ered 'riː'kɔŋ-k|ə*, -əz, -əriŋ, -əd
reconquest, -s 'riː'kɔnkwest, -s
reconsid|er, -ers, -ering, -ered 'riː-kən-'sid|ə* [ˌriː-kən-, -kn-], -əz, -əriŋ, -əd

reconsideration 'riː-kənˌsidə'reiʃən [-kn-]
reconstitut|e, -es, -ing, -ed 'riː'kɔnsti-tjuːt [-'---], -s, -iŋ, -id
reconstitution, -s 'riːˌkɔnsti'tjuːʃən, -z
reconstruct, -s, -ing, -ed 'riː-kəns'trʌkt [-kn-], -s, -iŋ, -id
reconstruction, -s 'riː-kəns'trʌkʃən [-kn-], -z
reconversion, -s 'riː-kən'vəːʃən [-kn-], -z
reconvey, -s, -ing, -ed 'riː-kən'vei, -z, -iŋ, -d
record (s.), -s 'rekɔːd, -z
record (v.), -s, -ing, -ed, -er/s; -able ri'kɔːd [rə'k-], -z, -iŋ, -id, -ə*/z; -əbl
recorder (musical instrument), -s ri-'kɔːdə* [rə'k-], -z
record-player, -s 'rekɔːdˌpleiə*, -z
recount (s.), -s 'riː'kaunt ['riː-kaunt], -s
recount (v.) (count again), -s, -ing, -ed 'riː'kaunt, -s, -iŋ, -id
recount (v.) (narrate), -s, -ing, -ed ri'kaunt, -s, -iŋ, -id
recoup, -s, -ing, -ed, -ment ri'kuːp, -s, -iŋ, -t, -mənt
recourse ri'kɔːs [rə'k-, -'kɔəs]
recov|er (get back, come back to health, etc.), -ers, -ering, -ered; -erable ri-'kʌv|ə* [rə'k-], -əz, -əriŋ, -əd; -ərəbl
recover (cover again), -s, -ing, -ed 'riː-'kʌvə*, -z, -riŋ, -d
recover|y, -ies ri'kʌvər|i [rə'k-], -iz
recreant (s. adj.), -s, -ly 'rekriənt, -s, -li
recreat|e (refresh), -es, -ing, -ed; -ive 'rekrieit, -s, -iŋ, -id; -iv
re-creat|e (create anew), -es, -ing, -ed 'riː-kri'eit, -s, -iŋ, -id
recreation (refreshment, amusement), -s; -al ˌrekri'eiʃən, -z; -əl
re-creation (creating anew), -s 'riː-kri'ei-ʃən, -z
recriminat|e, -es, -ing, -ed, -or/s ri'krimineit [rə'k-], -s, -iŋ, -id, -ə*/z
recrimination, -s riˌkrimi'neiʃən [rəˌk-], -z
recross, -es, -ing, -ed 'riː'krɔs [-'krɔːs, also 'riː-k- when contrasted with cross], -iz, -iŋ, -t
recrudesc|e, -es, -ing, -ed ˌriːkruː'des [ˌrek-], -iz, -iŋ, -t
recrudescen|ce, -t ˌriːkruː'desn|s [ˌrek-], -t
recruit (s. v.), -s, -ing, -ed, -er/s, -ment ri'kruːt [rə'k-], -s, -iŋ, -id, -ə*/z, -mənt
rectal 'rektəl [-tl]
rectangle, -s 'rek,tæŋgl ['rektˌæŋ-], -z
rectangular, -ly rek'tæŋgjulə* [rekt'æŋ-, -gjəl-], -li
rectification, -s ˌrektifi'keiʃən, -z

recti|fy, -fies, -fying, -fied, -fier/s;
-fiable 'rekti|fai, -faiz, -faiiŋ, -faid,
-faiə*/z; -faiəbl
rectiline|al, -ar ˌrekti'lini|əl [-nj|əl], -ə*
rectitude 'rektitju:d
recto 'rektəu
rector, -s; -ate/s, -ship/s 'rektə*, -z;
-rit/s, -ʃip/s
rectorial rek'tɔ:riəl
rector|y, -ies 'rektər|i, -iz
rect|um, -ums, -a 'rekt|əm, -əmz, -ə
Reculver, -s ri'kʌlvə* [rə'k-], -z
recumben|ce, -cy, -t/ly ri'kʌmbən|s
[rə'k-], -si, -t/li
recuperat|e, -es, -ing, -ed ri'kju:pəreit
[rə'k-, -'ku:-], -s, -iŋ, -id
recuperation riˌkju:pə'reiʃən [rəˌk-,
-ˌku:-]
recur, -s, -ring, -red ri'kə:* [rə'k-], -z,
-riŋ [ri'kʌriŋ], -d
recurren|ce, -ces, -t/ly ri'kʌrən|s [rə'k-],
-siz, -t/li
recursive (s. adj.), -s ri'kə:siv [ri:'k-], -z
recurv|e, -es, -ing, -ed ri:'kə:v, -z, -iŋ, -d
recusancy 'rekjuzənsi [ri'kju:z-, rə-
'kju:z-]
recusant, -s 'rekjuzənt [ri'kju:z-, rə-
'kju:z-], -s
red (s. adj.), -s; -der, -dest, -ness red,
-z; -ə*, -ist, -nis
redact, -s, -ing, -ed, -or/s ri'dækt, -s,
-iŋ, -id, -ə*/z
redaction, -s ri'dækʃən, -z
redbreast, -s 'redbrest, -s
redcap, -s 'redkæp, -s
Redcliffe 'redklif
redcoat, -s 'redkəut, -s
Reddaway 'redəwei
redd|en, -ens, -ening, -ened 'red|n, -nz,
-ŋiŋ [-niŋ], -nd
Redding 'rediŋ
reddish, -ness 'rediʃ, -nis
Redditch 'reditʃ
reddle 'redl
redecorat|e, -es, -ing, -ed 'ri:'dekəreit
[ri:'d-], -s, -iŋ, -id
redeem, -s, -ing, -ed; -able ri'di:m
[rə'd-], -z, -iŋ, -d; -əbl
redeemer (R.), -s ri'di:mə* [rə'd-], -z
redeliver, -s, -ing, -ed; -y 'ri:-di'livə*,
-z, -riŋ, -d; -ri
redemption (R.), -s ri'dempʃən [rə'd-], -z
redemptive ri'demptiv [rə'd-]
re-deploy, -s, -ing, -ed, -ment/s 'ri:-di-
'plɔi, -z, -iŋ, -d, -mənt/s
Red|fern, -field 'red|fə:n, -fi:ld
Redgauntlet red'gɔ:ntlit
red-handed 'red'hændid [-'--]

Redheugh (bridge in Newcastle upon
Tyne) 'redjəf
Redhill 'red'hil
red-hot 'red'hɔt ['--, -'- according to
sentence-stress]
re|-dial, -dials, -dialling, -dialled 'ri:|-
'daiəl, -'daiəlz, -'daiəliŋ, -'daiəld
rediffus|e, -es, -ing, -ed 'ri:-di'fju:z, -iz,
-iŋ, -d
rediffusion 'ri:-di'fju:ʒən
redintegrat|e, -es, -ing, -ed re'dintigreit
[ri'd-], -s, -iŋ, -id
redirect, -s, -ing, -ed 'ri:-di'rekt [-də'r-,
-dai'r-], -s, -iŋ, -id
rediscover, -s, -ing, -ed; -y 'ri:-dis'kʌvə*,
-z, -riŋ, -d; -ri
re|distribute, -distributes, -distributing,
-distributed 'ri:-|dis'tribju(:)t [-'distri-
bju:t], -dis'tribju(:)ts [-'distribju:ts],
-dis'tribjutiŋ [-'distribju:tiŋ], -dis-
'tribjutid [-'distribju:tid]
redistribution, -s 'ri:ˌdistri'bju:ʃən, -z
redivid|e, -es, -ing, -ed 'ri:-di'vaid, -z,
-iŋ, -id
redivivus ˌredi'vaivəs
red-letter 'red'letə*
Redmond 'redmənd
re|-do, -does, -doing, -did, -done
'ri:|'du:, -'dʌz, -'du(:)iŋ, -'did, -'dʌn
redolen|ce, -t 'redəulən|s, -t
redoub|le, -les, -ling, -led ri'dʌb|l
[ri:'d-], -lz, -liŋ [-ļiŋ], -ld
redoubt, -s; -able ri'daut [rə'd-], -s;
-əbl
redound, -s, -ing, -ed ri'daund [rə'd-],
-z, -iŋ, -id
redraft, -s, -ing, -ed 'ri:'drɑ:ft, -s, -iŋ, -id
re-draw, -s, -ing, redrew, redrawn
'ri:'drɔ:, -z, -iŋ, 'ri:'dru:, 'ri:'drɔ:n
redress (s. v.) (amends, make amends
for), -es, -ing, -ed ri'dres [rə'd-], -iz,
-iŋ, -t
redress (dress again), -es, -ing, -ed 'ri:-
'dres, -iz, -iŋ, -t
Redriff 'redrif
Redruth 'red-ru:θ
redshank, -s 'redʃæŋk, -s
redskin (R.), -s 'red-skin, -z
redstart, -s 'red-stɑ:t, -s
red-tapism 'red'teipizəm [red't-]
reduc|e, -es, -ing, -ed, -er/s ri'dju:s
[rə'd-], -iz, -iŋ, -t, -ə*/z
reducibility riˌdju:sə'biliti [rəˌd-, -si'b-,
-lət-]
reducible ri'dju:səbl [rə'd-, -sib-]
reduction, -s ri'dʌkʃən [rə'd-], -z
redundan|ce, -cy, -cies, -t/ly ri'dʌnd-
ən|s [rə'd-], -si, -siz, -t/li

redundantiz|e [-is|e], **-es, -ing, -ed** ri'dʌndəntaiz [rə'd-], -iz, -iŋ, -d

reduplicat|e, -es, -ing, -ed ri'dju:plikeit [rə'd-], -s, -iŋ, -id

reduplication, -s ri,dju:pli'keiʃən [rə,d-], -z

reduplicative ri'dju:plikətiv [rə'd-, -keit-]

redwood (R.) 'redwud

Reece ri:s

re-ech|o, -oes, -oing, -oed ri(:)'ek|əu, -əuz, -əuiŋ, -əud

reed (s. v.) (R.), -s, -ing, -ed ri:d, -z, -iŋ, -id

re-edit, -s, -ing, -ed 'ri:'edit, -s, -iŋ, -id

re-edition, -s 'ri:i'diʃən, -z

reed-pipe, -s 'ri:dpaip, -s

re-educat|e, -es, -ing, -ed 'ri:'edju(:)keit [ri:'ed-, -dʒu(:)-], -s, -iŋ, -id

re-education 'ri:,edju(:)'keiʃən [-dʒu(:)-]

reed-warbler, -s 'ri:d,wɔ:blə* ['-'-—], -z

reed|y, -ier, -iest, -iness 'ri:d|i, -ïə*, -iist, -inis

reef (s. v.), -s, -ing, -ed ri:f, -s, -iŋ, -t

reefer, -s 'ri:fə*, -z

reek (s. v.), -s (R.), -ing, -ed ri:k, -s, -iŋ, -t

Reekie 'ri:ki

reel (s. v.), -s, -ing, -ed ri:l, -z, -iŋ, -d

re-elect, -s, -ing, -ed 'ri:i'lekt, -s, -iŋ, -id

re-election, -s 'ri:i'lekʃən, -z

re-eligible 'ri:'elidʒəbl [ri:'el-, -dʒib-]

re-embark, -s, -ing, -ed 'ri:im'bɑ:k ['ri:em-], -s, -iŋ, -t

re-embarkation, -s 'ri:,embɑ:'keiʃən, -z

re-enact, -s, -ing, -ed, -ment|s 'ri:i'nækt ['ri:e'n-], -s, -iŋ, -id, -mənt/s

re-engag|e, -es, -ing, -ed, -ement/s 'ri:in'geidʒ ['ri:en-], -iz, -iŋ, -d, -mənt/s

re-enlist, -s, -ing, -ed 'ri:in'list ['ri:en-], -s, -iŋ, -id

re-ent|er, -ers, -ering, -ered 'ri:'ent|ə* [ri:'en-, ri'en-], -əz, -əriŋ, -əd

re-entrant ri:'entrənt [ri'en-]

re-entr|y, -ies ri:'entr|i [ri'en-], -iz

Rees ri:s

Reese ri:s

re-establish, -es, -ing, -ed, -ment 'ri:-is'tæbliʃ ['ri:es-], -iz, -iŋ, -t, -mənt

reeve (R.), -s ri:v, -z

re-examination, -s 'ri:ig,zæmi'neiʃən ['ri:eg-], -z

re-examin|e, -es, -ing, -ed 'ri:ig'zæmin ['ri:eg-], -z, -iŋ, -d

re-export (s.), -s 'ri:'ekspɔ:t, -s

re-export (v.), -s, -ing, -ed 'ri:eks'pɔ:t ['ri:iks'p-], -s, -iŋ, -id

re-fac|e, -es, -ing, -ed 'ri:'feis, -iz, -iŋ, -t

refashi|on, -ons, -oning, -oned 'ri:-'fæʃ|ən, -ənz, -niŋ [-əniŋ], -ənd

refection ri'fekʃən

refector|y, -ies ri'fektər|i [rə'f-, *also* 'refikt- *esp. in monasteries*], -iz

refer, -s, -ring, -red ri'fə:* [rə'f-], -z, -riŋ, -d

referable ri'fə:rəbl [rə'f-, 'refərəbl]

referee, -s ,refə'ri:, -z

reference, -s 'refrəns [-fər-], -iz

referendum, -s ,refə'rendəm, -z

referential ,refə'renʃəl

refill (s.), -s 'ri:-fil ['ri:'fil], -z

refill (v.), -s, -ing, -ed 'ri:'fil [ri:'fil], -z, -iŋ, -d

refin|e, -es, -ing, -ed, -er/s, -ement/s ri'fain [rə'f-], -z, -iŋ, -d, -ə*/z, -mənt/s

refiner|y, -ies ri'fainər|i [rə'f-], -iz

refit (s. v.), -s, -ting, -ted 'ri:'fit [ri:'f-], -s, -iŋ, -id

reflect, -s, -ing/ly, -ed, -or/s ri'flekt [rə'f-], -s, -iŋ/li, -id, -ə*/z

reflection, -s ri'flekʃən [rə'f-], -z

reflective, -ly, -ness ri'flektiv [rə'f-], -li, -nis

reflex (s. adj.), -es 'ri:-fleks, -iz

reflexed ri'flekst [ri:'f-, 'ri:-flekst]

reflexive ri'fleksiv [rə'f-]

refloat, -s, -ing, -ed 'ri:'fləut, -s, -iŋ, -id

refluent 'reflŭənt [-flwənt]

reflux, -es 'ri:flʌks, -iz

re-foot, -s, -ing, -ed 'ri:'fut, -s, -iŋ, -id

reform (s. v.) (*make better, become better, etc.*), -s, -ing, -ed, -er/s; -able ri'fɔ:m [rə'f-], -z, -iŋ, -d, -ə*/z; -əbl

reform (v.) (*form again*), -s, -ing, -ed 'ri:'fɔ:m, -z, -iŋ, -d

reformation (R.), -s ,refə'meiʃən [-fɔ:'m-], -z

reformative ri'fɔ:mətiv [rə'f-]

reformator|y (s. adj.), -ies ri'fɔ:mətər|i [rə'f-], -iz

refract, -s, -ing, -ed, -or/s; -ive ri-'frækt [rə'f-], -s, -iŋ, -id, -ə*/z; -iv

refraction, -s ri'frækʃən [rə'f-], -z

refractor|y, -ily, -iness ri'fræktər|i [rə'f-], -ili, -inis

refrain (s. v.), -s, -ing, -ed ri'frein [rə'f-], -z, -iŋ, -d

refresh, -es, -ing/ly, -ingness, -ed, -er/s, -ment/s ri'freʃ [rə'f-], -iz, -iŋ/li, -iŋnis, -t, -ə*/z, -mənt/s

refrigerat|e, -es, -ing, -ed, -or/s ri-'fridʒəreit [rə'f-], -s, -iŋ, -id, -ə*/z

refrigeration ri,fridʒə'reiʃən [rə,f-]

reft reft

refuge, -s 'refju:dʒ, -iz
refugee, -s ˌrefju(:)'dʒi:, -z
refulgen|ce, -t/ly ri'fʌldʒən|s [rə'f-],
-t/li
refund (s.), -s 'ri:-fʌnd, -z
refund (v.), -s, -ing, -ed ri:'fʌnd ['ri:'f-,
ri'f-], -z, -iŋ, -id
refurbish, -es, -ing, -ed 'ri:'fə:biʃ [ri:'f-],
-iz, -iŋ, -t
refurnish, -es, -ing, -ed 'ri:'fə:niʃ [ri:'f-],
-iz, -iŋ, -t
refusal, -s ri'fju:zəl [rə'f-], -z
refuse (s. adj.) 'refju:s
refus|e (v.), -es, -ing, -ed; -able ri-
'fju:z [rə'f-], -iz, -iŋ, -d; -əbl
refutability ˌrefjutə'biliti [ri,fju:t-,
rə,fju:t-, -lət-]
refutable 'refjutəbl [ri'fju:t-, rə'fju:t-]
refutation, -s ˌrefju(:)'teiʃən, -z
refut|e, -es, -ing, -ed ri'fju:t [rə'f-], -s,
-iŋ, -id
Reg (short for Reginald) redʒ
regain, -s, -ing, -ed ri'gein [ri:'g-], -z,
-iŋ, -d
reg|al, -ally 'ri:g|əl, -əli
regal|e, -es, -ing, -ed ri'geil, -z, -iŋ, -d
regalia ri'geiljə [rə'g-, -liə]
Regan 'ri:gən
regard (s. v.), -s, -ing, -ed ri'gɑ:d [rə'g-],
-z, -iŋ, -id
regardful ri'gɑ:dful [rə'g-]
regardless, -ly, -ness ri'gɑ:dlis [rə'g-],
-li, -nis
regatta, -s ri'gætə [rə'g-], -z
regenc|y, -ies 'ri:dʒəns|i, -iz
regenerate (adj.) ri'dʒenərit [rə'dʒ-,
-reit]
regenerat|e (v.), -es, -ing, -ed ri'dʒenə-
reit [rə'dʒ-], -s, -iŋ, -id
regeneration, -s ri,dʒenə'reiʃən [rə,dʒ-,
ˌri:dʒen-], -z
regent (R.), -s 'ri:dʒənt, -s
regentship, -s 'ri:dʒənt-ʃip, -s
Reggie 'redʒi
Reggio 'redʒiəu ('reddʒo)
regicidal ˌredʒi'saidl
regicide, -s 'redʒisaid, -z
régie rei'ʒi: ['reiʒi:]
regil|d, -ds, -ding, -t 'ri:'gil|d, -dz, -diŋ,
-t
régime, -s rei'ʒi:m [re'ʒ-, '--] (reʒim), -z
regimen, -s 'redʒimen, -z
regiment (s.), -s 'redʒimənt, -s
regiment (v.), -s, -ing, -ed 'redʒiment
[ˌ--'-], -s, -iŋ, -id
regimental (s. adj.), -s ˌredʒi'mentl, -z
regimentation ˌredʒimen'teiʃən [-mən-]
Regina ri'dʒainə

Reginald 'redʒinld
region, -s 'ri:dʒən, -z
re|gional, -gionally 'ri:|dʒənl [-dʒənəl,
-dʒṇl, -dʒṇl, -dʒənəl], -dʒnəli [-dʒṇli,
-dʒṇli, -dʒənəli]
Regis 'ri:dʒis
regist|er (s. v.), -ers, -ering, -ered
'redʒist|ə*, -əz, -əriŋ, -əd
registrant, -s 'redʒistrənt, -s
registrar, -s ˌredʒis'trɑ:* ['redʒistr-], -z
registrar|y, -ies 'redʒistrər|i, -iz
registration, -s ˌredʒis'treiʃən, -z
registr|y, -ies 'redʒistr|i, -iz
Regius 'ri:dʒəs [-dʒiəs, -dʒəs]
regnant 'regnənt
regress (s.) 'ri:gres
regress (v.), -es, -ing, -ed ri'gres [ri:'g-],
-iz, -iŋ, -t
regression, -s ri'greʃən [ri:'g-], -z
regressive, -ly ri'gresiv [ri:'g-, 'ri:'g-], -li
regret (s. v.), -s, -ting, -ted ri'gret
[rə'g-], -s, -iŋ, -id
regret|ful, -fully ri'gret|ful [rə'g-], -fuli
[-fəli]
regrettab|le, -ly ri'gretəb|l [rə'g-], -li
re-group, -s, -ing, -ed 'ri:'gru:p, -s, -iŋ,
-t
regular (s. adj.), -s, -ly 'regjulə* [-gjəl-],
-z, -li
regularity ˌregju'læriti [-gjə'l-]
regularization [-isa-] ˌregjulərai'zeiʃən
[-gjəl-, -ri'z-]
regulariz|e [-is|e], -es, -ing, -ed 'regju-
ləraiz [-gjəl-], -iz, -iŋ, -d
regulat|e, -es, -ing, -ed, -or/s 'regjuleit
[-gjəl-], -s, -iŋ, -id, -ə*/z
regulation, -s ˌregju'leiʃən [-gjə'l-], -z
regulative 'regjulətiv [-gjəl-, -leit-]
regul|us (R.), -i 'regjul|əs [-gjəl-], -ai
regurgitat|e, -es, -ing, -ed ri'gə:dʒiteit
[ri:'g-], -s, -iŋ, -id
rehabilitat|e, -es, -ing, -ed ˌri:ə'biliteit
[ˌri:hə-, riə-], -s, -iŋ, -id
rehabilitation, -s 'ri:ə,bili'teiʃən
['ri:hə-, riə-], -z
Rehan 'ri:ən, 'reiən
re-hash (s. v.), -es, -ing, -ed 'ri:'hæʃ, -iz,
-iŋ, -t
rehear, -s, -ing, reheard 'ri:'hiə*, -z,
-riŋ, 'ri:'hə:d
rehears|e, -es, -ing, -ed; -al/s ri'hə:s
[rə'h-], -iz, -iŋ, -t; -əl/z
Rehoboam ˌri:ə'bəuəm [ˌri:hə-, riə-]
re-hous|e, -es, -ing, -ed 'ri:'hauz, -iz,
-iŋ, -d
Reich raik [raix] (raiç)
Reichstag 'raikstɑ:g [-tɑ:k] ('raiçstɑ:k,
-tɑ:x)

Reid ri:d
Reigate 'raigit
reign (s. v.), -s, -ing, -ed rein, -z, -iŋ, -d
Reigny (in Cumberland) 'reini
Reikjavik 'reikjəvi:k ['rek-, -vik]
Reilly 'raili
reimburs|e, -es, -ing, -ed; -ement/s ,ri:im'bə:s ['ri:im'b-], -iz, -iŋ, -t; -mənt/s
reimport, -s, -ing, -ed 'ri:im'pɔ:t, -s, -iŋ, -id
reimpos|e, -es, -ing, -ed 'ri:im'pəuz, -iz, -iŋ, -d
reimpression, -s 'ri:im'preʃən, -z
Reims ri:mz
rein (s. v.), -s, -ing, -ed rein, -z, -iŋ, -d
reincarnate (adj.) 'ri:in'kɑ:nit [,ri:-, -neit]
reincarnat|e (v.), -es, -ing, -ed ri:'inkɑ:-neit [,ri:in'kɑ:n-], -s, -iŋ, -id
reincarnation, -s 'ri:inkɑ:'neiʃən [,ri:-], -z
reindeer 'reindiə*
reinforc|e, -es, -ing, -ed, -ement/s ,ri:in'fɔ:s ['--'-], -iz, -iŋ, -t, -mənt/s
reinstal|l, -ls, -ling, -led, -ment 'ri:in'stɔ:l, -z, -iŋ, -d, -mənt
reinstat|e, -es, -ing, -ed, -ement 'ri:in-'steit [,ri:-], -s, -iŋ, -id, -mənt
reinsur|e, -es, -ing, -ed; -ance/s 'ri:in'ʃuə* [-'ʃɔə*, -'ʃɔ:*, -'ʃə:*], -z, -riŋ, -d; -rəns/iz
reintroduc|e, -es, -ing, -ed 'ri:,intrə-'dju:s [-tru'd-], -iz, -iŋ, -t
reintroduction 'ri:,intrə'dʌkʃən [-tru'd-]
reinvest, -s, -ing, -ed 'ri:in'vest, -s, -iŋ, -id
reis (monetary unit) (sing.) reis, (plur.) reis [reiz]
reiss|ue (s. v.), -ues, -uing, -ued 'ri:-'iʃ|u: [-'iʃj|u:, -'isj|u:], -u:z, -u(:)iŋ, -u:d
reiterat|e, -es, -ing, -ed ri:'itəreit [ri'it-], -s, -iŋ, -id
reiterative ri:'itərətiv [ri'it-, -təreit-]
Reith ri:θ
reject (s.), -s 'ri:dʒekt, -s
reject (v.), -s, -ing, -ed, -or/s ri'dʒekt [rə'dʒ-], -s, -iŋ, -id, -ə*/z
rejection, -s ri'dʒekʃən [rə'dʒ-], -z
rejoic|e, -es, -ing/ly, -ings, -ed ri'dʒɔis [rə'dʒ-], -iz, -iŋ/li, -iŋz, -t
rejoin (answer), -s, -ing, -ed ri'dʒɔin [rə'dʒ-], -z, -iŋ, -d
rejoin (join again), -s, -ing, -ed 'ri:'dʒɔin [ri:'dʒ-, ri'dʒ-], -z, -iŋ, -d

rejoinder, -s ri'dʒɔində* [rə'dʒ-], -z
rejuvenat|e, -es, -ing, -ed ri'dʒu:vineit, -s, -iŋ, -id
rejuvenation ri,dʒu:vi'neiʃən
rejuvenesc|e, -es, -ing, -ed ,ri:dʒu:vi'nes [ri,dʒu:-, -və'n-], -iz, -iŋ, -t
rejuvenescen|ce, -t ,ri:dʒu:vi'nesn|s [ri,dʒu:-, -və'n-], -t
rekind|le, -les, -ling, -led 'ri:'kind|l, -lz, -liŋ [-ḷiŋ], -ld
re-lab|el, -els, -elling, -elled 'ri:'leib|l, -lz, -liŋ [-ḷiŋ], -ld
relaps|e (s. v.), -es, -ing, -ed ri'læps [rə'l-], -iz, -iŋ, -t
relat|e, -es, -ing, -ed, -er/s ri'leit [rə'l-], -s, -iŋ, -id, -ə*/z
relation, -s; -ship/s ri'leiʃən [rə'l-], -z; -ʃip/s
relatival ,relə'taivəl
relative (s. adj.), -s, -ly 'relətiv ['reḷtiv], -z, -li
relativity ,relə'tiviti
relax, -es, -ing, -ed; -able ri'læks [rə'l-], -iz, -iŋ, -t; -əbl
relaxation, -s ,ri:læk'seiʃən, -z
relay (s.) (fresh set of horses, relief gang), -s ri'lei ['ri:lei], -z
Note.—Always 'ri:lei in relay race.
relay (s.) (electrical apparatus), -s 'ri:'lei, -z
relay (v.) (lay again), -s, -ing, relaid 'ri:'lei, -z, -iŋ, 'ri:'leid
relay (s. v.) (broadcasting sense), -s, -ing, -ed 'ri:'lei [ri:'lei, 'ri:lei], -z, -iŋ, -d
release (s.) (liberation, discharge), -s ri'li:s [rə'l-], -iz
release (s.) (new lease), -s 'ri:'li:s ['ri:li:s], -iz
releas|e (v.), -es, -ing, -ed ri'li:s [rə'l-], -iz, -iŋ, -t
relegat|e, -es, -ing, -ed 'religeit, -s, -iŋ, -id
relegation, ,reli'geiʃən
relent, -s, -ing, -ed ri'lent [rə'l-], -s, -iŋ, -id
relentless, -ly, -ness ri'lentlis [rə'l-], -li, -nis
re-let (s. v.), -s, -ting 'ri:'let, -s, -iŋ
relevan|ce, -cy, -t/ly 'relivən|s [-ləv-], -si, -t/li
reliability ri,laiə'biliti [rə,lai-, -lət-]
reliab|le, -ly, -leness ri'laiəb|l [rə'l-], -li, -lnis
relian|ce, -t ri'laiən|s [rə'l-], -t
relic, -s 'relik, -s
relict, -s 'relikt, -s
relief, -s ri'li:f [rə'l-], -s

reliev|e, -es, -ing, -ed; -able ri'li:v
[rə'l-], -z, -iŋ, -d; -əbl
relievo ri'li:vəu
re|light, -lights, -lighting, -lighted, -lit
'ri:|'lait, -'laits, -'laitiŋ, -'laitid, -'lit
religion, -s ri'lidʒən [rə'l-], -z
religioni|sm, -st/s ri'lidʒəni|zəm [rə'l-,
-dʒni-], -st/s
religioso ri,lidʒi'əusəu [re,l-, rə,l-,
-'əuzəu]
religious, -ly, -ness ri'lidʒəs [rə'l-], -li,
-nis
relin|e, -es, -ing, -ed 'ri:'lain, -z, -iŋ, -d
relinquish, -es, -ing, -ed, -ment
ri'liŋkwiʃ [rə'l-], -iz, -iŋ, -t, -mənt
reliquar|y, -ies 'relikwər|i, -iz
reliques (in Percy's Reliques) 'reliks,
(otherwise) ri'li:ks [rə'l-]
relish (s. v.), -es, -ing, -ed 'reliʃ, -iz, -iŋ,
-t
reload, -s, -ing, -ed 'ri:'ləud [-'-], -z, -iŋ,
-id
reluctanc|e, -t/ly ri'lʌktən|s [rə'l-], -t/li
rel|y, -ies, -ying, -ied ri'l|ai [rə'l-], -aiz,
-aiiŋ, -aid
remain, -s, -ing, -ed ri'mein [rə'm-], -z,
-iŋ, -d
remainder, -s ri'meində* [rə'm-], -z
remak|e, -es, -ing, remade 'ri:'meik, -s,
-iŋ, 'ri:'meid
remand (s.), -s ri'mɑ:nd [rə'm-], -z
Note.—A variant pronunciation
'ri:mɑ:nd is used by some in
remand home.
remand (v.), -s, -ing, -ed ri'mɑ:nd
[rə'm-], -z, -iŋ, -id
remark (s. v.) (notice, comment), -s, -ing,
-ed ri'mɑ:k [rə'm-], -s, -iŋ, -t
re-mark (v.) (mark again), -s, -ing, -ed
'ri:'mɑ:k, -s, -iŋ, -t
remarkab|le, -ly, -leness ri'mɑ:kəb|l
[rə'm-], -li, -lnis
remarr|y, -ies, -ying, -ied; -iage/s
'ri:'mær|i, -iz, -iiŋ, -id; -idʒ/iz
Rembrandt, -s 'rembrænt [-rənt], -s
R.E.M.E. 'ri:mi
remediable ri'mi:djəbl [rə'm-, -dïəb-]
remedial ri'mi:djəl [rə'm-, -dïəl]
remed|y (s. v.), -ies, -ying, -ied; -yless
'remid|i, -iz, -iiŋ, -id; -ilis
rememb|er, -ers, -ering, -ered ri-
'memb|ə* [rə'm-], -əz, -əriŋ, -əd
remembrance, -s; -r/s ri'membrəns
[rə'm-], -iz; -ə*/z
re-militariz|e [-is|e], -es, -ing, -ed
'ri:'militəraiz, -iz, -iŋ, -d
remind, -s, -ing, -ed, -er/s ri'maind
[rə'm-], -z, -iŋ, -id, -ə*/z

Remington, -s 'remiŋtən, -z
reminisc|e, -es, -ing, -ed ,remi'nis, -iz,
-iŋ, -t
reminiscen|ce, -ces, -t ,remi'nisn|s,
-siz, -t
remis|e (s. v.) (thrust in fencing; carriage,
coach-house, etc.), -es, -ing, -ed
rə'mi:z [ri'm-], -iz, -iŋ, -d
remis|e (s. v.) (surrender), -es, -ing, -ed
ri'maiz [rə'm-], -iz, -iŋ, -d
remiss, -ly, -ness ri'mis [rə'm-], -li, -nis
remission, -s ri'miʃən [rə'm-], -z
remit, -s, -ting, -ted, -ter/s ri'mit
[rə'm-], -s, -iŋ, -id, -ə*/z
remittal, -s ri'mitl [rə'm-], -z
remittance, -s ri'mitəns [rə'm-], -iz
remnant, -s 'remnənt, -s
remod|el, -els, -elling, -elled 'ri:'mɔd|l,
-lz, -liŋ, -ld
remonetiz|e [-is|e], -es, -ing, -ed
ri:'mʌnitaiz, -iz, -iŋ, -d
remonstran|ce, -ces, -t/ly ri'mɔns-
trən|s [rə'm-], -siz, -t/li
remonstrat|e, -es, -ing, -ed 'remənstreit
[ri'mɔns-, rə'm-], -s, -iŋ, -id
remorse ri'mɔ:s [rə'm-]
remorse|ful, -fully ri'mɔ:s|ful [rə'm-],
-fuli [-fəli]
remorseless, -ly, -ness ri'mɔ:slis [rə'm-],
-li, -nis
remote, -ly, -ness ri'məut [rə'm-], -li,
-nis
remould, -s, -ing, -ed 'ri:'məuld, -z,
-iŋ, -id
remount (s.), -s 'ri:maunt ['-'-], -s
remount (v.), -s, -ing, -ed ri:'maunt
['ri:'m-], -s, -iŋ, -id
removability ri,mu:və'biliti [rə,m-, -lət-]
removal, -s ri'mu:vəl [rə'm-], -z
remov|e (s. v.), -es, -ing, -ed, -er/s;
-able ri'mu:v [rə'm-], -z, -iŋ, -d, -ə*/z;
Remploy, -s 'remplɔi, -z   [-əbl
remunerat|e, -es, -ing, -ed ri'mju:nəreit
[rə'm-, -'mjun-], -s, -iŋ, -id
remuneration ri,mju:nə'reiʃən [rə,m-,
-,mjun-]
remunerative ri'mju:nərətiv [rə'm-,
-'mjun-]
Remus 'ri:məs
Renaissance rə'neisəns [ri'n-, -sɑ̃:ns,
-sõ:ns, -sɑ:ns, -sɔ:ns] (rənesɑ̃:s)
renam|e, -es, -ing, -ed 'ri:'neim, -z, -iŋ,
-d
renascen|ce, -t ri'næsn|s [rə'n-], -t
Renault (car), -s 'renəu (rəno), -z
rend, -s, -ing, rent rend, -z, -iŋ, rent
rend|er, -ers, -ering/s, -ered 'rend|ə*,
-əz, -əriŋ/z, -əd

rendezvous (*sing.*) 'rɔndivuː: ['rɑ̃:nd-,
'rɔ̃:nd-, 'rɑ:nd-, 'rɔ:nd-, -deiv-]
(rɑ̃devu), (*plur.*), -z
rendition, -s ren'diʃən, -z
renegade, -s 'renigeid, -z
reneg(u)|e (*s. v.*), -es, -ing, -ed ri'niːg
[rə'n-, -'neig], -z, -iŋ, -d
ren|ew₀ -ews, -ewing, -ewed; -ewable
ri'njuː: [rə'n-], -uːz, -u(ː)iŋ, -uːd;
-u(ː)əbl
renewal, -s ri'njuː(ː)əl [rə'n-, -'njuːl], -z
Renfrew, -shire 'renfruː:, -ʃiə* [-ʃə*]
renin 'riːnin
rennet 'renit
Rennie 'reni
Reno 'riːnəu
Renoir rə'nwɑː* ['--, 're-] (rənwaːr)
renounc|e, -es, -ing, -ed, -ement
ri'nauns [rə'n-], -iz, -iŋ, -t, -mənt
renovat|e, -es, -ing, -ed, -or/s 'renəuveit,
-s, -iŋ, -id, -ə*/z
renovation, -s ˌrenəu'veiʃən, -z
renown, -ed ri'naun [rə'n-], -d
Renshaw 'renʃɔː
rent (*s. v.*), -s, -ing, -ed, -er/s rent, -s,
-iŋ, -id, -ə*/z
rent (*from* **rend**) rent
rental, -s 'rentl, -z
rent-free 'rent'friː [*also* '-- *when attributive*]
rentier, -s 'rɔntiei (rɑ̃tje), -z
Rentoul rən'tuːl [ren-]
rent-roll, -s 'rent-rəul, -z
renunciation, -s riˌnʌnsi'eiʃən [rə,n-], -z
Renwick 'renwik, 'renik
reoccupation, -s 'riːˌɔkjuː'peiʃən [ˌriɔk-],
-z
reoccup|y, -ies, -ying, -ied 'riː'ɔkjup|ai
[riː'ɔk-, ri'ɔk-], -aiz, -aiiŋ, -aid
reop|en, -ens, -ening, -ened 'riː'əup|ən
[riː'əu-, ri'əu-, -p|m], -ənz [-mz],
-niŋ [-ɳiŋ], -ənd [-md]
reorganization [*-isa-*], -s 'riːˌɔ:gənai'zeiʃən [riːˌɔ:-, riˌɔ:-, -gɳai'z-, -gəni'z-,
-gɳi'z-], -z
reorganiz|e [*-is|e*], -es, -ing, -ed
'riː'ɔ:gənaiz [riː'ɔ:-, ri'ɔ:-, -gɳaiz],
-iz, -iŋ, -d
rep rep
repaid (*from* **repay**, *pay back*) ri:'peid
[ri'p-, 'riː'p-], (*from* **repay**, *pay a
second time*) 'riː'peid
repair (*s. v.*), -s, -ing, -ed, -er/s ri'pɛə*
[rə'p-], -z, -riŋ, -d, -rə*/z
repairable ri'pɛərəbl [rə'p-]
reparability ˌrepərə'biliti [-lət-]
reparable 'repərəbl
reparation, -s ˌrepə'reiʃən, -z

repartee ˌrepɑ:'tiː:
repass, -es, -ing, -ed 'riː'pɑ:s [*also*
'riː-pɑ:s *when contrasted with* **pass**],
-iz, -iŋ, -t
repast, -s ri'pɑ:st [rə'p-], -s
repatriat|e, -es, -ing, -ed riː'pætrieit
[ri'p-, *rarely* -'peit-], -s, -iŋ, -id
repatriation 'riː:pætri'eiʃən [ˌriː-]
re|pay (*pay back*), -pays, -paying, -paid
riː|'pei [ri|'pei, 'riː|'pei], -'peiz,
-'peiiŋ, -'peid
re|pay (*pay a second time*), -pays, -pay-
ing, -paid 'riː|'pei, -'peiz, -'peiiŋ,
-'peid
repayable riː'peiəbl [ri'p-, 'riː'p-]
repayment, -s riː'peimənt [ri'p-, 'riː'p-],
-s
repeal (*s. v.*), -s, -ing, -ed ri'piːl [rə'p-],
-z, -iŋ, -d
repeat (*s. v.*), -s, -ing, -ed/ly, -er/s
ri'piːt [rə'p-], -s, -iŋ, -id/li, -ə*/z
repel, -s, -ling, -led; -lent ri'pel [rə'p-],
-z, -iŋ, -d; -ənt
repent, -s, -ing/ly, -ed ri'pent [rə'p-],
-s, -iŋ/li, -id
repentan|ce, -ces, -t/ly ri'pentən|s
[rə'p-], -siz, -t/li
repeop|le, -les, -ling, -led 'riː'piːp|l, -lz,
-liŋ [-liɳ], -ld
repercussion, -s ˌriː:pə'kʌʃən [-pə:'k-], -z
repertoire, -s 'repətwɑː* [-twɔ:*], -z
repertor|y, -ies 'repətər|i, -iz
repetition, -s ˌrepi'tiʃən, -z
repetitive ri'petitiv [rə'p-]
repin|e, -es, -ing, -ed ri'pain [rə'p-], -z,
-iŋ, -d
repiqu|e (*s. v.*), -es, -ing, -ed 'riː'piːk
[riː'p-, *also in contrast* 'riː-piːk], -s,
-iŋ, -t
replac|e, -es, -ing, -ed, -ement/s
ri'pleis [riː'p-], -iz, -iŋ, -t, -mənt/s
replaceable ri'pleisəbl [riː'p-]
replant, -s, -ing, -ed 'riː'plɑ:nt, -s, -iŋ,
-id
replay (*s.*), -s 'riː-plei, -z
replay (*v.*), -s, -ing, -ed 'riː'plei [riː'p-],
-z, -iŋ, -d
re-pleat, -s, -ing, -ed 'riː'pliːt, -s, -iŋ, -id
replenish, -es, -ing, -ed, -ment ri'pleniʃ
[rə'p-], -iz, -iŋ, -t, -mənt
replete, -ness ri'pliːt, -nis
repletion ri'pliːʃən
replevin ri'plevin [rə'p-]
replica, -s 'replikə [ri'pliːkə, rə'pliːkə], -z
repl|y (*s. v.*), -ies, -ying, -ied ri'pl|ai
[rə'p-], -aiz, -aiiŋ, -aid
repoint, -s, -ing, -ed 'riː'pɔint, -s, -iŋ, -id
repolish, -es, -ing, -ed 'riː'pɔliʃ, -iz, -iŋ, -t

repopulat|e, -es, -ing, -ed 'ri:'pɔpjuleit [ri:'p-], -s, -iŋ, -id

report (s. v.), -s, -ing, -ed, -er/s ri'pɔːt [rə'p-], -s, -iŋ, -id, -ə*/z

reportage ˌrepɔ:'tɑːʒ

repos|e (s. v.), -es, -ing, -ed ri'pəuz [rə'p-], -iz, -iŋ, -d

repose|ful, -fully ri'pəuz|fʊl [rə'p-], -fuli [-fəli]

repositor|y, -ies ri'pɔzitər|i [rə'p-], -iz

repoussé rə'puːsei [ri'p-] (rəpuse)

reprehend, -s, -ing, -ed ˌrepri'hend, -z, -iŋ, -id

reprehensible ˌrepri'hensəbl [-sib-]

reprehension ˌrepri'henʃən

represent, -s, -ing, -ed ˌrepri'zent, -s, -iŋ, -id

representation, -s ˌreprizen'teiʃən [-zən-], -z

representative (s. adj.), -s, -ly ˌrepri'zentətiv, -z, -li

repress, -es, -ing, -ed; -ible ri'pres [rə'p-], -iz, -iŋ, -t; -əbl [-ibl]

repression, -s ri'preʃən [rə'p-], -z

repressive ri'presiv [rə'p-]

repriev|e (s. v.), -es, -ing, -ed ri'priːv [rə'p-], -z, -iŋ, -d

reprimand (s.), -s 'reprimɑːnd, -z

reprimand (v.), -s, -ing, -ed 'reprimɑːnd [ˌrepri'm-], -z, -iŋ, -id

reprint (s.), -s 'riː'print ['riː-print], -s

reprint (v.), -s, -ing, -ed 'riː'print [riː'p-], -s, -iŋ, -id

reprisal, -s ri'praizəl [rə'p-], -z

reproach (s. v.), -es, -ing, -ed; -able ri'prəutʃ [rə'p-], -iz, -iŋ, -t; -əbl

reproach|ful, -fully, -fulness ri'prəutʃ|-fʊl [rə'p-], -fuli [-fəli], -fʊlnis

reprobate (s. adj.), -s 'reprəubeit [-prub-, -bit], -s

reprobat|e (v.), -es, -ing, -ed 'reprəubeit [-prub-], -s, -iŋ, -id

reprobation ˌreprəu'beiʃən [-pru'b-]

reproduc|e, -es, -ing, -ed, -er/s ˌri:-prə'dju:s ['ri:prə'd-, -pru'd-], -iz, -iŋ, -t, -ə*/z

reproduction, -s ˌri:prə'dʌkʃən ['ri:-prə'd-, -pru'd-], -z

reproductive, -ness ˌri:prə'dʌktiv ['ri:-prə'd-, -pru'd-], -nis

reproof (s.), -s ri'pru:f [rə'p-], -s

re-proof (v.), -s, -ing, -ed 'ri:'pru:f, -s, -iŋ, -t

reproval, -s ri'pru:vəl [rə'p-], -z

reprov|e, -es, -ing/ly, -ed, -er/s ri-'pru:v [rə'p-], -z, -iŋ/li, -d, -ə*/z

reptile, -s 'reptail, -z

reptilian (s. adj.), -s rep'tiliən [-ljən], -z

Repton 'reptən

republic, -s ri'pʌblik [rə'p-], -s

republican, -s; -ism ri'pʌblikən [rə'p-], -z; -izəm

republication, -s 'ri:ˌpʌbli'keiʃən, -z

republish, -es, -ing, -ed 'ri:'pʌbliʃ, -iz, -iŋ, -t

repudiat|e, -es, -ing, -ed, -er/s ri-'pju:dieit [rə'p-], -s, -iŋ, -id, -ə*/z

repudiation riˌpju:di'eiʃən [rə,p-]

repugnan|ce, -t/ly ri'pʌgnən|s [rə'p-], -t/li

repuls|e (s. v.), -es, -ing, -ed ri'pʌls [rə'p-], -iz, -iŋ, -t

repulsion ri'pʌlʃən [rə'p-]

repulsive, -ly, -ness ri'pʌlsiv [rə'p-], -li, -nis

reputability ˌrepjutə'biliti [-lət-]

reputable 'repjutəbl

reputation, -s ˌrepju(:)'teiʃən, -z

repute, -d ri'pju:t [rə'p-], -id

request (s. v.), -s, -ing, -ed ri'kwest [rə'k-], -s, -iŋ, -id

requiem, -s 'rekwiem [-kwiəm, -kwjəm], -z

requir|e, -es, -ing, -ed, -ement/s ri-'kwaiə* [rə'k-], -z, -riŋ, -d, -mənt/s

requisite (s. adj.), -s, -ly, -ness 'rekwizit, -s, -li, -nis

requisiti|on (s. v.), -ons, -oning, -oned ˌrekwi'ziʃ|ən, -ənz, -ŋiŋ [-əniŋ], -ənd

requit|e, -es, -ing, -ed; -al ri'kwait [rə'k-], -s, -iŋ, -id; -l

re-read (pres. tense), -s, -ing, re-read (past) 'ri:'ri:d, -z, -iŋ, 'ri:'red

reredos, -es 'riədɔs, -iz

res ri:z

resartus ri:'sɑ:təs [ri's-]

rescind, -s, -ing, -ed ri'sind [rə's-], -z, -iŋ, -id

rescission ri'siʒən [rə's-]   [-iŋ, -id

rescript, -s 'ri:skript, -s

resc|ue (s. v.), -ues, -uing, -ued, -uer/s 'resk|ju:, -ju:z, -ju(:)iŋ [-jwiŋ], -ju:d, -jŭə*/z [-jwə*/z]

research (s.), -es ri'sə:tʃ [rə's-, rarely -'zə:tʃ, 'ri:sə:tʃ], -iz

research (v.), -es, -ing, -ed, -er/s ri'sə:tʃ [rə's-, rarely -'zə:tʃ], -iz, -iŋ, -t, -ə*/z

reseat, -s, -ing, -ed 'ri:'si:t, -s, -iŋ, -id

resection, -s ri:'sekʃən [ri's-], -z

reseda, -s (plant) 'residə ['rezidə, ri'si:də], (colour) 'residə ['rezidə], -z

resell, -s, -ing, resold 'ri:'sel, -z, -iŋ, 'ri:'səuld

resemblance, -s ri'zembləns [rə'z-], -iz

resemb|le, -les, -ling, -led ri'zemb|l [rə'z-], -lz, -liŋ [-liŋ], -ld resent, -s, -ing, -ed, -ment; -ful, -fully ri'zent, -s, -iŋ, -id, -mənt; -fʊl, -fuli [-fəli]

reservation, -s ˌrezə'veiʃən [-zə:'v-], -z

reserv|e (s. v.), -es, -ing, -ed ri'zə:v [rə'z-], -z, -iŋ, -d

reservedly ri'zə:vidli [rə'z-]

reservist, -s ri'zə:vist [rə'z-], -s

reservoir, -s 'rezəvwɑ:* [-vwɔ:*], -z

reset, -s, -ting/s 'ri:'set, -s, -iŋ/z

reshap|e, -es, -ing, -ed 'ri:'ʃeip, -s, -iŋ, -t

reship, -s, -ping, -ped, -ment/s 'ri:'ʃip, -s, -iŋ, -t, -mənt/s

reshuff|le, -les, -ling, -led 'ri:'ʃʌf|l, -lz, -liŋ [-liŋ], -ld

resid|e, -es, -ing, -ed ri'zaid [rə'z-], -z, -iŋ, -id

residence, -s 'rezidəns, -iz

residenc|y, -ies 'rezidəns|i, -iz

resident, -s 'rezidənt, -s

residential ˌrezi'denʃəl

residual ri'zidjŭəl [rə'z-, -djwəl, -djul]

residuary ri'zidjŭəri [rə'z-, -djwəri, -djuri]

residue, -s 'rezidju:, -z

residu|um, -a ri'zidjŭ|əm [rə'z-, -djw|əm], -ə

resign (give up), -s, -ing, -ed, -edly ri'zain [rə'z-], -z, -iŋ, -d, -idli

re-sign (sign again), -s, -ing, -ed 'ri:'sain, -z, -iŋ, -d

resignation, -s ˌrezig'neiʃən, -z

resilien|ce, -cy, -t ri'ziliən|s [rə'zil-, ri'sil-, rə'sil-, -ljə-], -si, -t

resin, -s; -ous 'rezin, -z; -əs

resist, -s, -ing, -ed ri'zist [rə'z-], -s, -iŋ, -id

resistan|ce, -ces, -t ri'zistən|s [rə'z-], -siz, -t

resistless ri'zistlis [rə'z-]

resol|e, -es, -ing, -ed 'ri:'səul, -z, -iŋ, -d

resoluble ri'zɔljubl [rə'z-, 'rezəljubl]

resolute, -ly, -ness 'rezəlu:t [-zļu:t, -zəlju:t], -li, -nis

resolution, -s ˌrezə'lu:ʃən [-zļ'u:-, -zə'lju:-], -z

resolvability riˌzɔlvə'biliti [rəˌz-, -lət-]

resolv|e (s. v.), -es, -ing, -ed; -able ri'zɔlv [rə'z-], -z, -iŋ, -d; -əbl

resonan|ce, -ces, -t/ly 'rezŋən|s [-zənə-], -siz, -t/li

resonator, -s 'rezəneitə* [-zŋei-], -z

resort (s. v.), -s, -ing, -ed ri'zɔ:t [rə'z-], -s, -iŋ, -id

re-sort (sort out again), -s, -ing, -ed 'ri:'sɔ:t, -s, -iŋ, -id

resound, -s, -ing, -ed ri'zaund [rə'z-], -z, -iŋ, -id

resource, -s; -ful, -fully, -fulness ri'sɔ:s [rə's-, -'zɔ:s, -ɔəs], -iz; -fʊl, -fuli [-fəli], -fʊlnis

respect (s. v.), -s, -ing, -ed, -er/s ris'pekt [rəs-], -s, -iŋ, -id, -ə*/z

respectability risˌpektə'biliti [rəs-, -lət-]

respectab|le, -ly, -leness ris'pektəb|l [rəs-], -li, -lnis

respect|ful, -fully ris'pekt|fʊl [rəs-], -fuli [-fəli]

respecting (prep.) ris'pektiŋ [rəs-]

respective, -ly ris'pektiv [rəs-], -li

Respighi res'pi:gi (res'pi:gi)

respirable 'respirəbl [ris'paiərəbl, rəs'paiər-]

respiration, -s ˌrespə'reiʃən [-pi'r-], -z

respirator, -s 'respəreitə* [-pir-], -z

respiratory ris'paiərətəri [res'p-, rəs'p-, -'pir-, 'respirətəri, 'respireitəri]

respir|e, -es, -ing, -ed ris'paiə* [rəs-], -z, -riŋ, -d

respit|e (s. v.), -es, -ing, -ed 'respait [rarely -pit], -s, -iŋ, -id

resplenden|ce, -cy, -t/ly ris'plendən|s [rəs-], -si, -t/li

respond, -s, -ing, -ed; -ent/s ris'pɔnd [rəs-], -z, -iŋ, -id; -ənt/s

response, -s ris'pɔns [rəs-], -iz

responsibilit|y, -ies risˌpɔnsə'bilit|i [rəs-, -si'b-, -lət-], -iz

responsib|le, -ly, -leness ris'pɔnsəb|l [rəs-, -sib-], -li, -lnis

responsions ris'pɔnʃənz [rəs-]

responsive, -ly, -ness ris'pɔnsiv [rəs-], -li, -nis

rest (s. v.), -s, -ing, -ed rest, -s, -iŋ, -id

restart, -s, -ing, -ed 'ri:'stɑ:t, -s, -iŋ, -id

restat|e, -es, -ing, -ed 'ri:'steit, -s, -iŋ, -id

restaurant, -s 'restərɔ̃:ŋ [-rɑ̃:ŋ, -rɔ:ŋ, -rɑ:ŋ, -rɔŋ], -z, 'restərɔnt [-rənt], -s

restaurateur, -s ˌrestɔ(:)rə'tə:* [-tər-] (restɔratœ:r), -z

rest-cure, -s 'resʈkjuə* [-kjɔə*, -kjɔ:*], -z

rest|ful, -fully, -fulness 'rest|fʊl, -fuli [-fəli], -fʊlnis

rest-hou|se, -ses 'resthau|s, -ziz

resting-place, -s 'restiŋpleis, -iz

restitution ˌresti'tju:ʃən

restive, -ly, -ness 'restiv, -li, -nis

restless, -ly, -ness 'restlis, -li, -nis

restock, -s, -ing, -ed 'ri:'stɔk, -s, -iŋ, -t

restoration, -s ˌrestə'reiʃən [-tɔ:'r-, -tu'r-], -z

restorative (s. adj.), -s ris'tɔrətiv [res-, -'tɔ:r-], -z

restor|e, -es, -ing, -ed, -er/s; -able ris'tɔ:* [rəs-, -'tɔə*], -z, -riŋ, -d, -rə*/z; -rəbl

restrain (*hold back*), **-s, -ing, -ed, -er/s** ris'trein [rəs-], -z, -iŋ, -d, -ə*/z
re-strain (*strain again*), **-s, -ing, -ed** 'ri:'strein, -z, -iŋ, -d
restraint, -s ris'treint [rəs-], -s
restrict, -s, -ing, -ed; -ive ris'trikt [rəs-], -s, -iŋ, -id; -iv
restriction, -s ris'trikʃən [rəs-], -z
restrictionism ris'trikʃənizəm [rəs-, -ʃɲi-]
result (*s. v.*), **-s, -ing, -ed; -ant/s** ri'zʌlt [rə'z-], -s, -iŋ, -id; -ənt/s
resultative ri'zʌltətiv [rə'z-]
resum|e, -es, -ing, -ed ri'zju:m [rə'z-, -'zu:m], -z, -iŋ, -d
résumé, -s 'rezju(:)mei ['reiz-, -zu(:)-] (rezymə), -z
resumption, -s ri'zʌmpʃən [rə'z-], -z
re-surfac|e, -es, -ing, -ed 'ri:'sə:fis, -iz, -iŋ, -t
resurrect, -s, -ing, -ed ,rezə'rekt, -s, -iŋ, -id
resurrection (R.), **-s** ,rezə'rekʃən, -z
resuscitat|e, -es, -ing, -ed ri'sʌsiteit [rə's-], -s, -iŋ, -id
resuscitation, -s ri,sʌsi'teiʃən [rə,s-], -z
retail (*s. adj.*) 'ri:'teil [ri:'t-]
retail (*v.*), **-s, -ing, -ed, -er/s** ri:'teil [ri't-, 'ri:t-], -z, -iŋ, -d, -ə*/z
retain, -s, -ing, -ed, -er/s ri'tein [rə't-], -z, -iŋ, -d, -ə*/z
retake (*s.*), **-s** 'ri:teik, -s
retak|e (*v.*), **-es, -ing, retook, retaken** 'ri:'teik [-'-], -s, -iŋ, 'ri:'tuk [-'-], 'ri:'teikən [-'--]
retaliat|e, -es, -ing, -ed ri'tælieit [rə't-], -s, -iŋ, -id
retaliation ri,tæli'eiʃən [rə,t-]
retaliatory ri'tæliətəri [rə't-, -ljətəri, -lieitəri]
Retallack ri'tælək [rə't-]
retard, -s, -ing, -ed ri'tɑ:d [rə't-], -z, -iŋ, -id
retardation, -s ,ri:tɑ:'deiʃən, -z
retch, -es, -ing, -ed retʃ [ri:tʃ], -iz, -iŋ, -t
retell, -s, -ing, retold 'ri:'tel, -z, -iŋ, 'ri:'təuld
retention ri'tenʃən [rə't-]
retentive, -ly, -ness ri'tentiv [rə't-], -li, -nis
Retford 'retfəd
reticen|ce, -t/ly 'retisən|s, -t/li
reticle, -s 'retikl, -z
reticulate (*adj.*) ri'tikjulit [re't-, rə't-, -leit]
reticulat|e (*v.*), **-es, -ing, -ed** ri'tikjuleit [re't-, rə't-], -s, -iŋ, -id
reticulation, -s ri,tikju'leiʃən [re,t-, rə,t-], -z

reticule, -s 'retikju:l, -z
retin|a, -as, -ae 'retin|ə, -əz, -i:
retinue, -s 'retinju:, -z
retir|e, -es, -ing, -ed; -ement/s ri'taiə* [rə't-], -z, -riŋ, -d; -mənt/s
retold (*from* retell) 'ri:'təuld
retort (*s. v.*), **-s, -ing, -ed** ri'tɔ:t [rə't-], -s, -iŋ, -id
retouch (*s. v.*), **-es, -ing, -ed** 'ri:'tʌtʃ, -iz, -iŋ, -t
retrac|e, -es, -ing, -ed ri'treis [ri:'t-], -iz, -iŋ, -t
retract, -s, -ing, -ed ri'trækt [rə't-], -s, -iŋ, -id
retractation ,ri:træk'teiʃən
retraction, -s ri'trækʃən [rə't-], -z
retranslat|e, -es, -ing, -ed 'ri:'træns'leit [-trɑ:ns-, -trænz-, -trɑ:nz-, -trəns-, -trənz-], -s, -iŋ, -id
retranslation, -s 'ri:'træns'leiʃən [-trɑ:ns-, -trænz-, -trɑ:nz-, -trəns-, -trənz-], -z
re|tread, -treads, -treading, -trod 'ri:|'tred, -'tredz, -'trediŋ, -'trod
retreat (*s. v.*), **-s, -ing, -ed** ri'tri:t [rə't-], -s, -iŋ, -id
retrench, -es, -ing, -ed, -ment/s ri'trentʃ [rə't-], -iz, -iŋ, -t, -mənt/s
retrial, -s 'ri:'traiəl, -z
retribution ,retri'bju:ʃən
retribut|ive, -ory ri'tribjut|iv [rə't-], -əri
retrievab|le, -ly, -leness ri'tri:vəb|l [rə't-], -li, -lnis
retrieval ri'tri:vəl
retriev|e, -es, -ing, -ed, -er/s ri'tri:v [rə't-], -z, -iŋ, -d, -ə*/z
retrim, -s, -ming, -med 'ri:'trim, -z, -iŋ, -d
retroact, -s, -ing, -ed; -ive/ly ,re-trəu'ækt [,ri:t-], -s, -iŋ, -id; -iv/li
retroced|e, -es, -ing, -ed ,retrəu'si:d [,ri:t-], -z, -iŋ, -id
retrocession, -s ,retrəu'seʃən [,ri:t-], -z
retroflex, -ed 'retrəufleks, -t
retroflexion ,retrəu'flekʃən
retrograde 'retrəugreid
retrogression ,retrəu'greʃən [,ri:t-]
retrogressive, -ly ,retrəu'gresiv [,ri:t-], -li
retro-rocket, -s 'retrəu,rɔkit, -s
retrospect, -s 'retrəuspekt ['ri:t-], -s
retrospection, -s ,retrəu'spekʃən [,ri:t-], -z
retrospective, -ly ,retrəu'spektiv [,ri:t-, '--'--], -li
retroussé rə'tru:sei [ri't-] (rətruse)
retroversion, -s ,retrəu'və:ʃən [,ri:t-], -z
retrovert (*s.*), **-s** 'retrəuvə:t ['ri:t-], -s

retrovert (v.), -s, -ing, -ed ˌretrəʊ'vəːt [ˌriːt-], -s, -iŋ, -id

retr|y, -ies, -ying, -ied 'riː'tr|ai, -aiz, -aiiŋ, -aid

returf, -s, -ing, -ed 'riː'təːf, -s, -iŋ, -t

return (s. v.), -s, -ing, -ed; -able ri'təːn [rə't-], -z, -iŋ, -d; -əbl

Reuben 'ruːbin [-bən]

reunification, -s 'riːjuːnifi'keiʃən ['riːjun-], -z

reunion, -s 'riː'juːnjən [riː'j-, -nIən], -z

reunit|e, -es, -ing, -ed 'riːjuː'nait [-juː'n-], -s, -iŋ, -id

re-use (s.) 'riː'juːs ['riːjuːs]

re-us|e (v.), -es, -ing, -ed 'riː'juːz, -iz, -iŋ, -d ['riːjuːzd when attributive]

Reuter 'rɔitə*

Rev. 'revərənd

rev (s. v.), -s, -ving, -ved rev, -z, -iŋ, -d

reveal, -s, -ing, -ed, -er/s; -able ri'viːl [rə'v-], -z, -iŋ, -d, -ə*/z; -əbl

reveille, -s ri'væli [rə'v-, -'vel-], -z

rev|el (s. v.), -els, -elling, -elled, -eller/s 'rev|l, -lz, -liŋ, -ld, -lə*/z

revelation (R.), -s ˌrevi'leiʃən [-vl'ei-, -və'l], -z

revelr|y, -ies 'revlr|i, -iz

Revelstoke 'revəlstəuk   [-z

revendication, -s riˌvendi'keiʃən [rəˌv-],

reveng|e (s. v.), -es, -ing, -ed ri'vendʒ [rə'v-], -iz, -iŋ, -d

revenge|ful, -fully, -fulness ri'vendʒ|-ful [rə'v-], -fuli [-fəli], -fulnis

revenue, -s 'revinjuː [in old-fashioned legal usage ri'venjuː, rə'venjuː], -z

Note.—In Shakespeare both stressings occur, e.g. '— in 'Richard II', II. i. 226 and -'— in 'The Tempest', I. ii. 98.

reverberat|e, -es, -ing, -ed, -or/s ri'vəːbəreit [rə'v], -s, -iŋ, -id, -ə*/z

reverberation, -s riˌvəːbə'reiʃən [rəˌv-], -z

reverberatory ri'vəːbərətəri [rə'v-, -reitəri]

rever|e (R.), -es, -ing, -ed ri'viə* [rə'v-], -z, -riŋ, -d

reverenc|e (s. v.), -es, -ing, -ed 'revər-əns, -iz, -iŋ, -t

reverend (R.), -s 'revərənd, -z

reverent, -ly 'revərənt, -li

reverential ˌrevə'renʃəl

reverie, -s 'revəri, -z

revers (sing.) ri'viə* [rə'v-, -'vɛə*], (plur.) -z

reversal, -s ri'vəːsəl [rə'v-], -z

reverse (s.), -s ri'vəːs [rə'v-, 'riː'vəːs], -iz

revers|e (v.), -es, -ing, -ed; -ely ri'vəːs [rə'v-], -iz, -iŋ, -t; -li

reversibility riˌvəːsə'biliti [rəˌv-, -si'b-, -lət-]

reversible ri'vəːsəbl [rə'v-, -sib-]

reversion, -s ri'vəːʃən [rə'v-], -z

reversionary ri'vəːʃnəri [rə'v-, -ʃnə-, -ʃənə-]

revert, -s, -ing, -ed ri'vəːt [rə'v-], -s, -iŋ, -id

revet, -s, -ting, -ted, -ment/s ri'vet [rə'v-], -s, -iŋ, -id, -mənt/s

revictu|al, -als, -alling, -alled 'riː'vit|l, -lz, -liŋ, -ld

revi|ew (s. v.), -ews, -ewing, -ewed, -ewer/s ri'vj|uː [rə'v-], -uːz, -u(ː)iŋ, -uːd, -u(ː)ə*/z

revil|e, -es, -ing, -ed, -er/s ri'vail [rə'v-], -z, -iŋ, -d, -ə*/z

Revillon (English surname) rə'viljən

revis|e (s. v.), -es, -ing, -ed, -er/s ri'vaiz [rə'v-], -iz, -iŋ, -d, -ə*/z

revision, -s ri'viʒən [rə'v-], -z

revisit, -s, -ing, -ed 'riː'vizit [-'--], -s, -iŋ, -id

revisualiz|e [-is|e], -es, -ing, -ed 'riː'vizjuəlaiz [-zjwəl-, -zjul-, -ʒjʊəl-, -ʒjwəl-, -ʒuəl-, -ʒwəl-, -ʒul-], -iz, -iŋ, -d

revitaliz|e [-is|e], -es, -ing, -ed 'riː'vaitəlaiz [riː'v-, -tḷaiz], -iz, -iŋ, -d

revival, -s ri'vaivəl [rə'v-], -z

revivali|sm, -st/s ri'vaivəli|zəm [rə'v-, -vḷi-], -st/s

reviv|e, -es, -ing, -ed ri'vaiv [rə'v-], -z, -iŋ, -d

revivi|fy, -fies, -fying, -fied ri(ː)'vivi|fai, -faiz, -faiiŋ, -faid

reviviscence ˌrevi'visns [ˌriːvai'v-, -səns]

revocability ˌrevəkə'biliti [-vuk-, -lət-]

revocable 'revəkəbl [-vuk-], (when applied to letters of credit) ri'vəukəbl [rə'v-]

revocation, -s ˌrevə'keiʃən [-vu'k-], -z

revok|e (s. v.), -es, -ing, -ed ri'vəuk [rə'v-], -s, -iŋ, -t

revolt (s. v.), -s, -ing, -ed ri'vəult [rə'v-], -s, -iŋ, -id

revolution, -s ˌrevə'luːʃən [-vu'luː-, -vḷ'uː-, -və'lju:-], -z

revolutionar|y (s. adj.), -ies ˌrevə'luː-ʃnər|i [-vu'luː-, -vḷ'uː-, -və'lju:-, -ʃnər-, -ʃnr-, -ʃənər-], -iz

revolutioniz|e [-is|e], -es, -ing, -ed ˌrevə'luːʃnaiz [-vu'luː-, -vḷ'uː-, -və'lju:-, -ʃənaiz, -ʃnaiz], -iz, -iŋ, -d

revolv|e, -es, -ing, -ed ri'vɔlv [rə'v-], -z, -iŋ, -d

revolver, -s ri'vɔlvə* [rə'v-], -z
revue, -s ri'vju:[rə'v-], -z
revulsion, -s ri'vʌlʃən [rə'v-], -z
reward (s. v.), -s, -ing, -ed ri'wɔ:d
[rə'w-], -z, -iŋ, -id
reword, -s, -ing, -ed 'ri:'wə:d, -z, -iŋ, -id
rewrit|e, -es, -ing, rewrote, rewritten
'ri:'rait, -s, -iŋ, 'ri:'rəut, 'ri:'ritn
Rex reks
Reykjavik 'reikjəvi:k ['rek-, -vik]
Reynaldo rei'nældəu
reynard, -s 'renəd [-nɑ:d], -z
Reynard 'renəd, 'renɑ:d, 'reinɑ:d
Reynold, -s 'renḻd [-nəld], -z
Rhadamanthus ˌrædə'mænθəs
Rhae|tia, -tian 'ri:|ʃjə [-ʃiə, -ʃə], -ʃjən
[-ʃiən, -ʃən]
Rhaetic 'ri:tik
Rhaeto-Roman|ce, -ic 'ri:təurəu'mæn|s
[-ru'm-], -ik
rhapsodic, -al, -ally ræp'sɔdik, -əl, -əli
rhapsodiz|e [-is|e], -es, -ing, -ed
'ræpsədaiz, -iz, -iŋ, -d
rhapsod|y, -ies 'ræpsəd|i, -iz
rhea, -s riə ['ri:ə], -z
Rheims ri:mz
Rheinallt 'rainælt (Welsh 'hrəinaḻt)
Rhenish 'ri:niʃ ['ren-]
rheostat, -s 'riəustæt, -s
rhesus, -es 'ri:səs, -iz
rhetoric (s.) 'retərik
rhetoric|al, -ally ri'tɔrik|əl [rə't-], -əli
rhetorician, -s ˌretə'riʃən [-tɔ'r-], -z
rheum ru:m
rheumatic, -s, -ky ru(:)'mætik, -s, -i
rheumatism 'ru:mətizəm ['rum-]
rheumatoid 'ru:mətɔid ['rum-]
Rhine, -land rain, -lænd [-lənd]
rhino, -s 'rainəu, -z
rhinoceros, -es rai'nosərəs, -iz
rhinolog|ist/s, -y rai'nolədʒ|ist/s, -i
rhinoscope, -s 'rainəskəup, -s
rhizome, -s 'raizəum, -z
rho rəu
Rhoda 'rəudə
Rhode (biblical name) 'rəudi
Rhode (breed of fowls), -s rəud, -z
Rhode Island (state in U.S.A.)
rəud'ailənd [rəu'dai-, 'rəud,ailənd]
Note.—In U.S.A. the stress is -'--.
Rhode Island (breed of fowls), -s 'rəud-
ˌailənd, -z
Rhodes (Greek island, surname) rəudz
Rhode|sia, -sian rəu'di:|zjə [-ziə, -ʒjə,
-ʒiə, -ʒə, -sjə, -siə, -ʃjə, -ʃiə, -ʃə],
-zjən [-ziən, -ʒjən, -ʒiən, -ʒən, -sjən,
-siən, -ʃjən-, -ʃiən, -ʃən]
Rhodian, -s 'rəudjən [-diən], -z

rhodium 'rəudjəm [-diəm]
rhododendron, -s ˌrəudə'dendrən [ˌrɔd-,
-di'd-], -z
rhodomontade=rodomontade
rhomb, -s rɔm, -z
rhomboid, -s 'rɔmbɔid, -z
rhombus, -es 'rɔmbəs, -iz
Rhondda 'rɔndə ['rɔnðə] (Welsh 'hronða)
Rhone rəun
rhotacism 'rəutəsizəm
rhubarb 'ru:bɑ:b [old-fashioned -bəb]
Rhuddlan 'riðlən [-læn] (Welsh 'hriðlan)
rhumb, -s rʌm, -z
Rhyl ril (Welsh hril)
rhym|e (s. v.), -es, -ing, -ed, -er/s raim,
-z, -iŋ, -d, -ə*/z
rhymester, -s 'raimstə*, -z
Rhys (Welsh name) ri:s (Welsh hri:s),
(family name of Baron Dynevor) rais
rhythm, -s 'riðəm ['riθəm], -z
rhythmic, -al, -ally 'riðmik ['riθm-], -əl,
-əli
Riach riək ['ri:ək, -əx]
Rialto ri'æltəu
rib (s. v.), -s, -bing, -bed rib, -z, -iŋ, -d
ribald (s. adj.), -s; -ry 'ribəld, -z; -ri
Note.—A special pronunciation
'raibɔ:ld has to be used in Browning's 'Pied Piper' (to rhyme with
piebald).
riband, -s 'ribənd, -z
ribbon, -s 'ribən, -z
Ribston, -s 'ribstən, -z
Rica 'ri:kə
Riccio 'ritʃiəu
rice rais
Rice rais, ri:s
ricercata, -s ˌritʃə:'kɑ:tə [-tʃɛə'k-], -z
rich, -es, -er, -est, -ly, -ness ritʃ, -iz, -ə*,
-ist, -li, -nis
Richard, -s, -son 'ritʃəd, -z, -sn
Richelieu 'riʃəljə: [-lju:] (riʃəljø)
Riches 'ritʃiz
Richey 'ritʃi
Richmond 'ritʃmənd
rick, -s rik, -s
Rickard, -s 'rikɑ:d, -z
rickets 'rikits
Rickett 'rikit
ricket|y, -ier, -iest, -ily, -iness 'rikit|i,
-iə*, -iist, -ili, -inis
Ricksmansworth 'rikmənzwə:θ
rickshaw, -s 'rikʃɔ:, -z
Rico 'ri:kəu
ricoch|et, -ets, -eting, -eted 'rikəʃ|ei
[-kɔʃ-, -ʃ|et, ˌ-'-], -eiz [-ets], -eiiŋ
[-etiŋ], -eid [-etid]
rid, -s, -ding rid, -z, -iŋ

riddance 'ridəns
Riddell 'ridl, ri'del
Ridding 'ridiŋ
ridd|le (s. v.), -les, -ling, -led 'rid|l, -lz,
-liŋ [-liŋ], -ld
rid|e, -es, -ing, rode, ridden raid, -z, -iŋ,
rəud, 'ridn
Rideal ri'di:l
Ridealgh 'raidældʒ, 'ridiælʃ
Ridehalgh 'raidhælʃ, 'ridihælʃ
rider (R.), -s; -less 'raidə*, -z; -lis
ridge (R.), -s, -d ridʒ, -iz, -d
Ridg(e)way 'ridʒwei
ridicul|e (s. v.), -es, -ing, -ed 'ridikju:l,
-z, -iŋ, -d
ridiculous, -ly, -ness ri'dikjuləs [-kjəl-],
-li, -nis
Riding, -s, -hood 'raidiŋ, -z, -hud
riding-habit, -s 'raidiŋ,hæbit, -s
riding-master, -s 'raidiŋ,mɑ:stə*, -z
riding-mistress, -es 'raidiŋ,mistris, -iz
Rid|ley, -path 'rid|li, -pɑ:θ
Ridout 'ridaut
Rienzi ri'entsi
Rievaulx (abbey in Yorks.) 'ri:vəu
['ri:vəuz, 'rivəz]
Note.—'ri:vəu is the usual local
pronunciation.
rife raif
riff-raff 'rifræf
rif|le (s. v.), -les, -ling, -led 'raif|l, -lz,
-liŋ [-liŋ], -ld
rifle|man, -men 'raifl|mən [-mæn],
-mən [-men]
rifle-range, -s 'raiflreindʒ, -iz
rifle-shot, -s 'raiflʃɔt, -s
rift (s. v.), -s, -ing, -ed rift, -s, -iŋ, -id
rig (s. v.), -s, -ging, -ged rig, -z, -iŋ, -d
Riga 'ri:gə [old-fashioned 'raigə]
Rigby 'rigbi
Rigel (star) 'raigəl [rarely 'raidʒəl]
rigger, -s 'rigə*, -z
rigging (s.), -s 'rigiŋ, -z
right (s. adj. v. adv.), -s, -ly, -ness; -ing,
-ed rait, -s, -li, -nis; -iŋ, -id
rightabout 'raitəbaut
righteous, -ly, -ness 'raitʃəs [-tjəs], -li,
-nis
right|ful, -fully, -fulness 'rait|ful, -fuli
[-fəli], -fulnis
right-hand (attributive adj.) 'raithænd
right-handed 'rait'hændid
rightist, -s 'raitist, -s
righto 'rait'əu
Rigi 'ri:gi
rigid, -ly, -ness 'ridʒid, -li, -nis
rigidity ri'dʒiditi
Rigil Kentaurus 'raidʒil-ken'tɔ:rəs

rigmarole, -s 'rigmərəul, -z
Rigoletto ,rigə'letəu [-gəu'l-] (rigo-
'letto)
rigor (mortis) 'raigɔ:* ['rigə*]
rigorous, -ly, -ness 'rigərəs, -li, -nis
rigour, -s 'rigə*, -z
rig-out 'rig'aut ['--]
Rigveda rig'veidə ['-'--]
Rikki-Tiki-Tavi 'riki,tiki'tɑ:vi
ril|e, -es, -ing, -ed rail, -z, -iŋ, -d
Riley 'raili
rilievo ,rili'eivəu
rill, -s ril, -z
rim, -s rim, -z
Rimbault 'rimbəult [French poet
'ræmbəu] (rɛbo)
rime, -s raim, -z
Rimmon 'rimən
Rimsky-Korsakov 'rimski'kɔ:səkɔv [-ɔf]
('rjimskij'korsəkəf)
Rinaldo ri'nældəu
rind, -s raind, -z
Rind rind
rinderpest 'rindəpest
ring (s. v.) (encircle, put a ring on, etc.),
-s, -ing, -ed riŋ, -z, -iŋ, -d
ring (s. v.) (sound, etc.), -s, -ing, rang,
rung, ringer/s riŋ, -z, -iŋ, ræŋ, rʌŋ,
'riŋə*/z
ring-dove, -s 'riŋdʌv, -z
ring|leader/s, -let/s, -worm 'riŋ|-
,li:də*/z, -lit/s, -wə:m
Ringshall 'riŋʃəl
rink (s. v.), -s, -ing, -ed riŋk, -s, -iŋ, -t
[riŋt]
rins|e, -es, -ing, -ed rins, -iz, -iŋ, -t
Rio 'ri:əu ['riəu]
Rio de Janeiro 'ri:əudədʒə'niərəu ['riəu-]
Rio Grande (in North America) 'ri:əu-
'grændi ['riəu-, -'grænd]
riot (s. v.), -s, -ing, -ed, -er/s 'rai-ət, -s,
-iŋ, -id, -ə*/z
riotous, -ly, -ness 'rai-ətəs, -li, -nis
Riou 'riu: ['ri:u:]
rip, -s, -ping, -ped, -per/s rip, -s, -iŋ, -t,
-ə*/z
riparian rai'pɛəriən
ripe, -r, -st, -ness raip, -ə*, -ist, -li,
-nis
rip|en, -ens, -ening, -ened 'raip|ən, -ənz,
-ŋiŋ [-niŋ], -ənd
ripieno ,ripi'einəu
Ripley 'ripli
Ripman 'ripmən
Ripon 'ripən
ripost(e), -s ri'pɔst [-'pəust], -s
ripper, -s 'ripə*, -z
ripping (adj.), -est, -ly 'ripiŋ, -ist, -li

ripp|le, -les, -ling, -led 'rip|l, -lz, -ḷiŋ [-liŋ], -ld
ripple-mark, -s 'riplma:k, -s
ripply 'rip|i [-pli]
ripuarian ˌripju(:)'ɛəriən
Rip van Winkle 'ripvæn'wiŋkl
Risboro' [-borough] 'rizbərə
ris|e (s. v.), -es, -ing, rose, risen raiz -iz, -iŋ, rəuz, 'rizn
riser, -s 'raizə*, -z
risibility ˌrizi'biliti [ˌraiz-, -lət-]
risible 'rizibl ['raiz-]
rising (s.), -s 'raiziŋ, -z
risk (s. v.), -s, -ing, -ed risk, -s, -iŋ, -t
risk|y, -ier, -iest, -iness 'risk|i, -iə* [-jə*], -iist [-jist], -inis
rissole, -s 'risəul [old-fashioned 'ri:s-], -z
Rita 'ri:tə
ritardando, -s ˌrita:'dændəu, -z
Ritchie 'ritʃi
rite, -s rait, -s
Ritson 'ritsn
ritual, -s 'ritʃŭəl [-tʃwəl, -tʃul, -tjŭəl, -tjwəl, -tjul], -z
rituali|sm, -st/s 'ritʃŭəli|zəm [tʃwəl-, -tʃul-, -tjŭəl, -tjwəl, -tjul], -st/s
ritualistic ˌritʃŭə'listik [-tʃwə'l-, -tjŭə'l-, -tjwə'l-]
riv|al (s. v.), -als, -alling, -alled 'raiv|əl, -əlz, -ḷiŋ [-əliŋ], -əld
rivalr|y, -ies 'raivəlr|i, -iz
riv|e, -es, -ing, -ed, riven raiv, -z, -iŋ, -d, river, -s (R.) 'rivə*, -z   ['rivən
river-bank, -s 'rivə'bæŋk ['---], -s
river-basin, -s 'rivəˌbeisn, -z
river-bed, -s 'rivə'bed ['---], -z
riverside (R.) 'rivəsaid
rivet, -s, -(t)ing, -(t)ed, -(t)er/s 'rivit, -s, -iŋ, -id, -ə*/z
Riviera ˌrivi'ɛərə
Rivington, -s 'riviŋtən, -z
rivulet, -s 'rivjulit [-let], -s
rix-dollar, -s 'riks'dɔlə* ['riksˌd-], -z
Rizzio 'ritsiəu
roach (R.) rəutʃ
road, -s rəud, -z
road-block, -s 'rəudblɔk, -s
road-book, -s 'rəudbuk, -s
road-hog, -s 'rəudhɔg, -z
road-hou|se, -ses 'rəudhau|s, -ziz
roadmanship 'rəudmənʃip
road-mender, -s 'rəudˌmendə*, -z
road-sense 'rəudsens
roadside 'rəudsaid
roadstead, -s 'rəudsted, -z
roadster, -s 'rəudstə*, -z
road-test, -s 'rəudtest, -s
roadway, -s 'rəudwei*, -z

roadworth|y, -iness 'rəudˌwə:ði|i, -inis
roam, -s, -ing, -ed rəum, -z, -iŋ, -d
roan (s. adj.) (R.), -s rəun, -z
Roanoke ˌrəuə'nəuk
roar (s. v.), -s, -ing, -ed, -er/s rɔ:* [rɔə*], -z, -riŋ, -d, -rə*/z
roast (s. v.), -s, -ing, -ed, -er/s rəust, -s, -iŋ, -id, -ə*/z
roasting-jack, -s 'rəustiŋdʒæk, -s
rob (R.), -s, -bing, -bed, -ber/s rɔb, -z, -iŋ, -d, -ə*/z
Robb rɔb
robber|y, -ies 'rɔbər|i, -iz
Robbins 'rɔbinz
rob|e (s. v.), -es, -ing, -ed rəub, -z, -iŋ, -d
Robens 'rəubinz
Roberson 'rəubəsn, 'rɔbəsn
Note.—In Roberson's medium the usual pronunciation is 'rɔb-.
Robert, -s, -son 'rɔbət, -s, -sn
Roberta rə'bə:tə [rɔ'b-, rəu'b-]
Robeson 'rəubsn
Robespierre 'rəubzpjɛə* (rɔbɛspjɛ:r)
robin, -s 'rɔbin, -s
Robin, -son 'rɔbin, -sn
Robina rɔ'bi:nə [rəu'b-]
Robins 'rəubinz, 'rɔbinz
Robinson 'rɔbinsən
Roboam rəu'bəuəm
robot, -s 'rəubɔt ['rɔb-, -bət], -s
Robotham 'rəuˌbɔθəm
robotic rəu'bɔtik [rɔ'b-]
Rob Roy 'rɔb'rɔi
Robsart 'rɔbsa:t
Robson 'rɔbsn
robust, -ly, -ness rəu'bʌst, -li, -nis
Rochdale 'rɔtʃdeil
Roche rəutʃ, rəuʃ, rɔʃ
Rochester 'rɔtʃistə*
rochet, -s 'rɔtʃit, -s
rock (s. v.) (R.), -s, -ing, -ed, -er/s rɔk, -s, -iŋ, -t, -ə*/z
rock-bottom 'rɔk'bɔtəm
rock-bound 'rɔkbaund
Rockefeller 'rɔkifelə*
rocker|y, -ies 'rɔkər|i, -iz
rocket (s. v.), -s, -ing, -ed 'rɔkit, -s, -iŋ, -id
rocketry 'rɔkitri   [-id
rock-garden, -s 'rɔkˌga:dn, -z
Rockies 'rɔkiz
rocking-chair, -s 'rɔkiŋ-tʃɛə*, -z
Rockingham 'rɔkiŋəm
rocking-horse, -s 'rɔkiŋhɔ:s, -iz
rocking-stone, -s 'rɔkiŋ-stəun, -z
rock-plant, -s 'rɔkpla:nt, -s
rock-rose, -s 'rɔk'rəuz, -iz
rock-salt 'rɔk'sɔ:lt [-'sɔlt, in contrast 'rɔk-s-]

Rockstro 'rɔkstrəu
rockwork, -s 'rɔkwə:k, -s
rock|y, -ier, -iest, -iness 'rɔk|i, -iə*, -iist, -inis
rococo rəu'kəukəu
rod (R.), -s rɔd, -z
rode (from ride) rəud
rodent (s. adj.), -s 'rəudənt, -s
rodeo, -s rəu'deiəu ['rəudiəu], -z
Roderic(k) 'rɔdərik
Rodgers 'rɔdʒəz
Roding (several places in Essex) 'rəudiŋ [locally generally 'ruːdiŋ]
    Note.—The pronunciation 'rəudiŋ is being encouraged by the county council, and will doubtless become the accepted form before long.
Rod|ney, -way 'rɔd|ni, -wei
rodomontad|e (s. v.), -es, -ing, -ed ,rɔdəmɔn'teid [-'tɑːd], -z, -iŋ, -id
roe (R.), -s rəu, -z
roebuck (R.), -s 'rəubʌk, -s
Roedean 'rəudiːn
Roehampton rəu'hæmptən
Roentgen, see Röntgen
rogation (R.), -s rəu'geiʃən, -z
Roger, -s 'rɔdʒə*, 'rəudʒə*, -z
    Note.—The form 'rəudʒə* seems to occur chiefly as a surname in families of Scottish origin.
Roget 'rɔʒei
Rogozin rə'gəuzin [rɔ'g-]
rogue, -s rəug, -z
roguer|y, -ies 'rəugər|i, -iz
roguish, -ly, -ness 'rəugiʃ, -li, -nis
roil, -s, -ing, -ed rɔil, -z, -iŋ, -d
roist|er, -ers, -ering, -ered, -erer/s 'rɔist|ə*, -əz, -əriŋ, -əd, -ərə*/z
rok|e, -es, -ing, -ed rəuk, -s, -iŋ, -t
Rokeby 'rəukbi
Roker 'rəukə*
Roland 'rəulənd
role, -s rəul, -z
Rolf(e) rɔlf, rəuf
roll (s. v.), -s, -ing, -ed, -er/s rəul, -z, -iŋ, -d, -ə*/z
roll-back, -s 'rəulbæk, -s
roll-call, -s 'rəul-kɔːl, -z
roller-skat|e (s. v.), -es, -ing, -ed 'rəulə,skeit ['--'-], -s, -iŋ, -id
roller-towel, -s 'rəulə'tauəl [-'tauel, -'tauil, in contrast '--,--], -z
Rolleston 'rəulstən
rollick, -s, -ing, -ed 'rɔlik, -s, -iŋ, -t
rolling-pin, -s 'rəuliŋpin, -z
rolling-stock, -s 'rəuliŋ-stɔk, -s
Rollo 'rɔləu
Rolls rəulz

Rolls-Royce, -s 'rəulz'rɔis, -iz
roll-top (s.), -s 'rəul'tɔp, -s
roll-top (attributive adj.) 'rəul-tɔp
roly-pol|y, -ies 'rəuli'pəu|li, -iz
Romagna rəu'mɑːnjə (ro'maɲɲa)
Romaic rəu'meiik
Roman, -s 'rəumən, -z
romanc|e (s. v.) (R.), -es, -ing, -ed, -er/s rəu'mæns [ru'm-], -iz, -iŋ, -t, -ə*/z
Romanes (surname) rəu'mɑːniz (gipsy language) 'rɔmənes
romanesque ,rəumə'nesk
Romanic rəu'mænik
romani|sm, -st/s 'rəuməni|zəm, -st/s
romanization [-isa-], -s ,rəumənai'zeiʃən, -z
romaniz|e [-is|e], -es, -ing, -ed 'rəumənaiz, -iz, -iŋ, -d
Romansch rəu'mænʃ
romantic, -ally rəu'mæntik, -əli
romantici|sm, -st/s rəu'mæntisi|zəm, -st/s
Roman|y, -ies 'rɔmən|i ['rəum-], -iz
romaunt, -s rəu'mɔːnt, -s
Rome rəum
Romeike rəu'mi:ki
Romeo 'rəumiəu [-mjəu]
Romford 'rɔmfəd [old-fashioned 'rʌm-]
romic (R.) 'rəumik
Romish 'rəumiʃ
Romney, -s 'rɔmni ['rʌm-], -z
Romola 'rɔmələ
romp (s. v.), -s, -ing, -ed rɔmp, -s, -iŋ,
romper, -s 'rɔmpə*, -z   [-t [rɔmt]
Romulus 'rɔmjuləs
Ronald, -shay 'rɔn|d, -ʃei
Ronan 'rəunən
rondeau, -s 'rɔndəu, -z
rondel, -s 'rɔndl, -z
rondo, -s 'rɔndəu, -z
roneo (s. v.), -s, -ing, -ed 'rəuniəu [-njəu], -z, -iŋ, -d
Roney 'rəuni
Rongbuk 'rɔŋbuk
Ronson 'rɔnsən
Rontgen 'rɔntjən [-tgən]
Röntgen 'rɔntjən ['rʌnt-, 'rəːnt-, -tgən]
röntgenogram, -s rɔnt'genəgræm [rʌnt-, rəːnt-, 'rɔntjənəg-, 'rʌntjənəg-, 'rəːntjənəg-], -z
Ronuk 'rɔnək
rood, -s ruːd, -z
rood-loft, -s 'ruːdlɔft [-lɔːft], -s
rood-screen, -s 'ruːdskriːn, -z
roo|f (s.), -fs, -ves ruː|f, -fs, -vz
roof (v.), -s, -ing, -ed ruːf, -s, -iŋ, -t
roof-garden, -s 'ruːf,gɑːdn, -z

rook (s. v.), -s, -ing, -ed ruk, -s, -iŋ, -t

rooker|y, -ies 'rukər|i, -iz

room, -s ruːm [rum], -z

Room ruːm

-roomed -ruːmd [-rumd]

roomful, -s 'ruːmful ['rum-], -z

Rooms ruːmz

room|y, -ier, -iest, -ily, -iness 'ruːm|i ['rum-], -ɪə*, -iist, -ili, -inis

Roosevelt (American surname) 'rəuzəvelt ['ruːsvelt]

Note.—'rəuzəvelt is the pronunciation used in the families of the late Presidents of the United States. In England this name is often pronounced 'ruːsvelt.

roost (s. v.), -s, -ing, -ed, -er/s ruːst, -s, -iŋ, -id, -ə*/z

root (s. v.) (R.), -s, -ing, -ed; -y ruːt, -s, -iŋ, -id; -i

Rootham 'ruːtəm

rop|e (s. v.), -es, -ing, -ed rəup, -s, -iŋ, -t

rope-dancer, -s 'rəup,dɑːnsə*, -z

Roper 'rəupə*

rope-trick, -s 'rəup-trik, -s

rope-walker, -s 'rəup,wɔːkə*, -z

Ropner 'rɔpnə*

Roquefort, -s 'rɔkfɔː* (rɔkfɔːr), -z

roquet (s. v.), -s, -ing, -ed 'rəuki [-kei], -z, -iŋ, -d

Rorke rɔːk

Rosa 'rəuzə

rosace, -s 'rəuzeis, -iz

Rosalba rəu'zælbə

Rosalie 'rɔzəli, 'rəuzəli

Rosalind 'rɔzəlind

Rosaline (Shakespearian character) 'rɔzəlain

Rosamond 'rɔzəmənd

rosarium, -s rəu'zɛərɪəm, -z

rosar|y, -ies 'rəuzər|i, -iz

Roscius 'rɔʃɪəs [-ʃəs]

Roscoe 'rɔskəu

Roscommon rɔs'kɔmən

rose (R.), -s rəuz, -iz

rose (from rise) rəuz

roseate 'rəuziit [-zjit]

Rosebery 'rəuzbəri

rose-bud, -s 'rəuzbʌd, -z

rose-bush, -es 'rəuzbuʃ, -iz

rose-colour 'rəuz,kʌlə*

rose-garden, -s 'rəuz,gɑːdn, -z

Rosehaugh 'rəuzhɔː

rose-lea|f, -ves 'rəuzli:|f, -vz

rosemar|y (R.), -ies 'rəuzmər|i, -iz

Rosencrantz 'rəuzənkrænts

rose-pink 'rəuz'piŋk

rose-red 'rəuz'red

rose-tree, -s 'rəuztri:, -z

Rosetta rəu'zetə

rosette, -s rəu'zet, -s

rose-water 'rəuz,wɔːtə*

rosewood 'rəuzwud

Rosherville 'rɔʃə(:)vil

Rosicrucian, -s ,rəuzi'kruːʃjən [,rɔz-, -ʃɪən, -ʃən], -z

Rosier 'rəuziə* [-zɪə*, -zjə*]

rosin 'rɔzin

Rosina rəu'ziːnə

Roslin 'rɔzlin

Ross rɔs

Rossall 'rɔsəl

Rosse, -r rɔs, -ə*

Rossetti (English surname) rɔ'seti [rə's-]

Rossini rɔ'si:ni(ː) [rə's-] (ros'si:ni)

Rosslare 'rɔslɛə*, rɔs'lɛə*

Rosslyn 'rɔslin

Ross-shire 'rɔsʃiə* ['rɔʃʃiə*, -ʃə*]

roster, -s 'rəustə* ['rɔs-], -z

Rostrevor rɔs'trevə*

rostrum, -s 'rɔstrəm, -z

ros|y (R.), -ier, -iest, -ily, -iness 'rəuz|i, -ɪə* [-jə*], -iist [-jist], -ili, -inis

Rosyth rɔ'saiθ [rə's-]

rot (s. v.), -s, -ting, -ted, -ter/s rɔt, -s, -iŋ, -id, -ə*/z

rota, -s 'rəutə, -z

rotar|y (s. adj.), -ies 'rəutər|i, -iz

rotatable rəu'teitəbl

rotat|e, -es, -ing, -ed, -or/s rəu'teit, -s, -iŋ, -id, -ə*/z

rotation, -s rəu'teiʃən, -z

rotatory 'rəutətəri [rəu'teitəri]

rote rəut

Rothamsted 'rɔθəmsted

Rothenstein (English surname) 'rəuθən-stain, 'rəutən-, 'rɔθən-

Rothera 'rɔθərə

Rother|ham, -hithe 'rɔðə|rəm, -haið

Rothermere 'rɔðəmɪə*

Rotherston 'rɔðəstən

Rotherwick 'rɔðərik, -ðəwik

Rothes 'rɔθis

Rothesay 'rɔθsi [-sei]

Rothschild (English surname) 'rɔθtʃaild, 'rɔstʃ-, 'rɔθstʃ-

rotor, -s 'rəutə*, -z

rott|en, -enest, -enly, -enness 'rɔt|n, -nist, -nli, -nnis

rottenstone 'rɔtn-stəun

rotter, -s 'rɔtə*, -z

Rotterdam 'rɔtədæm [,--'-]

Rottingdean 'rɔtiŋdi:n

rotund, -ity, -ness rəu'tʌnd, -iti, -nis

rotunda (R.), -s, rəu'tʌndə, -z
rouble, -s 'ruːbl, -z
Rouen 'ruːɑ̃ːɳ [-ɔ̃ːɳ, -ɑːɳ, -ɔːɳ, -ɔɳ] (rwɑ̃)
roug|e (s. v.), -es, -ing, -ed ruːʒ, -iz, -iɳ, -d
rough (s. adj. v.), -s; -er, -est, -ly, -ness; -ing, -ed rʌf, -s; -ə*, -ist, -li, -nis; -iɳ, -t
roughage 'rʌfidʒ
rough-cast 'rʌfkɑːst
rough-hew, -s, -ing, -ed, -n 'rʌf'hjuː: -z, -iɳ [-'hjuiɳ], -d, -n
roughish 'rʌfiʃ
rough-rider, -s 'rʌf,raidə*, -z
rough-shod 'rʌfʃod
rough-spoken 'rʌf'spəukən [also '--,-- when attributive]
Rough Tor (in Cornwall) 'rau'tɔː*
roulade, -s ruː'lɑːd, -z
roulette ruː(ː)'let
Ro(u)mania, -n/s ruː(ː)'meinjə [-nïə], -n
Roumelia ruː(ː)'miːljə [-lïə]   [-n/z
rounceval, -s 'raunsivəl, -z
round (s. adj. v. adv. prep.), -s; -er, -est, -ly, -ness, -ish; -ing, -ed raund, -z; -ə*, -ist, -li, -nis [-aunnis], -iʃ; -iɳ, -id
roundabout (s. adj.), -s 'raundəbaut, -s
roundel, -s 'raundl, -z
roundelay, -s 'raundilei, -z
rounders 'raundəz
roundhand 'raundhænd
Roundhead, -s 'raundhed, -z
roundish 'raundiʃ
round-shouldered 'raund'ʃəuldəd ['-,--]
round-the-clock 'raundðəklɔk ['--'-]
round-up, -s 'raundʌp ['-'-], -s
Rourke rɔːk
Rous raus
rous|e, -es, -ing/ly, -ed rauz, -iz, -iɳ/li, -d
Rouse raus, ruːs
Rousseau 'ruːsəu (ruso)
Roussin 'rusin
rout (s. v.), -s, -ing, -ed raut, -s, -iɳ, -d
route, -s ruːt [in the army also raut], -s
route-march, -es 'ruːtmɑːtʃ ['raut-], -iz
Routh rauθ
routine, -s ruː'tiːn [ruː't-], -z
Routledge 'rautlidʒ [-ledʒ], 'rʌt-
Routley 'rautli
rov|e, -es, -ing, -ed, -er/s rəuv, -z, -iɳ, -d, -ə*/z
Rover, -s 'rəuvə*, -z
row (s.) (number of persons or things in a line), -s rəu, -z
row (s.) (excursion in a rowing-boat), -s rəu, -z

row (s.) (disturbance), -s rau, -z
row (v.) (propel boat with oars), -s, -ing, -ed rəu, -z, -iɳ, -d
row (v.) (reprimand), -s, -ing, -ed rau, -z, -iɳ, -d
Rowallan rəu'ælən
rowan (tree), -s 'rau-ən ['rəuən], -z
   Note.—In Scotland always rau-ən (or 'rʌuən with Scottish equivalent of au).
Rowan (surname) 'rəuən, 'rau-ən
Rowant (in Oxfordshire) 'rau-ənt
row-boat, -s 'rəubəut, -s
row-de-dow [rowdydow], -s 'raudi-'dau, -z
Rowden 'raudn
rowd|y (s. adj.), -ies, -ier, -iest, -ily, -iness, -yism 'raud|i, -iz, -iə* [-jə*], -iist [-jist], -ili, -inis, -iizəm
Rowe rəu
Rowed 'rəuid
rowel, -s 'rauəl, -z
Rowell 'rauəl, 'rəuəl
Rowena rəu'iːnə
rower (one who rows a boat), -s 'rəuə*, -z
rowing-boat, -s 'rəuiɳbəut, -s
Rowland, -s 'rəulənd, -z
Rowles rəulz
Rowley 'rəuli
rowlock, -s 'rɔlək ['rəulɔk, 'rʌlək], -s
Rowney 'rəuni, 'rauni
Rowntree 'rauntri(ː)
Rowridge 'rauridʒ
Rowse raus
Rowton 'rautn, 'rɔːtn
Roxburgh(e) 'rɔksbərə
Roy rɔi
roy|al, -ally 'rɔi|əl, -əli
royali|sm, -st/s 'rɔiəli|zəm, -st/s
royalt|y, -ies 'rɔiəlt|i, -iz
Royce rɔis
Royston 'rɔistən
Ruabon ruː(ː)'æbən (Welsh riu'abon)
rub (s. v.), -s, -bing, -bed rʌb, -z, -iɳ, -d
Rubáiyát 'ruː:baijæt [,--'-, -jɑːt]
rubato, -s ruː(ː)'bɑːtəu, -z
rubber, -s 'rʌbə*, -z
rubbish, -y 'rʌbiʃ, -i
rubb|le, -ly 'rʌb|l, -|li
Rubbra 'rʌbrə
rubefacient ,ruː:bi'feiʃjənt [-ʃïənt]
Rubens 'ruː:binz [-bənz, -benz]
Rubicon 'ruː:bikən [-kɔn]
rubicund 'ruː:bikənd
rubidium ruː(ː)'bidïəm [-djəm]
Rubinstein (Russian pianist) 'ruː:binstain
rubric, -s 'ruː:brik, -s
rub|y (R.), -ies 'ruː:b|i, -iz

ruche, -s ru:ʃ, -iz
ruck rʌk
rucksack, -s 'ruksæk ['rʌk-], -s
ruction, -s 'rʌkʃən, -z
rudd (R.), -s rʌd, -z
rudder, -s, -less 'rʌdə*, -z, -lis
Ruddigore 'rʌdigɔ:* [-gɔə*]
rudd|le (s. v.), -les, -ling, -led 'rʌd|l, -lz, -liŋ, -ld
rudd|y, -ier, -iest, -ily, -iness 'rʌd|i, -ïə* [-jə*], -iist [-jist], -ili, -inis
rude, -r, -st, -ly, -ness ru:d, -ə*, -ist, -li, -nis
Rudge, -s rʌdʒ, -iz
rudiment, -s 'ru:dimənt, -s
rudiment|al, -ary ,ru:di'ment|l, -əri
Rudmose 'rʌdməuz
Rudol|f, -ph 'ru:dɔl|f, -f
Rudyard 'rʌdjəd
rue (s. v.), -s, -ing, -d ru:, -z, -iŋ [ruiŋ], -d
rue|ful, -fully, -fulness 'ru:|ful, -fuli [-fəli], -fulnis
ruff (s. v.), -s, -ing, -ed rʌf, -s, -iŋ, -t
ruffian, -s, -ly; -ism 'rʌfjən [-fïən], -z, -li; -izəm
ruff|le (s. v.), -les, -ling, -led 'rʌf|l, -lz, -liŋ [-liŋ], -ld
Rufus 'ru:fəs
rug, -s rʌg, -z
Rugbeian, -s rʌg'bi(:)ən, -z
Rugby 'rʌgbi
Rugeley 'ru:dʒli ['ru:ʒli]
rugged, -ly, -ness 'rʌgid, -li, -nis
rugger 'rʌgə*
Ruhmkorff 'ru:mkɔ:f
ruin (s. v.), -s, -ing, -ed ruin ['ru:in], -z, -iŋ, -d
ruination rui'neiʃən [,ru:i'n-]
ruinous, -ly, -ness 'ruinəs ['ru:in-], -li, -nis
Ruislip (in Middlesex) 'raislip ['raizl-]
Ruiz ru(:)'i:θ
rul|e (s. v.), -es, -ing, -ed, -er/s ru:l, -z, -iŋ, -d, -ə*/z
ruling (s.), -s 'ru:liŋ, -z
rum (s. adj.), -mer, -mest rʌm, -ə*, -ist
Rumania (Ro-), -n/s ru(:)'meinjə [-nïə], -n/z
rumba, -s 'rʌmbə, -z   [-n/z
rumb|le (s. v.), -les, -ling/s, -led 'rʌmb|l, -lz, -liŋ/z, -ld
Rumbold 'rʌmbəuld
Rumelia ru(:)'mi:ljə [-lïə]
Rumford 'rʌmfəd
ruminant (s. adj.), -s 'ru:minənt, -s
ruminat|e, -es, -ing, -ed 'ru:mineit, -s, -iŋ, -id
rumination, -s ,ru:mi'neiʃən, -z

ruminative 'ru:minətiv [-neit-]
rummag|e (s. v.), -es, -ing, -ed 'rʌmidʒ, -iz, -iŋ, -d
rumm|y (s. adj.), -ier, -iest, -ily, -iness 'rʌm|i, -ïə*, -iist, -ili, -inis
rumour, -s, -ed 'ru:mə*, -z, -d
rumour-mong|er, -ers, -ering 'ru:mə-,mʌŋg|ə*, -əz, -əriŋ
rump, -s rʌmp, -s
rump|le, -les, -ling, -led 'rʌmp|l, -lz, -liŋ [-liŋ], -ld
rumptitum 'rʌmpti'tʌm
rumpus, -es 'rʌmpəs, -iz
rum-runner, -s 'rʌm,rʌnə*, -z
run (s. v.), -s, -ning, ran rʌn, -z, -iŋ, ræn
runabout, -s 'rʌnəbaut, -s
runagate, -s 'rʌnəgeit, -s
runaway (s. adj.), -s 'rʌnəwei, -z
Runciman 'rʌnsimən
Runcorn 'rʌŋkɔ:n
run-down, -s 'rʌndaun, -z
rune (R.), -s ru:n, -z
rung (s.), -s rʌŋ, -z
rung (from ring) rʌŋ
runic (R.) 'ru:nik
runnel, -s 'rʌnl, -z
runner, -s 'rʌnə*, -z
runner-up, -s 'rʌnər'ʌp ['rʌnə'ʌp], -s
running-board, -s 'rʌniŋbɔ:d [-bɔəd], -z
Runnymede 'rʌnimi:d
runt, -s rʌnt, -s
Runton 'rʌntən
runway, -s 'rʌnwei, -z
Runyon 'rʌnjən
rupee, -s ru:'pi: [ru'p-], -z
Rupert 'ru:pət
rupt|ure (s. v.), -ures, -uring, -ured 'rʌptʃ|ə*, -əz, -əriŋ, -əd
rur|al, -ally 'ruər|əl, -əli
ruridecanal ,ruəridi'keinl [-'dekənl]
Ruritania ,ruəri'teinjə [-nïə]
ruse, -s ru:z, -iz
rusé 'ru:zei (ryze)
rush (s. v.), -es, -ing, -ed, -er/s rʌʃ, -iz, -iŋ, -t, -ə*/z
Rushforth 'rʌʃfɔ:θ
rush|light/s, -like 'rʌʃ|lait/s, -laik
Rushmere 'rʌʃmiə*
Rusholme (near Manchester) 'rʌʃəm ['rʌʃhəum]
Rushton 'rʌʃtən
Rushworth 'rʌʃwə:θ
rushy 'rʌʃi
rusk (R.), -s rʌsk, -s
Ruskin 'rʌskin
Rusper 'rʌspə*
Russell 'rʌsl
russet (s. adj.), -s, -y 'rʌsit, -s, -i

Russi|a, -an/s 'rʌʃ|ə, -ən/z
russianism, -s 'rʌʃənizəm [-ʃɲi], -z
russianiz|e [-is|e], -es, -ing, -ed 'rʌʃənaiz
[-ʃɲaiz], -iz, -iŋ, -d
rust (s. v.), -s, -ing, -ed rʌst, -s, -iŋ, -id
rustic (s. adj.), -s, -ally 'rʌstik, -s, -əli
rusticat|e, -es, -ing, -ed 'rʌstikeit, -s,
-iŋ, -id
rustication ˌrʌsti'keiʃən
rusticity rʌs'tisiti
rust|le (s. v.), -les, -ling, -led 'rʌs|l, -lz,
-liŋ [-l̩iŋ], -ld
Rustum 'rʌstəm
rust|y, -ier, -iest, -iness 'rʌst|i, -iə*
[-jə*], -iist [-jist], -inis
Ruswarp (near Whitby) 'rʌzəp [-zwɔ:p]
Note.—Both forms are heard locally.
rut, -s, -ted rʌt, -s, -id
Rutgers 'rʌtgəz
ruth (R.) ru:θ
Ruthenian, -s ru(:)'θi:njən [-nïən], -z
Ruther|ford, -glen 'rʌðə|fəd, -glen
Ruthin 'riðin ['ru:θin] (Welsh 'hriθïn)

ruthless, -ly, -ness 'ru:θlis, -li, -nis
Ruthrieston 'rʌðristən
Ruthven (personal name) 'ru:θvən,
'rivən, (place in Angus) 'rivən, (place
in Aberdeenshire, loch in Inverness)
'rʌθvən
Note.—Baron Ruthven is 'rivən.
Ruthwell 'rʌθwəl [locally 'riðəl]
Rutland, -shire 'rʌtlənd, -ʃiə* [-ʃə*]
Rutter 'rʌtə*
rutt|y, -ier, -iest, -iness 'rʌt|i, -iə*, -iist,
-inis
Ruy Lopez 'ru:i'ləupez
Ruysdael 'raizdɑ:l
Ruyter 'raitə*
Rwanda ru(:)'ændə ['rwændə]
Ryan 'raiən ['rai-ən]
Ryde raid
rye (R.), -grass rai, -grɑ:s
Ryle rail
Rylstone 'rilstən [-stəun]
ryot, -s 'raiət ['rai-ət], -s
Ryswick 'rizwik

S

S (*the letter*), -'s es, -iz
Saba (*in Arabia*) 'sɑ:bə, (*in West Indies*) 'sæbə
Sabaean sə'bi(:)ən [sæ'b-]
Sabaoth sæ'beiɔθ [sə'b-, 'sæbeiɔθ, -əθ]
sabbatarian, -s, -ism ˌsæbə'tɛərïən, -z, -izəm
Sabbath, -s 'sæbəθ, -s
sabbatical sə'bætikəl
Sabin (*surname*) 'seibin, 'sæbin
Sabine (*Italian people*), -s 'sæbain, -z
Sabine (*surname*) 'sæbain, 'sæbin, 'seibin
Sabine (*river, lake, pass*) sə'bi:n [sæ'b-]
sable (*s. adj.*), -s 'seibl, -z
sabot, -s 'sæbəu, -z
sabotag|e (*s. v.*), -es, -ing, -ed 'sæbətɑ:ʒ [-tidʒ, -tɑ:dʒ], -iz, -iŋ, -d
saboteur, -s ˌsæbə'tə:* ['---], -z
sab|re (*s. v.*), -res, -ring, -red 'seib|ə*, -əz, -əriŋ, -əd
sabretache, -s 'sæbətæʃ, -iz
sabre-toothed 'seibətu:θt [-tu:ðd]
sabulous 'sæbjuləs
sac, -s sæk, -s
saccade, -s sæ'kɑ:d, -z
saccharine (*s.*) 'sækərin [-ri:n, -rain]
saccharine (*adj.*) 'sækərain [-ri:n]
sacerdot|al, -ally ˌsæsə'dəut|l [-sɔ:'d-], -əli
sachem, -s 'seitʃəm [-tʃem], -z
sachet, -s 'sæʃei (saʃɛ), -z
Sacheverell sə'ʃevərəl
sack (*s. v.*), -s, -ing, -ed, -er/s sæk, -s, -iŋ, -t, -ə*/z
sackbut, -s 'sækbʌt [-bət], -s
sackful, -s 'sækful, -z
sacking (*s.*) 'sækiŋ
Sackville 'sækvil
sacral 'seikrəl
sacrament, -s 'sækrəmənt [-krim-], -s
sacramental ˌsækrə'mentl
Sacramento ˌsækrə'mentəu
sacred, -ly, -ness 'seikrid, -li, -nis
sacrific|e (*s. v.*), -es, -ing, -ed 'sækrifais, -iz, -iŋ, -t
   Note.—An old pronunciation with -faiz is now probably obsolete.
sacrifici|al, -ally ˌsækri'fiʃ|əl, -əli
sacrilege 'sækrilidʒ

sacrilegious ˌsækri'lidʒəs [*rarely* -'li:dʒəs, -'li:dʒïəs, -'li:dʒəs]
sacristan, -s 'sækristən, -z
sacrist|y, -ies 'sækrist|i, -iz
sacrosanct 'sækrəusæŋkt
sad, -der, -dest, -ly, -ness sæd, -ə*, -ist, -li, -nis
sadd|en, -ens, -ening, -ened 'sæd|n, -nz, -ṇiŋ [-niŋ], -nd
sadd|le, -les, -ling, -led 'sæd|l, -lz, -ḷiŋ [-liŋ], -ld
saddleback (S.) 'sædlbæk
saddlebag, -s 'sædlbæg, -z
saddle-horse, -s 'sædlhɔ:s, -iz
saddler, -s; -y 'sædlə*, -z; -ri
Sadducee, -s 'sædjusi:, -z
Sade sɑd
Sadie 'seidi
sadi|sm, -st/s 'seidi|zəm ['sæd-, 'sɑ:d-], -st/s
sadistic sə'distik [sæ'd-]
Sadler 'sædlə*
Sadleir 'sædlə*
Sadowa 'sɑ:dəuə*
safari, -s sə'fɑ:ri, -z
safe (*s. adj*), -s; -r, -st, -ly, -ness seif, -s; -ə*, -ist, -li, -nis
safe-conduct, -s 'seif'kɔndʌkt [-dəkt], -s
safe-deposit, -s 'seifdiˌpɔzit, -s
safeguard (*s. v.*), -s, -ing, -ed 'seifgɑ:d, -z, -iŋ, -id
safe-keeping 'seif'ki:piŋ
safety 'seifti
safety-bicycle, -s 'seiftiˌbaisikl, -z
safety-bolt, -s 'seiftibəult, -s
safety-catch, -es 'seiftikætʃ, -iz
safety-curtain, -s 'seiftiˌkə:tn [-tən, -tin], -z
safety-lamp, -s 'seiftilæmp, -s
safety-lock, -s 'seiftilɔk, -s
safety-match, -es 'seiftimætʃ, -iz
safety-pin, -s 'seiftipin, -z
safety-razor, -s 'seiftiˌreizə*, -z
safety-valve, -s 'seiftivælv, -z
Saffell sə'fel
saffron (S.) 'sæfrən
sag (*s. v.*), -s, -ging, -ged sæg, -z, -iŋ, -d
saga, -s 'sɑ:gə, -z
sagacious, -ly, -ness sə'geiʃəs, -li, -nis

sagacity sə'gæsiti
sage (s. adj.) (S.), -s, -ly, -ness seidʒ, -iz, -li, -nis
sagitt|a, -ae sə'dʒit|ə, -i: [-ai]
Sagitta (constellation) sə'gitə [sə'dʒi-]
sagittal 'sædʒitl
Sagittarian, -s ˌsædʒi'tɛərɪən, -z
Sagittarius (constellation) ˌsædʒi'tɛərɪəs [ˌsægi-, -'tɑ:rɪəs]
sago 'seigəu
Sahara sə'hɑ:rə
sahib (S.), -s 'sɑ:hib [sɑ:b], -z
said (from say) sed (normal form), səd, sid (occasional weak forms)
Said (in Port Said) said [old-fashioned seid]
sail (s. v.), -s, -ing/s, -ed, -er/s, -or/s seil, -z, -iŋ/z, -d, -ə*/z, -ə*/z
sailor|man, -men 'seilə|mæn, -men
sailplane, -s 'seil-plein, -z
sainfoin 'sæn-fɔin ['sein-]
Sainsbury 'seinzbəri
saint (S.), -s seint [strong form], -s, sənt, sint, snt (weak forms)
St. Abb's snt'æbz [sənt-, sint-]
St. Agnes snt'ægnis [sənt-, sint-]
St. Alban, -'s snt'ɔ:lbən [sənt-, sint-, -'ɔl-], -z
St. Aldate's (street in Oxford) snt'ɔ:ldeits [sənt-, sint-, -'ɔl-, -dits, old-fashioned -'əuldz]
St. Ambrose snt'æmbrəuz [sənt-, sint-, -əus]
St. Andrew, -s snt'ændru: [sənt-, sint-], -z
St. Anne snt'æn [sənt-, sint-]
St. Anthony snt'æntəni [sənt-, sint-]
St. Asaph snt'æsəf [sənt-, sint-]
St. Augustine sintɔ:'gʌstin [sənt-, ˌsent-, ˌseint-, -tə'g-, rarely sənt'ɔ:gəstin, sint'ɔ:gəstin]
St. Austell snt'ɔ:stl [sənt-, sint-, locally -'ɔ:sl]
St. Bartholomew, -'s sintbɑ:'θɔləmju: [sənt-, -bə'θ-], -z
St. Bees snt'bi:z [sənt-, sint-]
St. Bernard, -s snt'bə:nəd [sənt-, sint-], -z
St. Blaize snt'bleiz [sənt-, sint-]
St. Blazey snt'bleizi [sənt-, sint-]
St. Bride's snt'braidz [sənt-, sint-]
St. Catherine [-thar-], -'s snt'kæθərin [sənt-, sint-, sŋ'k-], -z
St. Cecilia sintsi'siljə [sənt-, -lɪə]
St. Christopher snt'kristəfə* [sənt-, sint-, sŋ'k-]
St. Clair (surname) 'siŋklɛə* ['sink-], (place in U.S.A.) snt'klɛə* [sənt-, sint-]

St. Columb snt'kɔləm [sənt-, sint-]
St. David, -'s snt'deivid [sənt-, sint-], -z
St. Edmunds snt'edməndz [sənt-, sint-]
St. Elian snt'i:ljən [sənt-, sint-, -lɪən]
St. Elias sinti'laiəs [sənt-, -'laiæs]
St. Elmo snt'elməu [sənt-, sint-]
St. Francis snt'frɑ:nsis [sənt-, sint-]
St. Gall snt'gæl [sənt-, sint-, -'gɑ:l, -'gɔ:l]
St. Galmier sn'gælmiei [sŋ'g-, sənt'g-, sint'g-, -mjei] (sēgalmje)
St. George, -'s snt'dʒɔ:dʒ [sənt-, sint-], -iz
St. Giles, -'s snt'dʒailz [sənt-, sint-], -iz
St. Gotthard snt'gɔtəd [sənt-, sint-]
St. Helena (Saint) snt'helinə [sənt-, sint-], (island) ˌsenti'li:nə [sint-, sənt-]
St. Helen's snt'helinz [sənt-, sint-]
St. Helier, -'s snt'heljə* [sənt-, sint-, -lɪə*], -z
St. Ives snt'aivz [sənt-, sint-]
St. James, -'s snt'dʒeimz [sənt-, sint-], -iz
St. Joan snt'dʒəun [sənt-, sint-]
St. John, -'s (Saint, place) snt'dʒɔn [sənt-, sint-], -z, (surname) 'sindʒən
St. Joseph snt'dʒəuzif [sənt-, sint-, -zəf]
St. Kilda snt'kildə [sənt-, sint-]
St. Kitts snt'kits [sənt-, sint-]
St. Lawrence snt'lɔrəns [sənt-, sint-]
St. Leger (surname) snt'ledʒə* [sənt-, sint-], 'selindʒə*, (race) snt'ledʒə* [sənt-, sint-]
Note.—Most people bearing this name (including the Irish families) pronounce snt'ledʒə* [sənt-, sint-]. But there are members of the Doncaster family who pronounce 'selindʒə*.
St. Legers snt'ledʒəz [sənt-, sint-]
St. Leonards snt'lenədz [sənt-, sint-]
St. Levan snt'levən [sənt-, sint-]
saintlike 'seintlaik
St. Louis (city in U.S.A.) snt'luis [sənt-, sint-, -'lu:is], (places in Canada) -'lui [-'lu:i, -is]
St. Lucia snt'lu:ʃə [sənt-, sint-, rarely -ʃjə, -ʃɪə, -sjə, -sɪə]
St. Ludger snt'lu:dʒə* [sənt-, sint-]
St. Luke snt'lu:k [sənt-, sint-]
saintl|y, -ier, -iest, -iness 'seintl|i, -ɪə* [-jə*], -iist [-jist], -inis
St. Malo snt'mɑ:ləu [sənt-, sint-] (sēmalo)
St. Margaret, -'s snt'mɑ:gərit [sənt-, sint-], -s

St. **Mark** snt'mɑːk [sənt-, sint-]

St. **Martin, -'s** snt'mɑːtin [sənt-, sint-], -z

St. **Martin's le Grand** snt'mɑːtinzlə-'grænd [sənt-, sint-]

St. **Mary, -'s** snt'mɛəri [sənt-, sint-], -z

St. **Mary Axe** snt'mɛəri'æks [sənt-, sint-, old-fashioned 'siməri'æks]
Note.—The old form 'siməri'æks has to be used in Gilbert and Sullivan's opera 'The Sorcerer'.

St. **Marylebone** snt'mɛərilə'bəun [sənt-, sint-]
Note.—See also **Marylebone**.

St. **Matthew** snt'mæθju: [sənt-, sint-]

St. **Maur** (surname) 'siːmɔː* [-mɔə*]

St. **Mawes** snt'mɔːz [sənt-, sint-]

St. **Michael, -'s** snt'maikl [sənt-, sint-], -z

St. **Moritz** snt'mɔrits [sənt-, sint-]

St. **Neots** (in Hunts.) snt'niːts [sənt-, sint-, -'niːəts]

St. **Nicholas** snt'nikələs [sənt-, sint-, -kləs]

St. **Olaves** (in Suffolk) snt'ɔlivz [sənt-, sint-, -ləvz]

St. **Olave's** (hospital in London) snt-'ɔlivz [sənt-, sint-, -ləvz]

St. **Osyth** (in Essex) snt'əuziθ [sənt-, sint-, -'əusiθ]

St. **Pancras** snt'pæŋkrəs [sənt-, sint-, sm'pæŋkrəs]

St. **Patrick** snt'pætrik [sənt-, sint-]

St. **Paul, -'s** snt'pɔːl [sənt-, sint-], -z

St. **Peter, -'s, -sburg** snt'piːtə* [sənt-, sint-], -z, -zbəːg

St. **Regis** snt'riːdʒis [sənt-, sint-]

St. **Ronan** snt'rəunən [sənt-, sint-]

Saint-Saëns sæ̃ŋ'sɑ̃ːŋs [sæŋ-, -'sɑːns, -'sɔ̃ːŋs, -'sɔːns] (sɛ̃sɑ̃ːs)

St. **Salvator's** (college) sntsæl'veitəz [sənt-, sint-]

Sainsbury 'seinzbəri

Saintsbury 'seintsbəri

St. **Simon** snt'saimən [sənt-, sint-]

St. **Thomas, -'s** snt'tɔməs [sənt-, sint-], -iz

St. **Vincent** snt'vinsənt [sənt-, sint-]

St. **Vitus, -'s** snt'vaitəs [sənt-, sint-], -iz

saith (from say) seθ

sake, -s seik, -s

saké (Japanese wine) 'sɑːki

Sakhalin ˌsækə'liːn (səxa'ljin)

Saki 'sɑːki

salaam (s. v.), **-s, -ing, -ed** sə'lɑːm, -z, -iŋ, -d

salable 'seiləbl

salacious, -ly, -ness sə'leiʃəs, -li, -nis

salacity sə'læsiti

salad, -s 'sæləd, -z

Saladin 'sælədin

Salamanca ˌsælə'mæŋkə

salamander, -s 'sælə‚mændə* [-‚mɑːn-], -z

salami sə'lɑːmi(ː)

Salamis 'sæləmis

sal-ammoniac ˌsælə'məuniæk [-njæk]

salar|y, -ies -ied 'sælər|i, -iz, -id

Salcombe (in Devon) 'sɔːlkəm ['sɔl-]

sale (S.), -s seil, -z

sal(e)ability ˌseilə'biliti [-lət-]

saleable 'seiləbl

Salem 'seilem [-ləm]

Salesbury 'seilzbəri

sales|man, -men 'seilz|mən, -mən [-men]

salesmanship 'seilzmənʃip

salesroom, -s 'seilzrum [-ruːm], -z

Salford 'sɔːlfəd ['sɔl-]

Salian, -s 'seiljən [-lïən], -z

Salic 'sælik

salicional, -s sə'liʃənl [-ʃn̩], -ʃn̩, -ʃənəl], -z

salicylate sæ'lisileit [sə'l-]

salicylic ˌsæli'silik

salient (s. adj.), **-s** 'seiljənt [-lïənt], -s

saline (s.) **-s** sə'lain, -z

saline (adj.) 'seilain ['sæl-, sə'lain]

Saline (in Fifeshire) 'sælin, (in U.S.A.) sə'liːn

Salinger 'sælindʒə* ['sei-]

salinity sə'liniti

Salisbury 'sɔːlzbəri ['sɔlz-]

saliva sə'laivə [sl̩'ai-]

salivary 'sælivəri [sə'laivəri, sl̩'aiv-]

sallet, -s 'sælit, -s

sallow (s. adj.), **-s, -y, -ness** 'sæləu, -z, -i, -nis

Sallust 'sæləst

sall|y (s. v.) (S.), **-ies, -ying, -ied** 'sæl|i, -iz, -iiŋ, -id

sally-lunn, -s 'sæli'lʌn, -z

salmi, -s 'sælmi(ː), -z

salmon 'sæmən

Salmon (surname) 'sæmən, 'sælmən, 'sɑːmən, (river, etc., in Canada and U.S.A.) 'sæmən, (biblical name) 'sælmən [-mən]

Salome sə'ləumi [sl̩'əu-]

salon, -s 'sælɔ̃ːŋ [-lɔn] (salɔ̃), -z

Salonica (modern town) sə'lənikə [old-fashioned ˌsælə'niːkə], (in Greek history) ˌsælə'naikə

saloon, -s sə'luːn [sl̩'uːn], -z

Salop 'sæləp

Salopian, -s sə'ləupjən [sļ'əu-, -pɪ̆ən], -z
Salpeter (English name) 'sælpi:tə*
salpiglossis ,sælpi'glɔsis
Salsette sɔ:l'set [sɔl-]
salsify 'sælsifi
salt (s. adj.v.) (S.), -s ; -er, -est, -ly, -ness,
   -ish ; -ing, -ed, -er/s sɔ:lt [sɔlt], -s ;
   -ə*, -ist, -li, -nis, -iʃ; -iŋ, -id, -ə*/z
saltant 'sæltənt ['sɔ:l-, 'sɔl-]
Saltash 'sɔ:lt-æʃ ['sɔlt-]
saltation sæl'teiʃən
salt-cellar, -s 'sɔ:lt,selə* ['sɔlt-], -z
Salter, -ton 'sɔ:ltə* ['sɔl-], -tən
Saltfleetby 'sɔ:lt,fli:tbi ['sɔlt-, locally
   also 'sɔləbi]
Salting 'sɔ:ltiŋ ['sɔl-]
saltire, -s 'sɔ:ltaiə* ['sæl-], -z
Saltmarsh 'sɔ:ltmɑ:ʃ ['sɔlt-]
Saltoun 'sɔ:ltən ['sɔlt-]
saltpetre 'sɔ:lt,pi:tə* ['sɔlt-, -'--]
saltspoon, -s 'sɔ:lt-spu:n ['sɔlt-], -z
salt|y, -ier, -iest, -iness 'sɔ:lt|i ['sɔl-],
   -ɪə* [-jə*], -iist [-jist], -inis
salubrious, -ly, -ness sə'lu:brɪəs [sļ'u:-,
   sə'lju:-], -li, -nis
salubrity sə'lu:briti [sļ'u:-, sə'lju:-]
Salusbury (surname) 'sɔ:lzbəri
Salut (in Port Salut) sə'lu: (saly)
Salutaris ,sælju(:)'teəris [-'tɑ:r-]
salutary 'sæljutəri
salutation, -s ,sælju(:)'teiʃən, -z
salut|e (s. v.), -es, -ing, -ed sə'lu:t
   [sļ'u:t, sə'lju:t], -s, -iŋ, -id
salvable 'sælvəbl
Salvador 'sælvədɔ:* [,sælvə'dɔ:*]
salvag|e (s. v.), -es, -ing, -ed 'sælvidʒ,
   -iz, -iŋ, -d
salvarsan 'sælvəsən [-sæn]
salvation, -s sæl'veiʃən, -z
salvationi|sm,   -st/s   sæl'veiʃn̩i|zəm
   [-ʃəni-], -st/s
salv|e (s. v.) (anoint, soothe, etc.), -es,
   -ing, -ed sɑ:v [sælv], -z, -iŋ, -d
salv|e (save ship, cargo), -es, -ing, -ed
   sælv, -z, -iŋ, -d
Salve (Catholic antiphon), -s 'sælvi, -z
salver, -s 'sælvə*, -z
salvia, -s 'sælvɪə [-vjə], -z
Salviati ,sælvi'ɑ:ti
salvo, -es 'sælvəu, -z
sal volatile ,sælvə'lætəli [-vəu'l-, -vu'l-,
   -tļi]
Salzburg 'sæltsbə:g ['sɑ:l-] ('zaltsburk,
   -burç)
Sam sæm
Samarkand ,sæmɑ:'kænd
Samaria sə'mɛərɪə [sm̩'ɛə-]
Samaritan, -s sə'mæritn [sm̩'æ-], -z

same, -ness seim, -nis
samite 'sæmait ['seim-]
Sammy 'sæmi
samnite, -s 'sæmnait, -s
Samoa, -n/s sə'məuə [sɑ:'m-], -n/z
Samos 'seimɔs
Samothrace 'sæməuθreis
Samothracian, -s ,sæməu'θreiʃjən [-ʃɪən,
   -ʃən], -z
samovar, -s ,sæməu'vɑ:* ['---] (səma-
   'var), -z
Samoyed, -s (people) ,sæmɔi'ed, (dog)
   sə'mɔied, -z
sampan, -s 'sæmpæn, -z
samphire 'sæmfaiə*
samp|le (s. v.), -les, -ling, -led 'sɑ:mp|ļ,
   -lz, -liŋ [-ļiŋ], -ld
sampler, -s 'sɑ:mplə*, -z
Sampson 'sæmpsn
Samson 'sæmsn [-mps-]
Samuda sə'mju:də
Samuel, -s 'sæmjuəl [-mjwəl, -mjul], -z
samurai, -s 'sæmurai, -z
sanatorium, -s ,sænə'tɔ:rɪəm, -z
sanatory 'sænətəri
Sancho Panza 'sæntʃəu'pænzə [-kəu-]
sanctification ,sæŋktifi'keiʃən
sancti|fy, -fies, -fying, -fied 'sæŋkti|fai,
   -faiz, -faiiŋ, -faid
sanctimonious, -ly, -ness ,sæŋkti-
   'məunjəs [-nɪəs], -li, -nis
sancti|on (s. v.), -ons, -oning, -oned
   'sæŋkʃ|ən, -ənz, -ŋiŋ [-əniŋ], -ənd
sanctity 'sæŋktiti
sanctuar|y, -ies 'sæŋktjŭər|i [-tjwər-,
   -tjur-], -iz
sanctum, -s 'sæŋktəm, -z
Sanctus, -es 'sæŋktəs, -iz
sand sænd
sandal, -s ; -wood 'sændl, -z ; -wud
Sandbach 'sændbætʃ
sandbag, -s 'sændbæg, -z
sandbank, -s 'sændbæŋk, -s
sandboy, -s 'sændbɔi, -z
Sander|s, -son 'sɑ:ndə|z, -sn
Sanderstead 'sɑ:ndəsted
sandfl|y, -ies 'sændfl|ai, -aiz
Sand|ford, -gate 'sænd|fəd, -git [-geit]
sandhi 'sændhi: ['sʌn-, -di:] (Hind.
   səndhi)
sandhopper, -s 'sænd,hɔpə*, -z
Sandhurst 'sændhə:st
Sandling 'sændliŋ
sand|man, -men 'sænd|mæn, -men
San Domingo ,sændəu'miŋgəu [-dəu'm-,
Sandown 'sændaun   [-dɔ'm-]
sand-pap|er (s. v.), -ers, -ering, -ered
   'sænd,peip|ə*, -əz, -əriŋ, -əd

Sandra 'sændrə ['sɑːn-]
Sandringham 'sændriŋəm
sandstone 'sændstəun
sandstorm, -s 'sændstɔːm, -z
sandwi|ch (s. v.), -ches, -ching, -ched
  'sænwi|dʒ [-tʃ], -dʒiz [-tʃiz], -dʒiŋ
  [-tʃiŋ], -dʒd [-tʃt]
  Note.—Some people use -tʃ in the
  uninflected form and -dʒ- in the inflected forms of this word.
Sandwich (in Kent) 'sænwitʃ [-ndw-,
  -widʒ, old-fashioned 'sænidʒ]
sandwich|man, -men 'sænwidʒ|mæn
  [-itʃ-], -men
sand|y (S.), -ier, -iest, -iness 'sænd|i,
  -ïə* [-jə*], -iist [-jist], -inis
Sandys sændz
sane, -r, -st, -ly, -ness sein, -ə*, -ist, -li,
  -nis
Sanford 'sænfəd
sanforiz|e [-is|e], -es, -ing, -ed 'sæn-
  fəraiz, -iz, -iŋ, -d
San Francisco ˌsænfrən'siskəu
sang (from sing) sæŋ
Sanger 'sæŋgə*, 'sæŋə*
sang-froid 'sãː:ŋ'frwɑ: ['sɔ̃ː-, 'sɑː:ŋ*,
  'sɔ:ŋ-, 'sɔŋ-, 'sæŋ-, -'frwɔ:] (sãfrwɑ)
sanguinar|y, -ily, -iness 'sæŋgwinər|i,
  -ili, -inis
sanguine, -ly, -ness 'sæŋgwin, -li, -nis
sanguineous sæŋ'gwinïəs [-njəs]
Sanhedri|m, -n 'sænidri|m [-ned-, -nəd-,
  Jewish pronunciation sæn'hed-], -n
sanitar|y, -ily, -iness 'sænitər|i, -ili, -inis
sanitation ˌsæni'teiʃən
sanity 'sæniti
sank (from sink) sæŋk
Sankey 'sæŋki
San Marino ˌsænmə'riːnəu
Sanquhar 'sæŋkə*
San Remo sæn'reiməu [-'riː-m-]
sans (English word) sænz, (in French
  phrases) sãː:ŋ [sɔ̃ː:ŋ] (sã)
Sanscrit see Sanskrit
sanserif sæn'serif
Sanskrit 'sænskrit
sanskritic sæns'kritik
sanskritiz|e [-is|e], -es, -ing, -ed
  'sænskritaiz, -iz, -iŋ, -d
Santa Claus ˌsæntə'klɔ:z ['---]
Santa Fé ˌsæntə'fei
Santander ˌsæntən'deə* [ˌsæntæn'deə*,
  sæn'tændə*] (santan'der)
Santiago ˌsænti'ɑːgəu
Santley 'sæntli
Saône səun (soːn)
sap (s. v.), -s, -ping, -ped, -per/s sæp,
  -s, -iŋ, -t, -ə*/z

Sapele (place in Nigeria) 'sæpili,
  (mahogany from that district) sə'piːli
sapien|ce, -t/ly 'seipjən|s [-pïən-], -t/li
Sapir (Amer. linguist) sə'piə*
sapless 'sæplis
sapling, -s 'sæpliŋ, -z
saponaceous ˌsæpəu'neiʃəs
sapper, -s 'sæpə*, -z
Sapphic, -s 'sæfik, -s
Sapphira sə'faiərə [sæ'f-]
sapphire, -s 'sæfaiə*, -z
Sappho 'sæfəu
sapp|y, -iness 'sæp|i, -inis
Sapt sæpt
saraband, -s 'særəbænd, -z
Saracen, -s 'særəsn [-sin, -sen], -z
Saracenic ˌsærə'senik
Saragossa ˌsærə'gɔsə
Sarah 'seərə
sarai (palace), -s sə'rai [sɑː'rai], -z
Sarai (wife of Abram) 'seəreiai [-riai]
Sarajevo ˌsærə'jeivəu
Sarasate ˌsærə'sɑːti
Saratoga ˌsærə'təugə
Sarawak sə'rɑːwək [-wæk, -wə, ˌsærə-
  'wæk]
  Note.—Those who have lived in
  Sarawak pronounce sə'rɑːwək or
  sə'rɑːwə.
sarcasm, -s 'sɑː:kæzəm, -z
sarcastic, -ally sɑː'kæstik, -əli
sarcoma, -s, -ta sɑː'kəumə, -z, -tə
sarcopha|gus, -guses, -gi sɑː'kɔfə|gəs,
  -gəsiz, -gai [-dʒai]
Sardanapalus ˌsɑː:də'næpələs [-nə'pɑː:ləs]
sardine (fish), -s sɑː'diːn ['-'-, '--], -z
sardine (stone) 'sɑː:dain
Sardinia, -n/s sɑː'dinjə [-nïə], -n/z
Sardis 'sɑː:dis
sardius, -es 'sɑː:dïəs [-djəs], -iz
sardonic, -ally sɑː'dɔnik, -əli
sardonyx, -es 'sɑː:dəniks ['sɑː:d,ɔn-, -'--],
  [-iz
Sarepta sə'reptə
Sargant 'sɑː:dʒənt
sargasso (S.), -(e)s sɑː'gæsəu, -z
Sargeant 'sɑː:dʒənt
Sargent, -s 'sɑː:dʒənt, -s
sari, -s 'sɑː:ri(ː) (Hind. saṭi], -z
Sark sɑː:k
Sarma|tia, -tian/s sɑː'mei|ʃïə [-ʃïə,
  -ʃə], -ʃjən/z [-ʃïən/z, -ʃən/z]
sarong, -s sə'rɔŋ ['sɑː:r-, 'sær-], -z
Saroyan sə'rɔiən
sarsaparilla ˌsɑː:səpə'rilə
sarsenet 'sɑː:snit [-net]
Sartor 'sɑː:tɔ:*
sartorial sɑː'tɔ:rïəl
Sarum 'seərəm

sash, -es sæʃ, -iz
Saskatchewan səs'kætʃiwən [sæs-, -wɔn]
sassafras, -es 'sæsəfræs, -iz
Sassanian sæ'seinjən [-nɪən]
Sassenach, -s 'sæsənæk [-nək, -nəx], -s
Sassoon sə'suːn
sat (*from* sit) sæt
Satan 'seitən [*old-fashioned* 'sæt-]
satanic, -ally sə'tænik [sei't-], -əli
satchel, -s 'sætʃəl, -z
sat|e, -es, -ing, -ed seit, -s, -iŋ, -id
sateen, -s sæ'tiːn [sə't-], -z
satellite, -s 'sætəlait [-til-, -tl-], -s
satiable 'seiʃjəbl [-ʃiə-, -ʃə-]
satiat|e, -es, -ing, -ed 'seiʃieit [-ʃjeit], -s, -iŋ, -id
satiation ˌseiʃi'eiʃən
satiety sə'taiəti [-aiiti, 'seiʃjəti, 'seiʃiəti]
satin, -s, -y 'sætin, -z, -i
satinette ˌsæti'net ['sæti'n-]
satin-wood 'sætinwud
satire, -s 'sætaiə*, -z
satiric|al, -ally, -alness sə'tirik|əl, -əli, -əlnis
satirist, -s 'sætərist [-tir-], -s
satiriz|e [-is|e], -es, -ing, -ed 'sætəraiz [-tir-], -iz, -iŋ, -d
satisfaction ˌsætis'fækʃən
satisfactor|y, -ily, -iness ˌsætis'fæktər|i, -ili, -inis
satis|fy, -fies, -fying, -fied 'sætis|fai, -faiz, -faiiŋ, -faid
Satow 'sɑːtəu
satrap, -s; -y, -ies 'sætrəp, -s; -i, -iz
Satsuma 'sætsumə [sæt'suːmə]
saturat|e, -es, -ing, -ed 'sætʃəreit [-tʃur-, -tjur-], -s, -iŋ, -id
saturation ˌsætʃə'reiʃən [-tʃu'r-, -tju'r-]
Saturday, -s 'sætədi [-dei], -z
Saturn 'sætən [-təːn]
saturnalia (S.) ˌsætəː'neiljə [-tə'n-, -lɪə]
saturnian sæ'təːnjən [sə't-, -nɪən]
saturnine 'sætənain
satyr, -s 'sætə*, -z
satyric sə'tirik
sauce, -s sɔːs, -iz
sauce-boat, -s 'sɔːsbəut, -s
saucepan, -s 'sɔːspən, -z
saucer, -s 'sɔːsə*, -z
sauce-tureen, -s 'sɔːs-tə,riːn [-tu,r-, -tju,r-], -z
Sauchiehall ˌsɔːki'hɔːl ['---] (*Scottish* ˌsɔxi'hɔl)
sauc|y, -ier, -iest, -ily, -iness 'sɔːs|i, -ɪə* [-jə*], -iist [-jist], -ili, -inis
sauerkraut 'sauəkraut ('zauərkraut)
Saul sɔːl

Sault St. Marie (*in Ontario*) 'suː-seint-mə'riː:
sauna 'saunə ['sɔːnə]
Saunder|s, -son 'sɔːndə|z, 'sɑːndə|z, -sn
saunt|er, -ers, -ering, -ered 'sɔːnt|ə*, -əz, -əriŋ, -əd
saurian, -s 'sɔːrɪən, -z
sausage, -s 'sɔsidʒ, -iz
Sausmarez 'sɔməriz [-rez]
sauté, -s 'səutei, -z
Sauterne, -s səu'təːn [-'tɛən], -z
Sauvage (*Eng. surname*) 'sævidʒ, səu'vɑːʒ
savage (*s. adj.*) (S.), -s, -st, -ly, -ness; -ry 'sævidʒ, -iz, -ist, -li, -nis; -əri
savanna(h) (S.), -s sə'vænə, -z
savant, -s 'sævənt, -s
sav|e (*s. v. prep. conj.*), -es, -ing, -ed seiv, -z, -iŋ, -d
Save (*river in Jugoslavia*) 'sɑːvi
saveloy, -s 'sævilɔi [ˌsævi'lɔi, -və-], -z
Savels (*surname*) 'sævəlz
Savernake 'sævə(ː)næk
Savile 'sævil [-vl]
saving (*s. adj. prep.*), -s 'seiviŋ, -z
saviour (S.), -s 'seivjə*, -z
savitri (*Brahmin investiture*) 'sɑːvitri(ː) (*Hind.* savytri)
savoir faire 'sævwɑː'fɛə* [-vwɔː-] (savwarfɛːr)
Savonarola ˌsævənə'rəulə [-vn̩ə-]
savory (S.) 'seivəri
sav|our (*s. v.*), -ours, -ouring, -oured; -ourless 'seiv|ə*, -əz, -əriŋ, -əd; -əlis
savour|y (*s. adj.*), -ies, -ily, -iness 'seivər|i, -iz, -ili, -inis
savoy (S.), -s sə'vɔi, -z
Savoyard, -s sə'vɔiɑːd, -z
savvy 'sævi
saw (*s. v.*), -s, -ing, -ed, -n sɔː, -z, -iŋ, -d, -n
saw (*from* see) sɔː
sawbones, -es 'sɔːbəunz, -iz
Sawbridgeworth 'sɔːbridʒwəːθ
sawder 'sɔːdə*
sawdust 'sɔːdʌst
sawfish 'sɔːfiʃ
Sawney, -s 'sɔːni, -z
sawyer (S.), -s 'sɔːjə*, -z
Saxe - Coburg - Gotha (')sæks'kəubəːg-'gəuθə [-'gəutə]
saxhorn, -s 'sækshɔːn, -z
saxifrage, -s 'sæksifridʒ, -iz
Saxon, -s 'sæksn, -z
Saxone (*shoe company*) sæk'səun [*also* 'sæksəun *when attributive*]
Saxony 'sæksni [-səni, -sni]
saxophone, -s 'sæksəfəun, -z

saxophonist, **-s** sæk'sɔfənist ['sæksə-
fəunist], **-s**
*Note.—Professional saxophone players
use the first pronunciation.*
say (*s. v.*); **says; saying/s; said** sei; sez
(*normal form*), səz, siz (*occasional
weak forms*); 'seiiŋ/z; sed (*normal
form*), səd, sid (*occasional weak forms*)
Sayce seis
Saye and Sele 'seiən'si:l
Sayer, **-s** 'seiə*, sɛə*, -z
'sblood zblʌd
scab, **-s, -by, -biness** skæb, -z, -i, -inis
scabbard, **-s** 'skæbəd, -z
scabies 'skeibii:z [-bji:z, -bi:z]
scabious, **-es** 'skeibjəs [-bïəs], -iz
scabrous 'skeibrəs
Scafell 'skɔ:'fel [*also* 'skɔ:-fel, skɔ:'fel,
according to sentence-stress]
scaffold, **-s** 'skæfəld [-fəuld], -z
scaffolding, **-s** 'skæfəldiŋ, -z
Scala 'skɑ:lə
scalable 'skeiləbl
scald (*s. v.*), **-s, -ing, -ed** skɔ:ld, -z, -iŋ,
-id
scal|e (*s. v.*), **-es, -ing, -ed** skeil, -z, -iŋ,
-d
scalene 'skeili:n [skei'li:n, skæ'li:n]
Scaliger 'skælidʒə*
scallion, **-s** 'skæljən [-lïən], -z
scallop (*s. v.*), **-s, -ing, -ed** 'skɔləp, -s, -iŋ,
-t
scallop-shell, **-s** 'skɔləpʃel, -z
scallywag, **-s** 'skæliwæg, -z
scalp (*s. v.*), **-s, -ing, -ed** skælp, -s, -iŋ, -t
scalpel, **-s** 'skælpəl, -z
scall|y, **-ier, -iest, -iness** 'skeil|i, -iə*
[-jə*], -iist [-jist], -inis
Scammell 'skæməl
scamp (*s. v.*), **-s, -ing, -ed** skæmp, -s,
-iŋ, -t [skæmt]
scamp|er (*s. v.*), **-ers, -ering, -ered**
'skæmp|ə*, -əz, -əriŋ, -əd
scampi 'skæmpi
scan, **-s, -ning, -ned** skæn, -z, -iŋ, -d
scandal, **-s** 'skændl, -z
scandalization [-isa-] ˌskændəlai'zeiʃən
[-dˌai-]
scandaliz|e [-is|e], **-es, -ing, -ed**
'skændəlaiz [-dˌaiz], -iz, -iŋ, -d
scandalmong|er, **-ers, -ering** 'skændl-
ˌmʌŋg|ə*, -əz, -əriŋ
scandalous, **-ly, -ness** 'skændələs [-dˌəs],
-li, -nis
scandent 'skændənt
Scandinavia, **-n/s** ˌskændi'neivjə [-vïə],
-n/z
Scanlan 'skænlən

scansion, **-s** 'skænʃən, -z
scant, **-ly** skænt, -li
scant|y, **-ier, -iest, -ily, -iness** 'skænt|i,
-iə* [-jə*], -iist [-jist], -ili, -inis
Scapa Flow 'skæpə'fləu
scape, **-s; -goat/s, -grace/s** skeip, -s;
-gəut/s, -greis/iz
scapul|a, **-as, -ae, -ar** 'skæpjul|ə, -əz, -i:,
-ə*
scar (*s. v.*) (**S.**), **-s, -ring, -red** skɑ:*, -z,
-riŋ, -d
scarab, **-s** 'skærəb, -z
scarab|aeus, **-aeuses, -aei** ˌskærə-
'b|i(:)əs, -i(:)əsiz, -i:ai
scaramouch, **-es** 'skærəmautʃ [-mu:tʃ],
-iz
Scarborough [-boro'] 'skɑ:brə [-bərə]
Scarbrough 'skɑ:brə
scarc|e, **-er, -est, -ely, -eness; -ity**
skɛəs, -ə*, -ist, -li, -nis; -iti
scar|e (*s. v.*), **-es, -ing, -ed** skɛə*, -z,
-riŋ, -d
scarecrow, **-s** 'skɛə-krəu, -z
scaremong|er, **-ers, -ering** 'skɛəˌmʌŋ-
g|ə*, -əz, -əriŋ
scar|f, **-ves, -fs** skɑ:|f, -vz, -fs
scarf (*v.*), **-s, -ing, -ed** skɑ:f, -s, -iŋ, -t
scarf-pin, **-s** 'skɑ:fpin, -z
scarification ˌskɛərifi'keiʃən [ˌskær-]
scari|fy, **-fies, -fying, -fied** 'skɛəri|fai
['skær-], -faiz, -faiiŋ, -faid
scarlatina ˌskɑ:lə'ti:nə [-li't-]
Scarlatti skɑ:'læti (skar'latti)
scarlet 'skɑ:lit
scarp (*s. v.*), **-s, -ing, -ed** skɑ:p, -s, -iŋ, -t
scarves (*plur. of* scarf) skɑ:vz
Scase skeis
scath|e, **-es, -ing/ly, -ed; -eless** skeið,
-z, -iŋ/li, -d; -lis
scatt|er (*s. v.*), **-ers, -ering, -ered, -erer/s**
'skæt|ə*, -əz, -əriŋ, -əd, -ərə*/z
scatterbrain, **-ed** 'skætəbrein, -z, -d
scaveng|e, **-es, -ing, -ed, -er/s** 'skæv-
indʒ, -iz, -iŋ, -d, -ə*/z
Scawen 'skɔ:in ['skɔ:ən]
Scawfell 'skɔ:'fel [*also* 'skɔ:-fel, skɔ:'fel
according to sentence-stress]
scean dhu, **-s** 'ski:ən'du:, -z
Sceats ski:ts
scena, **-s** 'ʃeinə, -z
scenario, **-s** si'nɑ:riəu [se'n-], -z
scenarist, **-s** 'si:nərist, -s
scene, **-s** si:n, -z
scene-paint|er/s, **-ing** 'si:nˌpeint|ə*/z,
-iŋ
scenery 'si:nəri
scene-shifter, **-s** 'si:nˌʃiftə*, -z
scenic, **-ally** 'si:nik ['sen-], -əli

scent (s. v.), -s, -ing, -ed sent, -s, -iŋ, -id
scent-bag, -s 'sentbæg, -z
scent-bottle, -s 'sent,bɒtl, -z
sceptic (s. adj.), -s, -al, -ally 'skeptik, -s, -əl, -əli
scepticism 'skeptisizəm
sceptre, -s, -d 'septə*, -z, -d
Scharwenka ʃɑːˈveŋkə
schedul|e (s. v.), -es, -ing, -ed 'ʃedjuːl, -z, -iŋ, -d
Scheherazade ʃi,hiərəˈzɑːdə [ʃə,h-, -di]
Scheldt skelt [ʃelt]
schema, -s, -ta 'skiːmə, -z, -tə
schematic, -ally skiˈmætik [skiːˈm-], -əli
schem|e (s. v.), -es, -ing/ly, -ed, -er/s skiːm, -z, -iŋ/li, -d, -ə*/z
Schenectady skiˈnektədi
scherzando skɛətˈsændəu [skəːt-]
scherzo, -s 'skɛətsəu ['skəːt-], -z
Schiedam skiˈdæm ['--]
Schiehallion ʃiˈhæljən [-lïən]
Schiller 'ʃilə* (ʃilər)
Schipperke, -s 'ʃipəki ['ski-], -z ['ʃipək, -s]
schism, -s 'sizəm ['ski-], -z
schismatic, -al sizˈmætik, -əl
schist, -s, -ose ʃist, -s, -əus
schizophrenia ,skitsəuˈfriːnjə [,skidzəu-, -nïə]
schizophrenic, -s ,skitsəuˈfrenik [,skidzəu-], -s
Schleswig 'ʃlezwig [-zvig] ('ʃleːsviç)
schnap(p)s ʃnæps
Schofield 'skəufiːld
scholar, -s, -ly 'skɔlə*, -z, -li
scholarship, -s 'skɔləʃip, -s
scholastic, -ally skəˈlæstik [skɔˈl-], -əli
scholasticism skəˈlæstisizəm [skɔˈl-]
Scholes skəulz
scholiast, -s 'skəuliæst, -s
scho|lium, -lia 'skəu|ljəm [-lïəm], -ljə [-lïə]
Scholl (surname) ʃɔl, ʃəul
school (s. v.), -s, -ing, -ed skuːl, -z, -iŋ, -d
school-book, -s 'skuːlbuk, -s
schoolboy, -s 'skuːlbɔi, -z
schoolfellow, -s 'skuːl,feləu, -z
schoolgirl, -s 'skuːlgəːl [rarely -gəəl], -z
schoolhous|e, -ses 'skuːlhau|s, -ziz
school|man, -men 'skuːl|mən [-mæn], -mən [-men]
school-marm, -s 'skuːlmɑːm, -z
schoolmaster, -s 'skuːl,mɑːstə*, -z
schoolmate, -s 'skuːlmeit, -s
schoolmistress, -es 'skuːl,mistris, -iz

schoolroom, -s 'skuːlrum [-ruːm], -z
school-teacher, -s 'skuːl,tiːtʃə*, -z
school-time 'skuːl-taim
schooner, -s 'skuːnə*, -z
Schopenhauer 'ʃəupənhauə* ('ʃoːpən-hauər)
schottische, -s ʃɔˈtiːʃ [ʃəˈt-], -iz
Schouten (in Indonesia) 'skautn
Schreiner 'ʃrainə*
Schubert 'ʃuːbəːt [-bət]
Schumann 'ʃuːmən [-mæn, -mɑːn]
schwa, -s ʃwɑː, -z
Schwabe (English surname) ʃwɑːb
Schwann (English surname) ʃwɔn
Schweppe, -s ʃwep, -s
sciatic, -a saiˈætik, -ə
science, -s 'saiəns ['sai-əns], -iz
scientific, -ally ,saiənˈtifik [,sai-ən-], -əli
scientist, -s 'saiəntist ['sai-ən-], -s
scilicet 'sailiset
Scillonian, -s siˈləunjən [-nïən], -z
Scill|y, -ies 'sil|i, -iz
scimitar, -s 'simitə*, -z
scintilla sinˈtilə
scintillat|e, -es, -ing, -ed 'sintileit, -s, -iŋ, -id
scintillation, -s ,sintiˈleiʃən, -z
scioli|sm, -st/s 'sai-əuli|zəm, -st/s
scion, -s 'sai-ən, -z
Scipio 'skipiəu ['si-]
scire facias 'saiəriˈfeiʃiæs [-ʃjæs, -ʃjəs, -fjəs]
scirrhous 'sirəs [-ʃïəs]
scirrh|us, -i 'sir|əs, -ai
scission, -s 'siʒən ['siʃən], -z
scissors 'sizəz
scleros|is, -es skliəˈrəus|is [skliˈr-, skleˈr-, sklə'r-], -iːz
sclerotic skliəˈrɔtik [skliˈr-, skleˈr-, sklə'r-]
scoff, -s, -ing/ly, -ed, -er/s skɔf, -s, -iŋ/li, -t, -ə*/z
Scofield 'skəufiːld
scold, -s, -ing/s, -ed skəuld, -z, -iŋ/z, -id
scoliosis ,skɔliˈəusis
scollop (s. v.), -s, -ing, -ed 'skɔləp, -s, -iŋ, -t
sconc|e (s. v.), -es, -ing, -ed skɔns, -iz, -iŋ, -t
scone, -s skɔn [skəun], -z
Scone (in Scotland) skuːn
scoop (s. v.), -s, -ing, -ed, -er/s skuːp, -s, -iŋ, -t, -ə*/z
scoot (s. v.), -s, -ing, -ed skuːt, -s, -iŋ, -id
scooter, -s 'skuːtə*, -z
scope, -s skəup, -s
scorbutic skɔːˈbjuːtik
scorch (s. v.), -es, -ing/ly, -ed, -er/s skɔːtʃ, -iz, -iŋ/li, -t, -ə*/z

scor|e (*s. v.*), -es, -ing, -ed, -er/s skɔ:* [skɔə*], -z, -riŋ, -d, -rə*/z
scoria 'skɔ:rɪə ['skɔr-]
scoriaceous ˌskɔ:ri'eiʃəs [ˌskɔr-]
scorn (*s. v.*), -s, -ing, -ed skɔ:n, -z, -iŋ, -d
scorn|ful, -fully, -fulness 'skɔ:n|fʊl, -fuli [-fəli], -fʊlnis
Scorpio (*constellation*) 'skɔ:piəu [-pjəu]
scorpion, -s 'skɔ:pjən [-pɪən], -z
scot (S.), -s skɔt, -s
scotch (*s. v.*) (S.), -es, -ing, -ed skɔtʃ, -iz, -iŋ, -t
Scotch|man, -men 'skɔtʃ|mən, -mən
Scotch|woman, -women 'skɔtʃ|ˌwumən, -ˌwimin
scot-free 'skɔt'fri:
Scotia 'skəuʃə
Scotland 'skɔtlənd
Scots (*adj.*) skɔts
Scots|man, -men 'skɔts|mən, -mən
Scots|woman, -women 'skɔts|ˌwumən, -ˌwimin
Scott skɔt
scottice 'skɔtisi(:)
scotticism, -s 'skɔtisizəm, -z
scotticiz|e [-is|e], -es, -ing, -ed 'skɔtisaiz, -iz, -iŋ, -d
Scottish 'skɔtiʃ
scoundr|el, -els, -elly 'skaundr|əl, -əlz, -əli [-ḷi]
scour (*s. v.*), -s, -ing, -ed 'skauə*, -z, -riŋ, -d
scourg|e (*s. v.*), -es, -ing, -ed skə:dʒ, -iz, -iŋ, -d
scout (*s. v.*), -s, -ing, -ed skaut, -s, -iŋ, -id
scoutmaster, -s 'skautˌmɑːstə*, -z
scow, -s skau, -z
Scowen 'skəuən [-in]
scowl (*s. v.*), -s, -ing/ly, -ed skaul, -z, -iŋ/li, -d
scrabb|le, -les, -ling, -led 'skræb|ḷ, -lz, -liŋ [-liŋ], -ld
scrag (*s. v.*), -s, -ging, -ged; -gy, -gier, -giest, -gily, -giness skræg, -z, -iŋ, -d; -i, -iə*, -iist, -ili, -inis
scramb|le (*s. v.*), -les, -ling, -led 'skræmb|ḷ, -lz, -liŋ, [-liŋ], -ld
scrap (*s. v.*), -s, -ping, -ped; -py, -pier, -piest, -pily, -piness skræp, -s, -iŋ, -t; -i, -iə*, -iist, -ili, -inis
scrap|e (*s. v.*), -es, -ing/s, -ed, -er/s skreip, -s, -iŋ/z, -t, -ə*/z
scrap|y, -ier, -iest, -ily, -iness 'skreip|i, -iə* [-jə*], -iist [-jist], -ili, -inis

scratch (*s. v.*), -es, -ing, -ed; -y, -ier, -iest, -ily, -iness skrætʃ, -iz, -iŋ, -t; -i, -iə*, -iist, -ili, -inis
scrawl (*s. v.*), -s, -ing, -ed; -y, -ier, -iest, -ily, -iness skrɔ:l, -z, -iŋ, -d; -i, -iə* [-jə*], -iist [-jist], -inis
scray, -s skrei, -z
scream (*s. v.*), -s, -ing, -ed, -er/s; -y, -ier, -iest, -ily, -iness skri:m, -z, -iŋ, -d, -ə*/z; -i, -iə* [-jə*], -iist [-jist], -ili, -inis
scree, -s skri:, -z
screech (*s. v.*), -es, -ing, -ed, -er/s skri:tʃ, -iz, -iŋ, -t, -ə*/z
screech-owl, -s 'skri:tʃ-aul, -z
screed, -s skri:d, -z
screen (*s. v.*), -s, -ing, -ed skri:n, -z, -iŋ, -d
screen-play, -s 'skri:n-plei, -z
screen-writer, -s 'skri:nˌraitə*, -z
screw (*s. v.*), -s, -ing, -ed skru:, -z, -iŋ [skruiŋ], -d
screw-cap, -s 'skru:'kæp ['--], -s
screw-driver, -s 'skru:ˌdraivə*, -z
screw-steamer, -s 'skru:ˌsti:mə*, -z
screw-top, -s 'skru:'tɔp ['skru:-tɔp], -s
Scriabin 'skriəbin [skri'æbin] ('skrjabjin)
scribal 'skraibəl
scribb|le (*s. v.*), -les, -ling, -led, -ler/s 'skrib|ḷ, -lz, -liŋ [-liŋ], -ld, -ḷə*/z [-lə*/z]
scribbling-paper 'skribliŋˌpeipə* [-bliŋ-]
scribe, -s skraib, -z
Scriblerus skrib'liərəs
Scribner 'skribnə*
scrim skrim
scrimmage, -s 'skrimidʒ, -iz
scrimp, -s, -ing, -ed skrimp, -s, -iŋ, -t [skrimt]
scrip, -s skrip, -s
scripsit 'skripsit
script (*s. v.*), -s, -ing, -ed, -er/s skript, -s, -iŋ, -id, -ə*/z
scriptor|ium, -iums, -ia skrip'tɔ:r|iəm, -iəmz, -iə
scriptur|al, -ally 'skriptʃər|əl [-tʃur-], -əli
scripture (S.), -s 'skriptʃə*, -z
script-writer, -s 'skriptˌraitə*, -z
Scriven 'skrivən
scrivener (S.), -s 'skrivnə*, -z
scrofula 'skrɔfjulə
scrofulous, -ly, -ness 'skrɔfjuləs, -li, -nis
scroll, -s skrəul, -z
Scrooge skru:dʒ
Scroope skru:p
Scrope skru:p, skrəup
scrotum, -s 'skrəutəm, -z
scroung|e, -es, -ing, -ed skraundʒ, -iz, -iŋ, -d

scrub (s. v.), -s, -bing, -bed; -by, -bier,
-biest, -bily, -biness skrʌb, -z, -iŋ, -d;
-i, -ɪə*, -iist, -ili, -inis
scruff, -s skrʌf, -s
scrum, -s skrʌm, -z
scrummage, -s 'skrʌmidʒ, -iz
scrumptious 'skrʌmpʃəs [-mptʃəs]
scrunch, -es, -ing, -ed skrʌntʃ, -iz, -iŋ, -t
scrup|le (s. v.), -les, -ling, -led 'skru:p|l,
-lz, -liŋ [-liŋ], -ld
scrupulosity ˌskru:pju'lɔsiti
scrupulous, -ly, -ness 'skru:pjuləs
[-pjəl-], -li, -nis
scrutator, -s skru:'teitə*, -z
scrutineer, -s ˌskru:ti'niə*, -z
scrutiniz|e [-is|e], -es, -ing, -ed 'skru:-
tinaiz [-tn̩aiz], -iz, -iŋ, -d
scrutin|y, -ies 'skru:tin|i [-tn̩|i], -iz
scr|y, -ies, -ying, -ied skr|ai, -aiz, -aiiŋ,
-aid
Scrymgeour 'skrimdʒə*
Scrymsour 'skrimsə*
scud (s. v.), -s, -ding, -ded skʌd, -z,
-iŋ, -id
Scudamore 'skju:dəmɔ:* [-mɔə*]
scudo, -s 'sku:dou, -z
scuff|le (s. v.), -les, -ling, -led 'skʌf|l,
-lz, -liŋ [-liŋ], -ld
scull (s. v.), -s, -ing, -ed, -er/s skʌl, -z,
-iŋ, -d, -ə*/z
sculler|y, -ies 'skʌlər|i [-lr|i], -iz
scullery-maid, -s 'skʌlərimeid [-lri-], -z
scullion, -s 'skʌljən [-lɪən], -z
sculpsit 'skʌlpsit
sculpt, -s, -ing, -ed skʌlpt, -s, -iŋ, -id
sculptor, -s 'skʌlptə*, -z
sculptur|e (s. v.), -es, -ing, -ed 'skʌlp-
tʃə*, -z, -riŋ ['skʌlptʃriŋ], -d
scum (s. v.), -s, -ming, -med; -my
skʌm, -z, -iŋ, -d; -i
scupper, -s 'skʌpə*, -z
scurf, -y, -iness skə:f, -i, -inis
scurrility skʌ'riliti [skə'r-]
scurrilous, -ly, -ness 'skʌriləs, -li, -nis
scurr|y (s. v.), -ies, -ying, -ied 'skʌr|i,
-iz, -iiŋ, -id
scurv|y (s. adj.), -ier, -iest, -ily, -iness
'skə:v|i, -ɪə* [-jə*], -iist [-jist], -ili,
-inis
Scutari 'sku:təri [sku(:)'tɑ:ri]
scutcheon, -s 'skʌtʃən, -z
scutt|le (s. v.), -les, -ling, -led 'skʌt|l,
-lz, -liŋ [-liŋ], -ld
scut|um, -ums, -a 'skju:t|əm, -əmz, -ə
Scylla 'silə
scyth|e (s. v.), -es, -ing, -ed saið, -z,
-iŋ, -d
Scythia, -n/s 'siðɪə ['siθ-, -jə], -n/z

'sdeath zdeθ
se (note in Tonic Sol-fa), -s si:, -z
sea, -s si:, -z
sea-bird, -s 'si:bə:d, -z
seaboard 'si:bɔ:d [-bɔəd]
sea-borne 'si:bɔ:n [-bɔən]
sea-breeze, -s 'si:'bri:z ['si:bri:z], -iz
Seabright 'si:-brait
sea-captain, -s 'si:'kæptin ['-ˌ--], -z
sea-coast, -s 'si:'kəust ['si:-kəust], -s
sea-cow, -s 'si:'kau, -z
sea-dog, -s 'si:dɔg, -z
sea-elephant, -s 'si:'elifənt, -s
seafar|er/s, -ing 'si:ˌfɛər|ə*/z, -iŋ
sea-fog, -s 'si:'fɔg ['si:-fɔg], -z
Seaford (in Sussex) 'si:fəd [-fɔ:d]
Seaforth, -s 'si:fɔ:θ, -s
Seager 'si:gə*
Seago 'si:gəu
sea-going 'si:ˌgəuiŋ
sea-green 'si:'gri:n ['si:-gri:n]
sea-gull, -s 'si:gʌl, -z
seakale 'si:'keil, ['si:-keil, si:'keil]
seal (s. v.), -s, -ing, -ed, -er/s si:l, -z, -iŋ,
-d, -ə*/z
sealing-wax 'si:liŋwæks
sea-lion, -s 'si:ˌlaiən, -z
sealskin, -s 'si:l-skin, -z
Sealyham, -s 'si:lɪəm, -z
seam (s. v.), -s, -ing, -ed; -less si:m, -z,
-iŋ, -d; -lis
sea|man (S.), -men, -manship 'si:|mən,
-mən [-men], -mənʃip
Seamas 'ʃeiməs
sea-mew, -s 'si:-mju:, -z
seamless 'si:mlis
sea-monster, -s 'si:'mɔnstə*, -z
seamstress, -es 'semstris [-mps-], -iz
Seamus 'ʃeiməs
seamy 'si:mi
Sean ʃɔ:n
seance, -s 'seiɑ̃:ns [-ɔ̃:ns, -ɑ:ns, -ɔ:ns]
sea-pink 'si:'piŋk ⎨(seɑ̃:s), -iz
seaplane, -s 'si:-plein, -z
seaport, -s 'si:-pɔ:t, -s
sea-power 'si:ˌpauə*
sear, -s, -ing, -ed siə*, -z, -riŋ, -d
search (s. v.), -es, -ing/ly, -ed, -er/s
sə:tʃ, -iz, -iŋ/li, -t, -ə*/z
search-light, -s 'sə:tʃ-lait, -s
search-part|y, -ies 'sə:tʃˌpɑ:t|i, -iz
search-warrant, -s 'sə:tʃˌwɔrənt, -s
Searle sə:l
seascape, -s 'si:-skeip, -s
sea-serpent, -s 'si:ˌsə:pənt, -s
seashore 'si:'ʃɔ:* [-'ʃɔə*]
Seashore (surname) 'si:-ʃɔ:* [-ʃɔə*]
seasick, -ness 'si:-sik, -nis

seaside 'si:'said ['si:-said]
seas|on (s. v.), -ons, -oning, -oned 'si:z|n, -nz, -ɲiŋ [-niŋ], -nd
seasonab|le, -ly, -leness 'si:zŋəb|l [-znə-], -li, -lnis
seasonal 'si:zənl [-zŋ], -znl]]
seasoning (s.), -s 'si:zŋiŋ [-zniŋ], -z
season-ticket, -s 'si:zn,tikit ['--'--], -s
seat (s. v.), -s, -ing, -ed si:t, -s, -iŋ, -id
S.E.A.T.O. 'si:təu
Seaton 'si:tn
sea-trout 'si:-traut
Seattle si'ætl
sea-urchin, -s 'si:'ə:tʃin ['-,--], -z
sea-wall, -s 'si:'wɔ:l, -z
seaward 'si:wəd
sea-water 'si:,wɔ:tə*
seaweed 'si:wi:d
seaworth|y, -iness 'si:,wə:ð|i, -inis
sebaceous si'beiʃəs [se'b-]
Sebastian si'bæstjən [se'b-, sə'b-, -tiən]
Sebastopol si'bæstəpl [se'b-, sə'b-, -pɔl]
sec sek
secant, -s 'si:kənt, -s
secateurs ,sekə'tə:z ['səkətə(:)z]
seced|e, -es, -ing, -ed, -er/s si'si:d [si:'s-], -z, -iŋ, -id, -ə*/z
secession, -s si'seʃən, -z
secessionist, -s si'seʃnist [-ʃənist], -s
seclud|e, -es, -ing, -ed si'klu:d, -z, -iŋ, -id
seclusion si'klu:ʒən
second (s. adj. v.) (ordinary senses), -s; -ly; -ing, -ed, -er/s 'sekənd, -z; -li; -iŋ, -id, -ə*/z
second (military term), -s, -ing, -ed si'kɔnd [sə'k-], -z, -iŋ, -id
secondar|y (s. adj.), -ies, -ily 'sekəndər|i, -iz, -ili
second-class 'sekənd'klɑ:s [also '— when attributive]
second hand (of clock or watch), -s 'sekəndhænd, -z
second-hand (adj.) 'sekənd'hænd [when attributive 'sekəndhænd]
Secondi (town in Ghana) ,sekən'di:, (surname) si'kɔndi [sə'k-]
secondment si'kɔndmənt [sə'k-]
secondo, -s se'kɔndəu [si'k-], -z
second-rate 'sekənd'reit [also 'sekənd-reit when attributive]
second-rater, -s 'sekənd'reitə*, -z
secrecy 'si:krisi [-krəs-]
secret (s. adj.), -s, -ly 'si:krit, -s, -li
secretarial ,sekrə'tɛəriəl [-kri't-]
secretariat, -s ,sekrə'tɛəriət [-kri't-, -iæt], -s

secretar|y, -ies; -yship/s 'sekrətri|, [-krit-], -iz; -iʃip/s
secret|e, -es, -ing, -ed si'kri:t [si:'k-], -s, -iŋ, -id
secretion, -s si'kri:ʃən [si:'k-], -z
secretive, -ly, -ness si'kri:tiv ['si:kritiv], -li, -nis
Secrett 'si:krit
sect, -s sekt, -s
sectarian (s. adj.), -s, -ism sek'tɛəriən, -z, -izəm
sectar|y, -ies 'sektər|i, -iz
section, -s 'sekʃən, -z
sec|tional, -tionally 'sek|ʃənl [-ʃnəl, -ʃŋ], -ʃŋ, -ʃənəl], -ʃŋəli [-ʃnəli, -ʃŋli, -ʃŋli, -ʃənəli]
sector, -s 'sektə*, -z
secular, -ly 'sekjulə*, -li
seculari|sm, -st/s 'sekjuləri|zəm, -st/s
secularity ,sekju'læriti
secularization [-isa-] 'sekjulərai'zeiʃən [,sek-, -ri'z-]
seculariz|e [-is|e], -es, -ing, -ed 'sekjuləraiz, -iz, -iŋ, -d
secur|e (adj. v.), -er, -est, -ely; -es, -ing, -ed; -able si'kjuə* [sə'k-, -'kjɔə*, -'kjɔ:*, -'kjə:*], -rə*, -rist, -li; -z, -riŋ, -d; -rəbl
securit|y, -ies si'kjuərit|i [sə'k-, -'kjɔər-, -'kjɔ:r-, -'kjə:r-], -iz
Sedan si'dæn [sə'd-]
sedan-chair, -s si'dæn-tʃɛə* [sə'd-, [-'-'-], -z
sedate, -ly, -ness si'deit, -li, -nis
sedative (s. adj.), -s 'sedətiv, -z
Sedbergh (public school) 'sedbə* [-bə:g], (name of town) 'sedbə*
Sedd|ing, -on 'sed|iŋ, -n
sedentar|y, -ily, -iness 'sedntər|i, -ili, -inis
sedge, -s sedʒ, -iz
Sedge|field, -moor 'sedʒ|fi:ld, -muə* [-mɔə*, -mɔ:*]
sedge-warbler, -s 'sedʒ,wɔ:blə* ['-'--], -z
Sedgley 'sedʒli
Sedgwick 'sedʒwik
sedil|e, -ia se'dail|i [si'd-], -jə [-ĭə, -'diljə, -'diliə]
sediment, -s 'sedimənt, -s
sedimentary ,sedi'mentəri
sedition, -s si'diʃən [sə'd-], -z
seditious, -ly, -ness si'diʃəs [sə'd-], -li, -nis
Sedlescombe 'sedlskəm
Sedley 'sedli
seduc|e, -es, -ing, -ed, -er/s, -ement/s si'dju:s, -iz, -iŋ, -t, -ə*/z, -mənt/s
seduction, -s si'dʌkʃən, -z

seductive, -ly, -ness si'dʌktiv, -li, -nis
sedulous, -ly, -ness 'sedjuləs, -li, -nis
sedum, -s 'si:dəm, -z
see (s. v.) (S.), -s, -ing, saw, seen si:, -z,
   -iŋ, sɔ:, si:n
seed (s. v.), -s, -ing, -ed si:d, -z, -iŋ, -id
seed-cake 'si:dkeik
seedless 'si:dlis
seedling, -s 'si:dliŋ, -z
seed-pearl, -s 'si:d'pə:l ['--], -z
seed-potato, -es 'si:dpə'teitəu ['--,--], -z
seeds|man, -men 'si:dz|mən, -mən
   [-men]
seed-time, -s 'si:dtaim, -z
seed|y, -ier, -iest, -ily, -iness 'si:d|i, -ïə*
   [-jə*], -iist [-jist], -ili, -inis
seek, -s, -ing, sought, seeker/s si:k, -s,
   -iŋ, sɔ:t, 'si:kə*/z
Seel(e)y 'si:li
seem, -s, -ing/ly, -ed si:m, -z, -iŋ/li, -d
seeml|y, -ier, -iest, -iness 'si:ml|i, -ïə*
   [-jə*], -iist [-jist], -inis
seen (from see) si:n
seep, -s, -ing, -ed si:p, -s, -iŋ, -t
seepage 'si:pidʒ
seer (one who sees), -s 'si(:)ə*, -z
seer (Indian weight), -s siə*, -z
seersucker 'siə,sʌkə*
seesaw (Most v.), -s, -ing, -ed 'si:-sɔ:
   ['si:'sɔ:], -z, -iŋ, -d
seeth|e, -es, -ing, -ed si:ð, -z, -iŋ, -d
segment (s.), -s 'segmənt, -s
segment (v.), -s, -ing, -ed seg'ment
   ['--, səg'm-], -s, -iŋ, -id
segregate (adj.) 'segrigit [-geit]
segregat|e (v.), -es, -ing, -ed 'segrigeit,
   -s, -iŋ, -id
segregation ,segri'geiʃən
Seidlitz 'sedlits
Seigel 'si:gəl
seignior, -s 'seinjə* [-nïə*, rarely 'si:n-],
   -z
Seignior (surname) 'si:njə*
seignior|y, -ies 'seinjər|i [-nïər-, rarely
   'si:n-], -iz
seine (net), -s sein, -z
Seine (river in France) sein (sɛn, sɛ:n)
seis|ed, -in/s si:z|d, -in/z
seismic 'saizmik
seismograph, -s 'saizməgrɑ:f [-məug-,
   -græf], -s
seismograph|er/s, -y saiz'mɔgrəf|ə*/z,
   -i
seismographic ,saizmə'græfik [-məu'g-]
seismologic|al, -ally ,saizmə'lɔdʒik|əl
   [-məu'l-], -əli
seismolog|ist/s, -y saiz'mɔlədʒ|ist/s, -i
seismometer, -s saiz'mɔmitə*, -z

seizable 'si:zəbl
seiz|e, -es, -ing, -ed si:z, -iz, -iŋ, -d
seizin, -s 'si:zin, -z
seizure, -s 'si:ʒə*, -z
sejant 'si:dʒənt
Sejanus si'dʒeinəs [se'dʒ-]
selah, -s 'si:lə, -z
Selangor sə'læŋə* [-ŋɔ:*]
Sell|borne, -by 'sel|bɔ:n [-bən], -bi
Selden 'seldən
seldom 'seldəm
select (adj. v.), -ness; -s, -ing, -ed,
   -or/s; -ive/ly si'lekt [sə'l-], -nis; -s,
   -iŋ, -id, -ə*/z; -iv/li
selectee, -s ,selek'ti: [sil-], -z
selection, -s si'lekʃən [sə'l-], -z
selective si'lektiv [sə'l-]
selectivity silek'tiviti [,sel-]
Selena si'li:nə [sə'l-]
selenite (substance) 'selinait
Selenite (inhabitant of moon), -s
   si'li:nait [sə'l-], -s
selenium si'li:njəm [sə'l-, -nïəm]
Seleucia, -n/s si'lju:ʃjə [sə'l-, -'lu:-, -ʃïə,
   -sjə, -sïə], -n/z
Seleucid, -s si'lju:sid [se'l-, -'lu:-], -z
Seleucus si'lju:kəs [se'l-, -'lu:-]
sel|f, -ves sel|f, -vz
   Note.—Most compounds with self-
   have double stress, e.g. self-com-
   placent 'selfkəm'pleisənt, self-con-
   fidence 'self'kɔnfidəns, self-support-
   ing 'self-sə'pɔ:tiŋ. Only a few of the
   most important are given below.
self-centred 'self'sentəd
self-command 'selfkə'mɑ:nd
self-conscious, -ness 'self'kɔnʃəs, -nis
self-contained 'selfkən'teind
self-control, -led 'selfkən'trəul, -d
self-deception 'selfdi'sepʃən
self-defence 'selfdi'fens
self-denial 'selfdi'naiəl
self-denying 'selfdi'naiiŋ
self-determination 'selfdi,tə:mi'neiʃən
self-employed 'self-im'plɔid [-em-]
self-esteem 'self-is'ti:m [-es-]
self-evident 'self'evidənt
self-explanatory   'self-iks'plænətəri
   [-eks-, -nit-]
self-governing 'self'gʌvəniŋ [-vṇiŋ]
self - government   'self'gʌvnmənt
   [-vṃmənt, -vənmənt, -vəmənt]
self-importan|ce, -t 'self-im'pɔ:tən|s, -t
self-indulgen|ce, -t 'self-in'dʌldʒən|s, -t
self-interest 'self'intrist [-tərest, -trəst]
selfish, -ly, -ness 'selfiʃ, -li, -nis
self-made 'self'meid [also '-- when
   attributive]

self-possessed 'selfpə'zest [-pu'z-]
self-possession 'selfpə'zeʃən
self-preservation 'self,prezə(:)'veiʃən
self-relian|ce, -t 'self-ri'laiən|s [-rə'l-], -t
self-respect 'self-ris'pekt [-rəs-]
self-respecting 'self-ris,pektiŋ [-rəs-]
self-restraint 'self-ris'treint
Selfridge 'selfridʒ
self-righteous 'self'raitʃəs [-tjəs]
self-sacrifice 'self'sækrifais
selfsame 'selfseim
self-satisfaction 'self,sætis'fækʃən
self-satisfied 'self'sætisfaid
self-starter, -s 'self'stɑ:tə*, -z
self-styled 'self'staild ['self-staild]
self-sufficien|cy, -t 'selfsə'fiʃən|si, -t
self-taught 'self'tɔ:t
self-will, -ed 'self'wil, -d
self-winding 'self'waindiŋ ['self,waindiŋ]
Selim (Sultan of Turkey) 'si:lim ['sel-]
Selkirk 'selkə:k
sell (s. v.) (S.), -s, -ing, sold, seller/s
  sel, -z, -iŋ, səuld, 'selə*/z
Sellar 'selə*
Selous sə'lu:
Selsey 'selsi
Seltzer, -s 'seltsə*, -z
selvage, -s 'selvidʒ, -iz
selvedge, -s 'selvidʒ, -iz
selves (plur. of self) selvz
selvyt, -s 'selvit, -s
Selwyn 'selwin
semantic, -s, -ally si'mæntik [se'm-,
  sə'm-], -s, -əli
semanticism si'mæntisizəm [se'm-,
  sə'm-]
semanticiz|e [-is|e], -es, -ing, -ed
  si'mæntisaiz [se'm-, sə'm-], -iz, -iŋ, -d
semaphore, -s 'seməfɔ:* [-fɔə*], -z
semaphoric, -ally ,semə'fɔrik, -əli
semasiology si,meisi'ɔlədʒi [se,m-,
  sə,m-, -eizi-]
sematology ,semə'tɔlədʒi [,si:m-]
semblance, -s 'sembləns, -iz
semé 'semei
Semele 'semili
semen 'si:men
semester, -s si'mestə* [sə'm-], -z
semi- 'semi-
  Note.—Numerous compounds may
  be formed by prefixing semi- to
  other words. Compounds not entered
  below have double stress, i.e. a stress
  on semi- and the stress of the
  simple word. Examples: semi-
  detached 'semidi'tætʃt, semi-
  official 'semiə'fiʃəl, semi-tropical
  'semi'trɔpikəl.

semibreve, -s 'semibri:v, -z
semicircle, -s 'semi,sə:kl, -z
semicircular 'semi'sə:kjulə* [,semi's-]
semicolon, -s 'semi'kəulən ['semi,k-,
  -lɔn], -z
semi-final, -s 'semi'fainl, -z
seminal 'si:minl ['sem-]
seminar, -s 'seminɑ:* [,—'-'], -z
seminar|y, -ies 'seminər|i, -iz
Seminole, -s 'seminəul, -z
semi-precious 'semi,preʃəs ['--'--]
semiquaver, -s 'semi,kweivə*, -z
Semiramide ,semi'rɑ:midi
Semiramis se'mirəmis [si'm-]
Semite, -s 'si:mait ['sem-], -s
Semitic si'mitik [se'm-, sə'm-]
semitism 'semitizəm
semitone, -s 'semitəun, -z
semivowel, -s 'semi,vauəl ['semi'v-,
  -el, -il], -z
semmit, -s 'semit, -s
semolina ,semə'li:nə [-mu'l-]
Semon (surname) 'si:mən
Sempill 'sempl
sempiternal ,sempi'tə:nl
semplice 'semplitʃi
sempre 'sempri
sempstress, -es 'sempstris, -iz
sen sen
senary 'si:nəri
senate (S.), -s 'senit, -s
senator, -s 'senətə* [-nit-], -z
senatorial, -ly ,senə'tɔ:riəl, -i
senatus se'neitəs [si'n-, -'nɑ:-]
send, -s, -ing, sent, sender/s send, -z,
  -iŋ, sent, 'sendə*/z
send-off, -s 'sendɔf [-'ɔ:f, '-'-, also -'-
  when preceded by a stress], -s
Seneca 'senikə
Senegal ,seni'gɔ:l
Senegalese 'senigə'li:z [,sen-, -gɔ:'l-]
Senegambia ,seni'gæmbɪə [-bjə]
seneschal, -s 'seniʃəl, -z
senile 'si:nail
senility si'niliti [se'n-]
senior (s. adj.) (S.), -s 'si:njə* [-nɪə*], -z
seniorit|y, -ies ,si:ni'ɔrit|i, -iz
Senlac 'senlæk
senna 'senə
Sennacherib se'nækərib [si'n-, sə'n-]
sennight, -s 'senait, -s
señor se'njɔ:*
sensation, -s sen'seiʃən [sən-, sn-], -z
sensa|tional, -tionally sen'sei|ʃənl [sən-,
  -ʃnəl, -ʃn̩l, -ʃnl, -ʃənəl], -ʃnəli [-ʃnəli,
  -ʃn̩li, -ʃnli, -ʃənəli]
sensationali|sm, -st/s sen'seiʃnəli|zəm
  [sən-, -ʃnəl-, -ʃn̩l-, -ʃnl-, -ʃənəl-], -st/s

sense, -s sens, -iz
senseless, -ly, -ness 'senslis, -li, -nis
sensibility ˌsensi'biliti [-sə'b-, -lət-]
sensib|le, -ly 'sensəb|l [-sib-], -li
sensitive (s. adj.), -s, -ly, -ness 'sensitiv
  [-sət-], -z, -li, -nis
sensitivity ˌsensi'tiviti
sensitization [-isa-] ˌsensitai'zeiʃən
sensitiz|e [-is|e], -es, -ing, -ed 'sensi-
  taiz, -iz, -iŋ, -d
sensorial sen'sɔːrɪəl
sensor|y, -ily 'sensər|i, -ili
sensual, -ly, -ness, -ism, -ist/s 'sensjŭəl
  [-sjwəl, -sjul, -ʃŭəl, -ʃwəl, -ʃul], -i,
  -nis, -izəm, -ist/s
sensuality ˌsensju'æliti [ˌsenʃu-]
sensuous, -ly, -ness 'sensjŭəs [-sjwəs,
  -ʃŭəs, -ʃwəs], -li, -nis
sent (from send) sent
sentenc|e (s. v.), -es, -ing, -ed 'sentəns,
  -iz, -iŋ, -t
sententious, -ly, -ness sen'tenʃəs [sən-],
  -li, -nis
sentience 'senʃəns [-ʃïəns, -ʃjəns]
sentient, -ly 'senʃənt [-ʃïənt, -ʃjənt], -li
sentiment, -s 'sentimənt, -s
sentiment|al, -ally, -alism ˌsenti'ment|l,
  -əli [-ļi], -əlizəm [-ļizəm]
sentimentality ˌsentimen'tæliti [-mən-]
sentinel, -s 'sentinl, -z
sentr|y, -ies 'sentr|i, -iz
sentry-box, -es 'sentribɔks, -iz
sentry-go 'sentrigəu
senza 'sentsə
Seoul səul
sepal, -s 'sepəl ['siːp-], -z
separability ˌsepərə'biliti [-lət-]
separab|le, -ly, -leness 'sepərəb|l, -li,
  -lnis
separ|ate (adj.), -ately, -ateness
  'sepr|it [-pər-], -itli [-ətli], -itnis
  [-ətnis]
separat|e (v.), -es, -ing, -ed, -or/s
  'sepəreit, -s, -iŋ, -id, -ə*/z
separation, -s ˌsepə'reiʃən, -z
separati|sm, -st/s 'sepərəti|zəm, -st/s
Sephardi|c, -m se'faːdi|k, -m
sepia 'siːpjə
sepoy, -s 'siːpɔi, -z
sepsis 'sepsis
September, -s sep'tembə* [səp-, sip-], -z
septennial sep'tenjəl [-nïəl]
septet(te), -s sep'tet, -s
septic 'septik
septillion, -s sep'tiljən, -z
septime, -s 'septiːm, -z
septuagenarian, -s ˌseptjŭədʒi'nɛərïən
  [-tjwə-], -z

Septuagesima ˌseptjŭə'dʒesimə [-tjwə-]
Septuagint 'septjŭədʒint [-tjwə-]
sept|um, -ums, -a 'sept|əm, -əmz, -ə
septuple 'septjupl
sepulchral si'pʌlkrəl [se'p-, sə'p-]
sepulchre, -s 'sepəlkə*, -z
sepulture 'sepəltʃə* [-tjuə*]
sequel, -s 'siːkwəl, -z
sequel|a, -ae si'kwiːl|ə, -iː
sequence, -s 'siːkwəns, -iz
sequenti|al, -ally si'kwenʃ|əl, -əli
sequest|er, -ers, -ering, -ered si'kwest|ə*
  [sə'k-], -əz, -əriŋ, -əd
sequestrat|e, -es, -ing, -ed si'kwestreit
  ['siːkw-], -s, -iŋ, -id
sequestration, -s ˌsiːkwes'treiʃən [ˌsek-],
  -z
sequin, -s 'siːkwin, -z
sequoia, -s si'kwɔïə [se'k-], -z
serac, -s 'seræk, -s
seraglio, -s se'rɑːliəu [si'r-, sə'r-, -ljəu],
  -z
serai, -s se'rai [sə'r-], -z
Serampore ˌserəm'pɔː* [-'pɔə*, '—'-]
  (Bengali ʃrirampur, ʃirampur)
seraph (S.), -s, -im 'serəf, -s, -im
seraphic, -al, -ally se'ræfik [si'r-, sə'r-],
  -əl, -əli
Serapis 'serəpis
Serb, -s, -ia, -ian/s səːb, -z, -jə [-ïə],
  -jən/z [-ïən/z]
Serbonian sə:'bəunjən [-nïən]
sere (s. adj.), -s sïə*, -z
Seremban sə'rembən
serenad|e (s. v.), -es, -ing, -ed ˌseri'neid
  [-rə'n-], -z, -iŋ, -id
serenata, -s ˌseri'nɑːtə [-rə'n-], -z
serendipity ˌserən'dipiti [-ren-]
serene, -st, -ly si'riːn [sə'r-], -ist, -li
serenity si'reniti [sə'r-]
serf, -s, -dom səːf, -s, -dəm
serge (S.), -s səːdʒ, -iz
sergeant (S.), -s 'sɑːdʒənt, -s
sergeant-major, -s 'sɑːdʒənt'meidʒə*,
  -z
serial (s. adj.), -s 'sïərïəl, -z
seriatim ˌsïəri'eitim [ˌser-]
series 'sïəriːz [-riz, rarely -riːz]
serif [cer-], -s 'serif, -s
seringa, -s si'riŋgə [sə'r-], -z
Seringapatam sə,riŋgəpə'tɑːm [si,r-,
  -'tæm]
serio-comic 'sïərïəu'kɔmik
serious, -ly, -ness 'sïərïəs, -li, -nis
serjeant (S.), -s 'sɑːdʒənt, -s
Serjeantson 'sɑːdʒəntsn
sermon, -s 'səːmən, -z
sermonette, -s ˌsəːmə'net ['—'-], -s

sermoniz|e [-is|e], -es, -ing, -ed 'sə:mənaiz, -iz, -iŋ, -d
serous 'siərəs
Serpell 'sə:pl
Serpens (constellation) 'sə:penz
serpent, -s 'sə:pənt, -s
serpentine (s. adj.) (S.) 'sə:pəntain
serrate (adj.) 'serit [-reit]
serrated se'reitid [sə'r-, si'r-]
serration, -s se'reiʃən [sə'r-, si'r-], -z
serried 'serid
serum, -s 'siərəm, -z
servant, -s 'sə:vənt, -s
servant-girl, -s 'sə:vəntgə:l [rarely -gɛəl], -z
serv|e (s. v.), -es, -ing/s, -ed, -er/s sə:v, -z, -iŋ/z, -d, -ə*/z
servic|e (s. v.) (S.), -es, -ing, -ed 'sə:vis, -iz, -iŋ, -t
serviceability ˌsə:visə'biliti [-lət-]
serviceab|le, -ly, -leness 'sə:visəb|l, -li, -lnis
serviette ˌsə:vi'et, -s
servile, -ly 'sə:vail, -li
servility sə:'viliti
serving-spoon, -s 'sə:viŋ-spu:n, -z
servitor, -s 'sə:vitə*, -z
servitude 'sə:vitju:d
sesame (S.), -s 'sesəmi, -z
sesquialtera, -s ˌseskwi'æltərə, -z
sesquipedalian 'seskwipi'deiljən [ˌses-, -pe'd-, -lïən]
session, -s 'seʃən, -z
sessional (s. adj.), -s 'seʃənl [-ʃnəl, -ʃn̩l̩, -ʃn̩l̩, -ʃənəl], -z
sesterce, -s 'sestə:s, -iz ['sestəsiz]
sester|tium, -tia ses'tə:|tjəm [-tïəm, -ʃjəm, -ʃïəm], -tjə [-tïə, -ʃjə, -ʃïə]
sestet, -s ses'tet, -s
set (s. v.), -s, -ting set, -s, -iŋ
set-back, -s 'setbæk ['-'-], -s
Setebos 'setibɔs
Seth seθ
set-off, -s 'set'ɔf [-'ɔ:f], -s
seton (S.), -s 'si:tn, -z
set-out, -s set'aut, -s
set-square, -s 'setskwɛə* ['-'-], -z
settee, -s se'ti:, -z
setter, -s 'setə*, -z
setting (s.), -s 'setiŋ, -z
sett|le (s. v.), -les, -ling, -led, -ler/s, -lement/s 'set|l, -lz, -liŋ [-liŋ], -ld, -lə*/z [-lə*/z], -lmənt/s
set-to 'set'tu:
set-up, -s 'setʌp, -s
seven, -s, -th/s, -thly; -fold 'sevn, -z, -θ/s, -θli; -fəuld
sevenish 'sevn̩iʃ ['sevəniʃ]

Sevenoaks 'sevnəuks [-vnəu-]
seven|pence, -penny 'sevn|pəns [-vm|p-], -pəni
seventeen, -s, -th/s, -thly 'sevn'ti:n ['--, -'-, according to sentence-stress], -z, -θ/s, -θli
sevent|y, -ies, -ieth/s 'sevnt|i, -iz, -iiθ/s [-jiθ/s, -ïəθ/s, -jəθ/s]
sever, -s, -ing, -ed; -able, -ance 'sevə*, -z, -riŋ, -d; -rəbl, -rəns
sever|al, -ally 'sevr|əl, -əli
severe, -r, -st, -ly, -ness si'viə* [sə'v-], -rə*, -rist, -li, -nis
severit|y, -ies si'verit|i [sə'v-], -iz
Severn 'sevə(:)n
Severus si'viərəs [sə'v-]
Sevier 'seviə* [-vjə*]
Seville sə'vil [se'v-, si'v-, 'sevil, 'sevl]
Sèvres seivr [-və*] (sɛ:vr)
sew, -s, -ing, -ed, -n səu, -z, -iŋ, -d, -n
sewage 'sju(:)idʒ ['su(:)-]
Sewanee sə'wɔni
Seward 'si:wəd
Sewell 'sju:əl [sjuəl]
sewer (one who sews), -s 'səuə*, -z
sewer (drain), -s 'sjuə*, -z
sewerage 'sjuəridʒ
sewer-gas 'sjuəgæs ['-'-]
sewing-machine, -s 'səuiŋməˌʃi:n, -z
sewing|-woman, -women 'səuiŋ|ˌwumən, -ˌwimin
sex, -es, -less seks, -iz, -lis
sexagenarian, -s ˌseksədʒi'nɛərïən, -z
Sexagesima ˌseksə'dʒesimə
sex-appeal 'seks-əˌpi:l
sext(e) sekst
sextan 'sekstən
sextant, -s 'sekstənt, -s
sextet(te), -s seks'tet, -s
sextillion, -s seks'tiljən, -z
sexto, -s 'sekstəu, -z
sextodecimo, -s 'sekstəu'desiməu, -z
sexton, -s 'sekstən, -z
sextuple 'sekstjupl
sexual, -ly 'seksjŭəl [-ksjwəl, -ksjul, -kʃŭəl, -kʃwəl, -kʃul], -i
sexuality ˌseksju'æliti [-kʃu-]
Seychelle, -s sei'ʃel, -z
Seyfang 'si:fæŋ
Seymour 'si:mɔ:* [-mɔə*, -mə*], 'seim-
Note.—'seim- chiefly in families of Scottish origin.
Seys seis
sforzando sfɔ:t'sændəu
shabb|ly, -ier, -iest, -ily, -iness 'ʃæb|i, -iə*, -iist, -ili, -inis
shack|le (s. v.) (S.), -les, -ling, -led 'ʃæk|l, -lz, -liŋ [-liŋ], -ld

Shackleton 'ʃækltən
Shadbolt 'ʃædbəult
shaddock (S.) 'ʃædək
shad|e (s. v.), -es, -ing, -ed; -eless ʃeid, -z, -iŋ, -id; -lis
shadoof, -s ʃə'du:f [ʃæ'd-], -s
shad|ow (s. v.), -ows, -owing, -owed; -owy, -owiness 'ʃæd|əu, -əuz, -əuiŋ, -əud; -əui, -əuinis
shadowless 'ʃædəulis
Shadrach [-ak] 'ʃeidræk
　　Note.—Some Jews pronounce 'ʃædrɑːx.
Shadwell 'ʃædwəl [-wel]
shad|y, -ier, -iest, -ily, -iness 'ʃeid|i, -iə* [-jə*], -iist [-jist], -ili, -inis
shaft, -s ʃɑːft, -s
Shaftesbury 'ʃɑːftsbəri
shag, -s ʃæg, -z
shagg|y, -ier, -iest, -ily, -iness 'ʃæg|i, -iə*, -iist, -ili, -inis
shagreen ʃæ'griːn [ʃə'g-]
shah (S.), -s ʃɑː, -z
shaikh, -s ʃaik, -s
Shairp ʃɛəp, ʃɑːp
shak|e (s. v.), -es, -ing, shook, shak|en, -er/s ʃeik, -s, -iŋ, ʃuk, 'ʃeik|ən, -ə*/z
shakedown, -s 'ʃeik'daun ['--, also -'- when preceded by a stress], -z
Shak(e)spear(e) 'ʃeikspiə*
Shak(e)spearian ʃeiks'piərɪən
Shak(e)speariana ˌʃeikspiəri'ɑːnə [ʃeiks-ˌpiər-]
shake-up, -s 'ʃeik'ʌp ['--, also -'- when preceded by a stress], -s
shako, -s 'ʃækəu, -z
shak|y, -ier, -iest, -ily, -iness 'ʃeik|i, -iə* [-jə*], -iist [-jist], -ili, -inis
Shalders 'ʃɔːldəz
shale ʃeil
shall ʃæl (strong form), ʃəl, ʃl, ʃə, ʃ (weak forms)
　　Note.—The forms ʃə, ʃ, are chiefly used when we or be follows.
shallop, -s 'ʃæləp, -s
shallot (S.), -s ʃə'lɔt, -s
shall|ow (s. adj. v.) (S.), -ows, -ower, -owest, -owness, -owly 'ʃæl|əu, -əuz, -əuə*, -əuist, -əunis, -əuli
shalt (from shall) ʃælt (strong form), ʃəlt, ʃlt (weak forms)
shall|y, -iness 'ʃeil|i, -inis
sham (s. v.), -s, -ming, -med, -mer/s ʃæm, -z, -iŋ, -d, -ə*/z
shaman, -s, -ism 'ʃæmən, -z, -izəm
shamb|le, -les, -ling, -led 'ʃæmb|l, -lz, -liŋ, -ld
shambles (s.) 'ʃæmblz
sham|e (s. v.), -es, -ing, -ed ʃeim, -z, -iŋ, -d

shamefaced 'ʃeimfeist
shamefacedly 'ʃeimfeistli [-sidli, '-'---, -'---]
shamefacedness 'ʃeimfeistnis [-sidnis, '-'---, -'---]
shame|ful, -fully, -fulness 'ʃeim|fʊl, -fuli [-fəli], -fʊlnis
shameless, -ly, -ness 'ʃeimlis, -li, -nis
shammy 'ʃæmi
shampoo (s.), -s ʃæm'puː, -z
shampoo (v.), -(e)s, -ing, -ed ʃæm'puː, -z, -iŋ, [-'puiŋ], -d
shamrock (S.) 'ʃæmrɔk
Shan (state, language) ʃɑːn
Shandy 'ʃændi
shandygaff, -s 'ʃændigæf, -s
Shane ʃɑːn, ʃɔːn, ʃein
Shanghai ʃæŋ'hai ['-'-]
shank, -s ʃæŋk, -s
Shanklin 'ʃæŋklin
Shanks ʃæŋks
Shannon 'ʃænən
shan't ʃɑːnt
shantung (silk material) ʃæn'tʌŋ ['-'-]
Shantung ʃæn'dʌŋ [-'tʌŋ, -'duŋ, -'tuŋ, '-'-]
shant|y, -ies 'ʃænt|i, -iz
shap|e (s. v.), -es, -ing, -ed ʃeip, -s, -iŋ, -t
S.H.A.P.E. ʃeip
shapeless, -ness 'ʃeiplis, -nis
shapel|y, -ier, -iest, -iness 'ʃeipl|i, -iə*, -iist, -inis
Shapiro ʃə'piərəu
shar|e (s. v.), -es, -ing, -ed ʃɛə*, -z, -riŋ, -d
shareholder, -s 'ʃɛəˌhəuldə*, -z
share-out, -s 'ʃɛəraut ['ʃɛər'aut], -s
shark, -s ʃɑːk, -s
sharkskin 'ʃɑːk-skin
Sharon 'ʃɛərɔn [-rən]
sharp (s. adj. adv.) (S.), -s; -er, -est, -ly, -ness ʃɑːp, -s; -ə*, -ist, -li, -nis
Sharpe ʃɑːp
sharp|en, -ens, -ening, -ened 'ʃɑːp|ən, -ənz, -niŋ [-ṇiŋ], -ənd
sharpener, -s 'ʃɑːpnə*, -z
sharper (s.), -s 'ʃɑːpə*, -z
Sharples 'ʃɑːplz
sharp-set 'ʃɑːp'set
sharpshooter, -s 'ʃɑːpˌʃuːtə*, -z
sharp-sighted 'ʃɑːp'saitid
sharp-witted 'ʃɑːp'witid
Shasta (in California) 'ʃæstə
shatter, -s, -ing, -ed 'ʃætə*, -z, -riŋ, -d
Shaughnessy 'ʃɔːnəsi
Shaula (star) 'ʃəulə
Shaun ʃɔːn

shav|e (s. v.), -es, -ing/s, -ed ʃeiv, -z, -iŋ/z, -d

shaven 'ʃeivn

shaver, -s 'ʃeivə*, -z

Shavian 'ʃeivjən [-vïən]

shaving-brush, -es 'ʃeiviŋbrʌʃ, -iz

shaving-stick, -s 'ʃeiviŋ-stik, -s

shaw (S.), -s ʃɔ:, -z

shawl, -s ʃɔ:l, -z

shawm, -s ʃɔ:m, -z

shay, -s ʃei, -z

she ʃi: (normal form), ʃi (frequent weak form)

shea, -s ʃiə ['ʃi:ə, ʃi:], -z

Shea ʃei

shea|f, -ves ʃi:|f, -vz

Sheaffer 'ʃeifə*

shear (s. v.), -s, -ing, -ed, shorn ʃiə*, -z, -riŋ, -d, ʃɔ:n

Sheard ʃɛəd, ʃiəd, ʃə:d

shearer (S.), -s 'ʃiərə*, -z

Shearman 'ʃiəmən, 'ʃə:mən

Shearme ʃə:m

Shearn ʃiən, ʃə:n

shears (S.) ʃiəz

Shearson 'ʃiəsn

shea|th, -ths ʃi:|θ, -ðz [-θs]

sheath|e, -es, -ing, -ed ʃi:ð, -z, -iŋ, -d

sheaves (plur. of sheaf) ʃi:vz

Sheba 'ʃi:bə

Shebbeare 'ʃebiə*

she-bear, -s 'ʃi:'bɛə* ['—], -z

shebeen, -s ʃi'bi:n [ʃe'b-], -z

she-cat, -s 'ʃi:'kæt ['ʃi:-kæt], -s

Shechem 'ʃi:kem [among Jews also 'ʃekem, ʃə'x̣em]

shed (s. v.), -s, -ding ʃed, -z, -iŋ

she-devil, -s 'ʃi:'devl ['-,--], -z

Shee ʃi:

sheen (S.) ʃi:n

sheen|y (s. adj.), -ies 'ʃi:n|i, -iz

sheep ʃi:p

sheep-dip 'ʃi:pdip

sheep-dog, -s 'ʃi:pdɔg, -z

sheep-fold, -s 'ʃi:pfəuld, -z

sheepish, -ly, -ness 'ʃi:piʃ, -li, -nis

sheep-pen, -s 'ʃi:ppen, -z

sheep-run, -s 'ʃi:p-rʌn, -z

Sheepshanks 'ʃi:pʃæŋks

sheep-shearing 'ʃi:p,ʃiəriŋ

sheepskin, -s 'ʃi:p-skin, -z

sheer (s. adj. v. adv.), -s, -ing, -ed ʃiə*, -z, -riŋ, -d

Sheerness 'ʃiə'nes [also '—, -'-, according to sentence-stress]

sheet, -s, -ing ʃi:t, -s, -iŋ

sheet-anchor, -s 'ʃi:t,æŋkə*, -z

sheet-iron 'ʃi:t,aiən

sheet-lightning 'ʃi:t,laitniŋ

Sheffield 'ʃefi:ld [locally -fild]

she-goat, -s 'ʃi:'gəut ['ʃi:g- also ʃi:'g- when preceded by a stress], -s

sheik(h), -s ʃeik [ʃi:k, ʃek, ʃex], -s

Sheila 'ʃi:lə

shekel, -s 'ʃekl, -z

Shekinah ʃe'kainə [ʃi'k-]

Shelagh 'ʃi:lə

Sheldon 'ʃeldən

Sheldonian ʃel'dəunjən [-nïən]

sheldrake, -s 'ʃel-dreik, -s

shelduck, -s 'ʃeldʌk, -s

shel|f, -ves ʃel|f, -vz

shell (s. v.), -s, -ing, -ed ʃel, -z, -iŋ, -d

shellac (s. v.), -s, -king, -ked ʃə'læk [ʃe'l-, 'ʃelæk], -s, -iŋ, -t

Shelley 'ʃeli

shell-fish 'ʃel-fiʃ

shell-proof 'ʃel-pru:f

Shelmerdine 'ʃelmədi:n

shelt|er (s. v.), -ers, -ering, -ered ; -erless 'ʃelt|ə*, -əz, -əriŋ, -əd; -əlis

shelv|e, -es, -ing, -ed ʃelv, -z, -iŋ, -d

shelves (plur. of shelf, 3rd sing. pres. of shelve) ʃelvz

Shem ʃem

Shemeld 'ʃeməld

shemozzle, -s ʃi'mɔzl, -z

Shenandoah ,ʃenən'dəuə

Shennan 'ʃenən

Shenstone 'ʃenstən

she-oak, -s 'ʃi:'əuk, -s

shepherd (s. v.) (S.), -s, -ing, -ed 'ʃepəd, -z, -iŋ, -id

shepherdess, -es 'ʃepədis, -iz

Shepp|ard, -ey 'ʃep|əd, -i

Sheraton 'ʃerətn

sherbet 'ʃə:bət

Sherborne 'ʃə:bən [-bɔ:n]

Sherbrooke 'ʃə:bruk

sherd, -s ʃə:d, -z

Shere ʃiə*

Sheridan 'ʃeridn

sheriff, -s 'ʃerif, -s

Sherlock 'ʃə:lɔk

Sherman 'ʃə:mən

Sherriff 'ʃerif

sherr|y, -ies 'ʃer|i, -iz

Sherwood 'ʃə:wud

she's (=she is or she has) ʃi:z (normal form), ʃiz (occasional weak form)

Shetland, -s, -er/s 'ʃetlənd, -z, -ə*/z

shew, -s, -ing, -ed, -n ʃəu, -z, -iŋ, -d, -n

shewbread 'ʃəu-bred

Shewell ʃuəl ['ʃu:əl]

shewn (from shew) ʃəun

she-wol|f, -ves 'ʃiː'wul|f [in contrast '--],
-vz
Shewry 'ʃuəri
shibboleth (S.), -s 'ʃibələθ [-bəul-], -s
shield (s. v.) (S.), -s, -ing, -ed ʃiːld, -z,
-iŋ, -id
shieling, -s 'ʃiːliŋ, -z
shift (s. v.), -s, -ing, -ed ʃift, -s, -iŋ, -id
shiftless 'ʃiftlis
shift|ly, -ier, -iest, -ily, -iness 'ʃift|i, -ɪə*
[-jə*], -iist [-jist], -ili, -inis
shikaree, -s ʃi'kæri [-'kɑːr-], -z
Shillan ʃi'læn
shillela(g)h (S.), -s ʃi'leilə [-li], -z
Shilleto [-lito] 'ʃilitəu
shilling, -s; -sworth 'ʃiliŋ, -z; -zwəːθ
shilly-shall|y (s. v.), -ies, -ying, -ied
'ʃili,ʃæl|i, -iz, -iiŋ [-jiŋ], -id
Shiloh 'ʃailəu
shimmer (s. v.), -s, -ing, -ed 'ʃimə*, -z,
-riŋ, -d
shin (s. v.), -s, -ning, -ned ʃin, -z, -iŋ,
-d
shin-bone, -s 'ʃinbəun, -z
shind|y, -ies 'ʃind|i, -iz
shin|e (s. v.), -es, -ing, -ed, shone ʃain,
-z, -iŋ, -d, ʃon
shingle, -s 'ʃiŋgl, -z
shingly 'ʃiŋgli
Shint|o, -oism, -oist/s 'ʃint|əu, -əuizəm,
-əuist/s
shin|y, -ier, -iest, -iness 'ʃain|i, -ɪə*
[-jə*], -iist [-jist], -inis
ship (s. v.), -s, -ping, -ped, -per/s ʃip, -s,
-iŋ, -t, -ə*/z
shipboard 'ʃipbɔːd [-bəəd]
ship-build|er/s, -ing 'ʃip,bild|ə*/z, -iŋ
Shiplake 'ʃip-leik
Shipley 'ʃipli
shipload, -s 'ʃip-ləud, -z
ship-master, -s 'ʃip,mɑːstə*, -z
shipmate, -s 'ʃipmeit, -s
shipment, -s 'ʃipmənt, -s
ship-money 'ʃip,mʌni
ship-owner, -s 'ʃip,əunə*, -z
shipshape 'ʃipʃeip
Shipton 'ʃiptən
ship-way, -s 'ʃipwei, -z
shipwreck (s. v.), -s, -ing, -ed 'ʃip-rek,
-s, -iŋ, -t
shipwright (S.), -s 'ʃip-rait, -s
shipyard, -s 'ʃip-jɑːd, -z
Shiraz ʃiə'rɑːz
shire, -s ʃaiə*, -z
-shire (suffix) -ʃiə* [-ʃə*]
shirk (s. v.), -s, -ing, -ed, -er/s ʃəːk, -s,
-iŋ, -t, -ə*/z
Shirley 'ʃəːli

shirt, -s, -ing/s; -collar/s ʃəːt, -s, -iŋ/z;
-,kɔlə*/z
shirt-front, -s 'ʃəːtfrʌnt, -s
shirty 'ʃəːti
Shishak 'ʃaiʃæk [-ʃək, rarely 'ʃiʃ-]
Shiva 'ʃivə ['ʃiːvə] (Hind. ʃyva)
shiv|er, -ers, -ering/ly, -ered 'ʃiv|ə*,
-əz, -əriŋ/li, -əd
shiver|ly, -iness 'ʃivər|i, -inis
shoal, -s ʃəul, -z
shock (s. v.), -s, -ing/ly, -ed, -er/s ʃɔk,
-s, -iŋ/li, -t, -ə*/z
shockhead, -s, -ed 'ʃɔkhed, -z, -id
shod (from shoe v.) ʃɔd
shodd|y, -ier, -iest, -ily, -iness 'ʃɔd|i,
-ɪə*, -iist, -ili, -inis
shoe (s. v.), -s, -ing, shod ʃuː, -z, -iŋ
[ʃuiŋ], ʃɔd
shoeblack, -s 'ʃuː-blæk, -s
Shoeburyness 'ʃuːbəri'nes
shoehorn, -s 'ʃuːhɔːn, -z
shoe-lace, -s 'ʃuːleis, -iz
shoe-leather 'ʃuː,leðə*
shoeless 'ʃuːlis
shoe-maker, -s 'ʃuː,meikə*, -z
Shona (language of Mashonaland) 'ʃɔnə
[old-fashioned 'ʃəunə]
shone (from shine) ʃon
shoo (v. interj.), -s, -ing, -ed ʃuː, -z, -iŋ,
-d
shook (from shake) ʃuk
Shoolbred 'ʃuːlbred
shoot (s. v.), -s, -ing, shot ʃuːt, -s, -iŋ,
ʃot
shooter (S.), -s 'ʃuːtə*, -z
shooting-box, -es 'ʃuːtiŋbɔks, -iz
shooting-galler|y, -ies 'ʃuːtiŋ,gælər|i, -iz
shop (s. v.), -s, -ping, -ped ʃɔp, -s, -iŋ, -t
shop-assistant, -s 'ʃɔp-ə,sistənt, -s
shop-girl, -s 'ʃɔpgəːl [rarely -gɛəl], -z
shopkeeper, -s 'ʃɔp,kiːpə*, -z
shop-lift|er/s, -ing 'ʃɔp,lift|ə*/z, -iŋ
shop|man, -men 'ʃɔp|mən, -mən [-men]
shoppy 'ʃɔpi
shop-soiled 'ʃɔp-sɔild
shop-steward, -s 'ʃɔp'stjuəd [-'stjuːəd,
'--], -z
shop-walker, -s 'ʃɔp,wɔːkə*, -z
shop-window, -s 'ʃɔp'windəu, -z
shore, -s ʃɔː* [ʃɔə*], -z
Shore|ditch, -ham 'ʃɔː|ditʃ ['ʃɔə-], -rəm
shoreward 'ʃɔːwəd ['ʃɔə-]
shorn (from shear) ʃɔːn
Shorncliffe 'ʃɔːnklif
short (s. adj.) (S.), -s; -er, -est, -ly,
-ness ʃɔːt, -s; -ə*, -ist, -li, -nis
shortage, -s 'ʃɔːtidʒ, -iz
shortbread, -s 'ʃɔːtbred, -z

shortcake, -s 'ʃɔːtkeik, -s
short-circuit (s. v.), -s, -ing, -ed 'ʃɔːt-'səːkit, -s, -iŋ, -id
shortcoming, -s ʃɔːt'kʌmiŋ ['-,--], -z
short-dated 'ʃɔːt'deitid
short-eared 'ʃɔːt-iəd [rarely 'ʃɔːt-jəːd]
short|en, -ens, -ening, -ened 'ʃɔːt|n, -nz, -niŋ [-ŋiŋ], -nd
shortfall, -s 'ʃɔːtfɔːl, -z
shorthand 'ʃɔːthænd
short-handed 'ʃɔːt'hændid
shorthorn, -s 'ʃɔːthoːn, -z
short-lived 'ʃɔːt'livd [also 'ʃɔːt-livd when attributive]
short-sighted, -ly, -ness 'ʃɔːt'saitid, -li, -nis
short-tempered 'ʃɔːt'tempəd [also '-,— when attributive]
short-term 'ʃɔːttəːm
short-winded 'ʃɔːt'windid
shot (s. v.), -s ʃɔt, -s
shot-gun, -s 'ʃɔtgʌn, -z
shough, -s ʃʌf, -s
should ʃud (strong form), ʃəd, ʃd, ʃt (weak forms)
Note.—The form ʃt occurs only before breathed consonants.
should|er (s. v.), -ers, -ering, -ered 'ʃuld|ə*, -əz, -əriŋ, -əd
shoulder-blade, -s 'ʃuldəbleid, -z
shoulder-strap, -s 'ʃuldə-stræp, -s
shouldn't 'ʃudnt
shout (s. v.), -s, -ing, -ed ʃaut, -s, -iŋ, -id
shov|e (s. v.), -es, -ing, -ed ʃʌv, -z, -iŋ, -d
Shove (surname) ʃəuv
shov|el (s. v.) (S.), -els, -elling, -elled, -eller/s; -elful/s 'ʃʌv|l, -lz, -liŋ [-liŋ], -ld, -lə*/z [-lə*/z]; -lful/z
show (s. v.), -s, -ing, -ed, -n ʃəu, -z, -iŋ, -d, -n
show-business 'ʃəu,bizniz
show-case, -s 'ʃəu-keis, -iz
show-down, -s 'ʃəudaun, -z
shower (one who shows), -s 'ʃəuə*, -z
shower (s. v.) (fall of rain, etc.), -s, -ing, -ed; -y 'ʃau-ə*, -z, -riŋ, -d; -ri
shower-ba|th, -ths 'ʃau-əbɑː|θ, -ðz
show|man, -men 'ʃəu|mən, -mən [-men]
showmanship 'ʃəumənʃip
shown (from show) ʃəun
show-place, -s 'ʃəu-pleis, -iz
show-room, -s 'ʃəurum [-ruːm], -z
show|y, -ier, -iest, -ily, -iness 'ʃəu|i, -iə*, -iist, -ili, -inis
shrank (from shrink) ʃræŋk
shrapnel 'ʃræpnḷ [-nəl]
shred (s. v.), -s, -ding, -ded ʃred, -z, -iŋ, -id

shrew, -s ʃruː, -z
shrewd, -er, -est, -ly, -ness ʃruːd, -ə*, -ist, -li, -nis
shrewish, -ly, -ness 'ʃruːiʃ, -li, -nis
Shrewsbury 'ʃrəuzbəri ['ʃruːz-]
    Note.—'ʃrəu- is the pronunciation used by those connected with Shrewsbury School and by many residents in the neighbourhood, especially members of county families. The form 'ʃruː- is used by outsiders, and is the common pronunciation heard in the town.
shriek (s. v.), -s, -ing, -ed ʃriːk, -s, -iŋ, -t
shrievalt|y, -ies 'ʃriːvəlt|i, -iz
shrift ʃrift
shrike, -s ʃraik, -s
shrill, -er, -est, -y, -ness ʃril, -ə*, -ist, -i, -nis
shrimp, -s, -ing, -er/s ʃrimp, -s, -iŋ, -ə*/z
shrine, -s ʃrain, -z
shrink, -s, -ing/ly, shrank, shrunk, shrunken ʃriŋk, -s, -iŋ/li, ʃræŋk, ʃrʌŋk, 'ʃrʌŋkən
shrinkage 'ʃriŋkidʒ
shriv|e (S.), -es, -ing, shrove, shriven ʃraiv, -z, -iŋ, ʃrəuv, 'ʃrivn
shriv|el, -els, -elling, -elled 'ʃriv|l, -lz, -liŋ [-liŋ], -ld
Shropshire 'ʃrɔpʃiə* [-ʃə*]
shroud (s. v.), -s, -ing, -ed; -less ʃraud, -z, -iŋ, -id; -lis
Shrove ʃrəuv
shrub, -s ʃrʌb, -z
shrubber|y, -ies 'ʃrʌbər|i, -iz
shrubby 'ʃrʌbi
shrug (s. v.), -s, -ging, -ged ʃrʌg, -z, -iŋ, -d
shrunk (from shrink), -en ʃrʌŋk, -ən
Shubrook 'ʃuːbruk
shuck, -s ʃʌk, -s
Shuckburgh 'ʃʌkbrə
shudder, -s -ing, -ed 'ʃʌdə*, -z, -riŋ, -d
shuff|le, -les, -ling, -led, -ler/s 'ʃʌf|l, -lz, -liŋ [-liŋ], -ld, -lə*/z [-lə*/z]
shuffle-board, -s 'ʃʌflbɔːd [-bəəd], -z
shun, -s, -ning, -ned ʃʌn, -z, -iŋ, -d
shunt (s. v.), -s, -ing, -ed, -er/s ʃʌnt, -s, -iŋ, -id, -ə*/z
shut, -s, -ting ʃʌt, -s, -iŋ
Shute ʃuːt
Shutte ʃuːt
shutter, -s, -ed 'ʃʌtə*, -z, -d
shuttle, -s; -cock/s 'ʃʌtl, -z; -kɔk/s
sh|y (s. adj. v.), -ies, -yer, -yest, -yly, -yness; -ying, -ied ʃ|ai, -aiz; -ai-ə*, -aiist, -ai-li, -ai-nis; -aiiŋ, -aid

Shylock 'ʃailɔk
si (musical note) si:
Siam 'saiæm [sai'æm]
Siamese ˌsaiə'mi:z ['saiə'm-]
Siberia, -n/s sai'biərïə, -n/z
sibilant (s. adj.), -s 'sibilənt, -s
sibilation, -s ˌsibi'leiʃən, -z
Sible (in Essex) 'sibl
Sibley 'sibli
sibling, -s 'siblin, -z
Sibun 'saibən
sibyl (S.), -s 'sibil, -z
sibylline si'bilain ['sibil-]
sic sik
sice, -s sais, -iz
Sichel 'sitʃl
Sichem 'saikem
Sicilian, -s si'siljən [-lïən], -z
siciliano, -s siˌsili'ɑ:nəu [siˌtʃi-, ˌ—'—],
    -z
Sicilly, -ies 'sisilli, -iz
sick, -er, -est, -ness sik, -ə*, -ist, -nis
sick-bed, -s 'sikbed, -z
sicken, -ens, -ening (adj. v.), -ened,
    -ener/s 'sikn, -nz, -ɲiŋ [-niŋ], -nd,
    -ɲə*/z [-nə*/z]
sickish 'sikiʃ
sickle, -s 'sikl, -z
sick-list, -s 'sik-list, -s
sickily, -ier, -iest, -iness 'sikli, -ïə*,
    -iist, -inis
sickness 'siknis
sick-nurse, -s 'siknə:s, -iz
sick-room, -s 'sik-rum [-ru:m], -z
Siddeley 'sidəli
Siddons 'sidnz
side (s. v.), -es, -ing, -ed said, -z, -iŋ, -id
sideboard, -s 'saidbɔ:d [-bɔəd], -z
Sidebotham 'saidˌbɔtəm
side-car, -s 'saidkɑ:*, -z
sidelight, -s 'saidlait, -s
side-line, -s 'saidlain, -z
sidelong 'saidlɔŋ
sidereal sai'diərïəl
siderite 'saidərait
Sidery 'saidəri
side-saddle, -s 'saidˌsædl, -z
side-show, -s 'saidʃəu, -z
side-slip (s. v.), -s, -ping, -ped 'saidslip,
    -s, -iŋ, -t
sides|man, -men 'saidz|mən, -mən
    [-men]
side-stroke 'saidstrəuk
side-track (s. v.), -s, -ing, -ed 'said-
    træk, -s, -iŋ, -t
side-walk, -s 'said-wɔ:k, -s
sideways 'said-weiz
Sidgwick 'sidʒwik

siding (s.), -s 'saidiŋ, -z
sid|le, -les, -ling, -led 'said|l, -lz, -liŋ
    [-ˌliŋ], -ld
Sid|mouth, -ney 'sid|məθ, -ni
Sidon 'saidn [-dɔn]
Sidonian, -s sai'dəunjən [-nïən], -z
Sidonie si'dəuni
siege, -s si:dʒ, -iz
Siegfried 'si:gfri:d ('zi:kfri:t)
Sieglinde si:g'lində (zi:k'lində)
Siegmund 'si:gmund [-mənd] ('zi:k-
    munt)
sienna si'enə
Sien(n)a si'enə
Sien(n)ese ˌsie'ni:z
sierra (S.), -s 'siərə [si'erə], -z
Sierra Leone 'siərəli'əun [si'er-]
    Note.—An old-fashioned pronuncia-
    tion ˌsɑ:li'əun is now nearly obsolete.
siesta, -s si'estə, -z
siev|e (s. v.), -es, -ing, -ed siv, -z, -iŋ, -d
sift, -s, -ing, -ed, -er/s sift, -s, -iŋ, -id,
    -ə*/z
sigh (s. v.), -s, -ing, -ed sai, -z, -iŋ, -d
sight (s. v.), -s, -ing, -ed; -less sait, -s,
    -iŋ, -id; -lis
sightl|y, -iness 'saitl|i, -inis
sight-read|er/s, -ing 'saitˌri:d|ə*/z, -iŋ
sight-seeing 'saitˌsi:iŋ
sightseer, -s 'saitˌsi:ə* ['sait-siə*], -z
Sigismond [-mund] 'sigismənd
sigma, -s 'sigmə, -z
sign (s. v.), -s, -ing, -ed sain, -z, -iŋ, -d
sign|al (s. adj. v.), -als; -ally; -alling,
    -alled, -aller/s 'sign|l [-əl], -lz [-əlz];
    -əli; -liŋ [-əliŋ], -ld [-əld], -ələ*/z
signal-box, -es 'signlbɔks [-nəl-], -iz
signaliz|e (-is|e), -es, -ing, -ed 'signəl-
    aiz, -iz, -iŋ, -d
signal|man, -men 'signl|mən [-nəl|-,
    -mæn], -mən [-men]
signator|y, -ies 'signətər|i, -iz
signature, -s 'signitʃə* [-nətʃ-], -z
signboard, -s 'sainbɔ:d [-bɔəd], -z
signeme, -s 'signi:m, -z
signet, -s 'signit, -s
signet-ring, -s 'signit-riŋ, -z
significan|ce, -t/ly sig'nifikən|s, -t/li
signification ˌsignifi'keiʃən
significative sig'nifikətiv [-keit-]
signi|fy, -fies, -fying, -fied 'signi|fai,
    -faiz, -faiiŋ, -faid
Signior 'si:njɔ:*
signor (S.), -s 'si:njɔ:* (siɲ'ɲor), -z
sign-paint|er/s, -ing 'sainˌpeint|ə*/z, -iŋ
sign-post, -s 'sain-pəust, -s
Sigurd (English Christian name) 'si:gə:d,
    (Scandinavian name) 'siguəd [-gə:d]

Sikes saiks
Sikh, -s siːk (*Hind.* sikh), -s
Sikkim 'sikim
silage 'sailidʒ
Silas 'sailəs [-læs]
Silchester 'siltʃistə*
silenc|e (*s. v.*), -es, -ing, -ed 'sailəns, -iz, -iŋ, -t
silencer, -s 'sailənsə*, -z
silent, -ly 'sailənt, -li
Silenus sai'liːnəs
Silesia sai'liːzjə [si'l-, -ziə, -ʒjə, -ʒiə, -ʒə, -sjə, -siə, -ʃjə, -ʃiə, -ʃə]
Silesian, -s sai'liːzjən [si'l-, -ziən, -ʒjən, -ʒiən, -ʒən, -sjən, -siən, -ʃjən, -ʃiən, -ʃən], -z
silex 'saileks
silhouette, -s ˌsilu(ː)'et ['--'-, '---], -s
silic|a, -ate, -ated 'silik|ə, -it [-eit], -eitid
silicon 'silikən
silicone 'silikəun
silicosis ˌsili'kəusis
silicotic (*s. adj.*), -s ˌsili'kɔtik, -s
silk, -s -en silk, -s, -ən
silkworm, -s 'silk-wəːm, -z
silk|y, -ier, -iest, -iness 'silk|i, -iə* [-jə*], -iist [-jist], -inis
sill, -s (S.) sil, -z
sillabub 'siləbʌb [-bəb]
Sillence 'sailəns
Sillery 'siləri
Sillitoe 'silitəu
sill|y (*s. adj.*), -ies; -ier, -iest, -ily, -iness 'sil|i, -iz; -iə*, -iist, -ili, -inis
silo, -s 'sailəu, -z
Siloam sai'ləuəm [-'ləuæm]
silt (*s. v.*), -s, -ing, -ed; -y silt, -s, -iŋ, -id; -i
Silurian sai'ljuəriən [si'l-, -'luə-, -'ljɔər-, -'ljɔːr-]
Silva 'silvə
silvan 'silvən
Silvanus sil'veinəs
silv|er (*s. v.*), -ers, -ering, -ered; -ery, -eriness 'silv|ə*, -əz, -əriŋ, -əd; -əri, -ərinis
silver-gilt 'silvə'gilt [*also* '--- *when attributive*]
silver-grey 'silvə'grei
silver-plate 'silvə'pleit
silverside, -s 'silvəsaid, -z
silversmith, -s 'silvə-smiθ, -s
Silvertown, -s 'silvətaun, -z
Silvester sil'vestə*
Silvia 'silviə [-vjə]
Simenon 'siːmənɔ̃ːɳ [-nɔn] (simnɔ̃)
Simeon 'simiən [-mjən]
simian (*s. adj.*), -s 'simiən [-mjən], -z

similar, -ly 'similə*, -li
similarit|y, -ies ˌsimi'lærit|i, -iz
simile, -s 'simili, -z
similitude, -s si'militjuːd, -z
Simla 'simlə
simmer, -s, -ing, -ed 'simə*, -z, -riŋ, -d
Simmon(d)s 'simənz
simnel (S.), -s 'simnḷ [-nəl], -z
Simon 'saimən, *as surname also* si'məun
Simond 'saimənd, 'simənd
Simonds (*Lord*) 'siməndz
simoniacal ˌsaimə'naiəkəl [-məu'n-]
simony 'saiməni
simoom, -s si'muːm, -z
simper (*s. v.*), -s, -ing, -ed 'simpə*, -z, -riŋ, -d
Simpkin, -s, -son 'simpkin, -z, -sn
simp|le, -ler, -lest, -ly, -leness 'simp|l, -lə*, -list, -li, -lnis
simplehearted 'simpl'hɑːtid ['simpl,h-]
simple-minded 'simpl'maindid [*also* 'simpl,m- *when attributive*]
simpleton, -s 'simpltən, -z
simplicity sim'plisiti
simplification, -s ˌsimplifi'keiʃən, -z
simpli|fy, -fies, -fying, -fied 'simpli|fai, -faiz, -faiiŋ, -faid
Simplon 'sɛ̃ːmplɔ̃ːɳ ['sæmp-, -plɔːŋ, 'simplən] (sɛ̃plɔ̃)
simply 'simpli
Simpson 'simpsn
Sims simz
Simson 'simsn [-mps-]
simulacr|um, -a ˌsimju'leikr|əm, -ə
simulat|e, -es, -ing, -ed 'simjuleit, -s, -iŋ, -id
simulation, -s ˌsimju'leiʃən, -z
simultaneity ˌsiməltə'niəti [ˌsaim-, -mul-, -'niːiti, -'niːəti, -'neiiti]
simultaneous, -ly, -ness ˌsiməl'teinjəs [ˌsaim-, -mul-, -niəs], -li, -nis
sin (*s. v.*), -s, -ning, -ned, -ner/s sin, -z, -iŋ, -d, -ə*/z
sin (*in trigonometry*) sain
Sinai 'sainiai [-neiai, *old-fashioned* -ni]
sinapism, -s 'sinəpizəm, -z
Sinatra si'nɑːtrə
Sinbad 'sinbæd
since sins
sinceness 'sinsnis
sincere, -r, -st, -ly, -ness sin'siə* [sn-], -rə*, -rist, -li, -nis
sincerity sin'seriti [sn-]
sinciput, -s 'sinsipʌt [-pət], -s
Sinclair 'siŋkleə* ['sink-], 'siŋklə*
Sind sind
Sindbad 'sinbæd [-ndb-]
Sindh sind (*Hind.* syndh)

Sindhi 'sindi: (*Hind.* syndhi)
Sindlesham 'sindlʃəm
sine, -s sain, -z
sinecure, -s 'sainikjuə* ['sin-, -kjɔə*,
-kjɔ:*, -kjə:*], -z
sine die 'saini'daii(:) ['sini'di:ei]
Sinel 'sinəl
sine qua non, -s 'sainikwei'nɔn ['sini-
kwɑ:'nəun], -z
sinew, -s 'sinju:, -z
sinewy 'sinju(:)i
sin|ful, -fully, -fulness 'sin|fʊl, -fuli
[-fəli], -fʊlnis
sing, -s, -ing, sang, sung, singer/s siŋ,
-z, -iŋ, sæŋ, sʌŋ, 'siŋə*/z
singable 'siŋəbl
Singapore ,siŋgə'pɔ:* [,siŋə-, -'pɔə*, '--'-]
singe, -s, -ing, -d sindʒ, -iz, -iŋ, -d
Singer 'siŋə*, 'siŋgə*
Singhalese ,siŋhə'li:z [,siŋgə'l-, '--'-]
singing-ma ster, -s 'siŋiŋ,mɑ:stə*, -z
sing|le, -ly, -leness 'siŋg|l, -li, -lnis
single-handed 'siŋgl'hændid
singlehearted, -ly, -ness 'siŋgl'hɑ:tid
['siŋgl,h-], -li, -nis
single-minded 'siŋgl'maindid ['siŋgl,m-]
singlestick, -s 'siŋgl-stik, -s
singlet, -s 'siŋglit, -s
singleton (S.), -s 'siŋgltən, -z
singly 'siŋgli
singsong (*s. adj.*), -s 'siŋ-sɔŋ, -z
singular (*s. adj.*), -s, -ly 'siŋgjulə*
[-gjəl-], -z, -li
singularit|y, -ies ,siŋgju'lærit|i, -iz
sinh (*in trigonometry*) ʃain
Sinhalese ,siŋhə'li:z [,sinhə'l-, ,sinə'l-,
'--'-]
Sinim 'sinim ['sain-]
sinister 'sinistə*
sinistr|al, -ally 'sinistr|əl, -əli
sink (*s. v.*), -s, -ing, sank, sunk, sunken,
sink|er/s; -able siŋk, -s, -iŋ, sæŋk,
sʌŋk, 'sʌŋkən, 'siŋk|ə*/z; -əbl
sinless, -ly, -ness 'sinlis, -li, -nis
sinner, -s 'sinə*, -z
Sinnett 'sinit, si'net
Note.—*A. P. Sinnett, at one time
editor of the 'Pioneer', Allahabad,
pronounced* 'sinit.
Sinn Fein, -er/s 'ʃin'fein ['sin-], -ə*/z
sinologue, -s 'sinəlɔg [-ləug], -z
sinolog|y, -ist si'nɔlədʒ|i ['sai'n-], -ist
sinuosit|y, -ies ,sinju'ɔsit|i, -iz
sinuous 'sinjŭəs [-njwəs]
sinus, -es 'sainəs, -iz
sinusitis ,sainə'saitis
sinusoid, -s 'sainəsɔid, -z
Siobhan ʃi'vɔ:n [ʃə'v-]

Sion 'saiən ['zaiən]
Sioux (*sing.*) su:, (*plur.*) su:z
sip (*s. v.*), -s, -ping, -ped sip, -s, -iŋ, -t
siph|on (*s. v.*), -ons, -oning, -oned
'saif|ən, -ənz, -əniŋ [-ŋiŋ], -ənd
sir, -s sə:*, -z (*strong form*), sə* (*weak
form*)
Sirach 'siəræk
sirdar (S.), -s 'sə:dɑ:*, -z
sir|e (*s. v.*), -es, -ing, -ed 'saiə*, -z, -riŋ,
siren, -s 'saiərən [-rin], -z   [-d
Sirion 'siriən
Sirius (*star*) 'siriəs [*rarely* 'saiər-]
sirloin, -s 'sə:lɔin, -z
sirocco, -s si'rɔkəu, -z
sirrah 'sirə
sisal 'saisəl [*old-fashioned* 'sisl]
Sisal (*Mexican port*) si'sɑ:l (si'sal)
Sisam 'saisəm
Sisera 'sisərə
Siskin, -s 'siskin, -z
sisson 'sisn
siss|y, -ies 'sis|i, -iz
sister, -s; -ly 'sistə*, -z; -li
sisterhood, -s 'sistəhud, -z
sister-in-law, sisters-in-law 'sistərinlɔ:,
'sistəzinlɔ:
Sistine 'sistain [-ti:n]
sistrum, -s 'sistrəm, -z
Sisum 'saisəm
Sisyphean ,sisi'fi(:)ən
Sisyphus 'sisifəs
sit, -s, -ting/s, sat, sitter/s sit, -s, -iŋ/z,
sæt, 'sitə*/z
sit-down (s.) 'sitdaun
site, -s sait, -s
sitter-in, -s 'sitər'in, -z
Sittingbourne 'sitiŋbɔ:n [-bəən]
situate 'sitjueit [-tʃueit, -tjuit, -tʃuit]
situated 'sitjueitid [-tʃu-]
situation, -s ,sitju'eiʃən [-tʃu-], -z
Sitwell 'sitwəl [-wel]
Siva 'sivə ['ʃiv-, 'si:v-, 'ʃi:v-] (*Hind.* ʃyva)
Sivyer (*surname*) 'siviə* [-vjə*]
Siward 'sju(:)əd
six, -es; -fold siks, -iz; -fəuld
sixain, -s 'siksein, -z
sixer, -s 'siksə*, -z
six-foot (adj.) 'siksfut
six-footer, -s 'siks'futə*, -z
sixish 'siksiʃ
six|pence, -pences, -penny 'siks|pəns,
-pənsiz, -pəni
six-shooter, -s 'siks'ʃu:tə* ['sikʃ'ʃ-], -z
sixte sikst
sixteen, -s, -th/s, -thly 'siks'ti:n
['--, -'-, *according to sentence-stress*],
-z, -θ/s, -θli

sixteenmo [16mo] siks'ti:nmən

sixth, -s, -ly siksθ [-kstθ], -s, -li

Sixtus 'sikstəs

sixt|y, -ies, -ieth/s 'sikst|i, -iz, -iiθ/s [-jiθ/s, -ïəθ/s, -jəθ/s]

sizable 'saizəbl

sizar, -s; -ship/s 'saizə*, -z; -ʃip/s

siz|e (s. v.), -es, -ing, -ed saiz, -iz, -iŋ, -d

sizeable 'saizəbl

sizz|le, -les, -ling, -led 'siz|l, -lz, -ḷiŋ [-liŋ], -ld

sjambok (s. v.), -s, -ing, -ed 'ʃæmbɔk, -s, -iŋ, -t

Skagerrak 'skægəræk

skat|e (s. v.), -es, -ing, -ed, -er/s skeit, -s, -iŋ, -id, -ə*/z

skating-rink, -s 'skeitiŋriŋk, -s

skean dhu, -s 'ski:ən'du:, -z

Skeat ski:t

skedadd|le, -les, -ling, -led ski'dæd|l, -lz, -ḷiŋ [-liŋ], -ld

Skeggs skegz

Skegness 'skeg'nes ['—, -'-, according to sentence-stress]

skein, -s skein, -z

skeleton, -s 'skelitn, -z

skelter 'skeltə*

Skelton 'skeltn

sketch (s. v.), -es, -ing, -ed; -able sketʃ, -iz, -iŋ, -t; -əbl

sketch-book, -s 'sketʃbuk, -s

Sketchley 'sketʃli

sketch|y, -ier, -iest, -ily, -iness 'sketʃ|i, -ïə*, -iist, -ili, -inis

skew (s. adj.), -s skju:, -z

skewer (s. v.), -s, -ing, -ed skjuə*, -z, -riŋ, -d

Skey ski:

ski (s. v.), -s, -ing, -'d [ski-ed] ski:, -z, -iŋ, -d

skiagram, -s 'skaiəgræm, -z

skiagraph, -s 'skaiəgrɑ:f [-græf], -s

Skibo 'ski:bəu

ski-borne 'ski:bɔ:n [-bɔən]

skid, -s, -ding, -ded skid, -z, -iŋ, -id

Skiddaw 'skidɔ: [locally -də]

skier (one who skis), -s 'ski:ə ['ʃi:ə*], -z

skiff, -s skif, -s

skiffle 'skifl

ski-jump, -s 'ski:-dʒʌmp, -s

skil|ful, -fully, -fulness 'skil|ful, -fuli [-fəli], -fulnis

skill, -s, -ed skil, -z, -d

skilly 'skili

skim, -s, -ming, -med, -mer/s skim, -z, -iŋ, -d, -ə*/z

skim-milk 'skim'milk ['skimmilk]

skimp, -s, -ing/ly, -ed; -y, -ier, -iest, -iness skimp, -s, -iŋ/li, -t [skimt]; -i, -ïə* [-jə*], -iist [-jist], -inis

skin (s. v.), -s, -ning, -ned skin, -z, -iŋ, -d

skin-deep 'skin'di:p ['skindi:p]

skin-div|e, -es, -ing, -ed, -er/s 'skin-daiv, -z, -iŋ, -d, -ə*/z

skinflint, -s 'skin-flint, -s

skinner (S.), -s 'skinə*, -z

skinn|y, -ier, -iest, -iness 'skin|i, -ïə*, -iist, -inis

skip (s. v.), -s, -ping, -ped skip, -s, -iŋ, -t

skipper, -s 'skipə*, -z

skipping-rope, -s 'skipiŋrəup, -s

Skipton 'skiptən

skirmish (s. v.), -es, -ing, -ed, -er/s 'skə:miʃ, -iz, -iŋ, -t, -ə*/z

skirt (s. v.), -s, -ing/s, -ed skə:t, -s, -iŋ/z, -id

skirt-danc|er/s, -ing 'skə:t‚dɑ:ns|ə*/z, -iŋ

skirting-board, -s 'skə:tiŋbɔ:d [-bɔəd], -z

skit, -s skit, -s

ski-troops 'ski:-tru:ps

skittish, -ly, -ness 'skitiʃ, -li, -nis

skittle, -s 'skitl, -z

skiv|e, -es, -ing, -ed, -er/s skaiv, -z, -iŋ, -d, -ə*/z

Skrimshire 'skrimʃə*

Skrine skri:n

skua, -s 'skju:ə [skjuə], -z

skulk, -s, -ing, -ed skʌlk, -s, -iŋ, -t

skull, -s skʌl, -s

skull-cap, -s 'skʌl-kæp, -s

skunk, -s skʌŋk, -s

sk|y (s. v.), -ies, -ying, -ied, -ier/s sk|ai, -aiz, -aiiŋ, -aid, -ai-ə*/z

sky-blue 'skai'blu: [also 'skai-blu: when attributive]

Skye skai

sky-high 'skai'hai

skylark (s. v.), -s, -ing, -ed 'skailɑ:k, -s, -iŋ, -t

skylight, -s 'skailait, -s

sky-line, -s 'skailain, -z

skymaster, -s 'skai‚mɑ:stə*, -z

sky-rocket (s. v.), -s, -ing, -ed 'skai-‚rɔkit, -s, -iŋ, -id

skyscape, -s 'skai:-skeip, -s

skyscraper, -s 'skai‚skreipə*, -z

skyward, -s 'skaiwəd, -z

sky-writing 'skai‚raitiŋ

slab (s. v.), -s, -bing, -bed slæb, -z, -iŋ, -d

slack (s. adj. v.), -s; -er, -est, -ly, -ness; -ing, -ed, -er/s slæk, -s; -ə*, -ist, -li, -nis; -iŋ, -t, -ə*/z

slack|en, -ens, -ening, -ened 'slæk|ən, -ənz, -niŋ, [-niŋ, -əniŋ], -ənd
Slade sleid
slag, -gy slæg, -i
slain (from slay) slein
Slaithwaite 'slæθwət [-weit, locally also 'slauit]
slak|e, -es, -ing, -ed sleik, -s, -iŋ, -t
slalom, -s 'sleiləm ['slɑːl-], -z
slam (s. v.), -s, -ming, -med slæm, -z, -iŋ, -d
sland|er (s. v.), -ers, -ering, -ered, -erer/s 'slɑːnd|ə*, -əz, -əriŋ, -əd, -ərə*/z
slanderous, -ly, -ness 'slɑːndərəs, -li, -nis
slang (s. v.), -s, -ing, -ed; -y, -ier, -iest, -ily, -iness slæŋ, -z, -iŋ, -d; -i, -iə*, -iist, -ili, -inis
slant (s. adj. v.), -s, -ing/ly, -ed slɑːnt, -s, -iŋ/li, -id
slantwise 'slɑːnt-waiz
slap (s. v. adv.), -s, -ping, -ped slæp, -s, -iŋ, -t
slap-bang 'slæp'bæŋ [-iŋ, -t
slapdash 'slæpdæʃ
slap-stick, -s 'slæpstik, -s
slap-up (adj.) 'slæpʌp ['slæp'ʌp]
slash (s. v.), -es, -ing, -ed slæʃ, -iz, -iŋ, -t
slat, -s slæt, -s
slat|e (s. v.), -es, -ing, -ed, -er/s sleit, -s, -iŋ, -id, -ə*/z
slate-coloured 'sleit,kʌləd
slate-grey 'sleit'grei
slate-pencil, -s 'sleit'pensl, -z
Slater 'sleitə*
slattern, -s, -ly, -liness 'slætə(:)n, -z, -li, -linis
slaty 'sleiti
slaught|er (s. v.) (S.), -ers, -ering, -ered, -erer/s; -erous/ly 'slɔːt|ə*, -əz, -əriŋ, -əd, -ərə*/z, -ərəs/li
slaughterhou|se, -ses 'slɔːtəhau|s, -ziz
Slav, -s slɑːv [slæv], -z
slav|e (s. v.), -es, -ing, -ed, -er/s sleiv, -z, -iŋ, -d, -ə*/z
slave-driv|er/s, -ing 'sleiv,draiv|ə*/z, -iŋ
slave-owner, -s 'sleiv,əunə*, -z
slaver (slave-trader), -s 'sleivə*, -z
slaver (s. v.) (slobber), -s, -ing, -ed 'slævə*, -z, -riŋ, -d
slavery 'sleivəri
slave-ship, -s 'sleivʃip, -s
slave-trade, -r/s 'sleivtreid, -ə*/z
slavey, -s 'slævi ['sleivi], -z
Slavic 'slævik ['slɑːv-]
slavish, -ly, -ness 'sleiviʃ, -li, -nis
Slavonic slə'vɔnik [slæ'v-, slɑː'v-]
slay, -s, -ing, slew, slain, slayer/s slei, -z, -iŋ, slu:, slein, 'sleiə*/z

Slazenger 'slæzəndʒə*
sledg|e (s. v.), -es, -ing, -ed sledʒ, -iz, -iŋ, -d
sledge-hammer, -s 'sledʒ,hæmə*, -z
sleek, -er, -est, -ly, -ness sliːk, -ə*, -ist, -li, -nis
sleep (s. v.), -s, -ing, slept sliːp, -s, -iŋ, slept
sleeper, -s 'sliːpə*, -z
sleeping-car, -s 'sliːpiŋ-kɑː*, -z
sleeping-draught, -s 'sliːpiŋdrɑːft, -s
sleepless, -ly, -ness 'sliːp-lis, -li, -nis
sleepwalk|er/s, -ing 'sliːp,wɔːk|ə*/z, -iŋ
sleep|y, -ier, -iest, -ily, -iness 'sliːp|i, -iə* [-jə*], -iist [-jist], -ili, -inis
sleepyhead, -s 'sliːpihed, -z
sleet (s. v.), -s, -ing, -ed; -y, -iness sliːt, -s, -iŋ, -id; -i, -inis
sleeve, -s, -d; -less sliːv, -z, -d; -lis
sleigh (s. v.), -s, -ing, -ed slei, -z, -iŋ, -d
sleight (S.) slait
Sleights (in Yorks.) slaits
slender, -er, -est, -ly, -ness 'slendə*, -rə*, -rist, -li, -nis
slept (from sleep) slept
sleuth (s. v.), -s, -ing, -ed slu:θ [slju:θ], -s, -iŋ, -t
sleuth-hound, -s 'slu:θ'haund ['slju:θ-, '--], -z
slew (from slay) slu:
slic|e (s. v.), -es, -ing, -ed, -er/s slais, -iz, -iŋ, -t, -ə*/z
slick, -er, -est, -ly, -ness slik, -ə*, -ist, -li, -nis
slid (from slide) slid
slid|e (s. v.), -es, -ing, slid slaid, -z, -iŋ, slid
slide-rule, -s 'slaid-ru:l, -z
slide-valve, -s 'slaidvælv, -z
slight (s. adj. v.), -s; -er, -est, -ly, -ness; -ing/ly, -ed slait, -s; -ə*, -ist, -li, -nis; -iŋ/li, -id
slightish 'slaitiʃ
Sligo 'slaigəu
slim (adj. v.) (S.), -mer, -mest, -ly, -ness; -s, -ming, -med slim, -ə*, -ist, -li, -nis; -z, -iŋ, -d
slim|e (s. v.), -es, -ing, -ed slaim, -z, -iŋ, -d
slim|y, -ier, -iest, -ily, -iness 'slaim|i, -iə* [-jə*], -iist [-jist], -ili, -inis
sling (s. v.), -s, -ing, slung sliŋ, -z, -iŋ, slʌŋ
slink, -s, -ing, slunk sliŋk, -s, -iŋ, slʌŋk
slip (s. v.), -s, -ping, -ped slip, -s, -iŋ, -t
slip-carriage, -s 'slip,kæridʒ, -iz
slip-coach, -es 'slipkəutʃ, -iz
slip-knot, -s 'slipnɔt, -s

slipover, -s 'slip,əuvə*, -z
slipper, -s, -ed 'slipə*, -z, -d
slipper|y, -ier, -iest, -ily, -iness 'slipər|i,
-ïə*, -iist, -ili, -inis
slipp|y, -ier, -iest, -iness 'slip|i, -ïə*,
-iist, -inis
slipshod 'slipʃɔd
slipstream, -s 'slip-stri:m, -z
slipway, -s 'slipwei, -z
slit (s. v.), -s, -ting slit, -s, -iŋ
slith|er, -ers, -ering, -ered; -ery 'slið|ə*,
-əz, -əriŋ, -əd; -əri
sliver (s. v.), -s, -ing, -ed 'slivə* ['slaiv-],
-z, -riŋ, -d
Sloan(e) sləun
slobber (s. v.), -s, -ing, -ed 'slɔbə*, -z,
-riŋ, -d
slobber|y, -iness 'slɔbər|i, -inis
Slocombe 'sləukəm
Slocum 'sləukəm
sloe, -s sləu, -z
slog (s. v.), -s, -ging, -ged, -ger/s slɔg,
-z, -iŋ, -d, -ə*/z
slogan, -s 'sləugən, -z
sloid slɔid
sloop, -s slu:p, -s
slop (s. v.), -s, -ping, -ped slɔp, -s, -iŋ, -t
slop-basin, -s 'slɔp,beisn, -z
slop|e (s. v.), -es, -ing/ly, -ed, -er/s
sləup, -s, -iŋ/li, -t, -ə*/z
Sloper 'sləupə*
slop-pail, -s 'slɔppeil, -z
slopp|y, -ier, -iest, -ily, -iness 'slɔp|i,
-ïə*, -iist, -ili, -inis
slops (s.) slɔps
slosh (s. v.), -es, -ing, -ed; -y, -ier, -iest,
-iness slɔʃ, -iz, -iŋ, -t; -i, -ïə*, -iist,
-inis
slot (s. v.), -s, -ting, -ted slɔt, -s, -iŋ, -id
sloth, -s sləuθ, -s
sloth|ful, -fully, -fulness 'sləuθ|ful,
-fuli [-fəli], -fulnis
slot-machine, -s 'slɔtmə,ʃi:n, -z
slouch (s. v.), -es, -ing/ly, -ed slautʃ, -iz,
-iŋ/li, -t
slouch-hat, -s 'slautʃ'hæt, -s
slough (bog), -s, -y slau, -z, -i
slough (skin of snake), -s slʌf, -s
slough (v.) (cast off skin), -s, -ing, -ed
slʌf, -s, -iŋ, -t
Slough slau
Slovak, -s 'sləuvæk, -s
Slovakia sləu'vækïə [-'vækjə, -'vɑ:kïə,
-'vɑ:kjə, rarely -'veikïə, -'veikjə]
sloven, -s 'slʌvn, -z
Slovene, -s 'sləuvi:n [sləu'vi:n], -z
Slovenian, -s sləu'vi:nïən [-nïən], -z
slovenl|y, -iness 'slʌvnl|i, -inis

slow (adj. v.), -er, -est, -ly, -ness; -s,
-ing, -ed sləu, -ə*, -ist, 'sləuli
['sləu-li], 'sləu-nis; -z, -iŋ, -d
slow-coach, -es 'sləu-kəutʃ ['sləukəutʃ],
-iz
slow-motion 'sləu'məuʃən [also '-,--
when attributive]
slow-worm, -s 'sləuwə:m, -z
slug, -s slʌg, -z
sluggard, -s 'slʌgəd, -z
sluggish, -ly, -ness 'slʌgiʃ, -li, -nis
sluic|e (s. v.), -es, -ing, -ed slu:s, -iz,
-iŋ, -t
sluice-gate, -s 'slu:s'geit ['--], -s
slum (s. v.), -s, -ming, -med, -mer/s
slʌm, -z, -iŋ, -d, -ə*/z
slumb|er (s. v.), -ers, -ering, -ered,
-erer/s; -erless 'slʌmb|ə*, -əz, -əriŋ,
-əd, -ərə*/z; -əlis
slumland 'slʌmlænd
slumm|y, -ier, -iest, -iness 'slʌm|i, -ïə*,
-iist, -inis
slump (s. v.), -s, -ing, -ed slʌmp, -s, -iŋ,
-t [slʌmt]
slung (from sling) slʌŋ
slunk (from slink) slʌŋk
slur (s. v.), -s, -ring, -red slə:*, -z, -riŋ, -d
slush, -y, -ier, -iest, -iness slʌʃ, -i, -ïə*,
-iist, -inis
slut, -s slʌt, -s
sluttish, -ly, -ness 'slʌtiʃ, -li, -nis
Sluys slɔis
sly, -er, -est, -ly, -ness slai, 'slai-ə*,
'slaiist, 'slai-li, 'slai-nis
slyboots 'slaibu:ts
smack (s. v.), -s, -ing/s, -ed smæk, -s,
-iŋ/z, -t
Smale smeil
small (s. adj. adv.) (S.), -s; -er, -est,
-ness; -ish smɔ:l, -z; -ə*, -ist, -nis; -iʃ
smallage 'smɔ:lidʒ
Smalley 'smɔ:li
small-hold|er/s, -ing/s 'smɔ:l'həuld|-
ə*/z, -iŋ/z
smallpox 'smɔ:l-pɔks
small-talk 'smɔ:l-tɔ:k
Smallwood 'smɔ:lwud
smalt smɔ:lt [smɔlt]
smarm (s. v.), -s, -ing, -ed; -y, -iness
smɑ:m, -z, -iŋ, -d; -i, -inis
smart (s. adj. v.) (S.), -s; -er, -est, -ly,
-ness; -ing, -ed smɑ:t, -s; -ə*, -ist, -li,
-nis; -iŋ, -id
smart|en, -ens, -ening, -ened 'smɑ:t|n,
-nz, -ŋin [-niŋ], -nd
smartish 'smɑ:tiʃ
smash (s. v.), -es, -ing, -ed, -er/s smæʃ,
-iz, -iŋ, -t, -ə*/z

smash-and-grab 'smæʃən'græb ['—]
smatterer, -s 'smætərə*, -z
smattering, -s 'smætəriŋ, -z
smear (s. v.), -s, -ing, -ed; -y, -iness
smiə*, -z, -riŋ, -d; -ri, -rinis
Smeaton 'smi:tn
smell|l (s. v.), -ls, -ling, -t smel, -z, -iŋ, -t
smelling-bottle, -s 'smeliŋ,bɔtl, -z
smelling-salts 'smeliŋ-sɔːlts [-sɔlts]
smell|y, -ier, -iest, -iness 'smel|i, -iə*,
-iist, -inis
smelt (s. v.), -s, -ing, -ed smelt, -s, -iŋ,
-id
Smetana 'smetənə
Smethwick 'smeðik
Smieton 'smi:tn
Smike smaik
smilax, -es 'smailæks, -iz
smil|e (s. v.), -es (S.), -ing/ly, -ed smail,
-z, -iŋ/li, -d
Smiley 'smaili
Smillie 'smaili
smirch (s. v.), -es, -ing, -ed smə:tʃ, -iz,
-iŋ, -t
smirk (s. v.), -s, -ing, -ed, -er/s; -y
smə:k, -s, -iŋ, -t, -ə*/z; -i
Smirke smə:k
smit (from smite) smit
smit|e, -es, -ing, smote, smit, smitten,
smiter/s smait, -s, -iŋ, sməut, smit,
'smitn, 'smaitə*/z
smith (S.), -s smiθ, -s
Smith|ells, -er/s 'smiθ|əlz, -ə*/z
smithereens 'smiðə'ri:nz [,smiðə'r-]
Smithfield 'smiθfi:ld
Smithson 'smiθsn
Smithsonian smiθ'səunjən [-nïən]
smith|y, -ies 'smiθ|i ['smiθ|i], -iz
smitten (from smite) 'smitn
smock (s. v.), -s, -ing, -ed smɔk, -s, -iŋ, -t
smock-frock, -s 'smɔk'frɔk ['—], -s
smog smɔg
smokable, -s 'sməukəbl, -z
smok|e (s. v.), -es, -ing, -ed, -er/s
sməuk, -s, -iŋ, -t, -ə*/z
smoke-ball, -s 'sməukbɔ:l, -z
smoke-bomb, -s 'sməukbɔm, -z
smoke-box, -es 'sməukbɔks, -iz
smokeless 'sməuk-lis
smoke-room, -s 'sməuk-rum [-ru:m], -z
smoke-screen, -s 'sməuk-skri:n, -z
smoke-stack, -s 'sməuk-stæk, -s
Smokies 'sməukiz
smoking-carriage, -s 'sməukiŋ,kæridʒ,
-iz
smoking-compartment, -s 'sməukiŋ-
kəm,pɑ:tmənt, -s
smoking-concert, -s 'sməukiŋ,kɔnsət, -s

smoking-jacket, -s 'sməukiŋ,dʒækit, -s
smoking-room, -s 'sməukiŋ,rum
[-,ru:m], -z
smok|y, -ier, -iest, -ily, -iness 'sməuk|i,
-iə* [-jə*], -iist [-jist], -ili, -inis
Smollett 'smɔlit
smolt sməult
smooth (adj.), -er, -est, -ly, -ness
smu:ð, -ə*, -ist, -li, -nis
smooth|(e) (v.), -(e)s, -ing, -ed smu:ð,
-z, -iŋ, -d
smooth-faced 'smu:ðfeist
smote (from smite) sməut
smoth|er, -ers, -ering, -ered 'smʌð|ə*,
-əz, -əriŋ, -əd
smould|er, -ers, -ering, -ered 'sməuld|ə*,
-əz, -əriŋ, -əd
smudg|e (s. v.), -es, -ing, -ed; -y, -ier,
-iest, -ily, -iness smʌdʒ, -iz, -iŋ, -d;
-i, -iə*, -iist, -ili, -inis
smug (s. adj.), -s, -ly, -ness smʌg, -z, -li,
-nis
smugg|le, -les, -ling, -led 'smʌg|l, -lz,
-liŋ [-liŋ], -ld
smuggler, -s 'smʌglə*, -z
smut, -s, -ty, -tier, -tiest, -tily, -tiness
smʌt, -s; -i, -iə*, -iist, -ili, -inis
Smyrna 'smə:nə
Smyth smiθ, smaiθ
Smythe smaið, smaiθ
snack, -s snæk, -s
Snaefell 'snei-fel
snaff|le (s. v.), -les, -ling, -led 'snæf|l,
-lz, -liŋ [-liŋ], -ld
snag, -s snæg, -z
Snagge snæg
snail, -s; -like sneil, -z; -laik
snake, -s sneik, -s
snake-charmer, -s 'sneik,tʃɑ:mə*, -z
snak|y, -iness 'sneik|i, -inis
snap (s. v.), -s, -ping, -ped snæp, -s, -iŋ, -t
snapdragon, -s 'snæp,drægən, -z
snappish, -ly, -ness 'snæpiʃ, -li, -nis
snapp|y, -ier, -iest, -ily, -iness 'snæp|i,
-iə*, -iist, -ili, -inis
snapshot (s. v.), -s, -ting, -ted 'snæpʃɔt,
-s, -iŋ, -id
snar|e (s. v.), -es, -ing, -ed snsə*, -z,
-riŋ, -d
snark, -s snɑ:k, -s
snarl (s. v.), -s, -ing, -ed snɑ:l, -z, -iŋ, -d
snatch (s. v.), -es, -ing, -ed, -er/s
snætʃ, -iz, -iŋ, -t, -ə*/z
snatch|y, -ier, -iest, -ily 'snætʃ|i, -iə*,
-iist, -ili
sneak (s. v.), -s, -ing/ly, -ed; -y, -ier,
-iest, -ily, -iness sni:k, -s, -iŋ/li, -t;
-i, -iə* [-jə*], -iist [-jist], -ili, -inis

sneakers' sni:kəz

sneak-raid, -s ,-ing, -er/s 'sni:k-reid, -z, -iŋ, -ə*/z

sneer (s. v.), -s, -ing/ly, -ed sniə*, -z, -riŋ/li, -d

sneez|e (s. v.), -es, -ing, -ed sni:z, -iz, -iŋ, -d

Sneffels 'snefəlz

Snelgrove 'snelgrəuv

snell (S.), -s snel, -z

Snewin 'snju(:)in

Sneyd (in Staffs.) sni:d

Sneyd-Kinnersley 'sni:d'kinəsli

snick (s. v.), -s, -ing, -ed snik, -s, -iŋ, -t

snickersnee, -s 'snikə'sni:, -z

sniff (s. v.), -s, -ing, -ed; -y, -ier, -iest, -ily, -iness snif, -s, -iŋ, -t; -i, -iə*, -iist, -ili, -inis

snigger (s. v.), -s, -ing, -ed 'snigə*, -z, -riŋ, -d

snip, -s, -ping, -ped, -per/s snip, -s, -iŋ, -t, -ə*/z

snip|e (s. v.), -es, -ing, -ed ,-er/s snaip, -s, -iŋ, -t, -ə*/z

snippet, -s; -y 'snipit, -s; -i

sniv|el, -els, -elling, -elled, -eller/s 'sniv|l, -lz, -liŋ, -ld, -lə*/z

snob, -s; -bery, -bism snɔb, -z; -əri, -izəm

snobbish, -ly, -ness 'snɔbiʃ, -li, -nis

Snodgrass 'snɔdgrɑ:s

snood, -s, -ed snu:d [snud], -z, -id

snook (fish), -s snu:k, -s

snook (gesture), -s snu:k [snuk], -s

snooker 'snu:kə*

snoop, -s, -ing, -ed, -er/s snu:p, -s, -iŋ, -t, -ə*/z

snooz|e (s. v.), -es, -ing, -ed snu:z, -iz, -iŋ, -d

snor|e (s. v.), -es, -ing, -ed, -er/s snɔː* [snɔə*], -z, -riŋ, -d, -rə*/z

snorkel, -s 'snɔːkəl, -z

snort (s. v.), -s, -ing, -ed snɔːt, -s, -iŋ, -id

snorter, -s 'snɔːtə*, -z

snort|y, -ier, -iest, -ily, -iness 'snɔːt|i, -iə*, -iist, -ili, -inis

snot, -ty snɔt, -i

snout (S.), -s snaut, -s

snow (s. v.) (S.), -s, -ing, -ed snəu, -z, -iŋ, -d

snowball, -s, -ing 'snəubɔːl, -z, -iŋ

snow-blindness 'snəu'blaindnis

snow-boot, -s 'snəubu:t, -s

snow-bound 'snəubaund

snow-cap, -s, -ped 'snəu-kæp, -s, -t

Snow|den, -don 'snəu|dn, -dn

Snowdonia snəu'dəunjə [-niə]

snow-drift, -s 'snəu-drift, -s

snowdrop, -s 'snəudrɔp ['snəu-drɔp], -s

snowfall, -s 'snəu-fɔːl, -z

snow-field, -s 'snəu-fiːld, -z

snowflake, -s 'snəu-fleik, -s

snow-line, -s 'snəulain, -z

snow|-man, -men 'snəu|mæn, -men

snow-plough, -s 'snəu-plau, -z

snow-shoe, -s 'snəu-ʃuː, -z

snowstorm, -s 'snəu-stɔːm, -z

snow-white 'snəu'wait [-'hwait, '--]

snow|y, -ily, -iness 'snəu|i, -ili, -inis

snub (s. adj. v.), -s, -bing, -bed snʌb, -z, -iŋ, -d

snub-nosed 'snʌbnəuzd

snuff (s. v.), -s, -ing, -ed, -er/s snʌf, -s, -iŋ, -t, -ə*/z

snuff-box, -es 'snʌfbɔks, -iz

snuff-coloured 'snʌf,kʌləd

snuff|le, -les, -ling, -led, -ler/s 'snʌf|l, -lz, -liŋ [-liŋ], -ld, -lə*/z [-lə*/z]

snug, -ger, -gest, -ly, -ness snʌg, -ə*, -ist, -li, -nis

snugger|y, -ies 'snʌgər|i, -iz

snugg|le, -les, -ling, -led 'snʌg|l, -lz, -liŋ [-liŋ], -ld

so səu (normal form), sə (occasional weak form)

soak (s. v.), -s, -ing, -ed səuk, -s, -iŋ, -t

Soames səumz

so-and-so 'səuənsəu

Soane, -s səun, -z

soap (s. v.), -s, -ing, -ed; -y, -ier, -iest, -ily, -iness səup, -s, -iŋ, -t; -i, -iə* [-jə*], -iist [-jist], -ili, -inis

soap-bubble, -s 'səup,bʌbl, -z

soapstone 'səupstəun

soapsuds 'səupsʌdz

soar, -s, -ing, -ed sɔː* [sɔə*], -z, -riŋ, -d

Soares 'sɔːɑːriz

sob (s. v.), -s, -bing, -bed sɔb, -z, -iŋ, -d

sober, -er, -est, -ly, -ness 'səubə*, -rə*, -rist, -li, -nis

sobriety səu'braiəti

sobriquet, -s 'səubrikei, -z

sob-stuff 'sɔbstʌf

socage 'sɔkidʒ

so-called 'səu'kɔːld ['--, -'-, according to sentence-stress]

soccer 'sɔkə*

sociability ,səuʃə'biliti [-lət-]

sociab|le, -ly, -leness 'səuʃəb|l, -li, -lnis

soci|al, -ally 'səuʃ|əl, -əli [-li]

sociali|sm, -st/s 'səuʃəli|zm [-ʃli-], -st/s

socialistic ,səuʃə'listik [-ʃl'i-]

socialization [-isa-] ,səuʃəlai'zeiʃən [-ʃai-]

societ|y (S.), -ies sə'saiət|i, -iz

Socinian, -s səu'siniən [-njən], -z

socinianism səu'sinĭənizæm [-njən-]
Socinus səu'sainəs
sociologic|al,   -ally   ˌsəusjə'lɔdʒik|əl
[-sĭə-, -ʃjə-, -ʃĭə-], -əli
sociolog|ist/s, -y ˌsəusi'ɔlədʒ|ist/s, -i
sock, -s sɔk, -s
socket, -s, -ed 'sɔkit, -s, -id
Socotra səu'kəutrə [sɔ'k-]
Socrates 'sɔkrəti:z ['səuk-]
socratic, -ally sɔ'krætik [səu'k-], -əli
sod, -s sɔd, -z
soda, -s 'səudə, -z
soda-fountain, -s 'səudə,fauntin, -z
sodalit|y, -ies səu'dælit|i, -iz
soda-water 'səudə,wɔ:tə*
soda-water-bottle, -s 'səudə,wɔ:tə,bɔtl, -z
sodd|en (adj. v.), -enness; -ens, -ening,
-ened 'sɔd|n, -nnis; -nz, -ṇiŋ, -nd
sodium 'səudjəm [-dĭəm]
Sodom 'sɔdəm
sodom|y, -ite/s 'sɔdəm|i, -ait/s
Sodor 'səudə*
soever səu'evə*
sofa, -s 'səufə, -z
Sofala səu'fɑ:lə
Soffe (surname) səuf
soffit, -s 'sɔfit, -s
Sofia (in Bulgaria) 'səufjə ['səufĭə,
'sɔfĭə, səu'fi:ə, old-fashioned sə'faiə]
soft (s. adj.), -s; -er, -est, -ly, -ness
sɔft [sɔ:ft], -s; -ə*, -ist, -li, -nis
soft|en, -ens, -ening, -ened 'sɔf|n
['sɔ:f-], -nz, -niŋ [-ṇiŋ], -nd
softener, -s 'sɔfnə* ['sɔ:f-, -fnə*], -z
soft-headed 'sɔft,hedid ['sɔ:ft-]
soft-hearted 'sɔft'hɑ:tid ['sɔ:ft-, also
'-,--, esp. when attributive]
softish 'sɔftiʃ ['sɔ:ft-]
soft-ped|al (v.), -als, -alling, -alled
'sɔft'ped|l ['sɔ:ft-], -lz, -ḷiŋ, -ld
soft-spoken 'sɔft,spəukən ['sɔ:ft-, '-'--]
sogg|y, -ier, -iest, -iness 'sɔg|i, -ĭə*,
-iist, -inis
soh (note in Tonic Sol-fa), -s səu, -z
Soho 'səuhəu [səu'həu]
Sohrab 'sɔ:ræb
soil (s. v.), -s, -ing, -ed sɔil, -z, -iŋ, -d
soil-pipe, -s 'sɔil-paip, -s
soirée, -s 'swɑ:rei ['swɔr-] (sware), -z
sojourn (s. v.), -s, -ing, -ed, -er/s 'sɔ-
dʒə:n ['sʌdʒ-, -dʒən], -z, -iŋ, -d, -ə*/z
sol (S.), -s sɔl, -z
sola 'səulə
solac|e (s. v.), -es, -ing, -ed 'sɔləs [-lis],
-iz, -iŋ, -t
solamen, -s səu'leimen, -z
solanum səu'leinəm [-'lɑ:nəm]
solar 'səulə*

solarium, -s səu'lɛərĭəm, -z
solati|um, -ums, -a səu'leiʃj|əm [-ʃĭ|-],
-əmz, -ə
sold (from sell) səuld
sold|er (s. v.), -ers, -ering, -ered 'sɔld|ə*
['sɔ:d-, 'sɔd-, 'səuld-], -əz, -əriŋ, -əd
soldier, -s, -ing; -y 'səuldʒə* [rarely
-djə*], -z, -riŋ; -ri
soldierly 'səuldʒəli [rarely -djə-]
sold|o, -i 'sɔld|əu, -i:
sol|e (s. adj. v.) (S.), -es; -ely; -ing, -ed
səul, -z; -li; -iŋ, -d
solecism, -s 'sɔlisizəm [-les-, -ləs-], -z
solemn, -ly 'sɔləm, -li
solemnity sə'lemniti [sɔ'l-]
solemnization [-isa-], -s 'sɔləmnai'zeiʃən [ˌsɔl-, -ni'z-], -z
solemniz|e [-is|e], -es, -ing, -ed 'sɔləm-
naiz, -iz, -iŋ, -d
solenoid, -s 'səulinɔid ['sɔli-, -lən-], -z
Solent 'səulənt
sol-fa (S.) sɔl'fɑ: ['sɔl'fɑ:]
solfegg|io, -i sɔl'fedʒ|iəu, -i(:)
solferino (S.) ˌsɔlfə'ri:nəu
solicit, -s, -ing, -ed sə'lisit, -s, -iŋ, -id
solicitation, -s səˌlisi'teiʃən, -z
solicitor, -s sə'lisitə* [sḷ'is-, 'slistə*], -z
solicitous, -ly sə'lisitəs, -li
solicitude sə'lisitju:d
solid (s. adj.), -s; -est, -ly, -ness 'sɔlid,
-z; -ist, -li, -nis
solidarity ˌsɔli'dæriti
solidifiable sə'lidifaiəbl [sɔ'l-]
solidification səˌlidifi'keiʃən [sɔˌl-]
solidi|fy, -fies, -fying, -fied sə'lidi|fai
[sɔ'l-], -faiz, -faiiŋ, -faid
solidity sə'liditi [sɔ'l-]
solid|us, -i 'sɔlid|əs, -ai [-i:]
soliloquiz|e [-is|e], -es, -ing, -ed sə'lilə-
kwaiz [sɔ'l-], -iz, -iŋ, -d
soliloqu|y, -ies sə'liləkw|i [sɔ'l-], -iz
solipsism 'səulipsizəm
solitaire, -s ˌsɔli'tɛə* ['--'-, '---], -z
solitar|y (s. adj.), -ies; -ily, -iness
'sɔlitər|i, -iz; -ili, -inis
solitude, -s 'sɔlitju:d, -z
Sollas 'sɔləs
Solloway 'sɔləwei [-luw-]
solo, -s 'səuləu, -z
soloist, -s 'səuləuist, -s
Solomon 'sɔləmən
Solon 'səulən [-lən]
so-long 'səu'lɔŋ
solstice, -s 'sɔlstis, -iz
solubility ˌsɔlju'biliti [-lət-]
soluble 'sɔljubl
solus 'səuləs
solution, -s sə'lu:ʃən [sḷ'u:-, sə'lju:-], -z

solvability ˌsɔlvə'biliti [-lət-]
solv|e, -es, -ing, -ed; -able sɔlv, -z, -iŋ, -d; -əbl
solven|cy, -t 'sɔlvən|si, -t
Solway 'sɔlwei
Somali, -a, -s, -land səu'mɑːli, -ə [-ĭə, -jə], -z, -lænd
sombre, -st, -ly, -ness 'sɔmbə*, -rist, -li, -nis
sombrero, -s sɔm'breərəu [-'briər-], -z
some sʌm (strong form), səm, sm (weak forms)
somebody 'sʌmbədi [-ˌbɔdi, -bdi]
somehow 'sʌmhau [occasionally 'sʌmau in quick speech]
some more sə'mɔː* [-'mɔə*]
someone 'sʌmwʌn
Somers 'sʌməz
somersault, -s 'sʌməsɔːlt [-sɔlt], -s
Somerset, -shire 'sʌməsit [-set-], -ʃiə* [-ʃə*]
Somerton 'sʌmətn
Somervell 'sʌməvil [-vel]
Somerville 'sʌməvil
something 'sʌmθiŋ [-mpθ-]
sometime 'sʌmtaim
sometimes 'sʌmtaimz [səm'taimz]
somewhat 'sʌmwɔt [-mhw-]
somewhere 'sʌmwɛə* [-mhw-]
Somme sɔm
somnambuli|sm, -st/s sɔm'næmbju-li|zəm, -st/s
somniferous sɔm'nifərəs
somnolen|ce, -t/ly 'sɔmnələn|s [-nul-, -nəul-], -t/li
son (S.), -s sʌn, -z
sonagram, -s 'səunəgræm, -z
sonagraph, -s 'səunəgrɑːf [-græf], -s
sonalator, -s 'səunəleitə*, -z
sonant (s. adj.), -s 'səunənt, -s
sonar 'səunɑ:*
sonata, -s sə'nɑːtə [sʌ'ɑːtə], -z
sonatina, -s ˌsɔnə'tiːnə, -z
song, -s sɔŋ, -z
song-bird, -s 'sɔŋbəːd, -z
song-book, -s 'sɔŋbuk, -s
songster, -s 'sɔŋs-tə*, -z
songstress, -es 'sɔŋs-tris, -iz
song-thrush, -es 'sɔŋ-θrʌʃ, -iz
Sonia 'sɔnĭə [-njə]
sonic 'sɔnik
son - in - law, sons - in - law 'sʌninlɔː, 'sʌnzinlɔː
sonnet, -s 'sɔnit, -s
sonneteer (s. v.), -s, -ing, -ed ˌsɔni'tiə*, -z, -riŋ, -d
Sonning (near Reading) 'sɔniŋ ['sʌn-]
sonn|y, -ies 'sʌn|i, -iz

sonometer, -s səu'nɔmitə*, -z
sonorit|y, -ies sə'nɔrit|i [səu'n-], -iz
sonorous, -ly sə'nɔːrəs [səu'n-, 'sɔnərəs], -li
sonship 'sʌn-ʃip
soon suːn [rarely sun]
soot, -y, -ier, -iest, -iness sut; -i, -ĭə*, -iist, -inis
sooth suːθ
sooth|e, -es, -ing/ly, -ed suːð, -z, -iŋ/li, -d
soothsayer, -s 'suːθˌseiə* ['suː-ð-], -z
sop (s. v.), -s, -ping, -ped sɔp, -s, -iŋ, -t
soph, -s sɔf, -s
Sophia səu'faiə
Sophie 'səufi
sophi|sm/s, -st/s 'sɔfi|zəm/z, -st/s
sophister, -s 'sɔfistə*, -z
sophistic, -al, -ally sə'fistik [səu'f-], -əl, -əli
sophisticat|e, -es, -ing, -ed sə'fistikeit, -s, -iŋ, -id
sophistication səˌfisti'keiʃən
sophistr|y, -ies 'sɔfistr|i, -iz
Sophoclean ˌsɔfə'kliː(ː)ən
Sophocles 'sɔfəkliːz
sophomore, -s 'sɔfəmɔː* [-mɔə*], -z
Sophy 'səufi
soporific ˌsɔpə'rifik [ˌsəup-]
sopp|y, -ier, -iest, -iness 'sɔp|i, -ĭə*, -iist, -inis
sopran|o, -os, -i sə'prɑːn|əu, -əuz, -i(ː)
Sopwith, -s 'sɔpwiθ, -s
sorbet, -s 'sɔːbət [-bit]
Sorbonne sɔː'bɔn (sɔrbɔn)
sorcer|y, -ies; -er/s; -ess/es 'sɔːsər|i, -iz; -ə*/z; -is/iz [-es/iz]
sordid, -ly, -ness 'sɔːdid, -li, -nis
sordin|o, -i sɔː'diːn|əu, -i(ː)
sore (s. adj. adv.), -s; -r, -st, -ly, -ness sɔː* [sɔə*], -z; -rə*, -rist, -li, -nis
soroptimist, -s sɔ'rɔptimist, -s
sororit|y, -ies sə'rɔrit|i [sɔ'r-, sɔː'r-], -iz
sorosis (S.) sə'rəusis [sɔ'r-, sɔː'r-]
sorrel 'sɔrəl
sorr|ow (s. v.), -ows, -owing/ly, -owed, -ower/s 'sɔr|əu, -əuz, -əuiŋ/li, -əud, -əuə*/z
sorrow|ful, -fully, -fulness 'sɔrə|ful [-ru|f-], -fli [-fəli, -fuli], -fulnis
sorr|y, -ier, -iest, -ily, -iness 'sɔr|i, -ĭə*, -iist, -ili, -inis
sort (s. v.), -s, -ing, -ed, -er/s sɔːt, -s, -iŋ, -id, -ə*/z
sortie, -s 'sɔːti(ː), -z
sortilege 'sɔːtilidʒ
so-so 'səusəu
sostenuto ˌsɔstə'nuːtəu [-ti'n-, -'njuː-]

Sosthenes 'sɔsθəni:z [-θin-]
sot, -s sɔt, -s
Sotheby 'sʌðəbi ['sɔð-]
Sothern 'sʌðən
sottish, -ly, -ness 'sɔtiʃ, -li, -nis
sotto voce 'sɔtəu'vəutʃi (ˌsotto'vo:tʃe)
sou, -s su:, -z
soubrette, -s su:'bret [su'b-], -s
souchong 'su:'ʃɔŋ [-'tʃɔŋ, also '--, -'-, according to sentence-stress]
souffle (murmur), -s 'su:fl, -z
soufflé, -s 'su:flei, -z
sough (s. v.), -s, -ing, -ed sau, -z, -iŋ, -d
sought (from seek) sɔ:t
soul, -s səul, -z
Soulbury 'səulbəri
soul|ful, -fully, -fulness 'səul|ful [-fl], -fuli [-fəli, -f|i], -fulnis [-flnis]
soulless, -ly, -ness 'səullis, -li, -nis
sound (s. adj. v. adv.), -s; -er, -est, -ly, -ness; -ing/s, -ed saund, -z; -ə*, -ist, -li, -nis ['saunnis]; -iŋ/z, -id
sound-board, -s 'saundbɔ:d [-bɔəd], -z
sound-box, -es 'saundbɔks, -iz
sound-film, -s 'saundfilm, -z
soundless 'saundlis
sound-track, -s 'saundtræk ['sauntræk], -s
sound-wave, -s 'saund-weiv, -z
soup, -s; -y su:p, -s; -i
soupçon, -s 'su:psɔ̃:ŋ [-sɔŋ] (supsɔ̃), -z
soup-kitchen, -s 'su:pˌkitʃin, -z
soup-plate, -s 'su:ppleit, -s
soup-ticket, -s 'su:pˌtikit, -s
soup-tureen, -s 'su:ptəˌri:n [-tuˌr-, -tjuˌr-], -z
sour (adj. v.), -er, -est, -ly, -ness; -s, -ing, -ed 'sauə*, -rə*, -rist, -li, -nis; -z, -riŋ, -d
source, -s sɔ:s [sɔəs], -iz
sourdine, -s suə'di:n, -z
Sousa (Amer. conductor and composer) 'su:zə
sous|e, -es, -ing, -ed saus, -iz, -iŋ, -t
Souter 'su:tə*
south (s. adj. adv.) (S.) sauθ
sou|th (v.), -ths, -thing, -thed sau|ð [-θ], -ðz [-θs], -ðiŋ [-θiŋ], -ðd [-θt]
Southall 'sauðɔ:l ['sauθɔ:l]
Southampton sauθ'æmptən [sauθ'hæ-, sə'θæ-]
Southdown 'sauθdaun
south-east 'sauθ'i:st [in nautical usage also sau'i:st, also '--, -'-, according to sentence-stress]
south-easter, -s 'sauθ'i:stə*, -z
south-easterly 'sauθ'i:stəli
south-eastern 'sauθ'i:stən

south-eastward, -s 'sauθ'i:stwəd, -z
Southend 'sauθ'end [also '--, -'-, according to sentence-stress]
souther|ly, -n, -ner/s, -nmost 'sʌðə|li, -n, -nə*/z, -nməust [-nməst]
southernwood 'sʌðənwud
Southey 'sauði, 'sʌði
Southon 'sauðən
south-paw, -s 'sauθpɔ:, -z
Southport 'sauθpɔ:t
southron, -s 'sʌðrən, -z
Southsea 'sauθsi: [-si]
south-south-east 'sauθsauθ'i:st [in nautical usage also 'sau-sau'i:st]
south-south-west 'sauθsauθ'west [nautical pronunciation 'sau-sau'west]
southward, -s, -ly 'sauθwəd, -z, -li
Southwark 'sʌðək, 'sauθwək
    Note.—Some Londoners use 'sʌðək for the district, and 'sauθwək in S. Bridge, S. Bridge Road; others use one form (more usually 'sʌðək) in all cases.
Southwell (surname) 'sauθwəl, 'sʌðəl, (cathedral town in Notts.) 'sauθwəl [locally 'sʌðl]
    Note.—Viscount Southwell is 'sʌðəl.
south-west 'sauθ'west [nautical pronunciation sau'west, also '--, -'-, according to sentence-stress]
south-wester (wind), -s 'sauθ'westə* [in nautical usage also sau'westə*], -z
south-westerly 'sauθ'westəli [nautical pronunciation sau'w-]
south-western 'sauθ'westən
south-westward, -s 'sauθ'westwəd, -z
South|wick, -wold 'sauθ|wik, -wəuld
Soutter 'su:tə*
souvenir, -s 'su:vəniə* [-vin-, ˌ--'-], -z
sou'wester (hat), -s sau'westə*, -z
Souza 'su:zə
sovereign (s. adj.), -s 'sɔvrin, -z
sovereignty 'sɔvrənti [-rin-]
soviet (S.), -s; -ism 'səuviət ['sɔv-, -vjət, -vjet, səu'vjet, sɔ'vjet], -s; -izəm
sovran 'sɔvrən
sow (s.) (female pig, block of iron, trough for molten iron), -s sau, -z
sow (v.) (plant seed), -s, -ing, -ed, -n, -er/s səu, -z, -iŋ, -d, -n, -ə*/z
Sowerby (in Yorks. N. Riding) 'sauəbi [old-fashioned 'sɔ:əbi], (in Yorks. W. Riding) 'səuəbi ['sauəbi], (surname) 'səuəbi, 'sauəbi
Sowry 'sauəri
soy sɔi
soya 'sɔiə

spa, -s spɑ:, -z

Spa spɑ:

spac|e (s. v.), -es, -ing, -ed speis, -iz, -iŋ, -t

space-bar, -s 'speisbɑ:*, -z

space-craft, -s 'speis-krɑ:ft, -s

space|-ship/s, -shot/s 'speiʃ|ʃip/s, -ʃɔt/s

space-time 'speis'taim

spacious, -ly, -ness 'speiʃəs, -li, -nis

spade, -s; -ful/s speid, -z; -ful/z

spade-work 'speid-wə:k

spaghetti spə'geti [spɑ:'g-]

spahi, -s 'spɑ:hi: ['spɑ:i:], -z

Spain spein

spake (archaic past tense of speak) speik

Spalding 'spɔ:ldiŋ ['spɔl-]

spall (s. v.), -s, -ing, -ed spɔ:l, -z, -iŋ, -d

spam spæm

span (s. v.), -s, -ning, -ned spæn, -z, -iŋ,

spandrel, -s 'spændrəl, -z   [-d

spang|le (s. v.), -les, -ling, -led 'spæŋg|l,
-lz, -liŋ [-ḷiŋ], -ld

Spaniard, -s 'spænjəd, -z

spaniel, -s 'spænjəl, -z

Spanish 'spæniʃ

spank (s. v.), -s, -ing, -ed, -er/s spæŋk,
-s, -iŋ, -t [spæŋt], -ə*/z

spanking (s. adj.), -s 'spæŋkiŋ, -z

spanner, -s 'spænə*, -z

spar (s. v.), -s, -ring, -red spɑ:*, -z, -riŋ,
-d

spar|e (adj. v.), -ely, -eness; -es,
-ing/ly, -ed spɛə*, -li, -nis; -z,
-riŋ/li, -d

spark (s. v.) (S.), -s, -ing, -ed spɑ:k, -s,
-iŋ, -t

sparking-plug, -s 'spɑ:kiŋ-plʌg, -z

spark|le (s. v.), -les, -ling, -led 'spɑ:k|l,
-lz, -liŋ, -ld

sparklet, -s 'spɑ:klit, -s

spark-plug, -s 'spɑ:kplʌg, -z

sparring-match, -es 'spɑ:riŋmætʃ, -iz

sparrow, -s 'spærəu, -z

sparrowhawk, -s 'spærəuhɔ:k, -s

sparse, -ly, -ness spɑ:s, -li, -nis

Spart|a, -an/s 'spɑ:t|ə, -ən/z

spasm, -s 'spæzəm, -z

spasmodic, -ally spæz'mɔdik, -əli

spastic (s. adj.), -s 'spæstik, -s

spat (s.), -s spæt, -s

spat (from spit) spæt

spatchcock (s. v.), -s, -ing, -ed 'spætʃ-
kɔk, -s, -iŋ, -t

spate, -s speit, -s

spati|al, -ally 'speiʃ|əl [-ʃjəl, -ʃiəl], -əli

spatter (s. v.), -s, -ing, -ed 'spætə*, -z,
-riŋ, -d

spatul|a, -ae, -as 'spætjul|ə, -i:, -əz

spatulate (adj.) 'spætjulit [-leit]

spavin 'spævin

spawn (s. v.), -s, -ing, -ed spɔ:n, -z, -iŋ,
-d

Speaight speit

speak, -s, -ing, spoke, spoken, speaker/s
spi:k, -s, -iŋ, spəuk, 'spəukən,
'spi:kə*/z

speak-eas|y, -ies 'spi:k,i:z|i, -iz

speaking-trumpet, -s 'spi:kiŋ,trʌmpit,
-s

speaking-tube, -s 'spi:kiŋ-tju:b, -z

Spean spiən ['spi:ən]

spear (s. v.), -s, -ing, -ed spiə*, -z, -riŋ,
-d

spear-head, -s 'spiəhed, -z

spear|man (S.), -men 'spiə|mən, -mən
[-men]

spearmint 'spiəmint

spec spek

speci|al (s. adj.), -als, -ally 'speʃ|əl,
-əlz; -əli [-ʃi, -li]

speciali|sm, -st/s 'speʃəli|zəm [-ʃli-,
-ʃli-], -st/s

specialit|y, -ies ,speʃi'ælit|i, -iz

specialization [-isa-] ,speʃəlai'zeiʃən
[-ʃlai'z-, -ʃəli'z-, -ʃli'z-]

specializ|e [-is|e], -es, -ing, -ed 'speʃəl-
aiz [-ʃlaiz], -iz, -iŋ, -d

specialt|y, -ies 'speʃəlt|i, -iz

specie 'spi:ʃi: [-ʃi]

species 'spi:ʃi:z [-ʃiz]

specific (s. adj.), -s; -ally spi'sifik
[spə's-], -s; -əli

specification, -s ,spesifi'keiʃən, -z

specificity ,spesi'fisiti

speci|fy, -fies, -fying, -fied; -fiable
'spesi|fai, -faiz, -faiiŋ, -faid; -faiəbl

specimen, -s 'spesimin [-mən], -z

specious, -ly, -ness 'spi:ʃəs, -li, -nis

speck, -s, -ed spek, -s, -t

speckle, -s, -d 'spekl, -z, -d

speckless 'speklis

spectacle, -s, -d 'spektəkl [-tik-], -z, -d

spectacular, -ly spek'tækjulə*, -li

spectator (S.), -s spek'teitə*, -z

spectral 'spektrəl

spectre, -s 'spektə*, -z

spectrogram, -s 'spektrəugræm, -z

spectrograph, -s 'spektrəugrɑ:f [-græf],
-s

spectrographic ,spektrəu'græfik

spectrography spek'trɔgrəfi

spectrometer, -s spek'trɔmitə*, -z

spectroscope, -s 'spektrəskəup, -s

spectroscopic, -al, -ally ,spektrəs'kɔpik,
-əl, -əli

spectroscop|ist/s, -y spek'trɔskəp|ist/s,
-i

spectr|um, -a, -ums 'spektr|əm, -ə, -əmz
speculat|e, -es, -ing, -ed, -or/s 'spekju-
　leit, -s, -iŋ, -id, -ə*/z
speculation, -s ˌspekju'leiʃən, -z
speculative, -ly, -ness 'spekjulətiv
　[-leit-], -li, -nis
specul|um, -a, -ar 'spekjul|əm, -ə, -ə*
sped (from speed) sped
speech, -es spi:tʃ, -iz
speech-day, -s 'spi:tʃdei, -z
speechification, -s ˌspi:tʃifi'keiʃən, -z
speechi|fy, -fies, -fying, -fied, -fier/s
　'spi:tʃi|fai, -faiz, -faiiŋ, -faid, -fai-ə*/z
speechless, -ly, -ness 'spi:tʃlis, -li, -nis
speech-sound, -s 'spi:tʃsaund, -s
speed (s. v.) (S.), -s, -ing, -ed, sped; -y,
　-ier, -iest, -ily, -iness spi:d, -z, -iŋ, -id,
　sped; -i, -iə* [-jə*], -iist [-jist], -ili,
　-inis
speed-cop, -s 'spi:dkɔp, -s
speed-limit, -s 'spi:d,limit, -s
speed-merchant, -s 'spi:d,mə:tʃənt, -s
speedometer, -s spi'dɔmitə* [spi:'d-], -z
speedway, -s 'spi:d-wei, -z
speedwell (S.), -s 'spi:d-wel [-wəl], -z
Speen spi:n
Speigal 'spi:gəl
Speight speit
Speirs spiəz
speiss spais
spel|l (s. v.), -ls, -ling/s, -led, -t, -ler/s
　spel, -z, -iŋ/z, -t [-d], -t, -ə*/z
spellbound 'spelbaund
spelt (from spell) spelt
spelt|er (s. v.), -ers, -ering, -ered
　'spelt|ə*, -əz, -əriŋ, -əd
spence (S.), -s spens, -iz
spencer (S.), -s 'spensə*, -z
spen|d, -ds, -ding, -t, -der/s spen|d, -dz,
　-diŋ, -t, -də*/z
Spender 'spendə*
spendthrift, -s 'spendθrift, -s
Spens spenz
Spenser 'spensə*
Spenserian spen'siəriən
spent (from spend) spent
sperm, -s spə:m, -z
spermaceti ˌspə:mə'seti [-'si:t-]
spermatoz|oon, -oa ˌspə:mətəu'z|əuɔn
　[-əuən], -əuə
sperm-whale, -s 'spə:m-weil [-hw-], -z
spew, -s, -ing, -ed spju:, -z, -iŋ [spjuiŋ],
　-d
Spey spei
Spezia (Italian port) 'spetsiə [-tsjə,
　-dziə, -dzjə]
Spezzia (Greek island) 'spetsiə [-tsjə]
sphagnum 'sfægnəm

sphene (jewel), -s spi:n, -z
sphere, -s sfiə*, -z
spheric, -s, -al, -ally 'sferik, -s, -əl, -əli
spheroid, -s 'sfiərɔid, -z
spheroidal sfiə'rɔidl [sfe'r-]
spherometer, -s sfiə'rɔmitə*, -z
spherule, -s 'sferju:l [-ru:l], -z
sphincter, -s 'sfiŋktə*, -z
sphinx, -es; -like sfiŋks, -iz; -laik
Spica (star) 'spaikə
spic|e (s. v.) (S.), -es, -ing, -ed; -y,
　-ier, -iest, -ily, -iness spais, -iz, -iŋ,
　-t; -i, -iə* [-jə*], -iist [-jist], -ili,
　-inis
spick spik
spicule, -s 'spaikju:l ['spik-], -z
spider, -s; -y 'spaidə*, -z; -ri
Spiers spiəz, 'spaiəz
spiff|ing/ly, -y 'spif|iŋ/li, -i
spigot, -s 'spigət, -s
spik|e (s. v.), -es, -ing, -ed spaik, -s,
　-iŋ, -t
spikenard 'spaiknɑ:d
Spikins 'spaikinz
spik|y, -ier, -iest, -iness 'spaik|i, -iə*,
　-iist, -inis
spil|l (s. v.), -ls, -ling, -led, -t spil, -z, -iŋ,
　-d, -t
spiller (S.), -s 'spilə*, -z
spillikins 'spilikinz
Spilling 'spiliŋ
spilt (from spill) spilt
spin (s. v.), -s, -ning, span, spun,
　spinner/s spin, -z, -iŋ, spæn, spʌn,
　'spinə*/z
spinach 'spinidʒ [rarely -itʃ]
spinal 'spainl
spind|le, -les, -ly 'spind|l, -lz, -li
spindle-legged, -shaped 'spindl|legd,
　-ʃeipt
spindrier, -s 'spin-drai-ə* [-draiə*, '-'--],
spindrift 'spin-drift　　　　　　　　[-z
spine, -s, -d; -less spain, -z, -d; -lis
spinel spi'nel
spinet, -s spi'net ['spinet, 'spinit], -s
Spink spiŋk
spinney, -s 'spini, -z
spinning-wheel, -s 'spiniŋwi:l [-hwi:l], -z
spin|ose, -ous 'spain|əus, -əs
Spinoza spi'nəuzə
spinster, -s; -hood 'spinstə*, -z; -hud
spiny 'spaini
Spion Kop 'spaiən'kɔp
spiraea, -s spai'riə [-'ri:ə], -z
spir|al (s. adj.), -als, -ally 'spaiər|əl,
　-əlz, -əli
spirant (s. adj.), -s 'spaiərənt, -s
spire, -s, -d 'spaiə*, -z, -d

spirit, -s, -ed, -edly, -edness 'spirit, -s, -id, -idli, -idnis

spirit-gum 'spiritgʌm

spiritism 'spiritizəm

spirit-lamp, -s 'spirit-læmp, -s

spiritless, -ly, -ness 'spirit-lis, -li, -nis

spirit-level, -s 'spirit,levl, -z

spirit-rapping, -s 'spirit,ræpiŋ, -z

spirit-stove, -s 'spirit-stəuv, -z

spiritual, -ly 'spiritjŭəl [-tjwəl, -tjul, -tʃŭəl, -tʃwəl, -tʃul], -i

spirituali|sm, -st/s 'spiritjŭəli|zəm [-tjwəl-, -tjul-, -tʃŭəl-, -tʃwəl-, -tʃul-], -st/s

spiritualistic ,spiritjŭə'listik [-tjwə'l-, -tju'l-, -tʃŭə'l-, -tʃwə'l-, -tʃu'l-]

spiritualit|y, -ies ,spiritju'ælit|i [-tʃu-], -iz

spirituous 'spiritjŭəs [-tjwəs, -tʃŭəs, -tʃŭəs, -tʃwəs]

spiritus 'spiritəs ['spaiər-]   [-tʃwəs]

spirometer, -s ,spaiə'rɔmitə*, -z

spirt (s. v.), -s, -ing, -ed spə:t, -s, -iŋ, -id

spit (s. v.) (eject saliva, etc.), -s, -ting, spat spit, -s, -iŋ, spæt

spit (s. v.) (for roasting, etc.), -s, -ting, -ted spit, -s, -iŋ, -id

Spitalfields 'spitlfi:ldz

spit|e (s. v.), -es, -ing, -ed; -eful, -efully, -efulness spait, -s, -iŋ, -id; -ful, -fuli [-fəli], -fulnis

spitfire (S.), -s 'spit,faiə*, -z

Spithead 'spit'hed ['—, -'-, according to sentence-stress]

spittle 'spitl

spittoon, -s spi'tu:n, -z

Spitzbergen 'spits,bə:gən ['-'—, -'—]

spiv, -s; -vy spiv, -z; -i

splash (s. v.), -es, -ing, -ed, -er/s splæʃ, -iz, -iŋ, -t, -ə*/z

splash-board, -s 'splæʃbɔ:d [-bəəd], -z

splash|y, -iness 'splæʃ|i, -inis

splatter, -s, -ing, -ed 'splætə*, -z, -riŋ, -d

splay (s. v.), -s, -ing, -ed splei, -z, -iŋ, -d

spleen, -s; -ful, -fully, -ish, -ishly; -y spli:n, -z; -ful, -fuli [-fəli], -iʃ, -iʃli; -i

splendid, -ly, -ness 'splendid, -li, -nis

splendiferous splen'difərəs

splendour, -s 'splendə*, -z

splenetic (s. adj.), -s, -ally spli'netik, -s, -əli

splic|e (s. v.), -es, -ing, -ed splais, -iz, -iŋ, -t

splint (s. v.), -s, -ing, -ed splint, -s, -iŋ, -id

splinter, -s; -y 'splintə*, -z; -ri

split (s. v.), -s, -ting split, -s, -iŋ

splodd|y, -ier, -iest, -iness 'splɔd|i, -iə*, -iist, -inis

splodg|e, -es splɔdʒ, -iz

splodg|y, -ier, -iest, -iness 'splɔdʒ|i, -iə* [-jə*], -iist [-jist], -inis

splotch, -es, -y splɔtʃ, -iz, -i

splutter (s. v.), -s, -ing, -ed 'splʌtə*, -z, -riŋ, -d

Spode spəud

spoffish 'spɔfiʃ

Spofforth 'spɔfəθ [-fɔ:θ]

Spohr spɔ:* [spɔə*] (ʃpo:r)

spoil (s. v.), -s, -ing, -ed, -t, -er/s spɔil, -z, -iŋ, -t [-d], -t, -ə*/z

spoil-sport, -s 'spɔil-spɔ:t, -s

spoke (s.), -s spəuk, -s

spoke, -n (from speak) spəuk, -ən

spokes|man, -men 'spəuks|mən, -mən

spokes|woman, -women 'spəuks|-,wumən, -,wimin

spoliation ,spəuli'eiʃən

spoliator, -s 'spəulieitə*, -z

spondaic spɔn'deiik

spondee, -s 'spɔndi: [-di], -z

spong|e (s. v.), -es, -(e)ing, -ed, -er/s spʌndʒ, -iz, -iŋ, -d, -ə*/z

sponge|-cake/s, -finger/s 'spʌndʒ|-'keik/s, -'fiŋgə*/z

spong|y, -ier, -iest, -iness 'spʌndʒ|i, -iə* [-jə*], -iist [-jist], -inis

sponson, -s 'spɔnsn, -z

sponsor (s. v.), -s, -ing, -ed 'spɔnsə*, -z, -riŋ, -d

spontaneity ,spɔntə'ni:iti [-'niəti, -'neiəti]

spontaneous, -ly, -ness spɔn'teinjəs [spən-, -niəs], -li, -nis

spoof (s. v.), -s, -ing, -ed spu:f, -s, -iŋ, -t

spook, -s; -ish, -y, -iness spu:k, -s; -iʃ, -i, -inis

spool (s. v.), -s, -ing, -ed spu:l, -z, -iŋ, -d

spoon (s. v.), -s, -ing, -ed spu:n, -z, -iŋ, -d

spoonbill, -s 'spu:nbil, -z

Spooner 'spu:nə*

spoonerism, -s 'spu:nərizəm, -z

spoon|-feed, -feeds, -feeding, -fed 'spu:n|-fi:d, -fi:dz, -,fi:diŋ, -fed

spoonful, -s 'spu:nful, -z

spoon|y, -ier, -iest, -ily, -iness 'spu:n|i, -iə*, -iist, -ili, -inis

spoor, -s spuə* [spɔə*, spɔ:*], -z

Sporades 'spɔrədi:z

sporadic, -ally spə'rædik [spɔ'r-], -əli

spore, -s spɔ:* [spɔə*], -z

sporran, -s 'spɔrən, -z

sport (s. v.), -s, -ing, -ed spɔ:t, -s, -iŋ, -id

sportive, -ly, -ness 'spɔ:tiv, -li, -nis

sports|man, -men 'spɔ:ts|mən, -mən

sportsman|like, -ship 'spɔ:tsmən|laik, -ʃip

spot (s. v.), **-s, -ting, -ted** spɔt, -s, -iŋ, -id
spotless, **-ly, -ness** 'spɔtlis, -li, -nis
spotlight, **-s** 'spɔt-lait, -s
Spottiswoode 'spɔtizwud ['spɔtis-wud],
  'spɔtswud
spott|y, **-ier, -iest, -iness** 'spɔt|i, -ïə*,
  -iist, -inis
spouse, **-s** spauz, -iz
spout (s. v.), **-s, -ing, -ed, -er/s** spaut, -s,
  -iŋ, -id, -ə*/z
Spragge spræg
Sprague spreig
sprain (s. v.), **-s, -ing, -ed** sprein, -z, -iŋ,
  -d
sprang (*from* spring) spræŋ
Sprange spreindʒ
Sprangle 'spræŋgl
sprat (S.), **-s** spræt, -s
Spratt spræt
sprawl (s. v.), **-s, -ing, -ed, -er/s** sprɔ:l,
  -z, -iŋ, -d, -ə*/z
sprawl|y, **-ier, -iest, -iness** 'sprɔ:l|i, -ïə*
  [-jə*], -iist [-jist], -inis
spray (s. v.), **-s, -ing, -ed; -ey** sprei, -z,
  -iŋ, -d; -i
spread (s. v.), **-s, -ing, -er/s** spred, -z,
  -iŋ, -ə*/z
spread-eagl|e, **-es, -ing, -ed** 'spred'i:gl,
  -z, -iŋ [-liŋ], -d
spree, **-s** spri:, -z
sprig, **-s** sprig, -z
Sprigg sprig
sprightl|y, **-ier, -iest, -iness** 'spraitl|i,
  -ïə* [-jə*], -iist [-jist], -inis
Sprigings 'spriginz
spring (s. v.), **-s, -ing, sprang, sprung,**
  springer/s spriŋ, -z, -iŋ, spræŋ,
  sprʌŋ, 'spriŋə*/z
spring-balance, **-s** 'spriŋ'bæləns ['-ˌ--],
  -iz
spring-bed, **-s** 'spriŋ'bed ['--], -z
spring-board, **-s** 'spriŋbɔ:d [-bɔəd], -z
springbok, **-s** 'spriŋbɔk, -s
springe, **-s** sprindʒ, -iz
Springell 'spriŋəl, 'spriŋgəl
Springfield 'spriŋfi:ld
spring-gun, **-s** 'spriŋgʌn, -z
springlike 'spriŋlaik
Springpark 'spriŋ-pɑ:k
springtime 'spriŋ-taim
spring|y, **-ier, -iest, -ily, -iness** 'spriŋ|i,
  -ïə*, -iist, -ili, -inis
sprink|le (s. v.), **-les, -ling, -led, -ler/s**
  'spriŋk|l, -lz, -liŋ [-liŋ], -ld, -lə*/z
  [-lə*/z]
sprinkling (s.), **-s** 'spriŋkliŋ, -z
sprint (s. v.), **-s, -ing, -ed, -er/s** sprint,
  -s, -iŋ, -id, -ə*/z

sprit, **-s** sprit, -s
sprite, **-s** sprait, -s
sprocket, **-s** 'sprɔkit, -s
Sproule sprəul
sprout (s. v.), **-s, -ing, -ed** spraut, -s, -iŋ,
  -id
spruce (s. adj.), **-s; -r, -st, -ly, -ness**
  spru:s, -iz; -ə*, -ist, -li, -nis
sprue, **-s** spru:, -z
sprung (*from* spring) sprʌŋ
Sprunt sprʌnt
spry (S.), **-er, -est, -ness** sprai, 'sprai-ə*,
  'spraiist, 'sprai-nis
spud, **-s** spʌd, -z
spu|e, **-es, -ing, -ed** spju:, -z, -iŋ
  [spju:iŋ], -d
spum|e, **-es, -ing, -ed** spju:m, -z, -iŋ, -d
spun (*from* spin) spʌn
spunk; **-y, -ier, -iest** spʌŋk; -i, -ïə*, -iist
spur (s. v.), **-s, -ring, -red** spə:*, -z, -riŋ,
Spurgeon 'spə:dʒən |-d
spurious, **-ly, -ness** 'spjuərïəs [-jɔər-,
  -jɔ:r-, -jə:r-], -li, -nis
spurn (S.), **-s, -ing, -ed** spə:n, -z, -iŋ, -d
Spurr spə:*
Spurrier (*surname*) 'spʌrïə*
spurt (s. v.), **-s, -ing, -ed** spə:t, -s, -iŋ, -id
sputnik, **-s** 'sputnik ['spʌt-], -s
sputter (s. v.), **-s, -ing, -ed, -er/s**
  'spʌtə*, -z, -riŋ, -d, -rə*/z
sputum 'spju:təm
sp|y (s. v.), **-ies, -ying, -ied** sp|ai, -aiz,
  -aiiŋ, -aid
spy-glass, **-es** 'spai-glɑ:s, -iz
squab (s. adj.), **-s** skwɔb, -z
squabb|le (s. v.), **-les, -ling, -led, -ler/s**
  'skwɔb|l, -lz, -liŋ [-liŋ], -ld, -lə*/z
  [-lə*/z]
squad, **-s** skwɔd, -z
squadron, **-s** 'skwɔdrən, -z
squalid, **-est, -ly, -ness** 'skwɔlid, -ist, -li,
  -nis
squall (s. v.), **-s, -ing, -ed; -y** skwɔ:l, -z,
  -iŋ, -d; -i
squaloid 'skweilɔid
squalor 'skwɔlə*
squam|a, **-ae** 'skweim|ə, -i:
squam|ose, **-ous** 'skweim|əus, -əs
squand|er, **-ers, -ering, -ered, -erer/s**
  'skwɔnd|ə*, -əz, -əriŋ, -əd, -ərə*/z
squandermania 'skwɔndə'meinjə [-nïə]
squar|e (s. adj. v. adv.), **-es; -er, -est,**
  -ely, -eness; -ing, -ed skwɛə*, -z;
  -rə*, -rist, -li, -nis; -riŋ, -d
square-jawed 'skwɛə'dʒɔ:d ['-- *when*
  attributive]
square-toed 'skwɛə'təud ['-- *when*
  attributive]

squarish 'skwεərɪʃ

squash (*s. v.*), -es, -ing, -ed skwɔʃ, -iz, -iŋ, -t

squash-hat, -s 'skwɔʃ'hæt, -s

squash|y, -ier, -iest, -iness 'skwɔʃ|i, -ɪə*, -iist, -inis

squat (*s. adj. v.*), -s, -ting, -ted, -ter/s skwɔt, -s, -iŋ, -id, -ə*/z

squaw, -s skwɔ:, -z

squawk (*s. v.*), -s, -ing, -ed skwɔ:k, -s, -iŋ, -t

squeak (*s. v.*), -s, -ing, -ed, -er/s skwi:k, -s, -iŋ, -t, -ə*/z

squeak|y, -ier, -iest, -ily, -ness 'skwi:k|i, -ɪə* [-jə*], -iist [-jist], -ili, -inis

squeal (*s. v.*), -s, -ing, -ed, -er/s skwi:l, -z, -iŋ, -d, -ə*/z

squeamish, -ly, -ness 'skwi:miʃ, -li, -nis

squeegee (*s. v.*), -s, -ing, -d 'skwi:'dʒi: ['-'-], -z, -iŋ, -d

Squeers skwɪəz

squeez|e (*s. v.*), -es, -ing, -ed, -er/s; -able skwi:z, -iz, -iŋ, -d, -ə*/z; -əbl

squegger, -s 'skwegə*, -z

squelch (*s. v.*), -es, -ing, -ed skweltʃ, -iz, -iŋ, -t

squib, -s skwib, -z

squid, -s skwid, -z

squiff|y, -ier, -iest 'skwif|i, -ɪə*, -iist

squigg|le (*s. v.*), -les, -ling, -led 'skwig|l, -lz, -liŋ [-liŋ], -ld

squilgee (*s. v.*), -s, -ing, -d 'skwil'dʒi: ['-'-], -z, -iŋ, -d

squill, -s skwil, -z

squint (*s. v.*), -s, -ing, -ed skwint, -s, -iŋ, -id

squint-eyed 'skwint-aid

squire (S.), -s 'skwaɪə*, -z

squirearchy 'skwaɪərɑ:ki

squireen, -s ˌskwaɪə'ri:n, -z

squirm, -s, -ing, -ed skwə:m, -z, -iŋ, -d

squirrel, -s 'skwirəl, -z

squirt (*s. v.*), -s, -ing, -ed skwə:t, -s, -iŋ, -id

squish (*s. v.*), -es, -ing, -ed skwiʃ, -iz, -iŋ, -t

Srinagar sri:'nʌgə* [sri:'n-, -'nɑ:g-, 'sri:nəgə*] (*Hind.* syrinəgər)

s.s. 'es'es ['eses, 'sti:m-ʃip]

St. (=Saint) sənt, sint, snt [*rarely* sent, seint]

Note.—Names beginning with St. *are entered after* saint.

stab (*s. v.*), -s, -bing, -bed stæb, -z, -iŋ, -d

Stabat Mater, -s 'stɑ:bæt'mɑ:tə* [-bət-], -z

stability stə'biliti [-lət-]

stabilization [-isa-] ˌsteibilai'zeiʃən [ˌstæb-, -li'z-]

stabiliz|e [-is|e], -es, -ing, -ed, -er/s 'steibilaiz ['stæb-], -iz, -iŋ, -d, -ə*/z

stab|le (*s. adj. v.*), -les; -ly, -leness; -ling, -led 'steib|l, -lz; -li, -lnis; -liŋ [-liŋ], -ld

stable-boy, -s 'steiblbɔi, -z

stable|man, -men 'steibl|mən [-mæn], -mən [-men]

stabling (*s.*) 'steibliŋ

stablish, -es, -ing, -ed 'stæbliʃ, -iz, -iŋ, -t

staccato, -s stə'kɑ:təu, -z

Stac(e)y 'steisi

stack (*s. v.*), -s, -ing, -ed stæk, -s, -iŋ, -t

stadi|um, -ums, -a 'steidj|əm [-dï-], -əmz, -ə

staff (*s. v.*), -s, -ing, -ed stɑ:f, -s, -iŋ, -t

Staffa 'stæfə

Stafford, -shire 'stæfəd, -ʃiə* [-ʃə*]

Staffs. stæfs

stag, -s stæg, -z

stag|e (*s. v.*), -es, -ing, -ed steidʒ, -iz, -iŋ, -d

stage-craft 'steidʒkrɑ:ft

stage-effect, -s 'steidʒ-iˌfekt, -s

stager, -s 'steidʒə*, -z

stage-struck 'steidʒstrʌk

stagger (*s. v.*), -s, -ing, -ed, -er/s 'stægə*, -z, -riŋ, -d, -rə*/z

staghound, -s 'stæghaund, -z

stag-hunting 'stæg,hʌntiŋ

Stagirite, -s 'stædʒirait, -s

stagnan|cy, -t/ly 'stægnən|si, -t/li

stagnat|e, -es, -ing, -ed stæg'neit ['stægneit], -s, -iŋ, -id

stagnation stæg'neiʃən

stag|y, -ier, -iest, -ily, -iness 'steidʒ|i, -ɪə* [-jə*], -iist [-jist], -ili, -inis

staid, -ly, -ness steid, -li, -nis

stain (*s. v.*), -s, -ing, -ed, -er/s stein, -z, -iŋ, -d, -ə*/z

Stainer (*English name*) 'steinə*, (*German name*) 'stainə* ('ʃtainər)

Staines steinz

stainless, -ly, -ness 'steinlis, -li, -nis

stair, -s stεə*, -z

stair-carpet, -s 'stεəˌkɑ:pit, -s

staircase, -s 'stεəkeis, -iz

stair-rod, -s 'stεə-rɔd, -z

stairway, -s 'stεəwei, -z

Staithes steiðz

stak|e (*s. v.*), -es, -ing, -ed steik, -s, -iŋ, -t

stake-holder, -s 'steik,həuldə*, -z

stalactite, -s 'stæləktait, -s

stalagmite, -s 'stæləgmait, -s

Stalbridge 'stɔ:lbridʒ ['stɔl-]

stale, -r, -st, -ly, -ness steil, -ə*, -ist, -li, -nis

stalemat|e (s. v.), -es, -ing, -ed 'steil-'meit ['--], -s, -iŋ, -id
Stalin 'stɑ:lin ['stæl-] ('staljin)
Stalingrad 'stɑ:lingræd ['stæl-, -grɑ:d] (stəljin'grat)
stalinism 'stɑ:linizəm ['stæl-]
stalk (s. v.), -s, -ing, -ed, -er/s; -y stɔ:k, -s, -iŋ, -t, -ə*/z; -i
stalking-horse, -s 'stɔ:kiŋhɔ:s, -iz
Stalky 'stɔ:ki
stall (s. v.), -s, -ing, -ed; -age stɔ:l, -z, -iŋ, -d; -idʒ
stallion, -s 'stæljən, -z
stalwart (s. adj.), -s, -ly, -ness 'stɔ:lwət ['stɔl-, -wə:t], -s, -li, -nis
Stalybridge 'steilibridʒ
Stamboul stæm'bu:l
stamen, -s 'steimen [-mən], -z
Stamford, -ham 'stæmfəd, -əm
stamina 'stæminə
stammer (s. v.), -s, -ing, -ed, -er/s 'stæmə*, -z, -riŋ, -d, -rə*/z
stamp (s. v.) (S.), -s, -ing, -ed, -er/s stæmp, -s, -iŋ, -t [stæmt], -ə*/z
stamp-album, -s 'stæmp,ælbəm, -z
stamp-collection, -s 'stæmpkə,lekʃən, -z
stamp-collector, -s 'stæmpkə,lektə*, -z
stamp-dut|y, -ies 'stæmp,dju:t|i, -iz
stamped|e (s. v.), -es, -ing, -ed stæm-'pi:d, -z, -iŋ, -id
stamp-machine, -s 'stæmpmə,ʃi:n, -z
stance, -s stæns [stɑ:ns], -iz
stanch, -es, -ing, -ed stɑ:nʧ, -iz, -iŋ, -t
stanchion, -s 'stɑ:nʃən, -z
stand (s. v.), -s, -ing, stood stænd, -z, -iŋ, stud
standard, -s 'stændəd, -z
standardization [-isa-] ,stændədai'zeiʃən [-di'z-]
standardiz|e [-is|e], -es, -ing, -ed 'stændədaiz, -iz, -iŋ, -d
standard-lamp, -s 'stændədlæmp ['--'-], -s
stand-by, -s 'stændbai, -z   [-s
stand-in, -s 'stænd'in ['--], -z
standing (s.), -s 'stændiŋ, -z
standish (S.), -es 'stændiʃ, -iz
standoffish 'stænd'ofiʃ [-'ɔ:f-, -'--]
standpoint, -s 'stændpoint ['stæm-point], -s
standstill, -s 'stændstil, -z
stand-to 'stændtu: ['-'-]
stand-up (adj.) 'stændʌp
Stan|field, -ford 'stæn|fi:ld, -fəd
stanhope (S.), -s 'stænəp, -s
staniel, -s 'stænjəl [-niəl], -z
Stanis|las, -aus 'stænisl|əs [-ɑ:s], -ɔ:s
stank (from stink) stæŋk
Stanley 'stænli

stannar|y, -ies 'stænər|i, -iz
stann|ic, -ous 'stæn|ik, -əs
Stansfield 'stænzfi:ld [-nsf-]
Stanton 'stæntən, 'stɑ:n-
stanza, -s 'stænzə, -z
staple (S.), -s 'steipl, -z
Stapleton 'steipltən
Stapley 'stæpli, 'steipli
star (s. v.), -s, -ring, -red stɑ:*, -z, -riŋ, -d
starboard 'stɑ:bəd [-bɔ:d, -bəəd]
    Note.—The nautical pronunciation is 'stɑ:bəd.
starch (s. v.), -es, -ing, -ed; -y, -ier, -iest, -iness stɑ:tʃ, -iz, -iŋ, -t; -i, -Iə*, -iist, -inis
stardom 'stɑ:-dəm
star|e (s. v.), -es, -ing/ly, -ed, -er/s steə*, -z, -riŋ/li, -d, -rə*/z
starfish, -es, 'stɑ:-fiʃ, -iz
star-gaz|er/s, -ing 'stɑ:,geiz|ə*/z, -iŋ
stark (S.), -ly, -ness stɑ:k, -li, -nis
starland 'stɑ:-lænd
star|less, -light, -lit 'stɑ:-|lis, -lait, -lit
starling (S.), -s 'stɑ:liŋ, -z
Starr stɑ:*
starr|y, -iness 'stɑ:r|i, -inis
start (s. v.) (S.), -s, -ing, -ed, -er/s stɑ:t, -s, -iŋ, -id, -ə*/z
starting-point, -s 'stɑ:tiŋpoint, -s
start|le, -les, -ling, -led, -ler/s 'stɑ:t|l, -lz, -liŋ, -ld, -lə*/z
starvation stɑ:'veiʃən
starv|e, -es, -ing, -ed; -eling/s stɑ:v, -z, -iŋ, -d; -liŋ/z
stat|e (s. v.), -es, -ing, -ed, -ement/s steit, -s, -iŋ, -id, -mənt/s
statecraft 'steitkrɑ:ft
statel|y, -ier, -iest, -iness 'steitl|i, -Iə* [-jə*], -iist [-jist], -inis
stateroom, -s 'steit-rum [-ru:m], -z
states|man, -men 'steits|mən, -mən
statesman|like, -ly, -ship 'steitsmən|-laik, -li, -ʃip
Statham 'steiθəm, 'steiðəm
static, -s, -al, -ally 'stætik, -s, -əl, -əli
statice (plant), -s 'stætisi, -z ['stætis, -iz]
stati|on (s. v.), -ons, -oning, -oned 'steiʃ|ən, -ənz, -ŋiŋ [-niŋ], -ənd
stationar|y, -ily, -iness 'steiʃŋər|i [-ʃnər-, -ʃɳr-, -ʃənər-], -ili, -inis
stationer, -s 'steiʃnə* [-ʃɳə*], -z
stationery 'steiʃɳəri [-ʃnər-, -ʃɳr-, -ʃənər-]
station-master, -s 'steiʃən,mɑ:stə*, -z
station-wag(g)on, -s 'steiʃən,wægən, -z
statism 'steitizəm
statist, -s 'steitist, -s

statistic, -s, -al, -ally stə'tistik [stæ't-], -s, -əl, -əli

statistician, -s ,stætis'tiʃən, -z

statuary 'stætjŭəri [-tjwəri, -tjuəri]

statue, -s 'stætʃu: [-tju:], -z

statuesque ,stætju'esk

statuette, -s ,stætju'et, -s

stature, -s 'stætʃə*, -z

status, -es 'steitəs, -iz

status quo 'steitəs'kwəu ['stæt-]

statute, -s 'stætju:t [-tʃu:t], -s

statute-book, -s 'stætju:tbuk [-tʃu:t-], -s

statutory 'stætjutəri [-tʃut-]

staunch, -er, -est, -ly, -ness stɔ:ntʃ [stɑ:n-], -ə*, -ist, -li, -nis

Staunton (English surname) 'stɔ:ntən, 'stɑ:n-, (towns in U.S.A.) 'stæntən

Stavanger stə'væŋə*

stav|e (s. v.), -es, -ing, -ed, stove steiv, -z, -iŋ, -d, stəuv

stay (s. v.), -s, -ing, -ed, -er/s stei, -z, -iŋ, -d, -ə*/z [steə*/z]

stay-at-home 'steiəthəum

stay-down 'stei'daun ['--]

stay-in 'stei'in ['--]

staysail, -s 'stei-seil [nautical pronunciation 'steisl], -z

Steabben 'stebən

stead (S.) sted

steadfast, -ly, -ness 'stedfəst, -li, -nis

stead|y, -ier, -iest, -ily, -iness; -ies, -ying, -ied 'sted|i, -iə*, -iist, -ili, -inis; -iz, -iiŋ, -id

steak, -s steik, -s

steal (s. v.), -s, -ing, stole, stolen, stealer/s sti:l, -z, -iŋ, stəul, 'stəulən, 'sti:lə*/z

stealth, -y, -ier, -iest, -ily, -iness stelθ, -i, -iə* [-jə*], -iist [-jist], -ili, -inis

steam (s. v.), -s, -ing, -ed, -er/s -y, -iness sti:m, -z, -iŋ, -d, -ə*/z; -i, -inis

steamboat, -s 'sti:mbəut, -s

steam-engine, -s 'sti:m,endʒin, -z

steam-hammer, -s 'sti:m,hæmə*, -z

steam-launch, -es 'sti:m'lɔ:ntʃ [-'lɑ:ntʃ, in contrast '--], -iz

steam-power 'sti:m,pauə*

steam-roller, -s 'sti:m,rəulə* ['-'-], -z

steamship, -s 'sti:m-ʃip, -s

stearic sti'ærik

stearin 'stiərin

Stearn(e), -s stə:n, -z

steatite 'stiətait

steatopy|gia, -gous ,stiətəu'pai|dʒiə [-dʒiə], -gəs

Stedman 'stedmən

steed, -s sti:d, -s

steel (s. v.), -s, -ing, -ed; -y, -ier, -iest, -iness sti:l, -z, -iŋ, -d; -i, -iə* [-jə*], -iist [-jist], -inis

Steele sti:l

steel-plated 'sti:l'pleitid ['-,--]

steelyard, -s 'stilja:d ['sti:lja:d, 'stiljəd], -z

steenbok, -s 'sti:nbɔk ['stein-], -s

steep (s. adj. v.), -s; -er, -est, -ly, -ness; -ing, -ed sti:p, -s; -ə*, -ist, -li, -nis; -iŋ, -t

steep|en, -ens, -ening, -ened 'sti:p|ən, -ənz, -niŋ [-ŋiŋ], -ənd

steeple, -s, -d; -chase/s, -jack/s 'sti:pl, -z, -d; -tʃeis/iz, -dʒæk/s

steer (s. v.), -s, -ing, -ed, -er/s; -age; -sman, -smen stiə*, -z, -riŋ, -d, -rə*/z; -ridʒ; -zmən, -zmən [-zmen]

steering-gear 'stiəriŋgiə*

steering-wheel, -s 'stiəriŋwi:l [-ŋhw-], -z

steev|e (s. v.), -es, -ing, -ed sti:v, -z, -iŋ, -d

Steevens 'sti:vnz

Stein (English name), -itz stain, -its

steinbock, -s 'stainbɔk, -s

Steinway, -s 'stainwei, -z

stell|e, -ae 'sti:l|i(:), -i:

Stella, -land 'stelə, -lænd

stellar 'stelə*

stem (s. v.), -s, -ming, -med stem, -z, -iŋ, -d

stemma, -ta 'stemə, -tə

stemple, -s 'stempl, -z

stench, -es stentʃ, -iz

stenc|il, -ils, -illing, -illed 'stens|l [-il], -lz [-ilz], -liŋ [-iliŋ], -ld [-ild]

sten-gun, -s 'stengʌn, -z

stenograph, -s 'stenəgrɑ:f [-nəug-, -græf], -s

stenograph|er/s, -y ste'nɔgrəf|ə*/z [stə'n-], -i

Stent stent

stentorian sten'tɔ:riən

step (s. v.), -s, -ping, -ped, -per/s step, -s, -iŋ, -t, -ə*/z

step-aunt, -s 'stepɑ:nt, -s

step-brother, -s 'step,brʌðə*, -z

step|-child, -children 'step|tʃaild, -,tʃildrən [-,tʃuldrən]

step-dance, -s 'stepdɑ:ns, -iz

step-daughter, -s 'step,dɔ:tə*, -z

step-father, -s 'step,fɑ:ðə*, -z

Stephano 'stefənəu

stephanotis ,stefə'nəutis

Stephany (-ie) 'stefəni

Stephen, -s, -son 'sti:vn, -z, -sn

step-ladder, -s 'step,lædə*, -z

step-mother, -s 'step,mʌðə*, -z
Stepney 'stepni
steppe, -s step, -s
stepping-stone, -s 'stepiŋ-stəun, -z
step-sister, -s 'step,sistə*, -z
step-son, -s 'stepsʌn, -z
step-uncle, -s 'step,ʌŋkl, -z
stereo, -s 'stiəriəu ['ster-], -z
stereopticon, -s ,stiəri'ɔptikən [,ster-], -z
stereoscope, -s 'stiəriəskəup ['ster-], -s
stereoscopic, -al, -ally ,stiəri'skɔpik [,ster-], -əl, -əli
stereoscopy ,stiəri'ɔskəpi [,ster-]
stereotyp|e (s. v.), -es, -ing, -ed, -er/s; -y 'stiəriətaip ['ster-, -riəut-], -s, -iŋ, -t, -ə*/z; -i
sterile 'sterail
sterility ste'riliti [stə'r-]
sterilization [-isa-], -s ,sterilai'zeiʃən [-li'z-], -z
steriliz|e [-is|e], -es, -ing, -ed, -er/s 'sterilaiz, -iz, -iŋ, -d, -ə*/z
sterling 'stə:liŋ
stern (s.) (of ship), -s; -most stə:n, -z; -məust [-məst]
stern (adj.), -er, -est, -ly, -ness stə:n, -ə*, -ist, -li, -nis
Sterne stə:n
stern|um, -ums, -a 'stə:n|əm, -əmz, -ə
stertorous, -ly, -ness 'stə:tərəs, -li, -nis
stet stet
stethoscope, -s 'steθəskəup, -s
stethoscopic, -al, -ally ,steθə'skɔpik, -əl, -əli
stethoscopy ste'θɔskəpi
Steve sti:v
stevedore, -s 'sti:vidɔ:*, -z
Stevenage 'sti:vŋidʒ [-vənidʒ]
Steven|s, -son 'sti:vn|z, -sn
stew (s. v.), -s, -ing, -ed stju:, -z, -iŋ [stjuiŋ], -d
steward (S.), -s; -ess/es; -ship/s stjuəd ['stju:əd], -z; -is/iz [stjuə'des/iz]; -ʃip/s
Stewart stjuət ['stju:ət]
stew-pan, -s 'stju:-pæn, -z
Steyne sti:n
Steyning 'steniŋ
stg. 'stə:liŋ
stichomythia, -s ,stikəu'miθiə [-θjə], -z
stick (s. v.), -s, -ing, stuck, sticker/s stik, -s, -iŋ, stʌk, 'stikə*/z
stick-in-the-mud, -s 'stikinðəmʌd, -z
stickjaw, -s 'stikdʒɔ:, -z
stickleback, -s 'stiklbæk, -s
stickler, -s 'stiklə*, -z
stick-up (s. adj.), -s 'stikʌp, -s

stick|y, -ier, -iest, -ily, -iness 'stik|i, -iə*, -iist, -ili, -inis   [-nis
stiff, -er, -est, -ly, -ness stif, -ə*, -ist, -li, -nis
stiff|en, -ens, -ening, -ened 'stif|n, -nz, -ŋiŋ [-niŋ], -nd
Stiffkey (in Norfolk) 'stifki(:) [old-fashioned local pronunciation 'stju:ki]
stiff-necked 'stif'nekt [also '-- esp. when attributive]
stif|le, -les, -ling/ly, -led 'staif|l, -lz, -liŋ/li, -ld
Stiggins 'stiginz
stigma, -s, -ta 'stigmə, -z, -tə
stigmatic stig'mætik
stigmatization [-isa-] ,stigmətai'zeiʃən [-ti'z-]
stigmatiz|e [-is|e], -es, -ing, -ed 'stigmətaiz, -iz, -iŋ, -d
stile, -s stail, -z
stiletto (s.), -(e)s sti'letəu, -z
stilett|o (v.), -oes, -oing, -oed sti'let|əu, -əuz, -əuiŋ, -əud
still (s. adj. v. adv.) (S.), -s; -er, -est, -ness; -ing, -ed stil, -z; -ə*, -ist, -nis; -iŋ, -d
still-born 'stilbɔ:n
stillephone, -s 'stiləfəun, -z
still-room, -s 'stilrum [-ru:m], -z
stilly (adj.) 'stili
stilt, -s, -ed/ly, -edness stilt, -s, -id/li, -idnis
Stilton, -s 'stiltn [-tən], -z
stimie = stimy
stimulant, -s 'stimjulənt, -s
stimulat|e, -es, -ing, -ed, -or/s 'stimjuleit, -s, -iŋ, -id, -ə*/z
stimulation, -s ,stimju'leiʃən, -z
stimulative 'stimjulətiv [-leit-]
stimul|us, -i 'stimjul|əs, -ai [-i:]
stim|y (s. v.), -ies, -ying, -ied 'staim|i, -iz, -iiŋ, -id
sting (s. v.), -s, -ing, stung, stinger/s stiŋ, -z, -iŋ, stʌŋ, 'stiŋə*/z
stingo 'stiŋgəu
sting|y, -ier, -iest, -ily, -iness 'stindʒ|i, -iə* [-jə*], -iist [-jist], -ili, -inis
stink (s. v.), -s, -ing, stank, stunk stiŋk, -s, -iŋ, stæŋk, stʌŋk
stinker, -s 'stiŋkə*, -z
stink-pot, -s 'stiŋkpɔt, -s
stint (s. v.), -s, -ing, -ed stint, -s, -iŋ, -id
stipend, -s 'staipend [-pənd], -z
stipendiar|y (s. adj.), -ies stai'pendjər|i [sti'p-, -diə-], -iz
stipp|le, -les, -ling, -led 'stip|l, -lz, -ļiŋ [-liŋ], -ld
stipulat|e, -es, -ing, -ed, -or/s 'stipjuleit, -s, -iŋ, -id, -ə*/z

stipulation, -s ˌstipju'leiʃən, -z
stipule, -s 'stipju:l, -z
stir (s. v.), -s, -ring, -red, -rer/s stə:*, -z, -riŋ, -d, -rə*/z
Stirling 'stə:liŋ
stirp|s, -es stə:p|s, -i:z [-eiz]
stirrup, -s 'stirəp, -s
stirrup-pump, -s 'stirəppʌmp, -s
stitch (s. v.), -es, -ing, -ed stitʃ, -iz, -iŋ, -t
stith|y, -ies 'stiði|i, -iz
stiver, -s 'staivə*, -z
stoat, -s stəut, -s
Stobart 'stəubɑ:t
stochastic stɔ'kæstik [stə-]
stock (s. v.), -s, -ing, -ed stɔk, -s, -iŋ, -t
stockad|e (s. v.), -es, -ing, -ed stɔ'keid, -z, -iŋ, -id
stock-book, -s 'stɔkbuk, -s
stock-breeder, -s 'stɔkˌbri:də*, -z
stockbrok|er/s, -ing 'stɔkˌbrəuk|ə*/z, -iŋ
Stock Exchange 'stɔkiksˌtʃeindʒ
stock-farm, -s 'stɔkfɑ:m, -z
stockfish 'stɔkfiʃ
stockholder, -s 'stɔkˌhəuldə*, -z
Stockholm 'stɔkhəum
stockinet ˌstɔki'net ['--'-]
stocking (s.), -s, -ed 'stɔkiŋ, -z, -d
stock-in-trade 'stɔkin'treid
stockjobber, -s 'stɔkˌdʒɔbə*, -z
stock-market, -s 'stɔkˌmɑ:kit, -s
stockpil|e (s. v.), -es, -ing, -ed 'stɔkpail, -z, -iŋ, -d
Stockport 'stɔkpɔ:t
stock-pot, -s 'stɔkpɔt, -s
stock-raising 'stɔkˌreiziŋ
stock-still 'stɔk'stil
stock-taking 'stɔkˌteikiŋ
Stock|ton, -well 'stɔk|tən, -wəl [-wel]
stock|y, -ier, -iest, -iness 'stɔk|i, -iə*, -iist, -inis
Stoddar|d, -t 'stɔdə|d, -t
stodg|e (s. v.), -es, -ing, -ed; -y, -ier, -iest, -iness stɔdʒ, -iz, -iŋ, -d; -i, -iə*, -iist, -inis
stoep, -s stu:p, -s
Stogumber (in Somerset) stəu'gʌmbə*, (character in B. Shaw's 'Saint Joan') 'stɔgəmbə*
stoic (S.), -s, -al, -ally 'stəuik, -s, -əl, -əli
stoicism (S.) 'stəuisizəm
stok|e (S.), -es, -ing, -ed, -er/s stəuk, -s, -iŋ, -t, -ə*/z
Stoke Courcy [Stogursey] stəu'gə:zi
Stoke d'Abernon stəuk'dæbənən
stokehold, -s 'stəukhəuld, -z

stokehole, -s 'stəukhəul, -z
Stoke Poges stəuk'pəudʒiz
stole (S.), -s stəul, -z
stole (from steal), -n stəul, -ən
stolid, -est, -ly 'stɔlid, -ist, -li
stolidity stɔ'liditi [stə'l-]
Stoll (surname) stəul, stɔl
 Note.—Members of the family of the late Sir Oswald Stoll pronounce stɔl.
stomach (s. v.), -s, -ing, -ed 'stʌmək, -s, -iŋ, -t
stomach-ache, -s 'stʌmək-eik, -s
stomacher, -s 'stʌmələkə* [old-fashioned -ətʃə*, -ədʒə*], -z
stomachic stəu'mækik
stomatoscope, -s stəu'mætəskəup, -s
ston|e (s. v.) (S.), -es, -ing, -ed stəun, -z, -iŋ, -d
stone-blind 'stəun'blaind
stone-breaker, -s 'stəunˌbreikə*, -z
stone-cast, -s 'stəunkɑ:st, -s
stonechat, -s 'stəun-tʃæt, -s
stone-cold 'stəun'kəuld
stonecrop, -s 'stəun-krɔp, -s
stone-cutter, -s 'stəunˌkʌtə*, -z
stone-dead 'stəun'ded
stone-deaf 'stəun'def
stone-fruit 'stəun-fru:t
Stonehaven stəun'heivn
Stonehenge 'stəun'hendʒ [also '--, -'-, according to sentence-stress]
Stonehouse 'stəunhaus
stonemason, -s 'stəunˌmeisn, -z
stone-wall|er/s, -ing, 'stəun'wɔ:l|ə*/z, -iŋ
stone-ware 'stəun-wɛə*
stone-work 'stəun-wə:k
Stoney 'stəuni
ston|y (adj. adv.), -ier, -iest, -ily, -iness 'stəun|i, -iə* [-jə*], -iist [-jist], -ili, -inis
stony-hearted 'stəuniˌhɑ:tid
stood (from stand) stud
stoog|e (s. v.), -es, -ing, -ed stu:dʒ, -iz, -iŋ, -d
stook, -s stuk [stu:k], -s
stool, -s stu:l, -z
stoop (s. v.), -s, -ing, -ed, -er/s stu:p, -s, -iŋ, -t, -ə*/z
stop (s. v.), -s, -ping, -ped, -per/s stɔp, -s, -iŋ, -t, -ə*/z
stop|-cock/s, -gap/s 'stɔp|kɔk/s, -gæp/s
Stopford 'stɔpfəd
stop-go 'stɔp'gəu
Stopher 'stəufə*
stoppage, -s 'stɔpidʒ, -iz
stopper, -s 'stɔpə*, -z
stop-watch, -es 'stɔpwɔtʃ, -iz

storage 'stɔːridʒ ['stɔə-]

storage-heater, -s 'stɔːridʒ,hiːtə* ['stɔə-], -z

stor|e (s. v.), -es, -ing, -ed; -able; -age stɔː* [stɔə*], -z, -riŋ, -d; -rəbl; -ridʒ

store-hou|se, -ses 'stɔːhau|s ['stɔə*], -ziz

store-keeper, -s 'stɔː,kiːpə* ['stɔə-], -z

store-room, -s 'stɔːrum ['stɔərum, -ruːm], -z

storey (S.), -s, -ed 'stɔːri, -z, -d

storiated 'stɔːrieitid

storiette, -s ,stɔːri'et ['stɔːri'et], -s

stork, -s stɔːk, -s

storm (s. v.) (S.), -s, -ing, -ed stɔːm, -z, -iŋ, -d

storm-bound 'stɔːmbaund

storm-centre, -s 'stɔːm,sentə*, -z

storm-cloud, -s 'stɔːmklaud, -z

Stormont 'stɔːmənt

Stormonth (surname) 'stɔːmʌnθ [-mənθ]

storm-tossed 'stɔːmtɔst [old-fashioned -tɔːst]

storm-trooper, -s 'stɔːm,truːpə*, -z

storm|y, -ier, -iest, -ily, -iness 'stɔːm|i, -iə* [-jə*], -iist [-jist], -ili, -inis

Stornoway 'stɔːnəwei [-nuw-]

Storr, -s stɔː*, -z

Stortford (in Herts.) 'stɔːfəd [-ɔːtf-]

Storthing 'stɔːtiŋ

stor|y (S.), -ies 'stɔːr|i, -iz

story-book, -s 'stɔːribuk, -s

story-tell|er/s, -ing 'stɔːri,tel|ə*/z, -iŋ

Stothard 'stɔðəd

Stoughton (in Sussex, Leics.) 'stəutn, (in Somerset) 'stɔːtn, (in Surrey) 'stautn, (surname) 'stɔːtn, 'stautn Note.—'stautn in Hodder & S., the publishers.

stoup, -s stuːp, -s

Stour (in Suffolk, Essex) stuə*, (in Kent) stuə* [rarely 'stauə*], (in Hants) 'stauə*, stuə*, (in Warw.) 'stauə*, 'stəuə*, (in Dorset) 'stauə*

Stourbridge 'stauəbridʒ

Stourmouth (in Kent) 'stauəmauθ [rarely 'stuəmauθ]

Stourton (in Wilts., surname) 'stəːtn

stout (s. adj.), -s; -er, -est, -ly, -ness staut, -s; -ə*, -ist, -li, -nis

stout-hearted, -ly, -ness staut'hɑːtid ['-,-- when attributive], -li, -nis

stoutish 'stautiʃ

stove (s.), -s stəuv, -z

stove (from stave) stəuv

stove-pipe, -s 'stəuvpaip, -s

Stovold 'stɔvəuld

stow (S.), -s, -ing, -ed; -age stəu, -z, -iŋ, -d; -idʒ

stowaway, -s 'stəuəwei [-əuuwei], -z

Stowe stəu

Stowers 'stauəz

Stowey (in Somerset) 'stəui

Strabane strə'bæn

strabismus strə'bizməs [stræ'b-]

Strabo 'streibəu

Strabolgi strə'bəugi

Strachan strɔːn

Strachey 'streitʃi

Strad, -s stræd, -z

stradd|le (s. v.), -les, -ling, -led 'stræd|l, -lz, -liŋ [-liŋ], -ld

Stradivarius, -es ,strædi'vɑːriəs [-'vɛər-], -iz

straf|(e) (s. v.), -(e)s, -ing/s, -ed strɑːf, -s, -iŋ/z, -t

Strafford 'stræfəd

stragg|le, -les, -ling, -led, -ler/s; -ly, -liness 'stræg|l, -lz, -liŋ [-liŋ], -ld, -lə*/z [-lə*/z]; -li [-li], -linis [-linis]

Strahan strɑːn

straight (adj. adv.), -er, -est, -ness streit, -ə*, -ist, -nis [,edʒiz

straight-edge, -s 'streit-edʒ, 'streit-

straight|en, -ens, -ening, -ened 'streit|n, -nz, -niŋ [-ŋiŋ], -nd

straightforward, -ly, -ness streit'fɔːwəd ['streit'f-], -li, -nis

straightway 'streit-wei

strain (s. v.) (S.), -s, -ing, -ed, -er/s strein, -z, -iŋ, -d, -ə*/z

strait, -s (S.), -ened streit, -s, -nd

strait-jacket, -s 'streit,dʒækit, -s

strait-laced 'streit'leist

strait-waistcoat, -s 'streit'weiskəut [-stk-, old-fashioned -'weskət], -s

Straker 'streikə*

strand (s. v.) (S.), -s; -ing, -ed strænd, -z; -iŋ, -id

strange (S.), -r (adj.), -st, -ly, -ness streindʒ, -ə*, -ist, -li, -nis

stranger (s.), -s 'streindʒə*, -z

strang|le, -les, -ling, -led 'stræŋg|l, -lz, -liŋ, -ld

strangle-hold, -s 'stræŋglhəuld, -z

strangulat|e, -es, -ing, -ed 'stræŋgjuleit, -s, -iŋ, -id

strangulation, -s ,stræŋgju'leiʃən, -z

Strangways 'stræŋweiz

Stranraer stræn'rɑː* [-'rɑː*]

strap (s. v.), -s, -ping, -ped, -per/s stræp, -s, -iŋ, -t, -ə*/z

strap|hang, -hangs, -hanging, -hung, -hanger/s 'stræp|hæŋ, -hæŋz, -hæŋiŋ, -hʌŋ, -hæŋə*/z

Stras(s)burg 'stræzbəːg

strata (plur. of stratum) 'strɑːtə [-reit-]

stratagem, -s 'strætidʒəm [-tədʒ-, -dʒim, -dʒem], -z

strategic, -al, -ally strə'tiːdʒik [stræ't-, -'tedʒ-], -əl, -əli

strateg|ist/s, -y 'strætidʒ|ist/s, -i

Stratford 'strætfəd

Stratford-atte-Bowe 'strætfəd,æti'bəui [-ætə'bəuə]

strath, -s stræθ, -s

Strathcona stræθ'kəunə

Strathaven 'streivən

Strathavon stræθ'ɑːn

Strathmore stræθ'mɔː:* [-'mɔə*]

Strathpeffer stræθ'pefə*

strathspey (S.), -s stræθ'spei, -z

stratification ,strætifi'keiʃən

strati|fy, -fies, -fying, -fied 'stræti|fai, -faiz, -faiiŋ, -faid

stratocruiser, -s 'strætəu,kruːzə* ['strɑːt-, rarely 'streit-], -z

Straton 'strætn

stratosphere, -s 'strætəusfiə* ['strɑːt-, old-fashioned 'streit-], -z

stratospheric ,strætəu'sferik [,strɑːt-, old-fashioned ,streit-]

Stratton 'strætn

strat|um, -a 'strɑːt|əm [-reit-], -ə

stratus 'streitəs [-rɑːt-]

Straus(s) straus

Stravinsky strə'vinski (stra'vjinskij)

straw, -s, -y strɔː, -z, -i

strawberr|y (S.), -ies 'strɔː:bər|i, -iz

stray (s. adj. v.) **(S.), -s, -ing, -ed** strei, -z, -iŋ, -d

streak (s. v.), **-s, -ing, -ed; -y, -ier, -iest, -iness** 'striːk, -s, -iŋ, -t; -i, -iə* [-jə*], -iist [-jist], -inis

stream (s. v.), **-s, -ing, -ed, -er/s** striːm, -z, -iŋ, -d, -ə*/z

streamlet, -s 'striːmlit, -s

streamlin|e (s. v.), **-es, -ing, -ed** 'striːm-lain, -z, -iŋ, -d

Streatfeild 'stretfiːld

Streatfield 'stretfiːld

Streatham 'stretəm

Streatley 'striːtli

street (S.), -s striːt, -s

Strelitz 'strelits ('ʃtreːlits)

strength, -s streŋθ [-ŋkθ], -s

strength|en, -ens, -ening, -ened, -ener/s 'streŋθ|ən [-ŋkθ-], -ənz, -əniŋ [-ŋiŋ, -niŋ], -ənd, -ənə*/z [-ŋə*/z, -nə*/z]

strenuous, -ly, -ness 'strenjŭəs [-njwəs], -li, -nis

streptococc|us, -i ,streptəu'kɔk|əs, -ai

streptomycin ,streptəu'maisin

stress (s. v.), **-es, -ing, -ed** stres, -iz, -iŋ, -t

stress-group, -s 'stresgruː:p, -s

stressless 'streslis

stretch (s. v.), **-es, -ing, -ed, -er/s** stretʃ, -iz, -iŋ, -t, -ə*/z

Strevens 'strevənz

strew, -s, -ing, -ed, -n struː:, -z, -iŋ [struiŋ], -d, -n

stri|a, -ae 'strai|ə, -iː

striate (adj.) 'straiit [-aieit]

striated strai'eitid

striation, -s strai'eiʃən, -z

stricken (from strike) 'strikən

Strickland 'striklənd

strict, -er, -est, -ly, -ness strikt, -ə*, -ist, -li ['strikli], -nis ['striknis]

stricture, -s 'striktʃə*, -z

strid|e (s. v.), **-es, -ing, strode, stridden** straid, -z, -iŋ, strəud, 'stridn

strident, -ly 'straidənt, -li

strife straif

strigil, -s 'stridʒil, -z

strik|e (s. v.), **-es, -ing/ly, struck, stricken, striker/s** straik, -s, -iŋ/li, strʌk, 'strikən, 'straikə*/z

strike-break|er/s,-ing 'straik,breik|ə*/z, [-iŋ

strike-pay 'straikpei

Strindberg 'strindbəːg ('strindˌberj)

string (s. v.), **-s, -ing, -ed, strung, stringer/s** striŋ, -z, -iŋ, -d, strʌŋ, 'striŋə*/z

stringen|cy, -t/ly 'strindʒən|si, -t/li

stringendo strin'dʒendəu

Stringer 'striŋə*

string|y, -ier, -iest, -iness 'striŋ|i, -iə*, -iist, -inis

strip (s. v.), **-s, -ping, -ped, -per/s** strip, -s, -iŋ, -t, -ə*/z

strip|e (s. v.), **-es, -ing, -ed; -y, -iness** straip, -s, -iŋ, -t; -i, -inis

stripling, -s 'stripliŋ, -z

striv|e, -es, -ing/s, strove, striven, striver/s straiv, -z, -iŋ/z, strəuv, 'strivn, 'straivə*/z

strobilion, -s strəu'biliən [-ljən], -z

strobolion, -s strəu'bouljən [-liən], -z

stroboscope, -s 'strəubəskəup ['strɔb-], -s

stroboscopic ,strəubəu'skɔpik [,strɔ-]

stroboscopy strəu'bɔskəpi [strɔ'b-]

strode (from stride) strəud

strok|e (s. v.), **-es, -ing, -ed** strəuk, -s, -iŋ, -t

stroll (s. v.), **-s, -ing, -ed, -er/s** strəul, -z, -iŋ, -d, -ə*/z

Stromboli 'strɔmbəli [-bul-, -bəul-] ('stromboli)

strong (S.), -er, -est, -ly, -ish strɔŋ, -gə*, -gist, -li, -iʃ

strong-box, -es 'strɔŋbɔks, -iz
stronghold, -s 'strɔŋhəuld, -z
strong-minded 'strɔŋ'maindid [also
'-,-- when attributive]
strong-mindedness 'strɔŋ'maindidnis
strong-room, -s 'strɔŋrum [-ru:m], -z
stron|tia, -tian, -tium 'strɔn|ʃiə [-ʃjə,
-ʃə, -tiə, -tjə], -ʃiən [-ʃjən, -ʃən, -tiən,
-tjən], -tiəm [-tjəm, -ʃiəm, -ʃjəm,
-ʃəm]
Strood stru:d
strop (s. v.), -s, -ping, -ped strɔp, -s, -iŋ,
-t
strophe, -s 'strəufi ['strɔf-], -z
strophic 'strɔfik
Stroud straud
strove (from strive) strəuv
strow, -s, -ing, -ed, -n strəu, -z, -iŋ, -d,
-n
struck (from strike) strʌk
structur|al, -ally 'strʌktʃər|əl [-tʃur-],
-əli
structural|ism, -ist/s 'strʌktʃərəl|izm
[-tʃur-], -ist/s
structure, -s 'strʌktʃə*, -z
strugg|le (s. v.), -les, -ling, -led, -ler/s
'strʌg|l, -lz, -liŋ [-liŋ], -ld, -lə*/z
[-lə*/z]
strum (s. v.), -s, -ming, -med, -mer/s
strʌm, -z, -iŋ, -d, -ə*/z
strumpet, -s 'strʌmpit, -s
strung (from string) strʌŋ
strut (s. v.), -s, -ting, -ted strʌt, -s, -iŋ,
-id
Struthers 'strʌðəz
Strutt strʌt
Struwwelpeter (English) 'stru:əl,pi:tə*
strychnine 'strikni:n
Stuart, -s stjuət ['stju:ət], -s
stub, -s; -by, -bier, -biest, -biness
stʌb, -z; -i, -iə*, -iist, -inis
stubb|le, -ly 'stʌb|l, -li [-li]
stubborn, -er, -est, -ly, -ness 'stʌbən,
-ə*, -ist, -li, -nis
Stubbs stʌbz
stucco (s.), -(e)s 'stʌkəu, -z
stucco (v.), -es, -ing, -ed 'stʌkəu, -z, -iŋ,
-d
stuck (from stick) stʌk
stuck-up 'stʌk'ʌp [also '--, -'-, according
to sentence stress]
Stucley 'stju:kli
stud (s. v.), -s, -ding, -ded stʌd, -z, -iŋ,
-id
studding-sail, -s 'stʌdiŋseil [nautical
pronunciation 'stʌnsl], -z
Studebaker 'stu:dəbeikə*
student, -s 'stju:dənt, -s

studentship, -s 'stju:dənt-ʃip, -s
studio, -s 'stju:diəu [-djəu], -z
studious, -ly, -ness 'stju:djəs [-diəs], -li,
-nis
stud|y (s. v.), -ies, -ying, -ied 'stʌd|i, -iz,
-iiŋ, -id
stuff (s. v.), -s, -ing, -ed; -y, -ier, -iest,
-iness stʌf, -s, -iŋ, -t; -i, -iə*, -iist,
-inis
stuffing (s.), -s 'stʌfiŋ, -z
stultification ,stʌltifi'keiʃən
stulti|fy, -fies, -fying, -fied 'stʌlti|fai,
-faiz, -faiiŋ, -faid
stum stʌm
stumb|le (s. v.), -les, -ling, -led, -ler/s
'stʌmb|l, -lz, -liŋ, -ld, -lə*/z
stumbling-block, -s 'stʌmbliŋblɔk, -s
stump (s. v.), -s, -ing, -ed; -y, -ier, -iest,
-iness stʌmp, -s, -iŋ, -t [stʌmt]; -i,
-iə* [-jə*], -iist [-jist], -inis
stun, -s, -ning/ly, -ned stʌn, -z, -iŋ/li, -d
stung (from sting) stʌŋ
stunk (from stink) stʌŋk
stunner, -s 'stʌnə*, -z
stunt (s. v.), -s, -ing, -ed stʌnt, -s, -iŋ,
-id
stupe, -s stju:p, -s
stupefaction ,stju:pi'fækʃən [stjupi'f-]
stupe|fy, -fies, -fying, -fied 'stju:pi|fai
['stjup-], -faiz, -faiiŋ, -faid
stupendous, -ly, -ness stju(:)'pendəs, -li,
-nis
stupid (s. adj.), -s, -er, -est, -ly, -ness
'stju:pid ['stjup-, rarely 'stup-], -z,
-ə*, -ist, -li, -nis
stupidit|y, -ies stju(:)'pidit|i, -iz
stupor 'stju:pə*
Sturdee 'stə:di
sturd|y, -ier, -iest, -ily, -iness 'stə:d|i,
-iə* [-jə*], -iist [-jist], -ili, -inis
sturgeon, -s 'stə:dʒən, -z
Sturtevant 'stə:tivənt [-vænt]
stutter (s. v.), -s, -ing, -ed, -er/s 'stʌtə*,
-z, -riŋ, -d, -rə*/z
Stuttgart 'stutgɑ:t ('ʃtutgart)
Stuyvesant 'staivəsənt
st|y, -ies st|ai, -aiz
Styche staitʃ
stye, -s stai, -z
Stygian 'stidʒiən [-dʒjən]
styl|e (s. v.), -es, -ing, -ed stail, -z, -iŋ, -d
stylet, -s 'stailit, -s
stylish, -ly, -ness 'stailiʃ, -li, -nis
stylist, -s 'stailist, -s
stylistic, -s stai'listik, -s
stylite, -s 'stailait, -s
Stylites (Simeon S.) stai'laiti:z
stylograph, -s 'stailəugrɑ:f [-græf], -s

stylographic ˌstailəu'græfik
stymie = stimy
styrax, -es 'staiəræks ['stair-], -iz
Styria, -n/s 'stiriə, -n/z
Styx stiks
suable 'sju(:)əbl
Suaki|m, -n su(:)'ɑ:ki|m, -n
suasion 'sweiʒən
suave, -r, -st, -ly, -ness swɑ:v [old-
  fashioned sweiv], -ə*, -ist, -li, -nis
suavity 'swɑ:viti ['sweiv-, 'swæv-]
sub (s. prep.), -s sʌb, -z
subacid 'sʌb'æsid
subalpine 'sʌb'ælpain
subaltern, -s 'sʌbltən, -z
sub-bass, -es 'sʌb'beis, -iz
subclass, -es 'sʌbklɑ:s, -iz
subclassification, -s 'sʌbˌklæsifi'keiʃən
  ['-ˌ—ˌ—], -z
subclassi|fy, -fies, -fying, -fied 'sʌb-
  'klæsi|fai, -faiz, -faiiŋ, -faid
subcommittee, -s 'sʌbkəˌmiti, -z
subconscious, -ly, -ness 'sʌb'kɔnʃəs
  [sʌb'k-], -li, -nis
subcutaneous 'sʌbkju(:)'teinjəs [-niəs]
subdean, -s 'sʌb'di:n, -z
subdivid|e, -es, -ing, -ed 'sʌbdi'vaid
  ['sʌbdiˌv-], -z, -iŋ, -id
subdivision, -s 'sʌbdiˌviʒən, -z
subdominant, -s 'sʌb'dɔminənt, -s
subdual, -s səb'dju(:)əl, -z
subd|ue, -ues, -uing, -ued, -uer/s
  -uable səb'd|ju:, -ju:z, -ju(:)iŋ, -ju:d,
  -ju(:)ə*/z; -ju(:)əbl
sub-edit, -s, -ing, -ed 'sʌb'edit, -s, -iŋ -id
sub-editor, -s; -ship/s 'sʌb'editə* ['-ˌ—],
  -z; -ʃip/s
sub-famil|y, -ies 'sʌbˌfæmil|i [-məl-], -iz
subfusc 'sʌbfʌsk
subgroup, -s 'sʌbgru:p, -s
sub-heading, -s 'sʌbˌhediŋ, -z
sub-human (s. adj.), -s 'sʌb'hju:mən, -z
subjacent sʌb'dʒeisənt [səb-]
subject (s. adj.), -s 'sʌbdʒikt [-dʒekt], -s
subject (v.), -s, -ing, -ed səb'dʒekt
  [sʌb'dʒekt, 'sʌbdʒikt, 'sʌbdʒekt], -s,
  -iŋ, -id
subjection səb'dʒekʃən
subjective, -ly, -ness səb'dʒektiv
  [sʌb'dʒ-, sʌb'dʒ-], -li, -nis
subjectivism səb'dʒektivizəm [sʌb-]
subjectivity ˌsʌbdʒek'tiviti
subject-matter 'sʌbdʒiktˌmætə* ['-'—]
subjoin, -s, -ing, -ed 'sʌb'dʒɔin [sʌb'dʒ-],
  -z, -iŋ, -d
sub judice sʌb'dʒu:disi [sub'ju:diki]
subjugat|e, -es, -ing, -ed, -or/s 'sʌb-
  dʒugeit [-dʒəg-], -s, -iŋ, -id, -ə*/z

subjugation ˌsʌbdʒu'geiʃən [-dʒə'g-]
subjunctive (s. adj.), -s səb'dʒʌŋktiv, -z
sublease, -s 'sʌb'li:s ['sʌbli:s], -iz
subless|ee/s, -or/s 'sʌble's|i:/z, -ɔ:*/z
sublet, -s, -ting 'sʌb'let, -s, -iŋ
sub-librarian, -s 'sʌblai'brɛəriən, -z
sub-lieutenan|t/s; -cy, -cies 'sʌble-
  'tenən|t/s [-lə't-, -lef't-, -ləf't-]; -si,
  -siz (see note under lieutenancy)
sublimate (s.), -s 'sʌblimit [-meit], -s
sublimat|e (v.), -es, -ing, -ed 'sʌblimeit,
  -s, -iŋ, -id
sublimation ˌsʌbli'meiʃən
sublim|e (s. adj. v.), -er, -est, -ely,
  -eness; -es, -ing, -ed sə'blaim, -ə*,
  -ist, -li, -nis; -z, -iŋ, -d
subliminal sʌb'liminl [səb-]
sublimity sə'blimiti
submachine-gun, -s 'sʌbmə'ʃi:ŋgʌn
  [ˌsʌb-], -z
submarin|e (s. adj. v.), -es, -ing, -ed
  ˌsʌbmə'ri:n ['sʌb-mri:n, 'sʌbməri:n],
  -z, -iŋ, -d
submerg|e, -es, -ing, -ed; -ence səb-
  'mə:dʒ [sʌb-], -iz, -iŋ, -d; -əns
submersible (s. adj.), -s səb'mə:səbl
  [sʌb-, -sibl], -z
submersion, -s səb'mə:ʃən [sʌb-], -z
submission, -s səb'miʃən, -z
submissive, -ly, -ness səb'misiv, -li, -nis
submit, -s, -ting, -ted səb'mit, -s, -iŋ, -id
submultiple, -s 'sʌb'mʌltipl, -z
sub-normal 'sʌb'nɔ:məl [in contrast
  '-ˌ—]
suboctave, -s 'sʌbˌɔktiv, -z
subordinate (s. adj.), -s; -ly sə'bɔ:-
  dnit [-dənit, -dinit, -dnit], -s; -li
subordinat|e (v.), -es, -ing, -ed sə'bɔ:-
  dineit, -s, -iŋ, -id
subordination səˌbɔ:di'neiʃən
subordinative sə'bɔ:dinətiv [-dn̩-, -dən-]
suborn, -s, -ing, -ed, -er/s sʌ'bɔ:n
  [sə'b-], -z, -iŋ, -d, -ə*/z
subornation ˌsʌbɔ:'neiʃən
subpoena (s. v.), -s, -ing, -ed səb'pi:nə
  [sʌb'p-, sə'p-], -z, -iŋ [-nəriŋ], -d
sub-prefect, -s 'sʌb'pri:fekt [in contrast
  '-ˌ—]
subrogation ˌsʌbrəu'geiʃən
subscrib|e, -es, -ing, -ed, -er/s səb-
  'skraib [-bz'k-], -z, -iŋ, -d, -ə*/z
subscript 'sʌbskript [-bzk-]
subscription, -s səb'skripʃən [-bz'k-], -z
sub-section, -s 'sʌbˌsekʃən, -z
subsensible 'sʌb'sensəbl [-sib-]
subsequent, -ly 'sʌbsikwənt, -li
subserv|e, -es, -ing, -ed səb'sə:v [sʌb-],
  -z, -iŋ, -d

subservien|ce, -cy, -t/ly səb'sə:vjən|s [sʌb-, -vɪən-], -si, -t/li

subsid|e, -es, -ing, -ed səb'saɪd, -z, -ɪŋ, -id

subsidence, -s səb'saidəns ['sʌbsid-], -iz

subsidiar|y (s. adj.), -ies, -ily səb-'sidjər|i [-dɪə-], -iz, -ili

subsidiz|e [-is|e], -es, -ing, -ed 'sʌb-sidaiz, -iz, -iŋ, -d

subsid|y, -ies 'sʌbsid|i, -iz

subsist, -s, -ing, -ed; -ence səb'sist, -s, -iŋ, -id; -əns

subsoil, -s 'sʌbsɔil, -z

sub-species 'sʌb,spi:ʃi:z [-ʃiz]

substance, -s 'sʌbstəns [-bzt-], -iz

substanti|al, -ally, -alness səb'stæn-ʃ|əl [-bz't-], -əli [-|i, -li], -əlnis

substantiality səb,stænʃi'æliti [-bz,t-]

substantiat|e, -es, -ing, -ed səb'stæn-ʃieit [-bz't-, -ʃjeit], -s, -iŋ, -id

substantiation səb,stænʃi'eiʃən [-bz,t-, -nsi-]

substantival ,sʌbstən'taivəl [-bzt-]

substantive (s.), -s 'sʌbstəntiv [-bzt-], -z

substantive (adj.), -ly, -ness 'sʌbstən-tiv [-bzt-, səb'stæn-], -li, -nis

Note.—Generally səb'stæntiv *when applied to rank, pay, etc.*

substitut|e (s. v.), -es, -ing, -ed 'sʌb-stitju:t [-bzt-], -s, -iŋ, -id

substitution, -s ,sʌbsti'tju:ʃən [-bzt-], -z

substitu|tional, -tionally ,sʌbsti'tju:|ʃənl [-bzt-, -ʃnəl, -ʃŋl, -ʃnl, -ʃənəl], -ʃŋəli [-ʃnəli, -ʃŋli, -ʃnli, -ʃənəli]

substitutive 'sʌbstitju:tiv [-bzt-]

substratosphere, -s sʌb'strætəsfiə* ['sʌb's-, -'stra:t-, *rarely* -'streit-, -təus-], -z

substrat|um, -a 'sʌb'stra:t|əm [-reit-, '-,--], -ə

substructure, -s 'sʌb,strʌktʃə*, -z

subsum|e, -es, -ing, -ed səb'sju:m, -z, -iŋ, -d

subtangent, -s 'sʌb'tændʒənt, -s

subtenan|cy, -t/s 'sʌb'tenən|si, -t/s

subtend, -s, -ing, -ed səb'tend, -z, -iŋ, -id

subterfuge, -s 'sʌbtəfju:dʒ, -iz

subterranean ,sʌbtə'reinjən [-nɪən]

subterraneous ,sʌbtə'reinjəs [-nɪəs]

subtil(e) 'sʌtl

subtility sʌb'tiliti

subtiliz|e [-is|e], -es, -ing, -ed 'sʌtilaiz, -iz, -iŋ, -d

subtilty 'sʌtlti [-tilti]

sub-title, -s 'sʌb,taitl ['-'--], -z

subt|le, -ler, -lest, -ly, -leness 'sʌt|l, -lə* [-lə*], -list [-list], -li, -lnis

subtlet|y, -ies 'sʌtlt|i, -iz

---

subtopia sʌb'təupiə [-pjə]

subtract, -s, -ing, -ed səb'trækt, -s, -iŋ, -id

subtraction, -s səb'trækʃən, -z

subtrahend, -s 'sʌbtrəhend, -z

subtropical 'sʌb'trɔpikəl

suburb, -s 'sʌbə:b [-bəb], -z

suburban sə'bə:bən

suburbaniz|e [-is|e], -es, -ing, -ed sə'bə:bənaiz, -iz, -iŋ, -d

subvariet|y -ies 'sʌbvə,raiət|i, -iz

subvention, -s səb'venʃən [sʌb-], -z

subver|sion, -sive səb'və:|ʃən [sʌb-], -siv

subvert, -s, -ing, -ed sʌb'və:t [səb-], -s, -iŋ, -id

subway, -s 'sʌbwei, -z

succeed, -s, -ing, -ed sək'si:d, -z, -iŋ, -id

succentor, -s sək'sentə* [sʌk-], -z

success, -es; -ful, -fully sək'ses, -iz; -ful, -fuli [-fəli]

succession, -s sək'seʃən, -z

successive, -ly sək'sesiv, -li

successor, -s sək'sesə*, -z

succinct, -ly, -ness sək'siŋkt [sʌk-], -li, -nis

succory 'sʌkəri

succotash 'sʌkətæʃ

Succoth 'sʌkəθ

succour (s. v.), -s, -ing, -ed 'sʌkə*, -z, -riŋ, -d

succub|a, -ae, -us, -i 'sʌkjub|ə, -i:, -əs, -ai

succulen|ce, -t/ly 'sʌkjulən|s, -t/li

succumb, -s, -ing, -ed sə'kʌm, -z, -iŋ, -d

succursal, -s sʌ'kə:səl, -z

such sʌtʃ (*normal form*), sətʃ (*occasional weak form*)

such-and-such 'sʌtʃənsʌtʃ

suchlike 'sʌtʃlaik

suck (s. v.), -s, -ing, -ed, -er/s sʌk, -s, -iŋ, -t, -ə*/z

sucking-pig, -s 'sʌkiŋpig, -z

suck|le (s. v.), -les, -ling, -led 'sʌk|l, -lz, -liŋ [-liŋ], -ld

suckling (s.), -s 'sʌkliŋ, -z

suction 'sʌkʃən

Suda 'su:də

Sudan su(:)'dɑ:n [-'dæn]

Sudanese ,su:də'ni:z [*also* '--- *when attributive*]

Sudanic su(:)'dænik

sudarium, -s sju(:)'dɛərɪəm [su(:)-], -z

sudatory 'sju:dətəri ['su:-]

Sudbury 'sʌdbəri

sudd sʌd

sudd|en, -enest, -enly, -enness 'sʌd|n, -nist, -nli, -ŋnis

Sudeley 'sju:dli

sudorific (s. adj.), -s ˌsjuːdəˈrifik [ˌsuː-, -dɔˈr-], -s

suds sʌdz

sue (S.), sues, suing, sued sjuː [suː], sjuːz [suːz], ˈsju(ː)iŋ [ˈsu(ː)iŋ], sjuːd

suède sweid (sɥɛːd)   [[suːd]

suet, -y sjuit [suit, ˈsjuːit, ˈsuːit], -i

Suetonius swiːˈtəunjəs [swiˈt-, -nɪəs]

Suez ˈsu(ː)iz [ˈsju(ː)iz]

suff|er, -ers, -ering/s, -ered, -erer/s; -erable, -erance ˈsʌf|ə*, -əz, -əriŋ/z, -əd, -ərə*/z; -ərəbl, -ərəns

suffic|e, -es, -ing, -ed səˈfais, -iz, -iŋ, -t
  Note.—An old pronunciation səˈfaiz is now nearly obsolete.

sufficien|cy, -t/ly səˈfiʃən|si, -t/li

suffix (s.), -es ˈsʌfiks, -iz

suffix (v.), -es, -ing, -ed ˈsʌfiks [-ˈ-], -iz, -iŋ, -t

suffocat|e, -es, -ing/ly, -ed ˈsʌfəkeit, -s, -iŋ/li, -id

suffocation ˌsʌfəˈkeiʃən

Suffolk ˈsʌfək

suffragan (s. adj.), -s ˈsʌfrəgən, -z

suffrage, -s ˈsʌfridʒ, -iz

suffragette, -s ˌsʌfrəˈdʒet, -s

suffragist, -s ˈsʌfrədʒist, -s

suffus|e, -es, -ing, -ed səˈfjuːz [sʌˈf-], -iz, -iŋ, -d

suffusion, -s səˈfjuːʒən [sʌˈf-], -z

sufi, -s; -sm ˈsuːfi, -z; -zəm

sugar (s. v.), -s, -ing, -ed ˈʃugə*, -z, -riŋ,

sugar-basin, -s ˈʃugəˌbeisn, -z   [-d

sugar-cane, -s ˈʃugəkein, -z

sugarloa|f, -ves ˈʃugələu|f, -vz

sugar-plum, -s ˈʃugə-plʌm, -z

sugar-refiner, -s ˈʃugə-riˌfainə*, -z

sugar-refiner|y, -ies ˈʃugə-riˌfainər|i, -iz

sugar-tongs ˈʃugətɔŋz

sugar|y, -iest, -iness ˈʃugər|i, -iist, -inis

suggest, -s, -ing, -ed səˈdʒest, -s, -iŋ, -id

suggestion, -s səˈdʒestʃən [-eʃtʃ-], -z

suggestive, -ly, -ness səˈdʒestiv, -li, -nis

suicidal sjuiˈsaidl [ˌsjuːi-, sui-, ˌsuːi-, ˈ----]

suicide, -s ˈsjuisaid [ˈsjuːi-, ˈsui-, ˈsuːi-], -z

sui generis ˈsju(ː)aiˈdʒenəris [ˈsu(ː)-, -ˈgen-]

sui juris ˈsju(ː)aiˈdʒuəris [ˈsu(ː)-, -ˈdʒɔər-, -ˈdʒɔːr-, ˈsu(ː)iˈjuəris]

Suirdale [ˈʃəːdl [-dəl]

suit (s. v.), -s, -ing/s, -ed, -or/s sjuːt [suːt], -s, -iŋ/z, -id, -ə*/z

suitability ˌsjuːtəˈbiliti [ˌsuː-, -lət-]

suitab|le, -ly, -leness ˈsjuːtəb|l [ˈsuː-], -li, -lnis

suit-case, -s ˈsjuːtkeis [ˈsuːt-], -iz

suite, -s swiːt, -s

sulcal ˈsʌlkəl [-kl]

sulcalization [-isa-] ˌsʌlkəlaiˈzeiʃən

sulcaliz|e [-is|e], -es, -ing, -ed ˈsʌlkəlaiz, -iz, -iŋ, -d

Suleiman ˌsuleiˈmɑːn [ˈ---]

Suliman ˌsuliˈmɑːn [ˈ---]

sulk (s. v.), -s, -ing, -ed; -y, -ier, -iest, -ily, -iness sʌlk, -s, -iŋ, -t; -i, -iə* [-jə*], -iist [-jist], -ili, -inis

Sulla ˈsʌlə [ˈsulə]

sullen, -est, -ly, -ness ˈsʌlən [-lin], -ist, -li, -nis

Sullivan ˈsʌlivən

sull|y (S.), -ies, -ying, -ied ˈsʌl|i, -iz, -iiŋ, -id

sulphanilamide ˌsʌlfəˈniləmaid

sulphate, -s ˈsʌlfeit [-fit], -s

sulphi|de/s, -te/s ˈsʌlfai|d/z, -t/s

sulphur ˈsʌlfə*

sulphureous sʌlˈfjuəriəs [-ˈfjɔər-, -ˈfjɔːr-, -ˈfjəːr-]

sulphuretted ˈsʌlfjuretid [-fər-]

sulphuric sʌlˈfjuərik [-ˈfjɔər-, -ˈfjɔːr-, -ˈfjəːr-]

sulphurous ˈsʌlfərəs [-fjur-]

sulphury ˈsʌlfəri

sultan (S.), -s ˈsʌltən, -z

sultana (kind of raisin), -s səlˈtɑːnə [sʌl-], -z

Sultana (Sultan's wife, mother, etc.), -s sʌlˈtɑːnə, -z

sultanate, -s ˈsʌltənit [-neit], -s

sultr|y, -ier, -iest, -ily, -iness ˈsʌltr|i, -iə*, -iist, -ili, -inis

sum (s. v.), -s, -ming, -med sʌm, -z, -iŋ, -d

sumach, -s ˈsuːmæk [ˈsjuː-, ˈʃu:-], -s

Sumatra su(ː)ˈmɑːtrə [sju(ː)-]

Sumerian sju(ː)ˈmiəriən [su(ː)-]

summariz|e [-is|e], -es, -ing, -ed ˈsʌməraiz, -iz, -iŋ, -d

summar|y (s. adj.), -ies, -ily, -iness ˈsʌmər|i, -iz, -ili, -inis

summation, -s sʌˈmeiʃən, -z

summer, -s; -like ˈsʌmə*, -z; -laik

Summerfield, -s ˈsʌməfiːld, -z

summerhou|se, -ses ˈsʌməhau|s, -ziz

summertime ˈsʌmətaim

Summerville ˈsʌməvil

summery ˈsʌməri

summing-up, summings-up ˈsʌmiŋˈʌp, ˈsʌmiŋz-ʌp

summit, -s ˈsʌmit, -s

summon, -s, -ing, -ed, -er/s ˈsʌmən, -z, -iŋ, -d, -ə*/z

summons (s. v.), -es, -ing, -ed ˈsʌmənz, -iz, -iŋ, -d

Sumner 'sʌmnə*
sump, -s sʌmp, -s
sumpter (S.), -s 'sʌmptə*, -z
sumptuary 'sʌmptjŭəri [-tjwəri, -tjuri, -tʃŭəri, -tʃwəri, -tʃuri]
sumptuous, -ly, -ness 'sʌmptjŭəs [-tjwəs, -tʃŭəs, -tʃwəs], -li, -nis
Sumsion 'sʌmʃən
Sumurun ˌsumu'ru:n
sun (s. v.), -s, -ning, -ned sʌn, -z, -iŋ, -d
sun-ba|th, -ths 'sʌnbɑ:|θ, -ðz
sun-bath|e, -es, -ing, -ed, -er/s 'sʌn-beið, -z, -iŋ, -d, -ə*/z
sunbeam (S.), -s 'sʌnbi:m, -z
sunblind, -s 'sʌnblaind, -z
sun-bonnet, -s 'sʌnˌbɔnit, -s
sunburn, -s, -t 'sʌnbə:n, -z, -t
Sunbury 'sʌnbəri
Sunda 'sʌndə
sundae, -s 'sʌndei, -z
Sundanese ˌsʌndə'ni:z
Sunday, -s 'sʌndi [-dei], -z
sunder, -s, -ing, -ed 'sʌndə*, -z, -riŋ, -d
Sunderland 'sʌndələnd
sundial, -s 'sʌndaiəl, -z
sundown 'sʌndaun
sun-dried 'sʌn-draid
sundry 'sʌndri
sun-fish 'sʌn-fiʃ
sunflower, -s 'sʌnˌflauə*, -z
sung (from sing) sʌŋ
Sung (Chinese dynasty) suŋ [sʌŋ]
sun-hat, -s 'sʌnhæt, -s
sun-helmet, -s 'sʌnˌhelmit ['-'-'--], -s
sunk (from sink) sʌŋk
sun|less, -light, -like 'sʌn|lis, -lait, -laik
Sunningdale 'sʌniŋdeil
sunn|y, -ier, -iest, -iness 'sʌn|i, -iə*, [-iist, -inis
Sunnyside 'sʌnisaid
sunproof 'sʌn-pru:f
sunrise, -s 'sʌnraiz, -iz
sunset, -s 'sʌnset, -s
sunshade, -s 'sʌn-ʃeid, -z
sunshin|e, -y 'sʌnʃain, -i
sun-spot, -s 'sʌn-spɔt, -s
sunstroke, -s 'sʌn-strəuk, -s
sun-trap, -s 'sʌn-træp, -s
sun-worship, -per/s 'sʌnˌwə:ʃip, -ə*/z
sup (s. v.), -s, -ping, -ped sʌp, -s, -iŋ, -t
super (s. adj.), -s 'sju:pə* ['su:-], -z
superab|le, -ly, -leness 'sju:pərəb|l ['su:-], -li, -lnis ⌊ən|s [ˌsu:-], -t/li
superabundan|ce, -t/ly ˌsju:pərə'bʌnd-
superadd, -s, -ing, -ed ˌsju:pər'æd [ˌsu:-], -z, -iŋ, -id
superannuat|e, -es, -ing, -ed ˌsju:pə-'rænjueit [ˌsu:pə'r-, sjupə'r-, supə'r-], -s, -iŋ, -id

superannuation, -s ˌsju:pəˌrænju'eiʃən [ˌsu:-], -z
superb, -ly, -ness sju(:)'pə:b [su(:)-], -li, -nis
superbus (extra large bus), -es 'sju:pə-bʌs ['su:-, '--'-], -iz
Superbus sju(:)'pə:bəs [su(:)-]
supercargo, -es 'sju:pəˌkɑ:gəu ['su:-], -z
supercharg|e (s. v.), -es, -ing, -ed 'sju:pətʃɑ:dʒ ['su:-], -iz, -iŋ, -d
supercilious, -ly, -ness ˌsju:pə'siliəs [ˌsu:pə's-, sjupə's-, supə's-, -ljəs], -li, -nis
supererogation ˌsju:pərˌerə'geiʃən [ˌsu:-, -rəu'g-]
supererogatory ˌsju:pəre'rɔgətəri [ˌsu:-, -ri'r-]
superfici|al, -ally, -alness ˌsju:pə-'fiʃ|əl [ˌsu:pə'f-, sjupə'f-, supə'f-], -əli [-li], -əlnis
superficialit|y, -ies ˌsju:pəˌfiʃi'ælit|i [ˌsu:-], -iz
superficies ˌsju:pə'fiʃi:z [ˌsu:pə'f-, sjupə'f-, supə'f-, -ʃii:z]
superfine 'sju:pə'fain ['su:-,'--']
superfluit|y, -ies ˌsju:pə'flu(:)it|i [ˌsu:pə'f-, sjupə'f-, supə'f-], -iz
superfluous, -ly, -ness sju(:)'pə:fluəs [su(:)-, -flwəs], -li, -nis
superglottal 'sju:pə'glɔtl ['su:-, '--,--]
superhet, -s 'sju:pə'het ['su:-], -s
superheterodyne, -s 'sju:pə'hetərədain ['su:-, -rəud-], -z
superhuman, -ly ˌsju:pə'hju:mən [ˌsu:-, '--'--], -li
superimpos|e, -es, -ing, -ed 'sju:pər-im'pəuz ['su:-], -iz, -iŋ, -d
superintend, -s, -ing, -ed; -ence, -ent/s ˌsju:pərin'tend [ˌsu:-], -z, -iŋ, -id; -əns, -ənt/s
superior (s. adj.), -s sju(:)'piəriə* [su(:)'p-, sə'p-], -z
superiorit|y, -ies sju(:)ˌpiəri'ɔrit|i [su(:)-, sə,p-], -iz
superlative (s. adj.), -s, -ly, -ness sju(:)'pə:lətiv [su(:)-, -'pə:ˌtiv], -z, -li, -nis
super|man, -men 'sju:pə|mæn ['su:-], -men
supermarket, -s 'sju:pəˌmɑ:kit ['su:-], -s
supernal sju(:)'pə:nl [su(:)-]
supernatur|al, -ally ˌsju:pə'nætʃr|əl [ˌsu:pə'n-, sjupə'n-, supə'n-, -tʃur-, -tʃər-], -əli
supernormal 'sju:pə'nɔ:məl ['su:-]
supernumerar|y (s. adj.), -ies ˌsju:pə-'nju:mərər|i [ˌsu:-], -iz
superoctave, -s 'sju:pərˌɔktiv ['su:-], -z

superpos|e, -es, -ing, -ed 'sju:pə'pəuz ['su:-, ,--'-], -iz, -iŋ, -d

superposition, -s 'sju:pəpə'ziʃən ['su:-, -pu'z-, ,---'--], -z

superpriorit|y, -ies 'sju:pəprai'ɔrit|i ['su:-], -iz

superscrib|e, -es, -ing, -ed 'sju:pə-'skraib ['su:-, '---], -z, -iŋ, -d

superscript 'sju:pəskript ['su:-]

superscription, -s ,sju:pə'skripʃən [,su:pə's-, sjupə's-, supə's-], -z

supersed|e, -es, -ing, -ed ,sju:pə'si:d [,su:pə's-, sjupə's-, supə's-], -z, -iŋ, -id

supersession ,sju:pə'seʃən [,su:pə's-, sjupə's-, supə's-]

supersonic 'sju:pə'sɔnik ['su:-, ,--'--, *also* '--,-- when attributive]

superstition, -s ,sju:pə'stiʃən [,su:pə's-, sjupə's-, supə's-], -z

superstitious, -ly, -ness ,sju:pə'stiʃəs [,su:pə's-, sjupə's-, supə's-], -li, -nis

superstructure, -s 'sju:pə,strʌktʃə* ['su:-], -z

super-submarine, -s 'sju:pə'sʌbməri:n ['su:-, -'sʌb-mri:n], -z

supertax, -es 'sju:pətæks ['su:-], -iz

supertonic, -s 'sju:pə'tɔnik [*in contrast* '--,--], -s

superven|e, -es, -ing, -ed ,sju:pə'vi:n [,su:pə'v-, sjupə'v-, supə'v-], -z, -iŋ, -d

supervis|e, -es, -ing, -ed, -or/s 'sju:pə-vaiz ['su:-, ,sju:pə'v-, ,su:pə'v-, sjupə'v-, supə'v-], -iz, -iŋ, -d, -ə*/z

supervision, -s ,sju:pə'viʒən [,su:pə'v-, sjupə'v-, supə'v-], -z

supervisory 'sju:pəvaizəri ['su:-, ,sju:-pə'v-, ,su:pə'v-, sjupə'v-, supə'v-]

supine (s.), **-s** 'sju:pain ['su:-], -z

supine (adj.), **-ly, -ness** sju:'pain [su:'p-, '--], -li, -nis

supper, -s, -less 'sʌpə*, -z, -lis

supplant, -s, -ing, -ed, -er/s sə'plɑ:nt, -s, -iŋ, -id, -ə*/z

suppl|le, -leness, -ly 'sʌp|l, -lnis, -li [-li]

supplement (s.), **-s** 'sʌplimənt, -s

supplement (v.), **-s, -ing, -ed** 'sʌpliment [,--'-], -s, -iŋ, -id

supplement|al, -ary ,sʌpli'ment|l, -əri

supplementation ,sʌplimen'teiʃən

suppliant (s. adj.), **-s, -ly** 'sʌpliənt [-pljənt], -s, -li

supplicat|e, -es, -ing/ly, -ed 'sʌplikeit, -s, -iŋ/li, -id

supplication, -s ,sʌpli'keiʃən, -z

supplicatory 'sʌplikətəri [-keitəri]

suppl|y (s. v.), **-ies, -ying, -ied, -ier/s** sə'pl|ai, -aiz, -aiiŋ, -aid, -ai-ə*/z [-aiə*/z]

support (s. v.), **-s, -ing, -ed, -er/s; -able, -ably** sə'pɔ:t, -s, -iŋ, -id, -ə*/z; -əbl, -əbli

suppos|e, -es, -ing, -ed sə'pəuz [spəuz], -iz, -iŋ, -d

supposedly sə'pəuzidli

supposition, -s ,sʌpə'ziʃən [-pu'z-], -z

supposi|tional, -tionally ,sʌpə'ziʃ|ənl [-pu'z-, -ʃənəl, -ʃnl̩, -ʃnl̩, -ʃənəl], -ʃnəli [-ʃnəli, -ʃnl̩i, -ʃnl̩i, -ʃənəli]

supposititious, -ly, -ness sə,pɔzi'tiʃəs, -li, -nis

suppositor|y, -ies sə'pɔzitər|i, -iz

suppress, -es, -ing, -ed, -or/s; -ible sə'pres, -iz, -iŋ, -t, -ə*/z; -əbl [-ibl]

suppression, -s sə'preʃən, -z

suppurat|e, -es, -ing, -ed 'sʌpjuəreit, -s, -iŋ, -id

suppuration, -s ,sʌpjuə'reiʃən, -z

supra (in vide s.) 'sju:prə ['su:-]

supradental 'sju:prə'dentl ['su:-]

supra-national 'sju:prə'næʃənl [-ʃnəl, -ʃnl̩, -ʃnl̩, -ʃənəl]

suprarenal 'sju:prə'ri:nl ['su:-, '--,--]

suprasegmental 'sju:prəseg'mentl ['su:-]

supremac|y, -ies sju'preməsi [su'p-, sju:'p-, su:'p-], -iz

supreme, -ly, -ness sju(:)'pri:m [su(:)-], -li, -nis

sura, -s 'suərə, -z

surah 'sjuərə

surat (cotton fabric) su'ræt

Surat 'suərət ['su:rət, su'rɑ:t, su'ræt] (Hind. surət)

Surbiton 'sə:bitn

surceas|e (s. v.), **-es, -ing, -ed** sə:'si:s, -iz, -iŋ, -t

surcharge (s.), **-s** 'sə:-tʃɑ:dʒ ['sə:'tʃ-, sə:'tʃ-], -iz

surcharg|e (v.), **-es, -ing, -ed** sə:'tʃɑ:dʒ, -iz, -iŋ, -d

surcoat, -s 'sə:-kəut, -s

surd (s. adj.), **-s; -ity** sə:d, -z; -iti

sure (adj. adv.), **-r, -st, -ly, -ness; -footed** ʃuə* [ʃɔə*, ʃɔ:*, ʃə:*], -rə*, -rist, -li ['ʃɔ:-li, 'ʃɔə-li, 'ʃə:-li], -nis ['ʃɔ:-nis, 'ʃɔə-nis, 'ʃə:-nis]; -'futid

suret|y, -ies; -yship/s 'ʃuərət|i ['ʃuət-, 'ʃɔə-, 'ʃɔ:-, 'ʃə:-], -iz; -iʃip/s

surf sə:f

surfac|e (s. v.), **-es, -ing, -ed** 'sə:fis, -iz, -iŋ, -t

surf-bathing 'sə:f,beiðiŋ

surf-boat, -s 'sə:fbəut, -s

surfeit (s. v.), **-s, -ing, -ed** 'sə:fit, -s, -iŋ, -id

surf-riding 'sə:f,raidiŋ

surg|e (s. v.), **-es, -ing, -ed** sə:dʒ, -iz, -iŋ, -d

surgeon, -s 'sə:dʒən, -z
surger|y, -ies 'sə:dʒər|i, -iz
surgic|al, -ally 'sə:dʒik|əl, -əli
Surinam ˌsuəri'næm
surl|y, -ier, -iest, -ily, -iness 'sə:l|i, -ɪə*
  [-jə*], -iist [-jist], -ili, -inis
surmise (s.), -s 'sə:maiz [sə:'maiz], -iz
surmis|e (v.), -es, -ing, -ed sə:'maiz
  ['sə:m-], -iz, -iŋ, -d
surmount, -s, -ing, -ed; -able sə:-
  'maunt [sə'm-], -s, -iŋ, -id; -əbl
surnam|e (s. v.), -es, -ing, -ed 'sə:neim,
  -z, -iŋ, -d
surpass, -es, -ing/ly, -ed; -able sə:'pɑ:s
  [sə'p-], -iz, -iŋ/li, -t; -əbl
surplice, -s, -d 'sə:pləs [-plis], -iz, -t
surplus, -es; -age 'sə:pləs, -iz; -idʒ
surpris|e (v.), -es, -ing/ly, -ed,
  -edly sə'praiz, -iz, -iŋ/li, -d, -ɪdli
surreali|sm, -st/s sə'riəli|zəm [sju-, su-],
  -st/s
surrend|er (s. v.), -ers, -ering, -ered
  sə'rend|ə*, -əz, -əriŋ, -əd
surreptitious, -ly ˌsʌrəp'tiʃəs [-rip-,
  -rep-], -li
Surrey 'sʌri
surrogate, -s 'sʌrəgit [-rug-, -geit], -s
surround (s. v.), -s, -ing/s, -ed sə'raund,
  -z, -iŋ/z, -id
surtax, -es 'sə:-tæks, -iz
Surtees 'sə:ti:z
surtout, -s 'sə:tu: [sə:'tu:], -z
surveillance sə:'veiləns [sə'v-]
survey (s.), -s 'sə:vei [sə:'vei], -z
survey (v.), -s, -ing, -ed sə:'vei [sə'vei],
  -z, -iŋ, -d
surveyor, -s sə(:)'veɪə*, -z
surviv|e, -es, -ing, -ed, -or/s; -al/s
  sə'vaiv [sə:'v-], -z, -iŋ, -d, -ə*/z, -əl/z
Susan 'su:zn (rarely 'sju:zn)
Susanna su(:)'zænə
susceptibilit|y, -ies səˌseptə'bilit|i
  [-ti'b-, -lət-], -iz
susceptib|le, -ly sə'septəb|l [-tib-], -li
susceptive sə'septiv
suspect (s. adj.), -s 'sʌspekt, -s
suspect (v.), -s, -ing, -ed səs'pekt, -s, -iŋ,
  -id
suspend, -s, -ing, -ed, -er/s səs'pend,
  -z, -iŋ, -id, -ə*/z
suspens|e, -ible səs'pens, -əbl [-ibl]
suspensibility səsˌpensi'biliti [-sə'b-,
  -lət-]
suspension, -s səs'penʃən, -z
suspens|ive, -ory səs'pens|iv, -əri
suspicion, -s səs'piʃən, -z
suspicious, -ly, -ness səs'piʃəs, -li, -nis
Sussams 'sʌsəmz

Sussex 'sʌsiks
sustain, -s, -ing, -ed, -er/s; -able səs-
  'tein, -z, -iŋ, -d, -ə*/z; -əbl
sustenance 'sʌstinəns [-tnəns]
sustentation ˌsʌsten'teiʃən [-tən-]
susurration, -s ˌsjuːsə'reiʃən [ˌsu:-], -z
Sutherland 'sʌðələnd
Sutlej 'sʌtlidʒ [-ledʒ] (Hind. sətlwɹ)
sutler, -s 'sʌtlə*, -z
Sutro 'su:trəu
suttee, -s 'sʌti(:) [sʌ'ti:] (Hind. səti), -z
Sutton 'sʌtn
suture, -s 'su:tʃə* [-tjə*], -z
suzerain, -s 'su:zərein ['sju:-], -z
suzeraint|y, -ies 'su:zəreint|i ['sju:-,
  -rən-], -iz
svarabhakti ˌsvʌrə'bʌkti(:)   [ˌsvɑ:r-,
  -'bæk-] (Hind. svərəbhəkti)
svelte svelt
Svengali sveŋ'gɑ:li
Sverdlov 'sveədlɒv [-lɒf, -ləf] ('svjerdləf)
Sverdlovsk 'sveədlɒvsk [-ləvsk, -ləfsk]
  ('svjerdləfsk)
swab (s. v.), -s, -bing, -bed, -ber/s
  swɒb, -z, -iŋ, -d, -ə*/z
Swabia, -n/s 'sweibjə [-bɪə], -n/z
swadd|le, -les, -ling, -led 'swɒd|l, -lz,
  -liŋ [-liŋ], -ld
swaddling-clothes 'swɒdliŋ-kləuðz [-d|i-
  old-fashioned -kləuz]
Swadling 'swɒdliŋ
Swaffer 'swɒfə*
swag swæg
swag|e (s. v.), -es, -ing, -ed sweidʒ, -iz,
  -iŋ, -d
swagg|er (s. v.), -ers, -ering/ly, -ered,
  -erer/s 'swæg|ə*, -əz, -əriŋ/li, -əd,
  -ərə*/z
Swahili, -s swa:'hi:li [swə'h-], -z
swain (S.), -s swein, -z
swall|ow (s. v.), -ows, -owing, -owed
  'swɒl|əu, -əuz, -əuiŋ, -əud
swallow-tail, -s, -ed 'swɒləuteil, -z, -d
swam (from swim) swæm
Swami, -s 'swɑ:mi (Hind. svami), -z
swamp (s. v.), -s, -ing, -ed; -y, -ier,
  -iest, -iness swɒmp, -s, -iŋ, -t [swɒmt];
  -i, -ɪə* [-jə*], -iist [-jist], -inis
swan, -s swɒn, -z
Swanage 'swɒnidʒ
Swanee 'swɒni
swank; -y, -ier, -iest, -ily, -iness
  swæŋk; -i, -ɪə* [-jə*], -iist [-jist], -ili,
  -inis
swan-like 'swɒnlaik
swanner|y, -ies 'swɒnər|i, -iz
swan's-down 'swɒnzdaun
Swansea (in Wales) 'swɒnzi, (in Tasmania) 'swɒnsi [-si:]

swan-shot 'swɔn-ʃɔt

swan-song, -s 'swɔn-sɔŋ, -z

Swanwick 'swɔnik

swap (s. v.), -s, -ping, -ped swɔp, -s, -iŋ, -t

swaraj, -ist/s swə'rɑːdʒ [swɑːˈr-] (Hind. svəraɟ), -ist/s

sward, -s swɔːd, -z

sware (archaic past tense of swear) swɛə*

swarm (s. v.), -s, -ing, -ed swɔːm, -z, -iŋ, -d

swart swɔːt

swarth|y, -ier, -iest, -ily, -iness 'swɔːð|i [-ɔːθ|i], -iə* [-jə*], -iist [-jist], -ili, -inis

swash, -es, -ing, -ed; -buckler/s swɔʃ, -iz, -iŋ, -t; -ˌbʌklə*/z

swastika, -s 'swɔstikə, -z

swat, -s, -ting, -ted, -ter/s swɔt, -s, -iŋ, -id, -ə*/z

swath, -s swɔːθ, -s [swɔːðz]

swath|e, -es, -ing, -ed sweið, -z, -iŋ, -d

Swatow 'swɔtau

sway (s. v.), -s, -ing, -ed swei, -z, -iŋ, -d

Swaziland 'swɑːzilænd

swear (s. v.), -s, -ing, swore, sworn, swearer/s swɛə*, -z, -riŋ, swɔː*, [swɔə*], swɔːn, 'swɛərə*/z

swear-word, -s 'swɛəwəːd, -z

sweat (s. v.), -s, -ing, -ed, -er/s; -y, -iness swet, -s, -iŋ, -id, -ə*/z; -i, -inis

swede (S.), -s swiːd, -z

Sweden, -borg 'swiːdn, -bɔːg

Swedenborgian, -s ˌswiːdn'bɔːdʒjən [-dʒiən], -z

Swedish 'swiːdiʃ

Sweeney 'swiːni

sweep (s. v.), -s, -ing, swept, sweeper/s swiːp, -s, -iŋ, swept, 'swiːpə*/z

sweeping (s. adj.), -s 'swiːpiŋ, -z

sweepstake, -s 'swiːp-steik, -s

sweet (s. adj.) (S.), -s; -er, -est, -ly, -ness swiːt, -s; -ə*, -ist, -li, -nis

sweetbread, -s 'swiːtbred, -z

sweet-brier [-briar], -s 'swiːt'braiə*, -z

sweet|en, -ens, -ening, -ened, -ener/s 'swiːt|n, -nz, -niŋ [-ṇiŋ], -nd, -nə*/z [-ṇə*/z]

sweetheart, -s 'swiːthɑːt, -s

sweeting (S.), -s 'swiːtiŋ, -z

sweetish 'swiːtiʃ

sweetmeat, -s 'swiːtmiːt, -s

sweet-scented 'swiːt'sentid ['-,--]

sweet-tempered 'swiːt'tempəd ['-,--]

sweet|y, -ies 'swiːt|i, -iz

swell (s. v.), -s, -ing/s, -ed, swollen swel, -z, -iŋ/z, -d, 'swəulən

swell-box, -es 'swelbɔks, -iz

swelt|er, -ers, -ering/ly, -ered 'swelt|ə*, -əz, -əriŋ/li, -əd

swept (from sweep) swept

swerv|e (s. v.), -es, -ing, -ed swəːv, -z, -iŋ, -d

Swete swiːt

Swettenham 'swetṇəm

swift (s. adj. adv.) (S.), -s; -er, -est, -ly, -ness swift, -s; -ə*, -ist, -li, -nis

swift-footed 'swift'futid ['-,--]

Swiftsure 'swiftʃuə* [-ʃɔə*, -ʃɔ:*, -ʃə:*]

swig (s. v.), -s, -ging, -ged swig, -z, -iŋ, -d

swill (s. v.), -s, -ing, -ed swil, -z, -iŋ, -d

swim (s. v.), -s, -ming/ly, swam, swum, swimmer/s swim, -z, -iŋ/li, swæm, swʌm, 'swimə*/z

swimming-ba|th, -ths 'swimiŋbɑː|θ, -ðz

swimming-pool, -s 'swimiŋpuːl, -z

swim-suit, -s 'swimsjuːt [-suːt], -s

Swinburne 'swinbəːn [-bən]

swind|le, -les, -ling, -led, -ler/s 'swind|l, -lz, -liŋ, -ld, -lə*/z

Swindon 'swindən

swine, -herd/s swain, -həːd/z

swing (s. v.), -s, -ing, swung swiŋ, -z, -iŋ, swʌŋ

swing-boat, -s 'swiŋ'bəut ['--], -s

swinge, -s, -ing, -d swindʒ, -iz, -iŋ, -d

swingeing (adj.) 'swindʒiŋ

swing|le (s. v.), -les, -ling, -led 'swiŋg|l, -lz, -liŋ, -ld

swinish, -ness 'swainiʃ, -nis

swip|e (s. v.), -es, -ing, -ed, -er/s swaip, -s, -iŋ, -t, -ə*/z

swirl (s. v.), -s, -ing, -ed swəːl, -z, -iŋ, -d

swish (s. v.), -es, -ing, -ed swiʃ, -iz, -iŋ, -t

Swiss swis

switch (s. v.), -es, -ing, -ed switʃ, -iz, -iŋ, -t

switchback, -s 'switʃbæk, -s

switch-board, -s 'switʃbɔːd [-bɔəd], -z

Swithin 'swiðin [-iθin]

Switzerland 'switsələnd

swiv|el (s. v.), -els, -elling, -elled 'swiv|l, -lz, -liŋ [-liŋ], -ld

swizz|le (s. v.), -les, -ling, -led, -ler/s 'swiz|l, -lz, -liŋ [-liŋ], -ld, -lə*/z [-lə*/z]

swollen (from swell) 'swəulən

swoon (s. v.), -s, -ing, -ed swuːn, -z, -iŋ, -d

swoop (s. v.), -s, -ing, -ed swuːp, -s, -iŋ, -t

swop (s. v.), -s, -ping, -ped swɔp, -s, -iŋ, -t

sword, -s sɔːd [sɔəd], -z

sword-bearer, -s 'sɔːdˌbɛərə* ['sɔəd-], -z

sword-belt, -s 'sɔːdbelt ['sɔəd-], -s
sword-dance, -s 'sɔːddɑːns ['sɔəd-], -iz
Sworder 'sɔːdə*
swordfish 'sɔːdfiʃ ['sɔəd-]
swords|man, -men 'sɔːdz|mən ['sɔədz-],
  -mən
swore (from swear) swɔː* [swɔə*]
sworn (from swear) swɔːn
swot (s. v.), -s, -ting, -ted, -ter/s swɔt,
  -s, -iŋ, -id, -ə*/z
swum (from swim) swʌm
swung (from swing) swʌŋ
Sybaris 'sibəris
sybarite, -s 'sibərait, -s
Sybil 'sibil
sycamine, -s 'sikəmain [-min], -z
sycamore (S.), -s 'sikəmɔː* [-mɔə*], -z
syce, -s sais, -iz
sycophancy 'sikəfənsi [-kuf-]
sycophant, -s 'sikəfənt [-kuf-, -fænt], -s
Sycorax 'sikəræks
Sydenham 'sidŋəm [-dnəm]
Sydney 'sidni
Syed 'saied ['sai-əd]
syenite 'saiinait ['saiən-]
Sygrove 'saigrəuv
Sykes saiks
syllabar|y, -ies 'siləbər|i, -iz
syllabic, -ally si'læbik, -əli
syllabicat|e, -es, -ing, -ed si'læbikeit, -s,
  -iŋ, -id
syllabication si,læbi'keiʃən
syllabification si,læbifi'keiʃən
syllabicity ,silə'bisiti
syllabi|fy, -fies, -fying, -fied si'læbi|fai,
  -faiz, -faiiŋ, -faid
syllable, -s 'siləbl, -z
syllabus, -es 'siləbəs, -iz
syllogism, -s 'silədʒizəm [-ləudʒ-], -z
syllogistic, -ally ,silə'dʒistik [-ləu'dʒ-],
  -əli
syllogiz|e [-is|e], -es, -ing, -ed 'silə-
  dʒaiz [-ləudʒ-], -iz, -iŋ, -d
sylph, -s silf, -s
Sylva 'silvə
sylvan 'silvən
Sylvester sil'vestə*
Sylvia 'silvɪə [-vjə]
symbiosis ,simbi'əusis
symbol, -s 'simbəl, -z
symbolic, -al, -ally sim'bɔlik, -əl, -əli
symbolism 'simbəlizəm [-bul-, -bl-]
symbolization [-isa-] ,simbəlai'zeiʃən
  [-bul-, -bḷai'z-, -bəli'z-, -bḷi'z-]
symboliz|e [-is|e], -es, -ing, -ed 'sim-
  bəlaiz [-bul-, -bḷ-], -iz, -iŋ, -d
Syme saim
Symington 'saimiŋtən, 'sim-

symmetric, -al, -ally, -alness si'metrik,
  -əl, -əli, -əlnis
symmetry 'simitri
Symond 'saimənd
Symonds (surname) 'saiməndz, 'sim-
Symonds Yat 'siməndz'jæt
Symons 'saimənz, 'sim-
sympathetic, -al, -ally ,simpə'θetik, -əl,
  -əli
sympathiz|e [-is|e], -es, -ing, -ed 'sim-
  pəθaiz, -iz, -iŋ, -d
sympath|y, -ies 'simpəθ|i, -iz
symphonic sim'fɔnik
symphon|y, -ies 'simfən|i, -iz
symposium, -s sim'pəuzjəm [-'pɔz-,
  -zɪəm], -z
symptom, -s 'simptəm [-tim], -z
symptomatic ,simptə'mætik [-ti'm-]
synaer- = syner-
synagogue, -s 'sinəgɔg, -z
synaloepha sinə'liːfə
synapse 'sainæps [si'næps]
synchromesh, -es 'siŋkrəu'meʃ ['---], -iz
synchronic siŋ'krɔnik [sin'k-]
synchronism 'siŋkrənizəm [-krun-]
synchronistic ,siŋkrə'nistik [-kru'n-]
synchronization [-isa-], -s ,siŋkrənai-
  'zeiʃən [-krun-, -ni'z-], -z
synchroniz|e [-is|e], -es, -ing, -ed
  'siŋkrənaiz [-krun-], -iz, -iŋ, -d
synchronous, -ly, -ness 'siŋkrənəs
  [-krun-], -li, -nis
synchrony 'siŋkrəni [-krun-]
synchrotron, -s 'siŋkrəutrɔn, -z
syncopat|e, -es, -ing, -ed 'siŋkəpeit
  [-kəup-, -kup-], -s, -iŋ, -id
syncopation, -s ,siŋkə'peiʃən [-kəu'p-,
  -ku'p-], -z
syncope 'siŋkəpi [-kup-]
syncretic siŋ'kri:tik [sin'k-]
syncretism 'siŋkritizəm
syndic, -s 'sindik, -s
syndicali|sm, -st/s 'sindikəli|zəm [-kḷi-],
  -st/s
syndicate (s.), -s 'sindikit, -s
syndicat|e (v.), -es, -ing, -ed 'sindikeit,
  -s, -iŋ, -id
syndication ,sindi'keiʃən
syndrome, -s 'sindrəum [-drəmi,
  -,drəumi], -z
syne sain
synecdoche si'nekdəki
syneres|is, -es si'niərəs|is [-ris-], -i:z
Synge siŋ
synod, -s, -al 'sinəd, -z, -l
synodic, -al, -ally si'nɔdik, -əl, -əli
synonym, -s 'sinənim [-nɔn-, -nun-], -z
synonymous, -ly si'nɔniməs, -li

synops|is, -es si'nɔps|is, -i:z
synoptic, -s, -al, -ally si'nɔptik, -s, -əl, -əli
syntactic, -al, -ally sin'tæktik, -əl, -əli
syntagm, -s 'sintægəm, -z
syntax, -es 'sintæks, -iz
synthes|is, -es 'sinθis|is [-θəs-], -i:z
synthesiz|e [-is|e], -es, -ing, -ed 'sin-θisaiz [-θəs-], -iz, -iŋ, -d
synthetic, -s, -al, -ally sin'θetik, -s, -əl, -əli
synthetist, -s 'sinθitist [-θət-], -s [-əli
synthetiz|e [-is|e], -es, -ing, -ed 'sin-θitaiz [-θət-], -iz, -iŋ, -d
syphilis 'sifilis
syphilitic ,sifi'litik
syph|on (s. v.), -ons, -oning, -oned 'saif|ən, -ənz, -əniŋ [-n̩iŋ], -ənd
Syracusan ,saiərə'kju:zən
Syracuse (in classical history) 'saiərə-kju:z, (modern town in Sicily) 'saiərə-kju:z ['sir-], (town in U.S.A.) 'sirəkju:s

syren, -s 'saiərən [-rin], -z
Syria, -n/s 'siri̯ə, -n/z
Syriac 'siriæk
syringa, -s si'riŋgə, -z
syring|e (s. v.), -es, -ing, -ed 'sirindʒ [si'r-], -iz, -iŋ, -d
syrinx (all senses), -es 'siriŋks, -iz
syrophoenician 'saiərəufi'niʃi̯ən [-fi:'n-, -ʃi̯ən, -ʃən, -siən, -sjən]
syrt|is (S.), -es 'sə:t|is, -i:z
syrup, -s; -y 'sirəp, -s; -i
system, -s 'sistim [-təm], -z
systematic, -ally ,sisti'mætik [-tə'm-], -əli
systematization [-isa-] 'sistimətai'zei-ʃən [-təm-, -ti'z-]
systematiz|e [-is|e], -es, -ing, -ed, -er/s 'sistimətaiz [-təm-], -iz, -iŋ, -d, -ə*/z
systemic sis'temik [-'ti:mik]
systole 'sistəli
systolic sis'tɔlik
syzyg|y, -ies 'sizidʒ|i, -iz

T

T (*the letter*), -'s ti:, -z
ta (*Tonic Sol-fa name for diminished seventh from the tonic*), -s tɔ:, -z
ta (*syllable used in Tonic Sol-fa for counting time*) *generally* tɑ:, *but* tæ *in the sequence* **ta fe tay fe**, *q.v.*
ta (*thank you*) tɑ:
Taal tɑ:l
tab, -s tæb, -z
tabard (T.), -s 'tæbəd [-bɑ:d], -z
tabb|y, -ies 'tæb|i, -iz
taberdar, -s 'tæbə(:)dɑ:* [-də*], -z
tabernacle, -s 'tæbə(:)nækl, -z
Taberner tə'bə:nə*
tabes 'teibi:z
Tabitha 'tæbiθə
tablature, -s 'tæblətʃə* [-blitʃ-, -tjuə*], -z
tab|le (*s. v.*) (T.), -les, -ling, -led 'teib|l, -lz, -liŋ [-liŋ], -ld
tableau, -s 'tæbləu, -z
table-|cloth, -cloths 'teibl|klɔθ [-klɔ:θ], -klɔθs [-klɔ:ðz, -klɔ:θs]
table d'hôte 'tɑ:bl'dəut
table-kni|fe, -ves 'teiblnai|f, -vz
table-land, -s 'teibllænd, -z
table-leg, -s 'teiblleg, -z
table-linen 'teibl,linin
table-money 'teibl,mʌni
tablespoon, -s 'teiblspu:n, -z
tablespoonful, -s 'teiblspu:n,ful ['teibl-,spu:nful], -z
tablet, -s 'tæblit, -s
table-turning 'teibl,tə:niŋ
tabloid, -s 'tæblɔid, -z
taboo (*s.*), -s tə'bu:, -z
taboo (*v.*), -(e)s, -ing, -ed tə'bu:, -z, -iŋ [tə'buiŋ], -d
tabor, -s 'teibə* [-bɔ:*], -z
Tabor (*Mount*) 'teibɔ:* [-bə*]
tabouret, -s 'tæbərit [-bur-, -ret], -s
tabul|a, -ae 'tæbjul|ə, -i:
tabular 'tæbjulə*
tabulat|e, -es, -ing, -ed 'tæbjuleit, -s, -iŋ, -id
tabulation, -s ,tæbju'leiʃən, -z
tacet 'teiset ['tæs-]
tache, -s tɑ:ʃ [tæʃ], -iz
tachometer, -s tæ'kɔmitə*, -z

tachygraph|er/s, -y tæ'kigrəf|ə*/z, -i
tacit, -ly, -ness 'tæsit, -li, -nis
taciturn, -ly 'tæsitə:n, -li
taciturnity ,tæsi'tə:niti
Tacitus 'tæsitəs
tack (*s. v.*), -s, -ing, -ed, tæk, -s, -iŋ, -t
tack|le (*s. v.*), -les, -ling, -led, -ler/s 'tæk|l, -lz, -liŋ [-liŋ], -ld, -lə*/z [-lə*/z]
tacky 'tæki
Tacon 'teikən
tact tækt
tact|ful, -fully, -fulness 'tækt|ful, -fuli [-fəli], -fulnis
tactic, -s, -al, -ally 'tæktik, -s, -əl, -əli
tactician, -s tæk'tiʃən, -z
tactile 'tæktail
tactless, -ly, -ness 'tæktlis, -li, -nis
tactual, -ly 'tæktjuəl [-tjwəl, -tjul], -i
Tadcaster 'tædkæstə* [-kəs-]
Tadema 'tædimə
Tadhg taig
tadpole, -s 'tædpəul, -z
tael, -s teil ['teiəl], -z
ta'en (*dialectal for* taken) tein
ta fe tay fe (*syllables used in Tonic Sol-fa for counting four in a bar*) 'tæfi,tefi [-fə,t-]
Taff tæf
taffeta 'tæfitə
taffrail, -s 'tæfreil ['tæfril], -z
Taff|y, -ies 'tæf|i, -iz
taft, -s, -ing, -ed tæft, -s, -iŋ, -id
Taft (*surname*) tæft, tɑ:ft, (*town in Persia*) tɑ:ft
tag (*s. v.*), -s, -ging, -ged tæg, -z, -iŋ, -d
Tagore tə'gɔ:* [-'gɔə*] (*Bengali* ʈhakur)
tagrag 'tægræg
Tagus 'teigəs
Tahi|ti, -tian tɑ:'hi:|ti [tə'h-], -ʃən
tail (*s. v.*), -s, -ing, -ed; -less teil, -z, -iŋ, -d; -lis
tail-coat, -s 'teil'kəut [*in contrast* 'teil-kəut], -s
tail-end, -s 'teil'end ['teilend], -z
tailor (*s. v.*), -s, -ing, -ed 'teilə*, -z, -riŋ, -d
tailoress, -es ,teilə'res ['teiləres], -iz
tailor-made (*s. adj.*), -s 'teiləmeid, -z

tailpiece, -s 'teil-pi:s, -iz
tail-spin, -s 'teil-spin, -z
Taine tein (tɛːn)
taint (s. v.), -s, -ing, -ed; -less teint, -s,
  -iŋ, -id; -lis
Taiping (in Malaya) tai'piŋ ['-'-]
Tait teit
Taiwan tai'wæn [-'wɑːn, '-'-]
Taj Mahal 'tɑːdʒməˈhɑːl [-'hʌl] (Hind.
  taɪməhəl)
tak|e, -es, -ing, took, tak|en, -er/s
  teik, -s, -iŋ, tuk, 'teik|ən [-ŋ], -ə*/z
take-in, -s 'teik'in ['teik-in], -z
take-off, -s 'teik-ɔf [-ɔːf, '-'-], -s
take-over, -s 'teik‚əuvə*, -z
take-up, -s 'teik-ʌp, -s
takin, -s 'tɑːkin, -z
taking (s. adj.), -s, -ly, -ness 'teikiŋ, -z,
  -li, -nis
talbot, -s 'tɔːlbət ['tɔl-], -s
Talbot (surname) 'tɔːlbət ['tɔl-], (place)
  'tɔːlbət ['tɔl-], 'tælbət
  Note.—Both pronunciations are current at Port Talbot in Wales.
talc tælk
tale, -s teil, -z
tale-bearer, -s 'teil‚bɛərə*, -z
talent, -s, -ed, -less 'tælənt, -s, -id, -lis
tales (for completing a jury) 'teili:z
tales|man (person summoned to com-
  plete a jury), -men 'teili:z|mən [-lz-,
  -mæn], -mən [-men]
tale-teller, -s 'teil‚telə*, -z
Talfourd 'tælfəd
Taliesin ‚tæli'esin (Welsh tal'jesin)
talisman, -s 'tælizmən [-ism-], -z
talk (s. v.), -s, -ing, -ed, -er/s tɔːk, -s,
  -iŋ, -t, -ə*/z
talkative, -ly, -ness 'tɔːkətiv, -li, -nis
talkie, -s 'tɔːki, -z
talking-film, -s 'tɔːkiŋ'film [in contrast '---], -z
talking-to, -s 'tɔːkiŋtuː, -z
tall, -er, -est, -ness tɔːl, -ə*, -ist, -nis
tallage 'tælidʒ
tallboy, -s 'tɔːlbɔi, -z
Tallis 'tælis
tall|ow, -owy 'tæl|əu, -əui
tall|y (s. v.), -ies, -ying, -ied 'tæl|i, -iz,
  -iiŋ, -id
tally-ho (T.), -s 'tæli'həu, -z
tally|man, -men 'tæli|mən, -mən [-men]
Talman 'tɔːlmən
Talmud 'tælmud [-məd, -mʌd]
talmudic, -al tæl'mudik [-'mʌd-,
  -'mjuːd-], -əl
talon, -s 'tælən, -z
tam(e)ability ‚teimə'biliti [-lət-]

tam(e)able 'teiməbl
Tamaqua tə'mɑːkwə
Tamar (river in W. of England) 'teimə*,
  (biblical name) 'teimɑː* [-mə*]
tamarind, -s 'tæmərind, -z
tamarisk, -s 'tæmərisk, -s
tamber, -s 'tæmbə*, -z
tambour, -s 'tæmbuə* [-bɔə*, -bɔː*], -z
tambourine, -s ‚tæmbə'riːn, -z
Tamburlaine 'tæmbəlein
tam|e (adj. v.), -er, -est, -ely, -eness;
  -es, -ing, -ed, -er/s teim, -ə*, -ist, -li,
  -nis; -z, -iŋ, -d, -ə*/z
Tamerlane 'tæmə(:)lein
Tamil, -s 'tæmil [-ml], -z
Tammany 'tæməni
Tammerfors 'tæməfɔːz
Tamora 'tæmərə
tam-o'-shanter (T.), -s ‚tæmə'ʃæntə*, -z
tamp, -s, -ing, -ed tæmp, -s, -iŋ, -t
  [tæmt]
tamp|er, -ers, -ering, -ered 'tæmp|ə*,
  -əz, -əriŋ, -əd
tampon, -s 'tæmpən [-pɔn], -z
Tamworth 'tæmwə(:)θ
tan (s. adj. v.), -s, -ning, -ned, -ner/s
  tæn, -z, -iŋ, -d, -ə*/z
Tancred 'tæŋkred [-rid]
tandem, -s 'tændəm [-dem], -z
Tanfield 'tænfiːld
tang, -s tæŋ, -z
Tang (Chinese dynasty) tæŋ
Tanganyika ‚tæŋgə'njiːkə [-gæn-]
tangent, -s 'tændʒənt, -s
tangenti|al, -ally tæn'dʒenʃ|əl [-entʃ-],
  -əli
tangerine, -s ‚tændʒə'riːn ['tændʒə'r-,
  'tændʒər-], -z
tangibility ‚tændʒi'biliti [-dʒə'b-, -lət-]
tangib|le, -ly, -leness 'tændʒəb|l
  [-dʒib-], -li, -lnis
Tangier tæn'dʒiə* ['tændʒiə*]
tang|le (s. v.), -les, -ling, -led 'tæŋg|l,
  -lz, -liŋ [-liŋ], -ld
Tanglewood 'tæŋglwud
tangly 'tæŋgli
tango, -s 'tæŋgəu, -z
Tangye 'tæŋgi
tanh (mathematical term) θæn
tank, -s; -age, -er/s tæŋk, -s; -idʒ, -ə*/z
tankard, -s 'tæŋkəd, -z
tank-buster, -s 'tæŋk‚bʌstə*, -z
tanner (T.), -s 'tænə*, -z
tanner|y, -ies 'tænər|i, -iz
Tannhäuser 'tæn‚hɔizə* ('tan‚hɔyzər)
tanni|c, -n 'tæni|k, -n
Tanqueray 'tæŋkəri
tansy 'tænzi

tantalization [-isə-], -s ˌtæntəlai'zeiʃən; -z

tantaliz|e [-is|e], -es, -ing/ly, -ed, -er/s ˌtæntəlaiz, -iz, -iŋ/li, -d, -ə*/z

tantalum, -s 'tæntələm, -z

tantalus (T.), -es 'tæntələs, -iz

tantamount 'tæntəmaunt

tantiv|ly, -ies tæn'tiv|i, -iz

tanto 'tæntəu

tantrum, -s 'tæntrəm, -z

Tanzania ˌtænzə'niə [tæn'zeiniə, -njə]

Taoi|sm, -st/s 'tɑ:əui|zəm ['taui-], -st/s

tap (s. v.), -s, -ping, -ped tæp, -s, -iŋ, -t

tap-danc|e, -es, -ing, -ed, -er/s 'tæpdɑ:ns, -iz, -iŋ, -t, -ə*/z

tap|e (s. v.) (T.), -es, -ing, -ed teip, -s, -iŋ, -t

tape-machine, -s 'teipməˌʃi:n, -z

tape-measure, -s 'teipˌmeʒə* ['-'--], -z

taper (s. v.), -s, -ing, -ed 'teipə*, -z, -riŋ, -d

tape-recorder, -s 'teip-riˌkɔ:də*, -z

tapestr|y, -ies 'tæpistr|i [-pəs-], -iz

tapeworm, -s 'teip-wə:m, -z

tapioca ˌtæpi'əukə

tapir, -s 'teipə* [-piə*, rarely 'tæp-], -z

tapis 'tæpi: [-pi] (tapi)

tapist, -s 'teipist, -s

Tapling 'tæpliŋ

Tappertit 'tæpətit

tapping (s.), -s 'tæpiŋ, -z

tap-room, -s 'tæp-rum [-ru:m], -z

tap-root, -s 'tæp-ru:t, -s

tapster, -s 'tæpstə*, -z

tar (s. v.), -s, -ring, -red tɑ:*, -z, -riŋ, -d

taradiddle, -s 'tærədidl, -z

tarantella, -s ˌtærən'telə, -z

Taranto   tə'ræntəu   ['tɑ:rəntəu] ('tɑ:ranto)

tarantula, -s tə'ræntjulə, -z

taraxacum tə'ræksəkəm

tar-brush, -es 'tɑ:-brʌʃ, -iz

tard|y, -ier, -iest, -ily, -iness 'tɑ:d|i, -iə* [-jə*], -iist [-jist], -ili, -inis

tare, -s teə*, -z

Tarentaise ˌtærən'teiz (tarãtɛ:z)

Tarentum tə'rentəm

target, -s, -ed 'tɑ:git, -s, -id

targeteer, -s ˌtɑ:gi'tiə* [-gə't-], -z

tariff, -s 'tærif, -s

Tarkington 'tɑ:kiŋtən

Tarleton 'tɑ:ltən

tarmac, -s 'tɑ:mæk, -s

tarn, -s tɑ:n, -z

tarnish, -es, -ing, -ed 'tɑ:niʃ, -iz, -iŋ, -t

tarot, -s 'tærəu, -z

tarpaulin, -s tɑ:'pɔ:lin, -z

Tarpeian tɑ:'pi(:)ən

tarpon, -s 'tɑ:pɔn, -z

Tarquin, -s 'tɑ:kwin, -z

Tarquin|ius, -ii tɑ:'kwin|iəs [-jəs], -iai [-ii:]

tarradiddle, -s 'tærədidl, -z

tarragon 'tærəgən

Tarragona ˌtærə'gəunə

Tarring (surname) 'tæriŋ

tarrock, -s 'tærək, -s

tarry (adj.) (tarred, like tar) 'tɑ:ri

tarr|y (v.) (wait), -ies, -ying, -ied, -ier/s 'tær|i, -iz, -iiŋ, -id, -iə*/z

Tarshish 'tɑ:ʃiʃ

Tarsus 'tɑ:səs

tart (s. adj.), -s, -ly, -ness tɑ:t, -s, -li, -nis

tartan, -s 'tɑ:tən, -z

tartar (T.), -s 'tɑ:tə*, -z

tartaric tɑ:'tærik

Tartar|us, -y 'tɑ:tər|əs, -i

tartlet, -s 'tɑ:tlit, -s

Tarzan 'tɑ:zæn [-zən]

task (s. v.), -s, -ing, -ed tɑ:sk, -s, -iŋ, -t

Tasker 'tæskə*

taskmaster, -s 'tɑ:skˌmɑ:stə*, -z

task-mistress, -es 'tɑ:skˌmistris, -iz

Tasman 'tæzmən

Tasmania, -n/s tæz'meinjə [-niə], -n/z

Tass tæs

tassel, -s, -led 'tæsəl, -z, -d

Tasso 'tæsəu

tast|e (s. v.), -es, -ing, -ed, -er/s teist, -s, -iŋ, -id, -ə*/z

taste|ful, -fully, -fulness 'teist|ful, -fuli [-fəli], -fulnis

tasteless, -ly, -ness 'teistlis, -li, -nis

tast|y, -ier, -iest, -ily, -iness 'teist|i, -iə* [-jə*], -iist [-jist], -ili, -inis

tat (s. v.), -s, -ting, -ted tæt, -s, -iŋ, -id

ta-ta 'tæ'tɑ:

Tatar, -s 'tɑ:tə*, -z

ta tay fe (syllables used in Tonic Sol-fa for counting time) 'tɑ:tefi

Tate teit

Tatham 'teiθəm

Tatiana ˌtæti'ɑ:nə

tatler (T.), -s 'tætlə*, -z

tatter, -s, -ed 'tætə*, -z, -d

tatterdemalion ˌtætədə'meiljən [-di'm-, -liən]

Tattersall, -s 'tætəsɔ:l [-səl], -z

tatt|le (s. v.), -les, -ling, -led, -ler/s 'tæt|l, -lz, -liŋ [-liŋ], -ld, -lə*/z [-lə*/z]

tatt|oo (s. v.) (all senses), -oo(e)s, -ooing, -ooed, -ooer/s tə'tlu: [tæ't-], -u:z, -u(:)iŋ, -u:d, -u(:)ə*/z

tau tau
Tauchnitz 'tauknits ('tauxnits)
taught (from teach) tɔ:t
taunt, -s, -ing/ly, -ed, -er/s tɔ:nt, -s,
-iŋ/li, -id, -ə*/z
Taunton (in Somerset) 'tɔ:ntən [locally
'tɑ:n-]
Taurus (constellation) 'tɔ:rəs
taut, -ness tɔ:t, -nis
tautologic, -al, -ally ˌtɔ:tə'lɔdʒik, -əl, -əli
tautologism, -s tɔ:'tɔlədʒizəm, -z
tautologiz|e [-is|e], -es, -ing, -ed
tɔ:'tɔlədʒaiz, -iz, -iŋ, -d
tautologous tɔ:'tɔləgəs
tautolog|y, -ies tɔ:'tɔlədʒ|i, -iz
Tautpheus tɔ:t'fi:əs
tavern, -s 'tævən [-və:n], -z
Tavistock 'tævistɔk
taw (s. v.), -s, -ing, -ed tɔ:, -z, -iŋ, -d
tawdr|y, -ier, -iest, -ily, -iness 'tɔ:dr|i,
-ïə*, -iist, -ili, -inis
Tawell 'tɔ:əl
tawn|y, -ier, -iest, -iness 'tɔ:n|i, -ïə*
[-jə*], -iist [-jist], -inis
tax (s. v.), -es, -ing, -ed tæks, -iz, -iŋ, -t
taxability ˌtæksə'biliti [-lət-]
taxable, -ness 'tæksəbl, -nis
taxation, -s tæk'seiʃən, -z
tax-collector, -s 'tækskəˌlektə*, -z
tax-free 'tæks'fri: ['tæksfri:]
tax-gatherer, -s 'tæksˌgæðərə*, -z
taxi (s.), -s 'tæksi, -z
tax|i (v.), -ies, -ying, -ied 'tæks|i, -iz,
-iiŋ, -id
taxi-cab, -s 'tæksikæb, -z
taxiderm|al, -ic ˌtæksi'də:m|əl, -ik
taxidermist, -s 'tæksidə:mist [ˌtæksi'd-,
tæk'sidəmist], -s
taxidermy 'tæksidə:mi
taximeter, -s 'tæksiˌmi:tə*, -z
taxis (T.) 'tæksis
taxonomic, -ally ˌtæksəu'nɔmik, -əli
taxonomy tæk'sɔnəmi
tax-payer, -s 'tæksˌpeiə*, -z
tay (syllable used in Tonic Sol-fa in
counting time) generally tei, but te in
the sequence tay fe, q.v.
Tay tei
tay fe (syllables used in Tonic Sol-fa in
counting time) 'tefi, ˌtefi, see ta fe tay fe
Taylor 'teilə*
Taylorian tei'lɔ:rïən
T.B. 'ti:'bi:
Tchad tʃæd
Tchaikovsky (Russian composer)
tʃai'kɔvski [-'kɔfski] (tʃij'kofskij)
Tcherkasy tʃə:'kæsi
Tcherkessian, -s tʃə:'kesïən [-sjən], -z

tchick (s. v.), -s, -ing, -ed tʃik, -s, -iŋ, -t
tchick (interj.) ʬ [tʃik]
te (Tonic sol-fa name for leading-note),
-s ti:, -z
tea, -s ti:, -z
tea-cadd|y, -ies 'ti:ˌkæd|i, -iz
tea-cake, -s 'ti:-keik, -s
teach, -es, -ing/s, taught, teacher/s
ti:tʃ, -iz, -iŋ/z, tɔ:t, 'ti:tʃə*/z
teachability ˌti:tʃə'biliti [-lət-]
teachable, -ness 'ti:tʃəbl, -nis
tea-chest, -s 'ti:-tʃest, -s
teach-in 'ti:tʃ-in
tea-|cloth, -cloths 'ti:-|klɔθ [-klɔ:θ],
-klɔθs [-klɔ:ðz, -klɔ:θs]
tea-cup, -s; -ful/s 'ti:kʌp, -s; -ˌful/z
tea-fight, -s 'ti:-fait, -s
tea-garden, -s 'ti:ˌgɑ:dn, -z
tea-gown, -s 'ti:gaun, -z
Teague, -s ti:g, -z
tea-hou|se, -ses 'ti:hau|s, -ziz
teak ti:k
tea-kettle, -s 'ti:ˌketl, -z
teal ti:l
tea-lea|f, -ves 'ti:li:|f, -vz
team (s. v.), -s, -ing, -ed ti:m, -z, -iŋ, -d
teamster, -s 'ti:mstə*, -z
team-work 'ti:mwə:k
tea-part|y, -ies 'ti:ˌpɑ:t|i, -iz
tea-pot, -s 'ti:pɔt, -s
teapoy, -s 'ti:-pɔi, -z
tear (s.) (fluid from the eye), -s tiə*, -z
tear (s. v.) (pull apart, rend, rush, a rent,
etc.), -s, -ing, tore, torn teə*, -z, -riŋ,
tɔ:* [tɔə*], tɔ:n
tear-drop, -s 'tiə-drɔp, -s
tear|ful, -fully, -fulness 'tiə|ful, -fuli
[-fəli], -fulnis
tear-gas 'tiəgæs
tearless 'tiəlis
tea-room, -s 'ti:rum [-ru:m], -z
tea-rose, -s 'ti:rəuz, -iz
tear-shell, -s 'tiə'ʃel ['tiə-ʃel], -z
tear-stained 'tiə-steind
teas|e (s. v.), -es, -ing/ly, -ed, -er/s
ti:z, -iz, -iŋ/li, -d, -ə*/z
teas|el (s. v.), -els, -eling, -eled 'ti:z|l, -lz,
-əliŋ [-l̩iŋ], -ld
tea-service, -s 'ti:ˌsə:vis, -iz
tea-set, -s 'ti:-set, -s
tea-shop, -s 'ti:-ʃɔp, -s
teaspoon, -s 'ti:spu:n ['ti:-spu:n], -z
teaspoonful, -s 'ti:spu(:)nˌful, -z
tea-strainer, -s 'ti:ˌstreinə*, -z
teat, -s ti:t, -s
tea-table, -s 'ti:ˌteibl, -z
tea-things 'ti:θiŋz ['ti:-θiŋz]
tea-time 'ti:taim ['ti:-taim]

tea-tray, -s 'ti:trei ['ti:-trei], -z
tea-urn, -s 'ti:ə:n, -z
Teazle 'ti:zl
Tebay 'ti:bei
tec, -s tek, -s
technic, -s 'teknik, -s
technic|al, -ally, -alness 'teknik|əl, -əli
  [-ļi, -li], -əlnis
technicalit|y, -ies ˌtekni'kælit|i, -iz
technician, -s tek'niʃən, -z
technicolor 'tekniˌkʌlə*
technique, -s tek'ni:k ['--], -s
technocrat, -s 'teknəʊkræt, -s
technologic, -al ˌteknə'lɔdʒik, -əl
technolog|ist/s, -y tek'nɔlədʒ|ist/s, -i
tech|y, -ier, -iest, -ily, -iness 'tetʃ|i, -iə*,
  -iist, -ili, -inis
Teck tek
ted (T.), -s, -ding, -ded, -der/s ted, -z,
  -iŋ, -id, -ə*/z
Teddington 'tediŋtən
Teddy 'tedi
Te Deum, -s 'ti:'di(:)əm ['tei'deium],
  -z
tedious, -ly, -ness 'ti:djəs [-diəs], -li,
  -nis
tedium 'ti:djəm [-diəm]
tee (s. v.), -s, -ing, -d ti:, -z, -iŋ, -d
Teed ti:d
teem, -s, -ing, -ed ti:m, -z, -iŋ, -d
teen, -s ti:n, -z
teenager, -s 'ti:nˌeidʒə*, -z
teen|y, -iest 'ti:n|i, -iist [-jist]
Tees, -dale ti:z, -deil
tee-square, -s 'ti:-skwɛə* ['ti:'s-], -z
Teetgen 'ti:dʒən
teeth (pl. of tooth) ti:θ
teeth|e, -es, -ing, -ed ti:ð, -z, -iŋ, -d
teetot|al, -alism ti:'təut|l, -ļizəm
  [-əlizəm]
teetotaller, -s ti:'təutlə* [-tļə*], -z
teetotum, -s 'ti:təu'tʌm ['ti:təutʌm,
  ti:'təutəm], -z
tegument, -s 'tegjumənt, -s
Teheran tiə'rɑ:n [ˌtehə'r-, ˌteiə'r-]
Teign (in Devonshire) tin [ti:n]
Teignbridge 'tinbridʒ
Teignmouth 'tinməθ [locally also
  'tiŋməθ]
Teignton 'teintən
tekel 'ti:kel [-kəl]
telamon (T.), -s 'teləmən [-mɔn], -z
telautograph, -s te'lɔ:təgrɑ:f [-græf], -s
tele, -s 'teli, -z
tele-cine 'teli'sini
telecommunication, -s 'teli-kəˌmju(:)ni-
  'keiʃən, -z
telegenic ˌteli'dʒenik

telegram, -s 'teligræm, -z
telegraph (s. v.), -s, -ing, -ed 'teligrɑ:f
  [-græf], -s, -iŋ, -t
telegrapher, -s ti'legrəfə* [te'l-, tə'l-], -z
telegraphese 'teligrɑ:'fi:z [-græ'f-,
  -grə'f-]
telegraphic, -ally ˌteli'græfik, -əli
telegraphist, -s ti'legrəfist [te'l-, tə'l-],
  -s
telegraph-|line/s   -pole/s,   -post/s,
  -wire/s   'teligrɑ:f|lain/z   [-græf-],
  -pəul/z, -pəust/s, -ˌwaiə*/z
telegraphy ti'legrəfi [te'l-, tə'l-]
Telemachus ti'leməkəs [te'l-, tə'l-]
telemark (s. v.), -s, -ing, -ed 'telimɑ:k
  [-ləm-], -s, -iŋ, -t
telemeter (s. v.), -s, -ing, -ed 'telimi:tə*,
  -z, -riŋ, -d
telemetric ˌteli'mi:trik [-'met-]
telemetry ti'lemitri
telepathic, -ally ˌteli'pæθik, -əli
telepath|ist/s, -y ti'lepəθ|ist/s [te'l-,
  tə'l-], -i
telepathiz|e [-is|e], -es, -ing, -ed
  ti'lepəθaiz [te'l-, tə'l-], -iz, -iŋ, -d
telephon|e (s. v.), -es, -ing, -ed, -er/s
  'telifəun, -z, -iŋ, -d, -ə*/z
telephonee, -s ˌtelifəu'ni:, -z
telephonic, -ally ˌteli'fɔnik, -əli
telephonist, -s ti'ləfənist [te'l-, tə'l-,
  'telifəunist], -s
telephony ti'lefəni [te'l-, tə'l-]
telephoto, -s 'teli'fəutəu, -z
telephotograph,   -s   'teli'fəutəgrɑ:f
  [-græf], -s
telephotography 'telifə'tɔgrəfi
teleprinter, -s 'teliˌprintə*, -z
telerecord (s.), -s 'teliˌrekɔ:d, -z
telerecord (v.), -s, -ing/s, -ed 'teliri,kɔ:d
  [-rə,k-], -z, -iŋ/z, -id
telescop|e (s. v.), -es, -ing, -ed 'telis-
  kəup, -s, -iŋ, -t
telescopic, -ally ˌtelis'kɔpik, -əli
telescop|ist/s, -y ti'leskəp|ist/s [te'l-,
  tə'l-], -i
telescreen, -s 'teli-skri:n, -z
teletype, -s 'telitaip, -s
teletypesetter, -s 'teli'taip,setə* [ˌteli't-],
  -z
teleview, -s, -ing, -ed, -er/s 'telivju:
  ['--'-], -z, -iŋ [-juiŋ], -d, -ə*/z [-juə*/z]
televis|e, -es, -ing, -ed 'telivaiz, -iz, -iŋ,
  -d
television 'teliˌviʒən ['--'--, ˌ--'--]
televisor, -s 'telivaizə*, -z
tell (T.), -s, -ing, told, teller/s tel, -z, -iŋ,
  təuld, 'telə*/z
telling (adj.), -ly 'teliŋ, -li

telltale, -s 'tel-teil, -z
tellurium te'ljuəriəm [-jɔər-, -jɔ:r-]
telly, -ies 'telli, -iz
Telstar 'tel-stɑ:*
Telugu 'teləgu: [-lug-, ͵--'-]
Teluk Anson (in Malaya) ͵teləu'ænsn
[͵telu'æn-]
Teme ti:m
Téméraire ͵temə'rɛə* ['temə'r-]
(temerε:r]
temerity ti'meriti [te'm-, tə'm-]
Tempe 'tempi
temper (s. v.), -ers, -ering, -ered,
-erer/s 'temp|ə*, -əz, -əriŋ, -əd,
-ərə*/z
tempera 'tempərə
temperable 'tempərəbl
temperament, -s 'tempərəmənt, -s
temperament|al, -ally ͵tempərə'ment|l,
-əli [-ḷi]
temperance 'tempərəns
temperate, -ly, -ness 'tempərit, -li, -nis
temperature, -s 'tempritʃə* [-pər-,
-rətʃ-], -z
temperedly 'tempədli
Temperley 'tempəli
tempest (T.), -s 'tempist, -s
tempestuous, -ly, -ness tem'pestjŭəs
[təm-, -tjwəs], -li, -nis
Templar, -s 'templə*, -z
temple (T.), -s 'templ, -z
templet, -s 'templit, -s
Templeton 'templtən
templo, -os, -i 'templəu, -əuz, -i:
tempor|al, -ally 'tempər|əl, -əli
temporality ͵tempə'ræliti
temporar|y (s. adj.), -ies, -ily, -iness
'tempərər|i [-prər-], -iz, -ili, -inis
temporization [-isa-] ͵tempərai'zeiʃən
temporiz|e [-is|e], -es, -ing/ly, -ed, -er/s
'tempəraiz, -iz, -iŋ/li, -d, -ə*/z
tempt, -s, -ing, -ed, -er/s tempt, -s, -iŋ,
-id, -ə*/z
temptation, -s tempp'teiʃən, -z
tempting (adj.), -ly, -ness 'temptiŋ, -li,
-nis
ten, -s, -th, -ths, -thly ten, -z, -θ, -θs,
-θli
tenability ͵tenə'biliti [͵ti:n-, -lət-]
tenable, -ness 'tenəbl ['ti:n-], -nis
tenacious, -ly, -ness ti'neiʃəs [te'n-,
tə'n-], -li, -nis
tenacity ti'næsiti [te'n-, tə'n-]
tenanc|y, -ies 'tenəns|i, -iz
tenant, -s 'tenənt, -s
tenant|able, -less, -ry 'tenənt|əbl, -lis,
-ri
Ten|bury, -by 'ten|bəri, -bi

tench tenʃ [-ntʃ]
tend, -s, -ing, -ed tend, -z, -iŋ, -id
tendencious [-ntious] ten'denʃəs
tendenc|y, -ies 'tendəns|i, -iz
tend|er (s. adj. v.), -ers, -erer, -erest,
-erly, -erness; -ering, -ered 'tend|ə*,
-əz, -ərə*, -ərist, -əli, -ənis; -əriŋ, -əd
tenderfoot, -s 'tendəfut, -s
tender-hearted, -ly, -ness 'tendə'hɑ:tid
['tendə͵h-], -li, -nis
tenderloin, -s 'tendələin, -z
tendon, -s 'tendən, -z
tendril, -s 'tendril [-drəl], -z
tenebrae 'tenibri:
tenebrous 'tenibrəs
tenement, -s 'tenimənt [-nəm-], -s
Tenerif(f)e ͵tenə'ri:f
tenet, -s 'ti:net ['ten-, -nit], -s
tenfold 'ten-fəuld
tengku, -s 'teŋku:, -z
Teniers 'teniəz [-njəz]
tenish 'teniʃ
Tenison 'tenisn
Tennant 'tenənt
tenner, -s 'tenə*, -z
Tennessee ͵tenə'si: [-ni's-]
Tenniel 'tenjəl [-niəl]
tennis, -ball/s 'tenis, -bɔ:l/z
tennis-court, -s 'tenis-kɔ:t [-kɔət], -s
tennis-racket, -s 'tenis͵rækit, -s
Tennyson 'tenisn
tenon, -s 'tenən, -z
tenor, -s 'tenə*, -z
tenour 'tenə*
ten|pence, -penny 'ten|pəns, -pəni
tense (s. adj.), -s, -r, -st, -ly, -ness tens,
-iz, -ə*, -ist, -li, -nis
tensile 'tensail
tension, -s 'tenʃən, -z
tensity 'tensiti
tensor, -s 'tensə*, -z
tent (s. v.), -s, -ing, -ed tent, -s, -iŋ, -id
tentacle, -s 'tentəkl [-tik-], -z
tentacular ten'tækjulə*
tentative (s. adj.), -s, -ly 'tentətiv, -z, -li
tent-bed, -s 'tentbed ['-'-], -z
tenter, -s 'tentə*, -z
Tenterden 'tentədən
tenter-hook, -s 'tentəhuk, -s
tenth, -s, -ly tenθ, -s, -li
tent-pegging 'tent͵pegiŋ
tenu|is, -es 'tenju|is, -i:z [-eiz]
tenuity te'nju(:)iti [tə'n-, ti'n-]
tenuous 'tenjŭəs [-njwəs]
tenure, -s 'tenjuə* [-njə*], -z
tepee, -s 'ti:pi:, -z
tepid, -est, -ly, -ness 'tepid, -ist, -li, -nis
tepidity te'piditi

ter (*three times*) tə:*
Ter (*river in Essex*) tɑ:*
Terah 'tiərə [*rarely* 'terə]
teraph, -im 'terəf, -im
tercel, -s 'tə:səl, -z
tercentenar|y (*s. adj.*), -ies ˌtə:sen-
  'ti:nər|i ['tə:sen't-, -'ten-, tə:'sentin-],
  -iz
tercentennial ˌtə:sen'tenjəl ['tə:sen't-,
  -nɪəl]
tercet, -s 'tə:sit [-set], -s
terebene 'terəbi:n [-rib-]
terebinth, -s 'terəbinθ [-rib-], -s
terebinthine ˌterə'binθain [-ri'b-]
Terence 'terəns
Teresa tə'ri:zə [ti'r-, te'r-]
tergiversat|e, -es, -ing, -ed 'tə:dʒivə:-
  -seit, -s, -iŋ, -id
tergiversation ˌtə:dʒivə:'seiʃən
Terling (*in Essex*) 'tɑ:liŋ ['tə:l-]
term, -s tə:m, -z
termagant (*s. adj.*), -s 'tə:məgənt, -s
terminable, -ness 'tə:minəbl, -nis
terminal (*s. adj.*), -s 'tə:minl, -z
terminat|e, -es, -ing, -ed, -or/s 'tə:-
  mineit, -s, -iŋ, -id, -ə*/z
termination, -s ˌtə:mi'neiʃən, -z
terminative, -ly 'tə:minətiv [-neit-], -li
terminer 'tə:minə*
terminologic|al, -ally ˌtə:minə'lɔdʒik|əl,
  -əli
terminolog|y, -ies ˌtə:mi'nɔlədʒ|i, -iz
termin|us, -i, -uses 'tə:min|əs, -ai, -əsiz
termite, -s 'tə:mait, -s
tern, -s tə:n, -z
ternary 'tə:nəri
Ternate (*island*) tə:'nɑ:ti
terner|y, -ies 'tə:nər|i, -iz
Terpsichore tə:p'sikəri
Terpsichorean ˌtə:psikə'ri(:)ən [-kɔ'r-]
terra 'terə
terrac|e (*s. v.*), -es, -ing, -ed 'terəs
  [-ris], -iz, -iŋ, -t
terra-cotta 'terə'kɔtə [ˌ--'--]
Terra del Fuegian, -s 'terədel-fu'i:dʒjən
  [-dʒɪən, -dʒən], -z
Terra del Fuego 'terədel-fu'eigəu
  [-'fwei-]
terrain, -s 'terein [-'-], -z
terramycin ˌterə'maisin
terrapin, -s 'terəpin, -z
terrestrial, -ly, -ness ti'restrɪəl [te'r-,
  tə'r-], -i, -nis
terret, -s 'terit, -s
terrib|le, -ly, -leness 'terəb|l [-rib-], -li,
  -lnis
terrier, -s 'terɪə*, -z
terrific, -ally tə'rifik [ti'r-], -əli

terri|fy, -fies, -fying, -fied 'teri|fai, -faiz,
  -faiiŋ, -faid
territorial (*s. adj.*), -s, -ly ˌteri'tɔ:rɪəl, -z,
  -i
territorializ|e [-is|e], -es, -ing, -ed
  ˌteri'tɔ:rɪəlaiz, -iz, -iŋ, -d
territor|y, -ies 'teritər|i, -iz
terror, -s 'terə*, -z
terrori|sm, -st/s 'terəri|zəm, -st/s
terrorization [-isa-] ˌterərai'zeiʃən ['ter-,
  -ri'z-]
terroriz|e [-is|e], -es, -ing, -ed, -er/s
  'terəraiz, -iz, -iŋ, -d, -ə*/z
Terry 'teri
terse, -r, -st, -ly, -ness tə:s, -ə*, -ist, -li,
  -nis
tertian 'tə:ʃən [-ʃjən, -ʃɪən]
tertiary 'tə:ʃəri [-ʃjə-, -ʃɪə-]
Tertis 'tə:tis
tertium quid 'tə:tjəm'kwid ['tə:tɪəm-,
  'tə:ʃjəm-, 'tə:ʃɪəm-]
Tertius (*as Eng. name*) 'tə:ʃjəs [-ʃɪəs]
Tertullian tə:'talɪən [-ljən]
terylene 'terəli:n [-ri-]
terzetto, -s tə:t'setəu [tɛət-], -z
Tesla 'teslə
tessaract, -s 'tesərækt, -s
tessellat|e, -es, -ing, -ed 'tesileit [-səl-],
  -s, -iŋ, -id
tessellation ˌtesi'leiʃən [-sə'l-]
test (*s. v.*) (T.), -s, -ing, -ed; -able test,
  -s, -iŋ, -id; -əbl
testac|ean, -eous tes'teiʃ|ən [-jən, -ɪən],
  -əs [-jəs, -ɪəs]
testament (T.), -s 'testəmənt, -s
testament|al, -ary, -arily ˌtestə'ment|l,
  -əri, -ərili
testamur, -s tes'teimə*, -z
testate, -s 'testit [-teit], -s
testation, -s tes'teiʃən, -z
testator, -s tes'teitə*, -z
testatri|x, -ces, -xes tes'teitri|ks, -si:z,
  -ksiz
tester, -s 'testə*, -z
testicle, -s 'testikl, -z
testification, -s ˌtestifi'keiʃən, -z
testi|fy, -fies, -fying, -fied, -fier/s
  'testi|fai, -faiz, -faiiŋ, -faid, -faiə*/z
  [-faiə*/z]
testimonial, -s ˌtesti'məunjəl [-nɪəl], -z
testimonializ|e [-is|e], -es, -ing, -ed
  ˌtesti'məunjəlaiz [-nɪəl-], -iz, -iŋ, -d
testimon|y, -ies 'testimən|i, -iz
test-tube, -s 'testtju:b, -z
testud|o, -os, -ines tes'tju:d|əu [-'tu:-],
  -əuz, tes'tju:dini:z [tes'tu:dineiz]
test|y, -ier, -iest, -ily, -iness 'testi, -ɪə*
  [-jə*], -iist [-jist], -ili, -inis

tetan|us, -y 'tetən|əs [-tn̩-], -i
tetch|y, -ier, -iest, -ily, -iness 'tetʃ|i, -iə*, -iist, -ili, -inis
tête-à-tête, -s 'teitɑː'teit, -s
tether (s. v.), -s, -ing, -ed 'teðə*, -z, -riŋ, -d
tetrachord, -s 'tetrəkɔːd, -z
tetrad, -s 'tetræd [-rəd], -z
tetragon, -s 'tetrəgən, -z
tetrahedr|on, -ons, -a; -al 'tetrə'hedr|ən [-'hiːd-, 'tetrə,h-, tetrə'h-], -ənz, -ə; tetralog|y, -ies tə'trælədʒ|i, -iz   [-əl
tetrameter, -s te'træmitə*, -z
tetrarch, -s; -y, -ies 'tetrɑːk ['tiːt-], -s; -i, -iz
tetrasyllabic 'tetrəsi'læbik
tetrasyllable, -s 'tetrə,siləbl ['tetrə's-], -z
tetter 'tetə*
Teucer 'tjuːsə*
Teufelsdroeckh 'tɔifəlzdrek
Teutoburgian ,tjuːtəu'bəːgjən [-gɪən]
Teuton, -s 'tjuːtən, -z
Teutonic tju(ː)'tɒnik
teutonization [-isa-]   ,tjuːtənai'zeiʃən [-tɲai'z-, -təni'z-, -tɲi'z-]
teutoniz|e [-is|e], -es, -ing, -ed 'tjuːtən- aiz [-tɲaiz], -iz, -iŋ, -d
Teviot (river) 'tiːvjət [-vɪət], (Lord) 'tevɪət [-vjət]
Teviotdale 'tiːvjətdeil [-vɪət-]
Tewfik 'tjuːfik
Tewin 'tju(ː)in
Tewkesbury 'tjuːksbəri
Texan 'teksən
Texas 'teksəs [-sæs]
Texel 'teksəl
text, -s tekst, -s
text-book, -s 'tekstʃbuk, -s
textile, -s 'tekstail, -z
textual, -ly 'tekstjŭəl [-tjwəl, -tjul], -i
texture, -s 'tekstʃə*, -z
Teynham (Baron, place in Kent) 'tenəm
Thackeray 'θækəri
Thackley 'θækli
Thaddeus θæ'di(ː)əs
Thailand 'tailænd [-lənd]
Thalben 'θælbən, 'θɔːlbən
Note.—Dr. Thalben Ball, the organist, pronounces 'θælbən.
thaler, -s 'tɑːlə*, -z
Thales 'θeiliːz
Thalia, -n θə'laiə, -n
thalidomide θə'lidəumaid [θæ'l-]
thallium 'θælɪəm [-ljəm]
Thame (in Oxfordshire) teim
Thames (in England, Canada, New Zealand) temz, (in Connecticut) θeimz [temz]

than ðæn (strong form), ðən, ðn (weak forms)
thane (T.), -s θein, -z
Thanet 'θænit
thank (s. v.), -s, -ing, -ed, -er/s θæŋk, -s, -iŋ, -t [θæŋt], -ə*/z
Note.—The interjection Thank you (normally 'θæŋk-ju) has several other forms, the chief of which are 'hæŋk-ju, 'ŋk-ju, 'kkju. The first k of 'kkju has no sound, but the speaker feels the stress to be there.
thank|ful, -fully, -fulness 'θæŋk|ful, -fuli [-fəli], -fulnis
thankless, -ly, -ness 'θæŋklis, -li, -nis
thank-offering, -s 'θæŋk,ɔfəriŋ, -z
thanksgiving, -s 'θæŋks,giviŋ ['-'--, -'--], -z
thankworth|y, -iness 'θæŋk,wəːð|i, -inis
that (adj., demonstr. pron., adv.) ðæt
that (relative pron.) ðæt (strong form), ðət, ðt (weak forms)
Note.—The strong form is seldom used, except in very deliberate speech or when mentioning the word in isolation.
that (conj.) ðæt (strong form), ðət (weak form)
Note.—The strong form is not often used.
thatch (s. v.), -es, -ing, -ed, -er/s θætʃ, -iz, -iŋ, -t, -ə*/z
Thatcher 'θætʃə*
thaumaturge, -s 'θɔːmətəːdʒ, -iz
thaumaturgic ,θɔːmə'təːdʒik
thaumaturg|ist/s,   -y   'θɔːmətəːdʒ|- -ist/s, -i
thaw (s. v.), -s, -ing, -ed θɔː, -z, -iŋ, -d
thaw|y, -ily, -iness 'θɔː|i, -ili, -inis
the ðiː (strong form, also sometimes used as a weak form before vowels), ði (weak form before vowels), ðə, ð (weak forms before consonants)
theatre, -s 'θiətə* [θi'etə*], -z
theatre-land 'θiətəlænd [θi'et-]
theatric|al, -als, -ally, -alness θi'æ- trik|əl ['θjæ-], -əlz, -əli, -əlnis
theatricality θi,ætri'kæliti
theatrophone, -s θi'ætrəfəun, -z
Thebaid 'θi:beiid
Theban, -s 'θiːbən, -z
Thebes θi:bz
thee (accus. of thou) ðiː (normal form), ði (occasional weak form)
theft, -s θeft, -s
their ðɛə* (normal form), ðər (occasional weak form when a vowel follows)

theirs ðɛəz
thei|sm, -st/s 'θi:i|zəm, -st/s
theistic, -al θi:'istik, -əl
Thelusson (surname) 'teləsn
them ðem (strong form), ðəm, ðm
(weak forms), əm, m (occasional weak
forms)
thematic θi'mætik
theme, -s θi:m, -z
Themistocles θi'mistəkli:z [θe'm-,
θə'm-]
themselves ðəm'selvz
then ðen
thence ðens
thenceforth 'ðens'fɔ:θ
thenceforward 'ðens'fɔ:wəd
Theo 'θi(:)əu
Theobald 'θiəbɔ:ld [old-fashioned 'θibəld,
'tibəld]
Theobalds (in Herts.) 'tibldz ['θiəbɔ:ldz],
(road in London) 'θiəbɔ:ldz [formerly
'tibldz]
theocrac|y, -ies θi'ɔkrəs|i, -iz
theocratic, -al θiə'krætik [θiəu'k-], -əl
Theocritus θi'ɔkritəs
theodicy θi'ɔdisi
theodolite, -s θi'ɔdəlait, -s
Theodore 'θiədɔ:* [-dɔə*]
Theodoric θi'ɔdərik
Theodosi|a, -us θiə'dəusj|ə [θiə'd-, -sĭ|ə],
-əs
theologian, -s θiə'ləudʒjən [θiə'l-,
-dʒiən, -dʒən], -z
theologic, -al, -ally θiə'lɔdʒik [θiə'l-],
-əl, -əli
theolog|ist/s, -y θi'ɔlədʒ|ist/s, -i
theologiz|e [-is|e], -es, -ing, -ed θi'ɔlə-
dʒaiz, -iz, -iŋ, -d
Theophilus θi'ɔfiləs
Theophrastus θiə'fræstəs [θiəu'f-]
theorem, -s 'θiərəm [-rem, -rim], -z
theoretic, -al, -ally θĭə'retik ['θiə'r-], -əl,
-əli
theoretician, -s ,θiərə'tiʃən [-ri't-, -re't-],
-z
theorist, -s 'θiərist, -s
theoriz|e [-is|e], -es, -ing, -ed, -er/s
'θiəraiz, -iz, -iŋ, -d, -ə*/z
theor|y, -ies 'θiər|i, -iz
theosophic, -al, -ally θĭə'sofik ['θiə's-,
,θi:ə's-], -əl, -əli
theosoph|ism, -ist/s, -y θi'ɔsəf|izəm
[θi:'ɔ-], -ist/s, -i
theosophiz|e [-is|e], -es, -ing, -ed
θi'ɔsəfaiz [θi:'ɔ-], -iz, -iŋ, -d
Thera 'θiərə
therapeutic, -s, -ally ,θerə'pju:tik, -s,
-əli

therapeutist, -s ,θerə'pju:tist, -s
therap|ist/s, -y 'θerəp|ist/s, -i
there ðɛə* (normal form), ðə* (weak
form), ðr (alternative weak form before
vowels)
Note.—The weak forms occur only
when the word is used expletively,
as in there is, there are, there
was, there won't be, etc. The
form ðɛə* is also used in such
expressions.
thereabouts 'ðɛərəbauts ['ðɛərə'b-,
,ðɛərə'b-]
Note.—The form ,ðɛərə'bauts is always used in the expression there
or thereabouts. In other connec-
tions usage varies, the form 'ðɛərəbauts being apparently the most
frequent.
thereafter ðɛər'ɑ:ftə*
thereat ðɛər'æt
thereby 'ðɛə'bai ['--, -'- according to
sentence-stress]
therefor ðɛə'fɔ:*
therefore 'ðɛəfɔ:* [-fɔə*]
therefrom ðɛə'from
therein ðɛər'in [occasionally '—]
thereinafter ,ðɛərin'ɑ:ftə*
thereof ðɛər'ɔv [-'ɔf]
thereon ðɛər'ɔn
there's (= there is, there has) ðɛəz
(strong form), ðəz (weak form)
Theresa ti'ri:zə [tə'r-]
thereto ðɛə'tu:
thereunto ðɛər'ʌntu(:) [,ðɛərʌn'tu:]
thereupon 'ðɛərə'pɔn
therewith ðɛə'wið [-'wið]
therewithal ,ðɛəwi'ðɔ:l
therm, -s θə:m, -z
therm|al, -ally 'θə:m|əl, -əli
thermic, -ally 'θə:mik, -əli
Thermidor 'θə:midɔ:*
thermionic, -s ,θə:mi'ɔnik, -s
thermit 'θə:mit
thermodynamic, -s 'θə:məudai'næmik
[-di'n-], -s
thermogene 'θə:məudʒi:n
thermograph, -s 'θə:məugrɑ:f [-græf], -s
thermometer, -s θə'mɔmitə* ['θmɔm-],
-z
thermometric, -al, -ally ,θə:məu'metrik
[-mu'm-], -əl, -əli
thermopile, -s 'θə:məupail, -z
themoplastic (s. adj.), -s 'θə:məu-
'plæstik [,θə:-, -mə'p-], -s
Thermopylae θə:'mɔpili: [θə'm-]
thermos, -es 'θə:mɔs [-məs], -iz
thermostat, -s 'θə:məstæt [-məus-], -s

thermostatic ˌθəːməˈstætik [-məus-]

Thersites θəːˈsaitiːz

thesaur|us, -i, -uses θi(ː)ˈsɔːr|əs, -ai, -əsiz

these (plur. of this) ðiːz

Theseus (in Greek legend) ˈθiːsjuːs [-sjəs, -siəs], (Shakespearian character, and as name of ship) ˈθiːsjəs [-siəs]

Thesiger ˈθesidʒə*

thes|is (dissertation), -es ˈθiːs|is, -iːz

thesis (metrical term) ˈθesis [ˈθiːs-]

Thespian ˈθespiən [-pjən]

Thespis ˈθespis

Thessalian, -s θeˈseiljən [-liən], -z

Thessalonian, -s ˌθesəˈləunjən [-niən], -z

Thessalonica ˌθesələˈnaikə [-ˈniːkə]

Thessaly ˈθesəli

Thetis (Greek) ˈθetis, (asteroid, name of ship) ˈθiːtis

theurgic, -al θi(ː)ˈəːdʒik, -əl

theurg|ist/s, -y ˈθiːəːdʒ|ist/s, -i

thews θjuːz

they ðei (normal form), ðe (not infrequent as weak form esp. before vowels)

Note.—ðe occurs as a strong form in the single expression they are, when are has its weak form ə*. They are in this case is also written they're.

Theydon Bois ˈθeidnˈbɔiz

thias|us, -i ˈθaiəs|əs, -ai

thick (s. adj. adv.), -er, -est, -ly, -ness/es θik, -ə*, -ist, -li, -nis/iz

thick|en, -ens, -ening, -ened ˈθik|ən, -ənz, -ṇiŋ [-əniŋ, -niŋ], -ənd

thicket, -s ˈθikit, -s

thick-headed ˈθikˈhedid [also '-ˌ-- when attributive]

thickish ˈθikiʃ

thick-set ˈθikˈset ['-- when attributive]

thick-skinned ˈθikˈskind ['-- when attributive]

thick-skulled ˈθikˈskʌld ['-- when attributive]

thick-witted ˈθikˈwitid (also '-ˌ-- when attributive]

thie|f, -ves θiː|f, -vz   [-d; -əri

thiev|e, -es, -ing, -ed; -ery θiːv, -z, -iŋ,

thievish, -ly, -ness ˈθiːviʃ, -li, -nis

thigh, -s; -bone/s θai, -z; -bəun/z

thill, -s θil, -z

thimble, -s; -ful/s ˈθimbl, -z; -ful/z

thimblerig (s. v.), -s, -ging, -ged ˈθimblrig, -z, -iŋ, -d

thin (adj. v.), -ner, -nest, -ly, -ness; -s, -ning, -ned θin, -ə*, -ist, -li, -nis; -z, -iŋ, -d

thine ðain

thing, -s θiŋ, -z

thingam|y, -ies ˈθiŋəm|i, -iz

thingumabob, -s ˈθiŋəmibɔb [-məb-], -z

thingumajig, -s ˈθiŋəmidʒig [-mədʒ-], -z

thingumbob, -s ˈθiŋəmbɔb, -z

thingumm|y, -ies ˈθiŋəm|i, -iz

think, -s, -ing, thought, thinker/s θiŋk, -s, -iŋ, θɔːt, ˈθiŋkə*/z

thinkable ˈθiŋkəbl

Thinn θin

thinnish ˈθiniʃ

thin-skinned ˈθinˈskind [ˈθin-skind when attributive]

third (s. adj.), -s, -ly θəːd, -z, -li

third-rate ˈθəːdˈreit [also ˈθəːd-reit when attributive]

Thirsk θəːsk

thirst (s. v.), -s, -ing, -ed θəːst, -s, -iŋ, -id

thirst|y, -ier, -iest, -ily, -iness ˈθəːst|i, -iə* [-jə*], -iist [-jist], -ili, -inis

thirteen, -s, -th/s, -thly ˈθəːˈtiːn ['--, -ˈ- according to sentence-stress], -z, -θ/s, -θli

thirt|y, -ies, -ieth/s, -iethly, -yfold ˈθəːt|i, -iz, -iiθ/s [-jiθ/s, -ïəθ/s, -jəθ/s], -iiθli [-jiθli, -ïəθli, -jəθli], -ifəuld

this ðis

Note.—Some use a weak form ðəs in this morning (afternoon, evening).

Thisbe ˈθizbi

Thiselton ˈθisltən

thistle, -s ˈθisl, -z

thistle-down ˈθisldaun

thistly ˈθisl|i [-sli]

thither, -ward ˈðiðə*, -wəd [-wɔːd]

tho' ðəu

thole, -s θəul, -z

Thom (surname) tɔm

Thomas ˈtɔməs

Thomond (in Ireland) ˈθəumənd

Thompson ˈtɔmpsn

Thompstone ˈtɔmpstəun

Thomson ˈtɔmsn [-mpsn]

thong, -s θɔŋ, -z

Thor θɔː*

thoracic θɔːˈræsik [θɔːˈr-, θəˈr-]

thorax, -es ˈθɔːræks, -iz

Thoreau (American writer) ˈθɔːrəu

thorium ˈθɔːriəm

thorn, -s θɔːn, -z

Thornaby ˈθɔːnəbi

thornbush, -es ˈθɔːnbuʃ, -iz

Thorne θɔːn

Thorneycroft ˈθɔːnikrɔft [-krɔːft]

Thornhill ˈθɔːnhil

thornless 'θɔ:nlis
Thornton 'θɔ:ntən
thorn|y, -ier, -iest, -ily, -iness 'θɔ:n|i,
-iə* [-jə*], -iist [-jist], -ili, -inis
Thorold 'θɔrəld, 'θʌrəld
thorough, -ly, -ness 'θʌrə, -li, -nis
thorough-bass 'θʌrə'beis
thorough-bred, -s 'θʌrə-bred, -z
thoroughfare, -s 'θʌrəfɛə*, -z
thoroughgoing 'θʌrə,gəuiŋ
thorough-paced 'θʌrə-peist
thorp(e) (T.), -s θɔ:p, -s
Thor(r)owgood 'θʌrəgud
those (plur. of that) ðəuz
thou ðau
though ðəu
thought (s.), -s θɔ:t, -s
thought (from think) θɔ:t
thought|ful, -fully, -fulness 'θɔ:t|fʊl,
-fuli [-fəli], -fʊlnis
thoughtless, -ly, -ness 'θɔ:tlis, -li, -nis
thought-read|er/s, -ing 'θɔ:t,ri:d|ə*/z,
-iŋ   [-iŋ
thought-wave, -s 'θɔ:t-weiv, -z
Thouless 'θaules [-lis]
thousan|d, -ds, -dth/s, -dfold 'θauzən|d,
-dz, -tθ/s, -dfəuld
Thrace θreis
Thracian, -s 'θreiʃjən [-ʃiən, -ʃən], -z
thraldom 'θrɔ:ldəm
thrall (s. v.), -s, -ing, -ed θrɔ:l, -z, -iŋ, -d
thrash, -es, -ing, -ed, -er/s θræʃ, -iz, -iŋ,
-t, -ə*/z
thread (s. v.), -s, -ing, -ed; -bare θred,
-z, -iŋ, -id; -bɛə*
Threadneedle (street) θred'ni:dl ['-,--]
thread|y, -iness 'θred|i, -inis
threat, -s θret, -s
threat|en, -ens, -ening/ly, -ened
'θret|n, -nz, -ŋiŋ/li [-niŋ/li], -nd
three, -s θri:, -z
three-cornered 'θri:'kɔ:nəd ['-,-- when
attributive]
three-decker, -s 'θri:'dekə*, -z
three-dimensional 'θri:-di'menʃənl
[-dai'm-, -ʃnəl, -ʃn̩l̩, -ʃnl̩, -ʃənəl]
threefold 'θri:-fəuld
threeish 'θri:iʃ
three-legged 'θri:'legd ['-- when attributive, 'θri:'legid]
three|pence, -pences, -penny 'θre|pəns
['θri|p-, 'θrʌ|p-, 'θru|p-], -pənsiz,
-pəni [-pn̩i, -pni]
three-ply 'θri:-plai ['-'-]
three-quarter, -s 'θri:'kwɔ:tə* ['θri:-
,kw-, θri:'kw-, according to sentence
stress], -z
threescore 'θri:'skɔ:* [-kɔə*, 'θri:-sk-
when followed by a stress]

threesome, -s 'θri:səm, -z
threnod|y, -ies 'θrenəd|i ['θri:n-, -nəud-],
-iz
thresh, -es, -ing, -ed, -er/s θreʃ, -iz, -iŋ,
-t, -ə*/z
threshing-floor, -s 'θreʃiŋflɔ:* [-flɔə*], -z
threshold, -s 'θreʃhəuld, -z
threw (from throw) θru:
thrice θrais
thrift θrift
thriftless, -ly, -ness 'θriftlis, -li, -nis
thrift|y, -ier, -iest, -ily, -iness 'θrift|i,
-iə* [-jə*], -iist [-jist], -ili, -inis
thrill (s. v.), -s, -ing/ly, -ed θril, -z,
-iŋ/li, -d
thriller, -s 'θrilə*, -z
Thring θriŋ
thriv|e, -es, -ing/ly, -ed, throve, thriven
θraiv, -z, -iŋ/li, -d, θrəuv, 'θrivn
thro' θru:
throat, -s, -ed θrəut, -s, -id
throat|y, -ier, -iest, -ily, -iness 'θrəut|i,
-iə* [-jə*], -iist [-jist], -ili, -inis
throb (s. v.), -s, -bing/ly, -bed θrɔb, -z,
-iŋ/li, -d
throe, -s θrəu, -z
Throgmorton θrɔg'mɔ:tn ['θrɔg,m-]
thrombosis θrɔm'bəusis
thron|e (s. v.), -es, -ing, -ed θrəun, -z,
-iŋ, -d
throneless 'θrəunlis
throng (s. v.), -s, -ing, -ed θrɔŋ, -z, -iŋ,
-d
throstle, -s 'θrɔsl, -z
thrott|le (s. v.), -les, -ling, -led 'θrɔt|l,
-lz, -l̩iŋ [-liŋ], -ld
through, -ly, -ness θru:, -li, -nis
Througham (place) 'θrʌfəm
throughout θru:(')aut
throughput, -s 'θru:-put, -s
throve (from thrive) θrəuv
throw (s. v.), -s, -ing, threw, throw|n,
-er/s θrəu, -z, -iŋ, θru:, 'θrəu|n,
-ə*/z
throw-back, -s 'θrəubæk ['-'-], -s
thrum (s. v.), -s, -ming, -med θrʌm, -z,
-iŋ, -d
thrush, -es θrʌʃ, -iz
thrust (s. v.), -s, -ing θrʌst, -s, -iŋ
Thucydides θju(:)'sididi:z
thud (s. v.), -s, -ding, -ded θʌd, -z, -iŋ,
-id
thug, -s θʌg [rarely tʌg] (Hind. t̮həg), -z
thuggery 'θʌgəri
Thullier 'twiljə* [-liə*]
Thule 'θju:li(:)
thumb (s. v.), -s, -ing, -ed θʌm, -z, -iŋ,
-d

thumb-mark, -s 'θʌmmɑ:k, -s
thumbscrew, -s 'θʌm-skru:, -z
thumbstall, -s 'θʌm-stɔ:l, -z
thummim 'θʌmim [*in Jewish usage also* 'θum- *and* 'tum-]
thump (*s. v.*), **-s, -ing, -ed, -er/s** θʌmp, -s, -iŋ, -t [θʌmt], -ə*/z
thumping (*adj.*) 'θʌmpiŋ
Thun tu:n
thund|er, -ers, -ering/ly, -ered, -erer/s 'θʌnd|ə*, -əz, -əriŋ/li, -əd, -ərə*/z
thunderbolt, -s 'θʌndəbəult, -s
thunder-clap, -s 'θʌndə-klæp, -s
thunderous, -ly 'θʌndərəs, -li
thunder-storm, -s 'θʌndə-stɔ:m, -z
thunderstruck 'θʌndə-strʌk
thund|ery, -eriness 'θʌnd|əri, -ərinis
thurible, -s 'θjuəribl, -z
Thuringia, -n/s θjuə'rindʒiə [-dʒjə], -n/z
Thurloe 'θə:ləu
Thurlow 'θə:ləu
Thurn tə:n
Thuron (*English surname*) tu'rɔn [tuə'r-, tə'r-]
Thursday, -s 'θə:zdi [-dei], -z
Thurso 'θə:səu ['θə:zəu] (*Scottish* 'θʌrzo)
Thurston 'θə:stən
thus, -ness ðʌs, -nis
thwack (*s. v.*), **-s, -ing, -ed** θwæk, -s, -iŋ, -t
thwaite, -s θweit, -s
thwart (*of a boat*), **-s** θwɔ:t [*in nautical usage also* θɔ:t], -s
thwart (*v.*), **-s, -ing, -ed** θwɔ:t, -s, -iŋ, -id
thy ðai
Thyatira ,θaiə'taiərə
thyme, -s taim, -z
thymol 'θaimɔl ['taimɔl]
thymus, -es 'θaiməs, -iz
thymy 'taimi
Thynne θin
thyroid (*s. adj.*), **-s** 'θairɔid ['θaiər-], -z
Thyrsis 'θə:sis
thyself ðai'self
tiara, -s, -ed ti'ɑ:rə, -z, -d
Tibbitts 'tibits
Tibbs tibz
Tiber 'taibə*
Tiberias tai'biəriæs [-riəs]
Tiberius tai'biəriəs
Tibet ti'bet
Tibetan, -s ti'betən, -z
tib|ia, -iae, -ias 'tib|iə ['taib-], -ii:, -iəz
Tibullus ti'bʌləs [-'bul-]
tic tik
tic douloureux 'tikdu:lə'rə: (tik dulurø)
tic|e (*s. v.*), **-es, -ing, -ed** tais, -iz, -iŋ, -t

Ticehurst 'taishə:st
Tichborne 'titʃbɔ:n [-bən]
Ticino ti'tʃi:nəu (ti'tʃi:no)
tick (*s. v.*), **-s, -ing, -ed, -er/s** tik, -s, -iŋ, -t, -ə*/z
ticket (*s. v.*), **-s, -ing, -ed** 'tikit, -s, -iŋ, -ed
ticket-of-leave 'tikitəv'li:v
ticking (*s.*), **-s** 'tikiŋ, -z
tick|le, -les, -ling, -led, -ler/s 'tik|l, -lz, -liŋ [-liŋ], -ld, -lə*/z [-lə*/z]
Tickler 'tiklə*
ticklish, -ly, -ness 'tikliʃ [-liʃ], -li, -nis
tickly 'tikli [-kli]
tick-tack, -s 'tik'tæk ['tiktæk], -s
tidal 'taidl
tidbit, -s 'tidbit, -s
tiddledywinks 'tidldiwiŋks
tiddlywinks 'tidliwiŋks [-dli-]
tid|e (*s. v.*), **-es, -ing, -ed** taid, -z, -iŋ, -id
tide-waiter, -s 'taid,weitə*, -z
tidewater 'taid,wɔ:tə*
tidings 'taidiŋz
tid|y (*s. adj. v.*), **-ies; -ier, -iest, -ily, -iness; -ying, -ied** 'taid|i, -iz; -iə* [-jə*], -iist [-jist], -ili, -inis; -iiŋ [-jiŋ], -id
tie (*s. v.*), **ties, tying, tied** tai, taiz, 'taiiŋ, taid
Tien-tsin tjen'tsin ['-'-, *old-fashioned* (')tin-]
tier (*one who ties*), **-s** 'tai-ə*, -z
tier (*set of seats in theatre, etc.*), **-s** tiə*, -z
tierce (*in music, in fencing, cash*), **-s** tiəs, -iz
tierce (*in cards*), **-s** tə:s [tiəs], -iz
tiercel, -s 'tə:səl, -z
tiff (*s. v.*), **-s, -ing, -ed** tif, -s, -iŋ, -t
tiffany 'tifəni
tiffin, -s 'tifin, -z
Tiflis 'tiflis
tig, -s tig, -z
tige, -s ti:ʒ, -iz
tiger, -s 'taigə*, -z
tiger-cat, -s 'taigəkæt, -s
tigerish 'taigeriʃ
tiger-lil|y, -ies 'taigə,lil|i, -iz
tiger-moth, -s 'taigəmɔθ, -s
Tighe tai
tight, -er, -est, -ly, -ness tait, -ə*, -ist, -li, -nis
tight|en, -ens, -ening, -ened, -ener/s 'tait|n, -nz, -ŋiŋ [-niŋ], -nd, -ŋə*/z [-nə*/z]
tights taits
Tiglath-pileser 'tiglæθpai'li:zə* [-pi'l-]
tigon, -s 'taigən, -z
tigress, -es 'taigris, -iz

Tigris 'taigris
tike, -s taik, -s
tilbur|y (T.), -ies 'tilbər|i, -iz
tilde, -s tild ['tildi, -də], -z
til|e (s. v.), -es, -ing, -ed tail, -z, -iŋ, -d
Tilehurst 'tailhə:st
tiler, -s 'tailə*, -z
tiler|y, -ies 'tailər|i, -iz
till (s. v. prep. conj.), -s, -ing, -ed, -er/s; -able, -age til, -z, -iŋ, -d, -ə*/z; -əbl, -idʒ
tiller (of rudder), -s 'tilə*, -z
Tilley 'tili
Tilling, -s 'tiliŋ, -z
Tillotson 'tilətsn
Tilly (English name) 'tili, (German name) 'tili ('tili:)
tilt (s. v.), -s, -ing, -ed, -er/s tilt, -s, -iŋ, -id, -ə*/z
tilth tilθ
tilt-yard, -s 'tilt-jɑːd, -z
Timaeus tai'miːəs [ti'm-, -'miəs]
timbal, -s 'timbəl, -z
timbale, -s tæm'bɑːl ['timbəl] (tɛ̃bal), -z
timber, -s, -ing, -ed 'timbə*, -z, -riŋ, -d
timbre, -s tɛ̃:mbr [tæm-, -bə*, 'timbə*] (tɛ̃:br), -z
timbrel, -s 'timbrəl, -z
Timbuctoo ,timbʌk'tuː: [-bək-, '--'-]
tim|e (s. v.), -es, -ing, -ed, -er/s taim, -z, -iŋ, -d, -ə*/z
time-base, -s 'taimbeis, -iz
time-bomb, -s 'taimbɔm, -z
time-expired 'taimiks,paiəd [-mek-]
time-honoured 'taim,ɔnəd
timekeeper, -s 'taim,kiːpə*, -z
timeless 'taimlis
time-lock, -s 'taimlɔk, -s
timel|y, -ier, -iest, -iness 'taiml|i, -ɪə*, -iist, -inis
timeous 'taiməs
timepiece, -s 'taim-piːs, -iz
Times taimz
time-saving 'taim,seiviŋ
time-serv|er/s, -ing 'taim,sə:v|ə*/z, -iŋ
time-sheet, -s 'taim-ʃiːt, -s
time-table, -s 'taim,teibl, -z
time-work 'taim-wə:k
timid, -est, -ly, -ness 'timid, -ist, -li, -nis
timidity ti'miditi
Timon 'taimən [-mɔn]
Timor 'tiːmɔ:*
timorous, -ly, -ness 'timərəs, -li, -nis
Timotheus ti'məuθjəs [-θɪəs]
timothy (T.), -grass 'timəθi, -grɑːs
timous 'taiməs
timpan|o, -i 'timpən|əu, -i [-iː]

Timpson 'timpsn
tin (s. v.), -s, -ning, -ned tin, -z, -iŋ, -d
tinctorial tiŋk'tɔ:riəl
tinctur|e (s. v.), -es, -ing, -ed 'tiŋktʃə*, -z, -riŋ, -d
Tindal(e) 'tindl
Tindall 'tindl
tinder, -box/es 'tində*; -bɔks/iz
tine, -s tain, -z
tinfoil 'tin'fɔil ['tin-fɔil]
ting|e (s. v.), -es, -(e)ing, -ed tindʒ, -iz,
Tingey 'tiŋgi   [-iŋ, -d
ting|le (s. v.), -les, -ling, -led 'tiŋg|l, -lz, -liŋ [-liŋ], -ld
tink|er (s. v.), -ers, -ering, -ered 'tiŋk|ə*, -əz, -əriŋ, -əd
tink|le (s. v.), -les, -ling/s, -led, -ler/s 'tiŋk|l, -lz, -liŋ/z, -ld, -lə*/z
tin-minded 'tin,maindid ['-'--]
Tinnevelly ti'nevəli [,tini'veli]
        Note.—Both pronunciations were formerly in use by Anglo-Indians.
tinnitus ti'naitəs
tinny 'tini
tin-plate 'tin-pleit ['-'-]
tinsel 'tinsəl
tint (s. v.), -s, -ing, -ed, -er/s tint, -s, -iŋ, -id, -ə*/z
Tintagel tin'tædʒəl
Tintern 'tintə(:)n
tintinnabulation, -s 'tinti,næbju'leiʃən, -z
tintinnabul|um, -a, -ar, -ary, -ous ,tinti'næbjul|əm, -ə, -ə*, -əri, -əs
Tintoretto, -s ,tintə'retəu [-tɔ'r-], -z
tin|y, -ier, -iest, -iness 'tain|i, -ɪə* [-jə*], -iist [-jist], -inis
tip (s. v.), -s, -ping, -ped tip, -s, -iŋ, -t
tipcat 'tipkæt
Tippell 'tipəl
Tipperary ,tipə'reəri
tippet, -s 'tipit, -s
Tippett 'tipit
tipp|le, -les, -ling, -led, -ler/s 'tip|l, -lz, -liŋ [-liŋ], -ld, -lə*/z [-lə*/z]
tipstaff, -s 'tip-stɑːf, -s
tipster, -s 'tipstə*, -z
tips|y, -ier, -iest, -ily, -iness 'tips|i, -ɪə* [-jə*], -iist [-jist], -ili, -inis
tipsy-cake 'tipsikeik
tiptoe 'tiptəu ['tip'təu]
tiptop (s. adj.), 'tip'tɔp ['tipt-]
tirade, -s tai'reid [ti'reid, ti'rɑːd], -z
tirailleur, -s ,tirai'ə:* [-ai'jə:*, -ai'lə:*] (tirajœːr), -z
tirasse, -s ti'ræs, -iz
tir|e (s. v.), -es, -ing, -ed/ly, -edness 'taiə*, -z, -riŋ, -d/li, -dnis

tireless, -ly, -ness 'taiəlis, -li, -nis
Tiresias tai'ri:siæs [ˌtaiə'r-, -'res-, -sïəs, -sjəs]
tiresome, -ly, -ness 'taiəsəm, -li, -nis
tiro, -s 'taiərəu, -z
Tirzah 'tə:zə
'tis tiz
tisane, -s ti(:)'zæn, -z
Tishbite, -s 'tiʃbait, -s
Tissaphernes ˌtisə'fə:ni:z
tissue, -s 'tiʃu: ['tisju:, 'tiʃju:], -z
tit, -s tit, -s
Titan, -s 'taitən, -z
Titania ti'tɑ:njə [-nïə, old-fashioned ti'tein-, tai'tein-]
titanic (T.) tai'tænik [ti't-]
titanium tai'teinjəm [ti't-, -nïəm]
titbit, -s 'titbit, -s
tith|e (s. v.), -es, -ing, -ed taið, -z, -iŋ, -d
tithing (s.), -s 'taiðiŋ, -z
Titian, -s 'tiʃïən [-ʃjən, -ʃən], -z
titillat|e, -es, -ing, -ed 'titileit, -s, -iŋ, -d
titillation, -s ˌtiti'leiʃən, -z
titivat|e, -es, -ing, -ed 'titiveit, -s, -iŋ, -d
titivation, -s ˌtiti'veiʃən, -z   [-id
title, -s, -d ; -less 'taitl, -z, -d; -lis
titling (stamping a title), -s 'taitliŋ, -z
Titlis 'titlis
Titmarsh 'titmɑ:ʃ
tit|mouse, -mice 'tit|maus, -mais
Tito 'ti:təu
titter (s. v.), -s, -ing, -ed, -er/s 'titə*, -z, -riŋ, -d, -rə*/z
tittle, -s 'titl, -z
tittle-tattle 'titlˌtætl
titular (s. adj.), -s, -ly 'titjulə*, -z, -li
titular|y (s. adj.), -ies 'titjulər|i, -iz
Titus 'taitəs
Tiverton 'tivətn
Tivoli 'tivəli
Tivy (surname) 'taivi
Tizard 'tizəd
tmesis 'tmi:sis
T.N.T. 'ti:en'ti:
to (adv.) tu:
to (prep.) tu: (strong form, also occasionally used as weak form esp. in final position), tu (weak form, also used as strong form before vowels), tə, t (weak forms used before consonants only)
toad, -s təud, -z
toad-flax 'təudflæks
toad-in-the-hole 'təudinðə'həul
toadstool, -s 'təudstu:l, -z
toad|y (s. v.), -ies, -ying, -ied 'təud|i, -iz, -iiŋ [-jiŋ], -id
to-and-fro 'tu(:)ən'frəu

toast (s. v.), -s, -ing, -ed, -er/s təust, -s, -iŋ, -id, -ə*/z
toasting-fork, -s 'təustiŋfɔ:k, -s
toast-master, -s 'təust,mɑ:stə*, -z
toast-rack, -s 'təust-ræk, -s
tobacco, -s tə'bækəu, -z
tobacconist, -s tə'bækənist [-kṇi-], -s
tobacco-pipe, -s tə'bækəupaip, -s
tobacco-pouch, -es tə'bækəupautʃ, -iz
Tobago təu'beigəu
Tobias tə'baiəs [təu'b-]
Tobi|n, -t 'təubi|n, -t
tobogg|an (s. v.), -ans, -aning, -aned, -aner/s tə'bɔg|ən, -ənz, -əniŋ [-ṇiŋ], -ənd, -ənə*/z [-ṇə*/z]
Tobolsk tə'bɔlsk (ta'boljsk)
tob|y (T.), -ies 'təub|i, -iz
toccata, -s tə'kɑ:tə [tɔ'k-], -z
toco 'təukəu
tocsin, -s 'tɔksin, -z
tod (T.), -s tɔd, -z
today tə'dei [tu'd-]
Todd tɔd
todd|le, -les, -ling, -led, -ler/s 'tɔd|l, -lz, -liŋ [-liŋ], -ld, -lə*/z [-lə*/z]
toddy 'tɔdi
Todhunter 'tɔd,hʌntə* ['tɔdhəntə*]
Todmorden 'tɔdmədən ['tɔd,mɔ:dn]
to-do, -s tə'du: [tu'd-], -z
toe (s. v.), -s, -ing, -d təu, -z, -iŋ, -d
toe-cap, -s 'təu-kæp, -s
toe-nail, -s 'təuneil, -z
toe-strap, -s 'təu-stræp, -s
toff, -s tɔf, -s
toffee 'tɔfi
tog (s. v.), -s, -ging, -ged tɔg, -z, -iŋ, -d
toga, -s, -ed 'təugə, -z, -d
together, -ness tə'geðə* [tu'g-], -nis
toggery 'tɔgəri
toggle, -s, -d 'tɔgl, -z, -d
Togo, -land 'təugəu, -lænd
toil (s. v.), -s, -ing, -ed, -er/s tɔil, -z, -iŋ, -d, -ə*/z
toile, -s twɑ:l [twɔ:l] (twal), -z
toilet, -s 'tɔilit, -s
toilet-cover, -s 'tɔilit,kʌvə*, -z
toilet-paper 'tɔilit,peipə*
toilet-powder, -s 'tɔilit,paudə*, -z
toiletr|y, -ies 'tɔilitr|i, -iz
toilet-set, -s 'tɔilit-set, -s
toilet-table, -s 'tɔilit,teibl, -z
toilette, -s twɑ:'let (twalɛt), -s
toilsome, -ly, -ness 'tɔilsəm, -li, -nis
toilworn 'tɔilwɔ:n
tokay (T.) təu'kei [təu'kai, 'təukai] (Hung. 'to:kɑj)
token, -s 'təukən, -z
Tokharian tɔ'kɑ:rïən [təu'k-]

Tokley 'təukli
Tokyo [-kio] 'təukjəu [-kiəu]
Toland 'təulənd
tolbooth, -s 'tɔlbu:θ, -s ['tɔlbu:ð, -z]
told (*from* tell) təuld
toledo (*blade*), -s tɔ'li:dəu [tə'l-], -z
Toledo (*in Spain*) tɔ'leidəu [tə'l-, *old-fashioned* -'li:d-] (to'ledo), (*in U.S.A.*) tə'li:dəu
tolerability ˌtɔlərə'biliti [-lət-]
tolerab|le, -ly, -leness 'tɔlərəb|l, -li, -lnis
toleran|ce, -t/ly 'tɔlərən|s, -t/li
tolerat|e, -es, -ing, -ed 'tɔləreit, -s, -iŋ, -ed
toleration ˌtɔlə'reiʃən [-id
Tolkien 'tɔlki:n
toll (*s. v.*), -s, -ing, -ed, -er/s təul, -z, -iŋ, -d, -ə*/z
toll-booth, -s 'tɔlbu:θ, -s ['tɔlbu:ð, -z]
Tollemache 'tɔlmæʃ, -mɑ:ʃ
Tollesbury 'təulzbəri
Tolleshunt (*in Essex*) 'təulzhʌnt
toll-gate, -s 'təulgeit, -s
toll-hou|se, -ses 'təulhau|s, -ziz
Tolstoy 'tɔlstɔi (tal'stoj)
Toltec, -s 'tɔltek, -s
tolu (T.) təu'lu: [tə'lju:]
tom (T.), -s tɔm, -z
tomahawk (*s. v.*), -s, -ing, -ed 'tɔmə-hɔ:k, -s, -iŋ, -t
toman, -s təu'mɑ:n, -z
tomato, -es tə'mɑ:təu, -z
tomb, -s tu:m, -z
tombola, -s 'tɔmbələ [-bul-, tɔm'bəulə]
tomboy, -s 'tɔmbɔi, -z [-z
tombstone, -s 'tu:m-stəun, -z
tomcat, -s 'tɔm'kæt [*in contrast* 'tɔm-kæt], -s
tome, -s təum, -z
Tomelty 'tʌməlti
tomfool, -s 'tɔm'fu:l [tɔm'f-], -z
tomfoolery tɔm'fu:ləri
Tomintoul ˌtɔmin'təul
tomm|y (T.), -ies 'tɔm|i, -iz
tommy-gun, -s 'tɔmigʌn ['--'-], -z
tomogram, -s 'təuməgræm ['tɔm-], -z
tomorrow tə'mɔrəu [tu'm-]
   Note.—Variants with final -rə *or* -ru *are often used in the expressions* tomorrow morning, tomorrow night, *and with* -ru *in* tomorrow afternoon, tomorrow evening.
Tompion 'tɔmpjən [-piən]
Tompkins 'tɔmpkinz
Tomsk tɔmsk (tomsk)
tomtit, -s 'tɔm'tit [tɔm't-], -s
tom-tom, -s 'tɔmtɔm, -z
ton (*weight*), -s tʌn, -z
ton (*fashion*) tɔ̃:ŋ [tɔ̃:n, tɔ:ŋ] (tɔ̃)

tonal 'təunl [-nəl]
tonalit|y, -ies təu'nælit|i, -iz
Tonbridge 'tʌnbridʒ ['tʌmb-]
ton|e (*s. v.*), -es, -ing, -ed təun, -z, -iŋ, -d
toneless 'təunlis
tonematic, -s ˌtəuni'mætik, -s
toneme, -s 'təuni:m, -z
tonemic, -s təu'ni:mik, -s
tonetic, -s təu'netik, -s
tonetician, -s ˌtəuni'tiʃən [-ne't-], -z
tonga (*cart, medicinal bark*), -s 'tɔŋgə, -z
Tonga (*Friendly Islands*), -n/s 'tɔŋə [-ŋgə], -n/z
Tonga (*Bantu of Portuguese East Africa, language spoken there*), -s, -n 'tɔŋgə, -z, -n
Tongking tɔŋ'kiŋ ['-'-]
tongs tɔŋz
tongue, -s, -d; -less tʌŋ, -z, -d; -lis
tongue-tied 'tʌŋ-taid
tonic (*s. adj.*), -s 'tɔnik, -s
tonic-solfa ['Tonic Sol-fa] 'tɔnik-sɔl'fɑ:
tonight tə'nait [tu'n-]
tonnage, -s 'tʌnidʒ, -iz
tonological ˌtəunə'lɔdʒikəl
tonolog|ist/s, -y təu'nɔlədʒ|ist/s, -i
tonsil, -s 'tɔnsl [-sil]
tonsil(l)itis ˌtɔnsi'laitis [-sl'ai-]
tonsure, -s, -d 'tɔnʃə* [-ʃuə*], -z, -d
tontine tɔn'ti:n ['tɔnti:n]
tony (T.) 'təuni
Tonypandy ˌtɔni'pændi (*Welsh* tonə-'pandi)
too tu:
toodle-oo 'tu:dl'u:
took (*from* take) tuk
Tooke tuk
tool (*s. v.*), -s, -ing, -ed tu:l, -z, -iŋ, -d
tool-box, -es 'tu:lbɔks, -iz
tool-chest, -s 'tu:l-tʃest, -s
Toole tu:l
Tooley 'tu:li
toot (*s. v.*), -s, -ing, -ed, -er/s tu:t, -s, -iŋ, -id, -ə*/z
tooth (*s.*), teeth tu:θ, ti:θ
tooth (*v.*), -s, -ing, -ed tu:θ, -s, -iŋ, -t
tooth-ache 'tu:θ-eik
tooth-brush, -es 'tu:θbrʌʃ, -iz
toothcomb (*s. v.*), -s, -ing, -ed 'tu:θ-kəum, -z, -iŋ, -d
toothed (*having teeth*) tu:θt [tu:ðd]
toothless 'tu:θlis
tooth-paste, -s 'tu:θpeist, -s
toothpick, -s 'tu:θpik, -s
tooth-powder, -s 'tu:θˌpaudə*, -z
toothsome, -ly, -ness 'tu:θsəm, -li, -nis
toot|le, -les, -ling, -led 'tu:t|l, -lz, -liŋ [-liŋ], -ld

top (s. v.), -s, -ping, -ped tɔp, -s, -iŋ, -t
topaz, -es 'təupæz, -iz
top-boot, -s 'tɔp'bu:t, -s
top-coat, -s 'tɔp'kəut, -s
top-dressing 'tɔp'dresiŋ ['-,--]
top|e (s. v.), -es, -ing, -ed, -er/s təup, -s, -iŋ, -t, -ə*/z
Topeka təu'pi:kə
topflight 'tɔp-flait
top-gallant tɔp'gælənt [nautical pronunciation tə'gælənt]
Topham 'tɔpəm
top-hat, -s 'tɔp'hæt [also tɔp'h- when preceded by a stress], -s
top-heav|y, -iness 'tɔp'hev|i [tɔp'h-], Tophet 'təufet   [-inis
top-hole 'tɔp'həul
topi (topee), -s 'təupi, -z
topiary 'təupjəri [-pïə-]
topic, -s, -al, -ally 'tɔpik, -s, -əl, -əli
topicalit|y, -ies ,tɔpi'kælit|i, -iz
topknot, -s 'tɔpnɔt, -s
Toplady 'tɔp,leidi
topmast, -s 'tɔpmɑ:st [-məst], -s
topmost 'tɔpməust [-məst]
topnotch 'tɔp'nɔtʃ
topograph|er/s, -y tə'pɔgrəf|ə*/z [tɔ'p-, təu'p-], -i
topographic, -al, -ally ,tɔpə'græfik [,təup-, -pəu'g-], -əl, -əli
topper, -s 'tɔpə*, -z
topping (s. adj.), -s, -ly 'tɔpiŋ, -z, -li
topp|le, -les, -ling, -led 'tɔp|l, -lz, -liŋ [-liŋ], -ld
topsail, -s 'tɔpsl [-seil], -z
Topsham (near Exeter) 'tɔpsəm
topsyturv|y, -ily, -yness, -ydom 'tɔpsi-'tə:v|i [,tɔp-], -ili, -inis, -idəm
toque, -s təuk, -s
tor, -s tɔ:*, -z
Torah 'tɔ:rə [with some Jews 'təurɑ:, təu'rɑ:]
Torbay 'tɔ:'bei [-'-, also '-- when attributive]
torch, -es tɔ:tʃ, -iz
torch-light, -s 'tɔ:tʃ-lait, -s
torchon 'tɔ:ʃən [-ʃɔn] (tɔrʃɔ̃)
tore (from tear) tɔ:* [tɔə*]
toreador, -s 'tɔrïədɔ:* ['tɔ:r-], -z
toric 'tɔrik
torment (s.), -s 'tɔ:ment [-mənt], -s
torment (v.), -s, -ing/ly, -ed, -or/s tɔ:'ment, -s, -iŋ/li, -id, -ə*/z
torn (from tear) tɔ:n
tornado, -es tɔ:'neidəu, -z
Toronto tə'rɔntəu
torped|o (s. v.), -oes, -oing, -oed tɔ:'pi:d|əu, -əuz, -əuiŋ, -əud

torpedo|-boat/s, -net/s, -tube/s tɔ:-'pi:dəu|bəut/s, -net/s, -tju:b/z
Torpenhow (in Cumberland) 'tɔ:pənhau [also very commonly trə'penə locally, and sometimes tɔ:'penəu]
torpex 'tɔ:peks
Torphichen tɔ:'fikən [-'fixən]
Torphins tɔ:'finz
torpid, -s, -ly, -ness 'tɔ:pid, -z, -li, -nis
torpidity tɔ:'piditi
torpor, -s 'tɔ:pə*, -z
Torquay 'tɔ:'ki: [-'- when preceded by a
torque, -s tɔ:k, -s   [stress]
Torquemada (Spanish inquisitor) ,tɔ:ki'mɑ:də [-ke'm-, -kwi'm-, -kwe'm-] (torkə'mada), (pen name of E. P. Mathers, author and compiler of cross-word puzzles) ,tɔ:kwi'mɑ:də
torrefaction ,tɔri'fækʃən
torre|fy, -fies, -fying, -fied 'tɔri|fai, -faiz, -faiiŋ, -faid
torrent, -s 'tɔrənt, -s
torrenti|al, -ally tɔ'renʃ|əl [tə'r-], -əli
torrentiality tɔ,renʃi'æliti [tə,r-]
Torres 'tɔris [-iz]
Torricell|i, -ian ,tɔri'tʃel|i, -ïən [-jən]
torrid, -ness 'tɔrid, -nis
Torrington 'tɔriŋtən
torsion 'tɔ:ʃən
torso, -s 'tɔ:səu, -z
tort, -s tɔ:t, -s
tortious 'tɔ:ʃəs
tortoise, -s 'tɔ:təs, -iz
tortoiseshell 'tɔ:təʃel
tortuosity ,tɔ:tju'ɔsiti
tortuous, -ly, -ness 'tɔ:tjŭəs [-tjwəs, -tʃŭəs, -tʃwəs], -li, -nis
tor|ture (s. v.), -tures, -turing/ly, -tured, -turer/s 'tɔ:|tʃə*, -tʃəz, -tʃəriŋ/li, -tʃəd, -tʃərə*/z
tor|y (T.), -ies, -yism 'tɔ:r|i, -iz, -iizəm
Tosberry 'tɔsbəri
Toscanini ,tɔskə'ni:ni (toska'ni:ni)
tosh tɔʃ
toss (s. v.), -es, -ing, -ed tɔs [old-fashioned tɔ:s], -iz, -iŋ, -t
toss-up, -s 'tɔsʌp ['-'-, old-fashioned 'tɔ:s-], -s
tot (s. v.), -s, -ting, -ted tɔt, -s, -iŋ, -id
tot|al (s. adj. v.), -als, -ally; -alling, -alled 'təut|l, -lz, -li [-əli]; -liŋ [-əliŋ], -ld
totalisator, -s 'təutəlaizeitə* [-t̮ai-], -z
totalitarian, -ism ,təutæli'tɛərïən [təu,t-], -izəm
totality təu'tæliti
totaliz|e [-is|e], -es, -ing, -ed, -er/s 'təutəlaiz [-t̮aiz], -iz, -iŋ, -d, -ə*/z

tote, -s təut, -s
totem, -s; -ism 'təutəm, -z; -izəm
t'other 'tʌðə*
Tothill 'tɔthil ['tɔtil]
Totland 'tɔtlənd
Totnes 'tɔtnis [-nes]
Tottenham 'tɔtnəm [-tn̩əm]
totter, -s, -ing/ly, -ed, -er/s 'tɔtə*, -z, -riŋ/li, -d, -rə*/z
Totteridge 'tɔtəridʒ
tottery 'tɔtəri
toucan, -s 'tu:kən [-kæn, -kɑ:n], -z
touch (s. v.), -es, -ing, -ed tʌtʃ, -iz, touchable 'tʌtʃəbl   [-iŋ, -t
touch-and-go 'tʌtʃən'gəu [-əŋ'gəu]
touch-down 'tʌtʃdaun
touching (adj. prep.), -ly, -ness 'tʌtʃiŋ, -li, -nis
touch-line, -s 'tʌtʃlain, -z
touch-paper 'tʌtʃ,peipə*
touchstone (T.), -s 'tʌtʃstəun, -z
touchwood 'tʌtʃwud
touch|y, -ier, -iest, -ily, -iness 'tʌtʃ|i, -iə*, -iist, -ili, -inis
tough (s. adj.), -s, -er, -est, -ly, -ness tʌf, -s, -ə*, -ist, -li, -nis
tough|en, -ens, -ening, -ened 'tʌf|n, -nz, -n̩iŋ [-niŋ], -nd
toughish 'tʌfiʃ
Toulmin 'tu:lmin
Toulon tu:'lɔ̃:ŋ [-'lɔ:ŋ, -'lɔŋ] (tulɔ̃)
Toulouse tu:'lu:z (tulu:z)
toupée, -s 'tu:pei, -z
tour (s. v.), -s, -ing, -ed tuə* [tɔə*, tɔ:*], -z, -riŋ, -d
Touraine tu'rein
tourbillon, -s tuə'biljən [tə:'b-, 'tuəbilən, 'tɔ:bilən], -z
tour de force, -s 'tuədə'fɔ:s, -iz
tourist, -s 'tuərist ['tɔər-, 'tɔ:r-], -s
Tourle tə:l
tourmal|in/s, -ine/s 'tuəməl|in/z ['tə:m-], -i:n/z
tournament, -s 'tuənəmənt ['tɔ:n-, 'tɔ:n-, 'tə:n-], -s
Tourneur (Eng. surname) 'tə:nə*
tourney, -s 'tuəni ['tɔən-, 'tɔ:n-], -z
tourniquet, -s 'tuənikei ['tɔən-, 'tɔ:n-, 'tə:n-], -z [rarely -ket, -kets]
tournure, -s 'tuənjuə* ['tə:n-, also -'-] (turny:r), -z
Tours (French town) tuə* (tu:r), (English musical composer) tuəz
tous|le, -les, -ling, -led 'tauz|l, -lz, -l̩iŋ, -ld
tout (s. v.), -s, -ing, -ed taut, -s, -iŋ, -id
Tout (in Belle Tout in Sussex) tu:t, (surname) taut

Tovey 'təuvi, 'tʌvi
    Note.—Sir Donald Tovey, the musician, pronounced 'təuvi.
tow (s. v.), -s, -ing, -ed təu, -z, -iŋ, -d
toward (adj.), -ly, -ness 'təuəd, -li, -nis
toward (prep.), -s, tə'wɔ:d [tu'wɔ:d, twɔ:d, tɔ:d, təəd], -z
Towcester 'təustə*
towel, -s 'tauəl [taul], -z
towel-horse, -s 'tauəlhɔ:s, -iz
towelling, -s 'tauəliŋ ['tauil-], -z
tower (one who tows), -s 'təuə*, -z
tower (s. v.) (tall building, etc.), -s, -ing, -ed 'tauə* ['tau-ə*], -z, -riŋ, -d
Towle təul
Towler 'taulə*
town, -s taun, -z
Towne taun
townee, -s tau'ni:, -z
town|ish, -y 'taun|iʃ, -i
townscape, -s 'taun-skeip, -s
Townsend 'taunzend
townsfolk 'taunzfəuk
Townshend 'taunzend
township, -s 'taun-ʃip, -s
towns|man, -men 'taunz|mən, -mən [-men]
townspeople 'taunz,pi:pl
tow-pa|th, -ths 'təu-pɑ:|θ, -ðz
tow-rope, -s 'təurəup, -z
Towton 'tautn
Towyn 'tauin (Welsh 'təuɨn)
toxic, -al, -ally 'tɔksik, -əl, -əli
toixcolog|ist/s, -y ,tɔksi'kɔlədʒ|ist/s, -i
toxin, -s 'tɔksin, -z
toxophilite, -s tɔk'sɔfilait [-fəl-], -s
Toxteth 'tɔkstɛθ [-təθ]
toy (s. v.), -s, -ing, -ed tɔi, -z, -iŋ, -d
Toye tɔi
toyes, -es tɔiz, -iz
Toynbee 'tɔinbi
toy-shop, -s 'tɔi-ʃɔp, -s
Tozer 'təuzə*
trac|e (s. v.), -es, -ing, -ed, -er/s treis, -iz, -iŋ, -t, -ə*/z
traceab|le, -ly, -leness 'treisəb|l, -li, -lnis
tracer-bullet, -s 'treisə,bulit, -s
tracer-element, -s 'treisər,elimənt [-sə,el-], -s
tracer|y, -ies 'treisər|i, -iz
trachea, -s, -l, -n trə'ki(:)ə, -z, -l, -n
tracheae (alternative plural of trachea) trə'ki:i: [-'ki:ai]
tracheotomy ,træki'ɔtəmi
tracing (s.), -s 'treisiŋ, -z
tracing-paper 'treisiŋ,peipə*
track (s. v.), -s, -ing, -ed, -er/s træk, -s, -iŋ, -t, -ə*/z

trackless, -ly, -ness 'træklis, -li, -nis
tract, -s trækt, -s
tractability ˌtræktə'biliti [-lət-]
tractab|le, -ly, -leness 'træktəb|l, -li, -lnis
tractarian, -s, -ism træk'tɛərɪən, -z, -izəm
tractate, -s 'trækteit, -s
tractile 'træktail
traction 'trækʃən
traction-engine, -s 'trækʃənˌendʒin ['trækʃnˌen-], -z
tractor, -s 'træktə*, -z
Tracy 'treisi
trad|e (s. v.), -es, -ing, -ed, -er/s treid, -z, -iŋ, -id, -ə*/z
trade-mark, -s 'treidmɑːk, -s
trade-name, -s 'treidneim, -z
tradesfolk 'treidzfəuk
trades|man, -men 'treidz|mən, -mən
tradespeople 'treidzˌpiːpl
trade-wind, -s 'treid-wind, -z
tradition, -s trə'diʃən, -z
tradi|tional, -tionally trə'di|ʃənl [-ʃnəl, -ʃn̩l, -ʃnl̩, -ʃənəl]-ʃnəli [-ʃnəli, -ʃnl̩i, -ʃnli, -ʃənəli]
traditionalism trə'diʃnəlizəm [-ʃnəli-, -ʃnl̩i-, -ʃnli-, -ʃənəli-]
traduc|e, -es, -ing, -ed, -er/s, -ement trə'djuːs, -iz, -iŋ, -t, -ə*/z, -mənt
Trafalgar (in Spain) trə'fælgə* [archaic and poetical ˌtræfəl'gɑː*], (Square) trə'fælgə*, (Viscount) trə'fælgə* [ˌtræfəl'gɑː*], (House near Salisbury) ˌtræfəl'gɑː*
Note.—The present Lord Nelson pronounces the family name as trə'fælgə*. Previous holders of the title pronounced ˌtræfəl'gɑː*.
traffic (s. v.), -s, -king, -ked, -ker/s 'træfik, -s, -iŋ, -t, -ə*/z
traffic-jam, -s 'træfikdʒæm, -z
traffic-warden, -s 'træfikˌwɔːdn, -z
tragacanth 'trægəkænθ
tragedian, -s trə'dʒiːdjən [-dɪən], -z
traged|y, -ies 'trædʒid|i, -iz
Trager 'treigə*
tragic, -al, -ally 'trædʒik, -əl, -əli, -əlnis
tragi-comed|y, -ies 'trædʒi'kɔmid|i, -iz
tragi-comic, -al, -ally 'trædʒi'kɔmik, -əl, -əli
tragus, -es 'treigəs, -iz
Traherne trə'həːn
trail (s. v.), -s, -ing, -ed, -er/s treil, -z, -iŋ, -d, -ə*/z
train (s. v.), -s, -ing/s, -ed, -er/s trein, -z, -iŋ/z, -d, -ə*/z
train-band, -s 'treinbænd, -z

train-bearer, -s 'treinˌbɛərə*, -z
trainee, -s trei'niː, -z
train-ferr|y, -ies 'trein'fer|i ['-,--], -iz
training-ship, -s 'treiniŋʃip, -s
train-oil 'treinɔil
train-sick 'trein-sik
traips|e, -es, -ing, -ed treips, -iz, -iŋ, -t
trait, -s trei, -z [treit, -s]
traitor, -s 'treitə*, -z
traitorous, -ly, -ness 'treitərəs, -li, -nis
traitress, -es 'treitris, -iz
Trajan 'treidʒən
trajector|y, -ies 'trædʒiktər|i [trə'dʒektər|i], -iz
Tralee trə'liː
tram, -s træm, -z
tramcar, -s 'træm-kɑː*, -z
tram-line, -s 'træmlain, -z
tramm|el (s. v.), -els, -elling, -elled 'træm|əl, -əlz, -əliŋ [-liŋ], -əld
tramp (s. v.), -s, -ing, -ed, -er/s træmp, -s, -iŋ, -t [træmt], -ə*/z
tramp|le, -les, -ling, -led, -ler/s 'træmp|l, -lz, -liŋ [-liŋ], -ld, -lə*/z [-lə*/z]
trampolin(e), -s 'træmpəlin [-liːn], -z
tramway, -s 'træmwei, -z
trance, -s trɑːns, -iz
tranquil, -ly, -ness 'træŋkwil, -i, -nis
tranquillity træŋ'kwiliti
tranquillization [-isa-] ˌtræŋkwilai'zeiʃən
tranquilliz|e [-is|e], -es, -ing/ly, -ed, -er/s 'træŋkwilaiz, -iz, -iŋ/li, -d, -ə*/z
transact, -s, -ing, -ed, -or/s træn'zækt [trɑː-, trən-, -n'sækt], -s, -iŋ, -id, -ə*/z
transaction, -s træn'zækʃən [trɑː-, trən-, -n'sæk-], -z
transalpine 'trænz'ælpain ['trɑː-]
transatlantic 'trænzət'læntik ['trɑː-, -zə'tlæn-, -zæt'læn-, -zæ'tlæn-]
Transbaikalia 'trænzbai'kɑːljə ['trɑː-, -lɪə]
Transcaspian 'trænz'kæspjən ['trɑː-, -pɪən]
transcend, -s, -ing, -ed træn'send [trɑː-], -z, -iŋ, -id
transcenden|ce, -cy, -t/ly træn'sendən|s [trɑː-], -si, -t/li
transcendent|al, -ally ˌtrænsen'dent|l [ˌtrɑː-, -sən-], -əli [-li]
transcendentali|sm, -st/s ˌtrænsen'dentəli|zəm [ˌtrɑː-, -sən-, -tl̩i-], -st/s
transcontinental 'trænzˌkɔnti'nentl ['trɑː-]
transcrib|e, -es, -ing, -ed, -er/s træns'kraib [trɑː-], -z, -iŋ, -d, -ə*/z

transcript, -s 'trænskript ['trɑːn-], -s
transcription, -s træns'kripʃən [trɑːn-],
  -z   [-ns-], -z
transducer, -s trænz'djuːsə* [trɑːn-,
transept, -s 'trænsept ['trɑːn-], -s
transfer (s.), -s 'trænsfə(ː)* ['trɑːn-], -z
transfer (v.), -s, -ring, -red, -rer/s
  træns'fəː* [trɑːn-], -z, -riŋ, -d, -rə*/z
transferability trænsˌfəːrə'biliti [trɑːns-,
  ˌfəːrə'b-, ˌtrænsfərə'b-, ˌtrɑːnsfərə'b-,
  -lət-]
transferable træns'fəːrəbl [trɑːns'fəːrə-,
  'trænsfərə-, 'trɑːnsfərə-]
transferee, -s ˌtrænsfə(ː)'riː [ˌtrɑːn-], -z
transference, -s 'trænsfərəns ['trɑːns-
  fər-, træns'fəːr-, trɑːns'fəːr-], -iz
transfiguration (T.), -s ˌtrænsfigjuˈrei-
  ʃən   [ˌtrɑːnsf-, træns‚f-, trɑːnsˌf-,
  -gjuə'r-], -z
transfigur|e, -es, -ing, -ed, -ement/s
  træns'figə* [trɑːn-], -z, -riŋ, -d,
  -mənt/s
transfix, -es, -ing, -ed træns'fiks [trɑːn-],
  -iz, -iŋ, -t
transfixion, -s træns'fikʃən [trɑːn-], -z
transform, -s, -ing, -ed, -er/s; -able
  træns'fɔːm [trɑːn-], -z, -iŋ, -d, -ə*/z;
  -əbl
transformation, -s ˌtrænsfə'meiʃən
  [ˌtrɑːn-, -fɔː'm-], -z
transfus|e, -es, -ing, -ed, -er/s træns-
  'fjuːz [trɑːn-], -iz, -iŋ, -d, -ə*/z
transfusible træns'fjuːzəbl [trɑːn-, -zib-]
transfusion, -s træns'fjuːʒən [trɑːn-], -z
transgress, -es, -ing, -ed, -or/s træns-
  'gres [trɑːn-, -nz'g-], -iz, -iŋ, -t, -ə*/z
transgression, -s træns'greʃən [trɑːn-,
  -nz'g-], -z
tranship, -s, -ping, -ped, -ment/s
  træn'ʃip [trɑːn-], -s, -iŋ, -t, -mənt/s
transien|ce, -cy, -t/ly, -tness 'trænziən|s
  ['trɑːn-, -nzjən-, -nʒiən-, -nʒjən-,
  -nsiən-, -nsjən-, -nʃiən-, -nʃjən-], -si,
  -t/li, -tnis
transilient træn'siliənt [trɑːn-, -ljənt]
transistor, -s, -ized [-ised] træn'sistə*
  [trɑːn-,- nz-], -z, -raizd
transit, -s 'trænsit ['trɑːnsit, trænzit,
  'trɑːnzit], -s   [-n'ziʃən], -z
transition, -s træn'siʒən [trɑːn-, trən-,
tran|sitional, -sitionally træn|'siʒənl
  [trɑːn-, trən-, -'siʒnəl, -'siʒnl, -'siʒnl,
  -'siʒənəl, -'ziʃənl, -'ziʃnəl, -'ziʃnl,
  -'ziʃnl, -'ziʃənəl], -'siʒnəli [-'siʒnəli,
  -'siʒnl̩i, -'siʒnl̩i, -'siʒənəli, -'ziʃnəli,
  -'ziʃnl̩i, -'ziʃnl̩i, -'ziʃnl̩i, -'ziʃənəli]
transitive, -ly, -ness   'trænsitiv
  ['trɑːn-, -nzi-], -li, -nis

transitor|y, -ily, -iness 'trænsitər|i
  ['trɑːn-, -nzi-], -ili, -inis
Transjordan 'trænz'dʒɔːdn ['trɑːn-]
Transjordania, -n/s 'trænzdʒɔː'deinjə
  ['trɑːn-, -niə], -n/z
Transkei træns'kai [trɑːns-, trænz-,
  trɑːnz-, '-'-]
translat|e, -es, -ing, -ed, -or/s; -able
  træns'leit [trɑːns-, trænz-, trɑːnz-,
  trəns-, trənz-], -s, -iŋ, -id, -ə*/z; -əbl
translation, -s træns'leiʃən [trɑːns-,
  trænz-, trɑːnz-, trəns-, trənz-], -z
transliterat|e, -es, -ing, -ed, -or/s
  trænz'litəreit [trɑːn-, -ns'l-], -s, -iŋ,
  -id, -ə*/z
transliteration, -s ˌtrænzlitə'reiʃən
  [ˌtrɑːn-, -nsl-, -ˌ--'--], -z
translucen|ce, -cy, -t/ly trænz'luːsn|s
  [trɑːn-, -ns'l-, -'ljuː-], -si, -t/li
transmigrat|e, -es, -ing, -ed, -or/s
  'trænzmaiˈgreit ['trɑːn-, -nsm-, -'--],
  -s, -iŋ, -id, -ə*/z
transmigration, -s ˌtrænzmaiˈgreiʃən
  [ˌtrɑːn-, -nsm-], -z
transmissibility   trænzˌmisəˈbiliti
  [trɑːn-, -nsˌm-, -si'b-, -lət-, ˌ---'---]
transmissible trænz'misəbl [trɑːn-,
  -ns'm-, -sib-]
transmission, -s trænz'miʃən [trɑːn-,
  -ns'm-], -z
transmit, -s, -ting, -ted, -ter/s trænz-
  'mit [trɑːn-, -ns'm-], -s, -iŋ, -id,
  -ə*/z   [-ns'm-], -z
transmittal, -s trænz'mitl [trɑːn-,
transmittance, -s trænz'mitəns [trɑːn-,
  -ns'm-], -iz
transmogrification ˌtrænzmɔgrifi'keiʃən
  [ˌtrɑːn-, -nsm-, -ˌ---'--]
transmogri|fy, -fies, -fying, -fied trænz-
  'mɔgri|fai [trɑːn-, -ns'm-], -faiz,
  -faiiŋ, -faid
transmutability   trænzˌmjuːtə'biliti
  [trɑːnzˌm-, -nsˌm-, -lət-, ˌ---'---]
transmutation, -s ˌtrænzmjuː'teiʃən
  [ˌtrɑːn-, -nsm-, -mju't-], -z
transmut|e, -es, -ing, -ed, -er/s; -able
  trænz'mjuːt [trɑːn-, -ns'm-], -s, -iŋ,
  -id, -ə*/z; -əbl
transoceanic 'trænzˌəuʃi'ænik
transom, -s 'trænsəm, -z
transparenc|y, -ies træns'peərəns|i
  [trɑːn-, trən-, -nz'p-, -'pær-], -iz
transparent, -ly, -ness træns'peərənt
  [trɑːn-, trən-, -nz'p-, -'pær-], -li, -nis
transpir|e, -es, -ing, -ed træns'paiə*
  ['trɑːn-], -z, -riŋ, -d
transplant, -s, -ing, -ed; -able træns-
  'plɑːnt [trɑːn-], -s, -iŋ, -id; -əbl

transplantation, -s ˌtrænsplɑːnˈteiʃən [ˌtrɑːn-], -z
transpontine 'trænz'pɔntain
transport (s.), -s 'trænspɔːt ['trɑːn-], -s
transport (v.), -s, -ing, -ed; -able 'træns'pɔːt [trɑːn-], -s, -iŋ, -id; -əbl
transportability ˌtrænsˌpɔːtə'biliti [trɑːn-, -lət-, ˌ—'—]
transportation, -s ˌtrænspɔː'teiʃən [ˌtrɑːn-], -z
transpos|e, -es, -ing, -ed, -er/s; -able, -al/s træns'pəuz [trɑːn-], -iz, -iŋ, -d, -ə*/z; -əbl, -əl/z
transposition, -s ˌtrænspə'ziʃən [ˌtrɑːn-, -pu'z-], -z
trans-ship, -s, -ping, -ped, -ment/s træns'ʃip [trɑːn-, -nʃ'ʃ-, -nz'ʃ-, -nʒ'ʃ-], -s, -iŋ, -t, -mənt/s
Trans - Siberian 'trænzˌsai'biərĭən ['trɑːn-]
transubstantiat|e, -es, -ing, -ed ˌtrænsəb'stænʃieit [ˌtrɑːn-, -bz't-, -ʃjeit], -s, -iŋ, -id
transubstantiation, -s 'trænsəbˌstænʃi'eiʃən ['trɑːn-, -bzˌt-, -nsi-], -z
Transvaal 'trænzvɑːl ['trɑːn-, -nsv-, '-'-]
Transvaaler, -s 'trænzˌvɑːlə* ['trɑːn-, -nsv-, '-'—, -'-], -z
transversal, -s trænz'vəːsəl [trɑːn-], -z
transverse 'trænzvəːs ['trɑːn-, also '-'- esp. when not attributive]
transversely trænz'vəːsli [trɑːn-, '-'—, '-ˌ—]
Transylvania, -n ˌtrænsil'veinjə [ˌtrɑːn-, -nĭə], -n
tranter, -s 'træntə*, -z
trap (s. v.), -s, -ping/s, -ped, -per/s træp, -s, -iŋ/z, -t, -ə*/z
trap-door, -s 'træp'dɔː* [-'dɔə*], -z
trapes (v.), -es, -ing, -ed treips, -iz, -iŋ, -t
trapeze, -s trə'piːz, -iz
trapezium, -s trə'piːzjəm [-zĭəm], -z
trapezoid, -s 'træpizɔid, -z
trapp|y, -iness 'træp|i, -inis
Traprain trə'prein
Traquair trə'kwɛə*
trash (s. v.), -es, -ing, -ed træʃ, -iz, -iŋ, -t
trash|y, -ier, -iest, -iness 'træʃ|i, -iə*, -iist, -inis
Trasimene 'træzimiːn
trauma, -s 'trɔːmə, -z
traumatic trɔː'mætik
trav|ail (s. v.), -ails, -ailing, -ailed 'træv|eil, -eilz, -eiliŋ [-eliŋ, -iliŋ], -eild
Travancore ˌtrævən'kɔː* [-'kɔə*, '—'-]
trav|el (s. v.), -els, -elling, -elled, -eller/s 'træv|l, -lz, -liŋ [-ˌliŋ], -ld, -lə*/z [-ˌlə*/z]

travelator, -s 'trævələitə*, -z
travelogue, -s 'trævələg [-ləug], -z
Travers 'trævə(ː)z
travers|e (s. adj. v.), -es, -ing, -ed 'trævə(ː)s [trə'vəːs], -iz, -iŋ, -t
travest|y (s. v.), -ies, -ying, -ied 'trævist|i [-vəs-], -iz, -iiŋ, -id
Traviata ˌtrævi'ɑːtə
Travis 'trævis
travolator, -s 'trævələitə*, -z
trawl (s. v.), -s, -ing, -ed trɔːl, -z, -iŋ, -d
trawler, -s 'trɔːlə*, -z
tray, -s trei, -z
Traylee, -s trei'liː, -z
treacherous, -ly, -ness 'tretʃərəs, -li, -nis
treacher|y, -ies 'tretʃər|i, -iz
treacle, -s 'triːkl, -z
treac|ly, -liness 'triːk|li [-li], -ˌlinis [-linis]
tread (s. v.), -s, -ing, trod, trodden, treader/s tred, -z, -iŋ, trɔd, 'trɔdn, 'tredə*/z
treadle, -s 'tredl, -z
treadmill, -s 'tredmil, -z
Treanor 'treinə*
treason, -s 'triːzn, -z
treasonab|le, -ly, -leness 'triːznəb|l [-znə-, -zənə-], -li, -lnis
treasonous 'triːznəs [-znəs, -zənəs]
treas|ure (s. v.), -ures, -uring, -ured 'treʒ|ə*, -əz, -əriŋ, -əd
treasure-hou|se, -ses 'treʒəhau|s, -ziz
treasurer, -s 'treʒərə*, -z
treasurership, -s 'treʒərəʃip, -s
treasure-trove 'treʒə-trəuv
treasur|y, -ies 'treʒər|i, -iz
treat (s. v.), -s, -ing, -ed, -ment/s triːt, -s, -iŋ, -id, -mənt/s
treatise, -s 'triːtiz [-tis], -iz
treat|y, -ies 'triːt|i, -iz
Trebarwith tri'bɑːwiθ [trə'b-]
Trebizond 'trebizɔnd
treb|le (s. adj. v.), -les, -ly; -ling, -led 'treb|l, -lz, -li, -liŋ [-liŋ], -ld
Tredegar tri'diːgə* [trə'd-] (Welsh tre'degar)
Tredennick tri'denik [trə'd-]
tree (s. v.), (T.), -s, -ing, -d triː, -z, -iŋ, -d
tree-creeper, -s 'triːˌkriːpə*, -z
tree-fern, -s 'triː'fəːn, -z
treeless 'triː-lis
trefoil, -s 'trefɔil ['triː-f-], -z
Trefor 'trevə* (Welsh 'trevor)
Trefriw 'trevriu: (Welsh 'trevriu)
Trefusis tri'fjuːsis [trə'f-]
Tregaskis tri'gæskis [trə'g-]
Tregear (surname, place in Cornwall) tri'giə* [trə'g-]

Tregoning tri'gɔniŋ [trə'g-]
Treherne tri'hə:n [trə'h-]
trek (s. v.), -s, -king, -ked, -ker/s trek,
-s, -iŋ, -t, -ə*/z
Trelawn(e)y tri'lɔ:ni [trə'l-]
Treleaven tri'levən [trə'l-]
trellis, -es, -ed 'trelis, -iz, -t
trellis-work 'trelis-wə:k
Treloar tri'ləuə* [trə'l-], -'lɔə*
Tremadoc tri'mædək [trə'm-]
Tremayne tri'mein [trə'm-]
Trembath trem'bɑ:θ, 'trembɑ:θ
tremb|le, -les, -ling/ly, -led, -ler/s
'tremb|l, -lz, -liŋ/li, -ld, -lə*/z
trembly 'trembli
tremendous, -ly, -ness tri'mendəs
[trə'm-], -li, -nis
Tremills 'tremlz
tremolo, -s 'tremələu, -z
Tremont tri'mɔnt [trə'm-]
tremor, -s 'tremə*, -z
Tremoutha tri'mauðə [trə'm-]
tremulant, -s 'tremjulənt, -s
tremulous, -ly, -ness 'tremjuləs, -li, -nis
trench (s. v.) (T.), -es, -ing, -ed, -er/s
trentʃ, -iz, -iŋ, -t, -ə*/z
trenchan|cy, -t/ly 'trentʃən|si, -t/li
Trenchard 'trentʃɑ:d [-tʃəd]
trencher, -s 'trentʃə*, -z
trend (s.v.), -s, -ing, -ed trend, -z, -iŋ, -id
Trengganu (in Malaya) treŋ'gɑ:nu:
Trent trent
Trentham 'trentəm
trepan (s. v.), -s, -ning, -ned tri'pæn
[trə'p-], -z, -iŋ, -d
trephin|e (s. v.), -es, -ing, -ed tri'fi:n
[tre'f-, trə'f-, -'fain], -z, -iŋ, -d
trepidation ˌtrepi'deiʃən
Treshinish tri'ʃiniʃ [trə'ʃ-]
Tresilian tri'siliən [trə's-, -ljən]
Tresmeer 'trezmiə*
trespass (s. v.), -es, -ing, -ed, -er/s
'trespəs, -iz, -iŋ, -t, -ə*/z
tress, -es, -ed; -y tres, -iz, -t; -i
trestle, -s 'tresl, -z
Trethewy tri'θju(:)i [trə'θ-]
Trethowan tri'θəuən [trə'θ-, -'θauən],
-'θɔ:ən
Trevaldwyn tri'vɔ:ldwin [trə'v-]
Trevaskis tri'væskis [trə'v-]
Trevelga tri'velgə [trə'v-]
Trevelyan tri'viljən [trə'v-], -'veljən
Treves tri:vz
Trevethick tri'veθik [trə'v-]
Trevigue tri'vi:g [trə'v-]
Trevisa (John of) tri'vi:sə [trə'v-]
Trevithick 'treviθik
Trevor 'trevə* (Welsh 'trevor)

Trew tru:
Trewavas tri'wɔvəs [trə'w-]
Trewin tri'win [trə'w-]
trews tru:z
trey, -s trei, -z
triable 'trai-əbl
triad, -s 'trai-əd ['traiæd], -z
trial, -s 'traiəl, -z
    Note.—The reduced form trail is not
    used when the word is immediately
    followed by a word beginning with
    a vowel.
trialogue, -s 'trai-əlɔg, -z
triangle, -s, -d 'traiæŋgl, -z, -d
triangular, -ly trai'æŋgjulə* [tri-,
-gjəl-], -li
triangularity traiˌæŋgju'læriti [tri-,
ˌtraiæŋ-]
triangulat|e, -es, -ing, -ed trai'æŋgjuleit
[tri-], -s, -iŋ, -id
triangulation traiˌæŋgju'leiʃən [tri-,
ˌtraiæŋ-]
Triangulum trai'æŋgjuləm [-gjəl-]
triassic trai'æsik
trib|al, -ally, -alism 'traib|əl, -əli, -əlizəm
[-lizəm]
tribe, -s traib, -z
tribes|man, -men 'traibz|mən, -mən
[-men]
tribrach, -s 'tribræk, -s
tribrachic tri'brækik
tribulation, -s ˌtribju'leiʃən, -z
tribunal, -s trai'bju:nl [tri'b-], -z
tribunate, -s 'tribjunit [-neit], -s
tribune, -s 'tribju:n, -z
tributar|y (s. adj.), -ies 'tribjutər|i, -iz
tribute, -s 'tribju:t, -s
tricar, -s 'trai-kɑ:*, -z
trice trais
tricel 'traisel
triceps, -es 'traiseps, -iz
trichin|a, -ae, -as tri'kain|ə, -i:, -əz
Trichinopoli [-ly] ˌtritʃi'nɔpəli
trichinosis ˌtriki'nəusis
trichord (s. adj.), -s 'trai-kɔ:d, -z
trick (s. v.), -s, -ing, -ed, -er/s trik, -s,
-iŋ, -t, -ə*/z
tricker|y, -ies 'trikər|i, -iz
trickish, -ly, -ness 'trikiʃ, -li, -nis
trick|le (s. v.), -les, -ling, -led 'trik|l, -lz,
-liŋ [-liŋ], -ld
trickle-charger, -s 'trikl,tʃɑ:dʒə*, -z
trickly 'trik|li [-kli]
trickster, -s 'trikstə*, -z
trick|y, -ier, -iest, -ily, -iness 'trik|i,
-iə*, -iist, -ili, -inis
tricolo(u)r, -s 'trikələ* ['traiˌkʌlə*], -z
tricoloured 'traiˌkʌləd
tricot, -s 'trikəu ['tri:k-] (triko), -z

tricyc|le (s. v.), -les, -ling, -led 'traisik|l, -lz, -lin, -ld

trident, -s 'traidənt, -s

tried (from try) traid

triennial, -ly trai'enjəl [-nĭəl], -i

trier, -s 'trai-ə* ['traiə*], -z

trierarch, -s ; -y, -ies 'traiəra:k, -s; -i, -iz

tries (from try) traiz

Trieste tri(:)'est [-'esti] (tri'ɛste)

trif|le (s. v.), -les, -ling, -led, -ler/s 'traif|l, -lz, -lin [-l̩in], -ld, -lə*/z [-lə*/z]

trifling (adj.), -ly, -ness 'traiflin, -li, -nis

trifolium, -s trai'fəuljəm [-lĭəm], -z

triforium, -a, -ums trai'fɔ:rĭ|əm, -ə, -əmz

trig (s. v.), -s, -ging, -ged, trig, -z, -in, -d

trigam|ist/s, -ous, -y 'trigəm|ist/s, -əs, -i

trigger, -s 'trigə*, -z

triglyph, -s 'traiglif ['trig-], -s

trigon, -s 'traigən, -z

trigonometric, -al, -ally ˌtrigənə'metrik [-nəu'm-], -əl, -əli

trigonometr|y, -ies ˌtrigə'nɔmitr|i [-mət-], -iz

trigraph, -s 'traigrɑ:f [-græf], -s

trilater|al, -ally, -alness 'trai'lætər|əl [trai'l-], -əli, -əlnis

trilb|y (T.), -ies 'trilb|i, -iz

trilingual 'trai'lingwəl [trai'l-]

triliteral 'trai'litərəl [trai'l-]

trill (s. v.), -s, -ing, -ed tril, -z, -in, -d

trillion, -s, -th/s 'triljən, -z, -θ/s

trilobite, -s 'trailəubait, -s

trilog|y, -ies 'triləd3|i, -iz

trim (s. adj. v.) (T.), -mer, -mest, -ly, -ness; -s, -ming/s, -med, -mer/s trim, -ə*, -ist, -li, -nis; -z, -in/z, -d,

Trimble 'trimbl [-ə*/z

trimeter, -s 'trimitə, -z

Trincomalee 'trinkəumə'li:

Trinculo 'trinkjuləu

Trinder 'trində*

trine (T.) train

Tring trin

tringle, -s 'tringl, -z

Trinidad 'trinidæd [ˌ-ˌ-'-]

Trinidadian, -s ˌtrini'dædĭən [-'dei-, -djən], -z

trinitarian (T.), -s, -ism ˌtrini'tɛərĭən, -z, -izəm

trinitrotoluene trai'naitrəu'tɔljui:n ['trai,nai-]

trinit|y (T.), -ies 'trinit|i, -iz

trinket, -s 'trinkit, -s

trinomial trai'nəumjəl [-mĭəl]

trio, -s 'tri(:)əu, -z

triolet, -s 'tri(:)əulet ['traiəu-, -lit], -s

trip (s. v.), -s, -ping/ly, -ped, -per/s trip, -s, -in/li, -t, -ə*/z

tripartite, -ly 'trai'pɑ:tait [-'--, '-,--], -li

tripe, -s traip, -s

triphibious trai'fibĭəs [-bjəs]

triphthong, -s 'trifθɔn [-ipθ-], -z

triphthongal trif'θɔngəl [-ip'θ-]

triplane, -s 'trai-plein, -z

trip|le (adj. v.), -ly: -les, -ling, -led 'trip|l, -li; -lz, -lin [-lin], -ld

triplet, -s 'triplit, -s

triplex 'tripleks

triplicate (adj.) 'triplikit

triplicat|e (v.), -es, -ing, -ed 'triplikeit, -s, -in, -id

tripod, -s 'traipod, -z

tripoli (T.) 'tripəli [-pul-]

Tripolis 'tripəlis [-pul-]

Tripolitania ˌtripəli'teinjə [-pəl-, -nĭə]

tripos, -es 'traipos, -iz

triptych, -s 'triptik, -s

trireme, -s 'trairi:m ['traiər-], -z

Trisagion tri'sægiən [-gĭən]

trisect, -s, -ing, -ed, -or/s trai'sekt, -s, -in, -id, -ə*/z

trisection, -s trai'sekʃən, -z

Tristan (personal name) 'tristən [-tæn]

Tristan da Cunha 'tristəndə'ku:nə

Tristram 'tristrəm [-ræm]

trisyllabic, -al, -ally 'trai-si'læbik ['trisi-, ˌ-'--], -əl, -əli

trisyllable, -s 'trai'siləbl ['tri's-, -'--, 'ˌ-ˌ--] -z

trite, -r, -st, -ly, -ness trait, -ə*, -ist, -li, -nis

tritium 'tritĭəm [-tjəm]

Triton, -s 'traitn, -z

tritone, -s 'traitəun, -z

Tritonia trai'təunjə [-nĭə]

triumph (s. v.), -s, -ing, -ed, -er/s 'traiəmf [-ʌmf], -s, -in, -t, -ə*/z

triumphal trai'ʌmfəl

triumphant, -ly trai'ʌmfənt, -li

triumvir, -s tri'umvə* [trai'ʌmvə(:)*, 'traiəmv-], -z

triumvirate, -s trai'ʌmvirit [-vər-], -s

triumviri (alternative plur. of triumvir) tri'umviri: [trai'ʌmvirai, -vər-]

triune 'traiju:n

trivet, -s 'trivit, -s

trivial, -ly, -ness 'trivĭəl [-vjəl], -i, -nis

trivialit|y, -ies ˌtrivi'ælit|i, -iz

trivializ|e (-is|e), -es, -ing, -ed 'trivĭəl-aiz [-vjəl-], -iz, -in, -d

trivium 'trivĭəm

trizonal 'trai'zəunl [-nəl]

Trizone 'traizəun

Troa|d, -s 'trəuæ|d, -s

Trocadero ˌtrɔkəˈdiərəu
trochaic trəuˈkeiik [trɔ-]
troche (*lozenge*), -s trəuʃ, -iz [*rarely* trəuk, -s]
trochee, -s ˈtrəuki: [-ki], -z
trod, -den (*from* tread) trɔd, -n
troglodyte, -s ˈtrɔglədait [-ləud-], -s
troika, -s ˈtrɔikə, -z
Troilus ˈtrəuiləs [ˈtrɔil-]
Trojan, -s ˈtrəudʒən, -z
troll (*s.*), -s trəul [trɔl], -z
troll (*v.*), -s, -ing, -ed trəul, -z, -iŋ, -d
trolley, -s ˈtrɔli, -z
trolley-bus, -es ˈtrɔlibʌs ['—'-], -iz
trollop, -s ˈtrɔləp, -s
Trollope ˈtrɔləp
tromba, -s ˈtrɔmbə, -z
trombone, -s trɔmˈbəun [ˈtrɔmˈb-], -z
trombonist, -s trɔmˈbəunist, -s
Trondheim ˈtrɔnheim
Trondhjem (*old name of* Trondheim) ˈtrɔnjəm
troop (*s. v.*), -s, -ing, -ed tru:p, -s, -iŋ, -t
troop-carrier, -s ˈtru:pˌkæriə*, -z
trooper, -s ˈtru:pə*, -z
troop-ship, -s ˈtru:pʃip, -s
troop-train, -s ˈtru:p-trein, -z
trope, -s trəup, -s
trophic ˈtrɔfik
troph|y, -ies ˈtrəufʃi [*in the army also* ˈtrɔf-], -iz
tropic, -s, -al, -ally ˈtrɔpik, -s, -əl, -əli
troppo ˈtrɔpəu (ˈtrɔppo)
Trossachs ˈtrɔsəks [-sæks, -səxs]
trot (*s. v.*), -s, -ting, -ted, -ter/s trɔt, -s, -iŋ, -id, -ə*/z
troth trəuθ [trɔθ]
Trott, -er trɔt, -ə*
trottoir, -s ˈtrɔtwɑ:* [-wɔ:*] (trɔtwa:r), -z
troubadour, -s ˈtru:bəduə* [-dɔə*, -dɔ:*], -z
troub|le (*s. v.*), -les, -ling, -led, -ler/s ˈtrʌb|l, -lz, -liŋ [-ḷiŋ], -ld, -lə*/z [-ḷə*/z]
troublesome, -ly, -ness ˈtrʌblsəm, -li, -nis
troublous ˈtrʌbləs
Troubridge ˈtru:bridʒ
trough, -s trɔf [trɔ:f], -s
Note.—Some bakers pronounce trau, -z.
Troughton ˈtrautn
trounc|e, -es, -ing/s, -ed trauns, -iz, -iŋ/z, -t
Troup tru:p
troupe, -s tru:p, -s
Trousdell ˈtru:zdel [-dəl, -dl̩]
trousering, -s ˈtrauzəriŋ, -z

trousers ˈtrauzəz
trousse, -s tru:s, -iz
trousseau, -s ˈtru:səu, -z
trout traut
trout|let/s, -ling/s ˈtraut|lit/s, -liŋ/z
Trouton ˈtrautn
trove trəuv
trover ˈtrəuvə*
trow trəu [trau]
Trowbridge (*in Wilts.*) ˈtrəubridʒ
trow|el (*s. v.*), -els, -elling, -elled ˈtrau|əl [-el, -il], -əlz [-elz, -ilz], -əliŋ [-eliŋ, -iliŋ], -əld [-eld, -ild]
Trowell ˈtrəuəl
trowsers ˈtrauzəz
troy (T.) trɔi
truancy ˈtru(:)ənsi
truant, -s ˈtru(:)ənt, -s
trubeniz|e [-is|e], -es, -ing, -ed ˈtru:binaiz [-bən-], -iz, -iŋ, -d
Trübner ˈtru:bnə* (ˈtry:bnər)
truce, -s tru:s, -iz
trucial ˈtru:sjəl [-siəl]
truck (*s. v.*), -s, -ing, -ed; -age trʌk, -s, -iŋ, -t; -idʒ
truck|le, -les, -ling, -led ˈtrʌk|l, -lz, -liŋ [-ḷiŋ], -ld
truckler, -s ˈtrʌklə*, -z
truculen|ce, -cy, -t/ly ˈtrʌkjulən|s [ˈtru:k-], -si, -t/li
trudg|e (*s. v.*), -es, -ing, -ed trʌdʒ, -iz, -iŋ, -d
trudg|en (*s. v.*) (T.), -ens, -ening, -ened ˈtrʌdʒ|ən, -ənz, -əniŋ [-ṇiŋ], -ənd
Trudgian ˈtrʌdʒiən [-dʒən]
Trudy ˈtru:di
tr|ue (T.), -uer, -uest, -uly, -ueness tr|u:, -u(:)ə*, -u(:)ist, ˈtru:li, ˈtru:-nis
Truefitt ˈtru:fit
true-hearted ˈtru:ˈhɑ:tid [ˈ-ˌ--]
truffle, -s, -d ˈtrʌfl, -z, -d
trug, -s trʌg, -z
truism, -s ˈtru(:)izəm, -z
truly ˈtru:li
Truman ˈtru:mən
trump (*s. v.*), -s, -ing, -ed trʌmp, -s, -iŋ, -t [trʌmt]
trump-card, -s ˈtrʌmpˈkɑ:d [*in contrast* '--'], -z
Trumper ˈtrʌmpə*
trumpery ˈtrʌmpəri
trumpet (*s. v.*), -s, -ing/s, -ed, -er/s ˈtrʌmpit, -s, -iŋ/z, -id, -ə*/z
trumpet-call, -s ˈtrʌmpitkɔ:l, -z
trumpet-shaped ˈtrʌmpit-ʃeipt
truncat|e, -es, -ing, -ed ˈtrʌŋkeit [trʌŋˈk-], -s, -iŋ, -id
truncation, -s trʌŋˈkeiʃən, -z

truncheon, -s, -ed 'trʌntʃən, -z, -d
trundǀle (s. v.), -les, -ling, -led 'trʌndǀl,
-lz, -liŋ [-liŋ], -ld
trunk, -s; -ful/s trʌŋk, -s; -ful/z
trunk-hose 'trʌŋk'həuz
trunk-line, -s 'trʌŋk-lain, -z
trunnion, -s, -ed 'trʌnjən [-nɪən], -z, -d
Truro 'truərəu
Truscott 'trʌskət
Truslove 'trʌslʌv
truss (s. v.), -es, -ing, -ed trʌs, -iz, -iŋ, -t
trust (s. v.), -s, -ing/ly, -ed, -er/s trʌst,
-s, -iŋ/li, -id, -ə*/z
trustee, -s trʌs'ti: ['trʌs't-], -z
trusteeship, -s trʌs'ti:-ʃip, -s
trustǀful, -fully, -fulness 'trʌstǀful,
-fuli [-fəli], -fulnis
trustworthǀy, -iness 'trʌst,wə:ð|i, -inis
trustǀy, -ier, -iest, -ily, -iness 'trʌstǀi,
-ɪə* [-jə*], -iist [-jist], -ili, -inis
truǀth, -ths tru:|θ, -ðz [-θs]
truthǀful, -fully, -fulness 'tru:θful,
-fuli [-fəli], -fulnis
trǀy (s. v.), -ies, -ying, -ied, -ier/s trǀai,
-aiz, -aiiŋ, -aid, -ai-ə*/z
Tryon 'traiən
try-on, -s 'trai'ɔn ['--], -z
try-out, -s 'trai'aut ['--], -s
trypanosome, -s 'tripənəsəum, -z
trypanosomiasis ,tripənəusou'maiəsis
tryst (s. v.), -s, -ing, -ed traist [trist], -s,
-iŋ, -id
Trystan 'tristæn
Tsar, -s zɑ:* [tsɑ:*], -z
Tsarevitch, -es 'zɑ:rəvitʃ ['tsɑ:-, -riv-],
-iz
Tsarina, -s zɑ:'ri:nə [tsɑ:-], -z
tsetse 'tsetsi ['tetsi]
T-square, -s 'ti:-skwɛə*, -z
Tsushima 'tsu:ʃimə [tsu(:)'ʃi:mə]
T.T. 'ti:'ti: ['ti:-ti: esp. when attributive]
tub (s. v.), -s, -bing, -bed tʌb, -z, -iŋ, -d
tuba, -s 'tju:bə, -z
Tubal 'tju:bəl [rarely -bæl]
tubbǀy, -ier, -iest, -iness 'tʌbǀi, -ɪə*,
-iist, -inis
tube, -s tju:b, -z
tubeless 'tju:blis
tuber, -s 'tju:bə*, -z
tubercle, -s 'tju:bə:kl [-bəkl], -z
tubercular tju(:)'bə:kjulə* [-kjəl-]
tubercularizǀe [-isǀe], -es, -ing, -ed
tju(:)'bə:kjuləraiz [-kjəl-], -iz, -iŋ, -d
tuberculization [-isa-] tju(:),bə:kju-
lai'zeiʃən [-kjəl-, -li'z-]
tuberculizǀe [-isǀe], -es, -ing, -ed
tju(:)'bə:kjulaiz [-kjəl-], -iz, -iŋ, -d
tuberculosis tju(:),bə:kju'ləusis [-kjə'l-]

tuberculous tju(:)'bə:kjuləs [-kjəl-]
tuberose (s.) 'tju:bərəuz
tuberose (adj.) 'tju:bərəus
tuberous 'tju:bərəs
tubful, -s 'tʌbful, -z
tubiform 'tju:bifɔ:m
tubing, -s 'tju:biŋ, -z
tubular 'tju:bjulə* [-bjəl-]
tubule, -s 'tju:bju:l, -z
tuck (s. v.) (T.), -s, -ing, -ed tʌk, -s, -iŋ,
-t
tucker (T.), -s 'tʌkə*, -z
tuck-shop, -s 'tʌkʃɔp, -s
Tucson (in U.S.A.) tu:'sɔn ['tu:sɔn]
Tudor, -s 'tju:də*, -z
Tuesday, -s 'tju:zdi [-dei], -z
tufa 'tju:fə
Tufnell 'tʌfnl [-nəl]
tuft (s. v.), -s, -ing, -ed tʌft, -s, -iŋ, -id
tuftǀy, -ier, -iest, -iness 'tʌftǀi, -ɪə*
[-jə*], -iist [-jist], -inis
tug (s. v.), -s, -ging, -ged, -ger/s tʌg,
-z, -iŋ, -d, -ə*/z
tug-of-war, -s 'tʌgəv'wɔ:* [,--'-], -z
tugs-of-war (alternative plur. of tug-of-
war) 'tʌgzəv'wɔ:* [,--'-]
Tuileries 'twi:ləri(:) (tɥilri)
tuition, -s tju(:)'iʃən, -z
tuitionary tju(:)'iʃŋəri [-ʃnəri, -ʃŋri,
-ʃənəri]
Tuke tju:k
tulip, -s 'tju:lip, -s
tulle, -s tju:l (tyl), -z
Tullibardine ,tʌli'bɑ:din
Tullichewan ,tʌli'kju:ən [-i'xj-, -juən]
Tulloch 'tʌlək [-əx]
Tulloh 'tʌləu
Tulse tʌls
tumbǀle (s. v.), -les, -ling, -led 'tʌmbǀl,
-lz, -liŋ, -ld
tumble-down (adj.) 'tʌmbldaun
tumbler, -s; -ful/s 'tʌmblə*, -z; -ful/z
tumblǀy, -iness 'tʌmblǀi, -inis
tumbrel, -s 'tʌmbrəl, -z
tumbril, -s 'tʌmbril, -z
tumefaction ,tju:mi'fækʃən
tumeǀfy, -fies, -fying, -fied 'tju:miǀfai,
-faiz, -faiiŋ, -faid
tumescenǀce, -t tju:'mesn|s [tju'm-], -t
tumid, -ly, -ness 'tju:mid, -li, -nis
tumidity tju:'miditi [tju'm-]
tummǀy, -ies 'tʌm|i, -iz
tumour, -s 'tju:mə*, -z
tum-tum, -s 'tʌmtʌm, -z
tumular, -y 'tju:mjulə*, -ri
tumult, -s 'tju:mʌlt [-məlt], -s
tumultuous, -ly, -ness tju(:)'mʌltjŭəs
[-tjwəs], -li, -nis

tumul|us, -i, -uses 'tju:mjul|əs, -ai, -əsiz

tun (s. v.), -s, -ning, -ned tʌn, -z, -iŋ, -d

tuna, -s 'tu:nə, -z

Tunbridge 'tʌnbridʒ ['tʌmb-]

tundra, -s 'tʌndrə, -z

tun|e (s. v.), -es, -ing, -ed, -er/s tju:n, -z, -iŋ, -d, -ə*/z

tune|ful, -fullest, -fully, -fulness 'tju:n|fʊl, -fulist [-fəlist], -fuli [fəli], -fʊlnis

tuneless 'tju:nlis

tun(g)ku, -s 'tuŋku:, -z

tungsten 'tʌŋstən [-ten, -tin]

tunic, -s 'tju:nik, -s

tunicle, -s 'tju:nikl, -z

tuning-fork, -s 'tju:niŋfɔ:k, -s

Tunis 'tju:nis

Tunisia, -n/s tju(:)'niziə [-zjə, -sïə, -sjə], -n/z

Tunnard 'tʌnəd   [-liŋ [-əliŋ], -ld

tunn|el, -els, -elling, -elled 'tʌn|l, -lz,

tunny 'tʌni

Tuohy 'tu:i, 'tu:hi

Tupman 'tʌpmən

tuppence, -s 'tʌpəns [-pns, -pms], -iz

tuppeny 'tʌpɲi [-pni, -pəni]

tu quoque, -s 'tju:'kwəukwi, -z

Turandot (operas by Puccini and Busoni) 'tuərəndəu ['tjuə-, rarely -dɔt)

Turania, -n/s tjuə'reinjə [tju'r-, -nïə], -n/z

turban, -s, -ed 'tə:bən, -z, -d

turbid, -ly, -ness 'tə:bid, -li, -nis

turbidity tə:'biditi

turbine, -s 'tə:bin [-bain, rarely -bi:n], -z

turbo-jet, -s 'tə:bəu'dʒet ['---], -s

turbo-prop, -s 'tə:bəu'prɔp, -s

turbot, -s 'tə:bət, -s

turbulen|ce, -cy, -t/ly 'tə:bjulən|s, -si, -t/li

Turcoman, -s 'tə:kəmən [-mæn, -mɑːn], -z

tureen, -s tə'ri:n [tu'r-, tju'r-, tjə'r-], -z

tur|f (s.), -fs, -ves tə:|f, -fs, -vz

turf (v.), -s, -ing, -ed tə:f, -s, -iŋ, -t

turf|y, -ier, -iest, -iness 'tə:f|i, -ïə*, -iist, -inis

Turgenev tə:'geinjev [tuə'g-, -njef, -njif, -nev, -nəv] (tur'genjif)

turgescen|ce, -t tə:'dʒesn|s, -t

turgid, -ly, -ness 'tə:dʒid, -li, -nis

turgidity tə:'dʒiditi

Turin tju'rin [tjuə'r-]

Turk, -s tə:k, -s

Turkestan ˌtə:kis'tɑ:n [-'tæn]

turkey (T.), -s 'tə:ki, -z

turkey-cock, -s 'tə:kikɔk, -s

Turki 'tə:ki:

Turkish 'tə:kiʃ

Turkoman, -s 'tə:kəmən [-mæn, -mɑːn], -z

turmeric 'tə:mərik

turmoil, -s 'tə:mɔil, -z

turn (s. v.), -s, -ing, -ed tə:n, -z, -iŋ, -d

Turnbull 'tə:nbul

turn|coat, -s, -cock/s 'tə:n|kəut/s, -kɔk/s

turner (T.), -s 'tə:nə*, -z

turnery 'tə:nəri

Turnham 'tə:nəm

Turnhouse 'tə:nhaus

turning (s.), -s 'tə:niŋ, -z

turning-point, -s 'tə:niŋpoint, -s

turnip-tops 'tə:niptɔps

turnkey, -s 'tə:nki:, -z

Turnour 'tə:nə*

turn-out (assembly, equipage), -s 'tə:n'aut ['—, also -'- when preceded by a stress], -s

turnout (place for turning cars), -s 'tə:naut, -s

turnover, -s 'tə:n,əuvə*, -z

turnpike, -s 'tə:npaik, -s

turn-round, -s 'tə:nraund, -z

turnstile, -s 'tə:n-stail, -z

turntable, -s 'tə:n,teibl, -z

turn-up (adj.) 'tə:n'ʌp ['—]

turpentine 'tə:pəntain [-pmt-]

Turpin 'tə:pin

turpitude 'tə:pitju:d

turps tə:ps

turquoise, -s 'tə:kwɑ:z [-kwɔ:z, -kwɔiz], -iz

turret, -s, -ed 'tʌrit, -s, -id

turtle, -s 'tə:tl, -z

turtle-dove, -s 'tə:tldʌv, -z

turves (plur. of turf) tə:vz

Tuscan, -s, -y 'tʌskən, -z, -i

tush (s. interj.), -es tʌʃ, -iz

Tusitala ˌtu:si'tɑ:lə

tusk, -s, -ed, -y tʌsk, -s, -t, -i

tusker, -s 'tʌskə*, -z

Tussaud (surname) 'tu:səu

Tussaud's (exhibition) tə'sɔ:dz [tu's-, -'səuz]

tuss|le (s. v.), -les, -ling, -led 'tʌs|l, -lz, -liŋ [-liŋ], -ld

tussock, -s, -y 'tʌsək, -s, -i

tussore 'tʌsə* [-sɔ:*, -sɔə*]

tut (s. v.), -s, -ting, -ted tʌt, -s, -iŋ, -id

tut (interj.) ʒ [tʌt]

Tutankhamen ˌtu:təŋ'kɑ:men [-tæŋ-, -mən]

tutel|age, -ar, -ary 'tju:til|idʒ, -ə*, -əri

Tuthill 'tʌthil

tutor (s. v.), -s, -ing, -ed; -age 'tju:tə*, -z, -riŋ, -d; -ridʒ

tutorial, -ly tju(:)'tɔ:rɪəl, -i

tutorship, -s 'tju:təʃip, -s

tutti, -s 'tuti(:), -z

Tuttle 'tʌtl

tu-whit tu'wit [tu'hwit, tə-]

tu-whoo tu'wu: [tu'hwu:, tə-]

tuxedo (T.), -s tʌk'si:dəu, -z

TV 'ti:'vi:

Twaddell 'twɔdl, twɔ'del
  Note.—The Amer. linguist W. F. T. is twɔ'del.

twadd|le (s. v.), -les, -ling, -led, -ler/s 'twɔd|l, -lz, -liŋ [-liŋ], -ld, -lə*/z [-lə*/z]

twaddly 'twɔdli

twain (T.) twein

twang (s. v.), -s, -ing, -ed twæŋ, -z, -iŋ, -d

twang|le, -les, -ling, -led 'twæŋg|l, -lz, -liŋ, -ld

'twas twɔz (strong form), twəz (weak form)

tweak, -s, -ing, -ed twi:k, -s, -iŋ, -t

tweed (T.), -s twi:d, -z

Tweeddale 'twi:ddeil

Tweedie 'twi:di

tweed|le (s. v.), -les, -ling, -led 'twi:d|l, -lz, -liŋ [-liŋ], -ld

Tweedle|dee, -dum 'twi:dl|'di:, -'dʌm

Tweedmouth 'twi:dməθ [-mauθ]

Tweedsmuir 'twi:dzmjuə* [-mjɔə*, -mjɔ:*]

'tween twi:n

tween|y, -ies 'twi:n|i, -iz

tweeny-maid, -s 'twi:nimeid, -z

tweezers 'twi:zəz

twelfth, -s, -ly twelfθ, -s, -li

twelve, -s twelv, -z

twelvemo [12mo] 'twelvməu

twelvemonth, -s 'twelvmʌnθ, -s

twelvish 'twelviʃ

twent|y, -ies, -ieth/s, -iethly, -yfold 'twent|i, -iz, -iiθ/s, [-jiθ/s, -ɪəθ/s, -jəθ/s], -iiθli [-jiθli, -ɪəθli, -jəθli], -ifəuld

Twentyman 'twentimən

'twere twɔ:* [twɛə*] (strong forms), twə* (weak form)

twerp, -s twə:p, -s

twice twais

Twickenham 'twikŋəm [-knəm]

twidd|le, -les, -ling, -led 'twid|l, -lz, -liŋ [-liŋ], -ld

twig (s. v.), -s, -ging, -ged twig, -z, -iŋ, -d

Twigg twig

twiggy 'twigi

twilight, -s 'twailait, -s

twill (s. v.), -s, -ing, -ed; -y twil, -z, -iŋ, -d; -i

'twill twil (normal form), twəl, twl (occasional weak forms)

twin (s. v.), -s, -ning, -ned twin, -z, -iŋ, -d

twin|e, -es, -ing/ly, -ed, -er/s twain, -z, -iŋ/li, -d, -ə*/z

twing|e (s. v.), -es, -(e)ing, -ed twindʒ, -iz, -iŋ, -d

Twining 'twainiŋ

twink|le, -les, -ling, -led, -ler/s 'twiŋk|l, -lz, -liŋ [-liŋ], -ld, -lə*/z [-lə*/z]

twirl, -s, -ing, -ed twə:l, -z, -iŋ, -d

twirp, -s twə:p, -s

twist (s. v.) (T.), -s, -ing, -ed, -er/s twist, -s, -iŋ, -id, -ə*/z

Twistington 'twistiŋtən

twist|y, -ier, -iest, -iness 'twist|i, -ɪə* [-jə*], -iist [-jist], -inis

twit, -s, -ting/ly, -ted twit, -s, -iŋ/li, -id

twitch (s. v.), -es, -ing/s, -ed twitʃ, -iz, -iŋ/z, -t

twitt|er (s. v.), -ers, -ering, -ered 'twit|ə*, -əz, -əriŋ, -əd

'twixt twikst

two, twos tu: [also tu when the following word begins with ə], tu:z

two - dimensional 'tu:-di'menʃənl [-dai'm-, -ʃnəl, -ʃnl̩, -ʃnl̩, -ʃənəl]

two-edged 'tu:'edʒd ['tu:edʒd when attributive]

twofold 'tu:-fəuld

two-ish 'tu:iʃ

two-legged 'tu:'legd ['— when attributive, 'tu:'legid]

twopence, -s 'tʌpəns [-pms], -iz

twopenny 'tʌpṇi [-pni, -pəni]

twopenny-halfpenny 'tʌpṇi'heipṇi ['tʌpni'heipni, 'tʌpəni'heipəni]

twopennyworth, -s 'tu:'peniwə:θ ['tu:-'penəθ, 'tʌpṇiwə:θ, 'tʌpni-, 'tʌpəni-], -s

two-ply 'tu:-plai ['-'-]

two-seater, -s 'tu:'si:tə*, -z

two-step, -s 'tu:-step, -s

two-year-old, -s 'tu:'jər-əuld, -z

Twyford 'twaifəd

Tyacke 'tai-ək

Tyana 'tai-ənə

Tybalt 'tibəlt [-blt]

Tyburn 'taibə:n

Tychicus 'tikikəs

Tycho 'taikəu

tycoon, -s tai'ku:n, -z

Tydeus 'taidju:s [-djəs, -dɪəs]

Tydfil 'tidvil (*Welsh* 'tɨdvil)
tying (*from* **tie**) 'taiiŋ
Tyldesley 'tildzli
Tyler 'tailə*
tympanic tim'pænik
tympan|um, -ums, -a 'timpən|əm, -əmz, |-ə
Tynan 'tainən
Tynd|ale, -all 'tind|l, -l
Tyndrum tain'drʌm
Tyne tain
Tynemouth 'tainmauθ [-məθ, *old-fashioned* 'tinməθ]
  Note.–The pronunciation 'tinməθ *is now nearly obsolete.*
typ|e (*s. v.*), **-es, -ing, -ed** taip, -s, -iŋ, -t
type-bar, -s 'taipbɑ:*, -z
type-cutter, -s 'taip,kʌtə*, -z
type-founder, -s 'taip,faundə*, -z
type-foundr|y, -ies 'taip,faundr|i, -iz
type-set 'taipset
type-setter, -s 'taip,setə*, -z
typewrit|e, -es, -ing, typewrote, type-written, typewriter/s 'taip-rait, -s, -iŋ, 'taip-rəut, 'taip,ritn, 'taip-,raitə*/z
typhoid 'taifɔid
typhonic tai'fɔnik
typhoon, -s tai'fu:n ['tai'f-], -z
typh|ous, -us 'taif|əs, -əs
typic|al, -ally, -alness 'tipik|əl, -əli, -əlnis
typi|fy, -fies, -fying, -fied 'tipi|fai, -faiz, -faiiŋ, -faid

typist, -s 'taipist, -s
typo, -s 'taipəu, -z
typograph|er/s, -y tai'pɔgrəf|ə*/z, -i
typographic, -al, -ally ,taipə'græfik [-pəu'g-], -əl, -əli
typology tai'pɔlədʒi
typtolog|ist/s, -y tip'tɔlədʒ|ist/s, -i
tyrannic|al, -ally, -alness ti'rænik|əl [tai'r-], -əli, -əlnis
tyrannicide, -s ti'rænisaid [tai'r-], -z
tyranniz|e [-is|e], -es, -ing, -ed 'tirənaiz ['tirŋaiz], -iz, -iŋ, -d
tyrannosaurus, -i ti,rænə'sɔ:r|əs, -ai
tyrannous, -ly 'tirənəs ['tirŋəs], -li
tyrann|y, -ies 'tirən|i ['tirŋ|i], -iz
tyrant, -s 'taiərənt, -s
tyre (T.), -s 'taiə*, -z
Tyrian, -s 'tirīən, -z
tyro, -s 'taiərəu, -z
Tyrol 'tirəl [ti'rəul]
Tyrolean ti'rəuliən [,tirə'li(:)ən]
Tyrolese ,tirə'li:z [-rəu'l-, '--'-]
Tyrolienne, -s ti,rəuli'en [,tirəuli'en], -z
Tyrone ti'rəun
Tyrrell 'tirəl
Tyrrhenian, -s ti'ri:njən [-nīən], -z
Tyrtaeus tə:'ti:əs
Tyrwhitt 'tirit
Tyser 'taizə*
Tyson 'taisn
Tytler 'taitlə*
Tyzack 'taizæk [-zək], 'tizæk [-zək]

U

U (*the letter*), -'s ju:, -z
Uam Var 'ju:əm'vɑ:* ['juəm-]
Ubbelohde (*surname*) 'ʌbələud
ubiquitarian (U.), -s ju(:),bikwi'tɛərɪən,
 -z
ubiquitous ju(:)'bikwitəs
ubiquity ju(:)'bikwiti
U-boat, -s 'ju:bəut, -s
Uckfield 'ʌkfi:ld
udal (U.) 'ju:dəl
Udall 'ju:dəl
udder, -s 'ʌdə*, -z
Udolpho u:'dɔlfəu [ju:-]
udometer, -s ju(:)'dɔmitə*, -z
Uganda ju(:)'gændə [u:'g-]
ugh ɯːx, ɯh, ɯɣ, ʌx, uɸ, uh, əːh
Ughtred 'u:trid [-red]
uglification ˌʌglifi'keiʃən
ugli|fy, -fies, -fying, -fied 'ʌgli|fai, -faiz,
 -faiiŋ, -faid
ugl|y, -ier, -iest, -iness 'ʌgl|i, -ɪə*
 [-jə*], -iist [-jist], -inis
Ugrian, -s 'u:grɪən ['ju:g-], -z
u(h)lan, -s u'lɑ:n, -z
Uhland 'u:lənd [-lænd, -lɑ:nd] ('u:lant)
Uig 'u:ig ['ju:ig]
Uist 'ju:ist
Uitlander, -s 'eitlændə*, -z
ukase, -s ju:'keiz [-eis], -iz
Ukraine ju(:)'krein [-'krain]
Ukrainian ju(:)'kreinjən [-nɪən, *rarely*
 -'krain-]
ukelele, -s ˌju:kə'leili, -z
ulcer, -s, -ed 'ʌlsə*, -z, -d
ulcerat|e, -es, -ing, -ed 'ʌlsəreit, -s, -iŋ,
 -id
ulceration, -s ˌʌlsə'reiʃən, -z
ulcerous 'ʌlsərəs
ulema, -s 'u:limə, -z
ulex 'ju:leks
Ulfilas 'ulfilæs
Ulgham (*in Lincs. and Northumb.*) 'ʌfəm
Ulick 'ju:lik
ullage 'ʌlidʒ
Ullswater 'ʌlz,wɔːtə*
ulmus 'ʌlməs
uln|a, -ae, -ar 'ʌln|ə, -i:, -ə*
Ulrica (*English name*) 'ʌlrikə
Ulrich 'ulrik ('ulriç)

ulster (U.), -s, -ed 'ʌlstə*, -z, -d
ulterior, -ly ʌl'tiərɪə*, -li
ultim|ate, -ately 'ʌltim|it, -itli [-ətli]
ultimatum, -s ˌʌlti'meitəm, -z
ultimo 'ʌltiməu
ultra (*s. adj.*), -s 'ʌltrə, -z
ultra (*in* ne plus ultra), *see* ne plus ultra
ultra- 'ʌltrə-
 Note.—Numerous compound adjec-
 tives may be formed by prefixing
 ultra- *to adjectives. These com-*
 pounds have double stress, e.g.
 ultra-fashionable 'ʌltrə'fæʃənəbl
 [-ʃnə-]; *the pronunciation of all*
 such words may therefore be ascer-
 tained by reference to the simple
 words. When such adjectives are
 used as substantives they keep the
 double stress. (The words **ultra-**
 marine, ultramontane *given below*
 do not count as compounds.)
ultraism 'ʌltrəizəm
ultramarine ˌʌltrəmə'ri:n
ultramontane ˌʌltrə'mɔntein ['--'--]
ultramontanism ˌʌltrə'mɔntinizəm
 ['ʌltrə'm-, -tən-, -tein-]
ultrasonic 'ʌltrə'sɔnik
ultra vires 'ʌltrə'vaiəri:z ['ultrɑ:'viəreiz]
ululant 'ju:ljulənt
ululat|e, -es, -ing, -ed 'ju:ljuleit, -s, -iŋ,
 -id
ululation, -s ˌju:lju'leiʃən, -z
Ulverston 'ʌlvəstən
Ulysses ju(:)'lisi:z ['ju:lisi:z]
umbel, -s 'ʌmbəl [-bel], -z
umbellifer|ae, -ous ˌʌmbe'lifər|i: [-bə'l-],
 -əs
umber, -s, -y 'ʌmbə*, -z, -ri
umbilic, -s ʌm'bilik, -s
umbilical (*mathematical term*) ʌm'bilikəl,
 (*medical term*) ˌʌmbi'laikəl
umbilicus, -es ʌm'bilikəs [ˌʌmbi'laikəs],
 -iz
umble, -s 'ʌmbl, -z
umbo, -s, -nes 'ʌmbəu, -z, ʌm'bəuni:z
umbr|a, -as, -al 'ʌmbr|ə, -əz, -əl
umbrage 'ʌmbridʒ
umbrageous, -ly, -ness ʌm'breidʒəs, -li,
 -nis

umbrated 'ʌmbreitid
umbration, -s ʌm'breiʃən, -z
umbrella, -s ʌm'brelə, -z
Umbria, -n/s 'ʌmbriə, -n/z
umbriferous ʌm'brifərəs
umbril, -s 'ʌmbril, -z
Umfreville 'ʌmfrəvil
umiak, -s 'uːmiæk [-mjæk], -s
umlaut, -s 'umlaut, -s
umph m̩m̩ [ʌmf]
umpir|e (s. v.), -es, -ing, -ed 'ʌmpaiə*,
-z, -riŋ, -d
umpteen 'ʌmptiːn ['-'-]
umpty 'ʌmpti
un- ʌn-
Note.—The stressing of un- compounds depends on the meaning of
the prefix, the commonness of the
word, and other factors. Those
not included in the following list
are to be taken to have double stress
with single stress as a variant.
Thus undetachable is 'ʌndi'tætʃəbl
[,ʌn-], uncountenanced is 'ʌn-
'kauntinənst [ʌn-].

Una 'juːnə
unabashed 'ʌnə'bæʃt [,ʌn-]
unabated 'ʌnə'beitid [,ʌn-]
unable 'ʌn'eibl [ʌn-]
unabridged 'ʌnə'bridʒd [,ʌn-]
unaccented 'ʌnæk'sentid [,ʌn-,
-nək-, also '--,-- when attributive]
unacceptable 'ʌnək'septəbl [,ʌn-, -nək-]
unaccompanied 'ʌnə'kʌmpənid [,ʌn-,
also '--,--- when attributive]
unaccountable 'ʌnə'kauntəbl [,ʌn-]
unaccountab|ly, -leness ,ʌnə'kaunt-
əb|li, -lnis
unaccustomed 'ʌnə'kʌstəmd [,ʌn-]
unacknowledged 'ʌnək'nɒlidʒd [,ʌn-]
unacquainted 'ʌnə'kweintid [,ʌn-]
unacted 'ʌn'æktid
unadaptable 'ʌnə'dæptəbl [,ʌn-]
unaddressed 'ʌnə'drest
unadorned 'ʌnə'dɔːnd [,ʌn-]
unadulterated ,ʌnə'dʌltəreitid
unadvisability 'ʌnəd,vaizə'biliti [-lət-]
unadvisable 'ʌnəd'vaizəbl [,ʌn-]
unadvisableness ,ʌnəd'vaizəblnis
unadvised 'ʌnəd'vaizd [,ʌn-]
unadvisedly ,ʌnəd'vaizidli
unaffected (not influenced) 'ʌnə'fektid
unaffected (without affectation), -ly,
-ness ,ʌnə'fektid ['ʌn-], -li, -nis
unafraid 'ʌnə'freid
unaided 'ʌn'eidid [ʌn-]
unalienable 'ʌn'eiljənəbl [ʌn-, -liən-]
unalienably ʌn'eiljənəbli [-liən-]

unallotted 'ʌnə'lɒtid
unallowable 'ʌnə'lau-əbl [,ʌn-, -'lauəb-]
unalloyed 'ʌnə'lɔid [,ʌn-]
unalterability ʌn,ɔːltərə'biliti ['ʌn,ɔːl-,
-,ɔl-, -lət-]
unalterab|le, -ly, -leness ʌn'ɔːltərəb|l
['ʌn'ɔː-, -'ɔl-], -li, -nis
unaltered 'ʌn'ɔːltəd [ʌn-, -'ɔl-]
unambiguous, -ly 'ʌnæm'bigjŭəs [,ʌn-,
-gjwəs], -li
unanalysable 'ʌn'ænəlaizəbl
unanimity ,juːnə'nimiti [jun-, -næ'n-]
unanimous, -ly, -ness ju(ː)'næniməs, -li,
-nis
unannounced 'ʌnə'naunst
unanswerable ʌn'ɑːnsərəbl ['ʌn'ɑː-]
unanswered 'ʌn'ɑːnsəd [ʌn'ɑː-]
unappeas|able, -ed 'ʌnə'piːz|əbl [,ʌn-],
-d
unappetizing 'ʌn'æpitaiziŋ [ʌn-]
unapplied 'ʌnə'plaid [,ʌn-]
unappreciable ,ʌnə'priːʃəbl ['ʌnə'p-,
-ʃjə-, -ʃiə-]
unappreciated 'ʌnə'priːʃieitid [,ʌn-]
unapproachab|le, -ly, -leness ,ʌnə-
'prəutʃəb|l ['ʌnə'p-], -li, -lnis
unapproached 'ʌnə'prəutʃt [,ʌn-]
unappropriate (adj.) ,ʌnə'prəupriit
['ʌnə'p-]
unappropriated 'ʌnə'prəuprieitid [,ʌn-]
unapproved 'ʌnə'pruːvd
unarm, -s, -ing, -ed 'ʌn'ɑːm [ʌn-], -z,
-iŋ, -d
unascertain|able, -ed 'ʌnæsə'tein|əbl
[,ʌn-], -d
unashamed 'ʌnə'ʃeimd [,ʌn-]
unasked 'ʌn'ɑːskt [ʌn-]
unaspirated 'ʌn'æspəreitid [ʌn-, -pir-]
unassailable ,ʌnə'seiləbl ['ʌnə's-]
unassignable 'ʌnə'sainəbl [,ʌn-]
unassimilated 'ʌnə'simileitid [,ʌn-]
unassisted 'ʌnə'sistid [,ʌn-]
unassuming 'ʌnə'sjuːmiŋ [,ʌn-, -'suː-]
unattached 'ʌnə'tætʃt [,ʌn-]
unattainable 'ʌnə'teinəbl [,ʌn-]
unattempted 'ʌnə'temptid [,ʌn-]
unattended 'ʌnə'tendid [,ʌn-]
unattested 'ʌnə'testid [,ʌn-]
unattractive, -ly, -ness ,ʌnə'træktiv
['ʌnə't-], -li, -nis
unauthenticated 'ʌnɔː'θentikeitid
[,ʌn-]
unauthorized [-ised] 'ʌn'ɔːθəraizd
[ʌn-]
unavailing 'ʌnə'veiliŋ [,ʌn-, also '--,--
when attributive]
unavailingly ,ʌnə'veiliŋli
unavenged 'ʌnə'vendʒd [,ʌn-]

unavoidab|le, -ly, -leness ˌʌnə'vɔidəb|l
['ʌn-], -li, -lnis
unaware, -s 'ʌnə'wɛə* [ˌʌn-], -z
unbalanc|e, -es, -ing, -ed 'ʌn'bæləns
[ʌn-], -iz, -iŋ, -t
unbaptized 'ʌnbæp'taizd [ˌʌn-]
unbar, -s, -ring, -red 'ʌn'bɑː* [ʌn-], -z,
-riŋ, -d
unbearab|le, -ly, -leness ʌn'bɛərəb|l, -li,
-lnis
unbeaten 'ʌn'biːtn [ʌn-]
unbecoming, -ly, -ness 'ʌnbi'kʌmiŋ
[ˌʌn-, -bə'k-], -li, -nis
unbefitting 'ʌnbi'fitiŋ [-bə'f-]
unbegotten 'ʌnbi'gɔtn [ˌʌn-, -bə'g-]
unbeknown 'ʌnbi'nəun [ˌʌn-, -bə'n-]
unbelief 'ʌnbi'liːf [-bə'l-, '---, ˌ-'-]
unbelievable ˌʌnbi'liːvəbl ['ʌn-, -bə'l-]
unbeliever, -s 'ʌnbi'liːvə* [-bə'l-, '--ˌ--,
ˌ--'--], -z
unbelieving 'ʌnbi'liːviŋ [-bə'l-, '--ˌ--,
ˌ--'--]
unben|d, -ds, -ding, -ded, -t 'ʌn'ben|d
[ʌn-], -dz, -diŋ, -did, -t
unbeneficed 'ʌn'benifist
unbias(s)ed 'ʌn'baiəst [ʌn-]
unbidden 'ʌn'bidn [ʌn-]
un|bind (undo binding), -binds, -binding,
-bound 'ʌn|'baind [ʌn-], -'baindz,
-'baindiŋ, -'baund
unbleached 'ʌn'bliːtʃt [also 'ʌnb- when
attributive]
unblemished ʌn'blemiʃt ['ʌn'b-]
unblushing, -ly ʌn'blʌʃiŋ ['ʌn'b-], -li
unboiled 'ʌn'bɔild [also 'ʌnb- when
attributive]
unbolt, -s, -ing, -ed 'ʌn'bəult [ʌn-], -s,
-iŋ, -id
unborn 'ʌn'bɔːn ['ʌnb-, ʌn'b-, according to sentence-stress]
unbosom, -s, -ing, -ed ʌn'buzəm
['ʌn'b-], -z, -iŋ, -d
unbought 'ʌn'bɔːt [also 'ʌnb- when
attributive]
unbound (not bound) 'ʌn'baund [also
'ʌnb- when attributive]
unbounded ʌn'baundid
unbreathed 'ʌn'briːðd
unbridled ʌn'braidld
unbroken 'ʌn'brəukən [ʌn-]
unbuck|le, -les, -ling, -led 'ʌn'bʌk|l
[ʌn-], -lz, -liŋ [-liŋ], -ld
unburd|en, -ens, -ening, -ened ʌn-
'bəːd|n, -nz, -niŋ [-niŋ], -nd
unburied 'ʌn'berid [ʌn-]
unbusiness-like ʌn'biznislaik ['ʌn'b-]
unbutt|on, -ons, -oning, -oned 'ʌn-
'bʌt|n [ʌn-], -nz, -niŋ [-niŋ], -nd

uncalled for ʌn'kɔːldfɔː* ['ʌn'k-]
uncandid, -ly, -ness 'ʌn'kændid, -li, -nis
uncann|y, -ier, -iest, -ily, -iness ʌn-
'kæn|i, -iə*, -iist, -ili, -inis
uncanonical 'ʌnkə'nɔnikəl
uncared for 'ʌn'kɛədfɔː* [ʌn-]
uncatalogued 'ʌn'kætələgd
unceasing, -ly ʌn'siːsiŋ, -li
unceremonious, -ly, -ness 'ʌnˌseri-
'məunjəs [ˌʌn-, -niəs], -li, -nis
uncertain ʌn'səːtn ['ʌn's-, -tən, -tin]
uncertaint|y, -ies ʌn'səːtnt|i [-tən-,
-tin-], -iz
unchain, -s, -ing, -ed 'ʌn'tʃein [ʌn-], -z,
-iŋ, -d
unchallenged 'ʌn'tʃælindʒd [ʌn-]
unchangeability 'ʌnˌtʃeindʒə'biliti
[ʌn,tʃ-, -lət-]
unchangeable ʌn'tʃeindʒəbl ['ʌn'tʃ-]
unchangeab|ly, -leness ʌn'tʃeindʒəb|li,
-lnis
unchanged 'ʌn'tʃeindʒd [ʌn-]
unchanging ʌn'tʃeindʒiŋ ['ʌn'tʃ-]
uncharged 'ʌn'tʃɑːdʒd
uncharitab|le, -ly, -leness ʌn'tʃæritəb|l
['ʌn'tʃ-], -li, -lnis
uncharity 'ʌn'tʃæriti
uncharted 'ʌn'tʃɑːtid [ʌn-]
unchartered 'ʌn'tʃɑːtəd
unchaste, -ly 'ʌn'tʃeist [ʌn-], -li
unchastity 'ʌn'tʃæstiti [ʌn-]
uncheck|able, -ed 'ʌn'tʃek|əbl [ʌn-], -t
unchristian, -ly 'ʌn'kristjən [ʌn-,
-tʃən], -li
uncial (s. adj.), -s 'ʌnsiəl [-nsjəl, -nʃiəl,
-nʃjəl, -nʃəl], -z
unciform 'ʌnsifɔːm
uncinate 'ʌnsinit [-neit]
uncircumcised 'ʌn'səːkəmsaizd [ʌn-]
uncircumcision 'ʌnˌsəːkəm'siʒən ['ʌn-
ˌsəːkəm,s-]
unciv|il, -illy 'ʌn'siv|l [ʌn-, -il], -ili
unciviliz|ed [-is|ed], -able 'ʌn'sivilaiz|d
[ʌn-, -vˌlai-], -əbl
unclaimed 'ʌn'kleimd [also 'ʌn-k- when
attributive]
unclasp, -s, -ing, -ed 'ʌn'klɑːsp [ʌn-], -s,
-iŋ, -t
unclassifiable 'ʌn'klæsifaiəbl [ʌn-]
unclassified 'ʌn'klæsifaid [ʌn-]
uncle, -s 'ʌŋkl, -z
unclean, -ness 'ʌn'kliːn [ʌn-, also
'ʌn-kliːn when attributive], -nis
unclean|ly, -iness 'ʌn'klenl|i [ʌn-], -inis
unclos|e, -es, -ing, -ed 'ʌn'kləuz [ʌn-],
-iz, -iŋ, -d
unclothed 'ʌn'kləuðd [also 'ʌn-kləuðd
when attributive]

unclouded 'ʌn'klaudid [ʌn-]
unco 'ʌŋkəu
uncoffined 'ʌn'kɔfind [ʌn-]
uncoil, -s, -ing, -ed 'ʌn'kɔil [ʌn-], -z,
uncollected 'ʌn-kə'lektid   [-iŋ, -d
uncoloured 'ʌn'kʌləd
un-come-at-able 'ʌn-kʌm'ætəbl [,ʌn-]
uncomfortab|le, -ly, -leness ʌn'kʌm-
    fətəb|l, -li, -lnis
uncommercial   'ʌn-kə'mə:ʃəl   [also
    'ʌn-kə,m- when attributive]
uncommon ʌn'kɔmən ['ʌn'k-]
uncommon|ly, -ness ʌn'kɔmən|li, -nis
uncommunic|able, -ated 'ʌn-kə'mju:-
    nik|əbl [,ʌn-, -'mjun-], -eitid
uncommunicative, -ness 'ʌn-kə'mju:ni-
    kətiv [,ʌn-, -'mjun-, -keit-], -nis
uncomplaining, -ly 'ʌn-kəm'pleiniŋ
    [,ʌn-, also 'ʌn-kəm,p- when attri-
    butive], -li
uncompleted 'ʌn-kəm'pli:tid [,ʌn-]
uncomplimentary   'ʌn,kɔmpli'mentəri
    [,ʌn-k-]
uncompounded 'ʌn-kəm'paundid
uncompromising, -ly, -ness ʌn'kɔm-
    prəmaiziŋ [-prum-], -li, -nis
unconcealed 'ʌn-kən'si:ld [,ʌn-]
unconcern, -ed, -edly, -edness 'ʌn-
    kən'sə:n [,ʌn-], -d, -idli, -idnis
unconclusive 'ʌn-kən'klu:siv [,ʌn-]
uncondi|tional, -tionally 'ʌn-kən'di|ʃənl
    [,ʌn-, -ʃnəl, -ʃn̩l, -ʃn̩l, -ʃənəl], -ʃn̩əli
    [-ʃnəli, -ʃn̩li, -ʃn̩li, -ʃənəli]
unconditioned   'ʌn-kən'diʃənd   [,ʌn-
    kən'faind]
unconfined 'ʌn-kən'faind
unconfirmed 'ʌn-kən'fə:md
uncongenial 'ʌn-kən'dʒi:njəl [,ʌn-, -nïəl]
unconnected 'ʌn-kə'nektid [,ʌn-]
unconquerable ʌn'kɔŋkərəbl ['ʌn'k-]
unconquered 'ʌn'kɔŋkəd [ʌn-]
unconscionab|le, -ly, -leness ʌn'kɔn-
    ʃn̩əb|l [-ʃnə-, -ʃənə-], -li, -lnis
unconscious, -ly, -ness ʌn'kɔnʃəs
    ['ʌn'k-], -li, -nis
unconsecrated 'ʌn'kɔnsikreitid [ʌn-]
unconsidered 'ʌn-kən'sidəd [also '--,--
    when attributive]
unconstitu|tional, -tionally 'ʌn,kɔnsti-
    'tju:|ʃənl [,ʌn-, -ʃnəl, -ʃn̩l, -ʃn̩l, -ʃənəl],
    -ʃn̩əli [-ʃnəli, -ʃn̩li, -ʃn̩li, -ʃənəli]
unconstrain|ed, -edly 'ʌn-kən'strein|d
    [,ʌn-], -idli
unconsumed   'ʌn-kən'sju:md   [,ʌn-,
    -'su:md]   [[,ʌn-]
uncontaminated   'ʌn-kən'tæmineitid
uncontestable   ,ʌn-kən'testəbl   ['ʌn-
    kən't-]

uncontested 'ʌn-kən'testid [,ʌn-, also
    'ʌn-kən,t- when attributive]
uncontradicted 'ʌn,kɔntrə'diktid
uncontrollable   ,ʌn-kən'trəuləb|l   ['ʌn-
    kən't-]
uncontrollab|ly, -leness 'ʌn-kən'trəul-
    əb|li, -lnis
uncontrolled 'ʌn-kən'trəuld [,ʌn-]
unconventional 'ʌn-kən'venʃənl [,ʌn-,
    -ʃnəl, -ʃn̩l, -ʃn̩l, -ʃənəl]
unconventionalit|y, -ies 'ʌn-kən,ven-
    ʃə'næliti|i [-ʃn̩'æ-], -iz
unconverted 'ʌn-kən'və:tid [also 'ʌn-
    kən,v- when attributive]
unconvertible 'ʌn-kən'və:təbl [,ʌn-,
    -tib-]
unconvinced 'ʌn-kən'vinst [,ʌn-]
uncooked 'ʌn'kukt ['ʌn-k-, ʌn'k-,
    according to sentence-stress]
uncord, -s, -ing, -ed 'ʌn'kɔ:d [ʌn-], -z,
    -iŋ, -id
uncork, -s, -ing, -ed 'ʌn'kɔ:k [ʌn-], -s,
    -iŋ, -t
uncorrected 'ʌn-kə'rektid ['ʌn-kə,r-
    when attributive]
uncorroborated 'ʌn-kə'rɔbəreitid [,ʌn-]
uncorrupt, -ly, -ness 'ʌn-kə'rʌpt [,ʌn-],
    -li, -nis
uncountable 'ʌn'kauntəbl [ʌn-]
uncounted 'ʌn'kauntid [ʌn-]
uncoup|le, -les, -ling, -led 'ʌn'kʌp|l
    [ʌn-], -lz, -liŋ [-|iŋ], -ld
uncouth, -ly, -ness ʌn'ku:θ, -li, -nis
uncov|er, -ers, -ering, -ered ʌn'kʌv|ə*
    ['ʌn'k-], -əz, -əriŋ, -əd
uncreate, -d 'ʌn-kri(:)'eit, -id
uncritical, -ally 'ʌn'kritik|əl [ʌn-], -əli
uncrossed 'ʌn'krɔst [-'krɔ:st, also
    'ʌn-kr- when attributive]
uncrowned 'ʌn'kraund [also 'ʌn-kraund
    when attributive]
unction, -s 'ʌŋkʃən, -z
unctuosity ,ʌŋktju'ɔsiti
unctuous, -ly, -ness 'ʌŋktjŭəs [-tjwəs],
    -li, -nis
uncultivated 'ʌn'kʌltiveitid [ʌn-]
uncultured 'ʌn'kʌltʃəd [ʌn-]
uncurbed 'ʌn'kə:bd
uncurl, -s, -ing, -ed 'ʌn'kə:l [ʌn-], -z,
    -iŋ, -d
uncut 'ʌn'kʌt [also 'ʌn-kʌt, ʌn'kʌt,
    according to sentence-stress]
undamaged 'ʌn'dæmidʒd
undate 'ʌndeit
undated (wavy) 'ʌndeitid
undated (not dated) 'ʌn'deitid
undaunted, -ly, -ness ʌn'dɔ:ntid
    ['ʌn'd-], -li, -nis

undebated 'ʌn-di'beitid [‚ʌn-]
undeceiv|e, -es, -ing, -ed 'ʌn-di'si:v
[‚ʌn-], -z, -iŋ, -d
undecennial ‚ʌndi'senjəl
undecided, -ly, -ness 'ʌndi'saidid [‚ʌn-,
also '--‚-- *when attributive*], -li, -nis
undecipherable 'ʌndi'saifərəbl [‚ʌn-]
undecisive 'ʌndi'saisiv [‚ʌn-]
undecomposable 'ʌn‚di:kəm'pəuzəbl
undefended 'ʌndi'fendid [‚ʌn-, *also*
'--‚-- *when attributive*]
undefiled 'ʌndi'faild [‚ʌn-]
undefin|able, -ed ‚ʌndi'fain|əbl ['ʌn-
di'f-], -d
undelivered 'ʌndi'livəd [‚ʌn-]
undemonstrative 'ʌndi'mɔnstrətiv [‚ʌn-]
undeniable ‚ʌndi'naiəbl ['ʌndi'n-]
undeniably ‚ʌndi'naiəbli
undenomina|tional, -tionalism 'ʌndi-
‚nɔmi'nei|ʃənl [‚ʌn-, -ʃnəl, -ʃn̩l, -ʃn̩l,
-ʃənəl], -ʃn̩əlizəm [-ʃnəl-, -ʃn̩l-, -ʃn̩l-,
-ʃənəl-]
under (*s. adj. adv. prep.*), -s 'ʌndə*, -z
   Note.—Compounds with under- *not*
   included in the following list are to
   be taken to have double stress. Thus
   under-masticate *is* 'ʌndə'mæstikeit
underact, -s, -ing, -ed 'ʌndər'ækt
[-də'ækt], -s, -iŋ, -id
underbid, -s, -ding 'ʌndə'bid, -z, -iŋ
underbred 'ʌndə'bred
underbrush 'ʌndə-brʌʃ
under|buy, -buys, -buying, -bought
'ʌndə|'bai, -'baiz, -'baiiŋ, -'bɔ:t
undercarriage, -s 'ʌndə‚kæridʒ, -iz
undercast, -s 'ʌndəkɑ:st, -s
undercharge (*s.*), -s 'ʌndə'tʃɑ:dʒ
['ʌndətʃ-], -iz
undercharg|e (*v.*), -es, -ing, -ed 'ʌndə-
'tʃɑ:dʒ, -iz, -iŋ, -d
underclay 'ʌndə-klei
under-clerk, -s 'ʌndə'klɑ:k ['ʌndə-k-],
-s
undercliff, -s 'ʌndə-klif, -s
underclothed 'ʌndə'kləuðd
underclothes 'ʌndə-kləuðz [*old-fashioned*
-kləuz]
underclothing 'ʌndə‚kləuðiŋ
undercoat, -s 'ʌndəkəut, -s
under-colour, -s 'ʌndə‚kʌlə*, -z
under-coloured 'ʌndə'kʌləd
under-cover 'ʌndə‚kʌvə*
undercroft, -s 'ʌndə-krɔft [-krɔ:ft], -s
undercurrent, -s 'ʌndə‚kʌrənt, -s
undercut (*s.*), -s 'ʌndəkʌt, -s
undercut (*adj. v.*), -s, -ting 'ʌndə'kʌt,
-s, -iŋ
under-developed 'ʌndədi'veləpt

under|do, -does, -doing, -did, -done
'ʌndə|'du:, -'dʌz, -'du(:)iŋ, -'did,
-'dʌn ['ʌndədʌn *when attributive*]
underdog, -s 'ʌndədɔg ['--'-], -z
underdose, -s 'ʌndədəus, -iz
under|draw, -draws, -drawing, -drew,
-drawn 'ʌndə|'drɔ:, -'drɔ:z, -'drɔ:iŋ,
-'dru:, -'drɔ:n
under-dressed 'ʌndə'drest
under-driven 'ʌndə'drivn
underestimate (*s.*), -s 'ʌndər'estimit
[-də'es-, -meit], -s
underestimat|e (*v.*), -es, -ing, -ed
'ʌndər'estimeit [-də'es-], -s, -iŋ, -id
under-expo|se, -ses, -sing, -sed; -sure/s
'ʌndəriks'pəu|z [-dəiks-, -dəreks-,
-dəeks-], -ziz, -ziŋ, -zd; -ʒə*/z
under|feed, -feeds, -feeding, -fed 'ʌndə|-
'fi:d, -'fi:dz, -'fi:diŋ, -'fed
under-felt, -s 'ʌndəfelt, -s
underfoot 'ʌndə'fut ['ʌndə'f-]
undergarment, -s 'ʌndə‚gɑ:mənt, -s
under|go, -goes, -going, -went, -gone
‚ʌndə|'gəu ['ʌndə|'gəu], -'gəuz,
-'gəuiŋ, -'went, -'gɔn [-'gɔ:n]
undergraduate, -s ‚ʌndə'grædjuit
[-'grædʒŭət], -s
underground (*s. adj.*) (**U.**) 'ʌndəgraund
underground (*adv.*) ‚ʌndə'graund
['ʌndə'g-]
undergrown 'ʌndə'grəun ['ʌndə-grəun]
undergrowth 'ʌndə-grəuθ
underhand 'ʌndəhænd
underhanded, -ly, -ness ‚ʌndə'hændid
['ʌndə'h-, 'ʌndə‚h-], -li, -nis
Underhill 'ʌndəhil
underhung 'ʌndə'hʌŋ [*also* 'ʌndəh-
when attributive]
underlay (*s.*), -s 'ʌndəlei, -z
under|lay (*v.*), -lays, -laying, -laid
‚ʌndə|'lei ['ʌndə|'l-], -'leiz, -'leiiŋ,
-'leid
underlease, -s 'ʌndəli:s, -iz
underlet, -s, -ting 'ʌndə'let ['ʌndəl-], -s,
-iŋ
under|lie, -lies, -lying, -lay, -lain
‚ʌndə|'lai ['ʌndə|'l-], -'laiz, -'laiiŋ,
-'lei, -'lein
underline (*s.*), -s 'ʌndəlain ['--'-], -z
underlin|e (*v.*), -es, -ing, -ed ‚ʌndə'lain
['ʌndə'l-], -z, -iŋ, -d
underlinen 'ʌndə‚linin
underling, -s 'ʌndəliŋ, -z
under|man (*s.*), -men 'ʌndə|mæn, -men
underman (*v.*), -s, -ning, -ned 'ʌndə-
'mæn, -z, -iŋ, -d
undermentioned   'ʌndə'menʃənd
['ʌndə‚m-, ‚ʌndə'm-]

undermin|e, -es, -ing, -ed, -er/s ˌʌndə'main ['ʌndə'm-], -z, -iŋ, -d, -ə*/z

undermost 'ʌndəməust

underneath ˌʌndə'ni:θ ['ʌndə'n-]

underpass, -es 'ʌndəpɑːs, -iz

under|pay, -pays, -paying, -paid 'ʌndə|'pei, -'peiz, -'peiiŋ, -'peid [also 'ʌndəpeid when attributive]

underpayment, -s 'ʌndə'peimənt, -s

underpeopled 'ʌndə'piːpld

underpin, -s, -ning, -ned ˌʌndə'pin ['ʌndə'p-], -z, -iŋ, -d

underplay (s.) 'ʌndə-plei

underplay (v.), -s, -ing, -ed 'ʌndə'plei, -z, -iŋ, -d

underplot, -s 'ʌndə-plɔt, -s

underpopulated 'ʌndə'pɔpjuleitid

underprais|e, -es, -ing, -ed 'ʌndə'preiz, -iz, -iŋ, -d

underprivileged 'ʌndə'privilidʒd

underpriz|e, -es, -ing, -ed 'ʌndə'praiz, -iz, -iŋ, -d

underproduction 'ʌndə-prə'dʌkʃən [-pru'd-, '---,--]

underprop, -s, -ping, -ped ˌʌndə'prɔp ['ʌndə'p-], -s, -iŋ, -t

underrat|e, -es, -ing, -ed ˌʌndə'reit ['ʌndə'r-], -s, -iŋ, -id

under-ripe 'ʌndə'raip [also 'ʌndər-, ˌʌndə'r, according to sentence-stress]

under-roof, -s 'ʌndəruːf, -s

under|run, -runs, -running, -ran 'ʌndə|'rʌn [ˌʌndə|'r-], -'rʌnz, -'rʌniŋ, -'ræn

underscor|e, -es, -ing, -ed ˌʌndə'skɔ:* ['ʌndə's-, -'skəə*], -z, -riŋ, -d

undersea (adj.) 'ʌndəsi:

under-secretar|y, -ies; -yship/s 'ʌndə-'sekrətər|i, -iz; -iʃip/s

under|sell, -sells, -selling, -sold 'ʌndə|-'sel, -'selz, -'seliŋ, -'səuld

undersheriff, -s 'ʌndə'ʃerif ['--,--], -s

undershirt, -s 'ʌndəʃə:t, -s

undershot 'ʌndəʃɔt

underside, -s 'ʌndəsaid, -z

undersign, -s -ing, -ed ˌʌndə'sain ['ʌndə's-], -z, -iŋ, -d

undersigned (s.) 'ʌndəsaind ['--'-, ˌ--'-]

undersized 'ʌndə'saizd ['ʌndəsaizd]

underskirt, -s 'ʌndə-skə:t, -s

undersleeve, -s 'ʌndə-sli:v, -z

under|stand, -stands, -standing, -stood, -standed; -standable 'ʌndə|'stænd, -'stændz, -'stændiŋ, -'stud -'stændid; -'stændəbl

understat|e, -es, -ing, -ed 'ʌndə'steit, -s, -iŋ, -id

understatement, -s 'ʌndə'steitmənt ['ʌndə,s-], -s

understocked 'ʌndə'stɔkt

understood (from understand) ˌʌndə'stud

understrapp|er/s, -ing 'ʌndə,stræp|ə*/z -iŋ

understrat|um, -a 'ʌndə'strɑ:t|əm ['ʌndə,s-, -streit-], -ə

understud|y (s. v.), -ies, -ying, -ied 'ʌndə,stʌd|i, -iz, -iiŋ [-jiŋ], -id

under|take (take upon oneself), -takes, -taking, -took, -taken ˌʌndə|'teik, -'teiks, -'teikiŋ, -'tuk, -'teikən [-'teikŋ]

undertaker (one who agrees to perform), -s ˌʌndə'teikə*, -z

undertaker (one who arranges funerals), -s 'ʌndə,teikə*, -z

Undertaker (special historical sense), -s 'ʌndə,teikə*, -z

undertaking (s.) (enterprise, promise), -s ˌʌndə'teikiŋ ['--,--], -z

undertaking (s.) (arranging funerals) 'ʌndə,teikiŋ

undertenan|cy, -cies, -t/s 'ʌndə-'tenən|si ['ʌndə,t-], -siz, -t/s

under-the-counter 'ʌndəðə'kauntə*

undertime 'ʌndətaim

under-timed 'ʌndə'taimd

undertint, -s 'ʌndətint, -s

undertone, -s 'ʌndətəun, -z

undertook (from undertake) ˌʌndə'tuk

undertow, -s 'ʌndətəu, -z

undervaluation, -s 'ʌndə,vælju'eiʃən, -z

underval|ue, -ues, -uing, -ued 'ʌndə-'væl|ju: [-ju], -ju:z [-juz], -juiŋ [-jwiŋ], -ju:d [-jud]

under|vest/s, -wear 'ʌndə|vest/s, -wɛə*

underwent (from undergo) ˌʌndə'went

underwing, -s 'ʌndəwiŋ, -z [['ʌndə'w-]

underwood (U.), -s 'ʌndəwud, -z

underwork (s.) 'ʌndəwə:k

underwork (v.), -s, -ing, -ed 'ʌndə-'wə:k, -s, -iŋ, -t

underworker (subordinate worker), -s 'ʌndə,wə:kə*, -z

underworld (U.) 'ʌndəwə:ld

underwrit|e, -es, -ing, -underwrote, underwritten 'ʌndərait ['ʌndə'r-, ˌʌndə'r-], -s, -iŋ, 'ʌndərəut ['ʌndə'r-, ˌʌndə'r-], 'ʌndə,ritn ['ʌndə'r-, ˌʌndə'r-]

underwriter, -s 'ʌndə,raitə*, -z

underwrought 'ʌndə'rɔ:t

undescribable 'ʌndis'kraibəbl [ˌʌn-]

undeserv|ed, -edly, -edness 'ʌndi-'zə:v|d [ˌʌn-], -idli, -idnis

undeserving, -ly 'ʌndi'zə:viŋ [ˌʌn-], -li

undesign|ed, -edly, -edness 'ʌndi-'zain|d [ˌʌn-], -idli, -idnis
undesirability 'ʌndiˌzaiərə'biliti [-lət-]
undesirab|le, -ly, -leness 'ʌndi'zaiərəb|l [ˌʌn-], -li, -lnis
undesirous 'ʌndi'zaiərəs [ˌʌn-]
undetected 'ʌndi'tektid [ˌʌn-]
undeterminable 'ʌndi'tə:mınəbl [ˌʌn-]
undeterminate, -ly, -ness 'ʌndi'tə:-minit [ˌʌn-], -li, -nis
undetermination 'ʌndiˌtə:mi'neiʃən
undetermined 'ʌndi'tə:mind [ˌʌn-]
undeterred 'ʌndi'tə:d [ˌʌn-]
undeveloped 'ʌndi'veləpt [ˌʌn-]
undeviating ʌn'di:vieitiŋ ['ʌn'd-, -vjeit-]
undeviatingly ʌn'di:vieitiŋli [-vjeit-]
undid (from undo) 'ʌn'did [ʌn-]
undies 'ʌndiz
undigested 'ʌndi'dʒestid [ˌʌn-, -dai'dʒ-]
undignified ʌn'dignifaid ['ʌn'd-]
undiluted 'ʌndai'lju:tid [ˌʌn-, -di'l-, -'lu:t-]
undiminished 'ʌndi'miniʃt [ˌʌn-, also '--ˌ-- when attributive]
undimmed 'ʌn'dimd [ʌn-]
undine (U.), -s 'ʌndi:n [ʌn'd-, un'd-], -z
undiplomatic 'ʌnˌdiplə'mætik [ˌʌn-, -pləu'm-, -plu'm-]
undiscerning 'ʌndi'sə:niŋ [ˌʌn-, -i'zə:-]
undischarged 'ʌndis'tʃɑ:dʒd [also '--ˌ- when attributive, and ˌ--'- when not attributive]
undisciplined ʌn'disiplind ['ʌn'd-]
undisclosed 'ʌndis'kləuzd [ˌʌn-]
undiscouraged 'ʌndis'kʌridʒd [ˌʌn-]
undiscoverab|le, -ly 'ʌndis'kʌvərəb|l [ˌʌn-], -li
undiscovered 'ʌndis'kʌvəd [also 'ʌndisˌk- when attributive]
undiscussed 'ʌndis'kʌst
undisguised 'ʌndis'gaizd [ˌʌn-]
undismayed 'ʌndis'meid [ˌʌn-]
undisposed 'ʌndis'pəuzd [ˌʌn-]
undisputed 'ʌndis'pju:tid [ˌʌn-]
undissolved 'ʌndi'zɔlvd
undistinctive 'ʌndis'tiŋktiv
undistinguishab|le, -ly, -leness 'ʌn-dis'tiŋgwiʃəb|l [ˌʌn-], -li, -lnis
undistinguished 'ʌndis'tiŋgwiʃt
undistracted 'ʌndis'træktid
undisturbed 'ʌndis'tə:bd [ˌʌn-]
undivided, -ly, -ness 'ʌndi'vaidid [ˌʌn-], -li, -nis
un|do, -does, -doing, -did, -done, -doer/s 'ʌn|'du: [ʌn-], -'dʌz, -'du(:)iŋ, -'did, -'dʌn, -'du(:)ə*/z

undock, -s, -ing, -ed 'ʌn'dɔk [ʌn-], -s, -iŋ, -t
undomesticated 'ʌn-də'mestikeitid [ˌʌn-, -dəu'm-]
undoubted, -ly ʌn'dautid, -li
undraped 'ʌn'dreipt [also 'ʌn-dreipt when attributive]
undreamed of ʌn'dremtɔv ['ʌn'd-, -'drempt-, -'dri:md-]
undreamt of ʌn'dremtɔv ['ʌn'd-, -mptɔv]
undress (s.) 'ʌn'dres
undress (adj.) 'ʌndres
undress (v.), -es, -ing, -ed 'ʌn'dres [ʌn-], -iz, -iŋ, -t
undrinkable 'ʌn'driŋkəbl [ʌn-]
undue 'ʌn'dju: ['ʌnd-, ʌn'd-, according to sentence-stress]
undulat|e, -es, -ing/ly, -ed 'ʌndjuleit, -s, -iŋ/li, -id
undulation, -s ˌʌndju'leiʃən, -z
undulatory 'ʌndjulətəri [-leit-]
unduly 'ʌn'dju:li [ʌn-]
unduti|ful, -fully, -fulness 'ʌn'dju:ti|-ful [ʌn-], -fuli [-fəli], -fulnis
undying, -ly ʌn'daiiŋ, -li
unearned 'ʌn'ə:nd ['ʌnə:-, ʌn'ə:-, according to sentence-stress]
unearth, -s, -ing, -ed 'ʌn'ə:θ [ʌn'ə:θ], -s, -iŋ, -t
unearthl|y, -iness ʌn'ə:θl|i, -inis
uneas|y, -ier, -iest, -ily, -iness ʌn'i:z|i ['ʌn'i:-], -iə* [-jə*], -iist [-jist], -ili, -inis
uneatable, -ness 'ʌn'i:təbl [ʌn-], -nis
uneaten 'ʌn'i:tn [ʌn-]
uneconomic, -al 'ʌnˌi:kə'nɔmikl [ˌʌni:k-, 'ʌnˌek-, ˌʌnek-], -əl
unedifying 'ʌn'edifaiiŋ [ʌn-]
uneducated 'ʌn'edjukeitid [ʌn-, -dʒu-]
unelected 'ʌni'lektid
unembarrassed 'ʌnim'bærəst [-nem-]
unemo|tional, -tionally 'ʌni'məuʃ|ənl [ˌʌn-, -ʃnəl, -ʃn̩l, -ʃnl, -ʃənəl], -ʃn̩əli [-ʃnəli, -ʃn̩li, -ʃnli, -ʃənəli]
unemployable 'ʌnim'plɔiəbl [ˌʌn-, -nem-]
unemployed 'ʌnim'plɔid [ˌʌn-, -nem-]
unemployment 'ʌnim'plɔimənt .[ˌʌn-, -nem-]
unenclosed 'ʌnin'kləuzd [-niŋ'kl-, -nen'kl-, -n'tl-]
unencumbered 'ʌnin'kʌmbəd [ˌʌn-, -niŋ'k-, -nen'k-]
unending ʌn'endiŋ ['ʌn'en-]
unendowed 'ʌnin'daud [-nen-]
unendurable 'ʌnin'djuərəbl [ˌʌn-, -nen-, -'djɔər-, -'djɔ:r-, -'djə:r-]
un-English 'ʌn'iŋgliʃ [rarely -'eŋ-]

unenlightened 'ʌnin'laitnd [ˌʌn-, -nen-]
unenterprising 'ʌn'entəpraiziŋ [ʌn-]
unenviable 'ʌn'enviəbl [ʌn-, -vjə-]
unequal/s, -ally, -alness -alled 'ʌn'i:-
kwǀəl/z [ʌn-], -əli, -əlnis, -əld
unequitabǀle, -ly 'ʌn'ekwitəbǀl [ʌn-], -li
unequivocǀal, -ally, -alness 'ʌni'kwi-
vəkǀəl [ˌʌn-, -vuk-], -əli, -əlnis
unerring, -ly, -ness 'ʌn'ə:riŋ [ʌn-], -li,
-nis
unescapable 'ʌnis'keipəbl [ˌʌn-]
Unesco ju(:)'neskəu
unessential 'ʌni'senʃəl [ˌʌn-]
uneven, -ly, -ness 'ʌn'i:vən [ʌn-], -li, -nis
uneventǀful, -fully, -fulness 'ʌni'ventǀ-
ful [ˌʌn-], -fuli [-fəli], -fulnis
unexampled ˌʌnig'za:mpld ['ʌnig'z-,
-neg-]
unexceptionabǀle, -ly, -leness ˌʌnik'sep-
ʃnəbǀl ['ʌnik's-, -nek-, -ʃŋə-, -ʃənə-],
-li, -lnis
unexcepǀtional, -tionally 'ʌnik'sepǀʃənl
[ˌʌn-, -nek-, -ʃnəl, -ʃŋl, -ʃnl, -ʃənəl],
-ʃŋəli [-ʃnəli, -ʃŋli, -ʃnli, -ʃənəli]
unexcusable, -ness 'ʌniks'kju:zəbl
[ˌʌn-, -nek-], -nis
unexhausted 'ʌnig'zɔ:stid [ˌʌn-, -neg-]
unexpected, -ly, -ness 'ʌniks'pektid
[ˌʌn-, -nek-], -li, -nis
unexpired 'ʌniks'paiəd [ˌʌn-, -nek-]
unexplained 'ʌniks'pleind [ˌʌn-, -nek-]
unexplored 'ʌniks'plɔ:d [ˌʌn-, -nek-,
-'plɔəd]
unexposed 'ʌniks'pəuzd [-nek-]
unexpressibǀle, -ly ˌʌniks'presəbǀl
['ʌniks'p-, -nek-, -sib-], -li
unexpressive 'ʌniks'presiv [ˌʌn-, -nek-]
unexpurgated 'ʌn'ekspə(:)geitid [ʌn-]
unfading ʌn'feidiŋ
unfailing, -ly, -ness ʌn'feiliŋ, -li, -nis
unfair, -ly, -ness 'ʌn'fɛə* [ʌn-], -li, -nis
unfaithǀful, -fully, -fulness 'ʌn'feiθǀful
[ʌn-], -fuli [-fəli], -fulnis
unfaltering, -ly ʌn'fɔ:ltəriŋ ['-fɔl-], -li
unfamiliar, -ly 'ʌn-fə'miljə* [ˌʌn-,
-fm̩'i-], -li
unfamiliarity 'ʌn-fəˌmili'æriti [-fm̩,i-]
unfashionable 'ʌn'fæʃnəbl [ʌn-, -ʃŋə-]
unfastǀen, -ens, -ening, -ened 'ʌn-
'fɑ:sǀn [ʌn-], -nz, -niŋ [-ņiŋ], -nd
unfathomabǀle, -ly, -leness ʌn'fæðəm-
əbǀl, -li, -lnis
unfathomed 'ʌn'fæðəmd [ʌn-]
unfavourabǀle, -ly, -leness ʌn'feivərəbǀl
unfed ʌn'fed   [[ʌn-], -li, -lnis
unfeeling, -ly, -ness ʌn'fi:liŋ, -li, -nis
unfeigned ʌn'feind ['ʌn'f-]
unfeignedǀly, -ness ʌn'feinidǀli, -nis

unfelt 'ʌn'felt
unfermented   'ʌn-fə(:)'mentid   [also
'ʌn-fə(:),m- when attributive]
unfertilized [-ised] 'ʌn'fə:tilaizd [ʌn-]
unfetter, -s, -ing, -ed 'ʌn'fetə* [ʌn-], -z,
-riŋ, -d
unfilial, -ly 'ʌn'filjəl [ʌn-, -liəl], -i
unfinished 'ʌn'finiʃt [ʌn-, also '-,-- when
attributive]
unfit (adj.), -ly, -ness 'ʌn'fit [ʌn-], -li,
-nis
unfit (v.), -s, -ting, -ted ʌn'fit ['ʌn'f-],
-s, -iŋ, -id
unfitting (adj.) 'ʌn'fitiŋ [ʌn-]
unfittingly ʌn'fitiŋli
unfix, -es, -ing, -ed 'ʌn'fiks [ʌn-], -iz,
-iŋ, -t
unflagging ʌn'flægiŋ ['ʌn'f-]
unflattering, -ly 'ʌn'flætəriŋ [ʌn-], -li
unfledged 'ʌn'fledʒd [ʌn-, also 'ʌn-f-
when attributive]
unflinching 'ʌn'flintʃiŋ ['ʌn'f-]
unflinchingǀly, -ness ʌn'flintʃiŋǀli, -nis
unfold (open out folds, release sheep
from fold), -s, -ing, -ed 'ʌn'fəuld
[ʌn-], -z, -iŋ, -id
unfold (reveal), -s, -ing, -ed ʌn'fəuld
['ʌn'f-], -z, -iŋ, -id
unforeseeable 'ʌn-fɔ:'si:əbl [ˌʌn-]
unforeseeǀing, -n 'ʌn-fɔ:'si:ǀiŋ [ˌʌn-], -n
unforgettable 'ʌn-fə'getəbl [ˌʌn-]
unforgivǀable, -en, -ing 'ʌn-fə'givǀəbl
[ˌʌn-], -ən, -iŋ
unforgotten 'ʌn-fə'gɔtn
unformed 'ʌn'fɔ:md ['ʌn-fɔ:md when
attributive]
unfortified 'ʌn'fɔ:tifaid [ʌn-]
unfortunǀate, -ately -ateness ʌn'fɔ:-
tʃņǀit [-tʃņit, -tʃənǀit, -tʃņət], -itli
[-ətli], -itnis
unfounded 'ʌn'faundid [ʌn-]
unframed 'ʌn'freimd [also '-- when
attributive]
unǀfreeze, -freezes, -froze, -frozen
'ʌnǀ'fri:z, -'fri:ziz, -'frəuz, -'frəuzn
unfrequent, -ly ʌn'fri:kwənt, -li
unfrequented 'ʌn-fri'kwentid [ˌʌn-]
unfriendǀly, -liness 'ʌn'frendǀli [ʌn-],
-linis
unfrock, -s, -ing, -ed 'ʌn'frɔk [ʌn-], -s,
-iŋ, -t
unfruitǀful, -fully, -fulness 'ʌn'fru:tǀful
[ʌn-], -fuli [-fəli], -fulnis
unfulfilled 'ʌn-ful'fild [ˌʌn-]
unfurl, -s, -ing, -ed 'ʌn'fə:l ['ʌn'f-], -z,
-iŋ, -d
unfurnished 'ʌn'fə:niʃt [ʌn-, also 'ʌnˌf-
when attributive]

ungainl|y, -iest, -iness ʌn'geinl|i, -iist
  [-jist], -inis
ungarbled 'ʌn'gɑ:bld [ʌn-]
ungenerous, -ly 'ʌn'dʒenərəs [ʌn-], -li
ungenial 'ʌn'dʒi:njəl [ʌn-, -nïəl]
ungent|le, -ly, -leness 'ʌn'dʒent|l [ʌn-],
  -li, -lnis
ungentleman|ly, -liness ʌn'dʒentlmən|li,
  -linis
un-get-at-able 'ʌnget'ætəbl
ungird, -s, -ing, -ed 'ʌn'gə:d [ʌn-], -z,
  -iŋ, -id
unglazed 'ʌn'gleizd [also '-- when attri-
  butive]
unglorious 'ʌn'glɔ:rïəs [ʌn-]
ungloved 'ʌn'glʌvd [also 'ʌng- when
  attributive]
ungl|ue, -ues, -uing, -ued 'ʌn'gl|u:, -u:z,
  -u(:)iŋ, -u:d
ungodl|y, -ier, -iest, -iness ʌn'gɔdl|i,
  -ïə* [-jə*], -iist [-jist], -inis
Ungoed 'ʌŋgɔid
ungotten 'ʌn'gɔtn
ungovernab|le, -ly, -leness ʌn'gʌvən-
  əb|l [-vnə-], -li, -lnis
ungoverned 'ʌn'gʌvənd
ungown, -s, -ing, -ed 'ʌn'gaun, -z, -iŋ, -d
ungrace|ful, -fully, -fulness 'ʌn'greis|-
  ful [ʌn-], -fuli [-fəli], -fulnis
ungracious, -ly, -ness 'ʌn'greiʃəs [ʌn-],
  -li, -nis
ungrammatic|al, -ally 'ʌngrə'mætik|əl
  [,ʌn-], -əli
ungrateful ʌn'greitful ['ʌn'g-]
ungrate|fully, -fulness ʌn'greit|fuli
  [-fəli], -fulnis
ungrounded ʌn'graundid ['ʌn'g-]
ungrudging 'ʌn'grʌdʒiŋ [ʌn-]
ungrudgingly ʌn'grʌdʒiŋli
unguarded 'ʌn'gɑ:did [ʌn-]
unguarded|ly, -ness ʌn'gɑ:didli, -nis
unguent, -s 'ʌŋgwənt, -s
unguided 'ʌn'gaidid [ʌn-]
ungul|a, -ae 'ʌŋgjul|ə, -i:
ungulate (s. adj.), -s 'ʌŋgjuleit [-lit], -s
unhallowed ʌn'hæləud ['ʌn'h-]
unhampered 'ʌn'hæmpəd [ʌn-]
unhand, -s, -ing, -ed ʌn'hænd, -z, -iŋ,
  -id
un|hang (remove from hanging position),
  -hangs, -hanging, -hung 'ʌn|'hæŋ
  [ʌn-], -'hæŋz, -'hæŋiŋ, -'hʌŋ
unhapp|y, -ier, -iest, -ily, -iness ʌn-
  'hæp|i ['ʌn'h-], -ïə*, -iist, -ili, -inis
unharmed 'ʌn'hɑ:md [ʌn-]
unharness, -es, -ing, -ed 'ʌn'hɑ:nis
  [ʌn-], -iz, -iŋ, -d
unhatched 'ʌn'hætʃt

unhealth|y, -ier, -iest, -ily, -iness
  ʌn'helθ|i ['ʌn'h-], -ïə* [-jə*], -iist
  [-jist], -ili, -inis
unheard (not granted a hearing, etc.)
  'ʌn'hə:d
unheard of ʌn'hə:dɔv
unheed|ed, -ing 'ʌn'hi:d|id [ʌn-], -iŋ
unhesitating, -ly ʌn'heziteitiŋ, -li
unhing|e, -es, -ing, -ed ʌn'hindʒ ['ʌn'h-],
  -iz, -iŋ, -d
unhistoric, -al 'ʌnhis'tɔrik [occasionally
  'ʌnis-], -əl
unhitch, -es, -ing, -ed 'ʌn'hitʃ [ʌn-], -iz,
  -iŋ, -t
unhol|y, -iness ʌn'həul|i, -inis
unhook, -s, -ing, -ed 'ʌn'huk [ʌn-], -s,
  -iŋ, -t
unhoped for ʌn'həuptfɔ:*
unhors|e, -es, -ing, -ed 'ʌn'hɔ:s [ʌn-],
  -iz, -iŋ, -t
unhospitable 'ʌn'hɔspitəbl [ʌn-,
  'ʌnhɔs'p-, ,ʌnhɔs'p-]
unhous|e, -es, -ing, -ed 'ʌn'hauz [ʌn-],
  -iz, -iŋ, -d
unhuman 'ʌn'hju:mən [ʌn-]
unhung (not hung) ʌn'hʌŋ
unhurt 'ʌn'hə:t
Uniat, -s 'ju:niæt, -s
uniaxial, -ly 'ju:ni'æksïəl [,ju:-, -sjəl], -i
unicorn, -s 'ju:nikɔ:n, -z
unicycle, -s 'ju:nisaikl ['ju:ni's-], -z
unideal 'ʌnai'dɪəl [-'di:əl, -'di:l]
unidentified 'ʌnai'dentifaid [,ʌn-]
unidiomatic 'ʌn,idïə'mætik [-djə'm-
  -diu'm-, -dju'm-, -diəu'm-, -djəu'm-]
unifiable 'ju:nifaiəbl
unification, -s ,ju:nifi'keiʃən [jun-], -z
uniform (s. adj.), -s, -ed, -ly, -ness
  'ju:nifɔ:m, -z, -d, -li, -nis
uniformity ,ju:ni'fɔ:miti [jun-]
uni|fy, -fies, -fying, -fied 'ju:ni|fai, -faiz,
  -faiiŋ, -faid
unilater|al, -ally 'ju:ni'lætər|əl, -əli
uniliter|al, -ally 'ju:ni'litər|əl, -əli
unimaginab|le, -ly, -leness ,ʌni'mædʒi-
  nəb|l ['ʌn-], -li, -lnis
unimaginative, -ness 'ʌni'mædʒinətiv
  [,ʌn-], -nis
unimagined 'ʌni'mædʒind [,ʌn-]
unimpaired 'ʌnim'pɛəd [,ʌn-]
unimpeachable ,ʌnim'pi:tʃəb|l ['ʌn-
  im'p-]
unimpeachab|ly, -leness ,ʌnim'pi:tʃ-
  əb|li, -lnis
unimpeded 'ʌnim'pi:did [,ʌn-]
unimportan|ce, -t 'ʌnim'pɔ:tən|s [,ʌn-],
  -t
uninflated 'ʌnin'fleitid [,ʌn-]

uninflected 'ʌnin'flektid [ˌʌn-]
uninfluenced 'ʌn'influənst[ʌn-, -flwənst]
uninformed 'ʌnin'fɔːmd
uninhabitable, -ness 'ʌnin'hæbitəbl [ˌʌn-], -nis
uninhabited 'ʌnin'hæbitid [ˌʌn-]
uninitiated 'ʌni'niʃieitid [ˌʌn-, -ʃjeit-]
uninjured 'ʌn'indʒəd [ʌn-]
uninspired 'ʌnin'spaiəd
uninstructed 'ʌnin'strʌktid [ˌʌn-]
uninsured 'ʌnin'ʃuəd [-'ʃɔəd, -'ʃɔːd]
unintelligent, -ly 'ʌnin'telidʒənt [ˌʌn-], -li
unintelligibility 'ʌninˌtelidʒə'biliti [-dʒi'b-, -lət-]
unintelligib|le, -ly 'ʌnin'telidʒəb|l [ˌʌn-, -dʒib-], -li
uninten|tional, -tionally 'ʌnin'ten|ʃənl [ˌʌn-, -ʃnəl, -ʃn̩l, -ʃnl, -ʃənəl], -ʃnəli [-ʃnəli, -ʃn̩li, -ʃnli, -ʃənəli]
uninterest|ed, -ing 'ʌn'intrist|id [ʌn-, -trəs-, -tərəs-], -iŋ [-li
unintermitting,-ly 'ʌnˌintə'mitiŋ [ˌʌni-],
uninterrupted,-ly 'ʌnˌintə'rʌptid [ˌʌni-], -li
uninvit|ed, -ing 'ʌnin'vait|id [ˌʌn-], -iŋ
union (U.), -s 'juːnjən [-niən], -z
unioni|sm, -st/s 'juːnjəni|zəm [-niən-], -st/s
unipartite ˌjuːni'pɑːtait ['juːniˌp-]
unique, -ly, -ness juː'niːk [juː'n-], -li, -nis
unisexual 'ʌnːi'seksjuəl [ˌjuː-, -ksjwəl, -ksjul, -kʃuəl, -kʃwəl, -kʃul]
unison, -s 'juːnizn [-isn], -z
unissued 'ʌn'iʃuːd [ˌʌn-, -'iʃjuːd, -'isjuːd]
unit, -s 'juːnit, -s
unitable juː'naitəbl [juː'n-]
unitarian (U.), -s, -ism ˌjuːni'tɛəriən [jun-], -z, -izəm
unitary 'juːnitəri
unit|e, -es, -ing, -ed/ly, -er/s juː'nait [juː'n-], -s, -iŋ, -id/li, -ə*/z
unit|y (U.), -ies 'juːnit|i, -iz
univalve, -s 'juːnivælv, -z
univers|al, -als, -ally, -alness, -alism, -alist/s ˌjuːni'vəːs|əl [jun-], -əlz, -əli [-li], -əlnis, -əlizəm [-izəm], -əlist/s
universality ˌjuːnivəː'sæliti [[-list/s]
universaliz|e [-is|e], -es, -ing, -ed ˌjuːni'vəːsəlaiz [jun-, -s]aiz], -iz, -iŋ, -d
universe (U.), -s 'juːnivəːs, -iz
universit|y, -ies ˌjuːni'vəːsit|i [jun-], -iz
univocal (s. adj.), -s 'juːni'vəukəl, -z
unjust, -ly, -ness 'ʌn'dʒʌst [ʌn-, also '-- when attributive], -li, -nis
unjustifiab|le, -ly, -leness ʌn'dʒʌsti-faiəb|l ['ʌn'dʒ-, ʌnˌdʒʌsti'f-, 'ʌn-ˌdʒʌsti'f-], -li, -lnis

unkempt 'ʌn'kempt [ʌn-, also 'ʌn-k- when attributive]
unkept 'ʌn'kept
unkin|d, -der, -dest, -dly, -dness ʌn-'kain|d ['ʌn'k-], -də*, -dist, -dli, -dnis
unknot, -s, -ting, -ted 'ʌn'nɔt [ʌn-], -s, -iŋ, -id
unknowable 'ʌn'nəuəbl [ʌn-]
unknowing, -ly, -ness 'ʌn'nəuiŋ [ʌn-], -li, -nis
unknown 'ʌn'nəun [also 'ʌnn-, ʌn'n-, according to sentence-stress]
unlac|e, -es, -ing, -ed 'ʌn'leis [ʌn-], -iz, -iŋ, -t
unlad|e, -es, -ing, -ed 'ʌn'leid [ʌn-], -z, -iŋ, -id
unladylike 'ʌn'leidilaik [ʌn-]
unlamented 'ʌnlə'mentid [also '--ˌ-- when attributive]
unlash, -es, -ing, -ed 'ʌn'læʃ [ʌn-], -iz, -iŋ, -t
unlatch, -es, -ing, -ed 'ʌn'lætʃ [ʌn-], -iz, -iŋ, -t
unlaw|ful, -fully, -fulness 'ʌn'lɔː|ful [ʌn-], -fuli [-fəli], -fulnis
unleaded (without lead) 'ʌn'ledid [also '-ˌ-- when attributive]
unlearn, -s, -ing, -ed (p. tense, p. partic.), -t 'ʌn'ləːn, -z, -iŋ, -t [-d], -t
unlearned (adj.), -ly, -ness 'ʌn'ləːnid, -li, -nis
unleavened 'ʌn'levnd [ʌn-, also 'ʌnˌl- when attributive]
unled 'ʌn'led
unless ən'les, [ʌn'les, n̩'les, also 'ʌn'les for special emphasis]
unlettered 'ʌn'letəd
Unley 'ʌnli
unlicensed 'ʌn'laisənst [ʌn-]
unlike 'ʌn'laik ['ʌnl-, ʌn'l-]
unlikel|y, -ihood, -iness ʌn'laikl|i ['ʌn'l-], -ihud, -inis
unlikeness 'ʌn'laiknis [ʌn-]
unlimber, -s, -ing, -ed ʌn'limbə* ['ʌn'l-], -z, -riŋ, -d
unlimited ʌn'limitid ['ʌn'l-]
unlink, -s, -ing, -ed 'ʌn'liŋk [ʌn-], -s, -iŋ, -t [-'liŋt]
unliquidated 'ʌn'likwideitid [ʌn-, also 'ʌnˌlikwideitid when attributive]
unlit 'ʌn'lit [also 'ʌnlit when attributive]
unload, -s, -ing, -ed, -er/s 'ʌn'ləud [ʌn-], -z, -iŋ, -id, -ə*/z
unlock, -s, -ing, -ed 'ʌn'lɔk [ʌn-], -s, -iŋ, -t
unlooked for ʌn'luktfɔ:*
unloos|e, -es, -ing, -ed 'ʌn'luːs [ʌn-], -iz, -iŋ, -t

unloos|en, -ens, -ening, -ened ʌn'luːs|n ['ʌn'l-], -nz, -ŋiŋ [-iŋŋ], -nd

unlovel|y, -iness 'ʌn'lʌvl|i, -inis

unloving 'ʌn'lʌviŋ

unluck|y, -ier, -iest, -ily, -iness ʌn-'lʌk|i ['ʌn'l-], -iə*, -iist, -ili, -inis

un|make, -makes, -making, -made 'ʌn|'meik, -'meiks, -'meikiŋ, -'meid

unman, -s -ning, -ned 'ʌn'mæn [ʌn-], -z, -iŋ, -d

unmanageable ʌn'mænidʒəbl ['ʌn'm-]

unmanageab|ly, -leness ʌn'mænidʒ-əb|li, -lnis

unmanl|y, -ier, -iest, -iness 'ʌn-'mænl|i [ʌn-], -iə* [-jə*], -iist [-jist], -inis

unmanner|ly, -liness ʌn'mænə|li, -linis

unmarked 'ʌn'mɑːkt [also '--, -'-, according to sentence stress]

unmarried 'ʌn'mærid [also 'ʌn,m-, ʌn'm-, according to sentence-stress]

unmask, -s, -ing, -ed 'ʌn'mɑːsk [ʌn-], -s, -iŋ, -t

unmatched 'ʌn'mætʃt

unmeaning ʌn'miːniŋ ['ʌn'm-]

unmeaning|ly, -ness ʌn'miːniŋ|li, -nis

unmeasurable ʌn'meʒərəbl

unmeasured ʌn'meʒəd

unmentionable, -s, -ness ʌn'menʃŋəbl [-ʃnə-, -ʃənə-], -z, -nis

unmerci|ful, -fully, -fulness ʌn'məːsi|-ful, -fuli [-fəli], -fulnis

unmerited 'ʌn'meritid [ʌn-]

unmethodical 'ʌnmi'θɒdikəl [,ʌn-, -me'θ-, -mə'θ-]

unmind|ful, -fully, -fulness ʌn'maind|-ful, -fuli [-fəli], -fulnis

unmingled ʌn'miŋgld

unmistak(e)ab|le, -ly, -leness 'ʌnmis-'teikəb|l [,ʌn-], -li, -lnis

unmitigated 'ʌn'mitigeitid

unmixed 'ʌn'mikst [also 'ʌnm- when attributive]

unmodifiable 'ʌn'mɒdifaiəbl [ʌn-]

unmodified 'ʌn'mɒdifaid [ʌn-]

unmolested 'ʌnməu'lestid [,ʌn-]

unmoor, -s, -ing, -ed 'ʌn'muə* [ʌn-, -'mɔə*, -'mɔː*], -z, -riŋ, -d

unmounted 'ʌn'mauntid [also 'ʌn,m- when attributive]

unmourned 'ʌn'mɔːnd [ʌn-, -'mɔənd, rarely -'muənd]

unmov(e)able 'ʌn'muː'vəbl [ʌn-]

unmoved 'ʌn'muː'vd [ʌn-]

unmuff|le, -les, -ling, -led 'ʌn'mʌf|l [ʌn-], -lz, -liŋ [-liŋ], -ld

unmusic|al, -ally 'ʌn'mjuːzik|əl [ʌn-], -əli

unmuzz|le, -les, -ling, -led 'ʌn'mʌz|l [ʌn-], -lz, -liŋ [-liŋ], -ld

unnamed 'ʌn'neimd [also 'ʌnn- when attributive]

unnatur|al, -ally, -alness ʌn'nætʃr|əl ['ʌn'n-, -tʃur-, -tʃər-], -əli, -əlnis

unnavigable 'ʌn'nævigəbl [ʌn-]

unnecessarily ʌn'nesisərili [-səs-, -ser-, 'ʌn,nesi'ser-, 'ʌn,nesə'ser-]

unnecessar|y, -iness ʌn'nesisər|i ['ʌn'n-, -səs-, -ser-], -inis

unneighbourly 'ʌn'neibəli [ʌn-]

unnerv|e, -es, -ing, -ed 'ʌn'nəː|v [ʌn-], -z, -iŋ, -d

unnotice|able, -d 'ʌn'nəutis|əbl [ʌn-], -t

unnumbered 'ʌn'nʌmbəd [in contrast '-,--]

Uno 'juːnəu

unobjectionab|le, -ly 'ʌnəb'dʒəkʃŋəb|l [,ʌn-, -ʃnə-, -ʃənə-], -li

unobliging 'ʌnə'blaidʒiŋ [,ʌn-]

unobliterated 'ʌnə'blitəreitid [,ʌnə'b-, 'ʌnɔ'b-, ,ʌnɔ'b-]

unobservan|ce, -t 'ʌnəb'zəː'vən|s [,ʌn-], -t

unobserv|ed, -edly 'ʌnəb'zəː'v|d [,ʌn-], -idli

unobstructed 'ʌnəb'strʌktid [,ʌn-, also 'ʌnəb,s- when attributive]

unobtainable 'ʌnəb'teinəbl [,ʌn-]

unobtrusive, -ly, -ness 'ʌnəb'truːsiv [,ʌn-], -li, -nis

unoccupied 'ʌn'ɒkjupaid [ʌn-]

unoffending 'ʌnə'fendiŋ [,ʌn-, also 'ʌnə,f- when attributive]

unoffensive 'ʌnə'fensiv [,ʌn-]

unofficial 'ʌnə'fiʃəl [also 'ʌnə,f- when attributive]

unopened 'ʌn'əupənd [ʌn-, -pmd]

unopposed 'ʌnə'pəuzd [,ʌn-]

unordained 'ʌnɔː'deind

unordered 'ʌn'ɔːdəd [ʌn-]

unorganized 'ʌn'ɔːgənaizd [ʌn-, -gŋai-]

unorthodox 'ʌn'ɔːθədɒks [ʌn-]

unorthodoxy ʌn'ɔːθədɒksi ['ʌn'ɔː-]

unostentatious, -ly, -ness 'ʌn,ɒsten-'teiʃəs [-tən-], -li, -nis

unowned 'ʌn'əund

unpack, -s, -ing, -ed, -er/s 'ʌn'pæk [ʌn-], -s, -iŋ, -t, -ə*/z

unpaid 'ʌn'peid [also 'ʌnp-, ʌn'p-, according to sentence-stress]

unpaired 'ʌn'pεəd

unpalatable ʌn'pælətəbl ['ʌn'p-, -lit-]

unpalatableness ʌn'pælətəblnis [-lit-]

unparalleled ʌn'pærəleld [-r|eld, -rələld, -r|əld]

unpardonable ʌn'pɑːdņəbl ['ʌn'p-, -dnə-]

unpardonab|ly, -leness ʌn'pɑːdņəb|li [-dnə-], -lnis

unparliamentary 'ʌn,pɑːlə'mentəri [,ʌnp-, -li'm-, -ljə-]

unpatriotic 'ʌn,pætri'ɔtik [,ʌnp-]

unpaved 'ʌn'peivd [also 'ʌn-p- when attributive]

unpeeled 'ʌn'piːld [also 'ʌn-p- when attributive]

unperceiv|able, -ed ʌnpə'siːv|əbl [,ʌn-], -d

unperforated 'ʌn'pəːfəreitid [ʌn-]

unperformed 'ʌn-pə'fɔːmd [,ʌn-]

unpersua|dable, -sive 'ʌn-pə'swei|dəbl [,ʌn-], -siv [-ziv]

unperturbed 'ʌn-pə(ː)'təːbd [,ʌn-]

unperverted 'ʌn-pə(ː)'vəːtid

unphilosophic|al, -ally, -alness 'ʌn-,filə'sɔfik|əl [-ə'zɔ-], -əli, -əlnis

unpick, -s, -ing, -ed 'ʌn'pik [ʌn-], -s, -iŋ, -t

unpierced 'ʌn'piəst

unpiloted 'ʌn'pailətid [ʌn-]

unpin, -s, -ning, -ned 'ʌn'pin [ʌn-], -z, -iŋ, -d

unpitied 'ʌn'pitid [ʌn-]

unpitying ʌn'pitiiŋ ['ʌn'p-]

unpityingly ʌn'pitiiŋli

unplaced 'ʌn'pleist

unplait, -s, -ing, -ed 'ʌn'plæt [ʌn-], -s, -iŋ, -id

unplayable 'ʌn'plei əbl [ʌn-]

unpleasant ʌn'pleznt

unpleasant|ly, -ness ʌn'pleznt|li, -nis

unpleasing 'ʌn'pliːziŋ [ʌn-]

unpleasing|ly, -ness ʌn'pliːziŋ|li, -nis

unpliable 'ʌn'plai-əbl [ʌn-]

unpoetic|al, -ally, -alness 'ʌn-pəu'etik|əl [,ʌn-], -əli, -əlnis

unpolished 'ʌn'pɔliʃt [also 'ʌn,p-, ʌn'p- according to sentence-stress]

unpolite, -ly, -ness 'ʌn-pə'lait [-pəu'l-, -puˈl-], -li, -nis

unpolitic 'ʌn'pɔlitik [ʌn-, -lət-]

unpolluted 'ʌn-pə'luːtid [,ʌn-, -'ljuː-]

unpopular 'ʌn'pɔpjulə* [ʌn-, -pjəl-]

unpopularity 'ʌn,pɔpju'læriti [-pjə'l-]

unpractic|al, -ally 'ʌn'præktik|əl [ʌn-], -əli

unpracticality 'ʌn,prækti'kæliti

unpractised ʌn'præktist ['ʌn'p-]

unprecedented ʌn'presidəntid [rarely -'priːs-, -den-]

unpredictable 'ʌn-pri'diktəbl [,ʌn-, -prə'd-]

unprejudiced ʌn'predʒudist ['ʌn'p-]

unpremeditated 'ʌn-pri'mediteitid [,ʌn-]

unpreparation 'ʌn,prepə'reiʃən [,ʌn-p-]

unprepar|ed, -edly, -edness 'ʌn-pri'pεə|d [,ʌn-, -prə'p-], -ridli [-dli], -ridnis [-dnis]

unprepossessing 'ʌn,priː'pə'zesiŋ

unpresentable 'ʌn-pri'zentəbl [,ʌn-, -prə'z-]

unpresuming 'ʌn-pri'zjuːmiŋ [,ʌn-, -prə'z-, -'zuː-]

unpretending, -ly 'ʌn-pri'tendiŋ [,ʌn-pri't-, also 'ʌn-pri,t- when attributive], -li

unpretentious 'ʌn-pri'tenʃəs [,ʌn-, also '--,-- when attributive]

unpretentious|ly, -ness 'ʌn-pri'tenʃəs|li [,ʌn-], -nis

unpreventable 'ʌn-pri'ventəbl [,ʌn-]

unpriced ʌn'praist [-prəv-]

unprincipled ʌn'prinsəpld ['ʌn'p-, -sip-]

unprintable 'ʌn'printəbl [ʌn-]

unprinted 'ʌn'printid

unproclaimed 'ʌn-prə'kleimd [-prəu'k-, -pruˈk-]

unprocurable 'ʌn-prə'kjuərəbl [,ʌn-, -pru'k-, -'kjɔər-, -'kjɔːr-, -'kjəːr-]

unproductive, -ly, -ness ʌn-prə'dʌktiv [,ʌn-, -pru'd-], -li, -nis

unprofes|sional, -sionally 'ʌn-prə'fe|ʃənl [,ʌn-, -pru'f-, -ʃnəl, -ʃņl, -ʃnl, -ʃənəl], -ʃnəli [-ʃnəli, -ʃņli, -ʃnli, -ʃənəli]

unprofitab|le, -ly, -leness ʌn'prɔfitəb|l ['ʌn'p-], -li, -lnis

unprohibited 'ʌn-prəu'hibitid [-pru'h-]

unpromising 'ʌn'prɔmisiŋ [ʌn-]

unpronounceable 'ʌn-prə'naunsəbl [,ʌn-, -pru'n-, -prŋ'au-]

unprop, -s, -ping, -ped 'ʌn'prɔp [ʌn-], -s, -iŋ, -t

unpropitious, -ly, -ness 'ʌn-prə'piʃəs [,ʌn-, -pru'p-], -li, -nis

unprotected 'ʌn-prə'tektid [,ʌn-, -pru't-]

unproved 'ʌn'pruːvd

unprovided 'ʌn-prə'vaidid [,ʌn-, -pru'v-]

unprovok|ed, -edly 'ʌn-prə'vəuk|t [,ʌn-, -pru'v-], -idli [-tli]

unpublished 'ʌn'pʌbliʃt ['ʌn,p-, ʌn'p-, according to sentence-stress]

unpunctual, -ly 'ʌn'pʌŋktjŭəl [ʌn-, -tjwəl, -tjul, -tʃŭəl, -tʃwəl, -tʃul], -i

unpunctuality 'ʌn,pʌŋktju'æliti [-tʃu-]

unpunished 'ʌn'pʌniʃt

unqualified (without qualifications) 'ʌn'kwɔlifaid [ʌn-], (without reservation, downright) ʌn'kwɔlifaid

unquenchable ʌn'kwentʃəbl

unquestionab|le, -ly, -leness ʌn'kwes-tʃənəb|l [-eʃtʃ-, -tʃŋə-, -tʃnə-], -li, -lnis

unquesti|oned, -oning/ly ʌn'kwes-tʃ|ənd [-eʃtʃ-], -əniŋ/li [-niŋ/li]
unrav|el, -els, -elling, -elled, -eller/s ʌn'ræv|əl, -əlz, -ļiŋ [-əliŋ], -əld, -ļə*/z [-ələ*/z]
unread 'ʌn'red
unreadable, -ness 'ʌn'ri:dəbl [ʌn-], -nis
unread|y, -ily, -iness 'ʌn'red|i [ʌn-], -ili, -inis
unreal 'ʌn'riəl [ʌn-, -'ri:əl]
unrealit|y, -ies 'ʌnri'ælit|i [ˌʌn-, -ri:'æ-], -iz
unreason 'ʌn'ri:zn [*in contrast* 'ʌnˌr-]
unreasonable ʌn'ri:zŋəbl ['ʌn'r-, -znə-]
unreasonab|ly, -leness ʌn'ri:zŋəb|li [-znə-], -lnis
unreasoning ʌn'ri:zŋiŋ ['ʌn'r-, -zniŋ]
unreceipted 'ʌnri'si:tid [-rə's-, *also* '—ˌ— when attributive*]
unreceived 'ʌnri'si:vd [-rə's-]
unreciprocated 'ʌnri'siprəkeitid [ˌʌn-, -rə's-, -pruk-]
unreckoned 'ʌn'rekənd
unreclaimed 'ʌnri'kleimd [*also* '—ˌ- when attributive*]
unrecognizable [-isa-] 'ʌn'rekəgnaiz-əbl [ʌn'r-, 'ʌnˌrekəg'n-, -kig-]
unrecognized [-ised] 'ʌn'rekəgnaizd [ʌn-, -kig-]
unreconcilable 'ʌn'rekənsailəbl [ʌn'r-, 'ʌnˌrekən's-, -kn-]
unreconciled 'ʌn'rekənsaild [ʌn-, -kn-]
unrecorded 'ʌnri'kɔ:did [-rə'k-]
unrecounted 'ʌnri'kauntid [-rə'k-]
unredeemable 'ʌnri'di:məbl [ˌʌn-, -rə'd-]
unredeemed 'ʌnri'di:md [-rə'd-, *also* '— when attributive*]
unrefined 'ʌnri'faind [-rə'f-]
unreflecting 'ʌnri'flektiŋ [ˌʌn-, -rə'f-]
unreformed 'ʌnri'fɔ:md [ˌʌn-, -rə'f-]
unrefuted 'ʌnri'fju:tid [ˌʌn-, -rə'f-]
unregenerate 'ʌnri'dʒenərit [ˌʌn-, -rə'dʒ-]
unregistered 'ʌn'redʒistəd [ʌn-]
unrehearsed 'ʌnri'hə:st [ˌʌn-, -rə'h-]
unrelated 'ʌnri'leitid [-rə'l-]
unrelaxed 'ʌnri'lækst [ˌʌn-, -rə'l-]
unrelenting 'ʌnri'lentiŋ [ˌʌn-, -rə'l-]
unrelenting|ly, -ness ˌʌnri'lentiŋ|li [-rə'l-], -nis
unreliability 'ʌnriˌlai-ə'biliti [-rəˌl-, -lət-]
unreliable, -ness 'ʌnri'lai-əbl [ˌʌn-, -rə'l-], -nis
unrelieved 'ʌnri'li:vd [-rə'l-]
unremembered 'ʌnri'membəd [-rə'm-]
unremitting ˌʌnri'mitiŋ ['ʌn-, -rə'm-]
unremitting|ly, -ness ˌʌnri'mitiŋ|li [-rə'm-], -nis

unremovable 'ʌnri'mu:vəbl [ˌʌn-, -rə'm-]
unrepaid 'ʌnri'peid
unrepair, -able 'ʌnri'pɛə* [-rə'p-], -rəbl
unrepealed 'ʌnri'pi:ld [-rə'p-]
unrepentant 'ʌnri'pentənt [ˌʌn-, -rə'p-]
unreported 'ʌnri'pɔ:tid [ˌʌn-, -rə'p-]
unrepresented 'ʌnˌrepri'zentid [ˌʌnr-]
unrequested 'ʌnri'kwestid [ˌʌn-, -rə'k-]
unrequited 'ʌnri'kwaitid [-rə'k-]
unreserved 'ʌnri'zə:vd [ˌʌn-, -rə'z-, *also* '— when attributive*]
unreservedly ˌʌnri'zə:vidli [-rə'z-]
unresisting, -ly 'ʌnri'zistiŋ [ˌʌn-, -rə'z-], -li
unresolved 'ʌnri'zɔlvd [ˌʌn-, -rə'z-]
unresponsive 'ʌnris'pɔnsiv [ˌʌn-, -rəs-]
unrest 'ʌn'rest [ʌn-]
unrest|ful, -fully, -fulness 'ʌn'rest|ful [ʌn-], -fuli [-fəli], -fulnis
unresting 'ʌn'restiŋ [ʌn-]
unresting|ly, -ness ʌn'restiŋ|li, -nis
unrestored 'ʌnris'tɔ:d [ˌʌn-, -rəs-, -'tɔəd]
unrestrain|ed, -edly 'ʌnris'trein|d [ˌʌn-, -rəs-], -idli
unrestricted 'ʌnris'triktid [ˌʌn-, -rəs-]
unretentive 'ʌnri'tentiv [-rə't-]
unrevealed 'ʌnri'vi:ld [-rə'v-]
unrevoked 'ʌnri'vəukt [-rə'v-]
unrewarded 'ʌnri'wɔ:did [ˌʌn-, -rə'w-]
unrighteous, -ly, -ness ʌn'raitʃəs [*rarely* -tjəs], -li, -nis
unright|ful, -fully, -fulness 'ʌn'rait|ful [ʌn-], -fuli [-fəli], -fulnis
unripe 'ʌn'raip [*also* 'ʌnr-, ʌn'r-, *according to sentence-stress*]
unripeness 'ʌn'raipnis [ʌn-]
unrivalled ʌn'raivəld
unrob|e, -es, -ing, -ed 'ʌn'rəub [ʌn-], -z, -iŋ, -d
unroll, -s, -ing, -ed 'ʌn'rəul [ʌn-], -z, -iŋ, -d
unromantic, -ally 'ʌnrə'mæntik [ˌʌn-, -rəu'm-], -əli
unrop|e, -es, -ing, -ed 'ʌn'rəup [ʌn-], -s, -iŋ, -t
unruffled 'ʌn'rʌfld [ʌn-]
unrul|y, -ier, -iest, -iness ʌn'ru:l|i, -lə* [-jə*], -iist [-jist], -inis
unsadd|le, -les, -ling, -led 'ʌn'sæd|l [ʌn-], -lz, -liŋ [-liŋ], -ld
unsafe, -ly, -ness 'ʌn'seif [ʌn-], -li, -nis
unsaid 'ʌn'sed [ʌn'sed]
unsal(e)able, -ness 'ʌn'seiləbl [ʌn-], -nis
unsalted 'ʌn'sɔ:ltid [-'sɔl-]
unsanctified 'ʌn'sæŋktifaid
unsanitary 'ʌn'sænitəri [ʌn-]
unsatisfactor|y, -ily, -iness 'ʌnˌsætis-'fæktər|i [ˌʌn-s-], -ili, -inis

unsatisf|ied, -ying, 'ʌn'sætisf|aid, -aiiŋ
unsavour|y,-ily,-iness'ʌn'seivər|i[ʌn-],
-ili, -inis
uns|ay, -ays, -aying, -aid 'ʌn's|ei
['ʌn-s|ei], -ez, -eiiŋ, -ed
unscalable 'ʌn'skeiləbl [ʌn-]
unscathed 'ʌn'skeiðd [ʌn-, -eiθt]
unscented 'ʌn'sentid [in contrast 'ʌn,s-]
unscholarly 'ʌn'skoləli
unscientific 'ʌn,sai-ən'tifik [,ʌn-s-]
unscr|ew, -ews, -ewing, -ewed 'ʌn-
'skr|u: [ʌn-], -u:z, -u(:)iŋ, -u:d
unscriptur|al, -ally 'ʌn'skriptʃər|əl
[ʌn-, -tʃur-], -əli
unscrupulous ʌn'skru:pjuləs ['ʌn's-,
-pjəl-]
unscrupulous|ly, -ness ʌn'skru:pjuləs|li
[-pjəl-], -nis
unseal, -s, -ing, -ed 'ʌn'si:l [ʌn-], -z, -iŋ,
-d
unsearchab|le, -ly, -leness ʌn'sə:tʃəb|l,
-li, -lnis
unseasonab|le, -ly, -leness ʌn'si:znəb|l
['ʌn's-, -znə-], -li, -lnis
unseasoned 'ʌn'si:znd [also '-,-- when
attributive]
unseat, -s, -ing, -ed 'ʌn'si:t [ʌn-], -s, -iŋ,
-id
unseaworth|y, -iness 'ʌn'si:,wə:ð|i [ʌn-],
-inis
unsectarian, -ism 'ʌn-sek'tɛərɪən [,ʌn-],
-izəm
unsecured 'ʌn-si'kjuəd [-sə'k-, -'kjɔəd,
-'kjɔ:d, -'kjə:d]
unseeing 'ʌn'si:iŋ [ʌn-]
unseeml|y, -iness ʌn'si:ml|i, -inis
unseen 'ʌn'si:n [also 'ʌn-s-, ʌn's-,
according to sentence-stress]
unselfish, -ly, -ness 'ʌn'selfiʃ [ʌn-], -li,
-nis
unsensational 'ʌn-sen'seiʃənl [,ʌn-s-,
-sən-, -ʃnəl, -ʃnl, -ʃnl, -ʃənəl]
unsensitive 'ʌn'sensitiv ['ʌn's-, -sət-]
unsentimental 'ʌn,senti'mentl
unserviceable ʌn'sə:visəbl [ʌn-]
unsett|le, -les, -ling, -led 'ʌn'set|l [ʌn-],
-lz, -liŋ [-liŋ], -ld
unsevered 'ʌn'sevəd [ʌn-]
unshack|le, -les, -ling, -led 'ʌn'ʃæk|l
[ʌn-], -lz, -liŋ [-liŋ], -ld
unshakable ʌn'ʃeikəbl
unshaken 'ʌn'ʃeikən [ʌn-]
unshapely 'ʌn'ʃeipli [ʌn-]
unshaven 'ʌn'ʃeivn
unsheath|e, -es, -ing, -ed 'ʌn'ʃi:ð [ʌn-],
-z, -iŋ, -d
unship, -s, -ping, -ped 'ʌn'ʃip [ʌn-], -s,
-iŋ, -t

un|shod, -shorn 'ʌn|'ʃɔd, -'ʃɔ:n
unshrinkable 'ʌn'ʃriŋkəbl [ʌn-]
unshrinking, -ly ʌn'ʃriŋkiŋ, -li
unsighted 'ʌn'saitid [ʌn-]
unsightl|y, -ier, -iest, -iness ʌn'saitl|i,
-ɪə* [-jə*], -iist [-jist], -inis
unsigned 'ʌn'saind [also 'ʌn-saind when
attributive]
unskil|ful, -fully, -fulness 'ʌn'skil|ful
[ʌn-], -fuli [-fəli], -fulnis
unskilled 'ʌn'skild [also 'ʌn-skild when
attributive
unslaked 'ʌn'sleikt
unsociability 'ʌn,səuʃə'biliti [-lət-]
unsociab|le, -ly, -leness ʌn'səuʃəb|l
['ʌn's-], -li, -lnis
unsold 'ʌn'səuld [also 'ʌn-səuld when
attributive]
unsolder, -s, -ing, -ed 'ʌn'sɔldə* [-'sɔ:d-,
-'sɔd-, -'səuld-], -z, -riŋ, -d
unsolicited 'ʌn-sə'lisitid [,ʌn-]
unsolved 'ʌn'sɔlvd [also 'ʌn-s-, ʌn's-,
according to sentence-stress]
unsophisticated, -ly, -ness 'ʌn-sə'fis-
tikeitid [,ʌn-], -li, -nis
unsophistication 'ʌn-sə,fisti'keiʃən
unsorted 'ʌn'sɔ:tid
unsought 'ʌn'sɔ:t [ʌn's- in unsought for]
unsoun|d, -dly, -dness 'ʌn'saun|d, -dli,
-dnis
unsparing, -ly, -ness ʌn'spɛəriŋ, -li, -nis
unspeakab|le, -ly ʌn'spi:kəb|l, -li
unspecified 'ʌn'spesifaid [ʌn-]
unspent 'ʌn'spent [also 'ʌn-spent when
attributive]
unspoiled 'ʌn'spoilt [-ld]
unspoilt 'ʌn'spoilt
unspoken 'ʌn'spəukən [ʌn-]
unsporting 'ʌn'spɔ:tiŋ
unsportsmanlike'ʌn'spɔ:tsmənlaik[ʌn-]
unspotted 'ʌn'spɔtid [ʌn-]
unstability 'ʌn-stə'biliti [,ʌn-, -lət-]
unstable, -ness 'ʌn'steibl [ʌn-], -nis
unstack, -s, -ing, -ed 'ʌn'stæk [ʌn-], -s,
-iŋ, -t
unstamped 'ʌn'stæmpt ['ʌn-stæmpt
when attributive]
unstarched 'ʌn'sta:tʃt
unstatesmanlike 'ʌn'steitsmənlaik [ʌn-]
unsteadfast, -ly, -ness 'ʌn'stedfəst
[ʌn-], -li, -nis
unstead|y, -ier, -iest, -ily, -iness
'ʌn'sted|i [ʌn-], -ɪə*, -iist, -ili, -inis
un|stick, -sticks, -sticking, -stuck 'ʌn|-
'stik [ʌn-], -'stiks, -'stikiŋ, -'stʌk
unstinted ʌn'stintid
unstitch, -es, -ing, -ed 'ʌn'stitʃ [ʌn-],
-iz, -iŋ, -t

unstop, -s, -ping, -ped 'ʌn'stɔp [ʌn-], -s, -iŋ, -t

unstrap, -s, -ping, -ped 'ʌn'stræp [ʌn-], -s, -iŋ, -t

unstressed 'ʌn'strest [also 'ʌn-strest when attributive]

unstrung 'ʌn'strʌŋ [ʌn-]

unstudied 'ʌn'stʌdid [ʌn- when not attributive]

unsub|duable, -dued 'ʌn-səb|'dju(:)əbl [,ʌn-], -'dju:d

unsubmissive, -ly, -ness 'ʌn-səb'misiv [,ʌn-], -li, -nis

unsubstantial 'ʌn-səb'stænʃəl [,ʌn-, -bz't-]

unsubstantiality 'ʌn-səb,stænʃi'æliti [-bz,t-]

unsuccess 'ʌn-sək'ses ['ʌn-sək,ses]

unsuccess|ful, -fully, -fulness 'ʌn-sək-'ses|ful [,ʌn-], -fuli [-fəli], -fulnis

unsuitability 'ʌn,sju:tə'biliti [,ʌn-sju:-, 'ʌn,su:-, ,ʌn-su:-, -lət-]

unsuitab|le, -ly, -leness 'ʌn'sju:təb|l [ʌn-, -'su:-], -li, -nis

unsuited 'ʌn'sju:tid [ʌn-, -'su:-]

unsullied 'ʌn'sʌlid [ʌn-]

unsung 'ʌn'sʌŋ [ʌn-]

unsupportab|le, -ly, -leness 'ʌn-sə'pɔ:təb|l [,ʌn-], -li, -lnis

unsupported 'ʌn-sə'pɔ:tid

unsurmountable 'ʌn-sə(:)'mauntəbl [,ʌn-]

unsurpass|able, -ed 'ʌn-sə(:)'pɑ:s|əbl [,ʌn-], -t

unsusceptibility 'ʌn-sə,septə'biliti [-ti'b-, -lət-]

unsusceptible 'ʌn-sə'septəbl [,ʌn-, -tib-]

unsuspected, -ly, -ness 'ʌn-səs'pektid [,ʌn-], -li, -nis

unsuspecting, -ly, -ness 'ʌn-səs'pektiŋ [,ʌn-], -li, -nis

unsuspicious, -ly, -ness 'ʌn-səs'piʃəs [,ʌn-], -li, -nis

unsweetened 'ʌn'swi:tnd [also 'ʌn,s- when attributive]

unswerving, -ly ʌn'swə:viŋ, -li

unsymmetric, -al, -ally 'ʌn-si'metrik [,ʌn-], -əl, -əli

unsymmetry 'ʌn'simitri

unsympathetic, -ally 'ʌn,simpə'θetik, -əli

unsystematic, -al, -ally 'ʌn,sisti'mætik [,ʌn-sis-], -əl, -əli

untainted 'ʌn'teintid [ʌn-]

untamable 'ʌn'teiməbl [ʌn-]

untang|le, -les, -ling, -led 'ʌn'tæŋg|l [ʌn-], -lz, -liŋ [-liŋ], -ld

untarnished 'ʌn'tɑ:niʃt [ʌn-]

untasted 'ʌn'teistid

untaught 'ʌn'tɔ:t [also 'ʌn-tɔ:t when attributive]

untaxed 'ʌn'tækst [also 'ʌn-tækst when attributive]

unteachable 'ʌn'ti:tʃəbl [ʌn-]

untempered 'ʌn'tempəd [also 'ʌn,t- when attributive]

untenable 'ʌn'tenəbl [ʌn-, -'ti:n-]

untenanted 'ʌn'tenəntid

unthank|ful, -fully, -fulness 'ʌn'θæŋk|-ful [ʌn-], -fuli [-fəli], -fulnis

unthinkable ʌn'θiŋkəbl

unthinking 'ʌn'θiŋkiŋ [ʌn-]

unthinkingly ʌn'θiŋkiŋli

unthought|ful, -fully, -fulness 'ʌn-'θɔ:t|ful [ʌn-], -fuli [-fəli], -fulnis

unthought of ʌn'θɔ:tɔv

unthread, -s, -ing, -ed 'ʌn'θred, -z, -iŋ, -id

unthrift|y, -ily, -iness 'ʌn'θrifti [ʌn-], -ili, -inis

untid|y (adj. v.), -ier, -iest, -ily, -iness, -ies, -ying, -ied ʌn'taidi ['ʌn't-], -iə* [-jə*], -iist [-jist], -ili, -inis; -iz, -iiŋ [-jiŋ], -id

un|tie, -ties, -tying, -tied 'ʌn|'tai, -'taiz, -'taiiŋ, -'taid

until ən'til ['ʌn'til, n'til, also occasionally 'ʌntil, 'ʌntl when followed by a stress]

untimel|y, -iness ʌn'taiml|i, -inis

untinged 'ʌn'tindʒd

untiring, -ly ʌn'taiəriŋ, -li

unto 'ʌntu [-tu:, -tə]

  Note.—The form 'ʌntu: occurs chiefly in final position; the form 'ʌntə occurs only before consonants.

untold 'ʌn'təuld [ʌn't-, also occasionally 'ʌn-təuld when attributive]

untouchable, -s ʌn'tʌtʃəbl ['ʌn't-], -z

untouched 'ʌn'tʌtʃt [ʌn-]

untoward, -ly, -ness ʌn'təuəd ['ʌn-'təuəd, ,ʌn-tə'wɔ:d, ,ʌn-tu'wɔ:d, -tə-'wɔ:d, 'ʌn-tu'wɔ:d], -li, -nis

untraceable 'ʌn'treisəbl [ʌn-]

untrained 'ʌn'treind [also 'ʌn-t-, ʌn't-, according to sentence-stress]

untrammelled ʌn'træməld

untransferable 'ʌn-træns'fə:rəbl [-trɑ:ns-]

untranslat|able, -ed 'ʌntræns'leit|əbl [-trɑ:ns-, -trænz-, -trɑ:nz-, -trəns-, -trənz-], -id

untried 'ʌn'traid [also 'ʌn-traid when attributive]

untrimmed 'ʌn'trimd [also 'ʌn-trimd when attributive]

untrodden 'ʌn'trɔdn [ʌn-, also 'ʌn,t- when attributive]

untroubled 'ʌn'trʌbld [ʌn-]
un|true, -trueness 'ʌn|'truː [ʌn-], -'truː:-nis
untruly 'ʌn'truːli [ʌn-]
untrustworth|y, -ily, -iness 'ʌn'trʌst-ˌwəːð|i [ʌn-], -ili, -inis
untru|th, -ths 'ʌn'truː|θ [ʌn-], -ðz [-θs]
untruth|ful, -fully, -fulness 'ʌn'truːθ|-fʊl [ʌn-], -fuli [-fəli], -fʊlnis
untuck, -s, -ing, -ed 'ʌn'tʌk [ʌn-], -s, -iŋ, -t
unturned 'ʌn'təːnd [ʌn-]
untutored 'ʌn'tjuːtəd
untwist, -s, -ing, -ed 'ʌn'twist [ʌn-], -s, -iŋ, -id
unused (not made use of) 'ʌn'juːzd [ʌn-]
unused (not accustomed) 'ʌn'juːst [ʌn-, rarely -'juːzd]
unu|sual, -sually, -sualness ʌn'juː|ʒŭəl ['ʌn'j-, -ʒwəl, -ʒul, -ʒəl], -ʒŭəli [-ʒwəli, -ʒuli, -ʒəli, -ʒli], -ʒŭəlnis [-ʒwəlnis, -ʒulnis, -ʒəlnis]
unutterab|le, -ly, -leness ʌn'ʌtərəb|l, -li, -lnis
unuttered 'ʌn'ʌtəd
unvaccinated 'ʌn'væksineitid
unvariable ʌn'vɛərĭəbl ['ʌn'v-]
unvaried ʌn'vɛərid
unvarnished (not varnished) 'ʌn'vɑːniʃt [ʌn-], (simple) ʌn'vɑːniʃt
unvarying ʌn'vɛəriiŋ
unveil, -s, -ing, -ed, -er/s ʌn'veil ['ʌn'v-], -z, -iŋ, -d, -ə*/z
unventilated 'ʌn'ventileitid [ʌn-]
unversed 'ʌn'vəːst [ʌn-]
unvoic|e, -es, -ing, -ed 'ʌn'vɔis, -iz, -iŋ, -t [also 'ʌn'vɔist when attributive]
unwanted 'ʌn'wɒntid [also 'ʌn,w- when attributive]
unwari|ly, -ness ʌn'wɛəri|li, -nis
unwarlike 'ʌn'wɔːlaik [ʌn-]
unwarmed 'ʌn'wɔːmd [also 'ʌnw-when attributive]
unwarned 'ʌn'wɔːnd
unwarrantab|le, -ly, -leness ʌn'wɔrənt-əb|l, -li, -lnis
unwarranted (not guaranteed) 'ʌn-'wɔrəntid
unwarranted (unjustified) ʌn'wɔrəntid
unwary ʌn'wɛəri ['ʌn'w-]
unwashed 'ʌn'wɒʃt [also 'ʌnw- when attributive]
unwavering, -ly ʌn'weivəriŋ, -li
unwearable 'ʌn'wɛərəbl [ʌn-]
unwearied ʌn'wiərid
unwearying ʌn'wiəriiŋ
unwed 'ʌn'wed
unwelcome ʌn'welkəm ['ʌn'w-]

unwell 'ʌn'wel [ʌn-]
unwholesome, -ly, -ness 'ʌn'həulsəm [ʌn-], -li, -nis
unwield|y, -ier, -iest, -ily, -iness ʌn-'wiːld|i, -ĭə* [-jə*], -iist [-jist], -ili, -inis
unwilling 'ʌn'wiliŋ [ʌn-]
unwilling|ly, -ness ʌn'wiliŋ|li, -nis
Unwin 'ʌnwin
un|wind, -winds, -winding, -wound 'ʌn|'waind [ʌn-], -'waindz, -'waindiŋ, -'waund
unwiped 'ʌn'waipt
unwisdom 'ʌn'wizdəm
unwise 'ʌn'waiz [also 'ʌnw-, ʌn'w-, according to sentence-stress]
unwisely 'ʌn'waizli [ʌn-]
unwished for ʌn'wiʃtfɔ:* ['ʌn'w-]
unwitting, -ly ʌn'witiŋ, -li
unwoman|ly, -liness ʌn'wumən|li ['ʌn'w-], -linis
unwonted, -ly, -ness ʌn'wəuntid, -li, -nis
unworkable 'ʌn'wəːkəbl [ʌn-]
unworkmanlike 'ʌn'wəːkmənlaik [ʌn-]
unworn 'ʌn'wɔːn ['ʌnw- when attributive]
unworth|y, -ily, -iness ʌn'wəːð|i ['ʌn'w-], -ili, -inis
unwound (from unwind) 'ʌn'waund [ʌn-]
unwounded 'ʌn'wuːndid
unwrap, -s, -ping, -ped 'ʌn'ræp [ʌn-], -s, -iŋ, -t
unwritten 'ʌn'ritn [also 'ʌn,r- when attributive]
unwrought 'ʌn'rɔːt
Unyamwezi ˌunjæm'weizi [-jɑ:'mw-]
Unyanyembe ˌunjæn'jembi [-jɑ:'nj-]
unyielding, -ly, -ness ʌn'jiːldiŋ ['ʌn'j-], -li, -nis
unyok|e, -es, -ing, -ed 'ʌn'jəuk [ʌn-], -s, -iŋ, -t
up ʌp
up-and-down 'ʌpən'daun
Upanishad, -s u'pʌniʃəd [-'pæn-] (Hind. wpənyʃəd), -z
upas, -es 'juːpəs, -iz
upbraid, -s, -ing, -ed ʌp'breid, -z, -iŋ, -id
upbringing 'ʌp,briŋiŋ
upcast, -s 'ʌpkɑ:st, -s
Upcott 'ʌpkət [-kɔt]
upcountry (s. adj.) 'ʌp'kʌntri, (adv.) ʌp'kʌntri
Upernavik uː'pəːnəvik
Upham 'ʌpəm
upharsin juː'fɑːsin [uː-]
upheav|e, -es, -ing, -ed; -al/s ʌp'hiːv, -z, -iŋ, -d; -əl/z

upheld (*from* uphold) ʌp'held
uphill 'ʌp'hil ['ʌph-, ʌp'h-, *according to sentence-stress*]
up|hold, -holds, -holding, -held, -holder/s ʌp|'həuld, -'həuldz, -'həuldiŋ, -'held, -'həuldə*/z
upholst|er, -ers, -ering, -ered, -erer/s; -ery ʌp'həulst|ə* [əp-], -əz, -əriŋ, -əd, -ərə*/z; -əri
Upjohn 'ʌpdʒɔn
upkeep 'ʌpki:p
upland, -s; -er/s 'ʌplənd, -z; -ə*/z
uplift (s.) 'ʌplift
uplift (v.), -s, -ing, -ed ʌp'lift, -s, -iŋ, -id
Upminster 'ʌp,minstə*
upon ə'pɔn (*strong form*), əpən (*weak form*)
upper (s. adj.), -s; -most 'ʌpə*, -z; -məust [-məst]
uppercut, -s 'ʌpəkʌt, -s
Uppingham 'ʌpiŋəm
uppish, -ly, -ness 'ʌpiʃ, -li, -nis
Uppsala 'ʌpsɑːlə [,up-, ʌp's-, up's-]
uprais|e, -es, -ing, -ed ʌp'reiz, -iz, -iŋ, -d ['ʌp'reizd *when attributive*]
uprear, -s, -ing, -ed ʌp'riə*, -z, -riŋ, -d
Uprichard ju:'pritʃɑːd [-tʃəd], ʌp'ritʃəd
upright (s.), -s 'ʌp-rait, -s
upright (adj.) (honest) 'ʌp-rait ['ʌp'r-]
upright (adj. adv.) (erect) 'ʌp'rait [*also* -ʌp-r-, ʌp'r-, *according to sentence-stress*]
upright|ly, -ness 'ʌp,rait|li [ʌp'r-, 'ʌp'r-], -nis
uprising, -s ʌp'raiziŋ ['ʌp'r-, 'ʌp,raiziŋ],
uproar, -s 'ʌp,rɔː* [-rɔə*], -z   [-z
uproarious, -ly, -ness ʌp'rɔːriəs [-'rɔər-], -li, -nis
uproot, -s, -ing, -ed ʌp'ru:t, -s, -iŋ, -id
Upsala 'ʌpsɑːlə ['up-, ʌp's-, up's-]
upset (s.), -s ʌp'set ['ʌpset], -s
upset (adj., in upset price) 'ʌpset
upset (v.), -s, -ting, -ter/s ʌp'set, -s, -iŋ, -ə*/z
Upsher 'ʌpʃə*
upshot 'ʌpʃɔt
upside, -s 'ʌpsaid, -z
upside-down 'ʌpsaid'daun
upsilon, -s ju:p'sailən [up's-, 'ju:psilən], -z
upstairs 'ʌp'stɛəz ['ʌp-s-, ʌp's-, *according to sentence-stress*]
upstart, -s 'ʌp-stɑːt, -s
upstream 'ʌp'stri:m ['ʌp-stri:m]
upstroke, -s 'ʌp-strəuk, -s
upsurge (s.), -s 'ʌp-sə:dʒ, -iz
upsurg|e (v.), -es, -ing, -ed ʌp'sə:dʒ, -iz, -iŋ, -d

uptake, -s 'ʌpteik, -s
upthrust, -s 'ʌp'θrʌst ['ʌp-θrʌst], -s
uptilt, -s, -ing, -ed ʌp'tilt, -s, -iŋ, -id
Upton 'ʌptən
uptown 'ʌp'taun [ʌp't- *when preceded by a stress*]
upturn, -s, -ing, -ed ʌp'tə:n, -z, -iŋ, -d
upturned (adj.) 'ʌp'tə:nd ['ʌpt-, ʌp't-, *according to sentence-stress*]
upward, -ly, -s 'ʌpwəd, -li, -z
Upwey 'ʌpwei
ur (interj.), ʌ:, ə:
Ur ə:* [uə*]
uraemia juə'ri:mjə [ju'r-, jə'r-, jɔə'r-, jɔ:'r-, -mïə]
Ural 'juərəl ['jɔər-, 'jɔ:r-]
uralite 'juərəlait ['jɔər-, 'jɔ:r-, 'jə:r-]
Urania, -n juə'reinjə [ju'r-, jə'r-, jɔə'r-, jɔ:'r-, -nïə], -n
uranium ju'reinjəm [juə'r-, jə'r-, jɔə'r-, jɔ:'r-, -nïəm]
Uranus 'juərənəs ['jɔər-, 'jɔ:r-, juə'reinəs]
urate, -s 'juəreit ['jɔər-, 'jɔ:r-, -rit], -s
urban (U.) 'ə:bən
Urbana ə:'bænə [-'bɑ:n-]
urbane (U.), -ly ə:'bein, -li
urbanity ə:'bæniti
urbanization ,ə:bənai'zeiʃən
urbaniz|e, -es, -ing, -ed 'ə:bənaiz, -iz, -iŋ, -d
Urbevilles 'ə:bəvilz
urchin, -s 'ə:tʃin, -z
Urdu 'uədu: ['ə:d-, '-'-, -'-] (Hind. wrdu)
Ure juə*
urea, -l 'juərïə ['jɔər-, 'jɔ:r-, juə'riə], -l
urethra, -s juə'ri:θrə [ju'r-], -z
uretic (s. adj.), -s juə'retik [ju'r-, jə'r-], -s
urg|e (s. v.), -es, -ing, -ed, -er/s ə:dʒ, -iz, -iŋ, -d, -ə*/z
urgen|cy, -t/ly 'ə:dʒən|si, -t/li
Uriah juə'raiə [ju'r-, jə'r-]
uric 'juərik ['jɔər-, 'jɔ:r-]
Uriel 'juərïəl ['jɔər-, 'jɔ:r-]
Urim 'juərim ['jɔər-, 'jɔ:r-, 'uər-]
urin|al, -als, -ary 'juərin|l ['jɔər-, 'jɔ:r-, 'jə:r-, juə'rainl, jə'r-], -lz, -əri
urinat|e, -es, -ing, -ed 'juərineit ['jɔər-, 'jɔ:r-, 'jə:r-], -s, -iŋ, -id
urination ,juəri'neiʃən [,jɔər-, ,jɔ:r-, ,jə:r-]
urine, -s 'juərin ['jɔər-, 'jɔ:r-, 'jə:r-], -z
Urmia 'ə:mjə ['uəm-, -mïə]
urn, -s ə:n, -z
Urquhart 'ə:kət
Ursa (constellation) 'ə:sə
ursine 'ə:sain
Ursula 'ə:sjulə [rarely 'ə:ʃju-, 'ə:ʃu-]

Ursuline 'əːsjulain [-lin]
urtica 'əːtikə
urticaria ˌəːti'kɛərɪə
Uruguay 'urugwai ['jur-, 'juər-, 'jəːr-, -rəg-, ˌ—'—, old-fashioned 'urugwei, 'jurugwei, 'juərugwei, -rəg-]
Uruguayan, -s ˌuru'gwai-ən [ˌjuər-, ˌjur-, ˌjəːr-, -rə'g, old-fashioned -'gweiən], -z
Urumiah u'ruːmjə [-mɪə]
urus 'juərəs ['jɔər-, 'jɔːr-]
us ʌs (strong form), əs, s (weak forms)
usable 'juːzəbl
usage, -s 'juːzidʒ ['juːsi-], -iz
usance, -s 'juːzəns, -iz
use (s.), -s juːs, -iz
us|e (v.) (make use of), -es, -ing, -ed, -er/s juːz, -iz, -iŋ, -d, -ə*/z
used (adj.) (accustomed) juːst [rarely juːzd]
used (from use v.) juːzd
used (v.) (was or were accustomed) juːst (when followed by to), juːst (when not followed by to) [rarely juːzd]
use(d)n't 'juːsnt (when followed by to), 'juːsnt (when not followed by to)
use|ful, -fully, -fulness 'juːs|fʊl, -fuli [-fəli], -fʊlnis
useless, -ly, -ness 'juːslis, -li, -nis
usen't 'juːsnt (when followed by to), 'juːsnt (when not followed by to)
user, -s 'juːzə*, -z
uses (plur. of use s.) 'juːsiz
uses (from use v.) 'juːziz
Ushant 'ʌʃənt
usher (s. v.) (U.), -s, -ing, -ed 'ʌʃə*, -z, -riŋ, -d
usherette, -s ˌʌʃə'ret, -s
usquebaugh, -s 'ʌskwibɔː, -z
Ustinov 'juːstinɔf [-ɔv]
u|sual, -sually, -sualness 'juː|ʒŭəl [ʒwəl, -ʒul, -ʒəl], -ʒŭəli [-ʒwəli, -ʒuli, -ʒəli, -ʒli], -ʒŭəlnis [-ʒwəlnis, -ʒulnis, -ʒəlnis]
usufruct, -s 'juːsju(ː)frʌkt ['juːzj-], -s
usurer, -s 'juːʒərə*, -z

usurious, -ly, -ness juː'zjuərɪəs ['juz-, -'zjɔər-, -'zjɔːr-, ju(ː)'ʒuə-], -li, -nis
usurp, -s, -ing, -ed, -er/s juː'zəːp [ju'z-], -s, -iŋ, -t, -ə*/z
usurpation, -s ˌjuːzəː'peiʃən, -z
usury 'juːʒuri [-ʒəri, -ʒuəri]
Utah 'juːtɑ: [or -tɔ: as in U.S.A.]
utensil, -s ju(ː)'tensl [-sil], -z
uterine 'juːtərain
uter|us, -i, -uses 'juːtər|əs, -ai, -əsiz
Uther 'juːθə*
Uthwatt 'ʌθwɔt
Utica 'juːtikə
utilitarian (s. adj.), -s, -ism ˌjuːtili'tɛərɪən [ju(ː),tili't-], -z, -izəm
utility ju(ː)'tiliti
utilization ˌjuːtilai'zeiʃən [-li'z-]
utiliz|e [-is|e], -es, -ing, -ed, -er/s; -able 'juːtilaiz, -iz, -iŋ, -d, -ə*/z; -əbl
utmost 'ʌtməust [-məst]
Utopia, -n/s juː'təupjə [ju't-, -pɪə]
Utrecht 'juːtrekt [-trext, -'-]   [-n/z
utricle, -s 'juːtrikl, -z
utter (adj. v.), -ly, -ness; -s, -ing, -ed, -er/s; -able 'ʌtə*, -li, -nis; -z, -riŋ, -d, -rə*/z; -rəbl
utterance, -s 'ʌtərəns, -iz
uttermost 'ʌtəməust [-məst]
Uttoxeter juː'tɔksitə* [ʌ'tɔksitə*, 'ʌksitə*]
   Note.—'ʌksitə* is the pronunciation used by those connected with Denstone College and by members of county families in the neighbourhood. The common pronunciation in the town is juː'tɔksitə* or ʌ'tɔksitə*. The former is more frequent, and is the pronunciation of most outsiders.
uvula, -s 'juːvjulə [-jəl-], -z
uvular 'juːvjulə* [-jəl-]
Uxbridge 'ʌksbridʒ
uxorious ʌk'sɔːrɪəs
Uzzah 'ʌzə
Uzzell 'ʌzl
Uzziah ʌ'zai-ə

V

V (*the letter*), -**'s** viː, -z
v. (*versus*) viː ['vəːsəs], (*vide*) viː [siː, 'videi, 'vaidi]
vac, -s væk, -s
vacanc|y, -ies 'veikəns|i, -iz
vacant, -ly 'veikənt, -li
vacat|e, -es, -ing, -ed və'keit [vei'k-], -s, -iŋ, -id
vacation, -s və'keiʃən, -z
vaccinat|e, -es, -ing, -ed, -or/s 'væksineit [-ksn̩eit], -s, -iŋ, -id, -ə*/z
vaccination, -s ˌvæksi'neiʃən [-ksn̩'ei-], -z
vaccine 'væksiːn [-sin]
Vachel(l) 'veitʃəl
Vacher 'væʃə*, 'veitʃə*
vacillat|e, -es, -ing/ly, -ed, -or/s 'væsileit, -s, -iŋ/li, -id, -ə*/z
vacillation ˌvæsi'leiʃən
vacuity væ'kjuː(ː)iti [və'k-]
vacuo (*in in vacuo*) 'vækjuəu
vacuous, -ness 'vækjuəs [-kjwəs], -nis
vacuum, -s 'vækjŭəm [-kjwəm, -kjum], -z
vacuum-cleaner, -s 'vækjŭəmˌkliːnə* [-kjwəm-, -kjum-], -z
vade-mecum, -s 'veidi'miːkəm [-kʌm, 'vɑːdi'meikum], -z
vagabond (*s. adj*), -**s** 'vægəbɔnd [-bənd], -z
vagabondage 'vægəbɔndidʒ
vagar|y, -ies 'veigər|i [və'gɛər-], -iz
vagin|a/s, -al və'dʒain|ə/z, -əl
vagrancy 'veigrənsi
vagrant (*s. adj*.), -**s, -ly** 'veigrənt, -s, -li
vague, -r, -st, -ly, -ness veig, -ə*, -ist, -li, -nis
vail (**V.**), -**s, -ing, -ed** veil, -z, -iŋ, -d
Vaile veil
vain, -er, -est, -ly, -ness vein, -ə*, -ist, -li, -nis
vainglorious, -ly, -ness vein'glɔːrɪəs, -li, -nis
vainglory vein'glɔːri
Valais 'vælei (valɛ)
valance, -s, -d 'væləns, -iz, -t
vale (*s.*) (**V.**), -**s** veil, -z
vale (*good-bye*) 'veili ['vælei, 'vɑː-]

valediction, -s ˌvæli'dikʃən, -z
valedictory ˌvæli'diktəri
valence (*damask, short curtain*), -**s, -d** 'væləns, -iz, -t
valence (*in chemistry*) 'veiləns
Valencia -s və'lenʃɪə [-ʃjə, -ʃə, -sɪə, -sjə], -z
Valenciennes ˌvælənsi'en [-lɑ̃ːns-, -lɔ̃ːns-, -lɑːns-, -lɔːns-, -si'enz, -'sjen, -'sjenz] (valɑ̃sjɛn)
Note.—There was formerly a pronunciation ˌvælən'siːnz, which is now probably obsolete.
valenc|y, -ies 'veiləns|i, -iz
valentine, -s 'væləntain, -z
Valentine (*Christian name*) 'væləntain, -tain
Valentinian ˌvælən'tinɪən [-njən]
Valera və'leərə
valerian (**V.**), -**s** və'liərɪən, -z
Valerius və'liərɪəs
valet (*s.*), -**s** 'vælit, -s ['væli, 'vælei, -z]
valet (*v.*), -**s, -ing, -ed** 'vælit, -s, -iŋ, -id
valetudinarian, -s, -ism 'væliˌtjuːdi-'nɛərɪən [ˌvælitjud-], -z, -izəm
Valhalla væl'hælə
valiant, -ly, -ness 'væljənt, -li, -nis
valid, -ly, -ness 'vælid, -li, -nis
validat|e, -es, -ing, -ed 'vælideit, -s, -iŋ, -id
validation ˌvæli'deiʃən
validit|y, -ies və'lidit|i [væ'l-], -iz
valise, -s və'liːz [væ'l-, -iːs], -iz
Valkyrie, -s væl'kiəri ['vælkiri], -z
Valladolid ˌvælədəu'lid [-dɔ'l-] (baʎadoˈli)
Valletta və'letə
valley, -s 'væli, -z
Valois 'vælwɑː [-lwɔː] (valwa)
valorous, -ly 'vælərəs, -li
valour 'vælə*
Valparaiso ˌvælpə'raizəu [*old-fashioned* -'reizəu] (balparaˈiso)
Valpy 'vælpi
valse, -s vɑːls [vɔːls], -iz
valuable, -s, -ness 'væljŭəbl [-ljwəb-, -ljub-], -z, -nis
valuation, -s ˌvælju'eiʃən, -z

val|ue (s. v.), -ues, -uing, -ued, -uer/s
'væl|ju: [-ju], -ju:z [-juz], -juiŋ [-jwiŋ],
-ju:d [-jud], -jŭə*/z [-jwə*/z]
valueless 'væljulis
valve, -s vælv, -z
valvular 'vælvjulə*
vamoos|e, -es, -ing, -ed və'mu:s [-u:z],
-iz, -iŋ, və'mu:st [-u:zd]
vamp (s. v.), -s, -ing, -ed, -er/s væmp,
-s, -iŋ, -t [væmt], -ə*/z
vampire, -s 'væmpaiə*, -z
van (s. v.), -s, -ning, -ned væn, -z, -iŋ, -d
vanadium və'neidjəm [-dĭəm]
Vanbrugh 'vænbrə
  Note.—Sir John Vanbrugh, the seven-
  teenth-century dramatist and architect, is sometimes referred to as
  væn'bru:.
Vancouver væn'ku:və* [væŋ'k-]
vandal (V.), -s 'vændəl, -z
vandalism 'vændəlizəm
Vanderb|ilt, -yl 'vændəb|ilt, -ail
Van Diemen væn'di:mən
Vandyke [Van Dyck] (name of artist,
  picture by him), -s væn'daik, -s
vandyke (adj.) (brown, etc.) 'vændaik
vane (V.), -s, -d vein, -z, -d
Vanessa və'nesə
Van Eyck, -s væn'aik, -s
Vange vændʒ
van Gogh væn'gɔx [-'gɔk, -'gɔf]
vanguard, -s 'vænga:d, -z
van Homrigh væn'hɔmrig
vanilla və'nilə [vŋ'ilə]
vanish, -es, -ing, -ed 'væniʃ, -iz, -iŋ, -t
vanit|y, -ies 'vænit|i, -iz
vanquish, -es, -ing, -ed, -er/s; -able
  'væŋkwiʃ, -iz, -iŋ, -t, -ə*/z; -əbl
Vansittart væn'sitət [-ta:t]
  Note.—Lord Vansittart pronounced
  -tət.
van Straubenzee (English surname)
  ‚væn-strɔ:'benzi
vantage, -s 'va:ntidʒ, -iz
vapid, -ly, -ness 'væpid, -li, -nis
vapidity væ'piditi [və'p-]
vaporization [-isa-], -s ‚veipərai'zeiʃən
  [-ri'z-], -z
vaporiz|e [-is|e], -es, -ing, -ed, -er/s
  'veipəraiz, -iz, -iŋ, -d, -ə*/z
vaporosity ‚veipə'rɔsiti
vaporous, -ly, -ness 'veipərəs, -li, -nis
vapour (s. v.), -s, -ing/s, -ed; -y 'veipə*,
  -z, -riŋ/z, -d; -ri
vapour-ba|th, -ths 'veipəba:|θ ['--'-], -ðz
varec 'værek [-rik]
variability ‚veərĭə'biliti [-lət-]
variab|le, -ly, -leness 'veərĭəb|l, -li, -lnis

varian|ce, -t/s 'veərĭ'ən|s, -t/s
variation, -s ‚veəri'eiʃən [rarely ‚vær-], -z
varicella ‚væri'selə
varices (plur. of varix) 'værisi:z ['veər-]
varicose 'værikəus
varied 'veərid
variegat|e, -es, -ing, -ed 'veərigeit
  [rarely -rĭəg-, -riig-], -s, -iŋ, -id
variegation, -s ‚veəri'geiʃən [rarely
  -rĭə'g-, -rii'g-], -z
variet|y, -ies və'raiət|i, -iz
variform 'veərifɔ:m
variola və'rai-ələ
variole, -s 'veəriəul, -z
varioloid 'veəriəloid
variorum ‚veəri'ɔ:rəm [‚vær-]
various, -ly, -ness 'veərĭəs, -li, -nis
variphone, -s 'veərifəun, -z
varix, varices 'veəriks, 'værisi:z ['veər-]
varlet, -s 'va:lit, -s
Varley 'va:li
varmint, -s 'va:mint, -s
Varney 'va:ni
varnish (s. v.), -es, -ing, -ed, -er/s
  'va:niʃ, -iz, -iŋ, -t, -ə*/z
Varro 'værəu
varsit|y, -ies 'va:sit|i, -iz
varsovienne, -s ‚va:səuvi'en, -z
var|y, -ies, -ying, -ied 'veər|i, -iz, -iiŋ,
  -id
Vasco da Gama 'væskəudə'ga:mə
  [-da:'g-]
vascular 'væskjulə*
vascularity ‚væskju'læriti
vascul|um, -a 'væskjul|əm, -ə
vase, -s va:z [old-fashioned vɔ:z], -iz
vaseline 'væsili:n [-æs|-, -æsəl-, -æzil-,
  -æz]-, 'væsə'li:n, rarely 'va:zlin]
vaso-motor 'veizəu'məutə* ['veisəu-]
vassal, -s 'væsəl, -z
vassalage 'væsəlidʒ [-s|i-]
vast, -er, -est, -ly, -ness va:st, -ə*, -ist,
  -li, -nis
vasty 'va:sti
vat (s. v.), -s, -ting, -ted væt, -s, -iŋ, -id
vatful, -s 'vætful, -z
Vathek 'væθek
Vatican 'vætikən
vaticinat|e, -es, -ing, -ed væ'tisineit, -s,
  -iŋ, -id
vaticination, -s ‚vætisi'neiʃən [væ‚t-], -z
Vaud vəu (vo)
vaudeville (V.), -s 'vəudəvil ['vɔ:d-,
  -vi:l], -z
Vaudin (surname) 'vəudin
Vaudois (sing.) 'vəudwa: [-dwɔ:]
  (vodwa), (plur.) -z
Vaughan vɔ:n

vault (s. v.), -s, -ing/s, -ed, -er/s vɔ:lt [vɔlt], -s, -iŋ/z, -id, -ə*/z
vaunt (s. v.), -s, -ing/ly, -ed, -er/s vɔ:nt, -s, -iŋ/li, -id, -ə*/z
Vaux (English surname) vɔ:z, vɔks, vɔ:ks, vəuks, (in de Vaux) vəu
Note.—Brougham and Vaux is 'brum-ən'vɔ:ks
Vauxhall 'vɔks'hɔ:l ['vɔk'sɔ:l, also '--, -'-, according to sentence-stress]
vavasour (V.), -s 'vævəsuə*, -z
V.C., -'s 'vi:'si:, -z
V-day 'vi:dei
veal (V.), -y vi:l, -i
vector (s.), -s 'vektə* [-tɔ:*], -z
vector (v.), -s, -ing, -ed 'vektə*, -z, -riŋ, -d
vectorial vek'tɔ:riəl
Veda, -s 'veidə ['vi:d-], -z
Vedanta ve'dɑ:ntə [vi'd-, və'd-, -'dæn-] (Hind. vedanta)
vedette, -s vi'det [və'd-], -s
Vedic 'veidik ['vi:d-]
veer, -s, -ing/ly, -ed viə*, -z, -riŋ/li, -d
Vega (star) 'vi:gə, (foreign surname) 'veigə
vegetable (s. adj.), -s 'vedʒitəbl, -z
vegetal 'vedʒitl
vegetarian (s. adj.), -s, -ism ˌvedʒi-'tɛəriən, -z, -izəm
vegetat|e, -es, -ing, -ed 'vedʒiteit, -s, -iŋ, -id
vegetation, -s ˌvedʒi'teiʃən, -z
vegetative, -ly 'vedʒitətiv [-teit-], -li
vehemen|ce, -t/ly 'vi:imən|s ['vi:əm-, 'viəm-, 'vi:him-, 'vi:həm-], -t/li
vehicle, -s 'vi:ikl ['viək-], -z
vehicular vi'hikjulə* [-kjəl-]
veil (s. v.), -s, -ing/s, -ed veil, -z, -iŋ/z, -d
vein, -s, -ed ; -less, -like vein, -z, -d ; -lis, -laik
vein|y, -ier, -iest 'vein|i, -iə*, -iist
Veitch vi:tʃ
velar (s. adj.), -s 'vi:lə*, -z
velaric vi(:)'lærik
velarization [-isa], -s ˌvi:lərai'zeiʃən [-ri'z-], -z
velariz|e [-is|e], -es, -ing, -ed 'vi:ləraiz, -iz, -iŋ, -d
Velasquez (artist) vi'læskwiz [ve'l-, -kiz, -kwiθ]
veldt (V.) velt
velic 'vi:lik
velleity ve'li:iti
vellum, -s 'veləm, -z
veloce vi'ləutʃi [ve'l-, və'l-]
velocipede, -s vi'lɔsipi:d [və'l-], -z

velocit|y, -ies vi'lɔsit|i [və'l-], -iz
velours və'luə*
velum, -s 'vi:ləm, -z
velvet, -s, -ed 'velvit, -s, -id
velveteen, -s ven'velvi'ti:n [ˌ-'-'-, '---], -z
velvety 'velviti
Venables 'venəblz
ven|al, -ally 'vi:n|l, -əli
venality vi:'næliti [vi'n-]
vend, -s, -ing, -ed vend, -z, -iŋ, -id
vendee, -s ven'di: ['ven'd-], -z
vendetta, -s ven'detə, -z
vendible 'vendəbl [-dib-]
vendor, -s 'vendɔ:* [-də*], -z
veneer (s. v.), -s, -ing, -ed vi'niə* [və'n-], -z, -riŋ, -d
venerab|le, -ly, -ness 'venərəb|l, -li, -lnis
venerat|e, -es, -ing, -ed, -or/s 'venəreit, -s, -iŋ, -id, -ə*/z
veneration ˌvenə'reiʃən
venereal vi'niəriəl [və'n-, vi:'n-]
venery 'venəri
Venetian (s. adj.), -s vi'ni:ʃən [və'n-, -ʃjən, -ʃiən], -z
Venezuela, -n/s ˌvene'zweilə [ˌveni'z-, old-fashioned ˌvenezju'i:lə, ˌvenizju'i:-, viˌnezju'i:-], -n/z
vengeance 'vendʒəns
venge|ful, -fully, -fulness 'vendʒ|ful, -fuli [-fəli], -fulnis
venial, -ly, -ness 'vi:njəl [-niəl], -i, -nis
veniality ˌvi:ni'æliti
Venice 'venis
venison 'venzn [-nizn]
Venite, -s vi'naiti [ve'n-, -'ni:ti], -z
veni, vidi, vici 'veini:'vi:di:'vi:ki: [also with w for v]
Venn, -er ven, -ə*
venom, -s, -ed 'venəm, -z, -d
venomous, -ly, -ness 'venəməs, -li, -nis
venous 'vi:nəs
vent (s. v.), -s, -ing, -ed vent, -s, -iŋ, -id
ventilat|e, -es, -ing, -ed 'ventileit, -s, -iŋ, -id
ventilation ˌventi'leiʃən
ventilator, -s 'ventileitə*, -z
Ventnor 'ventnə*
ventricle, -s 'ventrikl, -z
ventricular ven'trikjulə*
ventriloquial, -ly ˌventri'ləukwiəl [-kwjəl], -i
ventriloqui|sm, -st/s ven'triləkwi|zəm, -st/s
ventriloquiz|e [-is|e], -es, -ing, -ed ven'triləkwaiz, -iz, -iŋ, -d
ventriloquy ven'triləkwi

vent|ure (*s. v.*), -ures, -uring, -ured, -urer/s 'ventʃ|ə*, -əz, -əriŋ, -əd, -ərə*/z

venturesome, -ly, -ness 'ventʃəsəm, -li, -nis

venturous, -ly, -ness 'ventʃərəs, -li, -nis

venue, -s 'venju:, -z

Venue (*in* Ben Venue) və'nju: [vi'n-]

Venus, -es 'vi:nəs, -iz

Vera 'viərə

veracious, -ly və'reiʃəs [vi'r-, ve'r-], -li

veracity və'ræsiti [vi'r-, ve'r-]

veranda(h), -s və'rændə, -z

verb, -s və:b, -z

verb|al, -ally 'və:b|əl, -əli

verbaliz|e [is|e], -es, -ing, -ed 'və:bəlaiz, -iz, -iŋ, -d

verbali|sm, -st/s 'və:bəli|zəm [-bļi-], -st/s

verbatim və:'beitim [-'bɑ:t-]

verbena, -s və(:)'bi:nə, -z

verbiage 'və:biidʒ [-bjidʒ]

verbose, -ly, -ness və:'bəus, -li, -nis

verbosity və:'bɔsiti

Vercingetorix ˌvə:sin'dʒetəriks

verdan|cy, -t/ly 'və:dən|si, -t/li

verd-antique 'və:dæn'ti:k [ˌvə:d-]

Verde və:d

Verdi 'veədi: ['və:d-, -di] ('verdi)

verdict, -s 'və:dikt, -s

verdigris 'və:digris [-gri:s]

verditer 'və:ditə*

Verdun (*in* France) 'veədʌn [-də:ŋ, -də:n, -'-] (verdœ̃), (*in* Canada) və:'dʌn

verdure 'və:dʒə* [-djə*, -djuə*]

Vere viə*

verg|e (*s. v.*), -es, -ing, -ed və:dʒ, -iz, -iŋ, -d

verger, -s 'və:dʒə*, -z

Vergil, -s 'və:dʒil, -z

veridical ve'ridikəl [vi'r-, və'r-]

verifiable 'verifai-əbl

verification, -s ˌverifi'keiʃən, -z

veri|fy, -fies, -fying, -fied, -fier/s 'veri|fai, -faiz, -faiiŋ, -faid, -fai-ə*/z [-faiə*/z]

verily 'verili

verisimilitude ˌverisi'militju:d

veritab|le, -ly 'veritəb|l, -li

verit|y (V.), -ies 'verit|i, -iz

verjuice 'və:dʒu:s

Vermeer, -s veə'miə* [və:'m-, -'meə*], -z

vermeil 'və:meil [-mil]

vermicelli ˌvə:mi'seli

vermicide, -s 'və:misaid, -z

vermicular və:'mikjulə*

vermiform 'və:mifɔ:m

vermilion, -s və'miljən [və:'m-], -z

vermin, -ous 'və:min, -əs

Vermont və:'mɔnt

vermouth, -s 'və:məθ [-mu:θ, *old-fashioned* -mu:t], -s

vernacular (*s. adj.*), -s, -ly və'nækjulə*, -z, -li

vern|al, -ally 'və:n|l, -əli

Verne (*French author*) veən [və:n] (vɛrn)

Verner (*English surname*) 'və:nə*, (*German grammarian*) 'və:nə* ['veənə*] ('vɛrnər)

Verney 'və:ni

vernier, -s 'və:njə* [-nĩə*], -z

Vernon 'və:nən

Verona vi'rəunə [və'r-, ve'r-]

veronal 'verənl

Veronese (*artist*) ˌverəu'neizi (vero'ne:ze)

veronese (*adj.*) ˌverə'ni:z [-rəu'n-, '--'-, '---]

veronica (V.), -s vi'rɔnikə [və'r-, ve'r-], -z

Verrall 'verɔ:l, 'verəl

Verrey 'veri

verruca, -s ve'ru:kə [vi'r-, və'r-], -z

verrucose ve'ru:kəus [vi'r-, və'r-]

Versailles veə'sai [və:'s-] (vɛrsɑ:j)

versant, -s 'və:sənt, -s

versatile, -ly, -ness 'və:sətail, -li, -nis

versatility ˌvə:sə'tiliti

Verschoyle 'və:skɔil

verse, -s və:s, -iz

versed və:st

verset, -s 'və:set [-sit], -s

versicle, -s 'və:sikl, -z

versification ˌvə:sifi'keiʃən

versificator, -s 'və:sifiˌkeitə*, -z

versi|fy, -fies, -fying, -fied, -fier/s 'və:si|fai, -faiz, -faiiŋ, -faid, -fai-ə*/z [-faiə*/z]

version, -s 'və:ʃən [-ʒən], -z

verso 'və:səu

verst, -s və:st, -s

Verstegan və:'sti:gən

Verstone 'və:stən

versus 'və:səs

vert (*s. adj.*) (V.), -s və:t, -s

vertebr|a, -ae 'və:tibr|ə, -i: [-ai, -ei]

vertebr|al, -ally 'və:tibr|əl, -əli

vertebrata ˌvə:ti'brɑ:tə [-'breitə]

vertebrate (*s. adj.*), -s 'və:tibrit [-breit], -s

vertebrated 'və:tibreitid

vertebration ˌvə:ti'breiʃən

vert|ex, -ices, -exes 'və:t|eks, -isi:z, -eksiz

vertic|al, -ally, -alness 'və:tik|əl, -əli, -əlnis

vertiginous vəː'tidʒinəs
vertigo 'vəːtigəu [vəː'taig-, *less commonly* vəː'tiːg-]
vertu vəː'tuː
Verulam 'veruləm
Verulami|an,   -um   ,veru'leimj|ən [-mĭ|ən], -əm
vervain 'vəːvein
verve vəːv [vɛəv]
very 'veri
Very 'viəri, 'veri
Vesey 'viːzi
Vesian 'veziən [-zjən]
vesica, -s 'vesikə [vi'saikə, 'viːsikə], -z
vesicle, -s 'vesikl, -z
Vespa 'vespə
Vespasian ves'peiʒjən [-ʒĭən, -ʒən, -zjən, -zĭən]
vesper, -s 'vespə*, -z
vespertine 'vespətain [-pəːt-]
vespiar|y, -ies 'vespĭər|i [-pjə-], -iz
vessel, -s 'vesl, -z
vest (*s. v.*), **-s, -ing, -ed** vest, -s, -iŋ, -id
vesta (**V.**), **-s** 'vestə, -z
vestal (*s. adj.*), **-s** 'vestl, -z
vestibular ves'tibjulə*
vestibule, -s, -d 'vestibjuːl, -z, -d
vestige, -s 'vestidʒ, -iz
vestigial ves'tidʒĭəl [-dʒjəl]
vestiture 'vestitʃə*
vestment, -s 'vestmənt, -s
vest-pocket, -s 'vest'pɔkit ['-,--], -s
Vestris 'vestris
vestr|y, -ies 'vestr|i, -iz
vesture, -s 'vestʃə*, -z
vesuvian (**V.**), **-s; -ite** vi'suːvjən [və's-, -'sjuː-, -vĭən], -z; -ait
Vesuvius vi'suːvjəs [və's-, -'sjuː-, -vĭəs]
vet (*s. v.*), **-s, -ting, -ted** vet, -s, -iŋ, -id
vetch, -es vetʃ, -iz
veteran (*s. adj.*), **-s** 'vetərən, -z
veterinar|y (*s. adj.*), **-ies** 'vetərinər|i ['vetnr|i], -iz
veto (*s.*), **-(e)s** 'viːtəu, -z
veto (*v.*), **-es, -ing, -ed** 'viːtəu, -z, -iŋ, -d
Vevey 'vevei ['vevi] (*in Switzerland* vəvɛ)
vex, -es, -ing, -ed veks, -iz, -iŋ, -t
vexation, -s vek'seiʃən, -z
vexatious, -ly, -ness vek'seiʃəs, -li, -nis
Vezian 'veziən [-zjən]
via [**viâ**] 'vaiə ['vai-ə]
viable 'vaiəbl ['vai-əbl]
viability ,vaiə'biliti [,vai-ə'b-, -lət-]
viaduct, -s 'vaiədʌkt [-dəkt], -s
vial, -s 'vaiəl [vail], -z
Vialls 'vaiəlz, 'vaiɔːlz
Via Mala 'viə'mɑːlə

viand, -s 'vai-ənd, -z
viaticum, -s vai'ætikəm [vi'æ-], -z
vibrant (*s. adj.*), **-s** 'vaibrənt, -s
vibrat|e, -es, -ing, -ed vai'breit ['vaib-], -s, -iŋ, -id
vibration, -s vai'breiʃən, -z
vibrational vai'breiʃənl [-ʃnəl, -ʃn̩l, -ʃnl, -ʃənəl]
vibrative vai'breitiv
vibrato, -s vi'brɑːtəu, -z
vibrator, -s vai'breitə*, -z
vibratory 'vaibrətəri [vai'breitəri]
viburnum, -s vai'bəːnəm, -z
vic (**V.**), **-s** vik, -s
vicar, -s; -age/s 'vikə*, -z; -ridʒ/iz
vicarial vai'kɛərĭəl [vi'k-]
vicarious, -ly, -ness vai'kɛərĭəs [vi'k-], -li, -nis
Vicary 'vikəri
vice (*s.*), **-s** vais, -iz
vice (*prep.*) 'vaisi
vice- (*prefix*) 'vais-
  Note.—Compounds with **vice-** *have, as a rule, double stress, and the pronunciation of those not entered below may be ascertained by referring to the simple words.*
vice-admiral, -s 'vais'ædmərəl, -z
vice-chair|man, -men 'vais'tʃɛə|mən, -mən
vice-chancellor,   -s   'vais'tʃɑːnsələ* [-slə*, -silə*], -z
vice-consul, -s 'vais'kɔnsəl, -z
vice-consulate,   -s   'vais'kɔnsjulit [vais'k-], -s
vicegerent, -s 'vais'dʒerənt [-'dʒiər-], -s
vice-president, -s 'vais'prezidənt, -s
vice-principal, -s 'vais'prinsəpəl [-sip-], -z
viceregal   'vais'riːgəl [vais'r-, *also* 'vais,ri:gəl *when attributive*]
vicereine, -s 'vais'rein ['vais-rein], -z
viceroy, -s 'vais-rɔi, -z
viceroyship, -s 'vais-rɔiʃip, -s
vice versa 'vaisi'vəːsə
Vichy 'viːʃi: ['viʃi] (viʃi)
vicinage 'visinidʒ
vicinity vi'siniti [vai's-]
vicious, -ly, -ness 'viʃəs, -li, -nis
vicissitude, -s vi'sisitjuːd [vai's-], -z
Vicker|s, -y 'vikə|z, -ri
Vicky 'viki
victim, -s 'viktim, -z
victimization [-isa-] ,viktimai'zeiʃən
victimiz|e [-is|e], **-es, -ing, -ed** 'viktimaiz, -iz, -iŋ, -d
victor, -s 'viktə*, -z
Victor 'viktə*

victoria (V.), -s, -n/s vik'tɔːrɪə, -z, -n/z
victorine, -s 'viktəriːn [,viktə'riːn], -z
Victorine 'viktəriːn
victorious, -ly, -ness vik'tɔːrɪəs, -li, -nis
victor|y (V.), -ies 'viktər|i, -iz
victu|al (s. v.), -als, -alling, -alled, -aller/s 'vit|l, -lz, -liŋ, -ld, -lə*/z
vicuna vi'kjuːnə [vai'k-]
vide 'vaidi(ː) ['videi]
videlicet vi'diːliset [vai'd-, vi'deiliket]
vie, vies, vying, vied vai, vaiz, 'vaiiŋ, vaid
Vienna vi'enə
Viennese ,viə'niːz [vɪə'n-]
Viet-cong 'vjet'kɔŋ [-'-]
Viet-minh 'vjet'min [-'-]
Viet-nam 'vjet'næm [-'nɑːm, -'-]
Vietnamese ,vjetnə'miːz ['--'-]
view (s. v.), -s, -ing, -ed, -er/s; -able vjuː, -z, -iŋ [vjuiŋ], -d, -ə*/z [vjuə*/z]; -əbl
Vieweg 'fiːveg
view-finder, -s 'vjuː,faində*, -z
viewless 'vjuːlis
Vigar 'vaigə*
Vigers 'vaigəz
vigil, -s 'vidʒil, -z
vigilan|ce, -t/ly 'vidʒilən|s [-dʒən-], -t/li
vigilante, -s ,vidʒi'lænti, -z
vignett|e (s. v.), -es, -ing, -ed vi'njet [-'net], -s, -iŋ, -id
Vigo (in Spain) 'viːgəu [old-fashioned 'vaigəu] ('bigo), (as name of ship) 'viːgəu, (street in London) 'vaigəu, (in Indiana) 'vaigəu ['viːgəu]
vigorous, -ly, -ness 'vigərəs, -li, -nis
vigour 'vigə*
viking (V.), -s 'vaikiŋ ['viːk-], -z
vilayet, -s vi'lɑːjet [vi'lɑːjət, vi'lai-ət, ,vilɑː'jet], -s
vile, -r, -st, -ly, -ness vail, -ə*, -ist, -li, -nis
vilification ,vilifi'keiʃən
vili|fy, -fies, -fying, -fied, -fier/s 'vili|-fai, -faiz, -faiiŋ, -faid, -faiə*/z [-fai-ə*/z]
villa (V.), -s 'vilə, -z
village, -s 'vilidʒ, -iz
villager, -s 'vilidʒə*, -z
villain, -s 'vilən [in historical sense also -lin], -z
villainage 'vilinidʒ
villainous, -ly, -ness 'vilənəs, -li, -nis
villain|y -ies 'vilən|i, -iz
villeg(g)iatura vi,ledʒɪə'tuərə [-dʒə't-, -dʒə't-, -'tjuər-, -'tjɔər-, -'tjɔːr-]
villein, -s; -age 'vilin, -z; -idʒ

Villette vi'let
Villiers 'viləz, 'viljəz [-lɪəz]
Vilna 'vilnə
vim vim
vinaigrette, -s ,vinei'gret [-ni'g-], -s
Vincennes væn'sen [væn's-] (vɛ̃sɛn)
Vincent 'vinsənt
Vinci 'vintʃi(ː)
vincul|um, -a, -ums 'viŋkjul|əm, -ə, -əmz
vindicability ,vindikə'biliti [-lət-]
vindicable 'vindikəbl
vindicat|e, -es, -ing, -ed, -or/s 'vindi-keit, -s, -iŋ, -id, -ə*/z
vindication ,vindi'keiʃən
vindicative 'vindikətiv ['vindikeitiv, vin'dikətiv]
vindictive, -ly, -ness vin'diktiv, -li, -nis
vine, -s vain, -z
vine-dresser, -s 'vain,dresə*, -z
vinegar, -s, -y 'vinigə*, -z, -ri
viner|y, -ies 'vainər|i, -iz
Viney 'vaini
vineyard, -s 'vinjəd [rarely -jɑːd], -z
vingt-et-un 'væntei'əːŋ ['væːnt-, -'əːn, -'uːn] (vɛ̃teœ̃)
viniculture 'vinikʌltʃə*
vinous 'vainəs
vint, -s, -ing, -ed vint, -s, -iŋ, -id
vintage, -s 'vintidʒ, -iz
Vinter 'vintə*
vintner, -s 'vintnə*, -z
viny 'vaini
viol, -s 'vai-əl [vail, viəl], -z
viola (flower), -s 'vaiələ ['viələ, 'vaiəulə, 'viəulə, vai'əulə, vi'əulə], -z
viola (musical instrument), -s vi'əulə ['viəulə], -z
Viola (Christian name) 'vaiələ ['vaiəulə, 'viəulə
violable 'vai-ələbl
violat|e, -es, -ing, -ed, -or/s 'vai-əleit ['vaiəul-], -s, -iŋ, -id, -ə*/z
violation, -s ,vai-ə'leiʃən [,vaiəu'l-], -z
violen|ce, -t/ly 'vaiələn|s, -t/li
violet (V.), -s 'vaiəlit, -s
violin (musical instrument), -s ,vaiə'lin, -z
violin (chemical substance) 'vaiəlin
violinist, -s 'vaiəlinist [,--'--], -s
violin-string, -s ,vaiə'lin-striŋ, -z
violist, -s (viola player) vi'əulist (viol player) 'vaiəlist, -s
violoncell|ist/s, -o/s ,vaiələn'tʃel|ist/s [rarely ,viəl-, -lin-], -əu/z
violone, -s 'vaiələun ['viəl-], -z
V.I.P., -'s 'viːai'piː, -z
Vipan 'vaipæn

viper, -s; -ish 'vaipə*, -z; -riʃ
virago, -(e)s vi'rɑːgəu [-'reig-], -z
Virchow 'vəːtʃəu ['viəʃəu] ('fïrço:)
vires 'vaiəriːz
Virgil, -s 'vəːdʒil, -z
Virgili|an, -us vəː'dʒilĭ|ən [və'dʒ-, -lj|ən], -əs
virgin, -s 'vəːdʒin, -z
virginal (s. adj.), -s 'vəːdʒinl, -z
Virginia, -s, -n/s və'dʒinjə [və:'dʒ-, -nïə], -z, -n/z
virginibus puerisque vəː'ginibəs-pŭə'riskwi [vəː'dʒin-, -pjŭə-]
virginity vəː'dʒiniti [və'dʒ-]
Virgo (constellation) 'vəːgəu ['viəg-]
viridescen|ce, -t ˌviri'desn|s, -t
viridity vi'riditi
virile 'virail ['vaiər-]
virility vi'riliti [ˌvaiə'r-]
virology ˌvaiə'rɔlədʒi
virtu vəː'tuː
virtual, -ly 'vəːtʃŭəl [-tʃwəl, -tʃul, -tjŭəl, -tjwəl, -tjul], -i
virtue, -s 'vəːtjuː, 'vəːtʃuː, -z
virtuosity ˌvəːtju'ɔsiti
virtuoso, -s ˌvəːtju'əuzəu [-'əusəu], -z
virtuous, -ly, -ness 'vəːtʃŭəs [-tʃwəs, -tjŭəs, -tjwəs], -li, -nis
virulen|ce, -t/ly 'virulən|s [-rju-], -t/li
virus, -es 'vaiərəs, -iz
vis vis
visa (s. v.), -s, -ing, -ed 'viːzə, -z, -iŋ ['viːzəriŋ], -d
visage, -s 'vizidʒ, -iz
vis-à-vis 'viːzɑːviː ['viz-, -zəv-, -zæv-, '--'-] (vizavi)
viscer|a, -al 'visər|ə, -əl
viscid 'visid
viscidity vi'siditi
viscosity vis'kɔsiti
viscount, -s; -ess/es, -y, -ies 'vaikaunt, -s; -is/iz, -i, -iz
viscountc|y, -ies 'vaikaunts|i, -iz
viscous, -ness 'viskəs, -nis
visé (s. v.), -s, -ing, -d 'viːzei, -z, -iŋ, -d
visibility ˌvizi'biliti [-zə'b-, -lət-]
visib|le, -ly, -leness 'vizəb|l [-zib-], -li, -lnis
Visigoth, -s 'vizigɔθ ['visi-], -s
vision, -s 'viʒən, -z
vi|sional, -sionally 'vi|ʒənl [-ʒnəl, -ʒṇl, -ʒnl, -ʒənəl], -ʒnəli [-ʒnəli, -ʒṇli, -ʒnli, -ʒənəli]
visionar|y (s. adj. -ies), 'viʒṇər|i [-ʒənə-], -iz
visit (s. v.), -s, -ing, -ed, -or/s 'vizit, -s, -iŋ, -id, -ə*/z
visitant (s. adj.), -s 'vizitənt, -s

visitation, -s ˌvizi'teiʃən, -z
visite, -s vi'ziːt [viː'z-], -s
visor, -s 'vaizə*, -z
vista, -s 'vistə, -z
Vistula 'vistjulə
visual, -ly 'vizjŭəl [-zjwəl, -zjul, -ʒjŭəl, -ʒjwəl, -ʒŭəl, -ʒwəl, -ʒul], -i
visualization [-isa-] ˌvizjŭəlai'zeiʃən [-zjwəl-, -zjul-, -ʒjŭəl-, -ʒjwəl-, -ʒŭəl-, -ʒwəl-, -ʒul-, -li'z-]
visualiz|e [-is|e], -es, -ing, -ed, -er/s 'vizjŭəlaiz [-zjwəl-, -zjul-, -ʒjŭəl-, -ʒjwəl-, -ʒŭəl-, -ʒwəl-, -ʒul-], -iz, -iŋ, -d
vita (glass) 'vaitə   [-d, -ə*/z
vit|al, -ally 'vait|l, -əli [-ļi]
vitality vai'tæliti
vitalization [-isa-] ˌvaitəlai'zeiʃən [-tļai-]
vitaliz|e [-is|e], -es, -ing, -ed 'vaitəlaiz, -iz, -iŋ, -d
vitals 'vaitlz
vitamin, -s 'vitəmin ['vait-], -z
vitamine, -s 'vitəmin ['vait-, -miːn], -z
vitiat|e, -es, -ing, -ed, -or/s 'viʃieit, -s, -iŋ, -id, -ə*/z
vitiation ˌviʃi'eiʃən
viticulture 'vitikʌltʃə* ['vait-]
vitreosity ˌvitri'ɔsiti
vitreous, -ness 'vitrïəs, -nis
vitrescen|ce, -t vi'tresn|s, -t
vitrifaction ˌvitri'fækʃən
vitrification ˌvitrifi'keiʃən
vitri|fy, -fies, -fying, -fied; -fiable 'vitri|fai, -faiz, -faiiŋ, -faid; -faiəbl
vitriol 'vitrïəl
vitriolic ˌvitri'ɔlik
Vitruvi|an, -us vi'truːvj|ən [-vĭ|ən], -əs
vituperat|e, -es, -ing, -ed, -or/s vi'tjuːpəreit [vai't-], -s, -iŋ, -id, -ə*/z
vituperation, -s vi,tiuːpə'reiʃən [vai,t-], -z
vituperative, -ly vi'tjuːpərətiv [vai't-, -pəreit-], -li
viva (s. interj.) (long live), -s 'viːvə, -z
viva (viva voce), -s 'vaivə, -z
vivace, -s vi'vɑːtʃi, -z
vivacious, -ly, -ness vi'veiʃəs [vai'v-], -li, -nis
vivacity vi'væsiti [vai'v-]
vivarium, -s vai'vɛəriəm [vi'v-], -z
vivat (s.), -s 'vaivæt ['viːv-], -s
viva voce 'vaivə'vəusi [-'vəutʃi]
vive viːv
Vivian 'vivïən [-vjən]
vivid, -est, -ly, -ness 'vivid, -ist, -li, -nis
Vivien 'vivïən [-vjən]
Vivienne 'vivïən [-vjən], ˌvivi'en
vivification ˌvivifi'keiʃən
vivi|fy, -fies, -fying, -fied 'vivi|fai, -faiz, -faiiŋ, -faid

viviparity ˌvivi'pæriti
viviparous, -ly, -ness vi'vipərəs [vai'v-], -li, -nis
vivisect, -s, -ing, -ed, -or/s ˌvivi'sekt ['vivisekt], -s, -iŋ, -id, -ə*/z
vivisection, ˌvivi'sekʃən
vivisectionist, -s ˌvivi'sekʃn̩ist [-ʃəni-], -s
vixen, -s 'viksn, -z
vixenish 'viksn̩iʃ [-səniʃ]
viyella vai'elə
viz. vi'di:liset [vai'd-, vi'deiliket, viz]
Note.—Most people in reading aloud substitute namely 'neimli for this word.
Vizard 'vizɑ:d
Vizetelly ˌvizi'teli
vizier, -s vi'ziə* ['viziə*], -z
Vladimir 'vlædimiə* [-mə*], (Russian vla'djimjir, Czech 'vladimir)
Vladivostock ˌvlædi'vostɔk (vladjivas-'tok)
vocable, -s 'vəukəbl, -z
vocabular|y, -ies vəu'kæbjulər|i [vu'k-, -bjəl-, -blr|i], -iz
voc|al, -ally 'vəuk|əl, -əli
vocalic vəu'kælik
vocalism 'vəukəlizəm [-k|i-]
vocalist, -s 'vəukəlist [-k|i-], -s
vocality vəu'kæliti
vocalization [-isa-], -s ˌvəukəlai'zeiʃən [-k|ai'z-, -kəli'z-, -k|i'z-], -z
vocaliz|e [-is|e], -es, -ing, -ed 'vəukəlaiz [-k|aiz], -iz, -iŋ, -d
vocation, -s vəu'keiʃən [vu'k-], -z
voca|tional, -tionally vəu'kei|ʃənl [vu'k-ʃnəl, -ʃn̩l, -ʃn̩l, -ʃənəl], -ʃn̩əli [-ʃnəli, -ʃn̩li, -ʃn̩li, -ʃənəli]
vocative (s. adj.), -s, 'vɔkətiv, -z
voce (in viva voce) 'vəusi, (in sotto voce) 'vəutʃi
vociferat|e, -es, -ing, -ed, -or/s vəu'sifəreit, -s, -iŋ, -id, -ə*/z
vociferation, -s vəuˌsifə'reiʃən, -z
vociferous, -ly, -ness vəu'sifərəs, -li, -nis
vocoid, -s 'vəukɔid, -z
vodka, -s 'vɔdkə, -z
Vogt (Eng. surname) vəukt
vogue vəug
voic|e (s. v.), -es, -ing, -ed vɔis, -iz, -iŋ, -t
voiceless, -ly, -ness 'vɔislis, -li, -nis
void (s. adj. v.), -ness; -s, -ing, -ed; -able, -ance vɔid, -nis; -z, -iŋ, -id; -əbl, -əns
voile vɔil
vol vɔl
volant 'vəulənt
Volapuk 'vɔləpuk ['vəul-]

volatile (adj.), -ness 'vɔlətail, -nis
volatile (in sal volatile) və'lætəli [vəu'l-, vu'l, -t|i]
volatility ˌvɔlə'tiliti
volatilization [-isa-] vɔˌlætilai'zeiʃən [vəu,læt-, və,læt-, ˌvɔlət-, -li'z-]
volatiliz|e [-is|e], -es, -ing, -ed vɔ'lætilaiz [vəu'læt-, və'læt-, 'vɔlət-], -iz, -iŋ, -d
vol-au-vent, -s 'vɔləu'vɑ̃:ŋ [-'vɔ̃:ŋ, -'vɑ:ŋ, -'vɔ:ŋ, -'vɔŋ] (volovɑ̃), -z
volcanic, -ally vɔl'kænik, -əli
volcanist, -s 'vɔlkənist, -s
volcano, -(e)s vɔl'keinəu, -z
vol|e (s. v.), -es, -ing, -ed vəul, -z, -iŋ, -d
volet, -s 'vɔlei (volɛ), -z
Volga 'vɔlgə
Volhynia vɔl'hiniə [-njə]
volition vəu'liʃən
volitive 'vɔlitiv
volks|lied, -lieder 'fɔlks|li:d ['vɔl-] ('fɔlks-li:t), -ˌli:də* ('fɔlks,li:dər)
Volkswagen (car), -s 'fɔlks,vɑ:gən ('vɔlks-), -z
voll|ey (s. v.), -eys, -eying, -eyed, -eyer/s 'vɔl|i, -iz, -iŋ, -id, -iə*/z
volplan|e (s. v.), -es, -ing, -ed 'vɔl-plein, -z, -iŋ, -d
Volpone vɔl'pəuni
Volsci 'vɔlski: ['vɔlsai]
Vol|scian, -s 'vɔl|skiən [-skjən, -ʃiən, -ʃən, -siən, -sjən], -z
Volstead 'vɔlsted
volt (electric unit), -s vəult [rarely vɔlt], -s
volt (movement of horse, movement in fencing), -s vɔlt, -s
volta (V.) 'vɔltə
voltage, -s 'vəultidʒ [rarely 'vɔl-], -iz
voltaic vɔl'teiik
Voltaire 'vɔltɛə* (vɔltɛ:r)
voltameter, -s vɔl'tæmitə*, -z
volte 'vɔlti
volte-face, -s 'vɔlt'fɑ:s [-'fæs] (vɔltəfas), -iz
voltmeter, -s 'vəult,mi:tə* [rarely 'vɔlt-], -z
volubility ˌvɔlju'biliti [-lət-]
volub|le, -ly, -leness 'vɔljub|l, -li, -lnis
volume, -s 'vɔljum [-lju:m, -ljəm], -z
volumeter, -s vɔ'lju:mitə* [və'l-, -'lu:-], -z
volumetric, -al, -ally ˌvɔlju'metrik, -əl, -əli
voluminous, -ly, -ness və'lju:minəs [vɔ'l-, -'lu:-], -li, -nis
voluntar|y (s. adj.), -ies, -ily, -iness 'vɔləntər|i [-lnt-], -iz, -ili, -inis
volunteer (s. v.), -s, -ing, -ed ˌvɔlən'tiə* [-ln̩'t-], -z, -riŋ, -d

voluptuar|y (*s. adj.*), **-ies** vəˈlʌptjŭər|i
[-tjwər-, -tjur-, -tʃŭər-, -tʃwər-,
-tʃər-], -iz
voluptuous, -ly, -ness vəˈlʌptʃŭəs
[-tʃwəs, -tjŭəs, -tjwəs], -li, -nis
volute, -s, -d vəˈljuːt [vɔˈl-, vəuˈl-,
-ˈluːt], -s, -id
volution, -s vəˈljuːʃən [vɔˈl-, vəuˈl-,
-ˈluː-], -z
Volvo (*car*), **-s** ˈvɔlvəu, -z
Volze vəulz [-id
vomit (*s. v.*), **-s, -ing, -ed** ˈvɔmit, -s, -iŋ,
vomitor|y (*s. adj.*), **-ies** ˈvɔmitər|i, -iz
Vondy ˈvɔndi
voodoo ˈvuːduː
Vooght (*surname*) vuːt
voracious, -ly, -ness vəˈreiʃəs [vɔːˈr-,
vɔˈr-], -li, -nis
voracity vɔˈræsiti [vɔːˈr-, vəˈr-]
vort|ex, -ices, -exes ˈvɔːt|eks, -isiːz,
-eksiz
vortic|al, -ally ˈvɔːtik|əl, -əli
vortices (*plur. of* **vortex**) ˈvɔːtisiːz
Vosges vəuʒ
votaress, -es ˈvəutəris [-res], -iz
votar|y, -ies ˈvəutər|i, -iz
vot|e (*s. v.*), **-es, -ing, -ed, -er/s** vəut, -s,
voteless ˈvəutlis [-iŋ, -id, -ə*/z
votive ˈvəutiv
vouch, -es, -ing, -ed vautʃ, -iz, -iŋ, -t
voucher, -s ˈvautʃə*, -z
vouchsaf|e, -es, -ing, -ed vautʃˈseif, -s,
Voules vəulz [-iŋ, -t
vow (*s. v.*), **-s, -ing, -ed** vau, -z, -iŋ, -d
vow|el (*s. v.*), **-els, -elling, -elled** ˈvau|əl
[-el, -il], -əlz [-elz, -ilz], -əliŋ [-eliŋ,
-iliŋ], -əld [-eld, -ild]

vowel-like ˈvauəllaik [-el-, -il-]
Vowles vəulz, vaulz
vox (**V.**) vɔks
vox celeste, -s ˈvɔkssiˈlest, -s
vox humana, -s ˈvɔkshju(ː)ˈmɑːnə, -z
voyag|e (*s. v.*), **-es, -ing, -ed** ˈvɔiidʒ
[ˈvɔidʒ], -iz, -iŋ, -d
voyager, -s ˈvɔiədʒə* [ˈvɔiidʒ-], -z
Voynich ˈvɔinik
vraisemblance ˌvreisɑ̃:mˈblɑ̃:ns [-sɔ̃:m-
ˈblɔ̃:ns, -sɑːmˈblɑːns, -sɔːmˈblɔːns,
-sɔmˈblɔns, -ˈ--, ˈ---] (vrɛsɑ̃blɑ̃:s)
Vryburg ˈvraibə:g
vulcan (**V.**) ˈvʌlkən
vulcanite ˈvʌlkənait [-kn̩ait]
vulcanization [-isa-] ˌvʌlkənaiˈzeiʃən
[-kn̩aiˈz-, -kəniˈz-, -kn̩iˈz-]
vulcaniz|e [-is|e], -es, -ing, -ed ˈvʌlkən-
aiz [-kn̩aiz], -iz, -iŋ, -d
vulgar, -er, -est, -ly ˈvʌlgə*, -rə*, -rist,
-li
vulgarism, -s ˈvʌlgərizəm, -z
vulgarit|y, -ies vʌlˈgærit|i, -iz
vulgarization [-isa-] ˌvʌlgəraiˈzeiʃən
[-riˈz-]
vulgariz|e [-is|e], -es, -ing, -ed, -er/s
ˈvʌlgəraiz, -iz, -iŋ, -d, -ə*/z
Vulgate ˈvʌlgit [-geit]
Vulliamy ˈvʌljəmi
vulnerability ˌvʌlnərəˈbiliti [-lət-]
vulnerable, -ness ˈvʌlnərəbl, -nis
Vulpecula vʌlˈpekjulə
vulpine ˈvʌlpain
vulture, -s ˈvʌltʃə*, -z
vultur|ine, -ous ˈvʌltʃur|ain [-tʃər-,
-tjur-], -əs
vying (*from* **vie**) ˈvaiiŋ

W

W *(the letter)*, **-'s** 'dʌb|ju(:), -z
Waaf, -s wæf, -s
Wabash 'wɔːbæʃ
wabble, *etc.*=**wobble,** *etc.*
Wace weis
Wacey 'weisi
wad *(s. v.)*, **-s, -ding, -ded** wɔd, -z, -iŋ, -id
Waddell wɔ'del, 'wɔdl
wadding 'wɔdiŋ
Waddington 'wɔdiŋtən
wadd|le, -les, -ling, -led, -ler/s 'wɔd|l, -lz, -liŋ [-'liŋ], -ld, -lə*/z [lə*/z]
wadd|y *(water-course)*, **-ies** 'wɔd|i, ['wæd-], -iz
wadd|y *(war-club)*, **-ies** 'wɔd|i, -iz
Waddy 'wɔdi
wad|e *(s. v.)* **(W.), -es, -ing, -ed** weid, -z, -iŋ, -id
wader, -s 'weidə*, -z
Wadey 'weidi
Wadham 'wɔdəm
Wadburst 'wɔdhəːst
wadi, -s 'wɔdi ['wæd-, 'wɑːd-], -z
Wadi Halfa 'wɔdi'hælfə ['wæd-, 'wɑːd-]
Wadman 'wɔdmən
Wadsworth 'wɔdzwəːθ
Wady 'weidi
W.A.F., -'s wæf, -s
Wafd wɔft [wæft, wɑːft]
Wafdist, -s 'wɔfdist ['wæf-, 'wɑːf-], -s
wafer, -s; -y 'weifə*, -z; -ri
waffle, -s 'wɔfl, -z
waffle-iron, -s 'wɔfl‚aiən, -z
waft, -s, -ing, -ed wɑːft [wɔft, wɔːft], -s, -iŋ, -id
wag *(s. v.)*, **-s, -ging, -ged** wæg, -z, -iŋ, -d
wag|e *(s. v.)*, **-es, -ing, -ed** weidʒ, -iz, -iŋ, -d
wage-earner, -s 'weidʒ‚əːnə*, -z
wag|er *(s. v.)*, **-ers, -ering, -ered, -erer/s** 'weidʒ|ə*, -əz, -əriŋ, -əd, -ərə*/z
wagger|y, -ies 'wægər|i, -iz
waggish, -ly, -ness 'wægiʃ, -li, -nis
wagg|le, -les, -ling, -led 'wæg|l, -lz, -liŋ [-liŋ], -ld
waggon, -s 'wægən, -z
waggoner, -s 'wægənə*, -z
waggonette, -s ‚wægə'net, -s
Waghorn 'wæghɔːn
Wagnall 'wægnl [-nəl]
Wagner *(English name)* 'wægnə*, *(German composer)* 'vɑːgnə* ('vɑːgnər)
Wagnerian, -s vɑːg'niəriən, -z
Wagneriana ‚vɑːgniəri'ɑːnə [vɑːg‚niə-]
wagon, -s 'wægən, -z
wagoner, -s 'wægənə*, -z
wagonette, -s ‚wægə'net, -s
wagon-lit, -s 'vægɔ̃ːn'li: ['wæg-, 'vɑːg-, -gɔːn-, -gɔn-] (vagɔ̃li), -z
Wagstaff 'wægstɑ·f
wagtail, -s 'wægteil, -z
Wahabi, -s wə'hɑːbi [wɑː'h-], -z
waif, -s weif, -s
wail *(s. v.)*, **-s, -ing/ly, -ed** weil, -z, -iŋ/li, -d
wain, -s wein, -z
wainscot, -s, -ing, -ed 'weinskət ['wen-], -s, -iŋ, -id
Wainwright 'weinrait
waist, -s weist, -s
waistband, -s 'weistbænd, -z
waistcoat, -s 'weiskəut [-stk-, *old-fashioned* 'weskət], -s
waist-deep 'weist'diːp ['--]
waist-high 'weist'hai ['--]
wait *(s. v.)*, **-s, -ing, -ed, -er/s** weit, -s, -iŋ, -id, -ə*/z
waiting-maid, -s 'weitiŋmeid, -z
waiting-room, -s 'weitiŋrum [-ruːm], -z
waitress, -es 'weitris, -iz
Waitrose 'weit-rəuz ['weitrəuz]
waiv|e, -es, -ing, -ed weiv, -z, -iŋ, -d
waiver, -s 'weivə*, -z
wak|e *(s. v.)*, **-es, -ing, -ed, woke, woken** weik, -s, -iŋ, -t, wəuk, 'wəukən
Wakefield 'weikfiːld
wake|ful, -fully, -fulness 'weik|fʊl, -fuli [-fəli], -fulnis
wak|en, -ens, -ening, -ened 'weik|ən, -ənz, -niŋ [-əniŋ, -niŋ], -ənd
Wal *(personal name)* wɔl [wɔːl]
Walbrook 'wɔːlbruk ['wɔl-]

Walcheren 'vɑ:lkərən ['vɑ:lxə-, 'wɔ:l-
kərən, *old-fashioned* 'wɔ:lʃərən, 'wɔl-
ʃərən]
Walcott 'wɔ:lkət ['wɔl-, -kɔt]
Waldeck 'wɔ:ldek ['wɔl-] ('valdɛk)
Waldegrave 'wɔ:lgreiv ['wɔl-], 'wɔ:ldə-
greiv ['wɔl-]
Note.—Earl Waldegrave is 'wɔ:lgreiv
['wɔl-]. *Some others with this name
pronounce* 'wɔ:ldəgreiv ['wɔl-], *In*
Waldegrave Hall *the pronunciation
is* 'wɔ:ldəgreiv ['wɔl-].
Waldemar 'væeldəmɑ:* ['vɑ:l-, 'wɔ:l-,
-dim:]
Walden 'wɔ:ldən ['wɔl-]
Waldo 'wɔ:ldəu ['wɔl-]
Waldorf 'wɔ:ldɔ:f ['wɔl-]
Waldstein (*American name*) 'wɔ:ldstain
['wɔl-], (*German name*) 'væeldstain
['vɑ:l-, 'vɔ:l-, 'vɔl-, 'wɔ:l-, 'wɔl-,
-dʃtain] ('valtʃtain)
wale, -s weil, -z
Waler, -s 'weilə*, -z
Waleran (*Baron*) 'wɔ:lrən ['wɔl-],
(*Buildings in Borough High Street,
London*) 'wɔlərən
Wales weilz
Waley 'weili
Walfish 'wɔ:lfiʃ ['wɔl-]
Walford 'wɔ:lfəd ['wɔl-]
Walhalla væl'hæelə
Walham 'wɔləm
walk (*s. v.*), **-s, -ing, -ed, -er/s** wɔ:k,
-s, -iŋ, -t, -ə*/z
Walker 'wɔ:kə*
Walkern 'wɔ:lkə:n [-kən]
Walkiden 'wɔ:kidn
walkie-talkie, -s 'wɔ:ki'tɔ:ki, -z
walkingstick, -s 'wɔ:kiŋ-stik, -s
walking-tour, -s 'wɔ:kiŋtuə* [-tɔə*,
-tɔ:*], -z
walk-over, -s 'wɔ:k,əuvə*, -z
wall (*s. v.*) (**W.**), **-s, -ing, -ed** wɔ:l, -z, -iŋ,
-d
wallab|y (**W.**), **-ies** 'wɔləb|i, -iz
Wallace 'wɔlis [-ləs]
Wallach, -s 'wɔlək, -s
Wallachia, -n/s wɔ'leikjə [wə'l-, -kɪə],
-n/z
walla(h), -s 'wɔlə, -z
Wallasey 'wɔləsi
Waller 'wɔlə*
wallet, -s 'wɔlit, -s
wall-eye, -s, -d 'wɔ:lai, -z, -d
wallflower, -s 'wɔ:l,flauə*, -z
wall-fruit 'wɔ:l-fru:t
Wallingford 'wɔliŋfəd
Wallis 'wɔlis

Walloon, -s wɔ'lu:n [wə'l-], -z
wallop, -s, -ing/s, -ed 'wɔləp, -s, -iŋ/z, -t
wall|ow (*s. v.*), **-ows, -owing, -owed,
-ower/s** 'wɔl|əu, -əuz, -əuiŋ, -əud,
-əuə*/z
wall-paper, -s 'wɔ:l,peipə*, -z
Wallsend 'wɔ:lzend
Wallwork 'wɔ:lwə:k ['wɔl-]
Walmer 'wɔ:lmə* ['wɔl-]
Walm(e)sley 'wɔ:mzli
Walmisley 'wɔ:mzli
Walney 'wɔ:lni ['wɔl-]
walnut, -s 'wɔ:lnʌt [-nət], -s
Walpole 'wɔ:lpəul ['wɔl-]
Walpurgis væl'puəgis [vɑ:l-, -'pə:g-]
(val'purgis)
walrus, -es 'wɔ:lrəs ['wɔl-, -rʌs], -iz
Walsall 'wɔ:lsɔ:l ['wɔl-, -sl]
Walsh wɔ:lʃ [wɔlʃ]
Walsham 'wɔ:lʃəm [*locally* 'wɔ:lsəm]
Walsingham (*surname*) 'wɔ:lsiŋəm
['wɔl-], (*place*) 'wɔ:lziŋəm ['wɔl-,
-lsiŋ-]
Walt wɔ:lt [wɔlt]
Walter (*English name*) 'wɔ:ltə* ['wɔl-],
(*German name*) 'vɑ:ltə* ('valtər)
Walters 'wɔ:ltəz ['wɔl-]
Waltham 'wɔ:ltəm ['wɔl-, -lθəm]
*Note.—The traditional local pronun-
ciation at Great Waltham and Little
Waltham in Essex is* 'wɔ:ltəm, *and
this is the pronunciation used by
those who have lived there for a long
time. Some new residents pronounce* -lθəm. *In telephoning to
these places from a distance it is
advisable to pronounce* -lθəm; *otherwise the caller is liable to be given*
Walton(-on-the-Naze), *which is in
the same county.*
Walthamstow 'wɔ:lθəmstəu ['wɔl-,
old-fashioned -ltəm-]
Walther (*German name*) 'vɑ:ltə* ('valtər)
Walthew 'wɔ:lθju: ['wɔl-]
Walton 'wɔ:ltən ['wɔl-]
waltz (*s. v.*), **-es, -ing, -ed, -er/s** wɔ:ls
[wɔls, wɔ:lts, wɔlts], -iz, -iŋ, -t, -ə*/z
Walworth 'wɔ:lwəθ ['wɔl-, -wə:θ]
wampum, -s 'wɔmpəm, -z
wan, -ner, -nest, -ly, -ness wɔn, -ə*, -ist,
-li, -nis
Wanamaker 'wɔnəmeikə*
wand (**W.**), **-s** wɔnd, -z
wand|er, -ers, -ering, -ered, -erer/s
'wɔnd|ə*, -əz, -əriŋ, -əd, -ərə*/z
Wandle 'wɔndl
Wandsworth 'wɔndzwəθ [-wə:θ]
wan|e (*s. v.*), **-es, -ing, -ed** wein, -z, -iŋ, -d

Wanganui (*in New Zealand*) ˌwɒŋə'nui [-ŋgə-]
Note.—The first is the form always used by those of Polynesian descent.
wang|le (*s. v.*), -les, -ling, -led 'wæŋg|l, -lz, -liŋ, -ld
Wann wɒn
Wanstall 'wɒnstɔːl
Wanstead 'wɒnstid [-sted]
want (*s. v.*), -s, -ing, -ed wɒnt, -s, -iŋ, -id
Wantage 'wɒntidʒ
wanting 'wɒntiŋ
wanton, -ly, -ness 'wɒntən, -li, -nis
wapentake, -s 'wæpənteik ['wɒp-], -s
wapiti, -s 'wɒpiti, -z
Wapping 'wɒpiŋ
Wappinger 'wɒpindʒə*
war (*s. v.*), -s, -ring, -red wɔː*, -z, -riŋ, -d
Warbeck 'wɔːbek
warb|le, -les, -ling, -led 'wɔːb|l, -lz, -liŋ [-liŋ], -ld
warbler, -s 'wɔːblə*, -z
Warburg (*Institute*) 'wɔːbəːg
Warburton 'wɔːbətn [-bəːtn]
war-cloud, -s 'wɔː-klaud, -z
war-club, -s 'wɔː-klʌb, -z
war-cr|y, -ies 'wɔː-kr|ai, -aiz
ward (*s. v.*) (W.), -s, -ing, -ed wɔːd, -z, -iŋ, -id
war-dance, -s 'wɔːdɑːns, -iz
warden (W.), -s 'wɔːdn, -z
warder (W.), -s 'wɔːdə*, -z
Wardlaw 'wɔːdlɔː
Wardle 'wɔːdl
Wardour (*street in London*) 'wɔːdə*
wardress (*female warder*), -es 'wɔːdris ['wɔːdres], -iz
war-dress (*war costume*), -es 'wɔː-dres, -iz
wardrobe, -s 'wɔːdrəub, -z
wardroom, -s 'wɔːd-rum [-ruːm], -z
wardship 'wɔːdʃip
ware (*s. interj.*) (W.), -s wɛə*, -z
Wareham 'wɛərəm
warehou|se (*s.*), -ses 'wɛəhau|s, -ziz
warehou|se (*v.*), -ses, -sing, -sed 'wɛə-hau|z [-s], -ziz [-siz], -ziŋ [-siŋ], -zd [-st]
warehouse|man, -men 'wɛəhaus|mən, -mən
warfare 'wɔː-fɛə*
war-god, -s 'wɔː-gɒd, -z
war-grave, -s 'wɔː-greiv, -z
Wargrave 'wɔːgreiv
Warham 'wɔːrəm
warhead, -s 'wɔːhed, -z

war-horse, -s 'wɔːhɔːs, -iz
wari|ly, -ness 'wɛəri|li, -nis
Waring 'wɛəriŋ
warlike 'wɔː-laik ['wɔːlaik]
warlock (W.), -s 'wɔːlɒk, -s
war-lord, -s 'wɔː-lɔːd, -z
warm (*s. adj. v.*), -er, -est, -ly, -ness; -s, -ing, -ed wɔːm, -ə*, -ist, -li, -nis; -z, -iŋ, -d
war-maker, -s 'wɔːˌmeikə*, -z
warm-blooded 'wɔːm'blʌdid ['-ˌ--]
warmer (*s.*), -s 'wɔːmə*, -z
warm-hearted 'wɔːm'hɑːtid [*also* '-ˌ-- *when attributive*]
warming-pan, -s 'wɔːmiŋpæn, -z
Warmington 'wɔːmiŋtən
Warminster 'wɔːminstə*
warmish 'wɔːmiʃ
war-monger, -s 'wɔːˌmʌŋgə*, -z
warmth wɔːmθ [-mpθ]
warn, -s, -ing/ly, -ed wɔːn, -z, -iŋ/li, -d
Warn|e, -er wɔːn, -ə*
warning, -s 'wɔːniŋ, -z
warp (*s. v.*), -s, -ing, -ed wɔːp, -s, -iŋ, -t
war|-paint, -path 'wɔː-peint, -pɑːθ
warrant (*s. v.*), -s, -ing, -ed, -er/s 'wɒrənt, -s, -iŋ, -id, -ə*/z
warrantab|le, -ly, -leness 'wɒrəntəb|l, -li, -lnis
warrantee, -s ˌwɒrən'tiː, -z
warrantor, -s 'wɒrəntɔː* [-tə*, ˌwɒrən-'tɔː*], -z
warrant|y, -ies 'wɒrənt|i, -iz
Warre wɔː*
warren (W.), -s 'wɒrən [-rin], -z
Warrender 'wɒrində*
Warrington 'wɒriŋtən
warrior (W.), -s 'wɒriə*, -z
Warsaw 'wɔːsɔː
warship, -s 'wɔː-ʃip, -s
Warsop 'wɔːsəp
Warspite 'wɔː-spait
wart, -s; -y wɔːt, -s; -i
wart-hog, -s 'wɔːthɒg ['-'-], -z
Warton 'wɔːtn
war-wearied 'wɔːˌwiərid
Warwick, -shire 'wɒrik, -ʃiə* [-ʃə*]
war-worn 'wɔːwɔːn
war|y, -ier, -iest, -ily, -iness 'wɛər|i, -iə*, -iist, -ili, -inis
was (*from* be) wɒz (*strong form*), wəz, wz (*weak forms*)
Wasbrough 'wɒzbrə
wash (*s. v.*) (W.), -es, -ing, -ed, -er/s; -able wɒʃ, -iz, -iŋ, -t, -ə*/z; -əbl
wash-basin, -s 'wɒʃˌbeisn, -z
washday, -s 'wɒʃdei, -z
washer, -s 'wɒʃə*, -z

washer|woman, -women 'wɔʃə|ˌwumən, -ˌwimin

wash-hou|se, -ses 'wɔʃhau|s, -ziz

washing 'wɔʃiŋ

washing-day, -s 'wɔʃiŋdei, -z

washing-machine, -s 'wɔʃiŋməˌʃiːn, -z

washing-stand, -s 'wɔʃiŋ-stænd, -z

Washington 'wɔʃiŋtən

washing-up 'wɔʃiŋˈʌp [ˌ—'-]

wash-out, -s 'wɔʃaut ['-'-], -s

wash-pot, -s 'wɔʃpɔt, -s

wash-stand, -s 'wɔʃstænd, -z

wash-tub, -s 'wɔʃtʌb, -z

wash|y, -ier, -iest, -iness 'wɔʃ|i, -ĭə*, -iist, -inis

wasn't 'wɔznt [also occasionally 'wɔzn when not final]

wasp, -s wɔsp, -s

waspish, -ly, -ness 'wɔspiʃ, -li, -nis

wasplike 'wɔsp-laik

wassail, -s 'wɔseil ['wæs-, -sl], -z

wassailing 'wɔsəliŋ ['wæs-, -sļiŋ, -seiliŋ]

Wassell 'wæsl

Wasson 'wɔsn

wast (from be) wɔst (strong form), wəst (weak form)

Wast, -water wɔst, -,wɔːtə*

wast|e (s. adj. v.), -es, -ing, -ed, -er/s; -age weist, -s, -iŋ, -id, -ə*/z; -idʒ

waste|ful, -fully, -fulness 'weist|ful, -fuli [-fəli], -fulnis

waste-paper-basket, -s weist'peipəˌbɑːskit ['-'-—,--], -s

waste-pipe, -s 'weistpaip, -s

wastrel, -s 'weistrəl, -z

Wat wɔt

watch (s. v.), -es, -ing, -ed, -er/s wɔtʃ, -iz, -iŋ, -t, -ə*/z

watch-case, -s 'wɔtʃkeis, -iz

watch-chain, -s 'wɔtʃ-tʃein, -z

watch-dog, -s 'wɔtʃdɔg, -z

watch|ful, -fully, -fulness 'wɔtʃ|ful, -fuli [-fəli], -fulnis

watch-glass, -es 'wɔtʃglɑːs, -iz

watch-key, -s 'wɔtʃkiː, -z

watch-maker, -s 'wɔtʃˌmeikə*, -z

watch|man, -men 'wɔtʃ|mən, -mən

watch-pocket, -s 'wɔtʃˌpɔkit, -s [[-men]

watch-spring, -s 'wɔtʃspriŋ, -z

watch-stand, -s 'wɔtʃstænd, -z

watch-tower, -s 'wɔtʃˌtauə*, -z

watchword, -s 'wɔtʃwəːd, -z

wat|er (s. v.), -ers, -ering, -ered 'wɔːt|ə*, -əz, -əriŋ, -əd

water-bed, -s 'wɔːtəbed, -z

water-borne 'wɔːtəbɔːn

water-bottle, -s 'wɔːtəˌbɔtl, -z

water-buck 'wɔːtəbʌk

Waterbur|y, -ies 'wɔːtəbər|i, -iz

water-butt, -s 'wɔːtəbʌt, -s

water-carrier, -s 'wɔːtəˌkærĭə*, -z

watercart, -s 'wɔːtəkɑːt, -s

water-chute, -s 'wɔːtəʃuːt, -s

water-closet, -s 'wɔːtəˌklɔzit, -s

water-colour, -s 'wɔːtəˌkʌlə*, -z

water-cooled 'wɔːtəkuːld

watercourse, -s 'wɔːtəkɔːs [-kɔəs], -iz

watercress, -es 'wɔːtəkres, -iz

water-diviner/s 'wɔːtədiˌvainə*/z

water-divining 'wɔːtədiˌvainiŋ

water-drinker, -s 'wɔːtəˌdriŋkə*, -z

waterfall, -s 'wɔːtəfɔːl, -z

water-finder, -s 'wɔːtəˌfaində*, -z

Waterford 'wɔːtəfəd

waterfowl 'wɔːtəfaul

water-gas 'wɔːtəˈgæs ['-—]

water-gate, -s 'wɔːtəgeit, -s

Watergate 'wɔːtəgeit

water-gauge, -s 'wɔːtəgeidʒ, -iz

waterglass 'wɔːtəglɑːs

water-glass, -es 'wɔːtəglɑːs, -iz

Waterhouse 'wɔːtəhaus

wateriness 'wɔːtərinis

watering-can, -s 'wɔːtəriŋ-kæn, -z

watering-cart, -s 'wɔːtəriŋ-kɑːt, -s

watering-place, -s 'wɔːtəriŋ-pleis, -iz

waterless 'wɔːtəlis

water-level, -s 'wɔːtəˌlevl, -z

water-lil|y, -ies 'wɔːtəˌlil|i, -iz

water-line, -s 'wɔːtəlain, -z

waterlogged 'wɔːtəlɔgd

Waterloo ˌwɔːtəˈluː [ˈ—'-, ˈ—]

Note.—The stressing '—— is that regularly used when the word is attributive (as in Waterloo Road). A minority use '—— in all cases.

water-main, -s 'wɔːtəmein, -z

water|man (W.), -men 'wɔːtə|mən, -mən [-men]

watermark (s. v.), -s, -ing, -ed 'wɔːtəmɑːk, -s, -iŋ, -t

water-nymph, -s 'wɔːtəˈnimf ['-—], -s

water-pipe, -s 'wɔːtəpaip, -s

water-power 'wɔːtəˌpauə*

waterproof (s. v.), -s, -ing, -ed 'wɔːtəpruːf, -s, -iŋ, -t

Waters 'wɔːtəz

watershed, -s 'wɔːtəʃed, -z

water-ski (s. v.), -s, -ing, -ed 'wɔːtəski:, -z, -iŋ, -d

waterspout, -s 'wɔːtə-spaut, -s

water-sprite, -s 'wɔːtə-sprait, -s

water-suppl|y, -ies 'wɔːtəsəˌpl|ai, -aiz

watertight 'wɔːtətait

water-wav|e (s. v.), -es, -ing, -ed 'wɔːtəweiv, -z, -iŋ, -d

waterway, -s 'wɔ:təwei, -z
water-wheel, -s 'wɔ:təwi:l [-təhw-], -z
water-wings 'wɔ:təwiŋz
waterworks 'wɔ:təwə:ks
water-worn 'wɔ:təwɔ:n
watery 'wɔ:təri
Wat|ford, -kin/s, -son 'wɔt|fəd, -kin/z, -sn
Wathen 'wɔθən
Watling (Street) 'wɔtliŋ
watt (W.), -s wɔt, -s
wattage 'wɔtidʒ
Watteau, -s 'wɔtəu, -z
wattle, -s, -d 'wɔtl, -z, -d
wattmeter, -s 'wɔtˌmi:tə*, -z
Watton 'wɔtn
Wauchope (surname, place in Scotland) 'wɔ:kəp [in Scotland 'wɔxəp]
Waugh wɔ: [in Scotland wɔx]
waught, -s wɔ:t [in Scotland wɔxt], -s
waul, -s wɔ:l, -z
wav|e (s. v.), -es, -ing, -ed ; -eless, -elet/s weiv, -z, -iŋ, -d; -lis, -lit/s
wave-length, -s 'weivleŋθ, -s
Wavell 'weivəl
wav|er, -ers, -ering/ly, -ered, -erer/s 'weiv|ə*, -əz, -əriŋ/li, -əd, -ərə*/z
Waverley 'weivəli
wav|y, -ier, -iest, -ily, -iness 'weiv|i, -iə* [-jə*], -iist [-jist], -ili, -inis
wax (s. v.), -es, -ing, -ed ; -en wæks, -iz, -iŋ, -t; -ən
waxwing, -s 'wæks-wiŋ, -z
waxwork, -s 'wæks-wə:k, -s
wax|y, -ier, -iest, -iness 'wæks|i, -iə* [-jə*], -iist [-jist], -inis
way (W.), -s wei, -z
wayfar|er/s, -ing 'wei,fɛər|ə*/z, -iŋ
Wayland 'weilənd
way|lay, -lays, -laying, -laid, -layer/s wei|'lei, -'leiz, -'leiiŋ, -'leid, -'leiə*/z
Wayn|e, -flete wein, -fli:t
wayside 'wei-said
wayward, -ly, -ness 'weiwəd, -li, -nis
W.C., -'s 'dʌblju(:)'si:, -z
Note.— When used as an abbreviation for the West Central District of London, some people pronounce in full 'west'sentrəl.
we wi: (normal form), wi (frequent weak form)
Note.—wi also occurs as a strong form in the single expression we are when are has its weak form ə*. We are in this case is also written we're.
weak, -er, -est, -ly, -ness wi:k, -ə*, -ist, -li, -nis

weak|en, -ens, -ening, -ened 'wi:k|ən, -ənz, -ŋiŋ [-niŋ, -əniŋ], -ənd
weakening (s. adj.), -s 'wi:kniŋ, -z
weakish 'wi:kiʃ
weak-kneed 'wi:k-ni:d ['wi:k'n-]
weakling, -s 'wi:k-liŋ, -z
weak-minded 'wi:k'maindid [also '-,-- when attributive]
weal, -s wi:l, -z
weald (W.), -s wi:ld, -z
wealden (W.) 'wi:ldən
wealth, -s welθ, -s
wealth|y, -ier, -iest, -ily, -iness 'welθ|i, -iə* [-jə*], -iist [-jist], -ili, -inis
wean, -s, -ing, -ed wi:n, -z, -iŋ, -d
weanling, -s 'wi:nliŋ, -z
weapon, -s ; -less 'wepən, -z; -lis
wear (s.) (corresponding to wear v.) wɛə*
wear (s.) (=weir), -s wiə*, -z
Wear (river) wiə*
wear (v.), -s, -ing, wore, worn, wearer/s wɛə*, -z, -riŋ, wɔ:* [wɔə*], wɔ:n, 'wɛərə*/z
wearable 'wɛərəbl
Wearing 'wɛəriŋ
wearisome, -ly, -ness 'wiərisəm, -li, -nis
Wearmouth 'wiəməθ [-mauθ]
Wearn wə:n
wear|y (adj. v.), -ier, -iest, -ily, -iness; -ies, -ying, -ied 'wiər|i, -iə*, -iist, -ili, -inis; -iz, -iiŋ, -id
weasand, -s 'wi:zənd ['wiz-, -znd], -z
weasel, -s 'wi:zl, -z
weather (s. v.), -s, -ing, -ed ; -beaten 'weðə*, -z, -riŋ, -d; -,bi:tn
weather-bound 'weðəbaund
weathercock, -s 'weðəkɔk, -s
weather-eye, -s 'weðərai, -z
weather-glass, -es 'weðəglɑ:s, -iz
Weatherhead 'weðəhed
weatherly (W.) 'weðəli
weatherproof 'weðə-pru:f
weather-tanned 'weðə-tænd
weatherwear 'weðəwɛə*
weather-wise 'weðəwaiz
weather-worn 'weðəwɔ:n
weav|e, -es, -ing, wove, woven, weaver/s wi:v, -z, -iŋ, wəuv, 'wəuvən, 'wi:və*/z
weazened 'wi:znd
web, -s, -bed web, -z, -d
Webb(e) web
webb|ing, -y 'web|iŋ, -i
Weber (English name) 'wi:bə*, (German composer) 'veibə* ('ve:bər)
webfooted 'web,futid
Webster, -s 'webstə*, -z
wed, -s, -ding/s -ded wed, -z, -iŋ/z, -id

Weddell (*surname*) wə'del, 'wedl, (*Sea*) 'wedl
Wedderburn 'wedəbə:n
wedding-cake, -s 'wediŋ-keik, -s
wedding-day, -s 'wediŋdei, -z
wedding-ring, -s 'wediŋriŋ, -z
wedg|e (*s. v.*), -es, -ing, -ed; -ewise wedʒ, -iz, -iŋ, -d; -waiz
wedge-shaped 'wedʒʃeipt
Wedgwood 'wedʒwud
wedlock 'wedlɔk
Wednesbury 'wenzbəri [*locally also* 'wedʒbəri]
Wednesday, -s 'wenzdi ['wedn-, -dei], -z
wee wi:
weed (*s. v.*), -s, -ing, -ed wi:d, -z, -iŋ, -id
Weedon 'wi:dn
weed|y, -ier, -iest, -iness 'wi:d|i, -ɪə* [-jə*], -iist [-jist], -inis
week, -s wi:k, -s
weekday, -s 'wi:kdei, -z
week-end, -s 'wi:k'end ['wi:k-end], -z
week-ender, -s 'wi:k'endə* [-'--], -z
Weekes wi:ks
Weekl(e)y 'wi:kli
weekl|y (*s. adv.*), -ies 'wi:kl|i, -iz
Weeks wi:ks
Weelkes wi:lks
Weems wi:mz
ween, -s, -ing, -ed wi:n, -z, -iŋ, -d
weep, -s, -ing/ly, wept wi:p, -s, -iŋ/li, wept
weeper, -s 'wi:pə*, -z
weever, -s 'wi:və*, -z
weevil, -s 'wi:vil [-vl], -z
weewee, -s, -ing, -d 'wi:wi:, -z, -iŋ, -d
weft weft
Weguelin 'wegəlin
Weigall 'waigɔ:l
weigh, -s, -ing, -ed; -able wei, -z, -iŋ, -d; -əbl ['weəbl]
weight (*s. v.*), -s, -ing, -ed weit, -s, -iŋ, -id
weightless, -ness 'weitlis, -nis
Weighton (*in* Market Weighton, *Yorks.*) 'wi:tn
weight|y, -ier, -iest, -ily, -iness 'weit|i -ɪə* [-jə*], -iist [-jist], -ili, -inis
Wei-hai-wei 'weihai'wei
Weimar 'vaimɑ:* ('vaimar)
weir (W.), -s wiə*, -z
weird, -er, -est, -ly, -ness wiəd, -ə*, -ist, -li, -nis
Weisshorn 'vaishɔ:n
Weland 'weilənd, 'wi:lənd
Welbeck 'welbek
Welch welʃ
Welcombe 'welkəm

welcom|e (*s. adj. v. interj.*), -es, -ing, -ed 'welkəm, -z, -iŋ, -d
weld (*s. v.*), -s, -ing, -ed, -er/s weld, -z, -iŋ, -id, -ə*/z
weldment 'weldmənt
Weldon 'weldən
welfare 'welfɛə*
Welford 'welfəd
welkin 'welkin
well (*s. adj. v. interj.*), -s, -ing, -ed wel, -z, -iŋ, -d
welladay 'welə'dei ['weləd-]
well-advised 'weləd'vaizd
Welland 'welənd
well-appointed 'welə'pointid
well-balanced 'wel'bælənst [*also* '-ᵢ-- *when attributive*]
well-behaved 'wel-bi'heivd [*also* '--ᵢ- *when attributive*]
well-being 'wel'bi:iŋ ['wel,b-]
well-born 'wel'bɔ:n
well-bred 'wel'bred [*also* '--, -'-, *according to sentence-stress*]
Wellby 'welbi
well-chosen 'wel'tʃəuzn [*also* '-ᵢ-- *when attributive*]
Wellcome 'welkəm
well-conducted 'wel-kən'dʌktid [*also* '--,-- *when attributive*]
well-connected 'wel-kə'nektid [*also* '--,-- *when attributive*]
well-cooked 'wel'kukt [*also* 'wel-kukt *when attributive*]
well-directed 'wel-di'rektid [-də'r-, -dai'r-, *also* '--,-- *when attributive*]
well-disposed 'wel-dis'pəuzd
well-do|er/s, -ing 'wel'du(:)|ə*/z, -iŋ
Welldon 'weldən
well-done 'wel'dʌn ['-- *when attributive*]
Weller 'welə*
Wellesley 'welzli
well-found 'wel'faund [*also* 'wel-faund *when attributive*]
well-groomed 'wel'gru:md ['-- *when attributive*]
well-grounded 'wel'graundid
well-informed 'welin'fɔ:md
Wellingborough 'weliŋbərə
Wellington, -s 'weliŋtən, -z
wellingtonia, -s ˌweliŋ'təunjə [-nɪə], -z
well-intentioned 'welin'tenʃənd [*also* '--,-- *when attributive*]
well-judged 'wel'dʒʌdʒd [*also* '-- *when attributive*]
well-known 'wel'nəun [*also* '--, -'-, *according to sentence-stress*]
well-made 'wel'meid [*also* '--, -'-, *according to sentence-stress*]

well-marked 'wel'mɑːkt [also '-- when attributive]

well-meaning 'wel'miːniŋ

well-meant 'wel'ment [also '--, -'-, according to sentence-stress]

well-nigh 'welnai

well-off 'wel'ɔf [-'ɔːf, also '--, -'-, according to sentence-stress]

well-ordered 'wel'ɔːdəd [also '-ı-- when attributive]

well - proportioned 'wel-prə'pɔːʃənd [-pruːˈp-, also '--ı-- when attributive]

well-read 'wel'red [also '--, -'-, according to sentence-stress]

well-rounded 'wel'raundid

Wells welz

well-spoken 'wel'spəukən [also 'wel-ıspəukən when attributive]

well-timed 'wel'taimd [also 'wel-taimd when attributive]

well-to-do 'wel-tə'duː [also '--- when attributive]

well-wisher, -s 'wel'wiʃə* ['-ı--], -z

welsh, -es, -ing, -ed, -er/s welʃ, -iz, -iŋ, -t, -ə*/z

Welsh, -man, -men welʃ, -mən, -mən [-men]

Welshpool 'welʃpuːl (Welsh 'welʃ'puːl)

welt (s. v.), -s, -ing, -ed welt, -s, -iŋ, -id

welt|er, -ers, -ering, -ered 'welt|ə*, -əz, -əriŋ, -əd

Welwyn 'welin

Wembley 'wembli

Wemyss wiːmz

wen, -s wen, -z

Wenceslas 'wensisləs [-səs-, -læs]

wench, -es wentʃ, -iz

wend, -s, -ing, -ed wend, -z, -iŋ, -id

Wend, -s, -ic, -ish wend [vend], -z, -ik, -iʃ

Wendell 'wendl

Wendover 'wen,dəuvə*

Wengen 'veŋən

Wengern Alp 'veŋən'ælp

Wenham 'wenəm

Wenish 'weniʃ

Wenlock 'wenlɔk

went (from go) went

Wentworth 'wentwəθ [-wəːθ]

wept (from weep) wept

we're (=we are) wiə*

were (from be) wəː* [wɛə*] (strong forms), wə* (weak form)

weren't wəːnt [wɛənt]

werewol|f, -ves 'wiəwul|f ['wəː], -vz

Wernher 'wəːnə*

wert (from be) wəːt (strong form), wət (weak form)

Weser (German river) 'veizə* ('veːzər)
Note.—'wiːzə* is necessary for rhyme in Browning's ' Pied Piper', but this pronunciation is exceptional.

Wesley 'wezli, 'wesli
Note.—It would seem that most people bearing the name Wesley pronounce 'wesli, but that they are commonly called 'wezli by others.

Wesleyan, -s; -ism 'wezliən ['wesl-, -ljən], -z; -izəm
Note.—'wesl- appears to be the more usual pronunciation among Wesleyans; with those who are not Wesleyans 'wezl- is probably the commoner form. There exists also an old-fashioned pronunciation [wes'liːən.

Wessex 'wesiks

west (s. adj. v.) (W.) west

Westbourne 'westbɔːn [-bən, esp. when attributive, as in W. Terrace]

West|brook, -bury 'west|bruk, -bəri

Westcott 'westkət

Westenra 'westənrə

Westerham 'westərəm

westering 'westəriŋ

wester|ly, -n, -ner/s 'westə|li, -n, -nə*/z

westeriz|e [-is|e], -es, -ing, -ed 'westənaiz, -iz, -iŋ, -d

westernmost 'westənməust

Westfield 'westfiːld

Westgate 'westgit [-geit]

Westlake 'westleik

Westmeath west'miːð

Westminster 'westminstə* [-'--]

Westmor(e)land 'westmələnd ['wes-mlənd]

west-north-west 'westnɔːθ'west [nautical pronunciation -nɔː'west]

Weston 'westən

Weston - super - Mare 'westən,sjuːpə-'mɛə* [-n,suːpə-, -nsjupə-, rarely -'meəri]

Westphalia, -n/s west'feiljə [-liə], -n/z

west-south-west 'westsauθ'west [nautical pronunciation -sau'west]

westward, -s, -ly 'westwəd, -z, -li

Westward Ho 'westwəd'həu

wet, -ter, -test, -ness wet, -ə*, -ist, -nis

wether, -s 'weðə*, -z

Wetherby 'weðəbi

wet-nurse, -s 'wetnəːs, -iz

Wetterhorn 'vetəhɔːn

wettish 'wetiʃ

Wexford 'weksfəd

wey (W.), -s wei, -z

Wey|bridge, -man, -mouth 'wei|bridʒ, -mən, -məθ

whack (s. v.), -s, -ing/s, -ed, -er/s wæk [hw-], -s, -iŋ/z, -t, -ə*/z

Whait weit [hw-]

whal|e, -es, -ing, -er/s weil [hw-], -z, -iŋ, -ə*/z

whalebone 'weilbəun ['hw-]

whale-fisher|y, -ies 'weil,fiʃər|i ['hw-], -iz

whale-oil 'weilɔil ['hw-]

Whaley (place near Buxton) 'weili ['hw-]

Whalley (surname) 'weili ['hw-], 'wɔːli ['hw-], (abbey near Blackburn) 'wɔːli ['hw-]

whang (s. v.), -s, -ing, -ed wæŋ [hw-], -z, -iŋ, -d

whangee 'wæŋ'giː [hw-]

Wharam 'wɛərəm ['hw-]

whar|f, -ves, -fs wɔːf [hw-], -vz, -fs

wharfage 'wɔːfidʒ ['hw-]

wharfinger, -s 'wɔːfindʒə* ['hw-], -z

Wharton 'wɔːtn ['hw-]

what wɔt [hw-]

what-d'you-call-it 'wɔtdju,kɔːlit ['hw-, -dʒu-]

whate'er 'wɔt'ɛə* [hw-]

Whateley 'weitli ['hw-]

whatever wɔt'evə* [hw-, rarely wət-, hwət-]

What|ley, -man 'wɔt|li ['hw-], -mən

Whatmough 'wɔtməu ['hw-]

whatnot, -s 'wɔtnɔt ['hw-], -s

what's-her-name 'wɔtsəneim ['hw-, -sneim]

what's-his-name 'wɔtsizneim ['hw-]

whatsoe'er ,wɔtsəu'ɛə* [,hw-]

whatsoever ,wɔtsəu'evə* [,hw-]

what-you-may-call-it 'wɔtʃəmə,kɔːlit

wheat, -en wiːt [hw-], -n [['hw-]

wheat-ear, -s 'wiːt-iə* ['hw-], -z

Wheathampstead (in Herts.) 'wiːtəmp-sted ['wet-, 'hw-]

Wheat|ley, -on 'wiːt|li ['hw-], -n

Wheatstone 'wiːtstən ['hw-, -stəun]

wheed|le, -les, -ling, -led, -ler/s 'wiːd|l ['hw-], -lz, -liŋ [-liŋ], -ld, -lə*/z [lə*/z]

wheel (s. v.), -s, -ing, -ed wiːl [hw-], -z, -iŋ, -d

wheelbarrow, -s 'wiːl,bærəu ['hw-], -z

wheel-chair, -s 'wiːl'tʃɛə* ['wiːl-tʃɛə*, 'hw-], -z

wheeler (W.), -s 'wiːlə* ['hw-], -z

wheelwright (W.), -s 'wiːlrait ['hw-], -s

Wheen wiːn [hw-]

wheez|e (s. v.), -es, -ing, -ed; -y, -ier, -iest, -iness wiːz [hw-], -iz, -iŋ, -d; -i, -iə* [-jə*], -iist [-jist], -inis

Whelan 'wiːlən ['hw-]

whelk, -s welk, -s

Note.—Not hwelk.

whelm, -s, -ing, -ed welm [hw-], -z, -iŋ, -d

whelp (s. v.), -s, -ing, -ed welp [hw-], -s, -iŋ, -t

when wen [hw-]

whence wens [hw-]

whene'er wen'ɛə* [hw-]

whenever wen'evə* [wən-, hw-]

whensoever ,wensəu'evə* [,hw-]

where wɛə* [hw-]

whereabouts (s.) 'wɛərəbauts ['hw-]

whereabouts (interrogation) 'wɛər-ə'bauts ['hw-, occasionally '— when followed by a stress]

whereas wɛər'æz [wər-, hw-]

whereat wɛər'æt [wər-, hw-]

whereby wɛə'bai [hw-]

where'er wɛər'ɛə* [wər-, hw-]

wherefore 'wɛəfɔː* ['hw-, -fɔə*]

where|in, -of, -on wɛər|'in [hw-], -'ɔv [-'ɔf], -'ɔn

whereso|e'er, -ever ,wɛəsəu'ɛə* [,hw-], -'evə*

whereto wɛə'tuː [hw-]

whereunder wɛər'ʌndə* [hw-]

whereunto ,wɛərʌn'tuː [,hw-]

whereupon ,wɛərə'pɔn [,hw-, '—'-, '—]

wherever wɛər'evə* [wə'r-, hw-]

wherewith wɛə'wiθ [hw-, -'wið]

wherewithal (s.) 'wɛəwiðɔːl ['hw-]

wherewithal (adv.) ,wɛəwi'ðɔːl [,hw-, '—'-, '—]

wherr|y, -ies 'wer|i ['hw-], -iz

whet (s. v.), -s, -ting, -ted wet [hw-], -s, -iŋ, -id

whether 'weðə* ['hw-]

whetstone (W.), -s 'wetstəun ['hw-], -z

whew ỹ: [ỹy:, ỹ:u:, hwu:]

Whewell 'hju(:)əl [-el, -il]

whey wei [hw-]

Whibley 'wibli ['hw-]

which witʃ [hw-]

whichever witʃ'evə* [hw-]

Whickham 'wikəm ['hw-]

whiff (s. v.), -s, -ing, -ed wif [hw-], -s, -iŋ, -t

Whiffen 'wifin ['hw-]

whig (W.), -s wig [hw-], -z

whigg|ery, -ism 'wig|əri ['hw-], -izəm

whiggish, -ly, -ness 'wigiʃ ['hw-], -li, -nis

Whigham 'wigəm ['hw-]

whil|e (s. v. conj.), -es, -ing, -ed wail [hw-], -z, -iŋ, -d

whilom 'wailəm ['hw-]

whilst wailst [hw-]

whim, -s wim [hw-], -z

whimper, -s, -ing/ly, -ed, -er/s 'wimpə* ['hw-], -z, -riŋ/li, -d, -rə*/z

whimsic|al, -ally, -alness 'wimzik|əl ['hw-, -msi-], -əli, -əlnis
whimsicality ˌwimzi'kæliti [ˌhw-, -msi-]
whin, -s win [hw-], -z
whinchat, -s 'win-tʃæt ['hw-], -s
whin|e (s. v.), -es, -ing/ly, -ed wain [hw-], -z, -iŋ/li, -d
whinger, -s 'wiŋə* [hw-], -z
whinn|y (s. v.), -ies, -ying, -ied 'win|i ['hw-], -iz, -iiŋ, -id
whin|y, -ier, -iest, -iness 'wain|i ['hw-], -iə*, -iist, -inis
whip (s. v.), -s, -ping/s, -ped wip [hw-], -s, -iŋ/z, -t
whip-cord 'wipkɔːd ['hw-]
whip-hand 'wip'hænd ['hw-, '--]
whipp|er-in, -ers-in 'wip|ər'in ['hw-], -əz'in
whippersnapper, -s 'wipəˌsnæpə* ['hw-], -z
whippet, -s 'wipit ['hw-], -s
whipping-boy, -s 'wipiŋbɔi ['hw-], -z
Whippingham 'wipiŋəm ['hw-]
whipping-top, -s 'wipiŋ-tɔp ['hw-], -s
Whipple 'wipl ['hw-]
whippoorwill, -s 'wippuəˌwil ['hw-, -pɔəˌw-, -pɔːˌw-], -z
Whipsnade 'wipsneid ['hw-]
whir (s. v.), -s, -ring/s, -red wəː* [hw-], -z, -riŋ/z, -d
whirl (s. v.), -s, -ing, -ed wəːl [hw-], -z, -iŋ, -d
whirligig, -s 'wəːligig ['hw-], -z
whirlpool, -s 'wəːl-puːl ['hw-], -z
whirlwind, -s 'wəːlwind ['hw-], -z
whirr (s. v.), -s, -ing/s, -ed wəː* [hw-], -z, -riŋ/z, -d
whisk (s. v.), -s, -ing, -ed wisk [hw-], -s, -iŋ, -t
whisker, -s, -ed 'wiskə* ['hw-], -z, -d
whiskey, -s 'wiski ['hw-], -z
whisk|y, -ies 'wisk|i ['hw-], -iz
whisp|er (s. v.), -ers, -ering/s, -ered, -erer/s 'wisp|ə* ['hw-], -əz, -əriŋ/z, -əd, -ərə*/z
whist wist [hw-]
whist-drive, -s 'wisʲdraiv ['hw-], -z
whist|le (s. v.), -les, -ling, -led 'wis|l ['hw-], -lz, -liŋ [-l̩iŋ], -ld
whistler (W.), -s 'wislə* ['hw-], -z
whit (W.) wit [hw-]
Whitaker 'witikə* ['hw-, -tək-]
Whit|bread, -by, -church 'wit|bred ['hw-], -bi, -tʃə:tʃ
whit|e (s. adj. v.) (W.), -es; -er, -est, -ely, -eness; -ing, -ed wait [hw-], -s; -ə*, -ist, -li, -nis; -iŋ, -id
whitebait 'waitbeit ['hw-]

whitebeard, -s, -ed 'waitbiəd ['hw-], -z, -id
whitecap, -s 'waitkæp ['hw-], -s
Whitechapel 'waitˌtʃæpl ['hw-]
Whitefield 'waitfiːld ['hw-], 'wit- ['hw-]
Whitefriars 'waitˌfraiəz ['hw-, '-'--]
Whitehall 'wait'hɔːl ['hw-, also '--, -'-, according to sentence-stress]
Whitehaven 'waitˌheivn ['hw-]
Whitehead (W.), -s 'waithed ['hw-], -z
white-heat 'wait'hiːt ['hw-]
white-hot 'wait'hɔt ['hw-, also '-- when attributive]
Whiteley 'waitli ['hw-]
white-livered 'waitˌlivəd ['hw-]
whit|en, -ens, -ening, -ened 'wait|n ['hw-], -nz, -niŋ [-n̩iŋ], -nd
whitening (s.) 'waitniŋ ['hw-]
whitethorn, -s 'waitθɔːn ['hw-], -z
whitethroat, -s 'waitθrəut ['hw-], -s
whitewash (s. v.), -es, -ing, -ed, -er/s 'wait-wɔʃ ['hw-], -iz, -iŋ, -t, -ə*/z
whitewood 'wait-wud ['hw-]
Whit|field, -gift 'wit|fiːld ['hw-], -gift
whither 'wiðə* ['hw-]
whithersoever ˌwiðəsəu'evə* [ˌhw-]
whiting (W.), -s 'waitiŋ ['hw-], -z
whitish, -ness 'waitiʃ ['hw-], -nis
whitleather 'witˌleðə* ['hw-]
Whitley 'witli ['hw-]
whitlow, -s 'witləu ['hw-], -z
Whit|man, -marsh, -ney, -stable, -stone 'wit|mən ['hw-], -maːʃ, -ni, -stəbl, -stəun
Whitsun 'witsn ['hw-]
Whitsunday, -s 'wit'sʌndi ['hw-, -sn'dei], -z
Whitsuntide, -s 'witsntaid ['hw-], -z
Whittaker 'witikə* ['hw-, -tək-]
Whittier 'witïə* ['hw-]
Whittingeham(e) 'witindʒəm ['hw-]
Whittington 'witiŋtən ['hw-]
whitt|le (W.), -les, -ling, -led 'wit|l ['hw-], -lz, -l̩iŋ [-liŋ], -ld
Whitworth 'witwə:θ ['hw-]
whit|y, -iness 'wait|i ['hw-], -inis
whiz, -zes, -zing, -zed wiz [hw-], -iz, -iŋ, -d
whizz (s. v.), -es, -ing, -ed wiz [hw-], -iz, -iŋ, -d
who (interrogative) huː [also hu when followed by a word beginning with ə or unstressed i]
who (relative) huː: (normal form), hu (frequent weak form), uː, u (occasional weak forms)
whoa wəu [wəuʔ]

whoe'er hu(:)'ɛə*
whoever hu(:)'evə* [occasionally u(:)-
    when closely connected to preceding
    word in the sentence]
whole, -ness həul, -nis
whole-hearted 'həul'hɑːtid
whole-hog, -ger/s 'həul'hɔg, -ə*/z
whole-meal 'həulmiːl
wholesale 'həul-seil
wholesaler, -s 'həul,seilə*, -z
wholesome, -st, -ly, -ness 'həulsəm, -ist,
wholly 'həulli ['həuli]   [-li, -nis
whom huːm (normal form), hum
    (occasional weak form)
whomsoever ,hu:msəu'evə*
whoop (s. v.), -s, -ing, -ed huːp, -s, -iŋ, -t
whoopee (s.)   'wupiː [-pi], (interj.)
    'wu'piː [-'-]
whooping-cough 'huːpiŋkɔf [-kɔːf]
whop, -s, -ping/s, -ped wɔp [hw-], -s,
    -iŋ/z, -t
whopper, -s 'wɔpə* ['hw-], -z
whor|e (s. v.), -es, -ing, -ed; -edom/s
    hɔː* [hɔə*], -z, -riŋ, -d; -dəm/z
whoreson, -s 'hɔːsn ['hɔəsn], -z
whorl, -s, -ed wəːl [hw-], -z, -d
whortle, -s 'wəːtl ['hw-], -z
whortleberr|y, -ies 'wəːtl,ber|i ['hw-,
    -bər|i], -iz
whose (interrogative) huːz
whose (relative) huːz (normal form), uːz
    (occasional weak form)
whoso 'huːsəu
whosoever ,hu:səu'evə*
why wai [hw-]
Whyle (surname) 'waili ['hw-]
Whymper 'wimpə* ['hw-]
Whyte wait [hw-]
Whytt wait [hw-]
wick (W.), -s wik, -s
wicked, -est, -ly, -ness/es 'wikid, -ist, -li,
Wickens 'wikinz   [-nis/iz
wicker, -work 'wikə*, -wəːk
wicket, -s 'wikit, -s
wicket-gate, -s 'wikit'geit, -s
wicket-keeper, -s 'wikit,kiːpə*, -z
Wickham 'wikəm
Wickliffe 'wiklif
Wicklow 'wikləu
wide (s. adj.), -s, -r, -st, -ly, -ness,
    waid, -z, -ə*, -ist, -li, -nis
wide-awake (s.), -s 'waidəweik, -s
wide-awake (adj.) 'waidə'weik
Widecombe 'widikəm
Widemouth 'widməθ
wid|en, -ens, -ening, -ened 'waid|n, -nz,
    -niŋ [-niŋ], -nd
wide-spread 'waidspred ['-'-]

widgeon, -s 'widʒən [-dʒin], -z
widish 'waidiʃ
Widnes 'widnis
widow, -s, -ed 'widəu, -z, -d
widower, -s 'widəuə*, -z
widowhood 'widəuhud
width, -s widθ [witθ], -s
wield, -s, -ing, -ed wiːld, -z, -iŋ, -id
Wiesbaden 'viːs,bɑːdn ['viːz,b-, viːs'b-,
    viːz'b-]   ('viːs,baːdən, locally vis-
                                'baːdən)
wi|fe, -ves waif, -vz
wife|hood, -less 'waif|hud, -lis
wife|like, -ly 'waif|laik, -li
Wiffen 'wifin
wig (s. v.), -s, -ging, -ged wig, -z, -iŋ, -d
Wigan 'wigən
wigging (s.), -s 'wigiŋ, -z
Wiggins 'wiginz
wigg|le (s. v.), -les, -ling, -led 'wig|l,
    -lz, -liŋ [-liŋ], -ld
wiggle-waggle 'wigl,wægl
wiggly 'wigli [-gli]
wight (W.), -s wait, -s
wig-maker, -s 'wig,meikə*, -z
Wigmore 'wigmɔː* [-mɔə*]
Wig|ton, -town 'wig|tən, -tən
wigwam, -s 'wigwæm, -z
Wilberforce 'wilbəfɔːs
Wilbraham 'wilbrəhæm [-brəm, -briəm]
Wil|bur, -bye 'wil|bə*, -bi
Wilcox 'wilkɔks
wild (s. adj. adv.) (W.), -s, -er, -est, -ly,
    -ness waild, -z, -ə*, -ist, -li, -nis
Wilde waild
wildebeest, -s 'wildibiːst, -s
Wilder 'waildə*
wilderness, -es 'wildənis, -iz
wildfire 'waild,faiə*
wilding (W.), -s 'waildiŋ, -z
wildish 'waildiʃ
wil|e (s. v.) (W.), -es, -ing, -ed wail, -z,
    -iŋ, -d
Wilfred [-rid] 'wilfrid ['wul-]
wil|ful, -fullest, -fully, -fulness 'wil|ful,
    -fulist [-fəlist], -fuli [-fəli], -fulnis
Wilhelmina (English name) ,wilhel-
    'miːnə, ,wilə'miːnə
Wilk|es, -ie, -ins wilk|s, -i, -inz
Wilkinson 'wilkinsn
Wilks wilks
will (s.) (W.), -s wil, -z
will (transitive v.), -s, -ing, -ed wil, -z,
    -iŋ, -d
will (auxil. v.) wil (strong form), l
    (normal weak form), wəl, əl (occa-
    sional weak forms)

Willard 'wilɑ:d [-ləd]

Willcocks [-cox] 'wilkɔks

Willes wilz

Willesden 'wilzdən

William, -s -son 'wiljəm, -z, -sn

Willie 'wili

willing (adj.) (W.), -ly, -ness 'wiliŋ, -li, -nis

Willing|don, -ton 'wiliŋ|dən, -tən

Willis 'wilis

will-o'-the-wisp, -s 'wiləðəwisp [-əðw-, '---'-], -s

Willoughby 'wiləbi

will|ow (s. v.), -ows, -owing, -owed; -owy 'wil|əu, -əuz, -əuiŋ, -əud; -əui

willowherb 'wiləuhə:b

willow-pattern 'wiləu₁pætən [-tn]

willow-wren, -s 'wiləu'ren ['---], -z

will-power, -s 'wil₁pauə*, -z

Wills wilz

Will|steed, -y 'wil|sti:d, -i

willy-nilly 'wili'nili

Wilma 'wilmə

Wilmcote 'wilmkəut

Wilmington 'wilmiŋtən

Wilmot(t) 'wilmət [-mɔt]

Wilmslow 'wilmzləu [locally 'wimzləu]

Wilna 'vilnə

Wilno (in Ontario) 'wilnəu

Wilsden 'wilzdən

Wilshire 'wilʃiə* [-ʃə*]

Wilson 'wilsn

wilt (from will, aux. v.) wilt (normal form), əlt, lt (occasional weak forms)

wilt (v.), -s, -ing, -ed wilt, -s, -iŋ, -id

Wilton, -s 'wiltən, -z

Wilts. wilts

Wiltshire 'wilt-ʃiə* [-ʃə*]

wil|y, -ier, -iest, -iness 'wail|i, -iə*, -iist, -inis

Wimble, -don 'wimbl, -dən

Wimborne 'wimbɔ:n [-bəən]

Wimms wimz

Wimperis 'wimpəris

wimple, -s 'wimpl, -z

Wimpole 'wimpəul

win (s. v.), -s, -ning, won, winner/s win, -z, -iŋ, wʌn, 'winə*/z

winc|e, -es, -ing, -ed wins, -iz, -iŋ, -t

wincey 'winsi

winceyette ₁winsi'et

winch, -es wintʃ, -iz

Win|chelsea, -chester 'win|tʃlsi, -tʃistə*

Winch|field, -ilsea, -more 'wintʃ|fi:ld, -lsi, -mɔ:* [-mɔə*]

wind (s.) (air blowing), -s wind [in poetry sometimes waind], -z

wind (v.) (go round, roll round), -s, -ing, wound waind, -z, -iŋ, waund

wind (v.) (blow horn), -s, -ing, -ed waind, -z, -iŋ, -id

wind (v.) (detect by scent, exhaust breath), -s, -ing, -ed wind, -z, -iŋ, -id

windage 'windidʒ

windbag, -s 'windbæg, -z

windcheater, -s 'wind₁tʃi:tə*, -z

wind-chest, -s 'windtʃest, -s

wind-cone, -s 'windkəun ['win-kəun], -z

Winder, -mere 'wində*, -miə*

windfall, -s 'windfɔ:l, -z

Windham 'windəm

Note.—The place in Vermont, U.S.A., is called locally 'windhæm.

windhover, -s 'wind₁hɔvə*, -z

winding (s. adj.), -s, -ly 'waindiŋ, -z, -li

winding-sheet, -s 'waindiŋʃi:t, -s

winding-up 'waindiŋ'ʌp

wind-instrument, -s 'wind₁instrumənt [-trəm-], -s

wind-jammer, -s 'wind₁dʒæmə*, -z

windlass, -es 'windləs, -iz

Windley 'windli

windmill, -s 'winmil [-ndm-], -z

window, -s 'windəu, -z

window-box, -es 'windəubɔks, -iz

window-dressing 'windəu₁dresiŋ

window-pane, -s 'windəupein, -z

window-seat, -s 'windəusi:t, -s

windpipe, -s 'windpaip, -s

windrow, -s 'wind-rəu, -z

wind-screen, -s 'windskri:n ['win-skr-], -z

Windsor 'winzə*

wind-swept 'windswept ['win-swept]

Windus 'windəs

windward (W.) 'windwəd

wind|y, -ier, -iest, -ily, -iness 'wind|i, -iə* [-jə*], -iist [-jist], -ili, -inis

wine, -s wain, -z

wine-bibber, -s 'wain₁bibə*, -z

wine-bottle, -s 'wain₁bɔtl, -z

wine-cellar, -s 'wain₁selə*, -z

wineglass, -es 'waingla:s ['waiŋg-], -iz

wineglassful, -s 'waingla:s₁ful ['waiŋg-], -z

wine-press, -es 'wainpres, -iz

wine-skin, -s 'wain-skin, -z

wing (s. v.) (W.), -s, -ing, -ed, -er/s wiŋ, -z, -iŋ, -d, -ə*/z

wing-commander, -s 'wiŋ-kə₁mɑ:ndə*, -z

wing-covert, -s 'wiŋ'kʌvət, -s

winged (adj.) wiŋd

-winged -wiŋd

Wingfield 'wiŋfi:ld

Winifred 'winifrid
wink (s. v.) (W.), -s, -ing, -ed, -er/s
 wiŋk, -s, -iŋ, -t [wiŋt], -ə*/z
Winkfield 'wiŋkfi:ld
Winkie 'wiŋki
winkle (W.), -s 'wiŋkl, -z
Winnepesaukee ˌwinəpə'sɔ:ki
winner, -s 'winə*, -z
Winnie 'wini
winning (s. adj.) (W.), -s, -ly 'winiŋ, -z,
 -li
winning-post, -s 'winiŋ-pəust, -s
Winnipeg 'winipeg
winn|ow, -ows, -owing, -owed, -ower/s
 'win|əu, -əuz, -əuiŋ, -əud, -əuə*/z
winnowing-fan, -s 'winəuiŋfæn, -z
Winslow 'winzləu
winsome, -ly, -ness 'winsəm, -li, -nis
Winstanley (in Lancs.) 'winstənli [win-
 'stænli, esp. by newcomers], (surname)
 'winstənli, win'stænli
Winston 'winstən
wint|er (s. v.) (W.), -ers, -ering, -ered
 'wint|ə*, -əz, -əriŋ, -əd
Winterbourne 'wintəbɔ:n [-bɔən, -buən]
wintertime 'wintətaim
Winterton 'wintətən
Winton 'wintən
Wintour 'wintə*
wintr|y, -iness 'wintr|i, -inis
winy 'waini
wip|e (s. v.), -es, -ing, -ed, -er/s waip,
 -s, -iŋ, -t, -ə*/z
wir|e (s. v.), -es, -ing, -ed 'waiə*, -z,
 -riŋ, -d
wire-cutter, -s 'waiəˌkʌtə*, -z
wire|draw, -draws, -drawing, -drew,
 -drawn, -drawer/s 'waiə-drɔ:, -drɔ:z,
 -ˌdrɔ:iŋ, -dru:, -drɔ:n, -ˌdrɔ:ə*/z
wire-haired 'waiəhɛəd
wireless (s. adj.), -es 'waiəlis, -iz
wire-pull|er/s, -ing 'waiəˌpul|ə*/z, -iŋ
wire-worm, -s 'waiəwə:m, -z
wiring 'waiəriŋ
wir|y, -ier, -iest, -iness 'waiər|i, -iə*,
 -iist, -inis
wis wis
Wisbech 'wizbi:tʃ
Wisconsin wis'kɔnsin
wisdom 'wizdəm
wise (s. adj.) (W.), -r, -st, -ly, -ness
 waiz, -ə*, -ist, -li, -nis
wiseacre, -s 'waizˌeikə*, -z
wisecrack, -s 'waizkræk, -s
Wiseman 'waizmən
wish (s. v.), -es, -ing, -ed, -er/s wiʃ, -iz,
 -iŋ, -t, -ə*/z
wishbone, -s 'wiʃbəun, -z

wish|ful, -fully, -fulness 'wiʃ|ful, -fuli
 [-fəli], -fulnis
wishing-bone, -s 'wiʃiŋbəun, -z
wish-wash 'wiʃwɔʃ
wishy-washy 'wiʃiˌwɔʃi
wisp, -s wisp, -s
wist wist
Wist|ar, -er 'wist|ə*, -ə*
wistaria, -s wis'tɛəriə, -z
wisteria, -s wis'tiəriə, -z
wist|ful, -fully, -fulness 'wist|ful, -fuli
 [-fəli], -fulnis
wit (s. v.), -s wit, -s
witch (s. v.), -es, -ing/ly, -ed witʃ, -iz,
 -iŋ/li, -t
witchcraft 'witʃkrɑ:ft
witch-doctor, -s 'witʃˌdɔktə*, -z
witch-elm, -s 'witʃ'elm ['witʃelm], -z
witcher|y, -ies 'witʃər|i, -iz
witch-hazel, -s 'witʃ'heizəl, -z
witch-hunt, -s 'witʃhʌnt, -s
witching 'witʃiŋ
witena gemot, -s 'witinə gi'məut [-tən-,
 -gə'm-], -s
with wið [occasionally also wiθ, esp.
 before words beginning with breathed
 consonants]
 Note.—In the N. of England the word
 is generally pronounced wiθ in all
 positions.
withal wi'ðɔ:l
Witham (surname) 'wiðəm, (river in
 Lincs.) 'wiðəm, (town in Essex)
 'witəm
with|draw, -draws, -drawing, -drew,
 -drawn wið|'drɔ: [wiθ|'d-], -'drɔ:z,
 -'drɔ:iŋ, -'dru:, -'drɔ:n
withdrawal, -s wið'drɔ:əl [wiθ'd-], -z
withe, -s wiθ, -s [wið, waið, -z]
with|er (W.), -ers, -ering/ly, -ered
 'wið|ə*, -əz, -əriŋ/li, -əd
withers (s.) (W.) 'wiðəz
with|hold, -holds, -holding, -held,
 -holden, -holder/s wið|'həuld
 [wiθ|'h-], -'həuldz, -'həuldiŋ, -'held,
 -'həuldən, -'həuldə*/z
within wi'ðin [wið'in]
without wi'ðaut [wið'aut]
with|-stand, -stands, -standing, -stood
 wið|'stænd [wiθ|'s-], -'stændz,
 -'stændiŋ, -'stud
with|y, -ies 'wið|i, -iz
witless, -ly, -ness 'witlis, -li, -nis
Witley 'witli
witness (s. v.), -es, -ing, -ed 'witnis, -iz,
 -iŋ, -t
witney (W.) 'witni
-witted -'witid [-ˌwitid]

Wittenberg 'vitnbə:g [-bɛəg, *old-fashioned* 'witnbə:g] ('vitənbɛrk)
witticism, -s 'witisizəm, -z
wittingly 'witiŋli
witt|y, -ier, -iest, -ily, -iness 'wit|i, -ɪə*, -iist, -ili, -inis
Witwatersrand (*usual pronunciation in England*) wit'wɔ:təzrænd ['wit,w-], (*pronunciation of English-speaking South Africans*) 'wit,wɑ:təz'rɑ:nd [-'rɑ:nt, 'vit,vɑ:təz'rɔnt, '-,--,-] (*Afrikaans* 'vit,vɑtərs'rɑnt)
wiv|e, -es, -ing, -ed waiv, -z, -iŋ, -d
Wiveliscombe 'wivəliskəm [*locally also* 'wilskəm
Wivelsfield 'wivəlzfi:ld
wivern, -s 'waivə:n, -z
wives (*plur. of* wife, *and from verb* wive) waivz
wizard (*s. adj.*), -s, -ry 'wizəd, -z, -ri
wizen, -ed 'wizn, -d
W.L.A. 'dʌbl̩ju(:)el'ei
w-ness 'dʌbl̩ju(:)nis
wo wəu [wəuʲ]
woad wəud
wo-back 'wəu'bæk [-'bæk°, -'bæʲ]
wobb|le (*s. v.*), -les, -ling, -led, -ler/s 'wɔb|l̩, -lz, -l̩iŋ [-liŋ], -l̩d, -l̩ə*/z [-lə*/z]
wobb|ly, -liness 'wɔb|l̩i [-li], -l̩inis [-linis]
Woburn (*place in Beds.*) 'wu:bə:n, (*street and square in London*) 'wəubən [-bə:n]
Wodehouse 'wudhaus
Woden 'wəudn
woe, -s wəu, -z
woe-begone 'wəubi,gɔn
woe|ful, -fully, -fulness 'wəu|ful, -fuli [-fəli], -fulnis
woke, -n (*from* wake) wəuk, -ən
Woking, -ham 'wəukiŋ, -əm
Wolborough 'wɔlbərə
Wolcot(t) 'wulkət
wold, -s wəuld, -z
Woldingham 'wəuldiŋəm
Woledge 'wulidʒ
wol|f (*s.*) (W.), -ves wul|f, -vz
wolf (*v.*), -s, -ing, -ed wulf, -s, -iŋ, -t
wolf-cub, -s 'wulfkʌb, -z
Wolfe wulf
Wolfenden 'wulfəndən
Wolff wulf, vɔlf
wolf-hound, -s 'wulfhaund, -z
wolfish, -ly, -ness 'wulfiʃ, -li, -nis
wolfram (W.) 'wulfrəm
wolf-skin, -s 'wulf-skin, -z
Wollaston 'wuləstən

Wollaton (*Nottingham*) 'wulətn
Wollstonecraft 'wulstənkrɑ:ft
Wolseley, -s 'wulzli, -z
Wolsey 'wulzi
Wolsingham 'wɔlsiŋəm
Wolstanton 'wulstæntən [*locally* 'wulstən]
Wolstenholme 'wulstənhəum
Wolverhampton 'wulvə,hæmptən ['wulvə'h-, ,wulvə'h-]
wolverine, -s 'wulvəri:n, -z
Wolverton 'wulvətn [-tən]
wolves (*plur. of* wolf) wulvz
woman, women 'wumən, 'wimin
woman-hater, -s 'wumən,heitə*, -z
womanhood 'wumənhud
womaniz|e [-is|e], -es, -ing, -ed, -er/s 'wumənaiz, -iz, -iŋ, -d, -ə*/z
womanish, -ly, -ness 'wuməniʃ, -li, -nis
womankind 'wumən'kaind ['wumənk-]
womanlike 'wumənlaik
womanl|y, -iness 'wumənl|i, -inis
womb, -s wu:m, -z
wombat, -s 'wɔmbət [-bæt], -s
Wombwell (*place in Yorks.*) 'wumwel [-wəl], (*surname*) 'wumwəl, 'wʌm-, 'wom-
women (*plur. of* woman) 'wimin
womenfolk 'wiminfəuk
won (*from* win) wʌn
wond|er, -ers, -ering/ly, -ered, -erer/s 'wʌnd|ə*, -əz, -əriŋ/li, -əd, -ərə*/z
wonder|ful, -fully, -fulness 'wʌndə|ful, -fli [-fuli, -fəli], -fulnis
Wonderland 'wʌndəlænd
wonderment 'wʌndəmənt
wonder-worker, -s 'wʌndə,wə:kə*, -z
wondrous, -ly, -ness 'wʌndrəs, -li, -nis
wonk|y, -ier, -iest, -ily, -iness 'wɔŋk|i, -ɪə*, -iist, -ili, -inis
wont (*s. adj.*), -ed wəunt, -id
won't wəunt [*also* wəun *when not final*, *also* wəump *before the sounds* p, b, m, *and* wəuŋk *before* k, g]
woo, -s, -ing, -ed, -er/s wu:, -z, -iŋ [wuiŋ], -d, -ə*/z [wuə*/z]
Wooburn 'wu:bə:n
wood (W.), -s, -ed wud, -z, -id
woodbind 'wudbaind
woodbine (W.), -s 'wudbain, -z
woodblock, -s 'wudblɔk, -s
Woodbridge 'wudbridʒ
Woodbury 'wudbəri
wood-carv|er/s, -ing 'wud,kɑ:v|ə*/z, -iŋ
woodchuck, -s 'wudtʃʌk, -s
woodcock (W.), -s 'wudkɔk, -s
woodcut, -s 'wudkʌt, -s
wood-cutter, -s 'wud,kʌtə*, -z

wooden, -ly, -ness 'wudn, -li, -nis
wooden-headed 'wudn,hedid
Wood|ford, -house 'wud|fəd, -haus
woodland, -s 'wudlənd, -z
wood-|louse, -lice 'wud|laus, -lais
wood|man (W.), -men 'wud|mən, -mən
wood-nymph, -s 'wud'nimf ['--], -s
wood-pavement 'wud'peivmənt ['-,--]
woodpecker, -s 'wud,pekə*, -z
wood-pigeon, -s 'wud,pidʒin [-dʒən], -z
Woodroffe 'wudrɔf, -rʌf
Woodrow 'wudrəu
woodruff (W.), -s 'wudrʌf, -s
Woods wudz
Woodside 'wud'said ['--]
Wood|stock, -ward 'wud|stɔk, -wəd
wood-wind, -s 'wudwind, -z
woodwork 'wudwə:k
wood|y, -ier, -iest, -iness 'wud|i, -iə*,
-iist, -inis
woof, -s wu:f, -s
Woof (surname) wuf
Wookey 'wuki
wool, -s wul, -z
Wooldridge 'wuldridʒ
Woolf wulf
Woolfardisworthy (near Bideford,
Devon) 'wulzəri [wul'fɑ:dis,wə:ði],
(near Crediton, Devon) wul'fɑ:dis,wə:ði
wool-gathering 'wul,gæðəriŋ
Woollard 'wulɑ:d
woollen 'wulən [-lin]
Woolley 'wuli
Woolliams 'wuljəmz
wooll|y (s. adj.), -ies, -ier, -iest, -iness
'wul|i, -iz, -iə*, -iist, -inis
woolly-headed 'wuli,hedid
Wooln|er, -ough 'wuln|ə*, -əu
woolsack 'wul-sæk
woolsey (W.) 'wulzi
Woolwich 'wulidʒ [-itʃ]
woolwork 'wulwə:k
Woolworth 'wulwəθ [-wə:θ]
Woomera 'wumərə ['wu:-]
Woorstead 'wustid [-təd]
Woosley 'wu:zli
Wooster 'wustə*
Wootton 'wutn
Worcester, -shire 'wustə*, -ʃiə* [-ʃə*]
Worcs. wə:ks
word (s. v.), -s, -ing/s, -ed ; -less wə:d,
-z, -iŋ/z, -id; -lis
word-book, -s 'wə:dbuk, -s
word-formation 'wə:dfɔ:,meiʃən
word-painting 'wə:d,peintiŋ
word-perfect 'wə:d'pə:fikt
word-picture, -s 'wə:d,piktʃə*, -z
word-splitting 'wə:d,splitiŋ

Wordsworth 'wə:dzwə(:)θ
Wordsworthian wə:dz'wə:ðjən [-ðiən]
word|y, -ier, -iest, -ily, -iness 'wə:d|i,
-iə* [-jə*], -iist [-jist], -ili, -inis
wore (from wear) wɔ:* [wɔə*]
work, -s, -ing/s, -ed, -er/s; -able/ness
wə:k, -s, -iŋ/z, -t, -ə*/z; -əbl/nis
workaday 'wə:kədei
work-bag, -s 'wə:kbæg, -z
work-basket, -s 'wə:k,bɑ:skit, -s
workbook, -s 'wə:kbuk, -s
work-box, -es 'wə:kbɔks, -iz
work-day, -s 'wə:kdei, -z
workhou|se, -ses 'wə:khau|s, -ziz
Workington 'wə:kiŋtən
workless 'wə:klis
work|man (W.), -men; -manlike
'wə:k|mən, -mən; -mənlaik
workman|ly, -ship 'wə:kmən|li, -ʃip
work-people 'wə:k,pi:pl
work-room, -s 'wə:k-rum [-ru:m], -z
workshop, -s 'wə:kʃɔp, -s
work-shy 'wə:kʃai
Worksop 'wə:ksɔp [-səp]
work-table, -s 'wə:k,teibl, -z
world, -s wə:ld, -z
worldling, -s 'wə:ldliŋ, -z
worldl|y, -ier, -iest, -iness 'wə:ldl|i,
-iə* [-jə*], -iist [-jist], -inis
worldly-minded 'wə:ldli'maindid ['--,--]
worldly-wise 'wə:ldli'waiz
world-wide 'wə:ld-waid [also '-'- when
not attributive]
worm (s. v.), -s, -ing, -ed wə:m, -z, -iŋ, -d
Worman 'wɔ:mən
worm-cast, -s 'wə:mkɑ:st, -s
worm-eaten 'wə:m,i:tn
worm-gear, -s 'wə:mgiə*, -z
worm-hole, -s 'wə:mhəul, -z
Worms (German city) vɔ:mz [wə:mz]
(vɔrms)
wormwood (W.) 'wə:mwud
worm|y, -iness 'wə:m|i, -inis
worn (from wear) wɔ:n
worn-out 'wɔ:n'aut ['-- when attributive]
Worple, -sdon 'wɔ:pl, -zdən
Worrall 'wʌrəl, wɔrəl
worr|y (s. v.), -ies, -ying/ly, -ied, -ier/s
'wʌr|i, -iz, -iiŋ/li, -id, -iə*/z
Worsborough 'wə:zbərə
worse wə:s
wors|en, -ens, -ening, -ened 'wə:s|n,
-nz, -niŋ [-ṇiŋ], -nd
Worsfold 'wə:sfəuld, 'wɔ:zfəuld
worship (s. v.) (W.), -s, -ping, -ped,
-per/s 'wə:ʃip, -s, -iŋ, -t, -ə*/z
worship|ful, -fully, -fulness 'wə:ʃip|ful,
-fuli [-fəli], -fulnis

Worsley (surname) 'wə:sli, 'wə:zli, (place near Manchester) 'wə:sli

Worsnop 'wə:znəp

worst (s. adj. v.), -s, -ing, -ed wə:st, -s, -iŋ, -id

Worstead 'wustid [-təd]

worsted (s.) (yarn, cloth) 'wustid [-təd]

worsted (v.) (from worst) 'wə:stid

Worswick (surname) 'wə:sik

wort, -s wə:t, -s

worth (W.), -s wə:θ, -s

Worthing, -ton 'wə:ðiŋ, -tən

worthless, -ly, -ness 'wə:θlis, -li, -nis

worth|y (s. adj.), -ies, -ier, -iest, -ily, -iness 'wə:ð|i, -iz, -iə* [-jə*], -iist [-jist], -ili, -inis

Wortley 'wə:tli

wot wɔt

Wotherspoon 'wɔðəspu:n

Wotton 'wɔtn, 'wutn
Note.—The place in Bucks. is called 'wutn.

would (from will) wud (strong form), wəd, əd, d (weak forms)

would-be 'wudbi: [-bi]

wouldn't 'wudnt

wound (s. v.), -s, -ing, -ed wu:nd, -z -iŋ, -id

wound (from wind, v.) waund

wove (from weave), -n wəuv, -ən

wow, -s wau, -z

wrack, -s ræk, -s

wraith, -s reiθ, -s

wrang|le, -les, -ling, -led, -ler/s 'ræŋg|l, -lz, -liŋ [-liŋ], -ld, -lə*/z [-lə*/z]

wrangler (candidate obtaining first class in mathematical tripos), -s 'ræŋglə*, -z

wrap (s. v.), -s, -ping/s, -ped ræp, -s, -iŋ/z, -t

wrapper, -s 'ræpə*, -z

wrasse, -s ræs, -iz

wrath rɔθ [rɔ:θ]

Wrath (Cape) rɔ:θ [in Scotland raθ, also rɑ:θ, ræθ]

wrath|ful, -fully, -fulness 'rɔθ|ful ['rɔ:θ-], -fuli [-fəli], -fulnis

Wratislaw (English surname) 'rætislɔ:

Wraxall 'ræksɔ:l

Wray rei

wreak, -s, -ing, -ed, -er/s ri:k, -s, -iŋ, -t, -ə*/z

wrea|th, -ths ri:|θ, -ðz [-θs]

wreath|e, -es, -ing, -ed ri:ð, -z, -iŋ, -d

Wreay (in Cumberland) rei [locally riə]

wreck (s. v.), -s, -ing, -ed, -er/s; -age/s rek, -s, -iŋ, -t, -ə*/z; -idʒ/iz

Wrekin 'ri:kin

wren (W.), -s ren, -z

wrench (s. v.), -es, -ing, -ed rentʃ, -iz, -iŋ, -t

Wrenn ren

wrest, -s, -ing, -ed rest, -s, -iŋ, -id

wrest|le, -les, -ling, -led, -ler/s 'res|l, -lz, -liŋ [-liŋ], -ld, -lə*/z [-lə*/z]

wretch, -es retʃ, -iz

wretched, -ly, -ness 'retʃid, -li, -nis

Wrexham 'reksəm

wrig|gle, -les, -ling, -led, -ler/s 'rig|l, -lz, -liŋ [-liŋ], -ld, -lə*/z [-lə*/z]

wright (W.), -s rait, -s

Wrigley 'rigli

wring, -s, -ing, wrung riŋ, -z, -iŋ, rʌŋ

wrink|le, -les, -ling, -led 'riŋk|l, -lz, -liŋ [-liŋ], -ld

wrinkly 'riŋkli

Wriothesley 'raiəθsli

wrist, -s rist, -s

wristband, -s 'ristbænd [old-fashioned 'rizbænd, 'rizbənd], -z

wristlet, -s 'ristlit, -s

wrist-watch, -es 'rist-wɔtʃ, -iz

writ (s.), -s rit, -s

writ (=written) rit

writ|e, -es, -ing/s, wrote, written, writer/s rait, -s, -iŋ/z, rəut, 'ritn, 'raitə*/z

with|e, -es, -ing, -ed raið, -z, -iŋ, -d

writing (s.), -s 'raitiŋ, -z

writing-case, -s 'raitiŋ-keis, -iz

writing-desk, -s 'raitiŋdesk, -s

writing-paper 'raitiŋ,peipə*

writing-table, -s 'raitiŋ,teibl, -z

written-off 'ritn'ɔf [-'ɔ:f]

wrong (s. adj. v.) (W.), -s; -ly, -ness; -ing, -ed rɔŋ, -z; -li, -nis; -iŋ, -d

wrong-doer, -s 'rɔŋ'duə* [-'du:ə*, 'rɔŋduə*, 'rɔŋ,du:ə*], -z

wrong-doing 'rɔŋ'du(:)iŋ ['rɔŋ,du(:)iŋ]

wrong|ful, -fully, -fulness 'rɔŋ|ful, -fuli [-fəli], -fulnis

wrongheaded, -ly, -ness 'rɔŋ'hedid, -li, -nis

Wrose rəuz, rəus

wrote (from write) rəut

wroth rəuθ [rɔ:θ, rɔθ]

Wrotham (in Kent) 'ru:təm

Wrottesley 'rɔtsli

wrought rɔ:t

wrought-|iron, -up 'rɔ:t|'aiən, -'ʌp

Wroxham 'rɔksəm

wrung (from wring) rʌŋ

wr|y, -ier [-yer], -iest [-yest], -yly, -yness r|ai, -ai-ə*, -aiist, -ai-li, -ai-nis

wryneck, -s 'rainek, -s

Wrythe raið
Wulf wulf
Wulfila 'wulfilə
Wulfstan 'wulfstən
Wurlitzer, -s 'wəːlitsə*, -z
Württemberg 'vəːtəmbɛəg ['wəːtəmbəːg]
 ('vyrtəmbɛrk)
Wuthering 'wʌðəriŋ
W.V.S. 'dʌbļju(ː)viː'es
Wyandotte, -s 'waiəndɔt, -s
Wyat(t) 'waiət
Wych waitʃ, witʃ
wych-elm, -s 'witʃ'elm ['witʃelm], -z
Wycherley 'witʃəli
wych-hazel, -s 'witʃ'heizəl ['-,--], -z
Wyclif(fe) 'wiklif
Wyclif(f)ite, -s 'wiklif-ait, -s

Wycombe 'wikəm
Wye wai
Wygram 'waigrəm
Wykeham, -ist/s 'wikəm, -ist/s
Wyld(e) waild
Wyl(l)ie 'waili
Wylly 'waili
Wyman 'waimən
Wymondham (*in Norfolk*) 'wiməndəm
 [*locally* 'windəm], (*in Leics.*)
Wyndham 'windəm Į'waiməndəm
Wynn(e) win
Wynyard 'winjəd
Wyoming wai'əumiŋ
Wysard 'waizɑːd
Wytham 'waitəm
wyvern (W.), -s 'waivə(ː)n, -z

X

X (*the letter*), **-'s** eks, -iz
Xanadu 'zænədu:
Xanthipp|e, -us zæn'θip|i [gz-, -n'ti-], -əs
Xanthus 'zænθəs ['gz-]
Xavier 'zævīə* ['zeiv-, -vjə*] (xa'bjer)
xebec, -s 'zi:bek, -s
xenogamy zi(:)'nɔgəmi [gz-]
xenon 'zenɔn ['gz-]
xenophobe, -s 'zenəfəub ['gz-, -nəuf-], -z
xenophobia ˌzenə'fəubjə [ˌgz-, -nəu'f-, -bīə]
Xenophon 'zenəfən ['gz-]
xerography ze'rɔgrəfi [ziə'r-]

Xerxes 'zə:ksi:z ['gz-]
Xhosa 'kɔ:sə ['kəusə] (*Kaffir* ʘhɔ:sa)
xi (*Greek letter*), **-'s** sai [gzai, zai], -z
Xmas 'krisməs [-stm-]
X-ray (*s. v.*), **-s, -ing, -ed** 'eks'rei ['--], -z, -iŋ, -d
xylograph, -s 'zailəgrɑ:f ['gz-, -ləug-, -græf], -s
xylograph|er/s, **-y** zai'lɔgrəf|ə*/z [gz-], -i
xylonite 'zailənait ['gz-, -ləun-]
xylophone, -s 'zailəfəun ['gz-, 'zil-], -z
Note.—'ziləfəun *is in common use among band players.*

Y

Y (*the letter*), -'s wai, -z
yacht (*s. v.*), **-s, -ing, -ed** jɔt, -s, -iŋ, -id
yachts|man, -men 'jɔts|mən, -mən
yah jɑ:
yahoo, -s jə'hu: [jɑ:'h-], -z
Yahveh 'jɑ:vei [jɑ:'vei, 'jɑ:və]
yak, -s jæk, -s
Yakutsk jæ'kutsk [jɑ:'k-, jə'k-] (ji'kutsk)
Yalding (*surname*) 'jældiŋ, (*house in London*) 'jɔ:ldiŋ
Yale jeil
Yalta 'jæltə
yam, -s jæm, -z
Yamuna (*river Jumna*) 'jʌmunə (*Hind.* jəmwna)
Yangtse-Kiang 'jæŋtsi'kjæŋ [-ki'æŋ]
yank (Y.), **-s, -ing, -ed** jæŋk, -s, -iŋ, -t [jæŋt]
Yankee, -s 'jæŋki, -z
yap, -s, -ping, -ped jæp, -s, -iŋ, -t
yappy 'jæpi
yard, -s jɑ:d, -z
yardarm, -s 'jɑ:dɑ:m, -z
Yardley 'jɑ:dli
yard-stick, -s 'jɑ:dstik, -s
Yare (*in Norfolk*) jɛə*, (*in the Isle of Wight*) jɑ:*
Yarico 'jærikəu
Yarmouth 'jɑ:məθ
yarn (*s. v.*), **-s, -ing, -ed** jɑ:n, -z, -iŋ, -d
yarrow (Y.) 'jærəu
yashmak, -s 'jæʃmæk, -s
yataghan, -s 'jætəgən, -z
Yate, -s jeit, -s
Yatman 'jætmən
yaw (*s. v.*), **-s, -ing, -ed** jɔ:, -z, -iŋ, -d
yawl, -s jɔ:l, -z
yawn (*s. v.*), **-s, -ing/ly, -ed** jɔ:n, -z, -iŋ/li, -d
yaws jɔ:z
yclept i'klept
ye (*you*) ji:(*normal form*), ji (*occasional weak form*)
ye (*the*) ji: [*or as* the, *q.v.*]
yea jei
Yeading 'jediŋ
Yealm jelm
Yealmpton 'jæmptən

Yeames ji:mz
yean, -s, -ing, -ed ji:n, -z, -iŋ, -d
yeanling, -s 'ji:nliŋ, -z
year, -s, -ly jə:* [jiə*], -z, -li
year-book, -s 'jə:buk ['jiəb-], -s
yearling, -s 'jə:liŋ ['jiəl-], -z
yearn, -s, -ing/s, -ed jə:n, -z, -iŋ/z, -d
yeast, -y, -iness ji:st, -i, -inis
Yeat(e)s jeits
Yeatman 'ji:tmən, 'jeitmən, 'jetmən
Yeddo (*old name of Tokyo*) 'jedəu
Yehudi je'hu:di [ji'h-, jə'h-]
yelk jelk
yell (*s. v.*) (Y.), -s, -ing, -ed jel, -z, -iŋ, -d
yellow, -s, -ed 'jeləu, -z, -d
yellow-ammer, -s 'jeləu,æmə*, -z
yellow-band 'jeləubænd
yellow-hammer, -s 'jeləu,hæmə*, -z
yellowish, -ness 'jeləuiʃ, -nis
yellowness 'jeləunis
yellowplush 'jeləu-plʌʃ
Yellowstone 'jeləu-stəun [-stən]
yellowy 'jeləui
yelp (*s. v.*), -s, -ing, -ed jelp, -s, -iŋ, -t
Yemen, -i, -is 'jemən, -i, -iz
yen, -s jen, -z
Yenisei ˌjeni'seii [-'sei, 'jenisei] (jenji-'sjej)
Yeo jəu
yeo|man, -men 'jəu|mən, -mən
yeoman|ly, -ry 'jəumən|li, -ri
Yeomans 'jəumənz
Yeovil 'jəuvil
Yerkes (*American name*) 'jə:ki:z
yes jes [jɛə, jeh]
yes|-man, -men 'jes|mæn, -men
yesterday 'jestədi [-dei, 'jestdi, ˌjestə-'dei]
yet jet
Yetholm 'jetəm
yew, -s ju:, -z
Yezo (*old name of Hokkaido*) 'jezəu
Yg(g)drasil 'igˌdræsl ['igdrəsil]
Y-gun, -s 'waigʌn, -z
Yiddish 'jidiʃ
yield (*s. v.*), -s, -ing/ly, -ed ji:ld, -z, -iŋ/li, -id
y-ness 'wai-nis
yod, -s jɔd, -z

yod|el (*s. v.*), **-els, -el(l)ing, -el(l)ed** 'jəud|l ['jɔd-], -lz, -l̩iŋ [-əliŋ], -ld

yog, -a, -i/s, -ism 'jəug, -ə, -i/z, -izəm

yoghourt 'jɔgə(:)t ['jəug-, -uət]

yo-ho jəu'həu

yoick, -s, -ing, -ed jɔik, -s, -iŋ, -t

yoicks (*interj.*) jɔiks

yok|e (*s. v.*), **-es, -ing, -ed** jəuk, -s, -iŋ, -t

yokel, -s 'jəukəl, -z

Yokohama ˌjəukəu'hɑ:mə

yolk, -s, -y jəuk, -s, -i

yon jɔn

yonder 'jɔndə*

Yonge jʌŋ

yore jɔ:* [jɔə*]

Yorick 'jɔrik

York, -shire jɔ:k, -ʃiə* [-ʃə*]

Yorke jɔ:k

yorker, -s 'jɔ:kə*, -z

Yorkist, -s 'jɔ:kist, -s

Yorks. jɔ:ks   [[-men]

Yorkshire|man, -men 'jɔ:kʃə|mən, -mən

Yosemite jəu'semiti

Yost, -s jəust, -s

yotization [-isa-], **-s** ˌjəutai'zeiʃən [-ti'z-], -z

yotiz|e [-is|e], **-es, -ing, -ed** 'jəutaiz, -iz, -iŋ, -d

you ju: (*normal form*), ju (*frequent weak form*), jə (*occasional weak form*)
Note 1.—*Sometimes when* **you** *is weakly stressed and is preceded by a word normally ending in* d, *the two words are joined closely together as if they formed a single word with the 'affricate' sound* dʒ *linking the two parts. Thus* **did you** *is often pronounced* 'didʒu: (*or* 'didʒu), *and* **behind you** bi'haindʒu(:).
Similarly when the preceding word normally ends in t; *for instance* **hurt you** *is sometimes pronounced* 'hə:tʃu: *or* 'hə:tʃu, *and* **don't you know** *as* 'dəuntʃu(:)'nəu *or* 'dəuntʃə'nəu. *See also* **what-you-may-call-it.**
Note 2.—*ju occurs as a strong form in the expression* **you are** *when* **are** *has its weak form* ə*. **You are** *in this case is also written* **you're.** *For other variants used in this case see* **you're.**

Youghal (*near Cork*) jɔ:l, (*on Lake Derg*) 'jɔkəl ['jɔxəl]

Youmans 'ju:mənz

young (*s. adj.*) (**Y.**), **-er, -est** jʌŋ, -gə*, -gist

Younger 'jʌŋə*, 'jʌŋgə*

Younghusband 'jʌŋˌhʌzbənd

youngish 'jʌŋiʃ [-ŋgi-]

Youngman 'jʌŋmən

youngster, -s 'jʌŋstə* [-ŋks-], -z

younker, -s 'jʌŋkə*, -z

your jɔ:* [jɔə*, juə*] (*normal forms*), jə* (*occasional weak form*)

you're (=**you are**) juə* [jɔə*, jɔ:*]

yours jɔ:z [jɔəz, juəz]

yoursel|f, -ves jɔ:'sel|f, [jɔə's-, juə's-, jə's-], -vz

you|th, -ths ju:|θ, -ðz

youth|ful, -fully, -fulness 'ju:θ|ful, -fuli [-fəli], -fulnis

you've (=**you have**) ju:v (*normal form*), juv, jəv (*occasional weak forms*)

yo-yo, -s 'jəujəu, -z

Ypres (*in Belgium*) i:pr̝ ['i:pəz, *sometimes facetiously* 'aipəz, 'waipəz] (ipr̝)

Ypres (*tower at Rye*) i:pr̝ ['i:prei, 'waipəz]
Note.—*The 'Ypres Castle', a public house near by, is called locally the* 'waipəz.

Ysaye i'zaii [i'zai]

Yser (*in Belgium*) 'i:zə* (izɛ:r)

Ystradgynlais ˌistræd'ginlais [ˌʌstræd-'gʌnlais] (*Welsh* əstrad'gənlais)

Ythan 'aiθən

ytterbium i'tə:bjəm [-biəm]

yttrium 'itriəm

Y-tube, -s 'wai-tju:b, -z

Yucatan ˌju:kə'tɑ:n [juk-, -'tæn]

yucca, -s 'jʌkə, -z

Yugoslav, -s 'ju:gəu'slɑ:v [-'slæv, '---], -z

Yugoslavia, -n 'ju:gəu'slɑ:vjə [-vɪə], -n

Yuill 'ju(:)il

Yukon 'ju:kɔn

Yule ju:l

yulery 'ju:ləri

Yuletide 'ju:l-taid

Yum-Yum 'jʌm'jʌm [-'- *when preceded by a stress*]

Yussuf 'jusuf [-səf]

Z

Z (*the letter*), -'s zed, -z
Zabulon 'zæbjulən [zə'bju:lən, zæ'bju:-]
Zacchaeus zæ'ki(:)əs [zə'k-]
Zachariah ˌzækə'raiə
Zacharias ˌzækə'raiəs [-'raiæs]
Zachary 'zækəri
Zadok 'zeidɔk
Zalmunna zæl'mʌnə
Zama 'zɑːmə
Zambez|i, -ia zæm'bi:z|i, -jə [-ïə]
Zambia 'zæmbïə [-bjə]
Zambra 'zæmbrə
Zangwill 'zæŋgwil
zan|y, -ies 'zein|i, -iz
Zanzibar ˌzænzi'bɑ:* ['zænzi'b-]
Zarathustra ˌzærə'θu:strə [ˌzɑ:r-]
zareba, -s zə'ri:bə, -z
Zarephath 'zærifæθ [-ref-, -rəf-]
Zaria 'zɑ:rïə
zeal zi:l
Zealand, -er/s 'zi:lənd, -ə*/z
zealot, -s, -ry 'zelət, -s, -ri
zealous, -ly, -ness 'zeləs, -li, -nis
Zebah 'zi:bə
Zebedee 'zebidi:
zebra, -s 'zi:brə ['zeb-], -z
zebu, -s 'zi:bu:, -z
Zebub 'zi:bʌb [-bəb, *rarely* zi'bʌb]
Zebulon 'zebjulən [ze'bju:lən]
Zechariah ˌzekə'raiə
zed, -s zed, -z
Zedekiah ˌzedi'kaiə
Zeeb 'zi:eb [zi:b]
Zeeland 'zeilənd ['zi:l-]
Zeiss, -es zais, -iz
Zeitgeist 'tsaitgaist ['zait-] ('tsaitgaist)
Zeller (*wine*) 'zelə*
Zelotes zi(:)'ləuti:z
zemindar, -s 'zemindɑ:*, -z
zemstvo, -s 'zemstvəu ('zjemstvə), -z
Zena 'zi:nə
zenana, -s ze'nɑ:nə [zi'n-], -z
Zend zend
zenith, -s 'zeniθ ['zi:n-], -s
Zeno 'zi:nəu
Zenobia zi'nəubjə [ze'n-, -bïə]
Zephaniah ˌzefə'naiə
zephyr (Z.), -s 'zefə*, -z
zeppelin (Z.), -s 'zepəlin [-p̣lin], -z

Zermatt 'zə:mæt
zero, -s 'ziərəu, -z
zerography ze'rɔgrəfi [ziə'r-]
Zerubbabel zi'rʌbəbəl [zə'r-, *in Jewish
   usage also* zi'ru:ˌbɑ:-, zə'ru:ˌbɑ:-]
Zeruiah ˌzeru'aiə [-rju-]
zest zest
zeta, -s 'zi:tə, -z
Zetland 'zetlənd
zeugma, -s 'zju:gmə ['zu:-], -z
Zeus zju:s
Zidon 'zaidn [-dɔn]
zigzag (*s. v.*), -s, -ging, -ged 'zigzæg, -z,
   -iŋ, -d
Ziklag 'ziklæg
Zilliacus ˌzili'ɑ:kəs, -'eikəs
Zimbabwe zim'bɑ:bwi
Zimri 'zimrai
zinc (*s. v.*), -s, -king, -ked ziŋk, -s, -iŋ, -t
zin(c)ky 'ziŋki
zinco, -s 'ziŋkəu, -z
zincograph, -s 'ziŋkəugrɑ:f [-græf], -s
zingar|o, -i 'ziŋgər|əu, -i(:)
zinnia, -s 'zinjə [-nïə], -z
Zion, -ism, -ist/s, -ward/s 'zaiən,
   -izəm, -ist/s, -wəd/z
zip, -s zip, -s
zip-fastener, -s 'zipˌfɑ:snə*, -z
zipper, -s 'zipə*, -z
Zippor 'zipɔ:* [zi'pɔ:*]
Zipporah zi'pɔ:rə [*rarely* 'zipərə]
zirconium zə:'kəunjəm [-nïəm]
zither, -s 'ziðə* ['ziθə*], -z
zloty, -s 'zlɔti, -z
Zoar 'zəuɑ:* ['zəuə*]
zodiac 'zəudiæk [-djæk]
zodiacal zəu'daiəkəl
Zoe 'zəui
zoetrope, -s 'zəuitrəup, -s
zoic 'zəuik
Zola 'zəulə
zollverein, -s 'tsɔl-fərain ['zɔlvərain]
   ('tsɔl-fərʔain), -z
zombie, -s 'zɔmbi, -z
zon|al, -ally 'zəun|l [-əl], -əli
zon|e (*s. v.*), -es, -ing, -ed; -eless zəun,
   -z, -iŋ, -d; -lis
Zoo, -s zu:, -z
zoograph|er/s, -y zəu'ɔgrəf|ə*/z, -i

zooks zuːks
zoolite, -s 'zəuəlait ['zəuᵊul-], -s
zoologic|al, -ally ˌzəuə'lɔdʒik|əl [zŭə'l-, zu'l-], -əli
Zoological Garden, -s zu'lɔdʒikəl'gɑːdn [zŭə'l-, zə'l-, zļ'ɔdʒ-, 'zlɔdʒ-, *rarely* ˌzəuə'l-], -z
zoolog|ist/s, -y zəu'ɔlədʒ|ist/s [zu'ɔ-], -i
zoom, -s, -ing, -ed zuːm, -z, -iŋ, -d
zoomorphic ˌzəuəu'mɔːfik
zo|on, -a 'zəu|ɔn, -ə
zoophyte, -s 'zəuəufait, -s
zoot, -s zuːt, -s
zootom|ist/s, -y zəu'ɔtəm|ist/s, -i
Zophar 'zəufɑː* [-fə*]
zoril, -s 'zɔril, -z
Zoroaster ˌzɔrəu'æstə*

Zoroastrian, -s, -ism ˌzɔrəu'æstrĭən, -z, -izᵊm
zouave (Z.), -s zu(ː)'ɑːv [zwɑːv, 'zuːɑːv], Zouch(e) zuːʃ   [-z
zounds zaundz [zuːndz]
Zuleika (*Persian name*) zu(ː)'leikə [-'laikə], (*as English personal name*) zu(ː)'leikə
Zulu, -s 'zuːluː, -z
Zululand 'zuːluː(ː)lænd
Zürich 'zjuərik ['zuə-] ('tsyːriç)
Zutphen 'zʌtfən
Zuyder Zee 'zaidə'zei [-'ziː]
zwieback, -s 'zwiːbæk [-bɑːk] ('tsviːbak), zygoma, -ta zai'gəumə [zi'g-], -tə   [-s
zymosis zai'məusis [zi'm-]
zymotic zai'mɔtik [zi'm-]

GLOSSARY OF PHONETIC TERMS

used in the Introduction and Explanations

Large-sized roman numerals refer to Sections of the Explanations

advanced (vowel or consonant), articulated with a more forward position of the tongue (than some other sound).

affricate (consonant), a variety of plosive consonant pronounced with relatively slow separation of the articulating organs, so that the effect of the homorganic fricative is audible during the release.

allophone, a member of a phoneme, q.v.

allophonic (transcription), a type of phonetic transcription containing special symbols to represent particular members of phonemes.

alveolar (consonant), articulated by the tip or the blade of the tongue against the upper gum.

aspirated (plosive), with a slight puff of breath following the release.

assimilation, replacement of a sound by another sound having greater resemblance to an adjoining sound in the word or sentence.

back (of the tongue), the part lying opposite to the soft palate.

back (vowel), one formed with a raising of the 'back' of the tongue, as shown in the Frontispiece.

bi-labial (consonant), formed by the two lips.

blade (of the tongue), the part which lies normally opposite the upper gum.

breathed (sound), pronounced with the vocal cords apart.

broad (phonetic transcription), a type of phonetic transcription which represents only the 'phonemes' of a language, and which uses for this purpose the minimum number of letter shapes of simplest romanic form together with such marks to denote length, stress, intonation and syllable separation as may be necessary for the avoidance of lexical ambiguity. See *Outline of English Phonetics*, 8th (1956) and subsequent editions, Appendix A, §5.

cardinal vowels, a set of vowel-sounds chosen to form a scale of reference. See XXIV A (p. xxxii) and Frontispiece.

central (vowels), neither 'front' nor 'back' nor 'open', but formed with a raising of the middle part of the tongue into a position which may be represented by a point within the central triangle shown in the Frontispiece and in the Table on p. xxxiii.

clear « l », a variety of « l » having as a secondary articulation a certain raising of the 'front' of the tongue towards the hard palate.

click, a type of plosive consonant in the formation of which air is sucked inwards.

close (vowels), formed with the 'front', 'back' or intermediate part of the tongue raised high towards the palate.

comparative (transcription), a form of phonetic transcription providing special symbols to show that sounds of the language transcribed differ from analogous sounds of another language or dialect. Synonymous with 'typographically narrow', q.v.

conditioned variant, an allophone.

dark « l », a variety of « l » having as a secondary articulation a certain raising of the 'back' of the tongue towards the soft palate.

dental (consonant), articulated by the tip of the tongue against the upper front teeth.

devoiced, modified by ceasing vibration of the vocal cords.

diaphone, a family of variant sounds used by different people but accepted as equivalents of an 'average' sound. See XXIV E (p. xxxvii).

diaphonic variant, a variant sound belonging to a diaphone.

digraph, a sequence of two letters used in a phonetic transcription to represent a single speech-sound.

digraphic (representation), representation of a single speech-sound by a sequence of two letters.

diphthong, a monosyllabic gliding sound beginning at one vowel and moving in the direction of another.

diphthongal, of the nature of a diphthong.

disyllabic, forming two syllables.

falling diphthong, a diphthong in which the initial part has greater 'prominence' than the final part.

flapped (consonant), formed like a rolled consonant, but consisting of one single tap of the articulating organ.

free variant, a member of a diaphone.

fricative (consonant), made by narrowing the air passage at some point, so that when air is expelled forcibly there is audible friction (hissing, etc.).

frictionless continuant, a consonant having the articulation of a fricative but pronounced with weak force so that little or no friction is audible.

front (of the tongue), the part lying normally opposite the hard palate.

front (vowel), one formed with a raising of the 'front' of the tongue, as shown in the Frontispiece.

fully voiced (sound), pronounced with vibration of the vocal cords continuing throughout the duration of the sound.

gliding (sound), formed by a gradual movement of the articulating mechanism.

glottal, formed in the glottis.

glottal stop, the plosive consonant formed by bringing the vocal cords together so that when they are separated the air from the lungs escapes suddenly causing audible plosion.

glottis, the vocal cords and the space between them.

half-close (vowel), formed with the tongue at about one-third of the distance between 'close' and 'open'. See Table on p. xxxiii.

half-open (vowel), formed with the tongue at about two-thirds of the distance between 'close' and 'open'. See Table on p. xxxiii.

hard (Russian consonant), having as a secondary articulation a raising of the 'back' of the tongue in the direction of the soft palate.

homorganic, having the same place of articulation (as another sound).

inclusive (transcription), a form of phonetic transcription which allows for more than one pronunciation of the words transcribed. See *Outline of English Phonetics*, 8th (1956) and subsequent editions, Appendix A, §§ *24–27*.

incomplete plosive (consonant), formed with complete closure of the air channel at some point, but without audible release.

internally comparative (transcription), a form of transcription containing a special symbol to show a comparison between the beginning of a digraphically represented sound and another sound occurring in the language.

intrusive « r », a « r » inserted at the end of a word normally ending in « ə », « iə », « ɛə », « ɔə », « uə », « ə: », « ɑ: » or « ɔ: », and not written with *r* in ordinary spelling, when a following word begins with a vowel. See XV (p. xxvi).

labial (consonant), bi-labial or labio-dental.

labialized (sound), one pronounced with added lip-rounding.

labio-dental (consonant), articulated by the lower lip against the upper teeth.

lateral (consonant), formed by a tongue-contact in the centre of the mouth, leaving a free passage for the air to escape on one or both sides.

lax (sound), one pronounced with relaxed muscles.

linguistically broad (transcription), phonemic, i.e. based on the principle 'one symbol per phoneme'.

linguistically narrow (transcription), allophonic, i.e. comprising special symbols to denote particular allophones (members of phonemes).

linking « r », a « r » inserted at the end of a word normally ending in « ə », « iə », « ɛə », « ɔə », « uə », « ə: », « ɑ: » or « ɔ: », and written with *r* in ordinary spelling, when a following word begins with a vowel. See XV (p. xxvi).

lip-rounding, protrusion or pursing up of the lips so that the opening between them is roundish in shape.

monophthongal (sound), a 'pure' vowel, i.e. one which is perceived as being of a stationary nature, and not of a gliding nature.

monosyllable, a sequence of speech-sounds forming a single syllable.

mouillé (consonant), French term for 'palatal' or 'palatalized'.

narrow (phonetic transcription), a form of phonetic transcription containing special symbols to denote allophones and/or to show comparisons between sounds of the language transcribed and analogous sounds of a foreign language or to show 'internal' comparisons.

nasal (consonant), formed by a complete closure in the mouth, the soft palate being, however, lowered so that air expelled by the lungs issues through the nose.

nasalization, pronunciation with simultaneous lowering of the soft palate, so that air issues through the nose as well as through the mouth.

nasalized (vowel), pronounced with simultaneous lowering of the soft palate, so that air issues through the nose as well as through the mouth.

norm (of a phoneme), the principal allophone (member) of a phoneme.

obscure (vowel), a sound of the type represented by « ə » (see Table on p. xxxiii), or having some acoustic resemblance to a vowel of this type.

open (vowel), formed with the body of the tongue in one of its lowest positions.

palatal (consonant), articulated by the 'front' of the tongue against the hard palate.

palatalized (consonant), having as a secondary articulation a raising of the 'front' of the tongue high towards the hard palate. On the release of such a consonant a « j »-glide is audible.

palato-alveolar (consonant), articulated by the blade, or tip and blade, of the tongue against the upper gum, with simultaneous raising of the main body of the tongue towards the palate.

phoneme, a family of related speech-sounds in a given language which count linguistically as if they were one and the same. The use of each member of the family (allophone) is determined by the phonetic context. See XXIX D (p. xxxvi), also my books *The Pronunciation of English*, 4th (1956) and subsequent editions, §§ 492–500, *Outline of English Phonetics*, 8th (1956) and subsequent editions, Chap. X, and *The Phoneme, its Nature and Use*, 3rd edition, 1967.

phonemic (transcription), a type of phonetic transcription which provides one and only one symbol for each phoneme of the language transcribed, and does not provide any special symbols to denote allophones.

phonetic (transcription), a system of alphabetic writing which provides a symbol for each phoneme of the language transcribed, with or without additional symbols or marks to denote allophones or to show comparisons between sounds of the language transcribed and those of another language or manner of pronouncing.

plosive (consonant), formed by complete closure at some point of the air channel followed by a release resulting in an audible plosion.

post-alveolar (consonant), articulated by the tip of the tongue against the hinder part of the upper gum.

pre-tonic (syllable), a syllable immediately preceding a syllable bearing strong stress.

prominent (sound or syllable), one which, by reason of its inherent quality, special length, stress or intonation, is heard more distinctly than other sounds or syllables which adjoin it in a word or other sequence.

retracted (vowel), articulated by raising a more backward part of the tongue (than some other vowel).

retroflex (consonant), made with the tip of the tongue curled back or retracted so as to articulate against the hard palate or against the back part of the upper gum. The sound called 'retroflex « ɽ »' (denoted by the phonetic symbol « ɽ ») is a 'retroflex flap'. In making it the tongue starts in a retroflex (curled back) position, with the tip near to the hard palate; it then performs a forward and downward movement during which its under side strikes the back of the upper gum.

rising (diphthong), a diphthong in which the final part has greater 'prominence' than the initial part.

rolled (consonant), formed by a rapid succession of taps of an elastic part of the speech mechanism.

rounded (sound), articulated with the lips protruded or pursed up so as to form an opening of roundish shape.

secondary stress, a degree of stress intermediate between strong stress and weak stress.

semi-vowel, a gliding sound in forming which the tongue and/or lips start in or near the position for a close vowel and immediately move away in the direction of the position for some other sound of equal or greater sonority. See *Outline of English Phonetics*, 8th (1956) and subsequent editions, §§ 800, 801, 802, 813.

single sound, an indivisible unit of speech utterance; a minimum section of a speech-chain, the subtraction or commutation of which can change a word into another word.

soft (Russian consonant), synonymous with 'palatalized'.

stop, the portion of a plosive consonant during which the articulating organs remain in contact.

stress, force of utterance (of a sound or syllable).

stressed (syllable), a syllable pronounced with strong force.

strong form (of a word), a pronunciation which the word has when said with strong stress.

syllabic (consonant), a consonant pronounced with such prominence (usually by length) as compared with adjacent sounds in a sequence as to make it sound like a separate syllable.

symbol (phonetic), a letter or digraph or accented letter employed to designate a single speech-sound.

tense (vowel), articulated with considerable muscular tension.

typographically broad (transcription), using the minimum number of letter shapes of simplest romanic form. See *Outline of English Phonetics*, 8th (1956) and subsequent editions, Appendix A, §§ 5, 13.

typographically narrow (transcription), using special symbols to show that sounds of the language transcribed differ from analogous sounds of another language or dialect. Synonymous with 'comparative', q.v. See *Outline of English Phonetics*, 8th (1956) and subsequent editions, Appendix A, § 6.

unrounded (vowel), pronounced with spread or neutral lips.

unstressed (syllable), pronounced with weak stress.

velar (consonant), articulated by the 'back' of the tongue against the soft palate (velum) or against the soft palate and the back part of the hard palate.

voice, sound made when the vocal cords are caused to vibrate.

voiced (sound), pronounced with vibration of the vocal cords.

voiceless (sound), pronounced without vibration of the vocal cords.

weak form (of a word), a pronunciation (differing from the strong form) which the word has or may have when said with weak stress.